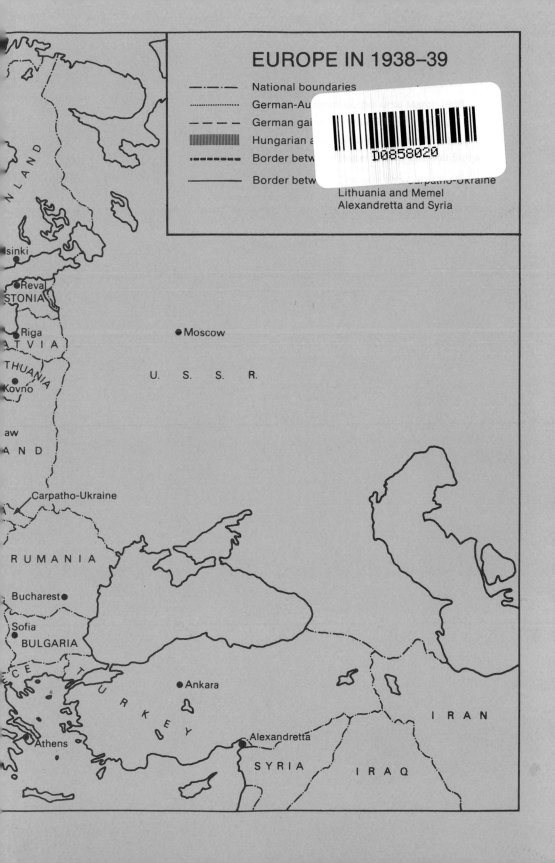

EUROPE IN 1938–39

- —·—·— National boundaries
- ················· German-Au...
- — — — German ga...
- ▓▓▓▓ Hungarian a...
- ▪▪▪▪▪▪▪ Border betw...
- ——— Border betw... ...patho-Ukraine
  Lithuania and Memel
  Alexandretta and Syria

...sinki

Reval
...STONIA

Riga
...TVIA

...THUANIA
Kovno

...aw
...AND

Carpatho-Ukraine

Moscow

U. S. S. R.

R U M A N I A

Bucharest

Sofia
BULGARIA

...CE
T U R K E Y

Ankara

Athens

Alexandretta

S Y R I A

I R A Q

I R A N

The Foreign Policy of Hitler's Germany

the foreign policy

Gerhard L. Weinberg

# of hitler's germany

Starting
World War II
1937–1939

The University of Chicago Press
Chicago and London

THE UNIVERSITY OF CHICAGO PRESS, CHICAGO 60637
THE UNIVERSITY OF CHICAGO PRESS, LTD., LONDON

86 85 84 83 82   5 4 3 2 1

Library of Congress Cataloging in Publication Data

Weinberg, Gerhard L
   The foreign policy of Hitler's Germany : starting
World War II, 1937–1939.

   Bibliography: p.
   Includes index.
   1.   Germany—Foreign relations—1933-1945.   I.   Title.
DD256.5.W418   327.43   79-26406
ISBN 0-226-88511-9

Gerhard L. Weinberg is the William Rand Kenan, Jr., Professor
of History at the University of North Carolina at Chapel Hill.
He is the author of numerous scholarly books and articles,
including the first volume of the present work, *The Foreign
Policy of Hitler's Germany: Diplomatic Revolution in Europe,
1933–1936,* published by the University of Chicago Press
in 1970.

for Wilma

Contents

	Preface	ix
1.	The Position of Germany in 1937	1
2.	Hitler's Preparations, 1937–38	18
3.	Britain and France Face the German Threat	52
4.	Another Attempt at a Settlement: The von Neurath and Halifax Visits	95
5.	Germany and the Civil War in Spain, 1937–39	142
6.	Germany, the Sino-Japanese War, and the Plans for a Tripartite Alliance	167
7.	Germany, Eastern Europe, Southeast Europe, and the Middle East	192
8.	Germany and the Western Hemisphere, 1937–38	249
9.	German-Italian Relations and the *Anschluss*	261
10.	War Denied: The Crisis over Czechoslovakia, Part 1	313
11.	War Denied: The Crisis over Czechoslovakia, Part 2	378
12.	Undoing Munich, October 1938–March 1939	465
13.	The Road to War	535
14.	Hitler Gets His War	628
15.	Conclusion	656
	Bibliography	678
	Index	709

Preface

The absence of a comprehensive treatment of international relations and the origins of World War II on which I commented in the preface to the preceding volume (1970), covering the years 1933–36, has not been remedied in the interim. There has been a great increase both in archives available and in literature published, but the problem of how the world came to be involved in a massive conflagration for the second time within a quarter of a century has continued to be a subject of great interest but of either very summary or limited monographic treatment. In the reassessment of the issues provided here, not only many archives but the works of other scholars have been freely drawn upon, even those with different perspectives or different conclusions.

While looking at the fateful question of how so great a disaster could befall humanity, I have been impressed by two considerations. The first is that the memory of what in the 1920s and 1930s was referred to as the ''Great War'' was of enormous significance, and that many decisions and choices were made in terms of what people rightly or wrongly thought to be the lessons of that conflict, its outbreak, its nature, and its outcome. All looked through that frame, often concentrating on different aspects or drawing contradictory inferences but still carrying the burden of that experience as each interpreted its relevance to current problems.

If this heritage of the past is a recurring theme, the focus for understanding the unfolding of new developments must be on German policy. It has become fashionable in some circles to reverse this perspective. It is at times suggested that Germany plunged Europe into war because she had been appeased too much by others—and that Japan thrust Asia into war because she was not appeased enough. The fact remains, however, that the initiative lay with Germany, and to a lesser extent with Italy, in Europe and with Japan in East Asia. After many years of studying the subject, I still believe that the most meaningful way to analyze how the whole world was plunged into war is to center attention on those who made the key choices and decisions. In these, they were affected both by domestic developments in their own countries and by the actions and reactions of others, but that in no way alters the source of the major trends. The idea that the historian can see better by walking on his hands instead of on his feet has the charm of novelty, but is apt to lead to misconceptions.

Of the three countries taking the initiative, Germany was the most important. Italy could start a colonial war in Africa, and Japan could initiate a limited war in East Asia. Terrible enough for those directly affected, neither of these conflicts would necessarily have spread around the globe. Only the initiative of Germany as Europe's most advanced and powerful industrial and military power could and did go beyond the immediate limits of one region or continent and explode into a worldwide catastrophe. Centering a study of the origins of World War II on the foreign policy of Hitler's Germany, therefore, still provides a useful, and I hope productive, approach. Since that war completed the process, initiated by the First World War, through which the Europeans destroyed the basis of power for their control of the globe at the beginning of the twentieth century, the issues are of significance not only for the larger and smaller countries of Europe, but for the world as a whole.

My earlier volume traced the diplomatic revolution by which the European situation was transformed. From a tolerated equal, Germany became by the end of 1936 the dominant power on the continent. Since that book appeared, some new material and many additional publications dealing with its period have become available, but little of it would require substantial change. The reviewers have been kind, and what criticism there has been has centered more on my reluctance to engage in debate with the latest schools of interpretation and lines of controversy in German scholarship than with the substance of the account. Since this study is designed to illuminate the events of the 1930s rather than the arguments of the 1960s that criticism may be validly applied to this book as well. There is, however, one significant difference between the two volumes. At the time that I wrote on the period 1933–36, there were very few studies dealing with the problems of those years in a detailed and scholarly way; and it was therefore necessary to base the bulk of that account on primary sources. For the years 1937–39, on the other hand, there is a vast scholarly literature, much of it of very high quality indeed. It has accordingly been possible in many places to follow other scholars across the mountains of evidence; I have tried to acknowledge my debt to these guides in the notes and to indicate where and why I have decided to go on a slightly different path.

By the end of 1936, the National Socialist regime had not only consolidated its hold on Germany, but had laid the foundations for the expansion toward which it was working. The initiation of rearmament, the launching of the Four-Year Plan, the remilitarization of the Rhineland, the creation of the Axis, the signing of the Anti-Comintern Pact; all these and other steps were in the past. Adolf Hitler, who was the unchallenged leader of the nation, could now move toward the goals he had charted by the means he preferred and in accordance with his assessments of other nations. These means and assessments, their origins and their nature, have been discussed in the preceding volume. Now he would have the opportunity to apply them. Germany's determination for war had become the central theme of world diplomacy. The way in which Hitler moved, how some tried to restrain him from doing so, how others hoped to benefit from his policies, and how the world situation evolved under these circumstances would be the theme of the following years and of this book.

In research of this type, the scholar accumulates obligations almost as rapidly as notes. I have been assisted in many ways by kind friends, Fritz T. Epstein, Joseph Anderle, Harold C. Deutsch, Donald C. Watt, and Jonathan Zorach. Hans-Adolf Jacobsen provided some important documents, and the late Howard M. Smyth helped in significant ways.

The Manuscript Division of the Library of Congress, the Historical Division of the Department of State, the Departmental Records Branch of the Adjutant General's Office—now the Military Archives Division of the National Archives—the Foreign Studies Branch of the Center for Military History, the Franklin D. Roosevelt Library at Hyde Park, the Wiener Library in London, the West German Federal Archives in Koblenz, the German military archives in Freiburg, the German foreign ministry archives in Bonn, and the Institut für Zeitgeschichte in Munich have all been most helpful. I happily join the numerous scholars who acknowledge the assistance of Patricia Dowling with the State Department Records in the National Archives. The staff of the Public Record Office in London was most generous with a demanding customer; all quotations from the Foreign Office, Cabinet, Lord Halifax, and Sir Nevile Henderson papers there are reproduced with the kind permission of the Controller of Her Majesty's Stationery Office.

Permission to use the papers of William E. Dodd was given by his family; the papers of Jay Pierrepont Moffat are used and quoted with the permission of his widow, Mrs. Albert Lévitt; the Houghton Library of Harvard University allowed access to the William Phillips papers; the University of Delaware Library permitted use of the George S. Messersmith papers; the London School of Economics allowed use of the Hugh Dalton papers; King's College of the University of London made available the papers of Lord Ismay, which are quoted with the permission of the Trustees of the Liddell Hart Centre for Military Archives; the Beaverbrook Library allowed use of the David Lloyd George papers, and Clare College of Cambridge University the Baldwin and Templewood (Sir Samuel Hoare) papers. A collection of microfilms of Milch papers was made available to me at the Imperial War Museum in London. I am especially grateful to Lord Lothian and to the Scottish Record Office for permission to consult and quote the Lothian muniments. Nicolaus von Below and Wolf Eberhard permitted use of materials at the Institut für Zeitgeschichte in Munich. Reference librarians and interlibrary loan specialists have been most helpful at the University of Michigan and at the University of North Carolina at Chapel Hill.

The scholar who attempts to work the vast and scattered mines of modern archives and to digest the masses of material gathered from them assuredly needs research grants. I want to express my appreciation for the support of the Kentucky Research Foundation of the University of Kentucky, the International Relations Program of the Rockefeller Foundation, the Social Science Research Council, the American Council of Learned Societies, the Horace R. Rackham School of Graduate Studies of the University of Michigan, the John Simon Guggenheim Foundation, the American Philosophical Society, and the William Rand Kenan, Jr., Trust research fund of the University of North Carolina at Chapel Hill.

The opinions, conclusions—and errors—of this work are the author's. For two decades the troubles, the chores, and the time demands of this project have called upon the patience of my wife. She has earned the dedication many times over.

Chapel Hill, North Carolina
May 1978

The Position of Germany in 1937

By the beginning of 1937 Germany was unquestionably the most powerful country in Europe. Although there were great gaps in her rearmament program, the head start she enjoyed over other powers provided not merely statistically measurable advantages in terms of divisions and airplanes; but, more important, it gave her an aura of strength and confidence in an apprehensive world.[1] The armaments boom had created full employment in Germany while others still struggled with the great depression; the Olympic games of 1936 had shown to large numbers of foreign visitors a united and determined country; and the confidence exuded by Germany's leaders contrasted markedly with the doubts and hesitations of others.

There was a self-reinforcing aspect to this situation. Success easily breeds confidence in those who attain it while discouraging both internal and external opponents. And the psychological dominance of Germany was all-pervasive. The new status of Germany was not some recondite development hidden from the eyes of all but the most observant. Quite the contrary, the world's news agencies sent their best international reporters to Germany, and the world press, radio, and newsreels were filled with impressive, even frightening, reports about the Third Reich. Any who had doubts could read or hear about the role of German planes in the Spanish Civil War, and even those in

1. An example is the memorandum of 18 November 1936 comparing the German with the Royal Air Force prepared in the Central Department of the Foreign Office, C 8249/2928/18, FO 371/19947. See also Committee of Imperial Defence, "The German Army: Its Present Strength and Possible Rate of Expansion in Peace and War," 13 January 1937, C 1134/136/18, FO 371/20731; Ian Colvin, *None So Blind* (New York: Harcourt, Brace & World, 1965), pp. 133–35.

other countries who were opposed to the National Socialist regime necessarily pointed to German strength as a key argument to underline their warnings about the future or their insistence on such measures as rearmament in the present.

The trading practices of the Third Reich impinged on those in the business world; her literary and artistic censorship was a subject for discussion by writers and artists. The religious persecutions in Germany had wide repercussions abroad; what was known or imagined about Germany's contacts with people of German background in other countries as close as Czechoslovakia and as far away as Chile excited apprehension everywhere. In short, Germany was news.

In the eyes of all inside and outside Germany, the figure of Adolf Hitler stood out as the embodiment of the Third Reich. A strange and ominous man, he had come seemingly from nowhere to incredible power; and while there were caricatures and jokes about this curious person, that merriment covered but thinly an underlying sense of admiration or apprehension, of fear or hate. Mad or sane, brilliant or confused, in full control or buffeted by conflicting advice, he was seen as without doubt the key figure, center stage in an extraordinary drama. No review of the specific details of Germany's position on the international scene of 1937 and no examination of the interaction between Germany and other powers leading to the outbreak of the Second World War can ever be complete unless those details and that interaction are seen within a framework of a world whose eyes and ears were focused on Germany and its leader.

Within Germany itself, the National Socialist regime was firmly in control. The other political parties had disappeared, independent political and other organizations were practically nonexistent, and a system of mass propaganda and indoctrination was reinforced by censorship and secret police. The originally narrow margin of popular support for the coalition that had placed Hitler in the chancellorship in 1933 had by 1937 swollen to an overwhelming majority. If jokesters referred to the theft of next year's election returns, all observers testified to the mass support enjoyed by the regime. The few doubters were silent, and if they complained, did so about specific aspects of the regime rather than the whole system.

The only possible internal challenger of the National Socialist movement was Germany's army, the air force being largely a creation of the new regime and the navy a small and peripheral structure. The army, in the process of rapid expansion, found the new regime far more congenial than its predecessor and contained few critics of the Hitler government. The circumstances surrounding the removal of the army's commander-in-chief early in 1938 followed by the pursuit of what looked like increasingly dangerous foreign policies opened a few eyes, but before that development, real enthusiasm, cautious professionalism, or determined blindness reigned supreme. The narrow perspectives of the German military leadership may be illustrated by an aspect of the murders of 30 June

1934. Included among the victims of the mass slaughter for which Hitler took personal responsibility were not only two generals but the wife of one of them, a woman who had been the wife of Germany's minister of defense and chancellor and who had never been accused of any allegedly illegal action whatever. This murder was not considered an affront to the army; but in 1938 the marriage of Field Marshal Werner von Blomberg—who had been implicated in the slaughter operation—to a woman with a "past" was considered incompatible with the army's "honor."[2] Officers who began by turning their "non-Aryan" comrades out of the army in 1934 would end up by turning their politically compromised comrades over to the hangman ten years later. By 1937, the first of these processes had been completed, but there were not yet any candidates for the second.

The domestic consolidation of National Socialist Germany was not only the background for the aura of power just described, it had been and continued to be the prerequisite for the expansionist policy Hitler preached before and after 1933.[3] He had seen and continued to see it as necessary for the foreign policies in which he believed, and these apparently domestic concerns, therefore, must be recognized as a part of German foreign policy. Because the National Socialist revolution came to Germany in stages after Hitler came to power, the process of consolidation continued in the very years when its earliest stages first enabled Hitler to mount aggression against his neighbors; that process would in fact continue into the last days of the Third Reich. The steps taken to strengthen National Socialist control and penetration of Germany's life and institutions must accordingly be recognized as the internal aspect of German foreign policy in the years immediately preceding the beginning of war in September 1939.

Germany's international position was specifically influenced by actions she herself had taken as well as by the policies of other powers.[4] She had left the League of Nations, but most of the disadvantages that step might have had for Germany in the long run had been obviated by the failure of Britain and France to give to the League the kind of success in the face of Italy's attack against Ethiopia that might alone have revived an institution already badly damaged by Japan's earlier flaunting of the rules and departure from the halls of Geneva.[5] The half-hearted sanctions imposed on

2. It is worth noting that even the brilliant book by Klaus-Jürgen Müller, *Das Heer und Hitler: Armee und nationalsozialistisches Regime 1933–1940* (Stuttgart: Deutsche Verlags-Anstalt, 1969) fails to make this comparison.

3. The most recent comprehensive treatment of the subject puts the issue beyond question: Norman Rich, *Hitler's War Aims: Ideology, the Nazi State, and the Course of Expansion* (New York: Norton, 1973).

4. A good summary is in André François-Poncet's report on the year 1936, *D.D.F.*, 2d, 4, No. 233.

5. The British government has begun publication of its diplomatic documents on the Ethiopian crisis with volume 14 of the second series of the *Documents on British Foreign Policy, 1919–1939*. There is a fine study of the crisis over Japan's challenge to the League over Manchuria in Christopher Thorne, *The Limits of Foreign Policy: The West, the League and the Far Eastern Crisis of 1931–1933* (New York: G. P. Putnam's Sons, 1973).

Italy had not merely failed to strengthen the League, but had torn the ties of France and England to Italy and had helped to push the latter to Germany's side; the real effect of sanctions had been to provide Germany with a form of political absolution from Rome for the National Socialist coup in Austria of 1934 and its attendant murder of Austrian Chancellor Engelbert Dollfuss. By the end of 1936 the joint intervention of Italy and Germany in the Spanish Civil War had given them a common cause—in spite of a certain rivalry there—and in any case prevented any real rapprochement between Italy and England regardless of endless negotiations and periodic agreements between them.[6] While German policy in Spain will be discussed in more detail in a later chapter, it should be noted here that Hitler's decision of December 1936 not to increase German support of Francisco Franco—at the time when Benito Mussolini decided on a very substantial increase in the Italian troop commitment to Spain[7]— practically guaranteed that the civil war would last a long time and thereby help assure that the German-Italian association cemented by their joint venture in the Iberian peninsula would not be easily broken.

The smaller European countries were afraid of Germany. Each hoped that by adroit maneuvering, preferably at somebody else's expense, it could avoid a dangerous confrontation with Berlin. Such states of intermediate strength like Poland and Yugoslavia did their best to get and remain on good terms with the German colossus. The major European powers other than Italy were uncertain about their relationship with the new Germany. The Soviet Union was alarmed at Germany's increasing might, and though she had no common border with that country, feared that at some point Germany might well attack her to seize some portion of Soviet territory. Once the Soviet leader, Joseph Stalin, had recognized this danger, he alternated between trying to come to an agreement with Germany and abetting the formation of some anti-German alliance; but neither policy had attained much success. Hitler as yet felt no need for an agreement with Russia, and the prospective allies of the latter were about as suspicious of her as they were of Germany.

The government of France was confronted by both domestic discord and foreign danger. The two forms of trouble reinforced each other. The internal quarrels of the Third Republic were accentuated by differences of opinion over foreign affairs, especially the policies to be followed toward the Spanish Civil War, the Soviet Union, the continuing aggravation with Italy, and the growing threat of Germany. The domestic turmoil in France, moreover, encouraged both Germany and Italy in the assumption

6. A useful survey in Jens Petersen, *Hitler-Mussolini: Die Entstehung der Achse Berlin—Rom 1933—1936* (Tübingen: Niemeyer, 1973).

7. Gerhard L. Weinberg, *The Foreign Policy of Hitler's Germany: Diplomatic Revolution in Europe, 1933–1936* (Chicago: University of Chicago Press, 1970) (hereafter cited as Weinberg, *Foreign Policy*), pp. 296–98.

that they had little to fear from France,[8] while the allies of France on the continent could not expect much help from a country quite likely to be without a government at just the moment when decisive action would be needed.

This concern extended to the British government. Though doubtful, as will be seen, about the ability of the French army to bring effective assistance to any part of Central or Eastern Europe, the British were still confident that the French army would be a match for the German if Germany attacked in the West. They were, however, justifiably alarmed about the weak state and inadequate expansion of the French air force. The evidence suggests that the French government was partly unaware and partly unconcerned about the problem in 1937—there would be a rude awakening in the crisis over Czechoslovakia—but the constant prodding from London reflects the anxiety felt there over French weakness in a critical area, a weakness inadvertently accentuated by the measures the French government had taken in 1936 to nationalize parts of the French aircraft industry and to reduce the work week.[9]

It is indicative both of the problems faced by the British and French in developing an effective policy in the face of a rising German threat and of the extent to which this threat eventually pushed the two powers together into a firm alliance that the London government was at first reluctant to raise this question in Paris for fear of then having to agree to joint Anglo-French staff talks.[10] Two considerations were at work here, both growing out of World War I. The British military and political leaders were very worried—and rightly so—lest the French then urge them to build up a large land army of the kind the British had developed in what was generally referred to as the "Great War." In the psychological atmosphere of 1936–37, such an idea was inconceivable to the English public and government alike. If there was one subject on which unanimity could be found in the United Kingdom, this was it. There might be differences over the wisdom of General Douglas Haig's conduct of the 1917 battle in Flanders; there were none over the conviction that Britain could never go to Passchendaele again.[11]

8. For French recognition of this aspect in the formulation of German foreign policy, see Bullitt (Paris) tel. 184 of 10 February 1937, U.S. National Archives, State Department Decimal File (hereafter cited as State), 862.014/203.

9. For some of the relevant documents, see C 3571, C 4601, C 5215, C6808/122/17, FO 371/20694; C 5604/185/1/8, FO 371/20734; R 6741/1/22, FO 371/21162; *D.D.F.*, 2d, 2, Nos. 308, 357, 419. For a French report on the German air force, see ibid., 4, No. 292. The French, prodded by the British, began to look at the question more seriously, especially when they concluded that Italy, to say nothing of Germany, was producing more modern warplanes than France (ibid., 7, Nos. 198, 213, 271). On the general problem, see Jacques Minart, *Le drame du désarmement française* (Paris: La Nef, 1959).

10. The subject is reviewed in detail in the papers included in the volume *Les relations franco-brittaniques de 1935 à 1939* (Paris: Editions du Centre de la Recherche Scientifique, 1975).

11. See, for example, the discussion between the British secretary of state for war, Leslie

The second factor holding back London from staff conversations was the great debate about responsibility for the outbreak of the World War. Britain's real or imagined share of that responsibility was generally tied to two aspects of British policy: the prewar staff conversations held by English military and naval officers with their French, and to a lesser extent Belgian, counterparts, and the fact that England had not made her own prospective position sufficiently clear to Germany to deter the latter from the gamble of war. Though more recent scholarship has largely eliminated the former and entirely removed the latter as factors in the outbreak of the war, both were very much in people's minds during the 1930s. The view that a clear British stand might have obviated war will be seen as repeatedly held up, first as an incentive to British firmness and later as an element of what it was hoped would be an effective warning to Germany once London had decided to take its stand; but the concern lest staff conversations involve Britain in war or even arouse domestic fears of such involvement long held back the coordination of British and French military planning.[12] With the Foreign Office taking the lead, and with the clearly growing menace of Germany providing the impetus, the United Kingdom moved from cool reluctance at the beginning of 1937 to an enthusiastic advocacy at the end of the year, with Prime Minister Neville Chamberlain himself taking the lead in urging on the French a coordination they had scarcely dared to hope for.[13]

Not only the arguments over the origins but also consideration of the course and outcome of the war had their effects on the policies of England and France. The terrible cost of the war and the apparent triumph of defensive over offensive weapons had produced an essentially defensive approach to warfare in both countries, with the French reluctant to consider any offensive land strategy and the British looking to a new blockade

---

Hore-Belisha, and the French military attaché on 10 February 1938 reported in *D.D.F.*, 2d, 8, No. 206.

12. Ibid., 9, No. 37.

13. This process—and the arguments—can be traced in C 6436, C 6790, C 7692, C 8237, C 8434, C 8468, C 8473, C 8474, C 8683/122/17, FO 371/20694; C 7717/18/17, FO 371/20687; C 7848/822/17, FO 371/20696; C 1141, C 1142, C 1634, C 1759, C 6941, C 7843/271/18, FO 371/20738. The British were stimulated at the beginning of 1937 by the report of a Royal Air Force mission to Germany, C 1450/185/18, FO 371/20733; Earl of Avon (Anthony Eden), *Facing the Dictators, 1923–1938* (Boston: Houghton Mifflin, 1962), pp. 548, 556. Eden did feel that perhaps the situation was not quite as serious as often presented. On 7 October 1937 he minuted on a report on the French air force: "I should like to add one word on the relation of these reports to policy. While it is no doubt true that there is much that is unsatisfactory about the state of the French Air Force and that of the French Navy, we should, I think, be careful not to exaggerate their weakness, while at the same time over-estimating the strength of the dictator States. We know of the shortcomings of the democracies; those of the totalitarian States are withheld from us, and I myself doubt whether, despite all their imperfections, the French Air Force and the French Navy are not today at least equal, and in the case of the latter superior to the respective Italian forces" (C 6436/122/17, FO 371/20694, f.159).

as the tool of victory if war did come.[14] Both countries thus pinned their hopes on strategies with two characteristics important for the international situation: neither could do anything effective to provide immediate assistance to any country that might be threatened by Germany, and both relied on a strategy geared to a long war. Both factors would operate to make them even more reluctant to take risks in the face of German moves, because any such move, if not directed against themselves, would require them to help a country which like Serbia in the previous conflict could be helped only by an allied victory in a long and costly war.

This reluctance to risk war with Germany was reinforced by the continuing feeling, especially in some circles in England, that the peace settlement at the end of the war had been unfairly harsh to Germany.[15] Whether or not correct, this attitude obscured from the eyes of many that a defeated Germany had emerged from the settlement relatively stronger than in 1914 and that in these circumstances any further concessions, however justified, that strengthened Germany would necessarily lead to an even greater unbalancing of the European situation.[16] The discrepancy between what many imagined had happened at Versailles to weaken Germany and the reality of a potentially enhanced German power position in Europe was so great that it took years of vehement shocks before the public in Great Britain, and to a lesser extent elsewhere, recognized that they faced the real, not the imagined, power relationships left by the peace settlement.

Outside Europe, the smaller countries were primarily affected by worry about German aims—especially if they contained citizens of German background—and by German trade practices. The possible doubts about the loyalty of a portion of their own citizens became an issue of increasing significance, especially in a number of Latin American nations. The triumph of National Socialist elements in the cultural and other organizations of these minorities, which was largely completed in 1937, seemed to point in alarming directions. Whatever the reality of the threat this process posed for the countries involved, the impressions created were damaging for both Germany and the people of German background abroad. The public posturing and secret agitation of organizations that came to look increasingly like local parts of a worldwide threat were a

14. The influence of somewhat exaggerated beliefs about the role of the blockade in the World War and the anticipated effects of its repetition in a future war on British thinking and planning in the interwar years remains to be examined in detail. There is a beginning in Donald C. Watt, *Too Serious a Business: European Armed Forces and the Approach to the Second World War* (Berkeley: University of California Press, 1975).

15. See essay 6 in Donald C. Watt, *Personalities and Policies* (Notre Dame, Ind.: University of Notre Dame Press, 1965), pp. 117–35.

16. I have dealt with this in "The Defeat of Germany in 1918 and the European Balance of Power," *Central European History*, 2, No. 3 (Sept. 1969), 248–60.

hindrance to good relations with Germany and to the domestic peace of the affected countries.[17]

Germany's trade practices had mixed effects on these nations. On the one hand, the German government was often willing to pay high prices for products otherwise difficult to sell in years when world trade was still in a depressed state.[18] On the other hand, the requirement that each trading partner of Germany use the proceeds of sales to Germany only or almost only for purchases there created all sorts of difficulties. If the Germans ran up large clearing debts, as they frequently did, the other country could either make what were in effect forced loans to Germany or reduce those debts only by increasing its imports from Germany, taking whatever Germany was willing to export at whatever prices Germany might ask.[19] This procedure, established at German insistence, reduced the other country's free foreign exchange available for purchases in third countries where it might have found lower prices as well as products it needed more than the German ones. The most disconcerting aspect of all this was that Germany at times reexported what she had imported, so that a country might find itself underbid in the world market for its products by its own earlier shipments to Germany.

An official in the British Foreign Office used a rough, but not unfair, example to show how this system worked:

Germany buys from Sweden, on *clearing* account, 1,000 tons of iron ore, out of which she makes 500 tons of iron. She buys from China, on *barter* terms, 10 tons of wolfram, and from Turkey, on *clearing* terms, 20 tons of chromium ore. Out of these materials, for which she had not paid a pfenning in currency, she makes 500 tons of fine steel. With her own resources of secondary raw materials, fuel, power, labour and

17. The best accounts of this question are in Alton Frye, *Nazi Germany and the American Hemisphere, 1933–1941* (New Haven: Yale University Press, 1967), and Hans-Adolf Jacobsen, *Nationalsozialistische Aussenpolitik 1933–1938* (Frankfurt/M: Alfred Metzner, 1968), chaps. II, 3, and IV, 4. The direct role of the foreign section (AO) of the National Socialist party in this process is described in Donald M. McKale, *The Swastika outside Germany* (Kent, Ohio: Kent State University Press, 1977). Documents for 1937 are to be published in *G.D.*, C, 6, Nos. 137, 168, 184, 237.

18. Or when circumstances made foreign sales difficult. Thus when British firms boycotted Mexican oil in retaliation for Mexican nationalization of the oil industry, the German navy took the oil and used it for its operations in Spanish waters in 1937–38. See Germany, Oberkommando der Kriegsmarine, "Ölversorgung der Kriegsmarine," 29 April 1941, pp. 6–8, Nuremberg document 984-PS, National Archives; *G.D.*, C, 6, Nos. 154, 386; D, 5, No. 600, n.4; cf. Josephus Daniels, *Shirt-Sleeve Diplomat* (Chapel Hill, N.C.: University of North Carolina Press, 1947), pp. 251–53; Wilhelm Meier-Dörnberg, *Ölversorgung der Kriegsmarine, 1935 bis 1945* (Freiburg: Rombach, 1973), pp. 39–42. In this fashion, one of the Spanish republic's best friends contributed substantially to its defeat.

19. A fine analysis of this process as it affected Latvia and Estonia is in Hans-Erich Volkmann, "Ökonomie und Machtpolitik: Lettland und Estland im politisch-ökonomischen Kalkül des Dritten Reiches (1933–1940)," *Geschichte und Gesellschaft*, 2, No. 4 (1976), 484–86. The whole range of issues is ably summarized in the same author's piece "Aussenhandel und Aufrüstung in Deutschland, 1933 bis 1939," in Friedrich Forstmeier and Hans-Erich Volkmann (eds.), *Wirtschaft und Rüstung am Vorabend des Zweiten Weltkrieges* (Düsseldorf: Droste, 1975), pp. 81–131.

technical skill, she makes, let us say, 10 tanks, 2 turbines, and 100 typewriters. The tanks are put into service, and (because she has nearly enough already) she releases four of last year's models for export. Two go to China, two to Turkey; and they pay not only for the wolfram and the chromium, but for ten bales of cotton and 100 tons of soya beans. The turbines go to Sweden, and more than balance the import of iron ore; while 99 of the typewriters are sold in the United Kingdom and bring in £200, which is spent on one of the relatively few raw materials which she cannot obtain through a clearing, such as copra. Thus the German army gets ten brand-new tanks in place of four obsolescent ones, and German industry gets ten bales of cotton, 100 tons of soya beans, one typewriter (times are hard, and there is room for economy here) and £200 worth of copra—all without any loss of [foreign] exchange. True, she has to do without her Turkish delight and birds' nest soup because Turkish cotton and Chinese wolfram are more important to her; but she has added six tanks to her collection, kept 1,000 men at work for two months, and, since the Swedes want to be paid for their iron ore, she has obliged them to buy German turbines where they would probably have preferred English ones.[20]

Although it is difficult to generalize about a multidimensional matter of this kind, it may be safe to say that in the first years of National Socialist foreign trade policies, many of her partners felt the advantages of the new system; but by 1937 the balance appeared to be turning as the disadvantages became more important in daily practice and as a slow recovery of world trade and prices occurred.[21]

A concrete example of the kind of difficulty that could easily arise out of these trade practices was the German dispute with Brazil and the United States over German-Brazilian trade in the spring and summer of 1937. Eventually an accommodation was worked out as a result of which Brazil in practice shifted to Germany exports previously sold in the United States and imports hitherto derived from England while re-equipping her own army with German artillery. The special limitations and subsidies that figured so largely in Germany's foreign trade practices, however, brought some friction into German relations with the largest country of South America and exacerbated her already bad relations with the United States, which favored freer rather than more restrictive trade practices.[22]

20. Note of 27 January 1938 in C 542/65/18, FO 371/21666, ff.37–38.
21. For British analyses of these procedures, especially when involving German credits, see C 2889/664/18, FO 371/20745; E 557/557/34, FO 371/20832. For warnings about the experiences of others, see London's explanation to Southern Rhodesia when considering a barter with Germany for tobacco, and to Thailand when considering a deal with Germany for tin (W 13574/816/50, FO 371/21227). On German policy in 1937, see *G.D.*, C, 6, No. 362.
22. Published documentation on this episode are *G.D.*, C, 6, Nos. 203, 406, 415, 421, 428, 440, 444, 445, 475, 482, 488, 512, 521; *U.S.*, 1937, II:332–43; *D.D.F.*, 2d, 5, No. 288; see also the arguments of Hjalmar Schacht and Herbert Feis in State 632.6231/216, and the entry in Pierrepont Moffat's diary for 21 July 1937, Moffat Papers, vol. 39. For an account of this issue relatively favorable to the German position, see Frank D. McCann, Jr., *The Brazilian-American Alliance, 1937–1945* (Princeton, N.J.: Princeton University Press, 1973),

The controversy produced between Germany and the United States in the example just cited was merely a continuation of the abrasive effects of German trade policies on her relationship with the United States. Although it was in this field that the two powers were actually most in contact on a regular basis, it would be quite erroneous to assume that the volume of records in the archives is a safe guide to the intrinsic historical importance of a subject.[23] As described in the preceding volume, German-American relations had deteriorated extraordinarily in the first years of the National Socialist regime, but this deterioration was primarily a result of political and ideological rather than economic factors. A series of incidents of minor practical but major symbolic importance during 1937 illustrate this aspect of the growing mistrust and disdain each country felt for the other. They all reflect an underlying hostility based on the extreme divergence of American from German institutions and perspectives. When the mayor of New York, Fiorello LaGuardia, made some nasty personal comments about Hitler in public, he could be sure of local approval; but the German government was incensed and protested officially in Washington. Secretary of State Cordell Hull formally expressed regret but tried to explain the American government's lack of authority to restrain such comments, an explanation the German authorities found hard to accept.[24]

A talk by Cardinal Mundelein to several hundred priests of the Chicago archdiocese in May 1937, in which the cardinal deplored the persecution of the Catholic church in Germany and referred to the "Austrian paperhanger," was used by Berlin not only as further grist for its animosity toward the Vatican but as the subject of a press campaign and diplomatic protests in Washington.[25] While that incident and the religious questions touched on in it occupied public attention, another competed with it: the exceedingly dubious circumstances surrounding the arrest, trial, death sentence, and execution of an American citizen in Germany for supposedly having some anti-Nazi leaflets in his possession.[26] As the new

chap. 6. The account in Hans-Jürgen Schröder, *Deutschland und die Vereinigten Staaten 1933–1939* (Wiesbaden: Steiner, 1970), pp. 247–56, though dubious in its basic approach, is useful for its material. The account of Stanley E. Hilton, *Brazil and the Great Powers, 1930–1939: The Politics of Trade Rivalry* (Austin: University of Texas Press, 1975) is extremely valuable, not only for its account of Brazil's economic relations with Germany and the United States, but also for its relating these matters to trade with Britain and Italy.

23. This is an area in which Schröder's book is defective.

24. A summary of this incident is in Arnold A. Offner, *American Appeasement: United States Foreign Policy and Germany, 1933–1938* (Cambridge, Mass.: Harvard University Press, 1969), p. 84; German documents will be published as *G.D.*, C, 6, Nos. 246, 278, 279. The U.S. was complaining at the same time about articles in German newspapers (ibid., No. 265).

25. *G.D.*, D, 1, Nos. 652–60, 665–69, 671–73, 683; Friedrich Engel-Jánosi, *Vom Chaos zur Katastrophe* (Vienna: Herold, 1971), p. 173. Parts of Cardinal Mundelein's speech in *New York Times*, 19 May 1937.

26. William E. Dodd, Jr., and Martha Dodd (eds.), *Ambassador Dodd's Diary* (New York: Harcourt, Brace, 1941), 22–27 April 1937, pp. 402–14, passim; *G.D.*, C, 6, Nos. 397,

German ambassador, Hans Heinrich Dieckhoff, wrote in a private letter to German Foreign Minister Constantin von Neurath about his first impressions of the United States: "That we can in any case count on little understanding, to say nothing of sympathy, here is shown by yesterday's speech by Cardinal Mundelein. Catholics, Protestants, Jews, Freemasons, Pacifists, Socialists, Democrats, Communists—all have something to object to about us."[27]

In the letter just quoted, Dieckhoff also mentioned an event that would provide the occasion for aggravations which should be mentioned here as symptomatic even though its main effect on German-American relations would not be felt until 1938. The German dirigible *Hindenburg* was destroyed in a terrible accident on 6 May 1937 as it was about to land at Lakehurst, New Jersey. The Germans thereupon decided to build no further zeppelins unless they could purchase noninflammable helium to replace the highly flammable hydrogen hitherto used for their dirigibles. Helium, however, was an American monopoly, controlled by the government, with its sale subject to license. In a long and acrimonious dispute, the American secretary of the interior, Harold Ickes, refused to approve a license and, almost a year to the day after the *Hindenburg* disaster, finally had his way.[28] There is some evidence now to show that Hitler did have ulterior military motives in mind in his interest in the helium purchase,[29] but certainly at the time ideological distaste was the key consideration. And with that feeling in the background, Ickes could stand his ground against President Franklin Roosevelt and all the other members of the cabinet. The two countries, which before 1933 were probably closer than any other major powers but which had become alienated in the first years of the new German regime, continued to move apart.

The two most important countries in East Asia, China and Japan, were both tied to Germany, the former by trade agreements and the presence of German military advisers, the latter by the Anti-Comintern Pact. Germany had not only made a successful comeback in the Far East but had developed good relations with the Nationalist government of China led by Chiang Kai-shek and with those elements that were by stages strengthening their grip on the government of Japan.

404; *U.S.*, 1937, 2:395–405. The Germans claimed that one reason they could not release Helmut Hirsch, the person involved, was that a previously released prisoner had made unfriendly speeches about Germany after returning to the U.S.

27. Dieckhoff to von Neurath, 20 May 1937, Deutsches Zentralarchiv Potsdam (hereafter cited as DZA), Büro RAM, Akte 60964, f.143. Since in this letter, Dieckhoff also complained that the area around the German embassy was becoming increasingly Black in population, it is hard to see whom, if anyone, he considered friendly.

28. There is a good summary of the helium controversy in Offner, pp. 239–44.

29. Fritz Wiedemann claims in his memoirs (*Der Mann der Feldherr werden wollte* [Dortmund: Blick und Bild Verlag, 1964], p. 103) that Hitler wanted to take helium in such small quantities that the U.S. would not recognize this violation of the license and use it for balloons.

The special agreements with China were providing Germany with important raw materials, especially wolfram, and foreign exchange, while China received military and industrial supplies.[30] The significance of this tie was underlined by an invitation to Chinese minister of finance Hsiang-hsi Kung to Berlin, where he conferred in well-publicized talks with Hitler, Hermann Göring, and Hjalmar Schacht in June 1937.[31] Within China, at the same time, in spite of the continuing internal friction between the military advisers and those Germans involved in trading operations, the position of the German advisers was as strong as ever and in fact given increased official recognition.[32] In regard to Japan, there was some consideration of the possibility of strengthening the Anti-Comintern Pact by more extensive German-Japanese agreements,[33] and by adding Italy to the Anti-Comintern Pact system.[34]

The apparently strong position of Germany was, however, threatened by several factors. In the first place, if the Chinese Nationalist movement consolidated its hold on the country and proceeded with the process of modernization—in which the Germans were aiding them—there was no guarantee that the Chinese might not eventually squeeze out the Germans as well as other foreigners. The war that started in 1937 kept this from happening, but the possibility was certainly in the background. Of more immediate significance was the presence in Japan of a considerable element that was dubious about the connection with Germany. These men had restrained the enthusiastic advocates of an alignment with Germany and would do so again. Especially in the first half of 1937, as the political parties made a final effort to influence Japanese policy in a moderate direction, the tie to Germany came into question.[35] Nothing practical grew out of the Anti-Comintern Pact; the commissions for combatting the Third International that were to have been established were stillborn, and the special functionary sent to the German embassy in Tokyo for that purpose ended up in charge of decorating the embassy on official holi-

30. *G.D.*, C, 6, No. 157; D, 1, 576; Emil Helfferich, *Ein Leben*, 4 (Jever, Oldenbourg: C. L. Mettcker & Söhne, 1964), 133–48. For 1937 material on HAPRO and the projects of Hans Klein (Weinberg, *Foreign Policy*, pp. 122–23, 125–26, 337–40), see *G.D.*, C, 6, Nos. 304, 314.

31. *G.D.*, C, 6, Nos. 409, 418, 429, 431, 434; D, 3, No. 292; "Bestellung aus der Pressekonferenz vom 10. Juni 1937," German Federal Archives Koblenz, Brammer collection (hereafter cited as Bundesarchiv, Brammer), Z.Sg. 101/9, f.429; *U.S.*, 1937, 3:287, 649–50.

32. *G.D.*, C, 6, Nos. 214, 349; Linnell (U.S. consul general, Canton) dispatch 42 of 3 March 1937, Gauss (consul general, Shanghai) dispatch 785 of 1 May 1937, Peck (counsellor in Peking) dispatch 482 of 28 May 1937, State 893.20/595, 598, 601.

33. The evidence on this subject for 1937 is very inadequate; see Theo Sommer, *Deutschland und Japan zwischen den Mächten 1935–1940* (Tübingen: J. C. B. Mohr, 1962), p. 54; *G.D.*, C, 6, Nos. 401, 359, 413; *D.D.F.*, 2d, 5, No. 261.

34. See n.37, below.

35. Sommer, pp. 54–55; *G.D.*, C, 6, Nos. 250, 294, 359, 442. The sending of the Japanese ambassador to Rome, Sugimura Yotaro, to Berlin in February 1937 to check up on developments there belongs in this context; von Hassell to von Neurath, 12 February 1937, DZA Potsdam, Büro RAM, Akte 60964, f.65; Drummond to Vansittart, 5 March 1937, C 2090/3/18, FO 371/20710.

days.[36] As for the plan to have Italy join the Anti-Comintern Pact, that was running into a whole series of difficulties, most of them generated by the ineptitude of Joachim von Ribbentrop, the enthusiastic proponent of the scheme, and by his feuding with the German foreign ministry and its regular officials.[37]

Even among Japanese supporters of closer ties to Germany there were few enthusiastic admirers of the Berlin regime; most were guided by the belief that an association with Germany strengthened Japan and threatened her potential enemies in the competition for empire. And if Japan secured the control of East Asia to which many of her leaders aspired, there was no assurance, as the Germans would soon discover, that any of the "co-prosperity" in the greater Japanese empire was to extend to them.

The most serious problem Germany had to face in East Asia, however, was the incompatibility of her ties to China with those to a Japan that was striving to halt the consolidation of China.[38] The half-open, half-concealed clash between the two East Asian countries had challenged German ingenuity in the period 1933–36. The outbreak of hostilities in July 1937 would confront the policymakers in Berlin with even more difficult problems.

There was another group of countries outside Europe whose relations with Germany and the European situation in general must be considered. These are the self-governing Dominions of the British Commonwealth. While the dissolution of the French colonial empire did not come about until during and after the Second World War, the First World War had hastened the process by which important portions of the British Empire attained an independent status in international relations as well as in the management of their internal affairs. The separate representation of the various Dominions in the League of Nations had been used by American opponents of that institution as a sign of excessive English influence when in reality it was a symbol of the weakening of London's power.[39]

36. Sommer, pp. 49–51; *G.D.*, C, 6, Nos. 192, 269, 325, 359, 450; James W. Morley (ed.), *Deterrent Diplomacy: Japan, Germany and the USSR, 1935–1940* (New York: Columbia University Press, 1976), p. 47. For material on German-Japanese intelligence contacts in 1937, see Case 3/2, PG 48900, Bundesarchiv/Militärarchiv.

37. Sommer, pp. 82–83; *G.D.*, C, 6, Nos. 235, 281, 292, 388; von Neurath to von Ribbentrop, 23 April 1937, DZA Potsdam, Büro RAM, Akte 60964, f.107; von Neurath to von Hassell, draft, not sent, of 1 June 1937, National Archives T-120, 3527/9175/E 645552; Morley, pp. 43–44. The British government was reading one of the relevant codes, apparently the Japanese one, and followed the negotiations, F 10344/26/23, FO 371/21028.

In April 1937 von Ribbentrop made arrangements for one of his assistants, Albrecht Haushofer, to go to East Asia, but paid no attention to his recommendations (Sommer, p. 124; *TMWC*, XXXIII, 169).

38. The dilemma is described in Trautmann's report 89 of 27 January 1937, *G.D.*, C, 6, No. 162; excerpts in Sommer, pp. 56–57.

39. One of the few historians who has paid attention to this subject is Donald C. Watt. Several of his essays relating to this issue are cited here. The opening of the British archives for the 1930s now provides substantial additional documentation. See the piece by Reinhard

The anniversary of the landing of Australian and New Zealand forces at Gallipoli in 1915 became, appropriately enough, a national holiday of Australia; and Parliament Hill in Ottawa was graced with a monument to the role of Canadian forces in the capture of Vimy Ridge in 1917; but Australians and Canadians alike were determined not to fight again at either location if there were any conceivable way to avoid it. Pressure from the Dominions had already influenced British policy in the Rhineland crisis of 1936.[40] As the menace from Germany increased, the government in the United Kingdom was increasingly interested in having the Dominions recognize the dangers this posed for themselves.[41] These dangers, combined with the implications of the American neutrality legislation of 1937 with its prohibition on the export of war materials to belligerents, underlined the importance of building up a munitions industry in the Dominions and India which would have the added advantage of immunity from German air attack.[42] But these very dangers led the Dominions to pressure the London government into concessions to Germany. At the Imperial Conference of 1937, the United Kingdom delegation did its best to explain the dangers confronting them and the policies London was following to deal with the situation, but the record shows the skepticism of the Dominion delegations.[43]

London had made its first tentative gestures to Germany on the colonial question. The broader policy aspects of this matter will be discussed later,

---

Meyers in *Tradition und Neubeginn* (Cologne: Heymann, 1975). The account in Ritchie Ovendale, *"Appeasement" and the English Speaking World: The United States, the Dominions, and the Policy of "Appeasement," 1937–1939* (Cardiff: University of Wales Press, 1975), is helpful but not definitive.

40. Weinberg, *Foreign Policy*, p. 258. Note the reference to the repercussions in Australia and New Zealand of Mrs. Simpson's presence alongside Edward VIII at the memorial at Gallipoli on the latter's Mediterranean trip, in the analysis of the abdication crisis by the French ambassador to London of 3 December 1936 (*D.D.F.*, 2d, 4, No. 92).

41. See the review of imperial defense prepared by the chiefs of staff subcommittee of the Committee of Imperial Defence on 22 February 1937 for the 1937 Imperial Conference in CAB 32/127. Cf. J. M. McCarthy, "Australia and Imperial Defence: Co-operation and Conflict, 1918–1939," *Australian Journal of Politics and History*, 17, No. 1 (April 1971), 19–32.

42. See the memorandum by Sir Thomas Inskip of 10 May 1937, C 3856/205/62, FO 371/20701. As Watt has pointed out (*Personalities and Policies*, p. 156), nothing substantial was then done about these schemes.

43. The account in Watt, *Personalities and Policies*, pp. 154–56, 165, 412–15, must now be supplemented by the minutes of the meetings of the conference in CAB 32/130, the proceedings and papers of the cabinet preparatory committee and of the United Kingdom delegation in CAB 32/127, and the related papers in FO 372/3200–3202. Unless otherwise noted, the discussion of the conference here is based on these records. Although the Canadian Department of External Affairs has published relevant documents in its series, *Documents on Canadian External Relations*, 6, *1936–1939* (Ottawa, 1972), esp. Nos. 125, 129, 137, 141, they add astonishingly little. The Australian collection, which includes documents from the Public Record Office as well as Australian archives, is considerably more informative. See especially Australia, Department of Foreign Affairs, *Documents on Australian Foreign Policy, 1937–49*, 1, *1937–1938* (Canberra: Australian Government Publishing Service, 1975) (hereafter cited as *Australian Documents*), Nos. 27, 28, 39.

but here was an issue that vitally and directly affected several Dominions. South Africa, Australia, and New Zealand all held former German colonies under mandate. After considerable soul-searching, the United Kingdom government decided to give the Dominion representatives a general outline of its thinking on this issue, though the record does not give a very clear picture of the reaction of the latter.[44] The English were especially interested in pushing General J. B. M. Hertzog, the prime minister of the Union of South Africa, who was always telling the British to make concessions to Germany on all issues, including the colonial field, but refused to give up former German Southwest Africa himself and also did not want German East Africa, now the British mandate of Tanganyika, returned either.[45] In fact, the Union government had just reiterated its determination to maintain control of Southwest Africa and would continue to do so, while indicating a willingness to pay Germany monetary compensation that the latter did not want.[46] Just precisely what the Germans did want other than lots of concessions in and outside Europe they were never prepared to specify, as will be recounted, but the Dominion leaders knew that Germany had various vaguely defined demands.[47]

The Commonwealth prime ministers strongly urged that Britain use her influence to pressure Czechoslovakia into concessions to its German minority, arrange some colonial concessions, and recognize the Italian conquest of Ethiopia.[48] Ray Atherton, the second man in the American embassy in London, summarized the import of the conference to Jay Pierrepont Moffat, chief of the European division of the Department of State, in terms the latter recorded in his diary:

> He said that the attitude of the Dominions at the Imperial Conference had made a very deep impression on the English Cabinet; that in effect the Dominions had said you fought once before to protect yourself from a threat in the low countries; we agree that this is a vital interest and would be prepared to help you again in that field. On the other hand, we would not be prepared to help if you became involved in Eastern Europe. As you cannot destroy Germany, make friends with her and if necessary buy her off in Eastern Europe.[49]

44. In addition to the records cited above, see C 3562, C 4135/37/18, FO 371/20221; C 2124/270/18, FO 371/20734, ff.55–56.

45. C 989/37/18, FO 371/20721. A tiny portion of German East Africa had been turned over to Portugal, a substantial piece had become a Belgian mandate, but most of it had become a British mandate.

46. *G.D.*, C, 6, Nos. 403, 500, 563; D, 1, No. 15; C 209/37/18, FO 371/20718.

47. Lord Lothian had sent all the Dominion prime ministers his report on his talks with Hitler, Göring, and Schacht in early May 1937.

48. U.S. Ambassador Bingham to Hull, 16 June 1937. Roosevelt's comment (of 7 July) was that this was "discouraging" (Library of Congress, Cordell Hull Papers, Folder 99-A).

49. Moffat Diary, 29 July 1937, Moffat Papers, vol. 39. To Moffat's comment that "it seemed that the tail was wagging the dog," Atherton responded that "one sensed the feeling that Britain had to take her Dominions into account in developing their policy or else weaken the bonds of Empire."

It should be noted that this attitude of the Dominions was known in Germany. The South African government relayed its impressions of the conference to Berlin, not only through conversations between Prime Minister Hertzog and the German minister in Pretoria, but also through the contacts of Oswald Pirow, the South African minister of defense, who had long been an advocate of concessions to Germany and who would still describe himself as a convinced adherent of National Socialism long after the Second World War.[50] The Union's secretary of state for external affairs even told the German minister that the Union would not go to war with Germany and had so informed the London government.[51]

The pressure of the Dominions, most strongly by South Africa but to a considerable degree by the others as well, was indeed understood in Berlin.[52] When Hitler referred to the divisions within the Commonwealth as restraining British intervention in Central Europe during the famous conference of 5 November 1937, he had substantial grounds for that opinion. The warning about the cohesion of the Commonwealth, if eventually it *did* come to war, that Canadian Prime Minister Mackenzie King had given Hitler on 29 June was disregarded as it did not fit in with the dictator's preconceptions.[53] The fears of the Dominions reinforced those of England and may be regarded as the British equivalent of the weakening effect that the horrendous and apparently vain suffering of World War I was having on the morale of the French.

This brings the survey back to Europe, where Germany stood unchallenged and still growing in strength. The initiative lay with her, and other countries would react to her measures or their fears and expectations of what those measures might be. This meant that during 1937 Germany could make her preparations as she saw fit for the execution of policies of her own choosing, policies which could involve either seizing

50. "I still support National Socialism because I consider it the appropriate form of government. I do not allow myself to be confused by the horror stories which are spread about National Socialism" (Pirow statement of 16 November 1961, Institut für Zeitgeschichte, Zeugenschrifttum [hereafter cited as IfZ, ZS] 283). See also Watt, *Personalities and Policies,* pp. 404ff.

51. *G.D.,* C, 5, No. 580.

52. Dertinger, "Informationsbericht Nr. 103," 1 July 1937, Bundesarchiv, Brammer, Z.Sg. 101/31, f.5. For British awareness that leaks from the Imperial Conference had encouraged Germany, see R 5224/770/67, FO 371/21140; R 4236/4067/67, FO 371/21141. For French knowledge of this encouragement to Germany, see *D.D.F.,* 2d, 6, No. 15; cf. ibid., No. 22.

53. Mackenzie King had promised the British Dominions secretary, Malcolm MacDonald, on 22 June that he would warn Hitler to this effect (C 6349/5187/18, FO 371/20750, f.354), and the record shows that he did so (C 5187/5187/18, FO 371/20750). It is obvious, however, that the Canadian prime minister was favorably impressed (C 6349/5187/18, FO 371/20750, ff.350–51). See also *G.D.,* C, 6, Nos. 370, 425. For a general survey of German-Canadian relations, based to a considerable extent on Canadian archives, see Fritz Genzel, "Die deutsch-kanadischen Beziehungen," in Manfred Funke (ed.), *Hitler, Deutschland und die Mächte: Materialien zur Aussenpolitik des Dritten Reiches* (Düsseldorf: Droste, 1977), pp. 327–38.

the initiative when it suited her or taking advantage of opportunities created by events and the actions of others. The following chapters will show what those preparations were like and to what purposes they were put. They will also show that the course of German policy was not to be substantially affected or diverted by any initiative for a settlement that might be advanced by others in the hope of stabilizing European peace and averting another war.

2 Hitler's Preparations 1937-38

By **1937,** Hitler's general views on Germany's future policy were firmly established, and the basis for implementing that policy was, in his judgment, being assured. Germany was not large enough to feed the existing, to say nothing of an increased, population, and her boundaries must therefore be expanded. That expansion he saw in terms far beyond the borders of 1914, which had been almost as inadequate as those established by the peace settlement. Revision of the Versailles settlement might be a subject of propaganda for consolidating opinion at home or undermining resistance to German moves abroad, but it could never be a guide for policy. In fact, the utilization of the revision theme was a two-edged sword: it might well bring concessions to Germany, but it implied limitations on those concessions, limitations that would hem Germany within borders that were not only too confined but that when broken would reveal the true nature of Hitler's aims. For this reason, general talk about the "wrongs" done Germany must pave the way not for righting those "wrongs" but for a series of wars for which the German people would be psychologically prepared by propaganda and the militarization of German life at the same time as the will of others to resist was being undermined by promises and threats.[1]

Only wars could secure for Germany the vast agricultural lands and areas providing raw materials she needed, but Hitler thought of such wars as entirely different from the last great conflict. It was this difference in the conception of war that gave him an advantage in foreign policy even as it would lead to trouble with some of his military leaders. Almost everyone else could conceive of another war only as a

1. Weinberg, *Foreign Policy,* chap. 1.

repetition of the recent conflict. Abroad, fear of such a disaster would incline potential enemies to great concessions in the hope of averting it, while attuning what military plans and preparations they did make to precisely that type of holocaust. Inside Germany, most of the military leaders also believed that another war, if it came, would be most likely to follow such a pattern; this was what made many reluctant to run the risk of a general war which they feared Germany would lose in the end as she had lost the last one.[2]

This was also the concern that led some of them, and of these General Georg Thomas, the leading specialist in the relationship of the economy to military affairs, was the most articulate, to argue that Germany ought to make her own military preparations conform to the needs of that kind of war—that is, to direct *all* her energies and resources to the establishment of a broad basis for a war of attrition. Few had wanted or expected that sort of war before 1914, but Germany had lost in part, it was thought, because her preparations had not been oriented toward the type of war she had in the event been obliged to fight and would surely be forced to fight if war came to Europe once more. There were, however, three fatal flaws in this point of view. In the first place, during the time it would take Germany to make adequate preparations of this kind, her potential enemies could easily catch up with the head start Germany's rushed rearmament had provided. Second, the reason that they would be likely to get ahead of Germany was that their economic base was already broader than Germany's—the very factor that had made a war of attrition so fatal for Germany in the past and would make it equally fatal in any future conflict. Finally, the kind of total internal economic mobilization required by preparation for a war of attrition would surely remind the German people of their former experience with such a project and could therefore be exceedingly detrimental to German morale.

The wars that Hitler had in mind, however, were of an entirely different type.[3] He was as doubtful of Germany's ability to win a war of attrition from her existing base as were most of his advisers, but he never meant to become involved in that kind of war. He neither wanted nor expected nor planned for such wars; even the later war against England that would follow German domination of continental Europe would be decided by the clash of battleships, not mutual strangulation by blockade.[4] For his first wars, he wanted to build up a quick and substantial head start over others in rearmament—a rearmament in breadth rather than depth—and to utilize the temporary military superiority in a short, isolated war that

2. One could add that this concern also affected German as well as French and British military thinking once war had started in 1939.

3. Weinberg, *Foreign Policy*, pp. 348–56.

4. See Jost Dülffer, *Weimar, Hitler und die Marine* (Düsseldorf: Droste, 1973), pp. 306 and 383ff., for Hitler's agreement with Raeder that submarines would be an important but essentially subordinate part of a German navy dominated by battleships, cruisers, aircraft carriers, and destroyers.

would strengthen Germany for the next such war by broadening her population or industrial base, giving her forces useful experience, and terrorizing potential opponents.

Such a policy—the *Blitzkrieg* theory—required two things: rapid rearmament and isolation of potential opponents. If the former fell into the sphere of domestic and the latter into that of foreign policy, the integral relationship of the two should not be overlooked. The specific requirements of Hitler's view of war for German rearmament and for Germany's relations with other countries must be discussed separately only because the sources and the issues make it convenient to do so. Most of this chapter will be devoted to rearmament needs, and subsequent chapters will deal with aspects of the foreign relations.

One should mention, however, that at least a few contemporary observers recognized Hitler's intentions. The British military attaché in Berlin reported at the beginning of 1937 that the German army was being prepared to fight both in the east and in the west in a series of "select little wars." The Foreign Office comments on this report point out the dilemma such a policy would create for the maintenance of collective security: the aggressor could start a little war and thereby shift the responsibility, if it turned into a big one, onto the friends of peace.[5] It was, of course, Hitler's hope and expectation, to be reinforced by threats and propaganda adapted to each occasion, that no one would be willing to assume that awesome responsibility.

The rearmament program Hitler wanted was then not merely one of increasing the size of the armed forces allowed Germany by the peace treaty. Internal restructuring of German society and its outlook would provide not only the basis for larger armed forces but the willingness to use those forces ruthlessly. The first years of National Socialist rule were designed to bring about this transformation of German society, and Hitler could feel confident by 1937 that much of it had indeed been accomplished.[6]

Even the potentially most difficult of the internal problems, the struggle with the Christian churches, did not substantially hamper the process.[7] The denunciation of the National Socialist regime in the papal encyclical "Mit brennender Sorge" ("On the Condition of the Catholic Church in the German Reich") in March 1937, though damaging German-Vatican relations, did no more than embarrass the government temporarily.

5. Memorandum by the British Military Attaché in Berlin, 25 January 1937, C 972/136/18, FO 371/20731. The Foreign Office wanted this report printed and circulated; the War Office objected because it considered the report too "political."

6. The best account of this process is in Karl Dietrich Bracher, Wolfgang Saur, and Gerhard Schulz, *Die nationalsozialistische Machtergreifung,* 2d ed. (Cologne: Westdeutscher Verlag, 1962).

7. John S. Conway, *The Nazi Persecution of the Churches, 1933–45* (London: Weidenfeld & Nicholson, 1968).

Without formally denouncing the concordat signed in 1933, Hitler simply went ahead with his policy of a step-by-step throttling of Christianity, which might otherwise compete with National Socialism's claim on the total allegiance of the German people.[8] There would be no ideological competition on the road to war.

Preparing for the wars Hitler anticipated fighting had implications for the size and composition of Germany's military establishment. In the first place, it must be big; big by comparison with the *standing forces* rather than the *reserves* of other countries, because Hitler expected to fight short wars in which the forces available at the outset, not the reserves that could be mobilized in a long drawn-out struggle, would be decisive. Rudolf Nadolny, the German delegate to the disarmament conference, had in April 1933 revealed Germany's intention of building up a standing army of 600,000.[9] If Hitler allowed a professional diplomat, whose advice he frequently ignored and whom he soon after let resign, to know this much of his intentions, the figure—which equaled the 1933 standing armies of France, Poland, and Czechoslovakia combined—must be taken as the lower limit of his original concept.[10]

The policy of rapidly building up a very large standing army, furthermore, would minimize the disadvantage of the Versailles requirement that Germany keep its soldiers on long-term enlistments, with a resulting (and intended) absence of large, trained reserves. That absence might retard the first stages of rearmament but would soon lose its significance in a situation where those who had—or would have had—their military training a decade earlier would not be called up anyway. It is in this context that the continuous pressure for building up the size of Germany's army with which Hitler hurried on his generals must be seen.

More than mere size, however, was affected by Hitler's views. There were implications for the composition of Germany's armed forces. If the military stalemate of the World War were to be avoided, the specific form which that stalemate had taken—the balance of offensive and defensive capability in trench warfare—had to be surmounted. Of the devices utilized during the war in efforts to break the stalemate, the artillery barrage in its various forms, gas canisters and shells, tunneling, airplanes, and tanks, the last two seemed the most likely means of shortening the war of the future.

8. The documentation for the crisis in German-Vatican relations is extensive; see the suggestions for further reading in Charles F. Delzell (ed.), *The Papacy and Totalitarianism between the Two World Wars* (New York: John Wiley, 1974); *G.D.*, C, 4, Nos. 482, 503; 6, Nos. 108, 215, 231, 242, 251, 260, 261, 271, 272; D, 1, Nos. 633–42, 647, 651, 661, 667–69, 671–73, 676–82, 684, 686, 705; 7, p. 516; Friedrich Engel-Jánosi, *Vom Chaos zur Katastrophe* (Vienna: Herold, 1971), pp. 174–76, 284–86.

9. Weinberg, *Foreign Policy,* p. 161.

10. No precise figures appear in Hitler's own earlier comments; he refers to a "decisive land power" and "vast military power" in Gerhard L. Weinberg (ed.), *Hitlers zweites Buch* (Stuttgart: Deutsche Verlags-Anstalt, 1961), p. 163.

Hitler himself was always enormously interested in problems and aspects of motorization. From the earliest years of political activity to his nightly ramblings during World War II, the subject fascinated him; he referred to it in 1928 as the "general motorization of the world, a matter of immeasurable significance for the future."[11] He not only roared around Germany in big automobiles, he campaigned repeatedly by airplane; and in this respect, the opening of the famous propaganda film "Triumph of the Will" by Hitler's arrival at the Nuremberg party rally by airplane quite accurately reflects an important theme in the Führer's life. It is no coincidence that of the few German generals with whom Hitler developed any close personal relationship and who reciprocated with strong sympathy for national socialism, the most prominent were Heinz Guderian, the advocate of armored warfare, and Albert Kesselring, the air force leader.[12]

The armored units of the German army were organized not as support groups integrated into regular infantry divisions—the fatal error of the French army in the face of the warnings of Charles de Gaulle—but as separate armored divisions, provided in 1937 with the first corps headquarters ever responsible solely for armored units.[13] The building of the air force had been entrusted to Hitler's friend and associate Herman Göring, an air ace in the war who had surrounded himself as much as possible with friends of similar background.[14] Together—knowing they had Hitler's full backing—Göring and his associates pushed forward with the rapid development of aircraft production, training units, active squadrons, and extravagantly elaborate headquarters buildings.[15]

The hurried buildup of the *Luftwaffe* was a means both of frightening

11. Ibid., p. 123; cf. Paul Kluke, "Hitler und das Volkswagenprojekt," *Vierteljahrshefte für Zeitgeschichte*, 8, No. 4 (October 1960), 341–83.

12. Clear traces of this affinity, combined with a distaste for the "old-fashioned" other generals, can be found in the postwar apologias of both: Heinz Guderian, *Erinnerungen eines Soldaten* (Heidelberg: Vowinckel, 1951), and Albert Kesselring, *Soldat bis zum letzten Tag* (Bonn: Athenäum, 1953); see also Müller, *Das Heer und Hitler*, p. 47. It was precisely this mutually understood relationship of loyalty and sympathy that made it possible for both men to retain Hitler's confidence in World War II in spite of differences on specific military questions that led Hitler to distrust others. Within the military as in the party hierarchy, Hitler was quite willing to tolerate differences as long as he was convinced of an individual's subjective loyalty to himself.

13. A brief summary in Larry H. Addington, *The Blitzkrieg Era and the German General Staff, 1865–1941* (New Brunswick, N.J.: Rutgers University Press, 1971), chap. 2. Such actions were taken by the French military attaché as sign of an intended attack on Czechoslovakia as soon as Germany was ready (*D.D.F.*, 2d, 5, No. 151).

14. Studies of the development and fate of the German air force before and during World War II have never adequately taken into account this very important personal factor in which Ernst Udet, Karl-Heinz Bodenschatz, Bruno Lörzer, Josef Veltjens, and others must be considered. There is a beginning in Edward L. Homze, *Arming the Luftwaffe: The Reich Air Ministry and the German Aircraft Industry, 1919–39* (Lincoln: University of Nebraska Press, 1976).

15. In spite of its apologetic tone, Karl-Heinz Völker, *Die Deutsche Luftwaffe 1933–1939* (Stuttgart: Deutsche Verlags-Anstalt, 1967) remains useful. Homze's work is far more substantial.

potential enemies into concessions without war[16] and of gaining a speedy
victory if war came by making possible sudden overwhelming attacks on
both military and civilian targets. We know now that the capabilities of
airpower were enormously overrated during the interwar years, but
contemporary expectations and terrors were very real.[17] And for those
who needed to have their expectations enhanced or their terrors exaggerated, the use of German planes in the destruction of Guernica, the holy
city of the Basques, in the spring of 1937 would serve as a shocking
stimulus at the time, with a frightening reminder in Pablo Picasso's famous painting. The first important memoirs of a German air force general
published after World War II were entitled "Trump or Bluff? Twelve
Years of the German Air Force."[18] Replacement of the word "or" by
"and" would provide an accurate description of the mission Hitler assigned his air force.

A most important by-product of the emphasis on motorization and the
largest possible air force was the extent to which it increased the difficulties of Germany's economic position. With no domestic sources of
natural rubber and almost no oil wells, Germany faced the problem of
either finding ways to finance vast imports of rubber and petroleum products or deriving these critical materials synthetically from raw materials
plentiful within her borders. The former meant dependence on foreign
trade; the latter a vast new industrial undertaking. The establishment of
the Four-Year Plan in 1936 and the appointment of Göring as its head
show how Hitler meant to answer this question.[19]

The Four-Year Plan took over the rudimentary synthetic oil and rubber
industries already in existence and expanded them rapidly, if not always
efficiently.[20] The accounts, which, with considerable justification,
criticize the deficiencies in these programs and stress the extent to which
they failed to cover Germany's total needs of the key raw materials they
were to provide, have overlooked three very significant aspects of the

16. Note Hitler's comment in June 1931 that Göring had told him that a few squadrons of
bombers over London—if it came to it—would suffice to have the English raise a white flag
and that the same thing held true for Paris (Edouard Calic [ed.], *Ohne Maske: Hitler-Breiting
Geheimgespräche 1931* [Frankfurt/M: Societäts-Verlag, 1968], p. 95). See also Homze, pp.
54–56, 106.
17. The persistence of myths about the effectiveness of air bombardment after the experience of World War II into the Vietnam conflict and beyond deserves, but awaits, its own
historian.
18. Herbert Joachim Rieckhoff, *Trumpf oder Bluff? 12 Jahre deutsche Luftwaffe* (Geneva:
Interavia-Verlag, 1945).
19. See above, n.3. The decision to try to improve domestic aircraft engine production,
rather than import engines, had been taken for similar reasons earlier (Homze, pp. 82ff.).
20. Dieter Petzina, *Autarkiepolitik im Dritten Reich: Der nationalsozialistische Vierjahresplan* (Stuttgart: Deutsche Verlags-Anstalt, 1968); Wolfgang Birkenfeld, *Der synthetische Treibstoff 1933–1945* (Göttingen: Musterschmidt, 1964). Petzina's analysis of the
financing of synthetic rubber (pp. 84–85) shows that considerations of military needs were
vastly more important than those of conserving foreign exchange. Homze, pp. 142ff., covers
the impact for the aircraft industry.

issue. In the first place, the needs themselves were steadily and rapidly rising as more motorization and a larger air force automatically required more rubber and oil. Any production level measured against a rising rather than a fixed demand level is likely to look inadequate even if substantial progress has been made and considerable technical experience with new processes acquired by a growing corps of experts. Second, the intended use of military power as a means of first threatening war and then fighting brief wars against selected and isolated enemies would reduce the importance of great stocks of supplies. One could give the impression of vast preparations and, if it came to war, one would have the ability to launch a vigorous first blow. Finally, in synthetic materials as in arms production and army expansion, the first stages are slow and cumbersome; dramatic results do not appear for years, and some of the early delays turn out to be blessings in disguise as they permit modifications of design or correction of other early mistakes.

The activities of the Four-Year Plan, moreover, were by no means limited to production of synthetic oil and rubber. A great variety of other projects was undertaken; but only three spheres of action became important and need to be discussed here: the production of synthetic fibers, the working of low-grade iron ore, and the effort to increase food production. Germany imported great quantities of fibers and pushed the output and use of synthetics in order to reduce her dependence on foreign suppliers and to conserve available foreign exchange for the importation and stockpiling of such strategic materials as nonferrous metals.[21] Some progress was made in this field, even if the dramatically successful competition of synthetic with natural fibers still lay in the future.

Certainly one of the most critical deficiencies of the German economy from the point of view of preparing for and waging war was the dependence on imports of Swedish iron.[22] As long as Germany controlled the Baltic Sea in the summer and could secure shipments along the Norwegian coast when the Gulf of Bothnia was frozen in the winter, all was well; but here was an obvious vulnerability. In this regard, there was, or at least appeared to be, the possibility of reducing dependence on imports by the massive utilization of low-grade domestic ores which would have the additional advantage of requiring less foreign exchange.

The expansion of Germany's iron and steel industry on the basis, at least in part, of greater exploitation of low-grade domestic ores was vehemently opposed by the leaders of German industry for two main reasons. In the first place, there could be no question that the utilization of what the industrialists referred to derogatively as "potting soil" *(Blumenerde)*

21. A summary in Petzina, pp. 86, 100–101.
22. On this subject, see Jörg-Johannes Jäger, *Die wirtschaftliche Abhängigkeit des Dritten Reiches vom Ausland dargestellt am Beispiel der Stahlindustrie* (Berlin: Berlin Verlag, 1969).

would require enormous capital investments for the production of preposterously expensive and necessarily noncompetitive steel products.
For an industry that had long played a key part in Germany's export
trade, this price problem was naturally a matter of great importance.
Second, the idea of a great increase in steel making capacity right after
several years in which the depression had left much of Germany's—and
other countries'—capacity idle, looked like an unreasonably risky policy
to men who were quite happy to see their existing plant utilized to capacity because of huge armaments contracts but doubted that such a situation
would continue indefinitely, and especially if capacity were further expanded.[23] Had the leaders of the Third Reich read the orthodox Marxist
analyses of national socialism as a tool of monopoly capitalism, they
would presumably have capitulated in the face of this opposition; but they
were, in fact, not hampered by such theories. As Göring explained to the
leaders of Germany's iron and steel industry on 17 March 1937, Hitler
considered it essential that Germany's domestic ores be utilized to an
extent sufficient to cover her needs in wartime;[24] and when his listeners
did not take this seriously, Göring moved forward on his own, leaving
Germany's industrial magnates to learn of the key decisions from the
newspapers.

On 15 July 1937 the "Reichswerke Hermann Göring" company was
established, with the German government providing the initial capital.
The industrialists were informed of this a week later and given the option
of cooperating or being left out. As for the management of what came to
be one of Europe's largest firms, Göring had a bureaucracy ready at hand.
The Prussian state ministry had no real functions to perform in the Third
Reich and was at Göring's disposal in his capacity as Prussian prime
minister. The agency that had once been Otto von Bismarck's tool in the
unification of Germany thus ended up in charge of excavating and processing "potting soil." Though all the extravagant goals set for Göring's
enterprise were not met, it performed a large and increasing role in Germany's preparations for and eventual conduct of war.[25]

23. A discussion of this issue from the point of view of the Vereinigte Stahlwerke, based
on the archives of the August Thyssen-Hütte, gives some (rather one-sided) information
about these problems. Wilhelm Treue and Helmut Uebbing, *Die Feuer verlöschen nie:
August Thyssen-Hütte 1926–1966* (Düsseldorf: Econ-Verlag, 1969), pp. 76ff.
    24. "Sitzung des Arbeitskreises der eisenschaffenden Industrie am 17.3.1937," Nurem-
berg document NI-090, National Archives.
    25. A history of the "A.G. für Erzbau und Eisenhütten Hermann Göring" and its succes-
sor organizations is greatly needed; for an introduction see Petzina, pp. 104–8, and Matthias
Riedel, *Eisen und Kohle für das Dritte Reich: Paul Pleigers Stellung in der NS-Wirtschaft*
(Göttingen: Musterschmidt, 1974). For a perceptive analysis of the meaning of Göring's new
powers in the economic field, see François-Poncet's report of 29 July 1937 in *D.D.F.*, 2d, 6,
No. 296. Some useful material is summarized in Anja E. Bagel-Bohlan, *Hitlers industrielle
Kriegsvorbereitung, 1936 bis 1939* (Koblenz: Wehr & Wissen, 1975).

The last major field that needs to be mentioned is the agricultural one. Here the corporative approach to economic and social issues had led to the creation of the *Reichsnährstand*, the Reich Food Estate, as the organization of all involved in agriculture.[26] Headed by the racialist dreamer R. Walther Darré, this organization had concentrated on maintaining the supposedly racially valuable peasantry on the land and raising the undoubtedly depressed prices of agricultural products. In Germany, as elsewhere during the years of the depression, the latter objective was seen as involving at least to some extent a *limitation* of production; only if the surplus stocks glutting the market were reduced could prices and farm income recover. Given the German need for food imports, this was potentially risky from the point of view of National Socialist foreign trade policy. And even before Göring assumed an increasing role in agricultural affairs from March 1937 on, the Reich Food Estate devoted considerable attention to *increasing* agricultural production—though most of the resulting increment was taken up by the increase in population that the regime was also stimulating as much as possible.[27] What was referred to as the "Battle of Food Production" *(Ernährungsschlacht)* was fought inside Germany indecisively until by military conquest she could impose starvation on others.

Thus with major emphasis on enormous investments in synthetic oil and rubber complexes, with an elaborate program in a variety of other areas including iron and steel, synthetic fibers, and other materials, the Four-Year Plan moved forward in 1937 and 1938 in the development and implementation of schemes to prepare Germany for the type of short war Hitler wanted to wage, and by which he expected to add to Germany areas that contained those raw materials she lacked and could not fully replace with synthetics.[28] These steps ran directly counter to the policies Hjalmar Schacht advocated, causing Schacht to give up the ministry of economics in the fall of 1937.[29] Göring's triumph, signalized by the appointment of his stooge Walther Funk as Schacht's successor, was complete. In foreign trade policy, this meant rejection by Germany of any participation in the world raw materials conference held at Geneva in 1937. Though proclaiming herself a "have-not" nation, Germany was interested in conquering, not sharing, the world's wealth; and Hitler forbade any German role in cooperative international approaches to the problem of access to adequate supplies of raw materials.[30]

26. See Bracher, pp. 647ff.
27. Summary in Petzina, pp. 91–96.
28. The best account is in Berenice A. Carroll, *Design for Total War: Arms and Economics in the Third Reich* (The Hague: Mouton, 1968), chaps. 5 and 7.
29. For Schacht's contemporary account of his resignation to an old acquaintance, Ernst Jaeckh, who passed on this account to the British government, see C 6900/3/18, FO 371/20711 (which went to the PM). Published documents are in *TMWC*, 36:282–91, 549–64, 567–78; *G.D.*, C, 6, No. 357.
30. The documentation on this issue and Germany's refusal to take part in any international approach to it is extensive. See *U.S.*, 1937, 1:638, 804–5, 806, 809, 819; *G.D.*, C, 6,

The policy line set by Hitler and implemented under Göring's direction also precluded any serious discussion by the German government of the colonial question. The details of this will be examined in the next chapter, but its relationship to the economic policy of preparation for a series of short continental wars should be noted here. Schacht had quite seriously, even if mistakenly, thought of colonies as at least a partial answer to Germany's trade and economic problems. He hoped for a revived German colonial empire, especially in West Africa, a region flowing with cocoa and vegetable oil if not with milk and honey. In the international setting of 1936–37, however, any such program presupposed German concessions in Europe; and Schacht's schemes would founder on Berlin's total unwillingness even to consider that possibility in 1937, just as they had been checked for the same reason in 1936.[31] German policy was oriented toward aggression, not concessions, in Central Europe, and her economic policy was to be oriented toward preparing for that. The organizational chaos in the economic field, even more pronounced in 1937 than in earlier and later years,[32] must be seen as the aftermath of Hitler's decision, foreshadowed in the establishment of the Four-Year Plan in 1936, to reject both the limiting of military production advocated by Schacht and the total mobilization of the economy urged by Thomas. The adopted line was rather to steer a course of rapid preparation in specific areas that would give Germany the means to fight the type of wars Hitler intended, wars that required limited autarchy through synthetics to make possible total autarchy by conquest.

The difficulties of a substantive as well as an organizational kind that existed during this period of internal turmoil were noticeable inside Germany and observed by other powers. The observations pointed to problems in the German economy that were largely self-created.[33] Inside Germany, the warnings of Schacht, Thomas, and others had the opposite effect from what they intended; as Berenice Carroll has aptly stated: "As the strain on the Germany economy increased in the late nineteen-thirties, . . . Hitler only grew the more certain that his own analysis was

---

Nos. 139, 334, 509; William E. Dodd, Jr., and Martha Dodd (eds.), *Ambassador Dodd's Diary* (New York: Harcourt Brace, 1941), 23 February 1937, p. 386; Dertinger, "Informationsbericht Nr. 62," 27 January 1937, Bundesarchiv, Brammer, Z.Sg. 101/30, ff.131–35; Memorandum on raw materials for Lord Halifax, 9 February 1937, C 1282/37/18, FO 371/20719. The German foreign ministry had agreed with Schacht in urging German participation (*G.D.*, C, 6, No. 113). The vast attention given to the problem at the time illustrates the extent to which the alleged economic roots of Germany's complaints were taken seriously, the expectation being that her policies would become more moderate if her "grievances" were met at least in part.

31. Weinberg, *Foreign Policy*, pp. 280–81.

32. Berenice Carroll used as a title for her chapter (8) dealing with this subject a quotation from Hugh R. Trevor-Roper: "A Confusion of Private Empires."

33. See, e.g., *D.D.F.*, 2d, 4, No. 243; *Hungarian Documents*, 1, Nos. 237, 324; Memorandum of Sir Robert Vansittart, 6 July 1937, C 5933/665/18, FO 371/20733.

correct: Germany could never achieve 'world power' with her own economic resources—she must expand them through conquest.''[34]

Before the development of the military basis for war inside Germany in
1937–38 can be examined further, it is necessary to show briefly how
Hitler's concept, with its refusal to consider the possibility of concessions
that might bring the return of colonies that Schacht wanted for economic
reasons, also temporarily cut across the strategic concepts of the German
navy.[35] Dedicated to the belief that Germany could win another war—
seen as waged first against France and the Soviet Union—only by an
offensive strategy against the Atlantic and Mediterranean supply routes of
France, the leaders of the German navy were convinced of the necessity
of acquiring bases outside Germany's limited coastline, bases from which
surface warships and submarines could attack those supply routes. They
hoped to seize some of these bases by surprise attack with combined
forces, the lightly defended French colonial possessions in North and
Central America being considered prime candidates for such operations.
The commander-in-chief of the German navy, Admiral Erich Raeder,
however, hoped that these potential conquests would be supplemented by
bases acquired before the outbreak of hostilities through negotiations with
friendly powers—here he thought of Portugal and Franco Spain—and by
the return of colonies to Germany.[36] While Schacht wanted the Cameroons to ease Germany's shortages of raw materials, the German navy
based its examination of naval strategy in wartime in the winter of 1937–38
on the assumption that the Cameroons would have been returned to Germany before a war started and would provide a naval base for operations
in the Atlantic.[37]

These ideas could not yet influence Hitler, and, furthermore, the navy
could at this time secure neither priority in armaments production for
naval construction nor full control of naval aviation.[38] On all these issues,
Hitler's insistence on a rapidly built up army and air force in line with his
own strategic concepts gave strength and success to the opponents of the
navy in the internal squabbles of the spring and summer of 1937. He

34. Carroll, p. 104. She also notes the irony in Thomas's gloomy memoranda probably
serving to spur Hitler on or to hasten his timetable when Thomas had intended the opposite.
This type of explanation appears to me to be more plausible than the concept of internal
concern over trouble with the working class discussed in the works of Timothy Mason.

35. The best survey is in Carl-Axel Gemzell, *Raeder, Hitler und Skandinavien: Der
Kampf für einen maritimen Operationsplan* (Lund: Gleerup, 1965); cf. Dülffer, pp. 374–76.

36. Raeder outlined his ideas to Hitler, Rudolf Hess, Lutz Schwerin von Krosigk, Joseph
Goebbels, and Constantin von Neurath on 3 February 1937, Jodl Diary, *TMWC*, 28:350;
excerpts from Raeder's presentation in Gemzell, pp. 49–57, 61–63, 95–96.

37. See Raeder's directive of 3 November 1937 for the "Kriegsspiel 1937/38" cited in
Gemzell, pp. 58–59.

38. On the problem of naval aviation, see in addition to Gemzell, p. 174, the study prepared after World War II: U.S., Office of Naval Intelligence, "German Naval Air, 1933 to
1945: A Report Based on German Naval Staff Documents," 15 January 1947 (Washington:
ONI, mimeographed). All studies of the war at sea stress Germany's deficiencies in this
regard.

pushed the navy to build up its strength—the immediate goal was the fourfold increase over the Versailles tonnage that would still leave it nominally in compliance with the Anglo-German Naval Agreement of 1935—but he was not willing to sacrifice rapid expansion of the army and air force to the material needs of the navy's construction program; that position would not be modified until later.

In only one field could the navy move forward essentially in accordance with its own preferences, which in this instance were largely shared by Hitler: the construction specifications for its ships. Since the initiation of the "pocket battleship" construction program in the Weimar years, these specifications had been oriented toward types suitable for offensive operations in the Atlantic. This aim continued with ships under construction in the mid-1930s, ships designed for attacks on French transoceanic supply routes and fleet action against the French navy being equally, and intentionally, suitable for similar action against Britain. The British Foreign Office and Admiralty with astonishing credulity continued to accept false German notifications of ship specifications as accurate. When asked after World War II, the former British naval attaché in Berlin could only explain his own and his associates' acceptance of false figures for the battleships *Bismarck* and *Tirpitz,* for example, by the fact that Raeder, though an inveterate liar, seemed very sincere, qualities that would stand him in good stead both when on trial and when writing his memoirs.[39] The British were misled enough not only to refrain from carefully checking out such clues to violations as came to them but to negotiate an additional naval agreement with Germany in 1937.[40] Disregarding the restrictions of her naval agreement with Britain, the German navy could move in this one area as its leaders thought best; ship specifications was one field in which it did not have to argue with the army or the air force and about which it was no longer necessary to deceive the German public.[41] Hitler

39. Donald McLachlan, *Room 39: A Study in Naval Intelligence* (New York: Atheneum, 1968), pp. 136–40. It should be noted that Raeder's lies served first to mislead the British, later to exculpate himself at the Nuremberg trial, and finally to provide a basis for German apologias for the German invasion of Norway. For a tabulation of the true as opposed to the announced tonnages of German warships as of 18 February 1938, see *TMWC*, 34:188; cf. Dülffer, p. 313. The inherent problem for Raeder's continuous deceptions was that during the war he wanted to stress that he had always thought and planned for a war with England, while after the war he wanted to prove the opposite. See also Albert Speer, *Spandauer Tagebücher* (Berlin: Propyläen, 1975), p. 472.

40. On this episode, which illustrates the final British attempt to limit the naval arms race on an international basis by a series of bilateral agreements as well as the German interest in building up a navy with pretended but no real regard for treaty limitations, see Donald C. Watt, "Anglo-German Naval Negotiations on the Eve of the Second World War," *Journal of the Royal United Service Institution*, 103 (1958), 201–7, 384–91; Dülffer, pp. 402–6, 410, 413–19; *G.D.*, C, 5, Nos. 571, 638; 6, Nos. 35, 40, 50, 68, 94, 136, 160, 179, 206, 260, 275, 282, 308, 367, 369, 399, 438, 451, 495; *D.D.F.*, 2d, 5, Nos. 15, 69, 81; 6, Nos. 91, 119, 143, 260, 298, 458.

41. The original "pocket battleship" program in the 1920s had been justified to the Reichstag by fairy tales about defending communications with East Prussia to preclude

himself, to be sure, was very interested in these technical matters, but once the concern about international repercussions which had occasionally enforced restraint in the earlier years was dropped, his pressure coincided with the inclination of the navy toward larger ships, heavier gun calibers, and shorter construction times.[42]

The main emphasis of German rearmament in the mid-1930s was concentrated on the air force and the army, with the navy receiving very substantial funds but not priority for the long lead-time required in the construction of large ships. Although Hitler wanted a large fleet in the not too distant future, the air and ground forces at first had priority. The emphasis on the army and air force, however, was also not without problems. While the many technical and organizational issues of rearmament had few implications for long-term policy,[43] the question of the proper command structure over all of Germany's armed forces had some very significant repercussions on policy issues, in part at least because it was never fully resolved in the Third Reich and therefore festered at times in the background and at times in the open.

During the years of the Weimar Republic the problem of how Germany's military forces were to be directed as a whole was not of great importance. There was no legal air force. The army tried, with some success, to assert its complete independence of all outside control. The navy wanted to do the same thing and—though this has been obscured by the emphasis of scholarship and publicity on the army—largely succeeded, at least in regard to planning and personnel. That success was to carry over at least partially into the National Socialist period. Two factors were responsible for the navy's success in both eras. One was the fact that all matters pertaining to the sea were outside the general experience of German government leaders of all parties; this gave the navy a partial immunity to outside interference. The reluctance of outsiders was reinforced by a second element: personal continuity. From 1928 until the end of World War II the German navy had only two chiefs, Admiral Erich

---

domestic and foreign opposition because of their true purpose of offensive naval warfare in the Atlantic.

42. Dülffer, rather than Michael Salewski, *Die deutsche Seekriegsleitung 1935–1945*, 1, *1935–1945* (Frankfurt/M: Bernard & Graefe, 1970), appears to me to understand Hitler's role in these matters correctly. On the trend toward bigger and bigger battleships, see Dülffer, pp. 383–86.

43. It might be argued that one important exception to this was the long-term impact of German emphasis—strongly urged by Hitler—on dive-bombers. Useful for tactical support operations, these planes were unsuited for distant and strategic operations; and the requirement that planes be able to dive-bomb posed technical obstacles to the development of the true four-engined bomber, the obvious long-range bomber type of the 1930s and 1940s. Germany's failure in this field—symbolized by the Heinkel 177 with its four engines mounted in tandem in two nacelles—had an impact on Germany's strategic capabilities, but this was unanticipated. Völker's discussion (pp. 207–9) is unconvincing; Homze, pp. 1–4, 121–28, 163–68, is much better.

Raeder until 1943 and Admiral Karl Dönitz thereafter. Having already served for five years as head of the navy when Hitler came to power, Raeder was in an excellent position to withstand any effort to make him and his naval staff subordinate to any over-all command structure.[44]

If personal continuity on the inside and diffidence about naval matters on the outside protected the navy, personal and political factors would protect the new air force. Hermann Göring was made air minister as well as commander-in-chief of the German air force from the very beginning, and in addition jumped in rank sufficiently to give him rank at first equivalent and later superior to that of the chiefs of the other branches of the armed forces. His cabinet status placed him on a par with war minister Werner von Blomberg, to whom, though not yet equal in rank, he could nevertheless give orders in certain areas as plenipotentiary for the Four-Year Plan. In any case, Göring's personal closeness to Hitler guaranteed that the air force, which was the former's pride and joy even more than the dozens of other agencies he accumulated, would be effectively independent of any military command structure below the chief of state himself.

The importance of these special factors assuring independence to the navy and air force will be seen in the impact of the attempt to establish a central overall command structure upon the relationship between that structure and the command and general staff of the army.[45] As first General Walther von Reichenau and after 1 October 1935 General Wilhelm Keitel together with his chief assistant Alfred Jodl attempted to create an armed forces command structure in the office of the minister of war, there followed a direct clash between them and the commander-in-chief and chief-of-staff of the army. Given the independence of the navy and the air force, the developing "Armed Forces Office" (Wehrmachtamt) with its "National Defense Section" (Abteilung Landesverteidigung) threatened to become a sort of competing army general staff at a higher level. In von Reichenau's time, the conflict was muted, in part because von Reichenau did not build up the National Defense Section to the point where it might, by the number, rank, and qualifications of its officers, be seen as an effective staff for directing German military operations. Whether von Reichenau missed the opportunity because of laziness—he was not a man for organizational busywork—or calculation—he still hoped to become commander-in-chief of the army himself; by the time he was shifted to command Military District VII in October 1935 the chance to do so before the outbreak of war had passed.[46] His successors, the team of Keitel and Jodl, were enthusiastic advocates of a centralized armed forces command structure and moved as rapidly as they could to effectuate that concept.

44. For Raeder's early success in securing direct access to Hitler, see Dülffer, pp. 246–47, 269.
45. The best survey is in Müller, chap. 5.
46. A serious study of von Reichenau is badly needed.

Their efforts produced a major clash with the army leadership in which organizational, ideological, and foreign policy issues were intertwined.[47]

The new team in the Armed Forces Office saw itself as new in more ways than one. They not only wanted to assume the role of staff planners for all the armed forces in theory and the army in practice, they saw the role of such a staff in a different way. The general staff tradition of the Prussian and then German army before, during, and after the World War had insisted on a major advisory role in broad strategic-political matters. The risks to be run, the basic nature of military deployment, and at times even the details of foreign policy had been considered within the proper sphere of general staff advice, if not direction.[48] If there had at times been a dangerously exaggerated tendency toward military control of decisions that were very properly political—a tendency personified by Erich Ludendorff—the orientation of Keitel and Jodl was in the opposite direction. Personally fascinated by Hitler and impressed by the dynamism of his movement, they now wanted the military to operate as a purely technical executive arm of the Führer; they would merely translate his commands as transmitted by the minister of war into formal military directives, the more detailed elaboration of which could then be left to the separate general staffs of the branches of the armed forces. No one along the route, neither they themselves nor most assuredly the staffs of the army, navy, or air force, had any business giving advice about the wisdom or unwisdom of the orders given. If Hitler with the *Führerprinzip*, the leadership principle, had transferred the rule of absolute obedience to superior orders from the infantry company to the political arena, they now wanted it returned to the military establishment at the very top. That in this attempt they would clash with an army leadership insisting on its own responsibility to give advice and weigh risks, and that they would find themselves in full accord with Hitler's preferences was to be expected.[49]

When the first outline for a German surprise attack on Czechoslovakia had gone in 1935 from the Armed Forces Office over von Blomberg's signature to the high command of the army, the army chief-of-staff, General Ludwig Beck, had rejected the whole idea and simply refused to work on it.[50] It was then, and continued to be, his judgment that any such attack would lead to a general war which Germany must lose. In June 1937 the Armed Forces Office once again prepared and von Blomberg issued an

47. The first author who recognized the interrelationship of the policy and organizational issues was Gemzell, but it has been most clearly discussed by Müller.

48. Gordon Craig, *The Politics of the Prussian Army, 1640–1945* (New York: Oxford University Press, 1956).

49. It should be noted that although there was a short clash between Hitler and Jodl in the fall of 1942, Keitel and Jodl both retained Hitler's confidence until 1945, a confidence they reciprocated more than fully.

50. Weinberg, *Foreign Policy*, p. 224. The interpretation of the directive of 1935 given (ibid.) has now been further substantiated in Dülffer, pp. 318–19, and all efforts to pretend that it was of a routine and precautionary rather than aggressive nature can be dismissed.

overall plan for the employment of Germany's armed forces, and once again this created difficulties.[51] The general directive stated that Germany had no need to be concerned about an attack from any quarter because of the opposition to war in almost every country and because of the inadequate preparations for war in the Soviet Union as well as other nations. Germany herself had no intention of launching a general European war, but there were certain specific situations in which she could take the initiative—presumably leading to a limited, not a general war. In addition, there were general deployment plans for a defensive war in the west against France, called "Red," and for an offensive war against Czechoslovakia, called "Green."

When this outline was sent to the high command of the German army, Beck, presumably with the support of the commander-in-chief Werner von Fritsch, simply ignored the portion which called for specific preparations for a German initiative called "Otto," which involved an invasion of Austria if there were an attempt to restore the Habsburgs there. The possibility of restoring Otto von Habsburg to the throne was much discussed at the time,[52] but Beck believed that under the circumstances of 1937 a German invasion of Austria would lead to a general war. Since von Blomberg and his staff had not consulted the army on the basic issue of the risks involved, Beck just disregarded the order.[53] Von Fritsch, moreover, went to the Armed Forces Office in person and complained.[54] He criticized the whole manner in which the Armed Forces Office operated and the way it was issuing orders such as the annual directives for the conduct of war, of which the one for 1937–38 had just come out, without prior consultation between the minister of war and the commander-in-chief of the army.[55] Since there appeared to be little inclination to accept

51. The "Weisung 1937/38" of 24 June 1937 is in *TMWC*, 23:733–45, and Walter Görlitz (ed.), *Generalfeldmarschall Keitel, Verbrecher order Offizier?* (Göttingen: Musterschmidt, 1961) (hereafter cited as *Keitel Papers*), pp. 115–23. It had been discussed in Hitler's presence as early as 27 January 1937 (Jodl Diary, *TMWC*, 28:249–50). A British estimate of German army strength at about this time in C 5456/136/18, FO 371/20731.

52. The subject of a possible Habsburg restoration is covered in chap. 9.

53. Wolfgang Foerster, *Ein General kämpft gegen den Krieg: Aus den nachgelassenen Papieren des Generalstabschefs Ludwig Beck* (Munich: Münchener-Dom Verlag, 1949), p. 63. This does not mean that Beck opposed the *Anschluss;* in 1938 he made the staff preparations when Hitler gave the order under circumstances in which Beck believed it was safe for Germany to move.

54. The date of this meeting between von Fritsch and Keitel was probably 15 July 1937 (see Jodl Diary, *TMWC*, 27:355). The record, from Jodl's papers and initialed by Keitel, is entitled "Ansichten und Äusserungen des Ob.d.H. gegenüber Chef WA (niedergeschrieben unmittelbar nach der Aussprache Juli 1937)," Nuremberg document 1781-PS, National Archives.

55. Von Fritsch also complained about the Armed Forces Office scheme to replace the military district commanders with armed forces commanders (Müller, pp. 231–32). This plan was dropped but later applied to some of the occupied areas in World War II and intended for the colonies Germany hoped to secure in Africa (Gerhard L. Weinberg, "German Colonial Plans and Policies, 1938–1942," *Geschichte und Gegenwartsbewusstsein: Festschrift für Hans Rothfels* [Göttingen: Vandenhoeck & Ruprecht, 1963], p. 487). This was clearly the

this view, von Fritsch further suggested that the minister of war himself take over the command of the army, thereby emphasizing the key role of the army in Germany's military posture, clarifying the command relationships, and—though he did not point this out—bringing von Blomberg into direct contact with the advice he would receive from Beck and the army general staff, not just the drafting assistance of Keitel and Jodl.

The arguments continued through the summer and fall of 1937, at this time focused more on the respective roles of the headquarters of the army and of the Armed Forces Office than on broader policy issues. Although he made a friendly visit to Paris in June 1937, Beck thought of France as Germany's most likely and most dangerous enemy.[56] He was, however, opposed to the risk of any war which was likely to become general, and this meant in effect, though not in theory, practically any war started by Germany at all. The problem of those risks and the probability of incurring them was, of course, in the background of the controversy as Keitel and Jodl argued for their position of unquestioning implementation of whatever inspiration the leader of Germany might pass on to his soldiers. While the argument among the latter over command structure was still in progress—and precluded any really united front among them—Hitler summoned the highest figures in the Reich to a conference at which he voiced the inspirations he wanted implemented.

As the foreign exchange and materials allocation crisis of 1936 had precipitated Hitler's decision to establish the Four-Year Plan in accordance with a detailed exposition of his views on the subject, so problems in the rearmament program led him to expound his views on the tasks immediately ahead to his chief military and foreign policy advisers in November 1937. The immediate occasion was the critical problem of steel allocation: the navy had pointed out to von Blomberg on October 25 that there was no prospect of completing its existing construction program unless there were substantial additional allocations both to firms directly engaged in naval contracts and to new Krupp steel works.[57] Hitler, of course, always saw such economic problems as aspects of Germany's need for *Lebensraum,* and his repeated references to that subject in his speeches in October and November 1937, as well as at the famous conference of 5 November, must be seen in this light.[58]

---

direction Hitler intended to take, but the issue properly belongs in the framework of Hitler's perception of the internal structure of his future empire.

56. On Beck's visit to Paris, see Müller, pp. 634–35; Foerster, pp. 47–49; Hans Speidel (ed.), *Ludwig Beck, Studien* (Stuttgart: K. F. Koehler, 1955), pp. 295–302; *D.D.F.*, 2d, 6, Nos. 94, 152. French General Maurice Gemelin was favorably impressed; and when Sir Orme Sargent in the British Foreign Office commented how the French appeared to get along better with the German general than the Polish colonel [Foreign Minister Josef Beck], Anthony Eden noted that this was not so curious for those who knew the colonel (C 4888/822/17, FO 371/20696).

57. Dülffer, pp. 446–47.

58. Note the reference to *Lebensraum* and the need to solve the problem soon while he himself was still alive in Hitler's talk to propaganda officials in late October 1937 (Max

Hitler's self-confidence had grown; the recent visit of Benito Mussolini, which will be discussed later, surely contributed to this. One of the results of that visit had been the dismissal of Hans Steinacher as head of the Association for Germandom Abroad (Volksbund für das Deutschtum im Ausland, VDA), and the assignment of full and open control over the organizations for those of German descent abroad to the SS. Steinacher had been dropped at Mussolini's request because of his continued support of the German element in South Tyrol in disregard of German promises to Italy; but as General Karl Haushofer explained to Rudolf Hess, the replacement of Steinacher by an SS officer with the obvious implication of total and direct German government control was a step that could be taken only if Germany felt strong enough to take gambles. After almost five years of National Socialist rule Berlin was prepared to run such a risk.[59] The open control of those of German ancestry, in addition to those of German citizenship, living in other countries, which was firmly established in 1937 represents a dropping of pretense as to future policy that can be compared with the open announcement of rearmament in 1935. It shows how secure the German government by then felt its position to be.[60]

When Hitler met with the minister of war, foreign minister, and the chiefs of the three branches of the armed forces, with his military adjutant, Friedrich Hossbach, taking the notes on which to base the record he wrote five days later, the man who controlled Germany gave his own assessment of the current situation and his future plans as far as he cared to reveal them.[61] He described what he was telling them as his considered views, to be looked upon as his last testament if he died—a personal

---

Domarus [ed.], *Hitler, Reden und Proklamationen, 1932–1945* [Neustadt a.d. Aisch: Verlagsdruckerei Schmidt, 1962], 1:745); the discussion of *Lebensraum* in his Augsburg speech of 21 November (ibid., 760); and the secret speech of 23 November (Henry Picker, *Hitlers Tischgespräche im Führerhauptquartier 1941–42* [Bonn: Athenäum, 1951], pp. 443–50).

59. Hans-Adolf Jacobsen (ed.), *Hans Steinacher Bundesleiter des VDA 1933–1937* (Boppard: Harald Boldt, 1970), pp. 380–81, 403–9, 413, 415–16, 469–73; *G.D.,* C, 6, No. 576. Steinacher asserted that if Germany gave up the minority in South Tyrol, no one would take her interest in the Sudeten Germans seriously (Jacobsen, *Steinacher,* pp. 451–53; Dertinger, "Informationsbericht Nr. 147," 23 October 1937, Bundesarchiv, Brammer, Z.Sg. 101/31, ff.341–43).

60. See Hans-Adolf Jacobsen, *Nationalsozialistische Aussenpolitik 1933–1938* (Frankfurt/M: Alfred Metzner, 1968), pp. 234ff., 495ff.; *G.D.,* C, 6, Nos. 141, 504.

61. The memorandum of Hossbach is printed in *G.D.,* D, 1, No. 19, and in *TMWC,* 25:403–13; a supplementary statement by Hossbach is in *TMWC,* 42:222–30. An important source is Hossbach's memoirs, *Zwischen Wehrmacht und Hitler* (Wolfenbüttel: Wolfenbütteler Verlagsanstalt, 1949). Jodl's references to the meeting are in his diary, *TMWC,* 28:355, 356, 376. For detailed analyses, see Müller, pp. 243–45; Walter Bussmann, "Zur Entstehung und Überlieferung der 'Hossbach Niederschrift,'" *Vierteljahrshefte für Zeitgeschichte,* 16, No. 4 (October 1968), 373–84; Hermann Gackenholz, "Reichskanzlei, 5. November 1937," *Forschungen zu Staat und Verfassung: Festgabe für Fritz Hartung* (Berlin: Duncker & Humblot, 1958), pp. 59–84; Peter Kielmansegg, "Die militärisch-politische Tragweite der Hossbach-Besprechung," *Vierteljahrshefte für Zeitgeschichte,* 8, No. 3 (July 1960), 268–74. The account in Deutsch, chap. 3, relies too heavily on the self-serving testimony and memoirs of Admiral Raeder. The silly speculations about postwar alterations of

element that Hitler repeatedly brought into policy discussions.[62] Germany, he asserted, needed space for her population which could not be fed from her present space, even if some of her raw materials needs could be covered. Dependence on world trade would not do; it limited independence and was in any case dubious in a world in which all countries were industrializing.[63] Germany would have to expand by seizing agriculturally useful land. This would involve war, and Germany had to decide where to seize the most with the least risk.

Britain and France would always oppose Germany and would yield no colonies unless they were faced by the threat of superior force. But they were both weaker than ever, Britain because of the process of dissolution of her empire and France because of her internal political troubles.[64] Force alone could solve Germany's problems, and the only questions to be answered were where and how.

In his discussion of the possible answers to these questions, Hitler threw together two types of considerations, the short-term one of "improving our military-political situation" which required the conquest of Austria and Czechoslovakia, and the long-term one of "solving the German space problem." Many have assumed that the two were identical, though it is clear that Hitler did not. He saw the short-term task as preliminary to the other; it would provide added food supply for "5–6 million"—assuming the expulsion of several million Czechs and Austrians—as contrasted with the long-term need to solve the space problem for "about 1–3 generations."[65] The short-term task would help with the bigger one by creating "a shorter better boundary, by freeing troops" and by making possible the recruitment of additional troop units "to the extent of about 12 divisions." The long-term goal of solving Germany's space problem would thus be aided by the prior seizure of Austria

---

the text in Göran Henrikson, "Das Nürnberger Dokument 386-PS (das 'Hossbach-Protokoll')," *Probleme deutscher Zeitgeschichte,* Lund Studies in International History, 2 (1970), 151–94, have been refuted in Bradley F. Smith, *Reaching Judgement at Nuremberg* (New York: Basic Books, 1977), pp. 140–42.

62. See, e.g., the comment recorded on 31 October 1937 that "he probably did not have very much longer to live; in his family the people did not live to an old age" (Domarus, 1:745) as well as his reference at the November meeting to the attitude of Italy depending on whether Mussolini were still alive. Hitler's comments in May and August 1939 were similarly focused on his own and the Duce's lifespan; Hitler's worry about the possibility that he might die before he could start the first of his wars was apparently accentuated by his fiftieth birthday in April of that year. For Hitler's decision to move more rapidly on Czechoslovakia in early May 1938 at the time he thought he was suffering from cancer, see p. 390 below.

63. This was an old theme of Hitler's; see *Hitlers zweites Buch,* p. 60 and n.1.

64. Note Hitler's expression of doubt at François-Poncet's assurance that France was not about to come apart (*D.D.F.,* 2d, 6, No. 250). In a way, Hitler's view of France was similar to Goerdeler's and Beck's perception of Germany: all overestimated the immediate difficulties but correctly saw the basic weaknesses of the two countries.

65. The population of Germany was growing at an annual rate of four to five hundred thousand at this time.

and Czechoslovakia; the troops freed by better borders and the additional divisions recruited in the annexed territory as well as the economic resources of the seized lands would strengthen Germany for its next war.

Hitler argued that the effort to reach the long-term goal would have to be launched by 1943–45; thereafter the odds would shift against Germany as her own stock of weapons became obsolete and her potential enemies rearmed, caught up with Germany, and would then be able to pick *their* time to act.[66] Germany's military forces would *all* have to be ready by 1943–45, therefore, and the decision made in the second portion of this meeting to allocate to the navy the steel it would need reflects Hitler's clear understanding that the long construction time of warships made such a decision necessary at this time if there were to be a substantial fleet ready when he planned to use it.[67] But the short-term goal might be reached much earlier, and Hitler gave a great deal of attention to the prospects and circumstances for that. Hitler thought it possible that the British had already written off Czechoslovakia and would be restrained by the difficulties within their empire and reluctance to become involved in a long European war. His assessment of pacifist sentiment in England and the leakage of information from the Imperial Conference could easily lead to this conclusion.[68] He deduced further that in the absence of British support, France would be unlikely to move in defense of Czechoslovakia. Italy would have no objection to the disappearance of Czechoslovakia; only her attitude in regard to the Austrian question was still uncertain. Poland would not move if Germany succeeded quickly; and the Soviet Union, unlikely to move because of the attitude of Japan, would be precluded from intervening by the speed of Germany's action. If the internal problems of France degenerated into civil war, Germany would move against Czechoslovakia immediately.

66. Any analysis of the incipient rearmament programs of England and France as well as the likelihood of some eventual American effort would suggest that from the perspective of 1937 this was a by no means unreasonable prediction. If Germany could not afford to scrap the stocks of planes and tanks on which her early rearmament program was based, replacing them with newer models even better than those on which Britain and France standardized their late efforts, there was indeed an element of time pressure.

67. Dülffer, pp. 447–51, gives the decisions and cites the appropriate sources. The fact that raw materials were discussed and that new allocations to the navy were decided upon were the only specifics of the meeting that the French ambassador in Berlin learned about at the time (*D.D.F.*, 2d, 7, No. 196).

68. As United States Assistant Secretary of State George S. Messersmith had written on 11 October 1937: "It is the fears of war and the horrors of war which persist in the democratic states, and understandably so, which are paralyzing our action. It is exactly this which the fascist states are deliberately capitalizing.... This fear of war in the democracies which has been accompanied by an extraordinary patience which does them credit may if carried beyond a certain point lead to their ruin.... The dictators hope and are playing their hand on the hope that the patience of the democracies will be carried beyond the point of safety." Messersmith went on to the aspect which led Hitler to set a date for war beyond which he would not wait: "The democracies hope that by the exercise of patience they will wear out the dictatorships and in the meantime are increasing their own strength through rearmament" (*U.S.*, 1937, 1:143–44).

The other potential opportunity for a sudden move might be created by
a war in the Mediterranean between Italy and France or Italy with England and France arising out of the struggle for control of that area or out
of the Spanish Civil War. A possible clash of Italy and France in the
Mediterranean was an idea that Hitler had long contemplated.[69] As for a
war arising out of the Spanish Civil War, this was a possibility on which
Hitler had speculated for some time, and which was in part responsible for
his decision in December 1936 to limit German aid to Franco in the hope
of prolonging the Civil War.[70] He had reaffirmed that position—helping
Franco a little to make sure he did not lose but not sending enough for a
quick and big victory—at the end of March 1937.[71] The possibility that
Germany was egging Italy on to a greater role in Spain in the hope of
precipitating a war between her and the Western Powers of which Germany could then take advantage by action in Central and Eastern Europe
had worried the British government all during 1937.[72] In his talk on 5
November, Hitler's cynical attitude was most explicit: Germany wanted a
long war in Spain, not a quick victory for Franco. To accentuate tension
in the Mediterranean which might precipitate a war between Italy and the
Western Powers, Italy should be urged to stay in the Balearic islands, an
action that could be justified only by the need for Italian assistance to
Franco in a continuing civil war, but that France and England could not
tolerate indefinitely. In fact, when in Rome ten days before, Joachim von
Ribbentrop had told the Italians that Hitler wanted them to keep the island
of Majorca in the Balearics; an assertion that surely reflects instructions
to this effect that von Ribbentrop had received from Hitler before this trip
and that followed the same line as the comments of Hitler to those
gathered on 5 November.[73]

In the discussion which followed, von Blomberg and von Fritsch argued
strongly that Britain and France might not stay out of a war Germany
started in Central Europe, and that Germany was not ready to face them.
Von Neurath expressed doubts about the imminence of a war between
Italy and the Western Powers in the Mediterranean. Hitler maintained his

69. *Hitlers zweites Buch,* p. 178 and n.1.
70. Weinberg, *Foreign Policy,* pp. 297–99.
71. See the entry in Jodl's diary for 30 March 1937, *TMWC,* 28:353.
72. Note that material on this possibility relayed by Norman Ebbutt, the *Times* correspondent in Berlin, was taken seriously in the Foreign Office in April (C 2845/3/18, FO
371/20710) and that in May the Foreign Office sent to the British embassies in Rome and
Berlin information—to be burned after reading—that Hitler and other National Socialist
leaders were speculating on a British-Italian war to enable them to seize what they wished in
Central and Eastern Europe without a war (C 3525/3/18, FO 371/20710).
73. Galeazzo Ciano, *Tagebücher 1937/38* (Hamburg: Wolfgang Krüger Verlag, 1949), 24
October 1937, p. 32. Cf. *G.D.,* D, 1, No. 86. The fact that a war in the Mediterranean did not
take place does not reduce the importance of Hitler's speculations as evidence for his views
and procedures. Clearly he was looking for opportunities to move; some that he anticipated
never came, while others he had not expected did turn up. The critical issue, surely, is
Hitler's intent to take advantage of whatever opportunities he considered suitable for
specific actions he planned to take.

own position; but when von Fritsch suggested that in view of what had been said he ought not to go through with his intended leave, Hitler responded that the probability of war was not quite that close.

In any analysis of this famous meeting several points must be stressed. The general line of argument with which Hitler justified his intention to go to war was the same as the one he had used in public before 1933 and repeatedly afterwards in meetings with his political associates and his military advisers. No one argued at the meeting with his long-term aims. With his short-term aims, no one argued either; all the objections raised dealt with his calculations as to the risks involved. All assumed that the annexation of Austria was a correct aim of German policy.[74] The destruction of Czechoslovakia was similarly considered appropriate. Göring had been preaching it for years.[75] Von Neurath had assured an old friend in March 1937 that Czechoslovakia would have to be destroyed.[76] Von Fritsch explained at the meeting that he was having exercises conducted to explore ways of attacking Czechoslovakia, while von Blomberg and Göring parroted large parts of Hitler's views two weeks later, von Blomberg to Lord Halifax and Göring to William Bullitt. On 20 November, von Blomberg told the British lord president of the council: "The vital questions for Germany with her expanding population and set as she was in the middle of Europe, were those which concerned her Central and Eastern European position. If everybody tried to sit on every safety value, there was bound to be an explosion." The colonial question was secondary, and the Czechs were a bad lot.[77] A few days before, Göring had told the American ambassador to Paris, who was visiting Berlin, that Austria would be annexed as would the Sudeten Germans (without referring to the fate of the Czechs),[78] though a few days later he referred to the destruction of the Czechoslovak state as a whole in his conversations with

74. Hitler had set the policy that Austria would be taken over from the outside, not the inside, some time before; and this was generally understood in the German government (see *G.D.*, D, 1, No. 216). The German minister to Vienna, Franz von Papen, had told the Hungarian minister there in May that both Austria and Czechoslovakia would disappear (*Hungarian Documents*, 1, No. 260, German text in Lajos Kerekes [ed.], "Akten des Ungarischen Ministeriums des Äusseren zur Vorgeschichte der Annexion Österreichs," *Acta Historica*, 7, Nos. 3–4 [1960], 378–79).
75. Weinberg, *Foreign Policy*, p. 318.
76. C 2337/3/18, FO 371/20710 (the friend was Ernst Jaeckh). Von Neurath's violent comments to the Austrian minister to Yugoslavia during his visit to Belgrade in June 1937 also alerted the British Foreign Office to his attitude (R 4087/493/3, FO 371/21118). I am inclined to give greater credence to the views von Neurath expressed in 1937 than to his protestations at the Nuremberg trial as evidence of his opinions at the time.
77. Lord Halifax's record in C 8161/270/18, FO 371/20736, f.341. Note that von Blomberg told Sir Ivone Kirkpatrick, the first secretary of the British embassy in Berlin, that he was afraid he might not have made himself sufficiently clear to Lord Halifax and wanted to repeat that "Germany had an expanding population and her expansion was inevitable. This was a fact. It would remain a fact even if Hitler died or disappeared. England could still sit on all the safety valves, but an explosion would eventually occur and no-one in Germany could prevent it" (ibid., f.345).
78. *U.S.*, 1937, 1:171–72.

the Hungarian prime minister and foreign minister.[79] Even the German
army chief of staff, Ludwig Beck, in his critique of Hitler's views expressed in a memorandum that comments point by point on the record of
the November conference, did not disagree with the aim of annexing
Austria and destroying Czechoslovakia.[80]

What Beck as well as von Fritsch, von Blomberg, and von Neurath
criticized was the assessment by Hitler that Britain and France would stay
out of a war that Germany might start in Central Europe. They doubted
that this was correct and were afraid that Germany would run the risk of a
general war. Beck, furthermore, was appalled at the whole line of reasoning which led Hitler to conclude that war was necessary; but Beck's
view was not shared by any of those present. Von Neurath had his
doubts, which he apparently expressed to Hitler again in January 1938,
but no vigorous argument could be expected from him.[81] As he explained
to Lord Halifax shortly after the conference, "the Nazi system was the
only thing to save Germany."[82]

Raeder said nothing in the first part of the November meeting. Since his
testimony at Nuremberg and his memoirs are unreliable, one can only
assume that he was—as usual—in general agreement with Hitler. On those
occasions when he disagreed or wished to arouse Hitler's interest in
policies and possibilities differing from those already contemplated,
Raeder never hesitated to express himself. The second part of the meeting
which was to deal with the immediate question of raw materials allocation
was the critical one for him, and he could be confident that Hitler's preference for war would bring the decisions the navy wanted—as indeed
happened.

Hitler did, however, have a plan to deal with the danger that some of his
advisers warned about. In this conference, as in all German internal plan-

79. *Hungarian Documents,* 1, No. 313 (German text in Kerekes, pp. 379–82); László
Zsigmond, "Ungarn und das Münchener Abkommen," *Acta Historica,* 6, Nos. 3–4 (1959),
261–62.

80. Beck was shown the memorandum by Hossbach himself since he was acting in von
Fritsch's place during the latter's leave. Beck's memorandum of 12 November 1937 is in the
Bundesarchiv, H 08-28/4, item 52. See the comments in Müller, pp. 249–51, and Deutsch,
pp. 72–74. An important aspect of Beck's memorandum from the historiographic point of
view is that it confirms the accuracy of the transmitted text of the Hossbach memorandum.
Hossbach himself told the three military adjutants about the meeting and read his memorandum to them (see the summary by David Irving of Oberst Nicolaus von Below, "Aufzeichnung aus dem Winter 1948/49; Zwischen Aufstieg und Absturz: Hitler und die
Luftwaffe," p. 3, Munich, IfZ).

As early as the beginning of March 1937 a German officer told the Lithuanian military
attaché in Berlin that Germany would build up her forces until the fall of 1938 and then go
after Czechoslovakia (*D.D.F.,* 2d, 5, No. 58). The general thrust of German plans was
widely understood.

81. Deutsch, pp. 71–72, argues for a firmer stand on von Neurath's part. In April 1937 von
Neurath had told the departing British ambassador, Sir Eric Phipps, that his own position
was secure, and that Hitler had promised to keep him beyond his 65th birthday (2 February
1938), but whether he was really that sure as the date approached is another matter (C
2841/165/18, FO 371/20732). See also *TMWC,* 40:447.

82. C 8161/270/18, FO 371/20736, f.338.

ning on the Czech question, emphasis was always on the destruction of Czechoslovakia as a state, not on the presence of the Sudeten Germans and their fate. On the contrary, as Hitler explained his views at the November meeting, the nationality problem of Czechoslovakia was the presence of *Czechs* who would have to be expelled *(zwangsweise Emigration)*, not Germans who needed help.[83] In the propaganda campaign leading up to what Hitler hoped and expected to be a war only against Czechoslovakia, however, all the stress was on the terrible persecution to which her German and other minorities were allegedly subjected. Such propaganda would assist in the moral and hence diplomatic isolating of Czechoslovakia from that assistance by the Western Powers which Hitler believed unlikely but his advisers claimed to be probable. This campaign will be examined subsequently, but its role as a method of shielding very different aims is certainly clarified by Hitler's comments on 5 November 1937.

There have been efforts since the record of those comments came to light to interpret them away or to pretend that they were unimportant or meaningless. Such efforts are solely of interest for an understanding of the methodology or politics of their authors.[84] They are irrelevant for an understanding of German foreign policy or military planning since none of those present at the meeting or immediately informed of Hitler's wishes could possibly know that there ever would be such a literature; they were much too busy trying to carry out what they took to be the dictator's orders.

Raeder was pleased to have been assured the steel allocations he needed and could now have the naval construction program move forward, especially the building of the larger warships, with the anticipation of added supplies in the future from new steel works for the even more enormous superbattleships planned for later.[85] Just in case the British needed further discouragement from supporting Austria or Czechoslovakia in the immediate future—or did in fact go to war—an immediate speeding up of submarine building was ordered on the very day of the meeting.[86] The new general construction plan for the navy that would reflect the November decisions would take a few weeks to prepare; it was issued on 21 December.[87]

Göring also immediately gave some new directives to the general staff of the air force. Both to assure a uniform approach by all branches of the armed forces—when each was working out its own implementing procedures—and in accordance with their concept of the military as being

83. After von Neurath was appointed *Reichsprotector* of Bohemia and Moravia, he proposed a plan for precisely such expulsions (*TMWC*, 33:252–59).

84. Such works are listed in notes 3 and 4 of the Bussmann's study cited in n.61, above.

85. Dülffer, p. 447.

86. Ibid., pp. 451–53. The critical point is again that of construction time: submarines could be ordered for service about two years later; cruisers and battleships took four to five years (see Rohwer's tabulation, ibid., pp. 570–79).

87. Ibid., p. 455.

purely an instrument and never an adviser of the political leader, Keitel
and Jodl now prepared a supplement to the general war directive of 24
June.[88] Von Blomberg's agreement to this approach, in spite of his reservations at the November meeting, may well have been caused by his
eagerness to utilize an expression of Hitler's will to override all objections
in the high command of the army to the issuance of such general directives. He had run into objections when he had issued these directives on
his own authority; once the revision of his own prior order had been
personally approved by Hitler, it could hardly be resisted without an open
break with the Führer himself.[89] The revision was accordingly prepared in
the Armed Forces Office by 7 December, approved by Hitler on the 13th,
and issued like the navy's new program on 21 December 1937.[90]

The directive of the previous June had left open the possibility of "military exploitation of politically favorable opportunities"; the new formulation called for an "aggressive war against Czechoslovakia." The timing
of such a move Hitler had not yet decided, as his response to von
Fritsch's question about going on leave reveals. The words, the orders,
and the procedures of this whole episode illuminate the combination of
predetermined planning and opportunistic execution in Hitler's approach
to foreign policy; he had picked his goal and alerted his generals to get
ready, but he would move forward as opportunity offered.

While Germany awaited the opportunity, her military forces proceeded
with the planning for aggressive action. The military concepts were fairly
simple. As and when the time was ripe, Austria would be occupied; and it
was not thought likely that this operation would require major military
action. Czechoslovakia, however, was in an entirely different category.
The bulk of Germany's army and air force would be directed against her
with the aim of a quick conquest of Bohemia and Moravia (Slovakia and
the Carpatho-Ukraine being left to presumptive allies, either Hungary or
Poland or both). While that conquest was in process, minimal German
forces would stand on the defensive in the west. If there were any prospect of surprise, the German air force would attack the Western Powers'
air forces at their bases, but otherwise just support the holding action in
the west. More important in supporting that holding action would be
fortifications constructed in the remilitarized Rhineland along Germany's
western frontier. Such fortifications would assist the smaller German
forces there and delay any attacking force until the main German army
could come to the western front after the crushing of Czechoslovakia.
Quite possibly the very existence of the fortifications would reinforce
French disinclination to attack Germany in the west at all, and thus leave

88. Müller, pp. 246–47. Note Jodl's subsequent reference to "Weisungen v. 24.6.
5.11.37. 7.12.37. 30.5.38" in his diary, *TMWC*, 28:376.
89. This probably explains the absence of a reaction by Beck; he was not yet psychologically ready for an open break.
90. *TMWC*, 28:356; 34:745–47; *G.D.*, D, 7:547–51.

France's eastern allies to their fate—a speculation that would prove largely sound.[91]

In a summary report on the German army in the fall of 1937, the British military attaché in Berlin suggested, in agreement with the ambassador, that the German army was strong enough for Germany to be immune to attack herself and that it could be ready to attack others by 1940 or possibly earlier. Only shortages of raw materials or an overthrow of the regime could avert this danger.[92] There were no signs of the latter, although the summer of 1937 did see the first serious contacts between British officials and Carl Goerdeler, who was becoming something of a leader of the opposition to Hitler inside Germany.[93] As for the former possibility, it confronted Britain with the risk of war with Germany when she was lean and angry or fat and ready.[94] As the British pondered this dilemma, the German preparations went forward.

If Hitler was willing to seize such opportunities as might arise to facilitate the annexation of Austria and Czechoslovakia, and to nudge the process if the opportunities did not come soon enough,[95] the occasion to make drastic changes among his military and diplomatic advisers arose, with at least some help from Hitler himself, at the beginning of 1938. On 12 January the German minister of war and commander-in-chief of the armed forces, Field Marshal Werner von Blomberg, married a young woman who turned out to have a police record of morals offenses. While Göring, who had had an important role in facilitating the marriage, hoped to utilize the opportunity he had helped create in order to become minister of war himself, Hitler seized the occasion to rid himself of a whole series of generals and diplomats, take over the position of commander-in-chief of the armed forces himself, and appoint his own special diplomatic sage, Joachim von Ribbentrop, to the post of foreign minister. The details of what has come to be known as the Fritsch-Blomberg crisis need not be

91. The details of German military preparations for the attack on Czechoslovakia will not be reviewed here. Only the broader policy aspects of the military plans will be taken up at appropriate points.

92. See n.94, below.

93. On Goerdeler's conversations in London, where he met with Sir Robert Vansittart, in June 1937, see C 4714, C 4882/165/18, FO 371/20733; Colvin, pp. 149–55. Goerdeler hinted that in a year or so there might be an army-supported government in Germany that would be friendly to Britain, but that Germany's border with Czechoslovakia should be changed and something done about the Polish Corridor. Goerdeler was in the United States in September, and the president was prepared to see him, but there is no record of any meeting in the president's appointment calendar (Dodd letter of 6 September 1937 and related documents in Hyde Park, OF 198-A).

94. C 6212/136/18, FO 371/20731. Eden and Vansittart both preferred the former. It should be noted that General Ironside noted in his diary on 11 October 1937 that his trip to the German maneuvers that fall had convinced him that Hitler would start a war (Roderick Maclead and Denis Kelly [eds.], *Time Unguarded: The Ironside Diaries, 1937–1940* [New York: David McKay, 1962], pp. 31–32).

95. The extent to which Hitler hastened the pace first in the case of Austria and subsequently of Czechoslovakia will be reviewed in chaps. 9–11.

recounted here, but certain aspects of it have an important bearing on the development of German foreign policy.[96]

Almost as soon as von Blomberg's "fault" was called to Hitler's attention, and before anyone had had an opportunity to discuss the matter with him, he decided to dismiss von Blomberg and also to use trumped up charges of homosexuality, that he knew to be false, to dismiss von Fritsch as commander-in-chief of the army. What has often been ignored in the literature on this crisis is that Hitler was perfectly willing to tolerate in his associates and officials all sorts of moral defects of a far more serious kind than the real or imagined ones of the two general officers. The notorious homosexual proclivities of Ernst Roehm had not bothered Hitler; they merely provided a handy additional explanation to give the German public for murdering him after he had for years led the Brown Shirts and had been made a cabinet minister. There can have been few morals charges of which Propaganda Minister Joseph Goebbels was not guilty, as Hitler well knew; but this did not keep Hitler from maintaining Goebbels in office until the end of the Third Reich.[97]

If Hitler, therefore, acted so quickly in the cases of von Blomberg and von Fritsch, it makes no sense to attribute that haste to the Führer's disappointment in von Blomberg or his initial belief in the charges against von Fritsch. Quite the contrary. Hitler immediately took advantage of what looked like wonderful excuses to get rid of these two under circumstances almost guaranteed to weaken any independence left to the military and to strengthen his own position. This was why he was so reluctant to allow the investigation which eventually showed that the charge against von Fritsch was a carefully planned frame-up, and why he could not allow the general's rehabilitation. The peculiar advantage of the supposed faults of the two generals, from Hitler's point of view, was that a strong reaction from the army leadership was practically precluded as long as the sordid circumstances of the whole operation could be kept concealed. Von Blomberg's marriage left him without support from his colleagues; he had enjoyed little enough before because he was seen as an advocate of National Socialist influence in the army. In any case, as a devoted admirer of Hitler, he could be depended upon to go quietly. Von Fritsch, though not uncritical, was equally unwilling to do anything himself or to encourage

96. Müller, chap. 6, is useful, but the author has been misled by too narrow a focus on the details without proper regard for the general pattern of Hitler's conduct. The account of Harold C. Deutsch, *Hitler and His Generals: The Hidden Crisis, January–June 1938* (Minneapolis: University of Minnesota Press, 1974), is both the most detailed and the most reliable.

97. Concern over the repercussions of knowledge about the allegations concerning Mrs. von Blomberg or General von Fritsch can hardly be advanced seriously for a Hitler who was perfectly willing to risk similar repercussions—of whatever character they might be—in the cases of the wife of von Fritsch's successor as well as in regard to the newly appointed minister of economics, Walther Funk.

those among the military who were inclined to act forcefully in behalf of a leader they admired and in whose downfall they sensed, even before they fully understood, a foul maneuver. In October 1926, when General Hans von Seeckt had been removed quite legally from a position equivalent to the one von Fritsch held now, the latter, then a lieutenant colonel, had urged von Seeckt to use force against the government of the Weimar Republic in order to maintain himself in office.[98] Now that von Fritsch himself was removed by Hitler in a filthy plot that involved a confrontation with a professional blackmailer in Hitler's presence, he submitted meekly to the indignity of Gestapo interrogation and discouraged those appalled by the political as well as personal implications of the incident from doing anything that went beyond purely legalistic steps to clear his name. In a way, von Fritsch continued to believe in Hitler as he had never been willing to support the Republic.

Given this loyalty to Hitler of the men removed, why did he drop them? It is too often forgotten that von Blomberg, like von Neurath, was not originally simply chosen by Hitler himself, but had been selected by President Paul von Hindenburg.[99] Although the appointment had been acceptable to Hitler—as had that of von Neurath—and though von Blomberg, again like von Neurath, had proved himself a capable and willing instrument of Hitler's will, he retained some independence, a quality both had shown in the conference of 5 November. Von Fritsch was even more obviously a man out of tune with Hitler's preferences. Like von Blomberg, he had been the choice of von Hindenburg when Hitler and von Blomberg himself would have preferred von Reichenau as commander-in-chief of the army.[100] Unlike von Blomberg, he had demonstrated considerable rigidity in resisting accommodation to the regime, and this had been recalled to Hitler not only on 5 November but also at a subsequent meeting of von Fritsch with Hitler on 9 November.[101] Now that Hitler felt ready to begin implementation of the aggressive policies he intended to pursue, he wanted not just willing instruments but totally dependent and pliant tools. Insight into this consideration of Hitler's can be gained not only from the military succession which will be examined later but also from the nature of the persons Hitler thought about in the diplomatic reshuffling that accompanied the military changes.[102]

98. Friedrich von Rabenau, *Seeckt: Aus seinem Leben, 1918–1936* (Leipzig: Hase & Koehler, 1940), p. 536. The discussion of von Fritsch's character by Deutsch does not come to grips with this important event for understanding von Fritsch's attitude toward governmental authority.

99. Summaries of the evidence in Müller, pp. 49–50; Deutsch, pp. 8–10.

100. Deutsch, pp. 11–13.

101. On von Fritsch and Hitler, see ibid., pp. 29–30; on the 9 November meeting, see ibid., pp. 71, 74–75.

102. The existing literature generally ignores the fact that the same individual, namely Hitler, was making both sets of changes simultaneously.

The Italians had asked some time before for the removal of Ulrich von Hassell from the German embassy in Rome; the person whom Hitler asked to take that position on 31 January was Hans Frank, his legal adviser from the time when Hitler was struggling for power in Germany; and it is worth noting that it was when asking Frank to go back to Rome, where he had previously represented Hitler on special missions, that Hitler also explained to Frank his ideas of making the army more National Socialist, settling the Austrian, Czechoslovak, Danzig, and Corridor questions, and making von Ribbentrop foreign minister.[103] Although the Rome embassy was eventually used as a consolation prize for moving von Neurath's son-in-law, Hans Georg von Mackensen, out of the position of state secretary in the foreign ministry, it is Hitler's perception of the relationship between policy and personnel that is informative.

The same kind of thinking was involved in the planned change at Vienna. Hitler had sent Franz von Papen there to get rid of him when von Papen had escaped being shot on 30 June 1934 and the Vienna post had become vacant because the German minister there had allowed himself to be publicly implicated in the abortive National Socialist coup of 24 July 1934.[104] Hitler was planning a more active policy in Austria and therefore intended to replace von Papen, though the speed of developments in this instance would leave the latter at his post even after his recall had been publicly announced.[105] Again the replacement was to have been an associate of Hitler's political struggles. At one point, Hitler considered Hermann Kriebel; later he promised the position to Albert Forster. The former had worked with Hitler in postwar Bavaria, was in Hitler's focus of attention at this time because of his post as consul general in Shanghai while Germany was trying to mediate in the Sino-Japanese war, and would receive an appointment as chief of the personnel and administrative section of the foreign ministry in 1939.[106] The latter, who was then Hitler's personal representative in Danzig, was told by Hitler that he would be sent to Vienna to arrange a coup in June or July, but had to content himself with taking more radical steps in the Free City of Danzig when

103. Hans Frank, *Im Angesicht des Galgens* (Munich: Friedrich Alfred Beck, 1953), pp. 280–82. Note that on 4 February the Reich press chief, Otto Dietrich, still included Frank's appointment to Rome among the changes to be made (Dr. Kausch, "Wichtige Bestellung für die Aufmachung und Behandlung der grossen personellen Veränderungen," Bundesarchiv, Brammer, Z.Sg. 101/11, f.83), and that the German ambassador to Poland still expected this change on 15 February (*Szembek Diary*, 15 February 1938, p. 272), although Frank (p. 282) claims that Hitler told him he would not be sent on 9 February. On Frank's earlier trips to Italy, see Weinberg, *Foreign Policy*, pp. 266–67, 333, 334.

104. Weinberg, *Foreign Policy*, pp. 106–7.

105. See chap. 9, below.

106. On Kriebel's pre-1938 career, see Weinberg, *Foreign Policy*, pp. 341–42; on his proposed appointment to Vienna, see the report by Dr. Kausch cited in n.103, above, and Dertinger's "Privater Sonderbericht," 7 February 1938, Bundesarchiv, Brammer, Z.Sg. 101/32, f.75.

Hitler was able to move more rapidly on the Austrian question than he had anticipated when he explained his hopes to Forster on 5 February.[107] While Herbert von Dirksen's real, not diplomatic, illness in Tokyo[108] and von Ribbentrop's removal from London to the position of foreign minister naturally touched off other changes in diplomatic personnel, the key point is that in those changes in which Hitler himself took some initiative, his first inclination was invariably to the appointment of men who were long-time political cronies and could be depended upon to be completely subservient instruments of his will. Frank, Kriebel, Forster, and von Ribbentrop *all* fit this description; von Blomberg, von Fritsch, and von Neurath could not be considered in the same category.

Who was to succeed them? The next ranking officer in the German armed forces was Göring, who very much wanted von Blomberg's spot and had played a major role in dumping von Blomberg and von Fritsch, the latter a possible appointee to the former's post. Hitler would not appoint Göring and decided to take over the position himself. The reasons why Göring was not appointed are only partly known; Foertsch's assertion that Hitler referred to Göring's laziness may well be based on Göring's notorious apathy of later years.[109] More plausible is the possibility that Hitler did not wish to give too much power to any single individual. Göring had been placed in charge of the Four-Year Plan in addition to control of the air force and multifarious lesser posts;[110] if he were also placed in control of the armed forces as a whole, his position would have become extraordinarily strong.[111] Hitler decided to take direct control of the armed forces himself and to use the staff which Keitel had been building up as his own.[112] There is some evidence that he had intended to

107. On the meeting between Hitler and Forster and Arthur Greiser in Berlin, which appears to have taken place on 5 February before or after the cabinet meeting, see C 4100, C 4359/197/55, FO 371/21801; Carl J. Burckhardt, *Meine Danziger Mission, 1938–1939* (Munich: Callwey, 1960), p. 133; Gallman (Danzig) dispatch 474, 9 May 1938, State 860K.00/323.

108. Von Dirksen was most upset at being grouped with all the others relieved of their posts on 4 February 1938, and he expected—and received—a new appointment. See Herbert von Dirksen, *Moskau-Tokio-London: Erinnerungen und Betrachtungen zu 20 Jahren deutscher Aussenpolitik, 1919–1939* (Stuttgart: Kohlhammer, 1950), pp. 194–95; Memorandum by von Mackensen, 20 December 1937, DZA Potsdam, AA, Büro RAM, Akte 60964, f.175.

109. Hermann Foertsch, *Schuld und Verhängnis: Die Fritschkrise im Februar 1938* (Stuttgart: Deutsche Verlags-Anstalt, 1951), p. 88.

110. Wiedemann (pp. 112–13) cites Göring as offering to give up the Four-Year Plan if he was placed in command of the armed forces.

111. Deutsch (pp. 118–19) comes to a similar conclusion. As a consolation prize, Göring was promoted to field marshal.

112. There is agreement that von Blomberg had made this suggestion to Hitler and had also recommended the use of Keitel as head of Hitler's staff in this new capacity (ibid., p. 119). What is easily overlooked now, but may well have occurred quite independently to both Hitler and von Blomberg at the time, is that Hitler's immediate predecessor as chancellor, Kurt von Schleicher, had retained his prior position as minister of war. If a minister of war could also be chancellor, why could a chancellor not also be minister of war?

do this eventually in any case,[113] and the moment was certainly opportune.

Hitler's daily contacts with Keitel during the whole crisis convinced him that here was a man he could work with and depend on the way he could depend on Frank, Kriebel, and Forster, a judgment that correctly assessed an officer who would remain in the same position until 1945. In this case, as in so many others, Hitler displayed an almost uncanny ability to sense the presence (or absence) of absolute devotion to himself. As a replacement for von Fritsch, Hitler wanted to appoint his favorite among the generals, Walther von Reichenau, Keitel's predecessor in the Armed Forces Office and at the time in charge of the Military District VII with headquarters at Munich. Keitel managed to dissuade Hitler by pointing to von Reichenau's failings in the one field where Keitel could detect mortal sin: von Reichenau was neither hard-working nor thorough. Furthermore, Keitel—whose objections to von Reichenau were supported for entirely different reasons by others—had a candidate who was likely to meet Hitler's needs even if Hitler did not know him well as yet. Walther von Brauchitsch was technically competent, had enough seniority to calm the army leadership, and was politically pliable. Before receiving the appointment—which a man of minimal decency would have refused except on an acting basis at a time when the charges against von Fritsch remained unproved—von Brauchitsch had to promise to bring the army "closer to the state and its ideology"; to make a string of key personnel changes including one in the position of chief of army personnel; to change his chief of staff, though that was postponed a while; and to agree to the centralized armed forces command structure Keitel had been pushing, though this also would be postponed a bit.[114]

Hitler was quickly, and correctly, convinced that in von Brauchitsch he had found the man he needed without the disadvantages that von Reichenau's appointment might have brought with it. About to resign from the army because of marital problems when the big prize dangled before his eyes, von Brauchitsch needed and received the assurance of financial assistance from Hitler to enable him to get out of his first and into a second marriage.[115] If the dependence on Hitler created by this secret subvention was not enough, the new commander-in-chief of the army turned out to be an anatomical marvel, a man totally without backbone,

113. See Müller, document 31, p. 636.

114. Müller, pp. 263–64. For an example of how this was done, see Georg Meyer (ed.), *Generalfeldmarschall Wilhelm Ritter von Leeb: Tagebuchaufzeichnungen und Lagebetrachtungen aus zwei Weltkriegen* (Stuttgart: Deutsche Verlags-Anstalt, 1976), pp. 41–42.

115. Müller, p. 268, n.65, leaves the issue open; Deutsch, chap. 7, has a full account, supplemented by conversations and correspondence with the author. Perhaps it was precisely the combination of financial difficulties that Hitler could solve and marriage to a woman for whose past Hitler could provide dispensation that made von Brauchitsch an attractive alternative to von Reichenau in Hitler's eyes. See also the letter, Hans Roschmann to Hildegard von Kotze, 25 May 1975, Bundesarchiv/Militärarchiv, M.Sg. 1/620.

who would be the despair of all who hoped for some sign of strength and leadership from him in the crises ahead. Whether by permanent inclination or because he knew himself to be personally and hopelessly compromised, and certainly in accord with the energetic preference of his new wife, a wildly enthusiastic worshipper of Hitler, von Brauchitsch would be a willing tool of Hitler from the day of his appointment until his final service when he was the scapegoat for the German army's defeat in Russia in December 1941 and Hitler took over the position of commander-in-chief of the army himself.

The circumstances surrounding the dismissal of von Fritsch opened the eyes of more among the military to the nature of the National Socialist system; but with no one to give a lead to action, the only significance of the incident for the opposition to Hitler lay in its bringing together of skeptics about the regime from both civilian and military spheres for the first time.[116] The man who would provide something of a rallying point later, the army chief-of-staff, General Ludwig Beck, felt restrained from playing any major part in pressuring von Brauchitsch into an active role in the spring of 1938, not only because his own position was clearly weak, but because he was worried about the efforts Keitel immediately made to follow up on the change in the *command personnel* with a change in the *command structure* along the lines he had long pushed.[117]

With Hitler now taking von Blomberg's place as commander-in-chief of the armed forces, those who argued for a more centralized command structure were, naturally, in a stronger position with Hitler. It was his immediate military staff whose prerogatives were at stake, and since Beck knew Keitel and Jodl to be slavish adherents of whatever brainstorms emanated from the Führer, it is not surprising that he should try, with a little success, to persuade von Brauchitsch to argue for a structure that allowed the high command of the army to retain a role in the decision-making process. It is also not surprising that Hitler should decide in favor of the direction Keitel urged, so that Beck could only comment at the end of July 1938 on suggested ways of coping with this problem as "too late."[118] The military apparatus was fully under Hitler's control as he moved to realize the first stages of his program of expansion. The questions raised by von Blomberg and von Fritsch at the November 1937 conference were symptomatic of their mental independence rather than direct causes for their dismissal; both were now gone from the scene.[119]

116. Well-presented in Müller, pp. 273–89. This is the thesis of the piece by Deutsch in Gerhard L. Weinberg (ed.), *Transformation of a Continent: Europe in the Twentieth Century* (Minneapolis: Burgess, 1975).

117. Deutsch stresses other factors; Müller's interpretation is closer to mine.

118. Draft letter (not sent) of Beck to von Manstein, 31 July 1938, Bundesarchiv, H 08-28/4; Müller, p. 665.

119. On 18 February Göring told Nevile Henderson that the military leaders had been purged in part because of opposition to Hitler's policy (C 1161/42/18, FO 371/21655). It will be noted that Erich Raeder, like Göring, was kept at his post.

Gone too was Hitler's chief armed forces adjutant, Colonel Friedrich
Hossbach, who had prepared the record of that famous meeting. Because
he had been too loyal to von Fritsch and too independent in his attitude,
he was replaced by the more complaisant Rudolf Schmundt, who would
stay until killed by the bomb of 20 July 1944.

The shift in diplomatic appointments carried out at the same time as the
military changes has already been alluded to. The most important of these
was undoubtedly the replacement of von Neurath by von Ribbentrop.
Although Hitler had reassured von Neurath about continuing him in office
beyond retirement age, reached with von Neurath's sixty-fifth birthday on
2 February 1938, he dismissed him two days later, sugar-coating the action by placing him in charge of a special advisory group—that never met.
The decision to combine this change with the other military and diplomatic ones (the evidence suggests that the replacement of von Hassell and
von Papen had been decided earlier) was apparently taken only just before
it was announced. The reasons for this timing must remain speculative.
Hitler may have thought that if he were going to make the military and
some of the diplomatic changes at one time, it would be just as well to
change foreign ministers too, especially because the appointment of von
Ribbentrop would open up the embassy in London.[120]

Another, and perhaps more important, consideration affecting the timing of Hitler's action may very well have been an important turning point
in German foreign policy. Just as the shifts at the Rome and Vienna posts
were associated with the policy of Germany toward Italy and Austria in
the winter of 1937–38, so the replacement of von Neurath at this particular
time was surely related to developments in German policy toward the
nations of East Asia. The details of those developments will be reviewed
in a subsequent chapter; but it must be noted here that von Neurath and
von Ribbentrop had long been on opposite sides of the argument over
German policy toward China and Japan, with the former favoring a continuation of Germany's strong ties to China and the latter enthusiastic
about an alignment with Japan. While Germany was acting as mediator in
the Sino-Japanese war, Hitler temporarily deferred public announcement
of an option for Japan; but in mid-January 1938 the mediation attempt
broke down when Japan decided not to deal with the Chinese Nationalists
any more. This opened the way for Hitler to adopt the policy von Ribbentrop had been advocating, first symbolized by the recognition of the
Japanese puppet state of Manchukuo, announced in Hitler's speech of 20

120. Note the evidence on plans to transfer von Papen to Spain and Eberhard von Stohrer,
the German ambassador to Franco, to London (Dertinger, "Privater Sonderbericht," 7
February 1938, Bundesarchiv, Brammer, Z.Sg. 101/32, f.75; Manfred Merkes, *Die deutsche
Politik im spanischen Bürgerkrieg 1936–1939*, 2d ed. [Bonn: Ludwig Röhrscheid, 1969], p.
342). With von Papen held over in Vienna, von Stohrer remained in Spain, and the London
embassy went to von Dirksen, whose recall (unlike von Stohrer's) had been publicly announced.

February in which he also talked about the personnel changes made earlier that month.

The coincidence of the ending of the German mediation effort with the Fritsch-Blomberg crisis may well have influenced Hitler in his decision to appoint the advocate of close relations with Japan as foreign minister at just the time when it seemed feasible to adopt his recommendations.[121] There can be little doubt, however, that the change in foreign ministers would have been made in any case; and the two members of the cabinet selected by von Hindenburg were thus replaced on the same day.[122]

The military and diplomatic changes of February 1938 can be seen as a whole as consolidating Hitler's power and surrounding him by more pliant tools in positions of influence. This was certainly the way the situation was interpreted by foreign observers who assumed that a more radical course would now be followed by Germany.[123] But this was, and would be, due not to the advice Hitler received from so-called radicals; it was because Hitler wanted such a course and picked advisers who would enthusiastically agree with him. Far from being driven by others, he was making certain that those in charge of oiling the machine he drove shared an unquestioning elation over wherever he wanted to go. As a shrewd contemporary German observer concluded: "By way of summary one may therefore assert objectively that the process of totalitarianization has once again moved to absolute effectiveness and that all the events proceed logically out of the concepts of the Führer. There has been no change of course, but rather the continuity of developments has been stabilized."[124]

121. When von Neurath told the new American ambassador, Hugh Wilson, about his dismissal on 19 February 1938, he said that Hitler had told him in January that he was to stay on, that he was then asked to resign, and that he had made no secret of his disapproval of German policy with respect to Japan (enclosure 2 to Gilbert dispatch 3889, 23 February 1938, State 762.00/185).

122. The appointment of von Ribbentrop very much upset Alfred Rosenberg, who had expected cabinet rank as well (Rosenberg to Hitler, 6 February 1938, in Theodor R. Emessen [ed.], *Aus Görings Schreibtisch* [Berlin: Allgemeiner Deutscher Verlag, 1947], pp. 68–70).

123. See *Hungarian Documents*, 1, No. 349; John F. Montgomery (U.S. minister Budapest) report 963, 9 February 1938, State 862.00/3753; Krofta's comments to the section chiefs of the Czechoslovak foreign ministry, No. 5/38 of 10 February 1938, Czechoslovak document in T-120, 1041/1809/414004–005).

124. Dertinger, "Privater Sonderbericht," 7 February 1938, Bundesarchiv, Brammer, Z.Sg. 101/32, f.79.

3   Britain and France Face the German Threat

The **increasingly** troubled European situation resulting from developments in Germany confronted the governments of Britain and France with grave problems. Several closely related problems loomed ahead, for the rearmament of Germany posed both military and economic issues. In an era when the debate over the origins of the World War stressed the role of the pre–1914 arms race in bringing on that conflict, the public in democratic countries was inclined to see in any return to competitive rearmament a step toward war. Especially in Britain, the pressure of public opinion retarded any idea of rebuilding the country's military strength.[1]

Neville Chamberlain, then chancellor of the exchequer, had provided most of what push there was for rearmament in the British government. This personal identification had both advantages and disadvantages. The advantages were threefold. The chancellor of the exchequer was the person who from the point of view of costs was always in an excellent position to hold back or assist the budget requests of the armed services; from that position, Winston Churchill had done

---

1. It is instructive to see how an article written to destroy the "myth" of the role of rearmament as an issue swinging the East Fulham by-election of October 1933 on close reading supports the basic accuracy of the old interpretation. Richard Heller, "East Fulham Revisited," *Journal of Contemporary History*, 6, No. 3 (1971), 172–96. See also the relevant materials from the papers of one of Baldwin's closest associates, in Robert Rhoads James (ed.), *Memoirs of a Conservative: J. C. C. Davidson's Memoirs and Papers, 1910–1937* (New York: Macmillan, 1970) (hereafter cited as *Davidson Papers*), pp. 397–99. The general issue is best treated in Reinhard Meyers, *Britische Sicherheitspolitik 1934–1938* (Düsseldorf: Droste, 1976), pp. 425ff.

as much to disarm Britain in the mid-1920s as Chamberlain did to rearm her in the mid-1930s.[2] It is quite true that there were limits to what Chamberlain thought feasible, but for some time he would push forward. Second, as an extremely energetic and well-organized person, Chamberlain could be expected to give great force to any policy he urged in a cabinet led by the retiring Stanley Baldwin. Finally, the fact that Chamberlain was the heir apparent who was expected to succeed Baldwin, originally in 1936 and then because of the constitutional crisis over the proposed marriage of Edward VIII, in the spring of 1937, gave to his views an added strength in government circles.

There was, however, a negative side to Chamberlain's identification with the rearmament program. As a combative politician who could be and often was mean in debate, supercilious in attitude, and self-righteous in his approach to problems, Chamberlain assured hostility to rearmament from those in the opposition parties who might otherwise have rallied to it in the face of a Germany of which they were most critical. If there were those on the French right who in fact remarked, as alleged, that they preferred Hitler to Léon Blum, they were matched by an attitude on the British left which preferred to trust Hitler rather than Neville Chamberlain. Labor members of Parliament voted against all funds for the military services in the years 1933–36. The realism of some like Hugh Dalton, and the too obvious inner contradiction between the call of Labor's left wing to send arms to the Spanish Republicans from a Britain that was not to have any arms itself, began to have an impact on Labor's parliamentary position in 1936–37. In March 1937 the Labor and Liberal members were still opposing Chamberlain's rearmament proposals,[3] but in July the parliamentary Labor party decided to abstain rather than vote against the estimates for the armed services. On the issue of conscription, however, they would still be unanimously opposed after Chamberlain and his associates had taken the plunge in the spring of 1939.[4]

A related aspect of opposition to rearmament, which was often voiced by Chamberlain himself as well as by his critics, was the diversion from

2. A detailed and detached study of Churchill's role as chancellor of the exchequer remains to be written. The account in Robert Rhoads James, *Churchill: A Study in Failure, 1900–1939* (New York: World, 1970), Part IV, is a useful introduction; the material on Churchill's role in disarming Britain is on pp. 181–86. On the "10-year rule" of keying arms budgets to the assumption of no major war being anticipated for ten years, and Churchill's role in its adoption and maintenance, see Meyers, pp. 388–97; Norman H. Gibbs, *Grand Strategy*, 1, *Rearmament Policy* (London: H.M. Stationery Office, 1976), chap. 2.

3. See Stephen Roskill, *Hankey, Man of Secrets*, 3, *1931–1963* (New York: St. Martin's, 1974), 289.

4. John F. Naylor, *Labour's International Policy: The Labour Party in the 1930's* (London: Weidenfeld & Nicolson, 1969), pp. 191–96. A sample of the problem posed by the contradiction between pacifism and distaste for National Socialism in the Labor party may be seen in James Griffiths, *Pages from Memory* (London: J. M. Dent, 1969), chap. 5, "The Pacifist Dilemma." A good survey is in Meyers, pp. 458–66. See also Peter Dennis, *Decision by Default: Peacetime Conscription and British Defence, 1919–1939* (Durham, N.C.: Duke University Press, 1972).

other possible expenditures that rearmament was thought to imply. While Hitler saw rearmament as good in itself and even better for having the side effect of reviving a stricken economy, Chamberlain and others saw it as competing for a place in the budget with outlays for health, housing, schools, and other public improvements. The key to Britain's economic revival in peacetime and her strength in war if it came was seen precisely in *not* spending her treasure on the wasteful and nonproductive costs of arms.[5]

An important factor in the debate over rearmament, both within the government at the time and in the literature on the subject as the British records have become available, was that of financial limitations on proposals for accelerating the rearmament program, particularly during 1937 and 1938.[6] Though possibly correct in some matters of detail, much of the post–World War II discussion has an unreal aspect because of its disregard of an issue central at the time. England had fought her earlier wars against great continental powers as a member of coalitions and alliances in which she provided financial assistance to her associates. Though there had been some change in this pattern in 1917–18, that change seemed to be more apparent than real. England had actually extended greater credits to her allies than she had herself obtained from the United States. Furthermore, the American Johnson Act which prohibited the extension of credit to countries like England which had defaulted on their war debts to the United States appeared to show that in any future war England would have to depend entirely on her own financial resources for herself as well as any support her allies might require. If those in the British government in 1937–38 did not stake the country's survival on American aid—on which England came to be dependent by the winter of 1940–41—there was certainly little at the time to indicate that this could be a safe course. The level of military effort Britain actually maintained in her next war with Germany was possible only because of the reversal of England's role into becoming a net recipient rather than granter of assistance; in the years of American isolationism the London government not surprisingly decided to limit its expenditures on arms to what it thought could be supported by her own economy.

What rearmament program there was in England was also slowed by confusions and hesitations about the question of a land army and the related inclination to do whatever seemed unavoidable in the least expensive manner. Nothing terrified both public and government more than the prospect of a land war on the model of 1914–18, a point of view which one can easily understand and which was certainly constantly reinforced by

5. Meyers, pp. 334ff.
6. Gibbs, chap. 8; Robert P. Shay, Jr., *British Rearmament in the Thirties* (Princeton: Princeton University Press, 1977); Martin Gilbert, *Winston S. Churchill, 5, 1922–1939: The Prophet of Truth* (Boston: Houghton Mifflin, 1977), chaps. 42, 43.

the flood of books about the war on the one hand and the gaping holes in the circle of every person's family and friends on the other. Yet there was a lurking uneasiness that such a thing might recur, if not in precisely the same form, at least in a form again requiring a substantial British land army. The beginnings of an agitated debate in British government circles over the role of the British army in any future war can be understood only as a reflection of this conflict between hope and insight.[7]

As the problem was discussed within government circles, culminating in a cabinet decision on 3 February 1937, the need to plan an expeditionary force to the continent as a last and least desirable resort had to be faced. Although the force sent would be small and take time both to equip with modern weapons and expand to more than nominal size, only the prospect of an expeditionary force could sustain Britain's diplomatic position in peace and offer any hope of safety in war. Without it there would be no credibility to her concerns in Europe and no substance to her alignment with France.[8] Chamberlain's appointment of the vigorous and imaginative Leslie Hore-Belisha as secretary of state for war infused energy and new ideas into a torpid army leadership, but there was a long way to go.[9]

An invasion of England itself was thought an unlikely danger, though only on the assumption that the Germans would have only their own North Sea ports from which to launch such a move.[10] The conclusion drawn, however, was not that no army would be needed, but that the slight danger of sea or airborne landing should not be allowed to tie down British troops in the home islands.[11] Such thinking reflects both the assumption that a war started by Germany was the one European contingency to be taken seriously by Britain and the flow of reports from British diplomats in Germany that before long—1938–40 are the years most commonly mentioned—Germany would launch the first aggression in an attempt to dominate Europe.[12] These worries about Germany, however,

7. C 205/205/62, FO 371/20701; Gibbs, chap. 12; Michael Howard, *The Continental Commitment* (London: Temple Smith, 1972).

8. Key documents are C 563/1/18, FO 371/20705; C 928, C 1050, C 1175/928/18, FO 371/20746. Cf. Roderick Macleod and Denis Kelly (eds.), *Time Unguarded: The Ironside Diaries, 1937–1940* (New York: David McKay, 1962) (hereafter cited as *Ironside Diaries*), p. 37. For a French review of arms production in major European powers, see *D.D.F.*, 2d, 4, No. 317.

9. On Hore-Belisha, see R. J. Minney (ed.), *The Private Papers of Hore-Belisha* (London: Collins, 1960); and the references to their cooperation in the *Memoirs* of Basil H. Liddell Hart (London: Cassell, 1965). For a French appreciation of Hore-Belisha's effect on the British army, see *D.D.F.*, 2d, 6, No. 174. The army leaders would get their revenge on the man who had woken them up by securing his dismissal in January 1940.

10. Joint Planning Sub-Committee of the Committee of Imperial Defence, "Sea-Borne and Air-Borne Land Attack on the British Isles," 7 January 1937, C 1479/205/62, FO 371/20701.

11. Ibid.

12. See the report of the British military attaché in Berlin of 12 January 1937 that was circulated to the cabinet, C 496/136/18, FO 371/20731; and the impressions of the chief of the

were compounded almost to the point of imposing a certain immobility on British strategic thought by the simultaneous danger in the Far East from Japan and, to a lesser extent, from Italy in the Mediterranean where disturbances in Palestine complicated the defense of Egypt against Italian forces in Libya. Risks run in one part of the globe threatened to create even greater risks in others; the dilemma of reconciling a continental defense against Germany with the need to defend a vast world empire, and to do so on the basis of inadequate strength against a multitude of challenges, seemed to defy resolution.[13]

In the naval field the London government felt more confident; a new program of construction was approved, but this was one area where the situation was thought to be more favorable to England than before the last war.[14] The greatest danger was seen as being in the air. British concern over this subject has already been alluded to;[15] it continued and even grew in 1937 as the threat of German bombing of England as well as the possible use of the German air force in offensives against other countries loomed ever larger in British calculations. The Foreign Office, conscious of risks at home and the dangerous loss of prestige abroad, pushed for greater expansion of the Royal Air Force, and new programs to accomplish this were approved in February and October 1937.[16] In the absence of the radar installations that would play such a key role in 1940, the London government's alarm is understandable, especially when it is seen against a background of an island state with a strong fleet whose near immunity from attack had been threatened only by the bombs of German dirigibles and planes in the very war which now threatened to repeat itself.

Such themes run through all the analyses of the military situation and its import for international affairs that were submitted by the British chiefs of staff to the cabinet in 1937. Britain was weak and would need years to rearm. Even the expanded programs for the air force would leave Britain

---

imperial general staff of the German maneuvers of September 1937 in C 7546/136/18, FO 371/20732. For British concern that the resignation of Ludwig Beck and his replacement by Walther von Reichenau, rumored in April 1937, meant a more aggressive German policy, see C 2967/6/18, FO 371/20710.

13. This is in large part the theme of Meyers's fine book; it is applied in detail to one area in Lawrence R. Pratt, *East of Malta, West of Suez: Britain's Mediterranean Crisis 1936–1939* (Cambridge: Cambridge University Press, 1975).

14. C 1516/205/62, FO 371/20701; Br. Cabinet 8 (37) of 17 February 1937, CAB 23/87, f.236; A 5459/6/45, FO 371/20649. The French were not so sure of this, *D.D.F.*, 2d, 9, No. 508; and as Pratt has pointed out, especially on the basis of the Chatfield papers, the reduced number of capital ships available for action in 1937–38 imposed severe restrictions on British naval strategy until the new ships could be ready and the older ones modernized.

15. See above, p. 5.

16. The course of the arguments and the conclusions reached can be traced in C 409, C 676/185/18, FO 371/20733; C 930, C 1585, C 1637, C 5102, C 7385, C 7817, C 8124/185/18, FO 371/20734; Br. Cabinet 9 (37) of 24 February 1937, CAB 23/87, ff.269, 276–77; C 8434/122/17, FO 371/20694. Key worries were the weakness of British air defenses (C 3821/205/62, FO 371/20701) and the need to escape the government's public pledge of air parity with Germany (Br. Cabinet 4 [37] of 27 January 1937, C 919/185/18, FO 371/20733).

behind in the race to catch up with a Germany that was continuing to build up its air force at an accelerating pace. The situation in regard to the formation of properly equipped land forces was even worse. Italy could attack Britain or parts of her empire only if assured of German support, while Japan could become dangerous by herself, especially if tempted by trouble for Britain in Europe. As for the prospects of the United Kingdom in a war with all three, that was so dire a matter that all possible attempts must be made to avoid it. The only bright spots in the picture were that Germany was not yet ready herself, and that Britain was finally starting a major rearmament program, including an expansion of plant capacity,[17] that would take time to show results but that offered the advantage of standardization on later and more modern weapons. The prospects for the immediate future, however, were extremely grim.[18] As General Edmund Ironside, then in charge of the Eastern Command, put it in his diary, Britain was so weak she could not bluff. The strong line that Winston Churchill was calling for was impossible. "We have nothing with which to fight—literally nothing—and will not have anything for two years."[19]

The hope that the effort Britain was making to remedy these deficiencies would in itself serve to help by its demonstration of serious purpose could not be relied upon; there was a general recognition that however great these efforts, it would be years before the results would be apparent, and in modern war these years just might not be available. The problem as posed by the military advisers of the government was how to postpone the danger of war and reduce the number of potential enemies, for the situation of Great Britain in the immediate future looked truly desperate.[20] And as the former chancellor of the exchequer who, since 1931, had rebuilt the confidence of Britain in its ability to survive the great depression as a world power, Neville Chamberlain was most unwilling to risk shaking that confidence by pointing out in public just how desperate the situation had become.

Compounding the problem faced by policymakers in London was their concern about France. The days when there were fears in Whitehall about French hegemony in Europe and belief in a need to moderate her supposedly harsh policies toward Germany must have seemed like a happy piece of ancient history as the British worried not only about the French

17. On this issue, which deserves a separate study, especially in comparison with Germany, see Meyers, p. 419, n.173.

18. The foregoing summarizes C 1406, C 1586/205/62, FO 371/20701; C 7851, C 8331/205/62, FO 371/20702; R 4963/78/22, FO 371/21160; J 4999/244/16, FO 371/20912; C 8124/185/18, FO 371/20734. Note the comments of Sir Thomas Inskip, minister for the coordination of defense, to members of Parliament that it could take until 1940 to complete the deficiency program, and that Britain was weak but would benefit from standardization on new weapons (Harold Nicolson, *Diaries and Letters, 1930–1939* [New York: Atheneum, 1966], 5 July 1937, p. 303.

19. *Ironside Diaries*, 24 June 1937, p. 25.

20. C 1760, C 2620/205/62, FO 371/20701; C 5697/205/62, FO 371/20702; R 2320/989/3, FO 371/21119.

air force but the French army as well. There was concern about the antiquated materiel—largely left over from the earlier war—and the unresolved riddle of what, if anything, France would and could do in the West if her allies in Central and Eastern Europe were attacked.[21] The comparison drawn by British military observers between the vigorous new German army, however disorganized by the process of rapid expansion, and the tired and poorly equipped French army was hardly reassuring to a country that had taken for granted a superior French army as a guarantor of its own defense and an excuse for dispensing with a substantial army itself.[22]

It is, therefore, not surprising that the recommendations made by the British chiefs of staff from the beginning to the end of 1937 were that every effort be made to reduce the number of potential enemies and increase the possible friends and neutrals, a viewpoint approved by both Chamberlain and Foreign Secretary Anthony Eden. Both also came to the conclusion that it would be useless and dangerous to attempt to buy off Germany, Italy, or Japan. It would be useless because the demands of the one bribed would only increase and the others would be the more tempted to move forward by such signs of weakness; it would be dangerous because such a policy might open the floodgates of drastic change—with an inherent danger of war—and because it would alienate France, the United States, and any other potential ally. Safety seemed to lie in delay and the hope that specific current difficulties could be resolved by negotiations.[23] How was this to be done?

One possibility that was left from the preceding year but looked less and less likely to lead to any useful conclusion was the effort to find a replacement for the Locarno system destroyed by Germany in March 1936. Unless a new pact served Hitler's concept of a complaisant England standing still while he conquered Central and Eastern Europe, there was nothing to be gained in his eyes by making what looked to him like retroactive concessions to obtain something he had already secured by the passive acquiescence of the Western Powers in the remilitarization of the

21. See especially the comparison of the French and German 1937 maneuvers in C 7703/136/18, FO 371/20732; *Ironside Diaries,* pp. 28–29; and Chamberlain's comments at the Committee of Imperial Defence on 5 July 1937, R 4963/78/22, FO 371/21160, p. 3.

22. The British dependence on the French army in the interwar years bears a certain resemblance to U.S. dependence on the British fleet in the nineteenth and early twentieth centuries. In both Britain and the U.S., the possibility of the "shield's" defeat played a key role in alerting policymakers to dangers ahead—though only in the U.S. did this lead to any literature reinterpreting the past in terms of this new insight.

23. The chiefs of staff appreciation, with Committee of Imperial Defence, cabinet, and Foreign Office comments, of 9 February is in C 1406/205/62, FO 371/20701. See also C 6124/185/18, FO 371/20734; R 4963/1/22, FO 371/21160. A survey of the issues may be found in Anthony Eden, *The Memoirs of Anthony Eden: Facing the Dictators* (Boston: Houghton Mifflin, 1962), chap. 9, which overstates the differences between Eden and Chamberlain. For an explanation by Admiral Chatfield of how this perception of Britain's dangers led to an effort at agreement with Italy, see his letter to Admiral Pound of 23 November 1937, quoted in Pratt, p. 114.

Rhineland. The negotiations for what was by now generally referred to as a Western Pact had accordingly been continuing for many months and, especially at English urging, were still in progress; but it was clear that nothing would come of the scheme. While Britain and France were interested in a security system to take the place of the one that had been torn up, Germany was willing to continue talks on the subject solely to please the British government, but would sign an agreement only if it would provide legal insulation from western hostility for a German attack in Central or Eastern Europe. As neither the French nor the British had any interest in such a scheme, there was no prospect of agreement, and by the summer of 1937, if not sooner, this was readily apparent to all.[24]

The evaporation of hopes for a new Locarno had effects that in the long run were precisely the opposite of those the Germans might have hoped for, and that would be fatal to Hitler's dreams of conquest. He had once hoped, and some historians argue that he long continued to hope, that he could detach England from France and bring her to his side. This conception, grounded in Hitler's view of the origins of the prewar Anglo-German rivalry and the postwar British concerns about France's supposed hegemony in Europe, could have some validity only as long as Germany was relatively weak and was not following an aggressive policy in Europe. The moment Germany destroyed the Locarno system and, by ending the demilitarization of the Rhineland, removed the most important bar to German aggression, she in fact riveted England to the side of France. But such a position for Britain did not mean that there would be no need or desire in England for an accommodation with Germany. On the contrary, while rearming and aligning Great Britain more closely with France, the government in London still hoped that the outstanding problems of Europe could be solved peacefully and by negotiation rather than by force. Given a failure to conceive, let alone credit, the idea that anyone might deliberately start another war, a basic preference for negotiated settlements, a horror of war based on the experience of 1914–18, a recognition of military weakness in the face of overextended commitments around the world, and a sense that at least some of Germany's grievances

24. No useful purpose would be served by recounting these tedious and abortive negotiations. The summary in Josef Henke, *England in Hitlers politischem Kalkül 1935–1939* (Boppard: Boldt, 1973), pp. 53–56, supports the interpretation given here. Relevant documents in *G.D.,* C, 6, Nos. 1, 6, 9, 24, 26, 33, 34, 47–49, 69, 79, 103, 107, 199, 201, 217, 223, 232, 241, 258, 263, 285, 287, 296, 420, 430, 474, 497, 505, 577; *D.D.B.,* 4, Nos. 163, 169, 202, 204; *D.D.F.,* 2d, 5, Nos. 51, 72, 98, 105, 112, 118, 123, 126, 137, 169, 372, 471; 6, Nos. 27, 44, 49, 85, 88, 94, 168, 207, 218, 243, 248, 379; *U.S.,* 1936, 1:374–75; 2:60–64; Wacław Jedrzejewicz (ed.), *Diplomat in Paris, 1936–1939: Papers and Memoirs of Juliusz Łukasiewicz* (New York: Columbia University Press, 1970), pp. 38–52; Krofta's comments to the section chiefs of the Czechoslovak ministry of foreign affairs, No. 7/37, 18 March 1937, Czechoslovak document in T-120, 1809/1041/414049–50; "Bestellung aus der Pressekonferenz vom 17. Juli 1937," and " . . . am 29. Juli 1937," Bundesarchiv, Brammer, Z.Sg. 101/10, ff.37, 63. For an account stressing the effort to extend the proposed new pact to Poland, see Marian Wojciechowski, *Die polnisch-deutschen Beziehungen 1933–1938* (Leyden: Brill, 1971), pp. 343ff.

were real, all combined to push the London government into renewed efforts toward some accommodation with Germany.

One step that was designed to bring England and Germany more closely together, but would have the effect of creating even more misunderstanding, was the appointment of a new British ambassador to Berlin. Though frequently associated with Neville Chamberlain in the public eye, Sir Nevile Henderson was actually appointed to the Berlin post by Stanley Baldwin on the recommendation of Anthony Eden and Permanent Undersecretary of Foreign Affairs Sir Robert Vansittart. Given the highly critical attitude of Sir Eric Phipps, who had been in Berlin since 1933, a new look by a new man might make for better contact; and since Vansittart had refused the Paris embassy, Sir Eric was shifted there to make way for the new appointee.[25]

Given the unpopularity of Joachim von Ribbentrop in London, where he spent little time in any case, the views of Sir Nevile Henderson were of special importance. In a memorandum of 10 May 1937 he set forth his views at the beginning of his mission to Germany as calling for British agreement to German expansion in Central and Eastern Europe provided that such expansion were carried out peacefully, in accord with the will of the people affected, and with proper regard for the independence of the non-German peoples of the area.[26] Apart from the inherent incompatibility of these conditions with each other in the Europe of the 1930s, what worried those in the Foreign Office most about these views was that without providing any assurance that Germany would in fact be satisfied with such concessions—certainly *Mein Kampf* indicated the contrary—any intimation by Great Britain that she approved such a policy could, as the commentators cited Chamberlain, be the word that would bring down the avalanche. It could be given in any case only if England were prepared to fight if the conditions were violated, and this she was in no position to do. Only delay, negotiations on specific issues, and rearmament could help. In the meantime, however, there was the danger that Henderson would voice his ideas: in fact, by the time he sent the

25. On the appointment of Henderson, see Thomas Jones, *A Diary with Letters, 1931–1950* (London: Oxford University Press, 1954), 15 February 1937, p. 315; Colvin, *None So Blind*, p. 146; Eden to Baldwin, 27 January 1937, Baldwin Papers, vol. 124; and the useful, but not very penetrating work of Rudi Strauch, *Sir Nevile Henderson, Britischer Botschafter in Berlin von 1937 bis 1939* (Bonn: Röhrscheid, 1959). Note the comment of Eden's private secretary: "There really is not anybody else obvious to send." John Harvey (ed.), *The Diplomatic Diaries of Oliver Harvey, 1937–1940* (New York: St. Martin's, 1970) (hereafter cited as *Harvey Diaries*), p. 41. Henderson presented his credentials on 11 May 1937; see Nevile Henderson, *Failure of a Mission, Berlin 1937–1939* (New York: G. P. Putnam's Sons, 1940), pp. 41–42; Domarus, 1:691–93.

26. The full text together with a covering letter of 20 July 1937 to Sir Orme Sargent and comments by Foreign Office officials, is in C 5316/270/18, FO 371/20736, ff.77–108. See also Henderson to Lord Lothian, 25 May 1937 (expressing agreement with the latter's views), Lord Lothian Papers, GD 40/17/204/351–2; and *D.D.F.*, 2d, 6, No. 6.

memorandum to the Foreign Office, he had already done so on several occasions.

In May and June 1937, Henderson expressed himself along the lines of his memorandum to the Austrian minister and the United States ambassador to Berlin as well as to Franz von Papen and George S. Messersmith, the German and American ministers to Vienna.[27] When such comments came back to London, and it turned out that in one case Henderson had even put them in writing, there was a considerable uproar, and the ambassador was recalled to be reprimanded.[28] The evidence suggests that he nevertheless continued talking about the inevitability of German expansion and the need for concessions to her to all he met, except for the Germans, though the latter could not long remain ignorant of his views.[29] Henderson believed that the sensible course for Great Britain to follow was to allow Germany to expand to the limits of her nationality border—i.e., to annex Austria, Danzig, Memel, the Sudeten area, and the portion of Silesia that had been awarded to Poland; that it would be appropriate for Germany to become a colonial power again, presumably in West Africa; and that she should be allowed to exercise some sort of peaceful hegemony in Central and Eastern Europe. He believed that British interests would not be threatened if this were allowed and even encouraged, and there was in any case no prospect of uniting the British public to fight a war against Germany, with all the costs and dangers a war would entail, unless Germany either went beyond such concessions to launch a war herself or directly threatened Great Britain.

As will be shown, all this was really not so far in substance from what both Chamberlain and Eden themselves believed, but there was a significant difference in emphasis: Henderson thought that Britain should openly take the initiative to approach Germany with such a program in exchange for a return to a changed League of Nations and a commitment to renounce force in international relations, while Chamberlain and Eden were unwilling to make an agreement at the expense of others, feared a slide to disaster if Great Britain declared itself disinterested in Central and Eastern Europe, and thought it wiser to delay rather than to hurry—and

27. On Henderson's comments to Tauschitz, see *Der Hochverratsprozess gegen Dr. Guido Schmidt vor dem Wiener Volksgericht* (Vienna: Österreichische Staatsdruckerei, 1947) (hereafter cited as *Guido Schmidt Trial*), pp. 493–94, 495–96, and *D.D.F.*, 2d, 6, No. 124; to Dodd, see *Dodd Diary*, 23 June 1937, p. 421, *U.S.*, 1937, 1:341, and Dodd to Phipps, 1 July 1937, C 5541/3/18, FO 371/20711; to von Papen, see *G.D.*, D, 1, No. 228; to Messersmith, see *Dodd Diary*, 12 July 1937, p. 422, and memorandum by Messersmith on his trip from Vienna to the U.S. via Berlin and London, pp. 7–10, Messersmith Papers. See also Henderson, pp. 29ff.
28. Dodd to Phipps, 1 July 1937, C 5541/3/18, FO 371/20711; C 5377/270/18, FO 371/20736.
29. When Hugh Dalton recounted Henderson's explication of his views to Eden, the latter commented: "I wish he would not go on like this to everybody he meets." Dalton Diary, 28 October 1937, Dalton Papers. See also C 5080/270/18, FO 371/20736; C 4975/270/18, FO 371/20735; R 7812/188/12, FO 371/21132.

most certainly not to approve—changes in Europe which England might
not like but could not prevent. But it would take shocks in Berlin rather
than admonitions from London to correct Henderson's approach. Eden
wrote him a personal note just before Lord Halifax went to Germany
saying: "I regard it of the greatest importance at the present time that no
encouragement whatsoever should be given the German government for
believing that His Majesty's Government would contemplate any settlement at the expense of the political independence of the nations of Eastern and Central Europe. I am confident that I can rely upon you to bear
this constantly in mind."[30] Henderson replied with long explications
about the wisdom of his own approach.[31]

What makes these views of Sir Nevile so important in spite of their
being disagreed with sharply in London was that they became known in
Berlin, partly through those to whom Henderson talked so freely, and
partly because the Germans had access to a large portion of the British
diplomatic correspondence and were therefore naturally more familiar
with the ambassador's opinions than with the objections noted on his
letters and reports within the Foreign Office.[32] When the German assessment of probable British reaction to their own possible moves is
examined, this aspect of the situation as it appeared to them must be
recalled.[33]

The replacement of Sir Eric Phipps was not the only personnel change
anticipated with pleasure in Berlin. For some time at least a few within the
German government had been looking forward to the retirement of
Baldwin after the coronation of George VI in May 1937. Neville Chamberlain was thought to be less hostile to Germany than his predecessor,
and there were hopes in Berlin that Anthony Eden might be dropped as
foreign secretary when the new prime minister took over.[34] More impor-

30. C 7725/270/18, FO 371/20736.
31. C 8293, C 8294/270/18, FO 371/20737.
32. The Italians were reading British diplomatic traffic and at times passed on choice
tidbits to the Germans (see Weinberg, *Foreign Policy*, p. 208). The Germans also decoded
some British telegrams, and apparently secured copies of some of the Berlin embassy
correspondence; see *G.D.*, C, 6, Nos. 344, 484, 487 (the last item may have been provided by
the Italians). In March 1937 the Yugoslav government transmitted to London conclusive
circumstantial evidence of the ability of the Italians to read British telegrams; but although
one official, Owen O'Malley, had his doubts, the Foreign Office eventually denied the
possibility (R 1687, R 1688/224/92, FO 371/21198).
33. Henke, pp. 56–65, discusses what he considers Hitler's slow turning away from a
desire for an alliance with England to shield an offensive eastward in the face of England's
unwillingness to accept the role this scheme allotted to her. The picture Henke presents
appears to me to be overdrawn, and also flawed by heavy dependence on the hopelessly
unreliable work of Dietrich Aigner, *Das Ringen um England* (Munich: Bechtle, 1969).
34. *D.D.F.*, 2d, 4, No. 430; 5, No. 39. On a final approach from Germany for a Baldwin-
Hitler meeting, see Jones, 3 January 1937, p. 299 (on the prior approaches, see Weinberg,
Foreign Policy, pp. 272–73; Henke, p. 34). Having now had the opportunity to examine the
Baldwin papers at Clare College, Cambridge, I am still incapable of imagining a conversation
between the two men.

tant in the long run was Hitler's complete misconception of most aspects of the British constitutional crisis itself.

Edward VIII had in fact shown himself more favorably disposed toward Germany than his father, George V. There was also some evidence that the woman over whose two prior marriages Edward would lose his throne was also rather pro-German and was known to have such views in the London society which included the German ambassador, Joachim von Ribbentrop.[35] There were, however, two related misconceptions in Hitler's appreciation of the events of December 1936 which culminated in the abdication of Edward VIII. In the first place, Hitler, like many other Germans, exaggerated the importance of the king's role in determining British policy. Perhaps the debate over the origins of the World War played a part in this misunderstanding; it was often held, especially in Germany, that Edward VII's anti-German attitudes and policies had contributed significantly to the forging of the Triple Entente, which had proved so fateful for the Second Reich. Even if there was some substance to that view, it had little bearing on the realities of power and influence in the world of the 1930s.

More astonishing is that von Ribbentrop was so totally ignorant of the currents of opinion in the country to which he was accredited that he believed and assured Hitler—who needed little convincing—that the whole marriage question was a false front that Baldwin had utilized to get rid of the king because of the latter's pro-German views.[36] Once Hitler was certain of the truth of this fairy tale, it developed in his mind, especially after the Duke of Windsor made a favorable impression on the Führer at a visit in October 1937, to a point where he imagined that Winston Churchill was responsible for the removal of England's pro-German ruler.[37] Given the erroneous impression that the duke had lost his throne because of his views on Germany, the even more preposterous idea that Churchill had arranged the clever use of the marriage issue to have him pushed out can be seen as a perfect example of how the imposition of preconceptions on reality can lead to total self-delusion. Such

35. The fairest account is Frances Donaldson, *Edward VIII* (London: Weidenfeld & Nicolson, 1974), chap. 15.

36. See *D.D.F.*, 2d, 4, Nos. 108, 140, and the very important record of a conversation between Sir Orme Sargent and Ernst Jaeckh, who had been shown von Ribbentrop's report to Hitler by Ernst Woermann, the second man in the German embassy in London, and who had been told by the latter that von Ribbentrop was unshakable in his views, in C 448/270/18, FO 371/20734. See also Henke, pp. 65–69; Dertinger, "Informationsbericht Nr. 53," 12 December 1936, Bundesarchiv, Brammer, Z.Sg. 101/29, ff.529–31; *G.D.*, C, 6, No. 84; Albert Speer, *Erinnerungen* (Berlin: Propyläen, 1969), p. 86. On 11 December 1936, the day the Abdication Act was passed, von Ribbentrop expected shooting in the streets of London, believed that Edward VIII would be restored to the throne, and discussed the matter with Hitler by telephone (*Davidson Papers*, p. 417)!

37. Wiedemann, pp. 153–56; Donaldson, chap. 27; Paul Schmidt, *Statist auf diplomatischer Bühne 1923–1945* (Bonn: Athenäum, 1950), pp. 373–76; *G.D.*, C, 6, Nos. 529, 553; Dr. Kausch, "Die Deutschlandreise des Herzogs von Windsor," 8 October 1937, Bundesarchiv, Brammer, Z.Sg. 101/10, ff.257–59.

delusions, of course, have their own subsequent impact, regardless of objective reality. The further deduction that Hitler drew was that the British, like the French, were permanent and implacable "hate opponents" *(Hassgegner)* of Germany as he told his leading advisers at the Hossbach conference of 5 November, a few days after he had entertained the Duke and Duchess of Windsor in Berchtesgaden.

These views were avidly shared by Joachim von Ribbentrop. Just before he became foreign minister, he wrote a lengthy memorandum for Hitler explaining his belief in the unrelenting hostility of Britain and in the need to concentrate Germany's diplomatic as well as military energies on the preparations for the inevitable war with England.[38] He alluded to having still had some slight hope of agreement with England when he went there as ambassador in 1936 in view of Edward VIII's opinions; once that monarch had been deposed by Baldwin lest he decline to go along with a policy hostile to Germany, all hope of a real German-English rapprochement was gone. "Every future day in which our political considerations are not basically determined by the thought of England as our most dangerous enemy—regardless of any tactical intermezzo of an understanding with us which might be attempted—would be a gain for our enemies."[39] In the face of such beliefs and attitudes, the efforts of the Chamberlain government to reach an accommodation with Germany could only fail.

Ironically, in view of Hitler's opinions, the circumstances of the constitutional crisis in England helped open rather than close the way to a British approach to Berlin. The beginnings of discontent within the ruling Conservative party about what was seen as an excessively complaisant policy toward Germany was severely undermined when the first major manifestations of this unease lost their impact because of Churchill's *support* of Edward VIII.[40] One of the key figures in the Conservative party who urged rearmament and a strong policy toward Germany, Churchill was just recovering some prestige in British public life from the isolation into which he had thrust himself in his long and bitter rearguard

38. Historians who argue that Hitler always wanted some agreement with England have never explained why Hitler appointed von Ribbentrop right after receiving this explication of the latter's views. Could it be that in this, as in so many other areas, von Ribbentrop was voicing what he correctly sensed were his master's preferences? A serious study of von Ribbentrop remains to be written.

39. Von Ribbentrop's memorandum for Hitler of 2 January 1938 summarizing a longer report is in *G.D.*, D, 1, No. 93. The man who soon after would become von Ribbentrop's chief assistant as state secretary, Ernst von Weizsäcker, found nothing to object to in all this; see ibid., No. 100. This voicing of full agreement with von Ribbentrop's general perception of the international situation at the time of his appointment as foreign minister is surely not irrelevant to von Weizsäcker's subsequent promotion. For background on von Ribbentrop's adoption of the line that Germany might fight soon against an England unwilling to accept Germany's ambitions in Eastern Europe, see Henke, pp. 64–65.

40. See especially Macmillan, pp. 440–41, on the Albert Hall rally of the "Arms and the Covenant" group on 3 December 1936, the day after news about the marriage plans of the king first appeared in the English press.

action in Parliament against the greater degree of self-government for
India embodied in the Government of India Act of 1935. Barely emerging
from that fiasco, he now threw himself into the lost cause of defending
Edward VIII in the face of a practically unanimous House of Commons.[41]
The very event which Hitler imagined was proof of a hopeless anti-
German policy in London in reality undermined for a long time the position of the most eloquent advocate of such a policy, and thereby helped
open the way for Neville Chamberlain and Anthony Eden to try to formulate and implement a policy of accommodation with the Third Reich.

In the summer of 1936 Phillip Kerr, Lord Lothian, had sent to Chamberlain and Eden a letter outlining his own proposals for British policy
toward Germany, a policy rather like that later advocated by Sir Nevile
Henderson, and hence not surprisingly receiving the latter's full approval.[42] Lord Lothian had participated in the Versailles peace conference and had become a critic of the treaty, advocating concessions to
Germany. He thought that Britain ought to let Germany annex Austria,
Memel, and Danzig, and should reconcile herself to a completion of the
unification of all Germans into one country, or otherwise face the possibility of war. Like others at the time, Lord Lothian believed that since
Germany's ostensible aims were subject to the limitation inherent in the
actual distribution of German-speaking people in Europe, the full application of the principle of self-determination to them—even if at the expense
of others—would right alleged wrongs done Germany and, without seriously harming British interests or the national rights of non-Germans,
preserve the peace.[43]

Again like many others, he failed to recognize that Hitler's aims included the displacement of non-Germans from areas that the latter considered suitable for German settlement; but Lord Lothian had put his
finger on a key issue that would prove the hinge of policy: if Germany ever
did go clearly beyond the existing nationality lines, then her ambitions of
European or world conquest would be proved in fact and not only anticipated in fear or speculation.[44] When that happened, Lord Lothian like

41. The point is made well, ibid., 7 and 8 December 1936, pp. 282, 284. Ironically, Chamberlain was one of the most vehement opponents of Edward VIII in the constitutional crisis
(*Davidson Papers*, pp. 415, 417); the Labor party leaders, outside the government at the
time, were equally vigorous in their hostility.

42. The text of Lord Lothian's proposal of 3 June 1936 has been published in J. R. M.
Butler, *Lord Lothian, 1882–1940* (London: Macmillan, 1960), pp. 215, 354–62.

43. See also Gottfried Niedhart, *Grossbritannien und die Sowjetunion, 1934–1939*
(Munich: Fink, 1972), pp. 104–9.

44. It is not suggested that the precise lines separating Germans from non-Germans were
always self-evident—quite the contrary; but if one distinguishes between detail and broad
areas, the matter becomes much simpler. Thus in the case of Czechoslovakia, there was
never any doubt that there were areas of compact German character on the fringes and of
compact Czech character in the center of Bohemia, whatever arguments one might make
about the location of the line dividing the two. It should be noted that from London's
perspective, the Polish Corridor was always, quite correctly, seen as inhabited overwhelmingly by Poles; it will be remembered that even Henderson referred only to the
Germans of Upper Silesia.

many others would turn to advocacy of a policy of opposition to Germany, but in the meantime his view implied extensive concessions.

The response of Neville Chamberlain, then still chancellor of the exchequer, to these ideas is characteristic and gives an outline of the policy he would follow when assuming the reins of power in 1937:

> I am afraid I have a lurking suspicion that there is no real bona fides in Germany, and that she is merely playing for time until she finds herself strong enough to make her next spring. At the same time, one must not let any opportunity slip by, and I am prepared to deal with her on the basis that she means what she says; and, if I could see a prospect of a real settlement, I would be prepared to go a long way to get it.[45]

More interested in foreign affairs than Stanley Baldwin, Chamberlain had worked closely with Eden on many issues,[46] but he had a suspicion that the foreign secretary was not as committed to a policy of negotiations as he was himself. This suspicion was fed by Sir Samuel Hoare, Eden's predecessor, who was personally much closer to Chamberlain and wrote him in March 1937:

> Do not let anything irrevocable or badly compromising happen in foreign politics until you are in control. I say this because I am convinced that the F[oreign] O[ffice] is so much biassed against Germany (and Italy and Japan) that unconsciously and almost continuously they are making impossible any European reconciliation.[47]

Though actually far more in agreement than was subsequently made to appear,[48] Chamberlain and Eden were of sufficiently differing temperament to assure some internal friction in the formulation, and even more in the conduct, of British policy. At the beginning, however, and it will be remembered that Baldwin remained prime minister until May, they worked together well on a policy both shared. Early in 1937, that was summarized by one Foreign Office official as being designed "to gain time," to which both Chamberlain and Eden would add, to secure peace.[49]

In the British government of 1937, the prospect of gaining time and securing peace was seen as lying in improving relations with Germany in order to restrain that power from moves that could start a war, and a major hope of accomplishing this objective rested on strengthening what were perceived to be the more cautious and moderate elements in the

45. Lord Lothian Papers, GD 40/17/445/47.
46. Eden, p. 501.
47. Templewood Papers, IX, 2.
48. Pratt (pp. 71–72) summarizes the evidence on Eden's favoring appeasement of Germany, and also shows (pp. 78–84) that it was Eden who originally persuaded Chamberlain to try for an agreement with Mussolini in 1937. See also Roy Douglas, "Chamberlain and Eden, 1937–38," *Journal of Contemporary History*, 13, No. 1 (Jan. 1978), 97–116.
49. Gladwyn Jebb's minute of 9 January 1937 on a memorandum on "Economic Appeasement" by Stanley Bruce (Australian high commissioner in London), W 373/5/50, FO 371/21215, f.7; cf. *Harvey Diaries*, p. 244.

German government: the army, the foreign office, and Hjalmar Schacht, then still minister of economics and head of the Reichsbank, the German central bank. In a perception of Germany that was in its own way as inaccurate as Hitler's view of England, the British government hoped that by strengthening what were believed to be moderate elements offering less radical advice to Hitler, the German leader could be deflected from more dangerous courses of action.[50] This would prove an illusory hope, but by tracing British and French policy in pursuit of this phantom, much can be learned about the background of World War II because, in the process, both sides of that conflict defined their views and revealed their objectives in concrete rather than theoretical terms.

The idea of attempting a settlement with Germany by colonial and economic concessions that Britain would make in exchange for German return to the League of Nations, respect for the independence of the Central and East European countries, and the prospect of a limitation of armaments had first been canvassed in the London government in the winter of 1935–36. Such schemes, originally developed and advocated by Sir Robert Vansittart, had never left the realm of internal discussion because of German refusal to negotiate with Britain about anything in the first months of 1936 as Hitler prepared to tear up the Locarno treaties.[51] The general idea of what one author has studied under the title of "economic appeasement" came up again when Schacht visited Paris and conferred with French Prime Minister Léon Blum in August 1936.[52] The possibility of agreement, at first apparent to both French and Germans, soon evaporated. Both the British and the French governments were unwilling to make colonial concessions to Germany except within a framework of a settlement to which Germany would also make some contribution. Schacht, however, was looking for free gifts to strengthen his own personal position in the struggle over control of the German economy and in the hope of diverting Hitler toward a more cooperative and less aggressive policy. The latter would not consider making any concessions in exchange for the restoration of former German colonies, and the episode ended without concrete results.[53]

There was, however, one significant after-effect of the informal soundings of 1936. There were some loose ends left over from the talks. The French had not passed on to Schacht the full text of the British government's response; and Schacht, though defeated in his project, had not given up all hope of success in either international negotiations or the

50. Br. Cabinet 1 (37) of 13 January 1937, C 506/270/18, FO 371/20734.

51. Weinberg, *Foreign Policy*, pp. 244–45; Niedhart, pp. 122–23.

52. Bernd Jürgen Wendt, *Economic Appeasement: Handel und Finanz in der britischen Deutschland-Politik 1933–1939* (Düsseldorf: Bertelsmann, 1971); C. A. MacDonald, "Economic Appeasement and the German Moderates, 1937–39: An Introductory Essay," *Past and Present*, 56 (Aug. 1972), 105–35.

53. Weinberg, *Foreign Policy*, pp. 280–81.

detouring of Hitler's ambitions from European conquests to colonial exploitation.[54] These factors, combined with the British and French interest in an effort to secure a rapprochement with Germany through an approach along lines possibly congenial to the "moderates" in Germany, led to a reopening of conversations with Schacht early in 1937.

As the British considered the hints from Schacht that he would like to talk with them, as they examined various proposals for economic appeasement that were submitted for internal review, and as they heard that Schacht might be visiting Paris again, a general review of the issues within the Foreign Office and with Chancellor of the Exchequer Neville Chamberlain produced preliminary agreement on several points.[55] There was some diffidence about answering in public the German colonial campaign lest the arguments against restituting colonies to Germany be subsequently used against the British government should it decide in favor of such a move. This point, as well as the need to be able to negotiate intelligently if the ocasion did arise, made it all the more important for the government to clear its own mind on the subject. Whatever might be offered to Germany, however, could be put forward only in return for a clearly specified quid pro quo. The Germans might well be asked to explain what they were prepared to offer in return, and in this fashion the government's rearmament program could be balanced with negotiations for an agreement. Such a procedure assumed the prospect of a genuine German contribution; and that, in British eyes, meant three things were required in addition to a more precise definition of their own position. The French must be restrained from making unilateral concessions, a policy toward which London thought Blum might be inclined. The British themselves would have to explore with Schacht the extent to which he was really authorized to begin negotiations. Finally, in view of the constant doubts about that authorization, the negotiations would have to be moved into regular diplomatic channels. All in London, furthermore, were agreed from the beginning on one point which Berlin previously had always rejected—and would continue to reject—namely, that there could be no unilateral concessions. A colonial settlement would make sense and could be made acceptable to the British public only if in return Germany provided guarantees of a change in policy that assured peace and security in Europe.[56]

54. On the confusion over the British message to Schacht, see C 156, C 369/37/18, FO 371/20718.

55. The documentation is very extensive. The following account is based on ibid.; C 207/37/18, FO 371/20718; C 1591/37/18, FO 371/20719; W 373/5/50, FO 371/21215; C 447/1/18, FO 371/20705; C 237/237/18, FO 371/20734; U.S., 1937, 1:31. For a partially accurate view by a German journalist at the time, see Dertinger's "Informationsbericht Nr. 58," 7 January 1937, Bundesarchiv, Brammer, Z.Sg. 101/30, ff.15–17.

56. It should be noted that Vansittart, who had originally pushed a plan for colonial restitution, was by now most skeptical that Germany could be deterred by it from adventures in Central Europe (R 659/419/22, FO 371/21178, f.209; G.D., C, 6, No. 182).

Eden and Chamberlain agreed on 18 January 1937 that an attempt to sound out Schacht on "a comprehensive settlement" should be made through Sir Frederick Leith-Ross, chief economic adviser of the government, with no clear indication of any intended British concessions, but with the expectation that Schacht would explain what "political undertakings and assurances" Germany would be prepared to give as its contribution to such a settlement. The samples listed in Sir Frederick's instructions include the key phrase, "abandonment of the policy of economic self-sufficiency and its corollary of territorial expansion."[57] When approached, Schacht said he would be happy to meet Leith-Ross, claimed to have Hitler's authorization for economic negotiations, and agreed that any negotiations would subsequently have to be transferred to the regular diplomats.[58]

On 2 February 1937 Leith-Ross had a secret meeting with Schacht, of which the French received both prior notice and a full record.[59] Schacht argued that only a policy of economic and colonial concessions could provide a viable alternative to the more radical policies being urged on Hitler. He claimed to have authorization from Hitler on economic and colonial matters, including a promise to accept restrictions on German sovereignty in any returned colonies. He further claimed to be familiar enough with the views of Hitler and von Neurath to be able to promise noninterference in Czechoslovakia, a commitment to refrain from any aggression against Russia, a return to a "reformed" League of Nations, and an arms limitations agreement as a part of a general settlement to be negotiated by Germany, Britain, and France. He urged that secret talks pave the way for formal negotiations, and that the British invite von Neurath to London in the later stages of these. He even thought that President Roosevelt might be persuaded to call the meeting at which the relevant agreements were to be signed and would be willing to urge American cancellation of the Allied war debts to the United States as the American contribution to a new world settlement.[60]

Although Schacht's comments suggested that the political guarantees Britain expected could be attained, authorities in London were exceedingly skeptical that this was in fact true. On the very day after Schacht's meeting with Leith-Ross, Hitler told the British ambassador in Berlin that he saw no prospect of agreement on a Western Pact, disarmament, or

57. Eden to Leith-Ross, 19 January 1937, C 475/1/18, FO 371/20705, f.66. The relevant documents, ibid., ff.58–59. It is significant that Chamberlain, not Baldwin, participated in this decision, and that the British, like Hitler, realized that full economic self-sufficiency could be secured by Germany only if she seized vast additional territories.

58. C 619/37/18, FO 371/20718.

59. The relevant papers are filed under C 1476/78/18, in FO 371/20726, ff.319–41; see also Sir Frederick Leith-Ross, *Money Talks: Fifty Years of International Finance* (London: Hutchinson, 1968), pp. 238–41.

60. There are hints in the records that Schacht had discussed this idea with William Bullitt, the American ambassador in Paris.

almost anything else; thus justifying a Foreign Office comment on Phipps's report that Hitler "would seem almost to have gone deliberately out of his way to put a spike in Dr. Schacht's wheel."[61] Leith-Ross himself was most dubious that Hitler would meet Britain's political requirements but thought it wise to continue the discussions.[62]

When Lord Halifax, as acting foreign secretary in Eden's temporary absence, met with Joachim von Ribbentrop on 11 February, the latter raised the German demand for the return of the colonies that Hitler had also voiced in his speech of 30 January. In the informal but lengthy conversation, the two contrasting positions which have already been alluded to and which would subsequently wreck all prospects for agreement emerged clearly. Halifax explained that the British-government could consider colonies for Germany only within the framework of a general settlement, while von Ribbentrop insisted that the colonies be returned without any concessions on Germany's part and that a German-British agreement, by omitting any reference to Central and Eastern Europe, in effect give Germany a free hand there. Whatever private musings pointed to such a concept, it was unacceptable to the government in London.[63]

Lord Halifax indirectly, but still clearly, made the point that von Ribbentrop chose to ignore until the two men as foreign ministers of their respective countries exchanged declarations of war over the issue in 1939:

> I told him—Halifax recorded—that Providence had decreed according to the present map of Europe that his country and Russia were not neighbours, and that if his Government could do anything in the direction of the effective preservation of the *status quo* of the intervening nations, this would at once both be a reassurance to Europe and, if it were required, be a reassurance to his own country vis-à-vis the only other European country of whom they professed to be in fear.

Von Ribbentrop's answer, in line with German expansionist aims, was to demand that any German-British agreement be limited to Western Europe.

In the following weeks, the British reviewed the problem of how to proceed both internally and with the French, while von Ribbentrop, in spite of Eden's cautions on the subject, proceeded to make a major public

61. Phipps tel. 74 (Saving) of 4 February 1937, C 989/1/18, FO 371/20706, ff.232–36.

62. Leith-Ross to Phipps, 4 February 1937 (enclosing a copy of his record of the talk with Schacht), C 1273/78/18, FO 371/20726, f.304. Phipps replied on 11 February warning that no German guarantees as to conditions under which she would run her colonies would be adhered to (ibid., ff.302–3).

63. Foreign Office memoranda for Halifax for this meeting are in C 1282/37/18, FO 371/20719. The British record is in C 1185/1/18, FO 371/20706; the German record in *G.D.*, C, 6, No. 201 (most of the German text is in Klaus Hildebrand, *Vom Reich zum Weltreich, Hitler, NSDAP und koloniale Frage, 1919–1945* [Munich: Fink, 1969], pp. 898–902). The information given on it to the French is in *D.D.F.*, 2d, 4, Nos. 435, 436. See also Jones, 12 February 1937, p. 313; Henke, p. 73.

speech on the colonial question, a procedure guaranteed to alarm British public opinion.[64] With French agreement to hold back on any further approaches until the British were clear in their own minds what if anything to offer Germany, and what specifically to ask in return, the London cabinet examined the problem. There was hope but little optimism that anything would come of it all. As the British leaders began their review, they could read a report on what the Japanese ambassador to Rome, Sugimura Yotaro, had told his British colleague on returning from a trip to Germany on behalf of the Japanese foreign ministry. Sugimura had learned that the Germans would give absolutely nothing for the return of their colonies, claimed to be afraid of Russia, and planned to destroy Czechoslovakia.[65]

The anguished soul-searching in London in March and April 1937 faced the problem of what to do about the approach from Schacht. Although it was doubted that he had authority to deal with the political issues that most interested the British government, and although all indications were that Hitler would not reverse himself on the positions he had taken on these questions, the feeling that no stone should be left unturned and no road untried in the search for peace led to a decision to try this route. It would obviously be necessary to coordinate any action with the French who had already discussed the general range of issues with Schacht and whose share of the former German colonial empire—the Cameroons and Togo—had been the focus of Schacht's demands and Blum's willingness to consider concessions. The lengthy internal deliberations lead to a communication to the French government which embodied tentative British decisions on the main issues involved as well as the approach to be followed, and which hence deserves careful examination.[66]

64. On the internal British discussions and consultation with the French, see C 1591/37/18, FO 371/20719; C 1328, C 1635, C 1806, C 1889/78/18, FO 371/20726. On Eden's meeting with von Ribbentrop on 26 February, see C 1638/1/18, FO 371/20706; *D.D.F.*, 2d, 5, No. 33. On von Ribbentrop's 1 March speech at Leipzig, see "Bestellungen aus der Pressekonferenz vom 1. März 1937," Bundesarchiv, Brammer, Z.Sg. 101/9, f.167; Hildebrand, pp. 508–9; C 1707/37/18, FO 371/20719; see also C 1428/136/18, FO 371/20731. On Eden's special warning to von Ribbentrop of 13 March, see C 2081/37/18, FO 371/20719, ff.152–56.

65. Drummond to Vansittart, 4 March 1937, and related documents, in C 2090/3/18, FO 371/20710, ff.146–54. Sugimura's comments to the French ambassador to the Vatican are in *D.D.F.*, 2d, 5, No. 67.

66. The final text of the instruction to Phipps, from which the extensive quotations here are taken, is in C 3260/270/18, FO 371/20735, pp. 4–7. Memoranda on the subject had been circulated to the cabinet Committee on Foreign Policy by Eden on 15 March (C 2124/270/18, FO 371/20734); by the secretary of state for the colonies, Ormsby-Gore, on 16 March (C 2302/37/18, FO 371/20720); and by the chancellor of the exchequer, Neville Chamberlain, on 2 April (C 2618/270/18, FO 371/20735).

It is worth noting that the Foreign Office thought Chamberlain's proposal the best—it was the firmest on the need for political concessions by Germany—and agreed to its being the basis for drafting the final text. The cabinet Committee on Foreign Policy met on the subject on 18 March (C 2303/37/18, FO 371/20720) and on 6 April (C 2619/270/18, FO 371/20735). Other relevant documents are C 2338, C 3243/37/18, FO 371/20720; C 2304/270/18, C 2763, C 2781, C 2948, C 3157/270/18, FO 371/20735; C 4135/37/18, FO 371/20721. On the broader

The communication of 27 April 1937, after briefly reviewing the earlier talks, repeated the caution that

> there is some uncertainty as regards the precise authority which Dr. Schacht may have from his government. . . . He was clearly not in a position to commit them on political questions, and before leaving Berlin gave Baron von Neurath an undertaking not to do so. Indeed, his observations on the readiness of the German Government to consider concessions in the political sphere were not very precise; and, although he intimated that the ideas he had expressed had received the approval of Herr Hitler, they did not bear any close relation either to the German Government's previously declared attitude on the questions to which he referred or to recent public and private statements by Herr Hitler himself.

Any further talks with Schacht might, therefore, at some point, have to be transferred "to more regular diplomatic channels." In spite of this difficulty, the British felt that

> every advantage should be taken of these overtures on the part of Dr. Schacht in order to explore the possibilities of a general agreement with Germany. They consider that the preponderant factor to be taken into account is the vital necessity, in the interests of every country in Europ [sic], of bringing about an appeasement of the political situation. No opportunity should . . . be missed of securing this object; and it would be desirable to start from the assumption that Dr. Schacht's proposals are to be regarded as indicating a genuine readiness on the part of the German Government for a general discussion which might develop into concrete negotiations.

If the French agreed with this view, then an answer to Schacht would have to be worked out. Schacht appeared to contemplate "a comprehensive settlement covering, on the one hand, certain economic and financial concessions to Germany, the most important of which related to the transfer of colonies; and, on the other hand, the acceptance of Germany of the political desiderata of the French and United Kingdom Governments." Schacht had formulated the German requirements; it would be up to the French and British to work out theirs. The British proposed that the answer to be given either Schacht or von Neurath be along the following lines:

> Before the French and United Kingdom Governments can judge whether the tripartite conversations on the basis suggested by Dr. Schacht would be useful, they would desire to know from the German Government whether, on the political side of the programme, the Ger-

issues of economic appeasement, see also W 6363, W 8976/5/50, FO 371/21215. The comments in *Harvey Diaries*, pp. 20, 21, 26, 29, 35–36, are unusually ill informed but a useful document is on pp. 407–9.

man Government are willing that the negotiations, of which these conversations would be the first stage, shall include the following objectives:—

(a) The conclusion of a treaty or treaties of non-aggression and guarantee for Western Europe to replace the Treaty of Locarno.

(b) Measures by Germany, in treaty form or otherwise, which will satisfy the Governments of Central and Eastern Europe with regard to Germany's intention to respect the territorial integrity and sovereign independence of all Central and Eastern European States. Confirmation will, in particular, be welcomed of Germany's readiness to negotiate a non-aggression and non-interference treaty with Czechoslovakia and to enter into some arrangement with regard to the Soviet Union.

(c) The return of Germany to the League of Nations. It would be desirable to learn whether the attitude of the German Government on this question is still as described in their Peace Plan of March 1936,[67] or whether they now consider it necessary to make any stipulations in this connexion.

(d) An international arrangement for the limitation of armaments.

It will be understood that the precise method by which each of these objectives can best be secured will be open to discussion, but the French [and British Governments] do not think it unreasonable to ask the German Government to give them a definite assurance that they intend to enter upon the discussion with a genuine desire to co-operate in achieving agreement upon these points, and that they would not seek to exclude any of the foregoing proposals on general grounds of principle.

If a basis of negotiation could be reached on the foregoing political questions, the French [and British Governments] would be ready to include in the discussions consideration of the question of assisting Germany to re-establish her financial and economic system on a sounder basis. They would not exclude from the discussion any proposal which the German Government might put forward in this connexion; but their examination of Germany's difficulties in this field suggests that the solution of these problems would depend not only on external assistance, but also on the readiness of the German Government to adopt the measures necessary to restore internal economic equilibrium, to reassure capital, and to play their part in a general relaxation of trade restrictions. All these questions would, therefore, be open to discussion.

In regard to colonies, the British had decided, largely at Chamberlain's urging, to make no specific reference "to the question of the transfer of

67. The reference here is to a public German offer to return to the League of Nations that accompanied the remilitarization of the Rhineland and was designed not to be implemented, but to be used as a means of restraining England in the crisis (Weinberg, *Foreign Policy*, pp. 250–51, 256).

colonial territories, on the importance of which Dr. Schacht has insisted, except in so far as it is stated that it is not intended to exclude any proposals from discussion." This was not only because Britain and France would first have to work out the details of a colonial offer, a subject of considerable difficulty that will be discussed later, but mainly because there could and would be no prospect of any colonial concessions to Germany unless the British and French political requirements were met by Germany; so that if the negotiations failed, it would be over Germany's refusal to meet these requirements rather than the refusal of colonial concessions. As the British message put it, colonial concessions "could only be contemplated if they were accepted by Germany as a full and final settlement of all her territorial claims, and if thereby a permanent basis could be found for European appeasement."

In any new colonial settlement, there would be several problems, regardless of which specific territories were involved. Would the territories be transferred within the mandate system or in full sovereignty? There were problems within the League as well as regarding other powers and their rights, especially if the latter course were considered. The whole problem of the protection of the rights of the native populations was especially difficult; having assumed obligations essentially similar to those of a trustee toward the inhabitants of these areas, how could Britain and France deal with the juridical and moral issues involved? Beyond these complications, there was the most touchy problem of all: what territory could be returned? It was known that Japan would never give back its share of the German empire, and the British Dominions had expressed themselves in similar terms about their mandates. A long list of "insuperable objections" was presented against the transfer of Tanganyika, the portion of German East Africa for which England was the mandatory, and some of these applied to a smaller portion that had become a Belgian mandate. That left the former German colonies in West Africa, Togo and the Cameroons, which were for the most part under French mandate and which had been discussed in the prior talks between Blum and Schacht. In those talks, Blum "appeared not to exclude the possibility of some colonial concession to Germany." If the French were willing to transfer their mandates as part of a general settlement, England would be willing to have the small portions of these former German colonies under her control returned also.

It was obvious that such a plan would mean "a much larger concession by France than by the United Kingdom." Further concessions would have to take the form "of economic measures, such as the assurance to Germany of supplies of raw materials or of outlets for German exports to British colonies." While this was not a particularly promising contribution on England's part, the internal debate in London suggests that those involved in it were fully aware of the inherent impossibility of having

France return all of her colonial gains, while Britain, which had secured
the literal as well as the figurative lion's share, contributed only the slivers
of Togo and the Cameroons.[68] Various suggestions for meeting this problem were put forth. One went in the direction of additional British political
commitments, apparently in the form of supplementary guarantees of
France's East European allies; a proposal made by Chamberlain that
should be noted as an important clue to his thinking which always included this as a possible, even if unpleasant, contingency. The others took
the form of possible colonial transfers to France by way of compensation.
The termination in favor of France of the British-French condominium
of the New Hebrides was mentioned, as was the transfer to France of the
British West Africa colony of Gambia, surrounded on all land sides by
French colonial possessions. Since there was no consensus, the evil day
of facing up to this problem was postponed.

When the British proposal is viewed as a whole, however, its thrust is
clear. The danger to the whole world, including the people of Africa, of
another war was so great that almost any effort must be made to avoid it.
The prospects did not look good, but if colonial concessions would bring
Germany back to the family of nations, especially by the maintenance of
the independence of the countries of Central and Eastern Europe and the
abandonment of German ambitions for an eventual attack on the Soviet
Union, the price—as perceived from London and Paris if not from Douala
and Lomé—would be worth paying. In any case, the attempt could serve
to strengthen the moderate elements in Germany and would, if rejected,
make clear where the fault lay. In later British plans of appeasement, the
same elements would recur. In the winter of 1937–38 and in the unofficial
contacts of the summer of 1939, there was always the hope, weak but not
to be neglected, that what were thought of as essentially economic concessions might deter Germany from an aggressive policy in Central and
Eastern Europe, a policy that would start a war into which all would be
drawn sooner or later. If Germany's problems were basically economic as
some Germans were arguing and some non-Germans believed, it seemed
to make sense to offer her a way out of those difficulties, even at considerable cost. Any such costs would be minute compared to those of
another world war.

In view of the mythology about alleged British attempts to direct German expansion eastward, it is worth noting that there is no evidence of
such efforts. On the contrary, it was precisely because the governments in
London as well as Paris realized that after the remilitarization of the

---

68. The British discussions of this time, as opposed to those of the winter 1937–38, show
no awareness of the fact that the French had reintegrated the "New Cameroons," the
territory ceded to Germany in the settlement of the Second Morocco Crisis of 1911, into
their central African colonial empire, and had successfully limited the application of the
mandate system to the pre-1911 portions of the Cameroons under their control.

Rhineland, Germany planned to remain temporarily quiet in the west while moving forward in Central and Eastern Europe that the plans reviewed here and those developed in the winter of 1937–38 and again in 1939 were prepared to deflect Germany from eastern adventures. Since the British had been given the impression that Germany might sign an agreement with Czechoslovakia directly, would not sign one with the Soviet Union, but would conclude an agreement that provided for an indirect German promise of nonaggression toward the latter power, they were pushing for that route—it was the substance, not the form, that mattered. The basic aim was clear: no German forcible expansion in Europe in return for which Britain and France would assist Germany economically by colonial, financial, and trade concessions.

The difficult question that the British had tried to avoid in preparing their views for the French—what colonial concessions they would make themselves if France were to give up her portion of the former German colonial empire—quickly came back to haunt them. In the talks between Sir Eric Phipps, the newly appointed British ambassador to Paris, Blum, French Foreign Minister Yvon Delbos, and François-Poncet, who was temporarily in Paris in early May 1937, the French expressed themselves in general agreement with the British view of how to proceed, though Blum as a Socialist wanted the idea of reassuring capital dropped. They also thought that the wishes of the Western Powers for political guarantees and the return of Germany to international economic cooperation would have to be satisfied before there could be any serious thought of returning colonies to Germany. They believed, and eventually succeeded in persuading London, that the best way to move forward in the immediate future was not to give the Germans anything in writing, but to take advantage of Schacht's planned trip to Paris in May to open the German pavillion at the international exposition for a talk with him at which the British would be represented and in which an effort would be made to see if there were any real prospects of agreement. If there proved to be, that would be the time to concert a formal communication to make to the German government. The French were doubtful that anything would come of it all, but wanted to keep trying; if there were any prospects of a real general settlement, surely the effort should be made even if the costs were great.

There were, however, two aspects to which further consideration would have to be given. The French might be willing to transfer territory under mandate, but would not agree to any transfer of colonies in full sovereignty. They were also quite explicit on the point that it would be almost impossible for France to make the bulk of the territorial concessions when, as the French public well knew, the British had acquired the bulk of Germany's colonial empire. Although Blum left himself an escape on the point—a sign of how strongly he really did want a detente with Germany—the French government expected the British to make some significant contribution in addition to the small portions of Togo and the Cameroons under British mandate.[69]

The resulting soul-searching in London as to whether there was any point in continuing the conversations with Schacht, if the French would not make colonial concessions unless there were an at least equivalent British contribution, led to agreement that Schacht should be sounded when he came to Paris and also to renewed investigation of the possibility of compensatory concessions to France rather than Germany. Gambia, which had been considered a candidate for cession to France several times since first coming under British control in the early seventeenth century, was the main candidate for transfer.[70] All such specifics, however, would depend on the extent to which Schacht appeared both inclined and authorized to indicate German willingness to meet the British-French political requirements. It quickly became apparent that neither condition would be met.[71]

As for any official authorization, it was soon obvious that Schacht had none. At Chamberlain's request, Lord Lothian asked Hitler at their meeting on 4 May what Schacht *was* authorized to discuss, only to be told that "Schacht was authorized to discuss economic questions, but that before he could trench on political issues he would have to get authority from [Hitler] himself."[72] The Foreign Office had already concluded that this was so, and von Neurath did what he could to spike Schacht's efforts by assuring Henderson and François-Poncet that the colonial question was of no importance and merely Schacht's hobby.[73] This lack of authority, combined with Schacht's own increasing reluctance to champion the political concessions Britain and France required, guaranteed that the talks held when he was in Paris at the end of May would lead nowhere. These talks are discussed in more detail at a later point in this chapter, but in any case, Schacht's report to Hitler did not move matters any further from the German side.[74] Before the subsequent British attempts to restart

69. C 3260/270/18, FO 371/20735, pp. 7–9; C 3469, C 3474, C 3476, C 3513/37/18, FO 371/20720; C 3664/37/18, FO 371/20721; C 3669/37/18, FO 371/20723; *D.D.F.*, 2d, 5, Nos. 420, 429. The French also wanted U.S. Ambassador Bullitt brought into the conversations, but the British successfully objected.

70. These discussions read like strange echoes of the late nineteenth century, but that does not remove their significance for understanding the participants. There is an echo in Stalin's attempts at appeasing Germany in the spring of 1941.

71. Foreign Office notes on C 3362/270/18, FO 371/20735; 10th meeting of the cabinet Committee on Foreign Policy, 10 May 1937, C 3590, and 11th meeting, 19 May 1937, C 3634/37/18, FO 371/20721; C 3664, ibid.; *D.D.F.*, 2d, 5, No. 429. With the Imperial Conference about to convene, the London government also had to consider the extent to which the Dominions were to be informed about talks on a subject that affected several of them most directly (C 3562/37/18, FO 371/20721).

72. Lothian to Chamberlain, Lothian Papers, GD 40/17/203/244.

73. C 3560/3/18, FO 371/20710; C 3741/37/18, FO 371/20721; *D.D.F.*, 2d, 5, No. 447.

74. The Schacht talks themselves are discussed on pp. 91–94 below. On the absence of replies or results, see C 3684/37/18, FO 371/20721; von Weizsäcker note, Pol. II 1537, of 29 May 1937, T-120, 3469/8915/E 622202; Wiedemann notes in *G.D.*, D, 7:545.

negotiations can be examined, however, it is necessary to retrace the Schacht negotiations and related developments from the perspective of their role in French foreign policy.

The remilitarization of the Rhineland had both ended a major factor in France's own security against aggression and eliminated the most important element in her ability to restrain Germany in Central and Eastern Europe. The report on his findings in Germany that Sugimura, the Japanese ambassador in Rome, gave to the French ambassador to the Vatican, namely, that Germany expected to annex Austria and then to crush Czechoslovakia while staying on the defensive in the west to hold off France, came as no surprise to the French government.[75] Their own diplomats had been reporting the same thing, and one had only to look at a map of Europe to see that this was the likely course of events.[76]

Amid the ever-receding hopes of arriving at a replacement for the Locarno agreements, the French government held all the more firmly to the tie with England, but it was clear to them that this tie provided safety for themselves alone and not for their allies. While the British would not disinterest themselves in Central and Eastern Europe, their public commitment to go to war was limited to the contingencies of aggression against France and Belgium.[77] The British position was understood in Paris; it was usually phrased in terms of an analogy to the policy of Britain before 1914. The possibility of British neutrality made war more likely, but a promise to go to war if Czechoslovakia, for example, were attacked, would divide the British public—and such a division would become known and invite war even more surely.[78] The French recognized Britain's growing concern about Germany, but they also realized that there were steps they would have to take themselves.[79]

The French proceeded to strengthen their defenses. They began the reequipment of their army, a lengthy and expensive process. It was obvious that this would take time; and the French government, furthermore, was very conscious of the fact that the French population base was only two-thirds that of Germany. Domestic strife in France accentuated the difficulties both because it diverted attention from foreign dangers and because budgetary troubles impeded the financing of rearmament. The French strengthened the Maginot Line—the system of fortifications along the border with Germany—and, responding somewhat to British pressure,

75. *D.D.F.*, 2d, 5, No. 67.
76. Ibid., 4, Nos. 360, 399.
77. A clear statement was made by Eden at Leamington on 20 November 1936, see Eden, pp. 539–41; *D.D.F.*, 2d, 4, Nos. 4, 15; John E. Dreifort, *Yvon Delbos at the Quai d'Orsay* (Lawrence: University Press of Kansas, 1973), chap. 5.
78. See R 1130/188/12, FO 371/21127; *U.S.*, 1937, 1:58–60, 84–86. This theme runs through the documents; aspects of it will be examined in connection with the war crises of 1938 and 1939.
79. For a French assessment, see *D.D.F.*, 2d, 4, No. 38.

also built up the French air force. The basic French military strategy, however, remained entirely defensive.[80]

On the diplomatic front, the French government had begun an effort in 1936 to strengthen the ties of the Little Entente.[81] That grouping was designed to protect its three members—Czechoslovakia, Rumania, and Yugoslavia—against the one danger which, in isolation, each could meet by itself: an attempt by Hungary to regain the territory lost by the Treaty of Trianon. It could not, however, even when all three were joined, protect them against one of the great powers. Rumania was concerned, and with good reason, about Russian attempts to regain Bessarabia.[82] Yugoslavia was worried, and with equally good reason, about Italian designs on portions of its territory. Czechoslovakia had excellent cause to fear German ambitions. What the French government attempted to do was to persuade the three countries to promise each other mutual assistance against any aggressor—meaning Germany or Italy—in which case they could be sure of France's coming to their support; the hope being that knowledge of the existence of such a combination would serve to deter aggression against any of them.

In spite of persistent efforts by both the French and Czechoslovak governments, nothing came of this plan. The major, but by no means only, obstacle was Yugoslavia. As Yugoslav Prime Minister Milan Stojadinović explained in December 1936 to a special French envoy sent to persuade him, Yugoslavia simply could not afford to expose itself to economic reprisals, having been forced to look to Germany for trade, first by the depression and later by her own adherence to sanctions against Italy. The internal tensions of the country, moreover, were such as to require a long period of peace, while in case of war, Yugoslavia would surely be overrun.[83] In the spring of 1937 Stojadinović was even more explicit with the French minister to Belgrade. France could defend herself behind the Maginot Line, but she could not really help the Little Entente powers if they were attacked unless herself assured of British help. Since

80. For the background of French military policy, see Judith M. Hughes, *To the Maginot Line: The Politics of French Military Preparations in the 1920's* (Cambridge, Mass.: Harvard University Press, 1971), and Volker Wieland, *Zur Problematik der französsischen Militärpolitik und Militärdoktrin zwischen den Weltkriegen* (Boppard: Boldt, 1973). On French and British reluctance to discuss disarmament publicly when the public was just coming around to support the rearmament effort and should not be lulled by hopes of disarmament, see *D.D.F.*, 2d, 5, Nos. 274, 450. For Admiral Darlan's concern that the reduction in French naval construction resulting from budgetary cuts would endanger France's position, see ibid., 6, Nos. 293, 354, 381.

81. Weinberg, *Foreign Policy*, p. 326; *D.D.F.*, 2d, 4 and 5, passim; Dreifort, pp. 132–40; R 2795/26/67, FO 371/21137.

82. No one as yet anticipated that Soviet territorial ambitions extended to other portions of Rumania.

83. *D.D.F.*, 2d, 4, No. 180; cf. Šeba (Bucharest) report 151/37, 17 March 1937, Czechoslovak document in T-120, 1809/1041/413846.

the latter assurance was not forthcoming, why provoke the Germans?[84] Little did he know that the situation was even worse than he imagined; for there was little that France would have done even if the British had given such assurances. It was left for the Poles to make that discovery in 1939.

In the meantime, however, the dilemma remained. If Yugoslavia was unwilling, no agreement could be reached. Knowing the strength of British influence in Belgrade, the French tried to enlist the London government in pressure on Yugoslavia, as well as to improve Czechoslovak-Polish relations.[85] The British were willing to try their hand at the latter of these projects, but they were most dubious about the former.[86] The whole scheme looked doubtful to the British. They were sure that both Yugoslavia and Rumania would say no anyway; Yugoslavia was not alone in objecting. The Rumanians had themselves told the British of their main worry: if Russian troops entered Rumania under a mutual assistance treaty, would they ever leave? The British, who believed that they might have to fight Germany as allies of the Soviet Union but would not care to have a Russian army in England, found this an obvious objection for Rumania to raise when the contingency contemplated was not an attack on Rumania herself but on one of two other countries by Germany or Italy.[87] Furthermore, the scheme threatened to push Germany and Italy more closely together while providing no practical help to anyone, as an examination of the geographic and military realities quickly revealed. The French would have to save Czechoslovakia; if they could not or would not, surely the Yugoslavs and Rumanians were in no position to do so. To these practical objections—which they could not rebut—the French would regularly reply with the broader political argument of stiffening the smaller nations, preventing a drift of those countries toward the Axis, and presenting a broad front to Germany.[88]

In the face of the French argument that the very reluctance of the small powers only underlined the greatness of the danger and hence of the need to meet it, the British remained convinced that the practical difficulties precluded an effective scheme. All the practical objections were present in 1939, but by then perspectives and attitudes had changed in London. It is most doubtful, moreover, that British pressure, even had it been forthcoming, would have succeeded in removing the objections of Belgrade and Bucharest. A timid France could not inspire the weakest of her allies to ostentatious bravery.[89] As for the intended first beneficiary of the

84. *D.D.F.*, 2d, 5, No. 235; cf. ibid., 6, No. 141.
85. R 189/26/67, FO 371/21136.
86. R 397, R 501, R 1021/26/67, FO 371/21136.
87. R 530/26/67, FO 371/21136.
88. R 838, R 1068/26/67, FO 371/21136; *D.D.F.*, 2d, 4, Nos. 404, 446.
89. The failure of the scheme was known quickly; see Slávik (Warsaw) report 2221 of 19 February 1937 on a conversation with the Soviet chargé, Czechoslovak document in T-120, 1809/1041/413765–66. The Italians passed information secured from British documents (see

whole scheme, Czechoslovakia, her government secretly assured Paris that it was prepared to adjust to the realities of the situation. In December 1936, when it was already evident that the projected new treaty system was unlikely to be realized, the Czechoslovak minister in Paris, Štefan Osuský, told French Foreign Minister Yvon Delbos that he and Czech President Eduard Beneš had discussed the dangers. They knew that Britain could not commit herself to them, and they wanted the French government to know that if it came to a situation where it looked as if Czechoslovakia and France were in a corner by themselves, Czechoslovakia would make the necessary sacrifices—even against her own interests—to avoid the risk of war.[90]

It is worth noting that the reluctance to take risks in the face of German and Italian strength was self-reinforcing. In this sense, the French argument had considerable validity. If countries too weak to stand up to Germany by themselves refused to get together for fear of provoking her, they would by definition each weaken themselves by a self-imposed isolation and weaken one another by the common knowledge that each stood alone. A somewhat similar dilemma was created by the international argument over the future status and role of Belgium in Europe.

In the years after the war, Belgium had been closely tied to France. The most recent regularization of her status had come in the Locarno arrangement by which her borders were guaranteed, she in turn guaranteed the German-French border, and Germany agreed to maintain the demilitarized status of the Rhineland. Domestic pressures in Belgium, originating in the objections of the Flemish element to the alignment with France; the renewed military strength of Germany, culminating in the remilitarization of the Rhineland; and the increasing signs of British and French weakness in the face of German moves, had all combined to produce a shift in Belgian policy toward one of an independent neutrality.[91] As the negotiations for a new Locarno, the so-called Western Pact, dragged on inconclusively, the question of Belgium's status and the possibility of some separate and independent regularization of it became increasingly acute. For about a year, from King Leopold's speech heralding the turn in Belgian policy in October 1936 to the German declaration about Belgium of October 1937, this issue stood forth as one of the most critical in Europe. Why was it so important?

n.32 above) to the Germans (*G.D.*, C, 6, No. 230). When there were rumors in the fall of 1937 that the scheme might be revived, nothing had changed that might have altered the negative outcome of the prior negotiations (R 6640/26/67, FO 371/21137; *Guido Schmidt Trial*, pp. 534–35).

90. *D.D.F.*, 2d, 4, No. 165. This is surely a document of great importance for an understanding of the events of 1938.

91. Weinberg, *Foreign Policy*, pp. 282–84. A detailed and very good review is in David O. Kieft, *Belgium's Return to Neutrality* (Oxford: Clarendon Press, 1972).

A series of geographic and military factors combined to make the position of Belgium in Europe more significant even than in the nineteenth century. Belgium's border with Germany was relatively short (about fifty miles, plus another fifty on the German-Luxembourg border) but it was close to Germany's most important industrial area. Furthermore, the German-French border was not only fairly short also but the southern portion of it ran along the Rhine River, and in any case covered no significant objectives on either side. If pressure were to be brought on Germany, either before or after a German attack on one of her Central or East European neighbors, the participation of Belgium was as essential to the Western Powers as it was dangerous for Germany. The same geographic factors made Belgium critical to the defense of France. If attacked by Germany, the combined borders of Belgium and France with Germany were not of inordinate length and might be held against an invasion, given adequate prior preparations. Lacking such Belgian-French cooperation, however, the problem of defense against Germany immediately became vastly more difficult, for the border between Belgium and France was more than three times as long as that between Belgium and Germany.

Here was a series of apparently insoluble conundrums. If the Belgians openly worked with the British and French after the German breach of Locarno, they risked internal dissension and German wrath. If they stayed out of things entirely, they might be overrun quickly by a Germany which had worked hard to establish an atrocious record as an occupying power in Belgium during the last war. Any Belgians inclined to forget this—there cannot have been many—were reminded of it by the continuing public controversy over the supposed Belgian provocation by guerrilla warfare of such German atrocities as the destruction of Louvain. If the Belgians took the third course, the one actually adopted, of arming themselves for defense but doing so independently while assuming that Britain and France would come to their aid if Germany staged a repetition of the earlier invasion, then they guaranteed the one thing they most wanted to avoid: that the country would become a battlefield subject to the destruction of modern warfare.[92] Moreover, having refused to allow France to move troops across Belgium in support of France's eastern allies, the Belgians would also make almost certain that when invaded, they would be invaded by a German army that had previously defeated enemies in the east and could concentrate its full might in the west.

The French, confronted with this puzzle, found equally unappealing alternatives. If they built fortifications along the lengthy Franco-Belgian border, they would appear to be writing off Belgium as well as all their eastern allies, and they would be assuming the need to defend a total border of impossible length against a country that could mobilize an

92. This point is aptly made in a French strategic appreciation of 14 April 1937, *D.D.F.*, 2d, 5, No. 275. It is also a main lesson of Brian Bond, *France and Belgium, 1939–1940* (London: Davis-Poynter, 1975).

eventually substantially larger army than her own. In the face of a situation in which the French already felt they needed larger forces to hold their defenses than the Germans—since the Germans could pick the spot to launch an offensive, while the French had no plans to attack in an early stage of a new war—this was a hopeless prospect.[93] If they did not build such a defense line by extending the Maginot Line to the sea, however, then they would have to depend on securing some sort of coordination with the Belgians. But everything in the development of Belgian policy suggested that such coordination, if possible at all, would be limited to the contingency of a German invasion of Belgium and would under no circumstances deal with the contingency that equally interested the French, namely, an action against Germany if the latter attacked Czechoslovakia or Poland.

Finally, the geographic element produced still another puzzle. With the development of air power, the question of air space, as distinct from surface space, raised a new problem of neutrality. If German planes flew over Belgium—or Holland for that matter—would that be considered by Belgium a sufficiently serious violation of neutrality to lead to her entering a war, or would Belgium consider that her neutral territory ended a given number of feet above the ground?[94] Because of the location of the United Kingdom and Germany in relation to each other, this was a topic of special interest to England and served to reinforce the already strong concern of the British government about Belgian policy.[95]

The French and British governments were, therefore, both very much interested in the closest possible ties with Belgium and did their utmost to persuade the Belgians not to take a completely neutral position.[96] While the Belgians thought that since Britain and France would in their own interest help them if Germany attacked, there was no need to provoke the Germans,[97] the British Foreign Office hoped that signs of concrete support for Belgium might arrest the drift to neutrality; accordingly on 13 January 1937, British cabinet approval was secured for a discussion of munitions supply and other matters with Belgium in case of war.[98] The German government, on the other hand, had an exactly opposite hope.

It was Hitler's view that every attempt should be made to complete the shift Belgium had started in October 1936 to the point where she was

93. C 4888/822/17, FO 371/20696.
94. The question of Luxembourg's neutrality will not be discussed here. Though the subject of interest and negotiations at the time, it was always subordinate to the Belgian question; i.e., if a war involved Belgium, it would involve Luxembourg as well, but no one seriously contemplated a contingency in which only Luxembourg might be involved.
95. On this subject, see C 3727/1/18, FO 371/20708; C 7378/1/18, FO 371/20709.
96. See D.D.F., 2d, 4, No. 2, Harvey Diaries, pp. 15–18, 21–22, 24, 31, 41–43; C 181/181/4, FO 371/20678; but compare Kieft, pp. 151–54.
97. D.D.F., 2d, 4, No. 301; D.D.B., 4, No. 188; C 1658/181/4, FO 371/20679.
98. C 212, C 318, C 1055/181/4, FO 371/20678; C 1142, C 2937, C 2938, C 6941/271/18, FO 371/20738. Kieft, pp. 161–66, stresses British responsibility for the decisions made by Belgium.

completely neutral like Switzerland. Not linked to France by military obligations and divested of whatever was left of her obligation under the covenant of the League of Nations to permit the transit of troops aiding an attacked League member, Belgium would serve as a barrier protecting Germany in the west.[99] Such a barrier would render French support of any countries Germany might attack in Central or Eastern Europe less likely and much more difficult if France did move. From his reference to Belgium in his 30 January speech,[100] to the German declaration of 13 October 1937[101] Hitler did what he could to reassure the Belgians about German intentions in the hope of facilitating a complete detaching of Belgium from any ties to Britain and France.

If in this process of making verbal and written promises to Belgium Hitler went further than von Neurath and others in the German foreign ministry thought wise,[102] the reason was the same as the one which had led him to make concessions to Poland and the Vatican in negotiations with them in the first years of his rule that also went beyond the foreign minister's preferences. While the latter thought that the arrangements arrived at might actually last, so that their terms were of real, long-term significance, Hitler never intended to keep them once they had served their original purpose. Since he did not have the slightest intention of keeping the promise to respect Belgium's independence and neutrality, any more than he intended to keep the treaties with Poland or the Vatican, it did not make much difference precisely what was promised as long as the key goal of the moment, in this case the neutrality of Belgium until Hitler was ready to attack in the west, was secured. When the moment for that attack came, some excuse would be found; and the barrier to western interference with his Central and East European adventures would become a corridor through which France could more easily be attacked.

The tug-of-war over Belgian policy continued through much of 1937. There were internal divisions in the Belgian government over the proper course to follow. The fear of provoking Germany, the belief that Britain would not have a land army to send to the continent,[103] the fear that the treaty obligations of France might involve Belgium in a war, and the

99. See *D.D.B.*, 4, Nos. 209, 217, 219, 221.

100. On the circumstances surrounding the reference to Belgium in Hitler's speech of 30 January 1937, and prior soundings, see ibid., Nos. 143, 154, 177, 185, 186, 189–92, 195, 200, 203; *G.D.*, C, 6, Nos. 39, 89, 166, 172, 174, 177, 196, 258, 266; Jacques Davignon, *Berlin 1936–1940, souvenirs d'une mission* (Brussels: Editions universitaires, 1951), pp. 47–53; C 1081, C 1126/181/4, FO 371/20678; C 1330/181/4, FO 371/20679.

101. For the negotiations leading to the October declaration, see *D.D.B.*, 4, Nos. 232, 235–37, 239, 240, 250; Davignon, pp. 59–60; *G.D.*, C, 6, Nos. 343, 363, 374, 384, 405, 454, 483, 506, 510, 528, 554, 555, 558, 560; *D.D.F.*, 2d, 7, Nos. 20, 29, 40, 46, 51, 63, 64, 66, 75, 78, 79, 83; *U.S.*, 1937, 1:116–17; "Bestellungen aus der Pressekonferenz vom 13. Oktober 1937," Bundesarchiv, Brammer, Z.Sg. 101/10, f.269.

102. *D.D.B.*, 4, Nos. 196, 198, 226.

103. Ibid., No. 228; General Robert von Overstraeten, *Albert I–Leopold III: Vingt ans de politique militaire belge 1920–1940* (Bruges: Desclée de Brouwer, 1949), 20 February and 5 March 1937, pp. 256, 257.

pressure of the Flemish element, all combined to give an edge to the advocates of neutrality. It is true that when the British and French governments accompanied their public declaration releasing Belgium from any obligation to themselves while promising to assist her in defending herself with a private communication that the effectiveness of this assistance would be greatly affected by the extent of prior concerted planning, the Belgian government agreed to unofficial staff contacts.[104] It is also true that Belgium never formally renounced her obligations under the covenant of the League. As a practical matter, however, Belgian policy was obviously oriented toward neutrality in any conflict other than one in which Belgium was invaded herself; and German policy, therefore, was successful in substance even if it fell slightly short in regard to form.[105]

In this case, as in the scheme to convert the ties of the Little Entente powers with each other and with France into a system of mutual assistance, the weakness of the participants to the discussion was self-reinforcing. The weakness of Britain and France contributed to the reluctance of Belgium; the fearful attitude of Belgium in turn threatened to immobilize the French. If French troops could not move through Belgium, how were they to come to the aid of Czechoslovakia or Poland? As Germany built fortifications along the Franco-German border, the prospects grew dimmer and dimmer.[106] As General Maurice Gamelin, the French chief of staff, put it to American Ambassador William Bullitt on 20 May 1937:

> . . . the ability of France to come to the assistance of Czechoslovakia or any other state of Eastern and Central Europe has been gravely diminished. France could no longer plan to march her troops through Belgium or base her planes on Belgian territory for attack on the Ruhr. Furthermore, as talks between the French and Belgian General Staffs had ceased there could be no certitude in making preparations for French support of Belgium in case Belgium should be attacked by Germany.[107]

When Bullitt asked Gamelin "if he did not believe that as soon as the French people began to realize the new position of Belgium, that the French soldiers would have to attack heavily fortified German lines on a

104. On the joint British-French declaration of 24 April and the supplementary warning and staff talks, see Kieft, pp. 167–72; *D.D.F.*, 2d, 5, Nos. 336, 349, 350, 370, 371, 400, 439, 446, 459; *G.D.*, C, 6, Nos. 329, 335, 342; *D.D.B.*, 4, Nos. 226, 228, 231, 233; C 3530/1/18, FO 371/20708.

105. *D.D.F.*, 2d, 5, Nos. 246, 255, 289, 367, 426, 463; 7, No. 289; *G.D.*, C, 6, Nos. 248, 268, 289, 446; D, 5, Nos. 473–79; *D.D.B.*, 4, Nos. 206, 214; Leonidas E. Hill (ed.), *Die Weizsäcker-Papiere, 1933–1950* (Frankfurt/M: Propyläen, 1974) (hereafter cited as *Weizsäcker-Papiere*), p. 118; C 1896/181/4, C 1923, C 2165, C 2316, C 2373/181/4, FO 371/20679; British cabinet meeting of 10 March 1937, CAB 27/622.

106. See *U.S.*, 1937, 1:77–78; Jean Szembek, *Journal 1933–1939* (Paris: Plon, 1952), 26 April 1937, pp. 227–28.

107. *U.S.*, 1937, 1:96, 97; see also ibid., 3:326.

short front, public opinion would begin to turn against such a horrible sacrifice of French lives,'' the latter replied that "public opinion rarely understood military questions.'' Bullitt had also received from Blum an emphatic expression of determination to go to war if Germany attacked Czechoslovakia, but the conclusion he drew was a shrewd one: "There is no doubt about the determination of the French Government at the present time to support Czechoslovakia in case of a German attack on Czechoslovakia but it is entirely conceivable that this determination will weaken during the coming months.''

It was the recognition of the decreasing effectiveness of any deterrent to German adventures eastward resulting from the remilitarization of the Rhineland and the effective neutralization of Belgium that led all observers of the international situation to assume—correctly as we now know—that Germany was planning to undertake such adventures in the near future.[108] But could there be an alternative deterrent in the east, if not from the Little Entente, perhaps from the Soviet Union, a country also potentially menaced by German expansion?

Russia was, in fact, tied to France by the 1935 Franco-Soviet agreement as well as by an alliance with Czechoslovakia that was dependent upon the Franco-Czechoslovak treaty of alliance. There were, however, very serious questions about the practical significance of these commitments. The reluctance of the Western Powers to place much faith in them is often attributed to ideological opposition to the Soviet regime, but there were far more practical obstacles to Soviet assistance to Czechoslovakia. The details of this issue will be examined in greater detail in the account of the crisis over Czechoslovakia, but some general aspects of the situation must be discussed in this broader review of French policy. If France was at least partially blocked from Germany by neutralized Belgium and a short, defended Franco-German border, the Soviet Union had no common border with Germany at all. Neither had she a common border with Czechoslovakia.[109] Poland and Rumania separated Czechoslovak from Russian territory, and neither was willing to allow Russian troops to cross for fear they would never leave.[110] There was, in fact, the real possibility that Poland would join Germany if France tried to pressure her into allowing Russian troops into the country.[111] Even had Poland and Rumania been willing, the transportation system in the area as well as in the adjacent parts of the U.S.S.R. was very poor—to say nothing of the

108. This was, of course, the reason for the British and French attempts to secure German restraint by economic and colonial concessions discussed elsewhere in this chapter.

109. It should also be noted that as soon as the Soviet Union and Czechoslovakia became contiguous at the end of World War II, the Soviet Union lost interest in Czechoslovakia's territorial integrity.

110. Dreifort, pp. 110–14, 119.

111. *D.D.F.*, 2d, 6, No. 35.

different railway gauges.[112] Massive land help was thus unlikely even in the remote contingency that it would be permitted.

The French, moreover, were not only dubious about Soviet ability to provide military help to Czechoslovakia by land forces; they also doubted that there could be effective assistance by air.[113] The French knew as well as the Germans that Czechoslovakia did not have the facilities to accommodate any substantial number of Russian planes.[114] If, however, the Czechs began to develop such facilities in peacetime—on the reasonable assumption that there would not be enough time to do so once Germany attacked—then the Germans would certainly find out and most likely launch a preventive attack. Thus work on the essential precondition for effective Soviet help would precipitate the very thing it was designed to avoid: a quick German invasion of Czechoslovakia.[115]

There were two further elements reducing in French eyes the prospects of effective support from the Soviet Union to restrain Germany. The reluctance of Britain, which itself was founded on doubts very similar to those of France, was one;[116] the internal turmoil of the Soviet Union was another. The great purge had begun to tear apart the Communist party of the Soviet Union in 1936; in 1937 it was destroying the command structure and effectiveness of the Red Army.[117] Hardly had Soviet Foreign Commissar Maxim Litvinov's Paris visit of May 1937 moved the French to technical military contacts with the Soviet Union when the purge moved into the Red Army hierarchy in June.[118]

These events not only dominated the newspaper headlines of the world but also came close to British and French leaders in a personal way. Marshal Mikhail Tukhachevsky, one of Russia's most prominent soldiers, headed the Soviet delegation at the funeral of George V and returned to the Soviet Union after conversations in Paris; he was shot in June 1937. Admiral Orlov was chief of the Soviet naval mission at the coronation

---

112. In World War II, the communications difficulties in this area showed up repeatedly; the need to improve them was a major factor in Hitler's decision to attack the Soviet Union in the spring of 1941 rather than the fall of 1940; again, in 1944–45, there were serious transportation difficulties in this region, and it was in this regard that the trucks and other vehicles provided by the U.S. under Lend-Lease were especially helpful to the Red Army.

113. For comments on the unlikely prospects of Soviet assistance to Czechoslovakia, see *U.S.*, 1937, 1:79, 97; Szembek, 26 April 1937, pp. 227–28; Bullitt tel. 192 of 11 February 1937, State 751.6111/185.

114. *D.D.F.*, 2d, 9, No. 199.

115. Ibid., 5, No. 275. The same analysis showed how feeble the hope of Polish assistance for Czechoslovakia really was: the Poles would have to help in the Těšín area, precisely the portion of Czechoslovakia they coveted for themselves!

116. This point is heavily stressed by Dreifort, pp. 116–17, but without regard to the fact that the British attitude was conditioned by the same practical considerations that affected the French also, *D.D.F.*, 2d, 9, No. 347; Pratt, p. 92.

117. On the purge, see John A. Armstrong, *The Politics of Totalitarianism* (New York: Random House, 1961), chaps. 4 and 5.

118. Dreifort, pp. 115, 119.

naval review for George VI at Spithead; he was called out of the official
dinner to go home to dismissal and execution.[119] In the face of the terrible
weakening the Soviet regime was inflicting on its own armed might, the
lack of confidence in that power's effectiveness in anything other than
self-defense should not surprise anyone.[120]

The doubts and hesitations are reflected in the diplomatic discussion of
possible Franco-Soviet military cooperation. When Blum asked Vladimir
Potemkin, the Soviet ambassador in Paris, on 17 February what aid Russia would provide in case of war, the latter answered that there would be
troops if Poland and Rumania allowed it, and otherwise a little assistance
by air and by ship. He stressed that in any case military protocols supple-
menting the Franco-Soviet treaty were needed to cover the various possible contingencies.[121] In the subsequent months, the French considered
this idea. On the one hand, there were their own doubts, growing out of
the knowledge of internal French opposition to closer ties with the Soviet
Union. Furthermore, they encountered resistance to the idea from the
British government; both Eden and Vansittart repeatedly warned of the
dangerous political implications in Europe of any such military
agreements.[122] On the other hand, there were the possible advantages in
regard to the defense of Czechoslovakia. Even more important in French
eyes as an argument in favor of maintaining Soviet goodwill by some
concessions on this point was the need to keep the Soviet Union from
aligning herself with Germany. This was the constant worry of the French
and one of the main arguments they used with the British.[123]

The French government, in view of these considerations, decided to
respond at least partially to Soviet wishes by authorizing the French

119. On this incident, see the memoirs of Sir Samuel Hoare, then First Lord of the
Admiralty, *Nine Troubled Years* (London: Collins, 1964), pp. 342–43. Hoare, later Lord
Templewood, had spent time in Russia, and, as the cabinet minutes for 1939 reveal, was the
strongest advocate of an alliance with the Soviet Union in the Chamberlain government. See
also Collier's note of 10 August 1937 on Chilston to Collier, 27 July 1937, N 3934/250/38, FO
371/21101.

120. *D.D.F.*, 2d, 8, Nos. 326, 343; Joseph E. Davies, *Mission to Moscow* (New York:
Simon and Schuster, 1941), pp. 167–68. On Soviet awareness of this situation, and the
resulting greater importance of Poland to France, see *G.D.*, D, 1, No. 73; for French reports
on the military purges and the—necessarily vain—attempts to impress on the Soviet government their devastating impact on French opinion, see *D.D.F.*, 2d, 6, Nos. 54, 65, 73, 144,
162; 7, No. 170; for the impact on Czechoslovak views of possible Soviet help, see ibid., 7,
No. 263.

121. Ibid., 4, No. 457. This whole issue is in need of further study. The Soviet government
attributed, or claimed to attribute, great importance to detailed and specific military arrangements with allies in 1937 and 1939; while actually fighting Germany during World War
II, however, the Soviet government in practice followed a policy of avoiding any such
procedures to the greatest extent possible.

122. Ibid., 5, No. 299; C 3620, C 3685/532/62, FO 371/20702.

123. *D.D.F.*, 2d, 5, Nos. 229, 299; Dreifort, p. 121; C 4888/822/17, FO 371/20696. For
Soviet hints of this possibility in December 1937, see *D.D.F.*, 2d, 7, Nos. 390, 436; for a
threat in 1938, see ibid., 9, No. 492. See also John A. Dreifort, "The French Popular Front
and the Franco-Soviet Pact, 1936–37," *Journal of Contemporary History*, 11 (1976): 217–36.

general staff to explore the possibilities of military assistance with the Soviet general staff through the military attachés.[124] Little is known about the results of any such contacts, but there is nothing to suggest that they amounted to much. The French were understandably reluctant to make detailed military arrangements with Red Army officers who were likely to be shot soon after for collaboration with Germany;[125] as has already been mentioned, the purges began to reach into the military sphere right after the French decision in favor of contacts at the military attaché level. The practical obstacles in the way of Franco-Soviet cooperation were enormous, and they were not surmounted in 1937, or later.[126]

If the prospects of effective resistance to German expansion in Central and Eastern Europe were so dim, what might be the possibility of a Franco-German agreement? Any such agreement would have the effect of stabilizing the situation in Europe. Pierre Laval had made the effort and failed in the face of Germany's persistent refusal to make the slightest concession.[127] It seemed inherently unlikely that what Laval had not accomplished could be attained by the Jewish prime minister of a Popular Front government, but Léon Blum was as determined to work for peace if there were any possibility of securing it as Chamberlain and Eden. The French left had been persistently critical of the Treaty of Versailles; though hostile to Hitler and all he stood for, there was a strong belief in the genuineness of German grievances and a predisposition, as would be expected from men who considered themselves Marxists, to look at both the problems of Germany and possible solutions for them in economic terms. That these should be discussed with a man like Schacht, therefore, seemed to make a good deal of sense.

The contacts Blum had had with Schacht in the summer of 1936 had not led anywhere, partly because there was no real prospect of German concessions in return for colonial cessions by France, but partly also because of other circumstances of the time. Germany had recently violated the Locarno agreements—not an auspicious moment for making a new agreement—and the hostility between a France sympathetic to the Spanish Loyalists and a Germany supporting Franco in the Spanish Civil War created a bad atmosphere. Although the passions aroused all over the

124. *D.D.F.*, 2d, 5, Nos. 285, 480; cf. C 3620/532/62, FO 371/20702; *G.D.*, C, 6, Nos. 360, 377; Anthony Adamthwaite, *France and the Coming of the Second World War, 1936–1939* (London: Frank Cass, 1977), pp. 48–50.

125. *D.D.F.*, 2d, 6, No. 35. In his thoughtful piece, "Léon Blum et l'Allemagne, 1930–1939," Jacques Bariéty argues that Blum did not want a military convention with the Soviet Union because of his worry that such agreements would bring on war as he and many others believed they had done before 1914 (*Les relations franco-allemandes, 1933–1939* [Paris: Editions du Centre National de la Recherche Scientifique, 1976], pp. 45, 50–51).

126. There was, nevertheless, no good reason for French Foreign Minister Delbos to snub Moscow during his East European trip in December 1937 (Dreifort, *Yvon Delbos*, pp. 148–49; *D.D.F.*, 2d, 7, No. 237).

127. Weinberg, *Foreign Policy*, pp. 219–20. For Laval's subsequent regrets over this failure, see Rosenberg to Göring, 22 May 1937, T-120, 5482/2621/E 382093–104.

world by that conflict lasted longer even than that protracted war, they were especially heated in those very months of 1936, August to November, when the first contacts with Schacht took place. At the end of 1936, a new phase in the Spanish Civil War appeared to offer an opportunity for reversing the situation; that is, for making that war an opportunity for a rapprochement instead of a source of friction.[128]

After the failure of Franco's forces to seize Madrid, evident by late November 1936, the apparent development of a stalemate between the two contesting sides suggested the possibility of ending the war by mediation. The course and failure of the mediation efforts in the winter of 1936–37 cannot be traced here. The aspect relevant to Franco-German relations is the idea put forward by the French government in December 1936 to have France and Germany cooperate (in concert with other powers) in settling the conflict in Spain, each in contact and sympathy with one party, and then to use that cooperation as a basis for wider discussion of economic and colonial questions.[129]

In December 1936 the French government put out a series of cautious feelers to see whether the German government was at all interested in a program that would start with a mediated settlement in Spain and then, whether or not that were secured, would utilize the Franco-German contacts developed in that effort to go on to a settlement of various outstanding issues. Economic topics to be worked on would include the Franco-German trade agreement which was in any case due for renegotiation, a reduction in trade barriers and other steps that would ease Germany's transition from a war economy to a peacetime economy participating more actively in normal world trade, and colonial concessions to Germany within the framework of a general political as well as economic settlement.[130] It became evident in the course of these soundings that von Neurath and the other officials in the German foreign ministry were not interested but that Schacht was, partly because it might help his own position in Germany, partly because he still hoped to divert Hitler from eastern conquests to international economic cooperation and colonial development in Africa. The German ambassador to France, Johannes von

128. The policy of Germany toward the Spanish Civil War has been touched on briefly in chap. 2; it will be examined in more detail in chap. 5.

129. The French archives for this period are quite fragmentary, and only a few French documents on these negotiations have survived and will be cited. There is, however, extensive British and German material, and since U.S. Ambassador Bullitt was in close touch with the French government, there is considerable information in American archives.

130. *D.D.F.*, 2d, 4, Nos. 174, 187, 193, 211, 230; *G.D.*, C, 6, Nos. 85, 93, 99, 123, 184; D, 1, Nos. 46, 56, 70–72, 91; D, 3, Nos. 150, 160, 162, 164, 167, 169, 173, 174, 179, 193; *U.S.*, 1936, 1:380–81, 382–83; 1937, 1:46–54; Edgar B. Nixon (ed.), *Franklin D. Roosevelt and Foreign Affairs* (Cambridge, Mass.: Harvard University Press, 1969), 3:528–30; *Dodd Diary*, pp. 380, 381; Dodd to Moore, 19 December 1936, Hyde Park, Moore Papers; Bullitt tels. 45 of 12 January, 50 of 13 January, 58 of 14 January, and 69 of 16 January 1937, State 751.62/ 386, 387, 391, 392; Dodd tel. 12 of 14 January 1937, State 751.62/388; Herbert L. W. Göring, "Vermerk," 28 December 1936, T-120, 5482/2621/E 382111.

Welczek, was also very strongly in favor of taking up the French offers.[131] It is entirely in keeping with other evidence about his views that von Welczek was later quoted as commenting in March 1937 that the French were now willing to negotiate; but that Germany was likely to miss the boat as she had done in the spring of 1918 when she had launched her great offensive in the west instead of negotiating for peace.[132]

The only result of the French soundings was that Schacht was to go to Paris again in January 1937, but even this trip was canceled because of a flare-up in German-French relations growing out of alarmist rumors of German troop landings in Spanish Morocco early in January.[133] The unresponsiveness of Hitler's 30 January speech to the overtures contained in Eden's speech of 19 January and Blum's of 24 January seemed to suggest that there would be no further talks at all.[134] In the meantime, however, the conversation between Schacht and Leith-Ross previously reviewed had been scheduled for 2 February, and the various problems as viewed by the French and British were examined in detail.[135] The British-French exchanges of February to May 1937 have already been reviewed. While the Western Powers were trying to clear their own minds on the prospects and possible terms of a settlement, Schacht went to Brussels to discuss world economic problems with Belgian Prime Minister Paul van Zeeland, who was trying to develop a program to improve world trade.[136] In his conversations in Brussels, and subsequently in Berlin with Maurice Frère, an assistant of van Zeeland, Schacht once more developed his projects for world trade and colonial concessions, throwing in a demand for the return of Eupen and Malmedy, Schleswig and Danzig, while asserting that Germany did not want Austria or Czechoslovakia.[137] Because Göring took an entirely different line with Frère, the French were left with the puzzle of who spoke for Germany. By that time, it had been decided

131. See especially his letter to von Neurath of 26 December 1936, stating that the French had reason to feel that they were now negotiating from a strong position, and urging the German government to accept the invitation, published in *Documents and Materials Relating to the Eve of the Second World War*, 2, *Dirksen Papers (1938–1939)* (Moscow: Foreign Languages Publishing House, 1948), Appendix II, No. 1, also to be published in *G.D.*, C, 6, No. 110.

132. C 2337/3/18, FO 371/20710, f.224.

133. Cf. "Bestellungen auf der Pressekonferenz am 13. Januar 1937," Bundesarchiv, Brammer, Z.Sg. 101/9, f.29. The flare-up may be considered to have been terminated with the brief Hitler–François-Poncet conversation of 3 February (*D.D.F.*, 2d, 4, No. 394).

134. *G.D.*, C, 6, Nos. 155, 156, 169, 171, 185, 188, 200; *D.D.F.*, 2d, 4, Nos. 346, 347, 351, 386, 389.

135. *D.D.F.*, 2d, 4, Nos. 311, 325; *U.S.*, 1937, 1:27–28, 29–31. A role in arranging German-French contacts that is not very clear from the evidence, was played at this time by Kurt Freiherr von Lersner (see the documents from Hyde Park cited in n.130; Bullitt tel. 152 of 3 February 1937, State 751.62/398; *G.D.*, C, 6, No. 178; cf. Weinberg, *Foreign Policy*, p. 173, n.78).

136. The van Zeeland project cannot be reviewed here. There are documents on it in the Belgian, French, and United States publications of diplomatic correspondence for 1937.

137. *G.D.*, C, 6, Nos. 307, 316, 328, 346, 352; *D.D.F.*, 2d, 5, Nos. 416, 432; *U.S.*, 1937, 1:823–24, 836–37; Kieft, p. 174.

that Schacht would make a trip to Paris at the end of May, so there was some hope that the question could be clarified. Certainly the French were highly skeptical; François-Poncet was sure that Schacht had no real influence any more and that the Germans were simply letting the talks with him go forward as a cover for their designs against Austria and Czechoslovakia, that Hitler would just accept whatever concessions he might get but make none in return.[138] Blum was not much more optimistic, but he was determined to give the attempt to start conversation another try.[139]

Just before Schacht left Berlin, about the middle of May 1937, he changed his tune completely. There is no direct evidence as to what happened. There is, however, good indirect evidence to suggest that Schacht saw Hitler and was given clear-cut instructions to stay away from political subjects.[140] In conversations with François-Poncet in Berlin a few days before leaving for Paris, Schacht announced that he would follow an entirely different approach from that of his earlier talks in Paris and from that of his recent conversations in Brussels and with Frère in Berlin. He had no offers to make; he would not talk about political subjects; he would merely listen on what would be in effect a courtesy visit. Given Schacht's earlier loquacity to all and sundry on the very subjects he now considered unmentionable, one can only assume that he had been restrained by his master's voice; the deprecating comments with which von Neurath regaled François-Poncet would have an impact in Paris and London, but they could never have restrained the self-assertive Schacht.[141]

In view of these preliminaries, little could be and was expected from Schacht's Paris visit of 25–29 May. Much of his time was devoted to negotiations about debts, and in his conversation with Blum—the only really political one of his stay—Schacht merely listened to Blum, whose presentation followed essentially the lines that the French and British had previously agreed upon, but to which Schacht had uncharacteristically

138. *D.D.F.*, 2d, 5, Nos. 311, 317, 325, 344; *U.S.*, 1937, 1:92.

139. *U.S.*, 1937, 1:93–95; see also Greiser to Göring, 5 April 1937, T-120, 5482/2621/E 382105–6.

140. Note that just before the trip to Brussels, Schacht had seen Hitler and received some instructions (Kieft, p. 174, n.2; and *U.S.*, 1937, 1:832–34). The detailed account of the colonial negotiations and discussions in the winter 1936–37 in Hildebrand, pp. 497–511, contains all manner of speculation, but is silent on the reversal in Schacht's attitude.

The reference to a new directive from Hitler to the effect that there was no prospect of agreement with Britain and that in view of England's unwillingness to support German space policy in Southeast Europe or German colonial policy, the propaganda and diplomacy of Germany should be carried out accordingly, in Dertinger's "Informationsbericht Nr. 92," of 27 May 1937, may reflect knowledge of the instructions behind Schacht's new approach (Bundesarchiv, Brammer, Z.Sg. 101/30, ff.447–49). It is also possible that Schacht's raising the Eupen-Malmedy question in Brussels after having been told *not* to do so by Hitler, who was anxious to nail down a neutral stance on Belgium's part, angered the Führer and produced an unmistakable order to stay out of all political matters on Schacht's next trip.

141. *D.D.F.*, 2d, 5, Nos. 436, 442, 447; *G.D.*, C, 6, No. 381; C 3736/3/18, FO 371/20710; C 3730/37/18, FO 371/20721; C 3666/78/18, FO 371/20727.

little to say.[142] He would carry back to Germany the expression of French and British willingness to negotiate a general settlement, in the latter stages of which colonial concessions to Germany would play a part if Germany were willing to meet the political precondition of abstention from aggression in Europe. The worry of some in Paris and London that a response Schacht might bring back from Hitler would leave the process of negotiations in unofficial as opposed to regular diplomatic channels was entirely unnecessary; if Hitler had not told Schacht to forget about any ideas of a general settlement before he went to Paris, he assuredly never authorized a reply to the suggestions Blum had put forward on behalf of the Western Powers.[143]

On various occasions later in 1937 there would be references back to these informal contacts.[144] Three themes dominate in these allusions. One was the continued interest of the French in negotiations that might lead to some settlement along the lines they and the British had suggested. The second was the absolute rejection by those in the German foreign ministry of any German interest in any such settlement; they clearly understood and for the most part shared Hitler's unwillingness to have his hands tied in Central and Eastern Europe. Finally, there is a current of anxiety on both sides, but especially the German one, that the records of the talks not show either one responsible for their breakdown—an anxiety obviously tied to concern over some future "war guilt" debate in which those records would be made public.

The whole thrust of Hitler's policy ran so directly counter to that of the concepts developed by France and Britain in connection with the Schacht soundings that there could be no prospect of agreement along the lines serious negotiations would necessarily have required. The very factor which made the British and French eager to have any negotiations transferred to regular diplomatic channels in the hope of reaching an agreement

142. Documents on the Schacht visit are in C 3751, C 4135/37/18, FO 371/20721; C 3861/3/18, FO 371/20710; C 3870, C 3886/237/18, FO 371/20734; *D.D.F.*, 2d, 5, Nos. 462, 470; *G.D.*, C, 6, No. 449; D, 1, Nos. 72, 83; *U.S.*, 1937, 1:106–7, 109; Bullitt tel. 705 of 31 May 1937, State 852.00/5567 (this is the portion of the telegram omitted from *U.S.*, 1937, 1:308). Cf. Dreifort, *Yvon Delbos*, pp. 173–74.

143. The summary of the negotiations prepared in the Foreign Office on 26 November 1937 for the visit of French ministers to London a few days later, "Developments in the Discussion with the French about the Colonial Question since the Despatch to Paris of the 27th April 1937," contains no reference to any meeting or exchange after the Schacht-Blum meeting of 28 May (C 8265/37/18, FO 371/20723, ff.116–20). The available evidence suggests that Schacht did not even get to see Hitler for a considerable period of time after returning from Paris (C 4068/1/18, FO 371/20708); see also C 4475/78/18, FO 371/20727, ff.243–48; *D.D.F.*, 2d, 6, No. 94.

144. Hemmen note of 13 July 1937, Hildebrand, p. 513; *G.D.*, C, 6, No. 430; D, 1, Nos. 7, 22, 35, 56, 63, 70, 71, 83 and n.1, 88, 90, 91; D, 3, No. 380; *U.S.*, 1937, 1:150, 158–59, 169. Some minor German-French agreements on radio, newspaper, and foreign correspondents were worked out in December 1937; see H. Merle Cochran (for Bullitt) dispatch 1452 of 30 December 1937, State 751.62/432.

that, whatever the details, would have to conform in outline to the type of arrangement they wanted, was the reason that Hitler would under no circumstances allow such formal negotiations to take place. We shall see how he thwarted subsequent efforts to make him specify his demands in a negotiating position where what was propagandistically defensible might set the limits of what he could actually demand. The one and only time he was maneuvered into such a situation—the negotiations of September 1938 culminating in the Munich agreement—he would regret to his last days alive; and in 1939 he would promise himself and his associates that no ''Schweinehund,'' no S.O.B. to use an appropriate equivalent, would ever do that to him again.

Whatever precise instructions Hitler actually gave Schacht before or after the latter's trip to Paris in May 1937, he was not going to risk being detoured from his immediate aggressive designs, and most assuredly not in talks inaugurated by a man whose advice he no longer followed and whom he would soon drop entirely. Schacht could trumpet German colonial demands and economic needs in a general way; that might help soften public resistance abroad and build up enthusiasm for aggression at home, but there must be no bargaining in which Germany would have to become specific in her demands and in her offers. Such a procedure threatened to tie her down to what others considered reasonable to concede to her and to what she herself promised in return.

Beyond showing once more German determination not to allow a negotiated settlement of alleged grievances, the Schacht talks must be placed in still another context from Hitler's perspective. Like the other efforts of the Western Powers to come to an agreement with him, they were interpreted by him—and by no means incorrectly—as signs both of opposition to German continental expansion and of a desperate reluctance to go to war to prevent it.[145] His comments to this effect of November 1937 have already been cited. In regard to colonies, he would get those for nothing when the continental expansion he intended had made Germany strong enough to demand them at the point of a gun. Ironically, the very attempts Britain and France made and were still to make to divert him from aggression in Europe by offering colonial and economic concessions encouraged him to take greater risks in a course of continental expansion which would, among other things, pave the way for what Hitler expected would become a later and even greater German colonial empire.

145. Hitler's view of a possibly imminent internal collapse of France played a role in the development of this attitude.

4   Another Attempt at a Settlement: The von Neurath and Halifax Visits

The collapse of the effort to develop the basis for a general settlement through the Schacht soundings of early 1937 did not put an end to such attempts. Two factors may be seen as primarily responsible for this continuation. In the first place, from the perspective of both London and Paris, but especially the former, the disadvantages of dealing with Schacht—unclear authority and unclear demands—were increasingly seen as outweighing the advantage of strengthening what was still considered a moderating influence on Hitler. The second element was peculiar to the political and personal situation in London as opposed to Paris. In both capitals the desire for the maintenance of peace and the willingness to make some sacrifices for it were present to an equivalent degree, but the political situation in the two capitals was different.

The end of the Schacht talks almost coincided with the end of Baldwin's service as prime minister. The new administration of Neville Chamberlain had behind it a solid majority in the House of Commons, an economy that had recovered considerable ground from the depression,[1] and the knowledge that the big rearmament program launched earlier in the year would eventually greatly strengthen the international position

1. Wendt, *Economic Appeasement*, pp. 426–36, stresses the role of the 1937 recession as a factor leading the Chamberlain government to the new attempt at appeasement. This is incorrect, at least in the form Wendt puts it, because the evidence clearly shows the British determination to go forward with the policy in May and June, several months before the new recession. Had von Neurath come to London as proposed, talks would have been under way long before the September stock market break and the October–November rise in unemployment. If these economic factors had any influence at all along the lines Wendt discusses, it would have been in strengthening the British in their purpose and going forward with the previously adopted course even after the cancellation of von Neurath's visit.

of England. While the British government could devote attention and energy to a new effort for an agreement with Germany, domestic problems kept the French government preoccupied. The Popular Front was in serious trouble throughout the summer of 1937, and Blum resigned in September. The new government of Camille Chautemps, in which Yvon Delbos remained as foreign minister, did not follow a foreign policy substantially different from its predecessor's; but there could be and were no French initiatives in the area of broader European policy in the summer and fall of 1937. Even in the continued troubles aroused by the Spanish Civil War, the diplomatic role of France was generally less active than that of England in those months.

Closely related to this political factor was a personal one. The new prime minister of England was determined to try for peace again and again.[2] As he became prime minister in name as well as in fact, his concern for foreign affairs was, as previously mentioned, well established.[3] Two months before, he had summarized his views in a special communication for the United States government, that had previously been reviewed with Baldwin and Eden and was formally addressed to Henry Morgenthau, the secretary of the treasury and hence Chamberlain's official counterpart.[4] Like the American government, the British was most interested in "preventing the outbreak of another war." That raised two questions: What were the causes and where was the menace? As to the causes, they were "both political and economic" and sometimes difficult to disentangle from one another. The source and nature of the menace seemed obvious to Chamberlain:

> The main source of the fears of Europe is to be found in Germany. No other country, not Italy . . . not Russia . . . certainly not France, England or any of the smaller Powers, is for a moment credited with any aggressive designs. But the fierce propaganda against other nations . . . the intensity and persistence of German military preparations, together with the many acts of the German Government in violation of treaties, cynically justified on the ground that unilateral action was the quickest way of getting what they wanted, have inspired all her neighbours with a profound uneasiness. Even these islands which could be reached in

2. Keith Feiling, *The Life of Neville Chamberlain* (London: Macmillan, 1946) is still extremely useful, especially for its quotations from the Chamberlain papers. Iain Macleod, *Neville Chamberlain* (New York: Atheneum, 1962), contains some additional excerpts. David Dilks is preparing a major work based on full access to the papers.

3. Jones, 30 May 1937, p. 350, says that Chamberlain means to be his own foreign minister; see also Colvin, chap. 8; Samuel Hoare (Lord Templewood), *Nine Troubled Years* (London: Collins, 1954), pp. 258–59. There is an excellent discussion of Chamberlain's position in Donald C. Watt, "British Domestic Politics and the Onset of War," *Les relations franco-britanniques de 1935 à 1939* (Paris: Centre National de la Recherche Scientifique, 1975), pp. 243–61.

4. Text in *U.S.*, 1937, 1:98–102. All the evidence this writer has seen supports the view that Chamberlain was expressing his own convictions as well as those of Eden, who in fact drafted some of the key passages (Eden, pp. 597–98). Baldwin agreed to the message, but it is difficult to know whether he would have expressed his own views in quite the same way.

less than an hour from German territory by an air force equipped with hundreds of tons of bombs cannot be exempt from anxiety.

The motive for this aggressiveness on the part of Germany appears to arise from her desire to make herself so strong that no one will venture to withstand whatever demands she may make whether for European or colonial territory.

With this intention in her heart she is not likely to agree to any disarmament which would defeat her purpose. The only consideration which would influence her to a contrary decision would be the conviction that her efforts to secure superiority of force were doomed to failure by reason of the superior force which would meet her if she attempted aggression.

This was why Britain was rearming, wished that the United States neutrality laws would be amended so that a victim of aggression could purchase weapons, and hoped that American-British cooperation in the Far East would restrain Japan and thus facilitate a firmer British position in Europe. But, as Neville Chamberlain saw it, there was also another path.

Although Chamberlain believed "it to be true that the political ambitions of Germany lie at the root of the economic difficulties in Europe," he was "by no means blind to the advisability of trying by all practicable means to ease the economic situation." He listed the various directions the British government was exploring to reach this goal. Included were the hoped for British-American trade agreement, the joint efforts with the French to explore a lowering of restrictions on international trade, and support of attempts made by Belgian Prime Minister van Zeeland at a project for improving worldwide economic activities. Finally there was, as Chamberlain put it, "a further matter that should be mentioned." He then referred to the talk Schacht had had with Blum the preceding year and with Leith-Ross the preceding month. Stressing the secrecy of these soundings, Chamberlain added that although complicated and difficult political and economic problems were involved, "it is possible that these conversations may lead to more formal contacts with the German Government through the normal channels."

Chamberlain was a determined and persistent, even stubborn, man, and he was not to be deterred by the fruitlessness of the contacts with Schacht in May from attempting to transfer the effort to "the normal channels." In this he was strongly supported by Eden. If the latter was more pessimistic about the chances of success, it was because of greater experience and familiarity with the difficulties rather than any divergence in basic approach.[5] At the conclusion of a series of internal Foreign Office minutes on the proper course for Britain to follow in the dangerous European situation, where both the moderates in Germany—here identified with the army—and the radicals around Hitler were seen as aiming for expansion

5. Wendt, pp. 437–38, properly stresses the basic congruence of Eden's views with Chamberlain's.

in Europe leading to a new war, the only difference apparently being the greater caution and inclination to delay of the former as opposed to the latter, Eden agreed with the view of Sir Alexander Cadogan that delay was most important for England. The situation in Germany might change in some way, and British rearmament could make progress. Eden thought that only a policy which accepted all opportunities to remove grievances and search for solutions gave any "scope for diplomatic effort by ourselves. The Leith-Ross–Schacht conversations, Mr. Van Zeeland's efforts are all on right lines for they at least gain time, and they might gain peace."[6]

Within the Foreign Office as a whole, views were crystallizing in the same direction. In April and May of 1937, the information from Germany which pointed to a German insistence that Britain take no interest in Central and Eastern Europe and suggested that an Anglo-German agreement would be possible only on that basis provoked the conclusion that Britain could never agree to such an arrangement. If any legitimate grievances of Germany could be identified—and the Germans were always conveniently hazy on this—then efforts should be made to meet them; but it would be dangerous for Britain to accept the sort of bargain Germany appeared to be offering (and Hitler might indeed have been interested in). It would divide the British public, alienate all actual or potential friends, mean writing off any prospect of future collaboration with the United States, and thus eventually leave an internally divided and internationally isolated Britain facing an immensely strengthened Germany. The preferable course was to negotiate such specific issues as could be identified, continue rearming, and show both the British and world public, by making every effort for peace, that war, if it came, was Germany's responsibility. The British government should attempt to find out just what the Germans wanted, if they were ever willing to specify what that was, but any scheme to divide the world between Germany and Britain was out.[7]

The conversations Lord Lothian had with Hitler, Göring, and Schacht early in May only confirmed the position of London. The Germans would not come forward with a specific program, unless it were one of British disinterest in Central and Eastern Europe; and that no one in the London government would agree to. Even Lord Lothian himself, though he thought there were prospects of progress, insisted with the Germans on

6. Eden's comment of 3 May 1937 on a Minute by Rex Leeper of 14 April 1937, C 2967/3/18, FO 371/20710, ff.269–77. In his first comments on 15 April, Eden had stressed the need for time and for careful examination of British tactics. He added that "we must clearly make much of Blomberg at the coronation" and wanted von Ribbentrop kept as well informed and entertained as possible. On von Blomberg's talks at the coronation—much pleasantry but little substance—see G.D., C, 6, Nos. 371, 380; Gerl to Hess, 4 June 1937, Nuremberg document 3752-PS, National Archives; Henke, p. 84; C 3555/270/18, FO 371/20735.

7. This is a summary based on C 2857, C 3317, C 3438, C 3825/3/18, FO 371/20710; C 2840/78/18, FO 371/20726; C 3793/270/18, FO 371/20735; D.D.F., 2d, 5, No. 436.

respect for the national identity of the peoples of Central and Eastern Europe. His circulation of the record of his talks to President Roosevelt as well as the Dominion prime ministers might shake the Foreign Office into paying more attention to these talks than it would have otherwise, but there was no substance to any of it. As one reads the records, it is obvious that the parties to the conversation were talking past each other, a fact that would only become obvious when Lord Lothian was awakened by the German action of 15 March 1939, and Philip Conwell-Evans, who had acted as interpreter, was shocked by German policy into advocacy of resistance rather than concessions to German demands. Lord Lothian's argument for a special German economic position vis-à-vis the countries to the south and east of Germany might have made sense within a framework of the kind that the British and French governments were themselves considering, but his constant coupling of this with an insistence on the national independence of the countries in that area was directly opposed to German aims, even if he did not realize it at the time.[8]

The opportunity for Chamberlain and Eden to put the attempted negotiations with Germany into "normal channels" came more quickly after Schacht's Paris trip than might have been anticipated. The bombing of the German pocket battleship *Deutschland* by Spanish Loyalist airplanes on the evening of 29 May 1937 led Hitler to decided on 30 May, a Sunday, to withdraw temporarily from the Non-Intervention Committee and have the German navy bombard the Spanish port town of Almería.[9] The attendant international uproar was the occasion for Eden to instruct Henderson to invite von Neurath for the beginning of the week of 7 June to discuss in London what might be needed for Germany's return to the Non-Intervention Committee and also for a general review of the international situation.[10] The fact that this invitation was sent on 1 June and contained a reference to the fact that "this occasion appears to provide useful opportunity for meeting without raising undue expectations and suspicions," suggests that the foreign secretary may have been thinking of such an

8. On Lord Lothian's trip, see C 3621/270/18, FO 371/20735; DZA Potsdam, Büro RAM, Akte 60964, ff.133–37; Lord Lothian to Norman Davis, 7 May 1937, enclosing reports of his Berlin interviews, Hyde Park, PSF Germany; Colvin, pp. 139–45; Henke, pp. 81–84; Butler, pp. 217–19, 337–53.

9. The account of Manfred Merkes, *Die deutsche Politik im spanischen Bürgerkrieg 1936–1939,* 2d ed. (Bonn: Röhrscheid, 1969), pp. 276–82, must be supplemented by the contemporary evidence in the diary of Alfred Jodl for 29–31 May 1937, "Angriff auf Panzerschiff Deutschland durch rotspanische Flieger," Nuremberg document 1955-PS, National Archives. (The identity of this as part of Jodl's diary is evident from his handwriting in the title and its inclusion in the "Verzeichnis der von Chef WFst abgegebenen Akten" in 1781-PS.) The French documents on the *Deutschland* incident have been published since the 2d edition of Merkes's book was prepared; *D.D.F.,* 2d, 6, Nos. 2, 5, 7, 12, 17, 18, 21, 23, 24, 29, 30, 32, 39, 40, 42, 43, 49. The German naval records were used by Werner Rahn, "Ibiza und Almería: Eine Dokumentation der Ereignisse vom 29. bis 31. Mai 1937," *Marine-Rundschau,* 68, No. 7 (July 1973), 389–406. See also Pratt, pp. 72–74; Henke, pp. 56–58.

10. Eden to Henderson, tel. 86 of 1 June 1937, C 4056/3976/18, FO 371/20748, ff.202–3. Most of the drafting of this document is in Eden's handwriting.

invitation even before the *Deutschland* incident, which thus provided the opportunity rather than the cause; but on this Eden's memoirs are as silent as the archives.

If the British were eager to have von Neurath come to London, the Germans were reluctant. Hitler, Göring, von Neurath, and some historians have often stressed the German interest in an agreement with England during the National Socialist period without ever facing up to the fact that whenever the British government offered the opportunity or even tried to start negotiations, Berlin refused.[11] The proposed trip of von Neurath was a casebook example illustrating Hitler's desire for British acquiescence in whatever he planned to do in Europe until he was ready to do it to England, as opposed to negotiations with the British government. For several weeks, von Neurath backed and filled, evaded answering, postponed a reply, and invented new conditions. In view of Sir John Simon's 1935 trip to Berlin, von Neurath owed a return visit; and finally, having apparently persuaded Hitler that because of British insistence on a visit, relations would suffer if he declined, von Neurath most reluctantly agreed to go. The Germans so informed the Italians while the British notified the French.[12] Hardly had Eden written an effusive letter to Henderson thanking him for his efforts to arrange the visit than the Germans found an excuse to call it off.[13]

As the undoubtedly real bombing of the *Deutschland* had provided the occasion for asking von Neurath to come to London, so an alleged torpedo attack on the German cruiser *Leipzig* on 19 June provided Hitler with an excuse to call the visit off. Whatever may be said about the concomitant German decisions to refuse any international investigation of this most questionable incident, and to withdraw from the international naval patrol scheme entirely, it is quite obvious that the incident was

11. Note the comment of von Ribbentrop's successor as ambassador in London, Herbert von Dirksen, in his memoirs: "During my term of office in London, Hitler never once took the trouble of following up on British offers of negotiations, even if only as a pretence. He never even answered" (*Moskau, Tokyo, London* [Stuttgart: Kohlhammer, 1950], p. 255). Henke's book is one of the few which shows an understanding of the incompatibility of Hitler's views with any and all British approaches (see esp. pp. 85–88).

12. On this curious, but instructive, charade, see C 4068/1/18, FO 371/20708; C 4185/270/18, FO 371/20735; C 4057, C 4058, C 4059, C 4070, C 4076, C 4096, C 4196, C 4213/3976/18, FO 371/20748; C 4047, C 4082/4047/18, FO 371/20749; *G.D.*, D, 3, Nos. 281, 284, 287, 288, 290–93, 298, 300, 303, 307–9, 311–15, 318–20, 323, 327–30, 334; Henderson, pp. 62–64; Henke, pp. 91–93; Ciano, *Diplomatic Papers*, pp. 122–23; "Informationsbericht Nr. 99," 18 June 1937, Bundesarchiv, Brammer, Z.Sg. 101/30, ff.491–95; Phillips Diary, 30 June 1937, Houghton Library, Phillips Papers, vol. 13, pp. 2115–18.

13. Eden to Henderson, 18 June 1937, Henderson Papers, FO 800/268, f.233. The text of Eden's letter is of interest. "Thank you very much indeed for your letter of June 17th in regard to Neurath's visit to London.

"I am very glad that the visit has now finally been arranged and I hope that it will lead to useful results. I have always thought that a frank talk would be extremely useful for clearing up any misconceptions which may exist in the German mind, whilst to us it should constitute a valuable opportunity of testing what German intentions really are.

"I am most grateful for your efforts in facilitating this visit."

seized upon as a heaven-sent pretext to call off von Neurath's trip. This was evident to everyone both inside and outside Germany at the time: if von Neurath could go to London after a real attack on the *Deutschland,* why not go after an imaginary attack on the *Leipzig?* Henderson pleaded with Hitler as well as with von Neurath, but Hitler remained obdurate. The London government learned that their distinguished guest was not coming a couple of days before hearing that Admiral von Fischel, the commander of the pocket battleships, had said that no torpedo tracks had been seen by the *Leipzig.*[14] In both London and Paris there was a combination of astonishment, regret, and annoyance; no National Socialist German foreign minister was invited to London again.[15]

The impression of a fundamental German distaste for negotiations with Britain created by the abortive visit is reinforced by what is now known about the preparations of both sides for that visit during the days when it still appeared as if it would take place. On the German side, the Balkan travels of von Neurath that had been one cause for postponing a trip to London, gave him a chance to speak to Prince Paul of Yugoslavia, who had just been in London himself. The Yugoslav regent assured von Neurath that Chamberlain and his government were sincere in their desire for peace with Germany, and warned him about the horrendous impression von Ribbentrop was making in London.[16] If the latter comment fitted in with von Neurath's predilections, the former left him unmoved; he told the Hungarian prime minister and foreign minister when in Budapest a few days later that there was little prospect of an agreement with England.[17] As it became more definite that von Neurath would go to London, materials were prepared for his conversations with British leaders.[18] These documents deal in some detail with the Spanish question and, in addition,

14. On the *Leipzig* incident and Hitler's decisions in connection with it, see *G.D.,* D, 3, Nos. 339–44, 346, 347, 349–51, 354; C 4458, C 4463/3976/18, FO 371/20749; 14th meeting of the cabinet Committee on Foreign Policy, 21 June 1937, CAB 27/622; *U.S.,* 1937, 1:336–37, 341, 343; *D.D.F.,* 2d, 6, Nos. 92, 95, 99, 101–3, 105, 107–13, 120, 171; Wiedemann, p. 157. Merkes, pp. 287–95, believes there really was an attack on the *Leipzig;* he fails to explain what the firing of torpedos which missed, even if it occurred, had to do with von Neurath going to London. Henke, pp. 93–94, believes in Hitler's real annoyance, but mainly on the basis of Merkes's account. The account of the incident in Hans-Henning Abendroth, *Hitler in der spanischen Arena* (Paderborn: Ferdinand Schöningh, 1973), pp. 170–73, ignores the proposed von Neurath visit. The British knowledge that there was no torpedo attack is in W 12285/7/41, FO 371/21338; their evidence that the *Leipzig* did run into something, though obviously no torpedo, is in W 12635/7/41, FO 371/21339; the evidence that the Italians did not believe in the incident is in R 4547/438/3, FO 371/21117.

15. C 4458, C 4463/3976/18, FO 371/20749; *U.S.,* 1937, 1:333. When Chamberlain was asked about a renewed invitation to von Neurath, he responded on 19 July that the government "did not consider the present moment appropriate" (5 Hansard 326, c. 1783). Is it a coincidence that the "appropriate" moment never came? Von Ribbentrop went to London in March 1938 after his appointment as foreign minister, but this was to say his farewells as ambassador.

16. RM 423 of 8 June 1937, T-77, 884/5632521–23.

17. *Hungarian Documents,* 1, No. 264.

18. *G.D.,* D, 3, Nos. 317, 333, 337.

cover a wide range of topics very briefly and without the slightest indication of substantive proposals.

At only one point did Ernst von Weizsäcker, head of the political department of the German foreign ministry, touch on the basic issue: "If England would let us do whatever we want where there are predominantly German interests and English [interests] are not touched, [and] if the British would take our raw materials situation seriously and help [us] improve it, then German-English cooperation for the purpose of maintaining peace would be assured."[19] Had von Neurath made this proposal, which elegantly combined Hitler's desire for a free hand on the continent with Schacht's hopes for trade and colonial concessions, he would have been quickly turned down. This scheme implied not an agreement between Germany and Britain but total British approval of whatever Germany wanted. As will be shown, Göring put this concept to Henderson later in the year, but in the summer of 1937 Hitler thought it best not to risk its exploration.[20]

The British government in its preparations for von Neurath's visit could draw upon the presentations of English policy that had been drafted for the imperial conference which overlapped with the efforts to bring the reluctant German foreign minister to London. In his briefing of the Dominion prime ministers at their first meeting on 19 May, Eden had indicated that the greatest risk of war in Europe was not in the east as both Poland and Rumania favored a policy of equilibrium and would not allow either neighbor the passage of troops for use against the other. "The danger of war was much greater in Central Europe in connection with countries such as Czechoslovakia and Austria. The countries of the Danube Basin afforded a natural field for Germany's economic development, but it was very doubtful whether Germany would be satisfied with such economic advantages." Eden pointed out that Italy had given up her interest in Austrian independence and that the situation in Central Europe was now like that in the Balkans just before the war. There were three courses open to England. She could disinterest herself in Central Europe altogether. "Such a policy would be unwise and would most certainly invite aggression." A second possibility would be to declare readiness to fight for Czechoslovakia or Austria if either became the victim of aggression. The British public would not be behind such a declaration, and it would be most dangerous for the government to announce a policy that did not have general support at home. "There remained the third possibility, namely,

19. "Würde England uns da gewähren lassen, wo überwiegend deutsche Interessen vorliegen und englische unberührt sind, würde England unsere Rohstofflage ernst nehmen und fördern helfen, so wäre die deutsch-englische Zusammenarbeit zum Zweck der Friedensbewahrung gesichert."

20. Note Dertinger's "Informationsbericht Nr. 100," of 26 June 1937, reporting that those still hoping for an understanding with England were going against the policy of Hitler and citing propaganda ministry directives supporting his interpretation (Bundesarchiv, Brammer, Z.Sg. 101/30, ff.505–9).

that without undertaking any military commitment we should make it clear that we were interested in events in Central Europe."[21]

At the twelfth meeting, Eden reiterated a similar view, reaffirming that Britain could not disinterest herself in Central Europe. "The United Kingdom Government desired a world settlement because they were conscious that a spark in some distant area might ignite a general conflagration but they were only prepared to undertake military commitments in definite and limited areas." At the same meeting, Eden expressed the view that the majority of Austrians were not in favor of annexation to Germany. If that really changed, Britain would not oppose an *Anschluss,* but she would not encourage it—which would be the practical effect of a public declaration of British disinterest in Central Europe. The knowledge by foreign governments of this attitude on the part of England would have the same effect; and this statement was, therefore, neither distributed for possible use in conversations with foreign diplomats nor included in what was to be said to von Neurath.[22]

Although one of Eden's comments in the archives states that he was "not entirely convinced of the truth" of the view held by Sir Orme Sargent and Sir Robert Vansittart that the *Anschluss* would change the whole situation in Central Europe to an extent that would be "inimical to peace and therefore to British interests," the decision on what precisely to say on this subject had not been made when the visit was canceled.[23] On other topics an agreed position had been developed. If there was the hope that better Anglo-German relations might have a salutary effect on the behavior of Italy, the main emphasis was on the issues between Germany and the United Kingdom. There would be a chance to review the latest developments in regard to Spain. Britain very much wanted good relations with Germany and hoped that the present talks would help. In regard to Central Europe, Eden would take the line he had just expounded to the Dominion prime ministers. The memory of the dispute over Serbia that had started the last war hung over British policy, and von Neurath was to be reminded of this: "The Great War took its rise from Central and S.E. Europe. Any violent disturbance would certainly lead to another war . . . .

21. Extract from Draft Minutes of the First Meeting of Principal Delegates, 10 May 1937, R 3903/770/67, FO 371/21139, ff.196–99. On the strategic discussions, see also Pratt, pp. 50–54.

22. Extract from Draft Minutes of the 12th Meeting of Principal Delegates, 3 June 1937, R 4048/770/67, FO 371/21139, ff.217–24. At this time, Henderson was instructed to try to ask Göring, who had complained about British interference with German policy, for a clearer explanation of where the Germans thought that Britain stood in Germany's way. For various reasons, the Henderson-Göring talk did not take place until October (C 4185/270/18, FO 371/20735). As part of the preparations for the visit, the Foreign Office was also trying to clear up all remaining confusion about the 1936 Schacht-Blum correspondence (C 4240/237/18, FO 371/20734; C 4700/37/18, FO 371/20721). See also C 4367/165/18, FO 371/20733.

23. The relevant papers, "Preparations for a visit of Baron von Neurath to London" are filed under C 5200/3976/18, FO 371/20749, ff.341–54. The discussion of an open door policy in the British colonies at the 13th meeting of the cabinet Committee on Foreign Policy on 16 June 1937 also belongs in this context (CAB 27/622).

A war that began in Central Europe could not possibly be limited, and would inevitably spread." Britain, therefore, could not disinterest herself in the independence of the countries of that area, but this did not mean that as part of a general European settlement Britain might not make commercial concessions in Germany's favor there.

Von Neurath might be asked whether any of Hitler's promises and offers of March 1936 about nonaggression pacts, a Western Pact, return to the League of Nations and other matters still held, and if so, on what terms. He should be told of British pressure in Prague in favor of better treatment of the German minority in Czechoslovakia but was to be contradicted if he repeated the German fairy tales of Soviet influence in that country. As for relations with the Soviet Union itself, von Neurath would be told that Britain "cannot join or countenance in any way the 'Anti-Communist front,' " and that she deplored the evidence of Russo-German friction. If von Neurath brought up the Danzig issue, he would be told that England wanted a peaceful evolution of events there, but that British public opinion would be sensitive to violent and unconstitutional acts in the Free City.

Should the occasion arise, von Neurath could be asked about the various conversations with Schacht to see whether the political aspects of those talks could now take place through diplomatic channels. On the colonial question, the German foreign minister would be given the same view both the British and the French had given Schacht, namely, that a general political settlement was the prerequisite of any consideration of colonial concessions. As in the talks with Schacht, the possibility of concessions in the fields of trade and finance would be mentioned. Furthermore, if Germany were interested, the British would be pleased to discuss having them join the British–French–United States currency stabilization agreement of September 1936. While this policy statement would be made to von Neurath, the technical discussions required for any implementation of the latter step would be held with Schacht; and in this way it was hoped in London that Schacht could be kept favorably disposed to the idea of a general settlement though excluded from the political discussions.[24]

The cancellation of von Neurath's visit made all these points academic, but the British policy reflected in them remained essentially unchanged until the outbreak of war in 1939. If war broke out in Central or Eastern Europe, it would surely spread. If, on the other hand, specific problems were discussed, a comprehensive settlement might be worked out. Since this was the last thing Hitler wanted, it is not surprising that he evaded talks on the possibility; orders were even given in Berlin that references to the invitation to von Neurath must be stricken from German press re-

24. On this aspect, see C 4475/78/18, FO 371/20727. See also the report on the Schacht-Henderson talk of 29 August 1937, in C 6206/270/18, FO 371/20736.

ports.[25] There was a further divergence of great importance that is implied rather than stated openly at this time. Hitler, as previously shown, thought that he could move step by step indefinitely and make war at times and against victims of his choosing. The British belief that any war would spread meant that a war once started would almost certainly involve them. This discrepancy in perception contributed equally to Hitler's unwillingness and England's eagerness for negotiations between them, Hitler operating on the hope and assumption of a series of isolated wars, while the British drew from 1914 the sad and fearful conclusion that they would be unable to remain outside any European war once it had started. Subsequent months would see the pattern of matched unwillingness and eagerness repeated.

Before the next major episode in the attempts at a British-German settlement—the visit of Lord Halifax to Germany in November—can be reviewed, the relationship of the United States to British and French policy toward Germany must be examined. The American aspect of the European diplomatic situation became important in the spring and summer of 1937 through the publicly well-advertised debate over the new neutrality legislation of the United States and the behind-the-scenes discussion of some American role in assisting a European settlement. The spring of 1937 saw a culmination of American efforts to legislate the danger of war away from the United States. As military leaders so often prepare to fight the last war, civilian leaders work to avoid it. This inherently rather questionable venture—it is, after all, impossible to keep out of a war you have already been in—was high on the priority list of isolationists and pacifists in the United States. In the congressional debate over the 1937 neutrality law, the assumption that the United States had been tricked, or had tricked herself, into war in 1917 was translated into proposals additional to those already on the books which were designed to keep the United States from being involved in a European conflict, it being assumed that any such involvement might come in the same way again.[26]

Allusion has already been made to Neville Chamberlain's letter calling attention to the dangerous implications of the neutrality law. If a potential aggressor knew that his victim could not buy weapons from the United States, the advantage his own armament gave him was doubled. The potential victim was not only unprepared but could not quickly remedy the deficiency. In fact, the general knowledge that this was so would encourage the aggressor to threaten or to strike, while discouraging the

25. "Bestellungen aus der Pressekonferenz vom 9. Juli 1937" (reference to "allerhöchste Anweisung"), Bundesarchiv, Brammer, Z.Sg. 101/10, f.19. See also Hess to Gerl, 31 August 1937, Nuremberg document 3752-PS, National Archives.

26. See Manfred Jonas, *Isolationism in America, 1935–1941* (Ithaca, N.Y.: Cornell University Press, 1966); William L. Langer and S. Everett Gleason, *The Challenge to Isolation, 1937–1940* (New York: Harper, 1952), chap. 1.

victim. Knowing that Germany had a head start in rearmament, Britain and France watched anxiously as proposals designed to keep war from coming to America seemed to make more likely the outbreak of war in Europe—and then engulf America anyway.[27] The Western Powers hoped that the legislation would at least leave some discretion to the president, but the final form of the law of 1 May 1937 left very little.

The prospect that, once war had broken out, the law might be changed provided little consolation if the Germans exploited their armaments advantage in a quick offensive. The old controversy over the Allied debts left over from the World War did nothing to make Americans more sympathetic to Britain and France, but it is unlikely that this was a very significant factor. The more dangerous the situation'in Europe appeared, the more public pressures mounted in the United States in favor of building a legislative Maginot Line against any danger of involvement. Ironically, in the United States (as in England), those most in favor of taking a strong line with Germany and Italy were among those equally fervent in demanding that anyone who took a strong line should be left in the lurch if that led him into trouble. In the face of these pressures, President Roosevelt, who was himself hopeful of keeping America out of any war, fought a rearguard action against only the more outlandish isolationist proposals, and the law eventually enacted offered little solace to British and French statesmen.

As in the examples mentioned in the preceding chapter, there was here another self-reinforcing process of undermining resolution in the face of danger. The British and French were necessarily more cautious in their attitude toward taking any risks in Europe in the knowledge that any deficiency in their armament could not be remedied by wartime purchases in the United States.[28] The more complaisant the attitude Britain and France adopted toward the dictators and the less their concern for the ideologically anti-Axis proclivities of an American public that wanted its own government's hands tied anyway, the more the isolationist tendencies in the American public and leadership grew.

This does not mean that London and Paris became uninterested in the development of American opinion and policy, but it did lead to a kind of petulance that was precisely the opposite of what was needed. Instead of looking for opportunities to assist the process of informing the American public about the dangers in Europe, the British government seemed to go out of its way to avoid that. It is true that in response to Roosevelt's and

27. For French observation, see *D.D.F.*, 2d, 4, No. 304; 5, Nos. 21, 54, 373, 399. For British observation, A 1895/448/45, FO 371/20666; Colvin, pp. 139–45.

28. An assessment of the dangers of the U.S. neutrality laws for Britain by the Chiefs of Staff Sub-Committee of the Committee of Imperial Defence of 13 May 1937 is in A 3587/448/45, FO 371/20666. See also A 4581 and A 4631/448/45, FO 371/20666.

Morgenthau's indications of a willingness to exchange information,[29] London became far more forthcoming in keeping Washington informed about current problems and negotiations. There was also the beginning of the negotiations that eventually led to the Anglo-American Trade Treaty, certainly the most important sign of a closer relationship between the two powers, and seen as such by the two countries.[30] On anything more elaborate, however, the British government tended to discourage rather than encourage feelers from Washington.

Already in 1936 President Roosevelt had considered the possibility of some broader step to assist a new European settlement, perhaps by calling a world conference.[31] The soundings made on his behalf with the London government early in 1937 were turned down there with a rather reasonable argument: having just alerted the British public to the need for a rearmament program, the British government would find itself having to start all over again if the heady prospect of disarmament were once again dangled before the people in circumstances where there was not the slightest chance of German cooperation. Furthermore, British agreement in or joint sponsorship of a conference at that point would look like a total retreat to the Germans.[32] If that made sense, the British handling of the alternative to which Roosevelt turned did not. As he cast about for some approach to the threatening danger of war,[33] the president decided to invite one of the British leaders to Washington.

When the idea of a visit was first broached, Baldwin was still prime minister, and either he, Chamberlain, or Eden was thought of as a possible guest. Over the following months, various ideas were put forth from Washington; and there was a considerable crossing of wires between the United States ambassador in London and Norman Davis, who was also there to represent the United States in naval negotiations. The outcome, however,

29. A 665/38/45, FO 371/20651.
30. On the Anglo-American trade negotiations, including the Foreign Office pressure for concessions to the U.S. because of the political importance of the negotiations, see A 1059/93/45, FO 371/20656; A 7450, A 7765/228/45, FO 371/20663; 12th meeting of the cabinet Committee on Foreign Policy, 11 June 1937, CAB 27/622; *U.S.*, 1937, 1:72–74; "Bestellungen aus der Pressekonferenz," 19 November 1937, Bundesarchiv, Brammer, Z.Sg. 101/10, f.367. There is a somewhat exaggerated account in Schröder, pp. 190–99.
31. Weinberg, *Foreign Policy*, p. 156. The most sophisticated analysis of the Roosevelt plan as well as of its fate in reality and in historical writing, is Francis L. Loewenheim, "An Illusion That Shaped History: New Light on the History and Historiography of American Peace Efforts before Munich," in *Some Pathways in Twentieth Century History: Essays in Honor of Reginald Charles McGrane*, ed. Daniel R. Beaver (Detroit: Wayne State University Press, 1969), pp. 177–220, 286–95. Though perhaps neglecting the "public relations" aspect of the president's project, Loewenheim has carefully assessed all the evidence available through 1967. Offner, chaps. 7 and 8, is far less satisfactory.
32. C 2614/3/18, FO 371/20710; W 4604/4604/98, FO 371/21254; *U.S.*, 1937, 1:640–41, 641–48, 72–74; Eden, pp. 599–600; *Dodd Diary*, 4 March 1937, pp. 388–89; *G.D.*, C, 6, No. 245; Bingham to Roosevelt, 24 March 1937, Library of Congress, Hull Papers, folder 98; Bingham tel. 135 of 12 March 1937, State 500.A 19/60.
33. See *D.D.F.*, 2d, 5, No. 270.

is certainly clear. No one went, neither Baldwin nor Chamberlain nor Eden.[34] There is no reason to believe that great results would have come from such a visit, but there would surely have been effects in three areas of some importance: a closer coordination between the deplorably divergent American and British policies in the Far East, an exchange of ideas and information that would have made it easier for the two governments to understand each other, and a clearer recognition of the problems facing both on the part of the American public.

Of those British officials whose views about the project can be determined from the record, Vansittart—who had been in charge of the American section of the Foreign Office during much of the 1920s—was most strongly in favor, and Neville Chamberlain was both most dubious and opposed. He thought nothing would come of it all anyway, failed to see the publicistic aspect of the whole problem, and was probably still influenced by his resentment over Roosevelt's actions toward the London Economic Conference of 1933 in which Chamberlain had, of course, played a major role on the British side. Eden's attitude is unclear. He had a vivid appreciation of the need for encouraging any American initiative, and was generally in agreement with Vansittart on the key importance of British-American cooperation.[35] He seems, however, not to have pushed very hard, and his memoirs sound rather apologetic on this point.[36]

It appears likely that Eden's reluctance to insist on working out something leading to an American visit at that time contributed to the dispute between him and Chamberlain over Roosevelt's January 1938 initiative in two ways. The lack of personal contacts made it more difficult for both Americans and British to clarify a proposal that was very nebulous in Roosevelt's own thinking originally—but might have been more specific and would certainly have been less of a surprise to London had there been some prior face-to-face discussions in which either Chamberlain or Eden would have had an opportunity to ask some pointed questions. In the second place, while Eden learned Chamberlain's views in the course of the British consideration of the invitation, the evidence suggests that Eden's own passive behavior kept Chamberlain from finding out how strongly the foreign secretary felt about not discouraging Roosevelt's initiatives.

34. On this episode, in addition to the evidence in Loewenheim and Offner, see Jones, pp. 327, 330, 337–38; Dorothy Borg, *The United States and the Far Eastern Crisis of 1933–1938* (Cambridge, Mass.: Harvard University Press, 1964), pp. 375–77; Janet Adam Smith, *John Buchan: A Biography* (Boston: Little Brown, 1966), pp. 444–47, 473–75; Bingham to Roosevelt, 1 July 1937, Roosevelt to Bingham, 16 July 1937, draft of letter, Norman Davis to Chamberlain, June 1937, all in Hyde Park, PSF Great Britain 1937; A 4412/228/45, FO 371/20661; A 6550, A 6869/228/45, FO 371/20663.

35. See the various Foreign Office comments on Sir Eric Phipps Berlin tel. 331 (Saving) of 6 November 1936 on his conversation with Dodd about a possible world conference, in A 8860/103/45, FO 371/19827, ff.314–21. Cf. A 5459/6/45, FO 371/20649.

36. Eden, p. 601.

It is, of course, doubtful that much could have been accomplished. The inability or unwillingness of Britain and the United States to cooperate effectively in the crisis in East Asia in the months following the outbreak of open hostilities between Japan and China in July 1937 certainly raises doubts about any possible cooperation in regard to European problems. At the Brussels conference as in the diplomatic contacts between the two powers—other than China—whose interests were most threatened by Japanese aggression, the hesitations of each reinforced the timidity of the other.[37] Roosevelt's "quarantine the aggressors" speech, made on 5 October 1937 at the dedication of Chicago's Outer Drive bridge in the shadow of the Tribune Tower did little more than stir a temporary excitement.[38] Roosevelt himself saw the speech as designed "to educate American opinion and to show the world in which direction that opinion is running," but did not feel that the "very difficult and restive American public opinion" would let him move ahead quickly.[39]

At the turn of the year, the president did, however, decide to move, if not quickly, certainly substantially. He authorized confidential discussions of naval contingencies in the Far East and sent Captain Ralph Ingersoll of the American navy on a special mission to London so that the United States and Britain could exchange information on their dispositions in case of war in the Pacific.[40] Chamberlain and Eden cooperated in responding blandly and without enthuasiasm to this overture, but

37. The point is well made by Loewenheim. See also Borg, chap. 14; Bradford A. Lee, *Britain and the Sino-Japanese War* (Stanford, Calif.: Stanford University Press, 1973); Nicholas Clifford, *Retreat from China—British Policy in the Far East, 1937–1941* (Seattle: University of Washington Press, 1967).

38. On the speech, see Dorothy Borg, "Notes on Roosevelt's 'Quarantine' Speech," *Political Science Quarterly,* 72 (Sept. 1957), 405–33; Borg, *United States and the Far Eastern Crisis,* chap. 13; Travis Beal Jacobs, "Roosevelt's 'Quarantine Speech,'" *The Historian,* 24 (Aug. 1962), 489–99; and a good general evaluation in Robert A. Divine, *Roosevelt and World War II* (Baltimore: Johns Hopkins University Press, 1969), pp. 16–19. British reaction in A 7186/448/45, FO 371/20667; French reaction in *U.S.,* 1937, 1:132–33; *D.D.F.,* 2d, 7, Nos. 33, 42, 53; German reaction in *G.D.,* D, 1, Nos. 412, 413, 416; "Bestellungen aus der Pressekonferenz," 6 October 1937, Bundesarchiv, Brammer, Z.Sg. 101/10, f.253.

For evidence that Roosevelt discussed the quarantine idea, phrased in terms of a financial blockade of Germany, with former Belgian Prime Minister Emile Francqui as early as 16 May 1934, see the British Foreign Office correspondence under C 3720/635/18, FO 371/ 18870, ff.388–93, and C 4982/635/18, FO 371/18871, ff.66–68. (The FDR Library informs me that the president had an off-the-record talk with Francqui following a luncheon, but has no account of the meeting or correspondence between Roosevelt and Francqui.)

39. Wickham Steed to Vansittart, in Mallet (Washington), tel. 344 of 13 October 1937, A 7441/228/45, FO 371/20663, ff.108–11. Wickham Steed had met Roosevelt and Hull on 12 October. Cf. A 7748/228/45, FO 371/20663.

40. On this episode, see Eden, pp. 617–20; Borg, *United States and the Far Eastern Crisis,* pp. 497–99; Pratt, pp. 57–61; Roskill, *Hankey,* 3:274–75, 309–10; *Cadogan Diary,* pp. 31–34, 37, 46, 49; F 11201, F 1748/9/10, FO 371/20961; F 95/84/10, FO 371/22106. The study by Lawrence R. Pratt, "The Anglo-American Naval Conversations on the Far East of January 1938," *International Affairs,* 47, No. 4 (Oct. 1971), 745–63, shows on the basis of the British records that the London government was exceedingly reticent about Roosevelt's approach.

they took differing positions on Roosevelt's next initiative.[41] He wanted
to summon an international conference to discuss a new program for a
conference of all governments at the White House to discuss the principles of international conduct and devise ways of assuring a reduction of
armaments and equality of economic opportunity. When he sounded the
British government—with a very short deadline for a response—Eden
was on a holiday; and Sir Alexander Cadogan, who had replaced Vansittart as permanent undersecretary but shared the latter's view of British–
United States relations, was unable to persuade Chamberlain to give a
positive response.[42] Chamberlain disregarded the publicity aspects of the
issue, looked at the rather vague and woolly scheme, and asked the president to defer action on his plan for a short time while he pursued his own
plans for better relations with Germany and Italy. Although Eden subsequently tried to reduce the negative tone of the first reply, the delay
requested by Chamberlain became a permanent one as Roosevelt never
brought this proposal forward again.[43] At a time when the British government was reviewing the results of Lord Halifax's visit to Germany and
was about to embark on a major new approach to Germany itself—the
same meetings of the cabinet Committee on Foreign Policy considered the
American overture and the planned proposal of colonial appeasement—
Chamberlain did not want to become involved in a scheme he saw as
running at cross-purposes with his own.[44]

There is little to suggest that much would have come of Roosevelt's
scheme had it been tried. The only discernible effect of the episode was on
the internal situation in London. Eden was most upset by Chamberlain's
action. He wanted to resign but could not because of the secrecy
Roosevelt had imposed on the existence of his project; nevertheless,
Eden's two strong letters of criticism and concern to the prime minister
probably mark the real breach between the two men.[45] The strong opposition expressed by Washington to the possibility of British recognition of
the Italian conquest of Ethiopia, a subject that was to be included in

41. Evidence on this proposal cited by Loewenheim will not be cited here. The origins and
history of the project can now be determined more precisely from the diaries of Adolf A.
Berle, *Navigating the Rapids, 1918–1971*, ed. Beatrice Bishop Berle and Travis Beal Jacobs
(New York: Harcourt Brace Jovanovich, 1973), 13 October 1937–7 February 1938, pp.
140–63 passim.

42. Cadogan to Chamberlain forwarding Lindsay's telegrams on the Roosevelt plan, 13
January 1938, FO 371/21526, ff.113–14; Cadogan to Eden, 13 January 1938, ibid., ff.110A–
112. Lindsay himself urged "a very quick and very cordial acceptance." (Most secret
telegram 42 of 12 January 1938, Premier 1/259, ff.73–74). Other documents on the original
plan in Premier 1/259; further details in *Cadogan Diary*, pp. 35–41, who insists, however,
that Vansittart opposed a favorable reply to Roosevelt.

43. Telegrams in Premier 1/259, ff.45–49, 59–60, 65–66; *Harvey Diary*, pp. 67–79, 88, 117.

44. The minutes of the 19th, 20th, and 21st meetings of the cabinet Committee on Foreign
Policy are in CAB 27/622, 623.

45. Eden to Chamberlain, 17 January 1938, Premier 1/259, ff.55–58; Eden to Chamberlain,
18 January 1938, FO 371/21526, ff.86A–88. Cf. Cadogan's entry in his *Diary*, 21 January
1938, p. 40.

British negotiations with Italy, touched on the general problem of how to conduct those negotiations over which the final break would come a few weeks later.

The evidence is clear that Chamberlain did want good relations with the United States, but in his approach he showed the same unbending attitude that so antagonized his domestic political opponents. Not even the hopes for a ministerial visit for the signing of the Anglo-American Trade Agreement of 17 November 1938 materialized.[46] In spite of the fact that as prime minister Chamberlain was mainly responsible for the concessions to the United States that were needed to bring about that agreement,[47] he could not look beyond the immediate diplomatic issues of the moment to the broader problem of allowing America to educate itself on the realities of a world that did not conform to the fantasies of those who feared that the United States might again be involved by its munitions makers in a war against the Kaiser. If President Roosevelt's leadership in foreign affairs in 1937–38 was faltering and vague as he was torn between a genuine hatred of war and a distaste for the aggression of Germany, Italy, and Japan, his casting about for ways and means of averting the drift to war testifies to a concern for the dangers ahead and a desire to move public opinion to a point where it might be led to a clearer appreciation of the new situation developing in Europe. He would receive no help in this endeavor from Chamberlain, who saw the dangers and problems clearly but had a stubborn confidence in his own ability to devise the means for coping with them and no confidence whatever in any American role.[48]

This determination was maintained after the refusal of von Neurath to visit London and took the form of a continued belief in personal contact with the dictators. Chamberlain's efforts at an arrangement with Mussolini will be mentioned later in this chapter but has to be seen as part of his general approach. The British prime minister believed that differences coud be settled by negotiations—or at least might well be—and that great differences required longer negotiations and greater patience. The possibility that anyone might in fact not want to negotiate at all but would prefer the arbitrament of war did not occur to him. Since he himself continued to believe that a war would spread, it did not seem possible to him either that anyone would run the risk of war voluntarily or that the very signs of eagerness to negotiate might encourage the willingness to run that risk. He was, therefore, pleased by Canadian Prime Minister Mackenzie King's report on his meeting with Hitler and other German

46. A 556/1/45, FO 371/21490.
47. The letter of Lord Runciman to Roosevelt of 18 February 1938 stressing Chamberlain's desire for a closer understanding with the U.S. and his support for a trade agreement may well have been inspired by Chamberlain himself. The letter, with Roosevelt's reply of 13 May, is in Hyde Park, PPF 4322. See also *U.S.*, 1938, 2:41, 44–45, 51–53.
48. There is no trace of this episode in the surviving French archives, *D.D.F.*, 2d, 7, No. 211, n.1.

leaders at the end of June 1937 and assured him that "we shall continue, with patience and persistence, our present endeavour to bring peace and order to a disturbed Europe."[49]

Difficulties in the Non-Intervention Committee and the sinking of ships by Italian submarines in the Mediterranean, which provoked the Nyon Conference, dominated the European, and the outbreak of war between China and Japan the Far Eastern diplomatic scene in July and August 1937, but London continued to examine the possibilities vis-à-vis Germany. The reports coming in from that country were anything but encouraging, but the cabinet thought that further exploration of the situation was desirable.[50] A long conversation between Henderson and Göring on 20 July certainly offered no encouragement. Göring talked about the Slavs as Germany's enemies, assured Henderson that Austria would have to join Germany and that Czechoslovakia would yield only to force, while the ultimate objectives of German policy could not be revealed.[51] Nothing the British learned through their embassy in Berlin about von Ribbentrop's views offered better hopes. Everything pointed to the German leaders having given up on an agreement with England and being engaged in planning for aggressive actions of their choice. As for Chamberlain's effort for a settlement, this was seen as temporizing until British rearmament was completed, an interpretation that was partially correct—but also partially mistaken.[52] As the firm line taken by the British government at the Nyon Conference of September 1937 against acts of piracy by Italian submarines showed, there were indeed prospects of a firmer posture once the British felt militarily capable of assuming it.[53] This did not mean, however, that Chamberlain was *only* playing for time; if settlements could be reached, he was all in favor.

The reports of Nevile Henderson in September and October of 1937 did not suggest that there was any greater prospect of agreement. His accounts of conversations with Hitler, Göring, and von Neurath made clear that Germany planned to move on Austria next, Czechoslovakia soon after, and subsequently to further expansion eastward. Britain could acquiesce in all this, in which case Germany would promise to leave her alone, at least for the time being. What was proposed, in effect, was the

49. Chamberlain to Mackenzie King, 29 July 1937, C 5187/5187/18, FO 371/20750, f.342. Material on the visit, ibid., ff.318–42; and C 6349/5187/18, FO 371/20750, ff.348–54. Cf. Dertinger's "Informationsbericht Nr. 103," 1 July 1937, Bundesarchiv, Brammer, Z.Sg. 101/31, ff.5–7.

50. C 5150/3/18, FO 371/20711; C 5138/165/18, FO 371/20733; Br. Cabinet 29 (37) of 8 July 1937, C 4966/270/18, FO 371/20735. Material summarizing a war scare in the summer of 1937 is in R 5224/770/17, FO 371/21140,

51. C 5314/270/18, FO 371/20736; the report of Henderson was stolen by the Italians from the British embassy in Rome and transmitted to the Germans, see Göring's Stabsamt, T-120, 5482/E 382022–33.

52. C 5957, C 6083/270/18, FO 371/20736; C 6301/3/18, FO 371/20711.

53. The British cabinet agreed on the line to be taken—sink submarines as needed—at the meeting of 8 September 1937, Cabinet 34 (37), W 17044/16618/41, FO 371/21405.

exact opposite of what the London and Paris governments had suggested in the Schacht talks. Instead of considering a return of colonies in exchange for German restraint in Europe, Göring—who alone put forth the idea in specific terms—wanted to have Britain (and France) agree to German expansion in Central and Eastern Europe in exchange for German restraint in colonial demands.[54] This suggestion, and Hitler's anti-British diatribes to the League high commissioner in Danzig, Carl J. Burckhardt, on 20 September hardly augured well for any formal negotiations along the lines developed in London and Paris, but the British government was not to be deterred.[55]

On 4 October Henderson had another lengthy conversation with Göring in which the latter declined to specify German demands and grievances. He repeated that the only workable proposal was a free hand for Germany in Europe and German respect for the security of the British Empire.[56] Two strains of development issued from this meeting. Within the British government, it was suggested that the impact of their rejecting this offer of an alliance might be softened by a unilateral British declaration that she would not attack Germany if the latter were attacked in Eastern Europe. Since there was not the slightest prospect of this contingency—everyone, including Göring, knew that the only probable source of attacks in Eastern Europe was Germany herself—this would have eliminated a fictitious German grievance while removing at the same time any danger of subsequent German complaints that no response had been made to any of her offers. After initial enthusiasm for this idea in London, Chamberlain and Eden agreed on 11 November that the scheme should be dropped.[57] The reasons are not fully evident from the record; concern for the reaction in France and the danger of misunderstanding in Germany and Eastern Europe appear to have been the main considerations. The other result of the Henderson-Göring talk in the end accomplished no more, but because in this instance, public action was taken, international interest of a very high degree was aroused. Almost certainly it was the discussion between the two men in Göring's hunting lodge at Rominten that produced the invitation to Lord Halifax to visit the international hunting expedition scheduled for Berlin in November 1937.

There had been discussion of a possible visit by Lord Halifax to Germany in 1936.[58] Lord Halifax, who in May 1937 had shifted from the post of lord privy seal to the equally unencumbered po-

---

54. Henderson-Hitler, 10 September 1937, C 6494/4222/18, FO 371/20749, ff.157–58; Henderson, p. 71; Henderson-Göring and Henderson-Neurath, 10–11 September 1937, Henderson, pp. 74–75; C 6494/4222, FO 371/20749, ff.159–64, 135–38.

55. C 7394/5/55, FO 371/20758; Burckhardt, pp. 97–103.

56. C 7027/270/18, FO 371/20736; R 6983/303/3, FO 371/21116.

57. Minute by William Strang of 11 November 1937, in C 7027/270/18, FO 371/20736, folio following f.157; see also R 7931/1/22, FO 371/21162.

58. Weinberg, *Foreign Policy*, pp. 272–73.

sition of lord president of the council, had periodically taken over Eden's responsibilities in the latter's absence. He was kept informed of significant developments in the diplomatic sphere by his membership on the Foreign Policy Committee of the cabinet and by the transmittal of important documents from the Foreign Office. He was personally close to Chamberlain—who had exceedingly few such associations—and also to Eden.[59] Though not always in agreement, Halifax and Eden worked together extremely well; their friendship survived the replacement of the latter by the former at the Foreign Office in February 1938 and the reversal of this succession in December 1940. Their differences reflected not so much a differing appreciation of the dangers in Europe as a great divergence in previous experience. Eden's formative experience in international affairs was in a Europe where the failure of disarmament, the collapse of collective security, and the rising threat of Germany left little room for optimism. He did not allow his personal distaste for Hitler and Mussolini to color his approach to them as much as Chamberlain feared, but it did make Eden exceedingly skeptical that any agreement worth the paper it was written on was likely to be secured. His strong advocacy of a policy of appeasement was, therefore, always tempered by doubts about the likelihood of success.

Halifax, on the other hand, had acquired his perspective on international affairs as viceroy of India. There he had applied his curiosity, energy, and political courage to a world as variegated as Europe but with one most important exception. Mohandas K. Gandhi was the recognized leader of the opposition to British rule, but Halifax had him released from jail, met him face to face, and worked out a settlement that did not eventually hold but that did show what could be accomplished if the protagonists sincerely tried to negotiate—even over the greatest imaginable gulf. As Halifax himself was to discover, however, there was a fatal flaw in the view that the viceroy who could talk usefully with Gandhi was surely the man who might talk usefully with Hitler. Though the German leader was seen by the mass of his followers in a way not unlike the regard millions of Indians had for Gandhi, the German leader was not interested in negotiations for an adjustment of differences and was most certainly no believer in nonviolence or civil disobedience. But it would take some hard experiences to bring this point home to Neville Chamberlain and Lord Halifax. In the meantime, the fact that Winston Churchill, the most vocal critic in British political life of talks with Gandhi, was almost as strongly opposed to conversations with Hitler only served to make a false analogy look more plausible. Lord Halifax fully understood that given the tensions between religions and races in India, Gandhi's agitation could lead to communal violence in spite of the nationalist leader's professions and

59. The most perceptive work on him is the Earl of Birkenhead's *Halifax: The Life of Lord Halifax* (Boston: Houghton Mifflin, 1966). Lord Halifax's own memoirs, *Fullness of Days* (New York: Dodd Mead, 1957), are helpful but very reticent.

preferences; it took him, like many others, a long time to realize that what was called communal violence in India was precisely what Hitler was determined to bring to Europe. Like Chamberlain, Halifax was able to see how a man's single-minded pursuit of cherished goals could lead him to ignore or underestimate the danger of touching off a bloodbath; it was inconceivable to them that the bloodbath itself could be anyone's goal.[60]

When the opportunity for Lord Halifax to visit Berlin arose in October 1937, therefore, there was initially agreement that this might provide a fine opportunity for a frank conversation with high-ranking Germans, including possibly Hitler.[61] In anticipation of the visit, there was again, as when von Neurath had been expected in London, anxious preparation in London and Berlin. The British studied both Burckhardt's report on his September talk with Hitler, which boded no good, and the Aga Khan's record of his conversation with the German leader on 20 October. Since Hitler had sounded a trifle more accommodating in the latter meeting, Eden thought that it might be used as a point of departure for Lord Halifax's talk.[62] Hitler had expressed an interest in the return of Germany's African colonies and suggested compensation in West Africa for former German East Africa, talked about a peaceful cultural and economic union with Austria and autonomy—whatever that meant—for the Germans of Czechoslovakia, and also indicated a willingness to return to the League. As the time for the visit actually approached, the generally negative attitude of von Ribbentrop and von Neurath reinforced the doubts in the Foreign Office that much of anything could be accomplished.[63] In particular, there was concern that Lord Halifax be most careful to warn the Germans about precipitate action, and that he elicit as specific as possible an elaboration of what Germany meant by her demands on Czecho-

60. For a shrewd observer's analysis of 4 October 1937 that the whole German colonial propaganda campaign of the fall of 1937 was solely a cover for planned expansion of German *Lebensraum* in Europe, see Dertinger's "Informationsbericht Nr. 141: Die österreichische Frage," Bundesarchiv, Brammer, Z.Sg. 101/31, ff.301–3; large part published in Hildebrand, p. 517.

61. C 7324/7324/18, FO 371/20751. The argument in the literature over the attitudes of Chamberlain, Eden, and Vansittart toward the idea of the visit is largely a product of confusion and hindsight. The contemporary evidence shows that all were originally in favor, that subsequently the prospect of a meeting of Eden with von Neurath at the Brussels conference on the Sino-Japanese conflict (see *G.D.*, D, 1, No. 13) made Eden dubious about Lord Halifax's going, but that by then Halifax was committed and von Neurath did not go to Brussels. Eden, pp. 576–81; *Harvey Diary*, pp. 59–60; Feiling, p. 332; Birkenhead, pp. 365–66.

62. C 74/3/18, FO 371/20712; R 7303/770/67, FO 371/21140; Paul Schmidt, *Statist auf diplomatischer Bühne, 1923–45* (Bonn: Athenäum, 1950), p. 382; Aga Khan III, *The Memoirs of Aga Khan* (New York: Simon and Schuster, 1954), pp. 276–77; cf. C 7232/3/18, FO 371/20712.

63. C 7506/37/18, FO 371/20722; C 7550/270/18, FO 371/20736; C 8293/270/18, FO 371/20737, f.62; C 7549/7324/18, C 7666/7324/18, FO 371/20751. On French information and reaction, see *D.D.F.*, 2d, 7, Nos. 229, 230, 232, 234, 238, 240, 246, 251; the French thought of this episode as analogous to Lord Haldane's trip to Berlin in 1912, and like Sir Robert Vansittart they hoped that it would prove as educational for Lord Halifax as the 1935 trip had been for Sir John Simon (ibid., No. 246).

slovakia, for example.[64] Similarly, the agitation in Germany on the colonial question suggested that the various aspects of this problem had better be examined further in London, while Halifax would have to make clear that no colonial concessions could be made except within the framework of a general settlement.[65]

In spite of an uproar over a leak about the planned visit, the British wanted to go ahead.[66] There is substantial evidence that the Germans tried to use this leak to call off the visit, as they had used the *Leipzig* incident, but the combined efforts of Sir George Ogilvie-Forbes, the British chargé in Berlin, Henderson, and Chamberlain kept the project alive in spite of a deliberately provocative communiqué Hitler arranged to have published in the party's news service, the *Nationalsozialistische Partei-Korrespondenz*.[67] This incident suggests that the Germans, knowing the general type of approach Halifax would take, were as uninterested as ever in negotiations along those lines; but it did not keep the key figures in London from arguing over detailed preparations for the talks.

Henderson urged a conciliatory attitude and concessions on the Austrian and Czech issues; Lord Halifax was inclined in that direction; and the permanent officials of the Foreign Office thought that a less complaisant attitude should be shown. But these differences revolved more around emphasis than substance. The basic question was whether there was any prospect of working out an agreement on the basis of German restraint in Europe if Britain and France would make concessions in the colonial sphere and whether such agreements might then lead to a general system of European security in which concessions to Germany might be made but would be limited by the national rights and independence of others.[68]

64. R 7303/770/67, FO 371/21140; R 7574/188/12, FO 371/21131.

65. C 7582, C 7595/37/18, FO 371/20722; *D.D.F.*, 2d, 7, Nos. 35, 37, 43; Dr. Kausch, "Mitteilung für die Redaktion," 5 November 1937, Bundesarchiv, Brammer, Z.Sg. 101/10, f.331.

66. There are no solid clues in the archives on the source of the leak; hints point to the Italian embassy in London or the Italian foreign ministry in Rome (see Eden's postscript to Vansittart to Henderson, tel. 198 of 15 November 1937, C 7732/7324/18, FO 371/20751, f.117; and *G.D.*, D, 1, No. 29).

67. See the material filed under C 7732/7324/18, FO 371/20751, ff.97–116; *G.D.*, D, 1, No. 25, 26; Dertinger, "Informationsbericht Nr. 163," 15 November 1937, Bundesarchiv, Brammer, Z.Sg. 101/31, ff.415–17. The latter document makes the analogy to the "welcome opportunity" of the *Leipzig* incident. It also suggests that the communiqué, aside from trying to discourage the visit altogether, was designed to reassure Rome and Tokyo on German policy. The full text of the communiqué, culminating in the question of "whether it would not be more helpful in the interests of a detente to postpone the visit" may be found in NSK, Folge 266, issued on 13 November but appearing under the release date of 16 November 1937. The analysis of this incident by the French ambassador in Berlin is in *D.D.F.*, 2d, 7, No. 277. Henke, pp. 109–13, agrees that Hitler wanted to avoid meeting Lord Halifax altogether, but exaggerates the interest of the German foreign ministry in the visit.

68. The notes Lord Halifax prepared for himself to take along to the meeting with Hitler are not in the Foreign Office files; he sent them to Chamberlain with a request for a meeting at which he wanted Vansittart present (see Halifax to Chamberlain, 8 November 1937, Premier 1/330, ff.174–87). The Foreign Office comments on these notes, which were discussed at a meeting between Chamberlain, Halifax, Eden, and Vansittart on 14 November,

Britain's French ally was reassured in several conversations; invitations to the French prime minister and foreign minister for a subsequent trip to London would provide the opportunity for providing them full information.[69] At the same time, Chamberlain's press secretary, obviously on orders from his chief, gave the Germans through the German News Agency, Deutsche Nachrichten Büro (DNB), representative in London a detailed reassurance of the British government's unified determination to try to come to an agreement with Berlin. The authorities there should disregard both the press leaks and all rumors of differences between Chamberlain and Eden; the conversation between Hitler and Lord Halifax was a good way to get things started, though all must realize that the development of a British-German rapprochement would be a slow process, taking years.[70]

This circumvention of regular channels was due not only to Chamberlain's great interest in having the process of talks started but also to a correct assessment of the opposition of the German ambassador to London, Joachim von Ribbentrop. In the days when the government to which he was accredited was preparing for the Halifax visit which was seen as the preliminary to serious Anglo-German negotiations, von Ribbentrop, who would later protest that all he ever wanted was Anglo-German friendship, was doing his best, or worst, to alienate the two countries from each other. Continuing his habit of spending much of his time away from his post, von Ribbentrop was devoting his efforts to bringing Italy into the Anti-Comintern Pact with Germany and Japan.[71] The details of those negotiations do not belong in this context, but von Ribbentrop's explanation to the Italians that he had failed to get along with the British and that this new scheme, seen by all participants and onlookers as directed against England, was the preliminary to a military alliance for the inevitable war against the Western Powers, suggests how far his perspectives were from those of the hosts of his infrequent stays in London.[72]

The fact that the proposed pact was, as Italian Foreign Minister Galeazzo Ciano put it, "ostensibly anti-Communist but in reality anti-British"[73] was understood in England. It did nothing to enhance von Ribbentrop's popularity in London, where, between his trips to Berlin,

---

are in C 7866/7324/18, FO 371/20751, ff.137–44. On the 14 November meeting, see also Harvey to Hendricks, 15 November 1937, C 7932/270/18, FO 371/20736, ff.261–62. On the London preparations for the visit, see further, R 7574, R 7653/188/12, FO 371/21131; C 7746, C 7799, C 7932/270/18, FO 371/20736; C 7834/226/18, FO 371/20734, ff.92–99.

69. See C 7785/3/18, FO 371/20712; C 7852/7324/18, FO 371/20751.

70. *G.D.*, D, 1, No. 29.

71. For a list of von Ribbentrop's travels in 1937 and early 1938, see T-120, 778/1562/378075–76.

72. Ciano, *Diplomatic Papers*, pp. 139–41; Ciano, *Tagebuch*, 24 October 1937, p. 32; Henke, pp. 95–96.

73. Ciano, *Tagebuch*, 2 November 1937, p. 37.

Munich, and Rome he preached about the dangers of communism to Eden.[74] While von Ribbentrop merely listened to the general views of Lord Halifax on his forthcoming trip,[75] the British government circularized its missions abroad instructing them to voice discreet British opposition to all ideological blocks if any government were solicited to join von Ribbentrop's Anti-Comintern Pact.[76] Unable to block the Halifax visit, von Ribbentrop then tried to persuade Hitler to have him participate in the meeting, but here the opposition of Henderson fitted in with the personal preferences of von Neurath, who was quite happy to exclude his rival from the spotlight.[77]

There is little evidence of detailed preparations in Germany for Lord Halifax's visit. The suggestions of the head of the political section of the German foreign ministry, Ernst von Weizsäcker, combine the demand for colonies with a free hand in Eastern Europe ("Kolonien und Aktionsfähigkeit im Osten") as in his plan when von Neurath was expected to go to London. The only new point is the caution that with Britain's rearmament program, time was running in England's favor, and Germany, therefore, should not delay negotiations indefinitely if she really wanted an agreement.[78] The key problem of negotiations, namely, that the British would consider colonial concessions only in the context of a general settlement which would limit Germany's freedom of action in Europe, was not grasped by von Weizsäcker, who imagined, in spite of the evidence brought back by Schacht, that the British might settle for German restraint in *Western* Europe. His superior, State Secretary von Mackensen, on the other hand, saw the point very clearly.[79] Hitler certainly understood it also; his comments in the Hossbach conference of 5 November

74. The latter suggested that "His Excellency would perhaps not be offended at the knowledge that we much desired that he would spend the greatest possible measure of time in his work with us in London. Herr von Ribbentrop appeared gratified at this aspect of the matter, which had not previously occurred to him and left assuring me once again of his satisfaction at the better relations between England and Germany. I refrained from telling His Excellency my view of the contribution which he had made to this alleged improvement." Eden to Henderson, No. 1288 of 27 October 1937, C 7451/270/18, FO 371/20736, ff.187–91; cf. Eden, pp. 571–72, 607.

75. *G.D.*, D, 1, No. 24.

76. F 9369/26/23, FO 371/21028. Note the decision *not* to hold up this instruction because of the Halifax trip.

77. Henderson tel. 290 of 16 November 1937, C 7853/7324/18, FO 371/20751, ff.129–31.

78. *G.D.*, D, 1, No. 21. Von Weizsäcker was here looking at the same issue from which Hitler drew the conclusion that a major war could not be postponed beyond a certain point (1943–45 was the time mentioned at the Hossbach conference five days before von Weizsäcker wrote his memorandum). After several years, Germany's armaments headstart would vanish; without the economic resources to scrap the existing stocks of weapons and to mass-produce newer models, Germany could go to war or try to negotiate before the diplomatic initiative passed out of her hands. Von Weizsäcker recommended negotiation; Hitler was determined on war.

79. See his directive on colonial policy to the German minister in Pretoria of 31 October 1937, *G.D.*, D, 1, No. 15, and his circular instruction on the colonial question on 11 November 1937, ibid., 7:518–21.

show that he understood that he could not have both voluntary colonial concessions and a free hand in Europe; and that he had decided to go ahead with the latter while postponing the former.[80] The fact that von Papen in a conversation with him three days later not only reported an attitude in France similar to that of the British but urged that it made sense for Germany to agree to such a policy of gradual and peaceful change in Europe in the expectation of colonial concessions probably had some influence on Hitler's decision to replace his minister in Austria at a time when a more active poicy there was to be implemented, and the general policy line von Papen urged ran in a directly contrary direction.[81] It is in this context that one must see the instructions to the German press to play down the Halifax visit and also the German attempt to spike the whole idea of conversations by the violent communiqué.[82] Hitler's subsequent comments to the Hungarian minister of foreign affairs on the visit placed the issue and his own perception of it in clear focus: "Halifax had suggested something might be done on colonies conditional on Germany binding itself to keep peace with Austria and Czechoslovakia and Hitler replied that there was no connection between the two subjects and he would not bargain on either."[83]

Lord Halifax was in Germany from 17 to 21 November, seeing Hitler and a number of other German leaders. In the long talk he had with Hitler, the fact that an agreement was most unlikely became evident.[84] Hitler explained that he would get what he wanted by negotiated agreement or by war—the free play of forces as he called it—but that he had no interest in the kind of comprehensive settlement that the British government hoped to secure. Hitler wanted colonies, but he would not make any concessions whatever in return for them. Those who had taken Germany's colonies could return them of their own free will now, and in that case he would accept suitable areas elsewhere in exchange for any they wished to keep. If Britain and France were disinclined to return them, then he would wait a few years and later take what he thought proper. As for the European situation, Hitler did not even put to Lord Halifax the

80. See above, pp. 35–37.

81. *G.D.*, D, 1, No. 22.

82. See above, p. 116, and Dr. Kausch, "Vertrauliche Bestellung an die Redaktion," 12 November 1937, Bundesarchiv, Brammer, Z.Sg. 101/10, f.349.

83. Montgomery (U.S. minister to Hungary) tel. 10, 26 January 1938, State 740.00/283.

84. The account of the visit is based primarily on the British and German records: C 8094/270/18, FO 371/20736; C 8279/270/18, FO 371/20737; *G.D.*, D, 1, Nos. 31, 33, 38. See also Birkenhead, chap. 20; Halifax, pp. 185–89; Eden, pp. 582–85; Henderson, pp. 93–96; *Harvey Diary*, pp. 61–62; Henke, pp. 113–17; Colvin, pp. 156–60; *TMWC*, 40:252–53; Lothar C. F. Wimmer, *Expériences et tribulation d'un diplomate autrichien entre deux guerres, 1929–38*, trans. Charles Reichard (Neuchâtel: Baconnière, 1946), pp. 206–8; Memorandum of Sumner Welles, 29 November 1937, State 741.62/206½ (not published in *U.S.*, presumably because it was kept out of the central files of the State Department and not inserted into them until 1948).

demand for a free hand that Göring had placed before Henderson. He simply pretended that all would work out all right and refused to be drawn out by any of the hints Lord Halifax put forward.

Two months earlier Lord Lothian had written to Henderson his view that the real issue was whether Germany or Russia or France were to be predominant in East Central Europe, "and if Germany is willing to accept the independence of nationality I think we ought to encourage her to assume that position, as it is the only way of preventing an explosion."[85] Though neither Chamberlain nor Halifax believed that Germany should be encouraged, there is good reason to believe that in other respects they agreed with this view, and that Hitler recognized this fact. Since it was precisely the "independence of nationality" that Hitler was not prepared to accept, however, there would be no advantage and actually great danger for Hitler's plans if he allowed any precise specification of delimitation of his ambitions in Europe.[86] The only hint that Lord Halifax was given about the new world Hitler hoped to create came not in response to suggestions of topics for a settlement, all of which Hitler waved off, but in an aside on the subject of India. Hitler told the former viceroy that the way to take care of problems there was to shoot Gandhi and a substantial number of his associates. No wonder Halifax thought that he and Hitler had a different sense of values, lived in different worlds, and spoke different languages.

Looking ahead, what conclusions were drawn from the talks? A side issue, of which a good deal was made but which in perspective does not appear nearly so important as it did at the time, would receive considerable further attention on both sides. This was the attitude of the press and of newspaper correspondents. The German minister of propaganda, Joseph Goebbels, promised to try for a better atmosphere. This was a promise he kept for a very short time indeed. There was also to be some restraint in the reciprocal expelling of newsmen, something the Germans could promise easily since they had already expelled the British newsman they most wanted to get rid of: Norman Ebbutt of *The Times* of London, a brilliant reporter whose accurate accounts of German developments had long annoyed Berlin and were often cut or entirely suppressed in London by Geoffrey Dawson, the editor of *The Times,* in agreement with Lord Astor, its owner.[87] In response to repeated German urging, Lord Halifax

85. Lothian to Henderson, 13 September 1937, Lord Lothian Papers, GD 40/17/347/331.
86. Henke takes a similar view.
87. On the expulsion of Ebbutt, see C 5830, C 6045, C 6120/305/18, FO 371/20740; Dertinger, "Informationsbericht Nr. 118," 19 August 1937, Bundesarchiv, Brammer, Z.Sg. 101/31, ff.155–57. On the attitude of Dawson and Lord Astor, see *The History of the Times,* vol. 4, pt. 2 (1952, Nendeln/Lichtenstein: Kraus Reprint, 1971), chap. 23; Evelyn Wrench, *Geoffrey Dawson and Our Times* (London: Hutchinson, 1955); Messersmith Notes on Conversations with Lord Astor and Geoffrey Dawson in 1937, Messersmith Papers. The often quoted letter of Dawson to his correspondent in Geneva of 23 May 1937 about how he could not understand German objections to *The Times* (Wrench, p. 361), has a close parallel in a letter to Lord Lothian of the same date: " . . . but I should like to get going with the Germans.

promised to take up with the British government the possibility of pleading for restraint with the English press, especially in regard to personal attacks on Hitler. Chamberlain did in fact touch on the problem in the House of Commons on 21 December and subsequently reminded British newspaper editors of their responsibility not to exacerbate an already delicate international situation.[88]

Because of a leak—apparently from the German side—from the talk between Lord Halifax and Schacht, in which the latter had proposed that a future German colonial sphere in West Africa be augmented by pieces of the Belgian Congo and Portuguese Angola, with Portugal compensated out of the southern part of Tanganyika, there was a great uproar in Portugal which the British government had to calm down as best it could. Since Portugal's colonies had in fact been discussed, and since Schacht's territorial concepts were not very far from some considered in London, this was no easy task; it was further complicated by Portuguese sensitivity in view of the prewar Anglo-German discussions about a possible partition of the Portuguese colonial empire and the postwar cession of a small sliver of German East Africa, the Kionga triangle, to the Portuguese colony of Mozambique.[89]

The main point, however, was whether there were to be any attempts at further negotiations. Göring had indicated interest in Anglo-German talks, but Hitler was not encouraging. On the other hand, he had tried in his own way to be a polite and charming host and had, therefore, not said a flat no. Lord Halifax thought that the political value of his talk with Hitler was not very high, that it had been valuable to make the contact, but that Hitler felt that time was on his side regarding European problems. The question to be answered by the British government was whether under these circumstances they should try to use colonial concessions as a lever for securing reassurance in Europe, to try once again for a bargain with colonies in order to make Hitler into a "good European," the assumption being that real as opposed to hypothetical offers might tempt the Führer. Lord Halifax was skeptical, but he believed that the attempt should be made. The comments within the Foreign Office on the accounts of his conversations were along the same lines. Extreme skepticism was coupled with a belief in the necessity of trying anyway and combined, in

---

I simply cannot understand why they should apparently be so much annoyed with *The Times* at this moment. I spend my nights in taking out anything which I think may hurt their susceptibilities and in dropping in little things which are intended to soothe them." Lord Lothian Papers, GD 40/17/337/340. It is typical of the tendentious character of Dietrich Aigner, *Das Ringen um England* (Munich: Bechtle, 1969), that he tries to discredit the self-description of Dawson (pp. 112–14, and esp. n.43).

88. On this subject, see C 8311/270/18, FO 371/20737.

89. W 20797, W 21667, W 21790, W 21794/1966/36, FO 371/21278; C 8375, C 8377/37/18, FO 371/20723; *G.D.*, D, 1, Nos. 52, 60, 61; von Neurath to von Ribbentrop, 8 December 1937, DZA Potsdam, Büro RAM, Akte 60964, f.174.

the case of both Eden and Vansittart, with highly favorable comments on the way Lord Halifax had handled himself.[90]

The discussion within the British government shows that there was general agreement on how to proceed; the only disagreement was on the prospects for success. Chamberlain's summary at the cabinet meeting of 24 November fairly states a position that had the support of both the cabinet members and the permanent officials in Whitehall: "For his part he would not make any offer in the colonial field except as a factor in a general settlement. The difficulty was to find what contribution the Germans could make. That would depend on the degree of conviction we felt as to their good faith. We should have to obtain some satisfactory assurance that they did not mean to use force in Eastern Europe."[91] Chamberlain's anticipation that there was some chance of agreement was not, however, shared by Eden or high officials in the Foreign Office; but since there was a basic agreement on how to proceed, this difference was of little practical importance.[92] The next steps were clearly first to inform the French and attempt to concert British and French views on the general prospects of agreement, and then to make a more definite approach to Germany.

As will be shown subsequently, the very weeks after Lord Halifax was in Germany during which the British government was working out its plans for negotiations with Berlin were a time when the German government was moving forward with its own designs against Austria. The fact that in its final stages that project moved slightly more rapidly than Berlin had anticipated must not be allowed to obscure the chronological realities. The soundings from London were taken in Germany not as the opening of a round of negotiations for a German agreement with England but as a confirmation of Hitler's view that Britain would not fight for Austria or Czechoslovakia, and that it was therefore safe for him to move. He had

90. In view of subsequent controversies, their contemporary expressions are worth quoting. Vansittart on 23 November: "Lord Halifax's paper [on his German trip] seems to me shrewd, and he appears to have handled the interview well and to have drawn some realistic conclusions" (FO 371/20736, f.312). Eden on 24 November "expressed great satisfaction with the way the Lord President had dealt with each point in his conversation with the Chancellor" (Br. Cabinet 43 [37] in CAB 23/90).

91. Br. Cabinet 43 (37), CAB 23/90, ff.165–70. Chamberlain also assumed that a return to the League and an agreement on armaments would be included in any settlement. For other information on internal British discussions at this time, see the Foreign Office materials on whether Hitler was seriously interested in German minorities abroad or merely wished to use some of them as excuses for expansion, in N 5764, N 5795/125/59, FO 371/21058; material on a possible visit of Göring to England in the continuation of the talks, in C 8067/3/18, FO 371/20712; and the discussions of the record of the Hitler-Halifax conversation in FO 371/20736, ff.310–16. Cf. the Hungarian minister in London's report of 19 November, *Hungarian Documents,* 1, No. 312; the Austrian minister in London's report of 22 November in *Guido Schmidt Trial,* pp. 526–27; the Austrian minister in Berlin's report of 26 November, ibid., pp. 499–501; the American chargé in London's report of 24 November, *U.S.,* 1937, 1:177–79.

92. Chamberlain's optimistic assessment is quoted at length from his papers by Feiling, pp. 332–33.

expressed his determination to do so at the Hossbach conference a few days before seeing Lord Halifax, and nothing he heard in that conversation deterred him in the slightest. On the contrary, the visit was used to further the interpretation that Britain would acquiesce in German designs; and this interpretation was then used to overawe the smaller states of Central and Eastern Europe.[93] If that calculation did not work out, Hitler would fight rather than change his plans: as he explained to an assemblage of National Socialist party officials on 23 November, Germany might well have to fight England to obtain the vast territories she needed.[94]

The Germans had to inform the Italians about the nature of the conversations, but the anxiety in Rome over the possibility of an Anglo-German rapprochement would vanish as it became evident that nothing of the sort was happening.[95] Italy's intention of leaving the League, communicated to the Germans at the same time, would provide an additional excuse for Germany to evade any British approaches on that subject. There was no need to be impolite, but nothing suggests that anyone in the German government seriously expected or desired progress toward an Anglo-German agreement along the lines of the general settlement the British appeared to them to want. Germany would go its own way without regard to any proposals from London; as agreement on terms dictated by Hitler was not possible, there was no point to even discussing whatever projects might emanate from London.[96] Contrary views have occasionally been expressed in postwar memoirs and other writings; they have no basis in contemporary evidence.

The French prime minister and foreign minister, invited to London to hear Lord Halifax report on his trip and to discuss possible future moves with their British colleagues, came to the meeting skeptical but hopeful. Like the permanent officials of the British Foreign Office, Chautemps and Delbos had little expectation that a general settlement with Germany could be realized but continued to hope for the best.[97] They believed, correctly, that direct exposure to Hitler would have proved a useful educational experience for Halifax and his British associates and that if there were any prospects for a settlement, these should certainly be explored. Furthermore, the French minister was about to go on a trip to the countries of East and Southeast Europe, and it was both important and useful

93. See *Hungarian Documents*, 1, No. 314, and compare Václav Král (ed.), *Das Abkommen von München* (Prague: Akademia, 1968) (hereafter cited as Král, *München*), No. 2.
94. Speech of 23 November 1937 in Henry Picker, *Hitlers Tischgespräche im Führerhauptquartier, 1941–42* (Bonn: Athenäum, 1951), pp. 443–50; cf. Domarus, 1:761–63; Speer, *Erinnerungen*, p. 539, n.5.
95. Ciano, *Tagebuch*, 23 November 1937, p. 50; *G.D.*, D, 1, No. 39.
96. Dertinger's "Informationsbericht Nr. 168," 22 November 1937, Bundesarchiv, Brammer, Z.Sg. 101/37, ff.437–39; *U.S.*, 1937, 1:167–69; Henke, pp. 118–19; Henderson's report on a conversation with von Neurath on 30 November 1937, C 8315/270/18, FO 371/20737.
97. French preparations for this meeting are in *D.D.F.*, 2d, 7, Nos. 264, 274, 275, 282.

for the two Western Powers to clarify and coordinate their own views before Delbos made his tour.[98]

The London talks of 28–30 November 1937 produced a wider range of understanding and agreement than might have been expected.[99] Lord Halifax gave a full account of his trip to Germany, and it is indicative of the extent of the frankness with which the French were treated that this was the account used to inform other departments of the British government as well as most British diplomatic missions abroad. Chamberlain expressed the opinion that he thought there was a possibility of agreement, that it could not be a purely Anglo-German one but would have to include France. It would be necessary to work out an approach and then see through diplomatic channels whether Britain and France could secure a general settlement, arrived at in good faith, in which colonial concessions would be exchanged for German good conduct in Europe. Delbos indicated that the information the French had of German aims was similar to that brought back by Lord Halifax, namely, that Germany was likely to move on Austria and Czechoslovakia next. To Chamberlain's question whether Germany could be stopped without resort to force, Delbos replied that if all really worked for a general settlement, there was some hope, but otherwise he feared that Europe would slide into another war.

Chamberlain warned the French leaders about the reluctance of the British public to go to war over the issue of Czechoslovakia, especially because of the impression that the Sudeten Germans had legitimate grievances. The French, who had hitherto been reluctant to do so, now agreed to urge concessions on the government of Czechoslovakia when Delbos visited Prague, but wanted the British to issue warnings in Berlin as well as in the Bohemian capital.[100] In prior internal British consideration of this question, the problem of granting autonomy to the Sudeten Germans had been canvassed, especially in view of the difficulties with public opinion in both the United Kingdom and the Dominions. Eden had reluctantly concluded that only British acceptance of a commitment in Central Europe in the form of a joint guarantee with France and Germany could lead to a settlement of this question;[101] but in the Anglo-French talks, the discussion was confined to the need to pressure Czechoslovakia, with Eden suggesting that any promises Czechoslovak President Eduard Beneš could be persuaded to make be used to secure assurances from Germany. In any case, the further the Czechoslovak government went, the better its international position would be; a point which will be

98. Král, *München*, No. 2; *G.D.*, D, 1, Nos. 37, 46; N 6024/5587/59, FO 371/21062.
99. The British record is in C 8234/270/18, FO 371/20736; the French record, given to the British on 20 December, is in C 8714/270/18, FO 371/20737, and published in *D.D.F.*, 2d, 7, Nos. 287, 291. A full report given by the French to the Czechoslovak minister in Paris, Osuský, is in Král, *München*, No. 6; American reports in *U.S.*, 1937, 1:180–88, 196–202. Cf. Eden, pp. 585–87; Dreifort, pp. 94–99.
100. For Foreign Office preparations on this subject, see R 8249/188/12, FO 371/21132.
101. R 8248/188/12, FO 371/21132.

further examined in the general discussion of the Czechoslovak crisis. There was agreement that an effort should be made to secure a German promise not to use force in her relations with Austria and also to make some commitment in regard to disarmament and a possibly reformed League of Nations.

Chamberlain summarized these matters as follows: "Whatever Germany's ultimate object—and we might assume that this was to gain territory—our policy ought to be to make this more difficult, or even to postpone it until it might become unrealizable." Here Chamberlain reflected on the terrible dilemma in Central Europe as seen from London. The French could not and the British would not fight for the status quo there; but even if they did, could they win? And even if they won, would and could they enforce a return to the status quo on Germany? But if Germany did secure control of Central Europe, would this not endanger the rest of Europe, including England? Would postponement combined with rearmament not ease the situation? In the face of these puzzles, should British policy be directed to letting developments take their course, to halting them, or to helping them?[102] Henderson and Lothian wanted the last-named course; Chamberlain opted for something midway between the first two; and the French, though reluctant to face the options, took a similar course.

On the colonial question, there was still agreement that concessions could be made only in the framework of a general settlement and that Britain as well as France would have to make a substantial contribution.[103] A number of schemes to cope with various aspects of this issue were touched on. Perhaps the use of chartered companies could circumvent the problem of transferring to the Germans authority over an indigenous population that might object to and suffer from such a transfer. Perhaps the difficulties caused for the British government by the dangers seen as inherent in any transfer of Tanganyika to Germany could be obviated by monetary compensation to Germany, or by territorial compensation in East Africa to powers *other* than Germany—presumably Belgium or Portugal, or both—in exchange for colonial concessions to Germany in West Africa by those countries. In any case, the British government would have to be clear in its own mind as to what it could and would do, and would then have to agree with the French on the conditions to be set before the Germans.

The Spanish problem and relations with Italy were among the other issues discussed; the public communiqué agreed upon at the end of the meeting, however, was noteworthy primarily because it indicated for the first time that the colonial issue was under review, a novelty hardly reduced by the reiteration of the position that colonies would be discussed

102. C 4757/3/18, FO 371/20711.
103. A summary of the status of the colonial question was prepared before the French ministerial visit, C 8265/37/18, FO 371/20723.

only within the framework of a general settlement and not in isolation.[104] Privately the British and French leaders had agreed to interpret the term "general settlement" as including a Western Pact that did not give Germany a free hand in Eastern Europe, a German commitment to England and France to abide by the July 1936 agreement affirming the independence of Austria, and German respect for the integrity of Czechoslovakia in exchange for concessions to the Sudeten Germans. Equal sacrifices would be made by England and France in the colonial portion of a settlement, but there would be no statement on any recognition of Germany's "right" to colonies.[105]

The highest officials of the British government could have saved themselves a great deal of time had they paid more attention to von Ribbentrop's negative reaction to all this; it was precisely the theoretical recognition of Germany's right to colonies and the total separation of the colonial from all other issues that he insisted on to Eden when briefed by the latter on the talks.[106] The British, however, did not deduce from von Ribbentrop's frequent absences in Germany that perhaps he was being kept continuously abreast of Hitler's thinking; instead they told both von Ribbentrop and von Neurath that the next step in the negotiations arising out of the Halifax visit would come through diplomatic channels and would take some time to prepare.[107] Von Ribbentrop recommended that the German government reject the expected British approach by refusing to relate the colonial question to any other issue, a position fully in accord with Hitler's and von Neurath's views at the time.[108] Nevile Henderson was apparently inclined to deprecate the idea of demanding a general settlement in the face of obvious German reluctance, but he was reprimanded repeatedly orally and in writing.[109] The London authorities were determined both to make an offer in the colonial field and to insist that Germany make a substantial political contribution in Europe.

104. FO 371/20736, ff.356, 422. It was at the end of the discussion that the British again pushed the French on the subject of air rearmament.

105. Foreign Office memorandum of 30 November 1937, C 8274/270/18, FO 371/20737, ff.16–23. On French pleasure with the results of the meeting, see C 8281/270/18, FO 371/20737; G.D., D, 1, No. 49. A thoughtful and very positive evaluation by the French ambassador in London is in D.D.F., 2d, 7, No. 299.

106. C 8280/270/18, FO 371/20737; Eden, pp. 587–88; G.D., D, 1, Nos. 47, 49, 50.

107. G.D., D, 1, No. 48; C 8280/270/18, FO 371/20737. Cf. N 6024/5587/59, FO 371/21062, reverse of f.402. The effort of Hildebrand to postulate a difference between Hitler and von Ribbentrop on the colonial issue is not convincing. The evidence suggests, on the contrary, that the views of the two men were essentially identical in the winter of 1937–38, a factor relevant to Hitler's appointment of von Ribbentrop to the position of foreign minister in February 1938. Given the importance of Anglo-German relations and colonial propaganda in those months, it is difficult to believe that Hitler would have taken this step if he had reason to believe there was any serious divergence of opinion.

108. G.D., D, 1, No. 51, Dertinger's "Informationsbericht Nr. 174," 2 December 1937, Bundesarchiv, Brammer, Z.Sg. 101/31, ff.473–75 (Hildebrand, pp. 540–41); D.D.F., 2d, 7, No. 296; cf. ibid., No. 321.

109. See C 8466, C 8634, C 8661/270/18, FO 371/20737.

As the British cabinet on 1 December 1937 began consideration of the offer to be made, it was apparent that the difficult problem of what to do about the reluctance to return the most important English mandate, Tanganyika, would have to be faced.[110] With most of the rest of the German colonies that had been turned over to the British Empire under the mandatory authority of various Dominions, London would have to face squarely the question of a British contribution, a question that had been left in merciful obscurity by the failure of the Schacht talks. Furthermore, it would be necessary to specify precisely what would be asked of Germany in return. Both the territorial issue and the broader political one were simpler for the French: for them the colonies involved were obviously Togo and the Cameroons, and the political demands were predetermined by the French treaty of alliance with Czechoslovakia. The cabinet agreed that the cabinet Committee on Foreign Policy would have to examine the whole question, develop an approach to Germany, and include in it possible economic concessions along with the colonial ones to be offered in exchange for the precise political concessions from Germany that would secure peace in Europe and justify to the British public the transfer of territory contemplated.[111]

Those involved in this whole project saw it as a serious undertaking that offered a slight—and perhaps the only—hope of an agreement with Germany that would avoid another war. Dominated by the experience of 1914–18, they seem to have thought of Lord Halifax playing a role not unlike Lord Haldane in 1912. The broader intentions of Germany would be tested, so to speak, by an attempt to settle what appeared to be the most difficult of the outstanding issues between the two powers, with the colonial question taking the place of the naval rivalry of an earlier day. The vehement colonial agitation in Germany, heavily augmented in 1937,[112] could be seen as whipping up German opinion in somewhat the same way that the propaganda of the *Flottenverein,* the Naval Society, had aroused German navalism in the early years of the century; and it remained to be seen whether the growth in the antagonism between Britain and Germany could be arrested and turned around by a general settlement. There was no expectation that an agreement would be reached easily or quickly. What Joseph Chamberlain had tried but failed to accomplish in his efforts for an English-German rapprochement at the turn of the century, what the British had subsequently worked out in long

110. Br. Cabinet 45 (37) of 1 December 1937, CAB 23/90, ff.215–23; C 8278/270/18, FO 371/20737.

111. On economic aspects, see C 8263/87/18, FO 371/20731; cf. R 4476/770/67, FO 371/21139.

112. Hildebrand, pp. 390ff.; Gerhard L. Weinberg, "Deutsch-japanische Verhandlungen über das Südseemandat," *Vierteljahrshefte für Zeitgeschichte,* 4, No. 4 (October 1956) (hereafter cited as Weinberg, "Südseemandat"), p. 390.

negotiations with the French, they would now try to work out with Germany: a negotiated resolution of outstanding differences that it was hoped would lead to a new relationship. The London government approached the prospect of a detente with Germany in a frame of mind that included the expectation of drawn out and difficult, but it hoped successful, months of negotiations, and they so intimated to the Germans.[113]

The British leaders were urged along the thorny path of prolonged negotiations by the harsh facts of the situation placed before them by their military advisers. Early in December, the Committee of Imperial Defence and the cabinet discussed the report of the chiefs of staffs summarizing the dangerous situation Britain would face in 1938.[114] The grim concluding sentence of the chiefs of staffs had been that "we cannot, therefore, exaggerate the importance, from the point of view of Imperial defence, of any political or international action that can be taken to reduce the number of our potential enemies and to gain the support of potential allies." Both Chamberlain and Eden believed that under the circumstances the right policy was one of delay, rearmament, and negotiations. Delay would be accompanied by the hope that rearmament would strengthen England, and that in any case, as Eden put it, "for periods in the past, Europe has managed to exist, under armed truce, without a general settlement, but without war." Rearmament, furthermore, would rally the smaller states of Europe to England's side and restrain Germany. Negotiations might alleviate tensions as long as no unilateral concessions were made. As Chamberlain phrased it: "He could see no prospect of success by methods which would shame us in the eyes of the world, alienate the good opinion of France and the United States of America and ultimately land us in worse difficulties than those which confront us at the present time. He preferred the policy that was at present being pursued by the Foreign Office, which was not one of doing nothing but of active diplomacy." They would try for better relations with Germany and with Italy; they would hope to resume the efforts at agreement with Japan that had been interrupted by Japanese aggression against China. They would hope to improve their relations with the smaller countries of Europe while expecting little help from a Soviet Union in internal upheaval but potentially capable of assistance to possible victims of Germany and also potentially a great menace if allied with Berlin.

113. C 8411/270/18, FO 371/20737; *G.D.,* D, 1, Nos. 74, 75, 81.

114. The CID meeting of 2 December 1937 in C 8704/205/62, FO 371/20702; the Cabinet 46 (37) of 8 December 1937 in C 8477, ibid. The text of the chiefs of staff sub-committee report of 12 November with the relevant Foreign Office comments and covering memoranda, is in C 7851, ibid., ff.195–213; it had been discussed in a preliminary way at the CID on 18 November, C 8331, ibid., ff.214–16. A further discussion took place in the cabinet on 22 December, Cabinet 49 (37), CAB 23/90, ff.356–77, with Foreign Office comments in C 42/42/18, FO 371/21654, f.448. A critical weakness of Germany in 1938, that of oil supplies, was not called to the attention of the cabinet (Roskill, 3:387); in 1939 it would be remedied by the Soviet Union.

As the government in London developed its approach, an important change of personnel was made. Sir Alexander Cadogan replaced Sir Robert Vansittart as permanent undersecretary of state for foreign affairs with the latter appointed to the new position of chief diplomatic adviser. Though still involved in key policy matters as the foreign secretary's representative on the Committee on Imperial Defence—and much involved in other diplomatic matters as the archives show—Vansittart's influence was substantially reduced. It is a double irony that this should be done at a time when the British government was pursuing an approach to Germany along lines he had himself originally proposed two years earlier and when the failure of that approach would see him play a most important role in the immediately ensuing Czechoslovak crisis. But he had warned too often, too vehemently, and too indiscriminately; and having earlier declined the Paris embassy, was now waved to the sidelines.[115] Certainly Eden's agreement with Chamberlain in this step shows the determination of both to move forward with the new project; and at his meeting with the Foreign Affairs Committee of the House of Commons on 9 December 1937, Eden at least claimed to be more optimistic about the chances of success in attaining what was still referred to as European appeasement.[116]

In December 1937 and January 1938 the British government considered the terms of an approach to Germany. The details of these internal deliberations are, for the most part, of no great importance in view of the fate of the approach; what is important is the earnestness with which the authorities in London examined the problem and the light shed on British policy by the final result.[117] If the Germans objected so strongly to the

115. Eden, pp. 590–91; Colvin, pp. 169–74; *Harvey Diary*, pp. 22, 44, 63–64, 101; Dalton Diary, 12 April and 4 November 1937; A. J. Sylvester to Lloyd George, 3 January 1938, Lloyd George Papers, G/22/4. Cf. *G.D.*, D, 1, Nos. 89, 95, 101.

116. Nicolson, pp. 314–15. On Chamberlain's determination to try, see *G.D.*, D, 1, Nos. 75, 81; on Eden's, see *U.S.*, 1938, 1:135–36.

117. On these discussions, see C 8682/148/62, FO 371/20700; C 8352, C 8406, C 8661/270/18, FO 371/20737; C 74, C 484/42/18, FO 371/21654; C 800, C 995/42/18, FO 371/21655; R 8128/188/12, FO 371/21132; W 22354/1966/36, FO 371/21278; C 157/85/18, FO 371/21672; C 1305/184/18, FO 371/21679; C 3775/184/18, FO 371/21680; C 13430, C 13657/184/18, FO 371/21682; C 508, C 515/184/18, FO 371/21678; C 448/448/18, FO 371/21700 (on possible Göring visit); Henderson to Halifax, 10 January 1938, and Halifax to Henderson, 14 January 1938, Henderson Papers, FO 800/269, ff.3–5; 21st meeting of the cabinet Committee on Foreign Policy, 24 January 1938, CAB 27/623; Cadogan to Horace Wilson, 22 January 1938, Premier 1/330, ff.83–110, 113; Feiling, pp. 322–24; Henderson, p. 113; *Cadogan Diary*, pp. 40–45; *Harvey Diary*, pp. 62–63, 78, 80, 81, 85; *G.D.*, D, 1, Nos. 78, 98, 99, 112; Earl R. Beck, *Verdict on Schacht* (Tallahassee: Florida State University, 1955), p. 111; Gilbert (U.S. chargé Berlin) tels. 16 of 17 January, 56 of 14 February, 70 of 21 February 1938, State 741.62/221, 225, 233; *U.S.*, 1938, 1:403; *Hungarian Documents*, 1, Nos. 318, 319.

The detailed examination of Chamberlain's African scheme in FO 371/21679, ff.154ff., was not *printed* until months later, but a copy was in Chamberlain's hands at the time, see Premier 1/247. Vansittart warned about the active role of Sir Horace Wilson in these matters; see C 484/42/18, FO 371/21654, ff.480–81.

term "general settlement," perhaps the way to phrase things would be to describe the process as "the contributions towards appeasement which, as the bases of a possible agreement, each country might be able to make in Europe and elsewhere."[118] That there could be no agreement without all making contributions was, however, agreed to by everyone, even Henderson, who was repeatedly in London for conferences during the discussion of the approach.[119] The contribution expected from Germany was primarily in terms of a nonagressive German policy toward Austria and Czechoslovakia. Because of the acceleration of German pressure on Austria, symbolized by Hitler's threats to Austrian Chancellor Kurt von Schuschnigg at their meeting of 12 February, during the weeks immediately preceding the British offer to Germany, the phraseology on this point was made even more explicit by Lord Halifax, Eden's successor. He instructed Henderson, over the ambassador's objections: "You should say that in our view appeasement would be dependent, among other things, on measures taken to inspire confidence in Austria and Czechoslovakia, and to establish better relations between those countries and Germany."[120]

A contribution seen as being made by all and being as beneficial for Germany as for Britain and France would be a beginning of arms limitation by the restriction or elimination of bombing and bombing places. This was a subject to which Hitler had alluded on a number of occasions in diplomatic conversations, and where it was thought—quite incorrectly as we now know—Hitler might be expected to consider British and German interests as coinciding.

On the colonial question, the discussions in London produced a new concept on which Henderson would be instructed to sound out the German government. Previous discussion had revealed the great difficulties Britain would face in making a contribution equivalent to that of France if the mandate of Tanganyika were not returned to Germany for fear of leaving Kenya between German and Italian territory. There was,

---

The subject of possible limitations on air warfare in general, and bombing in particular, is reviewed in Uri Bialer, " 'Humanization' of Air Warfare in British Foreign Policy on the Eve of the Second World War," *Journal of Contemporary History*, 13, No. 1 (Jan. 1978), 79–96.

118. Eden's instruction to Henderson, No. 164 of 12 February 1938, C 995/42/18, FO 371/21655, f.108. This is the official text on the basis of which Henderson saw Hitler on 3 March 1938; the supplements that Halifax sent him on 27 February and 2 March reinforced the warning about Austria and provided information about the steps being taken in London to try to restrain the British press and to coordinate British publicity abroad (ibid.).

119. See also François-Poncet on Henderson's optimism just before leaving Berlin for discussions in London at the end of January, *D.D.F.*, 2d, 8, No. 55.

120. This addition came in response to French and Austrian requests for a British demarche in Berlin on the Austrian crisis, see C 1095/42/18, FO 371/21655; R 1442/137/3, FO 371/22311; *D.D.F.*, 2d, 8, Nos. 185, 189, 190, 231, 258, 274, 276, 278, 301, 304, 403. It should be noted that the texts of the relevant documents directly contradict the assertion often found even in scholarly works (e.g., Hildebrand, p. 551), that England did not expect Germany to respect the independence of Austria as well as Czechoslovakia as part of an Anglo-German agreement.

moreover, the exceedingly difficult political and moral question posed by the rights of the population of any areas transferred. Would the public allow such transfers—to the National Socialists of all people—and what would be local reaction, and reactions elsewhere in the British Empire? The restrictions that might be imposed in protection of native rights— against forced labor and land alienation, for example—were the very ones that would hamper the economic exploitation for which Germany allegedly needed and wanted colonies. How could any such restrictions be enforced on a Germany that might at first agree to them and subsequently quietly violate or publicly renounce them like the demilitarization of the Rhineland? Moreover, was it not likely that the Germans would reject out of hand any special restrictions imposed on them by disinterring their ancient arguments about "equality of rights" (*Gleichberechtigung*) that had loomed large before German armaments had surpassed those of her neighbors?

In the recess of Parliament after Christmas, Chamberlain pondered these complexities and came up with an idea that looked to him, and to at least some other members of the government, like a possible solution to a substantial proportion of these puzzles. As he originally proposed it to the cabinet Committee on Foreign Policy, and as it came to be embodied in the scheme Henderson was to put before Hitler, Chamberlain envisaged a new colonial regime for all of Central Africa. The region south of the Sahara and north of the Zambezi River would be placed under a system in which all the powers holding territory there would be required to subscribe to certain principles for the well-being of the indigenous population; these would include demilitarization, provisions for the welfare of the inhabitants, and freedom of trade and communications. Germany would be allocated territory within this area, would be subject to the identical restrictions as all the other powers with lands there, and would be represented along with these others on a new international commission to observe the area. Thus Germany would hold colonies on the same basis as Britain, France, Belgium, and Portugal, and possibly Italy; there would be a new body to take the place of the Permanent Mandates Commission of the League of Nations; and, perhaps most important, both the area to be included and the restrictions to be imposed were essentially similar to the area and restrictions covered by the Congo Basin Treaties signed in Berlin in 1883.

Just which territory within the total area Germany would receive was not spelled out; Henderson was first to elicit a German reaction to the whole concept, with the details left to subsequent negotiations. The evidence as to what Chamberlain had in mind on the territorial question is not conclusive, but there are indications that he thought primarily of a German colonial empire in West Africa, based on the original German colonies of Togo and the Cameroons, enlarged by parts of Nigeria, French Equatorial Africa, and adjacent portions of the Belgian Congo and Portugese Angola. Belgium would be giving up this territory in exchange for keeping Ruanda-Urundi, her portion of former German East Africa; while Portugal would be compensated by the southern portion of Tanganyika, and France by other British colonial concessions, with the New Hebrides, islands in the West Indies, the northern portion of the Gold Coast, Gambia, and the remainder of Tanganyika figuring as possible candidates for transfer.

Some thought was also given to an alternative by which the area included in the new international system would extend only to the western border of Nigeria, in which case Togo would come under German sovereignty without any restrictions whatever. The idea was that this prospect would make the whole proposal more attractive to Germany, which, like Britain and France, would then have colonial territory both inside and outside the area subject to the new colonial regime. While none of these details was ever presented to the German government, such considerations do show how far the British were prepared to go in the attempt to make Hitler into a "good European."

As the British worked out the preliminary details of an offer to Germany, they had to notify their French allies, fit the offer into a general policy dealing with Italy as well as Germany, and modify as well as delay their offer to Germany because of the course of events in Europe. The French had agreed at the London meeting at the end of November that the British should take the lead in carrying forward the talks with Germany growing out of the Halifax visit. They were themselves in favor of an approach to Germany, and Delbos so explained to von Neurath when the latter met him briefly in Berlin as Delbos was passing through on his way to Warsaw and Southeast Europe.[121] On his trip, Delbos gave the Czechoslovak government the advice to make concessions to the Sudeten Germans that he had promised to make when in London;[122] after his return to Paris, he continued to hope for agreement with Germany, but like Prime Minister Chautemps was increasingly doubtful of the prospects of success.[123] The French began to urge the British to shift the nature of the approach to Germany; instead of attempting a comprehensive settlement, Britain and France should first try to get some smaller problems worked out and then use the better atmosphere created by such successes to move on to larger problems.[124] While the British rejected this idea, they

121. *G.D.*, D, 1, No. 55; C 8406/270/18, FO 371/20737; C 8730/7888/17, FO 371/20698; R 8546/26/67, FO 371/21137; *D.D.F.*, 2d, 7, Nos. 307, 319, 323, 324, 327, 340, 349; Dreifort, pp. 141–50.

122. *D.D.F.*, 2d, 7, No. 365.

123. *U.S.*, 1938, 1:2; Bullitt tels. 56 of 12 January and 136 of 25 January 1938, State 740.00/264, 277. On French consideration of publishing the correspondence on the Schacht talks, see C 157/85/18, FO 371/21672.

124. C 631/42/18, FO 371/21654; *U.S.*, 1938, 1:15–16; *D.D.F.*, 2d, 8, No. 35, pp. 68–69, No. 53. Note the similarity to the French concept of December 1936, when they hoped that

were far more sympathetic to the French request that detailed staff conversations were now needed for the contingencies of joint military operations should all peace projects fail.

In spite of the great reluctance of the British military leaders, the Foreign Office recommended' and the cabinet approved staff talks; although there would be no new formal commitments, Britain and France were drawing more closely together in the face of anticipated common dangers.[125] At the same time, the French sent a secret mission to the United States to remedy French deficiencies in air power by building up the American aircraft industry with a view toward the future purchase of planes on the assumption that if war in Europe once broke out, the American neutrality law would be amended.[126] On the issue of an approach to Germany, however, the French deferred to the British desire to go ahead, though with considerable reluctance.[127]

Fearing a leak of their scheme, the British gave the French only the vaguest hint of the proposal they planned to place before the Germans. If the Germans agreed in principle, the British would go into more detail with their allies; but if Berlin rejected the whole concept, there was little sense in risking a big ruckus over the proposed scheme.[128] The other colonial powers potentially affected, Portugal and Belgium, were left officially uninformed, though there is evidence that the Belgian government, or at least the Belgian king, was in fact aware of at least some of the specific ideas being considered.[129]

The weeks during which the approach to Germany was being worked out in London was also the time of decision for negotiations between England and Italy. Though still entertaining some hope that the Rome-Berlin Axis might yet be broken, the British government, and especially Chamberlain himself, wanted to improve relations with Italy as well as

---

joint mediation of the Spanish Civil War would open the way for a general settlement (see above, pp. 90–91.

125. C 8674/3285/17, FO 371/20698; C 841, C 1206/37/18, FO 371/21653; *Les relations franco-britanniques, 1935–1939*, p. 95; cf. *Ironside Diary*, pp. 46–48. The agreement between Chamberlain and Eden on this critical issue at the cabinet meeting of 16 February no doubt contributed to the surprise of many cabinet members at the split between the two a week later. See also Gibbs, pp. 624–36.

126. *U.S.*, 1938, 2:297–309; *D.D.F.*, 2d, 8, No. 447; John M. Haight, Jr., *American Aid to France, 1938–1940* (New York: Atheneum, 1970), pp. 1–12.

127. C 1287/42/18, FO 371/21655.

128. The text of the information to be given Paris was included in Eden's instruction to Henderson of 12 February (n.118, above).

129. *D.D.B.*, 5, No. 3. See the comment by the secretary of state for the colonies, William Ormsby-Gore, at the cabinet Committee on Foreign Policy on 24 January 1938, that "the King of Belgium, who had given considerable thought to the matter, had told him that while Belgium could not possibly contemplate the return to Germany of Ruanda-Urundi, she might be prepared to make some contribution in West Africa" (CAB 27/623, f.17), which appears to reflect discussions going into considerable detail.

Germany.[130] This aspect of the effort to secure peace by better relations with both Hitler and Mussolini—described at the time by Lord Halifax as "the broad question of getting onto closer terms with the gangsters"[131]—was being pushed by Chamberlain with the somewhat doubtful agreement of the French. Like the Anglo-Italian negotiations of a year before, these new talks would lead only to dubious agreements immediately violated by the Italians. The tedious details need not be recounted here; they show Chamberlain eager for some agreement and Mussolini quite unwilling to make any significant concession. There was really no way to bring the two powers together in the face of Mussolini's ambitions, his continued large-scale intervention in the Spanish Civil War, and his unwillingness to confront Hitler firmly over Austria.[132] The negotiations led to an agreement signed in April and put into effect in November 1938, but of little long-term significance; the talks did, however, have two exceedingly important immediate by-products. The prospect of negotiations with Italy as well as Germany was a major factor in Chamberlain's decision to ask Roosevelt to delay his planned call for a world peace conference.[133] The difference between Chamberlain and Eden on that specific issue was greatly increased by Eden's unwillingness to agree to formal negotiations with Rome until the Italians gave some small sign of complying with their earlier agreement with England. Over this essentially procedural issue, though it had some substantive overtones, the two men came to a break, with Eden resigning rather than going along with the procedure Chamberlain wanted.[134] Lord Cranborne, the parliamentary undersecretary, resigned with Eden and was replaced by R. A. B. Butler. Since Eden's successor, Lord Halifax, was in the House of Lords, Butler would play a more prominent role than his predecessor; but of greater significance was the fact that as a result of this situation, Chamberlain himself came to speak more frequently in the House of Commons on foreign affairs and thus became personally embroiled in contro-

130. As previously noted, Eden had originally urged the idea of negotiations with Italy on Chamberlain. The strategic factor—Britain's need to be able to send a fleet to the Far East without excessive risks in the Mediterranean—was more important than ever (see Roskill, 3:282–84).

131. See Lord Halifax's handwritten comment of 18 February 1938 on C 1324/42/18, FO 371/21656, f.264. See also *G.D.*, D, 1, No. 130; Gerl to Hess, 6 March and 15 April 1938, Nuremberg document 3752-PS, National Archives.

132. A brief account in Siebert, pp. 62–67. See *G.D.*, D, 1, No. 116; 2, No. 33; Eden, pp. 646ff.

133. See above, p. 110. Cf. *U.S.*, 1938, 1:122–24.

134. Eden's account is in his memoirs, chap. 13. See also *U.S.*, 1938, 1:136–39, 158–59; *Cadogan Diary*, pp. 44–55 passim; Nicolson, pp. 326–27; Feiling, pp. 337–38; *Harvey Diary*, pp. 91–97; Duff Cooper, pp. 211–13; Roskill, 3:298–305; Pratt, pp. 103–4; Nancy H. Hooker (ed.), *The Moffat Papers, 1919–1943* (Cambridge, Mass.: Harvard University Press, 1956), pp. 189–91; *G.D.*, D, 1, Nos. 111, 119, 120, 123, 126–28; Masaryk report No. 1 of 24 February 1938, Czechoslovak document in T-120, 1040/1809/412935–38 (excerpts in Berber, pp. 88–89); Douglas, pp. 105–14; *Australian Documents*, No. 127.

versy on a wider variety of subjects than might otherwise have been the case.

Eden's resignation delighted the Italians and Germans; Henderson wrote Lord Halifax that "coming from the Germans that is naturally a compliment to Eden. At the same time it must be admitted that it was unlikely that any understanding with Germany was possible as long as Eden was Secretary of State . . . . Eden and Hitler could never have agreed. I cannot therefore, since I regard an understanding with Germany as indispensable if we are not slowly or even rapidly to drift into war again, regard either Eden's resignation or your own appointment with anything but the utmost relief." [135] He would soon have the opportunity to discover whether an understanding with Germany would now be any easier to secure.

The situation in Germany itself had also changed during the winter months while the British offer was being prepared. The internal changes announced by Hitler on 4 February 1938 have already been discussed. [136] Beyond strengthening Hitler's position in Germany, these changes directly affected Anglo-German relations through the appointment of von Ribbentrop as German foreign minister. Von Ribbentrop's memorandum for Hitler summarizing his impressions as ambassador to the effect that war with England was inevitable has already been quoted. [137] In regard to the question immediately confronting Hitler, von Ribbentrop's assessment was in some ways quite shrewd, but it was fatal for any Anglo-German agreement both immediately along the lines London was then considering and, by implication, for any future agreement as well. "A clear English concession to [a settlement of] the Austrian and Czech questions as we see fit could have the effect of clearing the air in Europe. From my experiences here, I consider such a development unlikely and believe that at the most England might by circumstances be forced some day to tolerate such a solution. I am confirmed in the belief that this problem cannot be solved by official negotiations with England by the fact that in internal political as well as foreign affairs Chamberlain stands in a system (with France) which makes great decisions incredibly difficult to take." [138] In view of this attitude, it is not surprising that von Ribbentrop's replacement in London, Herbert von Dirksen, was a man of ability but without even the slightest influence in Germany. [139]

135. Henderson to Halifax, 27 February 1938, Henderson Papers, FO 800/269, f.35.

136. The internal German crisis, right after Chamberlain's request for postponement, was a factor in Roosevelt's further delaying his world peace project, *U.S.*, 1938, 1:124–25.

137. See above, p. 64. The U.S. chargé a.i. in London, Hershel Johnson, had a very accurate view of von Ribbentrop's experiences in London as well as knowledge that was generally accurate about both the existence and contents of von Ribbentrop's concluding report (Johnson's dispatch 3879 of 8 February 1938, State 862.00/3745).

138. *G.D.*, D, 1:135.

139. See von Ribbentrop's own postwar comments in *TMWC*, 35:145–46; see also C 2514/812/18, FO 371/21706.

The other major change in Germany's situation, that in German-Austrian relations, was closely tied to the Fritsch-Blomberg crisis of early February 1938. Hitler decided to increase the pressure on Austria; as Alfred Jodl noted in his diary on 31 January:"The Führer wants to divert the searchlight from the armed forces, keep Europe in suspense.... Schuschnigg is not to be allowed to gain courage, but [shall] tremble."[140] The Austrian chancellor was to do his trembling when Hitler, surrounded by the most fierce-looking of his generals, browbeat him into concessions at Berchtesgaden two weeks later, and then refused to acknowledge these concessions in a threatening speech on 20 February. In these weeks the Germans were simultaneously telling everyone except the British that both Eden and Lord Halifax had agreed to whatever Germany wanted to do with Austria, while they complained to the British about just the opposite, namely, that London was stiffening Vienna's resistance to Germany and encouraging von Schuschnigg to go back on his agreement with Hitler.[141] This form of duplicity was, of course, quickly registered in London; it hardly augured well for the forthcoming negotiations.

As the Germans considered the possibility of negotiations with Britain, how did they assess the prospects? In particular, how did the question of colonies and the idea of paying a price for them look to Berlin? On the colonial issue, the winter of 1937–38 saw the continued public demands for colonial restitution accompanied by examination of the issue within the German government. It was in the context of dealing with the two powers most favorable toward Germany among those who had acquired portions of her former colonial empire—the Union of South Africa and Japan—that the issue took a concrete as opposed to a theoretical form.

The Union of South Africa held the mandate for former German Southwest Africa; her government under Prime Minister James B. M. Hertzog was most kindly disposed toward Germany but simultaneously determined to hold on to Southwest Africa. There were apparently soundings about a possible South African purchase of German claims to the former German colony; nothing came of this as Berlin insisted that Germany would not give up her position calling for the return of her African empire.[142] As for the Japanese, they approached the Germans in December 1937 and January 1938 with schemes for a public Japanese acknowledgment of the right of Germany to her former colonies accompanied by an agreement on Germany's part to sell her former Pacific islands mandated to Japan to the latter power. Although the Germans were in principle prepared to agree to such an arrangement, Berlin feared that its whole colonial case would be weakened if any such agreement were made public and, therefore, allowed the subject to drop.

140. *TMWC*, 28:362. Müller (p. 269, n.71) doubts the connection.
141. R 1372/137/3, FO 371/22311; C 1237, C 1324/42/18, FO 371/21656; *Hungarian Documents*, 1, No. 397.
142. *G.D.*, D, 1, Nos. 15, 77, 79; 7:518–21; Weinberg, "Südseemandat," p. 392, n.8.

The Japanese tried to keep the negotiations going; in fact they were more interested than the Germans. The explanation for this curious reversal of roles, with Tokyo trying to lure back to Eastern Asia a Germany that, as Hitler proclaimed on 20 February had "no territorial interests whatever in East Asia," lies in the Japanese interest in the former German colonial empire in the Pacific that had come under Australian, New Zealand, and British mandate. Thinking that in any reopening of the colonial question Germany might recover these areas, Japan hoped to pave the way for acquiring them from Germany as well. In 1938 Berlin had no interest in such prospects; what colonial ambitions there were had a focus on Africa, not New Guinea, the Solomons, or Nauru. The relationship between Germany's "right" to the return of those territories and Japan's plans for expansion in the Pacific was left open until the negotiations for the Tripartite Pact of 1940.[143]

If the German government in the winter of 1937–38 looked to the recovery of a colonial empire in Africa, was there any willingness to consider making concessions for their return in the framework of some sort of general settlement? Although some technical preparations that looked to a continuation of the Halifax conversations were made in the German foreign ministry,[144] the general impression given by the German government at the end of 1937 was that there was no interest in a comprehensive settlement.[145]

In view of the postwar emphasis on disagreements with Hitler by many of the professional diplomats, it should be noted that for this critical juncture, such disagreement is restricted to imaginative memoirs and apologias. At the time, the views of Hitler's key diplomatic advisers were extraordinarily similar to his. Ernst von Weizsäcker wrote von Papen that he doubted there would be a settlement because Germany would not allow any restriction on her freedom of action in Central Europe, the price Britain and France would require for colonial concessions. In terms similar to those Hitler had used with Lord Halifax, von Weizsäcker explained that Germany would take what she wanted peacefully or by force.[146] He was at least willing to have the question of arms limitations explored; but Foreign Minister von Neurath would have none of that.[147] When Henderson saw von Neurath before going to London for consultations about the planned British offer, von Neurath was emphatic that there would be no

143. The whole subject is covered in Weinberg, "Südseemandat." Hildebrand found no space in his volume on Hitler's colonial policy for the only serious colonial discussions in which the German government engaged before World War II; there is merely an indirect reference (p. 533). See also *Australian Documents*, Nos. 3, 16, 37; German naval documents Case 3/2, PG 48901, ff.138–45, in Bundesarchiv/Militärarchiv.

144. *G.D.*, D, 1, Nos. 86, 100, 102.

145. Ibid., No. 87; C 8830/3/18, FO 371/22712; C 8719/270/18, FO 371/20737.

146. *G.D.*, D, 1, No. 96.

147. Ibid., Nos. 103, 105.

German contribution of any sort.[148] Hans Georg von Mackensen, von Neurath's son-in-law, who would soon be replaced as state secretary by von Weizsäcker, evidently held views essentially similar to those of both other men.[149] It is difficult to understand how, in the face of such unanimity, Henderson could write to Lord Halifax on 27 February: "Will Germany co-operate? Since you left here last November I have spoken to many Germans on the subject of co-operation. All appear to agree that she must, from Goering downwards, but I do not yet know the views of the only one who matters, namely Hitler."[150] Having asked for an appointment to see Hitler, Henderson would find out on 3 March.[151]

On 3 March 1938 Sir Nevile Henderson had his opportunity to present the British plan to Hitler in the presence of the newly appointed foreign minister, Joachim von Ribbentrop.[152] The British had given a brief prior notice to France and to the United States;[153] a fuller preview had been provided to the British cabinet.[154] An effort was also begun to try to restrain the British press and radio from excessive criticism, especially of Hitler personally, so that the latter could be informed of this by Henderson as a sign of British responsiveness on a subject that Hitler had often complained about.[155]

The accounts of the conversation between Hitler and the English ambassador show very clearly that there was an unbridgeable gulf and not the slightest prospect of agreement.[156] Hitler rejected the whole concept of a new regime for Central Africa. He would move forward in Central

148. Ibid., No. 108. Cf. Tauschitz report of 27 January 1938, *Guido Schmidt Trial*, pp. 507–8.

149. See his brief for von Ribbentrop's first meeting with François-Poncet, in *G.D.*, D, 1, No. 115; cf. ibid., No. 308. If von Mackensen ever had any original views when minister to Hungary, state secretary, or ambassador to Italy, they have escaped both contemporary observers and historical researchers.

150. Henderson Papers, FO 800/269, f.36.

151. *G.D.*, D, 1, No. 310. When Henderson saw von Ribbentrop on 1 March to set a date for the meeting on the colonial offer and to ask for a German contribution, the latter replied that there would be none (ibid., No. 131).

152. The notes Henderson prepared for himself to use at this meeting are in his papers, FO 800/270, ff.303–4.

153. *U.S.*, 1938, 1:31–32.

154. Br. Cabinet 10 (38) of 2 March 1938, C 1616/42/18, FO 371/21656.

155. C 1431/1261/18, FO 371/21709; circular to Dominion prime ministers, 10 March 1938, P 1259/4/150, FO 395/561; *G.D.*, D, 1, No. 148; *Australian Documents*, Nos. 133, 135.

156. See *G.D.*, D, 1, Nos. 135–39, 141, 142, 144; interrogation of von Dirksen, 8–13 December 1945, National Archives, State Department Special Interrogation Mission (Poole); Dirksen, pp. 207–10; C 1474, C 1475, C 1495, C 1502, C 1657/42/18, FO 371/21656; Henderson, pp. 113–18 (note that this portion of Henderson's memoirs was cut at the request of the Foreign Office, Cadogan to Henderson, 4 June 1940, Henderson Papers, FO 800/270, ff.323–24); *Harvey Diary*, pp. 108–9, 110–11; Massimo Magistrati, *L'Italia a Berlino (1937–1939)* (Verona: Mondadori, 1956), pp. 136–37; Wilson tel. 99 of 9 March 1938, State 741.62/242; Henke, pp. 130–34. For information given to the French, see *D.D.F.*, 2d, 8, Nos. 310, 407.

Hitler may conceivably have been influenced in his attitude by knowledge of a letter written by Lord Londonderry, once an advocate of good Anglo-German relations, who now recognized that there were no limits to German ambition (*G.D.*, D, 1, No. 104).

and Eastern Europe as he saw fit and at the risk of war; and he would continue to ask for the return of Germany's colonies, hoping—or threatening—that the day would come some years hence when they would be returned without any concessions on Germany's part.[157] He not only dismissed the British offer but reiterated earlier complaints about England's opposition to German aims in Vienna and Prague. He was urged on by a variety of nasty and misleading comments from von Ribbentrop, and only on Henderson's repeated insistence promised to give a written reply—which he never sent. As Henderson concluded:

> Hitler's whole attitude clearly shows how unpromising is the policy of those who think he may be deflected from his aims in Central Europe by French and British expressions of disapproval. If offer of British friendship and prospect of a colonial settlement are not sufficient to deter him or to secure even a temporary halt, how much less effective is likely to be an ambiguous warning which is not backed by a show of force.[158]

Since von Ribbentrop was coming to London to make his official farewell, there was an opportunity to show him how disappointed the British government was over the German rejection of the proposal, but this in no way altered the situation.[159] On the contrary, von Ribbentrop took the sincerity of British interest in a settlement as proof that it was safe for Germany to move rapidly against Austria and urged Hitler on to the annexation of Austria and, in effect, a rupture of negotiations with England.[160]

In the British cabinet on 9 March the failure of the attempt to initiate serious negotiations for a general settlement was reported. While no one wanted to give the impression that it was "now or never," the import of the meeting was essentially to that effect. Lord Halifax recalled that "conditions were now comparatively favorable and might not return"; Chamberlain said that this was not the last opportunity, "but that it was a more favorable opportunity than might occur again." The danger of war was ever greater, and Germany would have to be warned that "if once war should start in Central Europe it was impossible to say where it might not end or who might not become involved."[161] Lord Halifax informed the American government "that one of the twin efforts which His

---

157. Hitler had told Polish Foreign Minister Josef Beck on 14 January that he would certainly pursue the colonial question. "If the English were not yet ready to carry out a far-sighted policy, they would perhaps be forced into it in a little while" (*G.D.*, D, 5, No. 29; cf. *Lipski Papers*, No. 77).

158. Henderson tel. 71, 4 March 1938, C 1475/42/18, FO 371/21656, ff.328–33.

159. C 1524/42/18, FO 371/21656, ff.342–54; *Cadogan Diary*, pp. 58–59; *G.D.*, D, 1, Nos. 145, 147.

160. *G.D.*, D, 1, Nos. 146, 150, 151.

161. Br. Cabinet 11 (38), C 1766/42/18, FO 371/21656, ff.497–504. Note that this was the formulation used subsequently to warn Germany of the possibility of a war between England and Germany.

Majesty's Government were anxious to make to prepare the way for an appeasement, and on account of which we asked the President to postpone his initiative, has failed."[162] Henderson would not have an opportunity to refer back to his fateful conversation of 3 March in a meeting with Hitler until the eve of war—29 August 1939.[163]

The uproar over the annexation of Austria a week after the Hitler-Henderson meeting of 3 March assured that the negotiations would not be resumed for a long time; and in the event, they never were.[164] As Henderson wrote Lord Halifax on 16 March, "all the work of the past 11 months has crashed to the ground!"[165] Lord Halifax responded on the nineteenth that "our constructive efforts have suffered a pretty severe setback."[166] But it was more than a setback. When urged by Viscount Astor to renew negotiations in June 1938, Lord Halifax could only reply that "the Germans never seem to be able to grasp the dire effect of their action on public opinion here. The Anschluss, or rather the methods, by which it was brought about, shocked this country profoundly.... Such methods will always have such an effect here and will always be likely to block attempts to bring the two countries together."[167]

In February 1938 Hitler had a conversation with the German military attaché in Yugoslavia, Moriz von Faber du Faur. He told the latter: "In the immediate future I shall initiate an operation against Austria. It will go smoothly; I have come to agreement with [Yugoslav Prime Minister] Stojadinović. He prefers the *Anschluss* to the Habsburgs. Mussolini will put on a good face to a bad situation; he does not have much choice since he alienated England and France in his Abyssinian venture. It will be more difficult when I start on Czechoslovakia; but because Stojadinović has only a smile left for the Little Entente, that too will work. Only when I attack Poland will everyone jump on me." Asked why not then avoid an attack on Poland and let time work for Germany, Hitler responded that he could not afford to do that.[168] In none of this was there any room for an

162. *U.S.*, 1938, 1:132. Roosevelt, who had been doubtful about the whole scheme (*D.D.F.*, 2d, 8, No. 380), showed himself very accurately informed when reviewing it on 21 March (ibid., 9, No. 58, p. 113).

163. *B.D.*, 3d, 7, p. 387.

164. *G.D.*, D, 1, Nos. 381, 386, 400; C 2776/42/18, FO 371/21657; R 2659/137/3, FO 371/22316. A German foreign ministry circular of 31 March 1938 reaffirmed German opposition to a comprehensive settlement.

165. Henderson Papers, FO 800/269, f.50.

166. Ibid., f.56. One of the most prominent of the advocates of concessions to Germany, Lord Lothian, wrote to Lord Allen of Huntwood on 8 March 1938: "We have now got so much nearer to a position of collective justice for Germany that the problem of preventing Germany going beyond what is legitimate may soon become urgent" (Lord Lothian Papers, GD 40/17/352/28).

167. Halifax to Viscount Waldorf Astor, 23 June 1938, Halifax Papers, FO 800/309.

168. Moriz von Faber du Faur, *Macht und Ohnmacht: Erinnerungen eines alten Offiziers* (Stuttgart: Hans E. Günther, 1953), pp. 204–5. Note the astonishingly similar prediction of Chautemps on 21 February 1938, in *U.S.*, 1938, 1:27.

accommodation with the Western Powers on terms they could be expected to accept. Hitler would continue on his course, risking war where and when it seemed appropriate, and taking British and French expressions of interest in a rapprochement as signs of weakness to be exploited rather than as opportunities for a peaceful settlement.

If in the short run the effort of the British, supported by the French, was thus in a way counterproductive, in that it encouraged Hitler to think he could move forward without English opposition even if also without English approval, there was a long-range aspect to these abortive negotiations that ought not to be disregarded. Those who had spent many hours on these fruitless endeavors were hardly unaffected by having made them. Those who in 1939 made the decision to challenge Germany in war, a decision which would cost Britain its empire and them the world they knew and loved—something they sensed or knew as they made the decision—were the very same men who had tried so long and so patiently to devise ways to avoid it. When they faced that decision, they felt they had done their best and now had no choice, something no one else mustered up the courage to do in the face of Hitler either before or after them.

5   Germany and the Civil War in Spain 1937–39

The military uprising in Spain in July 1936 had not led to a quick change of the regime. Instead, the mixed success and failure of the plotters had forced them to ask for and depend on assistance from Italy and Germany to launch an effective military campaign against the government of the Spanish Republic. In a series of decisions in the summer of 1936 Hitler chose to aid the Spanish rebels, led by General Francisco Franco. The Germans had provided planes to airlift Franco's army from Morocco to the Iberian peninsula; had dispatched German armored, air force, and anti-aircraft units to Spain; were providing a steady stream of military supplies to the rebels; and publicly extended diplomatic recognition to the insurgents, thus fastening their own prestige to the eventual triumph of Franco's forces.[1]

The purposes that Hitler hoped to achieve by this support of Franco were several. The prospect of weakening the position of France by assuring that Spain was friendly rather than hostile to Germany was a welcome one to Hitler, who expected French interference with his plans for conquering living space in the East.[2] The cooperation with Italy in Spain would assure a continued alignment of Germany and Italy; any return of Italy to friendship with Britain and France after the rupture of that friendship in the Abyssinian crisis was made impossible by the joint intervention in Spain and the resulting friction with the Western Powers. Every effort made, especially from

1. Weinberg, *Foreign Policy*, pp. 284–95.
2. This point is especially stressed in the study of Hans-Henning Abendroth, *Hitler in der spanischen Arena* (Paderborn: Schöningh, 1973), esp. pp. 35–36, 319.

London, to heal the breach with Italy and thus possibly isolate Germany again was thwarted by Italy's involvement in the Spanish Civil War. A further possible advantage for the Germans was in the field of her armaments. Spain provided important raw materials, especially copper from the southern and iron from the northern part of the country. If these could be diverted from Britain—Spain's traditional customer for these ores—to Germany in exchange for aid in the civil war, both the raw materials and the foreign exchange situation of Germany would be helped.[3]

Finally, Germany's unhindered pursuit of her own ambitions in Central and Eastern Europe could only be assisted by the focus on Spain of governmental anxiety and public attention in the Western Powers. As the civil war developed into a massive conflict engaging worldwide sympathy for one side or the other, this could be the most valuable factor of all from the vantage point of Berlin, though this as well as the trying out of German weapons in a long war were the results of the unanticipated duration of a conflict that Hitler, like Franco and Mussolini, thought likely to end in a few weeks at most.

As the forces of Franco were stalled in the outskirts of Madrid in the last weeks of 1936, the issue facing the Germans and Italians was whether to add to their earlier assistance such substantial forces, including divisions of soldiers, as to enable him to win out quickly over the defenders of the Republic, now augmented by the International Brigades. Early in December Mussolini decided that Italy would respond to Franco's need by sending large land forces to Spain.[4] Hitler, however, did not follow this course. It is possible that he had already decided on his policy by the time he met von Blomberg on 3 December 1936, but the evidence on this meeting is indirect and inconclusive. Certainly at the conference in the Berlin chancellery on 21 December Hitler announced the lines to which he would adhere in the more than two years that the war continued in Spain. Against the recommendation of the German ambassador in Spain, General Wilhelm Faupel but in agreement with all his other military and diplomatic advisers, Hitler decided to send no divisional units of ground forces to Spain. Not only were the risks too great, not only would such action interfere excessively with Germany's own rearmament program, but massive aid was not in accord with Hitler's main objective, which was to focus European attention on Spain for a long time. A prolonged war, not a quick victory by Franco, was what German interests—as Hitler

---

3. Because so many other products that Spain traditionally exported, such as olive oil and oranges, were similar to those Italy produced, there was little danger that Germany would be outstripped by Italy in competition in the peninsula.

4. John F. Coverdale, *Italian Intervention in the Spanish Civil War* (Princeton, N.J.: Princeton University Press, 1975), pp. 156ff.

defined them—called for. This could best be accomplished by sending assistance not in a flood but in driblets.[5]

Almost a year after the meeting of 21 December, Hitler reiterated essentially the same view at the famous meeting of 5 November 1937, recorded in the Hossbach Memorandum. "According to the experience up to now in the course of military operations in Spain, the Führer did not expect their conclusion soon. If one takes into account the length of time Franco has used in his offensives up to now, the war could possibly last about another three years. On the other hand, from Germany's point of view a 100% [meaning immediate] victory of Franco is really not desirable; we are more interested in a continuation of the war and the maintenance of tensions in the Mediterranean."[6]

The comment on Franco's military procedure of slow offensives must be read as partly ironic; both the Germans and the Italians were periodically exasperated by the measured pace of the military operations of the Nationalist armies.[7] There is no reason to examine here the reasons which led Franco to adhere to this approach from the beginning to the end of the long and bitter conflict in Spain; the aspects of this procedure which are relevant to an understanding of German policy after the summer and fall of 1936 are that, first, it was seen as in accord with German interest in a drawn out rather than a rapidly concluded war and, second, that it was *not* in accord with Italy's hopes for a quick victory by Franco. The various recommendations by Faupel in December 1936 and the spring of 1937 must be seen as reflecting his personal belief that a quick victory by Franco was to be desired; this was why he so often urged on his government advice similar to or identical with that of Italy's representative in Spain; this was why he believed in interference in the internal affairs of Franco Spain for what he saw as the requirements of speedy victory; and this discrepancy between his approach and that of Berlin would be the basic cause of Faupel's recall in August 1937.[8]

5. Weinberg, *Foreign Policy*, pp. 297–99. The statement of Faber du Faur (pp. 160, 162), then German military attaché in Belgrade, that in the winter of 1937–38 von Fritsch told him that he wanted no German troops in Spain but suggested recruitment among White Russian émigrés in Yugoslavia probably belongs in this context. The émigrés in Yugoslavia had to wait until World War II to be recruited into the *Russische Schutzkorps Serbien*. Coverdale, p. 164, argues that the evidence on Hitler's policy should be read differently but merely concludes that "Hitler did not do everything he might have to shorten the war, but that is a far cry from deliberately prolonging it." Merkes, pp. 201–8, dates Hitler's meeting in the chancellery to 22 December 1936.

6. *G.D.*, D, 1:31.

7. Cf. Coverdale, pp. 172–73.

8. The comment by Menfred Merkes, *Die deutsche Politik im spanischen Bürgerkrieg 1936–1939*, 2d ed. (Bonn: Röhrscheid, 1969), p. 102, that the proposals of the German commanders in Spain with the object of bringing speedy victory to Franco "dissolve" the argument that Germany wanted a long war is similarly based on a confusion between the tactical proposals of men on the spot—who had no interest in seeing their soldiers killed in a drawn-out combat—and the broader policy objectives of Hitler.

The decision of Mussolini to send large contingents of Italian land forces to Spain placed Italy in the forefront of international concern.[9] The fact that major troop shipments took place immediately after the Anglo-Italian agreement of 2 January 1937, thereby violating it the day after it was signed, symbolizes the advantage for Germany in the continued estrangement of Italy from the Western Powers assured by a drawn out conflict in Spain.[10] The almost simultaneous war scare in France about alleged German troop concentrations in Spanish Morocco grew out of the suspicion and expectation in France that the two Axis powers were following identical policies in Spain. Since Italy was known to be sending army contingents in early January, it was thought likely that Germany was doing the same thing.

The uproar died down quickly—once it became obvious that Germany was in fact not dispatching land forces—but as an outgrowth of fears of German intentions in a tense international situation, the war scare over Spanish Morocco of January 1937 was the first of a series in which the May crisis of 1938 and the January crisis of 1939 must be grouped. If the German government invariably reacted with outraged protestations of innocence against the allegations made in those war scares, and used them as evidence of the unscrupulous warmongering of the press in other countries, it must be recalled that the atmosphere of sudden coups, lightning moves, and unheralded treaty violations had been created and was maintained by German policies. In November 1937 Hitler complained to Lord Halifax about the wild rumors in the press; why, they went so far as to have German troops suddenly appearing in Vienna or Prague . . .[11]

The real assistance of Germany to Franco, in accordance with Hitler's basic policy, was designed to assist the Nationalists in waging war, to keep them from losing to the Loyalists, but not to give them such great superiority as might produce a speedy victory. In practice, this meant an essentially even level of support, maintained at about the volume reached at the end of 1936. The Condor Legion, the German air force organization in Spain, was kept at approximately the same size from its arrival in the fall of 1936 until Franco's final victory in the spring of 1939.[12] In addition, Germany provided specialists, training officers, and military equipment.

A useful index of the volume of German assistance is provided by the German record of the costs involved. The secret accounting for internal purposes shows a rather steep rise in total outlay early in 1937, primarily

9. When Italian Ambassador Bernardo Attolico urged the dispatch of German troops to Spain on von Neurath on 13 January 1937, the latter again declined (G.D., D, 3, No. 200).

10. See Eden, pp. 484–87; Coverdale, pp. 200–202; D.D.F., 2d, 4, No. 242; Ciano, Diplomatic Papers, pp. 77–78, 78–80.

11. On the Morocco war scare of January 1937, see G.D., D, 3, Nos. 192, 195; D.D.F., 2d, 4, Nos. 248, 261, 265, 273, 274, 276–78, 282, 288; 5, No. 37; Merkes, pp. 209–13; Abendroth, pp. 145–49; Jodl Diary, 12 January 1937, TMWC, 28:348.

12. A good history of the Condor Legion remains to be written. There is a considerable amount of material in Merkes, but his interpretation of that evidence is often unconvincing.

because of substantial deliveries of equipment to Franco, but otherwise presents an almost straight line graph from the fall of 1936 to the end of May 1939.[13] Even if such a financial record necessarily obscures variations in the types of deliveries and has a built-in tendency toward stability because of the practically constant personnel costs of the Condor Legion, it nevertheless does provide a useful general indication of the trends in total German support of Franco.[14] The one major spurt in German aid, that of the spring of 1937, is faithfully reflected in the accounts. The Nationalists needed large shipments of German supplies, and Franco appealed directly to Hitler. In accord with his general policy, Hitler decided at the end of March to accede to Franco's wishes to a considerable extent, but not enough to assure a big victory.[15] Thereafter, the accounts reflect with equal faithfulness continued assistance without substantial variations for the next two years.

The support provided Franco was to provide Germany tangible returns beyond the political and diplomatic ones of drawing public attention away from German plans and actions. One of the factors in the German decision to intervene in Spain and a continuing element in her support of the Nationalists was the possibility of drawing on Spain's mineral riches for raw materials needed by Germany's rearmament program, and doing so without expending precious foreign exchange. The copper, iron, and pyrites of Spain might be diverted to German use either through some close economic association if Franco won quickly, or in repayment for German support if victory was delayed.

From the first days of German intervention, the machinery for supplying Franco and the mechanism for drawing on the Spanish economy for Germany's armaments program were in the same hands, both subordinated to the same German agency. Johannes Bernhardt[16] operated Hisma (Compañía Hispano-Marroquí de Transportes) in Spain and Rowak (Rohstoffe- und Waren-Einkaufsgesellschaft) in Germany for getting supplies to Franco and making purchases in Spain; all under the

13. Sonderstab W[ilberg], "Nr. 6789/39 IVa g. Kdos., Betr.: Übung Rügen," 12 June 1939, Bundesarchiv, Reichsfinanzministerium, R 2/23, f.214. This is the latest—and hence the most complete—of a series of periodic reports showing in graph form the total German expenditures, expenditures on deliveries to Franco, expenditures on the German forces in Spain, Spanish repayment, and the proportion of the latter in foreign exchange. Merkes, pp. 399–400, summarizes the financial statistics.

14. The figure of Merkes, p. 76, showing a total of about 18,000 German military men in Spain during the civil war with about one-third that number present at any given time is probably correct.

15. On this, see *G.D.*, D, 3, Nos. 204, 214–16, 222; Jodl Diary, 14 January, 27 March, 30 March 1937, *TMWC*, 28:349, 352–53; Merkes, pp. 219–21. It should be noted that German policy in the Non-Intervention Committee toward controls or shipments to Spain was keyed to the timing of these shipments (*G.D.*, D, 3, No. 212).

16. A study of Bernhardt's career would be most useful. He was important during World War II as well.

authority of Göring as plenepotentiary for the Four-Year Plan. Simultaneously, a World War associate of Göring, Josef Veltjens, was operating a
semiofficial gun-running business, shipping rifles and ammunition to Spain
for much-needed foreign exchange that the German government's Four-
Year Plan could use to purchase raw materials in other markets.[17]

This concentration of economic, military, and by implication diplomatic
power in organizations and agencies combined under direct government
control was a peculiar feature of German-Spanish relations. Marion
Einhorn, the East German historian of the economic aspects of German
intervention, was so blinded by catch-phrases about monopoly capitalism
that the extraordinarily close analogy to the Soviet foreign trade
monopoly conveniently eluded her.[18] Both from the side of German private economic interests and from the side of Spanish Nationalist government and private interests, efforts were made to break into the German
state monopoly of trade between Germany and Spain. All these attempts
were warded off, though a minor amount of trade on private accounts was
authorized by the state agencies.

The Spaniards wanted to use their foreign exchange to purchase
weapons and raw materials where available from countries other than
Germany. Furthermore, there are indications that they preferred to deal
with private German firms in order to play them off against Bernhardt,
and in any case to weaken the latter's exceedingly strong position in
demanding compliance with German economic requirements. This, of
course, was the very reason why the German government decided to
maintain the existing arrangement. Against the arguments of the
Spaniards and those German firms interested in entering or returning to
the field of German-Spanish trade, the arguments in favor of maintaining
the Hisma-Rowak monopoly were overwhelming. As an official of the
trade policy section of the German foreign ministry summarized them:

A. The undoubted success of Rowak/Hisma which has succeeded
because of its good relations with Franco in having Germany preferred

17. Although the Veltjens business is—because of its very nature—not wholly clear, those
accounts which show up in the ministry of finance files provide considerable insight into the
operation. In August 1937 the records refer to 30,000 rifles and 20 million rounds of infantry
ammunition (Bundesarchiv, R 2/20, ff.73, 100); in January 1939 there is reference to a further
shipment of rifles and ammunition (R 2/23, f.35); in February 1941 there is a reference to the
return of 50,000 carbine rifles (R 2/26, f.9); and a retrospective discussion of the financing of
the Veltjens operation of October 1941 refers to a total delivery of 87 million rounds of
infantry ammunition (R 2/26, ff.222–23). The finance ministry records also show that the
Veltjens deliveries were paid for in foreign exchange, with the last payment made in December 1939 (R 2/26, ff.148–50, 223). See also *G.D.*, D, 3, No. 213; Jodl Diary, 27 March 1937,
TMWC, 28:252–53. Merkes, pp. 49, 220, discusses Veltjens as a purely private arms merchant, an utterly ridiculous description. On Veltjens, see Weinberg, *Foreign Policy*, pp.
286–87, 288, n.106. His role in supplying defective weapons to the Loyalists is confirmed by
Abendroth, p. 181.

18. Marion Einhorn, *Die ökonomischen Hintergründe der faschistischen deutschen Intervention in Spanien 1936–1939* (Berlin-East: Akademie-Verlag, 1962), see esp. p. 140.

over all other countries in [Spain's] trade and in securing for Germany
the bulk of the raw materials available in Spain.

B. In order to assure the delivery of Spanish raw materials to Germany, steady pressure must be exerted on the Franco government,
which would prefer to sell these raw materials to other countries for
foreign exchange. Rowak/Hisma has the needed means of pressure because of the special [arms] deliveries which it can provide to the Franco
government.

C. Because of the special German deliveries to Spain, Germany has
acquired such a large credit balance that its repayment by Spanish
deliveries or by German [purchases of] shares in Spanish concerns will
be possible only over a long period of time. From this perspective there
is no great interest in having this credit balance further increased by any
additional other German exports.[19]

Under these circumstances, Göring secured the agreement of the foreign
ministry and even of Schacht to the full support of Bernhardt's system.[20]

Just as the monopoly of Hisma/Rowak was confirmed in Berlin, the
German embassy in Salamanca was instructed to urge Franco to agree to
the continuation of the existing system and to reverse the efforts of a
Spanish economic delegation that was demanding a clearing system in
which others could participate.[21] Franco agreed to the German request on
20 May 1937 and thus paved the way for a series of new German-Spanish
economic and trade agreements in the summer of 1937.[22]

Two aspects of the economic relationship were of primary significance
to Germany. In the first place, there was the actual current supply of raw
materials and food from Spain. In this regard, the Germans could feel very
satisfied with their accomplishments. Hisma was extremely successful in
acquiring raw materials from Franco Spain, even including those from the
Italian-occupied island of Majorca in the Balearics.[23] Very extensive
quantities of ores were shipped to Germany in 1937, and this pattern
largely continued.[24] In the first stages of the revolt in Spain, the area
containing the Rio Tinto copper mines had come under the control of
Franco, and the available ores from there had been confiscated for the
Germans with subsequent production also sent mainly to Germany. Since
the mines were British owned and the copper had previously been
supplied to England, this raised difficulties with London. These difficulties would continue for years and constituted one facet of the German

    19. *G.D.*, D, 3, No. 223; cf. Einhorn, p. 137.
    20. *G.D.*, D, 3, Nos. 213, 223, 231, 256; Merkes, pp. 233–37; Abendroth, pp. 128–34. See
also Wolfgang Schieder, "Spanischer Bürgerkrieg und Vierjahresplan," in Wolfgang
Schieder (ed.), *Der spanische Bürgerkrieg* (Munich: Nymphenburg, 1976), pp. 162–90.
    21. *G.D.*, D, 3, No. 256.
    22. Ibid., No. 263. On the economic agreements, see Merkes, pp. 234–40; Abendroth, pp.
135–36.
    23. See Merkes, p. 233, n.530.
    24. See *G.D.*, D, 3, No. 507.

concern over the competition with England in Spain that will be taken up subsequently.[25] The twin issues of raw materials for Germany and competition with Britain were present also in the area to which Spanish Nationalist military operations turned in the spring and summer of 1937.

The initial stalemate near Madrid in November 1936 had been followed by a succession of local Nationalist offensives in the vicinity of Madrid, each of which had been halted by the Loyalists after small advances.[26] The last of these offensives, one launched on Madrid from the north, came to be called the Battle of Guadalajara after the provincial capital north of which the attacking Italian units were defeated and pushed back a part of the distance to their starting position. Coming right after the prominent Italian role in the Nationalist victory at Málaga, this spectacular setback attracted international attention.[27]

If the army of the Spanish Republic was the victor of Guadalajara, Germany was the beneficiary. In the first place, Italian prestige in Spain dropped hopelessly below Germany's. In the second place, Mussolini now felt that Italy's very status as a world power and his own status as its leader were so deeply involved in the Spanish Civil War that there could be absolutely no turning back from that deeper and continued involvement in it which guaranteed the persistence of friction with England and France. If Germany's breach of Locarno had riveted Britain and France to each other, Italy's inability to extricate herself from Spain assured the maintenance of the Rome-Berlin Axis. In the third place, having so spectacularly failed to take Madrid either by frontal assault or by flanking attacks, Franco was obliged to shift his offensive capabilities from that section of the front to another, and this meant the northern section of Loyalist Spain, the Basque area around Bilbao.[28] This, in turn, was of great interest to the Germans because the area to be conquered contained the other major Spanish mineral resource Germany wanted: the rich iron mines that had hitherto supplied ores to United Kingdom smelters.[29]

If the offensive to conquer the northern portion of Republican Spain took longer than anticipated—a characteristic feature of the war—this was in no way due to the absence of German aid. On the contrary, it was in support of this Nationalist offensive that the Condor Legion perfected the technique of destroying towns from the air, first applied by them to Durango and Guernica for subsequent application to Warsaw, Rotterdam,

25. On the Rio Tinto ores, see ibid., Nos. 208, 218, 245, 381, 401; Einhorn, pp. 117–18, 145, 147, 198.

26. Brief accounts of these battles may be found in Hugh Thomas, *The Spanish Civil War* (New York: Harper & Row, 1977), secs. 28 and 34.

27. *G.D.*, D, 3, Nos. 220, 227, 229, 230, 236–38, 240, 246; "Informationsbericht Nr. 75," 24 March 1937, Bundesarchiv, Brammer, Z.Sg. 101/30, ff.285–95; *D.D.F.*, 2d, 5, No. 224; *Hungarian Documents*, 1, No. 254. For the Málaga campaign, see Coverdale, pp. 206–12; on the Guadalajara offensive, see ibid., pp. 212–60.

28. See Coverdale, pp. 277–84.

29. Abendroth, p. 237.

Coventry, and Belgrade—with an eventual return to the cities of Germany herself.[30]

The fall of Bilbao did not come until 19 June 1937; and the capture of the remaining portions of the Republic in the north, Santander and Asturias with its coal mines, was delayed until October by local resistance and a Republican offensive near Madrid. The Germans, however, had staked a claim to the Basque iron ores immediately, at least for a while diverting all the available ore to Germany.[31] The coal mines were of little interest to Germany, which itself exported coal to Spain, but the Basque iron mines added greatly to Germany's economic strength. Although iron ore could be shipped to Germany from Bilbao only during the last quarter of 1937, the volume was even then higher than the total annual German iron ore imports from all of Spain in the prewar period.[32] The Spanish campaign in the north, therefore, was of great benefit to the Germans and easily offset the troublesome affairs of the Non-Intervention Committee. The *Deutschland* and *Leipzig* incidents of May and June 1937 might attract great attention and arouse Hitler to frenzied denunciation of the Loyalists, but for Germany's long-term aims the vastly increased economic resources of Franco Spain were more important even if less spectacular.[33]

If substantial ore deliveries from Spain constituted one major concern of the German government, the other was the difficulties anticipated by Berlin in competing against Great Britain for future advantage in the Spanish economy. It was not only that Germany was taking copper and iron ores that had in large part previously gone to England and often originated in English-owned mines. As important, perhaps more important, was German recognition of her own lack of capital and England's ability to provide capital for the reconstruction that would be needed in Spain once the civil war was over. Hitler had told Faupel as early as November 1936 that Germany should use her present aid to Franco to establish firm trade relations; this would prevent England from subsequently using her strength in capital to take Germany's place.[34] A key element in all German economic negotiations with the Spaniards, therefore, became a determined effort so to anchor German economic interests in Spain as to preclude a subsequent return of Spain to that close economic relationship with Britain which had long characterized both Spanish mining and trade.

30. Of interest on the bombing offensive is the report by Martin Wronsky of Lufthansa, the German government-owned airline, cited by Einhorn, p. 131. See also *G.D.*, D, 3, Nos. 241, 247, 249, 251, 253, 258, 265; Merkes, pp. 397–98; Abendroth, pp. 158–60; Thomas, pp. 986–88; Klaus A. Maier, *Guernica, 26.4.1937* (Freiburg/Br.: Rombach, 1975).

31. See *G.D.*, D, 3, Nos. 390, 391.

32. Deutsche Revisions- und Treuhandaktiengesellschaft, "Bericht nebst Anlage über die bei der Rowak Handelsgesellschaft m.b.H., Berlin, vorgenommenen Prüfung des Jahresabschlusses zum 31. Dezember 1937," pp. 3, 5 (Bundesarchiv, Reichsfinanzministerium, R 2/27, ff.41, 43). See also Abendroth, p. 240.

33. On the *Deutschland* and *Leipzig* incidents, see pp. 99–101 above.

34. *G.D.*, D, 3, No. 132.

While the Germans wanted to take advantage of Franco's desperate need for military supplies to establish a permanent hold on the Spanish economy, the Spanish leader had every interest in resisting such a development. Both because of the importance of the British market and of British investors to the Spanish economy, and because he wanted to maintain the independence of Spain, Franco preferred to play Britain and Germany off against each other rather than allow the Spanish economy to come under German control. Through various channels, Franco assured the British and French governments that he had no intention of allowing Spain's independence or territorial integrity to be infringed by Germany or Italy.[35] He further encouraged the maintenance of some trade with both Western Powers, but especially with England. To the alarm of the Germans, there were frequent rumors of Spanish-English negotiations, especially about economic subjects; and the Germans immediately suspected that economic issues were behind the British de facto recognition of Franco in November 1937, which was accompanied by an exchange of diplomatic agents between the London and Nationalist governments.[36]

In the face of a possibility of Britain's return to a key role in the Spanish economy, the Germans were determined to use the economic leverage they had acquired and were continuing to acquire because of their aid to Franco's war effort. The strength of the German position was derived from two categories of aid. The value of the war materials supplied to Franco was credited to Hisma, which used the balances it was building up in Spain to pay for the ores and other materials Germany imported. Because the volume of deliveries to Spain exceeded those to Germany, Hisma had enormous excess funds which might be used to purchase shares of Spanish mining and other firms, so that in effect Germany would compete with Britain's export of capital by exporting war materials and using the Spanish payments for this aid to invest in the Spanish economy. This would become the major focus of German-Spanish friction.

The other significant category of aid to Spain was the services of the Condor Legion. The equipment, minus materials returned to Germany, was charged to Franco and included in the German official claims for repayment by Nationalist Spain; but the personnel costs were treated differently. The pay of the usually slightly over five thousand members of the Legion, together with the danger supplement added to it, was so high that the Germans thought it best not even to tell the Spaniards about it—as they would have had to if they had wanted to claim its inclusion in the accounts.[37] The German government did, however, secure a secret

35. *D.D.F.*, 2d, 4, No. 287; 5, No. 403; 6, No. 272.

36. *G.D.*, D, 3, Nos. 221, 244, 383, 389, 440, 454, 473; von Neurath to Faupel, 21 April 1937, DZA Potsdam, Büro RAM, Akte 60964, f.105; Coverdale, pp. 324–26; Abendroth, pp. 181–202. Sir Robert Hodgson was appointed British agent in Spain; the Duke of Alba became Franco's representative in London.

37. Reichsfinanzministerium, "Vermerke Wi 3735-449" and "450, g. Rs.," of 3 and 8 November 1938, Bundesarchiv, Reichsfinanzministerium, R 2/22, ff.156–57.

fund inside Spain through an aspect of the Condor Legion's pay. Half the danger pay supplement of the Legion members was made available to them individually for purchases in Spain in pesetas by the Franco regime in accounts with Hisma; but since the Germans serving in Spain did not use up all these funds, they received the equivalent of their unspent balances in marks in Germany.[38] This arrangement left the German government with the pesetas in Spain.

These so-called "savings pesetas" *(Sparpeseten)* came to over 90 million by 1939;[39] their existence was not known to the Spanish government; and they were kept in cash, first by Hisma, then by Bernhardt personally, and finally by the German embassy in Spain. A small portion of these funds was used during World War II to cover embassy expenses, but far larger sums were expended for German intelligence operations and for the activities of the German navy in supplying submarines from Spanish ports. Some amounts were in fact used for purchases in the Spanish economy and to provide German firms with Spanish currency, but the major use of this secret fund was for military purposes. Thus Germany could derive greater benefits from Franco's "benevolent neutrality" in World War II than the Spanish leader had imagined when financing the visits of Condor Legion members to Spanish brothels during the civil war.[40]

Most of the funds available to the German government for investment in Spain came from the deliveries of Hisma, and in its chief figure, Bernhardt, the Germans had a man determined to use these funds to establish German domination of Spain's economy. Starting in the summer of 1937, and almost certainly with Göring's prior approval, Hisma used parts of its balances to purchase mining rights and shares in mining firms or to establish firms of its own all over Nationalist Spain and Spanish Morocco.[41] Bernhardt moved more rapidly than the German diplomatic representatives in Spain realized and more extensively than the Spaniards were prepared to tolerate. The German-Spanish secret protocol on economic cooperation of 16 July 1937 was presumably seen by Bernhardt as the appropriate cover for these operations. Its concluding section had

38. Sonderstab W (Schweickhard) to Ministry of Finance, "2207/38 IVa g. Rs., Betr.: Sparpeseten," 2 June 1938, Bundesarchiv, R 2/22, f.54.

39. Stohrer, "Bericht Nr. 1007g., Sparpesetenguthaben der Legion Condor," 29 November 1937, Bundesarchiv, R 2/24, ff.294–98.

40. Documents on the usage of the "Savings Pesetas" during World War II may be found in the Bundesarchiv, R 2/24–26, passim. The relationship of these funds to the German submarine campaign remains to be investigated; see Salewski, 1:135.

41. Merkes, p. 229; Abendroth, pp. 241–56. Note that as early as 4 June 1937 the German press was forbidden to report on the purchase of shares of foreign mines, "Bestellungen aus der Pressekonferenz vom 4. Juni 1937," Bundesarchiv, Brammer, Z.Sg. 101/9, f.407. In April 1938 the official in the foreign ministry who handled aid to Spain suggested that Spain's debt to Germany be used in part for current repayment, in part for investment in Spain, and in part to assure future deliveries (*G.D.*, D, 3, No. 577).

provided, among other topics, that "the Spanish Nationalist Government will facilitate as far as possible the establishment of Spanish companies for the development and economic exploitation of minerals and other raw materials and for generally useful economic purposes with the participation of German citizens or German firms in accordance with the general Spanish legal regulations."[42]

In his characteristically cavalier manner, Bernhardt had neglected to look up the "general Spanish legal regulations" concerning mines; even by December 1937 the German embassy had not adequately studied the relevant texts.[43] Had they done so, they would have discovered, months before the Spaniards called it to their attention, that the Spanish regulations could be read to limit foreign ownership of mining claims and firms to 25 percent since the early 1930s. Because the qualifying phraseology in the German-Spanish protocol was not limited to the Spanish laws in effect at the time of its signing, there was the further possibility that the Spaniards might change the law whenever it suited them. In the fall of 1937 they decided to do so, and on 9 October by a new mining law suspended all changes in the control of Spanish mines since 18 July 1936, the date of the uprising against the Republic. This law would assure Franco a useful tool against any unwelcome changes in the area controlled by the Republican forces once he had conquered all of Spain, but it also threatened to destroy the whole German scheme for long-term control and exploitation of Spain's mineral resources—which was doubtless one of its main purposes.

The October decree alerted the Germans to their threatened position, though it was only during the subsequent agitated discussions with Spanish officials that they finally began to realize just how tenuous their legal standing really was. There is no need to review in detail the conferences among the interested agencies in Berlin and with the Spanish representatives. Repeatedly the Germans approached Franco personally; in their eyes, Spanish acceptance of the position Hisma had already secured through its holding companies for Spanish exploitation and mining was the key to future German-Spanish relations.[44] Göring—whose agencies in Spain were directly involved and whose responsibilities in the Four-Year Plan were affected by any problems in deliveries of raw materials to Germany—was greatly exercised by the Spanish actions, which he assumed were due to concessions to Britain. In order to enhance the position of Bernhardt in the negotiations, Göring gave him a new and

42. Text in *G.D.*, D, 3, No. 397.
43. Von Stohrer's own record of his 20 December meeting with Franco shows him ignorant of the details of the subject matter about which he was making an urgent demarche! (ibid., No. 491). Abendroth (pp. 245–47) puts the emphasis on confusion in the relevant Spanish regulations.
44. Accounts of these negotiations will be found in the books of Merkes, Einhorn, and Harper; a substantial selection of documents has been published in *G.D.*, D, 3.

special commission, something he had also done for Franz Neuhausen in Yugoslavia.[45]

All the titles of Bernhardt and all the urgings of the German ambassador only moved Franco to a promise to review the details of Hisma's acquisitions. The negotiations over these would drag on for a long time. Only in one subsidiary, though still important, area did Franco make a concession in response to Bernhardt's pressure. Starting in May 1938, the Franco government began to make monthly payments on a portion of its accumulating obligations to Hisma in foreign exchange.[46] On the mining control issue, however, Franco was obviously and deliberately stalling.

If the position of the Germans in Spain was not as strong as might have been expected from the enormous value of their assistance to Franco, certainly Franco's own attitude in his relations with Germany played a part. He was simply not the sort of person to be pushed around. A shrewd and cautious man, he admired the Germans, appreciated their support, was prepared to accommodate himself to German economic needs, but wanted above all to maintain control of the situation in Spain himself. It was not simply a matter of Franco's playing off the British and Germans against each other in order to protect Spain's independence; one cannot read the relevant records without getting the impression that Franco's pride and sense of propriety were offended by Bernhardt's grasping approach. Shipping ores to Germany was one thing; having Germany take advantage of his need for military aid at the moment to seize control of Spain's mineral resources for the future was quite another.

A second factor operating to weaken the position Germany might have secured was the almost interminable feuding among her own representatives. If there were real policy differences between Wilhelm Faupel, Germany's ambassador to Franco, Hugo Sperrle, the first commander of the Condor Legion, and Hans von Funck, the commander of the German army men in Spain as well as German military attaché, they are not apparent from the record. Probably the fact that Faupel himself was a military man increased rather than alleviated the problem. Whatever the real causes of friction, Faupel could not work with Sperrle and von Funck, and a great deal of German attention was devoted to their quarrel—which ended with the replacement of both Faupel and Sperrle, the former in August, the latter in October 1937.[47]

45. Ibid., No. 474, cf. No. 491. On Neuhausen's commission, see Weinberg, *Foreign Policy*, p. 325.

46. The payments in pounds sterling are analyzed in Robert Whaley, "How Franco Financed His War—Reconsidered," *Journal of Contemporary History*, 12, No. 1 (January 1977), 135–37, mainly on the basis of Spanish archival material.

47. See Jodl Diary for 5 January, 24 March, 4 October 1937, *TMWC*, 28:346, 352, 355; *G.D.*, D, 3, Nos. 386, 399, 411 n.1; Dertinger, "Informationsbericht Nr. 121," 23 August 1937, Bundesarchiv, Brammer, Z.Sg. 101/31, ff.167–75. There is a series of documents pertaining to Faupel's quarrels with Sperrle (referred to as "Sanders" in the correspondence) and von Funck in a file from von Neurath's office in the Potsdam archives, DZA Potsdam, Büro RAM, Akte 60964. Merkes, passim, discusses the quarrels at great length.

Differences over military tactics and arguments over the operations of Bernhardt had played some part in what appear to have been primarily personality clashes, but there was one facet of Faupel's activities in Spain that went beyond these matters and contributed to hints from the Spaniards that he be recalled. This was Faupel's dabbling in the internal politics of Franco Spain. What has not generally been recognized is that the internal developments in which Faupel was involved immediately preceded Hisma's attempts to control portions of the Spanish economy, almost certainly increased Spanish resistance to the latter, and may well have made Franco suspicious that his German friends might try their hand—or hands—at running the whole country.

The slow pace of Franco's military operations, the insufficient mobilization of the manpower resources of Nationalist Spain, and the political differences and rivalries within the Nationalist camp had long bothered the Germans.[48] Those German diplomats with experience in Spain, however, warned against any interference in internal affairs. Faupel's predecessor, Count Johannes Welczek, then German ambassador to Paris, reminded von Neurath of the dangers of trying to "reform" the Spaniards along German lines and thereby incurring the xenophobic reaction that any such procedure guaranteed.[49] He urged that the Germans in Spain be explicitly cautioned against involvement with the Falange, the political movement of Spanish fascism. It was precisely with this group, however, that Faupel and several other German representatives in Spain developed close relations, and so could easily be interpreted as siding with it in the rivalries over policy among the Nationalists.

Such rivalries were characteristic of both sides in the civil war. The important difference—a difference that may well have been decisive for the war's outcome—was that the divisions among the Republicans erupted repeatedly into what can only be called sub-civil wars and mass purges on their side, with such hostilities carried on about as ferociously as the fight against the Nationalists. The most spectacular of these internal conflicts broke out in Barcelona in April and culminated in the destruction of the POUM, the Spanish Trotskyite movement, in accordance with Soviet orders in June 1937.[50] At the very time of this grisly drama, Franco

The draft of a letter from von Blomberg to Hitler of 10 August 1937, which was prepared by Jodl but not sent, deals with Hitler's decision to replace Faupel and alludes to difficulties between the latter and Wilhelm Ritter von Thoma, the head of the German armored unit and of the training organization for Spanish officers and noncommissioned officers (National Archives, Nuremberg document 1955-PS).

48. A good comparison of the situation in Republican and Nationalist Spain by a German diplomat is in G.D., D, 3, No. 128.

49. Von Welczek to von Neurath, 27 December 1936, DZA Potsdam, Büro RAM, Akte 60964, ff.46–47 (this is the document cited in Einhorn, p. 128).

50. A good brief account in Thomas, secs. 37 and 39. Alexander Orlov, the NKVD chief in Spain at the time, conveniently omits his key role in these events in his memoirs, The Secret

was consolidating his own power by ending—or at least papering over—
the divisions on the Nationalist side in a manner characteristic of his
political style.

The major elements contending for influence in Nationalist Spain were
the Carlists and other species of monarchists, the Falange, and mis-
cellaneous clerical and military groups. Unlike the Republicans, Franco
generally preferred to apply the death penalty only to those on the *other*
side of the civil war; he simply exiled or jailed key figures who might be
actual or potential rivals for leadership of the Nationalist cause. With José
Antonio Primo de Rivera, the leader of the Falange, executed by the
Republicans, Franco jailed his successor, Manuel Hedilla Larres, and
exiled Manuel Fal Conde, the Carlist leader. Franco then combined all the
various elements into one single organization with himself as its leader.
This new creation, the Falange Española Tradicionalista y de las Juntas
Ofensivas Nacional-Sindicalistas, was as disparate as its name was long,
but Franco was the unchallenged leader of whatever it included. Whoever
was not included did not count in Nationalist Spain.

Though clear in their own minds that Franco was the only possible
person to lead the Nationalist cause, Faupel and several other German
representatives in Spain had been working with Hedilla and other Falan-
gist elements, both because they saw in them a spirit akin to German
National Socialism and because they believed that only the radical program of the Falange could succeed in mobilizing mass support behind
Franco and thereby assure a successful conclusion of the war. The consolidation of Franco's hold over the Falange, accompanied by considerable friction in April 1937, made Faupel's association with elements
Franco was pushing aside intolerable for the continuation of good
German-Spanish relations. The hints from Burgos met with Berlin's recognition that the situation had become impossible; Hitler decided to
recall both Faupel and Sperrle.[51]

In the face of these developments, it should not be surprising that
Franco was most cautious about the German economic demands and

---

History of Stalin's Crimes (New York: Random House, 1953).

It is not surprising that at a time when Stalin and the Soviet secret police were pulling
imaginary Trotskyites from under almost every bed in the Soviet Union, the very existence
of a real Trotskyite movement in "their" part of Spain stimulated Soviet ingenuity to the
forgery of POUM documents and the murder of the Trotskyite leader, Andrés Nin.

51. On Faupel's recall and the Hedilla affair, see Merkes, pp. 249–64. There were similar
problems about Italian interference, only in this case Mussolini was himself responsible
(Coverdale, pp. 190, 193–94). See also, James Joll, "Germany and the Spanish Civil War,"
in Max Beloff (ed.), *On the Track of Tyranny* (London: Vallentine, Mitchell, 1960), p. 133;
"Informationsbericht Nr. 99," 18 June 1937, Bundesarchiv, Brammer, Z.Sg. 101/30,
ff.491–95.

Eberhard von Stohrer was appointed Faupel's successor. He had been in Spain during the
World War and had been designated for the embassy in Madrid just before the outbreak of
the civil war. Some consideration was given to moving him to London in 1938 when von
Ribbentrop became foreign minister, but this plan was dropped and von Stohrer remained in
Spain until late in 1942.

allowed the talks concerning Hisma's control of mining firms to drag on for months. In the early part of 1938, the Germans and Spaniards argued over the mining concessions. While the Nationalists first retreated before the Republican offensive at Teruel and then retook the city, the Germans puzzled over the best ways to cope with Spanish legal and procedural obstruction.[52] Franco's need for more supplies during this phase of the war appeared to give the Germans added leverage, but the situation changed quickly.[53] The fighting around Teruel had weakened the Republican forces; and in March and April 1938 the Nationalist armies moved forward rapidly, cutting the Republic in two by reaching the Mediterranean on 15 April. For a moment it looked as if a total Nationalist victory were imminent, and the Spanish position in the mining controversy correspondingly stiffened,[54] only to soften again soon after when it became apparent that the Republic would hold in spite of the great setback it had received.[55]

These shifts reflect the inherent dilemma of both the Germans and the Spanish Nationalists. The Germans wanted Franco to get and keep his military operations moving, but they had a strong negotiating position only when Franco was stalled for lack of German (and Italian) support. Franco wanted both to win and to remain independent, but faced the demand that he mortgage Spain's independence for the aid he needed to win the civil war.

The interaction of military developments in Spain and diplomatic developments in Europe in the seven months of May to November 1938 temporarily resolved these problems. The euphoria of April soon gave way to gloom in the Nationalist camp as the Republic held in the summer. Assisted by a temporary opening of the French border (17 March–13 June), allowing substantial Soviet and French supplies to move through, the Republican forces regrouped and held firm. The continued internal dissension on the Loyalist side was temporarily offset by the exhaustion of the Nationalists. The final halting of the Nationalist offensive before Valencia in mid-July was soon followed by a Republican offensive from the northern region across the Ebro. The fighting near the Ebro would last from late July to mid-November; in its costs and character it resembled one of the great attrition battles on the Western Front in the World War. When the bloodbath on the Ebro was over, the northern Republican forces had been to all intents and purposes destroyed, but the Nationalist armies were so exhausted and weakened that only a complete surrender to German demands woud enable Franco to restore his offensive capabilities and avoid a compromise settlement of the civil war.

52. *G.D.*, D, 3, Nos. 499, 501–4, 508–10, 515, 516, 526; von Stohrer, No. 44 of 31 January 1938, T-120, 784/1557/377754. The accounts of Merkes and Abendroth already cited cover these talks; the latter is the more reliable.

53. *G.D.*, D, 3, Nos. 528, 532, 537, 539, 541, 542.

54. Ibid., Nos. 561, 566.

55. Ibid., Nos. 578–81, 584, 586.

In the summer of 1938, the Franco regime had tried to satisfy the Germans while containing their future role in the Spanish economy by a new mining law which increased permissible foreign participation from 25 to 40 percent and provided for possible exceptions to even this higher limit. The manner in which the new rules were prepared and promulgated annoyed the Germans—who could not understand that precisely because concessions were being made to their point of view the Spanish government was especially careful to use procedures free of outside interference—and friction over the application of the 6 June regulation continued into the fall.[56] While the Germans puzzled out ways to get around the new law and the Nationalists became increasingly desperate for more aid, the international situation accentuated the confrontation between Franco and the Germans.[57]

The crisis over Czechoslovakia in 1938 threatened to lead to a new world war at the very time when the fighting on the Ebro rcalled the horrors of the last. The possibility of war in Europe was most dangerous to the Spanish Nationalists. Since they had been unable to push on to victory in the spring of 1938, the possible outbreak of war between Germany and the Western Powers threatened all their gains since 1936. Aid from Germany and Italy would surely end, while the Republic could be expected to revive its strength in alliance with Britain and France. The French might, in fact, decide to clear up any doubts about their security in the Pyrenees and the Mediterranean by sending an army to the aid of the Loyalists; a possibility that could presumably be forestalled, if at all, only by a compromise peace in Spain.

As Franco saw this danger looming ahead, the absence of information from Berlin on the development of the crisis alarmed him all the more.[58] He decided to avert what must have looked to him as the greatest danger to his position and prospects—and to the Loyalists as the best hope of recovery—by assuring Britain and France in the most complete way that he would maintain absolute neutrality if a European war should break out. Although the Germans recognized the difficult situation Franco was in, they found his eagerness to proclaim neutrality in a war that had not broken out exceedingly offensive; and a considerable residue of resentment remained even after the Munich settlement had removed the fears of Franco and the hopes of the Republic.[59]

56. Ibid., Nos. 588, 591–93, 595, 596, 604, 606, 610, 612, 613, 632.

57. Ibid., Nos. 634, 642, 643, 651, 655, 663.

58. Merkes, p. 321, suggests that a reduction in the size of the Condor Legion in August and early September 1938 may have led Franco to believe that Germany was drawing back experienced crews for an imminent war.

59. G.D., D, 2, Nos. 622, 624, 638, 641, 659; 3, Nos. 656–59, 664–66, 669, 670, 704, 705; Merkes, pp. 320–28; Abendroth, pp. 217–24. Franco's own apologia to Hitler may be found in G.D., D, 7:501–4. Ciano, after expressing his disgust, recognized that Franco had little choice (Diary, 26 September 1938). Cf. U.S., 1938, 1:240–41, 255, 258, 260; D.D.F., 2d, 11, Nos. 369, 378.

In the period immediately following Munich, however, Franco faced the new danger of having to agree to a political settlement of the civil war. It was obvious that the Republican forces could not secure a victory, and many of their leaders would have been prepared to make peace; Franco wanted the unconditional surrender of his opponents but lacked the offensive power to break out of the stalemate to final victory.[60] The Germans had always feared that a compromise would be against their interests. A long war, as has been mentioned, was in accord with their preferences; but not if it led to a peaceful settlement of the civil war. Any such settlement involved the possibility—however remote—of elections, in which the Germans were sure the supporters of the Republic would win.[61] On the other hand, the German government was no longer willing to supply aid to Franco without commitments from him on the key issues outstanding in German-Spanish relations, and of these, the mining concessions problem was the most important to them. There was, therefore, agreement for once among the German authorities both in Berlin and in Spain that rigid conditions should be set for any future aid.[62]

As Spanish anxiety increased, Germany postponed a decision until it became obvious to Franco and his associates that only a complete surrender to German demands would enable them to secure the means of enforcing a complete surrender on their own domestic opponents. In mid-November 1938, accordingly, Franco decided to give in to Berlin. The needed exemptions from the restrictions of the mining law were voted by the cabinet; all other current issues were settled in accordance with German wishes; and the Germans were also assured that their desires for political agreements with Spain would be met when the military aid of the Axis had assured a speedy victory for Franco.[63] The happy Germans provided the support Franco needed to resume the offensive. As the Germans in December 1938 reviewed the great gains they had made and those that they still expected to make, Franco's forces crushed the northern portion of the Republic around Barcelona and prepared to complete the conquest of the southern portion around Madrid.[64]

One cannot say with absolute certainty why Franco decided to give in to German pressure at precisely this point in the civil war rather than risk a continued stalemate, but the signs of shock and fear at the prospect of a world war in the Czechoslovak crisis may well explain the decision of the Spanish leader. Who could know when Germany—again without the slightest notice to Franco—would run the risk of war? Might not some German move, about which he would learn from the newspapers, wreck all he

60. *G.D.*, D, 3, Nos. 660–72, 674, 685.

61. See, e.g., Faupel's analysis of May 1937, ibid., No. 254. The reasons for Franco's and Germany's opposition to a compromise peace are discussed by Merkes, pp. 119–22.

62. *G.D.*, D, 3, Nos. 679–82, 686, 687.

63. Ibid., Nos. 688, 690–93, 695, 697, 698, 700, 703; Merkes, pp. 329–32; Abendroth, pp. 226–29, 256–57.

64. *G.D.*, D, 3, No. 702; cf. Thomas, sec. 48.

had attained in over two years of war? Unlike Mussolini, who in May 1939 would sign an alliance with Hitler on the premise that there would be no war for several years, only to learn a few months later that Hitler was about to start one, Franco may have been frightened by the Czechoslovak crisis into taking radical steps to make certain that he would have finished his own war before Hitler started a conflict that was certain to jeopardize the prospects of Nationalist victory in the civil war if that war were not yet finished.[65] In other words, Franco felt that he had to take whatever measures might be necessary to win his war before the "campaign season" in Europe opened again in the summer of 1939.

The concessions to Germany of November 1938 were Franco's Brest-Litovsk. Like Lenin, he mortgaged a large portion of his country's future to Germany in order to obtain full control of the rest for himself. Each dictator was to be rescued from the implications of his own concessions by the subsequent victory of other powers over Germany. In the case of Lenin, the interval was less than a year; Franco would have to wait much longer—but then, he was a patient man.

The major aspect of German-Spanish relations other than the economic one in which the Spanish government shifted its position in November 1938 was that of a political alignment with Germany. This question had arisen before. In the spring of 1938 when Franco's success in splitting the Republic had suggested the possibility of an imminent Nationalist victory, there had been discussions of a possible German-Spanish political treaty and the adherence of Spain to the Anti-Comintern Pact. These discussions had gone hand in hand with consideration of a possible withdrawal of the Condor Legion and the Italian troops, but all such rosy prospects vanished with the restabilization of the front. The Nationalists had been worried about the anticipated British reaction if they adhered to the Anti-Comintern Pact even before the setbacks of mid-May 1938.[66] Thereafter, the difficult situation in the war left the Nationalists even more afraid of a public treaty with Germany—especially at a time when the French had opened the border for supplies to the Republic. They therefore told the Germans that a political treaty would have to be either secret until victory had been won or postponed until that time altogether. The German government was interested in the propaganda value of a public

65. It should be noted that Abendroth's interpretation (pp. 228–29) stresses the political prestige triumph of Munich as inclining Franco to Germany's side; an explanation hardly consonant with the subsequent hesitations about publicity for Spain's adhesion to the Anti-Comintern Pact. Abendroth's related view (p. 279) that Spain's colonial ambitions could be realized only at the expense of Britain and France does not appear convincing for this period, and when those ambitions were voiced by Franco in 1940, they collided with German and Italian as well as British and French colonial interests (Weinberg, "Colonial Plans," pp. 472–73).

66. G.D., D, 3, No. 582. For the negotiations up to that point, see ibid., Nos. 529, 544, 557–60, 564, 567, 570, 575, 576.

alignment of Spain with the Axis and accordingly expressed a preference for postponing the whole question.[67]

With the shift in Franco's policy in November 1938 and the resulting approach of military victory, the German-Spanish negotiations for a political agreement that had been suspended in May were resumed in December 1938. There were details to be settled—as well as a characteristically prolonged final military campaign—but the negotiations culminated in an agreement signed on 31 March 1939.[68] The treaty provided for consultation in international affairs, benevolent neutrality in case one partner were involved in war, abstention from international agreements hostile to one another, cooperation with the Italian government, and promises to cooperate in political, cultural, and economic relations.[69]

Although the Spaniards eventually also gave way on the subject of adherence to the Anti-Comintern Pact, that would be a longer and more difficult problem. It was not merely that the negotiations were complicated by the participation of Italy and Japan; there was a fundamental difference of interest and approach between Germany and Spain. Von Ribbentrop had always looked upon the Anti-Comintern system as his own brainchild, a gift of genius to a skeptical world. The propagandistic aspect of an imposing façade of unity, the appearance of a worldwide association of the rising nations as contrasted with the collapsing League of decaying democracies—these were the great merits of the Anti-Comintern Pact in the eyes of its creator. The early months of 1939 were, as will be examined later, the time when von Ribbentrop was attempting to convert the original association of Germany, Italy, and Japan into a formal military alliance; what better time could there be for a public association with those three wise powers of a Nationalist Spain that was conquering enemies of the new dispensation who had enjoyed such sympathies in the West? Only if seen in this context can the tremendous German pressure on Franco, personally and continually reinforced by von Ribbentrop, be understood.

Franco, on the other hand, could see no good reason to take a step, especially to take a public step, that was guaranteed to annoy Britain and France at a time when he was securing their formal diplomatic recognition and wanted a number of important concessions from them.[70] This was particularly so from his point of view as he could see nothing to be gained from adding such an action to the political treaty with Germany that he was willing to sign. Furthermore, he pointed out with understandable annoyance, he had surely given enough practical evidence of an anti-

67. Ibid., Nos. 587, 589, 590,

68. See ibid., Nos. 705–8, 714, 718–20, 725, 729, 733, 734, 741, 769; Merkes, pp. 335–37.

69. German and Spanish text in *G.D.*, D, 3, No. 773.

70. On British efforts to dissuade Spain from adhering to the pact, see C 2191/421/62, FO 371/22944; cf. Abendroth, pp. 286–87.

Communist orientation. In the face of this divergence of views, the talks dragged on from January to the end of March 1939. Only when victory in Spain was certain and German pressure most insistent did Franco agree to the signing on 27 March, but even then insisted that this action be kept secret. A leak, possibly arranged by the Germans, finally forced publication of Spain's adherence to the Anti-Comintern Pact on 7 April 1939.[71] Ironically, by then the German attempt to convert the German-Italian-Japanese association into a firm military alliance was seen in Berlin as unlikely to succeed so that the German government was beginning to give serious thought to an alignment with the Soviet Union. The publication of Spain's adhesion to the Anti-Comintern Pact would be the last act of the German government that could be interpreted as overtly anti-Soviet before the Nazi-Soviet Non-Aggression Pact.[72]

As the end of the civil war in Spain came into view early in 1939, the Germans thus reaped their political harvest. Having won major concessions from Franco in the economic field, they could afford to be generous in the concluding negotiations to secure their economic position in postwar Spain. These talks, it is true, lasted several months, but the Germans were delayed more by internal feuding of their own than by Spanish reluctance.[73] The outbreak of World War II in September 1939 would alter the whole situation, so that the details of these economic talks came to be of little practical importance.[74] German economic benefits from the intervention in Spain had either been already secured or would be completely transformed by the exigencies of war.

In a real sense, the same thing was also largely true of the political and military benefits to Germany. Franco had explained to the Italians that the long civil war had so weakened Spain that it would take years to rebuild the country; if a European war came in the near future, Spain would have to remain neutral.[75] The German government was fully aware of this fact and realized that for the time being the waning of the civil war had ended the favorable political effects Germany could draw from that conflict. These had, however, been very great. For years, public attention had been preoccupied with Spain. The continued estrangement of Italy from

71. The negotiations can be followed in *G.D.*, D, 3, Nos. 717, 721–24, 726, 728, 733, 734, 738, 741–43, 746, 748, 751, 752, 758, 760, 761, 767, 768, 770, 772, 775–79, 781, 782; Merkes, pp. 336–37.
72. Weinberg, *Germany and the Soviet Union*, pp. 21–22. On the publicity problems attendant upon the welcoming ceremonies for the returned Condor Legion in Germany at the end of May when anti-Soviet and anti-Communist themes had been banned because of the effort at a rapprochement with the Soviet Union, see Merkes, pp. 343–44, 346. See also Sommer, p. 182, n.36.
73. A good summary in Abendroth, chap. 12.
74. See *G.D.*, D, 3, Nos. 710, 753, 754, 756, 757, 759, 762, 764, 765, 783, 784, 786, 809. On internal German feuds, in which Bernhardt was again a center of controversy, see Abendroth, pp. 294–98.
75. *G.D.*, D, 3, Nos. 755, 763.

France and Britain had been successfully maintained. Every effort of London to rebuild a bridge to Rome had foundered over the problems of the Spanish Civil War.[76] Even if Mussolini was ever sincere in his desire for a rapprochement with England—and there is great doubt on that score[77]—nothing would come of the endless soundings and negotiations between London and Rome that cost Eden his position and Chamberlain and Halifax a good part of their reputation.[78] The Italians were encouraged to ever greater risks,[79] and the British and French had to worry about their Mediterrranean communications, the safety of Egypt, and the possibility of Italy's becoming permanently entrenched in the Balearic Islands.[80] At the same time, German and Italian authorities had accustomed themselves to working together in a wide variety of fields, in spite of occasional friction and rivalry.[81] As will be shown in chapter 9, it was this combination of factors that opened the door to Germany's annexation of Austria, which in turn facilitated the destruction of Czechoslovakia. In this sense, the Germans had already brought in their political harvest from the Spanish conflict long before the Condor Legion staged its triumphal return procession in Berlin.

There was a further advantage for the Germans to draw from the turmoil in Spain. The passions aroused by the conflict contributed both to internal divisions in France and Britain and to their estrangement from the Soviet Union. Inside the democracies, the question of intervention and nonintervention was debated bitterly; a study of the impact of this controversy on the United States is appropriately entitled *The Wound in the*

76. This is particularly striking when one reads the discussions on Spain in the British cabinet Committee on Foreign Policy during 1937 and 1938, CAB 27/622 and 623.

77. Thus at the end of October 1937, the Italian ambassador to Paris, Vittorio Cerruti, expressed the view that Mussolini was determined to make war on England and could not be detached from Hitler, a statement that was shown to Chamberlain (R 7531/1/22, FO 371/21162; cf. R 7469/1/22, ibid.).

78. R 2261/5/67, FO 371/21136; R 2376/1/22, FO 371/21158; R 4965, R 4976, R 4977, R 5137, R 5161, R 5176, R 5304, R 5186, R 5313/1/22, FO 371/21160; R 6096/1/22, FO 371/21161; R 6700, R 6907, R 7329, R 7776/1/22, FO 371/21162; R 8563/1/22, FO 371/21163 (this deals with Lady Ivy Chamberlain's visit to Rome in December 1937); R 6557/23/22, FO 371/22413; R 8513/23/22, FO 371/22414; Feiling, p. 330; *Hore-Belisha Papers*, pp. 101–2; Eden, pp. 535–37; Ciano, *Diary*, 10–11 September 1937, p. 13; 5 October 1937, p. 22; *U.S.*, 1938, 1:249–52; *G.D.*, D, 1, Nos. 116, 791; *Hungarian Documents*, 2, No. 209.

79. Ciano, *Diary*, 14 October 1937, p. 26.

80. W 18182/9549/41, FO 371/20588; Br. Cabinet 75 (1936), 16 December 1936, W 18354/9549/41, FO 371/20589; J 4324, J 4422/244/16, FO 371/20911; J 4995, J 5108/244/16, FO 371/20912; R 3076, R 4964/5/64, FO 371/21136; R 5290/1/22, FO 371/21160; R 6435/1/22, FO 371/21161.

81. Rintelen, p. 17; Merkes, pp. 173–74; *G.D.*, D, 3, Nos. 170, 209, 210, 255, 360–62, 376, 379, 423–25, 427–29, 433, 434, 444, 448, 456, 460, 489, 494, 495, 497, 498, 521, 616, 625, 631; C, 6, No. 350; D, 1, No. 2; Jodl Diary, 9 and 12 January 1937, *TMWC*, 28:347, 348; "Informationsbericht Nr. 59," 14 January 1937, "Informationsbericht Nr. 37," 21 May 1938, Bundesarchiv, Brammer, Z.Sg. 101/30, ff.33–37, 101/32, ff.339–41; Stohrer, "Bericht 259g," 17 February 1938, T-120, 784/1557/377841; Ciano, *Diplomatic Papers*, pp. 80–91, 115–17, 126–27, 128, 137, 144–46; Mussolini's instruction of 8 July 1938 to the Italian embassies in Paris, London, and Washington, in Moffat Papers, vol. 13.

Heart.[82] The bitterness of these divisions was to have no analogy until the American debate over Vietnam in the 1960s—though then the fronts would be reversed with the government practicing intervention and the critics urging nonintervention. Not unrelated to these controversies was the impact of the Spanish Civil War on relations between the Western Powers and the Soviet Union.

Though fully aware of the limited character of Soviet assistance to the Republic,[83] the Germans and Italians never ceased trumpeting their argument that Moscow controlled the Loyalists. The reluctance of Britain and France to aid the Republic had the effect of giving some truth to Axis propaganda by making the Republic dependent on Soviet aid. The Russian government, on the other hand, saw grounds for recognizing in the policies of London and Paris a complaisance toward Germany and Italy and a willingness to accept Franco's victory that could easily be made to fit into preconceived notions of a capitalist conspiracy against the U.S.S.R.[84] The firm position temporarily taken by Britain and France in the fall of 1937 at the Nyon Conference had produced an immediate Italian retreat, but that isolated incident only seemed to underline the flabbiness of Western policy the rest of the time.[85] The developments in Spain thus served to make a general alignment against Germany less likely by increasing the mistrust among the potential allies in the East and West.

The fighting itself was also to have favorable by-products for Germany. The Germans had an excellent opportunity to test their weapons and to train officers and men in their use under combat conditions, something especially useful for the German air force.[86] There was also the special role of Germany's air force as a means of bluffing potential victims into submission, of scaring potential enemies into acquiescence, and of achieving quick victory if war should come. The course of operations in Spain served to enhance the position of the Luftwaffe in these respects. The bombings of the Basque towns in 1937 and of Barcelona in 1938 not only horrified the world at the time but also heightened the sense of

82. Allen Guttmann, *The Wound in the Heart; America and the Spanish Civil War* (New York: Random House, 1962).

83. Ciano, *Diplomatic Papers,* p. 86; cf. W 12727/7/41, FO 371/21339; C 5049/122/17, FO 371/20694.

84. The suggestions of Abendroth (pp. 168–68) that the *Deutschland* incident was arranged by the Soviet Union in the hope of provoking conflict between the Western Powers and Germany over Spain by drawing Germany more deeply into the war there is based primarily on the fact that the bombers were piloted by Russians and belonged to a special squadron. It would be difficult to prove or disprove this thesis.

85. On Nyon, see *G.D.,* D, 3, Nos. 407–10, 413–19; "Informationsbericht Nr. 132," 9 September 1937, Bundesarchiv, Brammer, Z.Sg. 101/31, ff.211–13; Ciano, *Diplomatic Papers,* pp. 134–35; Ciano, *Diary,* 23 August 1937, p. 1; *D.D.F.,* 2d, 6, Nos. 338–500 passim, especially the records of the closed meetings of the conference in Nos. 423, 426, 447, 460; Dreifort, chap. 4; Pratt, pp. 72–74. Coverdale, pp. 306–10, takes a view of the conference somewhat different from that of most scholars.

86. A summary of the evidence is in Merkes, pp. 128–43, an excellent assessment in Homze, pp. 170–74.

menace that Germany hoped first to create and then to utilize.[87] The belief that another European conflict would probably begin, but certainly end, with the major cities of France and England destroyed from the air was to be a powerful influence on policy in Paris and London; it took much of its intensity from the events in Spain.

The Germans, like the Italians, could not impose on Franco the cession of bases since that would have undermined the position of the Nationalists and was in any case anathema to Franco. Even at the height of German triumphs in Western Europe in the summer of 1940 Franco would refuse German demands of that sort.[88] Von Blomberg's assurance that the German as well as the Italian contingents would leave Spain at the end of the fighting there was both meant sincerely and carried out in practice.[89] Nor could the Germans expect the Spaniards to repay their efforts with great affection. The British diplomatic agent in Franco Spain, Sir Robert Hodgson, reported perceptively on the Spanish reaction to Italian and German assistance in late August 1938:

There is . . . a subtle process at work to the detriment of Nationalist Spain's allies. So far as Italy is concerned this is of course long standing. The partnership has throughout been an uneasy one . . . . The general disposition is to refer to Italians with a certain amount of levity, to decry their performance in the field—where it surely would be too much to ask of them that they should display for a cause that is of no kind of interest to them the reckless gallantry that decimates the Spanish army—and to minimise the immense services their aviation and artillery have in fact rendered to "The Cause." No amount of propaganda or mellifluous phrasing can hide the fact that the two allies are heartily tired of one another and look forward to the day when their partnership in arms will be dissolved.

Relations with the Germans have been throughout, and continue to be, of a different character. The circumstances which were responsible for the Germanophil orientation of Spain at the time of the Great War are, to some extent, operative to-day. The immense respect which the efficiency of the German war machine then commanded in Spanish military circles made the Spanish army definitely Germanophil, still hypnotises soldiers . . . . Thus the German effort in Spain started under favorable auspices . . . . Nowadays a more critical attitude seems to be supervening. The Spaniards are not so sure as they were on which side the balance of indebtedness stands. Is it not arguable that it is Germany who is in debt to Spain? The fact that Germany—as Italy too—rushed to Spain's assistance was just as much to their own advantage as it was

87. There is considerable material on the Barcelona attacks in the various documentary collections and in the literature on the civil war, but a detailed study remains to be written and would be most useful.

88. Weinberg, "Colonial Plans," p. 481; Donald S. Detwiler, *Hitler, Franco und Gibraltar* (Wiesbaden: Steiner, 1962), chap. 4.

89. See, e.g., C 7228/3/18, FO 371/20712.

to hers. The three were fighting on a common front against a common foe . . . . But the land that was ravaged by the struggle was Spanish soil and the blood that was spilt in the course of it was Spanish blood. True, the Italians did a little blood letting too—at Guadalajara for instance—the Germans none, while the latter found in the Spanish battle-fields an extraordinarily convenient arena for trying out their latest military inventions . . . . No, on the whole the balance of indebtedness seems to be on the side of Germany, not on the side of Spain. And this makes it all the more annoying that the Germans should be advancing continual demands for payments . . . , should have swarms of their compatriots burrowing into every little business affair throughout the country and be doing their best to get their fingers into mining and other enterprises where they are not in the least wanted.[90]

Though written before Franco's policy switch of November 1938, there is little reason to believe that basic attitudes were greatly altered by those concessions to the needs of the moment.

The returns to Germany for her role in supporting Franco were thus not so much in later support from Spain, but in the immediate effects of the fighting itself. Ores for German rearmament, the diversion of attention from Central Europe, the strengthened alignment with Italy, all were hopes of Hitler and some of his associates in 1936; and all were realized. Like the Italo-Ethiopian war, the conflict in Spain was a disaster for the peoples immediately affected but a great boon for Hitler. He had seen the opportunities and made the most of them; if the Italians were stupid enough to pay the greater price in blood and treasure, that was their own, or rather Mussolini's, foolishness.[91] For almost three years civil war ravaged Spain; the tides of battle shifted this way and that; but only Berlin could call it all a gain.

90. Hodgson report of 24 August 1938, W 11582/29/41, FO 371/22624.
91. Coverdale, pp. 392–410, concludes that the price paid by Italy in money and materials was not very substantial and that no lessons learned in Spain were ever applied and no deficiencies discovered there subsequently remedied. Though the last two conclusions are undoubtedly correct, the former ignores the significance of marginal cost in a strained economy. Denis Mack Smith in his *Mussolini's Roman Empire* (New York: Penguin Books, 1976), p. 105, also concludes that "the war can be said to have been a very heavy burden on the far from flourishing Italian economy."

6   Germany, the Sino-Japanese War, and the Plans for a Tripartite Alliance

f the war that started in Spain in July 1936 was to prove of great advantage to the Third Reich, the hostilities which broke out between China and Japan in July 1937 were damaging to German policies and plans. As described in chapter 1, the relationship of Germany with the Nationalist regime in China as well as with the government of Japan was good. If Germany secured from China both raw materials and foreign exchange needed by Germany's war industries, she obtained from Japan the political advantage of having a power threaten by expansion in East Asia several of the same major powers whose interests might be affected by German expansion. As long as Sino-Japanese relations were peaceful, Germany's ties to both presented no problems; but even before the incident at the Marco Polo bridge near Peking on 7 July 1937, the friction between Nanking and Tokyo had repeatedly strained German ingenuity.

The difficulties of maintaining close relations with both China and Japan had been aggravated by policy disputes in Germany herself. Without reviewing the endless arguments, one might summarize the views of various contending elements inside the German government as follows: the ministry of war and the foreign ministry were, on the whole, pro-Chinese, with the ministry of war somewhat more willing to take steps helpful to Chiang Kai-shek. Von Ribbentrop and his special office, the *Dienststelle Ribbentrop,* were enthusiastically pro-Japanese; the foreign policy office of Alfred Rosenberg concentrated its interests on Afghanistan; and the foreign section of the National Socialist party, the A.O., never developed a clear policy line on East Asia. Göring was torn between what appears to have been great sympathy for Japan and equally great interest in the benefits to his economic projects of the raw materials and foreign exchange furnished by China, with the latter interest reinforced by the transfer in the fall of 1937 of HAPRO (Handels-gesellschaft für industrielle Produkte m.b.H.), the semiofficial German agency for trade with Nationalist China, from the supervision of the ministry of war to control by Göring's own Four-Year Plan.[1]

Hitler himself inclined more to the Japanese than the Chinese side.[2] Concentration on more immediate European issues had, however, led him to leave the multiple confusions of German policy in East Asia largely unresolved in the early years of National Socialist rule. It should be noted, nevertheless, that his basic sympathies would lead him, when pushed into a decision by events, to follow a policy of alignment with Japan. This proclivity could be seen in his agreement with von Ribbentrop's Anti-Comintern Pact, which had been opposed by the foreign ministry;[3] and it would reemerge in the winter of 1937–38. Until he reached that final decision, however, the first months of war between China and Japan would see German policy shifting from rebuffs to Japan to an attempt at mediation before a clear option for Tokyo.

Whether or not the Japanese intended a major expansion of their control of North China in July 1937 is not entirely clear. It has seemed to many that this was another in a series of expansionist moves, with the Japanese army determined to prevent the consolidation of China that appeared likely to follow the temporary cessation of civil war between the Nationalists and the Communists after the Sian incident involving the kidnapping of Chiang in December 1936. Others have pointed to evidence suggesting the unplanned nature of the incident and the very limited aims of the Japanese.[4] The latter interpretation, however, overlooks one most significant element: evidence of Japanese moderation and intended self-restraint might be unearthed by historians decades later, but it was certain to be invisible to the contemporary leaders of China. Faced by one more in a long series of aggressive and expansionist actions of the Japanese, the Chinese public and government determined to meet this last step as best they could. They would fight the Japanese, not only at places of Japan's choosing, but also in such locations as might offer greater hopes of success for themselves and support to the Chinese cause by others. If the

1. On Göring's views in 1936, see Weinberg, *Foreign Policy*, p. 340.
2. See ibid., pp. 20–21, and chap. 5.
3. On the negotiations for this pact, see now the supplementary information from the papers of Friedrich Wilhelm Hack in Bernd Martin, "Die deutsch-japanischen Beziehungen während des Dritten Reiches," in Manfred Funke (ed.), *Hitler, Deutschland und die Mächte* (Düsseldorf: Droste, 1977), pp. 460–62.
4. This view is the main burden of James A. Crowley, *Japan's Quest for Autonomy* (Princeton, N.J.: Princeton University Press, 1966). Bradford A. Lee, *Britain and the Sino-Japanese War, 1937–1939* (Stanford, Calif.: Stanford University Press, 1973), chap. 2, takes a midway position. This chapter is especially good for its delineation of Anglo-American differences in facing the situation, with Britain willing and the U.S. quite unwilling to pressure Japan toward a peaceful line of policy.

Japanese, therefore, both in North China and at Shanghai soon found themselves embroiled in a far larger conflict than they had intended, they had no one to blame but themselves. Austria-Hungary "only" wanted to crush Serbia in 1914; Germany "only" wanted to destroy Poland in 1939; and Japan may in 1937 have wanted "only" to protect against the possible resurgence of China her prior loot in Manchuria and her predominant position in North China; but those who deliberately let loose avalanches should not be surprised—though they usually are—by their own burial under the debris.

When the incident of 7 July was followed by further clashes in North China, the German government was most concerned about the impact of all this on German interests in East Asia. German diplomats anxiously observed developments.[5] Both in Tokyo and Nanking, the German representatives initially saw the dangers of the escalating conflict in a way similar to the perception of the German foreign ministry. Germany, having close ties to both sides, would want to stay neutral,[6] but a prolonged war between China and Japan was certain to have serious effects for Germany. German economic interests in China would be endangered, whatever happened. Japan would be weakened by what the Germans thought likely to become a long and drawn out war.[7] This weakening of Japan would reduce her value to Germany as a threat to the Western Powers and the Soviet Union, making all these powers freer to move in Europe. The longer the fighting in China, the more Japan would be drained and weakened. Furthermore, just as the Japanese political maneuvers in North China had brought the Chinese Nationalists and Communists closer together politically, so the military aggression of Japan could be expected to drive Chiang into the arms of the Soviet Union diplomatically. The longer the war, the more dependent on Russia he would become; the greater the disruption of China, the better the chances of a Communist victory in China afterwards.[8] On the other side of the globe, the Germans could see clearly in 1937 that the Japanese attack on China would open the door to Soviet expansion in Asia—just as the Japanese would see in 1939 that a German attack on Poland would open the door to Soviet expansion in Europe. Neither could persuade the other to recognize these realities.

In view of the German analysis of the situation in the summer of 1937, it should not be surprising that Berlin rebuffed all Japanese attempts to

5. *G.D.*, C, 6, Nos. 456, 457, 459, 460, 464, 466–68, 471, 481, 498; D, 1, Nos. 468, 477; Ernst L. Presseisen, *Germany and Japan* (The Hague: Nijhoff, 1958), pp. 127–28; Yu-hsi Nieh, "Die Entwicklung des chinesisch-japanischen Konfliktes in Nordchina und die deutschen Vermittlungsbemühungen 1937–38," Hamburg diss., Institut für Asienkunde, 1970, p. 134, n.420.

6. *G.D.*, C, 6, No. 480; D, 1, No. 463.

7. Ibid., D, 1, Nos. 465, 470, 471.

8. Ibid., C, 6, Nos. 470, 473, 478; D, 1, No. 476; *U.S.*, 1937, 3:481–84, 489–90.

secure diplomatic support by reference to the Anti-Comintern Pact. German diplomats explained to the Japanese that the conflict in China was helping, not hindering, the spread of communism; and that Germany, moreover, could not be expected to withdraw her military advisers to Chiang Kai-shek or suspend the trade which provided weapons to China in return for materials Germany needed.[9] On 16 August, Hitler himself at a meeting with von Neurath and von Blomberg confirmed this policy; he would have preferred to side with Japan but decided on a neutral policy with deliveries to China that were paid for in critically needed raw materials and foreign exchange being continued, though camouflaged as much as possible.[10] The German press, which had initially been instructed to take a neutral attitude, was lectured by the propaganda ministry about its pro-Chinese orientation and told to take a pro-Japanese view—only to be recalled to straight neutrality after Hitler's decision.[11]

From the perspective of Tokyo, the obvious alternative European power to which Japan might turn for support was Italy. If not as powerful as Germany, Italy's role was of interest to Japan for two main reasons. In the first place, Italy had been selling airplanes to China, and her officers were playing an important role in training the Chinese Nationalist air force. If Italy withdrew her training officers and ceased to supply China with planes, this would have both military and morale repercussions on the fighting in East Asia. Second, the location of Italy with her navy and African colonies astride Britain's Mediterranean communications would make any Italian alignment with Japan an asset in restraining Great Britain.

The Japanese accordingly approached the Italian government with requests that Italy cease all support of China. They also asked Italy to consider aligning herself politically with Japan through an Anti-Comintern agreement similar to that between Germany and Japan, the assumption being that Italy's taking such action at that moment would serve as a political reinforcement to Japan's position, especially because Italy was one of the signatories of the Nine-Power Pact guaranteeing the integrity and independence of China.

The Italians hastened to agree to the Japanese overtures. When the Chinese complained about the halting of airplane shipments, Italian Foreign Minister Ciano reminded them of China's participation in sanctions against Italy at the time of the Ethiopian war. Though officially

9. *G.D.*, C, 6, Nos. 465, 479; D, 1, Nos. 466, 467, 469, 472–74; *D.D.F.*, 2d, 6, Nos. 378, 386.

10. *G.D.*, D, 1, Nos. 478, 481. For Hitler's earlier comments on the value of Germany's trade with China, see ibid., C, 6, No. 429; *U.S.*, 1937, 3:287. For allusions by Hitler to heavy Japanese losses of officers in the fighting as recounted by Albert Forster to Carl Burckhardt, see the latter's letter of 1 December 1937 in Burckhardt, p. 119.

11. *G.D.*, D, 1, Nos. 480, 482; Nieh, pp. 126–29; "Bestellungen aus der Pressekonferenz," 21 July, 28 July, 29 July, 17 August 1937, Bundesarchiv, Brammer, Z.Sg. 101/10, ff.43, 61, 63, 117.

neutral, Italy was obviously siding with Japan.[12] In fact, Mussolini and Ciano began to push so hard for a close political alignment with Japan that the Japanese themselves became a bit worried and began to hold back.[13] How can one account for this Italian enthusiasm and the surprising reluctance of the Japanese to move forward with their own original suggestion? The answer is necessarily speculative but appears to lie in the different diplomatic styles and aims of the two powers. If the Japanese had originally sought Italian support as a means of exerting an indirect and subtle naval pressure on England, the Italians were enthusiastic about using the Japanese in the same way. Engaged in a serious and immediate naval controversy in the Mediterranean marked by ship sinkings, the Nyon Conference, and British naval orders to sink "pirate," i.e., Italian, submarines, the authorities in Rome were understandably eager to align themselves with one of the world's great naval powers that could divert British attention away from Mediterranean waters. This converse of Japan's interest in a naval diversion from the Pacific was accentuated by both the characteristic flamboyance of Mussolini's diplomatic style—which stressed loud gestures and dramatic forms—and a significant distinction in ultimate aim. Italy expected to fight Britain at some time and would be enormously assisted by an allied Japan.

The Japanese government, on the other hand, preferred low-key diplomacy and still hoped to accomplish its objectives in East Asia without a war with England. Once the Italians had taken their general position on the Sino-Japanese war, therefore, the Japanese had achieved most of what they had hoped for—without having to give anything in return—and were in no hurry to run risks that Mussolini was inviting them to share. It is even possible that the very eagerness of the Italians alarmed the Tokyo government by suggesting a possibly imminent Anglo-Italian war in which Japan certainly did not want to participate at the moment when her navy was preoccupied with supporting the Japanese landing force in and around Shanghai. It was the temporary lull in the Italian-Japanese negotiations which resulted from this divergence of perspective between Rome and Tokyo that provided the opportunity for a new initiative from within the German government.

Joachim von Ribbentrop was unhappy with Germany's attitude toward the conflict in East Asia from the start. As architect of the Anti-Comintern Pact he thought of himself as the advocate of close relations with Japan in Germany. He had originally hoped to convert the bilateral German-Japanese agreement into a broad front including Italy and possibly other countries, and therefore thought of himself with considerable justification as the originator of the concept of a tripartite German-Japanese-Italian

    12. Ciano, *Diplomatic Papers*, pp. 129–30, 130–31; Ciano, *Diary*, 23 August, 26 August, 7 October 1937, pp. 1, 4, 27; *G.D.*, C, 6, No. 508; D, 1, No. 464; Sommer, p. 84.
    13. *G.D.*, D, 1, No. 485.

alliance.[14] Neither the failure of von Ribbentrop's earliest attempts at the beginning of 1937 to broaden the German-Japanese agreement nor the discouraging report from the Far East of Albrecht Haushofer of his own *Dienststelle* dampened his enthuasiasm.[15] When in Berlin between visits to his London post, von Ribbentrop met with the Japanese ambassador and with his old friend Japanese Military Attaché Oshima Hiroshi to discuss the extension of the Anti-Comintern Pact and the situation in the Sino-Japanese conflict.[16]

Oshima persuaded von Ribbentrop—whose inclinations were in any case in that direction—that all was going well for Japan in the fighting and that Germany could look forward to wonderful economic prospects in a Japanese-controlled China. Von Ribbentrop transmitted these exciting, even if totally misleading, tidbits to Hitler and Göring. He persuaded these two to reverse Germany's position toward the conflict and secured Hitler's approval of an extension of the Anti-Comintern Pact to include Italy. The opponents of such policies in Germany, the foreign ministry and war ministry, succeeded in temporarily having the policy toward the Sino-Japanese war restored to its former status, and German deliveries to China were continued even after the flurry caused by Hitler's and Göring's actions of 18 October 1937.[17] In regard to the Anti-Comintern Pact, however, von Ribbentrop would get his way in spite of the contrary preferences of the German foreign ministry.[18]

On 18 October, the same day that the order to halt deliveries to China was issued, von Ribbentrop's assistant for East Asian affairs in the *Dienststelle Ribbentrop,* Hans von Raumer, flew to Rome to inaugurate new negotiations for the adhesion of Italy to the German-Japanese Anti-Comintern Pact, a proposal that reached Rome from Berlin at the same time as the Japanese finally responded to Italian pressure for an Italian-

14. See above, pp. 12–13; Sommer, pp. 82–83. Sommer (pp. 99–102) is in my opinion correct in stressing von Ribbentrop's role in pushing for a tripartite alliance as against the thesis of F. C. Jones and Mario Toscano that Japan took the initiative. Toscano's book on the Axis pact will be cited here from the English language version which contains the last revisions he made before his death, *The Origins of the Pact of Steel* (Baltimore: Johns Hopkins University Press, 1967). Although Sommer's book appeared between this version and the last Italian language edition, that of 1956, no account was taken of Sommer's findings.

15. Haushofer to Hess, von Ribbentrop, and von Dirksen, 1 September 1937, *TMWC,* 33:170–74; cf. *G.D.,* C, 6, No. 493. Hsi-huey Liang, *The Sino-German Connection: Alexander von Falkenhausen between China and Germany, 1900–1941* (Amsterdam: Van Gorcum, Assen, 1978), pp. 126–28, 132–33, is based on the von Falkenhausen papers, now in the Bundesarchiv/Militärarchiv in Freiburg.

16. *G.D.,* D, 1, Nos. 479 (note that in this document von Ribbentrop and the Japanese military attaché discussed the inclusion of Poland, not Italy, in the Anti-Comintern alignment), 486.

17. Ibid., Nos. 499, 500, 504; D, 7:521–22; *U.S.,* 1937, 3:625–26; Sommer, pp. 66–67; Nieh, pp. 136–37. It is possible that the propaganda ministry complaints of 16 October 1937 about the pro-Chinese tone of the German press should be seen in this context ("Bestellungen aus der Pressekonferenz," Bundesarchiv, Brammer, Z.Sg. 101/10, f.281).

18. *G.D.,* D, 1, Nos. 9, 488; Sommer, pp. 86–87.

Japanese political agreement by likewise suggesting a three-cornered Anti-Comintern treaty.[19] Oshima had apparently suggested this approach to Tokyo as a fine way out of the dilemma the Japanese had created for themselves by inspiring the Italians to be eager for a treaty with them. With the Italians and the Japanese both willing, and with the genial solution for salving Italy's pride by making her retroactively an "original" signer of the Anti-Comintern Pact, as opposed to a mere adherent to it, the road to the conclusion of a tripartite treaty seemed to be open.

The only remaining difficulty was that von Ribbentrop had failed to inform the foreign ministry about either of the decisions he had secured from Hitler and Göring. The foreign ministry and war ministry had immediately learned of the decision about deliveries to China when Göring ordered them stopped, and they had thereupon obtained a reversal of that action. Hitler's agreement to a tripartite Anti-Comintern Pact came to the foreign ministry's attention only when von Ribbentrop as well as von Raumer suddenly appeared in Rome to negotiate the new pact. There was a violent uproar in which the Italians to their interest and amusement learned that Hitler was fully behind von Ribbentrop's scheme—which he claimed as his own—but would have preferred for von Neurath to have been informed. Once that problem had been settled, the negotiations moved forward rapidly with the formal signing taking place in Rome on 6 November.[20]

The Italians had received some information about the secret protocols to the original German-Japanese agreement but did not become a party to them. Their contribution to the new alignment was instead to take the form of finally officially leaving the League of Nations, as Japan and Germany had done previously.[21] The new association would thereby present, as permanent, a solidarity they had already shown temporarily by all refusing to attend the Brussels Conference that had been called to discuss the Sino-Japanese war.[22] Whether or not the essentially propagandistic alignment of the Anti-Comintern Pact could be transformed, as von Ribbentrop hoped, into a tripartite military alliance for the inevitable war against the Western Powers remained to be seen.[23] Von Ribbentrop would find that the objections of important elements in the Japanese government to an anti-British coalition were not overcome as easily as those of the German diplomats whom Hitler had simply overruled.[24]

19. Toscano, pp. 8–9; Sommer, pp. 67, 86; Drechsler, pp. 62–66; cf. U.S., 1937, 3:612–14.
20. Ciano, Diplomatic Papers, pp. 138–46; Ciano, Diary, 20 October–5 November, passim.; G.D., D, 1, Nos. 10, 14, 17; Eden, pp. 571–72, 607; U.S., Japan 1931–1941, 2:160–61; Dertinger, "Informationsbericht Nr. 153," 2 November 1937, Bundesarchiv, Brammer, Z.Sg. 101/31, ff.347–49; C 7451/270/18, FO 371/20736. In this case, the British knew all about the Italian-Japanese negotiations, having obviously broken one of the relevant codes (F 10344, F 10616/26/23, FO 371/21028; U.S., 1937, 1:617; 3:668–70).
21. Ciano, Diary, 25 October 1937, p. 32. The official exit took place subsequently.
22. G.D., D, 1, Nos. 493–96, 503, 507, 13, 14.
23. Ciano, Diary, 24 October 1937, p. 32.
24. Sommer, pp. 86–93.

But before any thought could be given to more elaborate agreements between the three powers, the situation in the Far East had to be clarified. If even von Ribbentrop with his misplaced confidence in Japan's ability to conquer China realized that the war was weakening Japan, certainly the regular German diplomats could see how the continuation of hostilities sapped the strength of Japan and harmed German interests in China. In view of Germany's close ties to both contending powers, as well as her interest in a peaceful settlement between them, she was both the logical power to suggest mediation to Tokyo and Nanking and the country in which the two contestants might be prepared to confide.

As the war in East Asia continued into the fall and winter of 1937, there was an increasing interest in the possibility of a negotiated peace on both sides. Once the Japanese had surmounted the crisis in their military situation near Shanghai in August, Japanese military leaders became more and more concerned about the possibility of a long war; having defeated the Chinese both in the north and near Shanghai, they could contemplate a settlement without loss of prestige. Efforts had been made by Tokyo to secure a cessation of German military supplies to China, but these had failed as had the hopes for the recall of the German military advisers to Chiang Kai-shek. Although Berlin had instructed the advisers to stay away from the front, their activities were of great help to the Chinese who found their work useful not only in the basic training of officers and soldiers but also in drawing tactical lessons from the fighting in progress.[25] The German government thought it best to leave the advisers in China for the time being, lest they be replaced by Soviet officers and so that they might at an appropriate moment advise Chiang to make peace, as well as preserve the neutral position of Germany with good ties to both contending parties.[26] By this time the Chinese as well as the Japanese were beginning to consider the possibility of a peace settlement.

The fighting had not gone well for the Chinese Nationalist forces; Soviet aid was helpful but not nearly as great as the Chinese had been led to expect; and the Brussels Conference had produced much oratory but no

25. Considerable knowledge of the actual activities of the advisers can be secured from the translations of a series of papers and reports to the Chinese government from the advisers for the period 1937–38 which the United States military attaché Joseph Stilwell obtained early in 1939 and forwarded with his report No. 9766 of 27 April 1939 (National Archives, War Department Records 2009–255). Annotation on one of the documents indicates that Stilwell either translated the documents himself or went over the translations from the original German very carefully. These documents have, to the author's knowledge, not been exploited by students of the Sino-Japanese war; they are briefly cited in Charles F. Romanus and Riley Sunderland, *Stilwell's Mission to China* (Washington: Government Printing Office, 1953), p. 6, n.2, and they are used in Billie K. Walsh's "The German Military Mission in China, 1928–38," *Journal of Modern History,* 46, No. 3 (September 1974), 502–13, a useful but inadequately researched account.

26. *G.D.,* D, 1, Nos. 483, 487, 490, 491, 513, 519, 520. The British not only recognized the strength of the advisers' position with Chiang but feared that German naval advisers might displace their own (F 7911/1079/10, FO 371/21001).

concrete assistance to China's cause.[27] In this situation, the possibility of some accommodation between China and Japan appeared to exist, and the Germans strongly urged both sides to make peace.[28] Japanese Foreign Minister Hirota Koki gave the first set of Japanese terms to German Ambassador Herbert von Dirksen on 3 November 1937; and with von Neurath's transmittal of these for Chiang to Oskar Trautmann, the German ambassador in China, on the same day, the German mediation attempt may be said to have officially started.[29] The details of the negotiations which occupied the rest of 1937 and the first days of 1938 constitute a critical element in the modern history of both China and Japan but are of only tangential concern to the foreign policy of Germany.[30] From the point of view of Berlin, there were one minor and three major concerns.

The minor concern was that of keeping Germany distinct from all other powers as mediators. Berlin was unwilling to be associated in the mediation with Italy—which had already come down openly on the side of Japan.[31] The Germans were equally uninterested in using the visit of Lord Halifax to Germany during the mediation effort to associate Great Britain with themselves in this project.[32] The first of the major concerns was to be certain for Germany to act only as an intermediary, carrying messages back and forth, but never advancing concrete proposals herself. The record bears out German success in this regard. A second major concern was to urge both sides to a conciliatory position, the Japanese to keep their demands moderate, and the Chinese to go as far as possible to meet them. In this regard also the record shows consistent German adherence to such a line. The third, and most important, of the German interests was that the mediation succeed, i.e., that Japan and China reach an accommodation and end the hostilities. On this score, the Germans were unsuccessful.

During the course of the talks, the new military victories of Japan in China in November and December 1937, culminating in the capture of

27. *G.D.*, D, 1, Nos. 484, 492; *U.S.*, 1937, 3:827–28. An excellent account of the Brussels Conference is in Dorothy Borg, *The United States and the Far Eastern Crisis of 1933–1938* (Cambridge, Mass.: Harvard University Press, 1964), chap. 14; see also Lee, chap. 3.

28. *G.D.*, D, 1, Nos. 508–12; Joachim Peck, *Kolonialismus ohne Kolonien* (Berlin-East: Akademie-Verlag, 1961), No. 15; F 9307/9/10, FO 371/20959.

29. *G.D.*, D, 1, Nos. 514 (with an added sentence in Peck, No. 14), 515. On Hirota's role, see Richard Dean Burns and Edward H. Bennett (eds.), *Diplomats in Crisis: United States-Chinese-Japanese Relations, 1919–1941* (Santa Barbara, Calif.: ABC-Clio, 1974), pp. 244–45.

30. Accounts in Nieh, pp. 143–76 (with important evidence from Trautmann's diary); James T. C. Liu, "German Mediation in the Sino-Japanese War, 1937–1938," *Far Eastern Quarterly*, 8, No. 2 (February 1949), 157–81; Jones, pp. 59–70; Presseisen, pp. 124–47; Sommer, pp. 68–82; Peck, passim; Drechsler, pp. 42–48. In addition to the sources cited by these authors, the following documents have been used for the account given here: F 9764/9/10, FO 371/20959; *D.D.F.*, 2d, 8, Nos. 13, 31. Borg, chap. 13, discusses all the mediation efforts of 1937.

31. Ciano, *Diary*, 15 November, 30 November, 26 December 1937, 1 January 1938, pp. 45, 55, 72–73, 77; *U.S.*, 1937, 3:649–50, 788–89.

32. Peck, Nos. 25, 27; cf. *U.S.*, 1937, 3:687–88.

Nanking in mid-December, were used as an excuse to raise the previously communicated Japanese demands, which Chiang had been willing to accept as a basis for negotiations. In a long and bitter internal struggle in Tokyo, the generally perceived pattern of advocacy was reversed. While the Japanese military wanted peace with China on the 3 November terms, Japanese Prime Minister Konoye Fumimaro did not. In lengthy and devious maneuvers, he succeeded in tying the Japanese government to a new set of more extreme terms—which it was neither expected nor hoped that Chiang would accept—and then committed Japan to a course of total war against the Nationalist regime.[33] On 16 January 1938 the government of Japan announced that since the Nationalist regime would not make peace on Japan's terms—which were so harsh that the Germans had at first been hesitant about passing them on—Japan would fight on and would never deal with Chiang Kai-shek.[34] The one time in the decade between 1931 and 1941 that the civilian authorities in Tokyo mustered the energy, courage, and ingenuity to overrule the military on a major policy issue they did so with fatal results—fatal for Japan, for China, and for Konoye himself.

From the point of view of the Germans, the failure of the mediation effort created new problems. The Japanese tactic of changing terms they had previously asked the Germans to recommend to Chiang left a bad taste in the mouths of some German diplomats, but this was of short-term significance. More important was the fact that it left the Germans little choice but to take sides in the Far Eastern conflict.[35] They could try to remain neutral and to protect their interests in China by a gradual withdrawal from an exposed position there, or they could side clearly with either of the two warring powers. Of these three theoretically possible choices, one, namely, siding with China, had been ruled out by Hitler's personal preference for Japan and was, accordingly, never seriously considered. Adherence to an at least ostensible neutral position was advocated most strongly by Oskar Trautmann, the German ambassador in China, and appears to have been in accord with the preferences of von Neurath and von Mackensen, the two top figures in the German foreign ministry in mid-January 1938, as well as von Blomberg, the minister of war.[36] They stressed the maintenance of German interests in China in

33. The best account of this struggle is in Crowley, pp. 358–75. There had been hints of the more moderate view of the military from German sources (see Sommer, p. 73, and the sources cited there, as well as Peck, Nos. 78, 87, 113), but Crowley has been successful in clarifying the issue from Japanese sources. See also Lee, pp. 98–99.

34. Text in *U.S., Japan 1931–1941*, 1:437–38. When the Chinese government asked the Germans to reopen the mediation effort in April 1938, the German government replied by alluding to the Japanese decision not to negotiate with Chiang (Peck, Nos. 130, 131).

35. Note that on 17 January 1938 the German press was instructed to be pro-Japanese—but not anti-Chinese—in the Far Eastern conflict ("Bestellungen aus der Pressekonferenz," 17 January 1938, Bundesarchiv, Brammer, Z.Sg. 101/11, f.35; cf. 26 January, f.55).

36. For von Neurath's views at the time, see his comments to Polish Foreign Minister Beck on 13 January 1938 in *Lipski Papers*, No. 75, and compare with Hitler's confidence in a

what was likely to be a lengthy war; in the area controlled by the Chinese the Germans would be dependent on Chinese good will that could be quickly lost by siding with Japan, while in the area controlled by Japan the Germans as well as others would very likely be squeezed out by the conquerors. There was the further hope of countering Russian and British influence in China. Perhaps most important—though rarely expressed so precisely—was a great doubt that Japan could ever win the sort of victory she was now striving for, a victory that would give Japan complete control rather than a limited sphere of influence in China.[37]

On the other hand were the influences and arguments urging Germany to side openly and fully with Japan as Italy had already done. Herbert von Dirksen, the German ambassador in Tokyo, had argued that Germany should maintain her ties with Nationalist China only as long as there was some prospect of successful German mediation of the hostilities in the Far East. If mediation failed, a clear choice would have to be made; and shortly after the Japanese declaration on 16 January, he urged the German government in a lengthy dispatch to shift all economic interests in China to the northern area dominated by Japan, to recall the military advisers, to cease all military deliveries to China, and to extend formal diplomatic recognition to the puppet state of Manchukuo that the Japanese had formed out of the Manchurian provinces of China.[38] Even before this brief for a pro-Japanese line had reached Berlin on 17 February 1938, German policy was shifting in that direction.

This shift and the decisions implied by it can be understood in terms of the interaction of three elements: the pro-Japanese inclinations of Hitler, the agreement of Hitler and von Ribbentrop that a policy of German expansion in Europe could not count on permanent British acquiescence and therefore required additional means of threatening England, and the coincidence in time of the end of German mediation in East Asia with the personnel changes in Germany's military and diplomatic leadership.

The last of these three, the temporal and personnel factor, is the most obvious. Hardly had the Japanese declared that they would never negotiate with Chiang Kai-shek when von Blomberg was removed as German minister of war. Simultaneous shifts in the German foreign ministry would remove both Foreign Minister von Neurath and State Secretary von Mackensen; at least the former believed that differences of opinion on German policy in East Asia contributed to his dismissal at this

---

Japanese victory expressed to Beck on the following day (ibid., No. 77). These comments are not included in the German records of the conversations (*G.D.*, D, 5, Nos. 28, 29).

37. Indications of these views may be found in *G.D.*, D, 1, Nos. 519, 539, 546; C 7228/3/18, FO 371/20712 (on von Blomberg's views); Peck, No. 66. See esp. the detailed—and prophetic—critique by Trautmann of von Dirksen's advocacy of a pro-Japanese course in *G.D.*, D, 1, No. 573 (cf. Ciano's comments on Trautmann in his *Diary*, 1 January 1938, p. 77).

38. *G.D.*, D, 1, No. 564; cf. ibid., No. 565.

time.[39] There could be no doubt of the pro-Japanese proclivities of von Ribbentrop, the new German foreign minister, whose interest in closer German-Japanese relations went back several years, who was the architect of the German-Japanese Anti-Comintern Pact, and who by all indications approved the appointment of General Eugen Ott, the German military attaché in Tokyo, to the position of German ambassador there primarily in order to pave the way for the promotion of his old friend Oshima Hiroshi in a similar manner from military attaché to ambassador in Berlin.[40]

Von Ribbentrop had secured Hitler's agreement to the tripartite Anti-Comintern Pact as well as a halt in the shipment of military supplies to China as early as October 1937, and only the latter of these decisions had been reversed at the insistence of those who were now relieved of their high positions in the Third Reich. The negotiations on the Anti-Comintern Pact had reopened the question of recognizing Manchukuo, and it was around this symbolic issue that the turn in Germany's East Asian policy first became publicly apparent.[41] On this controversy, also, Hitler favored the Japanese position but had deferred formal action until after the conclusion of Germany's mediation attempt. If his agreement in principle to the recognition of Manchukuo of October 1937 was translated into a public action in February 1938, a new view of Germany's policy toward Japan was the basic reason, even if the end of mediation determined the timing of the formal announcement.

As described in earlier chapters, the British and French idea of a comprehensive European settlement had contemplated colonial and commercial concessions to Germany in exchange for German abstention from aggression in Central and Eastern Europe. All British and French efforts to push these schemes forward in 1937 had foundered on German unwillingness to contemplate any such concession on their part. The attempts of England and France had had, in a sense, the opposite effect of the intended one by encouraging Hitler to take greater risks in the face of such an obvious desire for peace. Nevertheless, the constant reiteration of a wish for Germany to respect the independence of the Central and East European states had shown Hitler and von Ribbentrop that Germany could not expect a free hand in Central and Eastern Europe from the

39. See above, p. 51 and the comments in Ciano's *Diary* for 21 and 24 November 1937, pp. 48–49, 51. It is also noteworthy that von Dirksen alone of those relieved of their posts on 4 February was given a promotion; in his case, ill-health was a genuine reason for removal from Tokyo, and appointment to the embassy in London a real step up in the traditional concept of diplomatic careers. The transfer of von Mackensen to the embassy in Rome, where he remained until 1943, might have been considered a promotion under normal circumstances, but hardly in the Germany of 1938.

40. See Sommer, pp. 107–8.

41. Gerhard L. Weinberg, "German Recognition of Manchoukuo," *World Affairs Quarterly*, 28, No. 2 (July 1957), 157–61. Several of the documents cited there from the German foreign ministry microfilm have since been published—from the German embassy China copies—by Peck. See also *D.D.F.*, 2d, 8, No. 208.

Western Powers; that those countries might acquiesce in what Germany did for fear of war, because of divisions at home, or because of threats to their interests elsewhere; but that there was no hope of positive agreement to German ambitions. It is in this context that Hitler's pro-Japanese views fitted so well with von Ribbentrop's idea of a German-Japanese-Italian alliance that would scare off Great Britain. Threats to her empire all around the globe might make England less willing to impede German expansion in Europe—or force her to face enormous dangers if she were rash enough to challenge a Germany with a Mediterranean and a Pacific ally.[42]

A firm German agreement with Japan, therefore, offered the hope that Britain could be intimidated into noninterference with German expansion on the continent of Europe, it being assumed that France—with her vulnerable Southeast Asian colony of Indochina—would be similarly intimidated, but would in any case not move without firm assurances of British support.[43] As both Hitler and von Ribbentrop contemplated these prospects in the first weeks of 1938, and as Hitler, intending to move soon against the very countries that the proposed general settlement was designed to protect, gave every sign that he would reject any steps toward such a settlement—as the English would learn on March 3—the real choice that the German leaders had to make was whether to make a full change in Germany's East Asian policy and then strive for agreement with Japan or whether to secure a firm commitment from Japan as a condition for the concessions to Japan implied by such a change.

Little is known about the reasons for the decision by Hitler and von Ribbentrop to move toward concessions to Japan without setting any conditions. Von Ribbentrop's specialist on East Asia, von Raumer, claims to have urged the opposite policy and to have broken with von Ribbentrop over this issue.[44] At a discussion within the German foreign ministry on 7 February, possible economic or political concessions to be asked of Japan in exchange for the recognition of Manchukuo were canvassed. Economic demands were dismissed as smacking of "horse-trading" (Kuhhandel); recognition of Germany's colonial claims was rejected as "not very useful"; only Japanese recognition of German expansion in Europe at the expense of Austria and Czechoslovakia looked like useful concessions to request as a security against any possible Anglo-Japanese rapprochement.[45] For several days, this view of the German foreign ministry appears to have been controlling,[46] but no negotiations

42. As indicated before, the British government was acutely aware of this danger. The subject is explored at length with reference to Japan by Lee and with reference to Italy by Pratt.
43. See above, n.14.
44. See Sommer, p. 103, n.3. Note also the contradictory references to this subject in G.D., D, 1, Nos. 523, 526.
45. Weinberg, "Recognition," pp. 160–61.
46. See ibid, p. 161, n.48; Peck, No. 126.

for this or any other concession preceded Hitler's announcement of the recognition of Manchukuo and general declaration in favor of Japan in his speech of 20 February 1938.[47] In notifying the Japanese officially of this step, the Germans expressed the hope that Japan would reward the German action by favorable treatment of German economic interests in Northern China, a hope that would never be realized.

Hitler had decided to go ahead without setting any conditions; one can only speculate that he and von Ribbentrop wanted a closer alignment with Japan, assumed that the Japanese had similar interests, and expected that once Germany had taken the necessary steps to dissociate herself from the League's policy of nonrecognition and to end German support of Chiang Kai-shek, the Japanese government would fall in with their wishes for a closer association to be evidenced by some new treaty of alliance as well as preferential treatment for Germany in Japan's East Asian sphere of influence. The extent to which Hitler and von Ribbentrop discussed these questions is not known. What evidence there is suggests that Hitler, who knew von Ribbentrop as an energetic advocate of the three-power alignment, left to the latter considerable discretion to proceed as seemed best to him. The new East Asian policy was being initiated in the weeks when Hitler was concentrating on the annexation of Austria, and the most far-reaching steps to liquidate Germany's position in China were taken in the subsequent months while the attack on Czechoslovakia was under preparation; it is easy to imagine that Hitler was pleased to be relieved of the lengthy bickering over German policy in East Asia that had obtained previously and was now replaced by von Ribbentrop's single-minded determination to charge ahead. The aura of German-Japanese cooperation which might deter Britain from intervening against German action on Austria and Czechoslovakia was in any case secured for the immediate future by a German policy of one-sided concessions to Japan.

The repeated interventions of Hitler in the disputes over German policy toward East Asia from July 1937 to February 1938 have no parallel in the subsequent months. Since his method of governing included running the details of subjects in which he was very interested, while allowing his subordinates great leeway in other areas—involving himself only when their conflicts of jurisdiction and policy became too urgent to ignore—the general subject of East Asian policy had come before him only intermittently in previous years.[48] Since von Ribbentrop moved forward in the general direction that Hitler wanted, and since the key figures who held different views either had been or soon would be removed from office, the details of German policy probably did not come before Hitler again for months. Nothing suggests that von Ribbentrop reported to Hitler the embarrassing troubles he would soon encounter, contrary to his own

47. Domarus, 1:798–99.
48. Weinberg, *Foreign Policy*, chap. 5.

predictions, in securing economic advantages for Germany in Japanese controlled parts of China.

The warnings of Oskar Trautmann probably never reached Hitler,[49] and anyway, Trautmann was recalled in the dispute over the withdrawal of the military advisers in June 1938. On that subject, Hitler's inclination had in fact been reinforced by the one important member of the German diplomatic corps who agreed with von Ribbentrop's China policy, Herbert von Dirksen, who saw Hitler in April in connection with his transfer from the Tokyo to the London embassy.[50] When the Japanese ambassador in Berlin alluded to von Ribbentrop's personal role in expressing thanks for the German recognition of Manchukuo, therefore, he was correctly interpreting Hitler's decision as one of allowing the new German foreign minister to implement Germany's new policy toward East Asia in accordance with his own judgment.[51]

The fact that the recognition of Manchukuo brought no special advantages to German trade with that area would not discourage von Ribbentrop. The first few months of the difficult negotiations for a friendship treaty and a trade agreement with the puppet state, concluded on 12 May and 14 September respectively—with neither document especially advantageous to Germany—were not taken as a clue to the fate of Germany's future negotiations with Japan.[52] On the contrary, von Ribbentrop persuaded Göring, presumably on the basis of Hitler's wishes, to have deliveries of German war supplies to China halted by a series of directives at the end of April and beginning of May 1938.[53] Because of the associated loss of foreign exchange, Göring was not very enthusiastic about this step. He suggested to Oshima that Japan might help make good Germany's losses, a forlorn hope.[54] More concrete relief for German foreign exchange needs could be expected from the continuation of industrial deliveries to China under HAPRO contracts, though it is doubtful that these could make up for the almost complete termination of arms deliveries.[55]

49. See, e.g., Peck, No. 127; *G.D.*, D, 1, Nos. 566, 567.

50. Interrogation of von Dirksen, 8–13 December 1945, State Department Special Interrogation Mission, National Archives; Dirksen, pp. 209–10.

51. *G.D.*, D, 1, No. 571.

52. See Weinberg, "Recognition," p. 162. The German press was instructed to give the German-Manchukuo agreement of 12 May great publicity ("Bestellungen aus der Pressekonferenz," 12 May 1938, Bundesarchiv, Brammer, Z.Sg. 101/11, f.361).

53. *G.D.*, D, 1, Nos. 576, 579, 581, 594; Sommer, pp. 108–10.

54. Göring to Oshima, 7 May 1938, Emessen, pp. 86–88; Oshima to Göring, ibid., pp. 89–90.

55. Göring's statements are summarized as follows on 2 May: "China-business: Military equipment deliveries which have not yet left a German port are to be held up. The industrial installations signed for via Hapro can continue to be worked on and delivered" (Aktenvermerk über die Besprechung am 2. Mai 1938 von 11:05 bis 12:25, London, Imperial War Museum, Milch Papers, folder 65, frame 7463). On 8 May: "Export . . . . *No* equipment is to be delivered any more" (Ergebnis der Besprechungen beim Herrn Generalfeldmarschall am 8.5.38, ibid., frame 7466).

The very repetition of orders to stop delivery supports the belief that at least some still continued. The assertion of Göring to Sven Hedin in October 1939 that Germany would

In spite of Chiang's strong protests that even the Italians had completed deliveries under existing contracts, the Germans stuck to their abrupt decision, at least formally.[56] Furthermore, von Ribbentrop next proceeded to order the recall of the German military advisers in China.

As long as the German officers who were under various personal contracts with the Nationalist government remained in China, Chiang was careful to restrain press and public reaction to the steps taken by Berlin. In the continuing war with Japan, the advisers were of great help to the Nationalist army, which was, of course, one reason that the Japanese had long been urging their recall to Germany.[57] In May 1938 von Ribbentrop ordered them home, offered to have the German government defray the costs, and threatened dire reprisals if they did not break their contracts and forfeit their livelihood. Chiang was most disturbed, and even Ott agreed with Trautmann that a recall in stages would be preferable to a dramatic breach. Von Ribbentrop, however, was by no means averse to spectacular steps; the man who was later to explain Germany's declaring war on the United States by asserting that it was a mark of great power status for a country to declare war on others rather than have them declare war on it, was quite willing to threaten a rupture of German diplomatic relations with China if the Chinese government did not immediately release the advisers from their contracts and speed them on their way to Germany. In the event, the German ambassador was recalled but diplomatic relations were maintained; the crude procedure employed, moreover, resulted not only in the end of the military advisers' role. Germany's position in China, carefully, laboriously, and successfully built up over a period of two decades, was liquidated by von Ribbentrop in less than six months.[58]

The German hope and expectation had been that they would secure some compensation for the losses in foreign exchange and war materials resulting from the sacrifice of their position in China to the ambitions of Japan by obtaining a special position in the trade and economic re-

---

"now" stop deliveries as reported in Sven Hedin's memoirs (*Ohne Auftrag in Berlin* [Buenos Aires, 1949], p. 49), on which Hartmut Bloss relies in his "Deutsche China-Politik im Dritten Reich" (Funke, p. 423) as evidence that Germany continued to send war materials until the outbreak of war in Europe in 1939 cannot, however, be accepted as controlling. Sven Hedin was strongly pro-Chinese, and Göring may have been trying to please his guest.

56. *G.D.*, D, 1, No. 582; Drechsler, pp. 50–54.

57. For a report by one of the advisers, explaining why he thought China would win, see Dr. Kausch's "Informationsbericht Nr. 45," 16 June 1938, Bundesarchiv, Brammer, Z.Sg. 101/32, ff.409–13.

58. On the recall of the military advisers, see Sommer, pp. 110–15, and the sources cited there; Drechsler, pp. 48–50; Dirksen, p. 210. See also Peck, No. 133; Kausch's "Vertraulicher Informationsbericht Nr. 48: Die zukünftige diplomatische Vertretung des Reiches in China," 15 July 1938, Bundesarchiv, Brammer, Z.Sg. 101/33, f.37; *D.D.F.*, 2d, 9, No. 461; 10, No. 105.

construction of Manchuria and Japanese controlled China. These expectations were disappointed, not only in regard to Manchuria and North China but in the broader field of German-Japanese economic relations as a whole.[59] As von Ribbentrop reminded Japanese Ambassador Togo Shigenori in their discussion of the recognition of Manchukuo that Hitler had announced two days earlier, he had not asked for any concessions from Japan in return; but he did expect the Japanese to recognize Germany's generous action by appropriate conduct on their part.[60] What the Germans wanted was treatment by the Japanese authorities in occupied China that was on a par with the treatment accorded Japanese firms and individuals.

As the German ambassador to China had warned and as the German government was quickly informed, there could be no hope that the Japanese government would seriously consider this possibility. On the contrary, the Tokyo government was hesitant about granting any status to the Germans that was superior to that of third countries—who were all being squeezed out—and merely hoped to use German interest in North China to secure German acceptance of Japanese control there by direct German-Japanese dealings on the specifics of the North China trade.[61] On 20 May 1938 Togo gave von Ribbentrop the text of a proposal outlining the situation that would obtain in Japanese-controlled China. He had received instructions on the subject from Tokyo, and the text clearly rejected the German expectation of a status which, if not one of parity with the Japanese, at least assured a distinct preference over third powers.[62]

When repeated efforts to alter this key factor failed, with Togo refusing to budge in the knowledge of Tokyo's position, von Ribbentrop tried to circumvent him by appealing to his friend Oshima, who promised to try to have the Japanese general staff intervene.[63] This procedure had worked the other way around when Oshima and von Ribbentrop had prepared the Anti-Comintern Pact behind the back of the German foreign ministry, but it did not work now. Von Ribbentrop would have done better to pay attention to Togo, who told him and his subordinates what the real position of Tokyo was, rather than to listen to Oshima, who wanted to be pleasant and helpful but could not bring about the least change in the firm determination of the Japanese government to maintain its position.

59. There is as yet no comprehensive study of this subject for the period 1937–41. Drechsler, pp. 55–60, has some details; Johanna Menzel Meskill, *Hitler and Japan: The Hollow Alliance* (New York: Atherton, 1966), chap. 4, covers the war years; Sommer decided to ignore the subject (p. 116, n.78); Presseisen, pp. 146–47, 156–60, gives an introductory survey. Bloss (Funke, pp. 423–24) asserts that Hitler had already dropped any idea of economic interest in China.

60. *G.D.*, D, 1, No. 571.

61. Ibid., Nos. 573, 575, 581.

62. Ibid., Nos. 587–90.

63. Ibid., Nos. 595, 603.

In a series of increasingly heated conversations in Berlin the negotiations were stalemated over German insistence on a clearly expressed preferential position vis-à-vis third powers that the Japanese government equally adamantly declined to allow.[64] German eagerness for the preferential position was heightened by reports on the actual situation in the areas controlled by Japan. German firms were being pushed out as ruthlessly as British, American, and other non-Japanese interests. Moreover, in their confiscations in China, the Japanese authorities were applying the same procedure that the Germans, as will be shown subsequently, had followed in Austria, namely, seizing the assets but refusing to honor attendant debts, including those to German firms. The fact, of course, was that the Germans had made all the concessions at their disposal to Japan unilaterally and now had no effective way to pressure the Japanese into deviating from their intentions in China. These intentions were obvious to everyone except von Ribbentrop. They aimed at the exclusion of all Western economic interests and activities with the sole exception of importing those items Japan herself needed and exporting those items Japan did not want—with the export-import business conducted by Japanese monopoly organizations. Neither the polite evasions of Togo nor the even more polite pleasantries of Oshima could alter these aims in the slightest.

In the face of such developments, the Germans themselves began to wonder whether a preferential position would in fact do them any good. If all except the Japanese were pushed out, the Germans' own acceptance of the concept that they could not have parity with the Japanese in reality settled the fate of German economic interests in China, and preferences over similarly excluded third powers would have only imaginary significance.[65] Given this assessment of what was really happening—that if all non-Japanese were excluded the relative legal status of those pushed out would make no difference to Germany's foreign exchange earnings—why were the Japanese so obdurate about conceding so worthless a gesture? The answer almost certainly lies, as the Germans suspected, in the reluctance of the Tokyo government to preclude the possibility of an agreement with Great Britain. As long as the Japanese were following the policy of driving *all* Westerners out of China, they could assure the British of equal treatment and commit themselves to give no third power any preference over British trade. The cheap concession of a largely imaginary preference for Germany could, therefore, be made

---

64. Ibid., Nos. 598, 602, 604–6. Cf. Drechsler, pp. 108–12, for 1939 negotiations. The assertion that the Japanese army tried to interest Germany in investing in North China, promising preferential treatment in exchange for German recognition of the special Japanese position, in Lincoln Li, *The Japanese Army in North China, 1937–1941* (Tokyo: Oxford University Press, 1975), p. 137, is contrary to the bulk of the evidence.

65. See the last paragraph of *G.D.*, D, 1, No. 606.

by Tokyo only by forgoing the equally cheap concession of promising no preference for third parties to the London government.[66] In the summer of 1938 the Tokyo government was not prepared to do this. As will be seen, the same reasoning was a determining factor in Tokyo's simultaneous unwillingness to agree to a tripartite military alliance potentially directed against Great Britain that the Germans were also pressing on them. The two sets of negotiations were, in fact, being conducted simultaneously and collapsed temporarily in August 1938 for identical reasons.

If the parallel economic and alliance negotiations of February to August 1938 have not generally been seen in a combined and coherent framework it is because most authors have ignored the economic talks in spite of adequate available evidence, while knowledge of the alliance negotiations has been limited by the dearth of relevant documentation. The German evidence is fragmentary, partly because von Ribbentrop was very secretive about his plans—even toward his own immediate assistants—and partly because some of the relevant files appear to have been destroyed.[67] The Italian archives are still closed, a portion of the record was in any case badly damaged by moisture, and the historian must depend on excerpts and summaries offered by Mario Toscano,[68] the late editor of the appropriate series of Italian foreign ministry documents in which the volumes for 1938 have still to appear. The Japanese diplomatic archives contain relatively little on this subject because a large portion of the negotiations was carried on by Oshima, then still military attaché, and by special courier; as a result much of the evidence from the Japanese side must be gleaned from the testimony of those involved at the Tokyo war crimes trial and from materials in private Japanese archives.[69] If the details of these negotiations are, therefore, still shrouded in some obscurity, the available information does allow us to ascertain the broad outlines of the policies pursued and to place the episode in the context of both German foreign policy and the international diplomatic situation.

The new German foreign minister, in agreement with Hitler, hoped to bring about a closer alignment of Germany with Italy and Japan, but his

66. This admittedly runs counter to the views of Sir Robert Craigie, the British ambassador to Tokyo at the time (see *B.D.*, 3d, 8, No. 99), but Craigie appears not to have known of the stalemate in the German-Japanese negotiations.

67. In addition to the *G.D.*, there are some documents used by Sommer. Useful for the German-Italian aspect of the negotiations is Donald C. Watt, "An Earlier Model for the Pact of Steel: The Draft Treaties Exchanged between Germany and Italy during Hitler's Visit to Rome in May 1938," *International Affairs* (London), 33, No. 2 (April 1957), 185–97.

68. *The Origins of the Pact of Steel*, pp. 6–41 (see above, n.14). Ferdinand Siebert's, *Italiens Weg in den Zweiten Weltkrieg* (Bonn: Athenäum, 1962), ignores the negotiations with Japan before October 1938.

69. The former has been done very well by Sommer (esp. pp. 116–39); the latter is the especial merit of Ohata Takushiro's piece "The Anti-Comintern Pact, 1935–1939," in James W. Morley (ed.), *Deterrent Diplomacy: Japan, Germany, and the USSR, 1935–1940* (New York: Columbia University Press, 1976).

steps to bring this about vis-à-vis Japan in his first months in office were necessarily indirect. As has been shown, in February–May 1938 von Ribbentrop took a series of actions designed to remove Japanese grievances over Germany's ties to Chiang Kai-shek. The evidence suggests that the brusque and abrupt manner in which this was done was due not so much to any special distaste for the Chinese government as to an eagerness to remove the obstacles to an agreement with Japan as quickly and in as conspicuous a manner as possible. In prior years, from his position as foreign policy adviser to Hitler with his own special staff and as ambassador to Great Britain with other official duties and responsibilities, von Ribbentrop had done what he could to further the cause of closer German-Japanese relations. In the process he had been hindered and at times thwarted by others; now that his triumph was complete he hastened to make up for what must have looked to him like lost time. If von Ribbentrop for several months took no actions aimed directly and explicitly toward the alliance with Japan that he had described in January 1938 to Hitler as of critical importance for Germany,[70] this was due to his belief that the obvious obstacles to such an alliance would have to be removed first. The decisions to remove those obstacles had been taken in Berlin by the end of April 1938, though it took two more months to have them fully implemented. It is thus understandable that von Ribbentrop should have turned formally to the question of a closer German-Japanese relationship in May and June, assuming that by this time Germany's conspicuous reorientation of her East Asian policy would be beginning to have some impact on Tokyo.

In the meantime, German actions in Europe had made a prior approach to Italy expedient. Italian acceptance of the annexation of Austria in March 1938 had been welcomed as a sign of true friendship in Germany, where the plans for an attack on Czechoslovakia were maturing and a closer relationship with Italy was seen as one way of forestalling Franco-British intervention against such an attack. The approach made to Italy early in May, when Hitler and von Ribbentrop were in Rome, did not produce a formal agreement. As will be discussed later, the Italians who were upset over the *Anschluss* and anxious about South Tyrol had just signed a new agreement with England and did not think this the right moment for a formal alliance with Germany.[71] Nevertheless, their expression of disinterest in Czechoslovakia encouraged Hitler to move forward.[72] The subsequent crystallization of Hitler's timetable for the attack on Czechoslovakia in mid-May 1938 led von Ribbentrop to return to his concept of a tripartite military alliance against Britain and France that might deter or defeat those powers.

70. *G.D.*, D, 1, No. 93.
71. See Watt, "An Earlier Model"; Sommer, pp. 116–19.
72. See pp. 308–10, 340 below.

In this endeavor, launched in June 1938, von Ribbentrop could be confident of Hitler's support. When the fate of General Ott had been under consideration, Hitler had expressed a desire to speak to him personally if he were to be appointed to a diplomatic post.[73] In view of Ott's previous association with the murdered General Kurt von Schleicher, Hitler's wish is easy to understand. When Hitler saw Ott at the end of May, he explained to the latter that because of the expected British opposition to Germany's conquest of *Lebensraum* in Eastern Europe, it was important to try to shift Japan from an anti-Russian to an anti-British policy. Hitler brushed aside Ott's view that Japan could assist Germany only if she were assured of American neutrality with a disquisition on the weakness and unimportance of the United States.[74] As for the general idea of securing a reorientation of Japan's policy along the lines Hitler desired, Ott reserved judgment. His excellent contacts with Japanese military leaders—a contributory factor to his appointment as ambassador—would presumably prove useful in this project.

Soon after this discussion, von Ribbentrop undertook to sound out both the Italians and the Japanese on a possible three-cornered alliance. On 17 June he touched on the project with Oshima, and on 19 June he discussed it at length with Italian Ambassador Bernardo Attolico.[75] Von Ribbentrop explained his view that only "a plain, open military alliance" would serve to deter England and France from interfering with the ambitions of Germany and Italy; he explained his conviction that Japan would also agree to participate for analogous reasons and informed Attolico that key figures in Japan were being sounded on this possibility. The Italian government was now more favorably disposed to the idea but, having been itself negotiating with Tokyo for closer ties,[76] wanted to know how far Japan really was willing to commit herself to Germany. At the moment, Oshima could give neither Attolico nor von Ribbentrop any information on that score; he was waiting for instructions from Tokyo himself.[77]

73. *G.D.*, D, 1, No. 574.
74. Sommer, pp. 122–23; Erich Kordt, *Wahn und Wirklichkeit: Die Aussenpolitik des Dritten Reiches*, 2d ed. (Stuttgart: Union Deutsche Verlagsgesellschaft, 1948), pp. 141–42. Subsequently, Hitler would somewhat revise his view of the interrelationship of German policy with the potential friction between Japan and the United States. In the summer of 1940 he expressed the view that a German attack on the Soviet Union, by freeing Japan from restraints imposed upon her by worry about her rear, would encourage Japanese expansion which in turn would immobilize the United States vis-à-vis Europe (Halder diary for 31 July 1940 quoted in Weinberg, *Germany and the Soviet Union*, p. 115).
75. On the von Ribbentrop-Oshima meeting we have only a brief German record (*G.D.*, D, 1, No. 595); for the von Ribbentrop-Attolico talk there is some rather misleading information in the German records (ibid., No. 784), but a full report by Attolico quoted and summarized in Toscano, pp. 27–33, with some supplementary details in Massimo Magistrati, *L'Italia a Berlino (1937–39)* (Milan: Mondadori, 1956), pp. 200–203. On the negotiations as a whole, cf. Presseisen, pp. 191–95.
76. The process is easily followed in the Ciano diary, beginning with 26 November 1937.
77. See Attolico's reports of 25 and 30 June and 2 July 1938, cited in Toscano, pp. 34–35.

At the end of June, Oshima received instructions from the Japanese general staff by courier. They included a draft military agreement to be concluded between the Japanese and German armies. The explicit limitation to the respective *armies* should have tipped off the Germans to expect resistance by the Japanese naval authorities to a Japanese commitment to fight Britain alongside Germany, since the burden of such a war would obviously fall on the navy; but this was not of immediate moment because the draft itself was directed solely against the Soviet Union. Similarly, the redrafting that State Secretary von Weizsäcker persuaded Oshima to accept when the latter handed him the text on 28 June still maintained an exclusively anti-Soviet orientation.[78]

Although the Germans used the Japanese proposal to make the Italians think that Japan had already agreed to Germany's concept,[79] von Ribbentrop was in reality dissatisfied with it. The anti-Soviet orientation ran directly counter to his and Hitler's desire to give the pact an anti-British character, and accordingly von Ribbentrop repeatedly explained to Oshima why a pact directed against *all* powers, not just Russia, was essential. As a rejoinder to the Japanese proposal, von Ribbentrop prepared and secured Hitler's approval for a three-power pact.[80] For the maintenance of secrecy, this text was sent to Tokyo by courier, a time-consuming procedure during which von Ribbentrop could pretend to all and sundry that the negotiations were going well and that Japan could be depended upon to side with Germany if the Czechoslovak crisis led to a world war.[81] The reality was quite different, since the new German proposal went beyond an agreement between the two armies and hence had to be submitted to the Japanese government as a whole.

When the Tokyo authorities received the German proposal at the beginning of August, debate immediately concentrated on the implications of an anti-British and possibly anti-American war inherent in the German draft. This was the last thing the Tokyo government wanted when the development of the crisis over Czechoslovakia suggested the real possibility that Germany might soon call on Japan to carry out her obligations under such a treaty.

The war with China had continued inconclusively, and their proud boasts of January were returning to haunt the Japanese leaders. Even more dramatic in its impact on Japanese consideration of their relations with Germany was the fighting with the Red Army at the border between Korea and the U.S.S.R. at Changkufeng (Lake Khasan).[82] Whatever the

78. Both texts in Sommer, pp. 129–30.

79. Ciano, *Diary*, 11 July 1938, p. 193.

80. See Sommer, pp. 130–32; Morley, pp. 50–51, where the text is quoted from Japanese archives.

81. *G.D.*, D, 2, No. 332.

82. On this conflict, see Max Beloff, *The Foreign Policy of Soviet Russia* (London: Oxford University Press, 1949), 2:191–94. There is a good account of the diplomatic negotiations

outcome of the argument over the causes of that incident, there can be no disputing the severity of the fighting and the fact that the agreement between Japan and the Soviet Union which produced a cease-fire on 11 August constituted a definite setback to Japan.

The contrast between Soviet firmness in 1938 and their earlier appeasement of Japanese ambitions by the sale of Russia's interest in the Chinese Eastern Railway to the puppet state of Manchukuo was dramatic. Only a year earlier, in June 1937, the Russians had been most conciliatory in an incident involving some islands in the Amur River.[83] The renewed militancy of the Soviet Union strengthened the desire of all factions in the Japanese government for an agreement with Germany directed against the Soviet Union. Simultaneously, it made the Japanese more cautious about antagonizing Great Britain; there were obvious dangers in adding to a continuing war in China and a threat of war with the Soviet Union the prospect of being precipitated by events in Europe into a war with Great Britain, especially since the latter might well secure the backing of the United States. It ought, therefore, to have been no surprise to the Germans that the instructions sent to Oshima urged a draft so revised as to aim the treaty primarily against the Soviet Union.[84] The Japanese ambassador in Germany, who had found out about the negotiations Oshima was carrying on behind his back with von Ribbentrop, warned against even a limited alliance with Germany and was transferred to Moscow for his pains. Even his replacement by Oshima himself could not, however, alter the basic facts.[85]

These were that Japan was most eager for a strengthening of the Anti-Comintern Pact with its various secret qualifications into a strong and explicit anti-Russian alliance.[86] Such an alliance could serve either to deter the Soviet Union or to strengthen Japan if all-out war between the two powers did start.[87] On the other hand, the very real likelihood that a Japan already engaged in a bitter conflict in China might at any moment find herself in a war with the Soviet Union, whether on the initiative of

---

centering on the role of Shigemitsu Mamuro in Burns and Bennet, pp. 255–67, with extensive notes citing the relevant evidence; for accounts of the conflict itself, see Morley, pp. 140–57; John Erickson, *The Soviet High Command* (London: Macmillan, 1962), pp. 488–99; Alvin D. Coox, *The Anatomy of a Small War: The Soviet-Japanese Struggle for Changkufeng/ Khasan, 1938* (Westport, Conn.: Greenwood, 1977).

83. On this incident, see Beloff, 2:179–80; Morley, pp. 137–40; *D.D.F.*, 2d, 6, No. 217.

84. The text of the instructions of 29 August 1938 is in the Saionji-Harada Memoirs under the date of 15 June 1939 (International Military Tribunal for the Far East, pp. 2554–55).

85. Sommer, pp. 133–39.

86. A picture of the complicated manner in which the secret protocols hollowed out the original German-Japanese Anti-Cominternpact is in Gerhard L. Weinberg (ed.), "Die geheimen Abkommen zum Antikominternpakt," *Vierteljahrshefte für Zeitgeschichte*, 2, No. 2 (April 1954), 193–201.

87. There is a useful account of the arguments in Tokyo in Morley, pp. 52–71.

either party or developing in unintended but inexorable escalation out of some border incident, made the Japanese government all the more reluctant to run still other risks. This meant that Tokyo would continue to push the British and Americans out of their positions in China, but would try to keep that process from becoming an open confrontation.

From the perspective of Tokyo, a clear economic *or* military alliance with Germany could lead to such a confrontation. Knowing how important the British considered their economic interests in China, the Japanese saw the German demand for a legally formulated preferential position in China primarily neither as a means of helping solve Germany's raw materials and foreign exchange needs nor as a real obstacle to the expulsion of all Europeans from Japanese-controlled China. The former problem left them cold, and as for the latter, once they had pushed all the Europeans out, it would make little difference what treaties or promises had been broken in the process.[88] What did matter was that formal Japanese agreement to a preferential position for Germany would be taken by the British as a signal of the end of all hopes for any present or future Anglo-Japanese rapprochement, and this the Japanese did not yet wish to give. If the authorities in Tokyo were unwilling to risk a rupture with Britain on this point, they were naturally even less enthusiastic about an open military alliance directed against "all powers."

From the point of view of Hitler and von Ribbentrop, the prospect of war with the Soviet Union was still remote: Germany had no common border with Russia, and neither did Czechoslovakia. Furthermore, as von Weizsäcker discussed the situation with reference to the purges then going on inside the Soviet Union in a letter at the end of May: "Russia hardly exists in our plans at the moment. As long as Stalin makes himself as useful as he is doing at present, we really need not have any special military worries about him."[89] The main interest of the German government was an alliance against England and France; having sacrificed their position in China to Japan, the Germans believed they had done all they could reasonably be expected to do for Tokyo—maybe more—and hardly thought it their business to support the Japanese in their border troubles with the Soviet Union.[90] The *appearance* of close relations with Japan as well as Italy, with the threats to Britain's world position implied thereby, was quite enough for Berlin, though naturally a strong alliance would have been most welcome.

88. Note the German reaction to the public assertion by the Japanese minister of the interior, Admiral Suetsugo Nobumasa, at the beginning of 1938 that all whites would be expelled from China in "Bestellungen aus der Pressekonferenz," 6 January 1938, Bundesarchiv, Brammer, Z.Sg. 101/11, f.9; Dertinger, "Informationsbericht Nr. 5," 5 January 1938, Z.Sg. 101/32, ff.17–19.
89. Von Weizsäcker to Trautmann, 30 May 1938, *G.D.*, D, 1, No. 586.
90. See the very perceptive "Informationsbericht Nr. 55," of 10 August 1938, in Bundesarchiv, Brammer, Z.Sg. 101/33, ff.71–75.

The eventual peaceful resolution of the dispute over Czechoslovakia appeared to bear out this calculation in spite of the fact that the actual negotiations between Germany and Japan had reached a stalemate in both the economic and military fields. Von Ribbentrop, in any case, believed that Japan's interests coincided with those of Germany and that a new world war would inevitably find them on the same side. If he was partially correct, he would still not succeed in working out a successful timing of the German-Japanese association. Though he resumed his efforts in the fall of 1938, these too, as will be seen, ended in failure. The German leaders wanted to expand Germany in Central and Eastern Europe. When they turned to Italy, the signals were always mixed. In London, they had found the light turned on red; when they looked to Tokyo, all they could see was a hazy yellow. It was not until they squinted toward Moscow that they found a light that was switched to green.

7 Germany, Eastern Europe, Southeast Europe, and the Middle East

n the preceding chapters, the international situation has been described in terms of German plans and preparations for expansion as contrasted with the efforts of Britain and France to avert war, and as affected by the two military conflicts of the time, the Spanish Civil War and the Sino-Japanese war. Before the German moves against Austria and Czechoslovakia are examined, the policy of Germany toward other countries not hitherto discussed will be reviewed. Not only is this necessary for a well-rounded picture of the way Germany moved in the world before the plunge into war, but significant aspects of German policy cannot be understood without such a survey. In some cases, German policy gives clues to long-term hopes, but in many instances the policy adopted by Berlin toward these other countries was very much affected by the desire to secure advantages for immediate goals elsewhere.

For these reasons, scrutiny of Germany's relations with such countries as Poland and Yugoslavia allows considerable insight into Hitler's sense of priorities as well as the way in which German policy tried to take advantage of the ambitions and fears of others. Furthermore, the divergence between Germany's perception of the international situation and that of other governments—with Hungary providing a particularly good example—will assist our understanding of subsequent developments in the relations between Germany and these European countries. Although in the years before the Second World War Germany's role in the Near East was essentially a marginal one, and she would fail entirely in that area during the war, some review of her relations with that portion of the globe is surely a necessary part of the whole story.

The interrelation of different facets of German foreign policy was especially evident in Germany's relations with Poland. Since the complete, even if temporary, reversal in German-Polish relations in 1933–34, the Berlin government had pursued a double line of conduct toward its eastern neighbor. On the most important issues—which meant those defined by Poland as being vital to *her*—the German government had been careful to avoid pushing Warsaw too far.[1] The cover for new policies at home and abroad which was provided for Hitler by the rapprochement with Poland was too valuable to give up yet. Accordingly, whenever the second political line, the nazification of the Free City of Danzig looking toward its eventual absorption by Germany, involved steps that Poland saw as excessively threatening, the German government pulled back and ordered the Danzig authorities to make such adjustments in their procedures as would satisfy Poland's concern for her own interests in the Free City.

The long-range thinking of Poland's leaders about the future of Danzig was not clear either to the Germans at the time or to historians subsequently. The special interest of Polish Marshal Edward Rydz-Śmigły in Danzig has been properly stressed by scholars who have examined the issue,[2] and his key role in post-Pilsudski Poland lent great weight to his views that were known in Berlin.[3] There are, on the other hand, various indications to suggest that Polish Foreign Minister Josef Beck was not nearly as certain of the importance of Danzig to Poland, hoped that in some way Polish leadership of a group of nations from the Baltic to the Black Sea could compensate for the prestige loss of a change in the status of Danzig, and was prepared to consider at some future time either a German-Polish condominium over Danzig or a partition of the territory of the Free City, with the latter procedure returning the city of Danzig and the bulk of the population to Germany while leaving the western third of the area to Poland.[4] The very fact that he was so closely associated personally with the rapprochement with Germany, however, made Beck, who knew how unpopular this policy was in Poland, particularly sensitive to German initiatives in Danzig that could be interpreted within Poland as resulting from his policy. For him, therefore, as well as others in the clique that governed Poland in the name of the deceased Pilsudski, Danzig was the barometer of German-Polish relations, and the maintenance of

1. Weinberg, *Foreign Policy*, pp. 57–74, 184–94, 302–10.
2. Anna M. Cienciala, *Poland and the Western Powers, 1938–1939* (London: Routledge & Kegan Paul, 1968); Hans Roos, *Polen und Europa; Studien zur polnischen Aussenpolitik 1931–1939* (Tübingen: Mohr, 1957); Marian Wojciechowski, *Die polnisch-deutschen Beziehungen 1933–1938*, trans. Norbert Damerau (Leyden: Brill, 1971).
3. See *G.D.*, C, 6, No. 59; and Hitler's telling Lipski in November 1937 to be sure to inform the marshal of his statements on Danzig (*Lipski Papers*, No. 73; *Szembek Diary*, 5 November 1937, p. 247).
4. The author summarized the evidence on this issue available at the time in "A Proposed Compromise over Danzig in 1939?" in *Journal of Central European Affairs*, 14, No. 4 (January 1955), 334–38; see now also *G.D.*, D, 7, No. 59; Cienciala, pp. 239–40. Ludwig Denne's superficial book, *Das Danzig-Problem in der deutschen Aussenpolitik 1934–39* (Bonn: Röhrscheid, 1959), ignores the subject.

Polish rights there a requirement of Polish as well as an indicator of German foreign policy.[5]

If Polish rights in Danzig constituted a subject that German initiatives might attempt to limit but could not terminate, the borders of the Corridor and Upper Silesia were obviously untouchable. On this subject all Poles were known to be in agreement, and Berlin would refrain from any questioning of the status quo. Hitler affirmed in public his belief that Poland needed an access to the sea, and he made similar statements to diplomats who might be expected to pass on their information to Warsaw.[6] Outstanding issues affecting current direct German-Polish relations, especially those concerning transit traffic across the Corridor and German-Polish trade, were settled in a series of successful negotiations in the winter of 1936–37; and although some important concessions were made in these by Poland, they also marked a further step away from the trade war that had once poisoned relations between the two countries.[7] On the basic issue of the German-Polish border, Göring was in Warsaw in February 1937 to reassure the Polish leaders that Germany had no desire for territorial revision and himself to hear assurances of Poland's adherence to the policies of Marshal Pilsudski.[8] Hitler, furthermore, repeated Göring's pledges when he received Polish Minister of Justice Witold Grabowski on 11 May 1937.[9]

The maintenance of good relations with Poland, moreover, limited the extent to which the German government could intervene in the fate of the remaining German minority inside Poland. It is true that the attitude of deference did not go to the same extreme as in the case of first Italy and later the Soviet Union where the German government agreed to the physical transfer of the people of German descent across the boundary.

5. A sign of Beck's own views of Danzig as less critical to Poland in the long run can be seen in his restraint toward the persistence with which Polish Ambassador Lipski pushed for a new German declaration on Danzig in 1937; Beck could not, of course, afford to appear uninterested in the subject at the time just as he could not reveal his real thoughts on this touchy issue in his memoirs.

6. This was presumably the purpose of Hitler's comments to the Rumanian minister on 20 November 1936 (*Lipski Papers*, No. 61; cited in Josef Beck, *Dernier rapport, politique polonaise, 1926–1939* [Neuchâtel: Editions de la Baconnière, 1951], p. 24, n.1).

7. On these negotiations, see the memorandum, seen by Göring, "Deutsch-Polnische Wirtschaftsverhandlungen," 2 December 1936, T-120, 2621/5481/E 382280–82; "Sitzung des Handelspolitischen Ausschusses vom 9. Februar 1937," T-120, 2612/5650/H 004102–4; "Bestellungen aus der Pressekonferenz," 17 December 1936, Bundesarchiv, Brammer, Z.Sg. 101/8, f.427; *G.D.*, C, 6, Nos. 106, 147; Kennard dispatches 6E of January 4 and 45E of 27 January 1937, C 169, C 754/30/18, FO 371/20717.

8. *Szembek Diary*, 16 February 1937, pp. 221–23; *Lipski Papers*, pp. 286–87; *G.D.*, C, 6, No. 227; Slávik reports 2220 of 19 February and 2674 of 2 March 1937, Czechoslovak documents in T-120, 1041/1809/413765–66 and 413767–68; Cudahy dispatch 1530 of 1 March 1937, State 760c.62/332; Wojciechowski, pp. 329–31; *D.D.F.*, 2d, 4, No. 461; 5, No. 9 (note that a leak from Paris of information the Poles had given the French encouraged the Poles to be even more secretive with their French ally, ibid., 5, No. 44).

9. *Szembek Diary*, 21 May 1937, pp. 230–31; *Lipski Papers*, p. 287; Wojciechowski, p. 339; Domarus, 1:693.

Nevertheless, the nationalistic and revisionist agitation of the pre-1933 period had given way to severe restrictions on the German press internally and cautious complaints to the Polish government externally. During 1937 this attitude of restraint was reinforced not only by broader political considerations which dictated good relations with Poland while Germany was preparing to move against Austria and Czechoslovakia but also by the special danger to a portion of the German minority resulting from the expiration of the Geneva Convention of 1922 that was scheduled to take place in July 1937.

This convention had been signed as a part of the settlement of the division of Upper Silesia between Germany and Poland following a plebiscite in the area. For a period of fifteen years it provided for extensive special protection for minorities on both sides of the new border.[10] In the period since Hitler came to power, international attention had been drawn to the convention in connection with an appeal to the League of Nations from the Jewish community in German Upper Silesia, an appeal generally referred to as the Bernheim case.[11] While the German government was eager to limit the application of the convention on German territory as much as possible, it had been happy to utilize the provisions of the convention to protect the German minority in the portion of Upper Silesia allocated to Poland. The approaching expiration of the convention was, therefore, contemplated in Berlin with a mixture of glee and apprehension—glee over the imminent possibility of subjecting German Upper Silesia's few hundred Jews to the same indignities already being visited on other German Jews, apprehension for the rights of the many thousands of German-speaking people in what the German documents sometimes refer to as "East Upper Silesia."

Within the German government, discussions on how to protect the German minority began in January 1937,[12] and von Neurath raised the subject with Beck when the latter stopped briefly in Berlin on 20 January 1937.[13] The Polish government, which had repudiated the League's role in the minorities problem earlier, was not in the least eager for a new treaty; and Beck at this meeting indicated a willingness to consider a number of technical questions in regard to the railways and mines of the region but coupled this with a clear hint that no new treaty about minority rights would be welcomed by Poland. The Germans, however, thought the issue

10. Though dated in parts, the best survey of the topic remains Georges Kaeckkenbeek, *The International Experiment in Upper Silesia: A Study in the Workings of the Upper Silesian Settlement, 1922–1937* (Oxford: Oxford University Press, 1942). K. had served as arbitrator under the terms of the convention. The broader issues are handled in Harald von Riekhoff, *German-Polish Relations, 1918–1933* (Baltimore: Johns Hopkins University Press, 1971).

11. An excellent account may be found in Eliahu ben Elissar, *La diplomatie du IIIe Reich et les Juifs (1933–1938)* (Paris: Juilliard, 1969).

12. Material is to be published as *G.D.*, C, 6, No. 134.

13. The Polish record is in *Lipski Papers*, No. 64; the German record will appear as *G.D.*, C, No. 148; cf. Wojciechowski, pp. 356–57.

of great importance and began to urge the Polish government to agree to such a treaty, simultaneously instructing the German press to maintain a moderate tone on the matter.[14] The German soundings met with a firm refusal in Warsaw, and Beck personally declined any bilateral minorities agreement.[15] In the face of this situation, the German authorities turned to a different approach. If Poland would not agree to a special treaty—presumably limited in its application to the area covered by the Geneva Convention of 1922—there was no means at hand to pressure her into it. On the other hand, desire to avoid a deterioration of relations with Germany and the hope of providing assistance to the large Polish minority in Germany might induce Warsaw to issue a governmental policy declaration to protect the rights of the German minority in Poland, with the German government promising to issue simultaneously an analogous declaration concerning the Polish minority in the Third Reich. If less binding than a treaty, such a declaration would be of broader territorial applicability and might serve to restrain local Polish authorities in their actions. After considerable internal discussion, Hitler approved this approach to the problem; and Hans Adolf von Moltke, the German ambassador to Poland, was instructed to ask Beck in Hitler's name to agree either to a new bilateral treaty or to separate governmental declarations.[16]

At the beginning of June 1937 the Polish government, after some internal discussion of the matter, told the Germans that a bilateral treaty was definitely out of the question but that they were prepared to consider favorably parallel policy declarations by the two governments.[17] The Germans thereupon began to transmit proposed texts to Warsaw, but there was no possibility of agreement before the Geneva Convention expired in July.[18] Although there is no direct evidence on the point, it would appear that this was not unwelcome to the Polish government since it improved their negotiating position. When the convention expired on 14 July, only minor technical agreements, dealing primarily with railway problems, had been signed; the major issue of the minorities was still open, and the Germans had to be exceedingly careful lest publicity or diplomatic pressure on their part provoke a reaction from which only the German minority in Poland would suffer.[19] Furthermore, the Poles now

14. *G.D.*, C, 6, Nos. 176, 194, 222, 277; *Szembek Diary*, 8 April 1937, pp. 224–25; "Bestellungen aus der Pressekonferenz," 19 March, 22 March, 15 April 1937, Bundesarchiv, Brammer, Z.Sg. 101/9, ff.219, 223, 279. Cf. *D.D.F.*, 2d, 5, No. 135; Slávik report 31 of 12 April 1937, Czechoslovak document in T-120, 1041/1809/413777–78. The whole subject is reviewed surprisingly briefly in Wojciechowski, p. 333, n.3.

15. *G.D.*, C, 6, No. 327.

16. Ibid., Nos. 331, 392–94.

17. Ibid., Nos. 402, 408.

18. Ibid., Nos. 432, 433, 435, 439; *Lipski Papers*, No. 65. Günter Wollstein's reference to a German-Polish minorities agreement of 5 July 1937 (Funke, p. 607, n.22) is based on a misunderstanding.

19. See *Szembek Diary*, 2 July 1937, pp. 232–33; "Bestellungen aus der Pressekonferenz," 4 June, 28 July 1937, Bundesarchiv, Brammer, Z.Sg. 101/9, f.407, and 101/10, f.61; but note *G.D.*, C, 6, No. 490.

used their stronger bargaining position to tie the minorities question to another issue: when Beck gave von Moltke the Polish counterdraft of a minorities declaration on 30 July, he also suggested that there be a joint declaration reaffirming the status quo in Danzig.[20] The negotiations over this combination of problems would drag on for more than three months, with Hitler eventually overruling the German foreign ministry and making a statement on Danzig; but this process cannot be properly analyzed unless the situation in Danzig and the attitudes toward the Free City of Hitler and the German foreign ministry are first placed in perspective.

German-Polish relations ought really not to have been troubled by the Danzig problem during 1937–38. The crisis over this in the summer and fall of 1936 had apparently been settled to the satisfaction of both parties. The Poles had succeeded in maintaining their rights in the Free City as well as its special international status, while the Germans could rejoice—though not too conspicuously—about the replacement of Sean Lester by Carl J. Burckhardt as the League's high commissioner in Danzig.[21] This change was both explicitly and implicitly a German triumph; Lester's attempts to maintain the constitution of the Free City had cost him the enmity of both the National Socialist leaders and Germany's diplomats. His removal, accompanied by instructions to his successor to exercise the greatest restraint and to try to mute rather than to hinder the nazification of the Free City should have opened a new era in Danzig in which the local National Socialist officials could ride roughshod over constitutional niceties as long as they neither made too much noise nor interfered too clearly in Polish rights. Because of Polish concern over a direct confrontation with Germany in Danzig questions, the position of high commissioner, which the British would as soon have dropped altogether, was maintained, but in a manner calculated to be satisfactory to Germany as well.[22] In addition to the settlement of the major double problem of the relationship of Danzig to the League and the appointment of a high commissioner, there had been a successfully completed series of complicated negotiations between Poland and Danzig on a variety of special and technical questions. Although it had looked for a moment as if

20. There is a reference to this meeting in *G.D.*, D, 5, No. 1, n.2; the full text of von Moltke's report will appear as *G.D.*, C, 6, No. 501.

21. See Weinberg, *Foreign Policy*, pp. 302–9. The instruction to the German press to restrain its joy over the Burckhardt appointment is in "Bestellungen aus der Pressekonferenz," 15 February 1937, Bundesarchiv, Brammer, Z.Sg. 101/9, f.131. For Poland's concentration on her own rights to the exclusion of all concern for the League's guarantee of the constitution, see *D.D.F.*, 2d, 8, No. 29.

22. For a review of the negotiations, see the "Memorandum by U.K. Delegation at Geneva: Free City of Danzig, Consideration of Danzig Affairs by the Council of the League of Nations in January 1937," C 1139/5/55, FO 371/20757. See also *G.D.*, C, 6, Nos. 140, 148, 158, 163, 165, 208; *Lipski Papers*, No. 64; Gallman (Danzig) dispatch 324 of 13 January, Gilbert (Geneva) tel. 45 of 27 January, and Cudahy dispatch 1480 of 29 January 1937, State 860K.00/274, 276, 280; Slávik report 5 of 2 February 1937, Czechoslovak document in T-120, 1041/1809/413758–59; C 1756, C 1781, C 1782/5/55, FO 371/20757.

these might produce serious German-Polish friction, by the end of January 1937 agreement had been reached between Danzig and Polish authorities.[23]

The new high commissioner, moreover, understood that his task was to be a conciliatory one. He would protect the Danzig opposition parties and the Jewish population as much as possible, but this was to be done with a minimum of friction and publicity. In other words, he was to make the inevitable as noiseless and painless as possible; and Burckhardt went about this role to the satisfaction of the Germans as well as the Poles and a special League committee consisting of the foreign ministers of England, France, and Sweden.[24]

If there were problems in Danzig in spite of all these auspicious developments, the explanation lies in the interaction of conflicting personalities in Danzig with contradictory policy impulses from the German government. The nominal head of the Danzig government was Arthur Greiser; the head of the National Socialist party was Albert Forster. The two could not abide each other, and the very fact that both were faithful followers of Hitler only made them rivals for the latter's affection and support. What one wanted, the other automatically rejected, and vice versa; only the occasional intervention of Hitler himself could bring them temporarily to the same course—until they parted company again on the next issue. Both wanted to return Danzig to the Reich and looked forward to successful careers in the party as a whole, as distinct from any local ambitions for Danzig itself. There was, nevertheless, a difference in temperament and perception between them which tended to determine which course each followed in regard to current problems. Forster, probably closer to Hitler personally, was a man of extremely violent temperament who did not particularly care about the day-to-day concerns of the people of Danzig. Greiser, always a trifle insecure about his relationship with Hitler, was a more restrained and thoughtful person with some interest in the impact of policy decisions on the life of the Danzig population.[25] Thus Forster was inclined to wild speeches, impetuous acts, and political experimentation regardless of the consequences, while Greiser leaned more to a cautious step-by-step approach to the nazification of Danzig. If Forster was eager to run risks, Greiser was more reluctant; and this difference was productive of perpetual turmoil in part because it was nourished rather than attenuated by the German government, which tended to speak to both of

23. On these problems and negotiations, see *G.D.*, C, 6, Nos. 28, 30, 63, 77, 100, 112, 117, 125, 140, 148, 158; *Lipski Papers*, No. 64; *Szembek Diary*, 4 December 1936, p. 218; "Anweisungen aus der Pressekonferenz," 8 December 1936, Bundesarchiv, Brammer, Z.Sg. 101/8, f.395.

24. *G.D.*, C, 6, Nos. 273, 303, 320; C 1756, C 1781, C 1782/5/55, FO 371/20757.

25. These contracts are drawn from the memoirs of Burckhardt and the reports of the various diplomats stationed in Danzig. They apply to the period up to the outbreak of war and do not necessarily apply to the respective wartime careers in occupation administration of the two men.

them on Danzig questions in three different tones: those of the foreign ministry, those of Hitler, and those of Göring.

The German foreign ministry officials were interested in a reasonably quiet short-term policy and, therefore, usually sided with Greiser in the continuing rivalry over specific actions to be taken in the Free City. In line with their traditional approach calling for a revision of the Versailles settlement as the proper aim of German foreign policy, they were, however, opposed both to concessions to Polish interests within Danzig and to any German action that might imply a reaffirmation of the legal status of the territory. Hitler's line was in general quite different. He was willing to have Forster try for short-term gains in Danzig as long as these did not create any problems for Hitler's broader aims. These, in turn, went infinitely beyond the revisionist views of the foreign ministry which he had ridiculed in *Mein Kampf* and in his second book and which looked to enormous additional living space in the east, something that was assuredly not to be found in the minuscule area of the Free City. If necessary, therefore, he was quite willing to give whatever formal reassurances might be needed to keep Poland quiet while he laid the foundations for an expansionist program that dwarfed the limited ambitions of his diplomats—and would require the breach of all reassurances at a time of his choosing. In the day-to-day affairs of the Free City, the foreign ministry was accordingly more conciliatory to Polish wishes than Hitler; in the intermediate span of commitments for a year or two, Hitler was more conciliatory than his diplomats; in the long run, however, Hitler took the most extreme view of all. He knew that he could depend on both Forster and Greiser to carry out his wishes and was content to let them feud with each other along the way. As for Göring, he had made relations with Poland one of his own special interests. Having visited Poland several times in Hitler's behalf, and personally well acquainted with Josef Lipski, the Polish ambassador to Berlin, Göring at least for a time looked on good relations with Poland as a personal policy the way von Ribbentrop identified himself first with a German tie to Japan and later to the Soviet Union.[26] On several occasions, therefore, Göring tried to mend local fences broken by Forster, attempted to move Forster to another assignment where his fence-breaking proclivities could be controlled more easily, and generally took a friendly view of Polish concerns.

It was in this confusion of rivalries and differing policy views that Forster wanted to push forward the nazification of Danzig, a process that involved incidents in Danzig and attracted world attention because of the relationship of the Free City to the League. Of these incidents, the one that received the most attention was the murder in 1937 of the leader of the Danzig Socialist party, Hans Wiechmann, right after he had seen the high commissioner. Although at first denied by the National Socialists,

26. Note Göring's comments to Bullitt in November 1937, *U.S.*, 1937, 1:172.

this Danzig equivalent of the Mateotti case—in which Mussolini had let the leader of Italy's Socialists be murdered a decade earlier—both discouraged any other contacts between the Danzig opposition and the high commissioner and focused public interest in England on the Danzig situation. Other incidents provoked by Forster, including plans to change the Danzig flag and to take various unconstitutional measures against the opposition parties and Jews in the Free City, kept the situation there boiling. Burckhardt attempted to restrain Forster by personal contact; the Polish government became increasingly worried; and Hitler finally intervened in July to restrain his overexuberant follower.[27] Since Hitler and Forster had met in late April, just before the new incidents, Hitler's orders not to change the Danzig constitution at this time must have seemed like a very slight tap on the wrist by Forster, who muted his antics but little.

Under these circumstances, the Germans had no reason to be surprised, as they claimed to be, when the Polish government took advantage of its strong negotiating position on the minorities question to raise the subject of a German declaration reaffirming the international status of Danzig. The possibility of the complete withdrawal of the League from Danzig was a contributing factor in bringing on this request,[28] but even that danger would not have forced a Polish move had not the constant agitation in Danzig suggested the risk of Poland's being faced by a fait accompli of some sort in the Free City. Ambassador Lipski took an especially active part in the attempt to secure a statement from the German government. He discussed the subject with von Moltke when the latter was temporarily in Berlin, and urged the Polish government to make the minorities declaration conditional on German compliance with this request.[29]

The negotiations on minorities and Danzig thus came to be joined in fact, if not legally. The view of the German foreign ministry was as its past position might lead one to expect. They would bargain hard over the text of a minorities declaration, making such concessions on this subject as might be needed to secure agreement; various Polish suggestions as to how the declarations by both sides might be made appropriately solemn and conspicuous were eventually agreed to. On the topic of Danzig, however, von Neurath was absolutely adamant. Von Moltke was instructed to

27. On these events, see *G.D.*, C, 6, Nos. 233, 340, 366, 379, 383, 389, 400, 411, 412, 419, 436, 447, 462; *Szembek Diary*, 8 and 10 May 1937, p. 227; Denne, pp. 77–90; Roos, pp. 295–98; Buckhardt, chaps. 3 and 4; Gallman dispatch 387 of 21 July 1937, State 860K.00/298; Lane to Roosevelt, 12 July 1937, Hyde Park, PSF Poland; Dr. Kausch, "Informationsbericht Nr. 90," 21 May 1937, Bundesarchiv, Brammer, Z.Sg. 101/30, ff.437–41; C 3893/3/18, FO 371/20711; C 3592, C 3905/5/55, FO 371/20757; C 5151/5/55, FO 371/20758.
28. Beck appears to have worried about the fate of Danzig in connection with the possibility of a new Locarno agreement. See Wojciechowski, pp. 343–68; *G.D.*, C, 6, Nos. 29, 533; *Szembek Diary*, 15 November 1936, pp. 216–17; *U.S.*, 1937, 1:120–21; C 4382, C 4751/1/18, FO 371/20708.
29. *Lipski Papers*, Nos. 66, 67.

tell Beck that the German government accepted the reality of the Free City and had no intentions of changing its status, but that a public declaration to this effect was out of the question. Such a declaration would be a voluntary reaffirmation of a portion of the Versailles settlement, something that von Neurath—who took such policy statements seriously—resolutely opposed. When Lipski tried to secure Göring's support in the face of the rebuff, the latter's inclination to agree with Lipski was thwarted by von Neurath's opposition. As Lipski continued to insist, the German foreign minister told him that the day would come when Danzig would have to be returned to Germany.[30]

Although the evidence suggests that Beck was less interested than Lipski in extracting a declaration on Danzig, the very fact that the issue had been pushed for so long now made him argue for it—while demonstrating his desire for continued good relations with Germany by disclaiming any formal connection between it and the minorities declaration. Under these circumstances, Hitler dropped his earlier reluctance, agreed to the inclusion of a reference to Danzig in the communiqué to be published along with the minorities declaration, and thus overruled his foreign minister. In fact, he would go even further and include in his speech of 20 February 1938 a eulogy to the wonderful state of German-Polish relations, with the marvelous situation of harmony in Danzig being held up by the Führer as an example for all.[31]

If one seeks the reasons for this willingness of Hitler to make a major concession to Poland, the dates of the two public pronouncements may unwittingly provide a significant clue. The date when Hitler received Lipski and representatives of the Polish minority in Germany for the declarations on minorities rights and Danzig, 5 November 1937, was also the day on which he told his key advisers in the secret conference recorded in the Hossbach memorandum about his intentions to move in the near future to the annexation of Austria and the destruction of Czechoslovakia. The speech of 20 February 1938, in which Hitler praised the wisdom of Poland's leaders and the happy situation in Danzig, was also the speech in which he spoke of the millions of Germans in Austria and Czechoslovakia whose fate was of great concern to him. Hitler's desire to maintain the benevolent neutrality of Poland toward his Austrian and

30. *G.D.,* C, 6, Nos. 513, 515, 530, 535, 537, 540, 541, 548; D, 5, Nos. 1, 2, 6–13; *Szembek Diary,* 25 August–4 October 1937, pp. 234–43 passim; *Lipski Papers,* Nos. 68–70; Dertinger, "Informationsbericht Nr. 130," 2 September 1937, Bundesarchiv, Brammer, Z.Sg. 101/31, f.205; Slávik report 62 of 28 August 1937, Czechoslovak document in T-120, 1041/1809/413817–18.

31. On the final stages of the negotiations and the relevant texts, see *G.D.,* D, 5, Nos. 13, 16, 18, 19; *Lipski Papers,* Nos. 70–73; Roos, pp. 298–301; Wojciechowski, p. 334; Richard Breyer, *Das Deutsche Reich und Polen* (Würzburg: Holzner, 1955), pp. 216–19, 297–331; "Bestellungen aus der Pressekonferenz," 5 and 8 November 1937, Bundesarchiv, Brammer, Z.Sg. 101/10, ff.329, 337; Slávik reports 79 and 80 of 9 and 13 November 1937, Czechoslovak documents in T-120, 1041/1809/413825–29; C 7684/372/18, FO 371/20744; *D.D.F.,* 2d, 7, Nos. 21, 214, 266.

Czechoslovak policies was presumably the key element in his decision to make the gesture that his foreign policy advisers had rejected.[32]

Whether or not this sort of gesture was worth anything is, of course, another matter entirely. In the short run, all it meant was that Hitler would restrain Forster's plans for the nazification of Danzig and the persecution of its Jews for a few months, though the leeway given Forster within these restraints was very considerable indeed. At their meeting in September 1937 Hitler had told Burckhardt, after long diatribes against the British and their interest in Danzig, that Forster would be told to hold back; and in the face of Polish protests over incidents in October and November the brakes were again applied from Berlin; but all of this represented not a change of policy but a temporary adjustment of approach.[33] Forster was told by Hitler that the Danzig situation had to be kept quiet for a little while longer because the Reich had to concentrate its immediate energies on Austria.[34] Forster himself was to make a goodwill visit to Poland.[35] As for the long run, Burckhardt for one was most dubious about the maintenance of the Free City; he felt that the Poles had undermined the League's role there and that Danzig was already practically a part of Germany.[36] Nothing suggests that Hitler seriously intended to adhere to his promises: he planned to move against Poland later and would then explain that Danzig was an issue of no importance. He wanted living space in the east, and the Danzig issue was as inconsequential in this regard in 1937 and 1938 as he would declare it to be in 1939.[37] As for promises of good treatment for minorities, it is as astounding as it is sad that anyone should have taken them seriously. Hitler would make his real opinion of the Poles explicit in 1939: they were to be "destroyed and exterminated."[38]

If the Polish government attached considerable value to German promises all the same, major reasons were fear of Germany combined with a lack of interest in the fate of Austria and a hope that German ambitions

32. Cf. *Szembek Diary*, 19 December 1937, p. 262.
33. On Burckhardt's role at this time, his meeting with Hitler, and his shielding of National Socialist activities in Danzig from scrutiny in Geneva, see *G.D.*, C, 6, Nos. 522, 531, 538; D, 5, Nos. 3–5, 668; *D.D.F.*, 2d, 6, No. 464; Burckhardt, pp. 97–103; Gallman dispatch 405 of 30 August 1937, State 860K.01–High Commissioner/41; Dertinger, "Informationsbericht Nr. 158," 8 November 1937, Bundesarchiv, Brammer, Z.Sg. 101/31, ff.383–87; C 6547, C 7394 (including Burckhardt's report on his 20 September meeting with Hitler), /5/55, FO 371/20758.
For National Socialist forward moves in Danzig, see *G.D.*, C, 6, No. 545; D, 5, Nos. 669, 15, 17, 24; C 7336/5/55, FO 371/20758; C 7966, C 8088/5/55, FO 371/20759; C 8384/165/18, FO 371/20733.
34. Gallman dispatch 439 of 16 November 1937, State 860K.00/315.
35. *Lipski Papers*, No. 74.
36. Slávik report 77 of 7 November 1937, Czechoslovak document in T-120, 1041/1809/413821–22 (an excerpt in Berber, pp. 80–81); cf. *D.D.F.*, 2d, 7, No. 155.
37. See below, p. 000.
38. Helmuth Groscurth, *Tagebücher eines Abwehroffiziers 1938–1940*, ed. Helmut Krausnick and Harold C. Deutsch (Stuttgart: Deutsche Verlags-Anstalt, 1970), p. 202.

might be satiated at the expense of Czechoslovakia.[39] There was, furthermore, doubt about the firmness of Britain and France in the face of German ambitions.[40] Poland would try to build up her own strength, as far as possible with French assistance,[41] and hoped to improve her diplomatic position by closer ties with Rumania and Hungary, however much this was complicated by the hostility between these two.[42] In any case, joining in resistance to Germany involved enormous risks, while standing aside might offer opportunities for Polish gains.[43] As will be seen, both the *Anschluss* of Austria and the imposition of territorial concessions on Czechoslovakia at Munich led to Polish advances. Whether these were worth making in the circumstances will long remain a subject of dispute. It should be noted, on the other hand, that Beck was as determined now as he had been earlier and would continue to be in 1939 that Poland should not become a German satellite. He would neither join the Anti-Comintern Pact nor establish any other formal ties with Germany.[44]

In the months after the minorities declarations of November 1937 German policy toward Poland continued to be determined by essentially the same factors as during the preceding year. Needless to say, the public declarations of Berlin and Warsaw did not end the minorities issue. Each side continued to complain to the other about instances of mistreatment and discrimination.[45] The Polish government had agreed to make a declaration in part in order to preclude having its German minority discussed publicly in Germany and elsewhere in the same context as the German minority in Czechoslovakia.[46] If the actual treatment of the German minority in Poland remained considerably worse than that of the Sudeten Germans, Berlin continued to be restrained in its interventions with the Warsaw authorities lest Poland be pushed into a common front with Czechoslovakia; the exigencies of the moment suggested the wisdom of restraint to both.

39. See *D.D.F.*, 2d, 4, Nos. 18, 96; 5, No. 245; *Szembek Diary*, 11 December 1936, p. 219, 7 October 1937, p. 243; *Lipski Papers*, p. 321.

40. This argument is repeatedly, and I believe excessively, stressed by Cienciala.

41. *D.D.F.*, 2d, 5, Nos. 402, 405, 414, 422; 6, Nos. 134, 150, 199, 343; but see Slávik's report of 13 March 1937, Czechoslovak document in T-120, 1041/1809/413769–71 (parts in Berber, pp. 73–74).

42. *D.D.F.*, 2d, 4, No. 369; *Hungarian Documents*, 2, No. 76; Slávik report 32 of 20 April 1937, Czechoslovak document in T-120, 1041/1809/413779–81; Korec (Bucharest) tels. of 25 and 27 April and 1 May 1937, ibid., 413848–50, 413852.

43. *Szembek Diary*, 21 and 31 December 1936, p. 220.

44. See *G.D.*, D, 1, Nos. 479, 18; 5, No. 34; *Lipski Papers*, p. 315 and No. 83; Wojciechowski, pp. 336, 341; R 7385, R 8162, R 8221/837/12, FO 371/21133. In September Beck briefly visited Paris on his own initiative; nothing much appears to have happened. There are no documents in *D.D.F.* See Černý (Czechoslovak chargé a.i. Paris) report 38 of 10 September 1937, T-120, 1040/1809/412954–55.

45. Some German complaints in *G.D.*, D, 5, Nos. 23, 27, 41, 44, 47, 48, 50, 51; Polish complaints, ibid., Nos. 39, 40, 42, 43.

46. *Szembek Diary*, 4 November 1937, p. 245.

Reassurances about future policy were exchanged when Beck was in Germany in January 1938 and Göring in Poland the following month.[47] In these meetings the Poles learned that Germany was likely to move against Austria soon but would respect Polish economic interests there (primarily as an export market for Polish coal) and that they would turn against Czechoslovakia thereafter. They also found the German government willing to continue restraining Forster in Danzig and otherwise eager to keep German-Polish friction to a minimum. The Germans for their part could feel confident that the eastern screen which Poland provided for actions against Austria and Czechoslovakia would be maintained. When the Poles, hoping for more explicit assurances, returned to a suggestion Hitler had made in May 1937 of extending the term of the 1934 agreement, Göring was favorable; but von Ribbentrop proved as dubious about new commitments to Poland as von Neurath; and nothing came of the project.[48] When Forster in his disappointment over not being designated von Papen's successor in Vienna once again became overly exuberant in Danzig, his earlier instructions to keep down the political temperature in the Free City were repeated.[49] With all now temporarily interested in keeping the high commissioner there, the situation in Danzig was kept reasonably calm, and Forster himself was invited to Warsaw for talks with Polish officials.[50] As neither Germany nor Poland wished any trouble in their relations, Danzig, the minorities problem, and all other current problems were subordinated to that desire.[51]

The annexation of Austria by Germany on 11 March 1938, though long expected in Warsaw, nevertheless surprised the Polish government by its timing.[52] Beck was in Italy in connection with his concept of some sort of

47. On Beck's trip to Germany, see *G.D.*, D, 5, Nos. 25, 28, 35 n.2, 29; *Hungarian Documents*, 2, No. 105; *Lipski Papers*, Nos. 75–77; *Szembek Diary*, 12 January 1938, p. 268; Wojciechowski, pp. 386–87, 404; Gallman dispatch 441 of 29 November 1937, State 760c.60K/362. On Göring's trip to Poland, see Wohlthat's briefing paper for him in T-120, 2621/5482/E 382269–74; *Lipski Papers*, Nos. 79, 80; *Szembek Diary*, 23 February 1938, pp. 275–78; *Hungarian Documents*, 2, No. 198; Wojciechowski, pp. 388–89, 404–7.

48. *G.D.*, D, 5, No. 34; *Szembek Diary*, 21 May 1937, pp. 230–31; *Lipski Papers*, Nos. 80–83.

49. Gallman dispatch 465 of 11 March 1938, State 860K.01–High Commissioner/47, and his dispatch 474 of 9 May 1938, State 860K.00/323; C 4100 (including Burckhardt to Walters, 27 April 1938), C 4359/197/55, FO 371/21801.

50. *G.D.*, D, 5, Nos. 36, 38; Gallman dispatches 446 and 448 of 18 and 21 December 1937, State 860K.01–High Commissioner/43, 45; C 8717, C 8917/5/55, FO 371/20759; C 4100, C 4359/197/55, FO 371/21801.

51. Wühlisch (Warsaw) report P 12c/12.37 of 7 December 1937, T-120, 1315/2371/D 496006; *G.D.*, D, 1, No. 68; 5, No. 49; "Bestellungen aus der Pressekonferenz," 17 December 1937, Bundesarchiv, Brammer, Z.Sg. 101/10, f.433 (the special propaganda directives concerning Poland mentioned in this document appear to be those reflected in Dertinger, "Informationsbericht Nr. 185," Z.Sg. 101/31, ff.547–49); "Bestellungen aus der Pressekonferenz," 11 May 1938, Z.Sg. 101/11, f.359; Gallman dispatch 487 of 17 June 1938, State 860K.00/329.

52. This surprise is well reflected in Szembek's diary for 11 March 1938 (pp. 286–87); but see *D.D.F.*, 2d, 8, Nos. 298, 305.

alignment joining Poland, Hungary, Yugoslavia, and Italy; and the other leaders of the Polish government waited a few days for his return before taking advantage of the situation for Polish aims. The rapidity of the German move precluded detailed planning on their part, but one of a long series of minor incidents on the Polish-Lithuanian border could be used as a pretext for action. Poland's relations with Lithuania had been poisoned from the beginning of both countries' independence in the wake of the war because of their dispute over Vilna and the surrounding territory. There were no diplomatic relations between the two neighbors who had once formed a single state by dynastic union. With the attention of Germany and other countries focused on Austria, the opportunity to settle accounts with Lithuania appeared to be at hand. There were apparently some in the Polish government who thought of bullying or forcing the small Baltic country into complete subservience; but Beck on returning to Warsaw kept the Polish demands to an insistence that official diplomatic relations between the two countries be established. An ultimatum to this effect was transmitted to the Lithuanian government which, advised to yield by all, agreed to the Polish demand.[53]

As the *Anschluss* had surprised the Polish government by its suddenness, so the Germans were startled to see a few days later that at any moment Polish troops might move into Lithuania. There were several unpleasant aspects to this from the perspective of Berlin. The Germans wanted a quiet period in Europe after the uproar caused by the annexation of Austria. They were concerned about the fate of the Memel territory that had been ceded by Germany as a result of the Treaty of Versailles and was under Lithuanian control. Finally, as long as Lithuania remained independent, there was always the possibility, however remote, of a German-Polish agreement by which Germany would acquiesce in a Polish annexation of Lithuania—with its access to the Baltic—in exchange for Polish agreement to return the Corridor to Germany. In the crisis, therefore, the German government cautioned the Poles about their own interests in Lithuania, simultaneously urging Lithuania to agree to the demand for establishing diplomatic relations. Internally, orders were given by Hitler not only to prepare for the occupation of the Memel territory as soon as Polish troops entered Lithuania but to push the German forces well beyond the 1914 border and seize a substantial part of the rest of the Baltic republic. These orders were, in the event, not implemented; but it should be remembered that in the 1939 negotiations with the Soviet Union the German government again hoped to secure a piece of Lithuania beyond the 1914 boundary, though slightly differently delineated. One can see, however, yet another indication that Hitler did not see himself as returning to the prewar borders of the Reich. Revision of the peace set-

53. Accounts of this incident may be found in Roos, pp. 305–16; Cienciala, pp. 49–53; Wojciechowski, pp. 390–401. The relevant French documents have since been published in *D.D.F.*, 2d, 8, Nos. 437, 487, 488, 492, 500–503, 505, 507, 514, 521–23; 9, Nos. 9, 15, 22, 38.

tlement might provide excuse or opportunity, but it in no way defined Hitler's aims.[54] The whole incident was settled in 1938 in a manner satisfactory to Poland as well as Germany, but although Poland had acted on her own initiative, she was obviously moving in Germany's wake, a situation that would soon be repeated.[55]

The sort of tacit cooperation between Germany and Poland that could be seen in the Polish-Lithuanian crisis was of far greater importance in the Czechoslovak crisis of 1938. The general development of that crisis will be examined subsequently, but the acquiescence of Poland in the hope of gains from the destruction of the Czechoslovak state must be seen as a most significant element in German-Polish relations and the general European situation in 1938. There was no formal German-Polish agreement on this subject at any time—though there is evidence that in return for German agreement to Poland's annexation of Danzig there could have been one.[56] A written agreement was not, however, necessary. As previously indicated, each made what it considered to be the concessions necessary to the other; Poland to keep from becoming Germany's immediate victim, Germany to restrain Poland from lining up in support of Czechoslovakia. The relations between Poland and Czechoslovakia had long been bad, and all attempts by France and England to help improve them failed. The Warsaw government accordingly left open the possibility of siding with her French ally if a general European war should ensue,[57] but in the meantime followed a policy predicated on the assumption that Czechoslovakia would fall apart under the pressure of her neighbors without such a war. The steps which the Polish government took in pursuit of this policy fitted in perfectly with German hopes even if there was no formal coordination between the two states.[58]

From the perspective of Warsaw, the hopes of securing territorial gains from the disintegration of Czechoslovakia focused primarily on Těšín,

54. For German policy in the Polish-Lithuanian crisis of 1938, see *Lipski Papers*, pp. 352–55; *G.D.*, D, 5, Nos. 33, 321–24, 337–39; Jodl diary for 11–18 March 1938, Nuremberg document 1781-PS (National Archives); Dertinger's reports of 15, 16, and 17 March 1938, Bundesarchiv, Brammer, Z.Sg. 101/11, ff.127–37.

It should be noted that the German plans for occupying a large part of Lithuania in case of a Polish-Lithuanian conflict remained in effect as contingency plans; for a 7 July 1938 reference to them see *TMWC*, 25:450, for a 21 October 1938 reference, see ibid., 34:481.

55. The Poles were, of course, also reminded by the German position in the incident of Berlin's interest in the future of Lithuania. See also *G.D.*, D, 5, No. 342.

56. Note Rydz-Śmigły's comments of 12 March 1938 in *Szembek Diary*, p. 289.

57. For Polish interest in maintaining the tie with France, see especially the visit of Delbos to Warsaw in Decmeber 1937: *US.*, 1937, 1:189–91; *G.D.*, D, 1, No. 64; Slávik report 84 of 6 December 1937, Czechoslovak document in T-120, 1041/1809/413830–36; Phipps tel. 233 of 20 December 1937, C 8730/7888/17, FO 371/20698; *D.D.F.*, 2d, 7, Nos. 319, 323 (note that Beck prevented a tête-à-tête of Delbos with Rydz-Śmigły).

58. During his Rome visit of May 1938, Hitler arranged a special audience for Alfred Wysocki, then ambassador to Italy, because of his services in Berlin on the German-Polish rapprochement (*Lipski Papers*, Nos. 85, 86; *Hungarian Documents*, 2, No. 185; Wojciechowski, p. 417).

the area that had been in dispute between Poland and Czechoslovakia in the period of upheaval after the collapse of Austria-Hungary. Included in Czechoslovakia, part of it was claimed by Poland on the ground of the national background of a substantial portion of its population—an exceedingly dangerous basis for Poland to suggest as the criterion of state boundaries. For this area to fall to Poland presupposed that Germany would secure the portions of Czechoslovakia inhabited by Germans, that Hungary would recapture those inhabited by Magyars, that Slovakia be returned to Hungary or left independent under Hungarian or Polish tutelage, and that no one do anything to save the Czechoslovak state. The way in which the Polish government might assist these various processes was to coordinate its policy with Hungary and promote an agreement between Hungary and Yugoslavia that would, by freeing Hungary from the threat of attack on her other borders, enable her to join in pouncing on Czechoslovakia. Furthermore, to keep any power from helping Czechoslovakia, Poland could use her ties to Rumania to stiffen the independence of the latter vis-à-vis the Soviet Union. Poland could further the same cause by striving for a rapprochement between Rumania and Hungary. If Rumania could by these means be encouraged to adhere to a policy of prohibiting the transit of Russian help to Czechoslovakia, a policy Poland was already following, then the prospect of a dismemberment of Czechoslovakia from which Poland might benefit would be that much closer. These are essentially the lines that the Warsaw government followed during the year from late 1937 to October 1938, and since they ran parallel to Germany's policies, it should not be surprising that they were agreeable to Berlin.[59]

Any analysis of German-Polish relations in 1937–38 with its partially conscious, partially unconscious, collaboration of the two nations would be incomplete without reference to the basic hopes and fears of these uneasy neighbors. The Polish government saw itself faced by a powerful and menacing Germany. Poland's leaders were very much afraid that at some point the danger they had thought themselves in during 1932–34— that Poland would be obliged by the great powers to make territorial and other concessions in order to preserve the peace—might recur.[60] If this became the fate of Czechoslovakia instead, that could be all to the good if

59. On these policies, see Roos, pp. 273ff.; Cienciala, chaps. 1 and 2; a survey by the British minister in Warsaw of 29 June 1937 is in C 1807/29/55, FO 371/20760. See also *Lipski Papers*, Nos. 75, 79; *G.D.*, D, 5, Nos. 25, 28; *Hungarian Documents*, 1, Nos. 357, 429; 2, Nos. 105, 123, 125, 135, 155, 172, 252, 274, 287; Lájos Kerekes (ed.), "Akten des Ungarischen Ministeriums zur Vorgeschichte der Annexion Österreichs," *Acta Historica*, 7, Nos. 3–4 (1960), document 13; Magda Ádám (ed.), "Documents relatifs à la politique étrangère de la Hongrie dans la période de la crise tchécoslovaque," *Acta Historica*, 10, Nos. 1–2 (1963), document 7; László Zsigmond (ed.), "Ungarn und das Münchener Abkommen," *Acta Historica*, 6, Nos. 3–4 (1959), 262–63, 267–68; *Szembek Diary*, 22 March 1938, p. 298; *D.D.F.*, 2d, 9, Nos. 244, 248, 511.

60. *Szembek Diary*, 14 December 1937, p. 261.

Poland secured her share and also attained a common border with Hungary. They felt that an independent policy was the country's best safeguard as opposed to subservience to any of the great powers, be it France, Germany, or the Soviet Union. That this very policy reinforced rather than reduced Poland's danger was a dilemma from which they found no exit. They were at first happy to see other countries, notably Belgium, follow their own example, only to realize that the implication of such a Belgian stance was that France would be gravely handicapped in fulfilling her treaty obligations to Poland—a handicap temporarily welcome in its equal impact on the French obligation to Czechoslovakia.[61] Nevertheless, the Polish government did, as indicated, try to keep its ties to France in existence; and Beck, in particular, undertook to improve Polish relations with England.[62] In his exaggerated self-esteem, he appears to have been unaware of his own unpopularity in English as well as French government circles.[63] He was pleased with the repeated German declarations of respect for Poland's interests and borders, culminating in Hitler's speech of 20 February 1938; but one may well doubt that he really believed this situation would always continue.[64]

Not only was Beck's policy of accommodation with Germany unpopular in Poland and limited by opposition within and without government circles,[65] but there were strict limits as to how far he himself would go. It appears to have been Beck's belief that Germany still had ambitions in Upper Silesia, Danzig, and the Corridor, and that she wanted a strong Poland only as a buffer against the Soviet Union while consolidating her own position in Central Europe. Thereafter he expected Germany to reach out for the Ukraine; this would menace Polish independence; and he believed that Poland would fight rather than allow German troops across her territory. He expected Poland to be defeated in such fighting; but equally unwilling to allow Russian or German troops into the country, he believed that France and Britain would eventually triumph over Germany.[66] If Hitler did in fact follow that route, the eventual result would be

61. See the comments of French Ambassador Noël on 1 June 1937, *D.D.F.*, 2d, 6, No. 4.
62. Roos, pp. 264–65; Wojciechowski, pp. 351–53, 361–63; Beck, pp. 293–95; Burckhardt, p. 165.
63. The comments to this effect in the Foreign Office records are numerous. On Kennard's survey cited in n.59, above, Eden noted: "We have certainly sought to do our best with Colonel Beck, but with little success I fear. He is an unsatisfactory individual to work with and shifty even to the extent of injuring his own country. AE July 20 [1937]." Cf. *D.D.F.*, 2d, 5, No. 430.
64. On the reception in Poland of Hitler's 20 February 1938 speech, see Winship (chargé a.i. Warsaw) dispatch 354 of 24 February 1938, State 762.00/183.
65. Note *G.D.*, D, 5, No. 53.
66. Biddle to Hull, 19 June 1938, State 740.00/441. The comment of Beck to Biddle that Poland would fight to prevent German troops from crossing Poland to take the Ukraine, because German control of the latter would menace Polish independence, was made before Beck went to Sweden on 24 May 1938. He had stated that although Poland would face the possibility of defeat in such a contingency, she would delay the Germans who would then be kept from their objective by a Franco-German war.

a catastrophe for Germany out of which Poland would reappear with great gains at German expense.[67] That the Polish catastrophe could be of even greater dimensions was hidden from his view.

Nothing suggests that Hitler's own views of the role of Poland had changed. The German-Polish rapprochement was useful for the moment; and it is easily understandable why he should have asked Hungarian Regent Miklós Horthy in late August 1938, at the height of the crisis over Czechoslovakia, to refrain from asking the Poles to return the Corridor to Germany.[68] The major aim of his East European policy was the eventual conquest of vast portions of the Soviet Union. While he prepared for that, he wanted Poland reassured rather than alarmed; once the time came to begin moving toward the main goal, Poland could either be a complaisant and truncated vassal of Germany or be crushed on the road to great conquests further East.[69]

As has been noted in the discussion of the Polish-Lithuanian crisis of March 1938, Germany was greatly interested in the fate of her other East European neighbor. German-Lithuanian relations in the years since Hitler came to power in Germany had been at first very tense and then somewhat calmer.[70] The new movements that had been organized by the Germans living in the Memel territory had been temporarily suppressed by the Lithuanian authorities. A spectacular court case in Kovno had been

---

Biddle was one of the few—if not the only—important foreign diplomat who got along well with Beck, and he appears to have been better informed on the Polish foreign minister's views than most others. This is evident when Biddle's reports are compared with those of other representatives in Warsaw; it was also known to the Germans (see *G.D.*, D, 6, No. 64). For Beck's own comments on Biddle, see *U.S.*, 1939, 1:114; cf. *B.D.*, 3d, 7, No. 48. A selection of Biddle's papers has been edited by Philip V. Cannistraro and others, *Poland and the Coming of the Second World War* (Columbus: Ohio State University Press, 1976).

67. See Burckhardt's report on his 23 July 1938 talks with Beck in Burckhardt, pp. 156–57.

68. *G.D.*, D, 5, No. 52. Note that when a Hungarian officer suggested that in the course of German-Polish-Hungarian cooperation against Czechoslovakia there might be some military cooperation between Germany and Poland, he was told by General Kurt von Tippelskirch, then chief of the section "Foreign Armies West" of the German army general staff (which handled intelligence against France, England, Belgium, and Poland), and by Admiral Wilhelm Canaris, head of the intelligence and counterintelligence office in the high command of the German armed forces, that such a procedure was out of the question. German military relations with Poland were unfriendly, and German espionage operations were directed very much against Poland (*Hungarian Documents*, 2, No. 252).

69. Hitler explained these views to Forster, who told Burckhardt about them on 29 November 1938 (Burckhardt, pp. 231–33). It is important to remember that Forster was himself so enthusiastic and devoted a believer in Hitler that he often repeated comments Hitler had made to him, frequently disregarding the possibility that the recipients of these confidences might not be as convinced of the brilliance of his leader's inspirations as he was himself. There are numerous examples of Forster's talking about his meetings with Hitler, and in this very special and limited way Forster is often an important witness for Hitler's views as expressed by the latter within the circle of his immediate associates. It is as if Rauschning had recounted Hitler's comments to others shortly after hearing them, instead of years later.

70. Weinberg, *Foreign Policy*, pp. 82–85, 300–302.

followed by a lengthy diplomatic and economic conflict that had finally been resolved, at least temporarily, in 1936.[71] The concessions made by the Lithuanian authorities had calmed the atmosphere, a trade agreement ended economic conflict, and the German press was instructed to restrain its attacks on the Baltic state.[72] The Lithuanian authorities had not allowed the process of nazification to proceed as openly as in Danzig, but the elected German representatives were again allowed to direct the internal affairs of the Memel area in accordance with the statute that governed Lithuania's relation to the territory.[73] A few of the prisoners of the Kovno trial were still in jail, but this was due to Berlin's refusal to accept them into Germany.[74]

It is true that there were still occasions for dispute. The operations of various German agencies in support of the Memel Germans certainly continued to cause apprehension in Kovno.[75] The Germans, on the other hand, objected to some small land expropriations in the Memel harbor area; and this question led to nasty comments and ruffled feelings in the fall of 1937.[76] The Memel Germans were, however, as well off as any minority in Europe, and it was obvious that Germany would start an international crisis over them only when it suited her other purposes.[77] To keep that possibility open, the German government was careful to ward off Lithuanian suggestions of actually signing the nonaggression pact that Hitler had offered them in his March 1936 speech. Good excuses to avoid implementing that promise could always be found by the exercise of a little ingenuity.[78]

As has been pointed out, when it looked as if Poland might invade Lithuania, Hitler planned to seize both Memel and adjacent portions of that country.[79] When the crisis of March 1938 passed peacefully, how-

71. For a review of the motives of both sides in settling this, see "Informationsbericht Nr. 173," 1 December 1937, Bundesarchiv, Brammer, Z.Sg. 101/31, ff.451–69.
72. "Bestellungen aus der Pressekonferenz," 17 December 1936, Bundesarchiv, Brammer, Z.Sg. 101/8, f.427.
73. See the contrast drawn by Arthur Bliss Lane in his letter to President Roosevelt of 12 July 1937, Hyde Park, P.S.F. State Department.
74. *G.D.*, C, 6, No. 256. N 131, N 3780/125/59, FO 371/21057. The British, as one of the signers of the statute, long followed the Memel issue with special interest.
75. See Felix-Heinrich Gentzen, "Die Rolle der 'Deutschen Stiftung' bei der Vorbereitung der Annexion des Memellandes im März 1939," *Jahrbuch für Geschichte der UdSSR und der Volksdemokratischen Länder,* 5 (1961), 92–93; *G.D.*, C, 5, No. 365; 6, Nos. 520, 524, 552. There appear to have been the usual problems of organizational rivalry, in this case involving the VDA, the Deutsche Stiftung, the Hitler Youth, Gauleiter Koch of East Prussia, and the Volksdeutsche Mittelstelle (Vomi).
76. On this problem, see *G.D.*, D, 5, Nos. 318, 319; N 5386, N 6193/125/59, FO 371/21058.
77. N 5764, N 5795/125/59, FO 371/21058. Cf. "Bestellungen aus der Pressekonferenz," 9 September 1937, Bundesarchiv, Brammer, Z.Sg. 101/10, f.187.
78. *G.D.*, D, 5, Nos. 343, 346, 347. German complaints are listed in ibid., Nos. 336, 340, 341, 350.
79. See above, p. 205. Another idea suggested at the time was German assistance to Lithuania to build a new port for Lithuania at Palanga, to be joined by canal to Memel, and thus create a sort of Lithuanian Gdynia (ibid., No. 335).

ever, German policy toward the situation in Memel was subordinated—like that toward Poland and Danzig—to the need for quiet in that part of Europe while Germany concentrated on destroying Czechoslovakia. When the Berlin-sponsored leader of the Memel National Socialists, Ernst Neumann, was given instructions after his release from jail, these were to the effect that the Memel Germans were to be most careful, disciplined, and quiet for the time being.[80]

There could not be much reassurance in this temporary calm for the Lithuanian authorities whose agents in the local National Socialist movement presumably kept them informed of the nature of Berlin's directives. The rather substantial demographic changes that were taking place in the urban area of Memel as a result of economic prosperity with an accompanying labor shortage and the immigration of thousands of Lithuanians in no way altered the political realities, though they might have done so over a longer period of time. As the Lithuanians quickly discovered during the crisis over Czechoslovakia in September 1938, when Hitler spoke publicly about being satisfied with Germany's other boundaries and having no more territorial demands to make, he meant only the next five minutes, and *not* whatever lands he might covet the following day.[81] Only the British ambassador to Berlin, Sir Nevile Henderson, appears to have credited these statements; the Lithuanians were quickly enlightened, though even they were not yet aware of how much further German ambitions with regard to them really went.

Germany's relations with the most important country of Eastern Europe, the Soviet Union, were simultaneously noisy and quiet in 1937–39. Each from time to time carried on loud propaganda campaigns against the other, but there was little substance to all this. The Germans denounced the U.S.S.R. as a dangerous world menace against whose machinations Germany had to protect herself and others—while also predicting the imminent collapse of the Soviet system into feebleness and anarchy.[82] The Soviet government reciprocated in kind. The fluctuations in these propaganda campaigns were sometimes taken as signs of a political rapprochement between the two countries, but since they did not coincide with the known Soviet approaches to Germany that will be reviewed subsequently, this interpretation would appear to have been incorrect.[83] More likely, the episodes of restraint were related to domestic consid-

80. Ibid., No. 349.
81. Ibid., Nos. 352, 355.
82. See the analysis by François-Poncet in *D.D.F.*, 2d, 6, No. 295; cf. "Informationsbericht Nr. 133," and "Nr. 135," 10 and 11 September 1937, Bundesarchiv, Brammer, Z.Sg. 101/31, ff.229–31, 235.
83. See *G.D.*, D, 1, Nos. 626, 627, 630; Gustav Hilger and Alfred G. Meyer, *The Incompatible Allies: A Memoir History of German-Soviet Relations, 1918–1941* (New York: Macmillan, 1953), p. 279.

erations in each country and to their desire for the maintenance of trade relations between them.[84]

German-Soviet trade was no longer at the levels reached in prior years, but it was still of importance to both countries. The negotiations for a new trade and payments agreement proved difficult; and there were occasional sharp arguments about specific items; but the importance of the exchanges to the economies of the two powers led each to make the concessions needed to prevent a rupture in trade. Thus, although no substantial increases or new German credits to the Soviet Union were agreed upon, in the economic as in the propaganda field, the noise level was not a very useful clue to the real situation.[85] All that one can safely conclude on the evidence of the economic relations is the point already stressed, namely, that each side thought them important. When the German government became alarmed about the widespread arrests of Germans in the Soviet Union in the summer of 1937, the German embassy was instructed to urge as many German citizens as possible to leave the country just as soon as possible, except those Germans temporarily in the country for business reasons lest German-Soviet trade suffer.[86] When the Soviet government changed its ambassadors in Germany in the course of the purge of the diplomatic corps, the new man sent to Berlin in the summer of 1938 was the former deputy people's commissar for foreign trade.[87]

The same contrast between surface disturbances and underlying continuity can be seen in two other aspects of German-Soviet relations. The arrests of Germans just mentioned took place during and in connection with the great purges shaking the U.S.S.R. These arrests led to considerable acrimony, charges, and countercharges, and Soviet demands for assistance from Germany in the repatriation of Soviet seamen kept in Spanish Nationalist prisons. There were months of argument, but in the end this matter, too, was settled quietly.[88] More troublesome were the twin problems of Soviet demands first that the German military and press attachés in Moscow be recalled and later that several of the German consular offices in the Soviet Union be closed. The attachés were allegedly implicated in some of the plots that the Soviet secret police was dreaming up in the purges, while the consulates were to be closed as part of a systematic effort to reduce contacts between all foreigners, not just Germans, and Soviet citizens. These problems were also eventually

84. *D.D.F.*, 2d, 6, No. 38.

85. Information on the trade relations and negotiations may be found in *G.D.*, C, 6, Nos. 129, 323, 336, 339; D, 1, Nos. 613, 619, 629; D, 7:534–38; Hencke to Dirksen, 2 March 1938, T-120, 1097/2082/450897–900; Hilger, pp. 284–85. Herbert Göring of the ministry of economics, a cousin of Hermann Göring, appears to have played a role in the economic negotiations as he had earlier (*Dodd Diary*, 20 March 1937, p. 397; Weinberg, *Foreign Policy*, p. 311).

86. These instructions will be published as *G.D.*, C, 6, No. 517.

87. See ibid., D, 1, No. 629.

88. Ibid., C, 6, Nos. 135; 146, 173, 187, 301, 351, 391, 491, 498, 511, 539, 575.

worked out, with the German military attaché remaining in Moscow; but in this case, there was for some time the real possibility that the post of German ambassador in Moscow might simply be left vacant.[89]

If these surface signs of calmed disturbances tell us so little about the policies of the two powers toward each other it is because the primary focus of both was on entirely different problems during this period. The general drive against foreigners in the Soviet Union, and the supposed complicity of German diplomats in various "plots" were manifestations of the internal upheaval of the U.S.S.R. in the era of the great purges.[90] This cataclysmic epoch in Soviet history had its roots in domestic, not foreign, policy issues. It had wide implications for Soviet relations with other countries, but cannot be explained by them. Thus the attacks on Germany and Japan as sponsors of various conspiracies might be used for purposes of domestic consolidation, but hardly made the Soviet Union a more attractive partner for any other enemies of those two powers. If both the diplomatic and military leaders who would have to negotiate political and military agreements with other potential enemies of Germany and Japan could be expected to disappear soon after for espionage in behalf of those very powers, there could be little incentive for anyone to enter into confidential negotiations with the U.S.S.R. Simultaneously, the wrecking of the Soviet military and diplomatic command structures weakened the Soviet Union greatly in international affairs.[91]

The extreme reticence of the Soviet regime in the Polish-Lithuanian crisis of March 1938, in which one of the very few European countries that had consistently maintained good relations with Moscow was publicly humiliated, may serve as an example of the general effect of a weakened Soviet position.[92] The dangerous developments in East Asia accentuated Soviet caution in Europe. With the outbreak of open war between Japan and China, the situation in Asia undoubtedly took up more of Moscow's attention; and the Soviet government took a firmer position there than in Europe, especially where its own borders were concerned.[93]

The one open conflict during these years was the civil war in Spain. For some time, the Soviet government followed in Spain a procedure not

89. On the question of the attachés, see Hermann Teske, *General Ernst Köstring: Der militärische Mittler zwischen dem Deutschen Reich und der Sowjetunion 1921–1941* (Frankfurt/M: Mittler, 1966); *G.D.*, C, 6, Nos. 213, 218, 221, 253, 301; on the consulates, see ibid., Nos. 489, 498, 544, 562, 564, 569–72, 578–80; D, 1, Nos. 614, 615, 620, 621; Hilger, pp. 279–80. For the possibility that von Schulenburg would be moved to either Warsaw or Tokyo in the revirement of February–March 1938 and the Moscow embassy left vacant, see Dertinger's "Privater Sonderbericht," of 7 February 1938, and his "Informationsbericht Nr. 27," of 24 March 1938, Bundesarchiv, Brammer, Z.Sg. 101/32, ff.75, 227; cf. *U.S., Soviet Union 1933–39*, p. 321.

90. See von Schulenburg's comments in *G.D.*, C, 6, Nos. 170, 578.

91. For French and British concern about this, see above, pp. 87–89. For German awareness of it, see above, p. 190, and *G.D.*, D, 1, Nos. 622, 623.

92. See *D.D.F.*, 2d, 8, No. 471.

93. See above, pp. 188–89.

entirely unlike that of the Germans, supplying the Loyalists, whom Russia was supporting, with enough equipment and other aid to keep them from losing but not sending enough to assure a victory.[94] The reasons for the maintenance of this posture by the Soviet Union, after the Nyon Conference of September 1937 had, in effect, assured safety to Soviet ships in the Mediterranean, remain to be satisfactorily explained. Whether the Soviet government was, as some have suggested, as interested in continuing friction between Germany and the Western Powers as Germany was interested in friction between the latter and Italy is by no means clear. In any case, in 1938, most likely during the summer, the Russian government decided to reduce its involvement in Spain so that the final German assistance to Franco was left unmatched and hence assured victory to the Nationalists.

In prior years, the Soviet Union had repeatedly attempted to come to a direct agreement with Hitler Germany, but these efforts had foundered in the face of German disinterest.[95] Stalin tried once more in February 1937 to open up negotiations for improving relations between Germany and the Soviet Union, once again using David Kandelaki of the Soviet Trade Delegation in Berlin and Hjalmar Schacht as contact points; but as in the previous instances, Hitler refused to take up the offered hand.[96] The German dictator was not yet interested in an accommodation with Stalin because his own immediate goals were shielded from Soviet interference or assistance by the position of Poland and Rumania. As long as that situation continued, there was nothing to be gained by an agreement with Russia, while the propaganda advantage of opposition to her would be lost.

The periodic rumors of a German-Soviet rapprochement during this period simply had no basis in fact; if Stalin was interested, Hitler was not.[97] The French may have thought that their pact with the Soviet Union restrained that power from aligning herself with Hitler, but the evidence indicates that this was not so; as the British ambassador to Moscow had pointed out to the Foreign Office, the 1926 German-Soviet Treaty of Berlin failed to keep the Russians out of the arms of the French when Moscow had considered that an appropriate policy.[98] The fact is that

94. Though in need of updating, the best study is David I. Cattell, *Soviet Diplomacy and the Spanish Civil War* (Berkeley: University of California Press, 1957); see also Thomas, pp. 940–42.

95. Weinberg, *Foreign Policy,* pp. 220–23, 310–12.

96. *G.D.,* C, 6, Nos. 183, 195 (published in Johann W. Brügel [ed.], *Stalin und Hitler, Pakt gegen Europa* [Vienna: Europaverlag, 1973], Nos. 7, 8); Walter G. Krivitsky, *In Stalin's Secret Service* (New York: Harper, 1939), pp. 37–39; Leonard Schapiro, *The Communist Party of the Soviet Union,* 2d ed. (New York: Random House, 1971), p. 490.

97. On these rumors, see *G.D.,* C, 6, No. 326; N 2064/45/38, FO 371/21095; Memorandum of the Czechoslovak Foreign Ministry, Nr. 90,903/III-4 of 20 June 1937, T-120, 1143/2028/444481.

98. N 546, N 1522/45/38, FO 371/21094; N 1934/45/38, FO 371/21095; cf. *D.D.F.,* 2d, 5, No. 192.

Stalin's most critical concerns were at home, and his interest in agreement with Germany should probably be seen in that framework. Hitler, on the other hand, looked in the immediate future to a strengthening of his position in Central Europe; and for that Poland, not the Soviet Union, was important as a neutral shield in the east, while Yugoslavia would assist in isolating his next victims from the south.

From the point of view of Germany, Yugoslavia was important as a neighbor of Austria and of Hungary. As a neighbor of Austria, Yugoslavia's attitude toward that country was of interest to Berlin. Would the South Slav state join others in any attempt to block the annexation of Austria or not? What would be her position if there were an attempted restoration of the Habsburgs in Vienna? The fact that Yugoslavia was Hungary's southern neighbor was significant for Germany because of the implications of the relationship between those two countries for Hungary's policy toward Czechoslovakia, Germany's other prospective victim. Because Hungary had lost territory to Czechoslovakia, Rumania, and Yugoslavia by the peace settlement of 1920, those three had joined in an alliance, the Little Entente, pledging support to each other in case Hungary attacked any one of them. This meant that the threat of a Hungarian attack on Czechoslovakia simultaneously with an attack by Germany could be credible only if the Little Entente were disrupted. As long as Hungary had to contemplate the possibility of an invasion by Yugoslav forces across her southern border, she could not consider attacking Czechoslovakia across her northern border. As will be seen, there were still other factors restraining Hungary, but this was both the most obvious and also the one most susceptible to an approach from Germany.

Internal and external factors had made Yugoslavia receptive to German approaches even before 1937.[99] The difficult problems of welding together into one state the disparate national elements constituting Yugoslavia have dominated its history. The predominantly Serb elite governing the country in the interwar years never came to a satisfactory arrangement with the Croat and Slovene components; and since both of these had been included in prewar Austria-Hungary, the possibility of a Habsburg restoration was greatly feared in Belgrade. As the power of Germany increased in the 1930s, Yugoslavia continued to prefer the maintenance of an independent and necessarily weak Austria on its border but, between a Habsburg restoration and German annexation of Austria, much preferred the latter in spite of the potential problems of having so powerful a neighbor. The internal nationality problem, especially in regard to Croatia, not only stimulated fear of a Habsburg restoration but also provided possible external enemies of Yugoslavia with a potential internal ally in the form of the Croatian nationalist movement.

99. Weinberg, *Foreign Policy*, pp. 116–18, 226–29, 313, 325–26.

The numerically predominant portion of Croatian nationalism was the Croatian Peasant party of Vladko Maček. Autonomist rather than separatist in orientation, this movement was willing to work within the framework of a Yugoslav state—though it was accorded very little opportunity to do so—and only occasionally flirted with outside powers, primarily Italy, though at times also Germany. A more radical group wishing to separate Croatia entirely from the South Slav state was the Ustasha. This extreme right-wing movement was led by Ante Pavelič, looked to Italy and Germany for inspiration as well as support, and, although hoping to use those powers for its own purposes, came to be used by them as a tool of their policies toward Yugoslavia.

The economy of Yugoslavia was almost as important as its nationality problem in inclining her to a course agreeable to Berlin. Germany was an increasingly important customer for the agricultural products Yugoslavia exported and had in fact become her most important trading partner as a result of the reduction of Yugoslavia's trade with Italy during the period of League sanctions against Italy. There were indeed problems attached to this economic situation, but there was no easy way out of Germany's economic embrace.

Belgrade had looked to the Western Powers and especially France for support. This had turned out to be a weak reed indeed. The immediate threat to Yugoslavia had long come from Italy, which dominated the Adriatic and through effective control of Albania practically cut off that sea. French hopes for a rapprochement with Italy had, however, made France a most reluctant ally against Yugoslavia's prospective foe. In the one important recent crisis with Italy, that touched off by the Italian-sponsored Ustasha's murder of the king of Yugoslavia in October 1934, the French government had dramatically subordinated the interests of Yugoslavia to hopes for an agreement with Mussolini. As for the more remote danger possibly emanating from Germany, the passivity of France in the face of German remilitarization of the Rhineland had shown how little hope there could be of effective French help. Although Prince Paul, the most important of the three regents designated by the late King Alexander for the period of his son's minority, was inclined to be pro-British, the retreat of England before Mussolini's Ethiopian venture followed by London's equally unremitting and undignified attempts to come to an agreement with him during Italy's open intervention in Spain suggested that little more than verbal support could be expected from Great Britain.

These factors constitute the background for Yugoslavia's interest in good relations with Germany and her resumption in the winter of 1936–37 of the efforts King Alexander had earlier made to try to work out a rapprochement with Italy. Urged on by the German government, which saw in this an opportunity to move Yugoslavia closer to the Axis and away from her prior association with France and the other members of the

Little Entente, the Belgrade government engaged in negotiations with Italy that culminated in an agreement in March 1937. The course of these talks will not be traced here, but certain aspects of them are important.[100]

The German government followed the negotiations with great interest, urged both sides forward, and hailed the conclusion of the settlement on 25 March 1937 as amounting to the disruption of the Little Entente.[101] This was not an unreasonable way to view the situation in spite of the fact that one motive for both parties to the agreement had been the notion that jointly they would carry more weight with Germany, "a difficult friend" as Ciano described her.[102] The extent to which the German assessment was correct in the long run, however, can be seen in the way the Yugoslav government kept the negotiations secret from their French and Little Entente allies until the very last moment, thus giving them meager opportunity to raise objections until it was too late.[103] When the Little Entente leaders met in Belgrade at the beginning of April, they could only note that the organization was very sick indeed.[104] Prince Paul had had the British government informed slightly earlier and in more detail, but the London authorities were in a difficult dilemma. They were quite happy to see a reduction in tension and some accommodation between Italy and Yugoslavia as part of a general calming of the European situation; on the other hand, they were very concerned lest Yugoslavia, Greece, and Turkey drift into the Italian orbit and by strengthening the position of the Axis encourage Italy and Germany to more daring adventures. British influence was therefore devoted primarily to making sure that Yugoslavia did not go too far, and in this regard, the caution of the Belgrade officials could be depended upon.[105]

Count Ciano's trip to Belgrade for the signing of the agreement with Yugoslavia was productive of more than the texts that dealt with the relations between the two countries, restricting the Ustasha, protecting national minorities, and other issues. The Yugoslav prime minister, Milan Stojadinović, at this time buried once and for all the plan for a mutual assistance treaty between France and the Little Entente that had been the

100. The best available account in Jacob B. Hoptner, *Yugoslavia in Crisis, 1934–1941* (New York: Columbia University Press, 1962), chap. 3. It is based to a considerable extent on Yugoslav sources made available to its author. Only the Ciano papers and diaries have been published; the Italian diplomatic document volumes for this period have not yet appeared.

101. *G.D.*, C, 6, Nos. 138, 143, 254, 274, 291, 297, 298; D, 3, No. 236; *D.D.F.*, 2d, 5, No. 166. The Germans had earlier been pleased by the Yugoslav-Bulgarian agreement (*G.D.*, C, 6, No. 132; *Hungarian Documents*, 2, No. 65).

102. Ivan Subbotić's report of 6 March 1937 to Stojadinović on his 3 March conversation with Ciano, quoted in Hoptner, p. 67. See also *Hungarian Documents*, 1, No. 220.

103. *D.D.F.*, 2d, 4, Nos. 326, 387, 395; 5, Nos. 89, 152, 154, 164; *U.S.*, 1937, 1:67–71; *G.D.*, C, 6, No. 302; *Hungarian Documents*, 2, Nos. 69, 71; Slávik report 30 of 8 April 1937, Czechoslovak document in T-120, 1041/1809/413772–76 (parts in Berber, pp. 74–75).

104. *D.D.F.*, 2d, 5, Nos. 211, 212, 221, 227; *G.D.*, C, 6, No. 309.

105. See R 650, R 1357/224/92, FO 371/21197; R 1623, R 1687, R 1688, R 1785, R 1896, R 2042/224/92, FO 371/21198; *Harvey Diaries*, pp. 24–25; cf. *Hungarian Documents*, 2, No. 73.

subject of lengthy negotiations in the preceding months.[106] Having signed with Italy, he could hardly be expected to sign an agreement with France that was designed to protect Yugoslavia against her new associate. Conversely, he could not promise to assist Czechoslovakia against Germany, Italy's Axis partner. Stojadinović could, therefore, now safely assure the Germans that there would be no Yugoslav assistance pact with France.[107] Furthermore, in view of the close relations that had obtained for some years between Italy and Hungary, the alignment with Italy provided yet one more link in the effort of the Axis to bring Yugoslavia and Hungary closer together.[108] More will be said about this subject later from the perspective of Germany and Hungary, but Italy's switch from working jointly with Hungary against Yugoslavia to working for better relations between her two Southeast European associates must be stressed. Finally, the personal meeting between Ciano and Stojadinović was to have some entirely unexpected results. Starting with it, and reinforced during Stojadinović's return visit to Italy in December 1937, Ciano developed a personal liking for the Yugoslav leader, while the latter became increasingly enamored of fascism as a form of government. If Ciano did not let his personal feelings interfere with later plots against the South Slav state, the new political proclivities of Stojadinović would contribute to his fall from power two years later.[109]

In regard to Yugoslavia's relations with Germany, the importance of the economic aspect has already been mentioned. This was of great significance to Germany, which drew agricultural products from Yugoslavia and was increasingly importing minerals and investing in mining companies as well.[110] There were political as well as economic aspects to this process; Yugoslavia was becoming dependent on the German market and was being forced to increase her imports from Germany, at the expense of other countries, in order to offset the clearing debts that the Germans ran up. One plan to limit German trade was vetoed by Stojadinović on political grounds; Yugoslavia might prefer not to become too closely tied to Germany but also could not afford to offend her.[111]

There were, in fact, various difficulties associated with German-Yugoslav trade. The appointment of Franz Neuhausen as Göring's special representative in Belgrade had caused friction among German agencies

106. Ciano, *Diplomatic Papers*, pp. 98–105.

107. *G.D.*, C, 6, Nos. 295, 300; D, 2, No. 37; von Neurath to Rümelin, 31 March 1937, DZA Potsdam, Büro RAM, Akte 60964, ff.86–88.

108. Ciano, *Diplomatic Papers*, pp. 98–105; *Hungarian Documents*, 2, Nos. 69, 70.

109. Hoptner, pp. 86–87, 126–29; Magistrati, p. 112; Lothar C. F. Wimmer, *Expériences et tribulations d'un diplomate autrichien entre deux guerres, 1929–1938,* trans. Charles Reichard (Neuchâtel: Baconnière, 1946), pp. 197–203; *D.D.F.*, 2d, 7, Nos. 332, 334, 335; R 590/147/92, FO 371/22475.

110. See Hoptner, chap. 4.

111. R 1623/224/92, FO 371/21198 (Vansittart passes on what appears to be secret service information about Yugoslav government proceedings).

earlier, and continued to do so.[112] Moreover, in a complicated series of trade transactions, that cannot yet be entirely unraveled, Gauleiter Erich Koch of East Prussia was involved in a series of barter operations that not only collided with regular German-Yugoslav trade but interfered in internal Yugoslav politics. Funds from these transactions were channeled to a far right political organization, the Zbor of Dimitrije Ljotić.[113] This was of great concern to Belgrade, especially because there was a fusion of the so-called Resurgence Movement within Yugoslavia's German community with the Zbor.[114] Stojadinović personally complained to the German minister about these and related mysterious activities of German agents; and von Neurath did what he could to secure restraint from the German side as well as to reassure the alarmed minister president.[115] New arrangements covering the current trade between Germany and Yugoslavia were successfully worked out in 1937, with Germany more pleased than the Yugoslavs by the consolidation of her new position in Yugoslavia's international commerce.[116]

It should be noted that whatever efforts Yugoslavia might make to avoid economic dependence on Germany were offset by the German annexation of Austria in March 1938. During December 1937, the Belgrade government tried to find other markets, hoped to limit the growth of its blocked Reichsmark balances in Germany by restricting exports to Germany, and used up some of the balances by selling blocked Reichsmark and by arms purchases. All this would be more than compensated for by the immediately increased role of Germany in Yugoslavia's foreign trade once Austria—third after Germany and Czechoslovakia in both export and import value in Yugoslavia—was included within the boundaries of Greater Germany.[117] If there had ever been an opportunity for the Western Powers to counter the drift of Yugoslavia into the Axis orbit by economic measures, it was largely wiped out by the *Anschluss*.[118]

112. Weinberg, *Foreign Policy*, pp. 229 n.102, 325; *G.D.*, C, 6, Nos. 249, 526, 561, 574.
113. Weinberg, *Foreign Policy*, p. 326 n.106; *G.D.*, C, 6, Nos. 150, 198, 211, 219, 252, 259; Hoptner, p. 103.
114. *G.D.*, C, 6, No. 234. On the Zbor movement, see Peter Sugar (ed.), *Native Fascism in the Successor States* (Santa Barbara, Calif.: Clio Press, 1971), pp. 131, 137–38.
115. *G.D.*, C, 6, Nos. 244, 293; von Neurath to von Heeren, 16 March 1937, DZA Potsdam, Büro RAM, Akte 60964, ff.71–72; cf. Wimmer, p. 204; Rudolf von Maltzahn, "Informationsbericht," received in Göring's office 16 February 1937, T-120, 2621/5482/E 382214–20.
116. *G.D.*, C, 6, Nos. 286, 345, 565; D, 5, No. 159; Lane to Moffat, 20 April 1938, Moffat Papers, vol. 13; Roland Schönfeld, "Deutsche Rohstoffsicherungspolitik in Jugoslawien 1934–1944," *Vierteljahrshefte für Zeitgeschichte*, 24, No. 3 (July 1976), 217–18, 224–27.
117. Compare the views of Neuhausen in his "Die Wirtschaftsbeziehungen Grossdeutschland-Jugoslawien," 5 May 1938, T-120, 2621/5482/E 382162–67, with the basically similar conclusions reached in the British Foreign Office in C 3249/772/18, FO 371/21705.
118. R 5338, R 5362/94/67, FO 371/22342; *D.D.F.*, 2d, 9, No. 177. An introductory survey in Wilhelm Treue, "Das Dritte Reich und die Westmächte auf dem Balkan," *Vierteljahrshefte für Zeitgeschichte*, 1, No. 1 (April 1953), 45–64.

German-Yugoslav economic relations constituted one of the subjects discussed when German Foreign Minister Constantin von Neurath visited Belgrade in June 1937. The possibility of such a visit had been canvassed earlier in the year, but the German government wanted to be certain that there would be no unpleasant surprises if von Neurath did indeed go. The elements needed to reassure Berlin were, first, a Yugoslav assurance that there would be no pact of assistance with France, second, that the planned visit of Count Ciano to Belgrade should work out properly, and third, that the meeting of the Little Entente Powers in Belgrade, scheduled for early April, would register the continuing disintegration rather than any revival of that institution. All these conditions were met, and the German foreign minister, who could not manage a couple of days in London, went off on a lengthy tour of the Balkans with Belgrade as his first stop.[119]

No important Yugoslav official had visited Berlin in recent years; von Neurath's trip—coming after previous visits by Göring and Schacht—must, therefore, be seen as an indication of how seriously the German government wanted to move Belgrade toward the Axis.[120] The conversations which von Neurath held in Belgrade produced no new agreements, but they did underline the fact that Germany and Yugoslavia were drawing closer together. Furthermore, the occasion gave von Neurath an opportunity to sound out the Yugoslavs on German-Austrian relations and to urge them toward an understanding with Hungary. Von Neurath's mixture of threats and reassurances appears to have left mixed feelings in Belgrade, but the open exchange of views was of a sort that Germany's leaders had hitherto engaged in only with the Italians from among their enemies in the World War.[121]

The converse of this development was the continuing estrangement of Yugoslavia from France. The French were annoyed by the lack of notice to them of von Neurath's visit—especially after the Yugoslav-Italian agreement—and by all the signs of closer ties between Belgrade and Berlin. Stojadinović's answer to the reproaches from Paris took two forms. On the one hand, he promised to remain faithful to the existing agreement with France[122] and to make no agreement with Hungary independently of his Little Entente partners. On the other hand, he had his representatives reproach the French for their passivity in March 1936, their unwillingness

119. On the background of the trip, see von Neurath to Rümelin, 31 March 1937, DZA Potsdam, Büro RAM, Akte 60964, ff.86–88; G.D., C, 6, No. 313 (DZA Potsdam, Büro RAM, Akte 60964, ff.93–94).

120. D.D.F., 2d, 6, No. 16.

121. Guido Schmidt Trial, pp. 545–48, and an additional report by Wimmer, the Austrian minister in Belgrade, in his memoirs, pp. 186–88 (Wimmer and von Neurath had been colleagues in London); G.D., C, 6, Nos. 410, 514; Hungarian Documents, 1, No. 262; D.D.F., 2d, 6, Nos. 51, 84; R 4087/439/3, FO 371/21118; R 4236, R 4272/4067/67, FO 371/21141; R 4418/3174/92, FO 371/21201.

122. Of November 1927 (League of Nations Treaty Series, 68:373).

to assist Yugoslavia either in rearmament or economically, and their general willingness to let Germany and Italy have their way. In other words, he claimed to have no choice; his policy was largely the result of French actions and inactions, and in any case, he would not go further than absolutely necessary.[123] When in Paris himself in October 1937, Stojadinović defended his policy as essential for the internal consolidation and strengthening of Yugoslavia which would, in case of war, be on the side of France but could not provoke Germany or Italy.[124]

The attempts of the French government to have Stojadinović removed in 1937 were as unsuccessful as their earlier hopes for Beck's dismissal in Poland, and the British were probably correct in thinking such activities unwise and counterproductive.[125] In any case, Stojadinović remained in power for the time being; and when French Foreign Minister Delbos himself was in Belgrade in December 1937, he could only put a good face on a bad situation.[126] The sole remedy was for France and Britain to rearm and assert their position in Europe vigorously; that would take time but was the only way to impress the Yugoslav leader. As the British government learned in December 1937, Stojadinović had told a Greek diplomat, in effect, that "whatever else happened, he was determined never to fight Germany. His country had tried it once and that was enough."[127]

As for the German hopes of getting Yugoslavia to come to a bilateral agreement with Hungary, however, that would prove a vastly more difficult project than either the Germans or the Italians, who were now urging the same thing, had anticipated. Four obvious, and one not so obvious, elements entered into the relations between the two neighbors. One was the boundary between the two; the question being, of course, whether Hungary was prepared to recognize once again the boundary established by the Treaty of Trianon, thus acknowledging the cession to Yugoslavia not only of Croatia-Slavonia but also of the Bácska and part of the Bánát with their Magyar minorities. Second, would Yugoslavia promise to allow this Magyar minority of over half a million in real life the rights supposedly guaranteed them by the minorities treaty that Yugoslavia, like the other successor states, had been required to sign when she acquired the lands the minorities inhabited. Third, would Yugoslavia, with or without the consent of her Little Entente partners, acquiesce

123. *D.D.F.*, 2d, 6, Nos. 25, 34, 114, 141; Osuský report of 6 May 1937, Czechoslovak document in T-120, 1041/1809/413853–54.

124. *D.D.F.*, 2d, 7, No. 58.

125. See Orme Sargent's very confidential letter to Phipps of 7 October 1937, R 6432/175/92, FO 371/21197.

126. *D.D.F.*, 2d, 7, No. 39; *G.D.*, D, 1, No. 85; Wimmer, pp. 211–14; C 8730/7888/17, FO 371/20698; R 4043/835/92, FO 371/21200; R 6737/175/92, FO 371/21197; R 147, R 590/147/92, FO 371/22475; Bullitt tel. 1771 of 23 December 1937, sec. 3, State 740.00/251 (this section omitted in *U.S.*, 1937, 1:206–7).

127. R 8116/3174/92, FO 371/21201.

formally in Hungary's repudiation of the restrictions imposed on her military strength by the Treaty of Trianon? Fourth, would Yugoslavia break openly with the Little Entente by assuring Hungary that she would remain neutral if Hungary used her newly enlarged and rearmed military forces to join Germany (and possibly Poland) in an attack on Czechoslovakia?

The negotiations between Belgrade and Budapest, carried on now openly, now secretly, at times directly, at times indirectly, were hampered not only by suspicions and reluctance on both sides, but also by still another factor, rarely mentioned but probably on the minds of the negotiators all the time. This was the problem of precedent. If the Yugoslav government promised to respect the rights of the Magyar minority, how could it refuse a reasonable accommodation with the other national components of the South Slav state? If Hungary formally renounced revision of the territorial provisions of the Treaty of Trianon vis-à-vis Yugoslavia, how could she maintain her claims against Czechoslovakia and Rumania? Although nothing suggests that the Slovaks were any more eager for a return of Hungarian domination than the Croats; and although the Magyar minority in Czechoslovakia was twice and that in Rumania three times as large as that in Yugoslavia, the principle was the same in all these cases.[128]

A satisfactory account of the tortuous negotiations remains to be written. Hungary alone of the participants has published a large collection of documents; there are bits and pieces from the German and Italian sides; but the Yugoslav documents remain closed.[129] From the point of view of the Germans, the most significant aspect of the negotiations was that Stojadinović was willing to consider the possibility, but could not quite see his way to a conclusion, and that the Hungarian government acted in an essentially similar fashion—willing to try but always hovering on the brink.[130] Even the personal blandishments of Germany's leaders failed to move the hesitant pair to the altar; when Hungarian Prime Minister Kálmán Darányi and Foreign Minister Kálmán de Kánya were in Berlin in November 1937, and when Stojadinović was regaled in the German capital in January 1938, their hosts urged on them once again the benefits of a bilateral agreement, but to no avail.[131]

128. A possible further factor on both sides was the concern of the government over possible objections from a public that in each country looked upon the other as a traditional enemy.

129. Hoptner, who is so informative on other aspects of Yugoslav foreign policy, is not only uninformed on this subject but has a somewhat misleading account of it (pp. 115–17).

130. Documents which illustrate this may be found in *Hungarian Documents*, 1, No. 254; 2, Nos. 66, 67, 72, 74, 75, 81, 85, 91, 97, 103, 107, 108, 121, 138, 217, 221, 225, 243, 247, 257, 259, 261, 274; *G.D.*, C, 6, No. 378; *D.D.F.*, 2d, 5, No. 361; Ciano, *Diplomatic Papers,* pp. 148–52; Ciano, *Diary,* 11 January 1938, p. 86. An excellent account in Carlyle A. Macartney, *October Fifteenth: A History of Modern Hungary* (Edinburgh: University Press, 1956), 1:151–54, 196–200, chap. 11, passim.

131. On the Hungarian visit, see *Hungarian Documents*, 1, No. 313 (German text, Kerekes, document 10); Zsigmond, pp. 261–62. On the Stojadinović visit, see *Hungarian*

The attention lavished on Stojadinović flattered his vanity and—by contrast with the prior less impressive reception of the Hungarians—annoyed Budapest, but the result was more a general improvement in the atmosphere of German-Yugoslav relations than concrete advances in the Yugoslav-Hungarian negotiations.[132] The maintenance of good German-Yugoslav relations was assured by Yugoslavia's lack of alternatives, German diplomatic adroitness in handling Stojadinović,[133] and Yugoslavia's calm acceptance of the *Anschluss*.[134] As for the negotiations with Hungary, however, Yugoslavia eventually remained in a common front with the other two powers of the Little Entente, while Hungary in spite of earlier reluctance decided at least to pretend to follow the course of working for agreement with all three simultaneously.

Ironically the resulting agreement, which could be read as trading Hungarian promises of nonaggression for Little Entente promises of better treatment for Magyar minorities and acquiescence in Hungarian rearmament, was reached on 23 August 1938, just as Hungary's leaders were on a state visit in Germany and the latter power was getting ready to launch a war of aggression against Czechoslovakia.[135] The agreement of Yugoslavia and Hungary, so long sought by Berlin, thus came in a framework most distasteful to Hitler and was seen by him as binding rather than freeing Hungary vis-à-vis Czechoslovakia and at the worst conceivable time.[136] If most of the German wrath for this was to be unloaded on the Hungarians, there was enough suspicion left over for a Yugoslavia which had maintained some real independence from Berlin in spite of years of determined effort to convert her into a German satellite.[137]

The minister president of Yugoslavia, like the foreign minister of Poland, had steered his country closer to the Axis against the inclinations of

---

Documents, 2, No. 107; *Guido Schmidt Trial*, pp. 503–5; *G.D.*, D, 5, Nos. 156, 158, 159, 162, 163, 165; *D.D.F.*, 2d, 8, Nos. 40, 49, 68, 70, 72, 74; Lane dispatch 124 of 10 February 1938, State 760H.65/776; "Bestellungen aus der Pressekonferenz," 12 and 17 January 1938, Bundesarchiv, Brammer, Z.Sg. 101/11, ff.25, 35.

132. Göring (see also *U.S.*, 1937, 1:170–77) had arranged the greater pomp for Stojadinović partly because he considered the rapprochement with Yugoslavia his personal work and partly because he remembered that the Hungarians had not received his wife-to-be officially in 1935 but the Yugoslavs had (Montgomery dispatch 959 of 9 February 1938, State 762.64/89).

133. See Lane to Moffat, 20 April 1938, Moffat Papers, vol. 13. For material suggesting that Prince Paul was also coming to a more favorable view of Germany, see Heinrich XXXIII. Reuss, "Aufzeichnung betr. Jugoslawien," June 1938, T-120, 2621/5482/E 382143–59; but cf. *G.D.*, C, 6, No. 448; *Hungarian Documents*, 2, No. 106.

134. See Hoptner, pp. 110–13; *Hungarian Documents*, 1, Nos. 304, 424, 446.

135. On the negotiations leading to the Bled agreement of 23 August 1938, see *Hungarian Documents*, 2, Nos. 75, 85, 87, 174, 175, 183, 208, 249, 255, 263, 271, 286, 287, 293, 294, 298, 301; *D.D.F.*, 2d, 7, Nos. 7, 12, 25, 73, 92, 317, 377; and n.130, above.

136. By a trick of fate, the same mischance befell the later German effort to arrange a Yugoslav-Hungarian agreement; hardly was the ink dry on the agreement of 12 December 1940 than Hungary was invited to join Germany in an attack on Yugoslavia. The Hungarian prime minister, Pál Teleki, committed suicide because of this dilemma.

137. See *Hungarian Documents*, 2, No. 267.

the public at large as well as those of other influential figures, Rydz-
Śmigły in the case of Poland, Prince Paul in the case of Yugoslavia. But
Stojadinović, like Beck, had shied away from any relationship of an
alliance type, realizing that in such circumstances the weaker partner
would necessarily become a mere appendage of the more aggressive and
powerful Germany. Though dubious about the efficacy of the ties to
France and the Little Entente, Stojadinović was as hesitant about giving
them up altogether as Beck was about abandoning entirely the Franco-
Polish alliance. Equally unwilling to be dominated from Berlin, both men
steered their countries into a policy of acquiescence in rather than resistance to German expansion, preferring the risks of the former to those of
the latter course. Simultaneously, each tried to find in other alignments
some semblance of balance and protection against the obvious threat of
German predominance in Central Europe; what Beck was hoping to secure by his policy of a "Third Europe" between Germany and the Soviet
Union, Stojadinović tried to attain through rapprochement with Italy. His
reluctance to move with similar speed to rapprochement with Hungary
reflected both the domestic problems of Yugoslavia and his assessment of
the danger of moving completely into the Axis camp. It would provide the
Hungarians with both a real reason and a welcome excuse for their own
caution about adhering too closely to Germany's policies.

Hungary's position in the pattern of German foreign policy had gone
through some ups and downs in the first years of National Socialist rule.
One of the few European countries which in 1933 was led by a government headed by an admirer of Hitler, the Hungary of Julius Gömbös had
hailed the advent of the new German ruler. Gömbös himself was the first
of Europe's leaders to visit Hitler, and for some time, German-Hungarian
relations appeared to be getting closer.[138] Although Gömbös had no intention of subordinating what he perceived to be Hungarian interests to
Germany, he believed that the revisionist aspirations of the two powers
could be harmonized. Furthermore, the collapse of the world market
prices for agricultural products had had a devastating effect on the Hungarian economy; it was the resulting political upheavals that had brought
Gömbös himself to the position of prime minister. New economic ties
with Germany opened up the possibility of ameliorating this desperate
situation; and in spite of some difficulties, German-Hungarian trade did in
fact provide a significant contribution to the slow but steady improvement
in Hungary's economic situation which culminated in the termination of
the League's financial mission in 1937.[139] By that time, Gömbös himself

138. Weinberg, *Foreign Policy*, pp. 110–16, 226–28, 321–23.
139. Macartney, 1:191–93. A review of German-Hungarian economic relations prepared in
the German foreign ministry before the visit of Darányi and de Kánya in Berlin in November
1937 is in *Documents secrets du ministère des affaires étrangère de l'Allemagne, 2, Hongrie:
La politique allemande 1937–1943* (Paris, 1946), No. 1; a survey of the statistics is in János

was dead, but even before his final illness, diplomatic and personal factors had combined to trouble German-Hungarian relations.

The diplomatic factors were largely inherent in the realities of the existing situation in Southeast Europe. The German element inside Hungary was angry about the continued efforts at Magyarization, while the Hungarian authorities were suspicious about the continuing loyalty of this element to Budapest. In the successor states, the German minorities were reluctant to cooperate with the Magyar element since even their worst grievances, real or imagined, in the current situation could not compare with their memories of Magyar oppression—the latter having firmly established themselves in first place as oppressors of national minorities in a part of Europe where the competition for that sad distinction was extremely keen. Moreover, as Gömbös himself had suspected, the more powerful Germany became, the less interested she was in Hungary. Yugoslavia and Rumania were sure to become and did become more interesting to a rearmed Germany, and only the possibility of joint operations against the Czechoslovakia both hated provided a basis for cooperation between Budapest and Berlin.

There was also a personal element in this situation. The Hungarian minister to Berlin, Constantin de Masirevich, was recalled at German insistence. Although his successor, Döme Sztójay, came to be both popular with the National Socialist authorities and a leading spokesman in favor of Hungary's following all German policies, the promotion of Masirevich to the legation in London and the subsequent hints to Berlin that the German minister in Budapest, Hans Georg von Mackensen, who was von Neurath's son-in-law, be recalled, hardly suggested the intimacy of close allies. Even more important than these matters of diplomatic personnel was the attitude toward Germany of the two men who, even while Gömbös was prime minister but more markedly after his death, played key roles in the setting of Hungary's foreign policy: the regent, Miklós Horthy, and the minister of foreign affairs from 1933 to 1938, Kálmán de Kánya.

Both men hoped that German actions in Europe would assist Hungary in reclaiming the lands lost by the Treaty of Trianon, but neither was sympathetic to the leaders of the Third Reich. Beyond a strong distaste that in the case of de Kánya went to the extent of nasty personal comments that got back, and may have been intended to get back, to the German subjects of them, a more fundamental divergence of views made both men dubious of staking their country's future on Germany's success.[140] Horthy as an admiral in the Austro-Hungarian navy had devel-

---

Tihanyi, "Deutsch-ungarische Aussenhandelsbeziehungen im Dienste der faschistischen Aggressionspolitik, 1933 bis 1944," *Jahrbuch für Wirtschaftsgeschichte,* 1972, No. 1, pp. 65–73.

140. See Szembek's comments in his diary, 5–9 February 1938, p. 270.

oped enormous respect for the role of the British navy in controlling the oceans; while de Kánya's long diplomatic experience, which included a term as Austro-Hungarian minister to Mexico during the war, had given him a recognition of the fact, often overlooked in Berlin, that the earth is round.[141] Their experiences and perceptions had convinced both men that in another world war, Germany would lose once again—with disastrous consequences for any allies dragged down with her.[142]

The caution of these two leaders of Hungary was, moreover, reinforced by their awareness of the fact that Hungarian disarmament as a result of the peace treaty left her at the mercy of her Little Entente neighbors should they go to war with her, and that any rearmament measures on Hungary's part—with rearmament begun seriously only after the departure of the League mission in 1937—would not show major results for several years. Although rarely alluded to in discussions or documents, this chronological discrepancy in the initiation of German and Hungarian rearmament was a critical factor in the intermittent discord between the two possible allies, whose relationship would culminate in bitterness and betrayal in 1944.[143]

The concern of the Germans over the possibility that the successor of Gömbös, Kálmán Darányi, might direct Hungary along new lines disagreeable for Berlin was demonstrated by press attacks on him and an article in the *Völkischer Beobachter*, inspired by Hitler, which asserted that not all borders needed revising, it being assumed that Hungary's claims to Transylvania were being referred to.[144] The Germans also increased their interest in the fate of the German minority inside Hungary and may have increased their contacts with various far right groups on the Hungarian political scene.[145] The main thrust of German policy, however, continued to be to urge the Budapest government to concentrate all re-

141. For a similar, but more detailed, discussion of Kánya, see Thomas L. Sakmyster, "Hungary and the Munich Crisis: The Revisionist Dilemma," *Slavic Review*, 32, No. 4 (December 1973), 728–29.

142. For an analysis of a somewhat similar kind, see R 7542/1644/21, FO 371/21154; cf. *D.D.F.*, 2d, 6, No. 382.

143. See also Nandor A. F. Dreisziger, "Civil-Military Relations in Nazi Germany's Shadow: The Case of Hungary," in Adrian Preston (ed.), *Swords and Covenants* (London: Croom Helm, 1976), p. 219.

144. Weinberg, *Foreign Policy*, pp. 323–24. Cf. *G.D.*, C, 6, No. 205. A year later, when the Goga government in Rumania seemed likely to secure German support, the Hungarians warned von Neurath that any German recognition of Rumania's border would have catastrophic implications for German-Hungarian relations (*Hungarian Documents*, 2, No. 115).

145. On the German minority at this time, see Macartney, 1:178–79; *G.D.*, C, 6, Nos. 280, 365, 437; D, 5, Nos. 144, 148, 189; *Hungarian Documents*, 1, Nos. 314, 427; Jacobsen, pp. 526–28; "Bestellungen aus der Pressekonferenz," 9 September 1937, Bundesarchiv, Brammer, Z.Sg. 101/10, f.187. See also L. Tilkovsky, "Volksdeutsche Bewegung und ungarische Nationalitätenpolitik (1938–1941)," *Acta Historica*, 12, Nos. 1–2 (1966), 59–112. The subject was discussed with von Neurath when he visited Budapest in June 1937 (*G.D.*, C, 6, No. 423; *Hungarian Documents*, 1, No. 264). German contacts with Hungarian political movements in those years await detailed scholarly investigation.

visionist aspirations on Czechoslovakia. On various occasions the Hungarians were reminded of this and the concomitant need to reach an agreement with Yugoslavia and some sort of temporary accommodation with Rumania.[146] The Magyar leaders understood both the significance and the implications of this advice, but it was not as easy for them to follow as for the Germans, and the Italians, to give.[147] The very idea of giving up hopes for revision in other directions, and especially toward Rumania, was not likely to excite enthusiasm in Budapest. Furthermore, the obvious way in which Hungarian agreement to such a procedure would make Hungary into a minor satellite of Germany, which could aid or abandon her client at will, aroused fears among Hungary's leaders.[148] They were at least equally fearful of more immediate risks. Unless Germany guaranteed Hungary against Yugoslav attack or assisted her in a rapid building up of her army, any Hungarian operation against Czechoslovakia could easily lead to a crushing defeat for Hungary. As has already been mentioned, the Hungarians tried to cope with part of this problem by lengthy negotiations with Yugoslavia, and when these did not work out, with all three members of the Little Entente.[149] Before these negotiations came to the conclusion that so annoyed Berlin, other questions had arisen between Germany and Hungary.

In the area of German-Hungarian economic relations, the occasional frictions were resolved without too much difficulty.[150] Any efforts Hungary might have made to reduce her dependence on Germany in this regard were, in any case, rendered pointless by the annexation of Austria, which greatly increased Germany's role in Hungary's foreign trade and also made her an important factor in regard to investments inside Hungary.[151]

The possibility of the incorporation of Austria into Germany had worried the Hungarians for some time; though preferring an independent Austria, they were reconciled to the probability of its disappearance.[152]

146. *G.D.*, D, 1, No. 181; *Hungarian Documents*, 1, No. 248.

147. Ciano, *Diplomatic Papers*, pp. 63–68.

148. The Hungarians were thus understandably alarmed about the rumors of German-Czechoslovak negotiations in the winter of 1936–37 and not fully reassured by von Neurath's promises in March 1937 (*G.D.*, C, 6, No. 238).

149. See above, pp. 221–23. For the 1937 portion of these negotiations, especially on Hungary's right to rearm, see also *Hungarian Documents*, 1, Nos. 222, 304; 2, Nos. 64, 68, 77, 80, 82–84, 86, 88, 90, 92–96; *G.D.*, C, 6, Nos. 181, 443; D, 5, Nos. 141, 143, 145; *D.D.F.*, 2d, 5, No. 479; 6, Nos. 3, 26, 71, 170, 211, 353, 380, 388, 392, 440; Jörg K. Hoensch, *Der Ungarische Revisionismus und die Zerschlagung der Tschechoslowakei* (Tübingen: Mohr, 1967), pp. 44–48, 72–75.

150. *G.D.*, C, 6, Nos. 131, 144, 257.

151. A good analysis is in *D.D.F.*, 2d, 8, No. 467; see also ibid., No. 498. For a broader analysis of the economic impact of the *Anschluss* on the German trade position in Southeast Europe as a whole see ibid., 9, No. 47.

152. *G.D.*, C, 6, No. 130; *Hungarian Documents*, 1, No. 203; Ciano, *Diplomatic Papers*, pp. 117–20; Macartney, 1:204–6.

They had, in fact, discussed it with von Neurath when the latter visited Budapest in the course of his Balkan journey of June 1937.[153] Nothing much on this or any other subject of importance appears to have been discussed when von Blomberg visited Budapest two weeks later,[154] but a whole range of issues, including the Austrian and Czechoslovak problems, were trouched on when Darányi and de Kánya went to Berlin in November.[155]

During the conversations between German and Hungarian leaders, outstanding economic questions were settled. The Hungarians complained about National Socialist propaganda among the German minority in Hungary, but Göring, von Neurath, and Hitler all placed the emphasis on the Austrian and Czechoslovak questions. They again urged Hungary to settle with Yugoslavia, work out something with Rumania,[156] and concentrate all her energies on Czechoslovakia. The Germans, however, did not respond to the Hungarian request for a German guarantee of Yugoslav neutrality if Hungary attacked Czechoslovakia. As for the Austrian issue, the Germans indicated their strong hostility to Austrian Chancellor Kurt von Schuschnigg and hinted that the *Anschluss* would come before long. Since Hitler had told his advisers of his general plans a few days earlier at the meeting recorded in the Hossbach memorandum, the Hungarian leaders received rather similar views from all their major conversations. Nevertheless, they appear not to have recognized how quickly the Germans might move.

If the possible return of Slovakia and the annexation of Ruthenia were dangled before the eager eyes of the Magyars as their loot from the destruction of Czechoslovakia, the annexation of Austria by Germany opened up the possibility of a return of the Burgenland area, ceded by Hungary to Austria under the terms of the peace settlement. The evidence on German offers of this area to Hungary and on Hitler's policy about the fate of the Burgenland is fragmentary and contradictory.[157] Until new information becomes available, the known details should probably be interpreted in terms of a pattern Hitler followed repeatedly. If another power

153. *G.D.*, C, 6, No. 423; *Hungarian Documents*, 1, No. 264; Travers (chargé a.i. Budapest) dispatch 711 of 17 June 1937, State 762.64/69; R 5254/4067/67, FO 371/21141.

154. *D.D.F.*, 2d, 6, No. 173; Kausch, "Informationsbericht Nr. 90," 21 May 1937, Bundesarchiv, Brammer, Z.Sg. 101/30, ff.437–41.

155. On this visit, see nn.131 and 139, above; Macartney, 1:202–4 and the sources cited there; *Hungarian Documents*, 1, No. 313; Zsigmond, pp. 261–62; Montgomery dispatch 891 of 2 December 1937 plus enclosures 9–12, State 762.64/84; Dodd dispatch 3767 of 6 December 1937, State 762.64/85; *D.D.F.*, 2d, 7, Nos. 231, 276, 329.

156. Note that when Göring was in Poland in February 1938, he and Beck agreed on the desirability of improving Hungarian-Rumanian relations, but Göring thought progress unlikely because of Hungarian intransigence (*Lipski Papers*, No. 79).

157. A good summary in Macartney, 1:206, esp. n.6. See also *Hungarian Documents*, 1, No. 391. This question is not touched on in the section dealing with Burgenland in *Austrian History Yearbook*, 8 (1972), 7–101; or Andrew F. Burghardt's, *Borderland: A History and Geographical Study of Burgenland, Austria* (Madison: University of Wisconsin Press, 1962).

would share the risks of drastic action, he would share the booty with them, and even do so generously from his point of view. If another power, however, declined to share the risks, or wanted additional benefits later, he would stubbornly decline. When the Hungarians refused to go along with him in the Czechoslovak crisis, they would get only scraps; and when they tried for more later, Hitler called a halt. When the Soviets agreed to go along with him in 1939, he was prepared to offer more than Stalin thought of asking; but when the Russians collected a part of their booty without risks in 1940, he was annoyed. When Lithuania declined to join in the attack on Poland in 1939, she was traded to the Soviet Union for a piece of Poland instead of becoming a German satellite expanded by the Vilna area she had so long hoped to recover. When Finland and Rumania played important roles in the attack on the Soviet Union, Hitler was willing to allot them generous shares of the vast lands he planned to conquer—having earlier been willing to sacrifice their interests in the deal with Stalin. There are other examples of this pattern, but no exceptions.

According to this manner of Hitler's procedure, it is probably best to assume that had Hungary moved in March 1938 simultaneously with Germany, thereby sharing the risks and opprobrium, Hitler would probably have left them with the Burgenland; but when they expressed a desire for it a few days later, Hitler was confident that the crisis was over and those who had not shared in the cooking could not expect to participate in the meal.[158] The best that Hungary could obtain from Berlin was a promise that Germany would respect the border of 1919.[159]

In subsequent months, Germany's relations with Hungary were dominated by the crisis over Czechoslovakia. Berlin continued to want Hungary's participation. The Hungarians were perfectly willing and even eager to do so but were held back by fear of Czechoslovakia's Little Entente allies, especially Yugoslavia, as well as their worry about a general war resulting from a German attack on Czechoslovakia. In regard to the latter issue, the Hungarians tried to maintain good relations with Britain and the United States.[160] They would even try during the state

158. This was an expression Hitler used on a similar occasion, referring to the attack on Czechoslovakia during the Hungarian state visit of August 1938 (*G.D.*, D, 2, No. 383). Macartney accepts a similar interpretation.

There had clearly been no follow-up in Budapest of the 28 May 1937 suggestion by the Hungarian minister in Vienna that Hungary make diplomatic preparations to substitute for German annexation of Austria a partition of that country in which Hungary would regain her pre-1919 western border, and the southern portion of Carinthia would be turned over to Yugoslavia in exchange for the retrocession of the Bácska to Hungary (Jedlicka and Neck, p. 202).

159. *Hungarian Documents,* 1, Nos. 438, 443; *G.D.*, D, 2, No. 182; 5, No. 183. There had been occasional talk about a German claim to adjacent parts of West Hungary.

160. Note that Hungary made its semiannual payment on its relief debt to the United States on 15 December 1937 and continued to do so until 1941 (*U.S.*, 1938, 2:553, n.4; cf. ibid., 555, 556). For a warning against a full alignment with Berlin from the Hungarian minister in London, see *Hungarian Documents,* 1, No. 447. Hungary also refused to leave the League (ibid., 2, No. 227).

visit of August 1938 to discourage Hitler from running the risk of what they were sure would be a losing world war. They continued the negotiations with Yugoslavia and the other Little Entente powers, hoping to keep a free hand toward Czechoslovakia but unable to do so completely.[161]

Although the German leaders repeatedly reproached the Hungarians about their diffidence, they would never take the one step which might have removed its most obvious cause—or revealed that the Hungarians were merely using it as an excuse: a German guarantee against the danger of Yugoslavia's coming to Czechoslovakia's aid. This issue had been brought up when Darányi and de Kánya were in Berlin; it was repeatedly raised by Hungarian military leaders with their German counterparts;[162] and it was placed before the Germans several times in 1938 through diplomatic channels.[163] Given the obvious military danger to Hungary, and Germany's interest in mobilizing additional enemies against Czechoslovakia, why were the Germans not willing to satisfy the Hungarian demand for a German guarantee of Yugoslav neutrality, especially after the Anschluss gave Germany a common border with Yugoslavia and hence a stronger position for threatening that country?

On this critical question, the German attitude is clear enough—Hitler refused—but the reasons must be inferred from indirect evidence.[164] Several factors may be adduced to explain the German policy. First, there was the personal element. Certainly Göring, and after the January meeting between Hitler and Stojadinović Hitler also greatly preferred the Yugoslav strong man to the Hungarian leaders they met. Von Neurath, and yet more strongly his successor von Ribbentrop, shared these sentiments. Stojadinović was a man after their own heart, while Darányi and de Kánya, Horthy and Imrédy (Darányi's successor) all appeared to them as hesitant, which was bad enough, but also as somehow not really pro-German, which was worse, and incidentally, true. A second factor, which will be examined in connection with the crisis over Czechoslovakia, was Hitler's belief that a German attack on that country would not in fact set off a general war, so that Hungary's fears were unwarranted. Third, there was concern that any German commitment to Hungary could easily have the opposite of the intended effect; instead of facilitating an agreement between Hungary and Yugoslavia that would split the Little Entente, it

161. See n.149, above. For the continued negotiations in 1938, see *Hungarian Documents*, 1, Nos. 399, 422; 2, Nos. 100, 102, 111, 113, 114, 116, 118, 122, 126, 130, 132, 134, 151, 153, 154, 156, 158, 159, 161, 165, 168–70, 184, 188, 195, 223, 230, 234, 236, 242, 248, 251, 253, 254, 256–88 passim; *G.D.*, D, 5, Nos. 176, 199, 216, 219, 221. Thoughout the documents, there are signs of British attempts to urge both sides to agreement.

162. Ádám, p. 92.

163. A summary in Macartney, 1:207, 210–11, 235. Key documents in *G.D.*, D, 2, No. 114; 5, Nos. 160, 161, 165 n.1, 173, 177, 178, 190–92; *Documents secrets*, 2, Nos. 10–12, 17.

164. Note that at one point Hitler was apparently willing to consider some sort of guarantee (*G.D.*, D, 5, No. 163).

might result in pushing the three more closely together than ever, especially frightening Yugoslavia back into the arms of her old associates. Finally, there may have been a feeling that Hungary, especially after the *Anschluss*, really had no choice but to line up with Germany; and that if the Hungarians were as eager to reclaim the ancient lands of the Crown of Saint Stephen as they always asserted, they would have to share in the moves and risks of German policy on whatever terms Germany might be pleased to allot them.[165]

In the face of the German refusal, the Hungarians tried in May and June 1938, but with not much greater success, to secure Italy's support against Yugoslavia to restrain the latter. Although perfectly willing to see Czechoslovakia destroyed, the Italian government was not willing to sacrifice its new relationship with Yugoslavia to Hungary's fears and would not commit itself as firmly as Budapest wanted.[166] The only other country in the area with which Hungary could concert her policy was Poland. This has already been touched on from the Polish side; from the standpoint of Budapest this meant cooperation with the one European country for which the Hungarians felt some real affection. From common antagonism to Habsburgs and Romanovs there had emerged a sympathy that now looked to a common border to result from the dissolution of Czechoslovakia, there being the rather unrealistic thought that such a common border would then make the Polish-Hungarian combination a barrier to both German and Soviet expansion. The fly in this ointment was that the Slovak separatists were much more inclined to lean to Poland than to Hungary—their bad memories of Magyar domination being even stronger than their sense of grievance against the Czechs—while Beck repeatedly toyed with the idea of some association of Slovakia with Poland. Nevertheless, the Hungarians secured at least ostensible Polish endorsement of their claim to almost all of Slovakia and Ruthenia, with only small border adjustments to be made in favor of Poland.[167] In spite of the pleasant words exchanged between Budapest and Warsaw, the Hungarians were probably not as confident of the intentions of their Polish friends as they pretended to be, so that in this direction also there were clouds over the bright hopes of revision accompanying any partition of Czechoslovakia.

As if Hungarian enthusiasm for throwing themselves into adventures on the side of Germany were not sufficiently dampened by all these factors, domestic worries provided additional problems. The new government of Béla Imrédy, who succeeded Darányi in May 1938, was in some ways

165. Cf. C 1872/132/18, FO 371/21674.

166. *Hungarian Documents*, 2, Nos. 119, 268, 269; *G.D.*, D, 5, Nos. 213, 315; Macartney, 1:233–35.

167. Kerekes, No. 13; *Hungarian Documents*, 1, No. 389 (German text in Zsigmond, pp. 262–63, nn.42 and 43); Ádám, No. 7; Zsigmond, pp. 267–68, n.53; Hoensch, pp. 58–67.

more sympathetic to Berlin than its predecessor, but the contacts of German intelligence and other agencies with the far right in Hungarian politics aroused the detestation of the regent as well as most members of the cabinet. The ruling elite of Hungary was still inclined to look with some favor on Hitler's regime; they found it hard to believe that anyone who in their eyes was so obviously correctly anti-Semitic could be wrong on anything else. Nevertheless, like many of Germany's conservative nationalists, they looked down distastefully at the rowdy young loud-mouths who were as conspicuous in their own as in Germany's fascist movement, and they bitterly resented the real and imagined ties of the Arrow Cross movement to Berlin.[168] The internal problems of the summer of 1938 must, therefore, be seen as another influence on Hungary's policy toward Germany.

The Hungarian explanation to the British that Horthy's visit to Germany in August 1938 was a purely ceremonial one was certainly incorrect.[169] Nevertheless, the refusal of Hungary at that time to join in a combined operation against Czechoslovakia, coming at the same moment as her agreement with the Little Entente—however that agreement might be explained by de Kánya—marked a real crack in German-Hungarian relations. The impact of this development on German policy toward Hungary during the Czechoslovak crisis will be reviewed in the context of the latter, but it had become obvious to Berlin that Hungary was simply not a reliable ally within the definition established by Hitler.

The fact that Horthy during his visit suggested to Hitler that he would be willing to urge the Poles to return the Corridor to Germany must have shown the German leader how hopelessly the Hungarian had misunderstood him. Hitler was trying to line up everybody and anybody on his side to gang up on Czechoslovakia for a quick and decisive little war that would smash that country and transfer the pieces to her neighbors; and here was the Hungarian regent talking about revising the Treaty of Versailles and in a manner almost calculated to split the very coalition against Czechoslovakia that Hitler was trying to form. The German record simply states that Hitler asked Horthy to refrain from making such a proposal;[170] what he thought was presumably about as courteous as the "nonsense, shut-up!" with which he interrupted Horthy's exposé of the danger of starting a war that would become general and that Great Britain would win in the end.[171]

168. Macartney, 1:210–30; cf. *Hungarian Documents*, 1, Nos. 440, 458; 2, Nos. 129, 197, 199. The German press was instructed to keep quiet about the Hungarian cabinet crisis, "Bestellungen aus der Pressekonferenz," 12 May 1938, Bundesarchiv, Brammer, Z.Sg. 101/11, f.361.

169. *Hungarian Documents*, 2, No. 276.

170. *G.D.*, D, 5, No. 52.

171. Macartney, 1:242.

The repeated, even if unwelcome, German suggestions to Hungary that she arrive at some agreement with Rumania must be seen as a symptom of Germany's changed policy toward the latter country. In the first years after Hitler came to power in Germany, Berlin had looked upon Rumania as aligned with France and the Little Entente against Germany. The identification of Nicolae Titulescu, Rumania's foreign minister, with the policy of collective security made him and his country the objects of German hostility; and all soundings for more friendly relations coming from Bucharest were rejected out of hand.[172] This was due to the belief that nothing could be usefully accomplished, not to any lack of interest in a change of Rumania's policy. German interests in Rumania were of two kinds, diplomatic and economic. The diplomatic interest was the concern that Rumania's ties to Czechoslovakia and France might lead her to an agreement with the Soviet Union analogous to those of the other two, thereby outflanking the barrier that Poland provided against Soviet help for Czechoslovakia. Germany had encouraged the elements in Rumanian politics opposed to any Rumanian treaty with the Soviet Union and rejoiced in the August 1936 dismissal of Titulescu, who had himself had serious reservations about such a treaty but had been the Rumanian leader most likely to approve a mutual assistance pact with Russia.

The economic interests of Germany in Rumania had been relatively small to begin with. Since Germany was buying substantial quantities of agricultural products from Yugoslavia and Hungary as part of her political and economic policy toward those countries, she was not so interested as yet in taking Rumania's wheat. There were, however, some factors drawing the Germans toward Rumania. The great deficit in meeting Germany's needs for vegetable fats and oils might be met in part by expanding soybean acreage in Southeast Europe, including Rumania, and efforts were being made in this direction. Even more important was Rumania's greatest natural asset beside her rich farms: Europe's most productive oil fields outside the Soviet Union. Because of high prices as compared with other petroleum exporters, Rumanian oil had not been shipped to Germany in large quantities in the past; but the future needs of the growing German air force may well have been a factor in Göring's adding Rumania to his other pet projects, Poland and Yugoslavia, about the time in 1936 when he was entrusted by Hitler with responsibility for Germany's raw materials and foreign exchange problems. A German-Rumanian trade agreement had already been signed in 1935, and after the dismissal of Titulescu, the road for strengthening both political and economic relations between Germany and Rumania appeared to be open.

One possible source of tension did not, in fact, cause the trouble that might have been expected. Although the German minority in Rumania

172. For German-Rumanian relations before 1937, see Weinberg, *Foreign Policy*, pp. 118–19, 230–31, 323–25.

was substantially larger than that in Hungary—about 800,000 as compared with a bit over half a million—there was practically none of the anxiety over them that frequently had such bad repercussions on German-Hungarian relations. This was not due either to the greater beneficence of the Rumanians to their national minorities or the stronger loyalty of those of German background in Rumania to their adopted country. The two elements of perhaps greatest significance in calming what could have been a great source of friction were the distance between Rumania and Germany—unlike the situation of Hungary with a substantial and dangerously compact area of German settlement adjacent to the border with Austria—and the internal bickering within the German minority, which was even more continuous and divisive than normally characteristic of these groups in Europe.[173]

The one special factor that did cast a cloud over German relations with Rumania was, even more than in the case of Hungary, the practice of various German National Socialist party and other agencies of dabbling in internal Rumanian politics. Alfred Rosenberg's National Socialist party foreign policy office (APA) and, from all appearances, a whole host of other German organizations were not only working at cross-purposes with each other in dealing with the German element in Rumania but were financing and attempting to influence, and were in various forms of contact with, a number of groups on the lunatic fringe of Rumanian politics. These contacts, especially those with the Iron Guard of Cornelius Codreanu, had greatly annoyed King Carol; they would serve as a continuing source of difficulties; and they were a cause of repeated protests to Berlin.

All the details of these contacts are not clear; but it is known that the Rumanian government found out about them and that various embarrassing documents fell into the wrong hands. Furthermore, those whom the Germans most favored, the tiny group around Octavian Goga, were in a position of real influence for only a few weeks in the winter of 1937–38, while the Iron Guard could secure no real position at all—until the Germans allowed a few of its members to set up a shadow "government-in-exile" after Rumania had gone over to the Allies in August 1944. German ties to the perennial losers of Rumanian politics, therefore, served to hinder rather than hasten closer German-Rumanian ties; their only im-

173. See Jacobsen, pp. 570–80, for a brief survey. Geza C. Paikert, *The Danube Swabians: German Populations in Hungary, Rumania and Yugoslavia and Hitler's Impact on Their Patterns* (The Hague: Nijhoff, 1967), contains considerable detail. Margot Hegemann, "Die Deutsche Volksgruppe in Rumänien—eine Fünfte Kolonne des deutschen Imperialismus in Südosteuropa," *Jahrbuch für Geschichte der UdSSR*, 4 (1960), 374–75, confirms the insignificance of these National Socialist groups in 1937–39. The important study by Philippe Marguerat, *Le IIIe Reich et le pétrole roumain, 1938–1940* (Geneva: A. W. Sijthoff, 1977), pp. 90–91, takes a similar view of the role of the German minority. A useful but superficial survey of their tiresome quarrels will be found in Wolfgang Miege, *Das Dritte Reich und die Deutsche Volksgruppe in Rumänien 1933–38* (Frankfurt/M: Peter Lang, 1972).

portance for an understanding of those ties in 1937–38 being that the progress of the rapprochement in spite of the constant aggravation shows how imperative the factors pushing the two countries together were perceived to be in Bucharest as well as Berlin.[174]

The German desire for better relations with Rumania was made evident by the assurances given to the Rumanian government when Georges Bratianu, leader of the Young Liberals, was in Berlin in the fall of 1936.[175] The key issue, then and later, was the attitude of Germany toward Hungary's desire for revision of her border with Rumania. Once the Berlin authorities had indicated that their friendship for Hungary did not extend to support for the return of Transylvania to Magyar control, they could be sure of making up for Hungarian disappointment by Rumanian gratitude. Although unwilling to make any public and explicit statement recognizing the existing border, for fear of excessive offense to Hungary,[176] Hitler did repeat to Mircea Djuvara, when he was appointed the new Rumanian minister to Berlin in April 1938, what he had previously told Bratianu in November 1936. Germany was not interested in the territorial disputes between the Balkan states, an assertion that Djuvara correctly interpreted as meaning that Germany would not support the revisionist aspirations of Hungary against Rumania.[177] Djuvara was the replacement for Nicolae Petrescu-Comnen who had been minister in Berlin since 1932 and had been appointed Rumanian foreign minister in the course of the upheaval in Rumanian domestic affairs; his appointment was actually a sign of King Carol's interest in good relations with Germany, a point of considerable importance in view of the nature of that upheaval.[178]

The Rumanian elections of 20 November 1937 had shown a decline in the public support for the Liberal government of Gheorghe Tatarescu, prime minister since 1934. King Carol thereupon appointed Goga prime minister. Goga's party, the Christian Nationalists, had not even secured 10 percent of the popular vote. Carol may have been trying to show up the

174. On the German ties to Goga and the Iron Guard, as well as Rumanian protests, see n.172, above, and Jacobsen, pp. 79–84; Marguerat, pp. 86–90; *G.D.*, D, 5, Nos. 157 n.3, 164, 186. The raids on Iron Guard headquarters after Carol's coup of 10 February 1938 produced evidence of ties to Germany, some of which was used in the subsequent trial of Codreanu and his associates; *G.D.*, D, 5, Nos. 203–5, 207–8; R 4515/9/37, FO 371/22450; Franklin Mott Gunther to Moffat, 19 May 1938, Moffat Papers, vol. 13. For an interesting effort to place the Iron Guard in the context of Rumanian history, see Stephen Fischer-Galati's piece "Fascism in Romania," in Peter F. Sugar (ed.), pp. 112–21.

175. Weinberg, *Foreign Policy*, p. 324.

176. The reference to the existing border in Goga's telegram of greetings to Hitler on 1 January 1938 was the main reason for neither its text nor Hitler's reply being published (*G.D.*, D, 5, No. 157; "Informationsbericht Nr. 2, Das deutsch-rumänische Verhältnis," 4 January 1938, Bundesarchiv, Brammer, Z.Sg. 101/32, f.6; *Hungarian Documents*, 2, No. 115). See also "Bestellungen aus der Pressekonferenz," 6 January 1938, Bundesarchiv, Brammer, Z.Sg. 101/11, f.9.

177. *G.D.*, D, 5, No. 196.

178. Ibid., No. 171. On Comnen, see his not always reliable memoirs, *Preludi del grande dramma* (Rome: Leonardo, 1947).

absurdity of Goga's pretensions, or he may have thought that the limitation this small popular base imposed on Goga would make him completely dependent on royal support. In any case, the apparent triumph of Hitler's voluble admirer was short-lived. Unprepared for office and untouched by any leadership ability, Goga neither broadened his base at home nor aroused enthusiasm abroad. At home the Iron Guard reluctantly tolerated him while all others stood aside, half amused, half appalled. Abroad, the Germans thought he lacked support,[179] while Britain and France protested against the anti-Semitic measures of the new government, pointedly reminding the Rumanians of their treaty obligations.[180] Even President Roosevelt expressed his concern, giving a warning message for King Carol to the departing Rumanian minister to Washington, who was himself going back to Bucharest to urge his government to keep out of the Axis orbit.[181] On 10 February 1938 King Carol dismissed Goga and in a coup replaced the constitution as well as the cabinet.[182] It was in the new government, now quite subservient to the king, that Petrescu-Comnen became foreign minister and under its direction that the Iron Guard leaders were tried and sentenced.

Both before and after this extraordinary drama, the Rumanians tried to improve their relations with Berlin. They shared with Yugoslavia in rejecting the plan supported by France and Czechoslovakia for the conversion of the Little Entente into a mutual assistance system.[183] The government in Bucharest wanted to keep its existing ties; like Stojadinović, King Carol was reluctant to give up the reinsurance provided by the agreements with France and the Little Entente, but he was willing to have them balanced by good relations with Germany.[184] He hoped for closer relations with Great Britain without France as intermediary. He admired and feared Germany, but feared and disliked the Soviet Union.[185]

179. Note Göring's comments to Beck on 23 February 1938, *Lipski Papers*, No. 79.

180. *U.S.*, 1938, 1:5–6. The exchanges between London and Bucharest protesting against Rumania's actions, reporting similar French steps, and urging a postponement of King Carol's planned trip to London are in R 36, R 109/9/37, FO 371/22447; R 924, R 926/9/37, FO 371/22448; R 1161/153/37, FO 371/22453. American reports on the situation are in *U.S.*, 1938, 2:672–83. For Rumanian efforts to maintain close relations with France even during the Goga period, see *D.D.F.*, 2d, 7, Nos. 400, 401; but the French government was still insistent on the issue of anti-Semitic legislation, see ibid., 8, Nos. 73, 152, 163.

181. Moffat Diary, 31 December 1937, Moffat Papers, vol. 39; R 324/9/37, FO 371/22447. The text of Rumanian Minister Davila's report of 29 December 1937 was intercepted and read by the Italians who passed it on to the Germans on 6 January 1938, DZA Potsdam, Büro RAM, Akte 60963, ff.141–42. Cf. *D.D.F.*, 2d, 7, No. 394.

182. For a German interpretation of the coup, see *G.D.*, D, 5, No. 179. See also Miege, pp. 237–39, 244, 328–33.

183. See above, pp. 79–81. See also *G.D.*, C, 6, Nos. 270, 305; D, 1, No. 65.

184. Ibid., C, 6, No. 197; D, 1, No. 69; 5, No. 145. On the visit of Delbos to Bucharest in December 1937, see *D.D.F.*, 2d, 7, No. 327; Veverka report of 11 December 1937, Czechoslovak document in T-120, 1041/1809/413866–67.

185. *D.D.F.*, 2d, 6, No. 286; Osuský to Krofta, 17 July 1937, and Masaryk to Krofta, 19 July 1937, Czechoslovak documents in T-120, 1316/2376/D 497048–55.

In the spring of 1937, the Rumanian government did sound the Soviet government on the possibility of a friendship pact, analogous to the Yugoslav-Italian settlement, in exchange for formal Soviet renunciation of Bessarabia, but Moscow was not willing to go along with such a project. The Soviet leaders would not renounce their claim to Bessarabia unless Rumania were more forthcoming, but their very rejection of the proposal undoubtedly heightened Rumanian suspicions of Soviet territorial ambitions.[186] This must be seen as part of the background to Rumania's continuing move toward the Axis. Bucharest was dubious about Germany's urging of a settlement with Hungary, and Rumanian objections to concessions in favor of the Magyar element in Transylvania proved a major delaying factor in the negotiations between Hungary and the members of the Little Entente that culminated in the Bled agreement of August 1938, but this reticence did not apply to her relations with Germany.[187] Especially after the coup of 10 February 1938, King Carol took pains to reassure the Germans and to try to keep the Iron Guard trials from damaging relations with Berlin.[188]

From the point of view of Germany, the advantages of improved relations with Rumania were obvious: politically there was the possibility of isolating Czechoslovakia; economically there was the hope of increased imports of petroleum. When von Neurath was in Rome in May 1937, he had explained to Count Ciano the desirability of bringing Rumania closer to the Axis.[189] In January 1938 he told Josef Beck, the Polish foreign minister, who had been working hard to strengthen even further the close relations between Poland and Rumania, that in the Titulescu years Germany had rejected all approaches from Bucharest, but that now the situation had changed and German-Rumanian relations were fine.[190] There was still the feeling that Germany had best not get too close to Rumania,[191] presumably because of the repercussions on German-Hungarian relations, but Berlin was well pleased with the situation where Rumania stood aside and hence helped shield German ambitions in Central Europe.

In the economic field, the agreement of 1935 worked satisfactorily, but during 1937, the German government wanted to broaden the basis and raise the level of German-Rumanian trade.[192] A series of negotiations

186. *D.D.F.*, 2d, 5, No. 396; Krofta circular of 3 June 1937, Czechoslovak document in T-120, 1041/1809/413874. By 1938 the situation would, as will be seen, be reversed. The Rumanians were so afraid of the Germans that they stated they would not agree to the transit of Russian troops in exchange for recognition of possession of Bessarabia.
187. On the negotiations leading to the Bled agreement, see above, pp. 221–23. Cf. *G.D.*, C, 6, No. 472.
188. Ibid., 5, Nos. 186, 203–5.
189. Ciano, *Diplomatic Papers*, pp. 115–17 (Italian text in DZA Potsdam, Büro RAM, Akte 60951, ff.105–9).
190. *Lipski Papers*, No. 75; cf. *Hungarian Documents*, 2, No. 114.
191. *G.D.*, D, 5, No. 189.
192. Ibid., C, 6, Nos. 142, 210.

ensued, and a special German economic delegation, headed by Helmuth Wohlthat of Göring's staff, was sent to Bucharest in November 1937 to work out an agreement. The Germans were willing to make considerable concessions, for political as well as economic reasons, in order to secure a new treaty with Rumania. Such a treaty was signed on 9 December 1937 and clearly marked a new stage in Germany's economic offensive in Southeast Europe as well as her hopes of realizing greater petroleum imports from Rumania.[193]

During the course of 1938, the Germans found that they wanted even more Rumanian oil, both to meet the needs of their growing air force and to keep the newly acquired oil refineries of Austria fully employed. The only way this could be accomplished was to increase German arms exports to Rumania and secure Rumanian agreement to additional oil exports. The Germans agreed among themselves to try for such a scheme, not only to obtain the oil supplies, but also to head off British and French economic moves designed to counter German economic influence. The fact that the Rumanians approved the extra oil shipments to Germany on 13 August 1938, just as the crisis over Czechoslovakia—Rumania's Little Entente partner—was reaching a culminating point may serve as an indication of the extent to which Germany had succeeded in winning Rumania to her side.[194]

As in the case of Yugoslavia, the strategic position of Rumania had induced the Germans to develop good relations with one of the successor states and to shift their position, at least temporarily, from backing revision of the 1919 peace settlement to effective endorsement of the status quo. In the case of Rumania, there was the additional lure of oil. This not only affected Germany's policy toward Hungarian revisionist aspirations in Transylvania but moderated Berlin's attitude toward Bulgaria. In the period before 1937, German-Bulgarian relations were good, though as yet not of great importance to either country.[195] The economic role of Germany in Bulgaria was already considerable and would grow further, as will be seen; but the political relations were affected by considerations only rarely alluded to in the record. Germany's open wooing of Yugoslavia meant that Bulgaria's aspirations for revision in that direction would get no support from Berlin. On the contrary, the Yugoslav-Bulgarian Friendship Pact of January 1937 was extremely welcome to Germany.[196]

193. On these negotiations, see Marguerat, p. 98; "Sitzung des Handelspolitischen Ausschusses vom 22. November 1937," T-120, 2612/5650/H 004113–15; *G.D.*, D, 5, Nos. 147, 154; *D.D.F.*, 2d, 8, No. 184.

194. *G.D.*, D, 5, Nos. 201, 212, 218; *Hungarian Documents*, 2, No. 262. Marguerat, pp. 15–21, 96–98, stresses Germany's interest in Rumanian oil, but he also shows how British and French influence in the Rumanian economy thwarted German efforts.

195. Weinberg, *Foreign Policy*, pp. 119, 231, 326–27.

196. *G.D.*, C, 6, No. 132; *Hungarian Documents*, 2, No. 65.

As for Bulgarian hopes of recovering the Dobruja from Rumania, this conflicted with Germany's hope of weaning the latter country away from her old ties. More important even than the friendship of Bulgaria in case of war would be Germany's need for Rumanian oil, and this higher priority, although mentioned only once by the German minister in Sofia, necessarily restrained German sponsorship of Bulgarian aims.[197]

The atmosphere of political relations between Germany and Bulgaria accordingly remained close in 1937–38, but without any dramatic developments. Von Neurath visited Sofia during his Balkan tour of June 1937; and though there were no special results, the visit demonstrated the harmony of old friends.[198] Within the limits set by Germany's relations with Rumania, this situation continued thereafter. The continuing evolution of German-Bulgarian economic relations was of major importance in this regard. Germany was a key market for Bulgarian tobacco but also began to pay more and more attention to the exploitation of Bulgarian ores. The Four-Year Plan's ROWAK as well as various German private firms became increasingly involved in the Bulgarian mining industry, though most of the impact of this on actual trade would not be felt until the period of World War II.[199] As German imports built up great clearing balances in favor of Bulgaria, the latter turned to Germany for military supplies.

Like the other powers defeated in the World War, Bulgaria had had restrictions imposed upon her army and armaments by the peace settlement; and like Hungary, she was now beginning to rearm. Even before 1937, Bulgaria had turned to Germany for equipment for her expanded army. This tendency was greatly accelerated in 1937–38, extensive negotiations taking place to provide both the materials and the credit terms Bulgaria wanted. King Boris took a direct personal interest in the matter, and an agreement was eventually signed on 12 March 1938. Political as well as financial reasons had motivated both sides in the talks, with the agreement marking a major step in the alignment of Bulgaria with Germany.[200] There were occasional minor frictions, but, on the whole,

197. *G.D.*, D, 5, No. 206.

198. On the von Neurath visit, see DZA Potsdam, Büro RAM, Akte 60964, ff.84–86; *G.D.*, C, 6, Nos. 416 (also T-77, 884/5632525–26), 417; *D.D.F.*, 2d, 6, No. 193.

199. "Bericht der Deutschen Revisions- und Treuhand-Aktiengesellschaft Berlin über die bei der Rowak Handelsgesellschaft m.b.H., Berlin vorgenommenen Prüfung des Jahresabschlusses zum 31. Dezember 1937," Anhang, p. 3, Bundesarchiv, R 2/27, f.65; Deutsche Revisions- und Treuhand-Aktiengesellschaft to Minister of Finance, 2 June 1937, ibid., ff.103–4; Klaus Sohl, "Die Kriegsvorbereitungen des deutschen Imperialismus in Bulgarien am Vorabend des zweiten Weltkrieges," *Jahrbücher für Geschichte der UdSSR und der volksdemokratischen Länder*, 3 (1959), 99–100.

200. On the negotiations, see *G.D.*, C, 6, No. 559; D, 5, Nos. 146, 166–68, 175, 181; Rümelin to von Neurath, 22 October 1937, DZA Potsdam, Büro RAM, Akte 60964, ff.157–58. For some details of German supplies to Bulgaria, see Sohl, pp. 110–13. It should be noted that Parvan Draganov, who played a key role in these negotiations on the Bulgarian side, was minister to Vienna at the time and was not transferred to Berlin until 22 April 1938.

Germany could be well satisfied that Sofia would adopt no policy hostile to her and that Bulgaria would continue to follow the lead of Berlin.[201]

The situation was by no means quite the same in Greece, appearances to the contrary.[202] German influence in Greece had been growing, and German willingness to take a substantial portion of the Greek tobacco crop had been an important element in creating a major role for Germany in Greek foreign trade. Furthermore, there was at least the presumption that the dictatorial regime of Jean Metaxas would look to Berlin for inspiration. The Greek government, nevertheless, wished to maintain good ties with Great Britain, and there was considerable resistance to German economic domination. Although at first skeptical, the authorities in London were eventually persuaded that the protestations of King George II of Greece were indeed genuine, and that the Athens regime was in fact desperately trying to fend off a German economic stranglehold on the country.[203] It would take the British government a long time to do anything about this; not until the winter of 1938–39 did London begin to move on the Greek requests for economic and political support.[204] In the meantime, the economic dependence of Greece on Germany as well as her need of arms imports from Germany—ironically wanted in part because of the German-assisted rearmament of Bulgaria as well as the threat of Germany's Italian ally—all combined to keep German influence in Greece high, even if it was unwelcome.[205]

In regard to Turkey, Germany was already in open competition for influence with Britain and France.[206] The strategic position of the country which controlled the Straits made it an eagerly sought associate, Turkey's desirability as a friend being further enhanced by her importance as a source of chrome ore. In the economic field, Germany had been trying to regain the strong position she once held in Turkey's internal economy and foreign trade with some success before 1937.[207] When German imports from Turkey had built up too large a clearing balance in favor of the latter,

201. *G.D.*, D, 5, Nos. 202, 206; Rümelin to von Neurath, 19 January 1938, DZA Potsdam, Büro RAM, Akte 60964, ff.181–82; *Hungarian Documents*, 2, No. 245; Hans-Joachim Hoppe, "Deutschland und Bulgarien, 1918–1945," Funke, pp. 605–7. For the French credit to Bulgaria in the summer of 1938 and Rümelin's calm comments, see *G.D.*, D, 5, Nos. 217, 222, 226.

202. For the 1933–36 period, see Weinberg, *Foreign Policy*, pp. 119, 231, 327.

203. R 2296, R 2346/349/19, FO 371/21147; R 2167/387/19, FO 371/21148; *D.D.F.*, 2d, 4, No. 237; Dimitri Kitsikis, "La Grèce entre l'Angleterre et l'Allemagne de 1936 à 1941," *Revue historique*, 238 (July–Sept. 1967), 93, 99–105; *D.D.F.*, 2d, 10, No. 189.

204. See below, p. 517. See also Ehrengard Schramm–von Thadden, *Griechenland und die Grossmächte im Zweiten Weltkrieg* (Wiesbaden: Steiner, 1955), pp. 10–11; Pratt, pp. 148–51, 155–56.

205. *G.D.*, C, 6, No. 396.

206. Very useful on the British effort to outbid Germany in Turkey in 1937–38 is Pratt, pp. 140–48.

207. Weinberg, *Foreign Policy*, pp. 119, 231, 327–28.

Berlin placed restrictions on them so that by the spring of 1938 a rough balance had been reached between Germany's exports of industrial goods and weapons for imports primarily of chrome ore, wheat, and tobacco.[208] Almost half of Turkey's foreign trade was with Germany, and the political as well as economic significance of this tie was underlined by the sending of the secretary general of the Turkish foreign ministry, Numan Menemencioglu, to Berlin in the summer of 1938 for the negotiation of a new trade agreement.

Numan was known in Berlin to be a leading, if not the leading advocate of close relations with Germany in the Ankara government. It is obvious from the record that to strengthen his position, the Germans were prepared to go further to meet his wishes than would otherwise have been the case. There was also the clear sense of competition with England, which had signed a credit agreement with Turkey in May and was trying hard to prevent German economic domination of that country. The German-Turkish agreement signed on 25 July 1938 went far to meet German wishes for assurances of chrome and wheat supplies in exchange for German concessions on technical questions of trade control.[209] Even the possibility of a German-Turkish credit agreement was discussed; but although nothing came of this until after Munich, the success of Numan's mission guaranteed Germany an exceedingly strong position in Turkey's foreign trade in spite of all Britain's efforts.[210]

On the political side, the competition was as keen, but Germany's success not quite as great. Turkey benefited from the rising power of Germany without herself having to make concessions to Berlin. The German remilitarization of the Rhineland had provided the occasion for Turkey to throw off some of the restrictions imposed on her control of the Straits by the Treaty of Lausanne. The new situation had been regulated by the Montreux convention, but the German effort to join this arrangement was delayed by Turkish legalisms and subterfuges of various sorts.[211] Von Ribbentrop had urged a settlement of this matter on Numan when the latter was in Berlin for the economic negotiations, but neither then nor when the Turkish official presented a plan to cope with this question in early 1939 was this issue settled.[212]

Just as the remilitarization of the Rhineland had enabled Turkey to secure revision of the peace settlement in one respect, so the continued growth of German power made it possible for her to obtain another major

208. *G.D.*, D, 5, Nos. 538, 545.

209. Ibid., Nos. 545–47, 549; Johannes Glasneck and Inge Kircheisen, *Türkei und Afghanistan—Brennpunkte der Orientpolitik im Zweiten Weltkrieg* (Berlin-East: VEB Deutscher Verlag der Wissenschaften, 1968), pp. 20–29, 36–40.

210. On the credit agreement talk in July 1938, see *G.D.*, D, 5, Nos. 552, 553. Germany was by far Turkey's most important trading partner; see Josef Ackermann's account in Funke, pp. 491–93.

211. *G.D.*, D, 5, Nos. 535–37, 540, 541, 543.

212. Ibid., Nos. 548, 550, 556, 558.

change in which she was interested—and again without having to make concessions to Germany. The one place in which a compact area of Turkish population had been cut off by the dismemberment of the Ottoman Empire was at the northeast corner of the Mediterranean where the Sanjak of Alexandretta with its substantial Turkish population had been included in the French mandate of Syria. In the face of the rising threat of Germany, the French government decided to accommodate Turkey in this regard; and exceedingly lengthy and complicated negotiations led to a Franco-Turkish agreement in July 1938 under which the province received first an autonomous status and was subsequently incorporated into Turkey.[213] The Germans would have liked to offset the Franco-Turkish agreement by a neutrality treaty with Turkey themselves, but the Turkish government in 1938 declined to go beyond official assurances of abstention from anti-German groups and neutrality in case of conflict.[214]

The Turks were presumably reluctant to do anything that might openly antagonize France, the power from which they hoped to secure Alexandretta; and the Germans had to content themselves for the time being with the economic agreement and the role in Turkey's trade that it assured them. The competition for Turkey's favor would continue after Munich; but in spite of pleasantries and assurances, Germany did not obtain the political guarantees of Turkish neutrality in case of war that she very much wanted to secure.[215] On the other hand, the Turkish government had been careful—and would continue to be careful—not to become involved in any arrangement pointed against Germany. When the Rumanian prime minister, acting on behalf of the Little Entente, was in Ankara in October 1937 to secure Turkish support for the Little Entente's assistance to Czechoslovakia he was flatly turned down.[216] The government in Ankara was trying hard to keep the country out of any possible involvement in war; and since this was really what Germany also wanted of Turkey at that time, the stand-off on the Bosporus could hardly be said to be damaging to German policy objectives.

German interests in the Near East beyond Turkey were slowly growing but not yet of great importance in 1937–38. There was some expansion of German trade with the area, but in no portion of it was it even nearly as

213. On these negotiations, see *D.D.F.*, 2d, 1–7 passim; the subsequent negotiations leading to incorporation are detailed by René Massigli in his memoirs, *La Turquie devant la guerre, mission à Ankara, 1939–1940* (Paris: Plon, 1964).

214. *G.D.*, D, 5, Nos. 548, 550, 551.

215. On German-Turkish relations in 1937–38, see also ibid., Nos. 543, 544; "Bestellungen aus der Pressekonferenz," 20 October, 2 November 1937, Bundesarchiv, Brammer, Z.Sg. 101/10, ff.289, 323.

216. R 7475/43/67, FO 371/21138. Tatarescu told Sir Percy Loraine, the British ambassador in Ankara, that only an English statement of support for Czechoslovakia would serve as a deterrent to Germany; Sir Percy pointed out that the British public would not allow such a statement.

significant as in Turkey.[217] German investment and credit policies, though not well coordinated, appear to have been designed to expand Germany's economic role in the area; but the development of the synthetic oil industry in Germany, together with the turn to increasing petroleum supplies from Rumania, suggested that there was a severe limit to Germany's interest in the oil of the Near East.[218] Although German progress in the field of synthetic fibers was not as dramatic as in the case of oil, the thrust of German economic policy was in the same direction and would at some point make her as independent of Egyptian cotton as of Arabian oil. The literature of German relations wih the Arab world does not generally touch on these matters, primarily because the available documents take them for granted rather than discussing their implications; but without the background of a situation in which Germany was trying as a matter of basic policy to make herself more and more independent of the Near East's most important export products, the limited success of German policy in that portion of the world would be difficult to explain.

An important factor in leading Germany to her policy of self-sufficiency was the influence of Britain in the Near East which would threaten to cut off supplies from Germany in case of war. It was this very influence of Britain, however, which also offered Germany opportunities in the area because it made Germany look like a promising ally against England, as well as against France, to some Arab leaders. An example of this can be seen in the efforts of Rosenberg's foreign policy office (APA) to develop ties with King Ibn Saud of Saudi Arabia. The basic element of the project appears to have been the shipment of German rifles and the construction of a cartridge factory on credit terms to Ibn Saud, the latter being interested in reducing his dependence on Great Britain.[219]

The German foreign ministry was willing to establish diplomatic relations with Ibn Saud, a project eventually accomplished by the accreditation of the German minister to Iraq to Saudi Arabia as well, but had doubts about the arms shipments. Not only would they bring no foreign exchange, at least in the ministry's opinion, but there was the apparently insurmountable problem of finding dependable Arab intermediaries and the probability that any arms shipped might end up being used against Germany in case of war. As the Saudi Arabian deputy foreign minister himself admitted in a visit to Berlin, the kingdom was so much under British influence that it might well have to go to war alongside England. In the face of this prospect, the foreign ministry, with the support of the war

217. For the period 1933–36, see Weinberg, *Foreign Policy*, pp. 328–30. A general discussion from a contemporary perspective in *D.D.F.*, 2d, 7, No. 159.

218. German efforts to secure a part in Iraqi oil concessions had foundered by 1936 (Meier-Dörnberg, pp. 34–39).

219. This episode is not discussed in Jacobsen's analysis of the APA, where only some projects in Turkey and Iran are mentioned (p. 70, n.13). See T-454, Roll 86; *G.D.*, D, 5, No. 583 n.3.

ministry, opposed both the arms deal and various related schemes discussed by the German minister to Iraq and Saudi Arabia after his first meeting with Ibn Saud.[220]

This policy was not reversed until the summer of 1939 when war with England looked increasingly likely. The foreign ministry recommended that the weapons deal now be handled through official channels and actually carried out, and a special emissary of Ibn Saud was assured by Hitler and von Ribbentrop in person of Germany's sympathy and willingness to build up Saudi military power.[221] It is not clear whether the promised rifles ever reached Saudi Arabia; but the long and complicated negotiations, further delayed by German concern for the sensitivity of Italy—which did nothing to help her with the Arabs—may serve as an example of the difficulties of converting German-Arab exchanges of assurances of friendship for each other and hostility to Britain and the Jews into concrete programs of collaboration.

This difficulty was particularly obvious in regard to the problem which dominated public attention in the Near East: the conflict in and over Palestine. The Arab rising of 1936 had led to the establishment of a special royal commission, the Peel Commission, to examine possible solutions to the conflicting claims of Arabs, Jews, and others in the Palestine mandate. Although the details were not revealed until July 1937, it was understood considerably earlier that the commission would recommend partition of the area. In the event, the proposed tripartite division into an Arab state, a small Jewish state, and a residual mandate, was never implemented in either its original or any amended form. The Arabs, who rejected the concept of partition entirely, succeeded in having the British drop any idea of partition. In the face of the rising German menace in Europe, the London government was reluctant to offend the Arab world and the Muslim inhabitants of the British Empire. As France tried to appease Turkey by territorial concessions on the Syrian-Turkish border, so Britain hoped to appease the Arabs by giving up the idea of establishing a Jewish state in Palestine and by imposing even stricter limits on Jewish immigration into the mandated territory (after previously closing the eastern three-fourths to Jewish immigration altogether). These gestures would not deter the leaders of the Arab uprising from siding with Germany during World War II, but they seemed to offer Britain some hope of ending the diversion of military resources to Palestine that interfered with the progress of British rearmament.[222]

220. *G.D.*, D, 5, Nos. 574, 578, 582–85, 588–90, 592.

221. Ibid., 6, Nos. 313, 422, 498, 541; Fritz Grobba, *Männer und Mächte im Orient* (Göttingen: Musterschmidt, 1967), p. 106; Werner Otto von Hentig, *Mein Leben eine Dienstreise* (Göttingen: Vandenhoeck & Ruprecht, 1962), pp. 346–47; "Informationsbericht Nr. 65," 21 June 1939, Bundesarchiv, Brammer, Z.Sg. 101/34, ff.325–27.

222. For a French view of this issue, see *D.D.F.*, 2d, 6, No. 174. For the broader problems, see Lukasz Hirszowicz, *The Third Reich and the Arab East* (London: Routledge & Kegan Paul, 1966), pp. 22–25; Michael J. Cohen, "British Strategy and the Palestine Ques-

When it looked, however, as if there were indeed the prospect of a Jewish state being created within a portion of Palestine, the Berlin government was greatly concerned; and there seemed to be a basis for cooperation with Arab opponents of the plan. As for the Arab side, there was no lack of approaches to Germany and expressions of hope for German assistance in scuttling the Peel Commission recommendations. The government of Iraq, in particular, sought German diplomatic support.[223] Haj Amin al-Husayni, the leader of the revolt in Palestine, tried to work out some agreement with Germany; it is not clear just when his contacts with Berlin started, but he was already well on the road to his World War II role of recruiter for Heinrich Himmler's armed units.[224]

If the German response to these gestures was not as enthusiastic as might have been anticipated, the obvious disunity among the Arabs as well as the German doubts about the reliability of those with whom they dealt were important factors. There was, moreover, some concern about the fate of the German Templer settlements in Palestine. These small nineteenth-century German Christian settlements were mostly located in the area provisionally assigned to the Jewish state in the partition plan; and as long as there appeared to be any chance that the plan would be implemented, it behooved Berlin to exercise some caution.[225] Germany certainly did not want a Jewish state to be established; Berlin saw in such a state a dangerous strengthening of world Jewish influence but without the prospect of all Jews being concentrated there.[226] On the other hand, as long as the German government was interested in the emigration of Jews from Germany, the Jewish community in Palestine was bound to be strengthened rather than weakened by German policy.

Both to hasten Jewish emigration from Germany and to blunt the possibility of a worldwide Jewish boycott of German exports, the German government had agreed in the summer of 1933 to the so-called Haavara agreement. Under its terms, Jews who emigrated from Germany to Palestine could secure the transfer to Palestine of at least some of their money

---

tion, 1936–39," *Journal of Contemporary History*, 7, Nos. 3–4 (July–Oct. 1972), 57–83 and "Appeasement in the Middle East: The British White Paper in Palestine, May 1939," *Historical Journal*, 16, No. 3 (Sept. 1973), 571–96; Pratt, pp. 126–28; *Australian Documents*, No. 328.

223. *G.D.*, D, 5, Nos. 567, 581.

224. Ibid., Nos. 566, 568, 572, 576; Hirszowicz, pp. 34–35. The material on German deliveries to the Arabs during the 1936–39 riot period published in Efraim Dekel, *Shai: The Exploits of Hagana Intelligence* (New York: Thomas Yoseloff, 1959), pp. 230–35, suggests that very little was actually sent.

225. *G.D.*, D, 5, Nos. 565, 569. For the history of the Templer settlements, see Alex Carmel, *Die Siedlungen der württembergischen Templer in Palästina, 1868–1918,* trans. Perez Leshem (Stuttgart: Kohlhammer, 1973); Carmel has summarized his findings in "The Political Significance of German Settlements in Palestine, 1868–1918," Jehuda Wallach (ed.), *Germany and the Middle East, 1835–1939* (Tel Aviv: Israel Press, 1975), pp. 45–71.

226. *G.D.*, C, 6, Nos. 387, 516; D, 5, Nos. 561, 564, 570, 571.

by arranging for the export of additional German goods to Palestine. The emigrant received proceeds from the sale of the additional German goods in Palestine in exchange for payments out of his blocked funds inside Germany to the German exporter.[227] This system had worked well from the German point of view. Of the approximately 120,000 Jews who had emigrated by the fall of 1937, one-third had fled to other European countries, one-third had gone to Palestine, and one-third had moved overseas to the United States, Latin America, South Africa, and elsewhere.[228] The prospects of further Jewish emigration were closely tied up with the maintenance of the Haavara system, even though it obviously contributed to the growth of the Jewish community in Palestine.

The prospect of a Jewish state being established within the Holy Land caused the German foreign ministry to reexamine the whole question. The Haavara agreement could be seen as contributing to the thing Berlin certainly did not want—a Jewish state—but there was no assurance that ending it would affect the British decision to go ahead with partition as Berlin expected. Furthermore, there was no certainty that it would make much difference to Jewish immigration into Palestine if Germany pushed her own emigrants in other directions. It was all very easy for Arab leaders to suggest that the Germans use their influence with Poland to keep that country from supporting the creation of a Jewish state to which Poland might drive *its* Jews. The plausibility of this request merely suggested that any space in Palestine not filled by Jews leaving Germany would simply be available for those from Poland.[229]

The National Socialist party's foreign section, the Auslands-Organisation (AO) had long been arguing for abolition of the Haavara system. The new German consul general in Jerusalem shared this point of view, and the head of the German foreign ministry's section dealing with the Jewish question, Vicco von Bülow-Schwante, argued in favor of more severe persecution of the Jews as a way to drive them out of Germany even if the special transfer system were ended. Others in the foreign ministry objected, and the conflict continued for most of 1937 and 1938.[230] Even the argument that at some point Arab newspapers might make in-

227. See Weinberg, *Foreign Policy*, p. 329 n.127. A detailed study of the system is in Werner Feichenfeld, Dolf Michaelis, and Ludwig Pinner, *Haavara-Transfer nach Palästina und Einwanderung deutscher Juden, 1933–1939* (Tübingen: Mohr, 1972).

228. A survey of the whole project by the Reichsstelle für Devisenbewirtschaftung, the government agency in charge of foreign exchange controls, which both administered and favored the system, was prepared in November 1937, *G.D.*, D, 5, No. 575. The arrangement also helped the Templer bank (Feilchenfeld, pp. 27, 72).

229. It must be recalled that all discussion of the subject in the 1930s and 1940s was affected by what subsequently proved to be absurdly low estimates of the "absorptive capacity" of Palestine.

230. On this subject, see *G.D.*, D, 5, Nos. 561–64, 579, 580, 587; Hirszowicz, pp. 30–33; Ernst Marcus, "The German Foreign Office and the Palestine Question in the Period 1933–1939," *Yad Washem Studies in the European Jewish Catastrophe and Resistance*, 2 (1958), 179–204.

formation about the arrangement public with serious results for German prestige in the Arab world did not move the Berlin authorities beyond a willingness to revise the scheme slightly.[231]

Although the evidence is indirect, it appears that Hitler decided in January 1938 that he wanted the emigration of Jews to continue and that emigration to Palestine was to remain a significant option for Jewish refugees from Germany.[232] By that time, the probability of a Jewish state being created by Great Britain had almost vanished, a consideration which may have contributed to Hitler's decision. In any case, the German desire to continue driving out Jews was greater than the interest in pleasing the Arabs. The only consolation the Arab nationalists appear to have received was a trickle of weapons, a remedy perhaps thought analogous to the quantities of aspirin Germany exported to the European countries whose leaders suffered headaches over Berlin's threats.[233]

The opportunities for the expansion of German influence were not in reality as great as they appeared to be. Germany could expand her trade in the area, but with not much capital to invest and no interest in great oil imports, there were severe limits to any such process.[234] The political divisions among the Arabs made them uncertain prospective allies for the Germans, and the alignment of Germany with Italy restrained the Arabs, who feared the expansion of Italian power, especially in the Red Sea area. If some elements of the Egyptian nationalist movement looked to National Socialist Germany for inspiration, they also soon became aware of Germany's subordination of her own policies in the Near East to those of Italy, which was correctly perceived as threatening Egyptian aspirations to the Sudan.[235] In the case of Egypt, as in the Near East as a whole, Hitler's view of what might be called a division of the world into spheres of *Lebensraum*, with the Mediterranean allocated to Italy, could only restrict German prospects.

231. *G.D.*, D, 5, Nos. 577, 579. This is also the conclusion of Eliahu ben Elissar, pp. 209–19.

232. See the references to a Hitler-Rosenberg meeting in *G.D.*, D, 5, No. 579. Marcus, p. 193, refers to a Hitler decision of the fall of 1938.

233. Another Near Eastern area in which there was some German interest in this period was Afghanistan, where the APA was very much involved. See Glasneck and Kircheisen, pp. 186–89, 194–97; Rosenberg to Wiedemann enclosing a note on Afghanistan by Malletke, 12 January 1937, Nuremberg document 1360-PS, National Archives.

234. For an analysis of a reduction rather than an increase of Germany's role in Iran during the National Socialist as contrasted with the Weimar period, see Yair Hirschfeld, "German Policy toward Iran: Continuity and Change from Weimar to Hitler," Wallach, pp. 117–40. On the other hand, the increasing role of Germany in Iran's foreign trade, until the Third Reich became the country's main trading partner by 1938–39, is demonstrated in Abolfazl Adli, *Aussenhandel und Aussenwirtschaftspolitik des Iran* (Berlin: Duncker & Humblot, 1960), pp. 49–50, 61, 65–66.

235. A useful summary is in Shimon Shamir, "The Influence of German National-Socialism on Radical Movements in Egypt," Wallach, pp. 200–208.

The supposed bond of Germans and Arabs in their common enmity to the Jews, furthermore, was on closer inspection a delusion. Germany wanted to drive out her Jewish population without allowing them to take their assets along in the form of foreign exchange; and in the era of the depression, the Haavara agreement was one of the few ways to do that. Many Arab nationalists, on the other hand, wanted no further Jewish immigration into Palestine, so that their interests on this issue ran directly counter to German policy. Hitler's own mental assignment of the whole area to Italy's appropriate sphere of *Lebensraum* made him most dubious about concessions to Arab requests if these in any way interfered with his more important priorities. In the years when British and French power in the Near East was beginning to wane, Germany found the region as difficult to deal with as have other outside powers before and since.

8 Germany and the Western Hemisphere 1937–38

German relations with the Western Hemisphere have been touched on in several respects. The special problems caused for British policy toward Germany by the attitude of the Dominions, including Canada; trade questions in Latin America, especially Brazil; and the questions posed by the relation of German agencies to people of German descent abroad have received attention. In regard to the United States, the major policy issues posed by the American tendency toward isolationism, as well as President Roosevelt's various abortive soundings that looked toward some attempt at settling European problems by an international conference have been discussed. In addition, a number of specific, essentially symbolic difficulties in Germany's relations with the United States have also been mentioned. What remains is to add some other elements to the picture and to fit the whole matter of German relations with the Western Hemisphere into the broader framework of German foreign policy and its impact abroad.

Germany's relations with the United States in 1937–38 followed if not in any straight linear fashion, the deteriorating course that had been set in 1933.[1] Many of the specific causes of friction previously present continued to contribute their share of aggravation. One that attracted great public attention at the time and assumed an importance out of all proportion to its intrinsic significance was the activity of the National Socialist sponsored organizations in the United States, primarily the "Friends of the New Germany," later reorganized as the "German-American Bund."

Always few in number, never mobilizing any appreciable proportion of the people of German back-

1. For the period 1933–36, see Weinberg, *Foreign Policy*, chap. 6.

ground in the United States, periodically torn by internal dissension, the Bund was an absolute disaster area in German-American relations. Its display of National Socialist symbols disturbed the American public and provided a perfect focus for anti-German sentiments and publicity. The combination of German and American citizens was a dangerous affront to American opinion, but there was no ready solution to this problem of combining citizens of different countries within the same organization, a necessary step if any viable organization at all were to continue. If the German citizens were told to withdraw from membership, as they eventually were, the Bund might well collapse because of its small size, inadequate leadership, and lack of financing—unless funds were provided by Germany in some clandestine fashion that was likely to become embarrassingly public. Even if it did not fall apart, the idea of a movement on National Socialist principles among German-Americans was not likely to do anything for Germany's popularity in the United States. The Bund, however organized, contributed to the internal divisions among the German-Americans, already very weak politically. It provided evidence for all those who argued that Germany threatened the United States. It also touched the sensitivity of an American public that expected assimilation of immigrants, if not culturally, at least to the American constitutional system, and resented the transplantation of European political parties to American soil, especially when such parties advocated a political system entirely opposite to that established by the founding fathers. And the Bund did all these things without any beneficial effect discernible to German diplomats or to Hitler's adjutant, Fritz Wiedemann, who returned from an American trip convinced of the harm being done by the Bund.[2]

If in spite of all warnings, troubles, and acrimonious discussions, Berlin could see its way only to ordering German citizens to leave the Bund, while a variety of clandestine German channels to what was now ostensibly a purely native American organization continued—with predictable results—the cause of this policy must be seen in the unwillingness of Hitler to give his deputy, Rudolf Hess, a clear mandate to terminate the

2. On the Friends of the New Germany and the Bund, see Jacobsen, pp. 528–49; Arthur L. Smith, *The Deutschtum of Nazi Germany and the United States* (The Hague: Nijhoff, 1965); *G.D.*, D, 1, Nos. 414, 420, 428, 433, 435, 437, 438, 441–43, 448, 453–55; *U.S.*, 1938, 2:461–64; Moffat Diary, 28 February 1938, Moffat Papers, Vol. 40; Gilbert to Moffat, 23 September 1937, Moffat Papers, Vol. 12. On the German-Americans in general, see *G.D.*, C, 6, Nos. 73, 81; D, 1, Nos. 430, 431. A useful study of the whole problem based on wide-ranging research, though not always sufficiently critical of the sources, is Klaus Kipphan, *Deutsche Propaganda in den Vereinigten Staaten, 1933–1941* (Heidelberg: Carl Winter, 1971). On the career of the most famous American apologist for the National Socialist regime, see Niel M. Johnson, *George Sylvester Viereck, German-American Propagandist* (Urbana, Ill.: University of Illinois Press, 1972). Sander Diamond's *The Nazi Movement in the United States, 1924–1941* (Ithaca, N.Y.: Cornell University Press, 1974), is the best general account of the Bund to date in spite of some inaccuracies. Diamond argues that Hitler did turn against the Bund in the end.

whole ridiculous operation. This in turn can be explained only by Hitler's general disregard for the potential importance of the United States to his own plans.

The same disregard of American susceptibilities characterized the German handling of other issues, big and small. The agreement that had been reached in Munich in the summer of 1936 on the American claims for German sabotage in the United States in the early years of the World War was never implemented by Berlin. Göring's special appointee for this issue, Franz von Pfeffer, could not secure the support of others in the German government to remove this sore in German-American relations.[3] One reason Göring had become interested in this problem was its possible relation to German trade with the United States; the situation in that regard continued to deteriorate as well.

The Germans had denounced the German-American trade treaty in order to eliminate its most-favored-nation clause. The German gamble that this would pressure Washington into a new trade agreement had failed utterly, and nothing occurred to change that situation. German diplomats reported that there was no real prospect of a new trade treaty, and they read the situation correctly.[4] Cordell Hull, the American secretary of state, who was a devotee of freeing the channels of world trade, believed strongly that this was an important aspect of preserving the peace and had only the most scathing comments for German trade practices.[5] An additional element of bitterness was introduced into Germany's economic relations with the United States by the German repudiation of Austrian debts in the United States after the *Anschluss*. The supposedly destitute and ailing Austrian economy had regularly met its international financial obligations, but once the assets of the Austrian economy had been seized by Germany, the latter claimed that it was too poor to continue payments. In the case of several other countries, whose trade accounts with Germany enabled them to threaten Berlin with the imposition of potentially harmful clearing mechanisms, the Berlin government found it expedient to work out special agreements. This was not done with the United States, however, and the repudiation of these obligations—after the assets built up with American help had been sequestered by Germany—provided still another source of acrimony.[6] German efforts to

3. The earlier phase of this issue is discussed in Weinberg, *Foreign Policy*, pp. 153–54. For the later period, see *U.S.*, 1937, 2:348–67; Dodd dispatch 3463 of 12 May 1937, Lester Woolsey to Green H. Hackworth, 24 May and 4 June 1937, State 462.11 L 5232/872, 878, 881. Karl Markau, the president of the German Chamber of Commerce in London, who had participated in the earlier negotiations, continued to do so, with Federico Stallforth representing American claimants; see C 9949/15/18, FO 371/22974.

4. *G.D.*, C, 6, No. 72; D, 1, No. 458; *U.S.*, 1937, 2:329–31; 1938, 2:422–25; Moffat Diary, 23–24 January 1938, Moffat Papers, Vol. 40.

5. *U.S.*, 1937, 2:328–29, 331; 1938, 2:441–46; *G.D.*, C, 6, No. 159; D, 1, No. 460.

6. *U.S.*, 1938, 2:483–502; 1939, 2:559–67; *G.D.*, D, 1, Nos. 756, 458.

tie the question of debts to a trade treaty only served to complicate an already deadlocked set of negotiations.[7]

What was happening in the United States during these years was a hardening of public attitudes. Although there was a general aversion to any direct American role in what were seen as European affairs, the generally positive attitude toward Germany that had replaced the anti-German hysteria of the war years had once again been replaced by negative feelings.[8] The persecution of the Catholic church as well as of the Jews had a strong impact.[9] Reports in newspapers, magazines, and newsreels on the militarization of German life, during the very years when pacifist sentiments were growing stronger in the United States, were repulsive to Americans, who were further angered by the public behavior of the German-American Bund. On the other hand, sympathy for Britain and France was clearly growing; surely these countries had done everything possible to satisfy any legitimate German grievances. If some segments of the American public thought the Western Powers too weak and yielding in the face of German moves, there was practically no one who credited either England or France with any desire to provoke Germany—a significant contrast with the attitudes of the 1920s. The result of these perceptions was that the prospect of another war was implicitly tied in the public mind with German aggression; if war did break out, it would be Germany's fault.[10] German representatives in Washington reported on this trend in American thinking. They warned Berlin that if war ever came, the United States could be expected to side with Germany's enemies sooner or later, and probably sooner.[11]

If none of this made any impact on Hitler, the explanation must be found in his assessment of the United States. Some day a German-dominated Eurasia would fight America; but until then he adjudged the United States as of no great importance as an actual or potential military power, and most certainly not one to be feared by Germany. In the 1930s, he believed

7. *U.S.*, 1938, 2:419–21; Hans-Jürgen Schröder, *Deutschland und die Vereinigten Staaten, 1933–1939* (Wiesbaden: Steiner, 1970), pp. 178–90.

8. Note Hugh Wilson's comments to Joseph Goebbels on 22 March 1938, *U.S.*, 1938, 2:434–38.

9. For State Department consideration of retaliatory action if Germany started seizing the property of American Jews, see Moffat Diary, 16 June 1938, Moffat Papers, Vol. 30.

10. This can be seen from the American reaction to the *Anschluss; U.S.*, 1938, 1:434–35, 442–45, 451–53; *G.D.*, D, 1, Nos. 391, 445; *Hungarian Documents*, 1, No. 460.

11. On this subject, see Manfred Jonas, "Prophet without Honor: Hans Heinrich Dieckhoff's Reports from Washington," *Mid-America*, 47 (July 1965), 222–23; Warren F. Kimball, "Dieckhoff and America: A German's View of German-American Relations," *The Historian*, 27 (February 1965), 218–43, both of which are very favorable to Dieckhoff. For some of the reports from Washington, see *G.D.*, C, 6, Nos. 207, 306, 338; D, 1, Nos. 419, 423, 427, 440, 444, 445, 447, 451; Dieckhoff to von Neurath, 20 May 1937, DZA Potsdam, Büro RAM, Akte 60964, f.143. For a French analysis, see *D.D.F.*, 2d, 3, No. 437; 6, No. 75. For an incident involving the German consul in Manila, see Moffat Diary, 22 August 1938, Moffat Papers, Vol. 41.

that there was no reason to have any special regard for American policy; on the contrary, he thought that the depression's impact on the country confirmed his own assessment of American debility.[12] The fact that the Americans did not like Germany's racial and religious policies only showed what dolts they were. He thought that an extraordinarily idiotic misassessment of the United States (which was sent to him in August 1937 by a German of dubious background, Baron Bernhard G. von Rechenberg, who had emigrated to the United States in 1924 and returned to become head of the foreign section of the National Socialist veterans organization) was such a wonderful document that he asked for extra copies to enlighten the foreign and propaganda ministries.[13] The misconceptions in this document about the decay of the United States fitted in so well with Hitler's own views that he would not allow them to be shaken. Soon after, his adjutant, Fritz Wiedemann, made an extensive tour of the United States during which he obtained a reasonably accurate impression of both the strength of the country and the degree of anti-German feeling. Appalled by what he had found, Wiedemann attempted to explain the situation to Hitler, but Hitler was so pleased by the confirmation he had just received of his prior views that Wiedemann's efforts were of no avail.[14] What Hitler would not learn from his friend and associate Wiedemann he was certainly not going to accept from the traditional diplomats.[15]

There was really nothing that American diplomats could do about this situation. Under circumstances which reflected no credit on President Roosevelt or on the higher officials of the State Department, Ambassador William E. Dodd was recalled from Berlin at the end of 1937.[16] Consideration of a successor involved several persons, but Roosevelt decided that if he was not to have a Jeffersonian Democrat in Berlin, he would

12. Gerhard L. Weinberg, "Hitler's Image of the United States," *American Historical Review*, 69, No. 4 (July 1964), 1010–13. A somewhat different perspective is to be found in Andreas Hillgruber, "Der Faktor Amerika in Hitlers Stategie 1938–1941," reprinted in his *Deutsche Grossmacht- und Weltpolitik im 19. und 20. Jahrhundert* (Düsseldorf: Droste, 1977), pp. 197–222.

13. *G.D.*, D, 1, Nos. 416–18. The memorandum of von Rechenberg is in T-120, 2568/5264/E 315836–72.

14. Wiedemann, pp. 215–18, 220–21; *G.D.*, D, 1, Nos. 427, 433 (the "Wohnbesuch" referred to in this document was Wiedemann); Gilbert tel. 303, 29 December 1937, State 811.00 Nazi/330; Speer, *Erinnerungen*, p. 135. Wiedemann claims in his memoirs that the one thing he persuaded Hitler to do was to participate in the New York World Fair; on that subject see also the meeting of Hitler with Sosthenes Behn referred to in Moffat Diary, 15–16 January 1938, Moffat Papers, Vol. 40.

15. Diamond's analysis of German, and especially Hitler's views of the United States is rather similar; he also shows how the sad fate of the Bund could be fitted into this perception. The very fact that Americans rejected the Bund illuminated their short-sightedness, and the signs of official action against the Bund proved that the United States was dominated by Jews.

16. The best account of the incident is in Offner, pp. 203–12.

emphasize the routine nature of the position by appointing a career diplomat. When Hugh Gibson declined the appointment, Hugh Wilson was appointed instead.[17] Dodd's critical attitude toward the National Socialist regime had so infuriated Hitler that he was at first unwilling even to receive his successor, but was persuaded after receiving reassuring words about the new ambassador.[18] Wilson was indeed prepared to do his best. He had spent more than a quarter of a century in the foreign service, and although certainly not pro-Nazi in any real sense of the term, looked with some sympathy on Germany.[19] But his appointment made no more difference in German-American relations than in the earlier replacement of Hans Luther by Hans Heinrich Dieckhoff in Washington.

During his months in Germany, Wilson could not bring about any more change in German policies than his predecessor. His tone may have been more amiable; and the higher regard in which he was held by the permanent officials of the German foreign ministry probably helped in the handling of current business of no major importance; but on the key issues of German-American relations, his short mission was as barren of success as Dodd's longer one.[20] He did contribute to the scare over Germany's air force by making an alarming report to President Roosevelt in July 1938,[21] but the president was in any case interested in assisting the French in building up their air force.[22] In October 1938, Wilson was trying hard, though entirely unsuccessfully, to make some contribution to an improvement in German-American relations by securing some concessions from Berlin on the subject of Jewish emigration.[23] Soon after, the anti-Jewish pogroms of November 1938 led the president to announce the recall of Wilson with a statement denouncing the German government. The ambassador never returned to Germany.

It is doubtful whether Wilson ever had much influence on President Roosevelt. The president had sensed a kindred spirit in Dodd and took the general thrust, if not the details, of Dodd's warnings seriously. As in prior years, Roosevelt continued to receive unofficial reports on the European situation from Samuel R. Fuller, Jr.[24] Unquestionably more important than the change in the Berlin embassy was the president's decision that the United States minister to Vienna, George S. Messersmith, who had

17. On the Gibson appointment, see U.S., 1937, 2:383; Dodd Diary, 23 and 30 November 1937, pp. 433–35; Moffat Diary, 13 May 1938, Moffat Papers, Vol. 40.
18. G.D., D, 1, Nos. 436, 439.
19. See Offner, pp. 214–16. Wilson's own works, Diplomat between Wars (New York: Longmans, Green, 1941), and A Career Diplomat: The Third Chapter, the Third Reich, ed. Hugh R. Wilson, Jr. (New York: Vantage Press, 1960), give a fair picture of the author's views.
20. See G.D., D, 1, Nos. 450, 456; U.S., 1938, 2:438–41.
21. Wilson to Roosevelt, 11 July 1938, Hyde Park, War Department.
22. Haight, pp. 6–8, 11.
23. G.D., D, 5, Nos. 645, 646.
24. See Hyde Park, PPF 2616 (Fuller's role is mentioned in Weinberg, Foreign Policy, pp. 143, 150 n.82, 156, 245 n.21, 279–80).

previously been consul general in Berlin, should return to Washington as assistant secretary of state in 1937.[25] Messersmith had observed the National Socialist accession to power in Berlin and had been at the center of the European crisis in Vienna; from these posts he had been warning Roosevelt and Hull of the dangers ahead. Unlike von Rechenberg, Messersmith was a shrewd observer, and his concern over the implications of German expansion in Europe reinforced the president's perception of those problems, just as von Rechenberg's delusions fed Hitler's concept of a weak and decaying United States. If the German dictator remained disdainful of the North American giant, the American president, though still hoping for the maintenance of peace in Europe, was very clear in his own mind about the nature of the dangers to it; and on this point, if almost no other, most Americans agreed with him.

German relations with the countries of Latin America took a decided turn for the worse in 1938. In the first years of National Socialist rule, the expansion of German trade with Latin America had been considerable, and the first stages of nazification among those of German descent abroad had not yet aroused any substantial antagonism in either the rest of the population or the governments of the countries in which they resided. Early in 1938, however, there was a distinct change in this situation, approximately simultaneous in several of the most important countries of South America. This shift was most dramatic in the largest, Brazil.

There were large numbers of Germans and descendants of German immigrants settled primarily in Brazil's southernmost three states, where they constituted between 10 and 20 percent of the population. Having arrived as settlers, these Germans had built up essentially homogeneous German communities, and their numerous children had then opened up adjacent areas, so that there were substantial areas of almost solid German settlement. The private school system of these areas, combined with a substantial Protestant population in an otherwise overwhelmingly Catholic country, made these Germans an obvious butt of those tendencies in the Brazil of Getulio Vargas which aimed at national assimilation through vast expansion of state-supported schools and restrictions on immigration, although the latter measure was directed more at Japanese than German immigrants. The acceleration of industrialization and urbanization during the Vargas era was no doubt transforming the German element, but at a rate that proved too slow for the government, especially when the Germans themselves drew attention to their separate cultural interests by taking steps to preserve them in the face of current social trends. These special characteristics of the situation in Brazil must be

25. Messersmith, whose prior service had been mainly in Latin America, had in fact been scheduled for appointment as minister to Uruguay, and the agrément for him had already been requested, when he was reassigned to Washington. Cf. *Hungarian Documents*, 1, No. 302.

kept in mind as the background for developments in German-Brazilian relations.[26]

Brazil had become an important trading partner of Germany in the mid-1930s, and political relations between Berlin and the government of Getulio Vargas were generally good.[27] There was even some discussion in November 1937 in both Berlin and Rome about asking Brazil to join the Anti-Comintern Pact. After the Vargas coup of 10 November 1937, by which he perpetuated his term in office, that project was dropped, largely in response to concerns expressed by Washington, but some sort of anti-Communist cooperation was discussed by the Brazilian and German governments.[28] In the first months of 1938, however, the Germans noticed that the Brazilian government was increasingly concerned about the activities of its German population and was taking more and more drastic steps against them and their institutions.[29] The November 1937 coup ended the period in which the German question in Brazil was essentially cultural; hereafter it would become a political and diplomatic issue of major proportions.

Here was the other side of Germany's use of racialist arguments in foreign policy. Since the German government was interested in the treatment of Germans outside the borders of the Reich and made louder and louder noises about their fate, the Brazilian regime, which looked forward to the assimilation of all immigrants, naturally became more and more alarmed about the activities of the German settlers in the south. The Germans were by now regimented by the National Socialist element among them, and their organizations and institutions could be seen as a threat to the unity of the country. The public activities of local National Socialist organizations were increasingly drawing the attention of the Brazilian press and parliament, and the very active Foreign Organization of the party (AO) thus drew the attention of those who were pushing the policy of "nationalizing" the country's minorities.[30] Many individuals who played important roles in the party were given to boastful statements, often had ties to various party and government agencies in Germany, and were an obvious affront to the Brazilian authorities.[31] The growth of

26. There is a fair and balanced account in Käte Harms-Baltzer, *Die Nationalisierung der deutschen Einwanderer und ihrer Nachkommen in Brasilien als Problem der deutsch-brasilianischen Beziehungen, 1930–1938* (Berlin: Colloquium Verlag, 1970).

27. See above, p. 000.

28. Frank D. McCann, Jr., *The Brazilian-American Alliance, 1937–1945* (Princeton, N.J.: Princeton University Press, 1973), pp. 54–55, stresses American objections in discussing the decision of Vargas to drop the idea of adhesion to the pact; see also ibid., pp. 69–70; Ciano, *Diplomatic Papers*, p. 147; Ciano, *Diary*, 9 November 1937, pp. 40–41; *G.D.*, D, 1, No. 97; D, 5, Nos. 593, 594; Harms-Baltzer, pp. 173–74 n.23.

29. *G.D.*, D, 5, No. 599; cf. ibid., No. 602.

30. Harms-Baltzer, pp. 30–37; Donald M. McKale, *The Swastika outside Germany* (Kent, Ohio: Kent State University Press, 1977), pp. 84–86.

31. Jacobsen, pp. 549–62; Alton Frye, *Nazi Germany and the American Hemisphere, 1933–1941* (New Haven: Yale University Press, 1967), pp. 65–70.

Germany's strength made the activities of the minority look more danger-ous than ever, and the influence of the United States began to be exerted to ward off such dangers from the Western Hemisphere. In the winter of 1937–38, a series of measures impinging upon the German schools and National Socialist organizations in southern Brazil were enacted, which indicated the direction in which the country was moving.[32]

A German step with fateful implications for most Latin American countries came on 10 April 1938. That was the date of the plebiscite in Germany and Austria on the annexation of Austria.[33] As a part of the ritual of ratification, the plebiscite was extended to include Germans overseas—many of them holding dual citizenship—who, in order to vote, either boarded German ships that then went outside the three-mile limit or entered their names on lists in German (or former Austrian) diplomatic or consular offices.[34] Whatever the propaganda value of such rituals and whatever the legal status of this procedure, here was a gesture guaranteed to alarm countries containing large numbers of immigrants. From the literature, press, and diplomatic documents of the time one can deduce something of the sense of shock which this action caused both govern-ment officials and the public. Suspicion of Germany and restrictions on the local organizations of the German community increased immediately and radically.

In the case of Brazil, this tendency was accentuated by the aftermath of the attempted coup of 10–11 May 1938 by the Integralists. This right-wing movement, the "Acção Integralista Brasileira," had supported Vargas in November 1937 but felt betrayed by him. Its philosophy had some re-semblance to fascism; it had certainly received strong electoral support from Brazilians of German descent; and German complicity in the coup was immediately suspected.[35]

The Brazilian authorities did not, in fact, secure evidence of ties be-tween several German officials and the Integralists until sometime later, but the extraordinarily rude and threatening behavior of German Ambas-sador Karl Ritter converted what was already a difficult and embarrassing situation into an impossible one. In spite of reprimands from Berlin,

32. McCann, pp. 71–72, 82–83.

33. Because of her focus on the German element in Brazil, Harms-Baltzer (p. 42) places the greatest emphasis on the nationalization measures following the 10 November 1937 coup as the turning point in German-Brazilian relations, but this ignores the great significance of the plebiscite, especially as viewed by people in Brazil and throughout Latin America. The chronological relationship between the plebiscite of 10 April and the Brazilian government's decree of 18 April barring all political activity by foreigners in Brazil is simply ignored by her otherwise excellent book. McCann (p. 88) lays heavy stress on an article of 21 March in the *Deutsche Diplomatische Korrespondenz* criticizing Brazilian measures.

34. For the voting in Chile (or rather offshore), see Frost (chargé a.i. Santiago) dispatch 960 of 13 April 1938, State 863.00/1721. A large number of similar reports from all over the world may be found in the 863.00 file. A summary of the worldwide extraterritorial plebiscite activities is in Arnold J. Toynbee, *Survey of International Affairs 1938*, 1:234.

35. Harms-Baltzer, pp. 63–66; McKale, pp. 145–48.

where the usually obstreperous von Ribbentrop was for once attempting to restrain one of his diplomats, Ritter, for reasons never fully explained, escalated the conflict—only to find himself declared *persona non grata* by the Brazilian government.[36] It is quite possible that those in the German embassy working with the Integralists really were doing so without Ritter's authorization, as he claimed; but when the Brazilian police secured some incriminating documents, he had already so compromised himself personally that no one in Rio de Janeiro believed a word he said.[37]

Once the Brazilian government had demanded Ritter's recall, Berlin retaliated by insisting on the recall of the Brazilian ambassador to Germany.[38] The relations between the two countries, once so good, had turned sour, and there was serious concern in Berlin that there would be an impact on the trade relations which were so important to Germany.[39] They were important to Brazil also, especially in regard to arms purchases in Germany.[40] Although there were further measures against the German settlers within Brazil, the Rio government took care not to let matters go too far. The needs of Brazil for export markets and the pressure of the Brazilian military leaders for the importation of German artillery provided strong motives for maintaining the tie to Berlin.[41]

Over the winter of 1938–39, the combination of interest in trade, consolidation of Vargas's rule, and German politeness made a rapprochement possible, and in June 1939 an exchange of ambassadors was again arranged.[42] The days of good German-Brazilian relations were, however,

36. The Brazilian government did not wish an abrupt deterioration of relations and utilized a home leave of Ritter in the fall of 1938 to suggest, at first informally, that he simply not return to his post. Note the letter of Oswaldo Aranha to Luis Sparano of 16 November 1938, from the Vargas papers, published in Hélio Silva, *1938: Terrorismo em Campo Verde* (Rio de Janeiro: Civilização Brasileira, 1971), pp. 314–17.

37. *G.D.*, D, 5, Nos. 604–7, 609, 610, 612, 617, 622, 623, 625, 627; McCann, pp. 86–91, 95–101; Hilton, pp. 168–76; Arnold Ebel, *Das Dritte Reich und Argentinien* (Cologne: Böhlau, 1971), pp. 277–88; Harms-Baltzer, pp. 69–80. The incriminating documents were, it would appear, concerned primarily with the attempts of several German organizations, especially the "Federação 25 de Julho," to operate in a manner that was contrary to Brazil's nationalizing legislation, as well as with the involvement of German embassy officials in those efforts. There was no evidence of sponsorship of the Integralist coup, a fact which may have influenced the Brazilian government to keep quiet after the discovery of the documents in connection with the arrest on 24 June 1938 of Federico Colin Kopp and his murder or suicide in jail soon after. The whole subject is still shrouded in mystery; the absence of any additional evidence to substantiate the assertions in Jürgen Hell's account in *Der deutsche Faschismus in Lateinamerika, 1933–1943* (Berlin-East: Humboldt-Universität, 1966), pp. 115–16, suggests that there is no material on the subject in the archives of the German Democratic Republic.

38. *G.D.*, D, 5, No. 628; Harms-Baltzer, pp. 105–11; McCann, pp. 103–4.

39. *G.D.*, D, 5, No. 629; cf. Dr. Kausch, "Informationsbericht Nr. 51," 20 July 1938, Bundesarchiv, Brammer, Z.Sg. 101/33, f.47; Harms-Baltzer, pp. 117, 120–23; McCann, pp. 165–68.

40. McCann, p. 111.

41. Hilton, pp. 176–82, 187–90.

42. *G.D.*, D, 5, Nos. 632 (note that von Levetzow, the German chargé, expressed in writing his belief that Brazilian Foreign Minister Oswaldo Aranha had been bought by the

clearly over. The repulsive behavior—even by National Socialist standards—of Ambassador Ritter served more as a focus than as a cause of this development. The basic issue was the incompatibility perceived by most Brazilians, both supporters and opponents of the "Estado Nôvo" of Vargas, between the national unity and modernization of Brazil and control by a Eurpean power over a substantial segment of Brazil's population. Since the attainment of that control was an aspect of National Socialist policy which Hitler was not prepared to renounce in Brazil—as he was in Italy—there could be no continuation either of good political relations between Germany and the largest country of Latin America or of the opportunities such a relationship might have offered.

Germany's relations with other Latin American countries took a somewhat similar course. In Argentina, the April 1938 plebiscite was taken very much amiss, and the German settlers in the country found themselves objects of suspicion.[43] There as in Brazil, the desire to develop a unified population out of a diverse immigrant population made the organizations of the German element appear most dangerous.[44] As in the case of the United States, the mixing of German citizens with Argentine citizens in these organizations was the subject of argument, with the problem complicated by the large numbers of people with dual nationality. Efforts were made to cope with these matters by new regulations of the Foreign Organization of the National Socialist party and by some reorganization of local groups, but to little avail.[45] The situation in Chile was developing in the same way.[46] If the Germans kept talking about the ethnic solidarity of all those of German descent, they could hardly be surprised when foreign governments became suspicious, not only of the party organizations abroad, but also of cultural activities that would have had no political significance but for the context in which the Germans themselves were placing them.

As the Latin American countries defined themselves and their independence against the North American colossus, they might—like some Arab nationalists—have looked to Germany as a counterweight. This possibility, however, was realized only to a very slight extent, the one instance being the sale of Mexican oil to Germany after the nationalization of the

United States), 636, 638, 639; Harms-Baltzer, pp. 111–16; McCann, pp. 115–16, 176–78; Hilton, pp. 190–91, 206–10.

43. Jacobsen, pp. 562–65; *G.D.*, D, 5, Nos. 613, 614, 621; cf. ibid., No. 595.

44. The memoirs of Eduardo Labougle, the Argentine ambassador to Germany 1932–39, concentrate very heavily on the question of Germans abroad which practically dominates the book; see his *Mision en Berlin* (Buenos Aires: Guillermo Kraft, 1946), pp. 12–144, passim, and 163ff. On the last days of Labougle's mission, see *Lipski Papers*, pp. 540–42.

45. See *G.D.*, D, 5, Nos. 624, 626, 630; Ebel, pp. 288ff.; McKale, pp. 149–52.

46. *G.D.*, D, 5, No. 603; cf. ibid., No. 637; Jacobsen, pp. 565–66; McKale, p. 145.

oil wells in 1938.[47] For the most part, however, the nations of Latin America did not turn to Germany as a counter to the United States. The church struggle in Germany automatically made the powerful Catholic church hostile to Germany. The fear of another war, which was generally associated with German initiative in South as in North America, inclined many to anti-German feelings.[48] The fear of what the local German population, regardless of citizenship, might do was a powerful factor in several countries, including Brazil and Argentina, the two largest.

It was in this framework that the efforts made by Washington were increasingly successful. The "Good Neighbor Policy" blunted many of the traditional—and frequently justified—complaints in Latin America against the United States, while the common threat of Germany provided a unifying consideration previously absent from consultations among the countries of the Western Hemisphere. At times, the countries of Latin America quite deliberately played on their possible ties with Germany to secure concessions from Washington, but the United States was in any case predisposed to such concessions by Hull's doctrinaire belief in the Good Neighbor Policy.[49] The Germans could only watch in displeased quiet as the Pan-American movement developed an increasingly close and anti-German character during 1937 and 1938.[50]

Until considerably more evidence on the clandestine relations between German agencies and their Latin American contacts becomes available, it will be exceedingly difficult to make a balanced judgment on the real nature of German policy in that part of the world. One thing, however, is sure. There was enough of an appearance of threats, enough evidence of obviously illegal and conspiratorial activity, to provide a common bond of fear of German aims, whatever they might be. For the first time, the peoples of North and South America thought of themselves as facing the same menace.[51]

47. See above, p. 8 n.18. It should be noted that William Rhodes Davis, who played a role in unofficial German-American peace soundings in the winter of 1939–40, was involved in these deals. There is considerable information on Davis in Klaus Volland, *Das Dritte Reich und Mexiko* (Frankfurt/M: Peter Lang, 1976), pp. 83–86, 125–27, 134–48, 154–56. The general subject of German oil purchases from Mexico is reviewed, ibid., pp. 86–164, passim. Vollard also argues that the timing of the Mexican nationalization decree of 18 March 1938 was influenced by the belief that the crisis over the annexation of Austria would limit the British reaction, the American one being in any case affected by the Good-Neighbor Policy (ibid., pp. 109–11).

48. Note the comments of the German minister in Peru in *G.D.,* D, 5, No. 619.

49. See, e.g., Hilton, chap. 5.

50. See *G.D.,* C, 6, No. 67; D, 5, No. 635; Offner, pp. 167–71. For a review of German discussion of the policies that might be adopted in the face of these trends during the summer of 1939, see Harms-Baltzer, pp. 132–45.

51. The survey by Reiner Pommerin, *Das Dritte Reich und Lateinamerika, Die deutsche Politik gegenüber Süd- und Mittelamerika 1939–1942* (Düsseldorf: Droste, 1977), is useful but by no means definitive.

9   German-Italian Relations and the *Anschluss*

The development of German-Italian relations that culminated in Italian Foreign Minister Galeazzo Ciano's visit to Germany in October 1936 and the subsequent public proclamation of the Axis by Benito Mussolini has been traced in my preceding volume.[1] A sequence of events largely unplanned by either power had brought together in an uneasy partnership a Germany and an Italy that both attracted and repelled each other. They were attracted to each other by what seemed to be similarities in ideology at home and in enemies—or imagined enemies—abroad. There was also at least the possibility of their expansionist aims being complementary. This concept, most strongly held by Hitler, posited German expansion into Eastern Europe and a natural sphere for Italy in the Mediterranean and North Africa.

Although Hitler clung to this view and allowed it to play an important role in his military strategy during World War II, the fuzziness, or self-contradiction, inherent in these supposedly complementary expansionisms was one of the major causes of difficulty between the two countries. There was, first of all, the question of Austria. Italy, out of fear and self-interest, found herself concerned for the independence of her own traditional enemy—Austria—where, in spite of Austrian dependence upon support from Rome, the feelings of hostility were heartily reciprocated. Two elements combined to inspire the Italian fear and self-interest which had made her the defender of

---

1. Weinberg, *Foreign Policy,* pp. 331–37; see also Jens Petersen, *Hitler-Mussolini: Die Entstehung der Achse Berlin-Rom, 1933–1936* (Tübingen: Niemeyer, 1973).

Austria. There was first the concern for Italy's own territorial integrity. The possibility that a large Germany rather than a small Austria might support an irridentist claim on the South Tyrol, or might even strive for a port on the Adriatic, was feared above all other conceivable dangers to Italy. Hitler had recognized this real obstacle to any German-Italian association and had publicly and repeatedly repudiated all claims to the South Tyrol, in spite of reluctance among his associates and revulsion among the German public at such cold-blooded sacrifice of a German minority.[2]

Although Hitler's understanding of this Italian worry would lead him to an even more extreme concession after the *Anschluss*—arrangements for the removal of the German population from the South Tyrol—he never recognized until well into World War II that implicit in German annexation of Austria was another source of conflict between German and Italian ambitions. Italy's interests were not confined to the southern and eastern shores of the Mediterranean, but extended to the Balkans. There the expansion of German influence, once firmly centered on Vienna, was as likely to clash with Italian as with French or British interests. This source of complications was more readily perceived by Rome than Berlin.[3]

If these two considerations of power and interest made an alignment of Germany and Italy difficult, there was a further factor, harder to define and document, but no less real. Insofar as one can speak of the likes and dislikes of the broader public, the Germans and Italians disliked and mistrusted each other. In England and France not wholly dissimilar popular antipathies were countered by substantial support for close relations between the two nations on the part of some portions of the public and by an awareness of the need for coordinated policies in government circles. In Germany and Italy that countervailing element, far more limited, but still decisive, was to be found in the attitudes of the two dictators.[4]

The first meeting between the two leaders at Venice in June 1934 had not been a particular success, though the attempted coup in Austria six weeks later had probably made it appear less fortunate in retrospect than it really was. The course of events since 1934, however, was seen by both as bringing them closer together. Because Hitler was determined to come to an agreement with Italy under almost any circumstances, he was not himself as influenced by the Italian reaction to the murder of Austrian

2. Weinberg, *Foreign Policy*, pp. 17–18, and the sources cited there. A survey of the issue in Jens Petersen, "Italien in der aussenpolitischen Konzeption Hitlers," *Historisch-politische Streiflichter*, ed. Kurt Jürgensen and Reimer Hansen (Neumünster: Wachholtz, 1971), pp. 212–17.

3. Petersen, "Italien in der aussenpolitischen Konzeption Hitlers," p. 208, comments that in Hitler's discussion of Italy's possible policies "there is nowhere the least mention of Italy's interests in the Balkans and Danubian area."

4. Manfred Funke refers to this very personal element on the part of Hitler as a sign of Hitler's power of autonomous decision making *(Entscheidungsautonomie)* in the face of the practically unanimous contrary view of party officials, diplomats, and military leaders (Funke, pp. 830–31).

Chancellor Engelbert Dollfuss as might have been expected.[5] Mussolini, on the other hand, would soon isolate himself from any possible coordination of his support of Austrian independence with Britain and France by the attack on Ethiopia. The conflict in East Africa may have brought the Italians temporary control of the somewhat meager resources of Ethiopia and the emotional euphoria of a successful defiance of world opinion, but its benefits for Germany were of a more substantial nature. The war opened opportunities for the expansion of German influence in the Balkans, provided a focus of attention elsewhere while her rearmament continued apace, and assured a division among the other Locarno powers when Germany remilitarized the Rhineland.[6]

Mussolini's abstaining from any concerted policy with England and France did not end when the Duce officially proclaimed the Ethiopian war over on 5 May 1936. By the time the long haggling over the ending of sanctions and the formal recognition of Italy's control of Ethiopia was over, other events had combined with Mussolini's own inclinations to rule out a rapprochement with the Western Powers. Though not subject to precise proof, there are indications that the advent of the Popular Front government of Léon Blum in France in June 1936 had a lasting effect on the Italian dictator. Representing everything in the world that Mussolini detested, Blum's government might well have been sincere in its desire for an accommodation with Italy, but the Duce was simply unwilling to consider the possibility.[7] France's permanent enmity toward what he considered the natural ambitions of Italy, an enmity which Hitler had always posited as the basis for a German-Italian alignment, appears to have impressed itself on Mussolini only in 1936. From Mussolini's perspective, this new view of France reinforced the clash of French and Italian interests that was opened up by the outbreak of civil war in Spain in July 1936.

The failure of the July uprising to secure immediate control over all of Spain resulted in requests to both Germany and Italy for assistance in moving the troops of General Francisco Franco from North Africa to the Spanish mainland. The essentially independent but simultaneous decisions of Hitler and Mussolini to grant such assistance involved them both in a venture that soon proved to be longer than either had originally anticipated. When the failure of Franco's offensive on Madrid in November 1936 raised the question of even larger German and Italian commitments in Spain, the two dictators, as previously described, decided on different responses. Mussolini, originally hoping to assure a speedy victory by Franco, sent Italian units to Spain whose share, first in the Nationalist

5. Weinberg, *Foreign Policy*, pp. 234–35.

6. The discussion of this topic too often overlooks that England and Italy were the intended joint guarantors of the Locarno settlement.

7. Dreifort (pp. 152–58, 177–80), on the other hand, argues that Blum and Delbos really did not expect or want better relations with Italy.

victory at Málaga, and then in the defeat at Guadalajara, firmly tied the
Italian leader's prestige to the fortunes of Franco throughout the long
conflict. This assured continued friction between Italy on the one hand
and France and England on the other, the latter two favoring non-
intervention, generally sympathizing with the Spanish Republic, and worrying about Italy's role in the Balearic islands.

It was the prospect of these very factors that helped incline Hitler to a
different decision. He would continue to assist Franco to prevent a
Nationalist defeat, but unlike Mussolini, he would not send substantial
regular land forces to Spain. As Hitler had concluded by late December
1936, a long rather than a short war in Spain was in Germany's interest.
Among the reasons for this view, besides the diversion of attention from
German policies elsewhere, that a long war might provide, was the fact
that the continued estrangement of Italy from Britain and France was seen
as pushing Italy to Germany's side.[8] Hitler even speculated that if a great
war did break out in the Mediterranean, it would provide an opportunity
for Germany to move in Central Europe, but this idea does not appear
until later. In any case, starting in the late summer of 1936, the cooperation of Germany and Italy in Spain, though often marked by rivalry and
friction, did serve to bring them closer together. It certainly precluded an
Italian return to the defense of Austrian independence.[9]

The German-Austrian agreement of 11 July 1936 had been both a
symptom of the German-Italian rapprochement and a sign of Germany's
ascendancy in Europe.[10] With Mussolini's encouragement, Austrian
Chancellor Kurt von Schuschnigg had made a series of agreements with
Germany that he considered the fixed basis for future policy of both
countries, while the Germans saw it as another step on the road to the
annexation of Austria. The subsequent months saw discussion over the
significance and international repercussions of the agreement as well as
arguments between the two parties over its practical application. Though
relieved at what appeared to be a relaxation of tension in Central Europe,
the Western Powers viewed the situation with concern.[11] What a high
Austrian official described to the Hungarians as a necessary evil,[12] was
seen by the Polish government as a prelude to the *Anschluss,* something
Warsaw thought of as a useful diversion of German attention from Eastern Europe.[13]

The German-Austrian negotiations over the implementation of the
agreement were complicated from the start by the differing perspectives

8. On this point, see the evidence cited in Weinberg, *Foreign Policy,* p. 298 n.148.
9. Cf. Siebert, pp. 51–53.
10. Weinberg, *Foreign Policy,* pp. 264–71.
11. *U.S.,* 1936, 1:325; *D.D.F.,* 2d, 2, No. 479; 3, No. 178.
12. Kerekes, No. 5 (the text in *Allianz Hitler-Horthy-Mussolini: Dokumente zur ungarischen Aussenpolitik [1933–44]* [Budapest: Akadémiai kiadó, 1966], No. 12, omits the
P.S.).
13. *D.D.F.,* 2d, 2, No. 458.

of the two parties, one seeing it as a possible bulwark of Austrian independence in spite of its concessions to Germany, the other viewing it as a shield for greater German control of Austrian affairs in spite of its recognition of Austrian independence. Parties holding such divergent views naturally could not arrive at further agreements quickly and easily.[14] The situation's inherent difficulty was compounded by special complications on each side. On the German side, it was the Austrian National Socialist party; on the Austrian side, it was the inclination of von Schuschnigg as well as some others in the Austrian government to use the prospect of a Habsburg restoration as a way of trying to strengthen Austria's bargaining position.

The National Socialist party of Austria had always been a caricature of the German one in its internal dissensions, never papered over effectively by a charismatic personality like Hitler. The amnesty granted many of its jailed leaders as a result of the German-Austrian agreement served to accentuate this situation by increasing both the number of those feuding as well as the subjects to feud about. A solidly founded history of the Austrian party remains to be written; but the performer of this labor of Hercules will have to deal not only with the purely internal complexities but also with the conflicting ties of the factions with party and state agencies inside Germany, the directives they received from these agencies, and the efforts of the Austrian National Socialists to play the agencies and personalities in the Reich off against one another for the benefit of their own policies and personal positions.[15] The efforts of Captain Josef Leopold to reassert his role in the Austrian party after his release from jail must be seen in this context, emphasizing as it did both the internal divisions in the party and the rivalry with Franz von Papen's attempts to push forward by diplomatic pressure.[16]

14. On the negotiations and concerns in the later summer and fall of 1936, see *G.D.*, D, 1, Nos. 156, 158–61, 163; von Papen to Hitler, A 4153 of 30 July 1936, T-120, 778/1549/376310–12; von Papen to Hitler, A 4801 of 1 September 1936, *TMWC*, 30:44–48; "Bestellungen aus der Pressekonferenz," 15 July, 16 September 1936, Bundesarchiv, Brammer, Z.Sg. 101/8, ff.29–31, 159; Wolfgang Rosar, *Deutsche Gemeinschaft: Seyss-Inquart und der Anschluss* (Vienna: Europa-Verlag, 1971), pp. 108–17. This book, though something of an apologia for Seyss-Inquart, is useful for many details turned up by the author.

15. The riot arranged by the Austrian National Socialists for the Olympic ceremonies in Vienna on 29 July 1936 will have to be fitted into the framework. See the description in G. E. R. Gedye, *Betrayal in Central Europe* (New York: Harper, 1939), pp. 192–93; Messersmith dispatch 848 of 31 July 1936, State 863.00/1298. A preliminary survey of the Austrian party is in Francis L. Carsten, *Fascist Movements in Austria: From Schönerer to Hitler* (London: Sage, 1977).

16. A good account in Jürgen Gehl, *Austria, Germany, and the Anschluss, 1931–38* (London: Oxford University Press, 1963), pp. 147–50.

It is indicative of the changed situation in Austria that Rost van Tonningen, the League commissioner for Austria, who had previously tried to mediate between Dollfuss and Mussolini, was now busy preparing for the Dutch National Socialist leader Anton Adriaan Mussert to meet—Hitler (Weinberg, *Foreign Policy*, p. 97 n.52; *G.D.*, C, 5, Nos. 539, 565; 6, No. 41).

On the Austrian side, von Schuschnigg was periodically tempted to go beyond the specific details of the negotiations over the economic, political, and press implementation of the 11 July agreement by alluding to the possibility of a Habsburg restoration.[17] Though von Schuschnigg was undoubtedly sincere in his personal dedication to a monarchical restoration, and although a theoretical case could indeed be made for the view that a restoration might serve as a barrier to the *Anschluss,* in practice the concept had serious disadvantages both abroad and at home.[18] Abroad it was more likely to unite Italy and Germany *against* Austria than to keep at least some Italian support for Austria. Precisely because of the theoretical implications of a restoration for the *Anschluss,* a restored monarchy was certain to be violently objected to by Berlin; in fact, it would be taken as a signal for a German invasion. This was not only the internal view of the German government, but had also repeatedly and emphatically been conveyed to von Schuschnigg.[19] As for Italy, the Habsburgs were hardly popular favorites with those who saw themselves as the heirs, if not the reincarnation, of the anti-Habsburg Risorgimento. When the government in Rome came to believe that von Schuschnigg might conceivably be serious about a restoration, Mussolini saw to it that appropriate articles in the official press enlightened the Austrian chancellor on Italy's objections to such experiments.[20] The fact that by this time von Schuschnigg could probably have counted on French agreement to a restoration, and might even have felt confident of the tacit consent of Czechoslovakia,[21] hardly outweighed these foreign dangers, accentuated as they were by the way in which the issue cemented Yugoslavia's new ties to the Axis powers.[22]

Even at home there was a serious defect to this ploy. The legitimists within Austria were in any case behind the government, but the main reservoir of potential additional supporters for the regime had other sympathies, and was likely to be even more alienated by such schemes. The Austrian Socialists viewed the government with sullen indifference, if not defiance, since the Dollfuss government had violently suppressed them on

17. *G.D.*, D, 1, Nos. 157, 195, 209; von Papen to Hitler, A 4153 of 30 July 1936, T-120, 778/1549/376310–12; von Papen to Hitler, 11 February 1937, T-120, 2500/4439/E 272552–53; *D.D.F.*, 2d, 4, No. 46.

18. A survey of the subject in Gordon Brook-Shepherd, *The Anschluss* (Philadelphia: Lippincott, 1963), pp. 111–15.

19. For German warnings of invasion to von Schuschnigg, see Berger to Schmidt, 30 January 1937, *Guido Schmidt Trial*, p. 516; the material on von Neurath's visit cited in n.46, below; also *Hungarian Documents*, 1, Nos. 217, 279.

20. Elizabeth Wiskemann, *The Rome/Berlin Axis*, 2d ed. (London: Collins, 1966), p. 100; cf. Gedye, p. 199. The survey of Blair R. Holmes, "Europe and the Habsburg Restoration in Austria, 1930–1938," *East European Quarterly*, 9, No. 2 (Summer 1974), 173–84, does not fill the need for a searching study of the subject.

21. Note the perceptive report of the Hungarian minister in Prague in *Hungarian Documents*, 1, No. 234; cf. ibid., No. 266.

22. See above, pp. 215–24.

12 February 1934. If von Schuschnigg had been at all perceptive about the possibility and feasibility of strengthening his government, it was in this direction that he might have made some gestures in the years between the military attack on the Socialists and his own trip to Berchtesgaden on the fourth anniversary of the shelling of Vienna's public housing. By flirting with a Habsburg restoration, he was deliberately facing the other way.

With the restoration scheme adding no real leverage to von Schuschnigg's negotiating position, all that was left for him was delay and careful maneuvering—often the same thing—in the face of German pressure. The months following the signing of the July agreement were, therefore, a period of complicated negotiations within Austria and between the German and Austrian governments.[23] If von Schuschnigg had hoped to use the threat of a restoration in these talks, the Germans had more immediate and concrete resources. A part of the July agreement had provided them with one certain and one possible ally within the Austrian government; Berlin made full use of the former and did its best to charm the latter. Edmund Glaise von Horstenau, the military historian, had been involved in the negotiations for the July agreement and was one of the members of the so-called National Opposition who were included in the Austrian cabinet under the terms of the agreement. Though not yet thinking of himself as a National Socialist—that would come later—Glaise did see himself as an officially recognized agent of the German within the Austrian government and was not above calling for pressure from Berlin in order to subvert the government he had sworn to support.[24] He also suggested that the other prospective agent for Berlin, the new state secretary in the Austrian foreign ministry, Guido Schmidt, be treated well by Germany and invited to Berlin for appropriate flattery and personal contact.[25]

In the trial conducted in post–World War II Austria, Guido Schmidt was acquitted of charges of treason.[26] Although the suspicion of treasonable relations with the Germans could not be proved, it was certainly shown that the vain and ambitious young man was indeed flattered by the attention paid to him in Germany, that he often followed German suggestions, and that he enjoyed—even if he did not earn by treason—the personal friendship of Hermann Göring, a friendship which secured him a well-paid post in the Four-Year Plan while his former colleagues in the

23. The best account is in Gehl, chap. 6. Some of the documents have been published in *G.D.*, D, 1, e.g., Nos. 168 and 171.

24. See ibid., No. 166. Note how, in a similar fashion, the new political movement designed to rally support for the regime, the Fatherland Front, worked to alienate the Protestants in the country; Irmgard Bärnthaler, *Die Vaterländische Front* (Vienna: Europa Verlag, 1971), pp. 177–86.

25. *G.D.*, D, 1, Nos. 163, 166. On Glaise, see also Ludwig Jedlicka and Rudolf Neck (eds.), *Österreich 1927 bis 1938* (Munich: Oldenbourg, 1973), pp. 198–99.

26. The transcript, documents, and verdict of the trial are published in *Guido Schmidt Trial*.

Austrian government languished in jails and concentration camps. Although Schmidt's personal integrity was eventually cleared in court, the fact that von Schuschnigg's closest adviser on foreign affairs was widely thought then and later to be an agent of the Germans may serve to show how tenuous the position of the Austrian government actually was once it agreed in 1936 to sup with the devil, as it was doing so with the demitasse spoon more appropriately used for stirring the famous Viennese whipped cream.[27]

The role of Hermann Göring in Austrian affairs was not confined to his wooing of Guido Schmidt.[28] Göring, in fact, took an increasingly active part in pushing for the annexation of Austria. His range of activities, spurred on by the hope of gaining economic resources for his Four-Year Plan, included a number of different but complementary procedures. He talked about closer relations with von Schuschnigg when they met at the funeral of Gömbös in October 1936.[29] He told all and sundry at every opportune and inopportune moment that the annexation of Austria by Germany was just a matter of time. This tactic, repeated too often to be anything other than calculated, must be seen as a form of psychological warfare, conditioning third parties to the inevitable and cajoling and threatening the Austrians into resignation in the face of what was certain to happen.[30] The most important recipients of Göring's views, however, were the Italians. Having repeatedly visited Rome earlier, Göring now had the added subject of the Spanish Civil War to discuss with the Axis partner. The Condor Legion was the main element in German support for Franco, so that as commander-in-chief of the German air force, Göring had every reason to take a hand in the discussion of Axis aid to Franco.

Before Göring appeared in Rome in January 1937, the stage for the next phase of German-Italian relations and their still differing attitudes toward Austria had been set by important meetings in November 1936. The Rome Protocols Powers—Italy, Hungary, and Austria—had met in Vienna to assess the new situation.[31] More important than the talks of the partici-

27. On Schmidt, see in addition to the trial, Dertinger's "Informationsbericht Nr. 141: Die oesterreichische Frage," 4 October 1937, Bundesarchiv, Brammer, Z.Sg. 101/31, ff.301–5; R 7270/303/3, FO 371/21116; cf. Filippo Anfuso, *Rom-Berlin im diplomatischen Spiegel*, trans. Egon Hyman (Essen: Pohl, 1951), pp. 58–59.

28. Letters exchanged between Göring and Schmidt are printed in *Guido Schmidt Trial*, pp. 302–17; their relationship was a major subject of the trial.

29. See *G.D.*, C, 5, Nos. 597 n.9; 600, D, 1, No. 169.

30. For examples of Göring's tactic, see his comments to Schmidt in November 1936 (Messersmith dispatch 983 of 4 December 1936, State 863.00/1324); his comments, direct and indirect, to Berger-Waldenegg in Rome in May 1937 (*G.D.*, D, 1, Nos. 203–5); his calculated "indiscretion" to Austrian industrialists in June 1937 (*D.D.F.*, 2d, 6, No. 167; von Papen to von Neurath, 19 June 1937, DZA Potsdam, Büro RAM, Akte 60964, ff.144–45; R 6541/139/3, FO 371/21115); his comments to Revertera in November 1937 (*Guido Schmidt Trial*, pp. 292–97, and Nachtrag, p. 4).

31. The Hungarian record is in *Allianz Hitler-Horthy-Mussolini*, No. 15; the Italian record in Ciano, *Diplomatic Papers*, pp. 63–68; see also Messersmith to Hull, 16 and 23 October 1936, Hull Papers, folder 93.

pants was the refusal of Germany to take part. Berlin wanted to handle its relations with each country bilaterally rather than risk dealing with a group.[32] They were to deal directly with Italy on economic issues,[33] and in like fashion to invite Guido Schmidt to Berlin, not only to secure additional specific concessions in direct German-Austrian negotiations, but above all to obtain an Austrian promise not to participate in any multilateral Balkan agreement without Germany.[34]

If Schmidt's visit to Berlin proceeded smoothly, it was because the Germans were satisfied to settle for minor concessions on current issues—Hitler urged but did not insist on Austria's leaving the League—as long as they received the one major concession that in their eyes really mattered: the promise of Austria not to join new economic (and potentially political) coalitions in the Balkan area without prior consultation with Berlin.[35] Schmidt's and von Schuschnigg's satisfaction with the visit[36] only shows their failure to understand the general thrust of German policy. If Austria were isolated, she could be effectively browbeaten and eventually absorbed by her large and powerful neighbor. The when and how of this absorption could be left open, and it was the subject of differing views within the German government, with Hitler himself leaving the precise details open; the essential prerequisite was the same regardless of which procedure was finally adopted.[37] An isolated Austria would fall to Germany sooner or later; only an Austria aligned with other countries might conceivably have maintained her independence longer.

A steady stream of official German visitors poured into Italy in late 1936, so that Göring came on the heels of such National Socialist notables as the Hitler youth leader Baldur von Schirach, Minister Hans Frank, State Secretary Erhard Milch with an air force delegation, police leader Kurt Daluege with Reinhard Heydrich and other SS officials followed by Heinrich Himmler himself, Gauleiter Wilhelm Bohle of the Foreign Section (AO) of the party, the chief press official of the government, Otto Dietrich, as well as other dignitaries of the Reich.[38] The Italians were

32. *G.D.*, C, 6, Nos. 16, 17.
33. See von Hassell to von Neurath, 13 November 1936, DZA Potsdam, Büro RAM, Akte 60964, ff.31–32; cf. *G.D.*, C, 6, No. 44.
34. On the preparations for the Schmidt visit, see Messersmith to Hull, 16 October 1936, Hull Papers, folder 93; *G.D.*, C, 6, No. 21; D, 1, Nos. 172–74, 176–80.
35. On the Schmidt visit, see Geyl, pp. 138–39; *G.D.*, D, 1, Nos. 181–85, 188. It was at this time that Schmidt invited von Neurath to visit Vienna.
36. The subsequent testimony of the two at the Schmidt trial (pp. 431–39), is confirmed by Schmidt's contemporary accounts to French Ambassador François-Poncet (*D.D.F.*, 2d, 4, No. 13) and to the American minister to Vienna (Messersmith dispatch 979 of 30 November 1936, State 762.63/331).
37. Note that in spite of recriminations over von Schuschnigg's Klagenfurt speech of 26 November 1936, von Neurath did go to Vienna in 1937 to further German aims. *G.D.*, D, 1, Nos. 186, 187, 190, 191; cf. *U.S.*, 1936, 2:8–9.
38. In his letter to von Neurath of 19 November 1936, enclosing lists of these visitors, von Hassell referred to them as an "avalanche" (DZA Potsdam, Büro RAM, Akte 60694, ff.33–36). Hitler's decree of 16 December 1936 concerning trips abroad by National Socialist

quite prepared to be cooperative, as they showed by agreeing to Germany's unilateral denunciation of the provisions governing the Rhine and Elbe rivers,[39] and by reinforcing the determination of the Germans not to come to any general agreement with France, as the French government was then suggesting.[40] That did not, however, mean that Göring's impassioned and impulsive demands for Italian acquiescence in the *Anschluss* were as yet received in Rome with enthusiasm.

Hermann Göring and his Italian hosts had little difficulty in coordinating their respective plans for intervention in the Spanish Civil War regardless of whether the then pending ban on foreign volunteers went into effect. Contrary to what Ciano had just been telling the Germans, Mussolini even said kind words about a possible Franco-German rapprochement, perhaps meaning this merely as a rejoinder to Göring's polite expression of approval of Italy's Mediterranean agreement with England (signed just before Göring's arrival). On the Austrian question, however, there was no such pleasant agreement—even if both sides afterwards professed satisfaction on all points. Göring stressed the inevitability of an *Anschluss* and urged the Italians in the immediate future to press Austria to adhere to the July agreement; i.e., to make concessions to the Germans, while in the long run reconciling themselves to the *Anschluss*.

In return, Göring implied that Germany would support Italy in any Mediterranean crisis—something of an echo of Hitler's views. Furthermore, although the evidence is not definitive on this, Göring most probably went beyond a simple promise to respect the Brenner border after an *Anschluss* by hinting at the evacuation to Germany of any persons in South Tyrol who wished to retain their German culture.[41] This idea of

---

officials appears to have been inspired by von Hassell's complaints (*Anordnungen des Stellvertreters des Führers*, pp. 386–88). It is known that von Hassell saw Hitler just before this (Akte 60964, ff.37–38), but no record of their talk has been found. Cf. Petersen, *Hitler-Mussolini*, p. 481.

39. See Weinberg, *Foreign Policy*, p. 276; excerpt of von Hassell's telegram of 1 December 1936, Germany, Auswärtiges Amt, *Aussenpolitische Dokumente*, 1936, No. 2 (Berlin: Reichsdruckerei, 1937), No. 38.

40. *G.D.*, C, 6, No. 90; D, 3, No. 161; cf. ibid., C, 6, No. 86.

41. Göring made this point quite bluntly to Ulrich von Hassell on 15 January when the two discussed Göring's forthcoming meeting with Mussolini (*G.D.*, D, 1, No. 199). In the absence of a full record of the Mussolini-Göring talk of 16 January (as opposed to that of 23 January), there is no way of knowing whether Göring touched on the subject. The fine study of Conrad F. Latour, *Südtirol und die Achse Berlin-Rom, 1938–1945* (Stuttgart: Deutsche Verlags-Anstalt, 1962) quite properly stresses the German government's shared responsibility for the radical decision to move the people as opposed to those who have insisted on Italian pressure as primarily responsible, but Latour does not refer to this important passage in von Hassell's memorandum. It should be noted that the memorandum itself was kept in the files of the German embassy in Rome, and there is no evidence to suggest that von Hassell informed officials in the German foreign ministry in Berlin of Göring's willingness—hardly given without Hitler's approval—to promise the Italians absolute security on the border, including a population transfer. Mario Toscano, in his book on the South Tyrol question, *Storia diplomatica della questione dell'Alto Adige* (Bari: Laterza,

moving people to fit borders, rather than the other way around, would play a most important role later, not only with respect to the South Tyrol, but also in the lives, and deaths, of millions. As in the other extreme measure of treating human beings as mere objects of policy—the mass extermination program—the leaders of the Third Reich applied their doctrines first to *Germans;* the resettlement of the South Tyroleans was in this sense analogous to the mass extermination of the tens of thousands of victims of the euthanasia program inaugurated in the fall of 1939.

The Italians, who at first seem to have thought that Göring meant that there was to be an immediate annexation of Austria, calmed down when reassured that the *Anschluss* was not that imminent, but Mussolini did make Göring understand that there was still great apprehension in Italy over any rapid change in the status of Austria. The agreement, reached orally rather than in writing, to the effect that Italy would urge Austria to base her policy on the July agreement while Germany would take no steps changing the status of Austria without consulting Italy, represented a reasonable accommodation between the two points of view, but in reality left many questions open.[42]

Three aspects of the conversations of Göring with Mussolini and Ciano must be mentioned if the development of the Axis and its practical import for German policy and international affairs are to be understood. Coming two weeks after the British-Italian gentlemen's agreement of 2 January 1937, the emphatic public cordiality of the Göring visit showed that those who did not sign gentlemen's agreements might be capable of cooperating (even if they did not claim to be gentlemen). The conversations themselves dealt with the Austrian question in a way astonishingly similar to that of Mussolini's talk with Pierre Laval about Ethiopia two years earlier. If after that earlier fateful meeting Laval had no reason to complain that Mussolini had left him with any doubts about Italy's real intentions toward Ethiopia, so Mussolini could not say that Göring had failed to explain the objectives of Hitler's policy toward Austria. If the details and timetable had been left open, and to this Mussolini's own objections contributed, it was not because Göring was concealing a specific plan, but

---

1967), pp. 129–31, notes this document, states that he found no reference to the transfer idea in the Italian records of the Göring-Mussolini talks, and on the basis of a comment by Göring in 1938 assumes that the suggestion was made on Göring's own initiative. See also Jedlicka and Neck, p. 201.

42. Sources on Göring's visit are: Jodl Diary, 9 January 1937, *TMWC*, 28:347; *G.D.*, C, 6, No. 164; D, 1, Nos. 199, 207, 208; 3, Nos. 209, 210; *Guido Schmidt Trial*, pp. 515–16; Ciano, *Diplomatic Papers*, pp. 80–91 (German text in DZA Potsdam, Büro RAM, Akte 60951, ff.75–97); information received by von Hassell, Akte 60951, ff.98–100. There are accounts in Gehl, pp. 139–40; Wiskemann, pp. 97–98; Toscano, *Questione dell'Alto Adige*, pp. 127–31; Schmidt (who confuses the January and May trips), pp. 345–47; Siebert, pp. 55–56. The conversation Mussolini-Liebitzky of 23 January 1938 (Jedlicka and Neck, pp. 202–3), reflects Mussolini's changing views.

because there was no specific plan. Mussolini, on the other hand, like Laval two years earlier, had hinted at acquiescence without giving a firm assurance.

Finally, the visit set the stage for what would become the turning point both in German-Italian relations and in the subsidiary question of Austria's future. Göring repeated, and Mussolini accepted in principle, Hitler's invitation for Mussolini to come to Germany and see the renewed Reich for himself. When Hans Frank had raised this possibility in September 1936, it had seemed best to send Ciano first; now that cooperation between Germany and Italy had progressed in many spheres, the Duce was willing to follow the path explored by his son-in-law. There would be considerable delay while other questions came to the forefront and preparations were made, but the signals had been set during Göring's visit. Upon returning, Göring realized that there were still obstacles to overcome, but he exuberantly assured—or threatened—the French ambassador on 7 February that *Anschluss* would surely come and that Czechoslovakia would have to be "operated on"; war would result if Germany were not allowed to have her way.[43]

In the spring and early summer of 1937, other issues dominated the international scene. The war in Spain, with the Italian defeat at Guadalajara, weakened the position of Italy, while the Italian-Yugoslav rapprochement served to restore the balance. During the first half of the year, the internal developments in Austria, along with the negotiations and relations between Germany and Austria, were characterized by extremely complex cross-currents. The details of these need not be recounted here. What does have to be noted are the main characteristics and trends, as well as those specific events which illuminate them.

The negotiations inside Austria and between the German and Austrian governments were marked by insistent pressure from Germany (stemming from Hitler himself), some attempted resistance by von Schuschnigg, and internal divisions among the Austrian National Socialists, though all were pushing for greater concessions from the Austrian government.[44] While von Schuschnigg did make some concessions, he did not go as far as the Germans wanted in terms of recognizing the Austrian National Socialist party, partly because of his own preferences and partly because of counter pressures from other elements in Austria. Certainly Berlin remained dissatisfied.[45]

German Foreign Minister Constantin von Neurath himself tried to obtain greater concessions from von Schuschnigg when visiting Vienna on

43. *D.D.F.*, 2d, 4, No. 423.

44. See *G.D.*, D, 1, Nos. 197, 198, 200–202, 206, 210, 211, 217–19; report on the internal situation in Austria, 14 January 1937, Nuremberg document 2831-PS, National Archives; von Papen to Hitler, A 482 of 21 January 1937, T-120, 2500/4939/E 272547–49; Messersmith dispatch 1022 of 18 January 1937, State 863.00/1328; Gehl, pp. 150–53.

45. *D.D.F.*, 2d, 4, No. 464; *Hungarian Documents,* 1, No. 202.

22–23 February 1937, but, aside from bullying the Austrian chancellor about any Habsburg restoration, accomplished little in spite of signing a cultural agreement.[46] It was at this time, however, that the closer cooperation between Germany and Italy became publicly evident. The Italian denunciation of the idea of a Habsburg restoration came on 26 February, right after von Neurath's visit, and must have shown von Schuschnigg which way the wind was blowing.[47] The Hungarians might give him fair words when he visited Budapest in March; the publication of the papal encyclical "Mit brennender Sorge" a few days later provided a measure of moral support; and the visit of Czechoslovak Prime Minister Milan Hodža to Vienna hinted at the possibility of cooperation with Prague; but none of these factors could make up for the defection of Italy.[48]

German-Italian relations in the period following Göring's January visit were marked by a further degree of cooperation. Both the German ambassador in Rome, Ulrich von Hassell, and the ambassador in Vienna, Franz von Papen, were advising Hitler to follow a cautiously steady policy in Austria in order to achieve better relations with Italy (which alone could facilitate an eventual *Anschluss*), and both—though separately—discussed the situation with Hitler in Berlin on 13 and 19 March 1937.[49] In the meantime, the German press had again been instructed to make no reference to Italian measures in South Tyrol.[50] The Italians, on the other hand, were beginning to reconcile themselves to what now seemed inevitable.

Count Ciano's share in the Italian rapprochement with Yugoslavia was inspired in part by a view of Italian-Yugoslav cooperation as barring any further German advance southward after the *Anschluss*.[51] A number of reports from this time show that the Italians actually held this attitude and

46. On von Neurath's visit, see *G.D.*, D, 1, Nos. 212–14; *Hungarian Documents*, 1, Nos. 204–7, 210, 211, 214; *D.D.F.*, 2d, 5, No. 19; Messersmith dispatches 1067 of 26 February, State 762.63/344, and 1078 of 8 March 1937, State 863.00/1337; Dodd tel. 35 of 1 March 1937, State 863.01/484; "Bestellungen aus der Pressekonferenz," 23 February 1937, Bundesarchiv, Brammer, Z.Sg. 101/9, f.151; "Informationsbericht Nr. 68," 26 February 1937, ibid., 101/30, ff.189–95 and 211–16.

47. See above, n.20; and *D.D.F.*, 2d, 5, No. 34; *Hungarian Documents*, 1, Nos. 210, 213, 215, 229, but see also No. 219.

48. On the Budapest visit, see *Hungarian Documents*, 1, Nos. 223, 225, 226; R 1949/989/3, FO 371/21119. On the Hodža visit, *D.D.F.*, 2d, 5, No. 183; *Hungarian Documents*, 1, Nos. 227, 228. On the papal encyclical, see above, p. 20; "Informationsbericht Nr. 75," 24 March 1937, Bundesarchiv, Brammer, Z.Sg. 101/30, ff.291–95; *Hungarian Documents*, 1, No. 216; *G.D.*, D, 1, No. 220.

49. Von Papen's memorandum is in *G.D.*, D, 1, No. 216; von Hassell's correspondence is in ibid., C, 6, Nos. 193, 216 (note von Hassell's request that this report be shown to Hitler, DZA Potsdam, Büro RAM, Akte 60964, f.67), 247, 312. On von Hassell's appointment to see Hitler, see Akte 60964, ff.67–70; I have been unable to find a report on the conversation. Hitler spent a longer than usual period in Berlin at this time.

50. "Bestellungen aus der Pressekonferenz," 3 March 1937, Bundesarchiv, Brammer, Z.Sg. 101/9, f.173.

51. This is properly stressed by Gehl, pp. 140–41.

were not merely using it as a tactical argument for the Yugoslavs.[52] The shift in Italy's position from absolute objection to the *Anschluss* toward preparing to cope with its implications once it had occurred had been hinted at to Göring when he was in Rome in January and was shown by Italian public denunciation of any Habsburg restoration in February; it was then made clear to the Southeast European countries in March and explained by Mussolini himself to von Schuschnigg when they met for the last time in April 1937.[53]

In the discussions of Mussolini and Ciano with von Schuschnigg in Venice on 22 and 23 April 1937, the Austrian chancellor found his hosts initially courteous but substantially changed. Their nice words could not offset, in fact they enhanced, the general thrust of their advice that Austria should continue to "work actively" in the direction of better relations with Germany.[54] Von Schuschnigg was warned against cooperation with Czechoslovakia—which he forswore—and was also required to explain his actions in playing around with the possibility of restoration. The studied discourtesy of the Duce in leaving his guest to go to the railway station by himself while the Italian leader visited a German cruise ship showed the world as well as the Austrian chancellor that Rome's priorities had changed. The text of the communiqué issued on the occasion of this visit contained no reference to the independence of Austria.

In their conversations with foreign diplomats, von Schuschnigg and Guido Schmidt might try to put a good face on the situation,[55] but no one was fooled. Before the meeting the Austrians had explained to the British government that an independent Austria needed real guarantees, not just kind words,[56] and afterwards the reports of Britain's representatives in Vienna and Rome helped to stimulate the London government to make a public declaration of interest in Central Europe in Parliament; but such declarations had little substantive effect.[57] When in London for the coronation of George VI, Guido Schmidt held detailed talks with Anthony Eden and Sir Robert Vansittart; but his message, that Austria's prospects would improve if Britain secured better relations with either Germany or Italy, was futile even if true.[58] As has already been explained, the British

52. *Hungarian Documents,* 1, Nos. 218, 229; Girsa (Belgrade) to Beneš, 1 April 1937, Czechoslovak document in T-120, 1041/1809/413847; *D.D.F.,* 2d, 5, No. 243.
53. See *Hungarian Documents,* 1, No. 231. Glaise had been to see Hitler just before and told von Schuschnigg and Schmidt about his impressions before the latter departed for Venice; von Papen to Hitler, tel. 37 of 22 April 1937, T-120, 2500/4939/E 272596.
54. Ciano, *Diplomatic Papers,* p. 113. On the Venice metting, see, in addition to the record in ibid., pp. 108–15, *G.D.,* C, 6, Nos. 319, 333; *D.D.F.,* 2d, 5, Nos. 254, 326, 334, 341, 343, 348, 354, 362, 376, 378, 380, 390; *Hungarian Documents,* 1, Nos. 238, 240, 243, 244, 246; Wiskemann, pp. 100–101.
55. *Hungarian Documents,* 1, Nos. 239, 241.
56. *G.D.,* D, 1, No. 220, Annex 1.
57. R 2967, R 3033, R 3108/438/3, FO 371/21117; R 3401/1979/3, FO 371/21119.
58. On Schmidt's London conversations, see R 3302/1979/3, FO 371/21119; *Guido Schmidt Trial,* pp. 520–21; *Hungarian Documents,* 1, Nos. 257, 258; *G.D.,* D, 1, No. 225.

efforts at better relations with Italy never accomplished anything in spite of such apparent successes as the gentlemen's agreement; and the long and complicated attempts to arrive at a settlement with Germany on the basis of colonial and economic concessions in exchange for German restraint in Central and Eastern Europe were making no progress at that time—when they were being carried on with Schacht—and were to be firmly rejected by Hitler ten days before the *Anschluss*.

Schmidt's soundings in Paris could not accomplish anything either.[59] French Foreign Minister Yvon Delbos had explained to American Ambassador William Bullitt in February that France would not fight for Austrian independence;[60] in late April he told the American in the presence of the British ambassador to Paris that Germany could take over Austria at any time.[61]

It should be easy to understand that the Germans were most pleased with the Venice meeting, and that German Foreign Minister von Neurath, who had accepted an invitation to visit Rome in early May, went with the attitude—explained to the Hungarian rather than the Italian government—that the main focus of strength in the Axis had shifted to Berlin.[62] During his stay in Rome, von Neurath had an opportunity to review with Mussolini and Ciano the progress made in the development of the Axis since his meeting with Ciano the preceding October.[63] The Axis leaders exchanged complaints about Franco's slow progress and agreed to continue coordinating their tactics in the Non-Intervention Committee. While the German foreign minister took up Göring's theme of urging Italy to pull out of the League of Nations, Mussolini repeated his own prior advice that the German government make peace with the churches. There was agreement that efforts should be made to try to bring Rumania closer to the Axis if that could be done without excessively antagonizing Hungary; a project to square the circle with which Germany and Italy would wrestle for years. The two powers reassured each other about their respective hostility to England, a touchy subject since each always suspected the other of scheming to sell out its interests for a deal with Great Britain. There was also agreement that the Austrian government should continue to be pressured into concessions to the National Socialists inside Austria, while the country's formal status would not change.

The proposed visit of Mussolini to Germany was discussed again. Von Neurath had talked this over with Hitler, who was anxious to impress the

59. On Schmidt's Paris visit in May 1937 see *Hungarian Documents*, 1, Nos. 245, 253, 257–59; *G.D.*, D, 1, No. 225. There is only the briefest summary in *D.D.F.*, 2d, 5, No. 448 and n.4.

60. *U.S.*, 1937, 1:46–54.

61. Ibid., pp. 84–86.

62. *Hungarian Documents*, 1, No. 242; cf. *D.D.F.*, 2d, 5, Nos. 330, 366; "Informationsbericht Nr. 86," 24 April 1937, Bundesarchiv, Brammer, Z.Sg. 101/30, ff.393–97.

63. On the visit, see *G.D.*, C, 6, Nos. 315, 341, 346, 347, 350, 354, 355; D, 1, Nos. 222, 650; D, 3, Nos. 246, 255; Ciano, *Diplomatic Papers*, pp. 115–17.

Duce with Germany's great might and hence suggested setting the trip to coincide with the German army maneuvers scheduled for September. Mussolini thought this a great idea, but reserved his final decision, which was affirmative and given to von Neurath at their farewell meeting on 5 May.[64]

Indicative in its own way of the correctness of von Neurath's view that Germany was the senior partner in the Axis was the fate of a proposal Ciano first made to him on 4 May and repeated at their final meeting the following day. Ciano wondered whether some new agreement on cooperation might not be signed at the time of Mussolini's visit. Von Neurath was doubtful about the idea then and became even more hesitant when Ciano developed his project during the summer. Securing the approval of Mussolini, Ciano suggested to the Germans through his brother-in-law, Massimo Magistrati, the counselor of the Italian embassy in Berlin, a four-power consultation pact among Italy, Germany, Austria, and Hungary. This was the last thing Germany wanted. Such an agreement would explicitly recognize the independence of Austria and implicitly recognize the Rome protocols with their emphasis on the same subject. There was also the possibility, probably a part of Ciano's motivation, that in any consultations under this agreement the Austrians and Hungarians might well side with Italy and thus enhance her position in the German-Italian partnership. Perhaps this was what Ciano had in mind when he told the Hungarian prime minister and foreign minister in Budapest on 21 May that though the *Anschluss* was inevitable, he hoped to delay it.[65] Von Neurath wanted no pacts of this sort; Hitler emphatically agreed, and von Hassell was left with the task of making the German refusal as palatable as possible to Count Ciano.[66] Germany would move forward according to her own preferences by dealing bilaterally with each of the other three countries; all the Italians would get for the time being was more visits, first by Göring again and then by German Minister of War von Blomberg.

Göring's second trip to Italy in 1937 was not of political importance, but

64. See von Neurath's handwritten addendum to his memorandum of 4 May in DZA Potsdam, Büro RAM, Akte 60951, f.113 (this is another copy of *G.D.*, C, 6, No. 355).

65. *Hungarian Documents*, 1, No. 254; this is not in Ciano's memorandum in his *Diplomatic Papers*, pp. 117–20.

66. The relevant documents, including the proposed text, from the foreign minister's files—RM 619 of 7 July, RM 637 of 12 July, and von Neurath to von Hassell of 13 July 1937—are in DZA Potsdam, Büro RAM, Akte 60951, ff.124–29; they will appear as *G.D.*, C, 6, Nos. 453, 458, and 461. The letter of von Hassell referred to in the last of these documents is his letter to von Neurath of 2 July 1937, DZA Akte 60951, ff.120–21. Von Hassell's subsequent views are in *G.D.*, C, 6, Nos. 469, 476; for confirmation of Mussolini's role, see ibid., No. 485. The subsequent fate of the project is discussed below. Magistrati's account in his memoirs, pp. 58–59, is not very informative.

in one way, von Blomberg's had a significant effect.[67] Although von Blomberg was dubious about what he saw of the Italian army in early June 1937, he was favorably impressed by the Italian air force and navy. Given the general skepticism of Germany's military leaders about the military potential of the Italians, the partial conversion of the Reich's highest officer served to restrain the doubts expressed by the German high command.[68]

Before the stream of German visitors to Rome was balanced out by Mussolini's trip to Germany, a new element had been introduced into the relations between Germany and Austria. The internal feuds of the Austrian National Socialists continued, as did their quarrels with von Papen's proclivity for intrigue rather than spectacle. The multifarious contacts of the Austrian with the German party also remained, serving as a constant embarrassment for the diplomats, since the conspiratorial habits of the National Socialists invariably dumped vast quantities of incriminating evidence into the hands of the Austrian government.[69] Similarly, there was no substantial change in the pattern of direct German-Austrian diplomatic contacts. There was pressure from Berlin and hesitant resistance from Vienna, with the visit of a special German commission to Vienna in July providing little more than a slight change in the terms of the arguments.[70] The new element was the introduction into the picture of two

67. On Göring's visit, see "Informationsbericht Nr. 84," 19 April 1937, Bundesarchiv, Brammer, Z.Sg. 101/30, ff.361–69; Dodd tel. 105 of 14 May 1937, State 762.65/308. On von Blomberg's visit, see Magistrati, pp. 41–46; *D.D.F.*, 2d, 6, Nos. 31, 52; Wiskemann, p. 103; Enno von Rintelen, *Mussolini als Bundesgenosse, Erinnerungen des Deutschen Militärattachés in Rom, 1936–1943* (Tübingen: Rainer Wunderlich, 1951), pp. 20–24; Vincenz Müller, *Ich fand das wahre Vaterland* (Berlin-East: Deutscher Militärverlag, 1963), p. 367; Enno von Rintelen, "Die deutsch-italienische Zusammenarbeit im II. Weltkrieg," 21 April 1947, Foreign Military Studies, B-495, p. 2, National Archives; von Hassell to von Neurath, 12 May 1937, DZA Potsdam, Büro RAM, Akte 60951, f.114.

68. On this whole subject, see Hans Meier-Welcker (ed.), "Zur deutsch-italienischen Militärpolitik und Beurteilung der italienischen Wehrmacht vor dem Zweiten Weltkrieg," *Militärgeschichtliche Mitteilungen*, 1970, No. 1, pp. 59–93.

69. On these tedious, and at times ludicrous, matters, see *G.D.*, D, 1, Nos. 223, 229, 231–33, 242, 248, 249, 257, 258; *Hungarian Documents*, 1, No. 269; von Papen to Hitler, A 2826 of 30 April 1937, T-120, 2500/4939/E 272603–5; von Papen to von Neurath, 19 June 1937, DZA Potsdam, Büro RAM, Akte 60964, ff.144–45; Rosar, pp. 125, 145.

70. The visit of the commission did provide an opportunity for Günther Altenburg to return to the scene of his 1934 conspiratorial activities (Weinberg, *Foreign Policy*, pp. 102–3, 105). On the commission's trip as well as the preceding and succeeding diplomatic talks, see *G.D.*, D, 1, Nos. 227, 234–38, 240; *D.D.F.*, 2d, 6, No. 237; *Hungarian Documents*, 1, Nos. 263, 268, 269, 275, 277, 278, 282; Leonidas Hill (ed.), *Weizsäcker-Papiere, 1933–1950* (Frankfurt/M: Propyläen, 1974), p. 117; "Bestellungen aus der Pressekonferenz," 6 July 1937, Bundesarchiv, Brammer, Z.Sg. 101/10, f.13; "Informationsbericht Nr. 106," of 13 July, and Nr. 107 of 15 July 1937, ibid., 101/31, ff.51–55; von Papen to Hitler, tel. 55 of 2 June 1937, T-120, 2500/4939/E 272617–18; von Papen to von Neurath, 19 June 1937, DZA Potsdam, Büro RAM, Akte 60964, ff.144–45; and a number of documents in the foreign ministry file "Pol. Abt. 09.01, Abkommen und Verträge mit Österreich," DZA Potsdam, AA, Akte 61147 (also in Dokumentationsarchiv des österreichischen Widerstandes, No. 2863).

individuals, one on the Austrian and one on the German side, who would play key roles in the ending of Austrian independence.

Arthur Seyss-Inquart was an Austrian attorney who belonged to various right-wing groups but had not officially joined the National Socialists, although he was sympathetic to them. He was known to Guido Zernatto, the general secretary of the Fatherland Front—a main source of von Schuschnigg's political strength—who introduced him to the chancellor in April 1937.[71] Von Schuschnigg was favorably impressed by Seyss-Inquart and came to depend upon the man who would betray both him and Austria. What apparently brought the two together was an overlap of views in which their agreements obscured their fundamental differences. Seyss-Inquart wanted the far right of Austrian politics to be decorously incorporated into the Fatherland Front and was prepared to join it himself. This meant abstention from the demonstrative activity of which Leopold and his followers were so fond and naturally appealed to von Schuschnigg. While Seyss saw this as a means of taking over Austria quietly from the inside with a "respectable" National Socialist government in Austria as the aim, von Schuschnigg thought of defusing the internal conflicts in Austria as a way of strengthening the Austrian state so that it could cooperate with Germany while maintaining its integrity as a separate country. For a short time the superficial similarity in method hid the divergent goals. The rowdy demonstration arranged at Wels in July by the Austrian National Socialists loyal to Leopold, which was designed to undermine the collaboration of von Schuschnigg with Seyss after Seyss had received a measure of support from Berlin, may well have served to bring the two even closer together.[72]

On the German side, the new entrant was Wilhelm Keppler. Keppler had for some years served Hitler on various special assignments in the economic sphere and had ties to both Göring and Himmler. He was assigned, it would appear at Hitler's request, to represent the National Socialist party's interests when the German commission went to Vienna in July 1937.[73] Keppler's initial participation in Germany's Austrian policies was quickly enlarged. When he and von Papen reported to Hitler about the Vienna negotiations, von Papen utilized the opportunity to complain about the feuding Austrian National Socialists and their multifarious contacts in Germany, so Hitler placed Keppler in charge of all party affairs in and about Austria.[74] This step had several significant

71. Geyl, pp. 154–55.
72. On Seyss-Inquart, see Rosar, passim, esp. pp. 122–60; *G.D.*, D, 1, Nos. 242, 257, 258; *Hungarian Documents*, 1, Nos. 267, 272; Seyss-Inquart to Keppler, 3 September 1937, Nuremberg document 3392-PS, National Archives; Brook-Shepherd, pp. 26–28. For his July 1937 trip to Germany, see Geyl, p. 156; for the demonstration at Wels, ibid., pp. 156–57; *Guido Schmidt Trial*, p. 415; von Papen to Hitler, A 4770 of 19 July 1937, T-120, 2500/4939/E 272635–37; *Hungarian Documents*, 1, No. 281.
73. Keppler to von Neurath, 13 August 1937, DZA Potsdam, AA, Akte 61147, f.45.
74. *G.D.*, D, 1, Nos. 241, 242; cf. *Guido Schmidt Trial*, p. 496.

implications. It would reduce the independence of the Austrian National Socialists by impairing their ability to maneuver among the contending factions in the German government and party. It served to bring the Austrian question even more into Hitler's immediate hands on a continuing basis than had been the case in the preceding years. Finally, it further reduced the role of the foreign ministry, which had been alarmed about von Papen's direct reporting to Hitler—and now often found out what was going on only when Keppler chose to share his knowledge.[75]

Keppler's assignment by Hitler must not, however, be taken as evidence of a less aggressive attitude on the part of von Papen and the foreign ministry than Hitler wanted. On the contrary, the evidence of the time shows that von Neurath and von Papen, von Mackensen and von Weizsäcker, were bullying the Austrians as much as possible at this time and made Guido Schmidt's visits to Berlin on 8 August and 13 September as unpleasant as they could.[76] Keppler's appointment represents much more Hitler's preference for his own personal representatives over the ministerial bureaucracy as well as his understandable interest in effective control of the Austrian National Socialists. Such control was especially important in view of the forthcoming visit of Mussolini. Hitler himself had suggested that the timing of this visit coincide with the German fall maneuvers; he hoped to make a maximum favorable impression on the Duce, and he certainly did not want that imperiled by some incident in Austria. There is no direct evidence on the subject, but the way in which the first meeting of the two dictators had been affected by their divergent views of the Austrian question was probably on Hitler's mind as he looked forward to the second. Leopold's failure even to secure a hearing for his case from Hitler in spite of lengthy written appeals shows Hitler's desire to avoid any disturbance of the atmosphere at this moment.[77]

In his memoirs, Filippo Anfuso, Mussolini's last ambassador to Hitler, asserts that the secret of the Axis is to be found in Mussolini's visit to Germany from 25 to 29 September 1937.[78] Although often tendentious and inaccurate, in this instance Anfuso, who himself took part in the visit as the head of Ciano's secretariat, is unquestionably correct. It was certainly not the case that any special agreements were signed between the two dictators. On the contrary, the Germans had rejected the proposal that Ciano originated and Mussolini drafted in its final form and that the Italians had hoped to have signed at the time of the visit. Unwilling to recognize Austrian independence again or to be bound to consultations in

75. See *G.D.*, D, 1, Nos. 244, 245.
76. On the views of those named, as well as Schmidt's visits, see *Hungarian Documents,* 1, Nos. 260 (German text in Kerekes, No. 9), 277, 287, 289–91; *G.D.*, D, 1, Nos. 239, 244, 245 n.1, 247, 250, 251; von Papen to von Neurath, 1 September 1937, Emessen, pp. 94–97; *D.D.F.*, 2d, 6, Nos. 59, 431; R 4087/439/3, FO 371/21118; "Informationsbericht Nr. 137," 18 September 1937, Bundesarchiv, Brammer, Z.Sg. 101/31, f.251.
77. Gehl, pp. 160–61.
78. Anfuso, p. 39.

which they might be confronted by a united front of Italy, Austria, and Hungary, the Germans had eventually suggested substitutes so speciously anodyne as to be meaningless; and the whole scheme was dropped when the Germans refused to consider all references to Austria and Hungary.[79] The development in economic relations which brought Germany and Italy closer together in 1937 at a time when Italy was eliminating the special trade preferences hitherto accorded Austria and Hungary also does not carry major implications.[80] On the contrary, during the very days that Italy was loosening her trade ties to Austria and Hungary—thereby making them even more economically dependent on Germany—the government in Rome was positively terrified lest the planned visit of von Neurath to London herald an Anglo-German agreement, possibly at Italy's expense. There was no need for the hysterics in Rome; Hitler was uninterested in the sort of agreement obtainable with the British and used the first handy, if unconvincing, excuse to cancel the trip. Hitler wanted Italian concurrence in the *Anschluss,* not a German commitment promising London to respect the independence of the countries of Central and Eastern Europe in return for economic and colonial concessions. But the reaction in Rome to the news of the intended visit reflects the lack of trust between the Axis partners at the time.[81] The significance and lasting repercussions of Mussolini's visit must be seen from an entirely different perspective.

The planning, like the timing, of the visit was keyed to the details of show and protocol, not to the preparation of specific agreements.[82] There is some evidence of a secret Italian approach to France just before the visit to Germany,[83] but the main concern of Mussolini, who alone counted among the Italians, appears to have been to see what the new Germany was like. He was willing to be impressed, but he was still a bit skeptical. His approval of the proposed agreement that would include some reference to Austria shows that before the visit he was by no means willing to endorse all German aspirations.

On the German side, there was no lack of touchy subjects that might be

---

79. *G.D.,* C, 6, Nos. 494, 496, 499, 502, 503. On Mussolini's not even receiving the Austrian and Hungarians ministers to Berlin during his visit, see Magistrati, pp. 63–64.

80. On German-Italian economic relations in the summer and fall of 1937, see *G.D.,* C, 6, Nos. 368, 390, 424, 523, 532, 536, 546; on the end of Italian trade preferences for Austria and Hungary, see ibid., Nos. 486, 556; *Hungarian Documents,* 1, Nos. 283, 284, 286, 308.

81. Ciano, *Diplomatic Papers,* pp. 122–25; *G.D.,* D, 3, Nos. 318–20, 327–29; Eden, pp. 506–11; *Hungarian Documents,* 1, No. 252.

82. *G.D.,* C, 6, Nos. 385, 441, 518, 527; Note by Weizšacker, 26 June 1937, DZA Potsdam, Büro RAM, Akte 60951, f.116; von Hassell to von Neurath, 2 July 1937, ibid., ff.120–21; von Neurath to Hitler, 5 July 1937, ibid., ff.122–23; "Wichtige Bestellung für die Redaktion: Das Programm des Mussolini-Besuches," 17 September 1937, Bundesarchiv, Brammer, Z.Sg. 101/10, f.217; "Informationsbericht Nr. 119," 20 August 1937, ibid., 101/31, f.163; Dertinger, "Vertrauliche Information," 23 September 1937, ibid., ff.259–61; Ciano, *Diary,* 27, 31 August 1937, pp. 4, 7; *U.S.,* 1937, 1:121–22.

83. *D.D.F.,* 2d, 6, Nos. 481, 491; cf. *G.D.,* D, 3, No. 421.

taken up. The hapless South Tyroleans even thought that Mussolini might be asked to pardon some deported co-nationals.[84] Ernst von Weizsäcker was worried lest Italy drag Germany into her own adventures or sell Germany out to Britain.[85] Von Neurath, von Papen, and von Mackensen discussed plans for taking up with Mussolini the most difficult subject of all: Austria.[86] While they wanted to get Mussolini's agreement to closer German-Austrian ties and the replacement of von Schuschnigg, leaving Austria only nominally independent, Hitler was more cautious and preferred to secure Mussolini's goodwill by moving more slowly at first.[87] This approach would work very well in the context of the visit. What Hitler wanted to do was to demonstrate to his people the end of German isolation; even though they had left the League and torn up Locarno, Germany could still have friends. He hoped to show Mussolini the organized might and industrial strength of Germany as well as the unified enthusiasm of the German people. Surely, if he saw these things, and if he was really the great leader that Hitler thought him, then Mussolini would align himself with Germany, and far from putting obstacles in her path, would consider it in his own and Italy's best interest to move forward alongside the Third Reich. As in other situations—relations with Poland and the Vatican to name only two—Hitler was quite prepared to be cautious for a while and appear more conciliatory than many of his advisers, if he saw the eventual prospect of more substantial gain.

In this respect the visit was a great success.[88] Mussolini was feted extravagantly wherever he went and greatly relished the public applause. Although his speech to the assembled multitudes was in a German his listeners found hard to understand, their disciplined enthusiasm was not dampened by the torrents of rain which accompanied the Duce's eloquence. In words that Hitler would echo half a year later, he assured the audience of his gratitude for Germany's refusal to join in sanctions at the time of the Ethiopian war: "We shall never forget that."[89] He was vastly impressed by what he saw of the German maneuvers in Mecklenburg,[90] though his subsequent insistence on introducing the goose-step, desig-

84. *G.D.*, C, 6, No. 549.
85. Ibid., No. 550.
86. Ibid., Nos. 551, 557; D, 1, Nos. 251, 252.
87. Ibid., D, 1, No. 256.
88. Accounts and details in Anfuso, pp. 39–58; Rintelen, p. 28; Siebert, pp. 56–59; Schmidt, pp. 364–70; Frank, pp. 268–69; Speer, *Tagebücher*, pp. 198–99; Wiskemann, pp. 104–8; *D.D.F.*, 2d, 6, Nos. 483, 497, 502; *G.D.*, C, 6, No. 568; D, 1, Nos. 1, 2; 3, No. 423 n.3; *Weizsäcker-Papiere*, pp. 117–18; Ciano, *Diary*, 29 September 1937, p. 20; *Hungarian Documents*, 1, No. 291; "Mitteilungen für die Redaktionen," 24 September 1937, Bundesarchiv, Brammer, Z.Sg. 101/10, ff.227–29; "Informationsbericht Nr. 140," 2 October 1937, ibid., 101/31, ff.295–99; R 6722/438/3, FO 371/21117; Gilbert (chargé Berlin) dispatch 3703 of 8 October 1937, State 762.65/346; Mack Smith, p. 97; Domarus, 1:732–39.
89. Domarus, 1:738.
90. It should be added that he was not the only one. The British impression is referred to on p. 58, above; for the great impact on the Belgians, see Overstraeten, pp. 263–64.

nated as the *passo Romano*, enhanced neither the popularity of the Germans in Italy nor the military effectiveness of the Italian army. A tour of the Krupp armament works in Essen and vast parades of military forces in Berlin and of party elements in Munich gave the Duce an impression of overwhelming strength. Here was a power with which Italy would do well to align herself.

It is too easily forgotten in this connection that Mussolini had taken over power in Italy when Germany was at her weakest—after defeat in the war. He had been the head of the Italian government at the time of the occupation of the Ruhr and for a full decade before Hitler became chancellor. His association with Germany since 1933 had been uneasy and a matter more of convenience than conviction. Under the impact of his visit, this was changed. The late chronicler of the Axis, Elizabeth Wiskemann, is surely correct in claiming that "the impression Nazi Germany made upon Mussolini was probably the most profound impression of his life."[91]

Closely tied to this changed attitude toward Germany was a changed relation to Hitler. Mussolini now sensed in Hitler what Hitler had long felt about him: that here was a man of destiny with whom he should, nay must, ally himself. And one should add that Hitler's own prior belief was reinforced by this experience. Whatever differences and aggravations might subsequently take place in German-Italian relations, the two dictators saw in each other—quite correctly—the guarantors of continued cooperation. Not friendship but mutual veneration was the tie. Perhaps each thought of the other as his mirror image, and in extolling the other man, each was reinforcing his perception of himself and his own role.

The outcome of the visit in specific terms, aside from the discussion of Spain, was mainly on the Austrian question. Precisely because Hitler had *not* asked for concessions in this regard, the happy and untroubled course of the visit left the impression that Mussolini had given the Germans a free hand. He had not really done so, as Frank and Hess learned when they visited Rome soon after,[92] but the very fact that everybody thought Mussolini had done so had its impact. Certainly the French and Poles thought this was the case.[93] Anthony Eden had commented on 22 September that Germany would now pay Italy nothing for Austria; Mussolini's policy of the two preceding years had made Germany's presence on the Brenner inevitable, and the Duce would rue the day if he lived.[94] It would in fact be

91. Wiskemann, p. 107. There is a good general discussion of Mussolini's conduct of foreign policy in Mack Smith, pp. 82–83.

92. Frank, pp. 274, 278.

93. See Lipski's comments in *Szembek Diary*, 4 October 1937, pp. 242–43; Blum's comment in R 6741/1/22, FO 371/21162; and Delbos's comment in Bullitt tel. 56 of 12 January 1938, State 740.00/264. See also Gordon (The Hague) tel. 11 of 5 February 1938, State 762.63/415; *D.D.F.*, 2d, 7, Nos. 6, 50.

94. C 6494/4222/12, FO 371/20749, f.137.

several months before the first part of this prophecy was fulfilled, but fulfilled it was before Hitler made the return visit in Rome to which his happy Italian guests had invited him.[95]

In the period from September 1937 to March 1938, the last months of Austrian independence, the critical issue was no longer whether that independence would be ended, but how. In chapters 3 and 4 we have already traced the failure of the British and French effort at a general settlement with Germany that might have preserved an independent status for Austria. Hitler merely took these efforts, of which the Halifax visit of November was the most visible aspect, as signs that he might be able to go forward in the first steps of his expansionist program without regard for the Western Powers. The intentional spreading of stories that Eden and Halifax had agreed to the *Anschluss*, like the impression that Mussolini had given Hitler a free hand, all combined to create an international climate in which it was assumed that Austria would be annexed.

The dilemma which faced the Western Powers in Central Europe was especially acute in regard to Austria. The French, who at one time did hint that they might mobilize if Germany took Austria, were unwilling to go to war for a country which quite possibly did not want to be independent—a problem the Italians also noted.[96] If war did come, the British public would hardly support entering it, while the Dominions had already made clear that they would not.[97] The Austrian issue posed for the first time the questions that would bedevil Britain and France over Czechoslovakia. If war came, could they win? Even if they won, would and could they reestablish the status quo and enforce its maintenance? But if they let Germany have her way, or even encouraged her, would not the subsequent danger from an enlarged and strengthened Germany be even greater? The internal British correspondence on these matters from the summer of 1937 points out the dilemma of the time and the direction of events. The British ambassador in Paris commented that he doubted the French would even mobilize for Austria; they might fight for Czechoslovakia, though it woud not do much good. The Austrians were not expecting a coup just then, and the Foreign Office thought a coup in the immediate future unlikely, though little could be done if one were to occur. It was also thought that internal German developments might precipitate events.[98]

Von Schuschnigg's comment to the French minister in Vienna, that only a British-French declaration that the political status quo in Central Europe was untouchable could avert all danger, was both unrealistic and

95. *G.D.*, D, 1, No. 5.
96. C 4757/3/18, FO 371/20711; C 7785/3/18, FO 371/20712; R 7948/303/3, FO 371/21116; *U.S.*, 1937, 1:152–53.
97. Note Göring's comments reflecting Hitler's and his own knowledge of this position in *Guido Schmidt Trial*, p. 295.
98. C 5126/3/18, FO 371/20711.

inaccurate.[99] It was unrealistic in that there was no prospect of such a declaration, and it was inaccurate because the status quo, especially in Austria, was crumbling steadily and could quite easily dissolve without the kind of overt international crisis in which any foreign power might usefully intervene. That the *Anschluss* eventually took precisely this form would be partly due to the unwise action of the Austrian chancellor himself. But even without the refusal of von Schuschnigg to reconcile his domestic socialist opponents, without his extraordinary willingness to make concessions to Seyss-Inquart even before his trip to Berchtesgaden, and without the plebiscite scheme, it is most doubtful that the outcome would have been different even if the details of the story had been otherwise. Hitler was determined to annex Austria by one means or another, and with no solid opposition to that aim either within or without that country, there was not much prospect of diverting him from his goal.

Inside Austria, the last months of 1937 saw a continuation of the feuding between the Austrian National Socialists and Seyss-Inquart, while Seyss as well as his German mentors were increasingly unhappy with the stalling tactics of von Schuschnigg. The various schemes and projects, which included plans for a visit by Göring to Vienna, contacts between the Austrian and the Czechoslovak governments, as well as a host of other activities, all merely served to indicate that a temporary stalemate had been reached. This stalemate was highlighted by the inability of the Rome Protocols Powers of Italy, Austria, and Hungary to reach any agreement at their last meeting on 10–12 January 1938 in Budapest.[100] The ability of the Germans to take advantage of this stalemate and to push the Austrian government further down the slipperly slope was assured by the maintenance of good German-Italian relations growing out of the Mussolini visit.

The closer relations between Germany and Italy were evidenced by a number of concrete measures in the months immediately following. After the Germans had made some concessions to meet a personal request of Mussolini, a new German-Italian economic agreement was signed on 18

99. *D.D.F.*, 2d, 6, No. 463.

100. On the planned Göring visit to follow Schmidt's visit, see *Hungarian Documents*, 1, Nos. 307, 309; Emessen, pp. 98–99; von Papen to von Neurath, 16 November 1937, DZA Potsdam, Büro RAM, Akte 60964, ff.168–69; *D.D.F.*, 2d, 7, Nos. 157, 298; Magistrati, p. 107; Rosar, pp. 169–70; *G.D.*, D, 1, Nos. 269, 273; R 7695/303/3, FO 371/21116. On the Austrian-Czechoslovak contacts, see *G.D.*, D, 1, Nos. 254, 259; *Hungarian Documents*, 1, Nos. 292, 294, 295, 299, 300; Wiley dispatch 138 of 25 February 1938, State 762.63/497. On the Seyss-Inquart–Leopold conflict and Keppler's role, see *G.D.*, D, 1, Nos. 255, 260, 267, 272, 275; Seyss-Inquart to Keppler, 1, 21, and 25 October, 2 November 1937, Nuremberg documents 3393-PS, 3394-PS, 3390-PS, and 3395-PS, National Archives; Seyss-Inquart to Keppler, 7 December 1937, Nuremberg document 3626-PS, National Archives; *TMWC*, 32:253–54. On the Rome Protocols Powers' meeting, see Ciano, *Diplomatic Papers*, pp. 148–49; Ciano, *Diary*, 10–12 January 1938, pp. 85–88; *Hungarian Documents*, 1, Nos. 323, 329. For other aspects of German-Austrian relations at this time, see *G.D.*, D, 1, Nos. 264, 268; *Hungarian Documents*, 1, Nos. 293, 301, 310, 311, 325, 327; *D.D.F.*, 2d, 7, No. 210; Wiley dispatch 53 of 10 December 1937, State 762.63/403; R 7842/303/3, FO 371/21116.

December.[101] What is revealing about this agreement is the implicit assumption that any joint war of Germany and Italy against other countries would be against the Western Powers. In case of "abnormal times," Germany and Italy's mutual support for "special circumstances" would be shipped exclusively over land, thus avoiding any possible interference with their communications by sea, something open only to England and France. If such plans were kept secret, equal care was exercised to draw public attention to others. The adherence of Italy to the Anti-Comintern Pact in November was accompanied by as much fanfare as her departure from the League of Nations. Closely related to this symbolic shift was the Italian recognition of the Japanese puppet state of Manchukuo. And all of these actions were accompanied by still more German visitors to Rome, including Hitler's deputy, Rudolf Hess, Hans Frank, the Prince of Hessen, and Joachim von Ribbentrop.[102]

While the German government was most careful to keep Rome informed about the Halifax visit, lest new Italian suspicions be aroused,[103] Ciano expressed to his German visitors the desirability of replacing von Hassell as German ambassador in Rome. Ciano thought von Hassell neither sufficiently enthusiastic about closer German-Italian relations nor influential enough with Hitler, and he wanted a party man as successor.[104] From the Italian point of view, there was substance to both complaints,[105] and Hitler had promised to change his own ambassador in Rome if requested to do so when he asked for Vittorio Cerruti's transfer from Berlin.[106] The change was, however, not made immediately, partly because von Hassell tried very hard to keep his post,[107] and partly because Hitler

101. "Sitzung des Handelspolitischen Ausschusses vom 8. Dezember 1937," T-120, 2612/5650/H 004119–20; Ciano, *Diary,* 18 December 1937, p. 64.

102. On the Anti-Comintern Pact and Italy's departure from the League, see above, pp. 170–73; see also Ciano, *Diary,* 22 November 1937, p. 50; *U.S.,* 1937, 1:194–95; *G.D.,* D, 1, Nos. 67, 76; "Bestellungen aus der Pressekonferenz," 8 November 1937, Bundesarchiv, Brammer, Z.Sg. 101/10, f.337; R 8244, R 8302/655/22, FO 371/21179; Magistrati entitled the chapter of his memoirs dealing with this and related episodes: "L'Italia si allontana dalla collaborazione internazionale." On Italian recognition of Manchukuo, see Weinberg, "Recognition," pp. 157–58; see also Magistrati, pp. 108–10. On the visits of Hess, Frank, and von Ribbentrop, see Frank, p. 274; Ciano, *Diary,* 27 and 30 October 1937, pp. 33, 35; Ciano, *Diplomatic Papers,* pp. 144–46; "Bestellungen aus der Pressekonferenz," 26 October 1937, Bundesarchiv, Brammer, Z.Sg. 101/10, f.303; "Informationsbericht Nr. 150," 27 October 1937, ibid., 101/31, ff.275–77.

103. See especially von Neurath to von Hassell, 25 November 1937, DZA Potsdam, Büro RAM, Akte 60964, ff.172–73; cf. *G.D.,* D, 1, No. 92; Magistrati, pp. 102–5.

104. Ciano, *Diary,* 27 and 30 October 1937, pp. 33, 35. There is a good retrospective analysis in *D.D.F.,* 2d, 8, No. 284.

105. Note von Hassell's advice to Henderson on 2 November that only a quick Anglo-German agreement could keep the Axis from becoming permanent (C 7550/270/18, FO 371/20736).

106. Weinberg, *Foreign Policy,* pp. 234–35.

107. Ciano, *Diary,* 4 and 6 January 1936, pp. 81, 82; von Hassell to von Neurath, 19 January 1938, DZA Potsdam, Büro RAM, Akte 60964, ff.177–80. Von Hassell's smuggling of art objects out of Italy for Göring (Emessen, pp. 28ff.) may belong in this context.

was not able to decide quickly on a replacement.[108] Eventually the change was included with those announced on 4 February 1938, and von Hassell, like his old rival von Neurath, was retired on that fateful day. Von Neurath remained a loyal minion of the Führer and ended up in the dock at Nuremberg, while von Hassell was active in the opposition to Hitler and was among those executed after 20 July 1944.

The successor to von Hassell was Hans Georg von Mackensen, an unimaginative diplomat of distinguished lineage whose brief service as state secretary ended with the removal of his father-in-law von Neurath from the post of foreign minister. He was to be on better terms with Ciano, in part no doubt because he was at all times faithful to the idea of the Axis. Ciano's happiness at the change was also probably enhanced by the fact that unlike his predecessor, who had enjoyed direct access to Mussolini in the years when the Duce had himself held the position of foreign minister, von Mackensen had to rely entirely on Ciano as foreign minister for his contacts and information.[109]

The Italian attitude toward Austria by this time was one of quiet resignation. As the Duce explained to von Ribbentrop on 6 November, in response to the suggestion that this question would "at a certain moment" have to be settled finally, Austria was a German country. Italy would do nothing if a crisis arose; the situation should be allowed to take its natural course. Independence could not be imposed on Austria.[110] Ciano, who was beginning the preparations for Hitler's visit the following May, noted in his diary that he had instructed the Italian minister in Vienna to administer oxygen to the dying Austrian government so that the German heir would not notice, but that the heir was more important than the dying. "The alliance with the Slavs," he noted in connection with the planning for the visit of Yugoslav Prime Minister Stojadinović, "allows us to view the eventual prospect of the *Anschluss* with equanimity."[111]

There is indirect evidence that the attitude of the foreign minister may well have been influenced by the belief that the South Tyroleans could be sent to Germany, never to return. Renato Prunas, the Italian chargé in Paris during the two-year period when there was no Italian ambassador to France, asserted to the American ambassador in January 1938 that agreement had been reached between the German and Italian governments for the transfer of the South Tyroleans.[112] Though presumably an exaggeration, this statement could reflect the internal Italian interpreta-

108. Note the Prince of Hessen's comment that von Dirksen would take von Hassell's place (Ciano, *Diary*, 18 December 1937, p. 64). For Hitler's consideration of prominent National Socialists for the post, see above, pp. 46–47. Cf. Magistrati, pp. 121–23.

109. Rintelen, p. 39. On Mussolini's isolation from contact with diplomats after Ciano became foreign minister, see R 8563/1/22, FO 371/21163.

110. Ciano, *Diplomatic Papers*, p. 146.

111. Ciano, *Diary*, 10, 24 November, 5 December 1937, 2 January 1938, pp. 41, 51, 57, 78; see also *D.D.F.*, 2d, 8, No. 15.

112. Bullitt tel. 55 of 12 January 1938, State 740.00/263.

tion of what they had been told by their German visitors, especially by Göring on his January 1937 trip.[113] Since there is definite evidence that Göring believed there was authorization to give such assurances to the Italians, it is not unreasonable to suppose that whether or not he himself did give them, the Italian government had learned of this German attitude by a year later.

The Italian view of a possible *Anschluss* may be more easily understood, then, if the presumed willingness of the Germans to accept those desiring to leave the South Tyrol is considered in conjunction with Ciano's comment on the agreement with Yugoslavia. As mentioned previously, not love of the Austrians, but fear of German territorial demands for the South Tyrol and perhaps an outlet to the Adriatic had been a primary factor in Rome's support of Vienna. Surely a Germany willing to agree to a population transfer in South Tyrol would not lay claim to Adriatic ports once under Habsburg control against the combination of those who had inherited them, Italy and Yugoslavia. Events were to bear out a large portion of the Italian government's expectations. After the *Anschluss*, the Germans did agree to the transfer of the South Tyroleans, and it was not until Yugoslavia had disappeared by partition and Italy herself had abandoned the Axis that Hitler moved in 1943 toward the annexation of South Tyrol and Trieste by the creation of "Operational Zones," *Alpenvorland*, and *Adriatisches Küstenland*.

In the last months of 1937 there was agreement in German government and party circles that some initiative, probably from the German side, would be needed to break what appeared to be a stalemate in German-Austrian relations. After Hitler's comments on his desire to annex Austria at the meeting of 5 November recorded in the Hossbach memorandum, all the key figures in Germany told foreign visitors that action against Austria was imminent.[114] The economic assets to be seized in Austria constituted an especially attractive lure at a time when German rearmament was causing increasing strains in the German economy.[115]

There were numerous indications that new steps were needed and that action would be taken early in the next year.[116] The difficult question to answer is what initiatives Hitler himself was thinking of. Keppler's comment that action would come in the spring may reflect what Hitler's special representative for Austrian questions was hearing from his mentor.[117] When von Papen talked to Hitler with Göring present on 14 December,

113. See above, pp. 270–71.

114. *U.S.*, 1937, 1:170–77; C 8830/3/18, FO 371/20712.

115. This point is heavily stressed by Norbert Schausberger, "Österreich und die nationalsozialistische Anschlusspolitik," in Funke, pp. 744ff. See also Forstmeier (ed.), p. 149.

116. Examples in *TMWC*, 32:253–54; *G.D.*, D, 1, Nos. 63, 273; *U.S.*, 1937, 1:158–59; *D.D.F.*, 2d, 8, No. 34.

117. *TMWC*, 32:253–54. Cf. the report of the Austrian consul general in Munich of 21 January 1938, *Guido Schmidt Trial*, p. 507.

Hitler wanted the question carried forward in such a manner as to avoid force as long as European considerations made that desirable.[118] Around 10 November, Danzig Gauleiter Albert Forster had learned that after January 1938 he was expected to keep the Free City quiet so that the Reich could concentrate on Austria.[119] Either at the same time or early in 1938, Forster was told by Hitler himself that he was to be transferred to Vienna—as von Papen's replacement—where he would be expected to stage a coup in June or July.[120] In view of the occasional references in the documents to following, in Austria, the Danzig model of a National Socialist government subordinate to but formally independent of Berlin, the possibility of using the very man who had been successful in Danzig and who belonged to the circle of Hitler's party associates must have looked very attractive to the Führer.[121]

In this context, the schemes for an uprising of Austrian National Socialists which are generally assumed to have had no support from Hitler should perhaps not be dismissed quite so readily.[122] The documents found by the Austrian police when they raided the Vienna party headquarters on 25 January and arrested Gauleiter Leopold Tavs, Leopold's deputy, provided for a planned series of provocative acts which would eventually lead to such stringent measures on the part of the government as to justify German intervention. The documents themselves have not been published, and it is difficult to prove or disprove whether, for example, Rudolf Hess had signed or initialed some of the documents as asserted by several reports.[123] What should be noted is that whether or not such schemes were authorized by the highest circles in Germany or merely reflected the enthusiastic strategy of Captain Leopold's efforts to gain control of the situation for himself and away from von Papen, this was the course Hitler had at his disposal if Forster had assumed his projected responsibilities in

118. *G.D.*, D, 1, No. 80.
119. Gallman dispatch 439 of 16 November 1937, State 860K.00/315.
120. C 4359/197/55, FO 371/21801; Gallman dispatch 474 of 9 May 1938, State 860K.00/323.
121. Note Seyss-Inquart's own admission that "Danzigfication" was the German policy, reported in Wiley tel. 53 and dispatch 148 of 8 March 1938, State 762.63/495 and 544.
122. For an example of a "Plan for an Uprising" ("Aufstandsplan") of Captain Leopold of early January 1938, see Wilhelm Canaris, "Aktenvermerk über Besprechung Leiter Abw.-Leiter Ausl. am 31.1.38," 2 February 1938, Nuremberg document 3574-PS, National Archives.
123. See *G.D.*, D, 1, Nos. 279, 280; *U.S.*, 1938, 1:385–87; *D.D.F.*, 2d, 8, No. 51; "Bestellungen aus der Pressekonferenz," 26 January 1938, Bundesarchiv, Brammer, Z.Sg. 101/11, f.55; "Informationsbericht Nr. 13," 26 January 1938, ibid., 101/32, f.59; Wiley dispatch 106 of 31 January 1938, State 863.00/1372. In view of his contacts in the Austrian government, the account of Gedye, pp. 209–10, cannot be dismissed out of hand. Gehl, pp. 167–68, bases his summary on the Zernatto memoirs, and concludes that "it seems most improbable, in view of the rest of the documentary evidence, that Hitler knew about it or even approved of it." Brook-Shepherd, pp. 15–18, also leaves the question open. Rosar, pp. 188–89, discusses the documents which he examined in the Austrian archives, but has nothing to say on this aspect.

Vienna.[124] Certainly Forster had not been designated by Hitler to keep things calm on the Austrian front; quite the contrary, it was the Danzig Gauleiter's penchant for violent words and drastic action that had led Göring to urge his removal from Danzig and recommended him to Hitler as just the right instrument to provoke the internal upheavals in Austria that would open the way for domination or annexation by Berlin.

Although pressure from the National Socialists inside Austria did not start the slide toward the *Anschluss,* it was used by the German government to assist the process. The initiative grew out of a combination of internal Austrian negotiations, pressures by the German on the Austrian government through von Papen, and internal developments in Germany that led Hitler to think the moment opportune for an external action.[125] The deadlock at the end of 1937 had discouraged Seyss-Inquart and Glaise-Horstenau, but Göring and Keppler worked to keep them from withdrawing; Göring and Keppler believed that Hitler was determined to move on the Austrian question in the spring or summer of 1938, and would need assistants within the Austrian government even if the details of procedure were still open.[126] Von Papen had suggested that the way to get things moving was to have von Schuschnigg meet Hitler, a suggestion which the Austrian chancellor had agreed to on 8 January only after von Papen had received Hitler's formal approval. Originally, the meeting was scheduled for the end of January, and the actions of the Austrian government in the period immediately after 8 January can be understood only in the framework of von Schuschnigg's expected visit to Berchtesgaden in the immediate future.

To strengthen his own position in the forthcoming meeting, von Schuschnigg moved dramatically on two fronts. The first concerned what he considered the most radical and dangerous of the domestic National Socialists, and the second was the reconciliation of the so-called moderate National Socialists with their Austrian allies. The action on the first front has already been mentioned. The government took the earliest convenient

124. The inclusion of the assassination of von Papen by the Austrian National Socialists as a provocation in what came to be known as the "Tavs Plan" does not speak for or against German official sanction. One source claims that the German military attaché, General Wolfgang Muff, was the originally intended victim and that this had been vetoed by Heinrich Himmler (Wiley dispatch 106 cited in the preceding note). It should be noted that the assassination of the German minister in Czechoslovakia was considered by Hitler in April 1938 as one possible provocation to excuse a German invasion of that country (*TMWC,* 25:416). Analogous arrangements for provocation, though involving concentration camp inmates as victims, were made for the invasion of Poland, and Hitler placed major emphasis on it in his speech announcing the beginning of the war.

125. The best accounts in Brook-Shepherd and Gehl. Sources cited in these accounts will generally not be cited here unless there are special reasons to do so. See also Král, *München,* No. 12.

126. *G.D.,* D, 1, No. 276; *TMWC,* 32:254–55, 332–34; cf. Rosar, pp. 180–88, where most of the blame for developments is laid to von Schuschnigg.

opportunity to raid the Vienna headquarters of the Austrian National Socialists, which had been operating openly for some time. It may be that the authorities found even more than they had anticipated; the large number of arrests and subsequent release of those against whom there was not sufficient evidence suggests a measure of surprise on the part of the police. Whatever the details, here was a serious blow to one segment of the Austrian National Socialists which also gave the government the option—which it never exercised—of publishing a collection of documents, similar to those of 1933 and 1934, which could embarrass the German government.[127]

If the raid on the Vienna National Socialists was accompanied by considerable publicity, even if the seized documents were never published, the other front on which von Schuschnigg moved—his negotiations, carried on through Zernatto, with Seyss-Inquart—was shrouded in secrecy for the time being.[128] It was von Schuschnigg's hope that if he could work out an agreement with Seyss before seeing Hitler, he could confront the Führer with a situation in which he had smashed one part and successfully appeased the other part of his domestic National Socialist opposition. He could then deal with whatever further proposals the Germans might present from a position of strength. It was for this reason that he tried to keep Seyss from knowing of his own forthcoming meeting with Hitler.

There were two basic flaws in von Schuschnigg's strategy. In the first place, his belief that Seyss was loyal was a pathetic delusion: Seyss was in constant contact with German party and state agencies. This meant that he learned of the forthcoming meeting between Hitler and von Schuschnigg and that the German government knew every detail of the concessions von Schuschnigg was prepared to make to Seyss. The other flaw in von Schuschnigg's strategy lay precisely in the concessions he was willing to offer. Imagining that in men like Seyss and Glaise he was dealing with honorable Austrians, and himself desirous of a settlement that would enable Austria to be closely associated with Germany and still retain a measure of independence, von Schuschnigg practically gave away the whole situation by agreeing to a vastly greater role for National Socialists in the Austrian government, including the appointment of Seyss as minister of the interior. The sole concession of Seyss was the promise

127. For the *Reichspost* revelations of August 1933 see Weinberg, *Foreign Policy*, p. 94; for the collection published after the July 1934 putsch, see ibid., pp. 89ff.

128. Gehl, p. 171, makes a major point of von Schuschnigg's decision to continue these on or about 8 February when the new date for his meeting with Hitler had been set; but the negotiations, as Gehl himself says (p. 173) had been going on "for about a fortnight" before 12 February. It appears to me that the sequence of events can be understood more easily if the *original* decision of von Schuschnigg to negotiate with Seyss is considered first—and by Gehl's own reckoning this about coincided with the raid on National Socialist headquarters—and the decision to continue on 8 February then becomes a reaffirmation of a prior conclusion which had been reached for the same reasons in a similar situation: strengthening von Schuschnigg's hand before what previously and now again was thought to be an imminent meeting with Hitler.

to make a public speech condemning illegal activities once the agreement were made public.[129]

The meeting of Hitler and von Schuschnigg, originally scheduled for late January, was postponed because of developments in Germany. The Fritsch-Blomberg crisis intervened, first to delay and then to speed up the course of German-Austrian negotiations. To a letter from von Papen about the scheduled meeting, von Neurath replied by telegram that Hitler was now willing to meet von Schuschnigg "in the first half of February," something von Papen transmitted to the Vienna authorities on the same day, suggesting "about the 15th of February" as the new time.[130] Von Schuschnigg accepted the proposed change on the understanding that Hitler would give his final decision on 30 January.[131] In the meantime, the session of the Reichstag at which Hitler was expected to speak on foreign policy was also postponed, to be held eventually on 20 February.[132] As Hitler concentrated on the internal changes in Germany, he combined the wholesale shifts in the military command structure with an almost equally large-scale set of changes in the diplomatic area.[133] Although this set was to include the removal of von Papen from Vienna at the same time as von Hassell, von Ribbentrop, and von Dirksen were recalled from their diplomatic posts, the Austrian question figured in Hitler's handling of the crisis in still another way.

The very time when Hitler was examining the various ways of dealing with the internal German situation was during the period when he had originally been scheduled to meet the Austrian chancellor. That meeting had now been postponed, but with the news stories on the Vienna police raid in the paper, Hitler thought it best to take steps which would prevent the Austrian chancellor from becoming too cocky and would simultaneously divert European attention from the internal German crisis to the Austrian question,[134] while also diverting the attention of the German public. When von Papen, therefore, saw Hitler on 5 February, the day after the announcement of his own recall, Hitler told him that the planned meeting should still go forward and sent the dismissed diplomat back to Vienna to make the necessary arrangements.[135] Thus von Papen's mis-

129. The full text in *Guido Schmidt Trial*, pp. 557–59. See also Canaris, "Zusammenstellung politischer Nachrichten aus Österreich," 1 February 1938, Nuremberg document 3582-PS, National Archives. Rosar, pp. 186–206, believes that the Seyss–von Schuschnigg negotiations were held specifically looking to the meeting with Hitler.

130. Von Neurath tel. 6 of 26 January 1938, T-120, 2500/4939/E 272688. The Austrian record of von Papen's conveying of the new schedule is in *Guido Schmidt Trial*, p. 557.

131. Note von Neurath to von Hassell, 26 January 1938, stating that Hitler was seeing no one before January 30 (DZA Potsdam, Büro RAM, Akte 60964, f.183).

132. See Dertinger's "Informationsbericht Nr. 12," 20 January and Nr. 14, 28 January 1938, Bundesarchiv, Brammer, Z.Sg. 101/32, ff.57, 63.

133. See above, pp. 43–51.

134. Jodl Diary, 31 January 1938, *TMWC*, 28:302; cf. *D.D.F.*, 2d, 8, Nos. 181, 182.

135. The story of von Papen's initiative in this, as well as of Hitler's having allegedly forgotten about the planned meeting with von Schuschnigg, rests only on assertions of von Papen at the trial of Guido Schmidt (p. 378) and in his memoirs, entitled with unconscious

sion ended as extraordinarily as it had begun: his appointment had been announced from Berlin before the Austrian government had given the agrément, and he returned to Vienna after his dismissal to arrange the details of von Schuschnigg's trip to Berchtesgaden to see Hitler.

Von Schuschnigg informed the Italian government on 10 February and notified the British, French, and Hungarians on the 11th that he was going to meet Hitler on the 12th.[136] When he arrived to meet the German dictator, he was confronted by Hitler, who laid down the ultimatum that von Schuschnigg agree to a set of terms which were essentially an expanded version of the very ones he had conceded tentatively to Seyss—hardly a coincidence since Seyss had had them transmitted to Hitler, but therefore all the more shocking to the trusting and overconfident von Schuschnigg. The terms of the conversations and the aura of military coercion reinforced by the summoning of German military figures, were designed by Hitler to put the utmost pressure on the Austrian leader. Von Schuschnigg was given to understand that the Germans would invade Austria. General Keitel, who had just been designated chief of the high command of the armed forces, General von Reichenau, who commanded the military district adjacent to Austria, and General Sperrle, who had been demonstrating his capacity for leveling cities in Spain, were brought into the meetings to overawe the Austrian chancellor.[137] Von Schuschnigg found himself forced to agree that the German demands would all be met by 15 February.[138]

Several aspects of this meeting need to be noted. The similarity between the Berchtesgaden agreement and the prior Seyss-Zernatto discussions should not obscure the difference between concessions made to a foreign government under the threat of force and concessions agreed to in domestic political negotiations. The threat of force was used by Hitler

---

irony, *Der Wahrheit eine Gasse* ("a narrow route for the truth"). In view of the contemporary evidence of Jodl (see the preceding note) that Hitler talked about "making von Schuschnigg tremble" on 31 January, I find this tale of von Papen's, like so many others, unconvincing.

136. Wiley dispatch 129 of 19 February 1938, State 762.63/484 (hereafter cited as Wiley Report). This is a detailed report on the background and course of the Berchtesgaden interview by the U.S. chargé in Vienna. On the first page is a comment by the former U.S. minister to Austria, then assistant secretary of state, George S. Messersmith: "This is a really excellent dispatch." With insignificant exceptions, all the details in the report have been substantiated since.

On the period just before von Schuschnigg's trip to Berchtesgaden, see also *Hungarian Documents*, 1, Nos. 350, 352, 353; *D.D.F.*, 2d, 8, Nos. 140, 144, 148, 203; Jedlicka and Neck, pp. 204, 235–36.

137. Jodl Diary, 11 February 1938, *TMWC*, 28:367; Rosar, pp. 206–15; *Keitel Papers*, p. 177; *Hungarian Documents*, 1, No. 356; *D.D.F.*, 2d, 8, Nos. 159–61; Král, *München*, Nos. 14, 15, 17, 18 (the bulk of the documents from the Czechoslovak archives pertaining to the *Anschluss* appear to have been kept separately and were not found by the Germans, see Mitis to Berber, 7 April 1939, T-120, 1039/1809/411929–30; from the sparse number in Král's work, it is possible that they have been lost).

138. Texts in *G.D.*, D, 1, Nos. 294, 295.

in direct German talks with another country for the first time on this occasion, and its success would inspire repetition. Von Schuschnigg's agreement to the inclusion of Seyss in his government as minister of the interior as a stooge of Hitler rather than as an Austrian politician, as well as a host of other changes, assured that the situation inside Austria, once it had started to slide, would continue sliding. To make sure of this, Hitler ordered military pressure on Austria during the days following the meeting of 12 February.[139]

While von Schuschnigg was busy implementing the Berchtesgaden agreement,[140] and still trusted Seyss-Inquart—hard though it is to believe such credulity[141]—the Germans could ward off all foreign protests by referring to the Austrian chancellor's public pretext that the meeting had been friendly. Hitler, furthermore, took two steps, one of which had few, but the other numerous repercussions. First, to assure the success of the combination of his own pressure from the outside and Seyss-Inquart's boring from the inside, he dismissed the protesting Leopold and temporarily held back the Austrian National Socialist rowdies.[142] His second step was to rescind the concession he had promised von Schuschnigg as the sole compensation for the agreement of 12 February. The Austrians correctly believed that they had been promised the inclusion in Hitler's speech of 20 February of appropriate passages praising the agreement and promising to respect the independence and to refrain from interfering in the internal affairs of Austria.[143] In the draft of this section of Hitler's speech (prepared by Günther Altenburg of the German foreign ministry after talking with Seyss in Berlin on 17 February immediately after Seyss's appointment to the von Schuschnigg cabinet), the kind words about the agreement and the promise not to interfere in internal affairs can still be found.[144] When Hitler spoke on 20 February, however, even this promise had vanished and only praise of the agreement remained.[145]

Although Guido Schmidt, as usual, professed himself pleased with whatever was done by the Germans, von Schuschnigg was very disappointed by this breach of promise and, in turn, decided that he himself would have to alter his approach. He adopted a far less friendly tone than he had planned in his own speech, scheduled for 24 February, and he began to consider a countermove of his own for a couple of weeks later,

139. Jodl Diary, 13 and 14 February 1938, *TMWC*, 28:367; Keitel to Hitler and response, 14 February 1938, 1775-PS, ibid., pp. 299–300.

140. Dertinger, "Vertraulicher Informationsbericht," 14 February, and "Abendmaterial, Wien," 15 February 1938, Bundesarchiv, Brammer, Z.Sg. 101/32, ff.101–7.

141. Palairet (Vienna) No. 22 of 15 February 1938, R 1442/137/3, FO 371/22311.

142. A good summary in Gehl, pp. 180–82.

143. *Hungarian Documents*, 1, Nos. 355, 361.

144. *G.D.*, D, 1, No. 307.

145. Domarus, 1:802–3. The noninterference promise was relegated to a circular by Hess (*G.D.*, D, 1, No. 304). Göring told François-Poncet that reference to Austrian independence had been omitted because it would end sooner or later anyway (*D.D.F.*, 2d, 8, No. 219; cf. ibid., No. 293).

possibly a sudden plebiscite.[146] Von Schuschnigg's speech of 24 February merely irritated the Germans; his decision to try a plebiscite, however, had more far-reaching implications.

While thinking about the possibility of calling for a plebiscite, von Schuschnigg did canvass the British, French, and Italians about the general situation, but the evidence suggests that he was only half-hearted in this. After the Berchtesgaden meeting, von Schuschnigg had done everything possible to reassure the British and French governments that all was well and had deprecated all expressions of concern about the situation. Instead of using the occasion of Hitler's bullying—about which a good deal had leaked out in spite of the good face put on it by Vienna—to arouse international support for Austrian independence, von Schuschnigg had done his best to dampen any such interest.[147] Once he had been confronted by Hitler with the threat of force, von Schuschnigg changed his whole approach, and his conduct in the crisis cannot be understood unless it is recognized that he was absolutely determined not to risk an outbreak of hostilities.

All the evidence of contemporary documents and observers as well as von Schuschnigg's own memoirs reveal this attitude; thus foreign assurances of support were of interest to him only if they served to deter a German invasion, not if they offered support in the case of hostilities. Since he knew that military support would neither be offered by others nor wanted by himself, the whole point of taking international soundings during the last half of February and the first days of March was to determine whether other powers would take positions in favor of Austrian independence that were so public, obvious, and convincing as to deter Hitler from further threats of using force, to say nothing about carrying out such threats. If von Schuschnigg still had any illusions about receiving that kind of public affirmation of support, he was to be quickly enlightened.

Neither the British nor the French government was willing to go beyond expressions of concern. The questions which loom so large in the documents, whether the representations in Berlin should be joint or separate, and whether the inclusion of references to Austria in the British approach were likely to have a deleterious effect on the planned British sounding of the Germans for a proposed general settlement, were of no substantial importance.[148] Whatever was said severally or jointly, and whatever the

---

146. Note Wiley's tel. 34 of 21 February 1938 in *U.S.*, 1938, 1:405. See also *Hungarian Documents*, 1, No. 378; Wiley tels. 48 of 3 March, State 762.63/481, and 49 of 4 March 1938, State 863.00/1393.

147. The details are summarized well in Brook-Shepherd, pp. 65–95. See also *D.D.F.*, 2d, 8, Nos. 166, 179, 215.

148. On French attitudes and perspectives, see *D.D.F.*, 2d, 8, Nos. 169, 185, 189, 190, 231, 258, 274, 276, 301, 304, 403; *G.D.*, D, 1, Nos. 291, 302, 124, 125, 133; *Hungarian Documents*, 1, No. 379; Bullitt tel. 269 of 18 February 1938, State 740.00/298. On the British attitude, see *G.D.*, D, 1, Nos. 305, 310; *Hungarian Documents*, 1, Nos. 365, 373, 394; C

British might be preparing to offer, Hitler could not care less; as has been discussed in connection wtih Hitler's turn to Japan at the end of the effort to mediate the Sino-Japanese war, it was his hope and expectation that Japan's advance in East Asia would help immobilize Britain, and hence France, in Europe.[149] Western statements and hopes were irrelevant to his intentions toward Austria.

The Italian government would have preferred the Germans to wait a bit, but not so much because of their position in Austria. That position had been written off,[150] but there was the possibility of securing concessions from London out of Britain's hope that an Anglo-Italian rapprochement might result in a stabilization of Austria's position.[151] Obviously, this bargaining position would vanish with Austria's disappearance,[152] and the frantic last-minute attempts to start Anglo-Italian talks—over which Eden resigned and during which the Italians refused to discuss Austria, which they had written off but pretended to the English might still be saved—should be viewed in this context. As previously mentioned, Göring was in Poland on 23 February to follow up Hitler's extravagant praise of the state of German-Polish relations in his speech of 20 February. It was clear that Germany had no need to worry about her eastern flank.[153] Nothing makes the isolation of Austria more evident than the fact that in these critical days, only Hungarian Foreign Minister Kálmán de Kánya had any encouraging words for the Austrian chancellor.[154]

It was thus at a time when the internal situation in Austria was deteriorating rapidly under continued German pressure,[155] and in the absence of either the promised German statement recognizing Austrian independence or strong outside support, that von Schuschnigg considered the possibility of holding a plesbiscite. A quickly held popular vote might

---

1095/62/18, FO 371/21655; British Cabinet 5 (38) of 16 February 1938, R 1623/137/3, FO 371/22311. On the idea of a joint approach, see *Hungarian Documents*, 1, Nos. 364, 377, 393, 408; Wiley tel. 31 of 19 February 1938, State 762.63/461; *U.S.*, 1938, 1:35–39; Foreign Office Memorandum of 16 February 1938, R 1442/137/3, FO 371/22311.

149. See above, pp. 178–79.

150. *D.D.F.*, 2d, 8, No. 263 (was Ciano trying to persuade himself?).

151. Gehl, pp. 178–80; *Hungarian Documents*, 1, Nos. 371, 382 (German text in Kerekes, No. 12); 2, No. 110; *G.D.*, D, 1, No. 129; *U.S.*, 1938, 1:418; *D.D.F.*, 2d, 8, No. 226; minutes of 24th meeting of British cabinet Committee on Foreign Policy, 1 March 1938, CAB 27/623.

152. See Ciano's instruction to the Italian ambassador in London of 16 February 1938, quoted in Renzo de Felice, "Betrachtungen zu Mussolinis Aussenpolitik," *Saeculum*, 1973, No. 4, p. 325.

153. *Lipski Papers*, No. 79; the whole subject is discussed in chap. 7, above.

154. Gehl, p. 184; *Hungarian Documents*, 1, Nos. 366, 387, 388, 392, 395; *G.D.*, D, 1, No. 332; cf. *Hungarian Documents*, 1, No. 381; 2, No. 110.

155. Wiley to Moffat, 21 February, 4 March 1938, Moffat Papers, Vol. 14; *G.D.*, D, 1, No. 313 (note that Keppler sent a copy of this report of his associate Veesenmayer to Göring, Nuremberg document 3576-PS, National Archives), 323, 333–35; *TMWC*, 32:329–31; *D.D.F.*, 2d, 8, Nos. 308, 347; Jodl Diary, 3 March 1938, *TMWC*, 28:369; Göring to Schmidt, 8 March 1938, Emessen, pp. 105–7. Rosar, pp. 215–57, disregards all German pressure, assumes that the Germans, especially Seyss-Inquart, remained loyal to their promises, and blames von Schuschnigg for the course of events.

well arrest the drift toward an *Anschluss;* the German government would either have to take overt action to interfere in the internal affairs of Austria or see von Schuschnigg strengthened and the situation substantially changed. The British Foreign Office comments on a 23 February report that the plebiscite idea originated in the Fatherland Front and had not yet been adopted by the Austrian government all show that a plebiscite looked from London like a good, and perhaps the only, way of saving Austria, but that it was precisely for this reason that Germany would never allow it.[156]

The Austrian chancellor prepared the way as best he knew how. He made a last-minute effort to conciliate the socialists whose votes he suddenly needed,[157] and informed the Hungarian government of his intentions on 7 March.[158] Because the Austrian minister to Rome no longer had direct access to the Duce since the latter had turned over the position of foreign minister to Ciano, only the Austrian military attaché could still go directly to Mussolini in his continuing capacity as minister of war. Von Schuschnigg, therefore, had him tell the Duce the real story of the Berchtesgaden meeting and inform him of the planned plebiscite. Mussolini still believed that he had Göring's firm assurance that there would be no German move against Austria without prior consultation—something that Hitler would take care of in his own way on 10 March. The Duce therefore mentioned the dangers inherent in the plesbiscite proposal but did not, as he later claimed to the Germans, advise against von Schuschnigg's project.[159] By the time von Schuschnigg learned Mussolini's views, he was in any case already committed and was reluctant to turn back. On the evening of 9 March he announced publicly that a vote would be held on 13 March with procedures likely to produce a favorable vote for "a free and German, independent and social, for a Christian and united Austria."

Seyss-Inquart and the Austrian National Socialists were unsure what to do when confronted by von Schuschnigg's move after they found out about it on or about 8 March, and consulted Hitler. Because Hitler had just imposed tighter control on the Austrian party, there was for once a situation in which the orchestration of German policy in Austria was undoubtedly completely in the hands of the Führer. Hitler ordered immediate preparation for the military occupation of Austria, drawing on the preliminary drafts of "Case Otto," the plan for a quick occupation of Austria to forestall a Habsburg restoration, a contingency which might have stabilized Austrian independence and which Hitler had intended to

156. Palairet tel. 39 of 23 February 1938, R 1713/137/3, FO 371/22313.

157. Gehl, pp. 183–84; Brook-Shepherd, pp. 105–11, 125–26; cf. *Hungarian Documents,* 1, Nos. 368, 372.

158. Hungarian Documents, 1, No. 398.

159. The postwar account of Colonel Emil Liebitzky, the Austrian military attaché in Rome 1933–38, is in *Guido Schmidt Trial,* pp. 222–24. The French government learned of this episode by June 1938; see the report in *D.D.F.,* 2d, 9, No. 537. Mussolini's denials to the Germans are in *G.D.,* D, 1, Nos. 349, 350.

react to by invasion. In May of 1937, the chief of staff of the army, General Ludwig Beck, had declined to prepare the implementing orders for "Case Otto" because he believed that such a German operation could lead to a general war he expected Germany to lose.[160] Now that there seemed to be a real possibility that the whole operation could be carried out without violent international complications, Beck improvised the necessary orders and the army prepared to move in.[161]

Hitler was under no circumstances going to tolerate von Schuschnigg's use of his own tactic of plebiscites. Even if the planned Austrian one was not rigged nearly as completely as those held in Germany, the very idea that anyone might use such tactics against him infuriated Hitler. He now gave orders to his Austrian followers that were the precise reverse of von Schuschnigg's strategy before Berchtesgaden. The radical Austrian National Socialists were now directed to put maximum pressure on the Austrian government, while Seyss-Inquart was to demand postponement and changes in the plebiscite under threat of German military action. The assumption was that von Schuschnigg would give way in the face of massive internal and external pressure. When he did so on 11 March, Göring believed that the situation was sufficiently fluid to permit even more far-reaching demands.

With Hitler's approval, Göring now instructed Seyss-Inquart to demand that von Schuschnigg resign and that the Austrian president ask Seyss himself to form a cabinet. Göring sent Seyss a list of cabinet members as well as instructions to send a request for German troops as soon as the new cabinet was installed.[162] The text of this request had already been sent to Seyss on 10 March in connection with the ultimatum on the plebiscite. Faced with the threat of an immediate German invasion, von Schuschnigg gave way. Last-minute consultations with other governments were essentially pro forma, and the diplomatic corps in Vienna knew it. In fact, their understanding of von Schuschnigg's position was such that the British minister did not even convey the frequently quoted passage that "His Majesty's Government cannot take the responsibility of advising the Chancellor to take any course of action which might expose his country to dangers against which H.M. Government are unable to guarantee protection." As Michael Palairet explained, "it would not have done any good."[163] It is not likely that the British believed Göring's promise that German troops sent to Austria would be withdrawn so that a truly free

160. Summary of the evidence in Müller, pp. 235–37.

161. *Keitel Papers*, pp. 178–79; Jodl Diary, 10 March 1938, *TMWC*, 28:371–72; ibid., 34:335–38, 774; *Hungarian Documents*, 1, Nos. 402, 405.

162. A major source for the development in these hectic days is the full record of Göring's telephone conversations, printed partly in *TMWC*, 31:354–84, and partly in G.D., D, 7: 504–15.

163. Note by Mr. Nichols, 11 March 1938, R 2478/137/3, FO 371/22315. The nondelivery of this message coud be inferred from the published documents (see *B.D.*, 3d, 1, No. 26), but scholars have overlooked what can now be confirmed from the archives.

plebiscite could be held; they were quite familiar with the free plebiscites conducted by the Germans in their concentration camps.[164] The Italian government asserted that since von Schuschnigg had not followed the advice they now claimed to have given him advising against the plebiscite, they would not involve themselves in the outcome of his plan.[165] The French government was immobilized by an internal political crisis.[166]

The Austrian chancellor knew all this, had lost all confidence in himself and in the support he could muster inside the country, and was in any case unwilling to risk an open conflict.[167] He submitted his own resignation to the president with the text of the latest German ultimatum—the existence of which, like the prior one about the plebiscite, the German government publicly denied. President Wilhelm Miklas, however, refused to appoint Seyss-Inquart as successor to von Schuschnigg.

From the confusing accounts of the details of developments on 11 March two things are clear.[168] Hitler wanted to cover any action with a veneer of legality in order to facilitate an internal *Gleichschaltung* of Austria on the Danzig model and an invasion by German troops. The first would have to be carried out by the constitutional or pseudoconstitutional transfer of power within Austria to men who had his confidence. This was the procedure he had used in Bavaria and Danzig and had previously tried unsuccessfully in Austria with Theo Habicht. Those efforts in 1933 and 1934 had been unsuccessful: pressure had not worked and a coup had failed. Now pressure was again to be the means. Once *Gleichschaltung* had been achieved, then the National Socialist government of Austria could itself take the second step of providing a legal cover for invasion by inviting German troops.[169] Hitler had seen the great political and psychological advantages, internally and externally, that pseudolegal procedures gave him; and he would try to use them in this case as in others, restraining the exuberant Göring when necessary.

Hitler's other major concern was the attitude of Mussolini. He knew that the Italian dictator was amenable to internal changes which would in effect transfer power to Hitler's agents, but that he was still hesitant about an end to Austria's formal separate status as a nominally independent state. Furthermore, there were the assurances Göring had given in Janu-

164. *G.D.*, D, 1, No. 376; *B.D.*, 3d, 1, No. 46; Weinberg, *Foreign Policy*, p. 166 n.38.

165. *Hungarian Documents*, 1, Nos. 406, 416, 417. The French diplomatic record is particularly skimpy at this point, a high proportion of the documents having been destroyed during the war; see *D.D.F.*, 2d, 8, Nos. 364, 366, 368, 369.

166. For the bad impression this made in London, see ibid., No. 416.

167. On the situation in Austria, Leiter Abwehr-Abteilung, "Nachrichten über Österreich," 27 January 1938, Nuremberg document 3583-PS, National Archives. Von Schuschnigg held the portfolio of minister of defense himself and issued the orders not to shoot; see Jedlicka and Neck, p. 247.

168. Gehl and Brook-Shepherd offer the best reconstructions of events.

169. The idea of the invitation may have originated with von Weizsäcker; at least he lays claim to having thought up this artifice on 10 March in his diary (*Weizsäcker-Papiere*, pp. 122–23).

ary 1937 and that had been reiterated to Mussolini on his visit in September to the effect that Germany would not change the formal status of Austria without prior consultation with Italy. Here was an issue calling for prompt resolution.

These two objectives, the legal cover for invasion and the acquiescence of Mussolini, were sought and obtained simultaneously. Since Miklas would not apoint Seyss-Inquart chancellor, Göring dreamed up the idea that, since Seyss had not joined in the resignation of the von Schuschnigg cabinet, he could, as the only remaining cabinet member, act on behalf of the rest by issuing the invitation to German troops. Seyss liked the implication that he was in charge but would have preferred to leave it at that and play Forster's Danzig role without the presence, at least for the time being, of German troops. This was hardly what Göring had in mind; so Seyss was declared to have sent the telegram requesting German troops when in fact he had not done so.[170] Because the telegram had been written in Germany in the first place, it was easy enough to produce the text afterwards as spurious evidence of its having been dispatched from Vienna. This thin veneer of "legality" was reinforced when a successful coup in the Austrian capital during the night of 11–12 March forced Miklas to agree to Seyss-Inquart's becoming chancellor. Seyss's preference for running Austria with his associates but without the presence of German troops could be ignored by Hitler because, by this time, Hitler had the faked invitation and also the agreement of Mussolini.

On the morning of the 11th, Hitler had sent the Prince of Hessen to Mussolini with a letter explaining both his belief in the need to occupy Austria and the reasons for giving such short notice. He also recalled Germany's attitude at the time of sanctions, assuring Mussolini of similar favors in the future, and reconfirmed the Brenner border with the reminder that this had always been his publicly recorded position.[171] The first soundings of the prince in Rome were apparently positive, and in the evening Mussolini personally assured him that there were no objections to Hitler's course. Hitler, when told on the phone, had the Prince repeat to Mussolini the words that Mussolini had himself used in September: "I will never forget this."

On 12 March German troops occupied Austria. Hitler himself entered the country to the cheering of vast crowds, while thousands were arrested by the temporarily ascendant Austrian National Socialists. The latter soon found themselves displaced, at least from the top positions, by Germans, who would institute a system of control analogous to that

170. Göring's persistent pressure for speed in the crisis is connected by Rosar (pp. 159–60) with his interest in the rapid seizure of Austria's economic assets; a lengthy crisis was sure to lead to the flight of the very Austrian capital Göring wanted to confiscate and utilize.

171. The German draft from Göring's files in Emessen, pp. 108–13; see also *G.D.*, D, 1, No. 352; Magistrati, pp. 143–45.

established in the rest of the Reich.[172] There would be only one significant exception to the pattern: while Prussia, Bavaria, Saxony, and the other former German states remained as nominal entities even under National Socialism, the very name of Austria was to disappear soon after its independence had been destroyed.[173]

All this was to be confirmed by a plebiscite in which a thoroughly rigged vote on the question of annexation was coupled with the election of those like Seyss-Inquart, Glaise-Horstenau, and the historian Ritter von Srbik as representatives to the Reichstag on the National Socialist ticket. Unlike the planned plebiscite of von Schuschnigg, this one was to be really free—meaning, of course, that everyone was not only free but compelled to vote yes. And for good measure, those in the rest of Germany would be called upon to vote yes also. For what would be the last time in the Third Reich, all were called upon to give their yes to the Führer. To the general chorus of approval orchestrated by Propaganda Minister Goebbels, a special voice was to be added on this occasion: that of Austria's Theodor Cardinal Innitzer.

The primate of Austria had ordered the Austrian churches to hoist swastikas and toll their bells as Hitler entered Vienna, had personally greeted the Führer, and then on 18 March had issued a proclamation, also signed by five other bishops, calling on Austria's Catholics to do their "obvious national duty" in the plesbiscite. This proclamation was sent to the man whom Hitler had charged with controlling the process of absorbing Austria into the Reich, Gauleiter Josef Bürckel. Having performed similar duties in the Saar, Bürckel was a logical choice from Hitler's point of view; his violent attacks on the Catholic church there endeared him to the Führer and should have inspired a little caution in the cardinal.[174] But Innitzer was himself an extreme nationalist, and even the best efforts of his authorized biographer could not convert him posthumously into any sort of humanitarian.[175]

172. Cf. *Hungarian Documents*, 1, Nos. 462, 463. The whole process is admirably described in Radomír Luža, *Austro-German Relations in the Anschluss Era* (Princeton, N.J.: Princeton University Press, 1975).

173. Some recent apologias for Seyss-Inquart, Neubacher, and others have stressed their alleged preference for an Austria only associated with rather than swallowed by Germany, and in this connection have cited evidence that Hitler himself originally probably intended a personal union of some sort with a special status for Austria. The Bavarian example certainly showed contemporaries how long such particularism was likely to endure.

174. See *G.D.*, D, 1, No. 663. For references to the idea of having Bürckel manage a plebiscite in Austria as early as 1936 (the year after he had done it in the Saar), see Rosar, pp. 107–8.

175. Viktor Reimann, *Innitzer: Kardinal zwischen Hitler und Rom* (Vienna, Munich: Molden, 1967). The author tries his best, but it is indicative of the theme of the book that the "Jews" for whom the cardinal exerted himself in the war years were always and only those who had converted to Catholicism. For Innitzer's effort to have the German bishops join the Austrian ones in an appeal to the voters, see Walter Adolph, *Kardinal Preysing und zwei Diktaturen* (Berlin: Morup, 1971), pp. 128–33.

The Vatican—which had issued its encyclical condemning National Socialism just a year earlier—was aghast at this public embrace. Innitzer was summoned to Rome and told off in no uncertain terms. The Vatican secretary of state, Cardinal Pacelli (later Pope Pius XII) even transmitted to President Roosevelt through Ambassador Kennedy a detailed written condemnation of the action.[176] But the damage had been done long before this document was published—presumably with the approval of the Vatican—in 1955, since over 99 percent of the Austrian people voted for Hitler. They would find the bed of roses in which they had joined Germany filled with more thorns than petals, and in being made to live, and die, as Germans, they discovered that they really were Austrians after all.

There were, however, plenty of petals for the German government. An analysis Keppler had prepared for von Ribbentrop on the economic aspects of the *Anschluss* claimed that it would be good for Austria, but all the examples he listed were of German needs that would be met.[177] The Germans took over the assets and repudiated the debts, thus creating some additional difficulties in their relations with Britain and the United States. Berlin eventually worked out an agreement with Italy to take care of the economic interests of its ally without creating a precedent for similar treatment of other claimants.[178] At the same time, the international trade effect of the *Anschluss* was to nullify any efforts on the part of Hungary and Yugoslavia to become less economically dependent on Germany.[179] As Hitler had gleefully anticipated at the Hossbach conference, Austria also provided the manpower base for additional German army divisions.[180] Furthermore, the Germans now outflanked the Czechoslovak border fortifications and also had common borders with Hungary and Yugoslavia, making both more susceptible to German pressure.

The disruption of all efforts on the part of the Western Powers for a general settlement with Germany has already been discussed. The British had been taking the initiative in this matter, and the methods used in the *Anschluss,* more than the event itself, shocked the government and public in Britain. Von Ribbentrop had been back in London at the time of the *Anschluss* to say his official farewell as ambassador and was warned by those with whom he spoke of the repercussions of a German resort to force.[181] He preferred not to take any of this seriously and to think, or

176. Text in *U.S.*, 1938, 1:474–76. See also *G.D.*, D, 1, Nos. 698, 701, 702; Wiley dispatch 176 of 2 April, and Phillips dispatch 857 of 8 April 1938, State 863.00/1705 and 1727; *Hungarian Documents*, 1, No. 459; *D.D.F.*, 2d, 8, No. 423; 9, Nos. 72, 114, 125, 134, 145, 209.

177. *G.D.*, D, 1, No. 281; cf. *Hungarian Documents*, 1, No. 431.

178. *G.D.*, D, 1, Nos. 747, 752, 754, 756, 765, 773; Magistrati, pp. 189–90.

179. See above, pp. 219, 227; *D.D.F.*, 2d, 9, No. 47; C 1872/132/18, FO 371/21674; C 3249/772/18, FO 371/21705.

180. For German acquisition of Austria's code-breaking capability, see Wiley to Moffat, 6 May 1938, Moffat Papers, Vol. 14.

181. *G.D.*, D, 1, Nos. 145, 147, 149, 359; *Hungarian Documents*, 1, No. 410.

claim to think, that "prospects of an Anglo-German understanding would not be affected." The Foreign Office comment was that if he really believed that, he must be "unbelievably dense."[182] If von Ribbentrop failed to understand the impact of German actions, the British ambassador to Germany, Sir Nevile Henderson, understood it all too well. The despairing comment of this advocate of a rapprochement with Germany to the new British foreign secretary, Lord Halifax, has already been quoted: "All the work of the past 11 months has crashed to the ground!" Halifax responded less dramatically but equally precisely: "Our constructive efforts have suffered a pretty severe set-back."[183]

The British, French, and Czechoslovaks themselves all feared that German designs on Czechoslovakia would be next.[184] This subject is the focus of the following chapters, but the interrelation of the two issues must be noted. The military impact of the *Anschluss* for any successful defense of Bohemia has already been mentioned. There was also the general contemporary belief that the two were in fact related questions. Not only did outside observers take this view,[185] but Hitler had mentioned the two jointly in his 20 February speech, and Göring—during the very days when he was giving spurious assurances of safety to the Czechoslovak minister in Berlin—explained to the Hungarian minister that Czechoslovakia would be next.[186] To be sure, a short pause was expected by all. Neville Chamberlain "likened Germany to a boa constrictor that had eaten a good meal and was trying to digest the meal before taking anything else."[187] But that there would be a next step was generally assumed. Finally, the German tactics in the *Anschluss*—moving quickly without warning while denying that they were moving; issuing ultimatums to another country while asserting to others that the ultimatums did not exist—created a situation of nervousness and public anxiety out of which the first international furor over Czechoslovakia, the May Crisis of 1938, would arise.[188]

The internal German repercussions of the *Anschluss* are also significant. The euphoria of the German public exceeded all previous heights.[189] All concern about the methods used was buried under the acclamation of an ecstatic populace. More important, perhaps, was the effective suppression of all doubts concerning the dramatic changes in

182. Mack (Vienna) tel. 133 of 15 March 1938, R 2659/173/3, FO 371/22316.
183. Henderson Papers, FO 800/269.
184. Ibid.; *Hungarian Documents*, 1, No. 452; *D.D.F.*, 2d, 8, Nos. 200, 248.
185. See the Messersmith memorandum of 18 February 1938, *U.S.*, 1938, 1:17–24.
186. *Hungarian Documents*, 1, No. 408 (German text in Kerekes, No. 14).
187. *U.S.*, 1938, 1:44.
188. Henderson, pp. 122–23; *B.D.*, 3d, 1, Nos. 18, 34; Gerhard L. Weinberg, "The May Crisis, 1938," *Journal of Modern History*, 29, No. 3 (September 1957), 213, 215. The book by Henderson B. Braddick, *Germany, Czechoslovakia and the 'Grand Alliance' in the May Crisis, 1938* (Denver: University of Denver, 1969), ignores the interrelation of the two events.
189. A good report in *U.S.*, 1938, 1:462–64.

personnel at the beginning of February. Both within the army and in the public at large, expansion abroad served to avert discontent at home. What Bismarck had done so successfully during the period of unification, and what the German annexationists had hoped to do in the World War—the substitution of expansion for domestic reform—was accomplished once again. If Bismarck could resort to bribery to secure the letter from the king of Bavaria offering an imperial crown to the king of Prussia, Hitler could use a faked telegram to justify sending troops into Austria to complete the greater Germany. There were even elaborate plans to issue a White Book which would demonstrate to the world the illegal character of the Schuschnigg regime, its oppressive nature, and its breach of domestic and international legal obligations. This grandiose project, however, was buried at the end of 1938 after the pogrom of November 1938 had presumably demonstrated beyond the need for further proof the superior quality of rule from Berlin.[190]

Hitler had won a triumph of enormous political and psychological significance. For the first time, one of the countries created by the peace settlement had disappeared. The first change in the territorial arrangement of 1919 had taken place, and it is worth noting that the land acquired by Germany had not been "lost" by the Treaty of Versailles. The threat of force had sufficed in this case, the only one in which Hitler himself preferred to avoid actual hostilities. Hitler's caution following the abortive coup of 1934 had been replaced at the last moment by a rush of action, but only as the opportunity for it appeared. Hitler's outrage at von Schuschnigg's daring to pretend that Austria was an independent country in which the government could hold a plebiscite when it wanted to—like Germany herself—was carefully contrived and controlled. As the American ambassador to Berlin wrote the secretary of state in discussing the *Anschluss:* "... in calling attention to Hitler's personal feelings in decisions of external policy, I do not wish to suggest that these decisions are made only on impulse or emotion. He has the profound political sagacity to give his resentment effective outlet only when conditions are propitious and when the most careful preparation has been made."[191]

That preparation had included, even if at the last minute, the notification of Mussolini. It was the reaction of Italy that had most concerned Hitler. He had completely disregarded the shock to England that interrupted—permanently, as it turned out—the British attempts at a rapprochement with Germany. But in spite of both his own occasional protestations and the fertile constructs of some historians, a rapprochement

190. See Altenburg to Wächter, 12 August 1938, and Altenburg to Megerle, 10 November 1938, in DZA Potsdam, AA Akte 61147 (Dokumentationsarchiv des österreichischen Widerstandes, Nr. 2863), ff.47–50. In view of Altenburg's role in the murder of Chancellor Engelbert Dollfuss, he was obviously the appropriate judge of Austrian legal niceties. For police documents on von Schuschnigg's incarceration in 1938, see T-84, Roll R-18.

191. Wilson to Hull, 24 March 1938, Cordell Hull Papers, folder 104.

with Britain was always a subject for purely speculative contemplation with Hitler and never an issue of serious policy to be taken into account in the conduct of German affairs. Relations with Mussolini were in an entirely different category. The great joy over Italy's attitude, expressed to Mussolini on Hitler's behalf by the Prince of Hessen, was genuine and was reiterated at length as the basis of future German policy when the Führer briefed Hans Georg von Mackensen, his new ambassador to Italy.[192]

The German government observed the repercussions of the *Anschluss* in Italian government circles with great care.[193] The concessions to Italy on economic questions growing out of the *Anschluss* belong in this framework, as do the kind words von Mackensen poured out to Mussolini, Ciano, and others upon his arrival in Rome.[194] It was this concern not to do the least thing that might annoy the Duce that appears largely responsible for the good face that the Germans turned toward the Italian-British negotiations which culminated in a new Mediterranean agreement on 16 April 1938. Kept informed by Rome about both the successful Italian negotiations with England and the warding off of French efforts at a similar agreement, the Germans accepted the new turn in British-Italian relations for what it was: a gesture of little practical significance.[195]

The fact, of course, was that once the independence of Austria had vanished, there was no way for Italy to make that country reappear. Under those circumstances, whatever one might think of the *Anschluss* in Italy, the maintenance of good relations with Germany afterwards did make sense. The willingness of the Italian government to make a new agreement with Britain can, however, be seen as an effort to strengthen the position of Italy after the shock of the *Anschluss* and before the visit of Hitler scheduled for the first week of May.[196] A factor of far greater importance in the eyes of the authorities in Rome was the question of South Tyrol. The *Anschluss* brought about some uneasiness on this score, and the assurances of Hitler and von Mackensen on the permanence of the Brenner border were accordingly welcome in Rome.[197] The agitation

192. On this conversation of 2 April 1938, see the references in *G.D.*, D, 1, Nos. 741, 745; Weizsäcker, *Erinnerungen*, p. 158; *Weizsäcker-Papiere*, pp. 125–26; Ádám, No. 4. Hitler's telegram of thanks to Mussolini sent from Linz on 13 March is in Domarus, 1:821; the section of his Reichstag speech of 18 March praising Mussolini, ibid., p. 831.

193. *G.D.*, D, 1, No. 399; Georg Dertinger, "Bemerkungen zur derzeitigen Politik Italiens," 30 March 1938, Bundesarchiv, Brammer, Z.Sg. 101/32, ff.251–59; cf. *Hungarian Documents*, 1, No. 433; Grant (Tirana) dispatch 600 of 30 March 1938, State 740.00/365.

194. *G.D.*, D, 1, No. 741. For some reports on negative public reaction to the *Anschluss* in Italy, see *D.D.F.*, 2d, 8, Nos. 388, 486, 525; 9, Nos. 85, 87.

195. *G.D.*, D, 1, Nos. 728, 733, 735, 737–40, 742, 755, 779; *D.D.F.*, 2d, 5, Nos. 278, 310; 8 and 9, passim; *U.S.*, 1938, 1:143–45; *Hungarian Documents*, 2, No. 201; Moffat Diary, 18 April 1938, Moffat Papers, Vol. 40. See also the discussion in the 25th and 28th meetings of the British cabinet Committee on Foreign Policy, CAB 27/623.

196. Perth to Halifax, 22 April 1938, R 4251/23/22, FO 371/22411.

197. *G.D.*, D, 1, Nos. 385, 396, 397, 741.

accompanying the annexation, however, followed as it was by the propaganda campaign for the 10 April plebiscite, aroused the wildest hopes, speculations, and rumors in South Tyrol. A variety of incidents took place, the understandable nervousness of the local Italian authorities now reinforcing their general tendency to repress the German element as much as possible. Under these circumstances, the extreme sensitivity of Mussolini and Ciano to any signs of trouble in or about South Tyrol was only to be expected, and the Germans were warned that everything must be done to assure absolute quiet in the area.[198]

At this time Ciano's brother-in-law, Count Magistrati, alluded to the possibility of transferring the South Tyrol Germans to Germany[199] and Ciano discussed the idea with the Duce on 3 April.[200] Scholars who have written on the subject consider these to be the earliest allusions to such a project,[201] but as previously mentioned, it had been discussed during or after Göring's Rome visit of January 1937. Against such a background, Ciano's decision to write a letter about the question to Magistrati for him to discuss with Göring, as well as Mussolini's agreement to the letter, Magistrati's meeting with Göring at which a population transfer was discussed, Ciano's additional request to the Prince of Hessen to talk about the South Tyrol with Göring, and the use of Mussolini's old contact to the German National Socialists, Giuseppe Renzetti, to review the matter with Göring,[202] can be fitted into a coherent picture.[203] If the Germans responded more by efforts to restrain any polemics concerning South Tyrol than by extensive negotiations about populations transfer, and if Hitler during his Rome visit tried to reassure Italian public and government opinion by assurances about the Brenner rather than by repeating the assurances of a transfer that Göring had been willing to make and repeat, this was not because of concern for the German element in South Tyrol, but because of an entirely different matter.[204]

198. Ibid., Nos. 118, 384, 729, 730, 734, 741, 744, 748, 749; Latour, pp. 22–25; Magistrati, pp. 160–64.

199. *G.D.*, D, 1, No. 384.

200. Ciano, *Diary,* 3 April 1938, pp. 137–38.

201. Latour, p. 23; very tendentious and erroneous, Winfried Schmitz-Esser, "Hitler-Mussolini: Das Südtiroler Abkommen von 1938," *Aussenpolitik*, 13, No. 6 (June 1962), 401–2; equally dubious, his "Die Genesis des Südtiroler Umsiedlungsabkommen vom 23. Januar 1939," in Franz Huter (ed.), *Südtirol: Eine Frage des europäischen Gewissens* (Munich: Oldenbourg, 1965), pp. 321–39.

202. Göring assured Renzetti that there was no great problem; those South Tyroleans who did not want to be Italian citizens would simply come to Germany; see Toscano, *Questione dell'Alto Adige*, pp. 145–46.

203. Latour, p. 25; Wiskemann, p. 134; Ciano, *Diary*, 17–21 April 1938, pp. 147–49. An account, including a portion of Ciano's letter, in Magistrati, pp. 163–67; the full text and related details may be found in Mario Toscano, *Pagine di storia diplomatica contemporanea*, 2 (Milan: A. Giuffré, 1963), 173–80. See also Hore-Belisha's account of Ciano's comments to him on 23 April in *Hore-Belisha Papers*, p. 119.

204. On the German efforts to restrain the situation in South Tyrol, see Latour, pp. 26–27; "Bestellungen aus der Pressekonferenz," 25 April 1938, Bundesarchiv, Brammer, Z.Sg.

By this time, Hitler had decided to use the Sudeten Germans as the pretext for the destruction of Czechoslovakia. He had met with Konrad Henlein, the leader of the German-financed and controlled element among the Sudeten Germans on 28 March and had instructed him on the tactics he was to follow. The details of this scheme and its application form the subject of the following chapters. In this context, however, it is essential to remember that Hitler was not only making such secret political preparations—and military ones as well—but that the whole publicity-conscious approach of Hitler to the *Anschluss* question and the alleged sufferings of the Germans in Czechoslovakia was based on the loud assertion that Germans should be allowed to live as they wanted—meaning as he wanted them to—wherever they were located. In this framework, any suggestion of population transfer would immediately vitiate his strategy against Czechoslovakia, and it was precisely the hope of securing Italian cooperation in that strategy which constituted one of the main objectives of Hitler's trip to Rome. It must be noted that the Germans did not reject the suggestion of a population transfer from South Tyrol at this time; they merely ignored the subject; and it is significant that it was Hitler himself who returned to it during a conversation with Mussolini in Munich in September 1938[205] and who in the spring of 1939, following the final destruction of Czechoslovakia, gave his full approval to a total population transfer.[206] In May 1938, however, Hitler's visit to Italy would as yet be only the occasion for a different handling of the question of South Tyrol.

Agreement on the schedule for Hitler's visit had been reached months before, and as a result of a leak in early January, the date had been announced officially in February.[207] The preparations on the Italian side were in Ciano's hands and were to be as elaborate as the imagination would allow. On the German side, the ceremonial preparations were concentrated on the numbers and uniforms of those who were to participate. As to the numbers, these were large enough to evoke memories of the Germanic invasions; with regard to uniforms, von Ribbentrop's foreign office entourage was now provided with a special garb. In spite of what can only be interpreted as soundings from the Vatican, it was agreed that Hitler should not visit the Pope while in Rome, and the Pope retaliated by closing the Vatican museum during the visit and making an unkind speech from his summer residence at Castel Gondolfo.[208] On the economic side, Hitler was cautioned against compromising the German position on eco-

---

101/11, f.313. There is no additional information on this aspect of the issue in Karl Heinz Ritschel, *Diplomatie um Südtirol* (Stuttgart: Seewald, 1964).

205. Latour, pp. 27–28.

206. Ibid., pp. 33–35.

207. "Informationsbericht Nr. 1," 3 January 1938, Bundesarchiv, Brammer, Z.Sg. 101/32, f.1; *U.S.*, 1938, 1:385.

208. *G.D.*, D, 1, Nos. 691–93, 695, 703, 708; Wiskemann, p. 135; *D.D.F.*, 2d, 8, Nos. 5, 41.

nomic questions growing out of the *Anschluss,* but there is no indication that this subject was actually discussed during the visit.[209]

The political preparations were more elaborate, though the surviving record is fragmentary.[210] In the German foreign ministry, a list of topics for possible discussion was drawn up; more significant was the preparation at von Ribbentrop's instructions of drafts of a German-Italian alliance in various formulations but all directed against Britain and France. Von Ribbentrop took several alternative drafts to Rome with him to hand over if the Italians appeared receptive, with the option of further redrafting during the visit itself, but with the hope of making the signing of a treaty the signal event of this visit. Although none of the drafts refer to it explicitly, the context of these preparations was evidently the forthcoming German attempt to destroy Czechoslovakia, just as the Germans would return more successfully to the alliance drafts in 1939 in the context of their plan to destroy Poland.

It is not known to what extent Hitler himself reviewed the alliance plans with von Ribbentrop before setting out for Rome. One may assume that the new foreign minister was acting with Hitler's approval, but in the absence of any evidence that Hitler ever even mentioned the project to the Italians, all comment on his views as to the importance of this treaty must remain speculative. The evidence shows that Hitler planned to discuss and did discuss the Czechoslovak question with the Duce and Ciano in general terms but left the alliance project to von Ribbentrop's negotiating skill. Hitler's intended discussion of Czechoslovakia in Rome was from the point of view that Germany could solve that question in the face of French and British objections only through a close alignment with Italy, which could be attained if Mussolini still had further ambitions in Africa requiring German support. Such an exchange of promises of support would enable him "to return with Czechoslovakia in his pocket," but the evidence that exists about Hitler's precise view of a German-Italian alignment is restricted to military contacts, and is not explicit about these.[211] Hitler himself, as we now know, was somewhat preoccupied with his own health in the days before his departure for Italy, and, concerned that a throat polyp—which must have been very bothersome considering his many public speeches in the plebiscite campaign—was a sign of cancer, wrote his last will before leaving Germany on the trip.[212]

209. *G.D.,* D, 1, No. 756; cf. ibid., No. 765.

210. The most complete discussion in Donald C. Watt, "An Earlier Model for the Pact of Steel: The Draft Treaties Exchanged between Germany and Italy during Hitler's Visit to Rome in May 1938," *International Affairs,* 33, No. 2 (April 1957), 185–97. The individual documents printed or cited in this article are not again cited separately here. For earlier internal German discussion, see *Weizsäcker-Papiere,* pp. 123–24.

211. Notes by Schmundt, evidently from late April 1938, *TMWC,* 25:414–15. Weizsäcker claims that at the 2 April meeting of Hitler and von Mackensen (see n.192), the former spoke of a treaty with Mussolini with each giving the other a free hand (*Erinnerungen,* p. 158).

212. Gerhard L. Weinberg (ed.), "Hitler's Private Testament of May 2, 1938," *Journal of Modern History,* 27, No. 4 (December 1955), 415. Cf. Speer, *Erinnerungen,* p. 118; William

During their stay in Italy from 3 to 9 May, the German guests were entertained spectacularly in Rome, Naples, and Florence. In addition to the usual parades, they were shown large portions of the Italian navy and air force. Although Hitler evidently enjoyed the sight-seeing, especially in Florence, and was very favorably impressed by what he saw of the Italian navy, the prominent role of King Victor Emmanuel III, the generally unfriendly attitude of court circles, and a number of minor incidents served to spoil his mood somewhat. Among these incidents, the one which attracted most attention—a scheduling mistake which caused him to review some troops while he was wearing a tuxedo—led to the dismissal of the German chief of protocol, who was later made the ambassador to Belgium. If correctly reported, a knife attack on his mistress, Eva Braun, would also not have improved Hitler's attitude.[213] The enthusiasm of the Italian crowds was also quite restrained to begin with. The shock of the *Anschluss* and concern over the South Tyrol were surely important factors in this attitude, a view that is corroborated by the change in atmosphere after Hitler's speech at the banquet of 7 May at the Palazzo Venezia.[214] In this speech, Hitler talked enthusiastically about the "natural frontier which Providence and history had clearly drawn for our two peoples." With the Alps as the permanent and inviolable border between the living spaces of the two, the Germans and Italians could live in permanent harmony. The way in which Hitler said this could not fail to impress his immediate as well as his greater audience, especially since the combination of an abandonment of the South Tyrol Germans with the concept of complementary living spaces reflected quite accurately what Hitler had been preaching for many years.

Accordingly, the conversations about the South Tyrol during the Rome visit concentrated on exchanges of verbal assurances. The border was final, the German government and party agencies would stop all agitation in or concerning the South Tyrol, while Mussolini promised to be more accommodating toward the German element in the South Tyrol out of his friendship for Germany.[215] The question of a population transfer was *not* discussed, presumably because the Italians felt reassured by Hitler's lyrical praise of the existing border and because the Germans were interested in sounding out the Italian government on the Czechoslovak ques-

---

S. Allen (Ed.), *The Infancy of Nazism: The Memoirs of Ex-Gauleiter Albert Krebs, 1923–1933* (New York: Franklin Watts, 1976), pp. 163–65. The possible implication of Hitler's fear of cancer, particularly acute at this time, on his urgency in considering military action against Czechoslovakia, is discussed on p. 390 n.52 below.

213. This incident is referred to in Domarus, 1:859; it is not mentioned in most accounts of the trip. The report in Nerin E. Gun, *Eva Braun, Hitler's Mistress* (London: Leslie Frewin, 1968), is somewhat skeptical about the attempt but leaves no doubt that Eva Braun went along on the trip.

214. Text in Domarus, 1:860–61; a good translation of most of it with some helpful comments in Wiskemann, pp. 136–37. Cf. *G.D.*, D, 1, No. 764.

215. *G.D.*, D, 1, Nos. 761, 767, 768; cf. Magistrati, p. 181.

tion.[216] The phraseology of the German foreign ministry's information telegram to German missions abroad makes the point evident by indirection. "As for the Sudeten German question, the discussions clearly showed that the Italians understand our concern about the fate of the Sudeten Germans."[217] If this maintains the fiction of Germany's interest in the Sudeten Germans—a fiction that would be difficult to uphold in public if agreement to transfer the South Tyrolean Germans had been reached simultaneously—the information on the visit recorded for internal use in the German foreign ministry is much more explicit about real German aims. State Secretary von Weizsäcker recorded that Italy would remain neutral in a German-Czechoslovak war and intended neither to hinder German aggression nor to support German pressure on Prague. The Germans concluded that Mussolini and Ciano did not consider the dangers attendant on a German-Czechoslovak war to be very great: Germany would handle it in such a way that a European war would not result, and the French and English were probably not willing to fight for Czechoslovakia anyway.[218] Ciano's subsequent comments to the American ambassador confirm the accuracy of this impression;[219] similar information on the forthcoming destruction of Czechoslovakia with the acquiescence of Italy reached the Hungarians.[220]

These tacit understandings about Czechoslovakia were not, however, reinforced by any written commitments. Von Ribbentrop first took up the possibility of a military assistance pact with Ciano during the trip to Naples for the naval inspection.[221] Ciano was skeptical and produced the draft of a vague treaty of friendship and mutual respect that he himself had worked out in the days before the arrival of the Germans when concern about the border and the South Tyrol had been uppermost in the minds of Mussolini and Ciano.[222] Although the German drafts dealt with Italy's worries about her northern border, there were other factors preventing agreement. The Germans wanted to secure Italian support if France and Britain came to the aid of Czechoslovakia when Germany attacked it, but at least some of the officials of the German foreign ministry were worried about being dragged by Italy into an adventure in the Mediterranean that could lead to war with the Western Powers on issues and at a time not in Germany's interest. It was, therefore, not until early 1939, when the civil war in Spain was clearly about to end, that Berlin was agreeable to a firm

216. Latour, p. 25 n.9; cf. Toscano, *Questione dell'Alto Adige*, p. 159 n.35.
217. *G.D.*, D, 1, No. 761.
218. Ibid., No. 762; cf. *Hungarian Documents*, 2, No. 163; Král, *München*, Nos. 72, 77.
219. *U.S.*, 1938, 1:53–54.
220. *Hungarian Documents*, 2, Nos. 177, 180.
221. Watt, "Earlier Model," pp. 191–92. The apparent conflict about dates in the evidence is most likely to be resolved by the explanation that von Ribbentrop did not give any draft text to Ciano on 5 May at all—Ciano's diary refers to an offer but not to an actual text—but only talked about the subject, withholding a text in the face of Ciano's objections and alternative pact proposal.
222. Toscano, *The Origins of the Pact of Steel*, pp. 10–13.

commitment to Italy. If these were the German reservations, there were
political and psychological ones on the part of Italy.

The Italians were not interested in the fate of Czechoslovakia and no
more eager to go to war with the Western Powers over the Sudeten
Germans than the Germans, in von Weizsäcker's words, wanted "to fight
for Majorca."[223] The prospect of League recognition of the conquest of
Ethiopia still debarred the Italians from an action that ran too obviously
counter to the agreement just reached with Great Britain. The short time
that had elapsed since the *Anschluss* may also have contributed to Italian
hesitations. Certainly the very bad impression von Ribbentrop made at
this time on both Mussolini—who was more favorably inclined to the
alliance project—and Ciano—who often let his attitude toward individuals
influence his diplomacy—had a restraining effect on the handling of the
alliance project.[224] Finally, the German information circular on the meetings asserts that the general situation in Southeast Europe was not discussed, but it may well be that Italian concern about possible future
conflicts of interest with Germany in that part of the world increased
Mussolini's reluctance to undertake a firm alliance with Germany at that
time.[225]

The result of this inability to come to an agreement on a treaty during
the state visit of the German leaders to Italy was that the alliance project,
for the time being, suffered the same fate as had the Italian proposal for a
German-Italian agreement prior to Mussolini's visit to Germany. What
had taken several months then took a few days now: the exchange of
views showed that the Axis partners were still too far apart on specifics
and on their respective assessment of the risks of an alliance, so that a
public show of solidarity was vastly more valuable than either a secret
agreement difficult to work out or a public agreement that would necessarily be so watered down as to undermine rather than reinforce the public
impression both wanted to make. For the time being, therefore, the project was allowed to languish.[226]

In spite of the fact that no formal agreement between Germany and
Italy was signed, both sides could be pleased about the outcome of the
meeting. The assurances Hitler had given about the Brenner border
satisfied the Italians, and the fact that they had been given in a manner
persuasive to the Italian public was especially gratifying to Mussolini,
who was sensitive to his standing with the people. Mussolini showed his
firm identification with Germany after the visit in both word and action.
The words were in a major speech in Genoa on 14 May in which he

223. Weizsäcker, *Erinnerungen*, p. 158.
224. Ciano, *Diary*, 6 May 1938, p. 157. Cf. Rintelen, pp. 44–45.
225. See the discussion of this topic in *G.D.*, D, 1, No. 745.
226. Watt, "Earlier Model"; Toscano, *The Origins of the Pact of Steel*, pp. 22–26; Anfuso, p. 66.

extolled the Axis and warned that in any ideological conflict, "the totalitarian states will immediately make common cause and march together to the end."[227] The deeds were in the one major field of domestic policy and ideology on which the German and Italian forms of totalitarianism had hitherto differed, that of anti-Semitism.

The National Socialists were hysterical anti-Semites in the face of a Jewish population in Germany of less than 1 percent; the Jewish population of Italy constituted perhaps one-tenth of 1 percent, and had never attracted similar attention from the fascist movement.[228] On the contrary, during the earliest months of Hitler's rule, Mussolini had intimated to the Germans that there might be wiser policies to follow; but now he paid Hitler the compliment of flattery by imitating German anti-Semitic legislation after Hitler's visit as he had copied the goose-step after his own visit to Germany. The history of the anti-Jewish measures of fascist Italy is not properly a part of an analysis of German foreign policy; what is relevant here is the deliberate adoption by Mussolini of a policy he had hitherto rejected and which had no basis of popular support in Italy—as it certainly did in Germany—solely as a means of demonstrating his solidarity with the German dictator. Nothing demonstrates the real power situation in the Axis more clearly than this reversal of imitation. Once Hitler had looked to Italian fascism and its leader as a model for his movement, including his own title and the form of salute that came to be identified with him; now the Duce attempted to persuade a skeptical Italy which had defied the world in the period of sanctions that its purity was threatened by the few thousand Italian Jews.[229]

On the German side, the visit confirmed that the close ties of the Axis had survived the shock of the *Anschluss*.[230] The assurances on the South Tyrol were easy for Hitler to give since they involved only a public reaffirmation of what he had always asserted. The close relationship of his policy on this question with the view of complementary German and

227. Full text in Edoardo and Ruilio Susmel (eds.), *Benito Mussolini, Opera Omnia* (Florence: La Fenice, 1959), 29:99–102; cf. *G.D.*, D, 1, Nos. 763, 764; *D.D.F.*, 2d, 9, Nos. 335, 339, 355, 360, 361, 372.

228. On fascist anti-Semitism, see A. James Gregor, *The Ideology of Fascism* (New York: Free Press, 1969), chap. 6; Renzo de Felice, *Storia degli ebrei italiani sotto il fascismo,* 3d ed. (Turin: Einaudi, 1972). Nicholas A. Stigliani and Antonette Margotto, "Fascist Anti-semitism and the Italian Jews," *Wiener Library Bulletin,* 28, Nos. 35–36 (1975), 41–49, provides a brief summary. See also Wiskemann, pp. 140–44; Funke, pp. 840–42. The article by Gene Bernardini, "The Origins and Development of Racial Anti-Semitism in Fascist Italy," *Journal of Modern History,* 49, No. 3 (Sept. 1977), 431–53, points out the role of issues in the Italian colonial empire in fascist racial thinking; but its argument that the inner dynamics of the system rather than the concept of drawing closer to Germany led to the turn of Italian policy in 1938 is unconvincing.

229. For an interesting analysis of Mussolini's turn toward Hitler, see the memorandum by Harold H. Tittmann of 2 June 1938, State 762.65/464. Cf. *Hungarian Documents*, 2, No. 202.

230. See Magistrati's comments, pp. 185–86.

Italian expansion into their respective living spaces made it logical to tie an affirmation of the Brenner border to the sounding of Italian opinion on German policy toward Czechoslovakia. As will become clearer in the context of Hitler's views and decisions about Czechoslovakia during the first half of 1938, the German leader could feel confident that the collapse of the Stresa front against German moves on Austria was permanent and would not be turned by the *Anschluss* into a new alliance of the Western Powers with Italy in defense of Czechoslovakia. Since this was really all he felt he needed, he could return to Germany secure in the knowledge that he could pursue his policy against Czechoslovakia without concern about a hostile coalition. There is also evidence that Hitler's own impression of Italian military power was very much affected, and his subsequent overestimation of Italy's armed forces is traced to this visit by Germany's military representative to Rome at the time.[231] The two dictators faced the world joined by personal ties and a public image of harmony. Whatever questions about a more formal relationship might have been left open in quiet talks during the visit, the people in both countries and the world at large were again presented with an image of solidarity that served the interests of Germany and Italy as the leaders of both perceived them at that moment.

231. Enno von Rintelen, "Die deutsch-italienische Zusammenarbeit im II. Weltkrieg," 21 April 1947, p. 4, Foreign Military Studies, B-495, National Archives.

10 War Denied: The Crisis over Czechoslovakia

Part 1

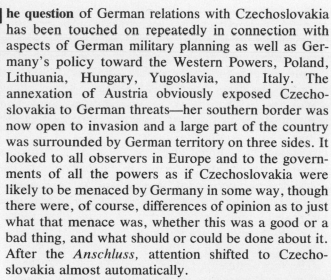

he question of German relations with Czechoslovakia has been touched on repeatedly in connection with aspects of German military planning as well as Germany's policy toward the Western Powers, Poland, Lithuania, Hungary, Yugoslavia, and Italy. The annexation of Austria obviously exposed Czechoslovakia to German threats—her southern border was now open to invasion and a large part of the country was surrounded by German territory on three sides. It looked to all observers in Europe and to the governments of all the powers as if Czechoslovakia were likely to be menaced by Germany in some way, though there were, of course, differences of opinion as to just what that menace was, whether this was a good or a bad thing, and what should or could be done about it. After the *Anschluss,* attention shifted to Czechoslovakia almost automatically.

The months of negotiations of 1938 and the hectic days that culminated in the Munich agreement have attracted enormous attention from scholars and have come to hold a certain symbolic significance. The Munich agreement in particular has come to have its own significance not necessarily based on an accurate reading of the events those who speak of the "lessons of Munich" have in mind. Here the focus is on German policy at the time and on the way that policy interacted with the situation inside Czechoslovakia and culminated in a temporary settlement seen by the public then and later as a victory for Germany but by Hitler as a great, perhaps the greatest, setback and mistake of his career. This paradox can be understood only if the perceptions, hopes, and actions of the main participants to the drama are analyzed separately, and the conclusions each drew from the same events are also separately viewed.

Hitler's antagonism toward the Czechs was profound and long-standing; it included the view that it was *their* presence in Bohemia and Moravia that constituted the key nationality problem of the area, and that their expulsion was the appropriate solution.[1] There was, of course, no prospect of implementing such a grandiose scheme in the first years of National Socialist rule in Germany, when Hitler, worried about Czechoslovakia's possibly joining with Poland and France in a preventive attack on Germany, followed a course of extreme caution toward his southern neighbor.[2] The Germans inside Czechoslovakia were to restrain themselves while Germany built up her own strength. The Berlin government did, however, begin to develop a different kind of tie to this German segment of the citizens of Czechoslovakia. During the Weimar years, the German government and a variety of semiofficial and private organizations had provided financial support for the German minority not only in Czechoslovakia but in a number of East and Southeast European countries, but the general nature of that support now changed in the Czechoslovak case.[3] Whatever the indirect political implications of the financial subventions in the past, they had been allotted directly to cultural, educational, and economic institutions. It was in the period preceding the Czechoslovak national elections of 1935 that the German government began to subsidize the campaign of a political party, the Sudeten German party of Konrad Henlein.[4] Inside that party various elements still contended for influence, but in the absence of any immediate desire on Hitler's part to move on the Czechoslovak question, there was as yet no need for Berlin to involve itself decisively into such matters.[5] It was enough for the Sudeten German party to grow in strength as a possible future tool.

The most immediate concern of the German government in the mid-1930s was the building up of Germany's armed might. While that process went forward, the first plans for an attack on Czechoslovakia were considered in Berlin but not fully developed because of the objections of General Beck, the army chief of staff.[6] Only diplomatic measures were

1. Summary in Gerhard L. Weinberg, "Germany and Czechoslovakia, 1933–1945," *Czechoslovakia Past and Present*, ed. Miloslav Rechcigl (The Hague: Mouton, 1969), 1:764–65. Pre-1933 German-Czechoslovak relations are described in F. Gregory Campbell, *Confrontation in Central Europe* (Chicago: University of Chicago Press, 1975).

2. Weinberg, *Foreign Policy*, pp. 27, n.7, 107–10.

3. For the mechanism of the Weimar period, see Norbert Krekeler, *Revisionsanspruch und geheime Ostpolitik der Weimarer Republik: Die Subventionierung der deutschen Minderheit in Polen, 1919–1939* (Stuttgart: Deutsche Verlags-Anstalt, 1973). John Hiden, "The Weimar Republic and the Problem of the Auslandsdeutsche," *Journal of Contemporary History*, 12 (1977), 273–89, is critical of this book. Some small payments for electoral purposes in Poland are noted in Riekhoff, p. 213.

4. Weinberg, *Foreign Policy*, pp. 225–26.

5. On this whole subject, see Ronald M. Smelser, *The Sudeten Problem, 1933–1939: Volkstumspolitik and the Formulation of Nazi Foreign Policy* (Middletown, Conn.: Wesleyan University Press, 1975).

6. Weinberg, *Foreign Policy*, p. 224.

taken. The Germans began a lengthy and persistent effort to persuade the Hungarians to reach an accommodation with Yugoslavia in the hope of focusing all of Hungary's revisionist aspirations against Czechoslovakia, while Hungary's accommodation with Yugoslavia and Germany's own better relations with the latter would disrupt the Little Entente.[7] The dramatic shift in German-Polish relations during the first year of Hitler's rule from open confrontation to tacit accommodation served to screen Germany's eastern border. If Czechoslovakia had never been interested in defending Poland's territorial integrity against German—or Soviet— ambitions, Poland was even less interested in defending Czecho- slovakia's. In fact, Poland had her own territorial dispute with her south- ern neighbor over Těšín, and at times thought of sponsoring the Slovak autonomists against Prague.[8] The German government, once Hitler had reoriented its Polish policy, was in a position to take advantage of the Polish-Czech antagonism, and we have already seen how German policy toward Poland in 1937–38 was carefully subordinated by Hitler to the needs of his aims against Czechoslovakia.

Germany's western frontier was open to invasion as long as the Rhine- land remained demilitarized; so there could be no German military ad- ventures in Central and Eastern Europe without French approval—which was not forthcoming. Only a remilitarized Rhineland and a defended western border could open up at least the possibility of German moves that risked French intervention; then the threat, or bluff, of a bloody battle on the western border could serve as a possible deterrent to any French move. It is in this sense that the German action of March 1936 of remilitarizing the Rhineland marks a major turning point in the interwar years. The Germans did not know that the French army had no plans to cope with such a step, and they did not know that there were no serious French plans to assist Czechoslovakia or Poland militarily either before or after March 1936; but Hitler could and did gamble on the belief that France was unlikely to move in 1936. Thereafter, he would do everything possible to reinforce French reluctance to march if he took other steps in Central Europe, until he was ready to move against France herself.

The impact of this German screening procedure in the east and west was not lost on the government of Czechoslovakia. With other possible sources of support dubious or even hostile, the leaders of Czechoslovakia participated during the winter of 1936–37 in an attempt at a direct accom- modation with Germany and were at one point confidently hopeful that

---

7. Ibid., pp. 226–27, 228–29.

8. On this effort in the spring of 1938, see Hoensch, *Ungarische Revisionismus,* pp. 65–66, and Thaddeus V. Gromada, "The Slovaks and the Failure of Beck's 'Third Europe' Scheme," in T. V. Gromada (ed.), *Essays on Poland's Foreign Policy, 1918–1939* (New York: Josef Pilsudski Institute of America, 1970), p. 60, n.5. By the summer of 1938, Warsaw had returned to the idea of Slovakia falling to Hungary in any disruption of the Czechoslovak state.

such an accommodation was attainable.[9] Hitler, however, had no interest in tying his own hands vis-à-vis Czechoslovakia and allowed the negotiations to peter out. Just as he refused the Italian attempts to commit him to new promises that implied respect for Austrian independence, so he would not agree to anything that might limit his freedom of action toward Czechoslovakia. He had been willing to follow a contrary procedure with Poland and concerning the status of Danzig; one can only conclude that in spite of the opportunistic shifts in his approach and the way he allowed events to influence his timing, Hitler did in fact have a sort of mental priority schedule in which Austria and Czechoslovakia were to disappear as independent countries in some fashion, but before Germany concerned herself directly with Poland. By the time knowledge of the secret German-Czechoslovak negotiations had reached the British and French governments, therefore, the whole project was already without any prospect of success.[10]

The building up of Germany's military forces was the main element in Hitler's policy toward Czechoslovakia during 1937, and the military planning to which this buildup was geared specified Czechoslovakia as the immediate target of Germany's aggressive designs. The work on these plans had been carried forward as part of the general development of Germany's new armed forces and the staff work for their employment. Hitler's discussion of his intentions concerning Czechoslovakia at the meeting of 5 November 1937 provides the historian with some insight into the way the German leader visualized the diplomatic and military aspects of the destruction of Czechoslovakia; it gave his military advisers both an impetus to further military preparations and a focus for their planning.[11] Hitler thought of the conquest of Czechoslovakia as a military operation that would shorten Germany's border, thereby freeing troops for other employment as well as providing the territorial and population basis for additional divisions, especially after the removal of many of the Czechs. It was his hope that the war which would accomplish this could be localized. This hope was based on several considerations. The reluctance of the French and British to go to war was obvious enough, and the efforts of France and Britain to obtain German assurances of restraint in Central and Eastern Europe in exchange for colonial and economic concessions were interpreted in this light. German knowledge of the objections to British involvement in Central Europe voiced by the Dominion prime

9. Weinberg, *Foreign Policy*, pp. 316–21.

10. For information reaching the French government, see *D.D.F.*, 2d, 5, Nos. 19, 104, 148, 231; the British government, see R 1655, R 1910, R 2021, R 2163/188/12, FO 371/21128; N 3287/461/38, FO 371/21104; the United States government, *U.S.*, 1937, 1:88–89; Dodd, *Diary*, 15 March 1937, p. 393, 3 April 1937, p. 296.

11. See above, pp. 35–41.

ministers at the Imperial Conference of 1937 contributed to Hitler's expectation of British unwillingness to assist France in a war for the defense of Czechoslovakia.[12]

The major diplomatic measure that might assist in the isolation of Czechoslovakia from potential support on the part of the Western Powers would be the stressing of the alleged grievances of the Sudeten Germans. Just as the German government had once used its debts in the United States to force Americans to subsidize German exports—while carefully avoiding a repudiation of the debts themselves—so now the Sudeten Germans would be utilized to isolate Czechoslovakia from outside support with every precaution being taken to make certain that the grievances would not be settled. Aspects of that strategy have already been touched upon; its full development and the way it succeeded in a manner contrary to Hitler's own intentions are major themes of this and the following chapter. The point which must be reiterated here is that at the beginning of the year which culminated in Munich, Hitler himself was quite explicit that the major issue was the destruction of Czechoslovakia, while the Sudeten Germans, far from being the focus of his concern, were to serve solely as the tool of broader aims. Those present at the meeting of 5 November fully understood this, and their arguments with Hitler at that meeting reflect their understanding. It was the war for the total destruction of Czechoslovakia that they feared might not be isolated; there is no sign that any of them expected interference with efforts to aid the Sudeten Germans. The idea that Czechoslovakia must be destroyed was, however, accepted and agreed to by all those present, and they parroted these sentiments to all who would listen in the weeks after the meeting.[13]

As for the military side of the operation, there were several ways in which Hitler's decisions and preferences expressed at the November meeting provided both an impetus to the German armed forces and a focus to their planning. Two interrelated aspects of this should be noted. The preparation and construction of a vast system of defensive fortifications on Germany's western border would serve a double purpose in shielding Germany during an attack on Czechoslovakia: it would provide a basis for the weaker German forces that could be used in the west to hold up any French offensive to relieve Czechoslovakia, and by its very existence—knowledge of which in a hopefully and intentionally exaggerated form would be allowed to become public—might serve to deter the French from even trying the difficult attempt to break through. As Hitler put it: "It is very unlikely that France would move forward without the support of England and in the expectation of having its offensive stalled at our western fortifications."[14]

12. See above, pp. 15–16.
13. See above, pp. 39–40.
14. *G.D.*, D, 1, No. 19, p. 30.

There was the further element in Hitler's views that only such a successful defense in the west, if France did move, would serve to keep
Poland from taking advantage of Germany's preoccupation with
Czechoslovakia and France to strike at East Prussia. The rapid building of
fortifications in the west would become one of Hitler's great interests in
1938: the appointment of Fritz Todt to replace the regular army construction chiefs on the Westwall (often referred to as the Siegfried Line), the
preparation by Hitler of a detailed memorandum on the fortifications—
one of the very few he ever wrote[15]—and his violent reaction to the
assertion of some of his generals in the summer of 1938 that the fortifications could hold out only a very short time are all aspects of Hitler's close
personal involvement in what he considered a key part of the military and
political preparation for the action against Czechoslovakia. Years later he
would recall the Westwall as the best example of the frustration of his
program for expanding Germany's army by the army's own leaders.[16] The
implications of the May Crisis of 1938 for the Westwall construction program, which will be discussed in connection with the account of that
crisis, also have to be seen in this context.

The other aspect of military preparations stressed at the meeting of 5
November was the problem of speed in dealing with Czechoslovakia
militarily, a major concern of Hitler's in 1938 the importance of which was
also reinforced by the May Crisis. Speed in the conquest of Czechoslovakia opened up the possibility of moving German troops rapidly back
from that front to the west if France did intervene, increased the possibility that hostilities might be finished even before French intervention
started if a few days of agitated diplomacy preceded a French declaration
of war, and would certainly help to deter any move to help Czechoslovakia on the part of the Soviet Union, which was in any case diverted
from risky involvement in European problems by the advance of Japan in
East Asia. The emphasis in German military planning for the actual operation against Czechoslovakia was, therefore, to be placed on speed in
breaching the border fortifications and gaining control of the main part of
Bohemia. The commander-in-chief of the German army, General von
Fritsch, mentioned that he had already ordered a study of this very problem; it would be a major theme in all the plans for an attack on Czecho-

---

15. The text of the "Denkschrift zur Frage unserer Festungsanlagen" of 1 July 1938 has
been published in Otto-Wilhelm Förster, *Das Befestigungswesen: Rückblick und Ausschau*
(Neckargemünd: Vowinckel, 1960), pp. 123–48; see also p. 98n. This memorandum has not
received the attention scholars have given Hitler's memorandum on the Four-Year Plan.
Useful for the progress of construction are the two top secret reports "Sechs Monate
Festungsbau" of 20 December 1938, and "Bericht vom Westwall," of 20 April 1940, in
Library of Congress, Prints and Photographs Division, Nos. 6893 and 6446. For good de-
scriptions of what the Westwall was actually like after construction, see First United States
Army, *Report of Operations 1 August 1944–22 February 1945* (Washington: Government
Printing Office, 1945), 1:51–54; and Charles B. MacDonald, *The Siegfried Line Campaign*
(Washington: Government Printing Office, 1963), pp. 30–35.

16. *Hitler's Table Talk* (Trevor-Roper, ed.), 16 August 1942, p. 634.

slovakia. The changes in German military planning immediately after the November conference reflect the view that a German move to crush the Czechoslovak state was to be prepared for the near future, possibly in 1938, and the revisions made were approved by Hitler on 13 December.[17]

The situation of Czechoslovakia in the face of these dangers was difficult indeed. Internally, the Czechs constituted just over half the population and were confronted by agitation for more autonomy from many of the Slovaks, to say nothing of the even more numerous Germans and the smaller Polish and Magyar minorities. Early in 1938, coinciding with the greater pressure from Germany, there was a substantial activation of Slovak demands which weakened and embarrassed the Prague government and to which it made no substantial response in the first part of the year.[18]

The Prague regime's treatment of the German minority of over three million had been simultaneously very good and very bad, very wise and very unwise. As for treatment as a cultural minority, these Germans were without doubt the best treated large group of Germans under foreign rule in Europe.[19] Nevertheless, they had been left with real grievances of obvious substance, especially over discrimination in the employment of government officials and the awarding of government contracts. Both of these areas were particularly sensitive issues during the depression, which hit hard at the Sudeten Germans with their involvement in the cyclically sensitive manufacturing and export fields. The political structure of Czechoslovakia was also a mixture of good and bad, wise forethought and dubious procedures. In theory, the rights of all citizens were protected by a democratic constitution; but in practice that constitution, drawn up without any participation from the German element, gave power to political parties organized along national lines, so that the German parties could always be outvoted. The years in which representatives of some of these parties, called Activists, particpated in the government could not obscure the fact that the government of the country was and would presumably always remain in the hands of Czechs and Slovaks, there being no parties which transcended nationality lines. Had there been a longer period of time for adjustments to be worked out and a clearer show of determination on the part of the Czechs to reconcile the German element in response to the pleadings of the Activist parties, the siren song from Berlin might have found a lesser echo within the

17. See above, pp. 41–42. The account in Boris Celovsky, *Das Münchener Abkommen von 1938* (Stuttgart: Deutsche Verlags-Anstalt, 1958), pp. 91–93, is still an excellent summary.

18. Hoensch, *Ungarische Revisionismus,* pp. 38–39, 70–72. See also *D.D.F.,* 2d, 10, Nos. 34, 106, 177.

19. This point is fully documented in Johann W. Brügel, *Tschechen und Deutsche, 1918–1939* (Munich: Nymphenburger Verlagshandlung, 1967) (the English language edition is deplorably inferior), and Radomír Luža, *The Transfer of the Sudeten Germans* (New York: New York University Press, 1964).

Czechoslovak state, as was true in Switzerland. Neither condition was fulfilled, and by 1938 it was perhaps already too late.

The government in Prague was unwilling to take a chance on the one tactic that might have worked by revealing the nature of Hitler's aims. Had the concessions offered in the fall (or anything like them) been made in the spring of 1938, the Sudeten leaders would have been forced to show their hand at a time singularly inconvenient for Berlin: they would have had to accept the offer or reject what they themselves had been demanding and hence destroy the credibility of their grievances before Germany was ready. The unwillingness of the Czechoslovak government to try such an approach was surely founded on the location of the German minority and the special problems inherent in that factor.

The German minority in Czechoslovakia was concentrated in a practically solid band along the border of Bohemia, a border that had hardly changed for many centuries. Disregarding the fluctuation of the nationality distribution in the center of Bohemia—fluctuations that were far more substantial than usually recognized—the critical question was that of the border areas where the population was predominantly German and was directly adjacent to Germany and the newly annexed Austrian provinces of the Reich. Here the Paris peace settlement had allowed economic, historical, and strategic factors to dominate.[20] If the critics of that settlement, especially John Maynard Keynes, had railed against the alleged insensitivity of the peacemakers to economic considerations, here was a good example of an effort to pay heed to such factors by maintaining the economic unity of the interdependent portions of Bohemia.[21] Any shift of the border that went beyond the transfer of small strips of land to affect the bulk of the German population would, however, not only disrupt the economic viability of the new Czechoslovak state but deprive it of its natural borders and its main railway arteries.

It was the fear that any grant to the Germans of special autonomous rights couched in territorial or national—as opposed to individual or personal—terms would be likely to lead to their secession from the Czechoslovak and adherence to the German state which held back the government in Prague. The defenses of the country were located in the very areas that might thus be lost, and the territorial configuration of Czechoslovakia after their loss would be indefensible. There was, furthermore, the very great probability that any major concessions made to the Germans under international pressure would be utilized by Czecho-

20. The best account is Dagmar H. Perman, *The Shaping of the Czechoslovak State* (Leyden: Brill, 1962). A historical memorandum on the problem, originally drafted by Sir James Headlam-Morley and put into clean form by Sir Maurice Hankey, was circulated to the Committee on Foreign Policy of the British cabinet by Lord Halifax on 21 March 1938 as "an instructive commentary on much with which we are now concerned" (C 2399/2399/18, FO 371/21754).
21. Ironically Keynes urged a modification of this border in the *New Statesman* of 26 March 1938.

slovakia's other minorities to make analogous demands with attendant analogous, if not equally dangerous, implications for the integrity of the Czechoslovak state.

At the peace conference, the demands of some Czechs for taking from Germany the territory of Lusatia, which had been lost to Bohemia in the seventeenth century, had been ignored, and there had been, on the other hand, no German demand for parts of Bohemia; but in the atmosphere of the 1930s the concept of national self-determination could be raised as a slogan by which the performance of Czechoslovakia and the wisdom of its borders could be measured and challenged. In an age when it was still thought appropriate to adjust boundaries to populations, rather than to shift people to fit boundaries, this was a difficult problem indeed. As has been mentioned in connection with Hitler's handling of the South Tyrol question, he was very careful to protect himself in 1938 against any undermining of this propaganda weapon by not agreeing formally to a transfer of the South Tyrolean Germans until after the Munich agreement. That such measures were still believed inconceivable at the time can be seen from the handling of a parliamentary inquiry in the House of Commons about the possibility of the Sudeten Germans who did not like living in Czechoslovakia simply leaving that country for Germany. The very idea was then still outside the realm of alternatives that might be considered.[22]

The strategy that Hitler followed in dealing with Czechoslovakia was both simple and clever. German propaganda would focus on the alleged injustices suffered by the Sudeten Germans. Insofar as these were real ones, they would be exploited; where there were none, they would be invented in sufficient detail to appear credible. When incidents could be provoked, they would form the basis for great publicity; when it proved impossible to provoke incidents, they would be fabricated. And all this would be carried forward in steadily increasing volume during the course of the year. Simultaneously, the Germans within Czechoslovakia would be harnessed to this campaign. They would furnish part of the basis for the propaganda and incidents, being given to believe that the German government was interested in their security and welfare. They would thus form the cover for an eventual German attack on Czechoslovakia that could be made to appear in the guise of defending Germans—rather than attacking Czechs—and which would find Czechoslovakia so isolated morally that she might also be isolated diplomatically and militarily.[23]

Before some of the major steps in this campaign are briefly outlined and documented, a word should be said about the receptivity of the public

22. The suggestion was formally raised in Parliament and dismissed as not serving any useful purpose by the parliamentary under-secretary (and later prime minister), R. A. B. Butler, on 22 June 1938, C 6243/1941/18, FO 371/21725.
23. The utilization of the Palestinian refugees by Israel's Arab neighbors in the 1950s and 1960s for similar purposes suggests that the technique has not been discredited by the ultimate fate of the Sudeten Germans.

inside and outside Germany to such a campaign. In an age when the triumph of the national over the dynastic principle of state organization was widely regarded as both good and necessary, when the questions of minority rights and national self-determination were very much to the fore, and when the public in Central and Western Europe had long heard of struggles of oppressed minorities from the Bulgarian to the Armenian massacres, from the Alsace-Lorraine to the Polish question, the possibility of arousing concern over the fate of the Sudeten Germans was clearly present. The other side of this coin was, of course, that Berlin could play its cynical tune credibly only once: when Hitler tried the same strategy again in the following year, to isolate Poland, almost or actually identical tales about the mistreatment of the German minority there failed to produce the same results. It was not just that there were fewer Germans in Poland than in Czechoslovakia; they were, after all, treated much less decently than those in Czechoslovakia. The real point was that having been tricked by faked concern about Germans in other countries once, no one was interested. One can read the record of the almost interminable discussions of the British and French governments in 1939 and practically never see a reference to the minority about which Berlin was then bleating into the wind.

A number of the main themes that would characterize the crisis over Czechoslovakia in 1938 were already well established before the annexation of Austria brought the Czechoslovak question to the fore. The isolation of Czechoslovakia from possible support was well advanced. The way in which Germany could rely on Poland to screen and even assist German moves against the Czechoslovak state has been described. From Warsaw, the possibility of the dissolution of Czechoslovakia was viewed with equanimity. Although there was no actual German-Polish agreement on the subject, the Poles looked forward to the prospect in terms of territorial gains for themselves, no great likelihood of a European war, and the possibility of a common border with Hungary.[24] It was equally clear that Czechoslovakia could not count on Yugoslavia for anything other than mild diplomatic interest.[25] Hungary hoped for territorial gains from the dissolution of Czechoslovakia and was restrained only by concern over involvement in any general European war or Yugoslav support for the Czechs. The latter possibility had, as previously explained, largely disappeared in view of the drift of Yugoslavia toward the Axis. The most spectacular sign of that reorientation had been the rapprochement of Yugoslavia and Italy.

24. *Hungarian Documents,* 1, No. 274; 2, Nos. 104, 117; *Lipski Papers,* Nos. 79–80; *Szembek Diary,* 14 November 1937, pp. 252–55; *D.D.F.,* 2d, 8, Nos. 307, 314, 355; 10, No. 95; R 7385/837/12, FO 371/21133; *U.S.,* 1938, 1:33–35; Gunther to Roosevelt, 10 December 1937, Hyde Park, P.S.F. France, 1937.

25. *D.D.F.,* 2d, 6, No. 11; *G.D.,* C, 6, No. 542; Koloman Gajan and Robert Kvaček (eds.), *Germany and Czechoslovakia, 1918–1945, Documents on German Policies* (Prague: Orbis, 1965), pp. 119–20.

The authorities in Rome, certainly, saw nothing to fear from a German move against Prague. Even before Italy acquiesced in the annexation of Austria by Germany, the Italian foreign minister had repeatedly stated that he thought Czechoslovakia an artificial state which had best be demolished. His comments to this effect were repeated by so many diplomats that it may be assumed Count Ciano meant them to be taken as Italy's position.[26] He let it be known to Czechoslovakia's partners in the Little Entente that there would be no help for Czechoslovakia from Rome;[27] he looked forward over the ruins of Czechoslovakia to that Rome-Belgrade-Budapest-Warsaw alignment from the south that Colonel Beck envisioned from the north.[28] The assumption in Rome appears to have been that Czechoslovakia would collapse under international pressure, her component parts becoming the booty of her neighbors without war.[29] With Italy still deeply involved in the fighting in Spain, the Italian leaders clearly did not expect that Italy herself would either play an active part or derive any direct or compensatory gains; the disappearance of another democracy from Europe would be a side benefit.[30]

Czechoslovakia did have a formal alliance with France which obligated the latter to come to her assistance in case of a German attack. There was, however, no staff agreement as to how such French assistance would be provided, an aspect frequently discussed in the literature in connection with the Franco-Soviet and Franco-Polish pacts but rarely mentioned in connection with Czechoslovakia.[31] Any resolution of this problem was complicated by the remilitarization of the Rhineland and the beginning of the construction of German fortifications there. The French, having suffered horrendously from the devastation of the last war, were determined to hold off the Germans from French territory in the initial stages of any future war and to move to the offensive only when, presumably as the result of a vast British continental army having been built up and sent to France, the Allies could advance into Germany. By that time, of course, the Germans would have overrun whatever Central and East European allies were faithful to France and could well be even stronger than at the

26. Girsa to Beneš, 1 April 1937, Czechoslovak document in T-120, 1041/1809/413847; *Guido Schmidt Trial*, p. 517; R 2802/26/67, FO 371/21137; *D.D.F.*, 2d, 10, No. 236.

27. Ciano, *Diplomatic Papers*, pp. 149–52.

28. Kerekes, No. 12; *Hungarian Documents*, 1, No. 382; 2, No. 120.

29. Cf. *G.D.*, D, 2, No. 24.

30. The contrast between Italian willingness to see German gains at the expense of Czechoslovakia unmatched by Italian ones in 1938, and her unwillingness to do so in 1939 can probably best be understood by reference to the fact that by March 1939 the Spanish Civil War was obviously in its final stage.

31. Note Gamelin's memorandum for Daladier of 28 April 1938, which opens with the statement that no military convention complementing the pact of mutual assistance existed and which contains a vague allusion to "moving offensively under the conditions foreseen by our operational plan" without any indication of what these might have been—as will be shown later, the conditions were not expected to obtain until long after Czechoslovakia had been overrun by the Germans. See Maurice Gamelin, *Servir* (Paris: Plon, 1946), 2:318–19.

outset of hostilities. Until the French archives are opened, the historian must depend upon the sketchy comments of General Maurice Gauché[32] for what must remain the most extraordinary failure of French intelligence: the preposterous overestimation of the progress in German construction of fortifications in the west. Perhaps the wish for a defensive military strategy was father to the thought that Germany's defenses would be terribly difficult and costly to breach; whatever the reason, the results would become evident diplomatically in 1938 and militarily in 1939.

Under these circumstances, French expressions of loyalty to the alliance and its commitment to go to war were phrased in broad and vague terms in 1937.[33] Implicit—and sometimes explicit—was the hope that such assertions would serve to deter Germany from aggression, and there was assuredly much sense in the view expressed by the French to their Polish ally that giving Germany any other impression was dangerous in the extreme.[34] Beyond the narrowly military question of how French help might in fact be given, however, there were two further problems. There was the very complicated question of what France would do if an internal upheaval in Czechoslovakia led to German intervention. Though in the event this contingency never arose, its discussion raised questions and doubts about French policy.[35] Even more difficult was the puzzle of British policy: would Britain support France in a war arising out of the latter's obligation to assist Czechoslovakia; and, inherently tied to this question, was the further one of whether the French posture of fidelity to her alliance was credible in the absence of assurances of British support.[36] French Foreign Minister Yvon Delbos was doubtless correct in his view that France would descend to the rank of a second-rate power if she abandoned Czechoslovakia, but if carrying out a stronger policy depended not on her own resolution but the expectation of English help, had not that descent already taken place?[37]

When Delbos told U.S. Ambassador Bullitt on 18 February 1938 that nothing could be done to keep Austria from being swallowed up by Ger-

32. *Le deuxième bureau au travail (1935–1940)* (Paris: Amiot-Dumont, 1953), pp. 141–42. The work of Georges Castellan, *Le réarmament clandestin du Reich 1930–1935* (Paris: Plon, 1954), which exploits the French records in far more detail, unfortunately does not deal with the period after the remilitarization of the Rhineland; and the documentary series *D.D.F.* is necessarily limited to including only a few important items from military and naval archives.

33. C 383/1/18, FO 371/20705; C 4757, C 5126/3/18, FO 371/20711; *G.D.*, D, 2, No. 21; *Guido Schmidt Trial*, pp. 572–73; *U.S.*, 1938, 1:35–39; Krofta circular of 10 October 1937, Czechoslovak document in T-120, 1041/1809/413878; Osuský telegram of 15 October 1937, ibid., frame 413861 (bits in Berber, No. 85); cf. Slávik report 85 of 10 December 1937, ibid., frames 413837–42 (distorted excerpt in Berber, p. 82).

34. *D.D.F.*, 2d, 5, No. 383.

35. Ibid., 7, Nos. 3, 18, 24, 94; *G.D.*, D, 2, Nos. 10, 13, 20–22, 24, 28; C 6875, C 6994/3/18, FO 371/20711.

36. *U.S.*, 1937, 1:89–92; 3:301–2; R 3718/770/67, FO 371/21139.

37. C 3685/532/62, FO 371/20702.

many, the latter noted the rapid spread in France of the view that the country should follow a purely defensive policy and abandon her friends and allies in Central and Eastern Europe. Bullitt commented in his report that "there may be a rapid reversal but at the present moment, for the first time since I arrived at this post, it is questionable that France would support Czechoslovakia, except in a case of direct and flagrant German invasion." He thought that peace might be maintained by acquiescence in German triumphs, that if the Germans followed a policy of *fortiter in re, suaviter in modo,* there might be no war because of the absence of resistance.[38] Under these circumstances, the development of the crisis over Czechoslovakia would depend heavily on two factors. First, how did the issue look to the British government; how did London see the situation in Czechoslovakia and its own interest in the position and strength of France? In the second place, would the Germans move with care and deliberation, or would they turn to "direct and flagrant" invasion?

The concern of the London authorities about the situation in and of Czechoslovakia was of long standing. Reports of the difficulties faced by the Sudeten Germans under Czech rule and the implications of the reaction of the Germans for the existence of Czechoslovakia in its 1919 borders had been arriving at the British Foreign Office with some regularity.[39] The conclusion reached there was, in Vansittart's words, "the plain fact is that the Sudetendeutsche are being oppressed by the Czechs."[40] This was not some abstract problem; as Eden asked, "What is to be the position of France if this problem leads to conflict between Germany and Czechoslovakia? and our position?"[41] What looked so troublesome from London was the obverse of the general German strategy previously described: "It may well be that Germany has designs on Czechoslovakia in any event, but it is quite certain that at present the Czechoslovak Government are providing them with an ever open door and a first-class pretext."[42]

One conclusion drawn in London was that it would be best to urge the Czechs to do their utmost—and certainly much more than hitherto—to remove the grievances of the Germans in their country; and such advice was given both in London and in Prague in the hope that the German case

38. Bullitt tel. 269 of 18 February 1938, State 740.00/298.
39. After Sir John Addison, the British minister in Prague, had sent a long and gloomy report to London on 25 August 1936 (R 5216/32/12, FO 371/20375), a collection of extracts of his prior warnings from 1931 to 1936 was pulled together on 7 October 1936 (R 6487/32/12, FO 371/20375). The subject is covered in detail in Jonathan Zorach, "The British View of the Czechs in the Era before the Munich Crisis," *Slavonic and East European Review,* 57, No. 1 (Jan. 1979): 56–70.
40. Minute of Sir Robert Vansittart of 12 September 1936 on R 5296/32/12, FO 371/20375.
41. Minute by Anthony Eden of 15 September 1936 on R 5337/32/12, FO 371/20375.
42. Vansittart's conclusion in the record of his meeting with Henlein on 20 July 1936 (R 4395/32/12, FO 371/20374).

against Czechoslovakia would thus not have such a strong basis, or, if carried forward nevertheless, would be clearly exposed.[43] There was the converse thought that the Czechs would be able to afford adoption of a more liberal internal policy if they could be absolutely certain of external military support in case of a crisis with Germany,[44] but there was great doubt in London that France would stand by her ally. This doubt lent strength to the other conclusion drawn in London, namely, that the French should be urged to use their influence in Prague in favor of concessions to the Sudeten Germans that might pacify the latter but would in any case remove the inner weakness of Czechoslovakia's diplomatic position.[45]

In January 1937 the British government accordingly made an effort to persuade the French to press concessions on the Czechs. The French ambassador in London and the French foreign minister were told that the British believed efforts needed to be made to meet the grievances of the Sudeten Germans, especially in the economic field.[46] The immediate response of the French was, however, the opposite of what London wanted. The French minister in Prague, Victor de Lacroix, warned against bilateral negotiations with Germany and argued to both the Czechoslovak and his own government that concessions made to the German government or the Sudeten Germans would only weaken Czechoslovakia in view of the inequality of the parties involved.[47] Lacroix's belief that any Czechoslovak-German agreement or concessions to the Sudeten Germans would be dangerous both for Czechoslovakia and for the position of France made sense, but *only* in a situation where either France by herself could and would stand by Czechoslovakia in a crisis or where France could count on British support and move jointly with England to defend Czechoslovakia. The first of these two contingencies was, however, excluded by a French policy that saw France as too weak to act by herself; and the Czechoslovak government itself had recognized this the preceding month.[48] As for the second alternative, that of British assistance, this too was recognized by Prague and Paris as doubtful,[49] and it was further recognized by Lacroix himself that the failure to reduce friction on the Sudeten issue would make it even less likely.[50]

43. Examples in R 2128, R 4487/32/12, FO 371/20374; cf. Weinberg, *Foreign Policy*, pp. 313–14; Masaryk to Krofta, 29 July 1937, Czechoslovak document in T-120, 1316/2376/D 497052–55.

44. Minute by Sargent of 15 October 1936 on R 6724/32/12, FO 371/20375.

45. See Vansittart's and Eden's comments, ibid.

46. *D.D.F.*, 2d, 4, No. 295; R 320/188/12, FO 371/21126; cf. *D.D.B.*, 4, No. 204.

47. *D.D.F.*, 2d, 4, Nos. 359, 375, 442, 474. It should be noted that this was the very time when, as became known later, the Czechoslovak government was secretly negotiating with Berlin.

48. *D.D.F.*, 2d, 4, No. 165.

49. Ibid.

50. Ibid., 5, No. 52.

The optimism about Czechoslovakia's prospects that Czechoslovak President Eduard Beneš habitually voiced was not rebutted by Lacroix.[51] When the French foreign minister became worried enough to have Lacroix sound Beneš out on some steps in the Sudeten German question, the hesitations of the latter were not met by any serious effort on the part of the French minister to urge action; on the contrary, he continued to warn against any German-Czechoslovak agreement.[52] Beneš was or professed to be hopeful that the agreement reached between the Prague government and the Activist parties which was announced by the government on 18 February 1937 would strengthen those parties, weaken Henlein's Sudeten German movement, and allow Czechoslovakia a breathing spell. The fact of the matter was, however, that Prague neither followed up the February agreement with major new steps nor created any momentum that might have changed the whole situation by shifting the initiative to the Czech leadership. The failure of anything substantial to come from the February agreement was soon evident to all, and the absence of French pressure at this critical juncture was a significant disservice to France's own ally. Given the unwillingness of the French government to make serious military plans to assist Czechoslovakia—to say nothing about determination to carry them out—it was hardly either fair or honest to leave Prague under the illusion that all might yet be well.[53]

Throughout the summer of 1937 the situation of Britain and France working at cross-purposes on Czechoslovakia continued. The London government urged Prague to initiate conversations with Henlein and to try to meet as many of the demands of the Sudeten Germans as possible, simultaneously urging the Sudeten German party to respond to any opportunity offered by the government, while Lacroix did what he could to reinforce the reluctance of the Czechoslovak authorities.[54] Although aware of the enormous importance of the minorities question for British public opinion, the French minister was still reluctant to urge concessions on the Czechs.[55] Fearful that this course would lead to an explosion, the British government began a major effort to convince the French that their own policy was one of lesser dangers than the rigid line which the French were still advocating in Prague.[56]

51. Ibid., 4, No. 393; 5, No. 149; for similar expressions by Krofta, see ibid., No. 40, and R 6804/154/12, FO 371/21125.
52. *D.D.F.*, 2d, 5, Nos. 202, 205, 228; 6, Nos. 28, 48, 139.
53. On the February 1937 agreement between the Czechoslovak government and the Activist parties, and subsequent events, see Brügel, pp. 308ff.; *D.D.F.*, 2d, 5, No. 22; *G.D.*, C, 6, Nos. 151, 220, 224; R 2886/188/12, FO 371/21128; R 3707, R 4408/188/12, FO 371/21129; R 5855/188/12, FO 371/21130.
54. *D.D.F.*, 2d, 6, Nos. 3, 222; R 4942, R 5708/188/12, FO 371/21130.
55. *D.D.F.*, 2d, 6, Nos. 222, 242.
56. R 5455, R 5986, R 6098/188/12, FO 371/21130.

This difference highlighted the French dilemma: they would neither advise their ally to make concessions that might leave Czechoslovakia subservient to Germany nor were they prepared to back up the Czechs if the situation became really dangerous. In September, October, and November 1937 the British government made a series of unsuccessful attempts to convince the French that Czechoslovakia would be strengthened, not weakened, by a settlement with the Sudeten Germans, and that in any case, a serious effort by Prague would weaken the German case. The simultaneous British efforts to persuade the Czechoslovak government of the wisdom of such a policy foundered on Czechoslovak opposition and the continuing contrary advice they were receiving from Paris. The Czechs and French repeatedly warned that there was no relying on German good faith, to which the British responded by agreeing that this was so, but that there was no prospect of demonstrating this fact unless the Czechoslovak government made—and was seen to make—a major effort and as a result became internationally less vulnerable.[57]

Although it was generally expected in Paris and Prague as well as London that Germany might find a way to swallow Austria, thereby opening up Czechoslovakia to invasion from the south, the English were alone in insisting that time was crucial; it might well be too late already, but the danger would become still greater if the situation were allowed to drift. By the end of 1937 the French were coming around to London's point of view and agreed to discuss the situation with the British leaders when visiting London to hear the report of Lord Halifax on his trip to Germany. The immediately following tour of the French foreign minister would provide an opportunity for him to discuss the matter with Beneš in Prague, but the evidence shows that little came of this. The last months of Austrian independence, therefore, did not see any new initiatives on the Sudeten question by the leaders of Czechoslovakia. They had sounded out Henlein in the fall, but they appear to have preferred the risks of delay to those of action, fearful that any action might set off a slide which could not be halted.[58]

If the attempt of the British government to move Prague by direct advice and indirect pressure during 1937 has been discussed at some length, it is because the conduct of Chamberlain's policy in 1938 cannot be understood without this background. The fact that world attention did

57. On this argument in the fall of 1937, see R 6258/188/12, FO 371/21130; R 7004, R 7005, R 7107, R 7357, R 7540, R 7705/188/12, FO 371/21131; D.D.F., 2d, 7, No. 136.

58. R 8196, R 8587/154/12, FO 371/21126; R 7705/188/12, FO 371/21131; R 7857, R 8128, R 8249, R 8261, R 8515/188/12, FO 371/21132; C 8730/7888/17, FO 371/20698; C 7852/7324/18, FO 371/20751; Václav Král (ed.), Die Deutschen in der Tschechoslowakei 1933–1947 (Prague: Československé Akademie Věd, 1964) (hereafter cited as Král, Die Deutschen), Nos. 80, 82; Robert Kvaček, "Zur Beziehung zwischen der Tschechoslowakei und den Westmächten vor dem Münchener Diktat," Acta Universitatis Carolinae, Philosophica et historica, 1968, pp. 209–12; Hungarian Documents, 2, No. 99; D.D.F., 2d, 7, Nos. 191, 193, 340, 365, 377; Veverka report, 11 December 1937, Czechoslovak document in T-120, 1041/1809/413866–67.

not focus on Czechoslovakia until 1938, and the subsequent decision of
the editors of the *Documents on British Foreign Policy, 1919–1939* to omit
internal comments and memoranda and to start the third series of their
volumes with the annexation of Austria in 1938 rather than, say, the
beginning of the Chamberlain cabinet in 1937, have joined to direct later
public and scholarly interest to the year of Munich. The perspective from
which the London government saw the problems of Czechoslovakia had,
however, been fairly precisely defined well before Hitler's initiative made
Czechoslovakia item number one on the diplomatic agenda.[59] And some
of the impatience with which the British leaders in 1938 treated both the
Czechoslovak and French governments on the matter of concessions to
the Sudeten Germans must be seen as an outgrowth of London's unsuccessful effort to make some progress on these questions before they
had become quite so acute.

From the beginning of 1937 the Foreign Office had believed that some
steps to conciliate the Sudeten Germans were needed. There was a clear
recognition that Germany might well want to end the independence of
Czechoslovakia altogether, but that was seen as no reason for not trying
to remove a major pretext and at least gain time.[60] The fear of German
aims that reinforced the reluctance of the Czechoslovak government was
also understood, but if Germany created an international crisis over the
grievances of the Sudeten Germans, France was seen as unlikely to fight
and Hitler as possibly willing to move aggressively on the assumption of
French abstention.[61] There were, in fact, few illusions in London. The
German press campaign about the Soviet airfields and the bolshevization
of Czechoslovakia were taken as preposterous efforts to whip up opinion
inside Germany and to frighten Czechoslovakia into weakening its ties to
the Soviet Union.[62] The fact that the Sudeten German party was finan-
cially supported from Germany was also known in London. When the
News Chronicle was advised not to publish internal correspondence it had
obtained showing German financing of the Sudeten German party in 1936,
it was noted in the Foreign Office that "they do not really tell us anything
very new." Henlein had, to be sure, asserted the contrary but was not
taken at face value. The critical issue was that publication of the documents in April 1937 would simply stir up the issue and reinforce the
pressures inside Czechoslovakia against any concessions to the Sudeten

59. Note the conversations between Colonel Christie and Hans Steinacher in Berlin in the
summer of 1937. Christie warned that there would be war if the Germans did not stop at the
nationality border, and that there were those in Germany who just pretended an interest in
the Sudeten Germans but in reality merely wanted to use them (Jacobsen, *Steinacher*, pp.
400–403).

60. See the Foreign Office comments on Bentinck's tel. 1 (Saving) from Prague of 5
January 1937 in R 133/133/12, FO 371/21125.

61. Note Orme Sargent's memorandum on the "Problem of Czechoslovakia" of 11 January 1937 in R 622/188/12, FO 371/21126.

62. R 278, R 287, R 433/188/12, FO 371/21126; cf. R 3710/188/12, FO 371/21129.

Germans.[63] When the situation of the Sudeten Germans, emphasizing
their economic suffering and political difficulties, were being presented to
the British public by such articles as those of Arnold J. Toynbee in the
Economist in July 1937, the way to show up Henlein as disloyal was for
the Czechoslovak government to make him a real offer which he would
either have to accept, thereby recognizing the willingness of the Prague
government to make meaningful concessions, or reject and thereby show
himself uninterested in agreement.[64] Such a development would not take
place until the very last stages of the 1938 negotiations.

In 1937 the London government was still hesitant about pressuring
Prague as contrasted with giving gentle warnings. Fearful of being embroiled in the Czechoslovak-German controversy, the British government
did not wish to mediate between the two countries and wanted neither to
push Prague into Berlin's arms nor to discourage the possibility of agreement. As to the Sudeten issue, London's policy was "to urge upon the
Czechoslovak Government the importance of a far-reaching settlement . . . not so much on the ground that such a settlement would make
an agreement with Germany possible . . . but because it would fortify
Czechoslovakia's reputation in the eyes of the world for humane and
generous treatment of her minorities in accordance with her treaty obligations."[65] It was this emphasis on the minorities issue as a critical weakness in Czechoslovakia's position that had induced the Foreign Office to
urge the *News Chronicle* to withhold publication of the incriminating
documents the newspaper had obtained and that led such officials as Sir
Robert Vansittart to maintain contact with Henlein and to meet with him
when he returned to England in mid-October 1937. The protestations of
the Sudeten leader were regarded with great skepticism, but the dilemma
of a real grievance which he represented remained.[66] What was so
threatening was the fact that the Sudeten Germans were both well organized and adjacent to a Germany which wished to utilize their grievances,
thus both creating a danger and rendering it difficult to remove by means

63. R 2979/188/12, FO 371/21128. For temporary optimism in April 1937, see R 2993, R
2994/188/12, ibid.
64. See Cadogan's letter to Newton of 7 July 1937 in reply to Newton's of 21 June, R
4400/188/12, FO 371/21129. Newton had reminded Cadogan that Beneš's playing off the
Activitists against Henlein might indeed be unwise, but what would the British do "if
Southern Ireland abutted on a potential enemy of kindred blood and most formidable
strength." Cf. R 7085/188/12, FO 371/21131. For Toynbee's bad impressions from his trip to
Czechoslovakia, see R 4023, R 4215/188/12, FO 371/21129; on his *Economist* articles, see R
5361/188/12, FO 371/21132.
65. Eden instructions for Newton of 12 March 1937, filed with related papers under R
1421/188/12, FO 371/21128. Cf. R 451/188/12, FO 371/21126; R 689, R 839/188/12, FO 371/
21127; R 5854/188/12, FO 371/21130; R 7376/188/12, FO 371/21131; R 3764/770/67, FO 371/
21139; Hugh Dalton, Diary, 24 June 1937, Dalton Papers.
66. On Henlein's October 1937 trip, see R 6733, R 6899, R 6900/154/12, FO 371/21125; R
6982, R 7574/188/12, FO 371/21131; Král, *Die Deutschen*, No. 78; Celovsky, pp. 118–19;
G.D., D, 2, Nos. 8, 14; Dalton Diary, 4 November 1937, Dalton Papers.

that decreased rather than increased the dimensions of the problem.[67] As they prepared Lord Halifax for his trip to Germany and as they hoped to persuade the French ministers on their subsequent visit to London of the wisdom of urging concessions on Czechoslovakia, the staff of the Foreign Office began to look at the specifics of Sudeten German demands.

The whole problem of autonomy for the Sudeten areas was canvassed in London seriously for the first time. Would the Czechs fight over this question? Could Czechoslovakia be expected to make so great a concession when the Sudeten German party was likely then to insist on the transfer of the territory to Germany once autonomy had been secured?[68] The only way of stabilizing such a situation was seen to be a guarantee by Britain, France, and Germany. Such a guarantee would secure the Sudeten Germans in their autonomy and Czechoslovakia in its borders and independence; but whether the Germans would accept such a restraint, whether France would agree to such a change in its commitment to Czechoslovakia, and whether the British public—to say nothing of the Dominions—would agree to "a new and extremely important commitment in Central Europe" were all extremely questionable.[69] Although agreement for Delbos to talk about the problem with the Czechoslovak government was reached at the London meeting, as has already been explained, nothing came of either that project or the subsequent British approach for a comprehensive settlement with Germany which followed in early 1938. In the very days when Hitler rejected that effort out of hand, the Austrian question was being rushed to a rapid conclusion by Hitler and Göring, in part to divert attention from the internal crisis over the dismissals of von Blomberg and von Fritsch. The Czechoslovak question would, therefore, come to the forefront of British concern again in circumstances when their own views were already rather clearly defined but in which any practical way out had become more difficult than ever.

The German government had carefully stayed away from the main issue in German-Czechoslovak relations—the nature of the future political relationship between the two—during 1937. The unofficial soundings on this

67. Note the Foreign Office brief for Lord De La Warr (Lord Halifax's successor as lord privy seal) of 4 November 1937, R 7036/188/12, FO 371/21131; cf. Král, *Die Deutschen,* No. 82.

68. R 7145, R 7574/188/12, FO 371/21131; R 7807/188/12, FO 371/21132.

69. Here is the germ of the idea of combining a settlement with a guarantee that became, in greatly modified form, the essence of the Munich agreement (Foreign Office memorandum of 26 November 1937, R 8248/188/12, FO 371/21132). Anthony Eden commented on this document: "This question is full of trouble but a further attempt to make progress with it is indispensable. We should start with the French. Ask M. Delbos to have a frank talk with M. Benes when he is in Prague and ascertain from him if he can—it will not be easy for M. Benes is a shrewd negotiator—the maximum that he will give. I am naturally reluctant to become committed in any way in Central Europe, but in the event we shall have to be associated in some form with any settlement reached, indeed none can be reached without our active collaboration. A.E. Nov. 28."

subject had foundered in the winter of 1936–37 because of German reluctance to accept commitments limiting the freedom of action of the Third Reich. Von Neurath gave the Czechoslovak minister in Berlin, Vojtěch Mastný, the definitive no of the German government on 20 March 1937.[70] A number of direct and indirect efforts made by the Czechoslovak government during 1937 to reopen the possibility of negotiating a political settlement were thwarted by the Berlin authorities, who were willing to take advantage of any concessions offered by Prague but did not want these to eventuate in an accommodation between the two neighbors.[71] Even Ernst Eisenlohr, the German minister in Czechoslovakia who though no friend of the Czechs was nevertheless personally in favor of an agreement that would have left the Czechoslovak state at least nominally independent,[72] fully recognized that his own government did not think that a political settlement of German-Czechoslovak relations was opportune.[73] A few days after the meeting recorded in the Hossbach memorandum, von Neurath noted that Eisenlohr was indeed correct in this regard.[74]

The delaying policy of thwarting all efforts at a permanent settlement until Germany was stronger was accompanied by a policy of hostile propaganda against Czechoslovakia, pressures on Prague for concessions, and a slow tightening of control over the Sudeten German party whose internal dissensions were not seen as a hindrance to Germany during this preliminary period. Little purpose would be served by a detailed chronicle of the phases of German propaganda operations in 1937 as complaints about mistreatment of the Sudeten Germans replaced attacks on mythical Soviet air bases, a recital of the alternation of threats and blandishments used by Berlin to try to push the Prague authorities into improving the lot

70. The German record will be published as *G.D.*, C, 6, No. 288; there is an English translation in Gajan and Kvaček, pp. 117–18.
71. In my judgment, the attempts of Mastný to work with Göring and Steinacher in 1937 and to have the VDA and AO legalized ought to be seen in this context; *D.D.F.*, 2d, 5, No. 273; Jacobsen, *Steinacher*, Nos. 110, 117, 141; *G.D.*, D, 2, Nos. 17, 63; "Bestellungen aus der Pressekonferenz," 8 November 1937, Bundesarchiv, Brammer, Z.Sg. 101/10, f.337; Krofta's comments to the section chiefs of the Czechoslovak foreign ministry, No. 7/37 and 3/38 of 13 May 1937 and 27 January 1938, Czechoslovak documents in T-120, 1809/1041/414051–52, 414003. It must also be noted that according to the introduction of Gajan and Kvaček (p. 31), Hubert Masařík, the head of the Czechoslovak foreign minister's cabinet, was in Germany on 15 and 16 October 1937 and heard a refusal of any basic agreement from State Secretary von Mackensen. Furthermore, the Germans used the excuse of Czechoslovak Prime Minister Milan Hodža's having talked about his plan for the economic development of the Danubian area in London to evade discussing it with him even informally (*G.D.*, C, 6, No. 373; on Hodža's London talks, and the text of the plan, see R 3445, R 4475/770/67, FO 371/21139).
72. On Eisenlohr's views, see the conclusion of *G.D.*, D, 2, No. 47. Brügel and other scholars also think him opposed to total German control of Czechoslovakia.
73. The point is made in Eisenlohr's report on his meeting with Beneš on 9 November 1937, *G.D.*, D, 2, No. 18; the Czechoslovak record of a portion of this conversation is in Král, *Die Deutschen*, No. 81. Note also Eisenlohr's comment in the second paragraph of *G.D.*, D, 2, No. 19; cf. ibid., No. 25; Celovsky, pp. 127–28.
74. See *G.D.*, D, 2, p. 31, n.1.

of the Sudeten Germans and worsening the lot of the political refugees from Germany in Czechoslovakia, or a review of the seemingly endless squabbles within the Sudeten German party.[75] A comment explaining one of the changes in the German propaganda line during 1937 can be applied with equal force to other temporary shifts in Germany's procedures: "The directive is accordingly of a purely tactical nature; it does not signify any basic change in German policy toward Czechoslovakia."[76]

In the last weeks of 1937 and the first two months of 1938 the German government was focusing on Austria, and hence left German-Czechoslovak relations in a quiet state.[77] It was during this period that Henlein sent Hitler his lengthy exposé explaining his own past policies and procedures.[78] He affirmed his own belief that it was impossible to reconcile Germans and Czechs to living in the same country and assured Hitler that his and his party's prior public declarations to the contrary had been tactical devices required by the current political situation. He wanted German support for himself among the Sudeten Germans, he urged that the German government place the Sudeten question high on its agenda, and he called for a discussion of future policy and procedures between the German government and himself.[79]

In the interval between Henlein's report and his receiving the requested instructions at meetings in Berlin there were new German steps in regard to Czechoslovakia only in the field of relations with the Hungarians. There were conversations by both Sudeten German leaders and von Ribbentrop and Keitel with Hungarian officials, but these contacts, looking to joint action within Czechoslovakia as well as against her from the outside,

75. On the propaganda campaign and discussion of a press truce, see *G.D.*, C, 6, No. 153; D, 2, Nos. 7, 11, 16; *D.D.F.*, 2d, 5, No. 65; 7, No. 188; Král, *Die Deutschen*, No. 81; Krofta's comments to the section chiefs of the Czechoslovak foreign ministry, No. 17/37, 25 November 1937, Czechoslovak document in T-120, 1041/1809/414070–72; "Bestellungen aus der Pressekonferenz," 3 March, 19 October, 5 November 1937, Bundesarchiv, Brammer, Z.Sg. 101/9, f.173, 101/10, ff.285, 329; "Informationsbericht Nr. 70," 4 March 1937, ibid., 101/31, ff.221, 223; Nr. 154, 4 November, and Nr. 155, 5 November 1937, ibid., 101/31, ff.367, 375.

On the efforts to secure practical concessions from the Czechoslovak government, see *G.D.*, C, 6, Nos. 226, 239, 240, 318; D, 2, Nos. 3, 6, 12, 15, 17, 19; Celovsky, pp. 126–27; *D.D.F.*, 2d, 7, No. 69; Král, *Die Deutschen*, No. 71.

On the internal affairs of the Sudeten German party, its squabbles, and its financing from Germany, see *G.D.*, C, 6, Nos. 200, 204, 228, 317, 519, 525; D, 2, No. 26; Král, *Die Deutschen*, Nos. 74, 84; Gajan and Kvaček, pp. 118, 123–24; *D.D.F.*, 2d, 5, No. 216; and the details in Smelser. It should be noted that Henlein was able to have a press attaché at the German legation in Prague transferred because of contacts with elements in the Sudeten German party opposed to himself (*G.D.*, D, 2, No. 26; Georg Vogel, *Diplomat unter Hitler und Adenauer* [Düsseldorf: Econ Verlag, 1969], pp. 27–28; Král, *München*, No. 42).

76. Dertinger, "Informationsbericht Nr. 70," 4 March 1937, Bundesarchiv, Brammer, Z.Sg. 101/30, f.223.

77. The discussions in this period and the reports from German diplomats on the visit of Delbos to Prague may be found in *G.D.*, D, 2, Nos. 29–68, passim; Celovsky, pp. 126–36.

78. The text of the 19 November 1937 document is in *G.D.*, D, 2, No. 23; a good discussion of it in Celovsky, pp. 116–17.

79. For a subsequent request, see *G.D.*, D, 2, No. 53.

were of a tentative nature. The Germans were as yet not ready to move; and, worried about Hungarian indiscretions and excessive speed, Berlin tended to hold back the Magyars at this point rather than to spur them on; Hitler wanted staff talks postponed until at least after his trip to Italy scheduled for early May.[80] When the Hungarian minister asked Göring at the time of the *Anschluss* why the German-Hungarian talks for cooperation against Czechoslovakia had been broken off just when it would be Czechoslovakia's turn, the response was that the Austrian question had to be fully settled first but that Czechoslovakia would surely follow. Göring added that the Germans were not quite ready for that operation, which would require greater strength.[81] In the days of the *Anschluss* itself, Germany was primarily interested in keeping Czechoslovakia quiet, and Göring himself assured the Czechoslovak government that no military action against them was contemplated.[82]

The opportunity for Henlein to receive the guidance and instructions he wanted came little more than two weeks after the *Anschluss* in a series of meetings in Berlin on 28 and 29 March.[83] Hitler told Henlein at a long meeting on 28 March that the question of Czechoslovakia would be "solved before very long" and prescribed the general tactic that the Sudeten German party was to follow: to raise demands that the Czechoslovak government could not agree to. Henlein himself repeated this formula to Hitler—"we must always demand so much that we cannot be satisfied"—to be sure he fully understood. Not only did he describe the Führer's instructions as requiring the constant raising of demands to preclude agreement in so many words to the officials of the German foreign ministry; but as early as 5 April the Hungarian foreign minister quoted Henlein as declaring that "whatever the Czech government might offer, he would always raise still higher demands.... he wanted to sabotage an

---

80. On this subject, see *Hungarian Documents*, 1, No. 407; Ádám, p. 91, n.8, and No. 6; *G.D.*, D, 2, Nos. 65, 66; *TMWC*, 31:110–13. On contacts between Henlein and the Slovak autonomists and the Hungarians at this time, see *Hungarian Documents*, 2, Nos. 112, 124; *G.D.*, D, 2, Nos. 54, 57–60.

81. *Hungarian Documents*, 1, No. 408 (German text in Kerekes, No. 14; French text in Ádám, No. 1).

82. On the promises of this moment, see *G.D.*, D, 2, Nos. 72, 74, 78, 80, 81; Czechoslovak foreign ministry notes of 12 March 1938, Czechoslovak documents in T-120, 1040/1809/412666, 412668; Mastný reports 42 and 43 of 12 March 1938, ibid., 1041/1809/414221–25 and 414218–20 (mostly in Berber, pp. 94–98); Krofta circular of 12 or 13 March 1938, ibid., 1040/1809/412669–70; Král, *München*, Nos. 33–38, 43; *D.D.F.*, 2d, 8, No. 398; Celovsky, pp. 151–55. Hitler set the tone for this effort to reassure the Czechoslovak government right after von Schuschnigg's trip to Berchtesgaden (Král, *München*, No. 16).

83. The sources for these meetings are *G.D.*, D, 2, Nos. 106, 107 (note that this is a document of *military* origin which appears not to have reached the German foreign ministry until 1939), 109 (the "annexed demands" not printed here may be found in Král, *Die Deutschen*, p. 162); Erich Kordt, *Nicht aus den Akten* (Stuttgart: Deutsche Verlags-Anstalt, 1950), p. 207. See also *G.D.*, D, 3, No. 559 which states that Hitler saw on 4 April what must have been D, 2, No. 109. Henlein had again requested a meeting in a letter to von Ribbentrop of 17 March 1938 (ibid., D, 2, No. 89; cf. Celovsky, pp. 161–63).

understanding by all means because this was the only method to blow up Czechoslovakia quickly."[84]

The more precise details of the demands Henlein was to make in this process were developed in a meeting at the German foreign ministry on 29 March; and these were then elaborated into Henlein's famous Karlovy Vary (Carlsbad) speech of 24 April 1938. In his Berlin meetings, Henlein also was granted freedom to coordinate his procedures with the other national minorities in Czechoslovakia, cautioned not to move more quickly than his mentors in the Reich desired, and given full assurance that he had Hitler's backing against any rival personalities and tendencies within the Sudeten German party.

It is important to emphasize that Hitler's instructions to Henlein not only dealt with the tactics to be followed inside Czechoslovakia to prevent any agreement but also touched on the other aspect of Hitler's plan. The Führer commended Henlein's successes in England and urged a further trip to London to aid in assuring nonintervention by Great Britain. He speculated on the possibility of some upheaval in France, a subject on which he often commented. It is this broader discussion that allows us to see that in the weeks after the *Anschluss* Hitler was defining his approach to the destruction of Czechoslovakia, not just in general terms as in the conference of 5 November 1937, but in terms of political and military procedures to be initiated forthwith.

The one thing most to be avoided was the very one which the British had been urging on Czechoslovakia and which the Czechoslovak government had been taking some steps toward in the winter: an agreement between the Sudeten German party and Prague. Everything possible had to be done to make sure that Germany's pretext was not removed. It is in this context that one must see Hitler's suggestion that the Sudeten German party demand separate German regiments with German officers and German as the language of command within the Czechoslovak army. Here was the issue on which the Dual Monarchy of Austria-Hungary had almost fallen apart in its greatest internal crisis between 1867 and 1918; and the fact that Henlein preferred to reserve this demand for later—and in the event did not make it—in no way detracts from the light that the proposal sheds on *Hitler's* thinking. From his experience of a multinational state, this was the one demand that the central government could not agree to grant.[85]

84. Zsigmond, pp. 267–68, n. The observant Dertinger had figured out this strategy by 27 April 1938: "The demands which will be put forward by the Sudeten Germans will in each situation be calculated to be a few percentage points above what in the worst [*sic*] possible situation the Czechoslovak government could accept" (Bundesarchiv, Brammer, Z.Sg. 101/32, f.295).

85. The Hitler-Henlein meeting, and especially this section, is completely misunderstood by Donald C. Watt ("Hitler's Visit to Rome and the May Weekend Crisis: A Study in Hitler's Response to External Stimuli," *Journal of Contemporary History*, 9, No. 1 [January 1974], pp. 23–32). He takes the demand for military units as something to be obtained instead

The hope Hitler expressed for British neutrality may or may not have been understood by Henlein in all its implications. After all, Henlein may at an earlier time in his career have been at least partially sincere in hoping for British support in securing concessions from the Prague government. That, of course, would require just the opposite of the nonintervention he was now expected to obtain. Hitler's desire for British nonintervention points clearly and directly to a German military attack on Czechoslovakia, which he hoped to keep isolated from intervention by England and France, with the neutrality of the former reinforcing internal turmoil in restraining the latter. The German military plans for the attack on Czechoslovakia, which are yet to be examined, were thus to be prepared in a context of the hope and expectation of a war that could be limited the way the Central Powers would have preferred to limit the war of 1914 to Austria-Hungary and Serbia. If at that time Austria's diplomatic and military delays had forfeited the unique opportunity of the Central Powers for limiting war that the assassination of Archduke Francis Ferdinand might have provided had Austria struck immediately, on this occasion Hitler would plan with greater care. The general political climate created by the demands of the Sudeten Germans would isolate Czechoslovakia so that she could be attacked with a minimum risk of general war. The timing of the final incident would not be left to chance or opportunity—as in the case of Sarajevo—but would be scheduled for the correct day and hour to maximize German tactical advantage. While Hitler and von Ribbentrop talked to diplomats about the possible need for German intervention in case of some bloody incident in Czechoslovakia (or, in 1939, in Poland), there was *never* even the slightest internal German discussion or planning for such a contingency. The way to control timing was, of course, to plan and arrange the incident for the moment considered appropriate for the planned attack; only if by some extraordinary stroke of good fortune there was a real incident at the "right" time could you dispense with the fake.[86]

These "finer" details of German planning were worked out at a later stage in the scenario—as would be the case in 1939 when the actual preparations for the attack on the Gleiwitz radio tower did not start until the first days of August. The most pressing problem in March and April of 1938 was the revision of what planning for an attack on Czechoslovakia had already been done in the light of the opening up of that country's

---

of what the text makes clear—something that might be asked *because* it was believed unobtainable. Watt has also reversed the time element: the text says that Henlein would run events in the immediate future *(zunächst)*, but that there would have to be close coordination. This scheme for steady escalation of demands to preclude agreement is converted by Watt into letting Henlein take the lead.

86. It is unfortunate that in his perceptive analysis of the German planning to take advantage of an incident that the Germans would probably have to arrange themselves, Celovsky (p. 159, esp. n.1) does not allude either to the outbreak of World War I or to the Gleiwitz incident staged by the Germans at the beginning of World War II.

southern border as a result of the annexation of Austria. The plans had just been revised after the conference of 5 November. Now they were to be redrawn again to take account of the new strategic situation. Time was not that pressing: as Göring had told the Hungarians and as Hitler appears to have said to his military entourage, "Austria had to be digested first."[87] The last week of March and the first ten days of April were devoted to the plebiscite on the annexation of Austria; thereafter the process of incorporating that country fully into Germany required only occasional decisions by Hitler, such as the formal appointment of Josef Bürckel on 23 April as the man in charge of that process.[88] Von Mackensen's interpretation of Hitler's view as being that a few months were needed for the digesting process before the Czechoslovak question could be made the focus for action is probably an accurate reading of Hitler's time schedule at the beginning of April 1938.[89]

Hitler's developing perception of how the operation against Czechoslovakia should be mounted can be seen in his discussion of the subject with Keitel on 21 April and the draft for an operational directive that the latter prepared on the basis of Hitler's comments at their meeting.[90] In

87. Jodl Diary, *TMWC*, 28:372. This undated entry probably reflects comments of Hitler about 20 March (the special section of Jodl's diary in Nuremberg document 1781-PS [National Archives] includes entries through 18 March). Watt repeatedly quotes the text of this portion of the published Jodl diary (pp. 46 and 47 of the original), but the references appearing between the entries of 11 March (preceding the unpublished 1781-PS) and 23 May 1938 can easily be misunderstood. The internal evidence of the diary shows that *all* the entries on these two pages were made *after* Jodl returned from leave on 24 July 1938. Like most scholars, the otherwise meticulous Watt has overlooked the fact that p. 48 of the original diary begins with an entry for 20 May which is followed immediately by an entry noting leave from 21 June to 24 July. Failure to pay careful attention to the original has obscured from most that the two inserted pages are a chronologically somewhat confused text, prepared long after the events; they begin with a sentence connecting with the separate (unpublished) portion of the diary about the *Anschluss* and Memel and end with a general discussion of the conflict between Hitler and his generals over the plan to attack Czechoslovakia in 1938. The interpretation given by Jodl in these pages must, therefore, be read in the context of his siding with Hitler in that dispute in the summer as he had sided with Hitler in the Fritsch-Blomberg crisis in the winter. If the Jodl diary pp. 46–47 are read in this way, they make sense as part of the version of events as perceived in the late summer by Hitler and those siding with him; if the point is disregarded, we find such absurdities as a reference to a past meeting of 9 June being included in something described as "an entry of 23 May" (Donald C. Watt, "The May Crisis of 1938: A Rejoinder to Mr. Wallace," *Slavonic and East European Review*, 44, No. 103 [July 1966], 478).

88. The decree is in Domarus, 1:853–54. There is considerable information on the subjects in Rosar and in Luža, *Austro-German Relations*.

89. Von Mackensen so told the Hungarian minister after seeing Hitler on 2 April, see Ádám, No. 4; cf. "Informationsbericht Nr. 27," 24 March 1938, Bundesarchiv, Brammer, Z.Sg. 101/32, ff.227–29.

90. The notes of Major Rudolf Schmundt, who had replaced Hossbach as Hitler's armed forces adjutant a few weeks earlier, are in *TMWC*, 25:415–18. These documents are a part of Schmundt's special file on "Fall Grün," the planned attack on Czechoslovakia, submitted at Nuremberg as document 388-PS and of critical importance for the insight they give into Hitler's policy. Several things of significance in interpreting these documents must be noted: Schmundt, like Keitel, was new at his post and was developing his competence at it. The documents in the file are *not* always in chronological order; thus the handwritten notes of

drawing on the account of the discussion and Keitel's subsequent drafting work, however, we must remember—as some historians have not—that Major Rudolf Schmundt himself appears not to have participated in the meeting and to have prepared his summary of the conversation on the basis of what Hitler or more likely Keitel told him,[91] and that Keitel was quite new to his position as something like a chief of military staff for Hitler in the reorganization of the German supreme command structure following the dismissal of von Brauchitsch and Hitler's assumption of the powers of the minster of war. In the case of the invasion of Austria, Keitel had simply turned to General Beck to prepare the necessary orders. Now he was asked by Hitler to take a hand himself, and he may well really have been as surprised as he claimed at his trial at Nuremberg.[92] The conclusions which some have drawn from the introductory wording of Keitel's 20 May draft as showing a change in Hitler's intentions before and after the May Crisis are certainly fallacious. The draft reflects not Hitler's views on the day Keitel submitted it but rather Keitel's formulation in language he thought appropriate for a general directive to the German armed forces of what he understood Hitler to have explained a month earlier at their 21 April meeting.[93] At that time Hitler had described himself as not intending to destroy Czechoslovakia by an unprovoked attack in the immediate future unless forced to in reaction to an incident inside Czechoslovakia—a phraseology for which no implementing planning took place—or tempted by a European situation that made an attack especially opportune, meaning presumably the sort of development Hitler often referred to on other occasions: an upheaval inside France or a war in the Mediterranean between Italy and the Western Powers.

In the days between the plebiscite on the annexation of Austria and the appointment of Bürckel as commissioner for the process of unification, Hitler thought of an attack on Czechoslovakia as not immediately imminent. He had explained part of his basic political strategy toward Czechoslovakia to Henlein; he explained other parts to Keitel. An attack out of the blue was too risky because it might lead to international complications when his primary hope was to isolate the conflict. It was on this hope that diplomatic and military planning had to focus. There would be a

---

item 2c (pp. 417–18) were clearly written before the clean typed version in item 2a (pp. 415–17). The assumption of Celovsky (p. 157, n.5) and others that item 1 (Hitler's discussion of his forthcoming trip to Italy) must antedate 21 April cannot be proven. The draft of Keitel, with a covering letter to Hitler, is on pp. 421–27.

91. Schmundt's preliminary notes are dated 22 April. Furthermore, although Keitel's attorney refers to Schmundt as being present (*TMWC*, 10:508), Keitel himself does not. In his memoirs (p. 182) Keitel dates the meeting with Hitler to 20 April.

92. *TMWC*, 10:508.

93. There is no evidence of any discussion between Hitler and Keitel on the subject between 21 April and 20 May. Keitel pictures himself as working on the 20 May draft without further contact with Hitler (ibid., pp. 508–9); the account in his memoirs (*Keitel Papers*, pp. 182–83) is similar.

slow escalation of tension which would justify Germany's military buildup and which would terminate in a German attack following either a decision by Germany that a surprise attack was now appropriate or an incident arranged inside Czechoslovakia that might provide a handy pretext.[94] In any case, once the attack had started, utmost speed of operations was the critical point. The first four days would be decisive in the sense that quick military action to breach the border defenses and penetrate the interior of Czechoslovakia would have the triple effect of encouraging Hungary and Poland to join in to secure their share of the booty, discouraging France and England from assisting Czechoslovakia and promoting the internal and morale collapse of the Czechoslovak state.[95] The army was to move as quickly as possible while trying to avoid having the defensive screen in the west appear provocative to the French; the air force was to help the army attain a speedy success by destroying the Czechoslovak air force and its bases as well as by tactical support operations; and the navy was to act as a security force in a manner that would avoid any unfavorable influence on the policies of the major European powers.

Although detailed operational plans were not yet spelled out,[96] the repeated references to having the air force spare Czechoslovakia's industrial installations as much as possible so that these could be utilized to enhance Germany's military economic strength show that Hitler intended, and Keitel understood him to intend, a complete and permanent occupation of Bohemia and Moravia. In his memoirs, Keitel claims that Hitler alluded to the sufferings of the Sudeten Germans as one reason for the attack on Czechoslovakia, but there is no trace of this in the contemporary documents. Instead, the ostensible beneficiaries of German action appear in a very different way. They are mentioned explicitly as recipients of instructions for assistance to the German military operations, and they are mentioned implicitly as useful "for placing the blame for war on the enemy" and for "providing the moral justification for military measures in the eyes of at least a portion of world opinion." The Sudeten Germans, in other words, were to help Germany, not the other way around.

As Hitler a few days after this meeting discussed his hopes for the trip

94. Hitler mentioned the possible murder of the German minister to Czechoslovakia. Later, on 30 August, a British Foreign Office official would speculate that "A spectacular method of creating the necessary conditions would be to arrange for the murder of Henlein—or even Lord Runciman—by a Czech 'Van der Lubbe'. With Himmler in charge such a plot cannot be ruled out as inconceivable" (Sargent memorandum, 30 August 1938, C 9041/1941/18, FO 371/21734, f.261). The reference to van der Lubbe reflects the general belief that the National Socialists themselves, not the Dutchman executed for it, had set fire to the Reichstag in 1933.

95. Note that on 24 April von Weizsäcker wrote in his diary that on 22 April Hitler had told the Hungarian minister that when Czechoslovakia was partitioned, the Hungarians would receive all the territory they had lost at the end of the war (*Weizsäcker-Papiere*, p. 126).

96. The exact timetable was still to be worked out with the army and air force according to a marginal comment (*TMWC*, 25:422).

to Italy scheduled for the beginning of May, one can see still a third way in which he phrased his plans toward Czechoslovakia in addition to those voiced to Henlein and Keitel.[97] If Mussolini had no further ambitions—a contingency it is difficult to imagine Hitler's believing likely—then the attack on Czechoslovakia would have to be postponed for a long time. The German border in the west would have to be completely closed off by fortifications first, and then one could tackle the project.[98] But with a close alignment or alliance with Italy, as a result of which Italy could move forward with her own ambitions, Germany could safely defy France and England by destroying Czechoslovakia quite soon. The Western Powers would then refrain from interfering. The alignment with Italy would enable Germany to pass safely through the four weeks required to redeploy her forces from the Bohemian theater of operations to the West. Italy should not make the mistake that Prussia had made in 1805 and 1806 in allowing her potential continental allies to be defeated by Napoleon only to be crushed herself when fighting him by herself in the following year. The armaments situation was in any case favorable to the Axis powers with their headstart over the rearmament programs of Britain and France.

Hitler, however, wanted his coordination with Italy limited to the political sphere—the implied threat of the Axis alignment would be sufficient. There would be no detailed staff conversations; he preferred to keep his military plans secret.[99] The implication is clear: there would be no occasion for joint military operations because a Germany aligned politically with Italy could expect to be allowed to attack Czechoslovakia without a general war. As the Germans learned in Rome, this was also the view of their Italian hosts.[100] When Hitler returned from his Italian trip, therefore, he was ready to review the plans for his next adventure as an operation for the immediate future. As von Weizsäcker noted in his diary on 13 May, Hitler interpreted Mussolini's attitude on the Czechoslovak question as expressed during the conversations in Italy as an encouragement for Germany to move forward; a week *before* the May Crisis von Weizsäcker records Hitler as wanting to settle with Czechoslovakia still in that year.[101]

97. Schmundt's undated notes, ibid., pp. 414–15.

98. The phrase "Grenze Westen schliessen, dann weitersehen" appears to me to mean that Hitler thought that actually completing the Westwall first was the alternative to moving while it was still being constructed.

99. Watt, who otherwise makes so much of the Italian trip, avoids citing this portion of Hitler's comments, which contradicts the thrust of his account ("Hitler's Visit to Rome," p. 29).

100. See above, p. 309. For a prior Italian view of the question, see the 20 March 1938 report of the Czechoslovak minister to Rome in Král, *München*, No. 51.

101. *Weizsäcker-Papiere*, pp. 127–28. This portion was omitted from the account of the Italian journey in von Weizsäcker's memoirs, perhaps because it is too obviously inconsistent with the theory that Hitler made his decision after and as a result of the May Crisis.

Hitler had sketched out the broad outlines for his plans against Czechoslovakia to the men who were to help him direct the tools of his strategy, Henlein and Keitel, in the weeks after the *Anschluss*. Now he thought that the time had come for working out the details. It was into his deliberations over the detailed plans that what has come to be known as the May Crisis burst. Before its impact on those deliberations can be assessed, it is necessary to turn to the reaction of other powers to the *Anschluss;* for if the German dictator turned from that success to the preparations for his next venture, others were seeking ways of coping with such a move on his part.

The main ally of Czechoslovakia was France, obliged by treaty to come to her defense in case of attack. It was the French who had been even more concerned about the impact of the *Anschluss* than the British, in part no doubt because of their recognition of the military implications of the opening up of Czechoslovakia's southern border.[102] The new government of Léon Blum which emerged from the French governmental crisis that coincided with the *Anschluss* was at least theoretically interested in the problem of what to do about Czechoslovakia, but the brief tenure of the cabinet—13 March to 9 April—sufficed only to illuminate the most critical point of all, namely, that the French thought or pretended to believe that in practice they could do nothing at all. At a meeting of the Permanent Committee of National Defense on 15 March, attended by the key figures of the French government and armed forces, there was agreement that France could hardly assist Czechoslovakia in her hour of danger.[103] French mobilization would, it was hoped, oblige the Germans to keep a substantial proportion of their forces in the west, but an attack in the west—clearly alluded to with utmost distaste—would be held up for a long time by the (at this time largely imaginary) German fortifications.[104]

There was little hope that the Soviet Union could help substantially, given the intervening territory of Poland and Rumania which might in fact themselves feel threatened by Russia. There were pious hopes that the British might be persuaded to pressure the Belgians into allowing an offensive across their country and the Rumanians to allow the Russians to send aid to Czechoslovakia.

Nothing suggests that there were serious expectations as to the prospects of either of these ideas. With good reason, the French had no faith in Belgian assistance.[105] The Belgians were doing everything possible to

102. See the French general staff assessment of 14 March 1938, *D.D.F.*, 2d, 8, No. 432. This may account for the new note in Lacroix's conversation with Hodža on 22 March 1938 (ibid., 9, No. 26).

103. The record is in Gamelin, 2:322–28; on this meeting, see also *D.D.F.*, 2d, 8, Nos. 331, 445, 446, 462.

104. For French self-delusion on this point as early as May 1936, possibly as a result of a German plant, see *D.D.F.*, 2d, 2, No. 172.

105. The documents cited in note 117 below show Daladier and Gamelin doubtful that Belgium would even resist a German attack.

maintain their neutral position.[106] King Leopold was at the time more worried about a French than a German attack, a form of delusion accentuated rather than removed by the *Anschluss*.[107] The Belgians were in fact telling the French government that they would deny transit to French troops even if the League asked for it under Article 16 of the Covenant and would prefer to give up the French guarantee than to assist France against Germany in any such move to support Czechoslovakia.[108] If British Foreign Office officials commented on a report to the same general effect from the British minister in Brussels that there was little else the Belgians could do until Britain and France were strong enough to protect Belgium, they were pointing to the reciprocal way in which the weaknesses of the Western Powers interacted with each other.[109] The Rumanians were known to share the views of the Belgians.[110] What is most obvious to the reader of the record of the March meeting is that there was simply no will or determination behind French public assurances of fidelity to the treaty with Czechoslovakia.

The impetus to this dispirited meeting had come from the question of the British to the French about what the latter really intended to do to defend their ally.[111] On 28 March Maurice Gamelin confirmed to Winston Churchill, who told Lord Halifax, what the British military attaché in Paris had already reported to his incredulous superiors in London the preceding month: if it came to a war over Czechoslovakia, the French could not attack the Germans in the west or the Italians in the Alps but would attack the Italians in Libya![112] The French had arrived at this project by eliminating an attack on Germany as too costly in lives and an attack on Italy as too difficult because of the terrain in the Alps and the weakness of the Yugoslav army,[113] while the growing Italian garrison in

106. See *D.D.B.*, 5, Nos. 4, 6–8, 15.

107. See Overstraeten, 25 February 1938, p. 272, and 12 March 1938, p. 273.

108. *D.D.B.*, 5, Nos. 10, 11; *D.D.F.*, 2d, 9, Nos. 34, 274.

109. Note Clive's letter to Sargent, 22 March 1938, C 1995/1378/4, FO 371/21565.

110. *U.S.*, 1938, 1:42; *D.D.F.*, 2d, 9, No. 225.

111. *B.D.*, 3d, 1, Nos. 62, 81; *D.D.F.*, 2d, 8, Nos. 400, 417. The holding of the 15 March meeting appears to have been precipitated in part by the repeated requests of Czechoslovak Minister Osuský for public reaffirmation of loyalty to the alliance by the French government, see Král, *München*, No. 30.

112. Gamelin's account in his memoirs (2:317) recounts only Churchill's comments. For a Foreign Office minute of 4 April 1938 on Churchill's report to Lord Halifax, see C 2580/2307/17, FO 371/21616. Note that the earlier French scheme of opening a front at Salonika appears to have been dropped, presumably because of doubts about Yugoslavia (See Weinberg, *Foreign Policy*, p. 362). Perhaps these indirect approaches have to be seen as the "lesson" learned by the French military from the disastrous failure of their Plan 17 offensive in 1914.

113. French concern about the weakness of the Yugoslav army may be seen in *D.D.F.*, 2d, 7, Nos. 81, 204, 325. Gamelin, it should be added, appears to have believed in April 1938 that in the spring of 1939 even the Italian army, to say nothing of the German, would be stronger than the French (ibid., 9, No. 121)!

Libya presented both a potential threat and an inviting target.[114] From what evidence there is, one must conclude that the plan to focus any French offensive operations on North Africa if war developed anywhere in Europe, crystallized in the winter of 1937–38.

The French military scheme, which in its logical lunacy bears an uncanny resemblance to General Alfred von Schlieffen's pre–World War I idea of defending Austria-Hungary against a Russian attack by invading Belgium, was received in London with a mixture of astonishment and disbelief. There was astonishment over what was thought to be— correctly as we now know—a vast overestimation of the strength of the German fortifications in the west as well as over the insistence on attacking Italy in North Africa when there seemed to be no point in bringing Italy in if neither Germany nor Italy could be attacked in Europe. There was some disbelief that the French really thought themselves already so weak; and the conclusion drawn was that British-French staff talks were surely necessary and that the French government would have to be asked formally once again what their plan for assistance to Czechoslovakia really was.[115]

With no continental army of their own, the British were to be greatly influenced throughout 1938 by their understanding that the French would in fact do nothing at all that could help Czechoslovakia except at the end of a long war of attrition. At the British-French meeting of 29 April in London, which will be discussed below, the French tried to avoid this point by stressing the need to present a united and determined front to the Germans,[116] but Gamelin himself had confirmed to the British secretary of state for war, Leslie Hore-Belisha, on 25 April that "it was impossible for France to give military assistance to Czechoslovakia."[117] It was in the face of these grim prospects that the British government viewed the immediate aftermath of the *Anschluss*.

114. See the minutes of the meeting of the Permanent Committee on National Defence of 8 December 1937, ibid., 7, No. 325. Alarmist reports about the Italian military buildup in Libya are scattered throughout this volume. Combined with the continuing civil war in Spain and Italian activity in the Balearic islands, these troop movements drew French attention to their territories and communications in the Mediterranean.

115. Some staff talks were already under way; on 3–4 March French and British air force officers met in Paris to arrange an exchange of target files and related information on Germany and Italy (ibid., 8, No. 316). Target files are the folders containing accumulated pictorial, geographic, statistical, espionage, and other information about possible industrial and other objectives of bombing raids. See also *D.D.F.*, 2d, 9, No. 144.

116. The relevant passage is in *B.D.*, 3d, 1:218.

117. C 3783/3474/17, FO 371/21617. The Foreign Office noted the contradiction. Gamelin's account of his talk with Hore-Belisha is in *Servir*, 2:317–18, and *D.D.F.*, 2d, 9, No. 238; it omits the point quoted. His report to Daladier (*Servir*, 2:318–19; *D.D.F.*, 2d, 8, No. 251) begs the question of what could be done to help Czechoslovakia, and thus in effect confirms Hore-Belisha's account. Gamelin's report to Daladier should in my opinion be seen in connection with the Anglo-French talks of 29 April.

When the Czechoslovak minister in London, Jan Masaryk, had his first meeting with Lord Halifax as the new British foreign secretary on 4 March, Masaryk noticed that Halifax had carefully reviewed the record of all his prior meetings with Eden and repeated the line that the more Czechoslovakia could do for its Germans, the stronger Czechoslovakia's international position would be. Though recognizing the efforts the Czechoslovak government had made, Halifax stressed the unfavorable geographic situation of the country.[118] Chamberlain and Lord Halifax were at this very time receiving the disappointing news of Hitler's rejection on the previous day of the British approach to Germany on colonial and economic concessions in return for German restraint in Europe—something of which Masaryk was aware. The need for a new orientation of British policy thus occurred under circumstances where the rejection of an attempt at appeasement, the acceleration of the crisis over Austria, and the moving of the Czechoslovak question to the immediate forefront of international interest coincided.[119]

The insistence of the Prague government on assurances from Paris and London at the time of the *Anschluss*, therefore, was greeted not only by constantly repeated expressions of loyalty to the alliance from Paris but also with considerable sympathy in London.[120] When Masaryk and Lord Halifax met again on 12 March, annoyance over German rejection of the British approach combined with horror and disgust over the German aggression against Austria to make the British foreign secretary sympathetic to the problems faced by Czechoslovakia.[121] Halifax had just told off von Ribbentrop in no uncertain language and repeated the substance of this to the Czech minister; but it is evident from the record that Lord Halifax failed to grasp that his own chagrin over the impact of Germany's actions as damaging the prospects of an Anglo-German agreement was not shared by the German foreign minister, who was not the least bit interested in such an agreement and had in fact just explained to Hitler why he thought such an agreement positively dangerous for Germany. To Masaryk's insistence that Germany's word could not be trusted and that concessions to Henlein would not alter the policy of Berlin, Halifax responded that he had learned a great deal in the last few days but that he did not wish to give up all hope of some day being able to negotiate with Germany. Though disagreeing about the long-term prospects for peace which Masaryk considered hopeless while Halifax preferred to retain a shred of

118. Král, *München*, No. 31 (excerpts in Berber, pp. 92–93).
119. The fact that it also coincided with negotiations with Italy right after the cabinet crisis that led to the replacement of Eden by Halifax helps explain the great determination with which the British pushed for an agreement with Italy in those days; note Masaryk's report on his conversation with Cadogan on 9 March, Král, *München*, No. 32 (a tiny excerpt in Berber, p. 93).
120. Král, *München*, No. 33; cf. *D.D.F.*, 2d, 8, Nos. 474, 475.
121. The account of Lord Halifax is somewhat restrained (*B.D.*, 3d, 1, No. 61); that of Masaryk is fuller (Král, *München*, No. 40, a tiny excerpt in Berber, p. 99).

hope, they agreed on the utility of some gesture for the immediate future; and it was out of this that there evolved the British public and diplomatic references to Göring's assurances to the Czechoslovak government in the days of the *Anschluss* that no attack on Czechoslovakia was intended.[122]

The basic issue which the British government reviewed in mid-March, however, was one not of temporary expedients but of basic commitments. In the ten days from 15 to 24 March the question to be faced in London was whether or not to give a further commitment, public or private, to Czechoslovakia either directly or indirectly by promising to help France if that country went to war under her treaty obligations to Czechoslovakia. As one reads the extensive documentation on the policy debates within the British government in those days, certain conclusions emerge. The members of the government, with almost no exceptions, were doubtful that anything much could be done to save Czechoslovakia from being overrun by Germany, so that if it came to war, only an eventual victory after a long and costly conflict offered any hope for Czechoslovakia at all. This view appears to have been held but not expressed earlier; it was strongly reinforced by a report of the Chiefs of Staff Sub-Committee of the Committee of Imperial Defence which is dated 21 March 1938 but the tenor of which was clearly anticipated for several days by key figures in the cabinet and the Foreign Office.[123] Sir Maurice Hankey, who served as secretary of both the cabinet and the Committee of Imperial Defence summarized its "dominant conclusion" as being "that no pressure which this country and its possible allies could exercise would suffice to prevent the defeat of Czecho-Slovakia [*sic*]."[124]

The memorandum and the discussion of it in the cabinet explored in great detail the poor military conditions for the allies if any war began in 1938. Not only could they do nothing for the Czechs, but during the long war that was anticipated, the German air force was likely to concentrate on bombing England at a time when her antiaircraft preparations were deficient and the radar screen as yet incomplete, while the French army could take shelter in the Maginot Line. The emphasis of this report, the discussion of the military prospects, and the repeated references to Germany's ability to throttle Czechoslovakia by economic measures even without war all point to a focus of attention on the practical problems of implementing any commitment if it failed to deter Germany from aggression and did then lead to war.

This concern over the practical problems tied back into the basic one that a war with Germany, especially at a time when neither France nor

122. Ibid.; *B.D.*, 3d, 1, Nos. 63, 71, 79. The German press was forbidden to print this portion of Chamberlain's House of Commons speech ("Vertrauliche Bestellung vom 14.3.38," Bundesarchiv, Brammer, Z.Sg. 101/11, f.121).

123. A full copy of the report, C.O.S. 698, "Military Implications of German Aggression against Czechoslovakia" is in C 2038/1941/18, FO 371/21713; cf. *Harvey Diaries*, 17–24 March 1938, pp. 118–23.

124. British Cabinet 15 (38) of 22 March 1938, C 2040/1941/18, FO 371/21713.

England thought herself militarily prepared for it, would be a lengthy and difficult one. This placed the dilemma in its cruelest form: if Germany were deterred by a British warning, well and good, but if she were not, was this the occasion to challenge her? On this point not only the military difficulties mentioned but doubts concerning British public opinion and the likelihood that Canada and South Africa would stay out of such a war were raised as objections. The latter considerations grew, of course, out of a focus of interest on the question of the Sudeten Germans. There were those who argued—correctly as we now know—that this was purely a German pretext and that Germany's real aims not only went far beyond the Sudeten Germans when it came to Czechoslovakia but that she would utilize the domination of Czechoslovakia and Central Europe for a subsequent assault from a strengthened position on Britain and France. Both Chamberlain and Halifax considered this a real possibility. If they were unwilling to assume the inevitability of war at this time, it was because of a combination of factors: reluctance to give up all prospect of an agreement with Germany that might prevent another world war; a failure to perceive the possibility that German expansionism might include the desire to seize territory inhabited by non-Germans with the intention of expelling or exterminating them; a real uncertainty over the prospects of Britain and France in a war with Germany; and a belief that there was a genuine grievance on the part of the Sudeten Germans that should have been removed earlier and might still be removed by negotiations. All these combined with the hope that something of Czechoslovakia's independence might be salvaged to restrain both the prime minister and the foreign secretary from supporting any new commitment to France or Czechoslovakia and secured them the full support of the British cabinet on this position.

There was, on the other hand, also the confirmed view, shared by all in the government, that as a practical matter and regardless of commitments or treaties, Britain could not afford to see France defeated by Germany and would have to come to her assistance if hostilities were to break out on the continent. It therefore seemed best, and this was the form of compromise on which the members of the government could unite in good conscience, to temper their refusal of any new commitment—which might encourage Germany and discourage France—through a public repetition by the prime minister of a warning similar to that which Lord Halifax had given von Ribbentrop in private at the time of the *Anschluss*. On 24 March Chamberlain said in the House of Commons:

> Where peace and war are concerned, legal obligations are not alone involved, and, if war broke out, it would be unlikely to be confined to those who have assumed such obligations. It would be quite impossible to say where it might end and what Governments might become involved. The inexorable pressure of facts might well prove more powerful than formal pronouncements, and in that event it would be well

within the bounds of possibility that other countries . . . would almost immediately be involved. This is especially true in the case of two countries like Great Britain and France.[125]

The hope was that the refusal of new promises of support combined with a warning of possible British involvement in any war that might break out would serve to nudge the French in their urging concessions on Czechoslovakia by withholding the certainty of British aid, and nudge the Germans away from enforcing their demands through military aggression by reminding them of the real possibility of British involvement if war did come.[126] It was Chamberlain's expectation that the French would welcome rather than resent such a policy; he found it "difficult to believe . . . the French would not be glad to find some method to relieve them of their engagement,"[127] an assessment that proved to be as correct in 1938 as it would have been in 1939 when British policy had been reversed.

The evidence suggests that both Chamberlain and Halifax at first favored a British commitment, and if they came down on the negative side of the issue in 1938 but the positive side in 1939 the intervening experience of a demonstration *ad oculos* of Germany's willingness to annex non-German territory must be seen as one critical factor. In 1938 it was a fear voiced by many,[128] in 1939 it was a reality in the face of solemn pledges to the contrary. If the use of German minorities as a pretext was not recognized in March 1938 as it would be in March 1939 it was again the contrast between warnings of future prospects—voiced in the Foreign Office and cabinet—and the harsh reality of German action. The fundamental problem was whether to try to take a democracy into a world war over a possible danger—which might or might not be realized—or over a danger already demonstrated for all to see.[129] Sir Alexander Cadogan in his "Memorandum on the Situation Created by the German Absorption of

125. *B.D.*, 3d, 1:97. The British government informed the United States and the Dominions ahead of time that this declaration would be made; *U.S.*, 1938, 1:40; C 2017/1941/18, FO 371/21713. For earlier drafts of the statement, in part the result of a parliamentary question, see C 1969/1941/18, FO 371/21712. I cannot agree with Celovsky's description of this statement as sophistry (p. 173). The prior internal British discussions, as well as subsequent developments, show that the final formulation was carefully prepared, seriously believed to be meaningful, and intended to be taken as an accurate description of British policy in the face of the contingency of war. It is worth recording that the Czechoslovak minister to London understood the nature and import of Chamberlain's speech and, though generally a bitter critic of the prime minister, was satisfied with it (Král, *München*, No. 56).

126. Note the corresponding interpretation by the German chargé in London in *G.D.*, D, 2, No. 104.

127. See n.124.

128. Note Henderson's comments in his letter to Lord Halifax of 16 March 1938: "Hitler has achieved the crown of his life's ambitions. Will success intoxicate him or tranquillize him? That is now the question. Most people will probably believe the first. In any case we have now to consider how to secure, if we can, the security of Czechoslovakia" (Henderson Papers, FO 800/269).

129. For two useful French analyses of the British position, see *D.D.F.*, 2d, 8, No. 318; 9, No. 222.

Austria and the Possibility of German Action on Czechoslovakia" of 17 March 1938, phrased his view of the puzzle in these words: "On the whole, I certainly feel that it would be a very difficult decision to choose any course of action that might plunge Europe into war now to avert what may be a worse war later on."[130]

At the meeting of the cabinet Committee on Foreign Policy on 18 March, Chamberlain, when asked whether Germany was likely to be satisfied with the Sudeten area or really wanted to absorb all of Czechoslovakia, responded "that it might be rash to forecast what Germany would do, but at the same time the seizure of the whole of Czechoslovakia would not be in accordance with Herr Hitler's policy, which was to include all Germans in the Reich but not to include other nationalities."[131] On the following day, Lord Halifax wrote:

> While I do not think the wise man ought to shrink in his own mind from preparing himself for any exhibition of German power politics, yet I do not think also that it is necessary to assume that Hitler's racial ambitions are necessarily likely to expand into international power lust. It is really on this that the thought on one side of the arena now turns, namely that when Germany has done this and that and the other in Central Europe, she will in overwhelming might proceed to destroy France and ourselves. That is a conclusion which I do not believe myself to be necessarily well founded and, if you do not necessarily believe this, it makes you look jealously at the remedies that are immediately proposed to forestall it.[132]

These views may be contrasted with the one Lord Halifax would expound for the benefit of a fellow peer in the summer of 1939:

> Last year the German Government put forward the demand for the Sudetenland on purely racial grounds; but subsequent events proved that this demand was only put forward as a cover for the annihilation of Czechoslovakia. In view of this experience... it is not surprising that the Poles and we ourselves are afraid that the demand for Danzig is only a first move towards the destruction of Poland's independence.[133]

As the British government reviewed the danger to Czechoslovakia and to the peace of Europe after the *Anschluss,* it was their judgment that the proof of German intentions was not yet clear enough in reality as distinct from speculation.[134] Certainly military considerations played a major part

130. C 1866/132/18, FO 371/21674; cf. *Cadogan Diary,* p. 63.
131. 26th meeting of the British cabinet Committee on Foreign Policy, 18 March 1938, C 1932/132/18, FO 371/21674.
132. Halifax to Henderson, 19 March 1938 (responding to the letter quoted in n.128, above), Henderson Papers, FO 800/269.
133. Halifax to the Earl of Bessborough, 20 July 1939, Halifax Papers, FO 800/316.
134. There is some evidence to suggest that the Russian call on 17 March for a conference, discussed later, tended to restrain rather than encourage the British. It looked all too obviously like an effort on the part of the Soviet Union, which had no common border with either

in the decision, and internally there would be comments later that this had been the first time that military weakness had compelled the British government to abandon a course initially thought proper—a commitment to come to the defense of Czechoslovakia—and instead adopt a more cautious approach;[135] but the political considerations were, in my opinion, the determining ones. Rearmament would be pushed and staff conversations would be held with the French, but the diplomatic efforts of Great Britain would be exerted in favor of trying for a peaceful solution of what was perceived as a German-Czech quarrel over the Sudeten Germans in the hope that the settlement which in British eyes should have been reached much earlier might still be attained without war on the one hand and without the destruction of Czechoslovakia—which might be jointly guaranteed after a Sudeten settlement—on the other.[136] Having made their choice, the British now had to put their view to the Czechoslovak government, discuss their policy with France, and see how Germany would respond.

The British government's public announcement of 24 March did have a certain steadying effect as they had hoped, but the refusal to assume new formal commitments was received by the French with considerable disappointment. French Foreign Minister Paul-Boncour immediately took the line that only a firm warning to Germany could avoid war, a view that Lord Halifax did not share.[137] As the latter told the French ambassador: "I felt there was a great difference of approach in these matters by the French and English minds. They were disposed, perhaps, to rate more highly than ourselves the value of strong declarations; we were naturally reluctant to make strong declarations unless we were in fact assured of

---

Czechoslovakia or Germany, to embroil the Western Powers in a war with Germany. See the comment of Chamberlain quoted in Feiling, p. 347, and the fact that the mandate to examine the question of war given to the Chiefs of Staff Sub-Committee assumed the neutrality of the Soviet Union.

135. See text and commentary of Creswell's memorandum of 22 April 1938, "Relative Strengths of British and German Air Forces," C 5874/1425/18, FO 371/21710.

136. In addition to other documents cited, I have relied on the following sources: *B.D.*, 3d, 1, No. 86 (Foreign Office comments in R 2755/152/12, FO 371/22337); Henderson to Halifax, 16 March 1938, Henderson Papers, FO 800/269; Memorandum of Lord Halifax, "Possible Measures to Avert German Action in Czechoslovakia," 18 March 1938, C 1865/132/18, FO 371/21674; Hadow Memorandum of 18 March 1938, FO 371/22337, ff.267–68; 27th meeting of the British cabinet Committee on Foreign Policy, 21 March 1938, C 2039/1941/18, FO 371/21713 (note that it was at this time that Lord Halifax circulated the historical memorandum on the borders of Czechoslovakia cited in n.20, above); Duff Cooper, p. 218; *Ironside Diaries*, pp. 53–54; Roskill, *Hankey*, 3:314; *D.D.F.*, 2d, 8, No. 480; 9, Nos. 3, 12; *Australian Documents*, Nos. 143, 149–58, 160–63; *Hungarian Documents*, 1, Nos. 436, 437.

It could be argued that a British intimation to Prague that extensive concessions to the Sudeten Germans would lead to a British guarantee might have produced such concessions by offering the Czechoslovak government some security against the risks attendant upon that course. The absence of any indication of new initiatives by Prague after the May Crisis, on the other hand, suggests that any such British step would have made little difference.

137. The British information for the French is in *B.D.*, 3d, 1, Nos. 106–9; Paul-Boncour's response, ibid., No. 112. But see also *D.D.F.*, 2d, 9, Nos. 42, 45.

being able to implement them should the need arise.''[138] It was this difference of view that would become a subject of discussion when he
leaders of the French government, by then Edouard Daladier and Georges
Bonnet as successors to Blum and Paul-Boncour, went to London at the
end of April to work out a coordinated approach on the Czechoslovak
question with the British. The meeting was to have been held earlier but
had been postponed because of another change in the French government; contemplated in mid-March for one French cabinet, it was held on
28 and 29 April with another.

In the interim, the French had worried considerably about the problem
of British support, fearful that its absence would encourage Germany and
undermine the credibility of their own assurances of loyalty to the alliance
with Czechoslovakia. Bonnet himself had told the American chargé before
becoming foreign minister that he believed that without a promise of
support it would not be possible. for France to come to the aid of
Czechoslovakia, and that this was the privately held opinion of the
Blum government, even though its members, like himself, had to affirm
the opposite in public.[139] If this was a correct assessment—and there is
considerable evidence that it was—the show of French confidence after
the 24 March statement that the British would come in on the side of
France in spite of the refusal of England to make a formal promise to this
effect, can only be interpreted as a device to "smoke out" British policy.
The subsequent clarification from London, underlining the indefinite nature of the British commitment and warning against reading into it an
unwarranted certainty that might retard the French in joining in the process of applying pressure for concessions on Prague, would have been
secretly welcomed rather than resented in Paris.[140] Certainly nothing the
British learned in the interval between the 24 March announcement in
Parliament and the meeting with the French five weeks later led them to
change their decision.

At the end of March, disquieting reports on the advance of German and
the lagging of British aircraft production upset the Committee of Imperial
Defence, and the subject was taken to the cabinet for discussion.[141] There

138. *B.D.*, 3d, 1, No. 109.
139. *U.S.*, 1938, 1:39–40; cf. 1936/132/18, FO 371/21674; *Hungarian Documents*, 2, No.
141.
140. C 2186/1941/18, FO 371/21713; *B.D.*, 3d, 1, Nos. 135, 138, 139.
141. C 3028/1425/18, FO 371/21710; cf. Charles A. Lindbergh, *The Wartime Journals of
Charles A. Lindbergh* (New York: Harcourt, Brace, Jovanovich, 1970), 2 and 27 April 1938,
pp. 11, 22. Note, however, the British Air Ministry's refusal to credit the performance of the
new German ME 109 fighter and to inform the cabinet in spite of Foreign Office prodding (C
1774/1425/18, FO 371/21710). A subsequent Foreign Office memorandum on the comparison
of air force strength underlined the devastating nature of the British situation. The new
permanent undersecretary, Sir Alexander Cadogan, quoted in his comments those of his
predecessor, Sir Robert Vansittart, that "for the first time within memory we have been
driven from our political course [on the question of Czechoslovakia] by sheer national
helplessness," and while suggesting that new diplomatic efforts should be made, fully agreed
with this description of the situation. See n.135, above; cf. *D.D.F.*, 2d, 9, No. 131.

the line to be taken with the French was approved, especially the concept of continued pressure on Czechoslovakia, which Lord Halifax thought was producing some real results.[142] In these days there were conflicting currents of advice. The Foreign Office was skeptical of suggestions that Czechoslovakia be urged to give up her ties to France and the Soviet Union;[143] Sir Nevile Henderson expressed the hope that Germany might calm down if the Sudeten issue were settled;[144] and earlier advocates of concessions to Germany like Lord Lothian were increasingly skeptical of the wisdom of continuing such a policy.[145] On the other hand, there was emphasis on the need to take the grievances of the Sudeten Germans seriously,[146] while the Canadian prime minister reinforced the belief that he favored concessions to avoid the danger of war.[147] Contradictory opinions were sometimes voiced by the same person: when Carl Goerdeler, one of the leading German opponents of Hitler, was in London at the beginning of April, he argued both that the British government should be clear and firm—and that the Sudeten area should be transferred to Germany.[148]

The efforts made by the Czechoslovak government in the weeks after the *Anschluss* to move toward a reconciliation with the Sudeten German party only accentuated the contradictory considerations before the British government. London was impressed by the slowness and lateness of the attempt as well as the resistance within Czechoslovak political circles.[149] There was dismay over the obduracy of the Sudeten German party in the negotiations;[150] suspicion that Henlein had been instructed from Berlin to raise impossible demands until Germany could annex the Sudeten area, create a vassal Czech duchy centered on Prague, and divide most of Slovakia between Poland and Hungary;[151] and the beginning of consid-

---

142. Cabinet 18 (38) of 6 April 1938, C 2664/1941/18, FO 371/21714. The effort that the Foreign Secretary thought was making progress came through informal contacts between Sir Samuel Hoare and Jan Masaryk which the latter utilized in pushing for concessions while in Prague at the beginning of April (Hoare, pp. 293ff.; *B.D.*, 3d, 1, Nos. 122, 124).

143. *B.D.*, 3d, 1, No. 134; comments in C 2989/1941/18, FO 371/21715.

144. *B.D.*, 3d, 1, No. 121; C 2777/1941/18, FO 371/21715; Henderson to Lothian, 22 April 1938, Lothian Papers, GD 40/17/396–98.

145. Lothian to the Aga Khan, 31 March, and to Henderson, 14 April 1938, Lothian Papers, GD 40/17/352/8 and GD 40/17/362/394–95.

146. C 3865/1941/18, FO 371/21717.

147. Feiling, p. 349.

148. Colvin, *None So Blind*, pp. 205–6; C 3448/541/18, FO 371/21702.

149. This is best pursued in the published British documents, *B.D.*, 3d, 1, Nos. 97–161, passim; cf. Král, *München*, Nos. 48, 50, 58, 62, 63 (excerpts in Berber, p. 107); *Cadogan Diary*, 5 April 1938, p. 67; *Harvey Diaries*, 1 April 1938, pp. 125–26. Note the comment of Kvaček (p. 215) on the poor tactics of the Czechoslovak government.

150. C 2774/1941/18, FO 371/21715.

151. See Creswell's comment on Newton's dispatch 119 of 20 April 1938 forwarding a record of a meeting between Henlein and Captain Victor Cazalet, M.P., on 19 April, C 3316/1941/18, FO 371/21716.

eration that a "neutral" British intermediary be sent to the scene.[152] Henderson's view that a settlement of the Sudeten issue on the basis of self-determination was the best way to restart the Anglo-German negotiations and need not imply the destruction of Czechoslovakia met with extreme skepticism.[153] On the other hand, the unfavorable reports on relative military strength suggested that this was a very poor time to run the risk of war. Chamberlain's speech in Birmingham on 8 April made in public a point he would repeat almost verbatim to the French three weeks later, that a warning to Germany was a gamble, not with money but with lives, and that he would not give the word to face "the stern necessity for war" unless he were "absolutely convinced that in no other way could we preserve our liberty."[154]

There was no realistic prospect that such perspectives would be changed by the proposal made by the Soviet Union on 17 March calling for international cooperative action against aggression and offering to participate in collective actions, explicitly referring to Czechoslovakia as the immediately menaced country. The Soviet Union was bound by treaty to assist Czechoslovakia if that country were attacked and already assisted by France. When asked by correspondents how the Soviet Union would implement any policy of support for Czechoslovakia, Foreign Commissar Maxim Litvinov responded to the effect that a way would be found, some sort of corridor would be used.[155] This last point, of course, went to the heart of the matter: having no common border with Czechoslovakia or Germany, the Soviet Union could neither assist the former nor attack the latter without the agreement of Poland—which was inconceivable—or Rumania. The latter contingency was almost as difficult both in theory and practice; in theory because the Soviet Union herself would not recognize the borders of Rumania and was suspected by that power, correctly as is now known, of having designs on portions of Rumania,[156] in practice because the actual system of communication and transportation that would have had to be utilized for any Soviet assistance to Czechoslovakia via Rumania was so complicated and primitive as to be

152. See the comments by Sargent (30 April), Cadogan (3 May), Halifax (3 May), and Vansittart (5 May) on the same document.

153. Henderson to Halifax, 21 April 1938, C 3445/1941/18, FO 371/21716. See also the comment's on Henderson's letter of 20 April (B.D., 3d, 1, No. 152) in A 4384/55/45, FO 371/21521.

154. Neville Chamberlain, The Struggle for Peace (London: Hutchinson, 1939), p. 171. In the meeting of 29 April, Chamberlain added to this comment on the gamble with lives rather than money the further one, which for obvious reasons he preferred not to state publicly, that it was necessary to consider whether Britain and France "were sufficiently powerful to make victory certain. Frankly, he did not think we were" (B.D., 3d, 1:221).

155. There is a good account in Celovsky, pp. 176–81. Only sources not listed in his footnotes will be cited here. See Hungarian Documents, 1, No. 449; 2, No. 131; New Documents on the History of Munich, Nos. 5, 9.

156. The possibility of Soviet recognition of Rumania's possession of Bessarabia in exchange for the right to move troops across Rumania to assist Czechoslovakia was discussed in the spring of 1938, but nothing came of it (D.D.F., 2d, 9, Nos. 112, 199).

almost useless.[157] These obstacles, which were as well known to the Soviets as to the Rumanians, may well have had something to do with the failure of the Russian government even to ask the Rumanians for permission for transit to assist Czechoslovakia, which was, after all, the Little Entente ally of Rumania.[158]

It is, however, most unlikely that anything would have come of such a request, had it been made. The Rumanian government was far too afraid of Germany to make any commitment prior to the outbreak of war—in the event of which they would first see whether anyone else came to Czechoslovakia's aid. On 9 May the Rumanian foreign minister told Bonnet that even recognition of the existing Rumanian-Russian border would not purchase a transit agreement; his simultaneous promise to be on the side of France in a war involving the latter left open the possibility of a later change in this policy but hardly provided any basis for serious contingency planning.[159]

Certainly few at the time anticipated that the Soviet government coveted a piece of Czechoslovakia and would proceed to annex it just as soon as a common Russian-Czechoslovak border, which did not exist in 1938, came into being at the end of World War II. In any assessment of Soviet foreign policy in the era of Joseph Stalin, however, one cannot simply ignore the fact that the two countries of East Central Europe with which the Soviet Union ever had good relations during the interwar years were Lithuania and Czechoslovakia, the two with which she had no common boundary; and that as soon as this fact changed, Stalin arranged for the annexation of all of one and part of the other into the U.S.S.R.[160] If the Soviet Union had an interest in Czechoslovakia in 1938 it was not in the territorial integrity of that country but rather in its role as a possible barrier to the expansion of Germany, unless the latter were involved in a war with the Western Powers. If that happened, the resulting war could only weaken any potential enemies of the Soviet Union without substantial involvement or danger to herself and regardless of the fate of Czechoslovakia.

Litvinov appears to have expected little from his proposal; he thought that the French had no confidence in the Soviet Union just as the latter

157. Prague had promised financial assistance for improvements Rumania was to make in the railway connecting the U.S.S.R. with Czechoslovakia, but little actual work had been done (ibid., Nos. 57, 199).

158. Note, e.g., the comment of the Russian chargé in Berlin cited in *U.S.*, 1938, 1:492. See also Krofta to Koreč (Bucharest), 8 April 1938, Czechoslovak document in T-120, 1039/1809/412305–6.

159. *D.D.F.*, 2d, 9, No. 306; see also ibid., Nos. 225, 467.

160. It should be noted that Soviet inability to translate her good relations with Lithuania into support for that country at the time of the Polish-Lithuanian crisis of March 1938 was hardly a sign of strength that might reassure Czechoslovakia, which was also on the other side of Poland from the Soviet Union; note Král, *München*, No. 51, and the report of Dr. Krno on a conversation with the Lithuanian minister on 22 June 1938, Czechoslovak document in T-120, 1040/1809/412737–38. There is a good defense of Soviet policy in this crisis in *D.D.F.*, 2d, 10, No. 110.

had no confidence in France, and thought it likely that the Czechs would cave in.[161] He expected Italy to turn away from Germany as she had abandoned her allies in World War I; and he responded to detailed questions from the Hungarian minister about the intent of his 17 March proposal to the effect that he had only wanted to sound things out, had expected little, had no great hopes for a favorable British response, had had no specific plan in mind, but had been primarily concerned to absolve the Soviet Union of any responsibility.[162] These comments, made on 23 March when the negative response of the British as well as others was already evident, if not yet officially communicated, might be taken as a form of "sour grapes." There is, however, another way to interpret his comments, namely, that he really had expected little, did want a cheap alibi, but would have been quite happy to be pleasantly surprised by a greater willingness of Britain to assume new commitments in Europe.[163] He could hardly be expected to anticipate that, as the following year showed, any such willingness of London to commit herself in Central or Eastern Europe would cost him his own position.[164]

The basic approach of the British and French governments was coordinated at their meeting in London on 28 and 29 April. In their preparations, the French expected a review of the Spanish situation, consideration of the relations of England and France with Italy, and an extensive discussion of Czechoslovakia. They correctly anticipated that the possibility of a general settlement with Germany—which had been a key subject of the

161. Litvinov's comments to Davies, the U.S. ambassador (Davies, p. 290; *U.S.*, 1938, 1:41–42) are in part the basis of the long and thoughtful letter Davies wrote to Marvin H. McIntyre, the secretary to the president, on 4 April, stressing that the Soviet Union was not that concerned about its isolation and asserting that if things in Europe did not work out as Chamberlain hoped, the day would come when the democracies would be glad of Russian help in spite of that country's "terrible tyranny over the human spirit and human life" (Hyde Park, P.P.F. 1381).
162. *Hungarian Documents*, 1, No. 450 (German text in Kerekes, No. 15); cf. Král, *München*, No. 49.
163. The official negative response of the British government was communicated on 24 March (*B.D.*, 3d, 1, No. 116). Note Halifax's comments to the French ambassador and the latter's similar views on 22 March (ibid., No. 109). Cf. *Hungarian Documents*, 1, No. 430. On the Soviet position, see also Celovsky, pp. 203–8.
It is very difficult to estimate the influence that Soviet Ambassador Maisky's vehemently anti-Chamberlain attitude had on assessments in Moscow; see *D.D.F.*, 2d, 8, No. 254, and, for 1939, *Soviet Documents* (hereafter cited as *S.U.*), Nos. 217, 218, 284, 301. See also his memoirs, Ivan M. Maisky, *Who Helped Hitler?* (London: Hutchinson, 1964).
164. For a summary listing sources for the general belief at the time that the Soviet Union would not move militarily except in self-defense, see Braddick, p. 12, n.73. For a number of differing French assessments of Soviet military power at this time, see *D.D.F.*, 2d, 8, No. 361; 9, Nos. 192, 228. Note the concern in the British Foreign Office in May 1938 over the *Times* stories about the Comintern which pictured the Soviet as greater than the German and Italian danger; like the spectacular "leader" on Czechoslovakia of 7 September, this opinion was an initiative of Geoffrey Dawson, objected to rather than sponsored by the Chamberlain government; N 2197, N 2495/97/38, FO 371/22288.

last such British-French meeting, that of November 1937—would hardly come up.[165]

It was a measure of the change in the international situation caused by the German rejection of the British approach to Berlin and by the *Anschluss* that what had only recently been viewed as the major topic for immediate consideration was now perceived as indefinitely postponed.[166] In their own preparations for the meeting, the British Foreign Office had written up a review of the developments on the colonial question since the Anglo-French meeting of 29–30 November;[167] the London cabinet, however, drew from recent developments the conclusion for future relations with Germany that they were "anxious to pursue the interrupted negotiations but that the present moment did not appear opportune."[168] The emphasis of this meeting as contrasted with the preceding one would be on whether and how to fight Germany rather than on how to come to a general settlement with her.[169]

French Prime Minister Daladier had asked Gamelin for a statement of the steps France could take militarily against Germany in favor of Czechoslovakia. Gamelin's written response adds up to practically nothing and is hedged about with such qualifications as to offer little hope.[170] The line Daladier would take in the London conversations was, accordingly, one of attempting to intimidate and restrain Germany by threats rather than any project of concrete military action. The British had been discussing the idea of themselves urging Czechoslovakia to make the utmost possible concessions and securing the support of the French in urging Prague to an accommodation. They were also considering informing the Germans of these measures in the hope of getting Berlin to be

165. *U.S.*, 1938, 1:44–46. French memoranda prepared in anticipation of the talks are in *D.D.F.*, 2d, 9, Nos. 231, 237, 239, 246, and the memorandum on the Cameroons cited in the next note. It was also at this time, in part as preparation for the meeting, that Léon Noël, the former French minister in Prague, then accredited to Warsaw, traveled in Czechoslovakia to prepare a report on the situation for his government (ibid., No. 256; Noël, *L'aggression allemande contre la Pologne* [Paris: Flammarion, 1946], pp. 198–202). Before the fall of the Blum government, Foreign Minister Paul-Boncour had summoned the French ambassadors in Moscow and Warsaw and the ministers in Prague and Bucharest to canvass the situation (*D.D.F.*, 2d, 9, No. 112).

166. It is indicative of the reversal of the diplomatic priorities that the U.S. chargé in Paris would repeatedly ask about the topic when none of the French officials mentioned it, only to be told each time that nothing was in prospect (Wilson's tels. 656, 658, and 694 in *U.S.*, 1938, 1:44–53). The French memorandum on the Cameroons (*D.D.F.*, 2d, 9, No. 229) was clearly prepared with a view to the possibility of the return of that colony to Germany being discussed in London. For prior British-French contacts on this question on 12 March, suggesting that there was now no prospect of a colonial settlement, see ibid., 8, No. 407; cf. ibid., No. 35, pp. 68–69, and No. 53.

167. C 3775/184/18, FO 371/21680.

168. Cabinet 21 (38) of 27 April 1938, C 3641/42/18, FO 371/21657.

169. Note the pessimistic tone of the French general staff preparations and notes; *D.D.F.*, 2d, 9, Nos. 230, 237.

170. The text is in his memoirs (2:318–19); see above n.117, also *D.D.F.*, 2d, 9, No. 238.

patient for a while as the Czechoslovak authorities tried to develop a new approach to the Sudeten question.[171] What the British did not understand, of course, was that this procedure fitted in perfectly with Hitler's own preference for the immediate future. It was important to him that the exuberance induced among the Sudeten Germans by the *Anschluss* be dampened a bit for now so that pressure could be built up over time. Precipitate action so soon after the *Anschluss* might bring on the general war Hitler wanted to avoid, while a slow but steadily increased drumbeat of propaganda and pressure, with all world attention centered on the real and imagined grievances of the Sudeten Germans, could lead up to a crisis in which quick and drastic German action against Czechoslovakia might be successfully isolated.[172]

If the British were developing this approach for the meeting with the French, it was in part because their earlier doubts about French military strength and the prospects of effective assistance for Czechoslovakia were being reinforced by the comments of Daladier and Gamelin to the British secretary of state for war in the very days of April that Henlein was moving publicly from a moderate line to the demands, previously concerted with Berlin, of his speech at Karlovy Vary on 24 April.[173] That speech and the attendant publicity served in an almost ideal fashion to focus interest on the Sudeten—as opposed to the Czech—question as the British cabinet discussed and approved on 27 April the line Chamberlain and Halifax were to take with the French.[174]

The British would ask the French to join in pressure on Czechoslovakia for concessions. If it came to war, there would be a long struggle and "even after a long war, it would be very difficult to re-establish Czechoslovakia in her old position." Germany should not be allowed to think she could do anything she liked; Beneš could not be left with the thought that he need make no great effort; and Britain and France should push for concessions without sponsoring any specific Czechoslovak proposals.

171. 29th meeting of the cabinet Committee on Foreign Policy, 7 April 1938, C 2770/1941/18, FO 371/21715; cf. *Hungarian Documents,* 2, No. 148; *G.D.,* D, 1, No. 750; *U.S.,* 1938, 1:486–87.

172. See the discussion of the Hitler-Keitel meeting of 20 April on pp. 337–39, above.

173. It was on his return from this trip that Hore-Belisha at a luncheon of the American Correspondents' Association in London on 27 April said that he expected Germany to take over all of Central Europe and parts of the Balkans and then attack England and France. He expressed the view that France would not honor her obligations to Czechoslovakia and that Italy (which he had just visited on the same trip) would in the end side with the Western Powers rather than Germany. London manager of the United Press to the UP vice-president for South America, 28 April 1938, attached to Weddell (Buenos Aires) to Hull, 7 June 1938, Cordell Hull Papers, folder 106. The Czechoslovak minister in London reported on this luncheon on the same day, Král, *München,* No. 66 (excerpt in Berber, p. 108).

On Henlein's speech, see "Bestellungen aus der Pressekonferenz," 23 and 25 April 1938, Bundesarchiv, Brammer, Z.Sg. 101/11, ff.311, 313; Král, *München,* Nos. 64, 69. British advice to him C 3510/1941/18, FO 371/21716.

174. On the British cabinet meeting 21 (38) of 27 April 1938, see C 3642/1941/18, FO 371/21716; C 4049/1941/18, FO 371/21718; C 3561/37/18, FO 371/21653. Cf. *Harvey Diaries,* 25–27 April 1938, pp. 132–33.

Some middle way was to be found between what the Germans wanted and what Prague was offering; the Germans would thereby avoid the risk of a European war and the Czechs save at least something of their independence. As for the French, they would be told that the British would make their main contribution if it came to war in the air and at sea. No land expeditionary force could be promised; but if one were sent, it could not exceed two divisions at the beginning of hostilities. On the assumption that this last was not a binding commitment, Anglo-French staff conversations about their possible deployment could be undertaken. The lengthy canvassing of this last topic, its obvious sensitivity, and the decision to inform the Germans and Italians of such staff talks if they did take place can be understood only in the context of the lengthy discussion in public and in print about the real or imagined role of Anglo-French military contacts in committing England to one side in the diplomatic background of World War I.[175] Hitler's suggestion to Henlein that he ask for separate regiments with German as the language of command in the Czechoslovak army reflects his memory of the great internal crisis of the Dual Monarchy in the years before the war and his desire that Henlein use that demand to obstruct any negotiated settlement of the Sudeten question; the willingness of the British government to brave the reopening of the staff talks controversy shows that there was a recognition, reluctant to be sure, that war was a real possibility.[176]

At the Anglo-French meeting of 28–29 April the two governments discussed the issues of the moment and eventually agreed upon a policy to which they adhered during the subsequent months.[177] After considerable argument over details, there was agreement on the subject of air, naval, and army staff talks; it was understood that the Germans and Italians would be informed of these. It was recognized by the French that the British promise to send two divisions to the continent in the first two weeks of war was on the one hand not a firm commitment but purely a possibility to be considered in staff planning but decided only by the

175. The most comprehensive treatment of prewar staff contacts is Samuel R. Williamson, *The Politics of Grand Strategy: Britain and France Prepare for War, 1904–1914* (Cambridge, Mass.: Harvard University Press, 1969). For some historical comparisons by Churchill, see Král, *München*, No. 61. On Chamberlain and Halifax "disregarding the views of many of their colleagues" in agreeing to staff conversations, see Duff Cooper, p. 220, whose comments are particularly interesting since he was a critic of the prime minister.

176. Note, however, Cardinal Pacelli's comment, cited in a 22 April 1938 statement of the Hungarian minister to the Vatican, that he expected the allies of Czechoslovakia to abandon her; because of the general fear of war, they would accept a *fait accompli* (*Hungarian Documents*, 2, No. 157).

177. The discussion is based mainly on the published British record of the meeting in *B.D.*, 3d, 1, No. 164, and the French record in *D.D.F.*, 2d, 9, No. 258. The two records are essentially identical, though the editors of the British series have deferred publication of the discussion of some issues other than Czechoslovakia to another volume. See also *Hungarian Documents*, 2, Nos. 162, 166; *U.S.*, 1938, 1:489–91, 47–53; *G.D.*, D, 1, No. 757; *Cadogan Diary*, 28 and 29 April 1938, pp. 71–74; *Harvey Diaries*, 28 April 1938, pp. 133–34 (parts of this entry were certainly written on the 29th or 30th).

British government of the day, while on the other hand it was, of course, entirely possible that in case of war larger forces would subsequently be sent.[178] There was, moreover, a recognition of the fact that the supplies from the United States which had been so important an element in sustaining the military effort of the Entente in the World War could not be taken for granted in any future war because of the American neutrality legislation; but both countries would nevertheless continue their attempts to hasten the buildup of their respective air forces by purchases in America.[179]

The critical question was that of Czechoslovakia. Here the approaches were at least superficially different. The French, who were committed to Czechoslovakia by treaty, argued that a strong and explicit promise of Britain and France to defend Czechoslovakia against aggression would rally the dubious countries like Yugoslavia and Rumania and perhaps even Poland and would thus offer the best hope of forestalling a war, a war which would surely come sometime under even worse conditions if the Germans were not told to stop now but were instead permitted to destroy the Czechoslovak state—their real aim—and to gain control of the resources of Southeast Europe. On the specifics of a war over Czechoslovakia if it did come in spite of hopes and expectations to the contrary, Daladier was optimistic but not very explicit. He praised the Czechoslovak army, spoke of the strength of the Soviet air force, but mentioned no French plan to assist the Czechs. Here was the crux of the situation, for Daladier advocated in 1938 the policy Chamberlain would adopt in 1939. With no plan to defeat Germany in war, or even to inflict serious damage on her while she destroyed Czechoslovakia, Daladier "could only profess his profound conviction that . . . war could only be avoided if Great Britain and France made their determination quite clear to maintain the peace of Europe by respecting the liberties and the rights of independent peoples."[180]

Chamberlain was not yet ready for what he described as a bluff: "Whatever the odds might be in favor of peace or war, it was not money but men with which we were gambling."[181] The military prospects looked grim indeed, and even if Britain and France did win a war, a subject on which he confessed to having some doubt, it would be a long war; and even then there would remain the question of whether it would "in fact be

178. Note Gamelin's comment at the meeting of the French Permanent Committee of National Defence of 8 December 1937 that he expected at first two and later four British divisions on the continent; the French leaders were, therefore, not surprised (*D.D.F.*, 2d, 7, No. 325); cf. ibid., 9, No. 230). Material on 1938 staff contacts, ibid., Nos. 444, 476, 484; see also No. 508.
179. In this connection, the influence of the World War experience on the thinking of those at the meeting is especially obvious; among other things, Daladier talked at length about the role of the Fokker planes built in the Netherlands during the war.
180. *B.D.*, 3d, 1:217; cf. *D.D.F.*, 2d, 9:579.
181. *B.D.*, 3d, 1:221.

possible to re-establish the Czechoslovak State on its present basis."[182] Since Chamberlain still thought that the German government, and Hitler in particular, were not committed to the total destruction of Czechoslovakia, he was suggesting that the main question was to save something for the Czechs, especially the existence of a Czechoslovak state.[183] To fight a war to keep the Sudetenland within Czechoslovakia hardly looked like a viable risk, especially if, as Chamberlain implied very strongly, you were unlikely to leave the Sudetenland inside Czechoslovakia after winning a war over Germany. War could be contemplated only if there really appeared to be no alternative at all.

The compromise which was drawn out of this difference of approach superficially resembles the British more than the French point of view. There would be renewed pressure on Prague to make the utmost concessions to the Sudeten Germans. Berlin would at the appropriate moment be informed by the London government of the efforts being made to settle the Sudeten German question peacefully. If the Germans seemed inclined to go beyond all reasonable bounds, however, the British government would give them as a formal and direct warning the statement of Chamberlain in the House of Commons to the effect that if Germany marched, France would honor her obligations to Czechoslovakia, and, in the ensuing war, Germany should not count on England's staying out. Berlin could thus either accept a reasonable compromise or run the risk of a general war, a general war which would then clearly grow not out of the problem of the Sudeten Germans but out of Germany's determination to destroy Czechoslovakia.[184]

If this procedure appeared to be closer to the British than the French position at the beginning of the talks, there are good reasons for believing that the French were pleased rather than disappointed by the outcome.[185] The French leaders expressed themselves as most satisfied with the meeting; they had to avow loyalty to their alliance in public while hoping

182. Ibid., p. 214.

183. In this connection, the comment of the Polish ambassador to France on Bonnet's statement that the annexation of the whole of Czechoslovakia by Germany would endanger Poland, is worth quoting: "I replied that in my opinion it was absolutely unreasonable to presume that in the twentieth century, after a great war, a result of which was the triumph of the national principle, any state, even one stronger than Germany, could annex territories inhabited by other nations against their will" (*Łukasiewicz Papers*, p. 96).

184. This policy was approved at the British Cabinet 22 (38) of 4 May 1938, C 4051/1941/18, FO 371/21718. It was explained in special detail to the prime minister of the Union of South Africa, who had complained about the British concessions to the French in almost hysterical terms on 5 May and had warned that the Union would not go to war on Britain's side under the circumstances (C 3928/1941/18, FO 371/21718; cf. C 6756/42/18, FO 371/21657).

185. A good exposition of this in Celovsky, pp. 188–90. Much of the available evidence has been cited there; I cannot, however, agree with Celovsky's view that the result of the meeting was a complete abandonment of Czechoslovakia. The threat of war against a German attack on Czechoslovakia as opposed to acting on the Sudeten issue was real—and it would in the end deter Germany in 1938. See also *Łukasiewicz Papers*, pp. 71–77.

that concessions from Prague would free them from the need to carry it out. But if the need did arise, prior diplomatic negotiations would have so redefined the issues as to assure them with almost complete certainty of the support from Great Britain which they believed necessary in war. The fact that the public show of determination which they had originally requested had been refused would, under these circumstances, make it more likely that Czechoslovakia would indeed offer concessions extensive enough to avert a conflict. If there was an element of dishonesty in the position of the French government, it was not so much in their accepting, and very willingly at that, the British position in the hope of evading treaty commitments they preferred not to implement, but rather in their unwillingness in the subsequent weeks to be as honest with their Czechoslovak allies as the latter had a right to expect.[186] A carefully phrased communication secretly conveyed to Beneš in early May instead of late July could have alerted him to take in the summer of 1938 the kind of steps he was ready to take in the fall. Only such a procedure might have shifted the initiative to Prague and then left the question of Germany's real aims answered in public rather than debated in private.[187] Instead of such a warning, the Czechs by a supreme irony would receive an exactly contrary impression when the May Crisis interrupted the diplomatic implementation of the procedure agreed to at the allied meeting. By calling forth the warning from England agreed to at the London talks for the contingency of a presumed imminent German attack, the crisis would leave the Czechoslovak government with a completely false impression of the situation.

In the weeks after the Anglo-French discussions, the two powers began to implement the policy on which they had agreed. They urged concessions to the Sudeten German party on Prague, while the British informed the German government of the effort being made. The British attempted to draw out the Germans as to the terms they thought appropriate, keeping in reserve the implied threat of war that had been decided upon in the London talks. Since Hitler had already set the policy of constant escalation of demands to preclude agreement, there could be no answer from Berlin to the request for specifics; any answer would have

186. Alexis Léger's urging speed on the Czechoslovak minister in Paris just *before* the London meeting was phrased in terms of internal French political considerations (Král, *München*, No. 63, excerpts in Berber, p. 107). The comments of Lacroix to Hodža on 22 March and to Beneš on 11 April (*D.D.F.*, 2d, 9, Nos. 26, 157) were certainly very different from those of 1937, but hardly particularly explicit.

187. The British minister did repeat to the Czechoslovak foreign minister the British view that the military prospects in a war were poor: Czechoslovakia would be overrun, there would be a long war, and at the end it was by no means sure that Czechoslovakia would be restored to her former borders; but this did not impress the Czechoslovak government enough to budge them (*B.D.*, 3d, 1, No. 195; Krofta's record is in T-120, 1039/1809/412188–94).

risked setting finite limits to what was expected of Prague. Instead, the Germans simply suggested that the demands voiced by Henlein in his Karlovy Vary speech would be a good place to start.

Some proposals of Prague which had been transmitted to Paris and London just before the April conference were considered quite inadequate there, and in the weeks immediately after that meeting, there were at first no signs that the Czechoslovak government was prepared to move in any way sufficiently dramatic to make a major impact on the situation within the country or on the attitude of the Western capitals.[188] The great dangers in this appearance of stubbornness were brought home to the Czechoslovak leaders by an urgent warning from Paris and a public report on the views of the British prime minister. The warning from Paris came from the long-time Czechoslovak minister there who reported that Sir Nevile Henderson was convinced of the sincerity of the Germans and was so reporting to London and that the reports of the French ambassador to Berlin about the situation were extremely upsetting for the French premier and foreign minister. He warned the Czechoslovak president, prime minister, and foreign minister of the absolute necessity for prompt action so that the French would not get the impression that the Czechs were postponing a settlement with the Sudeten Germans because they did not want such a settlement and preferred war.[189]

Although reaching the Czechoslovak authorities through newspaper stories rather than diplomatic dispatches, the warning from Britain was in some ways even more dramatic. Speaking to American newspaper correspondents on 10 May, the British prime minister took for "background information" an even more conciliatory line than he and Lord Halifax had come to advocate in the cabinet. He did not believe that France would take any military action to save Czechoslovakia, nor would Great Britain. As for the Sudeten German question, he said that since the cantonal system (on the Swiss model) would be very difficult to apply because of the Sudeten settlements being in a long, thin fringe along the frontier, the solution might be to move the frontier. If war did develop over Czechoslovakia and the allies defeated Germany, the Czechoslovak state would

188. Here and throughout the balance of this chapter, the tedious diplomatic steps which have been explained by many authors will not be retraced. The accounts of Celovsky, Eubank, Wheeler-Bennet, and Laffan cover the issues. For internal British discussion of these moves, see C 3837/1941/18, FO 371/21717; R 4494/1737/67, FO 371/22348. See also *Hungarian Documents*, 2, Nos. 189, 190, 194, 204; Král, *Die Deutschen*, Nos. 108, 112; Král, *München*, Nos. 73, 78; Mastný telegram, 18 May 1938, Czechoslovak document in T-120, 1039/1809/412150–51.

189. Osuský telegram of 14 May 1938, Czechoslovak document in T-120, 1039/1809/412013–15 (parts in Berber, pp. 108–9). The Czechoslovak foreign minister was sufficiently alarmed to respond the same day with instructions to reply with a denial to Daladier, ibid., frames 412341–42; Král, *München*, No. 74. Because of the fragmentary state of the surviving French record, there is some uncertainty about the reports of François-Poncet referred to. It is possible that *D.D.F.*, 2d, 9, Nos. 273 and 338 belong in this category.

still not be re-created along its present lines.[190] When stories about this gathering and Chamberlain's comments appeared in the newspapers, questions were raised in Parliament; and the prime minister refused to issue a denial. It is difficult to believe that Chamberlain would give a briefing of this sort to correspondents at Cliveden, the Astor country home, and not anticipate that his startling comments would come out in some form. Certainly his refusal to deny such views in the House of Commons, even if the whole episode was not so intended, must be seen as a form of pressure on Czechoslovakia to make the utmost concessions to the Sudeten Germans.

The British inclination in this direction was, if anything, strengthened further in those days by four factors. In the first place, the Czechoslovak minister in London had told Lord Halifax on 2 May that he thought Beneš "not only now fully realized the need of going to the very limit of reconciliation as regards the Sudeten but was even in fact prepared for a 'Swiss solution.'"[191] The belief that there was a real possibility of a Czechoslovak offer that would dramatically change the situation certainly provided an incentive for the London government to feel that a hard push from Britain and France might lead to such an offer's actually being made.[192] A second element of reinforcement came from a report of the British military attaché in Berlin of 9 May which expressed itself in very dubious terms about the ability of the Czechoslovak army to hold up a German invasion for any length of time.[193] Comments on this document made within the Foreign Office indicate that the negative assessment was

190. London manager of United Press to the UP vice-president for South America, 11 May 1938, enclosure to Weddell (Buenos Aires) to Hull, 7 June 1938, Cordell Hull Papers, folder 106. Chamberlain also alluded to a plan for a colonial settlement in exchange for a disarmament agreement. Cf. Gedye, pp. 391–95; Celovsky, p. 199; Macleod, pp. 231–32; and note that very similar views—suitably phrased—appear in the comments of Paul Reynaud, then French minister of Justice, in a talk with the German ambassador in Paris on 10 May (*G.D.*, D, 2, No. 152).

191. *Harvey Diaries*, 2 May 1938, p. 136; this is a summary of *B.D.*, 3d, 1, No. 166, a full account of the conversation in which Halifax gave Masaryk a report on the Anglo-French talks. Masaryk's own full report on this meeting is not available; a short telegram in T-120, 1039/1809/412128 (part in Berber, p. 108) gives a different view of the meeting and attributes such a comment to the British foreign secretary. The author is inclined to accept the British account as accurate, as does Celovsky, p. 195, n.1. See, on the other hand, *Cadogan Diary*, 6 May 1938, p. 75.

192. There is absolutely no evidence to this effect, but I cannot avoid stating my own belief that the comments of Lord Halifax after his 2 May meeting with Masaryk—of which the entry in the diary of his principal private secretary is a good reflection—led Chamberlain at the 10 May luncheon to go beyond what he had previously said with the intention of having a leak show the Czechoslovak government that if they thought major concessions *inside* Czechoslovakia were bad, things could get much worse.

193. *B.D.*, 3d, 1, No. 196. For diverging views of Czechoslovakia's military posture and the strength of her defenses, see H. C. T. Strong, "The Czechoslovak Army and the Munich Crisis: A Personal Memorandum," *War and Society: A Yearbook of Military History*, 1975, 162–77; Jonathan Zorach, "Czechoslovakia's Fortifications: Their Development and Role in the Munich Crisis," *Militärgeschichtliche Mitteilungen*, 17, No. 2 (1976), 81–94. The latter piece contains references to the relevant documents and literature; the former hardly accords with Strong's recommendations of 1938 as reported in *D.D.F.*, 2d, 10, No. 411.

shared there.[194] Whether or not correct, those views would discourage the taking of risks. In the third place, in these very days Henlein himself was in London again. He had taken the initiative for this visit, presumably in accordance with Hitler's instructions that he was to continue his efforts at keeping England neutral.[195] With the approval of Chamberlain and Halifax, Vansittart met with him as did a number of others, including Churchill.[196] The Sudeten leader claimed to be moderate and independent and asserted that autonomy and a fair deal for the German minority was all he wanted; indications are that his comments were discounted somewhat but generally believed. The implication was that the possibility of agreement did exist, especially since Henlein was also impressed by the general comments that if war did break out—with the initial fighting certain to take place in the Sudeten area itself—Britain would surely join in. There was also the thought that the recent experience of the Austrian National Socialists, who found themselves promptly superseded by National Socialists from Germany, would lead Henlein to prefer being important within Czechoslovakia to being shunted aside in the Reich.[197]

The fourth, and in some ways perhaps most critical, element was the reinforcement the British received from the French. Soon after the French ministers had returned to Paris, the French foreign minister met Lord Halifax again at and after the 9–14 May meeting of the League Council in Geneva. Daladier had already told the American ambassador to Paris that "it was impossible for France to go to war to protect Czechoslovakia," and that the reorganization of Czechoslovakia along Swiss lines might well be a step on the road to partition of the country.[198] Bonnet's views were even more defeatist; he had tried unsuccessfully to draw out Litvinov in Geneva[199] and had been told by both the Poles and

194. These comments are in C 4220/1941/18, FO 371/21719.
195. *Cadogan Diary*, 12 May 1938, p. 76.
196. On this visit, see ibid., 13 and 16 May 1938, pp. 76–77; Colvin, *None So Blind*, pp. 208–9; Nicolson, pp. 340–41; *B.D.*, 3d, 1, No. 219 and appendix 2; C 4510/1941/18, FO 371/21719; Gilbert, *Churchill*, 5:940–41; Czechoslovak Foreign Ministry to Mastný tel. 561 of 20 May 1938, Czechoslovak document in T-120, 1039/1809/412345; Kennedy to Moffat, 17 May 1938, Moffat Papers, Vol. 13; *U.S.*, 1938, 1:498–500; *Hungarian Documents*, 2, Nos. 203, 205, 216; *D.D.F.*, 2d, 9, Nos. 328, 350, 352, 356, 358, 363, 377, 441, 518, 535.
197. Note Masaryk's telegram of 14 May on the Henlein visit which, after recounting the details of the trip, concludes with: "All urge that our government take advantage of the favorable psychological moment [to come to an agreement]. I fully concur in this" (Czechoslovak document in T-120, 1039/1809/412185–86). Similarly Masaryk's report on his own talk with Henlein in Král, *München*, No. 75, and his comments to the American ambassador cited in the preceding note.
198. *U.S.*, 1938, 1:494. For discussion of the possibility of Czechoslovakia's surviving the amputation of the Sudeten areas, see *B.D.*, 3d, 1, Nos. 218 and 221, and the Foreign Office comments on these in C 4601, C 4614/1941/18, FO 371/21720.
199. For Litvinov's very different account of this conversation with Bonnet, see Fierlinger's report No. 4 of 28 May 1938, Czechoslovak document in T-120, 1039/1809/412444–59, and Litvinov's letter to the Soviet minister in Prague of 25 May 1938, *New Documents on the History of Munich*, No. 14. It should be remembered that the French merely said they would mobilize if Czechoslovakia were attacked; as we now know, they had no more intention of attacking Germany than the Soviet Union. For earlier arguments

Rumanians that they would fight rather than allow Russian troops across their borders to assist Czechoslovakia. A frontal attack on Germany would mean "the almost immediate death of the whole French youth."[200] In all these discussions, there is a despairing sense that in case of a clear and open German attack on Czechoslovakia, France would have to fight after all, but out of a fatalistic sense of obligation and with little prospect of receiving assistance or obtaining victory.

No wonder Bonnet urged Lord Halifax when they talked in Paris after the Council meeting to "work as hard as he could for a settlement in Czechoslovakia so that the French would not be faced with a crisis which they definitely did not want to face."[201] As Lord Halifax reported to the cabinet, Bonnet "wanted His Majesty's Government to put as much pressure as possible on Dr. Beneš to reach a settlement with the Sudeten-Deutsch in order to save France from the cruel dilemma between dishonouring her agreement or becoming involved in war."[202] At a time when the British and French thought that there was some real chance of a settlement being reached—though we now know that what would really have happened would have been a clear revelation of Germany's true aims—the May Crisis intervened. The warning that would be conveyed during that hectic weekend by the British to Hitler was preceded by an astonishingly similar warning to him from the chief of staff of his own army.

The first days of May 1938 were obviously a time when in German government circles the question of the destruction of Czechoslovakia was widely discussed. Keitel and Jodl might work on their draft of an order for the attack secretly, not even telling the army high command about it for fear of arousing the expected objections there;[203] but there is ample evidence of various other high military, diplomatic, and party officials discussing the likelihood of action against Czechoslovakia.[204] For the army's

---

between French Foreign Minister Delbos and Litvinov, in this case about French Communist party attacks on the French government, see *D.D.F.*, 2d, 8, Nos. 19, 32, 60.

200. *U.S.*, 1938, 1:500–504. Cf. ibid., pp. 507–8; *D.D.F.*, 2d, 9, No. 306. On the effort to rally Poland after the London meeting, see Král, *München*, No. 76 (part in Berber, p. 126); *D.D.F.*, 2d, 9, Nos. 285, 302, 307, 418, 495; cf. ibid., No. 130.

201. *U.S.*, 1938, 1:504. Bonnet may also have been affected by reports from François-Poncet that Mastný did not think Beneš was moving fast enough (*D.D.F.*, 2d, 9, No. 273; see also No. 338).

202. Cabinet 24 (38) of 18 May 1938, C 5115/1941/18, FO 371/21722; cf. *Harvey Diaries*, p. 142.

203. Note Keitel's comments, *Keitel Papers*, p. 183, and Klaus-Jürgen Müller's discussion of this, p. 300.

204. Müller, p. 301, cites several examples; the Hungarian minister in Berlin reported on such comments of Wilhelm Frick, the minister of the interior, on 6 May (*Hungarian Documents*, 2, No. 178); a planning study of the organization section of the High Command of the air force (OKL) of 2 May is clearly attuned to a war against England and refers to an interim planning date of 1 October 1938 (*TMWC*, 37:443–60); Gauleiter Röver of Oldenburg is quoted in the diary of the German minister to Norway as telling him in May that new space must be found in the east for the Germans, extending as far as the Caucasus, and that Czechoslovakia would have to disappear (Heinrich Sprenger, *Heinrich Sahm* [Cologne:

chief of staff, who had heavily criticized the views Hitler had expressed on 5 November 1937, who had seen and participated in the implementation of the first move called for in that meeting—the *Anschluss*—who had seen the commander-in-chief of the army dismissed in a disgraceful farce and replaced by a compromised second-rater, the indications that Hitler was now moving toward the next objective—an attack on Czechoslovakia—aroused the greatest concern.

On 5 May he prepared a warning memorandum which he submitted to the commander-in-chief of the army on 7 May.[205] In it Beck argued that Germany could get a great deal peacefully, in part because of the aversion to war in England and France; but if Germany did launch a military attack on Czechoslovakia, France would decide, however reluctantly, to honor her treaty obligation to go to war and that England, equally reluctantly, would join France out of her own interests either immediately or soon after. Equally correctly, he expected that the Western Powers would draw on American supplies and possibly intervention. He suggested that the Soviet Union would be hostile and Poland and Rumania might be also. In examining the military prospects, he again saw the French and British positions quite correctly: they might very well *not* launch an immediate attack in the west and see Czechoslovakia overrun, "leaving her reconstitution, like Serbia's earlier, to the general settlement at the end of a long war." Since he did not believe Germany could win such a war, he argued that Germany must not start a war in which England would be among Germany's enemies, a contingency he believed certain to arise if Germany attempted to force a solution of the Czechoslovak question in a manner contrary to Britain's preferences, i.e., by a military attack.

The new commander-in-chief of the army, General von Brauchitsch, took up the memorandum with Keitel before showing it to Hitler. Keitel—who was, it must be remembered, working under Hitler's instructions on a draft order for an attack on Czechoslovakia—urged von Brauchitsch not to show Hitler the portion of Beck's memorandum covering the international situation since he would get so angry that he would not even read the analysis of the military prospects in case of war. When von Brauchitsch followed this advice, Hitler still became angry and rejected Beck's views.[206]

Grote, 1969], p. 291); on 11 May the German press was directed to hold back a bit on attacks on Czechoslovakia, instructions for greater noise would come later ("Bestellungen aus der Pressekonferenz," Bundesarchiv, Brammer, Z.Sg. 101/11, f.359). These and other such developments point to the assumptions of those in the upper reaches of the German government in the first weeks of May.

205. Text in Gert Buchheit, *Ludwig Beck ein preussischer General* (Munich: List, 1964), pp. 133–38; see Müller, pp. 302–5; Foerster, pp. 81–87. A copy of Beck's memorandum was apparently transmitted to someone in the German foreign ministry; portions of it under the date of 7 May 1938 from the German foreign ministry files in the Deutsches Zentralarchiv Potsdam are printed in Král, *Die Deutschen*, No. 138.

206. The only account of this is in Keitel's memoirs, p. 184. The account appears creditworthy and is accepted by Müller (p. 305). Hitler's own subsequent references are to memoranda in the plural, presumably including Beck's later papers of the summer; see

The Führer's attitude at this time between the trip to Rome and the May Crisis was already set: the period of waiting for the international uproar over the *Anschluss* to die down was over. He would now prepare for the attack on Czechoslovakia, still in 1938, though as yet with no date specified.[207] Britain and France would not intervene, and Beck's views to the contrary were angrily rejected and would contribute to his further fall from grace as von Fritsch's objections at the meeting of 5 November 1937 had had a share in his dismissal. The evidence on Hitler's working on the details of plans for an attack as soon as he arrived back at the Obersalzberg after the Italian trip confirms this. The questions which his new armed forces adjutant Schmundt transmitted to the staffs in Berlin on 16 and 17 May[208] and the pressure of Schmundt on Keitel to send to Hitler in Berchtesgaden the draft order he was working on in accordance with Hitler's instructions,[209] must be seen as part of Hitler's preoccupation with the military details of the forthcoming operation. Those who attribute the wording of Hitler's 30 May revision of the draft Keitel sent to him to his anger over the May Crisis fail to take into account that the draft was based on a discussion of 20 April, and that Hitler's reaction to Beck's warning, as well as his work on the military details of an attack right after his return from Italy, shows very clearly that rightly or wrongly Hitler believed that the time to have the first of his short wars had arrived. The solidarity with Italy, which Beck questioned, was strong enough in Hitler's eyes to ward off any danger of a general war; and there was, therefore, no reason to postpone the action against Czechoslovakia which Hitler perceived as a military attack later in 1938 following a lengthy propaganda campaign.[210]

Wilhelm Treue (ed.), "Rede Hitlers vor der deutschen Presse (10. November 1938)," *Vierteljahrshefte für Zeitgeschichte*, 6, No. 2 (April 1958), 187; Helmut Heiber (ed.), *Hitlers Lagebespreuchungen* (Stuttgart: Deutsche Verlags-Anstalt, 1962), p. 786. The date of the Hitler-Brauchitsch meeting must have been about 12 May after Hitler returned from Italy to Berlin and before his departure for Berchtesgaden.

207. Note the comment of von Weizsäcker to the Hungarian minister reported in the latter's dispatch of 20 May that the timing for the settlement of the Czechoslovak question would be decided by Hitler, but it would take place no later than the following spring (*Hungarian Documents*, 2, No. 210). By that time Hitler had been away from Berlin for several days, working in Berchtesgaden on the plans for the attack. Von Weizsäcker was evidently conveying to the Hungarian minister an interpretation of what he had recorded in his own diary on 13 May (see above, n.101).

208. Schmundt's questions of 16 May and the answers of Zeitzler (the later army chief of staff, then a Lt. Col. in the OKW) are in *TMWC*, 25:418–20; for 17 May, only Zeitzler's answer has been printed in ibid., pp. 420–21.

209. *Keitel Papers*, p. 183.

210. The 12 May memorandum of von Weizsäcker quoted by Watt in his "Hitler's Visit to Rome and the May Weekend Crisis" (p. 30) to support a contrary interpretation simply does not do so. Since Hitler neither wanted nor requested Italian *military* assistance, the Italian expectation that Germany could "solve the Czechoslovak question without a European conflict" confirmed rather than contradicted Hitler's opinion. Watt asserts that Hitler was undecided before the May Crisis (p. 25), using as evidence the Hitler-Keitel meeting of 21 April and then attributes the indecision to Hitler's experience in Italy in early May. This not

In the middle of May 1938, therefore, the Western Powers were hopeful that an agreement could be reached without war, an agreement that would leave a Czechoslovak state, even if perhaps a truncated one. Hitler, on the other hand, thought that he had the opportunity to launch the first of his wars under circumstances where the strength of Germany, the weaknesses and reluctance of France and England, the military and political vulnerability of Czechoslovakia, and his alignment with Italy could assure him a short, isolated, and victorious war at the end of a period of German political and military preparations. He was busy working on the details of those preparations when the May Crisis produced developments which led to refinements in his planning.

The rumors of German troop movements which precipitated the war scare on the weekend of 19–22 May have given rise to vast speculation. Were they based on leaks about real intentions of the Germans for a coup? Were they based on minor German military moves designed to influence the elections in Czechoslovakia scheduled for that weekend? Were they planted on the British by the Czechs as a deliberate means at the least of clarifying the British position and at most to precipitate a war?[211] With the evidence now available, I still adhere to the view that "at a time of great international tension, reports of really routine German troop movements were mistaken as presaging an immediate attack on Czechoslovakia. When the times are appropriate for them, many omens or flying saucers will be seen."[212]

---

only inverts the chronology but ignores the fact that the evidence on Hitler's views and actions in the period between his Italian journey and the May Crisis shows him very much decided on the next move. Before the trip, Hitler had put the alternatives as an immediate move against Czechoslovakia or, if the Italians were hesitant in their diplomatic support, a substantial postponement. The 16 May question about which German divisions could move within twelve hours of mobilization hardly points to plans for the indefinite future—when German troop dispositions might be very different. Schmundt's repeated urgings that Keitel send the draft order also cannot be fitted in with Watt's view of an undecided Hitler. It is true that Keitel himself is the source for this last—for him potentially exculpatory—detail, but it is to be found in his memoirs (p. 183), not in his testimony in his own defense at his trial (*TMWC*, 15:508–9).

211. These theories are examined in Braddick's study. He leans to the last answer, but on very thin evidence. As the text shows, I do not agree with Braddick's conclusions.

212. Weinberg, "May Crisis," p. 224. The sources and details provided in that article will not generally be repeated here. See now also *Hungarian Documents*, 2, Nos. 207, 209, 211, 213, 214, 229; *Lipski Papers*, pp. 367–68; *D.D.F.*, 2d, 9, 378–459, passim, 494, 502, 507; 10, Nos. 77, 228; "Bestellungen aus der Pressekonferenz," 21 May, 24 May, 28 May, Bundesarchiv, Brammer, Z.Sg. 101/11, ff.379, 383, 391; "Informationsbericht Nr. 38," 23 May, Nr. 40, 28 May 1938, ibid., 101/32, ff.347–51, 361–67; Král, *München*, Nos. 79 (Berber, No. 127), 80, 81 (part in Berber, No. 130), 82, 83; Osuský tel. of 22 May 1938, Czechoslovak document in T-120, 1039/1809/412195–96; Masaryk tels. of 22 and 24 May, ibid., frames 412017–18; Gajan and Kvaček, No. 41; *Harvey Diaries*, 21 May 1938, pp. 142–43; *Cadogan Diary*, 19–22 May 1938, pp. 78–79; Transcript of Feis-Morgenthau telephone conversation, 23 May 1938, Morgenthau Papers, Vol. 125:393–97, Hyde Park; Trauttmannsdorff to Albrecht Haushofer, 23 May 1938, Haushofer Papers, Library of Congress Manuscripts Division Acc. No. 11249; *Australian Documents*, No. 209.

The fact that the British were so alarmed at what looked like an imminent German action should not be surprising: Henlein had just been in London, now on 19 May he broke off negotiations with the Czechoslovak government. Troop movements had been denied in the *Anschluss* crisis, as had the delivery of several German ultimatums to von Schuschnigg; that all those denials had been lies was both known in London at the time and recalled in May. At a time of great tension and repeated surprise moves there were several instances of erroneous anticipation; sometimes German moves were not expected, at other times they were mistakenly thought imminent. The alarms over alleged German troop landings in Morocco in January 1937 and supposed German plans for an invasion of Holland in January 1939 show that the May Crisis was neither the first nor the last instance of the latter type. Given the German habit of striking without warning, such scares were only to be expected. Certainly all the British records and materials currently available show that there was a genuine belief that Germany was about to move and that war was imminent. Furthermore, it was the bellicose statements of von Ribbentrop to the British and Czechoslovak representatives in Berlin which, when relayed to London, served to confirm and even heighten the fears there. It looked as if the withdrawal of Henlein from Czechoslovakia to Germany marked the end of what had looked like promising negotiations, which would now be replaced by a German military advance.

Under these circumstances, the British government decided to warn the Germans on 21 May and again the next day of the dangers inherent in any German attack. The French, who were also so informing Berlin, would honor their obligation under the alliance treaty, and under those circumstances Britain might well be forced to become involved also as the prime minister had warned on 24 March.[213] The angry tone with which von Ribbentrop greeted these warnings, his refusal to urge Henlein to resume negotiations, the generally threatening tone he assumed, and his professed indifference to a new world war all pointed toward future German

213. On the British warnings, see now also, in addition to the sources cited in the preceding note, *Hungarian Documents*, 2, Nos. 215, 218. Note the contrast between Deputy State Secretary Woermann's view on 14 May that Britain would not fight over Czechoslovakia (ibid., No. 196) and von Weizsäcker's on 20 May that prolonged Czechoslovak resistance in case of war could lead to English intervention (ibid., No. 210). On the French warning, see also François-Poncet's account to the American ambassador, Hugh Wilson, relayed by the latter in a personal letter to Pierrepont Moffat of 24 May 1938, Moffat Papers, Vol. 14.

An important document on Czechoslovak ideas about the need to mobilize quickly if war appeared imminent—in order to avoid having to complete mobilization while under German attack—is the note of the chief of the Czechoslovak general staff to General Gamelin of 7 April 1938, *D.D.F.*, 2d, 9, No. 128. This document provides a good clue to Czechoslovak general staff thinking during the May Crisis and in September; it also reveals the dilemma the Poles were pushed into by Germany's "silent mobilization" in 1939 as Czechoslovakia had been in 1938. A country could either await attack and be grievously hurt by Blitzkrieg tactics or, as would be necessary in an open society, announce mobilization measures in a period of crisis and thus *appear* to be provocative, especially in view of the debate about the sequence of mobilizations in the discussion of responsibility for the outbreak of war in 1914.

policy, since no German action was planned for that weekend; but they did nothing to calm the situation. What did lead to temporary quiet was the fact that the Germans were not yet ready to move and therefore did not do so, in spite of the fact that the Czechoslovak government called up one class of reservists and some specialists and moved these into the border areas to help assure calm during the elections.

The effect on Hitler of hearing first the warnings from London relayed to him in Berchtesgaden and subsequently the comments in the press that he had backed down before western pressure has often been described by others as pushing him into a decision to attack Czechoslovakia that fall.[214] Hitler himself—who knew of doubts and even opposition to his plans among the generals—at times used this explanation. It is, however, false. He had already decided before the weekend crisis, and he was quite capable of getting himself into a rage (which then became quite genuine) whenever it suited his purposes. This incident must not be examined in isolation. Hitler was pictured as backing down before Mussolini's movement of troops to the Brenner in July 1934—and not only postponed action against Austria for years but continued to woo the Italian dictator. Although he made angry comments to the French ambassador and others about the January 1937 stories concerning German troop shipments to Spanish Morocco, he never considered taking such action to spite the French, who had at first believed the reports. If he issued new orders on the Czechoslovak question after the May Crisis, it was because he was already working on them; some of the technical aspects, not the general thrust, were affected by developments in that crisis.

Hitler's work on the planned attack in which Schmundt gathered information for him was what had led to the urgings by Schmundt to Keitel to forward his draft to Berchtesgaden. Keitel did send this on 20 May with a covering letter explaining its role as a transitional text for the period until the new mobilization year began on 1 October. Reflecting the conversation of Hitler with Keitel a month earlier, the introductory statement on timing of course mirrors Hitler's comments of that time. In detail, the draft order merely amplifies the general plan for an attack designed to break Czechoslovak resistance quickly so that no one would come to the victim's help while Poland and Hungary might well join in on Germany's side. A long war could lead to international complications, and so all should be attuned to a speedy victory.[215] The general introductory statement which left the timing somewhat indefinite was by now out of date and would be replaced by one asserting that it was Hitler's "unalterable decision to destroy Czechoslovakia by military action in the forsee-

214. A good example of this sort is the story Karl Bömer of the propaganda ministry told a correspondent of the *Chicago Daily News* in the fall of 1938 (Wilson to Moffat, 22 October 1938, Moffat Papers, Vol. 14).
215. The text is in *TMWC*, 25:421–27.

able future."[216] In the details of implementing procedures, some changes were also made. When it was suggested, presumably by Keitel, that Hitler should brief the commanders in chief of the branches of the armed forces about his intentions,[217] the response characterized what the new orders would provide and the impact of the May Crisis on Hitler's thinking precisely enough to deserve quoting: "The Führer is engrossed with the Green [Czechoslovak plan]. The basic considerations are unaltered.[218] Surprise even more heavily emphasized. Conference with those concerned will take place after return [to Berlin] at the latest." After reporting that Hitler thought September too late a date for the army to hold exercises on the surprise capture of fortifications, the report concludes: "The Führer repeatedly emphasized the necessity of rapidly pushing ahead the construction of fortifications in the West."[219]

Hitler's strategic concept had not changed, but the orderly calling up of Czechoslovak reserves and their smooth movement into the border areas, combined with the Western show of solidarity reinforced the need for speed in breaching the Czechoslovak fortifications[220] as well as hurrying up the building of Germany's own fortifications in the west to deter, or if need be delay, the French. Even before Hitler met with his military leaders to explain his plans, he had seen Henlein on the Obersalzberg to give him further instructions. It would appear that Hitler told Henlein to hold to the Karlovy Vary program but not to let developments in Czechoslovakia to get out of hand because Germany first had to fill gaps in the fortifications on her western border. By the end of the summer or in the

216. Text of 30 May, ibid., p. 434 (full text on pp. 433–39).
217. Item 19 in the Green File, ibid., p. 432, is in my judgment a telegram from Keitel to Schmundt of 22 or 23 May 1938.
218. The German text reads "Grundgedanken unverändert," hardly the way Schmundt would have described Hitler's views to Keitel in response to a question about the Führer's intentions ("Absichten") if there had been any truth to the subsequent pretense that Hitler changed his intentions because of the events of the weekend.
219. Item 17, ibid., pp. 431–32. I believe this to be the document referred to in Jodl's diary under 23 May 1938 as follows: "Major Schmundt transmits views of the Führer (Appendix), further discussions which slowly develop the precise intentions of the Führer are held with the Chief of the OKW on May 28, June 3 and June 9. See Annexes (War Diary L)" (ibid., 28:373). This section of the diary, with its references to specific dates only in those cases where Jodl had documents in the OKW files, mostly referred to as annexes (which do not appear to have survived), is clearly a part of Jodl's subsequent reconstruction of events as discussed in note 87, above. The only *contemporary* entry Jodl made in his diary between March and August 1938 is the one of 20 May about a meeting he and Keitel had with Göring (ibid.), and this entry appears on a subsequent page of the original where it is followed by a reference to his own leave from 21 June to 24 July and then a reference to a meeting of 10 August. The discussion about the alleged relationship between the May Crisis and the decision to attack in this part of the diary dates to the time Jodl prepared his reconstruction, either just before going on leave, between 13 June (latest date in the reconstruction) and 21 June or, more likely after 24 July.
220. There was another aspect to timing in regard to the Czechoslovak border defenses: the longer Hitler waited to start an attack, the more likely it was that the Czechs would fortify the newly opened border with Austria (cf. *B.D.*, 3d, 1, No. 253). Note Hitler's comment in November 1938 that every postponement would merely have made an attack more difficult and more bloody (Treue, "Rede Hitlers," p. 183).

fall, the French would not be able to help Czechoslovakia and Hitler could then do as he wished.[221] In this fashion Hitler provided Henlein with a general idea of his schedule without being as specific on dates as he safely felt he could be with his own military.

Since Hitler was now setting his military timetable for an operation starting 1 October, with a complete breakthrough to be accomplished by 4 October, he had to return to Berlin, however briefly, to explain his offensive plans to the highest military leaders and to give a major push to the construction of the Westwall.[222] On 28 May Hitler spoke at length to a number of the highest military and political leaders, repeating much of what he had said on 5 November 1937 but pointing it more to the current situation. He pictured the planned attack on Czechoslovakia as preliminary to a later attack on the Western Powers to expand Germany to the English Channel, and he repeated his expectation that France and Britain would not intervene in a quick German war against Czechoslovakia. The Germans would have to figure out ways to break the Czechoslovak fortifications, and they would have to prepare the German public psychologically for war. At the same time, responsibility for construction of the Westwall was transferred from the military to Minister Todt, the man who had made his mark in the construction of the Autobahnen, Germany's superhighways.[223] The speech of 28 May and the official revised directive for the attack on Czechoslovakia issued on 30 May would precipitate a new crisis in the relations between Hitler and the army leadership, especially General Beck, but this will be discussed later. The point to be noted here is that by the end of May the top leaders of the German government and army were on notice that at the beginning of October Hitler expected to launch a short, successful, and isolated war against Czechoslovakia.

It has sometimes been asserted in the literature on the origins and course of World War II that the German navy was not designed for a war with England until after the May Crisis. This line was especially popular with the naval defendants at Nuremberg as well as apologists for them.[224]

221. Somewhat confused accounts of this conversation are reflected in Král, *Die Deutschen*, No. 151, and Florence Crane to Roosevelt, 5 July 1938, P.S.F. Cordell Hull, Hyde Park. In the reconstructed part of Jodl's diary, this is referred to as a basic ("Grundlegende Besprechung") meeting of 22 May on which Jodl saw a memorandum that, like the other annexes (see n.219, above) is apparently lost (*TMWC*, 28:373).

222. Green File, item 20, *TMWC*, 25:433. These are notes of Schmundt, apparently written between 23 and 27 May. On the Westwall, see also Müller, p. 307.

223. See Celovsky, pp. 216–17; Foerster, pp. 88–90; Müller, pp. 307–8; Wiedemann, pp. 127–28; Dülffer, pp. 466–68.

224. For deliberate efforts within the German navy to "cook" the record in this regard one can see not only Raeder's own wartime papers written as alibis but also such selective destruction of records as that noted in Dülffer, p. 439, n.24. Cf. ibid., p. 463, n.40. A good example of wartime alibi preparation is the memorandum on German submarine construction from Admiral Assmann's papers in *TMWC*, 35:561–62; on this document, see Bracher, *Machtergreifung*, p. 803, n.267.

It has already been shown that this was decidedly not the case, and that although some in the Naval High Command may have deluded themselves at the time, Admiral Raeder knew what was intended long before and acted accordingly (though not always informing his associates of Hitler's real intentions). Although the decision of 5 November allocated additional raw materials to the navy, in practice, shortages of labor, raw materials, and shipyard capacity as well as frequent changes of plans and the fact that even by the extravagant standards of the Third Reich the naval bureaucracy was incredibly overorganized and inefficient all combined to keep many of the projected warships from ever being constructed. The clues to policy, however, must be found in plans and projections, in naval matters more than others because of the longer lead time required for shipbuilding even under the best of circumstances. It was because he knew this that Raeder translated Hitler's November comments that war with England was possible as early as 1938 into an immediate effort to speed up the construction of submarines—the one type of vessel useful for such a war that could conceivably be constructed quickly.[225] Whatever the difficulties in implementing the new scheme, Raeder received Hitler's agreement for expanding the required shipbuilding capacity when the two reviewed the question before Raeder's order to this effect on 24 February 1938.[226] Although the expansion of the German navy in regard to larger ships would obviously take longer, the fact that war with England was anticipated was stressed by Raeder when the navy's war games for 1937 were discussed in a concluding conference on 12 April.[227]

The impact of the May Crisis on the navy, therefore, was not to turn that branch of the German armed forces toward planning for a war with England[228] but rather to refine and accelerate the existing plans as well as to make the realities clear to those in the High Command of the German navy hitherto in the dark.[229]

If the impact of the May Crisis on Germany was to influence the refinement of military preparations already ordered or under way, the impact on the governments in London and Paris was to accentuate the predisposition to urge Czechoslovakia to make concessions quickly and on a generous scale.[230] The belief that an imminent German invasion had barely

225. Dülffer, pp. 451–52.
226. Ibid., p. 454.
227. Ibid., pp. 461–62; Gemzell, pp. 63–66.
228. Watt in "Hitler's Visit to Rome and the May Weekend Crisis" attempts to maintain this thesis by quoting one document from the German naval archives.
229. Dülffer, pp. 466–70. The analysis of the meaning of Hitler's technical directives to the German navy at this time appears to be carried into greater refinement and precision than the evidence warrants.
230. None of this was due to any pro-German attitude in the government; the cabinet protocols and Foreign Office documents make this most obvious. When Henderson quoted von Neurath as saying the Communists controlled the Czechoslovak generals and had led them to start the May Crisis, no one in the Foreign Office believed it and Henderson was so

been averted itself served to reinforce the urgency of the situation, and the remedy seemed to be not more warnings to Berlin but some added military preparations[231] and heavier pressure on Prague. Chamberlain wrote at the time: "I cannot doubt in my own mind (1) that the German government made all preparations for a coup, (2) that in the end they decided after getting our warnings that the risks were too great, (3) that the general view that this was just what had happened made them conscious that they had lost prestige, and (4) that they are venting their spite on us because they feel that we have got the credit for giving them a check."[232]

The belief that Hitler might well react to any repetition of the warnings he had received during the May Crisis by taking immediate action against Czechoslovakia would restrain the British government from that course throughout the summer and until the very last moment when, after the Godesberg meeting, war was again seen as immediately imminent (and again in August 1939). The first of many suggestions from Germany urging a firm British stand to hold back Hitler, who wanted to obliterate Czechoslovakia rather than help the Sudeten Germans, was forwarded to Lord Halifax by Wickham Steed at this time,[233] but this was perceived as too risky a route.[234] Instead, the French were cautioned not to take the British warnings to Germany as anything more than an emergency measure to save the situation, while Czechoslovakia would be urged most strongly to make some really major concessions.[235] The permanent undersecretary in the Foreign Office went so far as to tell the Hungarian chargé in London on 24 May that the German demands—which at this point meant Henlein's Karlovy Vary speech—were justified and should

---

informed (C 5063/1941/18, FO 371/21722; cf. C 5425/1941/18, FO 371/21723). The strength of anti-German feelings in England at this time is commented on in a letter from Gerl to Hess, 1 May 1938, Nuremberg document 3752-PS, pp. 21–22, National Archives. (Note the 31 August 1936 statement of Hess that Dr. Franz Gerl's trips to and contacts in England were authorized by him and known to Hitler, ibid., p. 77).

231. C 5222/1941/18, FO 371/21722.

232. 28 May 1938, Feiling, p. 354. Cf. *Harvey Diaries,* 24 and 26 May 1938, p. 144. The discussion of the British cabinet meeting of Sunday, 22 May, in Ian Colvin, *The Chamberlain Cabinet* (New York: Taplinger, 1971), pp. 128–30, which concludes with the suggestion that the emergency meeting was perhaps a formality designed to impress the Germans, overlooks the fact that the meeting was called on 21 May when the situation looked very critical.

233. Henry Wickham Steed to Halifax, 23 May 1938, C 5117/1941/18, FO 371/21722.

234. At the time of the weekend crisis, the famous American flyer Charles Lindbergh was in London spreading tales about the German air force being ten times as strong as the British, French, and Soviet air forces put together (Nicolson, 22 May 1938, p. 343; the account in Lindbergh, p. 28, is not very useful).

235. An account in Celovsky, pp. 223–26. On the warning to the French, see also *Harvey Diaries,* 22 May 1938, p. 144. For the utter confusion in British military planning for the contingency of France coming to the aid of Czechoslovakia, see the War Office memorandum of 7 June 1938, C 5491/1941/18, FO 371/21723.

be granted practically in toto.[236] On the following day, Lord Halifax discussed the problem first in the cabinet and later with representatives of several of the Dominions.[237] He was clearly casting about for a way to find a solution that would deal with the Sudeten German problem preferably within Czechoslovakia but if necessary outside, one that would be accepted by the Czechs—under French pressure which he was certain would be forthcoming—and that would then lead to a situation in which the settlement of the Sudeten question would bring about a neutral status for Czechoslovakia, like that of Switzerland, in which Czechoslovakia would neither need nor want alliances with France and the Soviet Union. This would in turn both relieve France of a burden and Germany of an alleged grievance.

There was some optimism in London in view of a renewed contact between Henlein and the Czechoslovak authorities and considerable discussion of various possible schemes for bringing about a lasting settlement.[238] It must be added that at the same time that the British were trying very hard to have Prague move to a major offer, they were also using the channel between Sir Robert Vansittart and Henlein to urge restraint on the Sudeten Germans. Since Henlein claimed to be still willing to settle for what he had demanded when in London, and since the British had been given to understand by the Czechoslovak minister that these demands could be accepted, it is understandable that Sir Robert with the approval of Lord Halifax counseled Henlein to try to reach agreement, while the foreign secretary encouraged Prague to meet those demands.[239]

While the British returned to their effort to secure a Czechoslovak-

236. *Hungarian Documents*, 2, No. 222. There is no reference to this in the Cadogan diary, but it is entirely consistent with its general tenor. For 24 May it records: "H[alifax] wants to sever French-Czech and Czech-Soviet connections. He is quite right, but I tell him this can only be done by some form of 'neutralization'. We'll examine it" (p. 80).

237. The cabinet record 26 (38) is in C 5155/1941/18, FO 371/21722; the meeting with the Dominions representatives in C 5209/4815/18, FO 371/21770.

238. Note that the Foreign Office memorandum on the possibility of neutralizing Czechoslovakia printed in *B.D.*, 3d, 1, Appendix IV, was prepared at this time, see C 6039/1941/18, FO 371/21725. An earlier draft began with the statement, subsequently dropped, that in any European war over Czechoslovakia, "the outcome . . . in present circumstances would be at best doubtful and might be disastrous." Though sent to Phipps, Henderson, and Newton on 9 June, it had been drafted earlier. The comment on it by Vansittart, warning that Russia must be included among the guarantors of any status for Czechoslovakia lest the Soviet Union feel isolated as Germany wished, is dated 26 May (C 5235/1941/18, FO 371/21723). It was at this time that Sir William Strang, then head of the Central Department of the Foreign Office, was sent to Prague and Berlin to explore the situation; there is a brief reference in his memoirs, *Home and Abroad* (London: Andre Deutsch, 1956), p. 133, n.2.

239. Sir Robert's minute of 26 May and Halifax's telegram to Newton No. 125 of 27 May are in C 5260/1941/18, FO 371/21723. This telegram, like a number of documents on Vansittart's role in the Sudeten question in 1938, does not appear in the published British documents, but see *B.D.*, 3d, 1, No. 320. For Sudeten German party efforts through Colonel Christie and Vansittart to secure greater British pressure on Czechoslovakia at this time, see Král, *Die Deutschen*, Nos. 145–47.

German agreement with greater urgency but some confidence that agreement was possible, the French reacted to the weekend crisis with nothing less than panic.[240] They proclaimed fidelity to the alliance with Czechoslovakia in public while privately castigating the Prague government for calling up reserves without prior consultation.[241] Bonnet even appears to have deliberately read an at least slightly cooperative Polish attitude during the crisis as completely negative.[242] As soon as the immediate crisis of the weekend was over, the French government seconded the British efforts to pressure Czechoslovakia and took the lead in urging the prompt demobilization of those called up during the emergency.[243] The French government from this time on became even more insistent than the British, thus reversing the situation of 1937; but the collapse of French support was either not recognized or understood in Prague, or the authorities there believed that it could or should be disregarded.

It is not entirely clear whether the May Crisis did or did not give the Czechoslovak government a false sense of security. They most assuredly missed what turned out to be the last opportunity to seize the initiative.[244] The immediate aftermath of the show of internal unity and external support could be utilized by the government of Czechoslovakia in one of two ways: One was to see it as a chance to make a major offer from a position of strength in the hope that this would either settle the question or, if refused by Henlein, reveal to all beyond a doubt that Germany wanted the destruction of Czechoslovakia, not the welfare of the Sudeten Germans. The other route was to negotiate but with minor concessions, using the example of the weekend crisis as a sample to show how Germany could be made to back down if it came to a crunch. Evidence is not available as to whether both these alternatives were seriously considered in Prague;[245] all we know is that whether because of preference, fear of domestic opposition, or belief that once major concessions were made, the whole state

240. Celovsky, pp. 223–24; *Hungarian Documents*, 2, No. 225; Osuský tel. of 22 May 1938, Czechoslovak document in T-120, 1039/1809/412195–96. There is a useful account of Bonnet's general role in Adamthwaite, pp. 98–106.

241. *D.D.F.*, 2d, 9, Nos. 402, 414, 432, 439.

242. Lewis Namier, *In the Nazi Era* (London: Macmillan, 1952), pp. 183–86; *Łukasiewicz Papers*, pp. 81–99, 105–6. The seventh paragraph of Łukasiewicz's summary of the whole episode sent to Colonel Beck on 28 May (ibid., pp. 99–104) appears to give contemporary justification to the interpretation of Namier which is followed here; but see Celovsky, p. 235, n.3, and *D.D.F.*, 2d, 9, Nos. 418, 458.

243. The panic in Paris appears to have infected the American ambassador, William Bullitt; see his appeal of 22 May to Roosevelt in *U.S.*, 1938, 1:509–12; a subsequent report on French pressure on Czechoslovakia, ibid., pp. 517–19. It must be noted, however, that Bullitt's concern grew out of his conviction that France would indeed declare war on Germany if the Germans attacked Czechoslovakia.

244. See Hodža's meeting with Henlein and Karl Hermann Frank on 23 May 1938, Král, *Die Deutschen*, No. 140.

245. The long letter of Osuský to Krofta of 1 August 1938 (Král, *München*, No. 123; a snippet in Berber, No. 146) reviewing developments since March leaves one with the impression that there was no such consideration.

might well disintegrate, the Czechoslovak government in practice adopted the latter course.[246]

In spite of urgings from London and Paris, the Czechoslovak authorities made no immediate offer at all, using as explanation that they had not been given the formal demands of the Sudeten Germans in a written request, and thereby implicitly yielding the initiative to the Germans.[247] When the Sudeten German party handed in its demands on 8 June, the Czechoslovak government analyzed these and began lengthy negotiations about the details.[248] Actually submitting a formal set of demands was, of course, a very risky step for the Sudeten German party; there was always the danger that the Prague government would demolish the whole German strategy by simply saying yes to all or most of them.[249] After all, the Czechoslovak documents show that the Prague authorities believed the Sudeten German party's strategy to be one of ever increasing demands and thought Germany not yet ready to move militarily. The Sudeten leadership certainly feared that Prague might be tempted to take the risk of exposing their strategy. Henlein himself went to Germany again on 3 June, before taking the chance of having his demands granted, in order to ask what could be done to avoid agreement in that contingency.[250] His own proposal was that the Sudeten German party would then turn to a demand that Czechoslovakia's foreign policy be changed, in the anticipation that this would be refused, but no decision on that question was made at the time.[251]

246. Perhaps the Czechoslovak record of Beneš's conversation with Eisenlohr of 16 February 1938 is important evidence on the attitude of the president. At that time he said that he would never negotiate with Germany about the German minority, that he would not negotiate with Henlein or the Sudeten German party, nor would he negotiate about it with England and France. He would never agree to national autonomy nor would he negotiate about it with anyone (Král, *Die Deutschen*, No. 89; Eisenlohr's report in *G.D.*, D, 2, No. 57, does not make Beneš out to be quite so negative). The text does not sound as if this was simply a position assumed for negotiating purposes.

247. Král, *München*, Nos. 88, 90 (part in Berber, No. 139), 92. In the last of these documents, a report by Osuský of 13 June, Bonnet appears much more favorable to the Czechoslovak position than all other evidence suggests he was. Celovsky, pp. 226–27, 252–54, gives an account of the developments but overlooks the fact that the Prague government let the Sudeten Germans take the lead.

248. No useful purpose would be served by recounting these here; Czechoslovak documents on them are published in Král, *München*, Nos. 91, 93, 96.

249. Note the evasive responses to Czechoslovak Prime Minister Hodža on 6 April in this regard (Král, *Die Deutschen*, No. 113). Although the analogy to Serbia's fate during and after the World War often appears in the record, in no instance is the great diplomatic advantage accruing to Belgrade from its conciliatory response to the Austrian ultimatum mentioned.

250. *G.D.*, D, 2, No. 237. For earlier internal Sudeten German party discussion, see Král, *Die Deutschen*, No. 144.

251. The demands then being prepared all dealt with *internal* affairs. Von Weizsäcker commented that the answer to this puzzle had best be given when the situation actually occurred.

Henlein could have spared himself this anxiety; the Czechoslovak government did not say yes to his written demands. It was not until September that Beneš produced a program, referred to generally as the "Fourth Plan," which even at that late date threw the Sudeten German party into turmoil and which, if offered in some form in late May or early June, would have dramatically exposed Hitler's intentions at a time of Czechoslovakia's rather than Germany's choosing. Instead of taking such a route, if it was ever seriously considered, Prague trod the path of detailed negotiations on specific portions of the Sudeten German party's demands, thus unintentionally falling in with the strategy Hitler had prescribed.

11   War Denied:
The Crisis over
Czechoslovakia
Part 2

The three months following the May Crisis saw a continuation of anxious diplomatic concern with Czechoslovakia. What was the policy of Germany during this period? To the external world, Germany presented a picture of pacific assurances mixed with bellicose propaganda. On 12 June Rudolf Hess combined the two in a speech at Stettin that included both themes: a vehement denunciation of Czechoslovakia was accompanied by an equally vehement denial of warlike intentions.[1] Such tones did not convince everyone in the British Foreign Office, but the speech conformed so closely to the personal impressions and beliefs of Sir Nevile Henderson that he assured Lord Halifax he thought it "accurately represented Hitler's own views."[2] The German propaganda campaign against Czechoslovakia moved forward with constant emphasis on the question of the Sudeten Germans.[3] The acceleration of work on the German fortifications in the west, however, provides a better clue to Hitler's real intentions.

On 31 May the commander-in-chief of the German army transmitted to the German commander-in-chief

1. The text is in *Dokumente der deutschen Politik,* 6:289–92. Cf. *D.D.F.,* 2d, 10, No. 39.
2. Henderson's letter to Halifax, 16 June 1938, *B.D.,* 3d, 1, No. 419. In all fairness, it shoud be added that Henderson also relied on the fact that Germany was not yet ready for the major war that he himself believed would result from a German attack on Czechoslovakia. The ambassador's miscalculation was that he thought unnamed extremists rather than Hitler himself might engineer an incident that would precipitate a conflict. For a report on the negative reaction of the Foreign Office to the Hess speech, see the report from London, possibly by Karl Heinz Abshagen, of 18 June 1938, Bundesarchiv, Brammer, Z.Sg. 101/11, f.407.
3. Accounts in Hagemann, pp. 348–77; Joachim Leuschner, *Volk und Raum: Zum Stil der nationalsozialistischen Aussenpolitik* (Göttingen: Vandenhoeck & Ruprecht, 1958), pp. 51–54.

in the west, General Wilhelm Adam, Hitler's instructions to get 12,000 additional field fortifications built by the fall of the same year, a project Adam called impossible in spite of the promised support of the Todt organization and the National Labor Service *(Reichsarbeitsdienst)*.[4] Hitler, however, pursued the subject personally and with great energy. On 14 June Hitler reviewed the subject at length with Göring, who had just spent several days touring the western fortifications.[5] When General Adam reported on 30 June about the impossibility of the rapid progress demanded, Hitler insisted, gave a greater role—and subsequently greater credit—to Todt, and was moved to write his memorandum of 1 July on the fortification system.[6] Though it was of course designed to provide a real defensive cover for the attack on Czechoslovakia if a general war did take place, there was a substantial and deliberate element of bluff in this program: the hope that knowledge of the fortifications would discourage French intervention altogether.[7] The information on the extension of the German construction program in the west to include the Belgian and Dutch borders, officially given to the Belgians on 10 June, must surely be seen as a part of the general effort to give the impression of an invincible barrier which could no more be pierced there than any other portion of the border.[8] There is no need to trace this element in Hitler's strategy in detail; its culmination came at the Nuremberg party rally in September when Hitler boasted publicly and extensively about the enormous strength of the great barrier in the west—when he had just been told privately that it could not withstand a determined attack.[9]

Hitler's absolute conviction in the summer of 1938 that he could attack Czechoslovakia without precipitating a general war can be seen in his reaction to the reports of two close associates who went to London in July 1938. Albert Forster, the Gauleiter of the Danzig National Socialists, spent 8 to 15 July in England. Since he was known to be a personal associate of Hitler, the authorities in London made every effort to show him something of British industrial and naval strength and to point out to him the bad impression German persecution of the Jews and the Christian churches made in England. As for international affairs, he was told not

---

4. Adam's report in Munich, Institut für Zeitgeschichte, Z.S. 6, p. 1.

5. Sekretär des Führers, "Daten aus alten Notizbüchern": "14.6. [1938] Grosse Besprechung mit Göring über die West-Befestigung" (p. 24), Library of Congress, Manuscripts Division. On Göring's trip, see *Lipski Papers*, p. 370. Cf. *Engel Diary*, 25 June 1938, p. 26, 14 August 1938, p. 32; *D.D.F.*, 2d, 10, No. 97.

6. For the meeting of 30 June, see Adam's report cited in n.4, above. For Hitler's attention to the details of Westwall construction, see the material prepared in response to his questions of 9 June 1938 in 388-PS, *TMWC*, 25:443. For the memorandum of 1 July, see above, p. 318. Cf. *Engel Diary*, pp. 27–29.

7. Cf. *Keitel Papers*, pp. 193–94.

8. *D.D.B.*, 5, No. 18. See also ibid., No. 21.

9. Speech of 12 September 1938 in Domarus, 1:904; on Adam's prior warning, see his statement cited in n.4, above, and *Keitel Papers*, pp. 194–95; *G.D.*, D, 7:552–55.

only that Britain would prefer a quiet evolution of the Danzig issue but that the Sudeten German question would also have to be settled peacefully.[10] The German ambassador to London, Herbert von Dirksen, tried to impress the ardent National Socialist with the same general warning, namely, that England wanted peace but would fight if Germany attacked Czechoslovakia.

Forster was impressed by what he saw and heard; he returned to Germany determined to tell Hitler that Britain was not bluffing and would indeed go to war if Germany insisted on an invasion of Czechoslovakia—only to be confronted by Hitler's certainty that this was not so. Forster himself was converted back to Hitler's perception by 22 July, a few days after his return from England.[11] Ironically, Forster's initial worries about the likelihood of British intervention in any war initiated by a German invasion of Czechoslovakia induced Hitler to exert himself specially in order to persuade his friend of the opposite view. Hitler was so successful with his admirer that the Danzig party leader thereafter became an outspoken advocate of Hitler's view. In fact, he became so vehement in his assertions that Hitler was correct in his belief that England was bluffing that reports of Forster's assessment served to redouble British attempts in September to convince Hitler otherwise, while they alarmed those within the German government who were concerned over the imminent danger of a general war.[12]

If Forster was thus quickly reconverted to Hitler's belief that England could be disregarded as she was only bluffing, another close associate was not so readily influenced, but his failure to convert Hitler testifies to the constancy of the Führer's beliefs. Fritz Wiedemann, who had been Hit-

10. *B.D.*, 3d, 1:653–55; U.S.S.R., Ministry of Foreign Affairs, *Documents and Materials Relating to the Eve of the Second World War* (Moscow: Foreign Languages Publishing House, 1948) (hereafter cited as *D.M.*), 1, No. 13; *Cadogan Diary,* 14 July 1938, p. 86; C 6317/197/55, FO 371/21801; C 7024, C 7313/197/55, FO 371/21802. The Labor leader, Hugh Dalton, also saw Forster at Vansittart's request and warned the Germans not to repeat the mistake of 1914 (Dalton Diary, 13 July 1938). For Churchill's meeting with Forster, see Gilbert, *Churchill,* 5:955–57.

11. Dirksen, pp. 217–18; Burckhardt, pp. 169–73; *G.D.*, D, 2, No. 307; Dirksen report 2901 of 15 July 1938, T-120, 1315/2371/0496052–53 (cited in *G.D.*, D, 5, No. 49, n.1). The German press attaché in London, Fitz Randolph, attended some of the functions arranged for Forster. While he does not mention this in his memoirs, he does report on his own efforts to convince Goebbels that the British were not bluffing (Fitz Randolph, pp. 200–208).

12. *B.D.*, 3d, 2:689–92, and No. 775; *G.D.*, D, 2, Nos. 410, 416; 7:546; Weizsäcker, *Erinnerungen,* p. 179; Burckhardt, pp. 176–87. It should be noted that the report on Forster's recital of Hitler's opinion to Burckhardt was confirmed to the latter by von Weizsäcker, who urged him to have the British warn Hitler by a letter from Chamberlain, an idea discussed in London at a meeting on 9 September of Chamberlain, Halifax, Simon, Vansittart, Hoare, Wilson, and Cadogan. See the cover note to the first document cited in this footnote in C 9525/1941/18, FO 371/21737. The meeting is summarized in *Harvey Diaries,* 8–9 September 1938, pp. 171–73.

In a letter from Hugo Neumann to the magazine *Der Monat* of April 1953 (5:102–4), there is a report on a trip of Albert Forster and Ludwig Noé of the Danzig Shipbuilding Company to England on Hitler's behalf to assess whether or not the British were bluffing in their guarantee of Poland. I am inclined to think there is a confusion here with the 1938 trip.

ler's superior in the war, was appointed adjutant on Hitler's immediate staff in 1934. Interested in foreign affairs, he had been in London several times, most recently in May, when he had observed the May Crisis in the British capital, and again in June.[13] In June the idea of a visit by Göring to London was being advanced; it is not clear whether the idea originated in private British circles or with Göring himself. It is also not possible to reconstruct the relationship of the idea of a Göring visit to Forster's trip.[14] There is, however, no doubt that from the beginning a key figure in making arrangements for the trip by Wiedemann to explore the possibility of a visit by Göring to London was the Princess Stephanie Hohenlohe. A friend of Wiedemann who had contacts in London and was known to Hitler, the Princess was able to have the issue placed before Lord Halifax in such a fashion that Wiedemann could count on being received by the British foreign secretary.[15]

The British reserved comment on any visit by Göring, but they were willing to engage in a canvassing of the possibility in a manner that did not commit them. Everything points to the conclusion that Chamberlain, Halifax, and their advisers were willing to explore any avenue of approach but considered a peaceful settlement of the Czechoslovak question a prerequisite to any serious resumption of the Anglo-German negotiations that had been broken off by Hitler's rejection of the British approach in March.[16] It was in the context of such a possible resumption that the

13. See Wiedemann, p. 126; *Cadogan Diary,* p. 87, n.42; and *Hungarian Documents,* 2, No. 220. There are also some incidental references to these earlier trips in Wiedemann's own documents on his July 1938 visit. I found these documents in 1951 among Wiedemann's papers in the Manuscripts Division of the Library of Congress; they were then—since the appropriate volume of *G.D.* had already appeared—included in D, 7, as Appendix III, H.

14. Wiedemann's assertion in his memoirs (p. 158) that Forster brought the idea back from his London journey cannot be correct because Forster was still in England on the day Wiedemann asked Hitler for permission to go to England to check out the possibility of Göring's going. The suggestion of Wilhelm Höttl (under the pseudonym Walter Hagen), *Die geheime Front* (Linz: Niebelungen-Verlag, 1950), pp. 148–49, that Hitler took the initiative and that the purpose was to cut off Henlein's contacts in London by developing a private line of his own flies in the face of all the evidence. The suggestion of Helmuth K. G. Rönnefarth, *Die Sudetenkrise in der Internationalen Politik* (Wiesbaden: Steiner, 1961), 1:362–63, that Göring may have taken the initiative after reading a detailed report by Helmuth Wohlthat on his conversations in London during June (*G.D.,* D, 2, No. 279) is conceivably correct.

15. The fairest account of the background of the former wife of Prince Friedrich Franz Hohenlohe-Waldenburg-Schillingsfürst is in Celovsky, p. 277, n.1. For the Czechoslovak minister's view of the princess, see Král, *München,* No. 110. Lord Halifax's accounts of his conversations with Lady Snowden on 6 July, with Oliver Hoare (brother of Samuel Hoare) on 8 July, and with Princess Hohenlohe on 14 July 1938, together with comments by Samuel Hoare, Sargent, and Cadogan in C 7344/7262/18, FO 371/21781. The notes of Halifax for Chamberlain on the arrangements for Wiedemann's visit are in PREM 1/330, ff.60–62. See also *Harvey Diaries,* 11–16 July 1938, pp. 161–62.

16. Note the response of Lord Halifax on 23 June 1938 to Viscount Astor, who had cited von Dirksen's comment that Chamberlain's speech after the *Anschluss* closed the door to further negotiations: "German action itself closed it for the time being, and it will only be possible to open it again as the effect of that action wears off, and if there is some confidence that such methods will not be repeated." Halifax to Viscount Waldorf Astor, 23 June 1938, Halifax Papers, FO 800/309.

British leaders looked at the whole question of a Göring visit; von Neurath's planned trip to London had been canceled on a pretext, and the British had seen all they ever wanted of von Ribbentrop. The possibility of reopening contact with the German government through another route thus had some attraction, but much can be learned about the evolution of British policy by contrasting the extraordinary eagerness of Eden to have von Neurath visit London and the determination of Chamberlain to have Halifax see Hitler in 1937, with the cautious reaction to the 1938 soundings from Germany.[17] The intervening annexation of Austria and the contemporary dispute over Czechoslovakia now made the leadership in London quite insistent that any new visit must be carefully prepared. The various accounts of Wiedemann's conversation differ somewhat in detail, but they uniformly stress the importance attached by Lord Halifax to a pledge from Germany that there would be no precipitate action against Czechoslovakia. The implication was obvious and fully understood by Wiedemann: there could be no accommodation between England and Germany, and there was no point to trying to arrange one, if Germany launched a military attack on the Czechoslovak state.

It was, of course, at precisely this point that there was a great dilemma for the German emissary. Wiedemann had received Hitler's approval to go to London to sound out British attitudes, but he had himself been present at the meeting of 28 May at which Hitler had announced his determination to attack Czechoslovakia.[18] Wiedemann's rather tortuous effort in his memoirs to cover his duplicity in assuring the British that there was time for a peaceful settlement and that only outside and unforeseen developments could induce Germany to resort to force, must be understood as a reflection of his unwillingness to admit he deliberately misled the British on what they considered the key issue—a negotiated settlement of the Czechoslovak question—in what appears to have been his own as well as Göring's hope at the time that the resumption of Anglo-German negotiations would in turn bring about a dropping of Hitler's aggressive intentions. Wiedemann's and Göring's deliberate effort to avoid informing von Ribbentrop of the whole project would appear to be largely due to their recognition of von Ribbentrop's opposition to any agreement with England as well as their hope of moving Hitler in that direction by short-circuiting the key foreign policy adviser known to have other views.

The outcome of Wiedemann's conversation with Lord Halifax and Sir Alexander Cadogan was, however, quite different from what might have

17. It must be remembered that whatever the actual origins of the idea of a Göring visit, within the British government of the time it was thought that the approach originated from the German side.

18. Wiedemann's account of the 28 May meeting is in Nuremberg document 3037-PS, National Archives.

been expected.[19] The British were somewhat reassured by Wiedemann's protestations of German pacific intent; in spite of his refusal to give the British any hope that there would be a German renunciation of the use of force against Czechoslovakia, his own preferences and hopes deluded the British on the one point on which Wiedemann was lying. When Lord Halifax was in Paris—for the occasion of a royal visit to France—on the day after his meeting with Wiedemann, he and the French foreign minister could only contrast Wiedemann's assurances with the warnings they were all getting about German military activities.[20]

As for the possibility of any follow up in the diplomatic sphere, the various procedures for future Anglo-German negotiations that had been discussed in London by Wiedemann and Lord Halifax were quickly terminated by Hitler's total disinterest. In recollections written after Hitler had "exiled" him to the post of consul general in San Francisco, Wiedemann referred to this episode as a sign of the Führer's unwillingness to reach any agreement with England; Hitler had allowed Wiedemann only five minutes to report on his trip and had refused any visit by Göring as out of the question.[21] Those recollections were penned over a year after the event; when Wiedemann talked with the chief of staff of the German army, General Ludwig Beck, a few days after he had been in London and Berchtesgaden, he told Beck of Hitler's brusque rejection of any negotiations and confirmed the general's recognition that "the Führer remains of the opinion that a war must be conducted against Czechoslovakia, *even if France and England intervene*, something which he [Hitler] does not believe [will happen]."[22] The very mission that had been initiated with the hope of arranging negotiations for a settlement led to confusion on the side of the Western Powers, revealed Hitler's determination to go to war regardless of any danger of British and French intervention, and spurred on those inside the German government opposed to the risks Hitler was prepared to incur.

19. In addition to the sources previously cited, see *B.D.*, 3d, 1, Nos. 510, 511; 7, Annex IV, No. iv; Wiedemann, pp. 158–67; Dirksen, pp. 215–17; *G.D.*, D, 2:439, 445, 450; Feiling, p. 356; Fritz Hesse, *Das Spiel um Deutschland* (Munich: List, 1953), p. 125; *D.M.*, 2:155–56; *Cadogan Diary*, 17 and 18 July 1938, pp. 86–88; *Harvey Diaries*, 11–18 July 1938, pp. 161–64; Cabinet Conclusion 33 (38) of 20 July 1938, and Cadogan to Henderson, 21 July 1938, in C 7344/7262/18, FO 371/21781. The account in Keith Middlemas, *The Strategy of Appeasement* (Chicago: Quadrangle, 1972), pp. 264–66, provides some additional evidence but is not correct in its general outlines. General Beck's review of the Wiedemann mission, based on a conversation with the latter on 28 July, is discussed below; it is in Bundesarchiv, Nachlass Beck, H 08-28/4. Information on the visit received by the Czechoslovak government is in a short memorandum of 21 July 1938, T-120, 1041/1809/413989; cf. Král, *München*, No. 109.

20. *B.D.*, 3d, 1, No. 523. Cf. *G.D.*, D, 2, No. 308; *D.D.F.*, 2d, 10, No. 237.

21. *G.D.*, D, 7:545; cf. Wiedemann, p. 166.

22. Emphasis in the original, see above, n.19. The text of this document in Foerster, pp. 106–8, has been rearranged; in the original, the passage quoted here is the second sentence. See also Wiedemann's comments to von Weizsäcker on 22 August cited in *Weizsäcker-Papiere*, p. 137.

General Beck's warning of early May and Hitler's rejection of it have already been mentioned. Hitler's address of 28 May in which he expressed his determination to attack Czechoslovakia had been heard by Beck, who promptly responded in a detailed memorandum in which he expressed his basic agreement with Germany's need for space and the desirability of a forceful solution of the Czechoslovak question, but insisted that Germany was not ready for war, that the conflict would be general, and that the whole German military planning mechanism was faulty.[23] The anxiety of the chief-of-staff was heightened further when, almost in response to these warnings, Hitler's immediate staff—the High Command of the Armed Forces (OKW)—issued the revised version of the plan for the attack on Czechoslovakia on the following day.[24] Again Beck penned a critique of the proposed operation, now more vehement than earlier, and rejected both the general estimate of the political situation and the details of military planning contained in the order. In denouncing the directive to von Brauchitsch, the commander-in-chief of the army, Beck asserted that the whole scheme was so poorly conceived and developed that the general staff of the army would have to reject any and all responsibility for it.[25] Beck wanted von Brauchitsch to work for changes in both the military command structure as it was evolving in 1938 and the intention of attacking Czechoslovakia; and he attempted to reinforce these views by staging a general staff exercise which showed that the intended operation would entail disaster for Germany.[26]

There was, however, no prospect of rallying von Brauchitsch to any clear position that might thwart Hitler's policy. Beck had tried before, he would try again; and his successor as well as others inside and outside the German army would try to move von Brauchitsch. But the man without a backbone could not be provided with one by his associates. When taking over his position in February from the besmirched von Fritsch, the new commander-in-chief had sold himself and sold out the army to Hitler. Von Brauchitsch was accepting financial assistance from Hitler so he could divorce his wife and marry a woman whose past was hardly better than that of the woman whose marriage to von Blomberg had led to the latter's disgrace.[27] That event had provided the occasion for the dismissal of von

23. The memorandum of 29 May is in Bundesarchiv, H 08-28/3. Parts have been published in Foerster, pp. 90–94; there is a good summary and discussion in Müller, pp. 309–12; cf. *Engel Diary*, pp. 22–25.

24. This is the new version of "Operation Green" of 30 May 1938, text in *TMWC*, 25:433–39. The opening lines of Beck's memorandum of 3 June, cited below, refer explicitly to this document.

25. The full text has been published in Müller, pp. 651–54.

26. Ibid., pp. 313–14.

27. The fact that von Brauchitsch was tied to Hitler by a private scandal was known to at least some people at the time. Vansittart noted on 9 August 1938: "Hitler has a stranglehold on Brauchitsch of some private and discreditable kind; whether it is connected with the fact that Brauchitsch is billed for divorce, or with something dirtier and rifer still, I am at present unable to say." The conclusion Sir Robert drew, that the German army would do whatever it

Fritsch and von Brauchitsch's own appointment; he was therefore hardly the one to stand up to Hitler. It was accordingly quite in character for von Brauchitsch to assist Hitler in surmounting the crisis of confidence in the German army over the disgraceful treatment of von Fritsch at a special meeting held at Barth in Pomerania on 13 June.

Following the complete exoneration of von Fritsch, there were serious rumblings in the German officer corps about the shabby treatment accorded a man who was generally revered; and in late May and early June reports of such disaffection and the possibility of collective resignations by high level commanders reached Hitler. The Führer carefully used the international danger he was himself creating to head off disaffection.[28] First von Brauchitsch told the assembled high ranking officers that war with Czechoslovakia would soon come and that a vast program of building fortifications in the west would shield Germany in that operation. Under these circumstances no one should leave his post, and any who might be thinking of it should reconsider. After this shocker—for many of those present had not hitherto been given any such explicit indication that war was ahead—Hitler regaled the audience with a carefully contrived set of fairy tales about the von Fritsch case which appears to have gone over rather well. As Harold Deutsch has put it: "Hitler had again shown his exceptional insight into the tendency of men torn between conscience and self-interest to welcome what made it easier to opt for the latter."[29]

Once von Brauchitsch had totally identified himself in front of the officer corps with Hitler's handling of the two crises, one internal and the other external, and with this joining of the two, it is hardly surprising that he would not agree to Beck's logically opposite conclusions from the same junction. Von Brauchitsch, like Hitler, saw the imminent war against Czechoslovakia as a fine pretext for not reopening the messy scandal which he had ridden to the highest position in the army. Beck—who had not been present at Barth—was all the more alarmed about Hitler's insistence on going to war, and coupled this alarm with an increasing concern about the unscrupulous procedures and policies of the regime's domestic institutions. Beck's more vehement formulations of July stand as a memorial to his own courage and judgment, but they could not move von Brauchitsch. Beck's remonstrances culminated in the recommendation of 16 July that pressure be applied by a sort of general strike of the generals if Hitler persisted in his course; this may well have reminded von Brauchitsch of the mass resignation threats he had just

---

was told without resistance, was not entirely correct, however (C 9591/1941/18, FO 371/21737). For a subsequent reference to the matter by Hitler himself—clear evidence of the fact that the Führer was both aware of the situation of von Brauchitsch and quite willing to throw it up to him, even in front of subordinate officers—see the entry under 20 August 1941 in *Engel Diary*, pp. 109–10.

28. An excellent account of the meeting is in Deutsch, pp. 401–6.

29. Ibid., p. 406.

warded off and led only to Beck's resignation.[30] As Sir Lewis Namier commented on Beck's effort to inspire von Brauchitsch to a more responsible role: "Sense, courage, and character cannot be transmitted from him who has them to him who has not."[31]

Neither Beck's appeal and warning against the dangers of a world war seen as the unavoidable by-product of a German attack on Czechoslovakia nor similar warnings by Admiral Guse, the chief of staff of the German navy, and by Ernst von Weizsäcker, now the secretary of state in the German foreign ministry, altered the course Hitler was determined to follow.[32] Beck was allowed to resign; Guse was transferred by Raeder to an unimportant position.[33] Only von Weizsäcker remained at his post, encouraged by von Ribbentrop to have greater faith in Hitler's assessment of the situation but actually retaining his doubts. The state secretary as well as some of the other military opponents of Hitler's risky schemes would resort to other means of attempting to avert war, but in the meantime the military preparations moved forward.

Beck's opposition to the proposed attack on Czechoslovakia had not led to a refusal to participate in the needed preparatory work. On the contrary, the army was indeed going ahead with its preparations.[34] While at Hitler's headquarters the general problems of a war against Czechoslovakia with or without intervention of other powers were being examined,[35] German society as a whole was affected by the necessary acceleration of military preparations. A series of measures in June and July was designed to improve the utilization of German manpower resources, but such steps were only a portion of the broader reorganization necessitated by the impact of speeded up armaments programs on an economy already at full employment and one in which the government was reluctant to cut too deeply into civilian consumption and prestige projects. It is no coincidence that the months of June, July, and August 1938 saw a substantial redirection and reorganization of the structure of

30. On the developments of 13–29 July 1938, see Müller, pp. 317–33; cf. *Engel Diary*, 18 and 24 July 1938, pp. 27–28.

31. *In the Nazi Era*, p. 32.

32. Guse's memorandum of 17 July 1938 is quoted extensively by Helmut Krausnick in *Vollmacht des Gewissens* (Munich: Rinn, 1956), 1:311–13. Guse's operations officer, Helmut Heye, expressed similar doubts in even stronger language. Von Weizsäcker's memoranda of early June, 12 July, and 21 July, in *G.D.*, D, 2, Nos. 259 (cf. *TMWC*, 39:98), 288, 304, 374 (see also Namier, *In the Nazi Era*, pp. 72–74). For a contemporary appreciation by the French ambassador in Berlin, see *U.S.*, 1938, 1:61–62.

33. Dülffer's speculation (p. 476, n.18) that there was a connection between the effective end of Guse's naval career and his views on the implications of Hitler's plans is probably correct. The account in Salewski, 1:44–45, is rather weak. Cf. Walter Baum, "Marine, Nationalsozialismus und Widerstand," *Vierteljahrshefte für Zeitgeschichte*, 11, No. 1 (Jan. 1963), 22–23.

34. Beck alludes to this in his own memorandum of 16 July; the staff exercise he conducted shows, on the other hand, that he fervently hoped no such attack would actually be launched (cf. Müller, p. 313). Note the French strategic appreciation of 13 July 1938 in *D.D.F.*, 2d, 10, No. 202.

35. *TMWC*, 25:445–60.

Göring's Four-Year Plan with a shift of emphasis from long-term plans for autarchy to more immediate concerns of economic mobilization.[36]

The fact that Göring himself would as soon have seen Czechoslovakia succumb to Germany without war, or if by war, then only by a carefully isolated campaign, certainly did not mean that he was in any way holding back the preparations for a conflict. On the contrary, the German air force was carrying forward its own planning in the summer of 1938 on the assumption that a war over Czechoslovakia would entail war with England and France.[37] The record of Göring's own analysis of the situation on 8 July cannot be taken literally in all respects as he was speaking to a large group of aircraft industry leaders, but other evidence suggests that his comments generally reflected both his views at the time and his aspirations for the future.[38] Göring expressed the opinion that Germany had attained and could maintain superiority in airpower development and looked forward to the day when Germany had the kind of bombers that could fly to New York and return. Production had to be speeded up, and the aircraft industry would have to subordinate professional and commercial rivalry to the common endeavor.[39] As for the immediate future, Göring thought that there was a slight possibility of isolating a war against Czechoslovakia. He knew that France and Britain were reluctant to fight, but he recognized that attitudes in England were hardening, especially since the *Anschluss* and in anticipation of further German moves if Czechoslovakia were once destroyed. Göring, therefore, summarized both the short-run and long-term prospects of having the isolated small wars Hitler preferred at 10–15 percent as compared with an 80–90 percent chance of a world war.[40] In such a war, Germany could triumph and be the world's leading power, or lose and be crushed forever. Göring thought that Germany had a chance to win, or at least he claimed to have that belief. Certainly the German air force would be a major factor in any hope of victory the country might have, and he was not about to forgo any measure that could strengthen it.[41] Göring appears to have had res-

36. A useful account in Petzina, pp. 116–21.
37. The "Fall Rot" study of 2 June 1938 of a section of the German air force (Luftwaffengruppenkommando 3) is clearly based on this view, see *TMWC*, 38:412–19.
38. The text of the stenographic record is in ibid., pp. 376–401. No record of Göring's 14 June meeting with Hitler about the Westwall has come to light, and it is therefore impossible to determine to what extent that conversation influenced Göring's remarks on 8 July. See also *D.D.F.*, 2d, 10, Nos. 97, 270.
39. This point reflects the problem of competition within the German aircraft industry, a competition that was extraordinarily bitter at times, and of which Göring was very much aware in the years when he was quite actively involved in the building up of the Luftwaffe. The memoirs of Heinkel are one long refrain on the competition theme.
40. Göring refers to it as "einen grösseren Kladderadatsch" (a bigger mess); the context leaves no doubt as to his meaning.
41. The fragmentary character of the surviving record of the German air force has had a retarding influence on scholarly study of its history. Some information on 1938 developments may be found in Völcker, pp. 159–61, and in Karl Gundelach, "Gedanken über die Führung eines Luftkrieges gegen England bei der Luftflotte 2 in den Jahren 1938/39: Ein Beitrag zur Vorgeschichte der Luftschlacht um England," *Wehrwissenschaftliche Rundschau*, 10, No. 1 (Jan. 1960), 33–46. There is a useful survey in Homze, chap. 7.

ervations about the risk of war with England,[42] but the preparations of the Luftwaffe went forward. The basic plan of the air force would be a surprise attack on Czechoslovak airfields combined with a massive bombing of Prague.[43] The fate intended for Prague would befall Belgrade in 1941, but the Germans were certainly not bluffing in 1938.

The plans and construction programs of the German navy were also affected by the anticipation of an early war against Czechoslovakia that could precipitate a war with England. What Raeder really thought is not likely ever to be known; but he was quite willing to go along with whatever Hitler wanted, and the replacement of the doubting Guse by the unquestioning Schniewind as chief of the naval staff during 1938 cannot be interpreted in any way other than as a sign of Raeder's approval of Hitler's intentions as opposed to the doubts of Beck and Guse. It should be noted that Hitler appears not to have been aware of Guse's views; he certainly knew Beck's. If von Brauchitsch was hesitant about passing on the opinions of his chief of staff and did so only in a modified form, Raeder never even transmitted those of his chief of staff.[44]

When Hitler was developing the specifics of the planned attack on Czechoslovakia and reviewing Keitel's draft revision in May, the naval role in that operation was seen as rather small. This did not preclude Hitler from giving detailed attention to the naval construction implications of a war or the danger of a war with England.[45] Hitler was apparently thinking of using an accelerated submarine construction program against England somewhat the way the construction of the Westwall was to be used against France: as a means of discouraging intervention if possible, and as a useful tool of warfare if intervention took place after all.[46] In addition, the battleships *Bismarck* and *Tirpitz,* which were designed in part as oceanic shipping raiders, were to be finished earlier than originally scheduled and the six superbattleships of 56,000 tons originally planned for construction in sequence—with the keels of the last two laid in the

42. Beck's report on his conversation with Wiedemann on 27 July cites the latter as asserting that Göring was not one of those pushing for war, something Wiedemann had been able to confirm recently.

43. This emerges from the review of 24 August of the timing of the "incident" which would herald the German attack, *TMWC,* 25:460–61.

44. There is now general agreement, which I share, that Kurt Assmann's assertion in *Deutsche Schicksalsjahre* (Wiesbaden: Brockhaus, 1950), p. 45, that a naval memorandum along the lines of Guse's was shown to Hitler is incorrect. Assmann worked on the naval archives and may have seen Guse's and Heye's warnings—which never went outside the High Command of the navy. Speculation in the navy that England might enter a war started by a German attack on Czechoslovakia was expressly prohibited in the summer of 1938 (Munich, Institut für Zeitgeschichte, Z.S. Nr. 1809).

45. The most important source is a telegram from Hitler's naval adjutant, Jesko von Puttkammer, of 24 May 1938, containing both questions and wishes of Hitler concerning the naval construction program. See Gemzell, pp. 79–82; Dülffer, pp. 468–70. This document is the naval equivalent of the questions Hitler was simultaneously asking of the army.

46. This deterrent idea of massive submarine construction had already been a part of Hitler's projections in November 1937, see above, p. 41.

stocks previously used for the first two—were now to be constructed simultaneously (with more presumably to be built thereafter).

The details of the revised naval construction planning and of the strategic thinking within the naval staff need not be reviewed here.[47] Two points only should be included in a discussion of developments during the summer of 1938. In the first place, the discussions within the navy of various alternative construction programs and related strategies for battleships and possibly also battle cruisers all revolved around ships that could not be ready for a long time; only submarines and small surface vessels could be constructed in a short time span. In the second place, it was determined that the construction of large ships already under way was more likely to be delayed by shortages of men and materials rather than speeded up; in reality as opposed to planning, the big ships would be ready behind, not ahead of, schedule. This was due in part to overly optimistic estimates, but even more to the competition of other projects for manpower and other resources. The very same impulse which was driving the naval program forward was also responsible for the massive construction program on the Westwall with its insatiable demands for cement, steel, and labor, as well as the continued expansion of the air force. If the more ambitious projects of the navy were not moving forward as rapidly as Hitler and Raeder both wanted, competing demands for resources, not restraint or reluctance, were responsible.[48]

Hitler's insistence on going forward can only be taken as a measure of his self-confidence, a self-confidence that was combined with a great sense of urgency.[49] This personal element, the belief that only he could accomplish what he had in mind for Germany, that he must therefore move quickly using the generals now available for the first blows and a new set for the next ones,[50] and that all other considerations would have to be thrust aside in the rush to world power status, simply cannot be overlooked in any analysis of the extraordinary race for world empire as Hitler saw it, or to total disaster as others warned. By the time the agitated discussions of June and July showed Hitler the discrepancy between his views and those of Beck and others—Jodl characterized them as between "the recognition of the Führer that we *must* still [move] this year

47. Details in Dülffer, pp. 471–89.

48. I cannot omit recording my view that an extraordinary profusion of naval staff offices of diverse imaginable and unimaginable complexity contributed to delay. This was a disease that had afflicted the German navy as early as the Wilhelminian period. The problem of too many staffs for too few ships continued into the war.

49. Note that he was no more interested in talking to von Dirksen when the latter returned from London early in August than he had been in hearing out Wiedemann two weeks earlier (Dirksen, pp. 229–31). On 27 June he had done his best to assure French General Henri LeRond that France had nothing to worry about (*D.D.F.*, 2d, 10, No. 131; Adamthwaite, pp. 195–96). On 15 August, on the other hand, Hitler told the army commanders: "I am very much afraid that something could happen to me before I can carry out the necessary decisions. The most necessary decision: expanding living space." (Diary of Keitel's adjutant, Wolf Eberhard, Munich, Institut für Zeitgeschichte).

50. A comment of Hitler's quoted by Beck in his memorandum of 16 July.

and the view of the army that we cannot yet do it because the Western Powers will certainly intervene and we cannot yet stand up to them"[51]—the Führer must have had the medical opinion reassuring him that his fear of early May that he was suffering from cancer was groundless. Nevertheless, one may be permitted to speculate that such a reminder of mortality had some effect on an impatient man not too different from the one that would be produced by his fiftieth birthday in 1939.[52]

The summer of 1938 accordingly saw the military preparations of Germany pushed forward as rapidly as the country's resources, internal organizational rivalries and confusions, and reluctance to impose serious restrictions on civilian life allowed. These preparations were accompanied by a continuing propaganda campaign designed to isolate Czechoslovakia from external support. There were, in reality, relatively few incidents in the Sudeten area at the time, but as one contemporary German observer explained: "The tactics of the government of the Reich have hitherto provided for the utilization of the least significant incident in order to shake the conscience of the world."[53]

The great concern of the British government over the possibility of German military action that would precipitate a world war has been mentioned in connection with the Wiedemann mission. Throughout June and July the London authorities tried to urge a settlement. Their approach to the problem might fairly be described as consisting of four parallel lines pursued simultaneously.[54]

The first of these, appearing with great frequency and ever increasing vigor, was pressure on the Czechoslovak government to make extensive concessions to the Sudeten Germans.[55] One subsidiary aspect of this line

51. The entry is part of the subsequently inserted sheet in Jodl's diary; internal evidence suggests that it was written between 24 July and 10 August 1938 (*TMWC*, 28:373). A striking contemporary reflection of the confusion over fundamental responsibilities, the organization of the German military command structure, and the plans and risks of an attack on Czechoslovakia, may be found in General Erich von Manstein's letter of 21 July 1938 to Beck, urging the latter not to resign (full text in Müller, pp. 656–65).

52. The evidence is fragmentary but suggests that the decision to speed up the timetable on the Czechoslovak operation, which in the preceding chapter has been shown to antedate the May Crisis—and hence cannot be attributed to it—is quite possibly related to this health question, which at least coincides in time with the shift of early May. If this is so, it would also explain why Hitler found it convenient to refer to the May Crisis as an explanation. His own first recorded mention of the health problem of early May 1938 is dated from 29 March 1942 (Weinberg, "Hitler's Private Testament," p. 415; cf. Otto Dietrich, *12 Jahre mit Hitler* [Cologne: Atlas, 1955], p. 227). Perhaps the comments of Dr. Theodor Morell cited in *D.D.F.*, 2d, 10, No. 149 belong in this context.

53. "Informationsbericht Nr. 43," 14 June 1938, Bundesarchiv, Brammer, Z.Sg. 101/32, ff.395–97; cf. the report of 18 July in ibid., 101/33, f.41.

54. The diplomacy of the summer of 1938 has been covered extensively by Celovsky, Eubank, Rönnefarth, and Kvaček. Only the main outlines and additional information will be reviewed here. The account given the cabinet by Lord Halifax on 22 June provides a good summary of the situation as seen in London (C 6272/1941/18, FO 371/21725).

55. See C 5985/1941/18, FO 371/21724; C 6037, C 6055 (comment on *B.D.*, 3d, 1, No. 426)/1941/18, FO 371/21725; Cabinet 32 (38) of 13 July 1938, C 7072/1941/18, FO 371/21727; *Cadogan Diary*, 8 and 17 June 1938, pp. 82, 83. That there were limits to the pressure the British government was willing to apply on Czechoslovakia in the summer of 1938 can be seen in the Foreign Office's negative comments on Henderson's proposals of 30 June in

was the repeated—and usually successful—effort to have the French, as allies of Czechoslovakia, assume a position of almost blackmailing the Czechs by threatening a rupture of the alliance if Prague failed to comply. A second aspect of this approach was the attempt to take account of what was believed to be a difference of opinion within the Czechoslovak government where the prime minister, Milan Hodža, was reputed to be more amenable to concessions than President Beneš.[56]

The second major theme was to utilize the contact with Henlein to restrain him and his followers and to secure some insight into the conduct and prospects of the negotiations.[57] It is by no means very clear in this who was using whom, but on balance it must be said that Sir Robert Vansittart, who played the key role in these contacts, was misled by Henlein, who, it should be added, had also kept some of his own closest associates from knowledge of his real intentions and instructions.[58]

If these two lines dealt with the continuing negotiations between Czechoslovakia and the Sudeten Germans, the other two dealt with the contingency of these negotiations being broken off. On the one hand, the London government had once before, during the May Crisis, taken Henlein's breaking off talks with Prague as an occasion to warn Berlin that German military action could lead to a general war; and it found ways to get this same message explicitly and implicitly to the German government through Forster, Wiedemann, von Dirksen, and even Henderson.[59] On the other hand, if direct talks between Czechoslovak and Sudeten leaders were interrupted, the only possible alternative to a German invasion was seen in some other, indirect, form of German-Czechoslovak negotiations. For this purpose, the British government had at one point thought of some

---

B.D., D, 1, No. 458 under C 6600/1941/18, FO 371/21726, and again his proposals of 21 July in *B.D.*, 3d, 1, No. 532 under C 7375/1941/18, FO 371/21729. For French complaints about Henderson's comments in Berlin, see *D.D.F.*, 2d, 10, Nos. 130, 336, 338, 359.

56. C 5424/1941/18, FO 371/21723; C 5807/1941/18, FO 371/21724; C 7591/1941/18, FO 371/21729; Celovsky, pp. 257–61, 293. It is worth noting that Churchill privately expressed himself to Hubert Ripka in June in London along very similar lines, urging agreement with Henlein, referring to differences between Beneš and Hodža, and saying that while a critic of Chamberlain, he might himself act in the same way if he had the responsibility. Churchill also raised the question of a guaranteed neutral status for Czechoslovakia (Král, *München*, No. 94).

57. Vansittart's minute of 14 June, C 6643/1941/18, FO 371/21726; V.'s minute of 16 June, C 5989/1941/18, FO 371/21724; V.'s note of 21 June, C 6236/1941/18, FO 371/21725; V.'s minute of 27 June, C 6644/1941/18, FO 371/21726; V.'s memorandum of 12 July, C 7009/1941/18, FO 371/21727; V.'s minute of 22 July, C 7512/1941/18, FO 371/21729; V.'s minute of 26 July, C 7591/1941/18, ibid.; V.'s minute of 27 July, C 7634/1941/18, ibid.; V.'s minute of 3 August, C 7877/1941/18, FO 371/21730; Král, *Die Deutschen*, No. 172. Sir Robert's own very large role in unintentionally facilitating Henlein's deception of the British government may have had considerable influence on the violence of his subsequent anti-German attitude. Note his comments on Henlein in an essay on the Munich crisis in *Bones of Contention* (New York: Knopf, 1945), p. 122.

58. Celovsky, p. 289.

59. The meetings with Forster and Wiedemann have been discussed. On von Dirksen, see his report of 10 July in *G.D.*, D, 1, No. 793 (with a wrong date, see *D.M.*, 1:123). On Henderson, see *Hungarian Documents*, 2, No. 270.

sort of commission but turned increasingly to the idea of a British intermediary who would talk with both sides, examine the situation, and, it
was hoped, provide a mechanism for a peaceful solution. It was in this
context, of course, that the origins of the Runciman mission must be
found; and it was for this reason—that in case of a rupture in the talks
London saw such a mission as the only alternative to war—that such great
efforts were made to have both the Czechoslovak government and Henlein agree to his coming in the role of mediator.[60]

If one asks, just what did the British have in mind as a possible format
for a settlement, it is by no means easy to give an answer. The mass of
evidence, both published and unpublished, indicates that the British leaders thought that some form of autonomy would have to be accorded to the
Sudeten Germans and that this might lead to their secession from Czechoslovakia. It would also appear that Chamberlain and Halifax believed a
new international status would have to be found for Czechoslovakia at the
same time, a belief that, of course, assumes the continued existence of an
independent Czechoslovak state.[61] That status would take some neutralized form, possibly similar to that of Belgium since 1937, in which
Czechoslovakia would not have alliances (except possibly the Little Entente) but instead would receive guarantees of her independence from
other powers, including Great Britain.[62] It appears to have been thought
in London that Czechoslovakia might be nudged in this direction over a
period of time, with the Germans finding themselves having to agree to
such an arrangement with a general war as the alternative if they insisted
on more. That they wanted more was indeed suspected,[63] but whether
they would insist on it with all the risks involved was the big question.

60. A note by Sargent of 30 April first suggested a British mediator; see it and comments
on it in C 3316/1941/18, FO 371/21716; for subsequent developments, see the Foreign Office
comments on *B.D.*, 3d, 1, No. 359 in C 5297/1941/18, FO 371/21723; 31st meeting of the
cabinet Committee on Foreign Policy of 16 June 1938, CAB 27/624; Cabinet 29 (38) of 22
June 1938, C 6272/1941/18, FO 371/21725; Cabinet 31 (38) of 6 July 1938, C 6868/1941/18, FO
371/21727; C 7249/1941/18, FO 371/21728; Cabinet 33 (38) of 20 July 1938, C 7406/1941/18,
FO 371/21729; Vansittart's minute of 25 July, C 7560/1941/18, ibid.; V.'s minute of 26 July, C
7591/1941/18, ibid.; Cabinet 35 (38) of 27 July 1938, C 7707/1941/18, FO 371/21730; *D.D.F.*,
2d, 10, Nos. 237, 261, 266, 268, 276, 278.
61. There appears also to have been some thought given to the possible need for a politically less charged name for the country, but that presupposed the maintenance of its territorial integrity; see C 6600/1941/18, FO 371/21726, f.202.
62. Cabinet 27 (38) of 1 June 1938, C 5424/1941/18, FO 371/21723; C 5870/1941/18, FO
371/21724 (which should be compared with the less thoughtful earlier memorandum printed
in *B.D.*, 3d, 1, Appendix I); Cabinet 28 (38) of 15 June 1938, C 5980/1941/18, ibid.; C 6009, C
6010, C 6039/1941/18, FO 371/21725; 31st meeting of the cabinet Committee on Foreign
Policy, CAB 27/624; *Harvey Diaries*, 8 and 18 June 1938, pp. 151–52, 154. French criticism
of the British ideas revolved around their disadvantages for France (*D.D.F.*, 2d, 10, No.
170).
63. See the Foreign Office comments on Newton's 204 of 27 May (*B.D.*, 3d, 1, No. 327) to
the effect that the Sudeten German party no doubt received orders from Berlin to add new
conditions whenever there appeared to be the possibility of agreement (C 5083/1941/18, FO
371/21722), and on Henderson's 254 of 1 June (*B.D.*, 3d, 1, No. 359) that Hitler would not
like the removal "of a valuable grievance" (C 5297/1941/18, FO 371/21723).

It was on this last question, whether Hitler was determined on an attack on Czechoslovakia under any and all circumstances that London faced the gravest dilemma. It was precisely on this subject that a variety of sources from inside Germany were directing warnings to London, often with the implication or explicit assertion that a firm and clear warning to Hitler from the British government would lead the Führer to desist.

The concept of the British warning as a key to peace and the great role it played in the discussions in London as well as among some elements in Germany can be understood only with reference to the widely discussed opinion in government circles in both Britain and Germany that if the British foreign secretary had clearly and emphatically told the German government in 1914 that Great Britain would join France and Russia if Germany went to war, the German government would have pressured Austria into moderating its demands on Serbia or into accepting the Serb reply to their ultimatum, with war being averted as a result. More recent analyses of 1914 show, to my satisfaction, that the situation within the British cabinet made such a step by Sir Edward Grey impossible, and that even if he had made it, he would subsequently only have been accused of encouraging Russia and France to go to war since Germany's military plans and policies already assumed British intervention—though abstention would naturally have been preferred. But the leaders of governments act on their perceptions of the past, not the later arguments of scholars; and the belief in the importance and assumed efficacy of a formal British warning stands at the center of much of the debate in London as well as the unofficial contacts from Germans anxious to avert war.

The assumption, held especially in England by Chamberlain as well as others, that the British warning in May had stopped the Germans from moving at that time served to reinforce belief in the significance of such a step; but the real or feigned annoyance of Hitler at the subsequent public emphasis on his having backed down in the face of external threats was believed in London to make a repetition of such a warning dangerous because it was feared that Hitler's concern for prestige would lead him to take in defiance the very step that the warning was supposed to avert. It was out of this mixture of historical analogies and correct as well as incorrect assessments of the current situation that there emerged, first, the reluctance of the British to send a formal warning with its threat of general war and, second, the decision at the last minute to send such a warning after all but in what was thought to be a format least likely to provoke a negative reaction on Hitler's part, concern for which had contributed to the delay in sending it. As will be seen in the discussion of the final crisis in 1939, the written warning to Hitler then included specific reference to the allegation that if the British "had made their position more clear in 1914, the great catastrophe would have been avoided,"[64]

64. Chamberlain to Hitler, 22 August 1939, *B.D.*, 3d, 7, No. 145.

though in the event, Hitler was to disregard it for reasons that will be reviewed later—but one was his regret at having backed off in the face of such a warning in 1938.

The suggestions from some in Germany, telling the London government that Hitler intended an invasion of Czechoslovakia and that he could be deterred from this step only by a firm warning of British intervention, were by no means unanimous. The German state secretary, Ernst von Weizsäcker, would eventually come to that point of view, but during July he was in fact urging the British to *reduce* the appearance of commitment to fight if Czechoslovakia were attacked for fear that Beneš would not make great concessions unless left in doubt.[65] Von Weizsäcker's preference was clearly for the disintegration of Czechoslovakia under pressure rather than war, what he called a chemical rather than a mechanical solution.[66] During July, however, the London government began to hear from its intelligence sources that Germany would go to war in the fall.[67] Chamberlain's initial reaction was one of skepticism;[68] but later in July, as new and more specific information about a likely German attack reached London, frequently through Vansittart's sources, the threat began to be taken more seriously, though the planned German action was generally reported as scheduled from any time after the end of August, when it was actually planned for a month later.[69]

Early in August, London received two separate reports on a meeting of Hitler, Göring, and others at Berchtesgaden which in spite of some inaccuracies of detail reflected the realities of the situation rather precisely: the German determination to attack after the harvest, the insistence on moving forward regardless of risks and obstacles, and the doubts of the German military about the Westwall.[70] At the same time, that is, in the first days of August, the British began to get serious and specific warnings concerning Hitler's intentions from the opposition to Hitler inside Germany. The civilian opposition around Carl Goerdeler sent some details;[71] while the military opposition, centered in the Abwehr, the armed forces intelligence agency, warned of the attack scheduled for 28 September and announced the intention of sending a special emissary, Ewald von

65. *U.S.*, 1938, 1:528–29, and again ibid., p. 566.

66. *G.D.*, D, 1, No. 586; cf. *Hungarian Documents*, 2, No. 260. Similar views appear in von Weizsäcker's memoirs and in many other published documents.

67. C 7009/1941/18, FO 371/21727; C 7512/1941/18, FO 371/21729.

68. Note his comments at the cabinet meeting of 13 July, C 7072/1941/18, FO 371/21727.

69. C 7591, C 7614, C 7634/1941/18, FO 371/21729; cf. C 7461/42/18, FO 371/21657.

70. The meeting is dated to 4 July in one report and to 14 July in another (C 7871/1941/18, FO 371/21730; C 8189/1941/18, FO 371/21731). The report was thought plausible and seen by both Halifax and Chamberlain. Mastný reported on the meeting "around July 14" in his report 153 of 6 August 1938, Czechoslovak document in T-120, 1039/1809/412161–63. Whether or not such a meeting took place and on which date is unclear. If it did occur, the most likely original source of the leak would be General Karl Bodenschatz, who had a habit of telling all he knew to all he met.

71. C 8088/62/18, FO 371/21664.

Kleist-Schmenzin, to London.[72] By 9 August Sir Robert Vansittart had become convinced that Hitler did intend to move, thought that the army would follow orders regardless of the doubts of many of its leaders, and urged a program of warnings to the German government.[73]

Earlier in the summer, the authorities in London had been quite willing to use threats as a means of securing a policy change by the German government. As previously mentioned, after the Germans annexed Austria, they announced that they would no longer pay interest due on Austria's indebtedness abroad, an action that would leave the British government, which had guaranteed some of the bonds, with the obligation of paying the bondholders. Since Great Britain bought more from than she sold to Germany, the threat of imposing a clearing system on Anglo-German trade would force Germany to choose between paying the interest or losing foreign exchange earnings. At cabinet meetings on 1 and 15 June, the London government decided unanimously to use the threat. As Chamberlain said when the Germans responded by a conciliatory move: "This confirmed previous experience of the need of great firmness in negotiations with Germany."[74] An accommodation was reached in the signing of two agreements on 1 July; though some concessions were made by the British negotiator, the major ones came from the German side.

The idea that only a firm stand might influence Hitler was, thus, by no means unknown to those in charge in London; if they were reluctant to utilize this approach in spite of ever more insistent warnings about German intentions, it was due to an unwillingness to go that route until there was clearly no alternative; lives, not money, were at stake. This can be seen in the reaction to the warnings of early August. A fairly accurate report on Hitler's intention of attacking at the end of September, received by Lord Lloyd from a confidant in Germany, was transmitted to the Foreign Office, where it was seen as a confirmation of the comments of Ewald von Kleist-Schmenzin and transmitted to 10 Downing Street for that reason.[75] Von Kleist had been seen in London by Vansittart and Churchill with the approval of Chamberlain and Halifax.[76] The con-

72. Colvin, *None So Blind*, pp. 218–21 (Colvin to Lord Lloyd, 3 August 1938). Note, however, that some skepticism remained in the Foreign Office, see the comments of Victor Mallet on the report printed as *B.D.*, 3d, 2, No. 595 under C 8173/65/18, FO 371/21668, a document seen by Halifax and Chamberlain.

73. C 9591/1941/18, FO 371/21737.

74. Cabinet 27 (38) of 1 June 1938, C 5414/30/18, FO 371/21644. The appropriate extract from Cabinet 28 (38) of 15 June 1938 is in C 5992/30/18, FO 371/21645, and an important note by Ashton-Gwatkin of 29 June on the negotiations is in C 6579/30/48, FO 371/21646. See also Dirksen, p. 214; *D.D.F.*, 2d, 10, No. 144. A detailed account that rather overemphasizes the importance of the matter is in Wendt, *Economic Appeasement*, pp. 465–80, with references to Board of Trade and Treasury as well as Foreign Office records.

75. Lord Lloyd to Halifax, 10 August 1938, and related papers, in C 8189/1941/18, FO 371/21731. Lord Lloyd also informed the French (*D.D.F.*, 2d, 10, No. 352).

76. The background summary in *B.D.*, 3d, 2:683 is based on documents in C 8391/1941/18, FO 371/21731. Henderson's skepticism is reflected not only in his recommendation that von Kleist not be received but also in his telegram about another similarly inclined informant a few days later (*B.D.*, 3d, 2, No. 658).

servative opponent of Hitler accurately described the situation in Germany where Hitler was absolutely determined to attack Czechoslovakia, where the generals, including even von Reichenau, were opposed to such an adventure, and where a firm warning from Britain would lead either to a backdown by Hitler or a coup against him by the generals.[77]

Opinion on the accuracy of von Kleist's assertion that war would start on or after 28 September as well as on his recommendations for avoiding it was divided. Even those who accepted and understood the accuracy of von Kleist's description of Hitler's plans had doubts about the proposed remedy. The idea that Hitler's opponents might act seemed very doubtful; as one official put it, "We have had similar visits from other emissaries of the Reichsheer, such as Dr. Goerdeler, but those for whom these emissaries claim to speak have never given us any reason to suppose that they would be able or willing to take action such as would lead to the overthrow of the regime. The events of June 1934 and February 1938 do not lead one to attach much hope to energetic action by the Army against the regime."[78] More is now known about the planning of the German opposition for a coup against Hitler in the fall of 1938,[79] but it is difficult to blame the British government for its skepticism at the time about the military leaders whose obedience to Hitler might be reluctant but had hitherto been unvarying. The British could not know of the internal confusion of those in Germany who were considering acting against the regime, but the very fact that von Kleist was followed a few days later by another emissary, Hans Boehm-Tettelbach,[80] and still a week later by Theo Kordt, all urging a firm stand, all promising a coup in Germany—but all apparently unaware of the others—was not likely to impress anyone in London with the conspiratorial skills of those opposed to Hitler inside the Third Reich. It was at a discussion at the Foreign Office on 24 August that Chamberlain explained his identification of the opposition with the Jacobites which had first appeared in his letter of 19 August about von Kleist: "The arguments of the moderate elements in Germany resemble the arguments of the Jacobites at the Court of Louis XIV, who claimed that they would be able to

77. The reports of Vansittart and Churchill are in *B.D.*, 3d, 2, Appendix IV. See also Bodo Scheurig, *Ewald von Kleist-Schmenzin: Ein Konservativer gegen Hitler* (Oldenburg: Stalling, 1968).

78. Mallet comment of 22 August in C 8520/1941/18, FO 371/21732, f.174. Other comments on the von Kleist record are in the same file, which was used at the 24 August meeting referred to below. François-Poncet similarly thought the German army would march as ordered (*D.D.F.*, 2d, 10, Nos. 456, 459).

79. A forthcoming book by Harold C. Deutsch covering the period between his *Hitler and His Generals* and *The Conspiracy against Hitler in the Twilight War* will prove most helpful. For the time being, the best account is in Müller, chap. 8. For skepticism about the prospects and seriousness of a coup in 1938 from the German side, see Edgar Röhricht, *Pflicht und Gewissen: Erinnerungen eines deutschen Generals, 1932–1944* (Stuttgart: Kohlhammer, 1965), p. 114; Otto John, *Twice through the Lines* (New York: Harper & Row, 1972), pp. 32–33. For news about an emissary to London reaching the Czechoslovak government, see Král, *München*, No. 135.

80. On Boehm-Tettelbach, see Müller, pp. 207, 350–51.

overthrow William III if Louis was sufficiently threatening."[81] All in London knew that William III had not been overthrown. The recent tacit acceptance by the German army of the disgrace of its leaders did not inspire much confidence in the steadfastness of their successors.

The idea of some sort of further warning to the German government was, nevertheless, canvassed again; and it was decided to recall Henderson for consultations that were publicly announced as connected with the Czechoslovak crisis. It was also obviously necessary to consult more closely with the French government in the face of what looked like an imminent possibility of war, for by 24 August Chamberlain himself appears to have become convinced that Hitler had decided to attack Czechoslovakia probably right after the September National Socialist party rally.[82] The British therefore decided to approach the French at the very time that the French, equally alarmed, wanted to consult with London.[83] The results of deliberations in London will be reviewed in connection with the Runciman mission and the discussions of early September, but first the position of France and a number of other countries during the developing crisis must be examined.

Paris had also been receiving warnings that Germany was about to move. In fact, the French ambassador in Berlin had been given warnings by members of the opposition to Hitler urging a firm French stand similar to those given the British; but as François-Poncet told Sir Eric Phipps, the British ambassador to Paris, on 30 October, he had deliberately refrained from informing his government of these messages, partly because he thought them suspect, and partly because he feared they would strengthen the hands of the warmongers in France and of Beneš![84] In spite of this

81. The quotation is from Sargent's memorandum of 30 August 1938, C 9041/1941/18, FO 371/21734, f.263. Chamberlain's letter to Halifax is in *B.D.*, 3d, 2:686–87. For another warning to Chamberlain from a German industrialist via Robert Boothby, see C 9270/62/18, FO 371/21664. See also Wendt, *München*, pp. 32–35.

82. Sargent's memorandum of 30 August cited in the preceding footnote at f.261.

83. Foreign Office Memorandum, "Proposed Communication to the French Government," 24 August 1938, C 8718/1941/18, FO 371/21732. The record of the resulting meeting of Lord Halifax with the French chargé is in *B.D.*, 3d, 2, No. 691. See also *D.D.F.*, 2d, 10, Nos. 166, 188, 392.

84. Phipps to Halifax, 31 October 1938, Halifax Papers, FO 800/311. This is the section of the Phipps letter omitted from the published version in *B.D.*, 3d, 3:620. The full text of the omitted section is: "François-Poncet told me under the seal of secrecy that during August and part of September he received constant messages from emissaries of the Army, and even from officers, urging France to be firm and unyielding and declaring that in case of war the Nazi regime would collapse. *François-Poncet never informed his Government of these messages.* He felt that their origin made them suspect and that they might unduly strengthen the hands of the warmongers in France and of Benes & Co. He admitted, however, that this action, or rather non-action, of his had since formed a 'cas de conscience'. But he assured me solemnly that he would do the same again, for he is convinced that it would have been criminal folly to attach undue importance to messages from enemies of the régime. Moreover, whatever truth there might have been in them, once war was started all differences would have been swept away and all Germans would have united against the foreign enemy." The French ambassador did, of course, report quite accurately on the general situation as he saw it, including Hitler's desire for an attack and the reluctance of the

dubious action of François-Poncet, the Paris government was quite well informed about the situation; the puzzle was what to do about it.

There were some signs of a stiffening French attitude, but Paris simultaneously warned the Czechoslovak government to shift from arguing over details to making major concessions. At first, the pressure on Prague was still accompanied by a reluctance to threaten an end of the alliance.[85] With the continuing delays in the summer, however, French Foreign Minister Bonnet became increasingly exasperated. The French minister to Prague was recalled to Paris, where he was instructed on 17 July to warn Beneš that Czechoslovakia could not count on French military support if she became involved in war over the Sudeten question; and a few days later the Czechoslovak minister in Paris was told on behalf of the French cabinet that France could absolutely *not* go to war on this issue.[86] The Czechoslovak minister was insistent that this French position be kept absolutely secret; only French public assurances of loyalty to the alliance would enable the Prague government to secure a satisfactory settlement.

Beneš was understandably upset when told by Lacroix in person and Osuský by telegram that France would not fight.[87] He asserted that Czechoslovakia could not agree to all the demands of the Sudeten Germans; visibly shaken, he too was absolutely insistent that the German government must under no circumstances be allowed to know the real French position as there would otherwise be even greater pressure and a total collapse of Czechoslovakia, a development that would have implications for French security as well. The Paris government indeed followed this advice and continued to maintain a public posture of fidelity to their treaty obligation; but the Czechoslovak government, which may have thought that the third French government of 1938 might well be succeeded by a less pacifistic fourth, proceeded with its leisurely reactions to Sudeten German demands.[88]

---

generals (see *D.D.F.*, 2d, 10, Nos. 23, 150, 246, 312, 346; 11, Nos. 20, 38; *U.S.*, 1938, 1:61–62). A version of the warnings from Germany was given by Lord Lloyd to Gamelin on 16 September (Gamelin, 2:348–49). For a warning coming apparently from inside the German embassy in Moscow, see *D.D.F.*, 2d, 10, No. 449.

85. On French pressure, see *D.D.F.*, 2d, 10, Nos. 107, 115, 119, 121, 129. Reluctance to threaten a breach of the alliance is in the reply (ibid., No. 221) to a further British request (ibid., No. 163). For public signs of French firmness, see *U.S.*, 1938, 1:526–28, 529–30. A summer visit by Charles Lindbergh, the famous aviator, who touted the strength of the German air force, hardly encouraged the French; he would return with even gloomier messages in the fall (Lindbergh, 22 June 1938, p. 35).

86. *D.D.F.*, 2d, 10, Nos. 218, 222, 238, 266 n.2; Adamthwaite, pp. 197–99.

87. Lacroix's report on his 19 July meeting with Beneš is in *D.D.F.*, 2d, 10, No. 235 (see also *B.D.*, 3d, 2, No. 1); their meeting of 21 July, by which time Beneš had heard from Osuský, is in *D.D.F.*, 2d, 10, No. 242. Lacroix after this second meeting warned of the implications for French security of a collapse of Czechoslovakia; the Czechs might well submit to the Germans in view of their having survived under German domination for centuries, but what would happen to France (ibid., No. 245)?

88. A Czechoslovak compilation, dated 14 August, of French and other assurances is in Král, *München*, No. 133. There is other evidence that assessments made in Prague in the

During August, however, the development of the crisis and the information received by Paris led the French government, like the British, to believe that war was likely to break out in September.[89] The chief of staff of the French air force, General Vuillemin, was in Germany from 16 to 20 August, where he astonished Göring by assuring him that the French would indeed fight if Germany attacked Czechoslovakia and was himself impressed by the German air force. Every effort was made to intimidate Vuillemin and those with him, but though worried by what they saw, the French officers recognized that there was an element of bluff in what they were shown. Nevertheless, the very fact that the Germans had gone to such lengths to frighten off France only reinforced the belief of the French that Germany was indeed preparing to attack.[90] It was, of course, too late to do anything about the deplorable condition of the French air force, incapable of effective action of either a defensive or an offensive character. The results of neglect, confusion as to mission, and mass production of obsolescent equipment could not be remedied in short order; and the knowledge by both French and British governments of this terribly weak state of the French air force had a major effect on their worries in the crisis.[91]

With their thinking attuned more to the problems of land fighting, the French leaders were more likely to pay attention to the predictions of their army leaders. After the French cabinet had approved some minor steps designed to put the French army in a better state of readiness, Daladier asked once again, on 12 September, the question that had been put earlier in the year: what can France do on the ground to assist Czechoslovakia?[92] The answer of Gamelin and his top commanders was

---

summer of 1938 were overly optimistic, see *D.D.F.*, 2d, 10, No. 161. The Belgian ambassador in Paris, on the other hand, thought the French affirmations of loyalty were for political effect only, and that in a crisis the French would find a way to duck out (*D.D.B.*, 5, No. 17). Le Tellier also reported on French attempts at a rapprochement with Italy (cf. *U.S.*, 1938, 1:216).

89. *D.D.F.*, 2d, 10, Nos. 458, 506. Note Bonnet's comments on 12 August, *U.S.*, 1938, 1:62–63. Cf. *Hungarian Documents*, 2, No. 303.

90. On Vuillemin's visit, see *G.D.*, D, 2, No. 385; Stehlin, pp. 86–93; Heinkel, pp. 401–4; Celovsky, p. 307, n.4; Irving, *Milch*, p. 63; *U.S.*, 1938, 1:70; C 8693, C 8787/1425/18, FO 371/21710; *D.D.F.*, 2d, 10, Nos. 135, 203, 401, 402, 429, 440, 444, 537; Adamthwaite, pp. 238–40.

91. There is a useful summary, based partly on access to French archives, in Robert J. Young, "The Strategic Dream: French Air Doctrine in the Inter-War Period, 1919–39," *Journal of Contemporary History*, 9, No. 4 (Oct. 1974), 72–74. For a devastating comparison of the Luftwaffe with the British and French air forces which alarmed all in the Foreign Office, including Lord Halifax, see the memorandum of 26 August 1938, "Comparative Strength of the British and German Air Forces," C 9304/1425/18, FO 371/21710; cf. C 8950/1425/18, ibid. Vuillemin's own desolate report on the state of the French air force as of 26 September 1938 is in *D.D.F.*, 2d, 11, No. 377. See also Haight, chap. 1; Sholto Douglas, pp. 353–59, 364–65.

92. Gamelin, 2:344–47. In this very important document, the prime minister is referred to as "ministre" because Daladier was also minister of national defense. On this subject, see also Gauché, pp. 133–35.

simple and devastating. Practically nothing could be done to help Czecho-slovakia, which would have to await recovery until the peace treaty, as Serbia and other countries had had to do in the last war. It was not practical to cross the Rhine River at the southern half of the Franco-German border, and the Belgians would not allow the French to move across their country to attack the only portion of Germany with attractive objectives close to the border. Since the French were not willing to enter Belgium against that country's objections, the only alternative was an attack on the section of the Franco-German border dividing Lorraine from the Rhineland and Palatinate.

How did the French military assess this, the only real avenue of of-fensive operations against Germany? The record shows that the French general staff believed: (1) that this frontal assault on the Westwall would be a "modernized battle of the Somme,"[93] in other words, a bloody slogging operation not unlike the great engagement of 1916; (2) that this would be the case because even with German forces engaged in an attack on Czechoslovakia, the ground forces on the critical front in the west would be numerically approximately equal with fifty divisions on each side; and (3) that once the Germans had destroyed Czechoslovakia they could move the forces which had been engaged in that operation plus at least an additional fifteen newly formed divisions to the west. Once the main French army was already engaged in the attack on the Saar and Palatinate between the Mosel and the Rhine, the German reinforcement could be used for a thrust through Belgium to which no effective resis-tance could be offered.

These perspectives were based either on a subjectively honest or a deliberately extreme overestimation of the value of the German defenses in the west as well as the size of the German army, which in 1938 did not have fifty divisions altogether and was planning to use the bulk of its forces for the attack on Czechoslovakia. It is entirely possible that Game-lin believed the nonsense he was telling Daladier;[94] for himself as well as

93. The French generals had used the same terminology to Ambassador Bullitt, see Bullitt to Roosevelt, 13 June 1938, *Bullitt Letters*, pp. 267–68.

94. Note that in his memoirs Gamelin argues (p. 345, n.3, and pp. 347–48) that the events of 1944–45 when American and British forces attacked Germany from the west bore out his assessments of 1938. Regardless of the validity of the argument, the mere fact that Gamelin made it suggests that he may well have made his ridiculous predictions and analyses in 1938 in good faith, that he was stupid rather than devious. On Gamelin's contemporary reaction to a report by the French assistant air attaché in Germany on a conversation about the Westwall with General Bodenschatz at the end of June, see Stehlin, pp. 81–86, 94. The often lauded British military expert Sir Basil Liddell Hart was so opposed to a French attack on Germany in case of war that he thought the British should make the French promise not to launch one as a condition for sending an expeditionary force! (*Harvey Diaries*, 21 June 1938, p. 156). Possibly the terrible results of French underestimation of German army strength in 1914 had an effect on the calculations of later years. But by November 1938 the French assessment of German strength was more realistic (*D.D.F.*, 2d, 12, No. 461).

the French government it pointed to the absolute need for a defensive posture in the west, while only a long war in which Germany was somehow eventually throttled by her enemies offered hope of victory to France and of redemption to Czechoslovakia.[95] All the evidence shows that Bonnet at no time thought this a reasonable risk to run; Daladier appears to have contemplated it seriously but with great reservations in the last week of the crisis. One can, however, sympathize with his doubts about a course of action of such little promise if there were any way to avoid it; and as will become clear subsequently, Beneš himself would suggest though very late that the Czechoslovak government might be amenable to an alternative procedure. In any case, the French would under no circumstances move without British support, and the fact that there appeared to be little hope of securing substantial assistance from anybody else only redoubled French dependence on England.

An immediate problem for France in providing support for Czechoslovakia was the policy of Poland.[96] The role of Poland as the eastern shield of Germany's policy toward Czechoslovakia in 1938 has already been discussed. Separating both Germany and Czechoslovakia from the Soviet Union, Poland was unwilling to allow Russian troops to cross her territory to assist a neighbor upon whom Poland herself had demands, and because of the fear of herself becoming a victim of Soviet designs. The Warsaw government, on the other hand, faced a peculiar dilemma in its relations with France. Poland's leaders were skeptical about the resolution of France;[97] it seemed likely to them that the French would find a way to avoid helping Czechoslovakia if the latter were attacked, in part because they thought it unlikely that Czechoslovakia would fight.[98] Accordingly, if Czechoslovakia were abandoned, there was the possibility of Polish territorial gain by the annexation of Těšín and of Polish political gain by the expansion of Hungary to a common Polish-Hungarian border. The diplomatic steps Poland took in the summer of 1938 to further these aims,

95. See the evidence on the overassessment of Germany's western defenses and the absence of any fully developed program for an attack in the west in French mobilization plans, in Paul-Emile Tournoux, *Haute Commandement: Gouvernement et défense des frontières du nord et de l'est, 1919–1939* (Paris: Nouvelles Editions Latines, 1960), pp. 281–82, 298, 339–41. See also Král, *München*, No. 100 (parts in Berber, No. 138). The director of military operations and intelligence on the British General Staff noted in his diary on 25 September that according to British intelligence, the Germans had only nine divisions and two in reserve facing France; on the following day Gamelin told him that the French plan was "merely on advance to the Siegfried line and then withdrawal to the Maginot" (Pownall, 1:159, 163). For background on the British military assessment, see Patton (Consul General Singapore) dispatch 494 of 21 September 1939 on a conversation with one of the British officers on duty in the War Office in September 1938, State 760F.62/1969.

96. For aspects of this in early 1938, see *D.D.F.*, 2d, 8, Nos. 152, 163, 298, 305, 331. Many additional documents are in vols. 9 and 10.

97. For material on the French difficulties in supplying Poland with weapons, see ibid., 8, Nos. 11, 77, 162, 190, 205; 10, Nos. 12, 15, 48, 69; 11, No. 274.

98. See *U.S.*, 1938, 1:495–98; *G.D.*, D, 2, No. 228.

however, tended to accentuate the weaknesses on which they were predicated; for they encouraged the concentric pressure of Germany, Poland, and Hungary for the dissolution of Czechoslovakia, which looked all the more difficult to thwart because of its overwhelming nature. And Poland's ties to Rumania could be, and were, used to isolate Czechoslovakia from any possible Soviet aid on the one sector, however short, where Czechoslovakia bordered on an allied country.[99]

If Poland's role thus increased the likelihood of a peaceful settlement that was really a cold-blooded dismemberment of Czechoslovakia,[100] there was always the possibility, which Warsaw could not ignore, that the development of the crisis might take an entirely different turn and lead to war. In that contingency, the Polish leaders would not wish to find themselves on Germany's side if they could possibly help it. In cooperating with the hunters, they encouraged the hunt and discouraged prospective supporters of the victim;[101] at the same time they had to be ready to change sides and turn on their German fellow hunter if the victim were, at the last moment, forcibly assisted by the countries to which Poland herself had to look for support if and when Germany turned on her.[102] The French and British governments, on the other hand, were interested in having Poland refrain from a policy which they believed encouraged Germany to attack Czechoslovakia by giving her the prospect of an isolated victory;[103] but at the same time they themselves were hoping for a peaceful settlement that in their opinion could come about only if Czechoslovakia made substantial concessions.

At the time of the May Crisis and thereafter, the Warsaw government followed a kind of double policy toward Paris. The Poles insisted that Czechoslovakia make concessions to them equivalent to those made to

99. Cf. *Lipski Papers*, p. 373 and No. 88.

100. In a conversation with the leader of the Hungarian minority in Czechoslovakia in June 1938, Beck expressed himself as expecting a peaceful solution, with Slovakia and the Carpatho-Ukraine falling to Hungary, the former but not the latter hopefully receiving some autonomy. Beck professed to be worried that the Germans would move beyond the ethnographic line and occupy all of Bohemia and Moravia; he would prefer some independent residual Czech state which would be dependent upon the Berlin-Rome-Warsaw circle (*Hungarian Documents*, 2, No. 250). As the Canadian high commissioner in London had written on 26 May 1938: "'Partition' is a word with tragic associations for Poland. When applied to a neighbouring state, however, the idea behind it seems to have some attractive features!" *Documents on Canadian External Relations*, 6, No. 883, p. 1084.

101. Note the Lipski-Göring conversation of 17 June, *Lipski Papers*, No. 87.

102. The element of duplicity inherent in this policy may or may not have been necessary, but it was not likely to make friends for Poland either among contemporary leaders or subsequent analysts. See the Foreign Office comments on Kennard's report of 4 June from Warsaw (*B.D.*, 3d, 2, No. 375) in C 5394/1941/18, FO 371/21723. A memorandum by Vansittart of 31 August according to which a member of Rydz-Śmigły's entourage asserted that Poland's policy would depend on that of the Western Powers—if they aided Czechoslovakia Poland would fight alongside them, but if not, she would seize her share of Czechoslovakia—was considered as confirming previous estimates by most Foreign Office officials (C 9072/1941/18, FO 371/21734).

103. Cf. Cienciala, pp. 69–73; Slávik report 23 of 9 May 1938, Czechoslovak document in T-120, 1040/1809/413034–37.

the Germans by implying that they might join in a German attack,[104] while trying to maintain their ties to France by implying that they would side with her—or at least stay neutral—if it came to a general war over Czechoslovakia.[105] That such a policy only half pleased the Germans should be evident; at all times complications with Poland in case a German attack on Czechoslovakia did not produce a prompt victory remained a real possibility in German thinking.[106] On the other hand, as the Poles could excuse their own doubts by the weakness of France, so the French could and did see in the attitude of Poland still another obstacle to effective help for the isolated Czechoslovak state.[107]

Relations between Poland and Germany in the summer of 1938 were accordingly characterized by continuing contact on current minor problems accompanied by mutual reassurances of common views toward Czechoslovakia. Both powers believed, or professed to believe, in the wicked character of Czechoslovak policy, the necessity for a peaceful disintegration of the Czechoslovak state, the great benefits to be derived by all from such a happy development, and the need to keep all outsiders—the Soviet Union in particular—from interfering with it.[108] The efforts of the Western Powers to enroll Poland in defense of Czechoslovakia could be and were used by Warsaw with the Germans as a reminder of Poland's importance to the Third Reich and of the need for the latter to be careful in Danzig.[109] The Germans, on the other hand, went to considerable lengths to reassure the Poles that once the question of Czechoslovakia was settled, Poland would *not* be next on the list of German targets.[110] In a suggestion similar to the one he appears to have made to the Italians

104. It seems to me that this is the only reasonable way to interpret Beck's instructions to the Polish ambassador in Paris. Asked to confirm that Beck had told the French ambassador in Warsaw "that in any event the Polish government does not anticipate Poland's aggression against Czechoslovakia," Beck responded that "I only told Ambassador Noël that Poland would certainly not be the factor on whose initiative the final crisis in the Czechoslovak situation would occur" (*Łukasiewicz Papers,* pp. 108, 110).

105. The Poles were responding to the threat of an end of the Franco-Polish alliance, Osuský report 83 of 29 June 1938, Czechoslovak document in T-120, 1040/1809/412942–43 (portion in Berber, No. 136); but see *D.D.F.,* 2d, 9, No. 511.

106. This contingency has been discussed in connection with German military planning for the attack on Czechoslovakia; see also *G.D.,* D, 2, Nos. 259, 277, 282; *D.D.F.,* 2d, 10, No. 95. Note Biddle's tel. 168 of 5 September 1938 on German suspicions of closer British-Polish relations, State 760F.62/660 (portion omitted from *U.S.,* 1938, 1:577).

107. The account in Cienciala, chaps. 2 and 3, is very useful but tends to overlook the extent to which Polish policy contributed to the strength of Germany's diplomatic position. Important documents from the Polish side are printed in *Łukasiewicz Papers,* pp. 108–26; from the French side in *D.D.F.,* 2d, 10, Nos. 12, 15, 48, 158, 219. See also the account in Wojciechowski, pp. 431–50.

108. Note Lipski's report to Beck of 11 August in *Lipski Papers,* No. 89; cf. ibid., No. 91; *G.D.,* D, 2, No. 255.

109. *Lipski Papers,* Nos. 90–92.

110. It was precisely on this score that the French had warned Warsaw; the Poles claimed to be realists, but what would they do when Germany appeared on their southern as well as their western and northern border and when Germany demanded the return of Germans in Poland after those in Austria and Czechoslovakia? *D.D.F.,* 2d, 8, No. 314.

about transferring the Germans of South Tyrol to Germany as a means of reassuring Rome about the annexation of Austria, Göring suggested to Polish Ambassador Lipski on 24 August 1938 that perhaps the best thing would be "if German minorities in Poland were to return to Germany, and vice versa."[111]

Such words were as cheap as those asserting that Germany had no designs on Polish territory, but there appears to have been no real German willingness to give more formal assurances to Poland.[112] Forster was once again summoned to Germany and told to restrain his activities in Danzig in the light of Germany's desire for good relations with Poland during the crisis over Czechoslovakia, but Berlin would go no further in substantive concessions.[113] In public, however, the wonderful state of German-Polish relations was stressed by Hitler in his 12 September speech at the Nuremberg party rally as an obvious contrast to the terrible suffering allegedly inflicted on the poor Sudeten Germans by the government of the incorrigible Czechoslovakia: "Because a great patriot and statesman in Poland [Pilsudski] was willing to make an accord with Germany, we immediately proceeded to follow up on it and arrived at an agreement which means more for peace in Europe than all the jabbering in the temple of the League in Geneva."[114] Ambassador Lipski expressed his satisfaction with these remarks, but also voiced the opinion that some formal acknowledgment of the frontier with Poland—analogous to the one Hitler had made in his speech in Florence near the end of his Italian journey in May—would be most desirable.[115] Berlin did not follow up on this suggestion, and the course of German-Polish relations after the Czechoslovak crisis of 1938 would take a very different turn from that suggested by the Polish ambassador on 13 September. For a few critical weeks, however, Germany and Poland would continue their informal collaboration in the dismemberment of Czechoslovakia.[116]

During the summer of 1938, the Polish government did what it could to coordinate its policy with Hungary in the hope that the active revisionist policy of the latter would serve three purposes. The encouragement of

111. *Lipski Papers*, p. 386; Cienciala, pp. 96–99. Göring repeated this suggestion on 16 September, *Lipski Papers*, pp. 404–5.

112. These were discussed by Lipski and Göring, see *Lipski Papers*, Nos. 91–93; cf. *G.D.*, D, 2, No. 271. At this time, the "German-Polish Society" was activated, see *Groscurth Diary*, 29 August 1938, p. 101; Kleist, p. 14. Those who assert that the German claims on Poland raised in October 1938 were reasonable conveniently overlook the fact that the Germans only a few weeks before had solemnly promised the Poles not to make these claims.

113. On Forster, see *Lipski Papers*, p. 394; Levine, pp. 138–39. On Danzig in general and other specific issues in German-Polish relations, see Cienciala, pp. 62, 94–95.

114. Domarus, 1:902.

115. Lipski–von Moltke talk of 13 September 1938, *Lipski Papers*, pp. 399–400. Note that von Ribbentrop, during Hitler's Italian journey, explained that Hitler's recognition of Germany's borders applied to all of them except that with Czechoslovakia, but he made this statement to the *Hungarian* minister in Rome (*Hungarian Documents*, 2, No. 182).

116. Hoensch, *Ungarische Revisionismus*, pp. 76–77, n.119.

Hungarian demands would emphasize the grievances of minorities inside Czechoslovakia *other* than the Germans, thereby lending credibility to Poland's interest in the Polish minority in Czechoslovakia without raising embarrassing questions about national minorities within Poland. In the second place, now that Austria had been annexed by Germany, the whole southern border of Czechoslovakia would be menaced by Hungary's role, thus making it all the less likely that the dismemberment of Czechoslovakia would be resisted by force. Finally, the successful detaching of Slovakia and the Carpatho-Ukraine from Prague's control and their direct or indirect control by Budapest would establish a common Polish-Hungarian border and thus tie together the "Third Europe" of Beck's dreams.[117] Given the fact that the elements within Slovakia who wanted greater autonomy from Prague were often no more enthusiastic about Magyar than about Czech domination,[118] this policy was by no means a simple one to implement, even without the peculiar relationship with France that such an anti-Czechoslovak policy entailed.

The Hungarian government was itself torn by conflicting desires, emotions, and expectations. In the immediate situation, there was the hope that the substantial Magyar minority in Czechoslovakia—about 650,000 in Slovakia and the Carpatho-Ukraine—would benefit from concessions made to all national minorities. More significant, at a time when the possibility of an attack or the threat of an attack on Czechoslovakia opened up the prospect of that country's dismemberment, there was the hope that Hungary's aspirations for territorial revision might be at least partially realized. The resulting common border with Poland looked as welcome from Budapest as it did from Warsaw, but there were, nevertheless, some doubts and reservations. The reluctance of many Slovaks to return to Magyar control does not appear to have been perceived as a major obstacle; a combination of self-confidence and self-delusion reduced this to a matter for maneuver, bribery, and—if need be—repression.[119] More important was the fear that the disintegration of Czechoslovakia might not be peaceful.[120]

As long as the combined pressure by Czechoslovakia's neighbors seemed likely to lead to a quiet throttling of the hated state, the Hungarian government was both eager for its portion of the spoils and willing to do its share of saber rattling and diplomatic noise making. If war came, however, there were enormous dangers. In the first place, as previously mentioned, the Hungarian government was worried that Yugoslavia might attack her from the rear if Hungarian troops moved northward in a military campaign; and all Hungarian attempts to secure from Berlin some

117. *Hungarian Documents*, 2, Nos. 173, 187, 191 (German text in Zsigmond, pp. 270–71), 192, 200, 219, 235, 237–39, 241, 244, 246.
118. For discussion of this issue between Poland and Hungary, see ibid., Nos. 200, 246, 250, 278, 331.
119. Hoensch, *Ungarische Revisionismus*, pp. 62–63.
120. See *Hungarian Documents*, 2, No. 171.

form of guarantee against that contingency had been rejected.[121] Direct
negotiations with Yugoslavia and Rumania, which were a possible
alternative means of simultaneously improving the lot of Magyar
minorities in those two countries and restraining these two Little Entente
powers from coming to the aid of their Czechoslovak ally against a Hungarian attack dragged on all through the spring and summer of 1938. The
Hungarians, however, never quite succeeded in excluding Czechoslovakia herself from the purview of these negotiations and eventually arrived
at an agreement with all three Little Entente powers that renounced the
use of force in their relationship in exchange for recognition of Hungary's
right to rearm and the promise of agreements on the treatment of
minorities.[122] The fact that this agreement was announced on 22 August
1938, while Hungary's leaders were on a state visit in Germany, can only
be interpreted as a breach in German-Hungarian joint or parallel action
against Czechoslovakia resulting from Hungary's fear of a danger even
greater than the possible hostility of Yugoslavia and Rumania, namely,
the outbreak of a general European war.

The leaders of Hungary were willing to concert with Germany in the
diplomacy of the spring and summer of 1938, and they listened with pleasure to comments such as those of Göring on 1 June and 5 July urging
combined military operations against Czechoslovakia.[123] To Göring's
comments that Hungary could not count on Germany to handle all the
problems for her, the Hungarian minister could only combine his expression of agreement in principle with references to the dangers for Hungary
in practice. The more acute the crisis over Czechoslovakia became in August 1938, the more difficult the dilemma faced by the Hungarian government. If Czechoslovakia made concessions, Hungary wanted her own
minority included; if Czechoslovakia were peacefully partitioned, Hungary wanted what she considered her share; but if war broke out, Hungary
wanted no part.[124] Not only was Hungary militarily incapable of standing
up to Yugoslavia and Rumania if they combined forces against her, but
the Hungarian regent, prime minister, and foreign minister were all convinced that in a general war Germany would again be defeated and that

121. The Hungarians were not reassured by Italian promises of support; if it came to a
general war, Italy's main forces would be needed on the border with France and in Africa
while the Italo-Yugoslav border offered little but steep mountains where, as the Hungarians
well knew, Italy had been unable to move forward substantially in the fighting of 1915–17
(see *G.D.*, D, 2, No. 402).

122. See especially *Hungarian Documents*, 2, No. 176; *B.D.*, 3d, 2, No. 690; *D.D.F.*, 2d,
10, No. 448.

123. *G.D.*, D, 2, Nos. 232, 248, 284; *Allianz*, No. 48; but note *Hungarian Documents*, 2,
No. 186, and *G.D.*, D, 2, No. 296, for pushing from the Hungarian side.

124. Hoensch, *Ungarische Revisionismus*, pp. 73–75. Note *Hungarian Documents*, 2,
No. 289; *D.D.F.*, 2d, 10, No. 68. This concern of the Hungarians played a part in their
refusal at this time to follow Italian urgings to leave the League (Ciano, *Diary*, 17 July 1938,
p. 147).

Hungary would be crushed beyond all hope of recovery if she were allied with the Third Reich in such a conflict.

The German government, on the other hand, wanted to utilize Hungary's aspirations for territorial revision at the expense of Czechoslovakia as a means of assisting her own strategy of a quick isolated war in which Hungary—as a possible major beneficiary—would just have to share in the risks incurred for great rewards. From that point of view, the fact that Horthy had accepted an invitation to come to Germany for the christening of the heavy cruiser *Prinz Eugen* scheduled for 22 August would provide an excellent opportunity to see just how closely the two countries could work together.[125]

As the Hungarian regent, prime minister, foreign minister, and minister of defense headed for their meetings with Hitler and other German leaders, the negotiations with the Little Entente had just reached the point of agreement, so that the Hungarians found themselves parties to public announcements about the renunciation of force in the very days when they were expected by the Germans to agree to participate in a war six weeks later.[126] As if this public "distance from Germany's policy toward Czechoslovakia,"[127] as von Ribbentrop called it, were not enough, the Hungarians were almost frantic about the danger of a general war, having been warned by Helmuth Groscurth on behalf of Admiral Canaris of Hitler's intention of attacking Czechoslovakia.[128] From this and other warnings, the Hungarians had a clear picture of the dissension within the German leadership, a dissension caused by the belief of many of the generals that the war against Czechoslovakia Hitler was determined to launch would quickly become a general war that Germany would lose.[129] In their meetings with Hitler, von Ribbentrop, and the German military leaders, therefore, the Hungarians stressed that they believed there would indeed be a general war and urged Germany not to start one. Hungary was not yet militarily ready to face her Little Entente neighbors, and she could

125. The cruiser was originally to be named *Admiral Teggetthoff* in honor of the most famous Austrian naval commander—it was in this connection that the participation of Horthy as an admiral of the former Austro-Hungarian navy had seemed particularly appropriate—but Italian objections to naming a German cruiser for the man whose laurels had been won at Italy's expense led to a last-minute substitution of the more "neutral" name (see "Informationsbericht Nr. 55," 10 August 1938, Bundesarchiv, Brammer, Z.Sg. 101/33, f.179).

126. *Hungarian Documents*, 2, Nos. 295, 296; cf. ibid., Nos. 305–7, 314 (French text in Ádám, No. 10).

127. *G.D.*, D, 2, No. 383. The strong German negative reaction is shown in the circular instruction of von Weizsäcker about the agreement, especially its "undesirable" renunciation of the use of force (ibid., 5, No. 221).

128. *Groscurth Diary*, 20 August 1938, p. 102.

129. *Hungarian Documents*, 2, No. 292 (German text in Zsigmond, p. 277, n.78, together with another similar warning). This episode is examined in Thomas L. Sakmyster, "The Hungarian State Visit to Germany of August, 1938: Some New Evidence on Hungary in Hitler's Pre-Munich Policy," *Canadian Slavonic Studies*, 3, No. 4 (Winter 1969), 679. Documents used in this article will generally not be cited again here.

either herself be ready to join an attack in a year or two—if Germany were willing to postpone action—or would have to wait to see whether an immediate German attack on Czechoslovakia were indeed localized, in which case they could join in after a couple of weeks.[130]

This position of the Hungarians, voiced repeatedly in conversations with von Ribbentrop, Keitel, and Hitler himself, was, of course, directly contrary to what those three wanted and expected.[131] While Keitel appears simply to have listened, von Ribbentrop scolded and warned his Hungarian visitors. Hitler made a major effort to persuade the Hungarians to change their minds. In his meeting with Horthy, Hitler explained his plan for an attack on Czechoslovakia and offered to let Hungary have Slovakia and the Carpatho-Ukraine if she joined promptly in the action. Horthy declined participation in a combined attack and maintained his refusal in a subsequent conversation with Hitler. The latter was, however, so interested in the concept of a quick, joint, concentric attack on Czechoslovakia that he made still another attempt to persuade the Hungarians, this time in a talk with the Hungarian minister of defense.[132] Hitler expressed confidence that the Western Powers would not intervene in the war and that the Little Entente allies of Czechoslovakia would not move either. The one country that would move, he claimed, was Poland; and if Hungary did not participate, the Poles might end up not only with Těšín but with Slovakia as well. Even this possibility did not move the Hungarian minister, though it was a shrewd act on Hitler's part to remind the Hungarians of a contingency of which they certainly had their suspicions. Hitler told the Hungarian minister that the World War could have been localized if a swift attack on Serbia had been launched; the implication for 1938 was obvious, but no reply to this revelation of Hitler's perception of the past as a lesson for the future is recorded. Hitler further assured his guest that "he doesn't listen to his generals, because they always say they are not ready and they are always worrying, as they did over the proclamation of military sovereignty and the occupation of the

130. This appears to me to be the fairest reading of the then available evidence summarized by Sakmyster and the new evidence from Hungarian records provided by him. *Hungarian Documents*, 2, No. 297, not cited by S., seems to reflect the confusion in German military circles. Important independent evidence confirming the account of S. is in the report on the subsequent (6 September) visit of Hungarian Chief of Staff Keresztes-Fischer prepared after World War II by Erich Hansen, who had been present at the meeting in the High Command of the German army (Hansen to Hillgruber, 23 March 1957, Munich, Institut für Zeitgeschichte, Z.S. 1130, pp. 13–14). Cf. Hoensch, *Ungarische Revisionismus*, p. 71; Král, *München*, No. 169; Sakmyster, "Hungary and Munich," pp. 734–36; *D.D.F.*, 2d, 10, Nos. 361, 503; 11, No. 1.

131. Note that Horthy went so far as to warn the Polish ambassador to Germany about the dangers of war (*Lipski Papers*, p. 381). See also the account in *Weizsäcker-Papiere*, pp. 137–39.

132. Sakmyster, "Hungarian State Visit," p. 684, correctly observes that Hitler's vigorous efforts to persuade the Hungarians contradicts A. J. P. Taylor's thesis that Hitler did not want war in 1938; why go to all this trouble to secure Hungarian participation in a war he did not intend to wage?

Rhineland,"[133] an indirect answer to the advice Hitler suspected the Hungarians were getting from some of his generals.

All these efforts of the Germans were in vain. Hungary was not ready and was afraid to move. The Magyar leaders regretted the necessity of having to turn the Germans down, since revision of the border with Czechoslovakia was one of their dearest hopes and aims.[134] The Germans correctly read Hungarian policy as one of waiting in case war did break out to see how things went before committing themselves. They had warned the Hungarians that "those who wished to share in the meal would have to help with the cooking,"[135] but Hitler recognized that Hungary was not prepared to help in the kitchen. He would subsequently often refer back to this refusal to take risks. In the short run, it meant that Hitler could not count on immediate Hungarian participation in war; in the intermediate situation, it meant that Hungary could count on German support only for minor revisions of the Hungarian-Czechoslovak border; with the long-term future of Slovakia left for Germany's later decisions. Hungary, in any case, had not met Hitler's test of will.[136] A month later, when it looked as if the war Hitler wanted might be obviated by a peaceful settlement on the basis of the cession of the Sudetenland to Germany, Hitler would try to utilize the aspirations of Hungary as well as Poland once more in the hope of bringing on the rupture he wanted, but the fact that he himself had to push the Hungarians forward would reinforce rather than diminish his contempt and distrust of the Hungarians after August 1938.

If Poland could serve as a shield and Hungary was but a dubious ally to German policy, what about Italy? Neither Axis partner had fully clarified its own thinking on this point. The Germans had discussed the Czechoslovak question only briefly with their Italian hosts in May. The Italians had declared themselves disinterested in the fate of Czechoslovakia but were left with the impression that the Germans were unlikely to resort to force in the near future, but that if they did, hostilities would be isolated. In fact, Count Ciano was to note in his diary on 19 August that the Germans had said there would be no war for several years.[137] As the Germans increased the volume of their propaganda campaign, however, the Italians wanted to know more precisely what Germany intended, and

133. Sakmyster, "Hungarian State Visit," p. 688.

134. *G.D.*, D, 2, No. 402.

135. Hitler's comment to Prime Minister Imrédy, ibid., No. 383; *Weizsäcker-Papiere*, p. 138. Note that Hitler agreed to general staff contacts (*G.D.*, D, 2, No. 383), but instructed the German chief of staff to give no hints about the timing of Germany's planned attack on Czechoslovakia to the Hungarian chief of staff (Jodl diary, 6 September 1938, *TMWC*, 28:375).

136. Note also Göring's comments in *Lipski Papers*, pp. 384–85, 395–96, and *G.D.*, D, 2, No. 402; Kánya's comments to the French minister on 8 September 1938 in *D.D.F.*, 2d, 11, No. 47.

137. *Diary*, p. 208. The same divergence in timetable would recur in an even more extreme form after the meetings of May 1939.

starting in late May they repeatedly asked the Germans for specific information about their plan. The responses given by the Germans were vague, stressing the iniquities of the Czechs and the possibility of a German response to Czechoslovak provocation, but without specificity as to plans or timing.[138]

Mussolini himself seemed unable to make up his mind what he wanted to do. As one scholar has phrased it, "it is difficult to discover a constructive policy aim seriously pursued in Mussolini's thinking and will during those weeks and months."[139] The Duce may have hoped that the April agreement with England would be followed by even further concessions from London; but as he was himself unwilling to reduce the Italian involvement in the civil war raging in Spain or to make an agreement with France analogous to that with England, friction between Italy and the Western Powers continued. To reassure the Germans that this was so, the Italian government kept Berlin informed of the stages in the inconclusive and unsuccessful talks with the British;[140] and in the course of these negotiations, Mussolini more and more talked himself into a position of alignment with Germany, in war if necessary, and preferably in alignment with Japan as well.[141]

The repercussions of the *Anschluss,* however, hung over the prospect of a German-Italian alliance. The economic and financial problems arising out of the German annexation of Austria were settled to Italy's satisfaction by an agreement reached on 28 May,[142] and the time when Germany was using the Sudeten Germans as a pretext for the dismemberment of Czechoslovakia was not the time to make much noise about the Germans in South Tyrol.[143] Nevertheless, Mussolini realized that it would take the Italian public a good deal of time and propagandistic preparation to warm up to the idea of a firm military alliance with Germany.[144] The discussion of that subject in the summer of 1938 accordingly would see some exchanges of drafts and comments; but although Mussolini was very much interested, he was also sure that the subject would have to be approached slowly and carefully.[145] All the same, the hardening of Italian resolve in

138. Ciano, *Diary,* 27, 28, 31 May, 3, 18 June 1938, pp. 171–72, 175, 177–78, 213; *G.D.,* D, 2, Nos. 220, 223, 229; cf. *Hungarian Documents,* 2, No. 240.

139. Siebert, p. 72.

140. *G.D.,* D, 1, Nos. 777, 782, 788, 792, 799; Ciano, *Diary,* 22 June, 2, 12 July 1938, pp. 184, 191, 194.

141. Ciano, *Diary,* 12, 26 May 1938, pp. 161, 170–71; Magistrati's information for Wiskemann in Wiskemann, pp. 152–53. On the possible tie to Japan, see Ciano, *Diary,* 6, 21 June 1938, pp. 178, 184.

142. *G.D.,* D, 1, No. 773; Ciano, *Diary,* 28 May 1938, p. 173.

143. The subject almost disappeared from view between May and September 1938. See *G.D.,* D, 1, No. 780; Latour, p. 27.

144. It must be noted that there were still obstacles in the field of diplomatic personnel even after the removal of Cerrutti and von Hassell. The Italian military attaché in Berlin, General Marras, was really more pro-French than pro-German. See *D.D.F.,* 2d, 9, No. 181.

145. *G.D.,* D, 1, Nos. 774, 781.

the summer of 1938 to annex Albania at an opportune moment as well as the initiation of a major anti-Semitic campaign in mid-July both had the real effect of pushing the Axis partners closer together.[146]

From the German point of view, there were equivalent hesitations but still a real concern for closer relations with Italy. The Germans and Italians not only kept each other informed of relevant diplomatic developments[147] but on 19 June von Ribbentrop, who had had prior conversations about the subject with Italian Ambassador Bernardo Attolico, proposed a formal and public military alliance.[148] The German foreign minister had been the architect of the Anti-Comintern Pact, had proposed some public treaty action during the May visit, and favored agreements of great propaganda value; now he wanted an alliance worked out in meetings with Ciano, involving the Japanese but *excluding* the problem of war arising out of the Czechoslovak crisis. Presumably he thought that the Italians would find the scheme more attractive if they were free but not obligated to intervene in that contingency. Subsequent negotiations in late June and early July revealed the Italians to be interested in principle but desirous of moving carefully and slowly. They felt that the Italian public would have to be prepared and they were as yet not informed of any German timetable.[149] This last was evidently very much a matter of concern to Rome; the Italians discussed with their new-found Yugoslav and their old Hungarian friends the proper sequence of events by which Hungary, if she attacked Czechoslovakia a bit after rather than before the Germans, could assure Yugoslavia's remaining neutral.[150]

There is, nevertheless, a curious ambiguity in the Italian position, and there is evidence that the Germans were aware of it. When the Italian chief of staff, General Alberto Pariani, was in Germany in July, he was given a frank exposition of the situation by Göring and was enormously impressed by the great strides German rearmament had made.[151] Right after the return of Pariani, however, Mussolini—who as minister of defense had presumably heard from his chief of staff—told the Hungarian

146. Ibid., No. 778; *U.S.*, 1938, 2:583ff.; Ciano, *Diary*, 10, 14 July 1938, pp. 192–93, 195. The Albanian issue illustrates the accuracy of Hitler's belief that Italian territorial aspirations would drive her to Germany's side.

147. *G.D.*, D, 2, No. 260. Hans Frank was in Rome for a public address on 21 June, but there is no evidence of any diplomatic conversations (Ciano, *Diary*, p. 184).

148. The Italian records provide the main source on this; see Toscano, *Origins*, pp. 27–32; cf. *G.D.*, D, 1, No. 784.

149. Ciano, *Diary*, 27 June, 11, 12 July 1938, pp. 187, 193, 194; *G.D.*, D, 1, No. 786; Toscano, *Origins*, pp. 32–35. For Attolico's arrangements to sound out the Japanese—which resulted in the discovery that in that quarter all was as yet open—see the documents from the Italian archives cited in Toscano, *Origins*, pp. 34–35.

150. Note *Hungarian Documents*, 2, Nos. 247, 257, 284; Ciano, *Diary*, 24 June 1938, pp. 186–87.

151. The most complete account appears to be that in the memoirs of Rintelen (pp. 48–50), who accompanied Pariani. See also Ciano, *Diary*, 15 July 1938, p. 195; and the intercepted instruction of Mussolini of 8 July 1938, in Moffat Papers, Vol. 13.

prime minister and foreign minister that he did not expect a European war over the Czechoslovak question, but that Italy would support Germany if one broke out and that he had so informed the Germans.[152] Two comments by Mussolini recorded by Ciano in his diary may provide a clue to the Duce's conflicting emotions. On 17 July Mussolini insisted that there be no Italian measures the Germans might think questionable; if it ever came to it, he wanted to be able to accuse the Germans of deserting him rather than the other way around—a sure reflection of his sensitivity to German charges that Italy had betrayed her Triple Alliance partners in the war.[153] A few days later, on 21 July, on the other hand, he was angry on learning from the newspapers about the Wiedemann mission to London and wondered what the Germans would say if he sent his secretary to Paris for conversations with the French foreign minister.[154]

The Italian leader might incline more and more to a definite alignment with Germany; but the idea of serving as junior partner to a great power that would not even take him into its confidence and was likely to confront him with unpleasant surprises left a residue of reluctance, symbolized by Ciano's declining an invitation by von Ribbentrop to the September National Socialist party rally in Nuremberg when progress might be made on the alliance negotiations.[155] The wildly enthusiastic report of Marshal Italo Balbo on his trip to Germany of 9–14 August during which Göring had urged the conversion of the Axis into a formal alliance appears to have alarmed rather than pleased.[156] Attolico and von Weizsäcker had already discussed the possible imminence of general war in mid-July; a few days after Balbo's return the Italians received from within the German general staff a warning analogous to that provided the Hungarians to the effect that a German attack on Czechoslovakia had been decided upon, that it would take place at the end of September, and that all was ready for war.[157] The Italians preferred to have things develop along the lines of their interpretation of the May conversations that war was some years off and immediately instructed Attolico to ask the Germans for precise information. Having decided to join Germany if a general war took place, they felt entitled to know whether and when it was to occur; but von Ribbentrop, who must have sensed the uneasiness of his prospective

152. Ciano, *Diplomatic Papers*, p. 228; Ciano, *Diary*, 18, 20 July 1938, pp. 197–99. Attolico told von Ribbentrop about the conversation and the Duce's position on 26 July when the two again discussed the proposed alliance (*G.D.*, D, 2, No. 334; Toscano, *Origins*, pp. 37–38).

153. *Diary*, p. 197. Ironically, Hitler himself thought Italy's conduct in 1914–15 had been very sensible and that the view of Italy as disloyal was a characteristic stupidity of his own domestic opponents (*Hitlers zweites Buch*, pp. 93ff.).

154. *Diary*, pp. 199–200.

155. *G.D.*, D, 1, No. 797; Toscano, *Origins*, pp. 38–40.

156. Magistrati, pp. 212–14; Ciano, *Diary*, 16 August 1938, p. 206; cf. *G.D.*, D, 1, No. 798; *D.D.F.*, 2d, 10, Nos. 360, 364, 391.

157. *G.D.*, D, 2, No. 295; Ciano, *Diary*, 19 August 1938, p. 208.

ally and who may well have had instructions from Hitler not to reveal exact details, merely assured Attolico that no decisions had been reached and that the Italians would be the first to know.[158]

It should be easy to understand that Mussolini and Ciano found this situation both extraordinary and alarming. Substantial Italian forces in Spain might be immediately affected by the outbreak of a general war even if Italy did not join in right away, while if she did, all sorts of problems would arise. There is a certain frantic quality to the subsequent repeated Italian requests for information from the Germans, requests that received no clear answer but were interpreted in Berlin as reflecting doubts in Rome.[159] The Prince of Hessen was once again called in, this time by the Italians, to find out from Hitler directly what was going on lest there be another surprise like the *Anschluss*.[160] The prince brought back a lengthy memorandum Hitler had dictated to him on 4 or 5 September, but in this the Führer only reiterated his general views and provided no clue to his actual plans.[161] Ciano correctly deduced that Hitler was simply unwilling to give precise information to the Italians, a fact that left Italy free to make its own decisions.[162] Hitler may well have thought it best to leave some uncertainty about Italy's position. He wanted and expected a short, isolated war in which there would be no need for Italian intervention, and uncertainty as to Italy's role might help restrain prospective supporters of Czechoslovakia. A visit to Italy by Admiral Canaris at the same time in early September that the Prince of Hessen was in Germany convinced the German chief of intelligence that the Italians were dubious about war and planned to stay out if one started, a view that impressed so ardent an admirer of Hitler's as Alfred Jodl.[163] Hitler would claim that Italy was in fact going to come in—the Duce only suffered from generals as obstinate as his own—but whether or not he was quite as certain as he claimed is a little doubtful; Mussolini's first encouraging and then discouraging him would affect the final denouement of the Czechoslovak crisis.

If Hitler was even the least bit unsure of Italy, he was correct in his doubts. Like the Hungarians who were eager to talk about revision at Czechoslovakia's expense but dubious when they saw the Germans not

158. Ciano, *Diary*, 20, 21, 26 August 1938, pp. 208–9, 212; *G.D.*, D, 2, No. 384; cf. Ciano, *Diary*, 25 August 1938, pp. 211–12; *Hungarian Documents*, 2, No. 302.

159. See *G.D.*, D, 2, Nos. 401, 409, 414; Ciano, *Diary*, 29, 30 August 1938, pp. 213–14.

160. Ciano, *Diary*, 2 September 1938, pp. 215–16; the diary of Wolf Eberhard, Munich, Institut für Zeitgeschichte, mentions a meeting of Hitler, von Brauchitsch, Keitel, and the prince on 3 September at 10:15.

161. Hitler's memorandum for Mussolini is *G.D.*, D, 2, No. 415. See Ciano, *Diary*, 6, 7 September 1938, p. 222.

162. Ciano, *Diary*, 3, 5, 10 September 1938, pp. 217, 218, 222. See also *D.D.F.*, 2d, 11, Nos. 63, 77.

163. *Groscurth Diary*, 6 September 1938, p. 113; Jodl diary, 8 September 1938, *TMWC*, 28:376. Cf. *Hungarian Documents*, 2, No. 324. The report of indications from a member of the Italian embassy in Washington that Italy might stay neutral in a major war in *G.D.*, D, 2, No. 421, was initialed by von Ribbentrop and von Weizsäcker (T-120, 1321/2410/511044). Cf. *G.D.*, D, 2, No. 436.

just shouting and waving their arms on the brink but definitely about to go over, the leader of Italy was all for public pronouncements about the virtues of the Axis and private declarations of the need for war and the inevitability of the dictators crushing the democracies, but very hard of hearing when the trumpet sounded for battle. On 12 September the Germans finally gave the Italians the information they claimed to want: Göring told them in Hitler's behalf that the Führer wanted to have a secret meeting with the Duce at the Brenner pass at any time that was convenient—but *before* 25 September. With Europe on the brink of war, and with Italy pressing for details of Germany's intentions, here was both a clue to Germany's timetable and an opportunity to find out more. The Italians, however, either failed or deliberately refused to grasp the implications of this message. Ciano offered to make more propaganda for the Germans—an offer they happily accepted—but Mussolini coupled a polite expression of interest with a comment that he had planned a trip into some Italian provinces and would prefer an October meeting![164] Ciano's statement to the Yugoslav minister on 13 September that "it was premature" to speak of Italy going to war but that Italy maintained her solidarity with Germany, shows that as the crisis reached its height, the government in Rome was a reluctant dragon, useful to Germany for frightening potential enemies with its shadow but not to be relied on for breathing fire.[165]

If the role of Poland was to be one of diplomatic assistance to Germany combined with possible Polish seizure of portions of Czechoslovakia—but only if there were no general war—and if Berlin had good reason to be skeptical about the immediate military participation of Hungary and to have some residual doubts about that of Italy, how was the German government to assess the possible role of the Soviet Union? In the period June to September 1938, as the crisis over Czechoslovakia mounted, the role or possible role of Russia in case of a German attack on Czechoslovakia was often the focus of discussion, and the issue has continued to exercise a fascination for historians and those who wish to argue the meritorious or sinister character of Soviet policy. Since the Soviet government has yet to allow open access to scholars to Russian diplomatic records of the eighteenth century, it is not likely that some of the critical questions can be answered with any assurance in the lifetime of our contemporaries. That need not mean, however, that the evidence from a variety of available sources does not allow us to state with considerable confidence what *other* governments believed to be the intent and policy of Russia; and these beliefs, correct or mistaken, are themselves important since it was they, rather than conclusions that might be drawn on the basis

164. Ciano, *Diary*, 12, 13 September 1938, pp. 222–23, 224. Celovsky (p. 329, n.5) misunderstood the evidence when he asserted that Mussolini accepted the invitation.
165. Ciano, *Diplomatic Papers*, p. 233.

of new evidence centuries hence, which influenced the policies and actions of those governments.[166]

The dominant element in the assessment of Soviet policy by those who might be on either side of a German-Czechoslovak conflict as well as those who might remain neutral was the geographic reality of Russia's separation from Czechoslovakia by Poland and Rumania. Just what the Soviet Union could or might want to do in the face of this reality was interesting, but not necessarily nearly as important as the voluminous speculation on the subject might lead one to expect. If the Soviet Union did not honor her treaty obligation to assist Czechoslovakia when France had come to the aid of the latter, then there would clearly be nothing the Western Powers could do about a situation in which they were left to fight Germany by themselves—just as they had been in 1918, though now without the American help that had been so important then. If, on the other hand, the Soviet government did declare war, the situation would be little different. The Russians might send some planes by flying them over Rumania, and much of the diplomatic documentation deals with this subject.[167] Such action, if carried out, would be helpful to Czechoslovakia—assuming the Germans did not succeed in destroying the Czechoslovak airfields in the first stages of a conflict—but was not likely to keep the country from being overrun by the Germans, who would then turn west on France, since the same area that separated Russia from Czechoslovakia would then separate German-occupied Czechoslovakia from Russia.[168] Were the Red Army to move across Rumania and Poland, how-

---

166. There is a good summary of the evidence available by 1957 in Celovsky, pp. 311–26. An earlier, but useful, survey is in John A. Lukacs, *The Great Powers and Eastern Europe* (New York: American Book Co., 1953), pp. 172–89; see also Cienciala, pp. 116–17. Documents cited by Celovsky will generally not be cited here. There are additional details in *Hungarian Documents*, 2, Nos. 231, 233, 258, 290, 304, 313; *New Documents on the History of Munich* (Prague: Orbis, 1958), and a useful critique of the latter publication by František Vnuk, "Munich and the Soviet Union," *Journal of Central European Affairs*, 21, No. 3 (Oct. 1961), 285–304.

167. The material on this subject and on any Rumanian offer to look the other way if Russian planes flew over her territory (perhaps because there was nothing Rumania could do about them anyway) can be read in several ways. Litvinov stressed the importance of obtaining transit rights for troops in spite of the knowledge of both the physical inadequacy of the route and the opposition of Bucharest; when the French relayed Rumanian tacit agreement to overflight, the Russian response always coupled air with land transit rights. This can be read as a means of insisting on land transit rights—or as a means of avoiding any aid to Czechoslovakia even by air. See *D.D.F.*, 2d, 9, No. 199; 10, Nos. 6, 182, 511, 534; 11, Nos. 17, 29, 38, 95, 96, 165; *Hungarian Documents*, 2, Nos. 330, 336. See also the detailed discussion of the problems in Fierlinger's report No. 5 of 18 June 1938, Czechoslovak document in T-120, 1039/1809/412508–15; and Coulondre's complaint about the French breaking off a project to purchase planes in the Soviet Union (*D.D.F.*, 2d, 10, No. 18).

168. Note the comments by British Foreign Office officials on a claim by Fierlinger that he had assurances of Soviet aid. Not only was Lord Chilston doubtful, but in London it was recalled that the Chinese had hoped for extensive Soviet aid in their conflict with Japan only to receive little help in fact (C 9186/1941/18, FO 371/21734, commenting on *B.D.*, 3d, 2, No. 761).

ever, and no one detected signs of this being intended, both countries were practically certain to declare war on Russia; and France and Czechoslovakia would then find themselves fighting alongside one ally and against another.[169]

From the perspective of the Western Powers and Czechoslovakia, therefore, Soviet intervention, even if it occurred, was unlikely to be particularly helpful in the immediate situation and was likely to produce more problems rather than to help in the long run. On the other hand, from the point of view of the Soviet government, there was much advantage to a war that broke out in the west. If the French and British fought the Germans, that could be all to Russia's advantage whether or not she joined in. If she joined in, there was the possibility of gains in Eastern Europe, but there was also the risk that the French would not fight offensively and leave Germany the option of turning eastward for further expansion. If, however, she stayed out and France and Britain did fight and crush Germany, there was still the possibility that the resulting upheaval would open up the possibility for Soviet territorial gain at least in the Baltic area and possibly elsewhere. From Moscow's point of view, therefore, there was a premium on keeping options open, and the repeated emphasis in Soviet statements as the crisis became *more* urgent on the role of the League in securing cooperative action against Germany is certainly open to the interpretation that this complicated route was thought of as a means of making it possible to postpone a decision as long as possible.[170]

It is worthy of note that the one area of armaments policy in which there is a record of Stalin's taking a personal interest during the summer of 1938

169. Note Osuský's comment to this effect on 30 May 1938, *U.S.*, 1938, 2:523. The French, British, and Czechoslovak representatives in Poland all agreed that if Germany atacked Czechoslovakia and there was no war, Poland would seize Těšín; if there were a general war, Poland would stay out unless Russian troops entered Polish territory in which case she would fight the Soviet Union. If Soviet troops did not enter, then there was the prospect of Poland's later coming in on the allied side (Noël report of 11 September 1938, *D.D.F.*, 2d, 11, No. 90). The Polish ambassador in Paris asserts that Bonnet never asked the Poles to allow the Russians to send their armies across Poland (*Łukasiewicz Papers*, p. 107); and Comnen, the Rumanian foreign minister, insists in his memoirs (p. 31) that he was never asked for troop transit rights either; but this is surely a formality as in both cases it was known that the answer would be no. It might be argued, of course, that Germany would disregard the objections of Poland and Rumania to pursue a war against Russia, but given the distance at which Germany would then have to operate from home bases threatened by a much closer France, a return to the west first was surely more likely—and so the Germans themselves figured in military planning in 1938 as Hitler had anticipated in *Mein Kampf*.

170. See also Fierlinger's telegrams of 9, 10 June 1938, Czechoslovak documents in T-120, 1039/1809/412149, 412152–53, and Krofta to Osuský, 15 June 1938, ibid., frame 412364. Fierlinger's reports during September reflect his belief in Soviet adherence to her alliance with Czechoslovakia; but when the prospect of war was most imminent, on 27 September, he cautioned about any Czechoslovak effort to secure Polish neutrality or assistance because he had "the impression that in case of a favorable development the Soviets would try to secure a common border with us" (Fierlinger tel. 961 of 27 September 1938, 13:50 p.m., Czechoslovak document, ibid., frame 412088). Such a common border could, of course, be secured only by Soviet seizure of Galicia from Poland.

concerns the Russian desire to order a battleship to be built in the United States.[171] In his meeting with U.S. Ambassador Davies, his first ever with a foreign diplomat, Stalin predicted that Chamberlain's policy would fail because "the fascist dictators would drive too hard a bargain" and that "the Soviet Union had every confidence that it could defend itself." A major investment in the construction of a modern battleship which would not be available for three or four years at the earliest, however, hardly suggests that the need for Russia to defend herself in a major war against Germany or Japan was considered a contingency of the immediate future. It was accordingly simple enough for the Russians to blame others for not standing up to the Germans under circumstances in which there was no danger of having to do so on a major scale themselves.[172]

When that danger arose in the following year, Stalin preferred alignment with Hitler to either neutrality or alliance with Hitler's enemies; nevertheless, whether it was wise for Britain and France to treat the Soviet Union as coolly as they did in 1938 is another matter. Such treatment might easily be explained by the fears—real or unreal—of the leaders of the Western Powers; but it was also likely to reinforce the fears—real or unreal—of Russia's leaders as well. The former were afraid of Soviet expansion and subversion, the latter of some great hostile coalition. Looking backward from 1938, the latter fear had some justification; looking forward from 1938, it is the former fears that have been validated by events.[173] The situation in 1938 would only play into the hands of a Germany which had imagined and convinced herself and many others that the European settlement of 1919 was terribly harmful to her, when the situation of that year ought to have demonstrated the exact opposite.

Germany was, in fact, facing a Czechoslovakia that had no common border with Russia and in her calculations took advantage of this situation. German military planning reckoned with the possibility of some Soviet air support for Czechoslovakia, but was in general based on the assumption that Russia would do very little in a military way, whether or not she formally entered hostilities. German diplomatic reports from Moscow confirmed the absence of major military preparations during the summer and early fall of 1938; and, after the crisis was over, noted that

171. Stalin-Davies meeting of 5 June 1938, *U.S., The Soviet Union, 1933–1939*, pp. 572–73; cf. ibid., pp. 694ff. See also Franz Knipping, *Die Amerikanische Russlandpolitik in der Zeit des Hitler-Stalin Pakts, 1939–1941* (Tübingen: Mohr, 1974), pp. 16–17.

172. Cf. Maisky's comment on 17 August that he did not think the French would fight for Czechoslovakia, *U.S.*, 1938, 1:548; see also ibid., pp. 65–68, 68–69; *D.D.F.*, 2d, 10, No. 474.

173. I am dubious about the alleged importance of an anti-Bolshevik line in British and French policy in this regard. See the extensive discussion of the issue in Gottfried Niedhart, *Grossbritannien und die Sowjetunion, 1934–1939* (Munich: Fink, 1972). Collier's memorandum of 16 August 1938 appears to summarize the British view: National Socialist, Fascist, and Communist systems were different in theory but similar in practice; however, National Socialist Germany was the immediate danger to Britain (N 4071/97/38, FO 371/21659). See also Donald Lammers, "Fascism, Communism, and the Foreign Office, 1937–39," *Journal of Contemporary History*, 6, No. 3 (1971), 66–86; *D.D.F.*, 2d, 9, No. 347.

the Soviet Union had not even undertaken the limited mobilization precautions thought necessary by such countries as Holland, Belgium, and
Switzerland.[174] From the perspective of Berlin, it made little difference
whether the Soviet Union did or did not intervene.

Under these circumstances, Hitler's plans could be implemented, or at
least so it appeared. The massive construction projects on the Westwall
went forward; and Hitler, who toured the fortifications 26–29 August,
expressed himself as highly pleased with the situation and utilized the
opportunity for nasty comments to and about those of his generals, especially Adam and von Wietersheim, who had expressed skepticism about
the strength of the fortified zone.[175] The desire not only to have the
harvest completed but to have as much time as possible for the construction program—while still leaving a short campaign season in 1938—had
induced Hitler to order the preparations for the attack on Czechoslovakia
completed by the end of September 1938.[176] The initiation of a war against
Czechoslovakia would, as Hitler perceived it, come during a period of
constant incidents within Czechoslovakia, with one at a time previously
picked for the attack being utilized as the official pretext. This, of course,
was all something that could not—as in 1914—be left to chance.[177] On 26
August Hitler passed instructions to the Sudeten German party through
Karl Hermann Frank calling for the provocation of incidents in Czechoslovakia.[178] These incidents would, it was hoped, isolate Czechoslovakia
diplomatically and subsequently provide the excuse for war; orders actually to start the incidents on 4 September were given the day before, the
assumption presumably being that ten days would have sufficed for any
needed preparations.[179]

The German need for provocation inside Czechoslovakia was underlined a few days later by the first challenge to Hitler's scenario: the
Czechoslovak "Fourth Plan" of 5 September which threatened to deprive
Hitler of his pretext for war by granting all the essentials of Henlein's
demands in his Karlovy Vary speech. Before the origins and setting of this

174. *G.D.*, D, 4, No. 477. Cf. *U.S.*, 1938, 1:557–58.

175. Jodl diary, 10, 26–29 August 1938, *TMWC*, 28:374, 375; Munich, Institut für Zeitgeschichte, Z.S. 6 (Adam), pp. 2–4. Note also *D.D.F.*, 2d, 10, No. 456.

176. Note Jodl's comment of 15 September that the attack could not be launched any
earlier than originally intended; the original timetable and the railway schedule attached to it
had been set "by the Führer with reference to the longest possible continuation of
[fortification] work in the West" (Jodl diary, *TMWC*, 28:380).

177. According to later testimony by Keitel, Hitler had himself referred to the Sarajevo
assassination (ibid., 10:507).

178. *Groscurth Diary*, 27 August 1938, p. 104 and n.26.

179. Ibid., 3 September 1938, p. 111. See also Král, *Die Deutschen*, Nos. 211, 212. It will
be noted that this procedure obviated any need to take the Sudeten leaders into Hitler's
confidence on the timing of the planned attack. They would start a series of incidents not
knowing which one the German government would elevate to the role of casus belli. The
advantage of this procedure was that there was no danger of a leak about this critical point;
the disadvantage was that the Sudeten leaders might run out of incidents too soon. Hitler's
procedure for dealing with this problem is reviewed later.

step by Beneš are discussed, it might be best to note that the Sudeten German party was up to the challenge. New incidents were immediately staged at Moravská Ostrava; and the Czechoslovak reaction to these, however restrained, could then provide the excuse for breaking off negotiations between the Sudeten German party and the Czechoslovak government.[180] It was almost certainly the success of the Sudeten German party in enthusiastically following Hitler's instructions to create incidents at a time when his generals were continually sounding warnings against war that led Hitler to drop his original intention of having the final incidents staged by the armed forces in favor of the establishment of the Sudeten German Free Corps right after his first meeting with Chamberlain. The Führer retained his desperate desire for war—Long Live War ("Es lebe der Krieg") he had said to Henlein—and the Sudeten leaders rather than the cautious and defeatist generals appeared to be the right ones to help get it started, and started at the correct moment.[181]

How had it happened that Hitler had had to face the challenge of Beneš's "Fourth Plan"? This last-minute effort by the Czechoslovak government may have been presented in the belief that it would be rejected by the Germans, thereby unmasking the true strategy of Berlin—in which case it was a belated effort to accomplish what could have been more easily and usefully done earlier. It is also entirely possible that Beneš saw this as a final alternative to the two other possibilities: territorial concessions and war. Whatever the motive, and on this there is and will continue to be room for debate, there is general agreement that the decision to present a plan that conceded the major demands publicly made by the Sudeten German party was largely the result of British and French pressure on Prague.[182] As has been pointed out, the London government was very much worried that direct negotiations between the Sudeten Germans and the Czechoslovak government might break down, and they had anticipated the possibility of sending some mediator, originally a commission, subsequently an individual, as a focus for continued indirect

180. *Groscurth Diary*, 8 September 1938, p. 115; Král, *Die Deutschen*, No. 215. The literature on the incidents is extensive; it is briefly summarized in *Groscurth Diary*, p. 115, n.78. For Groscurth's statement that the Czechs were not letting themselves be provoked, see ibid., 11 September 1938, p. 117. Smelser, who thinks that the incident at Moravská Ostrava (Mährisch-Ostrau) may have been one of a staged series but was actually *not* designed as a direct response to the "Fourth Plan" says that "the SdP leaders immediately seized upon it as a drowning man seizes a life raft" (p. 237).

181. *Groscurth Diary*, 4 September 1938, pp. 111–12; cf. *Hungarian Documents*, 2, No. 322. For an analysis of the critical importance of timing the particular incident that would be utilized to justify an attack not only on the proper day but also at the correct hour, see Jodl's memorandum of 24 August 1938, *TMWC*, 25:460–62.

182. Note Krofta's own interpretation in transmitting the plan to the Czechoslovak legations in Paris, London, and Moscow on 6 September 1938, Král, *München*, No. 163. See also *D.D.F.*, 2d, 11, Nos. 37, 44. The French, like the British, had been very upset when on 29 August Beneš had withdrawn concessions he had promised to make on 24 August (ibid., 10, No. 520).

negotiations should the direct ones be threatened with rupture. It was this concept that gave rise to the famous mission of Lord Runciman to Czechoslovakia and to his efforts to maintain a diplomatic, as opposed to military, method of dealing with the dispute over the Sudeten Germans.

By mid-July London had come to the conclusion that some such mission would be needed, lest negotiations be broken off, and was encouraged by the discussions with Wiedemann that there was hope of accomplishing something useful. The reluctant lord was, therefore, sent to the equally reluctant Czechs to examine the situation, talk with them and the Sudeten leaders, and attempt to facilitate a negotiated solution. The details of the Runciman mission need not be recounted here. They are in any case not as important as the fact that the mission itself in one way played into Hitler's hands by focusing public attention on the real and imagined grievances of the Sudeten Germans, but on the other hand also paved the way toward diverting Hitler's policy by securing a peaceful settlement—the purpose of the mission, but the last thing Hitler wanted.[183] Even after the incidents utilized to break off negotiations following the Czechoslovak "Fourth Plan," the members of the Runciman mission were trying hard to get Henlein's representatives to keep negotiating, and the supposedly required presence of the Sudeten leaders at the Nuremberg party rally had to serve as an alternative excuse for leaving Prague. Most would not return until the following year. Henlein himself had been warned by the British that a general war would follow a German invasion of Czechoslovakia—and that the Sudeten Germans were the surest first victims of any hostilities—but the man who once imagined he was leading was now only following events.[184]

If the Czechoslovak offer of the "Fourth Plan" sent the Sudeten Germans into a panicky search for excuses to break off negotiations, it confronted the British government with the question of whether or not to put pressure on the German government to accept what they had previously

183. The account in Celovsky, pp. 278ff. is helpful. Other accounts of the Runciman mission in Eubank, Smelser, Rönnefarth, and Thompson. There is additional information in *Harvey Diaries*, 11–16 July, p. 162; *Cadogan Diary*, pp. 87, 89; C 8431/1941/18, FO 371/21731; C 8918/1941/18, FO 371/21733 (refers to *B.D.*, 3d, 2, No. 711); C 8949/1941/18, FO 371/21733; *Hungarian Documents*, 2, Nos. 272, 273, 275, 283, 291, 299; Král, *Die Deutschen*, Nos. 168, 173, 174, 176, 184, 187, 188, 196, 200, 203, 217; Král, *München*, Nos. 111, 112 (part in Berber, No. 143), 113 (Berber, No. 144), 114–19, 122 (a bit in Berber, No. 145), 123 (a bit in Berber, No. 146), 125 (part in Berber, No. 147), 128, 129, 130 (part in Berber, No. 149), 134, 136, 138 (part in Berber, No. 150), 140, 141, 145 (part in Berber, No. 152), 148, 150–55, 156 (part in Berber, No. 154), 157, 159–61, 165, 181; Krofta tel. 777 to London, 26 July 1938, Czechoslovak document in T-120, 1039/1809/412074; Memorandum of 18 August 1938, "Das Wochenende bei Kinsky," ibid., frame 412147; Memorandum on a conference with a member of the Runciman mission, 22 August 1938, ibid., frame 412158 (distorted part in Berber, No. 151); Krofta to Masaryk, No. 884 of 25 August 1938, ibid., frames 412038–39; Masaryk tel. 713 of 31 August 1938, ibid., frames 412022–23 (part in Berber, No. 153); Osuský tel. 788 of 15 September 1938, ibid., frames 411971–72; *D.D.F.*, 2d, 10, Nos. 297ff., passim.

184. C 8118/1941/18, FO 371/21731. See also C 8949/1941/18, FO 371/21733.

pressured the Prague government into offering.[185] Such pressure could take the form of a new warning along the lines of that delivered during the May Crisis and now being urged by some in the British government as well as by those of the German opposition who thought that a firm British stand would either deter Hitler or encourage the generals to action if an attack on Czechoslovakia were actually ordered. But this was not so simple a matter. As Lord Halifax commented on 29 August, "The difficulty does not arise from doubt as to whether or not H.[itler] has made up his mind [to go to war] but as to whether the only thing that might be an effective deterrent should be employed."[186] With Henderson recalled to London to participate in the discussions, the question of a formal warning was again canvassed in the British government and the subject of a special meeting of the cabinet on 30 August. The advocates of a warning received an unexpected assist from Professor Philip Conwell-Evans, a key figure in the Anglo-German Society, and a leading exponent of concessions to Germany. Having just returned from Germany where he had seen von Ribbentrop and others, he was now certain that Hitler had decided to attack Czechoslovakia and occupy the main parts of that country, starting between the end of September and mid-October, in spite of the doubts of his generals but in expectation of British and French neutrality. Only a formal warning would restrain him.[187]

The British ambassador to Berlin, however, argued most vehemently against any formal warning, fearing that it would produce the opposite reaction from that hoped for; it would infuriate rather than inhibit the German leader whom Henderson thought undecided and influenced by divergent views among his associates.[188] In the lengthy cabinet review, the danger of dividing the British public, the unlikelihood of influencing Hitler, and the attitude of several of the Dominions were argued in opposition as well, and it was decided for the time being not to add to Sir John Simon's reiteration, in his speech at Lanark on 27 August, of Chamberlain's statement of 24 March in Parliament.[189] It was thought best to await

185. The point was made—in anticipation—in a plea by Vansittart to Lord Halifax on 25 August 1938, C 9608/1941/18, FO 371/21737. See also C 9004/1941/18, FO 371/21734; Král, München, Nos. 167, 168.

186. C 9005/1941/18, FO 371/21734, f.227. Note that Lord Halifax learned of another German call for a warning, this one by Karl-Heinz Abshagen, on the same day that he made the foregoing response to a memorandum by Vansittart, C 9271/1941/18, FO 371/21735. Cf. Colvin, None So Blind, pp. 233–34; U.S., 1938, 1:549–51.

187. Vansittart's minute, 30 August 1938, C 9377/1941/18, FO 371/21735.

188. Within the Foreign Office Henderson's view that Hitler had not made up his mind was not accepted. It was generally believed that Hitler had decided on war—and that the great problem in getting big Czechoslovak concessions was the resulting need for a British guarantee of Czechoslovakia (C 9023/1941/18, FO 371/21734). Cf. D.D.F., 2d, 10, No. 524.

189. Celovsky, pp. 302–3. The record of the cabinet meeting is in C 9192/1941/18, FO 371/21735. Duff Cooper, who alone advocated a formal warning, gives his impressions in his memoirs, pp. 224–25; Hore-Belisha, who opposed a warning, on p. 138 of his papers. A useful summary by Sargent in C 9041/1941/18, FO 371/21734; cf. Hoare, p. 299. A good report on Chamberlain's views at the time is in U.S., 1938, 1:560–61. A report on the impact of Simon's speech in Germany is in D.D.F., 2d, 10, No. 484.

the results of the new plan Beneš was expected to present, while urging him to make it as generous as possible, and to maintain the regular diplomatic route until after the Nuremberg party rally.[190]

Whatever effect Simon's speech and a subsequent amplification in a press statement might have had was quickly obliterated by the famous *Times* leader of 7 September suggesting in an analysis of the Czechoslovak "Fourth Plan" which had just been offered that it might be well for the Czechoslovak government to consider the advantages of becoming a more homogeneous state by the secession of the fringe areas.[191] The article, and especially the implication that the editor, Geoffrey Dawson, had put into it by suggesting British government approval of territorial cession—he had written that the project "has found favor in some quarters"—was promptly repudiated by the British government. Although there was certainly a willingness by both Chamberlain and Halifax to consider the possibility of territorial concessions as a part of a negotiated settlement, as Chamberlain had himself indicated in May, the public ventilation of the concept at this time was believed singularly inopportune in that it might serve to encourage Hitler to rash action at the very time when the British government, in the interval between a generous Czechoslovak offer and Hitler's forthcoming speech at Nuremberg, was primarily interested in restraining his exuberance.[192]

Both Simon's speech and the press statement amplifying it had been in part a response to the urgings for a firm British warning that so many had mentioned as necessary. One great problem kept concealed at the time but potentially even more likely to encourage Hitler than the *Times* leader was the attitude of France. Although the French government repeatedly urged a new British warning to Germany, the London government could not be certain that this was really what Paris wanted.[193] As soon as

190. This meant having Henderson tell von Ribbentrop that Britain would fight, though von Ribbentrop continued not to believe it (see *U.S.*, 1938, 1:570). The German minister of finance did believe it (*TMWC*, 36:492–98).

191. Celovsky, pp. 305–6, has an interpretation which can no longer be accepted and missed the early clue in Jones, p. 407. There is a full account in *The History of the Times*, 4, *The 150th Anniversary and Beyond*, part 2, *1941–1948* (London, 1952; Nendeln/Lichtenstein: Kraus Reprint, 1971), pp. 929–37. A scholarly study placing the piece in its setting on the basis of substantial research in the archives of *The Times* and several other British newspapers is Franklin Gannon, *The British Press and Germany, 1936–1939* (Oxford: Clarendon Press, 1971), pp. 176–83. Information secured by the French is in *D.D.F.*, 2d, 11, No. 59.

192. See *U.S.*, 1938, 1:545, 549–51, for accurate reports on British views as passed on to the United States in August. Chamberlain's statement to the press that the German government should be under no illusion that there could be a brief war against Czechoslovakia without the danger of French and British intervention is printed in *B.D.*, 3d, 2, Appendix III. In telling Bullitt on 8 September of Halifax's repudiation of *The Times* leader, Bonnet explained that he himself thought the Sudeten area should be transferred to Germany but peacefully and claimed that both the French and British governments wanted this done peacefully but that both would fight if Germany resorted to force (Bullitt tel. 1415 of 8 September 1938, State 760F.62/702).

193. On the French requests to London, see *D.D.F.*, 2d, 10, Nos. 432, 454, 455, 526; 11, Nos. 33, 34, 41, 42, 55.

Chamberlain briefed the press, and Lord Halifax in statements on 11 and 12 September repeated the likelihood of British intervention in a war started by a German invasion of Czechoslovakia, French Foreign Minister Bonnet became hysterical and told off the British ambassador with the reproach that such announcements increased the risk of a war that must be avoided.[194] The collapse of the French position as reported to London after this conversation will be examined later; the point that must be noted is that the French strategy of urging firmness on the British, while using the alleged unwillingness of Britain to be firm as an argument with Prague, was most risky. The British might be persuaded to issue the formal warnings to Germany that the French ostensibly wanted—and thereby make more difficult the French idea that Czechoslovakia would have to make the concessions needed for a peaceful settlement at almost any cost. This convoluted version of London's strategy for pushing Berlin and Prague toward a settlement was not without its own danger. Since the French government, in response to the request of the Czechoslovak government, had never told the British about their threat to abandon Czechoslovakia, there was the possibility, realized in September, that revelation of the true French position might serve not only to bring on greater German demands or a sudden Czechoslovak collapse—as Prague had feared—but also a reorientation of British policy. All these contradictory currents were coming together in the second week of September, but new assessments had to be made not only in London but in Berlin as well.

Hitler was receiving alarming reports from his diplomats in the days before his speech scheduled for 12 September. These reports from both London and Paris suggested that an open German attack on Czechoslovakia would force a most reluctant France to honor her obligation to come to the assistance of Czechoslovakia, and that Britain would then be drawn in, a view that correctly reflects what we now know to have been the French and British attitude at the time. As Helmut Groscurth noted in his diary, Hitler had pushed aside Ambassador Welczek's report to this effect—he was not interested.[195] On 30 August Hitler had asserted that the British were merely bluffing to gain time, but if they and the French came in, Germany was ready. The best time for an attack on Czechoslovakia had arrived.[196] It was a few days after this that Hitler said to Henlein "Long Live War" and expressed readiness for one lasting two to

194. Ibid., 11, Nos. 88, 112, 125. This confirms the account in John W. Wheeler-Bennett, *Munich: Prologue to Tragedy* (New York: Viking, 1964), p. 97, n.1, while contradicting the version in the text, p. 98.

195. *Groscurth Diary*, 4 September 1938, p. 112. Note that this action of Hitler's was reported to Conwell-Evans by his German sources and repeated by him to Lord Halifax, who recounted it to the British cabinet on 12 September as part of the evidence that "Herr Hitler was possibly or even probably mad," meaning that he had made up his mind to go to war regardless of any warnings from France, Britain, or anyone else, C 9818/1941/18, FO 371/21736, f.397.

196. *Groscurth Diary*, 2 September 1938, p. 109. See also *D.D.F.*, 2d, 11, No. 22.

eight years, thus obviously implying the possibility of British and French intervention. He preferred not to give the British and French time until the spring,[197] a dim echo of the later date for an attack on Czechoslovakia that he had once contemplated. Discouraging reports were simply not to be circulated, and Hitler asserted his belief that the negative reports on the prospects of Italian intervention were untrue and the result of a conflict of views between Mussolini and the Italian generals similar to his own quarrel with his generals.[198] It is worth noting the views within the Hitler-adoration society of Keitel and Jodl: Keitel was as sure of the Führer's inspiration as ever; Jodl entrusted the first slight worry to his diary on 8 September.

Jodl considered the fact that the original basis for the German plan had been that the Western Powers would take no decisive action. Now it appeared that Hitler was holding to his intention although he was no longer sure of that point. Jodl confessed to being "not without worry" but insisted that it was essential to maintain one's nerves and firmness in the face of pressure from abroad.[199] Hitler's speech on 12 September was certainly firm enough; he denounced the Czechs in the most violent possible language.[200] If he did not burn all his bridges at this point it was not because he was averse to war[201] but because he was still arguing with his military advisers over the details of the operational plans for the attack which could not, in any case, be launched for another two and a half weeks.

The final German military preparations and the stepped up propaganda campaign mounted in the days right after 12 September must be seen as integral parts of the same scheme: there would indeed be an attack on Czechoslovakia, and the propaganda campaign might yet isolate the prospective victim from assistance by the West.[202] If, however, it did not accomplish the latter purpose, there was still another function to which Hitler would refer after the crisis and which was clearly of great importance to him in 1938 as it would be in 1939. The propaganda campaign was directed to the home front as well as abroad; should there be a general war, the German public with its memories of the last war must be con-

197. *Groscurth Diary,* 4 September 1938, pp. 111–12, 5 September 1938, p. 113.

198. Ibid., 8 September 1938, pp. 114–15.

199. *TMWC,* 28:376. For Keitel's views, see ibid., 13 September 1938, p. 378, and Ulrich von Hassell, *Vom anderen Deutschland* (Zurich: Atlantis, 1946), p. 18.

200. Text in Domarus, 1:897–906.

201. Note Groscurth's summary of Halder's comment on his return from the first part of the Nuremberg party meeting: "One insists on war.... The next step—Rumania, Ukraine, etc.—is already being considered" (11 September 1938, p. 117).

202. Should one not place into this context Frank's account in his memoirs that at the end of the party congress in Nuremberg Hitler mentioned that he might use him in Prague (p. 320)—presumably the way he later used Frank in Poland? Frank claims to have been astonished by the reference to Prague rather than the Sudetenland; whether this assertion is true or not, the reference to Hitler's thinking about an occupation regime of some sort is surely illuminating.

vinced of the absolute necessity of another general war if the sacrifices such a war would entail were to be shouldered willingly.[203]

The days immediately after Hitler's speech saw further troubles in the Sudeten area which were utilized by the leaders of the Sudeten German party for a final rupture of negotiations followed by the dissolution of the party by Henlein's orders. It is quite possible that Laurence Thompson is correct in rejecting the idea that Hitler's speech was a signal to insurrection, an otherwise widely held view, but that does not lead to the conclusion that perhaps Beneš precipitated the breach by stampeding the Sudeten German party.[204] Beneš had every incentive to maintain the process of negotiations as long as possible; it was the Sudeten German party that was in the highly embarrassing position of having run out of demands—Prague had just granted their major ones—before Hitler's timetable called for an attack. The Sudeten leaders had not been given the precise date any more than the Hungarians or Italians, presumably for fear of a leak, and they had for obvious reasons not been secretly warned by opponents of Hitler's project as the two prospective allies had been cautioned. They therefore had to find a way to bridge the time to that point "still in September" by which Hitler had told Henlein he would act.[205] That Hitler himself fully approved the actions of the Sudeten leaders can be seen from the fact, already mentioned, that immediately after the first visit of Chamberlain to Germany, Hitler would entrust the creation of a new set of incidents within Czechoslovakia to them rather than the military, whom he had originally assigned that task. In this fashion, they would be used to help him out of the difficulty that had been produced in part by their own prior activities, namely, the danger posed by Chamberlain's visit that a negotiated rather than a military settlement might evolve.

The idea of a visit by Chamberlain was one that had developed in London in the days at the end of August when alarming news of Hitler's decision to attack Czechoslovakia in late September was coming in from all quarters and the possibility of a formal warning was discussed as one means of deterring him from such a course. Chamberlain thought of it as a last-minute move designed for a contingency when German military action was immediately imminent, so that war would not break out, as it had in 1914, without a last personal contact. In an age of perpetual summitry and constantly airborne government leaders, the novelty of the approach is not so easy to appreciate. There had, of course, been personal meetings of European leaders both under the auspices of the League and at such special gatherings as Locarno. Nevertheless, one cannot deny a certain

203. Hitler's 10 November speech to the German press is discussed below. For the hysterical campaign of September 1938, see Celovsky, pp. 335–38; Groscurth, 17 September 1938, pp. 120–21.

204. Thompson, pp. 140–45.

205. *Groscurth Diary*, 4 September 1938, p 112. The inadvertent discrepancy in the timetable was recognized by François-Poncet (*D.D.F.*, 2d, 11, No. 151).

shrewdly calculated daring quality in Chamberlain's idea that by offering to board a plane for the first time in his life at the age of sixty-nine to see Hitler, he would impress on the Germans the gravity of the situation and would surely make Hitler postpone an attack on Czechoslovakia until he had at least found out what the prime minister of Great Britain had to say. Success of such a venture would depend on two factors, surprise and timing; surprise so that the shock effect would deter immediate hostilities, timing so that the effort would not be wasted. Surprise was to be achieved by keeping the whole scheme secret from all but a tiny number. The details of the project were worked out after the cabinet meeting of 30 August with only Chamberlain, Halifax, Simon, Henderson, and Sir Horace Wilson present.[206] The belief that secrecy was the key to surprise, which in turn was seen as the key to holding Hitler back, led to serious consideration of not telling the Germans that the prime minister was coming until after his plane had left London, but this idea was dropped. The timing of Plan Z, as it was called, would depend on Chamberlain's assessment of the urgency of the situation.[207]

In the first week of September, discussion in London continued to revolve around the idea of a formal warning to Hitler. The suggestion that this be done was reinforced by Theo Kordt, counsellor of the German embassy in London, who was acting secretly for State Secretary von Weizsäcker and the German opposition to Hitler.[208] The continuing discussion was also affected by a message from Burckhardt reporting Forster's repetition of Hitler's decision for war; von Weizsäcker had asked Burckhardt to relay this message to London with a request that the British send a warning letter to Hitler.[209] All this led to the decision to add to prior public comments a further statement Henderson was instructed to make about the fact that Britain would be drawn in by French intervention. In the event, however, this was made only to von Ribbentrop and not to Hitler.[210]

While Chamberlain was still dubious about a formal warning to Hitler, something he clearly thought of as a last resort to be used after and not

206. Note by Horace Wilson of 30 August 1938 in PREM 1/266A, f.363. Cf. Colvin, *None So Blind*, pp. 231–32; Feiling, p. 357. Chamberlain told Samuel Hoare, the other ex-foreign secretary in the cabinet, about the plan on 10 September (Hoare, p. 300).

207. Chamberlain explained the background to the cabinet on 14 September after he had notified Hitler but before Hitler accepted. His account in C 9950/1941/18, FO 371/21738 appears to be full and frank. See also *B.D.*, 3d, 2:647–49.

208. Colvin, *None So Blind*, pp. 235–36. Kordt saw Wilson and Halifax on 5 and 7 September.

209. See above, p. 380; *Harvey Diaries*, 8 September 1938, pp. 171–72; C 9525/1941/18, FO 371/21737; *B.D.*, 3d, 2, Appendix IV, iv. Soon after, the British learned of an unofficial feeler by Helmuth Wohlthat to the United States raising the question of protecting Germany against a peace even harsher than that of Versailles if a European war led to an overthrow of the German government and the defeat of Germany (C 9934/1941/18, FO 371/21738).

210. C 9378, C 9384/1941/18, FO 371/21735; C 9818/1941/18, FO 371/21736, ff.393–95; *Harvey Diaries*, 9 September 1938, pp. 172–73; *Cadogan Diary*, 4–8 September 1938, pp. 94–96; *B.D.*, 3d, 2, No. 765 and comments in C 9182/1941/18, FO 371/21734. Cf. *Hungarian Documents*, 2, No. 321; Colvin, *None So Blind*, pp. 237–38; *U.S.*, 1938, 1:584–86.

before a trip of his own to Hitler, but on which he could not explain his full reasoning to the cabinet without risking the secrecy of Plan Z, the prime minister was certainly not blind to the need for some military preparation. Anglo-French staff talks for cooperation in case of war had been going on since mid-June, and by 6 September arrangements for the transfer of an advance air striking force to France were complete.[211] The available material on the initial orders of the British bomber command shows, on the whole, both that the possibility of war was seen as real and that anticipation of a likely shift of targets from narrowly defined military to more broadly defined industrial ones was rather realistic.[212] On 8 September, the same day on which a new warning was discussed, there also began a series of special meetings of ministers and others on defense measures, authorized by the prime minister to act on certain matters without reference to the cabinet. These gatherings, held from that date until 29 September, reflect a pattern of getting the British navy, air force, and army ready both in actuality and to impress the British public as well as the Germans, but without alarming everyone.[213] The announcement of the first steps concerning the navy at least served to alarm the German naval attaché when he learned to what he claimed was great surprise that such preparations were being made on the assumption which was taken for granted in England that if France were involved in war, Britain would be also.[214]

Conflicting pressures were bearing in on the prime minister. There was a certain hardening of public opinion in England, especially after the Czechoslovak "Fourth Plan" became known.[215] There was on the other hand strong pressure for concessions to avoid war coming from the British Commonwealth. The South Africans had insisted they would not join in any war over Czechoslovakia. Similar views were voiced by the Australian government, and the Canadian government was consistent in its opposition to any position that might lead to war. In a variety of ways, these points of view were put to the London government during the first two weeks of September; and although one might argue that this was as much an excuse as a reason for British policy, there was certainly a case

211. C 9407/37/18, FO 371/21654. Background documents in *D.D.F.*, 2d, 9, Nos. 444, 476, 484, 508; 10, Nos. 73, 86, 409.

212. Air Ministry to Foreign Office, 14 September 1938, with comments and enclosure, C 9753/1941/18, FO 371/21736.

213. See the file "Committee of Imperial Defence, Measures Taken in Connection with the Czechoslovak Crisis—Record of Ministerial Conferences, September–October 1938," CAB 16/189. On 8 September the British embassy in Berlin asked for advice on procedures for destroying its archives and proceeded to burn practically all its records for 1933–36 (L 6487/453/402, FO 370/564; L 7380/453/402, FO 370/565).

214. C 9818/1941/18, FO 371/21736, ff.395–96; *Cadogan Diary*, 10 September 1938, p. 96; *Harvey Diaries*, 11 September 1938, p. 175; U.S. Naval Attaché London No. 890 of 20 September 1938, Hyde Park, PSF Probability of War H. But compare the report of the German naval attaché in *G.D.*, D, 2, No. 451.

215. Note the firm position advocated by Lord Astor—host of Cliveden—on 11 September as recorded in C 9916/5302/18, FO 371/21776, f.30.

to be made for extreme care lest the Commonwealth be divided if war came.[216]

During the days from 9 to 13 September, London hoped to restrain the Germans by the appearance of resolution without further official warning.[217] When the cabinet met on 12 September, the developments since 30 August were reviewed and there was agreement that no further steps should be taken until after Hitler's speech that evening. The cabinet was informed about consultations with the Labor party as well as with Eden and Churchill, but no reference was made to Plan Z.[218] It was at that time thought that if Hitler had decided to move, it would be between 18 and 29 September, so that London's planning was, in a sense, ten days out of phase with what is known of German intentions—the various warnings from Germany had in the end confused more than enlightened London. This mistaken sense of the time element helps explain the decision to move late in the evening of the following day (13th) when news of further incidents in Czechoslovakia suggested that if the step were not taken at once, it would be too late because Hitler might have given the order to march.

The British prime minister was confirmed in his choice of timing by what sounded to London like panic in the French government on 12 and 13 September. One could argue that the French collapse was itself influenced by earlier British reluctance to promise to assist France if war started, but a more searching reading of the evidence suggests that the key element was the reality—as opposed to the theory—of the imminence of a great war that reinforced not only the inclinations of Bonnet, who had long favored maximum concessions, but also of Daladier to call frantically for steps to avert a situation where France would have to choose between dishonoring herself and fighting a war she had no confidence of winning. Certainly the anguished cries of the French prime minister on 13 September for some sort of action to avert war were due in part to a closer look at what now loomed ahead, a look influenced by Lindbergh's gloomy predictions concerning the defeat about to be inflicted on France by the German air force, and the publicly and privately announced determination of the Belgians not to allow French troops to march through the country.[219]

216. The subject was first reviewed in some detail by Donald C. Watt in an essay that appeared in 1958 in the *Vierteljahrshefte für Zeitgeschichte* and in a revised version in 1965 as essay 8 in *Personalities and Policies*. For British documents on this, see especially C 10023/1941/18, FO 371/21738; C 9916/5302/18, FO 371/21776. See also Eric M. Andrews, *Isolationism and Appeasement in Australia: Reactions to the European Crises, 1935–1939* (Columbia, S.C.: University of South Carolina Press, 1970), pp. 138–40; James Eayrs, *In Defence of Canada: Appeasement and Rearmament* (Toronto: University of Toronto Press, 1965), pp. 63–65; *Documents on Canadian External Relations*, 6, Nos. 881–86; *Australian Documents*, Nos. 242, 245, 246, 253, 256, 276–79.

217. See Feiling, p. 360, quoting Chamberlain's letter to his sister of 11 September 1938.

218. Cabinet minutes in C 9818/1941/18, FO 371/21736; cf. Duff Cooper, p. 227.

219. On Lindbergh's stay in France on 9 September see his *Journal*, pp. 69–70 (Thompson, pp. 109–10, confuses this with the August visit); *Harvey Diaries*, 15 September 1938, p. 180; *U.S.*, 1938, 1:581–83; *B.D.*, 3d, 2, Nos. 814, 855; 5, No. 1; cf. Jones, p. 411;

Among the ideas Daladier suggested at the last minute was a joint British-French appeal to Hitler, which Chamberlain obviated by a direct telegram to Hitler from himself, and the idea of a three- or four-power conference of France, Britain, Germany, and possibly Italy, which had also been canvassed in London before 13 September but dropped, in part because of objections to the exclusion of the Soviet Union.[220]

The ideas Chamberlain took with him to Germany can be seen in the briefing paper prepared for his trip and the discussion in the British cabinet on the morning of 14 September when Chamberlain told his colleagues that he had sent a telegram the night before offering to go to Germany but had not yet received an answer from Hitler.[221] Chamberlain had originally thought of using the Czechoslovak "Fourth Plan" as a basis, keeping Czechoslovakia within its old borders, and substituting a guarantee by France and the Soviet Union for the existing mutual assis-

---

Adamthwaite, pp. 240–42. For a critical review of Lindbergh's report, which turned out to be based on information he had gathered on a trip two years before, and for the British effort to restore French self-confidence in view of that fact, see the material filed under C 10025/1425/18, FO 371/21710 and subsequent documents on Lindbergh's distortions in C 10674 and C 13079; cf. Lindbergh, pp. 72–73; *U.S.*, 1938, 1:72–73. On the French military assessment of 12 September, see above, pp. 399–401, and *Łukasiewicz Papers*, p. 126.

On the attitude of Belgium (and other neutrals) in early September, see *D.D.B.*, 5, Nos. 24–27; *G.D.*, D, 2, No. 454. The big worry of King Leopold during the Czechoslovak crisis was that the French might move on Brussels (Overstraeten, pp. 294–97)! A British survey of 13 September of the attitudes of various countries if Germany attacked Czechoslovakia is in R 7671/106/67, FO 371/22353.

The evidence on the collapse of the French position as reported to London is now fully confirmed from the French documents; see *D.D.F.*, 2d, 11, Nos. 125 (reported in *B.D.*, 3d, 2, No. 855), 129, 131, 168. It should be noted that Gamelin had prepared a memorandum on the military situation of a smaller and reorganized Czechoslovakia by 9 September (ibid., No. 65). French fears that war was imminent were doubtless reinforced by accurate reports from François-Poncet; predicting an attack order around 25 to 27 September, they showed how serious the situation was (ibid., Nos. 114, 115). On the general impact of French actions on Chamberlain's decision, see *B.D.*, 3d, 2, Nos. 852, 855–58, 861; Cabinet 38 (38) of 14 September 1938, C 9950/1941/18, FO 371/21738, ff.87–89; *Cadogan Diary*, 13 September 1938, pp. 97–98; *Harvey Diaries*, 13–14 September 1938, pp. 177–79; Feiling, pp. 363–64; Thompson, pp. 147–49; *U.S.*, 1938, 1:594–96. The record of Bullitt's telephone message for Roosevelt dated as "probably May 9, 1938" in *Bullitt Letters*, pp. 260–61, should be dated 13 September and belongs in this context. The Czechoslovak government learned about the French collapse, see Masaryk tel. 785 of 14 September 1938, Czechoslovak document in T-120, 1039/1809/412032–33 (excerpt in Berber, No. 160); Osuský tel. 788 of 15 September 1938, ibid., frames 411971–72; Král, *München*, Nos. 180, 185; *D.D.F.*, 2d, 11, No. 166. Having been warned in July, Prague could hardly claim surprise.

220. Colvin, *None So Blind*, pp. 248–49; C 9966/1941/18, FO 371/21738 (note that this document was read at a meeting of Chamberlain, Halifax, Simon, Hoare, and Cadogan on 13 September); *Harvey Diaries*, 11 and 12 September 1938, p. 176; Osuský tel. 793 of 15 September 1938, Czechoslovak document in T-120, 1039/1809/412131. For military preparations ordered on 13 September, see Hore-Belisha, p. 139; C 9779/429/62, FO 371/21632.

221. The briefing paper and comments on it are in R 8044/113/67, FO 371/22344. The minutes of the cabinet meeting of 14 September are in C 9950/1941/18, FO 371/21738 (cf. Duff Cooper, pp. 228–29; Hore-Belisha, pp. 139–40). Material on the planning for sending the telegram to Hitler was turned up in 1950 and was filed with the document published as *B.D.*, 3d, 2, No. 866, in C 9708/1941/18, FO 371/21736; cf. *Cadogan Diary*, 10–11 September 1938, p. 96. An earlier draft, apparently prepared on 7 and 8 September (ibid. 7–8 September, p. 95), has not been found.

tance treaties, so that Czechoslovakia, like Belgium, would be assisted if attacked but not obligated to aid others herself. By 14 September the prime minister thought it more likely that instead of either such a scheme or agreement on Lord Runciman as arbitrator, Hitler would now demand a plebiscite. This was a demand which would in practice be extremely difficult to implement, but it would be even more difficult for a democracy to go to war to prevent the holding of one. Perhaps a period of autonomy could be followed by a plebiscite in a calmer atmosphere, perhaps in mixed areas a population transfer would prove the only safe approach; and if the plebiscite did eventually lead to a territorial change, Czechoslovakia could be persuaded to agree on the promise of a guarantee by Britain, France, the Soviet Union, and Germany with no obligation on her part to assist the guarantors.[222] This would be a new liability which he realized would not save Czechoslovakia if Germany decided to attack, but would have value as a deterrent. If Germany was seriously interested in friendship with Britain, here would be a chance to work for it. Although the prime minister did not explicitly say so at the cabinet meeting, he obviously believed, and so told the American ambassador right after the meeting, that at least this effort would show that everything had been done to avoid war and that if Hitler insisted on hostilities in the face of a possible peaceful settlement, the British would tell him that they would fight alongside France.[223]

With differing degrees of enthusiasm and reluctance, the members of the cabinet except for the first lord of the admiralty, Duff Cooper, approved Chamberlain's line of thinking, but all were strongly in favor of the trip and hoped that the prime minister's step would be met by an invitation from Germany. Fear of a war for which the country was not prepared on an issue of dubious merit in the eyes of the public at home and in the Commonwealth clearly gave a major impetus to the strength of feeling with which those present looked upon this venture.[224] It would take extra hours to obtain a reply from Germany, in part because of the large number of high officials absent from Berlin.[225] How did the idea of a visit by Chamberlain strike Hitler?

222. The idea of a British guarantee as the concomitant of pressure on Czechoslovakia had been canvassed repeatedly, e.g., in the discussion of the visit of von Kleist in late August (*B.D.*, 3d, 2, Appendix IV, discussion in C 8520/1941/18, FO 371/21732); cf. Král, *München*, No. 177. The idea of a neutralized Czechoslovakia had, on the other hand, always worried the French because of its military implications for them.

223. Kennedy tel. 923 of 14 September 1938, State 760F.62/797.

224. The Chiefs of Staff Committee had been asked on 12 September for their appreciation of the situation in case of war; their response of 14 September was gloomy and asserted that Czechoslovakia could be restored only at the end of a long war (C 9776/1941/18, FO 371/21736). For British deficiencies in the air arm and in anti-aircraft protection in September 1938 see Meyers, pp. 302–3; Sholto Douglas, pp. 353–59, 364–65. The statistics are summarized in Homze, p. 241.

225. Hugh R. Wilson to Moffat, 19 September 1938, Moffat Papers, Vol. 14.

In the German government, preparations for war against Czechoslovakia and also against England and France if necessary were going forward in those days.[226] Still another attempt was being made to persuade Hungary that it would be safe to join in the attack, but the efforts of von Weizsäcker, von Ribbentrop, and Göring were thwarted by another warning reaching the Hungarians from German military leaders which confirmed the Budapest government in its doubts about Germany's fate in a long war.[227] Hitler, however, was not worried; he approved Henlein's step of 13 September in breaking off negotiations with Prague and dissolving his negotiating team.[228] Hitler was certainly completely surprised by Chamberlain's approach. He was apparently prepared to hear a warning of British intervention if war came and was then quite willing to contemplate that possibility.[229] A telegram indicating a willingness to meet the British prime minister was sent, but there is no contemporary evidence for any discussion by Hitler of what he himself planned to say or why he agreed to the trip. Hitler did, however, approve Henlein's proclamation calling for the Sudetenland to be annexed by Germany—the slogan "Home to the Reich" *(Heim ins Reich)* was to be fulfilled in a manner few contemporaries anticipated. The decision of Hitler to push on this point simultaneously with the conversation with Chamberlain surely indicates a determination to proceed under any circumstance.[230] He obviously felt, nevertheless, that his whole propaganda line both at home and abroad would collapse unless he at least agreed to meet the British leader. Given the sensitivity of the issue of responsibility for the outbreak of war, constantly debated since 1914, Chamberlain had calculated correctly on this point, even if he had been misled on the issue of timing.

In the meeting of Hitler and Chamberlain at Berchtesgaden on 15 September, the British prime minister argued that a way should be found to settle the outstanding issues peacefully, while Hitler repeatedly insisted that he intended to solve the Sudeten problem forthwith, by military attack if necessary, and without regard to the possibility of such action leading to a world war. A British warning, he said, could not deter him from acting; and when reminded that the London government had been reproached for not making its position clear in 1914, Hitler asserted his

226. *TMWC*, 25:462–64; 28:337; 29:319–27; 33:190. Note the discussions between Hitler, von Brauchitsch, and Halder on 9 and 10 September 1938, ibid., 28:378, and 25:464–69; and the last-minute German efforts to purchase trucks (C 9434/1425/18, FO 371/21710) and to secure oil from the Western Hemisphere (Nuremberg document 983-PS, National Archives).

227. *Hungarian Documents*, 2, No. 327 (von Weizsäcker), 328 (Bodenschatz for Göring), 329 (von Ribbentrop), 310 (warning of German army leaders), 338 (Kánya does not share Polish optimism, Germany cannot win a long war, push for a plebiscite; German text in Zsigmond, p. 278, n.79).

228. Gajan and Kvaček, No. 44, p. 136.

229. See Lipski's account of his conversation with Hitler on 20 September, quoting the latter "that he was taken aback to a certain extent by Chamberlain's proposition to come to Berchtesgaden" (*Lipski Papers,* No. 99, p. 408).

230. *G.D.,* D, 2, Nos. 489, 490.

belief that even then things had already gone too far toward war for anything Britain might say to hold up developments. Challenged by an angry Chamberlain over why he had let him come to Germany when he was determined on war in any case, the Führer responded that war could be averted if the principle of self-determination were recognized. Chamberlain responded that while he could agree to that personally, he would have to secure the agreement of his government as well as that of the French and of Czechoslovakia; he argued that Hitler would need to take measures to calm the situation while he himself tried to secure approval of a scheme of territorial cession and until he could meet Hitler once more to report on these efforts. Since Chamberlain had been led to believe that Germany was about to march into Czechoslovakia, a belief reinforced by Hitler's demeanor in their meeting, while Hitler in reality did not intend to move for another two weeks, it was easy enough for the latter to make what looked like a concession by promising not to launch an attack right away.[231] Chamberlain returned to England to see whether he could secure agreement to a peaceful cession of the Sudeten area as the only possible alternative to war, Hitler having been obliged to his own great regret to confine himself to a demand for the German areas.

The days immediately following the Berchtesgaden meeting, accordingly, saw the two participants moving in diametrically opposite directions. Chamberlain was convinced that he had halted at least temporarily the outbreak of war, which he assumed would be a world war, and which he thought might be averted entirely if he could get the British, French, and Czechoslovak governments to agree to a territorial transfer of the Sudeten area to Germany. Believing at this point in Hitler's good faith on this issue, he would work energetically to secure such agreement. Hitler was confident that Chamberlain could not get it. As he told von Ribbentrop and von Weizsäcker right after the meeting, "by his brutally announced intention to solve the Czech [sic] question now even at the risk of a European war, as well as by the promise that he would be satisfied in Europe, Chamberlain had been induced to make the promise that he would work for the cession of the Sudetenland. He [Hitler] would not refuse a plebiscite. If the Czechs refused, the road would be clear for the German invasion."[232] If by any chance Czechoslovakia gave in on the Sudeten areas, the main portion of Czechoslovakia would be taken over later, perhaps the following spring. Somehow, however, there would have to be a war, and during his own lifetime.[233]

231. For the Berchtesgaden meeting, see G.D., D, 2, No. 487; Hungarian Documents, 2, No. 350; Feiling, pp. 366–67; Schmidt, pp. 394–98; Groscurth Diary, 17 September 1938, pp. 119–20. Of great interest is Hitler's assertion, reported by Lord Halifax to the French but not otherwise in the record, that if war were coming he preferred to fight it at age forty-nine rather than when older (D.D.F., 2d, 11, No. 188).

232. Von Weizsäcker, Erinnerungen, p. 184. Von Weizsäcker here quotes his own contemporary notes.

233. Weizsäcker-Papiere, p. 143; this section was omitted from the memoirs.

Hitler's determination to go ahead with the conquest of Czechoslova-kia, even at the risk of a general war, was noted by others in the German government at the time.[234] If he was still willing to run the risk of a general war, he was certainly going to do what he could to minimize the chances of being cheated out of at least a little war. Though expecting the negotia-tions to fail over the demands he had already made, Hitler wanted to be as safe as possible from the "danger" of having them met. The first and simplest step he took to protect himself from the danger that the Berchtesgaden meeting might make war politically impossible was to deny the British government a record of the meeting; they might have tricked him by making it necessary for him to agree to meet with Cham-berlain, but he had a few tricks of his own. Only the famous German interpreter Paul Schmidt had been present; and when the British who had known Schmidt as a dependable interpreter for years asked for their copy of the record, they were informed that it would not be given to them! There is no need to go into the ensuing tempest in this particular teapot; but although an abbreviated version was finally handed over after a great deal of agitated—and from the British side annoyed—discussion had taken place, the fact that Hitler personally ordered this extraordinary action makes it important as a clue to his thinking and policy right after the meeting. Far from being eager to nail down the commitment of Cham-berlain, he was fearful of recording his own, thinking perhaps that he could subsequently claim to have asked for more or promised less.[235]

The second step Hitler took to make sure there would be a war as soon as his military preparations were completed was to arrange for the in-cidents within Czechoslovakia that would provide the needed pretext, thus doing the precise opposite of what Chamberlain had asked. While Hitler repeatedly asserted to foreign statesmen and diplomats that some incident provoked by the Czechs might touch off German intervention at any moment, no one has yet located a shred of evidence in the voluminous German record suggesting that the slightest consideration was actually ever given to planning for such a contingency. On the contrary, the Ger-mans were very conscious of the fact that timing was a key factor in their war plans, and since April 1938 it had always been clear to them that only a staged incident or a specific one in a series of staged incidents could guarantee them the choice of date, hour, and minute for the initiation of

234. Contemporary evidence to this effect from the days right after Berchtesgaden is in the Groscurth diary for 17 September, p. 120; Erich Kordt, *Nicht aus den Akten* (Stuttgart: Deutsche Verlags-Anstalt, 1950), p. 259. The French ambassador in London noted that Hitler had rejected Chamberlain's effort at the beginning of their meeting to discuss Anglo-German relations in general (*D.D.F.*, 2d, 11, No. 460).

235. See Erich Kordt's comment in *Nicht aus den Akten*, p. 259. Schmidt himself (pp. 398–99) claims to have thought that this was von Ribbentrop's way of taking revenge for his own exclusion from the meeting, but the evidence of the German documents is explicit on Hitler's personal decision (*G.D.*, D, 2, Nos. 522, 532, 537, 544). See also *B.D.*, 3d, 2, Nos. 895–97, 930, 931, 949, 983, 985.

hostilities. The calmness which prevailed in the Sudeten areas after Henlein and some of his associates left the country for Germany, therefore, threatened to undermine the general political pretext of disorder in the Sudeten areas at the very time when the constant warnings and objections of the generals appear to have raised doubts in Hitler's mind about the reliability of the military in staging the specific incidents that he needed as the properly timed excuse for invasion.[236]

Since Henlein's proclamation had not produced any spontaneous upheaval, something else was needed to create the continued uproar which would provide the general political excuse as well as the specifically timed incident. On 16 September, therefore, Hitler ordered the establishment of the Sudeten German Free Corps, and he confirmed this by having it formally organized on the following day.[237] The task assigned by Hitler to this collection of Sudeten German men who had fled to Germany was the "maintenance" *(Aufrechterhaltung)* of disorder, the arranging of clashes, and the mounting of terrorist attacks on Czechoslovak border posts and other installations. Terrorist activities were to be conducted along the whole length of the German-Czechoslovak frontier. The operation was designed to fit into the pattern of pretense that the situation in Czechoslovakia—instead of the policy and plans of Hitler—was responsible for the danger and eventual outbreak of war. Just before Chamberlain was scheduled to return to Germany, and when the Czechoslovak acceptance of Hitler's ostensible demands was known in Germany, the Free Corps units were instructed to conduct at least ten forays in each district. The details of the attempts to meet the quota of incidents assigned to the Free Corps are not of special importance; the critical point is that this represented the application by Hitler of a device which could assure him of the needed pretext for war without dependence on the army, which was most unenthusiastic about the Free Corps. The incidents provoked by this special collection of cutthroats in the meantime provided Hitler with plenty of stimulus for all sorts of imaginary Czechoslovak atrocities with which he unsuccessfully regaled Chamberlain at their meeting at Bad Godesberg and which formed an important element in his public speeches and the German press campaign.[238]

236. The calm situation in the Sudeten area on 15–17 September, as well as the sense of the Germans there of being deserted by Henlein, is evident from the published German and British documents; e.g., *G.D.*, D, 2, Nos. 516, 518; *B.D.*, 3d, 2, No. 916.

237. The best account is Martin Broszat, "Das Sudetendeutsche Freikorps," *Vierteljahrshefte für Zeitgeschichte*, 9, No. 1 (Jan. 1961), 30–49. There is considerable additional information in the Groscurth diary, pp. 120ff.; the material supports Broszat's account. See also the important documents of the Sudetendeutsche Freikorps published in Král, *Die Deutschen*, Nos. 227, 229, 238; and Standartenführer Altenburg, "Aufzeichnungen über die Tätigkeit der Wasser-Fahr-Abteilung des Freikorps Konrad Henlein," 14 September–11 October 1938, Library of Congress, Manuscripts Division, Acc. No. 9918. In addition, see *D.D.F.*, 2d, 11, Nos. 203, 278, 279; Diary of Wolf Eberhard, 16 and 20 Sept. 1938, Munich, Institut für Zeitgeschichte.

238. For examples of instructions to the German press on 19 and 20 September designed to show that the Czechoslovak state should disappear from the map of Europe, see the reports on the press conferences in Bundesarchiv, Sammlung Traub, Z.Sg. 110/9, ff.200–203.

The third measure Hitler took to avoid any risk of what he called "the danger that the Czechs might accept everything" was to try to activate Hungary and Poland against Czechoslovakia to the point of extreme demands at the very least and hopefully to parallel military action.[239] Neither Poland nor Hungary needed much encouragement as long as it was simply a matter of making demands on Czechoslovakia. Both powers had been demanding for some time that their respective minorities within Czechoslovakia be accorded whatever concessions were allowed the Sudeten Germans.[240] Whether or not this was an intelligent policy on the part of Poland, in which the percentage of Poles was about the same as the percentage of Czechs and Slovaks in Czechoslovakia, does not appear to have worried the Polish leaders at this time. They raised their own demands in a manner parallel to the Germans, insisted after the Berchtesgaden meeting on a plebiscite for the Poles if there was to be one for the Germans, denounced their arbitration treaty with Czechoslovakia, and in general needed very little nudging from Berlin in order to fall in with Hitler's strategy. There is no doubt that they were ready to move militarily into Těšín if the occasion arose; whether or not they would have attacked Czechoslovakia as an associate of Germany without first awaiting the reaction of France and Britain to the German invasion of Czechoslovakia is not entirely certain.[241]

From the point of view of Germany, the important thing is that Poland was fully playing her part, not only by warding off Russia, urging Rumania not to allow transit aid to Czechoslovakia, and herself increasing demands for concessions from Prague, but also was falling in with Hitler's desire for a more insistent and rapid escalation of pressure right after the Berchtesgaden meeting. From Hitler's perspective, the question of whether Beck was doing this on his own and without needing any German urging was entirely subordinate to the fact that Poland was helping to provide a basis for him to raise new demands and resort to a military solution even if his Berchtesgaden demands were by some mischance to be met.[242] To the extent that the Poles were eager on their own even without German urging, they merely relieved the Germans of any need to consider making concessions on the Danzig and German-Polish frontier

239. *G.D.*, D, 2, No. 554, p. 689. See also *Hungarian Documents*, 2, No. 361; Ádám, Nos. 12–16; *U.S.*, 1938, 1:614.

240. Cienciala, pp. 92ff.; *Hungarian Documents*, 2, Nos. 308, 309, 312, 315, 318, 326.

241. See above, n.169. Cienciala (p. 118, n.35) argues that Poland would have moved only in a war limited to Germany and Czechoslovakia. She may well be correct, but since the Western Powers were certain that this was the one contingency that would not occur, the matter is not that important.

242. The literature on Poland's role in the period 12–22 September is immense. A defense of Polish policy may be found in Cienciala (pp. 102ff.), where Beck's interest in German concessions on the Danzig issue is given greater prominence than his interest in the Těšín question. See also, in addition to the material cited by Cienciala, the English translations of relevant documents from the Lipski (pp. 401–12) and Łukasiewicz (pp. 127–36) papers; Wojciechowski, pp. 429–31, 451–80; Roos, pp. 344–49; Krofta circular tel. 1170–71 of 22 September 1938, Czechoslovak document in T-120, 1040/1809/412588 (Berber, No. 169).

confirmation issues that the Poles would have liked to obtain in return for falling in with German policy.[243] When Hitler personally talked with the Polish ambassador to Germany on 20 September, Hitler, like Göring a few days earlier, warded off Polish requests for concessions on Danzig and the recognition of the frontier by alluding to such German demands as the superhighway across the Corridor; but the two could agree that Polish demands would enable Hitler to reject agreement with Chamberlain on the Czechoslovak question by raising new obstacles involving Poland and Hungary.[244]

If the Germans found the Poles enthusiastic about the strategy of increasing the pressure on Czechoslovakia, they found the Hungarians willing in theory but still reluctant in practice, something the Poles had also discovered.[245] The vastly greater territorial interest Hungary might have in a dissolution of Czechoslovakia whetted their appetite and had given urgency to their expressions of interest in the extension to the Magyar minority of whatever might be conceded to the Sudeten Germans. The very fact, however, that Hungarian aspirations extended to all of Slovakia and the Carpatho-Ukraine and hence involved the complete destruction of Czechoslovakia made them more aware of the danger of a general war, something for which they were not only unprepared but which they thought Germany would lose.[246] The Germans did their best, or worst, to move them. Hitler complained on 20 September to the Hungarian prime minister and foreign minister, whom he had summoned to Berchtesgaden, about the indecisive attitude of Hungary. Asserting that war was the best solution, he urged them to demand a plebiscite right away. If they raised such demands and agreed with the Germans not to guarantee Czechoslovakia until everyone's demands had been met, Hitler could use that point with Chamberlain at their next meeting. There remained the danger that the Czechoslovak government might accept whatever was asked of them, but the Hungarian visitors could certainly

243. There can be no doubt in view of the current available evidence that Cienciala is correct in asserting that Beck's instruction to Lipski which included a demand for a plebiscite came before and independently of Göring's suggestion that the Poles make that demand. She has, however, failed to note that this independently raised demand also reduced Poland's ability to secure concessions from Berlin. For Polish pressure on Hungary to move fast, see *Hungarian Documents*, 2, Nos. 316, 343, 348, 354.

244. The record of the Hitler-Lipski talk is in *Lipski Papers*, No. 99 (the copy of this document published in *D.M.*, 1, No. 23, is the one circulated in the Polish foreign ministry). There appears to be no full German record, *G.D.*, D, 2, No. 555. Cf. *Hungarian Documents*, 2, No. 377.

245. *Hungarian Documents*, 2, Nos. 355, 357.

246. It is not clear whether the Hungarian government was influenced in these critical days by obvious signs that neither the Slovak autonomists nor the leaders of local movements in the Carpatho-Ukraine were particularly enthusiastic about the prospect of incorporation in Hungary, preferring at least at that time a future within a less centralized Czechoslovakia to a return to rule from Budapest. The evidence is ably summarized in Jörg K. Hoensch, *Die Slowakei in Hitlers Ostpolitik* (Cologne: Böhlau, 1965), pp. 83–98, and Hoensch, *Ungarische Revisionismus*, p. 86.

read between the lines that Hitler would find a road to war out of that dilemma.[247]

While it was precisely this that alarmed the Hungarians—unlike Hitler, they did not want to run the risk of a general war—they also did not want to lose out on any gains that might be made by pressure and bluster alone. They would, accordingly, proclaim to all and sundry that Hungary expected concessions on a par with those accorded Germany and Poland, and in this fashion fitted their approach somewhat to Hitler's immediate plan.[248] There was, nevertheless, an undertone of worry in the Hungarian reaction to Hitler's presentation which the latter correctly read as a sign of their fear of war. He would use their demands to get out of his commitment to Chamberlain, but when it came time to divide the meal, he would remember that once again Hungary had been a reluctant assistant in the cooking process.[249]

Whereas Hitler had not known what to expect from Chamberlain when the two were first to meet, he did know what the alternatives might be when the prime minister returned. If the answer was no, Hitler had his excuse to march. If the answer was yes, he would be ready to use the troubles created by his Sudeten German Free Corps to demand immediate transfer of the Sudeten areas and he would use the demands of Poland and Hungary to insist on their immediate settlement as well. Surely these new demands would not all be granted, and hence he could go to war. If they were all granted, the Führer no doubt trusted in his own ingenuity for a way to escape the danger of a peaceful settlement.[250]

Chamberlain in the meantime was trying to secure agreement to the idea of a plebiscite for the Germans in Czechoslovakia from his own colleagues, the French, and Czechoslovakia. At an informal meeting immediately after his return to London on 16 September, the prime minister discussed the talk with Hitler with some of his colleagues. There was informal agreement that it would be necessary to support self-determination, probably via a plebiscite. Runciman, who had just re-

247. *G.D.*, D, 2, No. 554; 5, No. 272. See also *Hungarian Documents*, 2, Nos. 334, 341, 342, 346, 347, 349, 368, 373, 375; Ádám, No. 11; Sakmyster, "Hungary and the Munich Crisis," pp. 737–38; *D.D.F.*, 2d, 11, Nos. 227, 238, 256.

248. *Hungarian Documents*, 2, Nos. 351, 352, 358, 359 (*Horthy Papers*, No. 25), 362 (French text in Ádám, No. 15), 363; Hoensch, *Ungarische Revisionismus*, pp. 81ff.; Krofta circular tel. 1172–75 of 22 September 1938, Czechoslovak document in T-120, 1040/1809/412587.

249. *Hungarian Documents*, 2, No. 345; Hoensch, *Ungarische Revisionismus*, pp. 90–91; Sakmyster, "Hungary and the Munich Crisis," p. 738. There was a Polish-Hungarian "gentlemen's agreement" to coordinate their respective anti-Czech policies, but this had no substantial effect in practice (*Hungarian Documents*, 2, Nos. 317, 319, 320, 325).

250. It is worth noting that on 20 September the pocket battleship *Deutschland* left Spanish waters for the Atlantic, equipped to carry out cruiser warfare for several months, with a second pocket battleship scheduled to follow in October (Dülffer, p. 489). The cruiser warfare was presumably not to be directed against Czechoslovak shipping. Hitler's projects to escalate the crisis between Berchtesgaden and Godesberg were summarized by François-Poncet in *D.D.F.*, 2d, 11, No. 291.

turned from Czechoslovakia, expressed the view that Beneš would very likely agree.[251] On the following day, Chamberlain gave a detailed and accurate report on his meeting with Hitler to the full cabinet.[252] He reported himself as persuaded that Hitler had intended to march into Czechoslovakia momentarily but had held his hand for a short time.[253] As for his own reaction to the likelihood of war, he explained that he had told Hitler that Britain did not wish to be open to the reproach, leveled after 1914, of not having made her own situation clear if war did come, and that he had tried to make Hitler recognize that this was not a threat but simply a way of avoiding any misunderstanding of the situation. If war were now averted, however, the road to better Anglo-German relations might be open. The prime minister concluded that Hitler would indeed limit himself to the demand for self-determination for the Sudeten Germans; this was to be the end, not the beginning, of German demands on Czechoslovakia.

Hitler's aims, the prime minister believed, were "strictly limited." This view, it would appear, had combined with the apparent urgency of the situation to lead him to omit discussion of any details or conditions with regard to the application of the principle of self-determination. He had simply agreed for himself and suggested a second meeting after he had had an opportunity to consult others. As for the Poles and Hungarians, Chamberlain and Halifax both recognized that there were problems in that regard; but believing as they did that a German invasion was imminent, they appear to have been of the opinion that those questions could be left for later settlement. There was agreement that a final British position should not be formally arrived at until after conversations with the French, but the record shows the cabinet in general agreement with the prime minister. Duff Cooper, the first lord of the admiralty, expressed his concern over a slide to surrender in a situation where more demands would doubtless follow agreement to those currently before them.[254] He added, however, that war was a terrible option and that no one could predict the future with certainty; he was therefore prepared to agree to the

251. Minutes of this meeting at 6:30 p.m. on 16 September in CAB 27/646. Present were Chamberlain, Halifax, Simon, Hoare, Vansittart, Cadogan, Horace Wilson, and Runciman. Cadogan's account is in his diary, p. 99.

252. Cabinet 39 (38) of 17 September 1938, C 9956/1941/18, FO 371/21738. See also Duff Cooper, pp. 229–30; Hore-Belisha, pp. 140–42; *Harvey Diaries,* 17 September 1938, pp. 182–84; *U.S.,* 1938, 1:607–14.

253. A very similar view that Hitler had postponed an already ordered attack was held by François-Poncet. *D.D.F.,* 2d, 11, No. 151; Král, *München,* No. 178 (the key phrase has been carefully omitted from Berber, No. 161).

254. The same issue arose that evening at a meeting of Chamberlain, Halifax, and Wilson with leaders of the Labor party. When Hugh Dalton suggested that it would be best to hold firm now since otherwise one would constantly have to yield to new threats and would finally be left alone to fight or give in, the prime minister admitted to being "often haunted by fears like this" but would not agree to war being inevitable. If war were avoided now, it might be avoided altogether (Dalton Diary, 17 September 1938). This, of course, was the point on which Chamberlain would change his views in 1939.

principle of self-determination as a basis for negotiations but would insist on careful conditions for its application. Lord Halifax took an essentially similar view, though he was both a bit more optimistic about the future and more obviously convinced that some permanent settlement of the conflict between Czechs and Germans in Bohemia had to be found, hardly a surprising view for one who had spent the last few months concentrating on this problem. There was in the cabinet something of a reluctant consensus that a guarantee would have to be given to Czechoslovakia to make the acceptance of self-determination acceptable to her, and there was an equally reluctant consensus that while Britain could not go to war to oppose self-determination, it was entirely possible that she would have to anyway if unacceptable implementing procedures were insisted on by the Germans.[255] But first there had to be consultations with the French.

For some thirteen hours, interrupted only for meals and for discussions within each delegation, the British and French leaders met in London on 18 September.[256] The British gave a full account of the Berchtesgaden meeting, told the French of their own belief that only agreement to self-determination would avert war, and argued that the French and British jointly would have to urge the Czechoslovak government to acquiesce. The French, who had welcomed the prime minister's trip to Germany,[257] were hardly enthusiastic over the outcome. To their reminiscences of past promises by Hitler to limit his demands, the British could counter with reminiscences about past opportunities Beneš had had to make concessions when the situation was not so critical. The point if it came to war was that Czechoslovakia would be overrun in the early stages, and that once victorious, the allies were unlikely to reconstitute Czechoslovakia in her present borders anyway.

French Prime Minister Edouard Daladier was firm in the assertion that if Germany attacked, Czechoslovakia would fight and France would fight with her.[258] He was also very much opposed to a plebiscite, as that would open up all sorts of other dangers; but he was equally explicit on his own desire to find a peaceful solution "other than a plebiscite" and on his

255. On 16 September, General Ironside had noted in his diary: "It would be madness to expose ourselves to annihilation for the sake of the Czechs" (p. 61). The Foreign Office's assessment of Soviet actions in case of a German attack on Czechoslovakia was equally discouraging. On 17 September it was believed that there would be no extensive help at the outset, that no decisive action could be taken because of the recent purges, and that the Soviet Union would wait on the war weariness of others. On the other hand, there appeared to be no signs of a German-Soviet rapproachement. Cadogan commented on 21 September: "Yes, Pray God we shall never have to depend on the Soviet, or Poland or—the U.S." (N 4601/533/63, FO 371/22276).

256. The British record is in *B.D.*, 3d, 2, No. 928; the French record is in *D.D.F.*, 2d, 11, No. 212; see also Hoare, pp. 304–7; Thompson, pp. 165–67.

257. *U.S.*, 1938, 1:600–602.

258. Cf. *Hungarian Documents*, 2, Nos. 353, 360. Daladier had been given a very shrewd analysis of Hitler's policy on 15 September; see *D.D.F.*, 2d, 11, No. 169.

preference for peace "without destroying the existence of Czechoslova-kia." What was the origin of this stress on opposition to a plebiscite, combined with a willingness to contemplate alternative solutions as long as they preserved the "existence" of Czechoslovakia, a phraseology open to the interpretation that this was not necessarily the same as preserving her territorial integrity?[259]

The origin of the French view is to be found in the fact that a way out of their desperate dilemma of choosing between dishonoring their obligation and becoming involved in war had been suggested to them by Beneš himself. In the days after putting forward the "Fourth Plan" the Czecho-slovak president evidently considered other possible alternatives. On the afternoon of 14 September, he reviewed with the British minister the general situation in the negotiations with the Sudeten Germans, asserted that he was prepared to continue talks, insisted on opposition to plebi-scites, but instead alluded to the possibility of small territorial concessions, although he ruled these out under the existing circumstances.[260] It is important to note that this conversation *preceded* Beneš's learning of Chamberlain's forthcoming visit to Berchtesgaden and thus reflects his thinking before the pressures generated by that development.[261]

The Czechoslovak president was considerably more explicit with the French. Having stressed repeatedly the danger of any plebiscites, which would disrupt the whole country, Beneš appealed to the French govern-ment on 15 September, the day of the Hitler-Chamberlain meeting, to remain loyal to her alliance. He was, however, by now most doubtful that the response would be positive; even while receiving a reply from Paris that referred back to the warning of July, he worked on a project for

259. Cadogan's account in his diary (p. 100) calls attention to this aspect of Daladier's choice of words; the passage itself is in *B.D.*, 3d, 2:387.

260. *B.D.*, 3d, 2, Nos. 884, 888. Hodža made an even more explicit statement on the possibility of a limited territorial cession, ibid., No. 902. Cf. David Vital, "Czechoslovakia and the Powers, September 1938," *Journal of Contemporary History*, 1, No. 4 (1966), 40–41.

261. Celovsky (p. 347), who reviewed this incident with great care on the basis of the evidence available when he wrote, mistakenly dated the conversation to 15 September. Newton's telegram 583 of 14 September (*B.D.*, 3d, 2, No. 884), however, refers to the conversation as having taken place "this afternoon."

Beneš learned about Chamberlain's forthcoming trip from a telephone call from the Czechoslovak minister in London at 9:49 p.m. on the 14th. The transcript of this telephone conversation, which was intercepted by the Germans, is included at ff.221–22 in a batch of intercepts from the *Forschungsamt* handed by General Bodenschatz, Göring's adjutant, to the British embassy in Berlin on 27 September 1938 and forwarded that day to the Foreign Office. They were filed under C 11002/1941/18, FO 371/21742. These transcripts as a group sound authentic on the basis of internal and external evidence—they fit with other docu-ments and contain many unflattering comments about the Germans. It should be re-membered that the telephone lines from London and Paris to Czechoslovakia went through Germany. There may well, of course, have been other conversations either not intercepted by the Germans or intercepted but not included among those handed to the British. The Beneš-Newton conversation, it must also be noted, took place before Masaryk's telegram re-porting on the French collapse (No. 785 of 14 September cited in n.219, above) arrived in Prague.

territorial concessions which he sent (along with relevant maps) to Paris by the hand of a Social Democratic member of the cabinet, Jaromír Nečas, who was to give it to Léon Blum for Daladier.[262] As he discussed that proposal with the French minister on 16 September when the latter brought the formal French answer to Beneš's appeal, it provided for a cession of land outside the ring of fortifications with about a third of Czechoslovakia's German population; the transfer to Germany of another third; and for the remaining third to stay inside Czechoslovakia as a far less dangerous minority since a high proportion of these would be people politically opposed to National Socialism and Jews.[263] Nečas took the project to Paris where he was to repeat Beneš's insistence that a plebiscite meant disaster—and that the origin of the proposal was never to be revealed. By the time it was given to Daladier as he was about to leave for London, the French foreign ministry had already prepared briefs for the French ministers which dealt with the details of such a project.[264]

Beneš's concept, which harked back to suggestions he had made at the peace conference in 1919 and to which certainly Hodža and possibly other members of the government were privy, was a cession of the Sudeten area outside the belt of fortifications on the condition that much of the balance of the Sudeten German population be transferred out of the remaining parts of Czechoslovakia. A plebiscite would disrupt the whole country, whereas a redrawn frontier accompanied by a large population transfer could leave a defensible and more homogeneous state. Far from being the warmonger of German propaganda, Beneš was trying to find a way that

262. On opposition to a plebiscite, see *D.D.F.*, 2d, 11, Nos. 87, 103. The appeal of Beneš is ibid., No. 150. Bonnet's reply is No. 157; his comments to Osuský to the effect that a territorial transfer would be necessary are in No. 177 (see also No. 166).

In the afternoon of the 15th, Beneš was told by René Brunet, a Socialist deputy who acted as an unofficial French emissary in Czechoslovakia in 1938, that the French would not fight even if the British were willing. Beneš responded that then Germany would dominate Central Europe, ally herself with the Soviet Union, and then fight England and France (ibid., No. 178). On Brunet, see ibid., p. 166, n.2; Thompson, p. 117; *G.D.*, D, 2, Nos. 340, 493.

263. The details as given by Beneš to Lacroix mention a larger territorial and a smaller population change than the written text given to Nečas. Compare *D.D.F.*, 2d, 11, No. 180 with No. 192. See also ibid., No. 175; Adamthwaite, pp. 212–13; Celovsky, pp. 345–47.

264. *D.D.F.*, 2d, 11, No. 195; Adamthwaite, p. 213. See also *D.D.F.*, 2d, 11, No. 196; Celovsky, pp. 347–49; Thompson, pp. 164–65; Luža, *Transfer of the Sudeten Germans*, p. 141, n.146; Bruegel, p. 623, n.82; Cienciala, p. 114, n.23; *U.S.*, 1938, 1:686. The instructions of Beneš for Nečas were first published in *Mnichov v dokumentech* [Munich in documents] (Prague: Orbis, 1958), 2:209–10. In London, where he went from Paris, Nečas took a very belligerent line with Labor party officials, see Dalton Diary, 18 September 1938. There is a cryptic reference to Nečas going to see only Attlee in the Masaryk-Beneš telephone conversation of 19 September, FO 371/21742, f.227. Nečas may have been instructed to make in London a communication similar to that made in Paris (*D.D.F.*, 2d, 11:288, n.1), but unless further evidence is found, he either did the opposite on his own—or had a very different set of instructions for the British capital.

There may have been a plan of Beneš to make with Hungary an arrangement analogous to that he was proposing to make with Germany (Hoensch, *Ungarische Revisionismus*, p. 102, n.87); but Beneš told Lacroix that even President Masaryk had been unable to obtain approval of a cession to Hungary (*D.D.F.*, 2d, 11, No. 180).

might preserve independence within defensible borders for Czechoslovakia without war—and without most of its Germans—while providing some territorial cession to Germany. The project itself makes a good deal of sense if one accepts any massive population transfer to accompany a territorial cession; and it would have left a far stronger and more unified Czechoslovakia than the "Fourth Plan," had the latter been accepted and implemented. Advanced by Prague as a means of seizing the diplomatic initiative after the May Crisis or the French warning of July, it might conceivably have changed the situation considerably, but in September the project played a very different role.

The French leaders were careful not to tell the British about the approach Beneš had made,[265] but their confidence that the Czechoslovak government would accept a cession of territory as long as there was no plebiscite and their insistence on this approach was surely a reflection of their knowledge of Beneš's views. During the break for lunch, furthermore, Daladier assured Chamberlain that "while he saw the most serious objections to recognizing the general principle of self-determination, which would involve other minorities, he thought that he could get M. Benes to agree to a cession of territory in the particular case of the Sudeten Germans."[266] The French went further concerning territory to be ceded than Beneš had indicated because they shared the opinion of the British that there was no alternative, but they insisted on a British guarantee of what would be left of Czechoslovakia once the areas with the belt of fortifications had been turned over to the Germans, a danger for Czechoslovakia being implicit in any such drastic change of the border. Since Daladier did not wish to reveal the fact that he had maps showing what Beneš felt he could safely yield and what would be likely to happen if majority decisions were arrived at by plebiscites, the French prime minister brought forth some extraordinarily feeble and unconvincing arguments for a British guarantee with which he could then feel justified in shifting from the map Beneš had favored to one very like the map Beneš feared and rejected. The British waved aside the spurious arguments but

265. The British record is in *B.D.*, 3d, 2, No. 928; the French in *D.D.F.*, 2d, 11, No. 212. Daladier, who knew Bonnet to be very much inclined to concessions, may not have informed his foreign minister about the written Nečas proposal; but the latter was thinking along similar lines (see the important letter of Osuský to Beneš of 17 September, Král, *München*, No. 185), and so interpreted the remarks of Beneš to Lacroix (see Osuský tels. 839 and 845 of 19 September, Czechoslovak documents in T-120, 1039/1809/412124–25 and 412121–23; also Král, *München*, No. 255). Daladier claims to have mentioned the Czechoslovak message of a willingness to concede territory in a private talk with Chamberlain *before* the formal Anglo-French session (*Les Evénements survenues en France de 1933 à 1945*, Annexes I:33–34), but unlike Vital (p. 41, n.6) and Adamthwaite (p. 214), I am doubtful about this assertion. It does not fit together with the things Daladier said at the meeting, but it does fit with his strategy before the Parliamentary Commission.

266. The quotation is from Chamberlain's account of the meeting to the cabinet on 19 September in FO 371/21744, f.174.

recognizing the strength of French opinion in the matter, and in line with their own prior discussion of the issue, agreed to the guarantee.

Subject only to the approval of his colleagues in Paris—which he secured with little·difficulty on the following day—Daladier concurred in a joint approach to Prague. The Czechoslovak government would be told that they could have a plebiscite, but as it was believed that they preferred simply to cede specific areas, they would be called upon to yield those with a majority of Germans in them. This drastic change entitled them to "some assurance of their future security" and this would take the form of Great Britain joining in an international guarantee against unprovoked aggression and the substitution of a general guarantee for the existing treaties with their obligations for mutual assistance.[267]

Daladier had, as already mentioned, little trouble persuading the French cabinet to concur in the joint approach to Czechoslovakia—after some discussion, the members agreed unanimously.[268] Chamberlain was still faced with serious reservations in his cabinet about the wisdom and efficacy of the guarantee he had offered on behalf of England, but there also unanimity was eventually secured.[269] There were two issues open: would the implied decision to ignore the demands of Poland and Hungary for the time being work out in practice, and would Czechoslovakia agree to turn over the border areas including both the Germans and the fortifications to Germany?

As for Poland and Hungary, the days after the Anglo-French conversations of 18 September, especially as word leaked out that territorial cessions were under consideration, saw those countries energetically pushing for concessions to themselves, immediately and on the same basis as those being contemplated for Germany. In this regard, the two were doing exactly what Hitler hoped they would, and what Czechoslovakia's leaders had feared they might. Both the British and French governments were aware of the problem and were forcefully reminded of it by the diplomatic representatives of Poland and Hungary. If there was reluctance to agree to such proposals as well as an expectation that the demands might be worked out over a period of time as opposed to those few days, three reasons appear to have been important. In the first place,

267. The text is in *B.D.*, 3d, 2, No. 937. Cf. *U.S.*, 1938, 1:618–19.

268. Celovsky, p. 351. This writer does not share Celovsky's belief (pp. 352–53) that the opponents of concessions to Hitler in the French cabinet agreed in anticipation of Czechoslovakia's rejection of the proposal; confronting Beneš with a unanimous (as opposed to a divided) French government was hardly the way to encourage him to turn down the proposal! Cf. *U.S.*, 1938, 1:620–21.

269. The record of the cabinet meeting of 19 September is in FO 371/21744, ff.171–93. Chamberlain had given a report on the talks with the French in a meeting with a Labor delegation, who had been very much impressed, or rather depressed, by hearing of the French military situation and the intention of the Soviet Union to take the issue to Geneva if France honored her obligation to go to war. See also *U.S.*, 1938, 1:621–22; Hore-Belisha, pp. 142–43.

the repeated references in the documents to speed regarding Germany and delay regarding the others surely reflects a perception in London and Paris that the Sudeten question could touch off a world war at any moment while the other issues were of a sort susceptible to solution in a calmer atmosphere. Although unmentioned, there may well have been a reluctance to ask too much of Czechoslovakia at one time. Finally, there is a third aspect to which no one appears to have referred at the time, partly no doubt out of politeness, but partly because everyone knew it, took it for granted, and therefore saw no reason to discuss it. Surely Poland with her German, Lithuanian, Belorussian, and Ukrainian minorities was not the country to argue seriously that the boundaries of East Central Europe should be redrawn. As for the Magyars, they were notorious in Europe for having achieved the dubious distinction of treating national minorities worse than anyone else. They might also be expected to anticipate that any insistence on their part on the dismemberment of Czechoslovakia would surely return Yugoslavia to her Little Entente obligations.[270] Under these circumstances, London and Paris hoped that the Polish and Hungarian issues could be postponed, and Chamberlain agreeed with his colleagues that if Hitler used these problems to make new demands the prime minister would refuse to discuss them without consulting his cabinet.[271]

The Czechoslovak government now faced the difficult choice between agreement to the cession of the Sudeten areas in exchange for a dubious guarantee and the doubtful hope of being left alone by Germany on the one hand, and defiance and war on the other. During the period from noon on 19 September to the early hours of the twenty-first the Czechoslovak government examined the problem. The French and British ministers insistently urged prompt acceptance and predicted that it would be forthcoming. Beneš and Hodža apparently both thought it best to agree to the Anglo-French plan. There was no doubt about the reality of German plans to attack; there was no doubt that Czechoslovakia would be battered and overrun in the early stages of any conflict. If the Western Powers did not move, all of Czechoslovakia would remain the spoil of her enemies. If they did move, and if the Soviet Union joined in, the allies of Czechoslovakia would win after a long war, but they would hardly thank Czechoslovakia for appearing to have involved them in it by her obstinacy, and they were very likely to have her emerge at the end of such a war with borders

270. See *Hungarian Documents,* 2, Nos. 366, 375, 385; Hoptner, pp. 116–18; *D.D.F.,* 2d, 11, No. 335.
271. The cabinet meeting record is in C 10711/1841/18, FO 371/21741; cf. Duff Cooper, p. 231. On Polish and Hungarian representations and activities during the days from 18 to 22 September, see *Hungarian Documents,* 2, Nos. 364, 365, 367, 369–74, 376–81, 383, 384, 387, 388; *B.D.,* 3d, 3, chap. 1. For later actions, see *Hungarian Documents,* 2, Nos. 391, 392, 394, 398, 399, 405; *U.S.,* 1938, 1:650–54. For a Yugoslav effort to mediate the Hungarian-Czechoslovak conflict, see *Hungarian Documents,* 2, Nos. 396, 407; Hoensch, *Ungarische Revisionismus,* p. 101. Cf. *D.D.F.,* 2d, 11, No. 137.

much like those implied in the proposal now before the Prague government. Neither the Czechoslovak public nor the members of the coalition government had, however, been prepared for the possibility of extensive territorial concessions, so that the government felt it could signalize its agreement only following a great show of French and British pressure. This pressure was provided by Paris and London, but it is ironic that after months—in the case of London even years—of pressure for concessions that had been resented in Prague, the final installment of that pressure was to all intents and purposes solicited by the Czechoslovak leaders themselves.[272] The only hope that may have held Beneš back in those critical days was the possibility of new currents coming to the fore in the Western capitals; but as it became obvious that in spite of reservations and objections and even shame in London and Paris there would be no reversal of policy, there was no alternative to surrender.[273]

Chamberlain could return to Germany for his second meeting with Hitler bringing British, French, and Czechoslovak agreement to the demands Hitler had voiced at Berchtesgaden. As those demands and the agreement to them became known, there was a hardening of public opinion in England and France, a hardening reflected in the discussion in the cabinet in London on 21 September. There was some anticipation that further demands would be made. The day before, Sir Orme Sargent had noted in the Foreign Office:

> If Hitler is true to form, we must be prepared at his forthcoming meeting with the Prime Minister for him to make further demands under

272. Daladier put this point frankly to objecting French cabinet members, who informed Osuský. The latter asked Beneš to deny this assertion (Osuský tel. 882 of 22 September 1938, Czechoslovak document in T-120, 1039/1809/412118–19), which Beneš promptly did (Beneš to Osuský, 23 September 1938, ibid., frames 412132–33).

273. The summary in Thompson, chap. 18, is excellent. There is also a good account—though somewhat exaggerating Czechoslovak military strength—in Vital, pp. 41–57. See also the evidence collated in Celovsky, pp. 356–74, which, though very helpful, is much influenced by the arguments over the post–World War II validity of the territorial cession. In addition, see Chvalkovský's comments to Phillips on 22 September 1938, Phillips diary, pp. 2745–47, Phillips Papers, vol. 17; intercepted telephone conversations in FO 371/21742, ff.231–43 (see esp. Osuský-Beneš, 21 September 1938, 10:32 a.m. in which Osuský wants acceptance postponed as long as possible in hopes of a change in Paris, and Beneš is doubtful); *Cadogan Diary*, 19 and 20 September 1938, pp. 101–2; *Harvey Diaries*, 19–21 September 1938, pp. 187–91; Heidrich (Geneva) tel. 826 of 18 September 1938, Czechoslovak document in T-120, 1039/1809/412093; Osuský tel. 827 of 18 September 1938, ibid., frame 412126; *D.D.F.*, 2d, 11, Nos. 217–52, passim; Adamthwaite, pp. 215–17; Gilbert, *Churchill*, 5:977–78.

There was a good deal of discussion and denial at the time about alleged Czechoslovak efforts to assist in the overthrow of the French and British governments with the purpose of displacing the Anglo-French plan for a cession of the Sudeten territories. The Germans at the time claimed to the British and French that they had transcripts of telephone conversations of Czechoslovak diplomats talking between London and Paris and Prague to prove this point. It is, therefore, of special interest that in the collection of transcripts handed by the Germans to the British it is precisely this critical point which is covered *not* by verbatim transcripts but by a summary in paragraph form (FO 371/21742, ff.233–34), although almost all the other conversations in the collection are in transcript format.

threat of war. On the last occasion he invented a massacre of 300 Sudeten to justify his abandonment of autonomy, which he had previously demanded, and its replacement by his present claim for annexation.

If he wishes now to make further demands, he will no doubt be able to invent a state of affairs which will enable him to maintain that the situation has deteriorated since the Berchtesgaden meeting in such a way that he is no longer able to accept as a settlement what he had then demanded.[274]

Such possibilities were canvassed in the cabinet, where Hitler's adherence to his own prior position as set forth at Berchtesgaden was seen as a test of his sincerity. There would be no further concessions. Discussion revolved primarily around the new status of Czechoslovakia: there should be a German-Czechoslovak nonaggression treaty accompanied by British, French, and Soviet guarantees of Czechoslovakia against aggression.[275] There was, or at least appeared to be, a clear sense that everything possible and reasonable had been done; if the Germans were not willing to settle peacefully under these conditions, war would come, but of Germany's choosing.[276]

When Chamberlain met Hitler again at Bad Godesberg on 22 September, he reviewed recent developments, explained that he had secured approval for territorial transfer, and proceeded to elucidate some suggestions and conditions under which such territorial cessions might be worked out. Presumably to retain some leeway in the negotiations, he suggested that the figure of 65 percent German population provide the basis for a commission to draw the new border rather than the 75 percent Lord Runciman had originally recommended or the bare majority that was provided by the Anglo-French plan.[277] He also explained to Hitler the idea of new guarantees for Czechoslovakia to replace its current security system.

274. Memorandum by Sargent, 20 September 1938, C 10329/1941/18, FO 371/21739.

275. The minutes are in C 10711/1941/18, FO 371/21741. On the stiffening of the British and French positions on 20 and 21 September, see *U.S.*, 1938, 1:631–32, 636; 8th and 9th informal meetings of British ministers, 21 and 22 September 1938, CAB 27/646; *Cadogan Diary*, 21 September 1938, p. 102; *Harvey Diaries*, 22 September 1938, p. 191; *B.D.*, 3d, 2, Nos. 1009, 1010, 1015, 1016, 1026; *D.D.F.*, 2d, 11, No. 277.

276. The British and French reaction to reports of the Sudeten German Free Corps occupying some Czechoslovak territory on 22 September, which included the decision to withdraw their earlier caution against Czechoslovak mobilization (though temporarily again suspended), must be seen in this context; Celovsky, pp. 401–8; Král, *München*, Nos. 215 (part in Berber, No. 170), 216, 218, 219 (part in Berber, No. 219); *D.D.F.*, 2d, 11, Nos. 308, 313, 134. Hugh Dalton, one of the leaders of the Labor party, was in Paris on 23 September and was told by Phipps about the difficult situation where in the early stages of war all would go in favor of Germany and only in the long run would this be reversed (Dalton Diary, 23 September 1938).

277. In the telephone conversation Masaryk-Beneš of 19 September, 7:00 p.m., Masaryk said with reference to the original Anglo-French plan after Berchtesgaden: "If it only said 75%, but 50%, that is impossible." Beneš's response was "terrible." FO 371/21742, f.229. On Runciman's reaction to the 50 percent figure, see the Masaryk-Beneš conversation of 23 September, 10:05 a.m., ibid., f.246.

Hitler's response was based on the strategy he had developed after the Berchtesgaden meeting. He professed—perhaps genuine—astonishment at what Chamberlain had managed to do, but he used the conditions he himself had created in the meantime to justify rejection of a settlement on the basis of his prior demands. The activities of the Free Corps provided the pretext for asserting that things were so bad inside Czechoslovakia that he had to move in right away, there could and would be no discussion about properties, commissions, refugees, and such. Huge stretches would be occupied forthwith, and plebiscites—presumably on the recent Austrian model—would be held in them after German occupation, with several additional areas subject to plebiscites as well. In regard to the German-Czechoslovak nonagression pact Chamberlain had suggested, nothing like that was feasible even after Germany's territorial demands had been met until after the Polish and Hungarian demands Hitler had been stimulating had also been accommodated.[278]

The new demands were obviously designed to prevent the peaceful agreement toward which Chamberlain was pushing. Hitler had previously expressed to the Hungarians his own fear that the Czechs might accept everything, and von Ribbentrop told Schmundt after the Bad Godesberg meeting that acceptance of the memorandum containing the German demands was the most painful thing that could happen to the German government.[279] One official in the British Foreign Office was to suggest that since the Germans would doubtless invent new demands as soon as this list was accepted, it might be as well to show them up by agreeing now, thereby exposing Hitler's tactics all the more effectively.[280] Such an approach did not occur or appeal to the British prime minister. He was obviously shocked and upset. Rather than simply break off talks and return to England, he did get into some discussion of the new German ultimatum. Under the impression of Chamberlain's firmness and the news of the Czechoslovak mobilization—which arrived during the later stages of the Bad Godesberg talks after Britain and France had withdrawn their objections to such a step as a result of learning Hitler's newest demands—the Führer changed the timetable for the occupation by a few days and some other minor modifications were also made, but the substantive situation remained unchanged. Dictation was to replace negotiation, and Czechoslovakia was to be punished rather than rewarded for agreeing to the cession of the Sudeten areas.

278. The British record is in *B.D.*, 3d, 2, No. 1033; the German in *G.D.*, D, 2, No. 562. Chamberlain had taken along his own interpreter to avoid a repetition of the fiasco about the Berchtesgaden record. Also important is *Lipski Papers*, No. 107 (*D.M.*, 1, No. 32). For further details, see Celovsky, pp. 393–98; Thompson, pp. 186–96; *Harvey Diaries*, 22 and 24 September 1938, pp. 191–95.

279. *Groscurth Diary*, 27 September 1938, p. 125; cf. Dirksen, pp. 232–33.

280. Sargent's memorandum of 28 September 1938 in C 11294/1941/18, FO 371/21744. Cadogan noted that the cabinet on the 27th (meeting 46) had definitely decided against such a line.

Chamberlain merely agreed to pass on to the Czechoslovak government the new German demands.[281] As he returned to England disappointed at what certainly looked like the failure of his efforts, he appears to have clutched at the minor concessions that Hitler had made during the Bad Godesberg talks as a possible route to further concessions leading to an agreement after all. Only in this way can one understand the slow but continuous hardening of his attitude after Godesberg.[282] In his first meeting with ministers right after returning and in the following cabinet meeting, the prime minister inclined to the view that some way might be found to work on the basis of the new terms, though his own words show him doubtful about that, while many in the cabinet were convinced it was impossible. It was in this regard that there was an advantage in the prime minister and foreign secretary not having both participated in the sessions in Germany; the prime minister remembered the discussion *after* Hitler's original rejection, while the foreign secretary was naturally most impressed by the outcome of the Godesberg meeting as a whole. That was unacceptable, and he so explained his view at the cabinet meeting on 25 September. Chamberlain fell in with this judgment and so did the whole cabinet with those most dubious about firmness and those equally dubious about concessions for once in agreement.[283]

If the hardening of public opinion in England contributed to this view, so did the similar process in France which was reflected in the attitude of the French ministers, who again came to London to confer with their British counterparts. The English ministers put them through a difficult few hours as they inquired about the military measures which the French proposed to back up their proclaimed support of Czechoslovakia; but after reading these tough exchanges one can also see that they represent

281. A detailed Czechoslovak "Analyse du mémorandum allemand de Godesberg" prepared on or about 25 September 1938, and showing the impossibility of Czechoslovak acceptance is in T-120, 1039/1809/412519–52. The analysis is summarized in Král, *München*, No. 229. The full text was presumably the material Prague at one point thought of sending Masaryk by airplane (Král, *München*, Nos. 225, 226, 228). For a Czechoslovak explanation of the problems of the Godesberg terms for the French, see ibid., No. 231. Similar analyses by the French themselves in *D.D.F.*, 2d, 11, Nos. 350, 354, 355.

282. Interesting on this is the report of the Canadian high commissioner on a talk with Chamberlain on 26 September between the two meetings of Horace Wilson with Hitler: "Was struck by point in Prime Minister's statement when he said although he had been inclined at first to be impressed by view that German proposals for occupation of Sudetenland was largely a matter of method, he had come to the conviction that there was more to it than that. If matter was merely one of method, why was Hitler so determined not to modify terms? Prime Minister is convinced that proposals reveal ambitions more far-reaching than Hitler has been prepared to admit" (*Documents on Canadian External Relations*, 6, No. 897, p. 1097). See Eayrs, pp. 67–69, which reflects the Dominion pressure on England to compromise further. See also *Australian Documents*, Nos. 283, 304.

283. For the report of Chamberlain and the subsequent internal British discussions, see Birkenhead, pp. 398–401; Hore-Belisha, pp. 144–46; Nicolson, pp. 366–68; *Cadogan Diary*, 24 and 25 September 1938, pp. 103–6; 13th informal meeting of ministers, 24 September, 3:30 p.m., CAB 27/646; Cabinet 42 (38), 24 September, 5:30 p.m., C 11441/1941/18, FO 371/21744, ff.145–67; Cabinet 43 (38), 25 September, 10:30 a.m., C 10929/1941/18, FO 371/21742; *U.S.*, 1938, 1:652.

the canvassing of last doubts before firm resolution is arrived at. The Czechoslovak government would not be urged to accept the new terms; and in the hope of deterring Hitler from taking the plunge, Sir Horace Wilson would be sent first to suggest a supervised territorial transfer, but also to warn Hitler that if Germany marched, France would honor her alliance and England would fight on her side.[284]

One of the advocates of a firm line, Duff Cooper, who had not participated in the talks with the French or the informal meeting of ministers, commented in his diary about Chamberlain's statement at the subsequent cabinet meeting that England would fight with France that "the Prime Minister made this announcement casually and I could hardly believe my ears."[285] Chamberlain was not the fist-pounding type, but his quiet shift from doubt to resolution was therefore all the more convincing to his colleagues and to the French. They now set about getting ready for war in earnest. The French were beginning to mobilize their army, and Great Britain announced the mobilization of the fleet at the very time on 27 September when Sir Horace was in Germany.[286] The British warned the Dominions that war was practically certain. Whatever the grimness of the predictions made by French and British military leaders, the political leaders in both countries were ready—reluctantly ready, but ready nevertheless—to go to war if Czechoslovakia as expected rejected the new German demands and Germany attacked.[287] The repeated statements of the Russian government asserting loyalty to their treaty commitments and the agreement reached at the Anglo-French meeting in London formed the basis of the British public statement on the evening of the 26th that France, Britain, and the Soviet Union would all be involved in a war initiated by Germany.[288] The French plan in case of war appears to have been to make a token advance into Germany, then withdraw to the

284. On the Anglo-French meetings and the decision to send Horace Wilson to Germany, see *B.D.*, 3d, 2, Nos. 1093, 1096; *D.D.F.*, 2d, 11, Nos. 356, 375; Birkenhead, pp. 401–3; Hore-Belisha, pp. 146–48; *Cadogan Diary*, 26–27 September 1938, pp. 106–7; *Harvey Diaries*, 25 September 1938, pp. 196–98; Thompson, chap. 20; Celovsky, pp. 412–17; Cabinet 44 (38), 25 September, 12:00 p.m., C 10930/1941/18, FO 371/21742; Cabinet 45 (38), 26 September, noon, C 10931/1941/18, ibid.; *U.S.*, 1938, 1:641–50; Hull-Kennedy telephone conversation, 26 September, 9:30 a.m., State 760F.62/1362. For efforts of some French officials to undermine Daladier's firm position, see *D.D.B.*, 5, No. 35, but cf. *U.S.*, 1938, 1:656–57, 666–69.

285. P. 237.

286. On the military preparations at this stage, see Hore-Belisha, pp. 148–51; Ismay, pp. 92–93; John Wheeler-Bennett, *John Anderson, Viscount Waverly* (New York: St. Martin's, 1962), pp. 205–7; *Cadogan Diary*, 27 September 1938, p. 107; Pownall, pp. 160–63; *B.D.*, 3d, 2, No. 1075; *D.D.F.*, 2d, 11, Nos. 293, 294, 343, 458; *G.D.*, D, 2, No. 604; C 10607/1941/18, FO 371/21740. For other indications that Britain and France were set to go to war, see *U.S.*, 1938, 1:659–60, 662; R 7762/899/22, FO 371/22438 (blockade of Italy in event of war).

287. For gloomy military comments, see Ironside, pp. 61–62; *D.D.F.*, 2d, 11, No. 377; the devastating comparison of French and German air forces in C 10163/36/17, FO 371/21596; Gamelin's views in *B.D.*, 3d, 2, No. 1143. For evidence that the Belgians preferred giving up the British and French guarantee to letting the French army through in any attack on Germany as well as on Belgian determination to shoot at the French if they tried to push through, see Overstraeten, p. 298.

288. Celovsky, pp. 421–22; *D.D.F.*, 2d, 11, No. 484; Adamthwaite, p. 151.

Maginot Line for the winter and devastate the area evacuated the way the Germans had done in their 1917 planned retreat to the Hindenburg Line. For 1939, a combined French and British attack on Italy was intended. Gamelin assumed that Czechoslovakia could hold out for a few weeks and that the Soviet Union would provide air assistance.[289]

Along with these military plans and preparations, there was a critical diplomatic one. As war appeared practically certain, the Czechoslovak government, which was now convinced that it could count on British and French aid if Germany attacked, offered territorial concessions to Poland, an offer which Britain and France tried to use to secure Poland's neutrality or even assistance against Germany if war came.[290] This effort proved unavailing, but it shows how the prospective allies perceived the coming of war and attempted to place themselves in the best possible position for what they recognized would be a long and difficult struggle. As these military and diplomatic preparations went forward, Sir Horace Wilson was in Germany on the mission assigned him as a result of the Anglo-French talks.

On 27 September Hitler received the news of the British public announcement of the likelihood of general war and, in a second meeting with Wilson, the warning in formal terms that Britain and France would stand by Czechoslovakia. The day before he had been so set on his plan for attacking Czechoslovakia that he had almost walked out on Sir Horace in the middle of their first conversation and had been only with difficulty

289. C 10722/10722/18, FO 371/21782 (this was a meeting chaired by Inskip on 26 September with Gamelin explaining his views; cf. Gamelin, 2:351–52); *D.D.F.*, 2d, 11, Nos. 376, 405; Adamthwaite, pp. 231–32; Pownall, p. 163; Thompson, pp. 206–8. For a Franco-Soviet military contact on 26 September, see *D.D.F.*, 2d, 11, No. 380.

290. *B.D.*, 3d, 2, Nos. 1096, 1102; *G.D.*, D, 2, Nos. 606, 629, 639, 652; *Hungarian Documents*, 2, Nos. 402, 412; *Łukasiewicz Papers*, pp. 138–39; Wojciechowski, pp. 486–88; Roos, pp. 350–52; Cienciala, pp. 125–33, 198–210; *D.D.F.*, 2d, 11, Nos. 328, 344, 346, 351, 357, 371, 395; Namier, *Europe in Decay*, pp. 284ff.; Slávik tel. 906, 24 September 1938, Czechoslovak document in T-120, 1039/1809/412089; Krofta circular 1356–57, 26 September 1938, T-120, 1040/1809/412608 (Berber, No. 178); Král, *München*, No. 222; *Harvey Diaries*, 26 September 1938, p. 198. The Polish attitude and actions as well as their results will be further examined in the following chapter. The evidence of Slávik's detailed report on the circumstances surrounding the Czechoslovak effort to transmit the offer of territorial concessions to Poland (and also the French diplomatic documents) certainly supports the suspicion voiced by several scholars that Beck deliberately accentuated the crisis. Slávik report 57 of 26 September 1938, T-120, 1040/1809/412981–91 (one sentence in Berber, No. 178).

The indirect effort made through Sir Thomas Hohler to get Hungary to stand aside on the basis of a British promise to champion her cause belongs in this context, see the material under C 11418/2319/12, FO 371/21569. Rumania was prepared to join the allies if Hungary attacked Czechoslovakia (*D.D.F.*, 2d, 11, No. 457).

On the 27th the British relayed to the French information contradicting some of Lindbergh's pessimistic statistics after deciding that they did indeed wish to encourage the French, C 10025/1425/18, FO 371/21710. The U.S. naval attaché in London reported that "on the afternoon of 28 September [war] was considered a certainty" (No. 947 of 8 October 1938, Hyde Park, PSF Probability of War H). The preparations for the dispatch of members of the British Legion to Czechoslovakia to assist in the territorial transfer grew out of the Berchtesgaden meeting, and though continuing in the subsequent days, were scrapped as it became clear that the original transfer concept was being abandoned (Wootton, pp. 230–42, 330–31).

recalled to the fact that as host he really had to hear out his visitor.[291] Having worked himself into a frenzy for the speech he was to deliver that night, Hitler was not about to engage in diplomatic niceties. The speech itself must be read in terms of Hitler's own purposes. Having decided to order mobilization at 2:00 p.m. on 28 September and to attack on the 30th, Hitler now wanted to isolate Czechoslovakia from potential allies and to rally the German public for war, limited if possible, worldwide if necessary. The violent and even hysterical attacks on Beneš covered the latter point; the insistence that Germany did not want any Czechs and that this was Germany's last territorial demand was to assist with the former.[292] The warning that on instructions from London Sir Horace gave Hitler on the 27th produced an unpleasant scene but still did not shake the German leader out of his decision to move.[293] The fact that on the 27th and after the second meeting with Wilson Hitler decided to write an answer to the letter from Chamberlain the reading of which he had almost walked out on the day before can be seen either as the first sign of a shift away from his determination to go to war or, more likely, as a maneuver designed to try to split Britain and France from Czechoslovakia in war.[294]

A development of the 27th that would contribute to Hitler's change of mind on the following day was the reception accorded by the Berlin crowds to a military demonstration on the late afternoon of that day. Motorized units moved through the capital at Hitler's orders, but this grim sign of the imminence of war produced just the opposite reaction from the one Hitler expected after his rousing speech of the night before and the crescendo of press and radio propaganda.[295] The viewing public was anything but enthusiastic, and the propaganda minister himself would

291. Schmidt, pp. 407–8; *B.D.*, 3d, 2, Nos. 1115, 1116, 1118; *G.D.*, D, 2, No. 634. On the background, see *D.D.F.*, 2d, 11, No. 349.

292. Text of the speech of 26 September in Domarus, 1:923–33. Comments on its hysterical tone by the Prussian minister of finance Johannes Popitz in von Hassell, p. 21; by Groscurth, in his diary, p. 124. On the reference in the speech to not wanting any Czechs and possibly guaranteeing the remainder of Czechoslovakia, see *B.D.*, 3d, 2, No. 1162, n.2, and Celovsky, p. 419.

293. *B.D.*, 3d, 2, Nos. 1128, 1129; *G.D.*, D, 2, No. 634; *Lipski Papers*, No. 109. The reports of Sir Horace on his meetings with Hitler were discussed at the 15th informal meeting of ministers on 27 September, 4:30 p.m. (CAB 27/646) and at the cabinet meeting 46 (38) at 9:30 p.m. (C 11443/1941/18, FO 371/21744).

294. The letter is in *B.D.*, 3d, 2, No. 1144 and *G.D.*, D, 2, No. 635. The timing shows that the decision to send the letter and the drafting preceded the military demonstration of 27 September. It should be noted that Göring, who was opposed to war at this time, is recorded in the Jodl diary on 28 September as still thinking it could hardly be avoided (*TMWC*, 28:389).

295. On the propaganda of the last days of the crisis, see the reports on the press conferences of 24 and 27 September 1938, Bundesarchiv, Traub, Z.Sg. 110/9, ff.204–5, 209. On the troop movement through central Berlin and Hitler's reaction to the attitude of the public, the account and sources cited in Celovsky, pp. 425–26, can now be supplemented by *Engel Diary*, pp. 39–40; *Weizsäcker-Papiere*, p. 145. See also the report on a conversation with Canaris on 28 September 1938 in the diary of Wolf Eberhard, Munich, Institut für Zeitgeschichte.

remind Hitler of the public's attitude on the following day.[296] All the same, throughout the 27th of September, in spite of the disappointing public response, the warning of Sir Horace Wilson, and the renewed refusal of Hungary to join immediately in war on Czechoslovakia,[297] Hitler was still resolute in his determination to go to war. His comments late that evening to von Ribbentrop and von Weizsäcker of whom the former favored and the latter opposed military action, that he would now destroy Czechoslovakia by war cannot be dismissed as bluff—there was surely no point in bluffing his own immediate advisers of whom one would continue to argue for war after Hitler had changed his mind and the other had argued against it and continued to do so.[298]

On 28 September Hitler did change his mind.[299] The events of the preceding day now had some new elements added to them. In the morning the news of the mobilization of the British fleet reached Berlin. Such signs of the reality of an imminent world war went along with reports on Chamberlain's speech of the preceding evening, which had on the one hand talked of war as an immediately imminent contingency but on the other hand pointed out how minor the *ostensible* issue was: a short time difference in carrying out a territorial cession already agreed to. Combined with the evident lack of enthusiasm in Germany and the concurrence of Göring and Goebbels with the arguments of the generals this appears to have given Hitler some pause. The British government had been putting forward some new compromise ideas to bridge the gap between the Berchtesgaden and Godesberg terms,[300] and the French were even more inventive in trying to get some immediate concessions that would satisfy Hitler without quite accepting the Godesberg demands. In the late morning of the 28th the French ambassador saw Hitler for the first time in several weeks and presented these ideas to him. A message from Mussolini, appealing to Hitler to postpone the mobilization scheduled for that

296. On Goebbels, see also the incident mentioned in Fitz Randolph, pp. 230–31, 257–58, which appears to refer to the transmittal by Goebbels of a warning to Hitler based on a report from the propaganda minister's representative in London.

297. *Hungarian Documents*, 2, Nos. 397, 401, 411, 413; Hoensch, *Ungarische Revisionismus*, p. 100; *D.D.F.*, 2d, 11, No. 364; cf. *Groscurth Diary*, 30 September 1938, p. 129. Note also von Ribbentrop's asking Lipski on the 26th whether Poland would join in war immediately and Lipski's evasive reply (*Lipski Papers*, No. 107, p. 421; cf. ibid., pp. 426–27; there appears to be no German record).

298. *Weizsäcker-Papiere*, pp. 145, 170. For von Ribbentrop's views, see also *G.D.*, D, 2, No. 374, and his comment in June that Albrecht Haushofer's warning that Britain and France would fight if Germany attacked was British Secret Service propaganda (ibid., No. 270); *Groscurth Diary*, 29 September 1938, p. 128, n.142. It is not certain whether the entry of Groscurth that Hitler wanted any general who did not reach his objective shot reflects a comment made on the 28th (when he entered it in his diary) or earlier (*Groscurth Diary*, p. 127).

299. Groscurth's diary entry: "It is hard to grasp this change. The Führer has finally given in (nachgegeben), and thoroughly" (p. 128).

300. The British cabinet, led on this issue by Lord Halifax, had, however, at its meeting of 27 September refused to urge the Czechoslovak government to withdraw tacitly to the line demanded by the Germans (C 11443/1941/18, FO 371/21744).

afternoon, interrupted the meeting with François-Poncet; and soon after the resumed meeting was concluded, Mussolini urged on Hitler Chamberlain's idea of a conference to work out the details of territorial cession instead of resorting to war.[301] This sign that Mussolini himself really preferred peace and would not go to war alongside Germany appears to have been the final factor tipping Hitler in the direction of peace. How had this development come about?

As previously shown, German-Italian cooperation in the Czechoslovak crisis had been considerable but not complete. The Italian government had provided propaganda support for the German cause. They were also happy to push Hungary forward, though remaining cautious enough to warn the Magyars that Yugoslavia could be neutralized only if Hungary waited for some time after Germany attacked Czechoslovakia before joining in.[302] After the Berchtesgaden meeting, when Hitler was eager to stir up more trouble to avoid a settlement on the basis he and Chamberlain had discussed, the Italians readily fell in with German requests for further propaganda support and some additional pushing of the Hungarians.[303] In these matters there was continued cooperation between Germany and Italy, but there was, nevertheless, a most important point on which the policies of Hitler and Mussolini diverged; and after the Godesberg meeting this difference would become crucial.

While Hitler was generally reassuring in public in the first years after 1933, he planned and hoped for war and fashioned his preparations and policies accordingly. Mussolini tended to do the reverse: he was always speaking publicly and privately about the virtues of war and the need to fight Britain and France, but his plans and policies were geared to postponing such heroics, quite possibly to the Greek calends. When the reality—as opposed to the theoretical possibility—of the immediate outbreak of world war stared Italy in the face after Godesberg, Mussolini was not willing to fight for Germany's aims in Czechoslovakia, especially at a time when Italy had given a hostage to fate in Spain that would surely be an early casualty of any wider war.[304] He was still reluctant to make this point clear to the Germans, perhaps because he was worried about being

301. The sequence of events on the morning of the 28th is most accurately stated in the account Attolico gave American Ambassador Hugh Wilson on 21 October 1938, *U.S.*, 1938, 1:727–29. See also the reconstruction by François-Poncet, *D.D.F.*, 2d, 11, No. 450.

302. *Hungarian Documents*, 2, Nos. 368, 374, 380, 382, 389, 413, 417, 419; *G.D.*, D, 2, No. 627; Celovsky, pp. 384ff.

303. See Ciano, *Diplomatic Papers*, pp. 234–36; Ciano, *Diary*, pp. 226, 227, 229, 230; Král, *München*, No. 213; *G.D.*, D, 2, Nos. 571, 577; *Lipski Papers*, No. 103.

304. Note that in mid-September Mussolini had informed Brazilian President Getulio Vargas that Italy would join on Germany's side in war only if Russia came in or France moved in Spain (*U.S.*, 1938, 1:600). This was not necessarily either a truthful or an accurate statement of Mussolini's true intentions, but it does give a reflection of the Italian leader's weighing of war possibilities and alternatives. Another such rumination is recorded in Ciano's diary for 17 September (pp. 227–28). The British chiefs of staff in response to a question from Lord Halifax had expressed the view that it would be better if Italy remained neutral in any war, even if this damaged the blockade system, and the Foreign Office concurred (R 7762/899/22, FO 371/22438).

thought cowardly, perhaps because he still could not believe that the "decadent democracies" would take the plunge. On the contrary, when the Prince of Hessen was sent to Mussolini after the Godesberg meeting to enlighten the Duce about the stalemate in the negotiations, the imminence of war, and Germany's willingness to risk a general war, Mussolini expressed doubt that Britain and France would move but promised that Italy would come into the war as soon as England did.[305] Ciano's comment that this statement urged Germany neither toward war nor away from it is surely inaccurate; Hitler could only take it as encouragement. That such assurances of support would, at the critical moment a few days later, be followed by urgent telephoned requests first to postpone mobilization, and second to agree to a conference must have been read as a last minute reversal by Hitler, who had every reason to think up to this moment that he had Mussolini at his side.

During the hours of the greatest international tension, when on 27 and 28 September it looked to governments and public alike that war would start in a few days, the idea of an appeal for peace was widely canvassed. President Roosevelt had launched one and was thinking of another. The president was sympathetic to the Western Powers and willing to let them know that they would have American political support, but he was very much opposed to any war and still hopeful one could be avoided.[306] Since Hitler was generally assumed to be the one who would start hostilities, and since it was believed that Mussolini might have some influence with him, the concept of asking Mussolini to urge Hitler to postpone action and participate in a conference appeared to be an obvious avenue of approach.[307] This was the route Roosevelt took, urging Hitler to agree to working out the details of transfer by conference instead of war and calling on Mussolini to use his influence with Hitler in favor of that approach. The appeal of the American president arrived in Rome about the same time as an essentially similar appeal from the British prime minister.[308]

305. Ciano, *Diary*, 25 September 1938, pp. 233–34. French assessments of Italy's position in *D.D.F.*, 2d, 11, Nos. 120, 163, 164, 337, 373, 374, 454.

306. On United States policy, see *U.S.*, 1938, 1:565–66, 568, 657–58; 2:56–57; *Moffat Papers*, pp. 196–97; Morgenthau Diary, 19 September 1938, Vol. 141, p. 115, Hyde Park; Robert A. Divine, *Roosevelt and World War II* (Baltimore: Johns Hopkins Press, 1969), pp. 20–23; *G.D.*, D, 1, No. 462; *D.D.F.*, 2d, 11, Nos. 523, 529, 436. The special message from Roosevelt via Lindsay printed in *B.D.*, 3d, 7:627–28 was circulated at the end of the 8th informal meeting of ministers on the morning of 21 September (CAB 27/646).

307. An official in the Foreign Office on 27 September suggested that Chamberlain appeal to Roosevelt to urge Mussolini to summon a peace conference in Rome; now that all other hopes for peace were gone, this looked like the only route (C 11130/1941/18, FO 371/21744).

308. See *U.S.*, 1938, 1:675–80, 684–85, 689, 699; *Bullitt Papers*, pp. 287–300; *Berle Papers*, pp. 186–88; Phillips to Roosevelt, 29 September 1938, Hyde Park, PSF Phillips; Phillips to Roosevelt, 6 October 1938, State 760F.62/1462½. The argument over whether Mussolini received the British or the American appeal first does not appear significant to me; he called Attolico after receiving both. Celovsky, p. 455, n.2, summarizes the evidence, but with an interpretation (also given on p. 449) that I consider incorrect. My reading of the evidence is that Roosevelt acted because he believed war imminent and hoped to contribute to averting

The British, like the French, government had been casting about for a way out of what indeed would look like a ridiculous situation if one took Hitler's ostensible demands for his real aims. A world war in which many millions would surely lose their lives was to start over the timetable for implementing a previously agreed plan of territorial transfer; it was under these circumstances that the British Dominions were doing their best to get London to change its position of supporting Czechoslovak rejection of the Godesberg terms.[309] It was, on the other hand, precisely the fixed determination to go to war if Germany moved militarily that made both Chamberlain and Daladier hopeful that a negotiated settlement could still be worked out, but the poor state of Franco-Italian relations made it impossible for the French to appeal to Mussolini.[310] Chamberlain therefore asked Mussolini to intervene with Hitler, something the Italian dictator did immediately, first to obtain a twenty-four-hour postponement of mobilization and then to secure agreement to a conference at Munich in which Mussolini himself promised to participate.[311] Ciano was in favor of a peaceful solution and Mussolini also appears to have fallen in with Chamberlain's request quickly and willingly.[312] If Ciano claimed that it was impossible to refuse Chamberlain's appeal because Hitler would otherwise draw upon himself the hatred of the whole world and the whole responsibility for war, this hardly explains Mussolini's sudden reversal. We cannot know the reason for Mussolini's action with certainty, but it is difficult to avoid the conclusion that in 1938—as in 1939—his realism triumphed over his preferences, but on both occasions his pride restrained him from counsels of prudence until the very last moment.[313] One must

---

it, not, as Celovsky suggests, because he feared to be left out of the picture when the turn to peace was already evident.

309. On the last-minute pressure from the Dominions, see C 11443/1941/18, FO 371/21744; C 10298/4770/18, FO 371/21766; C 10938/5302/18, FO 371/21777; C 12029/5302/18, FO 371/21778; *Harvey Diaries*, 27 September 1938, pp. 199–200.

310. Daladier's views on what he was himself sure was the eve of war late on 27 September 1938 is best and most accurately reflected in Bullitt's telegram of 11:00 p.m. in *U.S.*, 1938, 1:686–88. On Franco-Italian relations at this point, see *B.D.*, 3d, 2, No. 1168; Ciano, *Diary*, 27 September 1938, p. 239. On the last-minute French efforts to maintain peace, see *D.D.F.*, 2d, 11, Nos. 385, 388, 390, 393, 400, 401, 403, 404, 415, 422, 464. The final French offer is ibid., No. 413; François-Poncet's reports on 28 September ibid., Nos. 420, 421.

311. *B.D.*, 3d, 2, No. 1125 and n.2 with its instructions of 27 September 1938, 11:00 p.m., which Perth carried out early on the 28th (ibid., Nos. 1161, 1192, 1231; *G.D.*, D, 2, No. 661; *U.S.*, 1938, 1:693–94). A further British appeal to Mussolini was sent on the morning of the 28th (*B.D.*, 3d, 2, No. 1159) even before London had heard the results of the prior demarche. The combination of certainty that general war would ensue if Germany moved militarily and the desperate hope that surely some way to obviate that could be found is reflected in Horace Wilson's comments on the morning of 28 September cited in *G.D.*, D, 2, No. 657.

312. See *B.D.*, 3d, 2, Nos. 1187, 1192; Ciano, *Diary*, 28 September 1938, pp. 238–39.

313. One cannot in this instance use the argument that Mussolini wanted to play a great public role. He was happy to do so, but the idea of Mussolini's personal participation was not included in the original conversations about the conference and was injected as a requirement by Hitler. It is possible that the first request of Mussolini—the one for a twenty-four-hour postponement—was the result of his having misunderstood the German timetable (see *G.D.*, D, 2, No. 611).

look at this procedure from Hitler's point of view to understand the impact of what had to look to him like a last-minute Italian change of heart.

Although we do not possess a record of the Prince of Hessen's report to Hitler on the results of his conference with Mussolini and Ciano on 25 September, it can surely be assumed that having been sent by Hitler on this urgent trip, the prince reported to the Führer on 26 or 27 September.[314] Furthermore, on the 27th the Italians themselves suggested that the Germans and Italians coordinate their political strategy for war by having Ciano and von Ribbentrop meet immediately, to which the Germans added the idea of military consultations, so that Keitel, Pariani, and Valle were added to a gathering that was, ironically enough, scheduled for Munich at noon on the 29th.[315] Certainly the exchanges concerning this meeting left Hitler, through the evening of 27 September, with the impression of an Italy ready to move.

It is with this background of a renewed belief by Hitler that if it did come to a general war, Italy would be at his side—and what this meant for the policies of Yugoslavia and Hungary as well—that the impact of Mussolini's requests to postpone mobilization and to agree to a conference must be considered.[316] In the face of dubious generals, warning diplomats, hesitant allies, and a gloomy public, Hitler changed his policy. He would not risk a general war for what he really wanted, the destruction of Czechoslovakia, but would settle for what he had said he wanted and what everyone now assured, promised, even guaranteed he would get. In a way, he was trapped by his own propaganda strategy, and the attempt to escape the route of peaceful settlement by the policies he had followed after the Berchtesgaden meeting had failed. The determination of the Western Powers to fight if he went after his real aims and their eagerness to accommodate the ostensible ones had created a situation in which Hitler decided not to fight. He would afterwards regret his retreat, as we shall see, and he would even pretend to others and perhaps persuade himself that he had simply bullied concessions out of others; but he had also made concessions himself. He would not test the warnings against military action by Germany, at least not in 1938.[317]

314. The mission of the prince had been announced to the Italians by von Mackensen on 22 September (Ciano, *Diplomatic Papers*, p. 234); Berlin had telephoned on the afternoon of the 24th that the prince was flying to meet the Duce (Ciano, *Diary*, p. 233). The fact that the German files do not contain material on the trip reflects the peculiarity of the procedure, not any lack of importance in the mission. The diplomatic historian must always be cautious not to assume that the volume of surviving evidence is a safe indication of the significance of an issue to the participants.

315. Ciano, *Diary*, 27 September 1938, p. 237 (note the reference to this meeting's being canceled, ibid., 28 September, p. 239). See also *Groscurth Diary*, 28 September 1938, p. 127, where Innsbruck is given as the proposed meeting place. Cf. *Hungarian Documents*, 2, No. 410; *Lipski Papers*, No. 127, pp. 466–67.

316. Note also Attolico's report on Mussolini's views to von Ribbentrop at the end of July in *G.D.*, D, 2, No. 334.

317. See von Weizsäcker's comments of 9 October 1938 in his diary, *Weizsäcker-Papiere*, pp. 145, 171; *Harvey Diaries*, 29 September 1938, pp. 201–2.

Hitler's acceptance of the conference idea in reality ended the danger of war because, whatever the details of the settlement, there could be no doubt that the Czechoslovak government would have to accept the terms agreed to by Britain, France, Germany, and Italy; and the differences between the various schemes then under discussion for the transfer of the Sudeten areas were not sufficient to cause any serious difficulty in arriving at an agreement. Now that Hitler had reversed himself on the issue of war, he was no longer interested, as he had been after Berchtesgaden, in using the Polish and Magyar minorities as obstacles to a settlement, and it was left to Mussolini to put in a word for them.

Hitler and Mussolini met beforehand, and Hitler discoursed at some length on the need for a general war against Britain and France at an appropriate time when the two of them were still alive, a message which in this context was surely Hitler's way of answering whatever arguments had led Mussolini to change his mind and of inoculating him against a repetition the next time. Mussolini already had a set of demands for the Munich conference, limited to the German areas, which he presented as his own although it had been drafted by Göring, von Neurath, and von Weizsäcker and transmitted to Rome via Attolico.[318] After several hours of discussion, in which the British prime minister brought forward the largest number of objections and reservations on details,[319] agreement was reached on a series of texts that provided for cession of territory in stages, an international commission to arrange the implementation and related details, the dropping of all plebiscite projects and special areas, a time limit for settlement of Polish and Hungarian territorial claims (with a new four-power conference if the time expired without agreement), and British and French guarantees of Czechoslovakia against unprovoked aggression immediately, to be followed later by German and Italian guarantees when the Polish and Hungarian border issues had been settled. All this was done without the participation of any Czechoslovak representative; the Prague government could accept or take the consequences.[320]

318. There are accounts of the Mussolini-Hitler meeting in Anfuso, pp. 75–79, and Ciano, *Diary,* 29–30 September 1938, p. 240. On the origins of the text produced by Mussolini at the meeting, see Celovsky, p. 462, n.1, though I have followed the interpretation of Leonidas Hill, "Three Crises, 1938–39," *Journal of Contemporary History,* 3, No. 1 (Jan. 1968), 119–20, which is confirmed by *D.D.F.,* 2d, 12, No. 19.

319. On the 29th Vansittart received information from Goerdeler via Christie that British mobilization was having an effect on the German public which was turning against Hitler (C 11164/62/18, FO 371/21664). Halifax relayed this information to Chamberlain at Munich as it might help him hold a firmer line in the negotiations (*B.D.,* 3d, 2, No. 1216). The British had also received appeals for firmness from Prague (*D.D.F.,* 2d, 11, Nos. 430, 431, 435).

320. The discussions and agreements are summarized by Celovsky. See also "Informationsbericht Nr. 65," 4 October 1938, Bundesarchiv, Brammer, Z.Sg. 101/33, ff.191–207. An analysis of the relative advantages of the agreement for Czechoslovakia by François-Poncet is in *D.D.F.,* 2d, 11, No. 485. For the attempts of the Hungarians to influence the discussions by calling attention to their own demands, see *Hungarian Documents,* 2, Nos. 415, 420, 422, 423, 428; Hoensch, *Ungarische Revisionismus,* pp. 103–5.

War had been averted to the universal relief of vast numbers. The very way in which the crisis had built up into a deadlock from which a new world war appeared to be the most likely issue had brought the memory of 1914, and of what followed, vividly to the minds of people for whom that war was the greatest horror of their lives. The signs of this were numerous. The extraordinary scene in the House of Commons when Chamberlain was handed Hitler's invitation to Munich in the middle of his speech on 28 September and the members and gallery alike stood and cheered;[321] the telegram from Roosevelt as Chamberlain departed for Munich: "Good Man"; the crowds of Germans cheering Chamberlain and Daladier in obvious contrast to the glum crowds that had watched the military demonstration in Berlin; the euphoric crowd that greeted the shame-faced Daladier on his return to Paris; all show a burst of feeling of relief that war had been averted.[322] Having in resignation steeled themselves to do for Czechoslovakia in 1938 what no one even suggested thinking about thirty years later, the population in England and France reacted to the situation in a way that is surely easy to understand.

For the German people, the peaceful settlement also meant something they could not know at the time. The plan of some of those opposed to the regime to overthrow Hitler had been geared to his willingness to risk a world war to get his way, and the peaceful settlement of the Sudeten question thus removed the basis for the intended action. The plot was called off at the last moment, and whether or not it would have succeeded, most of those involved were not to pull themselves together again for another attempt for a long time. By his last-minute change of policy, Hitler averted an internal crisis; by their willingness to work out a peaceful settlement with Hitler—which was what made Hitler's change of policy possible—the Western Powers removed the basis on which Hitler's internal opponents planned to try to take action.[323] As Sir Nevile Henderson, who could fairly claim to be one of the architects of the settlement,

321. The earlier accounts are now supplemented (and partially corrected) by the one in Thompson, pp. 231–32, and *Cadogan Diary*, 28 September 1938, p. 109; *Harvey Diaries*, 28 September 1938, p. 201. The speech, which was to have included a threat of war in its concluding passage, had been discussed in the cabinet the night before (C 11443/1941/18, FO 371/21744).

322. In reviewing his actions in Rome on the morning of 28 September, the Earl of Perth wrote Lord Halifax on 30 September: "... there came vividly to my mind the efforts made by Sir Edward Grey in the critical days preceding the outbreak of the war in 1914—efforts which unhappily failed—to assemble the statesmen of the Great Powers directly interested round a table" (*B.D.*, 3d, 2, No. 1231, p. 644). For the happy greeting of Mussolini as the peacemaker in Rome, see Anfuso, pp. 87–88.

323. An excellent account of the last stages of the conspiracy in September may be found in Müller, pp. 374–77. I believe Wendt's interpretation of a British choice for Hitler as against an opposition perceived as being "Prussian" to be mistaken. There were, however, doubts in the Foreign Office about encouraging a last-minute coup by German generals by promising not to take advantage of a coup and perhaps making some concession (C 11614/62/18, FO 371/21664; Sargent's concluding comment on the matter on 4 October was: "Bring up next time"). It is my opinion that with von Brauchitsch invariably coming down on Hitler's side at the critical moment, the attempted coup would probably have failed.

wrote Lord Halifax on 6 October after some very anxious moments in the International Commission:

> I never want to work with Germans again— For some days last week I believed war to be inevitable . . . . In my blackest pessimism I tried to console myself with two thoughts (a) that war w'ld rid Germany of Hitler and (b) that it [would] remove me from Berlin. As it is by keeping the peace we have saved Hitler and his regime and I am still in Berlin. Perhaps both objectives can be attained by other means. You can move me from Berlin and the Germans themselves can get rid of Hitler.[324]

Another side of the issue may be found in the observation of a Foreign Office official on the complaint of a German consul in Yugoslavia against Munich as giving Hitler a new lease on life: "It is really intolerable that anti-Nazi Germans should make a reproach to His Majesty's Government out of the fact that they have not been rescued from the oppression of their own Government—at the cost of a world war—when they themselves lack the courage to raise a finger."[325]

For Czechoslovakia, agreement first to the Anglo-French plan after Berchtesgaden and submission later to the imposition of the Munich agreement meant the loss of the Sudeten areas, soon followed by the loss of land to Poland and Hungary, under the most humiliating circumstances. These circumstances, combined with the shame and regret they inspired in the Western Powers, led the latter to resent and turn away from those they had treated rather shabbily—a not uncommon reaction—and to refuse to make any real effort to assist Czechoslovakia in its desperate attempt under new leaders and new policies to work out a new life for its people within the new boundaries.[326] The international political repercussions of this, surely the most avoidable, failure of Britain and France will be reviewed in their diplomatic context; but the immediate repercussion for the Czechs and Slovaks was to make the adjustment for them even more difficult than it would have been under the best of circumstances; and eventually it left them completely at the mercy of the Germans. This last, however, would, for some time at least, have been their fate in any case. Barring a successful revolt inside Germany— and this writer at least remains skeptical of the success of what some would have tried but to little avail—there was no serious doubt that Czechoslovakia would have been overrun in the initial German onslaught,

324. *B.D.*, 3d, 3:615. Others who subsequently claimed parentage of the Munich solution appear to me to have had an entirely peripheral role; Lord Allen of Hurtwood belongs in this category (Arthur Marwick, *Clifford Allen: The Open Conspirator* [Edinburgh: Oliver & Boyd, 1964], pp. 178–79, 183–86; *B.D.*, 3d, 2:647; *G.D.*, D, 2, Nos. 351, 366, annex 3; Král, *München*, Nos. 138 [p. 195], 139).

325. C 12287/184/18, FO 371/21681.

326. The Hodža government had resigned during the crisis and been replaced by one led by the old military hero Jan Syrový. Beneš resigned and left the country soon after Munich. A new arrangement was also made for the relationship of Slovakia and the Carpatho-Ukraine to the central government.

as Poland would be in the following year, and that liberation would come only at the end of a long and bitter war. Beneš's recognition of this fact was a major element in his agreement to the territorial cessions. Another factor had been the certainty that at the end of such a war—in which Czechoslovakia would surely suffer much—the Sudeten areas would be lost anyway. The Western Powers had repeatedly made this point clear; there could not in any future peace settlement be a return to the borders of 1919, with the prospect of still another war against Germany to maintain that border later. At the height of the crisis, even as they agreed with the Czechoslovak government's rejection of the Godesberg terms, the British urged Prague to accept an alternative procedure for implementing the agreed territorial cession on the basis that if Germany invaded and a general war ensued, "there is no possibility that at the end of that conflict, whatever the result, Czechoslovakia could be restored to her frontiers of today."[327]

Had there been no agreement for the cession of the land with over three million Germans to Germany, an agreement which the German government itself later tore up to reveal its real ambitions, there would certainly not have been the subsequent agreement of the Allies that Czechoslovakia should receive back the territory she had yielded along with permission to expel the Germans who had lived there for centuries. It was, after all, the Germans who had proclaimed to the world that they could not live in the same country with Czechs. By a tragic irony, it was by giving up the Sudeten areas to a Germany governed by Hitler that Czechoslovakia came to be in a position to reclaim them permanently and with universal agreement. The Soviet Union, the one major power to denounce the Munich agreement, would be the one to insist in 1945 that Czechoslovakia yield to her that portion of the country now adjacent to herself in which the population could be claimed to have a greater affinity to that on the Soviet side of the border—precisely the basis of the Munich settlement.

The British and French governments were immensely relieved by the avoidance of war. There was a sense of the need to remedy some of the military weaknesses that had contributed to their reluctance to fight and their doubts about the outcome of war. But there was also, at least for a short time, a sense of hope that with this great crisis resolved, there could be a new beginning in Europe.[328] Although these hopes would soon be dashed, the policies of Britain and France in the months after Munich

327. *B.D.*, 3d, 2, No. 1138. There is not the slightest evidence that if a German invasion had touched off a coup inside Germany and that coup had been successful, the outcome would have been very different for Czechoslovakia. Britain and France would still have insisted on the cession of the Sudeten area; only the details would have been different. Both the London and the Paris governments were determined not to be placed in the position of having to fight against as opposed to for self-determination in the future.

328. Surely the quixotic scheme for the French to buy German engines for French air force planes in the winter of 1938–39 belongs in this framework. See Lindbergh, pp. 119–48, passim; Haight, pp. 110–11; Stehlin, pp. 129–32; *Bullitt Papers*, pp. 312–15.

were certainly influenced by the view that, war having been averted when it had appeared unavoidable, it should surely be possible to arrive at peaceful solutions of other issues. This expectation was symbolized by the Anglo-German declaration that Chamberlain and Hitler signed right after the Munich agreement[329] and the Franco-German declaration issued when von Ribbentrop visited Paris in December 1938; and it should not be surprising that Neville Chamberlain, who had so personally and dramatically identified himself with the peaceful resolution of the Czechoslovak crisis, should long remain the most persistently and stubbornly optimistic of the participants.

The Soviet Union was offended by its exclusion from the Munich conference and could draw comfort from its ability to denounce the weakness of others in not standing up to the dictators under circumstances where its own risks had been minimal.[330] The question of what to do in the new situation created by the Munich agreement was an open one, and there is considerable evidence that in the weeks after Munich the subject was reviewed from a variety of angles in Moscow.[331] It was assumed that Germany would continue on her aggressive course, but Soviet concern continued to be focused primarily on domestic affairs. The international situation would be watched with care, but the most recent developments reinforced the tendency to concentrate on internal problems.

The situation in Southeast Europe was indeed altered by the diplomatic triumph of Germany. To the smaller nations of the area, Munich symbolized the ascending power of Germany and the declining role of France. In one way or another, these countries had best find a way to get along with the new colossus; they would be well advised not to count on outside support except in the most extraordinary circumstances. Poland and Hungary, of course, believed that they had a green light for their demands on Czechoslovakia, and they would try, each country in its own way, to take advantage of the situation. The repercussions of their policies would play a major part in the international situation during the winter of 1938–39.

In the United States, the initial sense of relief would give way to a sense of unease and disapproval even greater than among the opponents of Munich in Britain and France.[332] Not having faced the danger of war

329. On this development, see now *Engel Diary*, 1 October 1938, p. 40.

330. The exclusion of the Soviet Union had been at the insistence of Germany. Whether or not Beneš was correct in asserting, as he did in February 1938, that the Germans were doing this to isolate the Soviet Union so that they themselves could make an agreement with her and then end the independence of the smaller countries of East Central Europe and threaten Britain and France is not clear from the available evidence (*U.S.*, 1938, 1:410–14).

331. See the evidence summarized in Weinberg, *Germany and the Soviet Union*, pp. 6–7. Note also *D.D.F.*, 2d, 11, Nos. 184, 201; 12, No. 17.

332. Note the memorandum of Messersmith of 29 September 1938, *U.S.*, 1938, 1:704–7; *Moffat Papers*, pp. 218–19. The most thoughtful analysis of the evidence is in Francis L. Loewenheim, "The Diffidence of Power—Some Notes and Reflections on the American Road to Munich," *Rice University Studies*, 58, No. 4 (Fall 1972), 11–79.

themselves, it was much easier for Americans to be indignant about concessions made to Germany. For Americans perhaps more than any others Munich came to be a symbol of surrender to pressure, of capitulation before threats. The idea that it was Hitler who had backed down was and remained inconceivable to American observers then and subsequently. Instead, the supposed lesson of Munich was that firmness at the risk of war was the only reasonable policy in the face of a threatening situation; a view which came to be known as a domino theory of international relations where one concession necessarily led to another and the fall of one barrier necessarily promoted the fall of the next.[333]

For Hitler himself, and hence for the Germany he continued to direct, the Munich agreement was a flawed triumph. It was a triumph in the sense that Germany had got, or rather would get in the next few days, what she claimed she wanted, and would get it under circumstances that conspicuously accentuated the leading role of Germany in Europe. The flaw, of course, was that Hitler had been trapped into settling for what he had publicly claimed rather than what he really wanted and had persistently told his associates he would get. He had had to abandon his plan for a war to destroy Czechoslovakia; and the very fact that his diplomatic triumph was so great could easily lead him to even greater annoyance over having refrained from war, because it suggested that perhaps he had been right after all in insisting that Britain and France would not come to Czechoslovakia's aid. In fact, many National Socialists so maintained afterwards, and those in Germany who had warned of a general war were discredited for their warnings, when in reality the accuracy of their predictions had never been put to the test when Hitler himself had dropped his plan to attack.[334] Because of this shift of the facts—with the warners weakened and discredited because of their concern over a general war when it was Hitler who had at the last moment balked at running the risk against which they had cautioned him—Hitler was able to gain an even greater ascendancy over the country's military structure. Since none of the warners among the military or the diplomatic advisers ever mustered the nerve to point out that their predictions had *not* been tested, Hitler could successfully project onto them his own weakness of resolve.

The many recorded expressions of Hitler's dissatisfaction with the Munich agreement not only reflect his regret over having abandoned his original intentions but also reveal an attitude that helped shape his subsequent policies. The next chapter will show that even before the occupation of the ceded territory was completed, Hitler was talking about the total destruction of the rest of Czechoslovakia, and his insistence on

333. The logical alternative, that concessions at one point might be compensated for by immediate strengthening either of the country that has been obliged to make concessions and/or adjacent areas, appears not to have occurred to many either then or later.
334. This point is correctly made by von Weizsäcker in *Weizsäcker-Papiere*, pp. 145, 146, 149, 168–69.

giving that project priority over the Polish question can be understood most readily as an indication of the degree of his annoyance at having been thwarted. His denunciations of the Hungarians for having refused to go along with a joint attack on Czechoslovakia would influence his policy toward that country when its appetite proved greater than its readiness to help in the kitchen.[335] Above all, he resented Chamberlain's success in maneuvering him into a peaceful solution.[336]

The insistence that he would under no circumstances be cheated out of a war against Poland in 1939 cannot be understood in any way other than as a determination not to repeat the 1938 experience. The only thing he would then worry about, as he told his generals, was that at the last minute some "Schweinehund," some S.O.B., would come along with a compromise to prevent war; there can be no doubt that it was the British prime minister that he had in mind. Hitler would never again make what he came to think of as his greatest mistake: specifying demands that could be propagandistically justified at home and abroad, but which he thereby risked having granted. In 1939 von Ribbentrop would be personally and strictly instructed by Hitler not to let the German demands on Poland out of his hands; they were written to be used to justify a war, and under no circumstances was anyone to have a chance to accede to them. To the last days of his life Hitler regretted his change of plan in 1938. Musing in his Berlin bunker in February 1945 about the causes of his failure, he would regret that the Western Powers had made it so difficult for him to begin war as early as 1938. "We ought to have gone to war in 1938.... September 1938 would have been the most favorable date."[337]

In view of the intention of the French in 1938 to follow essentially the same military strategy that they adhered to in 1939, namely, to do next to nothing, it is possible to argue that even given Hitler's erroneous assumption that a war in 1938 would have been an isolated one, his assessment of the military consequences of postponement was correct. A German offensive in the west in 1939 rather than 1940 would hardly have found the French stronger, and it would have met an England without the radar screen and fighter planes so important in the Battle of Britain. Germany,

335. Note the vehement denunciation of 21 October 1938 reported by Groscurth, who was present, in his diary (p. 151 and n.254).

336. For Hitler's dissatisfied comments on Munich, see François-Poncet, p. 334; Dietrich, p. 55; *Keitel Papers,* p. 195; Frank, p. 353. As he told a group of high-ranking officers on 10 February 1939, he had had to pull back the preceding September and had not reached his goal, but he would surely start a war in his lifetime (*Groscurth Diary,* p. 166).

337. Hugh R. Trevor-Roper (ed.), *The Testament of Adolf Hitler: The Hitler-Bormann Documents* (London: Cassell, 1961), 21 February 1945, pp. 84–85. The contrast with his opponent is striking. On resigning from office, Chamberlain wrote King George VI, 30 September 1940: "It has been my fate to see the failure of all my efforts to preserve peace.... Yet I do not feel that I have anything to reproach myself for in my attempts to avoid the present war, which might well have succeeded if they had not come up against the insatiate and inhuman ambitions of a fanatic" (Feiling, p. 452). See Chamberlain's own account of the final crisis, ibid., pp. 375–77.

of course, also became militarily stronger in the interval; there is here still another of the many ironies of the time: Germany's use on a considerable scale of Czechoslovak tanks during World War II.[338]

The subject of the military balance of 1938 versus 1939 can be argued indefinitely; the political side is, however, clear-cut. In 1938 whatever might be said about Hitler's prior actions, the question of whether or not they warranted a world war with all its costs and horrors on the basis of belief—however well founded—concerning his future actions was open to much debate. And in a long war, any democracy would find that debate a very difficult one indeed. After Hitler's deliberate destruction of the Munich agreement, however, the picture changed.[339] Assessments of Hitler's intentions in international affairs were now based on solid and sobering experience. As Churchill expressed it during the war when speaking of Chamberlain in the House of Commons after the latter's death in 1940: "Herr Hitler protests with frantic words and gestures that he has only desired peace. What do these ravings and outpourings count before the silence of Neville Chamberlain's tomb? Long and hard, hazardous years lie before us, but at least we entered upon them united and with clean hearts."[340]

338. Fridolin M. von Senger und Etterlin, *German Tanks of World War II*, trans. J. Lucas (New York: Galahad Books, 1969), pp. 29–30. Hitler referred to such tanks in the situation conference of 27 April 1945 (*Der Spiegel*, 10 Jan. 1966, p. 41)! On the other hand, British license fees for the famous Bren-gun helped finance the Czechoslovak government in exile during the war (Walter Hummelberger, "Die Rüstungsindustrie der Tschechoslowakei 1933 bis 1939," ed. Forstmeier, pp. 320–21).

339. For Hitler's own later recognition of this, see *The Testament of Adolf Hitler*, p. 85.

340. *Hansard*, 12 November 1940.

12   Undoing Munich
        October 1938–March 1939

The European situation, in fact the world, had been changed by the Munich agreement. War had been averted at the very moment when it appeared inevitable, but the circumstances surrounding the settlement gave a clear appearance of German triumph and of British and French humiliation. The question was whether the agreement would lead to a period of peace during which Germany would enjoy the advantages she had gained and quietly gather the fruits of her recently recognized status as the leading power in Europe, or whether Germany would take such vehement advantage of her enhanced position as to arouse greater opposition and the risk of war. In a sense, the question was whether Hitler indeed meant what he promised in signing the Anglo-German declaration on the day after Munich: that there would be no war between those two countries as they consulted together to solve old issues that remained and new ones that might arise.

The critical point for the future of Europe and the world was that after Munich Hitler would move in the direction exactly opposite from that he had indicated to Chamberlain, repeating in a way between October 1938 and 15 March 1939 exactly what he had done between their meetings at Berchtesgaden and Godesberg, only now on a larger scale. Even that, however, was not all. Since Hitler's interest in the destruction of Czechoslovakia had always been a subsidiary, short-term goal on the road to the larger aim of securing living space in the east, the next step toward that long-term aim, namely preparing elimination of the resistance by the west to his subsequent conquest of living space, would now have to take place simultaneously with the completion of the preliminary action interrupted at Munich. The months from October 1938 to March 1939, therefore, would be a time when German foreign policy was directed to the simultaneous accomplishment of two objectives: the elimination of Czechoslovakia and the staging for a war with England and France. As will be seen, Hitler would attempt to make a virtue of necessity by so arranging the former as to assist with the latter.

The Munich agreement had deprived Hitler of the little war he had wanted—and subsequently persuaded himself he might have had—as well as the complete control of the Czech part of Czechoslovakia that he had expected to seize in the first days of hostilities. The little war would obviously have to wait; there was no prospect of trying out the German army on what was left of Czechoslovakia after she had yielded her border fortifications. But the seizure of the rest of the Czech areas might still be attained by other means, and Hitler immediately set out to do so. It was obvious that Czechoslovakia was now at Germany's mercy, and Hitler insisted that full advantage be taken of this. There was to be no generosity or forbearance shown to the humiliated Czechs; Hitler's instructions to the German negotiators on the International Commission handling the implementation of the Munich agreement as well as the various sub-committees of the commission were consistently to take the harshest possible line. There were repeated ultimatums, new conditions, and additional demands, all part of a general process of hounding Czechoslovakia in the strongest possible way.[1]

That all this would provide only a temporary respite to Czechoslovakia, even if she agreed to every demand from Berlin, soon became obvious. The plans, for which agreement was also extorted, for superhighways and canals across Czech territory surely point in the direction of intended annexation.[2] The persistence of German press attacks on the Czechs, the endless reproaches leveled at the conciliatory new Czechoslovak foreign minister, František Chvalkovsky, and the absolute refusal under various

1. Examples in *G.D.*, D, 4, Nos. 12, 17, 53, 108. On the International Commission, see the documents ibid., chap. 1; *B.D.*, 3d, 3; Erich Hansen's account in IfZ, ZS 1130. ff.104–7; Stehlin, pp. 112–3; *U.S.*, 1938, 1:721–22. Mastný's reports are in Král, *München*, Nos. 276, 280; see also ibid., Nos. 248, 253, 254, 257, 258, 261; Král, *Die Deutschen*, Nos. 248, 257; *D.D.F.*, 2d, 11, Nos. 488, 496; 12, Nos. 12, 14, 21, 25–27, 45, 52, 53, 62, 63, 65, 78, 102, 107, 342, 365, 373. A good survey of the activities of the commission is in Theodore Procházka, "The Delimitation of the Czechoslovak-German Frontiers after Munich," *Journal of Central European Affairs*, 21, No. 2 (July 1961), 200–218. The special research office *(Forschungsamt)* of Göring appears to have concluded on the basis of intercepts that the British were playing an obstructionist role in the commission; it is difficult to assess the import of this erroneous finding; see the text in David Irving (ed.), *Breach of Security: The German Secret Intelligence File on Events Leading to the Second World War* (London: William Kimber, 1968), p. 49. Von Weizsäcker asserts in his memoirs, p. 195, that he was too soft as chairman of the commission to suit Hitler (see also *Weizsäcker-Papiere*, p. 146), but I cannot find any trace of the slightest effort on his part to ameliorate the lot of the Czechs; on the contrary, the state secretary appears to have maintained the strong anti-Czech animus so evident in both contemporary documents and his posthumously published papers.

2. See *G.D.*, D, 4, Nos. 103, 108. Note the instruction not to refer to this arrangement as a "corridor" in the press conference of 29 October 1938, Bundesarchiv, Traub, Z.Sg. 110/10, f.79.

pretexts to give Czechoslovakia the guarantee promised at Munich all indicate Germany's fixed determination not to allow the Czechoslovak state to consolidate itself within its new boundaries.[3]

In the circle of his immediate advisers, Hitler made no secret of his intentions. The day after the Munich agreement was signed, he revealed his intention to annex the remaining Czech territory at the first opportunity.[4] Contemporary evidence shows that as early as 3 October the commander of the 10th Army in the occupation of the Sudetenland, General von Reichenau, was repeating Hitler's decision to occupy the rest of Czechoslovakia to visiting staff officers, and there is other evidence reporting Hitler's determination dating from this time.[5] Hitler now wanted to handle the political preparations for the destruction of Czechoslovakia through internal subversion, in which the Slovaks would play the role that the Sudeten Germans had played earlier. German procedures to activate the Slovaks were well under way by the time that the various territories ceded under the Munich agreement had been fully occupied by German troops.[6] As for the details of the military invasion of the rest of Czechoslovakia, these were being worked on as early as 10 and 11 October, it being assumed that the German army would not be resisted.[7]

There were, however, advocates of alternative courses of action in Germany. One leading member of the Sudeten German party developed a plan in mid-October leaving the Czechs a state of their own, though one totally dependent on Germany.[8] Later on, Ernst von Weizsäcker suggested that the German claims on Poland should be brought forward

3. German documents on this are in chap. 1 of *G.D.*, D, 4. See also *Hungarian Documents*, 3, Nos. 274, 384.

4. Kordt, *Wahn und Wirklichkeit*, p. 137.

5. *Groscurth Diary*, p. 133. Cf. von Hassell, 10 October 1938 (but referring to 4 or 5 October), p. 25. The Hungarian minister in Berlin had a clear view of Hitler's intentions by 15 October (*Hungarian Documents*, 2, No. 539).

6. See Hoensch, *Slowakei*, p. 60; *Groscurth Diary*, pp. 334, n.42, 345; *Hungarian Documents*, 2, No. 534; Ferdinand Durčansky, "Mit Tiso bei Hitler," *Politische Studien*, 7 (1956), pp. 2, 9; Hoettl, pp. 166–78, 180–86; Henry Delfiner, *The Vienna Broadcasts to Slovakia* (New York: Columbia University Press, 1974).

7. *TMWC*, 25:520–22; Müller, p. 387, n.45; Diary of Wolf Eberhard, 11 Oct. 1938, Munich, IfZ. For the subsequent order of 21 October 1938, see *TMWC*, 34:477–81. On 4–5 December, Hitler, after an inspection of the Czechoslovak fortifications told some twenty or thirty German military leaders at lunch of his determination to adhere to his original plan of incorporating all of Bohemia and Moravia into Germany. Interrogation of Walter Warlimont by Harold Deutsch on 22 September 1945; DeWitt Poole Mission (exact date derived from "Daten aus alten Notizbüchern," p. 34). Vojtech Mastny in his "Design or Improvisation? The Origins of the German Protectorate of Bohemia and Moravia in 1939," *Columbia Essays in International Affairs: The Dean's Papers, 1965* (New York: Columbia University Press, 1966), pp. 127–53, fails to take account of the real problem of breaking the Munich agreement right after it was signed. Hitler was not that crude or careless; he obviously wanted to prepare the way with careful attention to a pretext.

8. One version of Hans Neuwirth's memorandum is dated 15 October 1938; it is in *Groscurth Diary*, pp. 334–40 and p. 39, n.103. Another version is in Král, *Die Deutschen*, No. 256.

and settled before any final steps were taken against the Czechs.[9] There was also a scheme to formalize in treaty form Czechoslovakia's incorporation into Germany's sphere as a satellite.[10] None of these concepts appealed to a Führer who felt he had been cheated and was determined to seize Bohemia and Moravia as he had originally intended. The process of internal dissolution under German pressure took time, and was affected by the interests of other countries as well as by Hitler's manipulations of those interests for purposes other than the takeover of Czechoslovakia; but there could be no turning back from the main course. The interaction of Hitler's policy toward Czechoslovakia with these other factors will be reviewed at least in outline, but first it is essential to note how closely, clearly, and consistently the Führer adhered to his main purpose.

In view of the opinion of some that Hitler never knew from one day to the next what he was doing, it may be worth recalling that even before Munich he had specified that if he should be obliged to settle for less than the destruction of Czechoslovakia, he would complete the process in the following spring. The promise he had reluctantly given that he would guarantee Czechoslovakia after her territorial questions with Poland and Hungary had been settled was one he was determined not to keep. His attitude in this was especially obvious in his denial of it to Chvalkovsky, the Czechoslovak foreign minister who did the most to obtain Czech agreement to everything the Germans asked for.[11] On 13 February 1939, Hitler informed his associates that he intended to move in mid-March.[12] Under these circumstances, the attempts of the Czechoslovak government to retain some minimal measure of autonomy by offering to convert the country into a German satellite with a representative of Hitler in the cabinet were ingenious but in vain. The German officials would not even discuss such ideas with Hubert Masarýk, the special emissary sent for

9. *Weizsäcker-Papiere*, pp. 150–52, 173. This is probably the matter referred to in Kordt, *Wahn und Wirklichkeit*, pp. 138–39; cf. *G.D.*, D, 4, No. 83.

10. The details are set forth in Heinrich Bodensieck, "Der Plan eines 'Freundschaftvertrages' zwischen dem Reich und der Tschecho-Slowakei in Jahre 1938," *Zeitschrift für Ostforschung*, 10 (1961), 462–76. See also Stephan Dolezel, "Deutschland und die Rest-Tschechoslowakei," in Karl Bosl (ed.), *Gleichgewicht, Revision, Restauration* (Munich: Oldenbourg, 1976), pp. 253–64.

11. See esp. *G.D.*, D, 4, No. 158; cf. Král, *München*, No. 266; Ciano, *Diary*, 5 October 1938, p. 248; *U.S.*, 1939, 1:34–35. Note that while the Germans were eager to get the International Commission out of the picture as quickly as possible and to have all questions handled by bilateral German-Czechoslovak talks in which Germany could bully unhindered and unobserved (*G.D.*, D, 4, No. 53), once it came to those direct negotiations, the Germans lost all interest in speed—the longer the delay, the better the excuse for more demands as prerequisites for the never to be granted promise to leave the rest of Czechoslovakia alone (ibid., No. 166).

12. *Weizsäcker-Papiere*, p. 150. Note the directive issued to the German press two days later banning reports on improved German-Czechoslovak relations ("Bestellungen aus der Pressekonferenz," 15 February 1939, Bundesarchiv, Brammer, Z.Sg. 101/12, f.48). Other, even earlier, references to the idea of moving in March will be found in Hitler's December statement to Neumann and January statement to Csáky cited below.

the purpose.[13] The Berlin government was under no circumstances going to risk starting talks which might lead to a settlement. The final stages were to be directed from Berlin with Czechoslovakia responding to German initiatives, not the other way around. Although it took pressure first on the Slovaks and then on the frightened Czechoslovak president, everything was to be managed by German command. Even a request for German troops had been concocted in Berlin as in the Austrian case.[14] In the end German troops were to move in as ordered on 14 March even before the arrangements designed to provide some pseudo-legal cover had been completed.[15]

If one asks the reason for this insistence on humiliating and crushing a people who had already surrendered, there can only be speculative answers. Hitler's anti-Czech sentiments were strong indeed, and they appear to go back to his early years in Austria, where it was the Czechs who were the immediate butts of Germanic racialism, just as the Poles provided such a target for the Prussians. The fact that Hitler had been thwarted in his plans would appear to be a critical element, in my opinion. Hitler was a vengeful man with a long memory, as Gustav von Kahr would discover: he was murdered in 1934 for his conduct in November 1923. The Czechs were to be made to suffer for their role in upsetting Hitler's plans; ironically enough, the outbreak of a general rather than a limited war in 1939 would leave them relatively less molested than other victims of National Socialist domination. As the American consul general in Prague predicted on 23 May 1939, "the Germans will probably hold the upper hand without undue difficulty as long as the broad basis of national-socialist power remains intact. But they will have no happy time of it, and if the tide ever turns, Czech retaliation will be fearful to contemplate."[16]

13. On this episode, see *G.D.*, D, 4, Nos. 177, 178, 185; 5, No. 111; Kordt, *Wahn und Wirklichkeit*, pp. 142–43; Hoettl, pp. 166–69; Hans Schiefer, "Deutschland und die Tschechoslowakei vom September 1938 bis März 1939," *Zeitschrift für Ostforschung*, 4 (1955), 57–58.

14. The German-prepared draft of a Slovak request for protection is in *G.D.*, D, 4, No. 209. An ultimatum had also been planned (ibid., No. 188) which was to have been handed to a Czechoslovak plenipotentiary whose appearance von Ribbentrop would demand even while German troops occupied the country (text in Král, *Die Deutschen*, No. 279). Hácha's trip kept von Ribbentrop from a full rehearsal of the procedure applied in August to Poland.

15. On the final stages, see esp. *G.D.*, D, 4, Nos. 188, 193; *U.S.*, 1939, 1:60–61; *Hungarian Documents*, 3, Nos. 411, 418; *TMWC*, 35:173–79; Hagemann, pp. 377–87; "Bestellungen aus der Pressekonferenz," 10 and 11 March 1939, Bundesarchiv, Brammer, Z.Sg. 101/12, ff.70, 71; "Informationsbericht," No. 20 of 7 March, No. 23 of 10 March, No. 24 of 13 March 1939, ibid., 101/34, ff.91, 105–7, 109–13. On the early invasion steps, see Keitel, p. 200; Gajan and Kvaček, pp. 151–52; Wagner, p. 81. A record of the last military steps is in the war diary with annexes of the 5th (Transport) Section of the General Staff of the German Army on the occupation of Bohemia and Moravia, 10 March–21 April 1939, folders H 25/47 and 48, T-78/269/6252043–217.

16. *U.S.*, 1939, 1:68. This document is printed as No. 28 in George F. Kennan, *From Prague after Munich: Diplomatic Papers, 1938–1940* (Princeton, N.J.: Princeton University Press, 1968). There were, of course, also the economic resources of Bohemia and Moravia; but since these were open to German control in any case, they do not provide an adequate explanation.

If the Czechoslovakia that remained after Munich was to disappear, and the Czech portions of it were to be taken over by Germany, what did Hitler want to do about the other parts of that state, Slovakia and the Carpatho-Ukraine? During the Czechoslovak crisis of 1938, Hitler had perceived this issue in terms of the dismemberment of Czechoslovakia by her three neighbors. Poland would receive her share. To Hitler that meant primarily the Těšín area, and he would support Polish demands there because the Polish government followed a procedure toward Czechoslovakia that was sufficiently brutal to fit in with his own. Where German and Polish territorial ambitions conflicted, he would try to use the issues involved in his effort to harness Poland to the German chariot. But on the whole, he was willing for Poland to secure the land she wanted. Hungary, the third prospective partner in partition, had, however, held back at the critical moment.

Hitler's own unwillingness to risk a general war by a military invasion of Czechoslovakia might have given him at least some basis for understanding the hesitations of a much less powerful associate in such a risky venture, but Hitler saw only the opposite side of this coin. It was Hungary's diffidence that had contributed to the abandonment of a military solution, and he would not forget or forgive this dereliction. From his point of view, the very fact that Hungary's appetite had not diminished in proportion to her reluctance to help cook the meal made the conduct of Budapest all the more reprehensible. If he had once been quite willing, even eager, for Hungary to take over both Slovakia and the Carpatho-Ukraine, that was now no longer the case. On 14 October he told the former Hungarian prime minister, Kálmán Darányi, whom Horthy had sent to Germany to ask for support of Hungary's claims, that "if there had been a war, Hungary would have gotten all of Slovakia."[17] He had warned the Hungarian leaders in August and September that they would have to move energetically, and that whoever did not do so would come out short. "Poland had recognized the right moment, struck out, and reached her goal." Hungary had failed to do so, and it was now too late. Through negotiations a new border would have to be found between Hungary on the one hand and Slovakia and the Carpatho-Ukraine on the other; but like the Sudeten German question, this would have to be on a supposedly ethnographic basis.

Beyond such temporary expedients and border adjustments, what did Hitler have in mind for the Slovak and Carpatho-Ukrainian portions of the doomed state? In conversations with both Hungarian and Slovak leaders, he would claim to have thought earlier that the Slovaks wanted to return to Hungary, and that his new-found sympathy first for the Slovaks' autonomy and then for their "independence" under German aegis was the

17. *G.D.*, D, 4, No. 62. Other material on Darányi's visit to Germany is in ibid., Nos. 63ff.; *Hungarian Documents*, 2, Nos. 522 (*Horthy Papers*, No. 28) and following; Hoensch, *Ungarische Revisionismus*, pp. 141–46.

result of his discovery that the Slovaks preferred not to be returned to Magyar rule.[18] One may be permitted some skepticism about this explanation.[19] Whether or not Hitler had held the mistaken earlier impression of Slovak preferences, he never considered the views of those Slovaks who preferred to be a part of the Czechoslovak state and who were certainly a very substantial proportion of the population. This preference was symbolized by the fact that in 1938 the prime minister of Czechoslovakia, Milan Hodža, was a Slovak. If that was not to prevent his desire for Slovakia to be annexed by Hungary before Munich, the autonomist preferences Hitler claimed to have discovered thereafter would not keep him, as will be shown, from considering transfer of the Slovaks to Polish control or a partition between Poland and Hungary in the winter of 1938–39 when his policy toward Poland made such a project look like a possible inducement for Warsaw to fall in with his plans. Hitler hinted as much to Darányi on 14 October 1938. Near the end of their conversation, the Führer said that "if Germany were to form a great bloc with Hungary and Poland, nothing was final and border changes could always still be made."[20] This passage surely indicates that Hitler thought of Slovakia and its people purely as an instrument to be used, not as a region whose inhabitants' wishes ought to be respected.

During the last days before the destruction of Czechoslovakia, the Slovaks were made to assist in the process; in fact Hitler would then threaten a reluctant Jozef Tiso, who had been relieved from his position as Slovak prime minister, with Hungarian occupation if he did not fall in with German plans by an immediate declaration of independence.[21] In the interim, however, the control that Germany exercised over Prague made it expedient to keep Slovakia at least nominally a part of Czechoslovakia. It could thereby remain temporarily at Berlin's disposal rather than being handed over free to the Hungarians, who had been so reluctant about paying their share of the costs.[22]

Slovakia, as far as the Germans were concerned, was to have a status independent of Prague but within Czechoslovakia, and hence available for future disposition by Berlin.[23] Germany would therefore support only

18. Hitler took this line with Darányi (*G.D.*, D, 4, No. 62), Tuka (ibid., No. 168), and Tiso (ibid., No. 202).

19. Macartney, however, accepts a good part of it (1:335).

20. *G.D.*, D, 4, No. 62, p. 71.

21. Ibid., No. 202; Hoensch, *Slowakei*, pp. 286–96; *U.S.*, 1939, 1:60–61. Von Ribbentrop threatened that Germany would take a part of Slovakia with the rest being divided between Hungary and Poland. He also handed Tiso the draft text of the Slovak declaration of independence; Fratišek Vnuk, "Slovakia's Six Eventful Months (October 1938–March 1939)," *Slovak Studies*, 4, *Historica*, 2 (1964), 105–20.

22. Hitler in fact used this very terminology to Darányi, citing what he claimed the Czechoslovak crisis had cost the German budget and asking how much Hungary had paid. See also *Hungarian Documents*, 2, No. 613.

23. The first version of the memorandum for Hitler of Ernst Woermann, head of the political section of the German foreign ministry, was prepared on 5 October, before the Sillein agreement on Slovak autonomy of 6 October; it is cited in Hoensch, *Ungarische*

territorial adjustments in favor of Hungary at Slovakia's expense. During
the complicated negotiations over this subject between the Czechoslovak
government—which very intelligently let the Slovaks defend their own
interests—and the government in Budapest, Berlin urged both sides to
accept a prompt compromise. When this proved impossible, Germany
insisted on a peaceful solution and arranged for a joint German-Italian
arbitration procedure by which an award was made in Vienna on 2
November 1938. This award gave substantial areas to Hungary, but by no
means all Budapest had wanted or expected. Italy had been obliged under
German pressure to reduce its support for Hungary, and in the settling of
details the German government was willing to endorse considerable cessions to Hungary but insisted on Slovakia's retaining some important
areas under dispute.[24]

A small but strategically important piece of Slovak territory had been
taken by Germany herself, and the Poles—who had hoped to play a part in
the settlement—promptly alienated the Slovaks by insisting on a series of
territorial concessions to themselves.[25] When the dust had settled, three
things were evident: first, there was an autonomous Slovakia within the
nominal bounds of a Czecho-Slovak state (as it now came to be more
properly called); second, the Slovaks were not likely to yearn for closer
relations with either Hungary or Poland after the experience of territorial
mutilation; and third, Germany, by restricting Italy's role as sponsor of
Hungarian revisionism and by entirely excluding the other two Munich
powers, Britain and France, as well as Poland, from any part in arranging
the new settlement, had demonstrated for all who cared to look that *her*
will would dominate the fate of those in the area.

If the fate of Slovakia, here recounted in a very abbreviated form,
presented problems of some complexity, these were charmingly simple
compared with those of the easternmost extremity of Czechoslovakia, the
Carpatho-Ukraine. This largely mountainous and undeveloped area,

---

Revisionismus, p. 117, and summarized in Wojciechowski, p. 530. A second version was
prepared on 7 October; it is published in *G.D.*, D, 4, No. 45 (Hoensch, *Ungarische Revisionismus*, p. 128). Hitler's decision is recorded in *G.D.*, D, 4, No. 46; see also ibid., No.
53.

24. On the negotiations culminating in the Vienna award, see Hoensch, *Ungarische Revisionismus*, Section II, and the sources cited there; *Hungarian Documents*, 2, Nos. 429–
624, passim; Vnuk, pp. 43–51; Cienciala, pp. 149–65; *Lipski Papers*, No. 125; Král, *München*, Nos. 273, 278; Macartney, 1, chap. 13.

25. The territory annexed by Germany, consisting of the areas of Engerau and Theben,
enabled the Germans to dominate the capital of Slovakia, Pressburg-Bratislava. There is an
excellent account in Hoensch, *Ungarische Revisionismus*, pp. 211–15; see also Vnuk, pp.
33–38; Procházka, pp. 215–16; *Hungarian Documents*, 2, No. 470; "Informationsbericht Nr.
76," 9 November 1938, Bundesarchiv, Brammer, Z.Sg. 101/33, f.347. On the cession of
pieces of Slovak territory to Poland, see Hoensch, *Ungarische Revisionismus*, pp. 198–211;
Vnuk, pp. 58–63; Cienciala, pp. 164–65; Roos, p. 365. The territorial changes are most easily
understood by reference to the map included in Hoensch, *Ungarische Revisionismus*, or the
maps in Vnuk between pp. 32 and 33.

sometimes referred to as Ruthenia, had been a part of Hungary until the end of the World War, when it had been incorporated into the new state of Czechoslovakia. Its special importance, and the attention it would therefore draw, derived from two of its characteristics: geographical location and national composition. Geographically, this territory provided the only direct link between Czechoslovakia and her Little Entente ally, Rumania. This was Czechoslovakia's one border with a friendly power. But though the area joined two allies, Czechoslovakia and Rumania, it separated two friends, Hungary and Poland. Hungary and Poland, joint enemies of Czechoslovakia, could have a common border only if Hungary regained at least the Carpatho-Ukraine (the regaining of Slovakia, of course, providing for a longer common border). Such a common border might in theory provide a barrier to German expansion eastwards by shutting her off territorially from Rumania—once Germany was in a position to dictate Czecho-Slovak policy—somewhat in the way the common border of Poland and Rumania had closed the Soviet Union off from Czechoslovakia.

The national composition of the Carpatho-Ukraine was mixed; there were substantial numbers of Magyars, especially in the lower lying southern portions, and there were some Rumanians in the easternmost villages, but the majority of the population, the so-called Ruthenians, were in fact Ukrainians. As such, they were more closely related to the large Ukrainian minority in the southern part of the revived Poland and to the large population of the Ukrainian Soviet Socialist Republic than to the Czechs and Slovaks with whom they were united in one state by the peace settlement.[26] As long as they were within that state, the various and usually divergent currents of centralist, autonomist, pro-Magyar, and pro-Russian sentiment within the area could hardly be of wider European concern, but the moment the Czechoslovak state was likely to fall apart, the nationality question would be of great importance. Once Slovakia secured autonomy from Prague, the fate of the Carpatho-Ukraine would attract general attention: separated from Prague by the intervening Slovak entity, the Carpatho-Ukraine might disappear within Hungary, or it might provide a convenient and safe focus for the aspirations of the dissident Ukrainians within both Poland and the Soviet Union, among whom there were substantial nationalistic currents in the face of national repression.[27]

The Hungarians wanted to recover the Carpatho-Ukraine and knew that Poland strongly favored such a development. After Munich, the less likely it became that Hungary would be allowed to seize Slovakia, the

26. There were also some Ruthenians within the administrative borders of Slovakia; but this problem, and the related one of the seizure of parts of eastern Slovakia by Hungary in March 1939, cannot be examined here. It will be touched on in the following chapter.

27. I have used the term "disappear" in the sense that within the Austro-Hungarian empire it had been the Ruthenians in Galacia, not the much smaller group within Hungary, who had defined the issue. The nationality problems of Hungary had been perceived as involving Croats, Rumanians, Slovaks, Serbs, and Germans.

more eager she became to secure at least this former Hungarian territory, and the more important this annexation looked to Warsaw. Even the Soviet Union was moved by concern over the implications of a focus for Ukrainian nationalist agitation to favor the inclusion of the Carpatho-Ukraine in Hungary. The interest the Soviet regime shared with Poland in the repression of Ukrainiàn national hopes provided one element in the rapprochement between those two powers after Munich which was signalized by the Polish-Soviet declaration of 27 November 1939, reaffirming their nonaggression pact of 1932 and calling for better economic relations.[28]

One country that was opposed to the Hungarian annexation of the Carpatho-Ukraine was Rumania. Not only was Bucharest in general apprehensive about anything that enhanced the size and potential power of Hungary—hardly a surprising attitude in view of Rumania's own holdings of vast stretches of territory formerly included in Hungary—her army was also heavily dependent on weapons imported from Czechoslovak factories. These arms would have to move across the territory of a hostile Hungary once the Carpatho-Ukraine had been annexed by Budapest. Although in the end the Vienna arbitration award would give Hungary control of the only east-west railway on which the products of the Skoda works could reach Rumania, during the critical days of October 1938 before that award, Rumania opposed the idea of a common Polish-Hungarian border. Even the efforts of her Polish ally to soften this resistance, in part by suggesting that the easternmost part of the Carpatho-Ukraine with its small Rumanian population be ceded to Rumania, could not persuade Bucharest to drop its objections.[29] In the final analysis, however, the determining element in the fate of the Carpatho-Ukraine in 1938–39 was not the preference of Hungary or Poland, of the Soviet Union or of Rumania, but the will of Germany.

In trying to analyze German policy toward the Carpatho-Ukraine, one must distinguish among those in Germany with sympathies for the Ukrainians or Poles, those who thought they saw real military and political importance in a Polish-Hungarian common border as a possible obstacle to future German expansion eastwards, and the views, preferences, and

28. Cienciala, pp. 183–84; Roos, pp. 385–87; Bohdan B. Budurowycz, *Polish-Soviet Relations, 1932–1939* (New York: Columbia University Press, 1963), pp. 127–33; Wojciechowski, p. 527, and esp. the comments of Soviet diplomats cited in n.3; *Lipski Papers*, No. 123, p. 453; *Hungarian Documents*, 2, Nos. 535, 553; *S.U.*, Nos. 30, 32, 39, 51, and see also Nos. 61, 85; Fierlinger tel. 1350 of 30 November 1938, Czechoslovak document in T-120, 1039/1809/412231; *D.D.F.*, 2d, 12, Nos. 412, 415, 429.

29. On Rumania's interest, and on Beck's effort to win Rumanian support for a common border by territorial cession, see Hoensch, *Ungarische Revisionismus*, pp. 118, 158–59; Henryk Batowski, "Le Voyage de Joseph Beck en Roumanie en octobre 1938," *Annuaire Polonais des Affaires Internationales 1959–1960*, pp. 149–56; Cienciala, pp. 159–61; Roos, pp. 370–72; *Łukasiewicz Papers*, pp. 147–48; *Lipski Papers*, Nos. 120 (Batowski, pp. 152–55), 121; *Harvey Diaries*, 22 October 1938, p. 215; *Cadogan Diary*, 6 October 1938, p. 114; *Hungarian Documents*, 2, Nos. 471, 479, 513, 517, 528, 543, 558, 564, 572; *D.D.F.*, 2d, 12, Nos. 39, 178, 182, 201; *Les relations franco-allemands, 1933–1939*, p. 350.

decisions of Hitler. At times, as will become apparent, these perspectives were all temporarily congruent, but on other occasions they diverged, and the key point remains that it was Hitler who decided the course Germany would try to follow. There certainly was an element of concern for Ukrainian aspirations among at least some of those who worked with Ukrainian nationalist organizations in Germany. These contacts, designed primarily for intelligence purposes and hence conducted mainly by German intelligence agencies, could only benefit from a semiautonomous Carpatho-Ukraine as a basis for intelligence operations against Poland or the Soviet Union, or both.[30] Those elements in the National Socialist party who identified with Alfred Rosenberg's concept of a "decomposition" of the Soviet Union into its constituent nationalities, and who maintained some contacts with Ukrainians primarily through Rosenberg's Foreign Policy Office (APA), also had some interest in Ukrainian aspirations.[31] The high command of the German armed forces recorded its opposition to a common Polish-Hungarian border on 5 October, putting forward military and political objections and favoring a continued tie of the area to Prague.[32] Göring, on the other hand, had taken a proprietary interest in German relations with Poland; and since the Poles strongly desired a common border with Hungary, he leaned in the direction of allowing the Hungarians to go ahead and seize the area.[33] The German foreign ministry's 7 October brief to Hitler recommended opposition to a common Polish-Hungarian border and favored an autonomous status for the Carpatho-Ukraine.[34]

Hitler had assumed that if there were a joint German-Polish-Hungarian campaign against Czechoslovakia, Hungary would receive the Carpatho-Ukraine; there is no evidence pointing to any reluctance or doubts in that regard. When Hitler encouraged the Poles and Hungarians after Berchtesgaden to push demands that he could utilize to prevent a peaceful

30. On this aspect, see John A. Armstrong, *Ukrainian Nationalism, 1939–1945*, 2d. ed. (New York: Columbia University Press, 1963), chap. 1; *G.D.*, D, 5, No. 82; W. Mühlberger, "Zwischenbericht über die ukrainischen Sendungen am Reichssender Wien," 1 February 1939, T-120, 2621/5482/E 382227–37; and scattered material in *Groscurth Diary* and the Lahousen diary (Institut für Zeitgeschichte, Munich).

31. An excellent discussion of the "decomposition" theory is to be found in Alexander Dallin, *German Rule in Russia, 1941–1945* (New York: St. Martin's, 1957), pp. 46–49, 51–56. For a discussion of the APA and its Ukrainian contacts, see Jacobsen, *NS Aussenpolitik*, pp. 87–88, 449ff. See also *Lipski Papers*, No. 126.

32. *G.D.*, D, 4, No. 39. Since this document of 6 October and the one of 5 October to which it refers were both drafted in Abteilung Ausland, it is probably safe to assume that it was Admiral Canaris, the chief of armed forces intelligence, who persuaded Keitel of this view and the advisability of informing the foreign ministry of it.

33. Göring responded favorably to Lipski's comments on the subject on 10 August (*Lipski Papers*, No. 89, p. 378), on 24 August (ibid., No. 91, p. 385), on 16 September (ibid., No. 96, p. 403), and on 1 October (Lipski's report of 3 October cited in Wojciechowski, p. 528, noted as missing from Lipski's files in *Lipski Papers*, p. 437, n.18). I do not share Wojciechowski's interpretation (loc. cit.) that Göring's expressions represented some prearranged tactic to encourage the Poles, or Cienciala's opinion (p. 162) that Göring's similarly favorable view on 21 October was designed to restrain Poland.

34. *G.D.*, D, 4, No. 45.

agreement, the Polish ambassador discussed Poland's interest in Hungary's acquiring the Carpatho-Ukraine at great length, but in their conversation of 20 September Hitler appears not to have committed himself on the subject.[35] Similarly, the encouragement that Hitler gave the Hungarian prime minister and foreign minister on the same day did not include an explicit reference to the Carpatho-Ukraine.[36] It is presumably safe to conclude that if the Hungarians had finally abandoned what Hitler considered their timidity and had boldly moved in, he would have happily approved their annexation of the area, it always being clear that Germany had no interest in that portion of the hated Czechoslovak state. It is entirely possible that at the time of Munich he would have been willing to see Hungary move into the Carpatho-Ukraine—the way the Poles seized Těšín—but thereafter he was to change his approach.[37] The fact that the Italians continued to support the Hungarian position and therefore had to be rather dramatically restrained by Hitler only makes his new view of the issue more obvious and distinctive.[38]

By 8 October Hitler had decided that the Carpatho-Ukraine would not be allowed to fall to Hungary just then. It should remain an autonomous part of Czechoslovakia, thereby staying under at least indirect German control.[39] There would be no common Hungarian-Polish border for the time being. What did Hitler have in mind? The evidence on the subject is mainly circumstantial, but in my opinion conclusive all the same. Hitler, far from being sympathetic to Ukrainian aspirations, was surely the most dangerous enemy the Ukrainians ever had. The Magyars might wish to Magyarize any Ukrainians they could annex; the Poles wished at least to control and perhaps to Polonize the Ukrainians within the borders of Poland; the Soviet leaders wished to impose total control and a measure of Russification on the Ukrainians in the U.S.S.R.; and the Czechs and Rumanians wanted to rule their Ukrainians with a minimum of fuss and bother. Only Hitler conceived of the extension of another people's living space, that of the Germans, into a Ukrainian area in which German settlers would over time displace the expelled or exterminated Ukrainians. Such schemes, explicated in *Mein Kampf* and Hitler's second book, would not see even the first stages of implementation until after 22 June 1941, but there is no evidence to suggest that in the years between devel-

35. *Lipski Papers*, No. 99.
36. *G.D.*, D, 4, No. 554.
37. Hoensch (*Ungarische Revisionismus*, p. 116) believes that Hitler would have been willing to see Hungary seize both Slovakia and the Carpatho-Ukraine in the first days of October. In view of his disgust with the Hungarians, I am not so sure about Slovakia, but the Carpatho-Ukraine would have looked like a minimum reward for last-minute boldness. Macartney (1:276) leaves the question of Hitler's opinion open.
38. On the Italian support of Hungarian ambitions in the Carpatho-Ukraine, as well as related issues, and the withdrawal of this support in the face of German objections, see *Hungarian Documents*, 2, Nos. 456, 461, 480, 497, 519, 526, 529 (French text in Ádám, No. 24), 530, 531, 533, 541, 551, 555, 559, 566, 573, 577, 589, 598, 604, 614, 615; 3, Nos. 22, 39, 41, 42, 52, 56, 59, 62, 63, 69, 90, 103; Cienciala, pp. 158–59; Macartney, 1:288–99.
39. *G.D.*, D, 4, Nos. 46, 50. Cf. *Hungarian Documents*, 2, No. 516.

oping and attempting to carry out these horrendous ideas Hitler acquired a temporary affection for Ukrainians. If he allowed his own associates and officials to maintain contacts with Ukrainians and if he tolerated a limited amount of Ukrainian propaganda in the winter of 1938–39, it was surely not because of a suddenly discovered love for the people who occupied the soil his agrarian expansionism craved for his own "aryan" farmers.[40]

There is also no evidence that Hitler thought of the Carpatho-Ukraine as some sort of a wedge against the Soviet Union. The speculations to this effect ascribe to Hitler Rosenberg's ideas that Hitler himself was careful to keep Rosenberg from implementing after June 1941. Disdainful of Soviet power and Slavic peoples, Hitler was not interested in using the population of the U.S.S.R. against their own government, and the tiny population of the Carpatho-Ukraine could hardly play a role he was unwilling to assign the incomparably greater population of the Soviet Ukraine.[41] As for the strategic picture, Hitler knew enough geography to realize that the mountainous terrain of the Carpatho-Ukraine did not offer an invasion route to the east any more than it had presented a serious threat of Soviet aid across Rumania to Czechoslovakia westward.

Hitler temporarily preserved the Carpatho-Ukraine's autonomy, which was a result of the Munich agreement, solely because he saw it as a useful instrument of his diplomacy toward Poland and Hungary, and he saw no reason to give it away for nothing.[42] He would repeatedly keep the Hungarians from seizing it—both on 20 November 1938 and 12 February 1939 only German vetoes prevented Hungarian military invasions of the Carpatho-Ukraine.[43] Yet a month after the second veto, on 12 March 1939, Hitler not only lifted his ban but actually instructed the Hungarians to seize the area, ignoring the appeals of those in the area who preferred German to Magyar overlordship.[44]

Surely Hitler's comment to Darányi on 14 October 1938, that "nothing was final" and that border changes could be made if Hungary and Poland joined Germany in a bloc, explains his attitude. The Carpatho-Ukraine

40. Weinberg, *Foreign Policy*, pp. 85–86; Wojciechowski, pp. 533–34; Roos, pp. 369–70; Cienciala, p. 197, n.77; Hoensch, *Ungarische Revisionismus*, pp. 251–52.

41. It is worth noting that those who stress Hitler's interest in the Soviet Ukraine as a reason for his earlier vetoes of Hungarian occupation do not claim the converse, that his instruction to Hungary to occupy the Carpatho-Ukraine meant that Hitler had given up his territorial aspirations on Soviet Ukrainian land. Note Kleist's citing of Hitlers views in *S.U.*, No. 149.

42. Note also von Ribbentrop's comment on the conversation of 24 November between Hitler and King Carol of Rumania, who had expressed the strongest opposition to annexation of the Carpatho-Ukraine by Hungary, that Hitler had been careful not to commit himself on this issue (*G.D.*, D, 5, No. 254, pp. 284–85).

43. On the German vetoes, see *G.D.*, D, 4, Nos. 128–34, 167; 5, No. 252; Hoensch, *Ungarische Revisionismus*, pp. 216–44; *Hungarian Documents*, 3, Nos. 48, 50 (French text in Ádám, No. 27), 57, 58. Germany had allowed Hungary pieces of the Carpatho-Ukraine with Magyar population (as in the case of Slovakia).

44. *G.D.*, D, 4, Nos. 198, 199, 215, 218, 235–37; *Hungarian Documents*, 2, Nos. 413, 458; Hoensch, *Ungarische Revisionismus*, pp. 258ff.; Macartney, 1:336–39; Kennan, No. 11. Other documents are summarized in *G.D.*, D, 6:75.

was a pawn to be utilized in negotiations with Hungary and Poland; the area would be turned over to Hungary, but only when it suited Hitler. Had Poland been willing to pay the right price, she might have secured all or part of Slovakia for herself and succeeded in getting the Carpatho-Ukraine under Hungarian control at an earlier date.[45] As it was, the area would be turned over to Hungary under circumstances in which the advantages this might have had for Poland and Hungary were more than offset by Germany's simultaneously acquiring direct control of Bohemia and Moravia as well as indirect but fully effective control of Slovakia. This resolution of the issue, so different from the one Hitler had held before Darányi, was the result of developments in Germany's relations with Poland.

The German government had, on the whole, every reason to be pleased with Poland's conduct in the early stages of the Czechoslovak crisis. In a way, even the reaction of the Polish government to the Munich conference had been satisfactory to Berlin. Because of fears that some four-power European council might someday tell *them* what to do to preserve the peace, the Polish government was upset about not being included among those invited to Munich and was determined to secure its share of the Czechoslovak booty by independent action rather than at the hands of the great powers. Beck arranged for an ultimatum with a very short time limit to be handed to the Prague government. The Těšín territory was to be handed over immediately, and with all sorts of dire consequences threatened, the Czechoslovak government agreed to the Polish demands. By thus abruptly and deliberately seizing a portion of Czechoslovakia, Beck could try to create the appearance of an independent Polish action, secure an area long coveted by Poland, and contribute to the popularity within Poland of a regime whose basis in the country was never especially firm.[46]

There were, of course, incidental by-products of the Polish action. Poland made herself even more unpopular in Britain and France than she already was; stabbing Czechoslovakia in the back and doing so in the most nasty fashion possible was not likely to increase affection for Poland either among the Western Powers or in the United States.[47] The efforts of Beck to keep his troubles with Germany in October and November 1938 as quiet as possible were probably in part due to a recognition of this

45. It is even possible that if the Slovak autonomists had been more enthusiastically cooperative, Hitler might have let them have the Carpatho-Ukraine as Woermann had argued in the first draft of his memorandum on the Slovak and Carpatho-Ukrainian questions (see above, n.23).

46. Accounts in Wojciechowski, pp. 486–513; Cienciala, pp. 140–45; Roos, pp. 354–57.

47. For British reaction to the Polish moves, see *B.D.*, 3d, 3, chap. 1; *Cadogan Diary*, 1 October 1938, p. 111; *Hungarian Documents*, 2, Nos. 435, 478; *Lipski Papers*, Nos. 108, 115. On the French reaction see *Łukasiewicz Papers*, pp. 142–44; *D.D.F.*, 2d, 11, Nos. 440, 466, 500, 502–7, 510, 512. On the U.S. reaction, see *U.S.*, 1938, 1:708–10; Roosevelt memorandum for Hull, 29 September 1938 ("It reminded him of a fight between a very big boy and a very little boy. The big boy had the little boy on the ground and a third boy stepped forward and kicked the little boy in the stomach"), Hyde Park, PSF Cordell Hull 1938.

western reaction, as was the advice of von Weizsäcker that Germany take advantage of the situation by leaving Czechoslovakia autonomous but dependent while concentrating all German pressure on Poland. It was Hitler's insistence on the total destruction of Czechoslovakia that would largely obliterate the memory of Poland's actions from the policy formulation process of the Western Powers.

From the German point of view, however, the Polish move was welcome. Anything that hastened the process of weakening Czechoslovakia, regardless of whether Poland acted separately or jointly with Germany, had the same effect.[48] Because there had been parallel but not coordinated action against Czechoslovakia, Germany and Poland did have to work out their respective territorial demands in the Silesian area where the projected annexations of the two powers could conceivably overlap. The critical point here was the town of Oderberg (Bohumin), important as a major railway center and greatly desired by Poland. There is substantial evidence that among German diplomats and military leaders there was hope that the area would be annexed by Germany, but Hitler overruled all such attempts and agreed to Poland's occupying the town.[49] The Germans living there were out of luck; they were to find the new masters far worse than those they had complained about earlier, and many of them fled to Germany.[50] In this case Hitler was quite willing to sacrifice mere people to his hope for Polish agreement to his larger objectives; he was unwilling, however, to let Poland have the nearby area of Moravská-Ostrava. Its mineral and industrial importance was such that the Germans preferred the Czechs to retain it temporarily, and they were to start their own occupation of Czechoslovakia on 14 March 1939 with this portion.[51]

Some wider questions of German-Polish relations had arisen in the summer and fall of 1938 in connection with the discussion by the two countries of their policies toward Czechoslovakia. The German ambassador to Warsaw had suggested at the beginning of July that Polish policy in the Czechoslovak crisis might be bent in a direction more favorable to Germany's aims by such German concessions as an extension of the term of the 1934 German-Polish agreement, a guarantee of Poland's western

48. See *Lipski Papers*, pp. 437–38.
49. On the Oderberg (Bohumin) issue, see *G.D.*, D, 4, No. 17; 5, Nos. 57, 60–62, 65, 66; Roos, pp. 355–56; Cienciala, pp. 149–52; *Lipski Papers*, Nos. 101, 108–12, 116–18; *D.D.F.*, 2d, 12, Nos. 71, 84, 85, 422. It could be argued that because the map which accompanied the Godesberg ultimatum included the Oderberg area in the territory to be occupied by Germany, Hitler, who approved that map, originally intended to have Oderberg go to Germany. My reading of the evidence is that those who drafted the map drew the line to include Oderberg without explaining to Hitler that this was an area claimed by Poland.
50. *G.D.*, D, 5, No. 63. See the file on these Germans in T-120, 1321/2391/D 500101–262. Their fate, like that of the Germans in other parts of Czechoslovakia occupied by Poland, would provide the subject for many German protests to Warsaw.
51. *G.D.*, D, 4, No. 53; 5, No. 58, cf. ibid., Nos. 59, 68, 69; *Lipski Papers*, p. 438, and No. 119; Cienciala, p. 152. Göring's suggestion that if the area had to be ceded to Poland, it should be traded for Danzig should, in my opinion, be read as his reaction to talk about recovering Danzig then current among Germany's leaders and his belief that Hitler was willing to be generous with Poland in the distribution of the spoils of Czechoslovakia.

border, the promise of Těšín, and possibly agreement on Polish interests in Lithuania or the Soviet Union.[52] The Poles themselves had repeatedly brought up their own wishes for steps Germany should consider as part of the coordinated anti-Czechoslovak program. These had included extension of the 1934 agreement, German recognition of the finality of the German-Polish border similar to that which Hitler had extended to the German-Italian border in May, and a new agreement covering the maintenance of something very like the status quo in Danzig to replace the vanishing role of the League.[53] Beck was willing to go to Germany to meet Göring or Hitler to discuss these issues. In making these approaches, the Polish foreign minister hoped to secure what the Polish historian Marian Wojciechowski has aptly called "the freezing of the status quo" in German-Polish relations at the point reached in 1934, even though Beck himself was helping Germany change the European situation in which the 1934 agreement had been signed.[54] When the conference at Munich removed the immediate danger of war, Beck found another way to put before the Germans the general question of German-Polish relations, still hoping, it would appear, for a permanent fixation of the status quo.[55]

As the German reaction to Beck's approach as well as their own proposals would quickly show, the maintenance of the status quo was the last thing Germany wanted, although it is not known whether German evasion of Beck's soundings before Munich was in anticipation of future changes in the relationship between the two countries. Ironically, the one point on which Beck himself wanted a major change was one that the Germans tried to use to have him fall in with their own plans, and the more Beck emphasized this point, the more it became a useful bargaining counter for the Germans. This was the question of the common Polish-Hungarian border that the Poles had raised with the Germans before Munich and were to put forward again later. As already mentioned, Poland very much wanted Hungary to annex the Carpatho-Ukraine and to do so on her own without turning to the four Munich powers. In the months after Munich, the Warsaw government repeatedly urged the Hungarians to act; the record is full of attempts by the Poles to push the Magyars forward, now offering assistance and support for a Hungarian advance, now threatening the withdrawal of Polish friendship if Hungary continued to hesitate.[56]

52. *G.D.*, D, 2, No. 277.

53. See above, pp. 404, 435f. The most recent formulation of the Polish position had been Beck's instruction of 19 September for Lipski's meeting with Hitler after Berchtesgaden (*Lipski Papers*, No. 98).

54. Wojciechowski, p. 471. W. quotes the full text of Beck's 19 September instruction from the Polish archives and cites some places where it has been published (pp. 468–69).

55. Like Cienciala (pp. 142–43, n.114), I find Wojciechowski's interpretation (pp. 505–11) of Beck's conduct on 30 September along these lines as the one most likely to be correct.

56. The Hungarian documents reflect Polish alternation between offers of help and disgust with Hungary's inactivity very well; see *Hungarian Documents*, 2, Nos. 463 (French text in Ádám, No. 21), 475, 499, 501 (French text in Ádám, No. 22), 504, 512, 518, 521, 537, 550, 556, 557, 583, 587, 588, 591, 595, 596, 601, 608, 611; see also *G.D.*, D, 5, Nos. 76, 79, 80. Note Poland's strong opposition to any Hungarian appeal to the four Munich powers, *Hungarian Documents*, 2, Nos. 524, 527, 536.

When the Polish government had raised the Carpatho-Ukraine issue before Munich, Göring had been favorable, but Hitler had been noncommittal. Even Göring had been reluctant about the other aspects of a new German-Polish settlement that the Poles had suggested, and Hitler also had declined any discussion of details. After all, it was unnecessary for the Germans to tie their own hands in this fashion when Poland's own leaders were already following a policy essentially favorable to Germany. They were also reluctant to run the risk of driving Poland into a possible coalition with Czechoslovakia and the Western Powers by formally rejecting the Polish suggestions and making demands of their own at a time when all German efforts were bent on maintaining the front of Germany, Poland, and, they hoped, Hungary against Czechoslovakia. That situation had now changed.

The near outbreak of war with the Western Powers had, as will be explained in more detail, made Hitler eager to subordinate Poland to Germany in a new settlement, and the way was now free for demands that had previously only been hinted at, as much to ward off Polish requests as to invite serious negotiations. The eagerness of the Poles to secure a common border with Hungary provided an opportunity for the Germans to present their demands in a context in which Poland might be willing to make a bargain. On 22 October, Polish Ambassador Lipski reaffirmed Poland's urgent desire for a common border with Hungary.[57] When he was received by German Foreign Minister von Ribbentrop on the 24th, he was to receive the German demands for a return of Danzig to Germany, an extraterritorial road and railway across the Corridor to East Prussia, and Poland's adherence to the Anti-Comintern Pact. In return, Poland was to receive special rights in Danzig, a German guarantee of her western border, and an extension of the 1934 agreement. German approval of a common Polish-Hungarian border was also hinted at.[58]

Before the German demands, their origin, significance, and repercussions, can be analyzed in the detail their fateful importance merits, a word must be said about Hitler's role in their being put forward at this time. It has sometimes been suggested, and Beck at first believed, that all this was von Ribbentrop's own idea and that Hitler was not yet ready to formulate his own position definitively. All the evidence shows the contrary. The Germans realized that negotiations with Poland might well be prolonged and delicate, and there might be an advantage to a preliminary stage of talks the details of which would not have to be considered binding on the two parties, but the strategy was Hitler's own. In mid-October Hitler had suggested a possible redrawing of the map of Czechoslovakia if Germany, Poland, and Hungary formed a solid block. Just before offering

57. On the Lipski–Woermann conversation of 22 October see *G.D.*, D, 5, No. 80.

58. On the Lipski–von Ribbentrop conversation of 24 October, see ibid., No. 81; *Lipski Papers*, No. 124; Cienciala, pp. 162–63, 177–81; Wojciechowski, pp. 542–46; Burckhardt, pp. 226, 231–32; Roos, pp. 380–82; Biddle tel. 260, 6 December 1938, State 862.4016/1980; C 15393/197/55, FO 371/21804.

this proposal to former Hungarian Prime Minister Darányi, Hitler had ordered that no commentaries or news unfriendly to Poland appear in the German press.[59] On 23 October, the day before the Lipski–von Ribbentrop conversation, Hitler himself discussed the projected road and railway across the Corridor with the man who was expected to build them, Minister Fritz Todt, and explained to him that a guarantee of the Corridor would be a part of the agreement for this project.[60] It is also known that on the 24th Hitler conferred in Munich with Albert Forster, his associate and gauleiter in Danzig, about the policies to be adopted there in the immediate future.[61] Forster, who later referred to von Ribbentrop's demands as "Hitler's message,"[62] was trying to get approval for some new anti-Jewish decrees in Danzig that Greiser, the leader of the Danzig senate, and Böttcher, the foreign affairs specialist of Danzig, were concerned might lead to international complications, and that von Weizsäcker had earlier indicated should be handled in a manner that would not annoy the Poles. Hitler told Forster to go ahead with the decrees; he apparently expected Polish agreement to the incorporation of Danzig within the Reich and wanted the internal situation there as similar as possible to that in Germany as a whole.[63] Hitler's conversations with Todt and Forster about German relations with Poland are documented more precisely than his instructions to von Ribbentrop.[64] The whole thrust of von Ribbentrop's demands reflects close instruction by Hitler himself. It has too often been overlooked that during these very days von Ribbentrop was receiving Hitler's detailed instructions on future policies toward Britain and France for transmittal to the Italians by the foreign minister on Hitler's behalf.[65] It is surely safe to assume that when receiving these directives von Ribbentrop was given the guidelines for his conversation with Lipski.[66]

59. *G.D.*, D, 5, No. 70.

60. Ibid., No. 86. This letter of Todt to von Ribbentrop of 27 October refers to the meeting with Hitler having taken place "last Saturday." That would have been 23 October. According to the record in "Daten aus alten Notizbüchern," Hitler was in the Munich-Berchtesgaden area from late on 20 October to 24 October. Hitler had himself mentioned the road project to Lipski on 20 September, and Lipski in reporting on that had referred to it as a project with which Beck was familiar (*D.&M.*, 1:183).

61. On Forster's stay in Berchtesgaden on 24 October, see Kuykendall (Danzig) dispatch 78 of 9 December 1938, State 860K.01/104; C 15393/197/55, FO 371/21804; Burckhardt, pp. 226, 231–32; Wojciechowski, p. 541; *G.D.*, D, 5, No. 672.

62. Biddle tel. 260, 6 December 1938, State 862.4016/1980.

63. *G.D.*, D, 5, Nos. 73, 77, 670–77. The issue of anti-Jewish legislation in Danzig as seen by the high commissioner is recounted in chap. 6 of Burckhardt's memoirs. There is an excellent account in Ben Elissar, pp. 323–38.

64. It is worth noting that von Ribbentrop thought Hitler so interested in the details of the negotiations with Poland that he carefully had the relevant documents sent to the Führer, see, e.g., *G.D.*, D, 5, Nos. 113, 115, 131.

65. On these instructions we have the most interesting memorandum by Count Ciano of von Ribbentrop's recital of them in Rome in his *Diplomatic Papers*, pp. 242–46.

66. In his generally unreliable memoirs, von Ribbentrop states that Hitler "wanted to reach a formal settlement with Poland, and he instructed me in October, 1938, to negotiate

If one examines the German demands one must consider first specific details and then the total impact. The return of Danzig must have come as a particularly shocking demand to Lipski because less than a month earlier Hitler had announced in his speech of 26 September that the Sudetenland was Germany's last territorial demand in Europe.[67] If it was suggested that such speeches were not to be taken literally—whatever Hitler wanted at the moment was always the only and final demand—the fact remained that Hitler himself had formally reaffirmed the status quo in Danzig less than a year before. If both of those assurances, one general and the other made specifically to the Polish government, meant nothing, then what was the value of new German assurances about the German-Polish border once Poland had agreed to the current set of German demands?[68] The Danzig issue was once again to be a focus of German-Polish relations and would become the subject of considerable discussion.

The idea of what was sometimes referred to as a corridor across the Corridor, the highway and railway project, was not new. This issue had been raised before in German-Polish relations, partly because of the convenience it would provide for Germany and partly because it would conserve German foreign exchange by eliminating the transit payments to Poland that had been a complicating factor in German-Polish trade relations. The various prior discussions had not led anywhere, but the Polish government could hardly claim to be surprised. Whether or not such a transportation system would or would not have extraterritorial status would be a particularly important question, but it is not likely that the fact that the negotiations over this issue were contemporaneous with Germany's insistence on such facilities across Czechoslovakia encouraged Polish enthusiasm for being treated in the same way.[69]

The prolongation of the German-Polish agreement of 1934 was something the Poles themselves had periodically suggested, but its meaning would be quite substantially changed if such a prolongation were agreed upon in the context of an entirely new arrangement. The most important portion of such a new arrangement, in reality if not in appearance, would

---

with the Polish Ambassador with a view to settling all pending questions" (*The Ribbentrop Memoirs* [London: Weidenfeld and Nicolson, 1954], p. 97). There is considerable evidence, however, that the Poles originally thought von Ribbentrop was acting on his own without full authorization from Hitler, and perhaps for tactical purposes the German foreign minister may have encouraged this belief.

67. Burckhardt reported on 12 October that Forster was describing the phrase of "last territorial demand" as a purely tactical maneuver (Burckhardt to Walters, quoted in Burckhardt, p. 189). Was this also a reflection of what Hitler had told Forster?

68. The guarantees mentioned by the Germans were always purely bilateral; Cienciala (pp. 178–79) is surely mistaken in referring to international guarantees.

69. On this issue, see *G.D.*, D, 5, Nos. 14, 86; *Biddle Papers*, p. 43; Wojciechowski, pp. 547–48, n.1. For subsequent reports on the negotiations, see Biddle's dispatches 782 and 814 of 4 and 23 November 1938, State 760c.62/407 and 415.

be Poland's adherence to the Anti-Comintern Pact.[70] Poland had repeatedly rejected this proposal earlier, most recently when von Ribbentrop had suggested it on 27 September.[71] As will become clear in the
account of German-Polish negotiations in 1938–39, Beck was more adamant in his opposition to *this* German demand than to any other, and would
never allow even internal Polish foreign ministry discussion of any compromise on it.

Since the pact Beck refused to join provided solely for opposition to the
international organization of Communism, and Poland was vehemently
anti-Communist as well as on the least friendly terms possible with the
Soviet Union, why the reluctance of Poland to join and why the insistence
of Germany that she do so? The answer to the question of Poland's
attitude is that adherence to the Anti-Comintern Pact was seen as a form
of policy subservience to Germany, a subservience not only in regard to
the Soviet Union but in every other respect as well. This was no idle
speculation on Beck's part. Once Poland took the step Germany wanted,
she would be at Germany's mercy because she would have ruptured her
tie to France while exposing herself to the wrath of her great eastern
neighbor. It was, of course, this very subservience that Hitler wanted.
For his ambitions further east he needed either Poland's acquiescence or
that country's destruction; any truly independent Poland would be a bar
to his aims, and in the immediate future he especially wanted Poland quiet
while he settled with England and France.

In the weeks after the 24 October meeting, therefore, Hitler tried to
obtain Polish agreement to German demands, and he was prepared to
make it worthwhile for Poland by making concessions on the Carpatho-
Ukrainian and possibly the Slovakian questions.[72] He was enough interested in not unduly alarming Poland that he held back for a while with
German plans for the annexation of Memel. Here was another territorial
demand to which Hitler's renunciation presumably did not apply.[73] At his
Berchtesgaden meeting with Chamberlain, Hitler had claimed to want
only Lithuanian adherence to the Memel Statute, but that reference appeared only in the British, not the German, record of the conference. No
one in London believed Hitler's promise on this subject worth anything.[74]
The Lithuanian government attempted to conciliate Germany by making
concessions to the Germans in Memel, but Berlin was not interested in

70. Is it entirely a coincidence that this is the one point of the 24 October discussion that
von Ribbentrop, the originator of the Anti-Comintern Pact, "forgot" in his account of the
conversation in his memoirs (p. 98)?

71. *Lipski Papers,* p. 427, and No. 113.

72. As on other occasions, the adoring Forster repeated his master's views with great
accuracy, in this case to Burckhardt on 29 November 1938 (Burckhardt, p. 232).

73. The Latvian acting minister of foreign affairs indicated on 28 September that in spite of
Hitler's statement two days earlier, the Führer would ask for Danzig and Memel after the
Sudetenland with the Corridor coming next (*U.S.,* 1938, 1:77).

74. N 4658, N 4885/2/59, FO 371/22220. There were some steps by the British and French
as signatory powers during the winter of 1938–39, but these made no difference any more.

any accommodation. The Lithuanian relaxation of restrictions only meant a full nazification of the Memel territory, and the authorization to hold elections on 11 December 1938 merely produced the anticipation that, immediately after the election, Memel would be integrated into the Reich.

As the agitation for annexation to Germany proceeded in Memel during November and early December, the government in Berlin was deciding whether or not to move for annexation immediately or to restrain the exuberance of the Memel Germans when the expected results of the 11 December elections led them to a public petition for annexation. Early in December, Hitler decided to postpone annexation unless the Lithuanian government willingly agreed—as they were not yet prepared to do. There is evidence that reluctance about compensation that might have to be arranged for Poland and concern over the risk of driving Lithuania into Poland's arms were important considerations in the German decision to keep Memel quiet for a while, but the key element appears to have been the general uncertainty over whether any German-Polish agreement was likely to be reached together with a desire to avoid action that might interfere with arriving at one.[75]

After the 11 December elections, the enthusiastic Memellanders were restrained on orders from Berlin, but by mid-December it was assumed that the area would be seized, it was hoped by an agreement with Lithuania under which pressure would be combined with generous promises of free trade via Memel to induce Lithuania to become a satellite of Germany, possibly in a customs union.[76] The timing was tied by Hitler to his other plans. When he spoke to the leader of the Memel National Socialists, Ernst Neumann, following the elections about 17 December, Hitler told him that the Memel question would be settled by annexation in 1939 at the end of March or preferably in mid-April, and that he wanted no acute crisis before that time.[77] Negotiations with Poland were still under way—the Polish foreign minister himself was expected in Germany early

75. On the Memel issue in October–December 1938, see *G.D.*, D, 5, Nos. 359–75; Lorenz to Göring enclosing material on Memel, 25 November and 3 December 1938, T-120, 2621/5482/E 382250–59; "Informationsbericht Nr. 82," 2 December 1938, Bundesarchiv, Brammer, Z.Sg. 101/33, f.379; German press conference of 3 December 1938, Bundesarchiv, Traub, Z.Sg. 110/10, f.187; Plieg, pp. 193–202; Memorandum by Collier on the Memelland, 9 December 1938, N 6135/2/59, FO 371/22222. See also "Bestellungen aus der Pressekonferenz," 9 January 1939, Bundesarchiv, Brammer, Z.Sg. 101/12, f.10; Kirk (Moscow) tel. 35 of 26 January 1938, State 860M.01(Memel)/557.

76. *G.D.*, D, 5, Nos. 380, 395 n.3.

77. The reception of Neumann by Hitler is reported in a letter of the head of the German foreign ministry department responsible for the Baltic States, Werner von Grundherr, to the German minister to Lithuania, Erich Zechlin, of 2 January 1939 (*G.D.*, D, 5, No. 381). The exact date is not known as the meeting was kept out of the press (ibid., No. 382); but Neumann had been scheduled to visit Germany on or about 17 December (ibid., No. 372). It is clear that Germany's policy options were being reviewed on or about that date; note the final sentence of Ritter's memorandum of 16 December (ibid., No. 380). Plieg, p. 202, refers to the Hitler-Neumann meeting as having taken place "at the end of December" but gives no reason for this dating.

in January—and Hitler wanted to arrange the final stages of the Czecho-slovak and Memel questions in a manner coordinated with his policy toward Poland.

The prospects of an agreement with Poland were perceived as slight in Germany by the time Hitler wanted to act against Czechoslovakia in March, so that German action in both cases was taken without regard for Poland's interests; indeed, it was taken in order to put pressure on Poland from both flanks. Memel was taken from Lithuania under pressure a few days after the occupation of Prague.[78] Germany eventually tried to get Lithuania to become her ally in a quick war against Poland, the way she had once hoped to use Poland and Hungary in a quick war against Czechoslovakia, and offered the old Lithuanian capital of Vilna as bait; but the Lithuanian government refused. As punishment, Germany, which had previously assured herself the right to occupy Lithuania by agreement with Moscow,[79] was to trade Lithuania to the Soviet Union for a portion of central Poland while retaining claim only to a small piece of Lithuanian territory for herself.[80] Although these events took place well after the time under consideration here, they are referred to not only because they complete the story of German policy toward Memel and Lithuania up to September 1939 but because they illuminate Hitler's general procedure in such matters and, more specifically, show how Hitler subordinated his policies in this area to his broader aims toward Poland.

Other matters were handled in the same way. The repeated German protests over the treatment of Germans in those areas of Czechoslovakia annexed by Poland were kept muted for the time being, even though there is evidence to show that Hitler himself was quite upset about this issue.[81] When, after the enactment of a new Polish passport regulation, the Germans took the occasion to arrest and deport under horrible circumstances thousands of Polish Jews living in Germany, and the Poles retaliated by deporting Germans, the Berlin government quietly gave way.[82] The son of one of the deported families shot a staff member of the German embassy in Paris, and the German government used this as an excuse for a national program of burning synagogues, wrecking stores, arresting many thousands of German Jews, and promulgating a vast series of anti-Jewish

78. *G.D.*, D, 5, Nos. 399, 405; Plieg, pp. 203–12.

79. Note that Hitler's war directive *(Weisung)* 4 of 25 September 1939 still looked toward the occupation of Lithuania, by force if necessary (Walther Hubatsch [ed.], *Hitlers Weisungen für die Kriegführung, 1939–1945* [Frankfurt/M: Bernard & Graefe, 1962], p. 28).

80. Weinberg, *Germany and the Soviet Union*, pp. 58–59; Leonas Sabaliūnas, *Lithuania in Crisis: Nationalism and Communism, 1939–1940* (Bloomington, Ind.: Indiana University Press, 1972), pp. 147–49; *U.S.*, 1939, 1:443; *G.D.*, D, 6, No. 328; 7, Nos. 410, 419, 429, 459, 481. The experience of Lithuania must be compared with that of Slovakia, which will be discussed in the next chapter. The Slovak government eventually agreed to join in hostilities against Poland and received territorial rewards appropriate for a willing satellite.

81. See *G.D.*, D, 5, No. 99 for a comment of Hitler to General Haushofer, and Burckhardt, p. 232, for a comment of Hitler to Forster.

82. *G.D.*, D, 5, Nos. 84, 88, 89, 91, 92, 95, 97, 98, 107, 127; Ben Elissar, pp. 301–21; *Lipski Papers*, No. 126.

decrees. But the international repercussions of the notorious November pogrom were to be felt in Germany's relations with the Western Powers rather than with Poland, and will be examined in that context.[83]

While the Germans waited for a Polish response to their demands, there was reluctance in Berlin to reprove Warsaw for its support of Hungary's annexation of the Carpatho-Ukraine, since in German eyes the Vienna award of 2 November had settled this matter at least for the time being.[84] Only after the attempted Hungarian coup of 20 November did the Germans inform the Poles of their strong objections at that time to the action Poland had been hoping for—and von Moltke was careful to tell Beck at the same time that von Ribbentrop could not see why the Ukrainian question should cause difficulties for German-Polish relations.[85]

Considerable light on both Hitler's policies and the hopes and preferences of the Polish government can be shed by aspects of the negotiations between Germany and Poland after von Ribbentrop had initially presented the German demands on 24 October. The Polish ambassador, Josef Lipski, had immediately warned in that meeting about Germany's raising the Danzig issue, but he promised to inform Beck of the German demands and to present the official Polish response. Lipski returned to Berlin on 1 November from conferences in Warsaw which culminated in instructions dated 31 October for his response to von Ribbentrop's proposals.[86] Von Ribbentrop, however, would not see Lipski until 19 November.[87] Although there were some circumstances which might be adduced to explain the delay of the foreign minister as purely technical and coincidental, these hardly provide an adequate explanation for a man who was otherwise not averse to summoning diplomats to meetings in the middle of the night upon very short notice.

The matter is necessarily speculative, but it is probable that Lipski's immediate reaction and some signals received in Germany in the days after 24 October showed von Ribbentrop that the Polish response was almost certain to be generally negative.[88] During the period of delay, German exercise of its new power over Czechoslovakia symbolized by the Vienna award of 2 November and the planned German-French declaration which would show Poland her isolation, might lead to second

83. For von Moltke's report on the Polish reaction see *G.D.*, D, 5, No. 103.

84. Note the reference in Woermann's note of 12 November on the subject, stating that the connection with the "well-known other question" probably ruled out a German demarche in Warsaw (ibid., No. 100).

85. Ibid., No. 104. On Polish-Hungarian interaction in the crisis over Hungary's attempted seizure of the Carpatho-Ukraine with Polish support in November, see *Hungarian Documents*, 3, Nos. 2, 7, 9, 12, 13 (French text in Ádám, No. 26), 14, 28, 29, 40, 46, 54, 55, 60, 61, 65, 67, 80, 109; Roos, pp. 373–75.

86. On Lipski's stay in Warsaw, see Szembek, 29 October 1938, p. 366. The instructions of 31 October are *Polish White Book*, No. 45, plus a sentence omitted from the published version to be found in *Lipski Papers*, p. 458.

87. See *Lipski Papers*, Nos. 126, 127.

88. See also Lipski's own speculations on this point in his 12 November letter to Beck, ibid., No. 126.

thoughts in Warsaw, and at this stage in the German-Polish talks (unlike the earlier talks with Czechoslovakia) Berlin did actually want to reach agreement. In the Tripartite Pact negotiations with Japan, which proceeded concurrently, von Ribbentrop repeatedly operated on the assumption that instructions from Tokyo might be modified under the impact of internal debate in Japan and remonstrances from the Japanese ambassadors in Berlin and Tokyo. He may have expected a similar development in the negotiations with Warsaw. If so, he was to be disappointed. Lipski, who actually thought of resigning after the 24 October meeting, was if anything more obdurate than Beck about concessions to Germany—just the opposite of the Japanese envoys who were pressuring the Tokyo government to fall in with German wishes.[89]

The instructions Lipski carried out when he finally saw von Ribbentrop on 19 November reflected the Polish government's general position.[90] The question of better communications across the Corridor might be considered, though there was no willingness to make any new routes extraterritorial. On Danzig, the Polish position was a double one. They would not agree to annexation by Germany, but there was an interest in a new German-Polish treaty covering the status of Danzig and replacing the League's role. At this stage of the negotiations, Beck was apparently willing to let Danzig assume control of its own foreign affairs and to make other concessions in a new treaty, but he was quite insistent on maintaining a special status for the Free City.[91] By a supreme irony, the two countries that had done most to undermine the League's position in Danzig now both wanted the high commissioner kept there—each preferring to deal with the problems in Danzig via a mediator until a new permanent settlement could be worked out in accordance with its own preferences.[92] During the last weeks of 1938 and in early 1939, therefore, both Germany and Poland tried to keep the League high commissioner's position in existence and worked out arrangements to convince the suspicious British and French governments of the undesirability of withdrawing all League connections with the Free City at that time.[93] Regard-

89. On Lipski's consideration of resignation after 24 October, and on his formal application for reassignment after 15 March 1939, see ibid., p. 501.

90. Lipski's account, ibid., No. 127; the German record is in *G.D.*, D, 5, No. 101. To facilitate German propaganda to the effect that the Poles had assumed an uncompromising position *after* the British guarantee of March 1939, Lipski's warning about the danger of an annexation of Danzig for German-Polish relations as well as von Ribbentrop's response were excised from the text of the German record as published in the *German White Book*, No. 198. Now that the full text has long been available, the use of it or the doctored version provides a handy test for the *bona fides* of those writing on the subject.

91. Biddle dispatch 755 of 20 October 1938, State 760K.62/55; Kuykendall dispatch 78 of 9 December 1938, State 860K.01/104; *G.D.*, D, 5, No. 102; Burckhardt, p. 229.

92. Kuykendall dispatch 78 of 9 December 1938, State 860K.01/104; Burckhardt, pp. 229–30, 233.

93. This complicated issue is treated at length in Burckhardt's memoirs; see also Cienciala, pp. 186–88; Denne, pp. 159–75; Roos, pp. 388–89, 394–95; *G.D.*, D, 5, Nos. 96, 117, 118, 123, 124, 129, 133, 135; Kuykendall dispatch 85 of 21 December 1938, State 860K.01/112; C 15953, 15954/197/55, FO 371/21804. On Polish insistence that the League play a role

ing the German demand that Poland join the Anti-Comintern Pact, however, the earlier Polish refusals were simply reiterated; on this subject there was no possibility of compromise. Beck offered to discuss German-Polish relations in personal conversations, but held out no hope on this German proposal.

There were further German-Polish discussions in November and December 1938, but both parties appear to have hoped that the other would modify its position. In any case, there was no progress aside from an agreement that von Ribbentrop would return the earlier formal visit of Beck by going to Warsaw, while Beck would stop over in Germany to meet Hitler early in January 1939 in the hope of preparing some possible agreements that might be signed when von Ribbentrop made his official visit to Poland.[94]

Lipski had warned the German government at the beginning of these talks that Berlin's demands raised the greatest dangers. All close observers were convinced that Poland would fight rather than give in to Germany on issues she considered vital to her independence; Burckhardt was of this opinion, and American Ambassador Anthony Biddle, probably the only foreign diplomat close to Beck, was also sure of it.[95] Even German Ambassador von Moltke had some doubt that his own government recognized the strength of Polish feeling and determination.[96]

During this period, Hitler appears to have wavered between the hope that Poland would agree to a peaceful incorporation of Danzig by Germany—either as part of a new settlement or by indicating a willingness to acquiesce in a German fait accompli—and the expectation that his demands could be obtained only by war.[97] In order to increase pressure on Poland, the restrictions on the German press regarding that country were eased somewhat on 5 December;[98] the general impression one gets is that Hitler, who had seen Czechoslovakia buckle after a show of firmness, simply could not believe at first that the Poles would not do the same.[99] In January 1939 he would himself discuss the problems with Beck—whose

---

until a new German-Polish agreement could be reached, see also the note by Böttcher of 4 November 1938, T-120, 1315/2371/D 496126.

94. On the rest of the November and December negotiations, see Cienciala, pp. 180–86; Roos, pp. 389–90; *G.D.*, D, 5, Nos. 112, 113, 115, 116; *Lipski Papers*, Nos. 128–31.

95. Biddle tel. 260 of 6 December 1938, State 862.4016/1980; Biddle dispatch 872 of 28 December 1938, State 860K.01/109; C 15954/197/55, FO 371/21804.

96. Biddle dispatch 872 of 28 December 1938, State 860K.01/109; cf. Kuykendall dispatch 82 of 15 December 1938, State 860K.01/110. But note von Weizsäcker's certainty on 14 December that there would be war with Poland in which Britain and France would remain neutral (*Groscurth Diary*, pp. 158–59).

97. On Hitler's thinking about war with Poland soon after the 24 October von Ribbentrop–Lipski talk, see *Keitel Papers*, pp. 196–97; for his contingency orders to occupy Danzig but on the assumption that there would be no war with Poland, see the orders of 24 November in *TMWC*, 34:481–82, and of 8 December, ibid., pp. 416–22.

98. *G.D.*, D, 5, No. 110.

99. See Wojciechowski, p. 549, citing a report on Forster's comments in Danzig after he had seen Hitler.

courteous treatment by the Germans contrasted sharply with the vituper-
ation accorded Beneš—but those negotiations cannot be seen in isolation. By the beginning of 1939 other German moves consolidating her hold
on Southeast Europe in the wake of Munich were beginning to yield
results; and although not pointed directly toward Poland, these developments cannot but have increased German confidence in the success of
their Polish policy.

Of the countries of Southeast Europe, Bulgaria as a nation defeated in
the World War was, naturally enough, most inspired by what looked like a
season of revision after Munich. The Bulgarian government looked to
Berlin for support of its own revisionist hopes, primarily by asking for
credits to rebuild its armed forces. The government in Berlin could take
such approaches in stride; they held some earlier French credits against
the Bulgarians and in general thought it best to restrain Bulgarian exuberance lest hostilities develop as a result. The German government might
wish to start wars at times of its own choosing, but it did not want inconvenient hostilities started by others. In the case of Bulgaria, that
meant hostilities against Rumania with which Germany herself was trying
to develop better relations. In spite of the restraint that these attitudes
imposed on German-Bulgarian relations, however, there was a determination in Berlin to keep Bulgaria as much in the German orbit as
possible; and if arms credits were a necesssary ingredient of that, Berlin
would eventually grant them.[100]

The rapprochement between Germany and Yugoslavia that had preceded Munich continued thereafter, although the fate of her Little Entente
ally naturally alarmed public opinion in the South Slav state. Nevertheless, as long as Hungary was restricted by Germany to the annexation of
ethnographically Magyar portions of Czechoslovakia—as opposed to the
historic borders—and as long as Stojadinović remained in power, Berlin
could depend on the maintenance of good relations with Yugoslavia. The
fall of Stojadinović over internal problems on 4 February 1939 introduced
a new and uncertain element from the perspective of Berlin. The new
government reaffirmed its adherence to friendly relations with Germany,
an intention underlined by the appointment of the minister to Berlin,
Aleksander Cincar-Marković, to serve as the new foreign minister. Efforts were made from the German side to offset the possible weakening of
political ties by the beginning of arms deliveries that would tie Yugoslavia
to Germany, but any fruits of such a policy lay in the future. For the time
being, Belgrade's attitude was unexpectedly an open question for Berlin.
Stojadinović would never return to power, and with him an element that

---

100. On German-Bulgarian relations in the period November 1938–March 1939, see *G.D.*,
D, 5, Nos. 240, 241, 250, 251, 263, 270, 274, 301–3, 312, 314, 315; *D.D.F.*, 2d, 12, Nos. 72,
362. Marguerat, pp. 121–22, emphasizes German use of Bulgarian demands as a lever on
Rumania.

both Berlin and Rome had counted on in the Balkans disappeared permanently from the scene.[101]

A compensating strengthening of Germany's position occurred as a result of developments in her relations with Rumania. The collapse of France's position in Europe with the mutilation of Czechoslovakia probably had a greater effect on Rumania than on any other country in Europe other than Czechoslovakia herself. In view of the traditional ties going back to the beginnings of Rumanian independence and manifested in the way in which the elite of Rumania looked to France as the model for everything from fashion to government, the revelation of France's abdication was particularly shocking. Worry over Hungarian gains at Czechoslovakia's expense—the revision of the border originally established by the Treaty of Trianon being considered a dangerous precedent by Rumania—combined with an ever present fear of Russian territorial ambitions to suggest a change in policy that would move Bucharest's position closer to Berlin's.[102]

Feelers from Rumania were put out in behalf of King Carol as soon as the Munich conference was announced. From the beginning of this new development, the German minister in Rumania, Wilhelm Fabricius, urged that Germany take advantage of the trend and concentrate on the economic sphere. Arms deliveries from Germany might help, but the key element in his view was always the building up of vast German debts to Rumania by massive German orders for wheat and oil, with such debts tying Rumania almost permanently to Germany.[103]

There was a positive response from Germany, where von Ribbentrop was interested, where there was a desire for exploiting the general situation to develop better political and economic relations, and where the Rumanian objections to Hungary's seizure of the Carpatho-Ukraine provided a temporary symmetry of political purpose.[104] An especially important motive for Germany at this time was her obvious need for Rumanian oil. Anticipating war with the Western Powers, Germany was building up her armed forces, a buildup which implied the need for more and more petroleum products in the face of as yet inadequate synthetic production and the practically certain interruption of supplies from overseas

101. On German-Yugoslav relations, see *G.D.*, D, 5, Nos. 229, 232, 276, 285, 288, 290, 291, 296, 307, 308; 6, No. 205; Neuhausen to Prince Paul, 17 December 1938, and annexed memorandum on the problems of the Germans in Yugoslavia, T-120, 2621/5482/E 382120–41; Hoptner, p. 133 (whose account of the fall of Stojadinović on pp. 121–33 is most useful); *Hungarian Documents*, 3, Nos. 296, 309, 315, 323; report by Sir Ronald Campbell on Yugoslavia's foreign relations under the new government, 27 February 1939, R 1435/409/92, FO 371/23883.

102. See Batowski, pp. 143–44; *D.D.F.*, 2d, 12, No. 242.

103. *G.D.*, D, 5, Nos. 227, 228, 230, 231, 234; Hillgruber, pp. 23–24; but see Marguerat, p. 120, n.2.

104. On von Ribbentrop's interest, see *G.D.*, D, 5:259, n.1; see also ibid., Nos. 235, 236. The Rumanian foreign minister since March 1938, Nicolas Comnène, had been Rumania's minister in Berlin for the preceding ten years.

in case of war. Under these circumstances, a major German effort to secure control of Rumania's economy, especially her oil industry, was clearly indicated.[105]

As a mechanism for developing closer relations with Germany, King Carol hinted that he would himself like to stop there and perhaps see Hitler, a suggestion to which the latter responded favorably.[106] As in 1936, the king arranged for Georges Bratianu, a member of one of Rumania's most influential families, to test the waters in Berlin during a visit from 2 to 12 November 1938.[107] At almost the same time, difficult economic negotiations between Germany and Rumania seemed to have at least some chance of resulting in agreement; Carol made the needed concesssions, but he demonstrated his concern for his country's independence by driving a very hard bargain.[108] As a matter of fact, the strong economic position of the Western Powers, especially Great Britain, in Rumania's economy enabled Rumania to operate with considerable effectiveness in restraining any substantial German advance there for a considerable time.[109] The agreement reached between Germany and Rumania on 10 December 1938 had some advantages for Germany but in no way came up to Berlin's original hopes.[110]

While the negotiations for the economic agreement were still under way, King Carol visited Germany. His talks with Hitler on 24 November and with Göring two days later show a similar combination of desire for better relations with Germany and an insistence on an independent status for Rumania. Hitler was all sweetness and light, declaring disinterest in any but the German minority in Rumania, but refused to commit himself to leaving the remainder of the Carpatho-Ukraine with Czechoslovakia. The prospect of a further shift of Rumania to the German orbit nevertheless existed, particularly through trade relations. If these prospects were not immediately realized, it was because of steps King Carol took right after the visit to consolidate his domestic position.[111]

In his talks in Berlin the king had already signalized his concern about the internal situation in Rumania, where he intended to remain in charge, by asking for the recall of Arthur Konradi, one of the leaders of the German minority. The king was willing to adapt his foreign policy some-

105. A very useful survey of this aspect in Marguerat, pp. 95–103.

106. *G.D.*, D, 5, Nos. 237–39, 243; Marguerat, p. 120.

107. On Bratianu's 1936 visit, see Weinberg, *Foreign Policy*, p. 324; on his 1938 visit, see *G.D.*, D, 5, No. 242; Hillgruber, p. 25; Marguerat, p. 121.

108. *G.D.*, D, 5, Nos. 246–48; cf. *Hungarian Documents*, 3, No. 19; Marguerat, pp. 101–3.

109. A detailed analysis in Marguerat, pp. 103–19, which supersedes the relevant portions of Wendt, *Economic Appeasement*. See also Adamthwaite, p. 275; *D.D.F.*, 2d, 12, Nos. 278, 350, 407.

110. Marguerat, pp. 122–25.

111. On the royal visit to Germany and the conversations held there, see *G.D.*, D, 5, Nos. 254, 257; *Hungarian Documents*, 3, Nos. 99, 107, 117, 133; *D.D.F.*, 2d, 12, Nos. 449, 450, 452; *Lipski Papers*, No. 128; Hillgruber, pp. 25–28; Marguerat, pp. 120–21. On the desire of King Carol to have Wohlthat lead an economic mission to Bucharest, see *G.D.*, D, 5, No. 257.

what more to German preferences, but he obviously wished to secure himself against domestic pressures that might undermine his rule. After the recent experience of Czechoslovakia, he probably saw in the Rumanian Iron Guard with its ties to German National Socialist organizations the potential of Henlein's Sudeten Germans. Immediately after his return to Bucharest, on 30 November, King Carol had Corneliu Codreanu, the head of the Iron Guard, and thirteen of its other leaders shot. He was to discover, like von Schuschnigg, that the Third Reich considered imitation a form not of flattery but of impertinence. The murdering of political opponents, like the holding of questionable plebiscites, was to be a German monopoly, and Hitler was, or pretended to be, enraged over the murders. Coming so soon after his meeting with the king, it looked as if the killing of the Rumanian fascist leaders had his approval. Although there is only indirect evidence on the subject, Hitler may also have been upset over the weakening of an important pro-German element in Rumanian political life. In any case, the German government professed to be shocked, and the German press was instructed to expatiate at length on the evils of such treatment of political opponents.[112]

The setback to German-Rumanian relations did not last long. Rumania still wanted to sell her surplus wheat, and Germany still needed to buy Rumanian oil. The Rumanians wanted to reinsure themselves with the ever more powerful Germany, which always had the option of supporting the revisionist demands of Hungary and Bulgaria against them; and the Germans wanted very much to draw Rumania with its natural riches and strategic position closer to themselves. For a while, a British economic counteroffensive prevented a reorientation of Rumania's trade system; but while this determined and at least partially successful British effort helps to explain the reaction of London to the eventual German success in pressuring Rumania in March, it could not prevent that success.[113]

In the first weeks of 1939, German-Rumanian relations improved again. The new Rumanian foreign minister, Grigore Gafencu, did what he could to overcome the real or imagined bad impression left by the murders, and the Germans were receptive to the economic prospects involved in a closer alignment of Rumania with Berlin.[114] Once again Bratianu went to Germany with the king's approval, and once again as in November Gö-

112. *G.D.*, D, 5, Nos. 260, 261; *Lipski Papers,* Nos. 128, 129; *D.D.F.*, 2d, 12, No. 455; *Hungarian Documents,* 3, Nos. 107, 112, 151, 171, 324; "Informationsbericht Nr. 82," 2 December 1938, Bundesarchiv, Brammer, Z.Sg. 101/33, f.379; German press conferences of 1, 2, 3, 8, 10 December, Bundesarchiv, Traub, Z.Sg. 110/10, ff.177, 184, 188, 198, 210; Hillgruber, pp. 28–30; Marguerat, p. 123.

113. Marguerat, pp. 125–30.

114. *G.D.*, D, 5, Nos. 264, 275, 279–81, 286, 287, 289; *Hungarian Documents,* 3, Nos. 331, 343, 397; Hillgruber, pp. 30–31. By this time the Rumanians also realized that with the railway cut by Hungarian territorial gains, the Carpatho-Ukraine was no longer of such importance to them (cf. *Hungarian Documents,* 3, No. 214). A rather different picture of Gafencu's views in January 1939 is presented by A. Chanady and J. Jensen, "Germany, Rumania and the British Guarantees of March-April, 1939," *Australian Journal of Politics and History,* 16, No. 2 (Aug. 1970), 205.

ring's special trade assistant Helmuth Wohlthat was asked to come to Bucharest for economic negotiations.[115] This time Wohlthat did go, and he found the Rumanians extremely cooperative. Here was a great opportunity for Germany to secure something very much like economic domination of Rumania, and there was no further hesitation about political murders. Expansion of soybean planting, in which Germany had long been interested, increased purchases of wheat, and a share in Rumania's oil production were all far more real than sentimental regrets about admirers of the Third Reich. By the end of February 1939 there were clear signs of a possible new Rumanian economic alignment with Germany, an alignment that could not but have repercussions on Germany's relations with Bulgaria, which have already been mentioned, with Poland, Rumania's ally, and with Hungary, Rumania's hostile neighbor.[116]

The Hungarians had had plenty of opportunity since Munich to learn that they had drawn Germany's disfavor upon themselves.[117] The signs of Czechoslovakia's becoming more and more a dependency of Germany, which in turn would not allow Hungary to seize as much of that country as she wanted, were too obvious to overlook. The German veto of Hungary's planned occupation of the Carpatho-Ukraine on 20 November was soon followed by reports that the Czechoslovak government was considering adherence to the Anti-Comintern Pact and would thereby enter the German orbit.[118] The first signs of a rapprochement between Germany and Rumania were even more frightening for Budapest. It was certainly not entirely a coincidence that within days of the German veto and King Carol's meeting with Hitler there was a major reorganization of the Hungarian government in which István Csáky replaced Kálmán de Kánya as foreign minister.[119] The new foreign minister was known for his pro-German sympathies, and he immediately developed further the policy of a closer relationship with Berlin which Kánya had found it expedient to adopt on the morrow of Germany's veto.[120]

Csáky was invited to Berlin to review the unfortunate way in which German-Hungarian relations had been developing in recent months, and he hastened to accept.[121] Even before going to meet von Ribbentrop,

---

115. *G.D.*, D, 5, No. 282.

116. Ibid., Nos. 284, 293–95, 297, 298, 306. Note that the Germans became concerned about British countermeasures that might interfere with German predominance and thought of sending Wohlthat back to Bucharest before 15 March (ibid., No. 309). See also Marguerat, pp. 130–33; Chanady and Jensen, pp. 206–7.

117. Even in the area of supplying armaments the Germans were uncooperative, although this had been an important factor in Hungarian reluctance to risk war (Macartney, 1:245).

118. *Hungarian Documents*, 3, No. 68.

119. Roos, p. 379; Hoensch, *Ungarische Revisionismus*, p. 230. For a short interim, from 28 November to 10 December, Prime Minister Béla Imrédy also held the portfolio of foreign minister. An extensive and useful account of the interaction of Hungarian internal affairs with the German veto of the invasion of the Carpatho-Ukraine to produce a change of government and the replacement of Kánya is in Macartney, 1:305–17.

120. Kánya had made a violent enemy of von Ribbentrop by his sharp comments; see Macartney, 1:241.

121. *Hungarian Documents*, 3, Nos. 115, 119, 121; *G.D.*, D, 5, Nos. 244, 252, 255.

Count Csáky pushed forward with the project already started under his predecessor for Hungary's adherence to the Anti-Comintern Pact.[122] During December 1938 the Hungarian government coordinated its planned adhesion with Germany and Italy, and also decided at the urging of the Axis powers to leave the League of Nations.[123] Difficulties about the German minority in Hungary continued,[124] but the Budapest government was obviously doing its utmost to fall in with German preferences.[125]

The decision to join the Anti-Comintern Pact and leave the League would not turn out quite the way the Hungarians had calculated. They lost considerable sympathy in the West and they found themselves very much at odds with the Soviet government. The Russians decided to make a major issue of the adherence to the Anti-Comintern Pact and retaliated by closing the Soviet legation in Budapest and the Hungarian legation in Moscow.[126] The precise motives for this policy—not extended to other signatories of the pact—are not known. Moscow may well have felt that the Hungarian action was inappropriate at the time the Soviets themselves were supporting Hungarian aspirations for the Carpatho-Ukraine,[127] or they may well have meant the whole gesture as a warning to Poland under no circumstances to follow the Hungarian example. As it turned out, the Budapest government was to discover that solidarity with the Axis was often a one-way street. The other parties to the Anti-Comintern Pact were unwilling to respond to Hungarian requests for demonstrative action in Moscow.[128] They did not understand that Berlin's view of the Anti-Comintern Pact was entirely different from Budapest's, that Berlin was interested in its use against the Western Powers and had not the least desire for trouble with the Soviet Union. Only telegrams of congratulations would recompense Hungary when, like the puppet state of

122. On Kánya's taking the decisive steps on 13 October before his replacement by Csáky, see Macartney, 1:288; for further offers to join the Anti-Comintern Pact during Kánya's remaining time in office, see ibid., pp. 312–14.

123. *Hungarian Documents,* 3, Nos. 47, 123, 131, 155 (French text in Ádám, No. 33), 156, 166, 176, 184, 208; *G.D.,* D, 4, No. 408; 5, Nos. 256, 258, 259, 265–69, 271, 283; Ciano, *Diary,* 19–20 December 1938, p. 299; Macartney, 1:317–19; Thomas L. Sakmyster, "Army Officers and Foreign Policy in Interwar Hungary, 1918–41," *Journal of Contemporary History,* 10, No. 1 (Jan. 1975), 30.

124. *G.D.,* D, 5, No. 253; "Informationsbericht Nr. 89: Zur Lage des Deutschtums in Ungarn," 17 December 1938, Bundesarchiv, Brammer, Z.Sg. 101/33, ff.405–9; cf. *Hungarian Documents,* 3, No. 305.

125. Note the explanation of Hungary's policy provided to the Poles, who were skeptical about Hungary's new reticence on the Carpatho-Ukraine, in *Hungarian Documents,* 3, No. 132.

126. Ibid., Nos. 177, 181, 194 (French text in Ádám, No. 34), 202, 213, 222, 224, 231, 232, 236, 239, 248, 269, 285, 288, 306; 4, Nos. 61, 65, 67, 72.

127. Note Macartney, 1:292, n.4, 322.

128. *Hungarian Documents,* 3, Nos. 287, 293, 297, 298, 308, 312, 317, 329, 335, 336, 338, 339, 341, 342, 349, 368, 387; *G.D.,* D, 4, No. 412; 5, No. 283. The Hungarians believed that German dependence on raw materials from the U.S.S.R. was responsible for Berlin's attitude (*Hungarian Documents,* 3, Nos. 369, 376). This was certainly an aspect of the impact of any severance of Germany's relations with the Soviet Union that worried Berlin, see *G.D.,* D, 4, No. 488; Weinberg, *Germany and the Soviet Union,* p. 11, n.37.

Manchukuo, she joined the Anti-Comintern Pact formally on 22 February 1939.[129]

The troubles over Hungary's acts of symbolic obeisance to Germany—joining the Anti-Comintern Pact and leaving the League—still lay in the future when the Hungarian foreign minister met Hitler and von Ribbentrop on 16 January.[130] Hitler complained at length about Hungary's policy in the fall, insisting that it would have been so much better to have settled with Czechoslovakia then, once and for all. That opportunity had been lost because of Hungary's reticence, but now new paths had to be found. Hitler was willing to give the Hungarians another chance, but they would have to do things his way. As to what that might be, Hitler was specific on three things. First, Czechoslovakia would be made to disappear, second, this would be done through the joint actions of Germany, Hungary, and Poland—which he obviously still thought amenable to subordinating herself to Germany.[131] And finally Hitler gave Csáky the same view of timing he had given Ernst Neumann the preceding month, though in this case we have a fuller record of precisely what was said: "He had come to the conclusion that between October and March nothing of a military sort could be carried out in Europe."

What was meant, although the Hungarian government did not understand it immediately, was that if Hungary worked closely with Germany at times and in ways determined by Berlin, she could expect a further share of the Czechoslovak booty. Once Budapest had decided to march to Berlin's tune, she would have to make her moves conform precisely; the Germans were accustomed to a very exacting standard of drill, a point Hitler had tried to explain to his Magyar visitors by referring to the coordination of a soccer team as a model. This meant that all Hungarian efforts to speed up the process would be unavailing and in fact resented by Berlin.[132]

The Germans were also interested in restraining the Hungarians in their relations with Rumania. Although the Magyars resented this, they were expected by Berlin and Rome to be at least civil to the country in which Germany was developing a greater stake.[133] It was also assumed that

129. *Hungarian Documents*, 3, Nos. 218, 344, 348, 350, 353–58, 361, 362. On the restoration of Soviet-Hungarian relations, see ibid., 4, Nos. 225, 236, 258, 410.

130. On the meeting, see ibid., 3, Nos. 212, 230; *G.D.*, D, 5, Nos. 272 (Hitler-Csáky), 273, 278; *Lipski Papers*, No. 132; Macartney, 1:319–21.

131. The comments Hitler and von Ribbentrop made separately to Csáky about Poland need not have been subjectively dishonest. Von Ribbentrop was less definite than Hitler, and both may well have thought that there was a real possibility of agreement at least until von Ribbentrop 's trip to Warsaw ten days after Csáky's visit to Berlin, and possibly even after that.

132. For Hungary's unsuccessful attempts to hasten the process, see *Hungarian Documents*, 3, Nos. 254, 268, 280, 294, 303, 313, 318, 340, 351, 366, 385, 388, 390 (French text in Ádám, No. 36, erroneously dated May instead of March), 401, 404 (French text in Ádám, No. 37).

133. Ibid., Nos. 230, 245, 256, 259, 261, 264, 310, 311, 337, 367.

Magyar revisionist aspirations would not be turned on Yugoslavia, especially at a time when the future course of that country was in doubt after the fall of Stojadinović.[134] Whatever the Hungarians thought of all this, and there are considerable signs of continued minor frictions between Germany and Hungary,[135] having made their peace with Germany the Magyars had to stick to their new policy if they did not want Germany herself to take over the Carpatho-Ukraine and possibly much of Slovakia when Czechoslovakia disappeared. By the time Hitler was ready to move on the timetable he had mentioned earlier, he had given up on Poland, at least for the time being; but the Hungarians would finally receive their reward. And that reward would be doubly sweet. Not only were they instructed by the Germans on 13 March to march into the Carpatho-Ukraine,[136] but they could have the satisfaction of seizing the whole area without having to turn a bit of it over to the hated Rumanians.[137]

The first steps toward closer German ties with Rumania and far more decisive measures to bring Hungary back into Germany's good graces had been taken by the time Polish Foreign Minister Josef Beck stopped in Germany on his return to Warsaw from the Riviera. On 5 January he met with Hitler in the presence of von Ribbentrop and the two ambassadors, and on the following day had a conversation just with the German foreign minister.[138] Hitler reviewed the Czechoslovak crisis from his perspective, expressing regret over the way Chamberlain and Daladier had pushed him away from liquidating Czechoslovakia. He repeated his familiar complaints about the hesitations of the Hungarians, but asserted that Hungary as well as Poland and Germany would have to participate in the future destruction of Czechoslovakia. His lengthy discussion of the Carpatho-Ukrainian question shows his recognition of its importance to Poland.

134. Ibid., Nos. 250, 252, 256, 259, 260, 262, 265, 266, 273, 275, 277, 337.

135. Ibid., Nos. 251, 257, 267, 333, 334; "Bestellungen aus der Pressekonferenz," 22 February 1939, Bundesarchiv, Brammer, Z.Sg. 101/12, f.55. Note Horthy's comments to the U.S. minister on 28 January, Montgomery tel. 18, State 740.00/557. On German-Hungarian economic relations, see Forstmeier (ed.), p. 109.

136. See above, p. 477; *Hungarian Documents,* 3, Nos. 414, 415, 427–30, 432, 435, 439, 440. For evidence that the Hungarian government was determined to move into the Carpatho-Ukraine as soon as Germany occupied Bohemia, with or without Berlin's approval, see Macartney, 1:334, n.7. I do not share Macartney's reading of this evidence; had Hitler actually wanted to keep the Hungarians out of the Carpatho-Ukraine, he could easily have restrained them by threatening to reopen the question of the border between German and West Hungary.

137. *Hungarian Documents,* 3, Nos. 426, 438, 442, 451–53, 459, 461, 466, 468, 471, 472, 474, 475, 477, 481, 482, 485, 486, 493, 494; 4, Nos. 12, 26; *G.D.,* D, 6, Nos. 2, 4, 6, 13, 29, 39; Macartney, 1:333–34. A critical issue was the easternmost corner of the Carpatho-Ukraine with its segment of the railway connecting Poland and Rumania as well as some villages with Rumanian population; a summary of the developments is in *B.D.,* 3d, 5, No. 28.

138. On Beck's talks in Germany, see *G.D.,* D, 5, Nos. 119–21; *Polish White Book,* Nos. 48, 49; Beck, pp. 182–83; Cienciala, pp. 188–90; Szembek, pp. 404–8; *Hungarian Documents,* 3, Nos. 200, 215, 221; *Biddle Papers,* pp. 43–45, 300–9; Biddle tel. 4 of January 1939, State 862.5016/2052; von Weizsäcker to Consul General Danzig, tel. 239 of 9 January 1939, T-120, 1215/2371/D 496171.

Here was part of the bait for his proposed new settlement with Warsaw. The demands for Danzig and the route across the Corridor were put forward in the context of a German guarantee of Poland's western border and special rights in Danzig as von Ribbentrop had put them in October, though Hitler left the question of the Anti-Comintern Pact for von Ribbentrop on the following day. On the Danzig issue Beck stressed the great difficulties of acceding to the German demand, but it is worth noting that he was far more definite in rejecting any Polish adherence to the Anti-Comintern Pact. Otherwise he just promised to consider the German demands, and it was agreed that von Ribbentrop would come to Warsaw later that month. What conclusions were drawn by the Germans and Poles from these talks, and how were these hopes confirmed or refuted by von Ribbentrop's visit to Warsaw?

Hitler and von Ribbentrop were disappointed by Beck's reluctance to place the future of his country at Germany's mercy, but they do not appear to have given up all hope that Poland would yet give in. There was certainly greater doubt that agreement would be reached than earlier, but von Ribbentrop went to Warsaw still hopeful that a combination of kind words, tempting offers, and German pressure might produce an agreement along the lines Berlin wanted. The conversation in Warsaw apparently convinced him that friendly words would be of no avail. Only direct and vehement pressure could accomplish anything.[139] The change in Germany's assessment and approach would be evident immediately after the conclusion of von Ribbentrop's visit on 26 January.

The German procedure in moving toward the destruction of Czechoslovakia in the six weeks from the beginning of February to 15 March shows that, on the basis of his own talks with Beck and now von Ribbentrop's report on his experiences in Warsaw, Hitler had shifted his perception of Poland considerably. Although he had probably not yet given up all hope of drawing Poland into the German orbit, it was pressure, not compromise, that would now be the essence of German strategy. While Hungary would be allowed a share of the spoils in spite of her disappointing performance of the year before, Poland was rigidly excluded even though she had played a role Germany liked in 1938. There were two distinct facets to this procedure. Poland was not allowed to play a part or secure a share, and the early seizure of Moravská-Ostrava by the Germans was largely designed to preclude any last-minute effort by Poland to gain by the final dissolution of Czechoslovakia. Furthermore, the insistence of the

139. On the Warsaw visit of 24–26 January 1939, see *G.D.*, D, 5, Nos. 122, 125, 126; *Polish White Book*, Nos. 50–56; *Lipski Papers*, No. 133; Szembek, pp. 411–17; Winship (U.S. chargé a.i. Warsaw) dispatches 912, 923, 930, of 20, 28 January, 3 February 1939, State 760c.62/439, 442, 445; Kuykendall dispatch 116 of 6 February 1939, State 860K.01/120; *Biddle Papers*, pp. 310–14; Cienciala, pp. 194–96; Kleist, pp. 19–23; *S.U.*, No. 125; "Informationsbericht Nr. 9," 30 January 1939, Bundesarchiv, Brammer, Z.Sg. 101/34. Himmler visited Poland in February 1939.

Germans on a military protectorate of Slovakia posed a direct and obvious threat to Poland, not unlike the way the German occupation of Austria had outflanked Czechoslovakia from the south in the preceding year. When the Germans repeated their demands after 15 March, therefore, they thought themselves in a stronger position to exercise pressure, and though more hostile as well as doubtful, may still have had some hope that Poland would succumb to their demands peacefully.[140]

Beck's reaction was entirely different. The maintenance of Poland's independence from foreign dictation was axiomatic with him, and he was therefore very much alarmed by the German demands. As long as these had been presented only by von Ribbentrop, there was always the possibility that in the face of a firm Polish stand the Germans would withdraw or modify them in order to pursue other aims, perhaps in the colonial field. Now that he had heard them from Hitler himself, von Ribbentrop's insistence sounded even more ominous. The slight easing of Polish relations with the Soviet Union signalized by the Polish-Soviet declaration of 27 November had probably been in part a means of strengthening Poland's independent position vis-à-vis Germany. There was, however, no way in which the Polish government of the time believed it could develop really close relations with the Soviet Union safely, partly for fear of Soviet ambitions, partly for fear of provoking a violent German response.

Beck's attempts to further his scheme for a Third Europe through a common border with Hungary and close ties with Italy should also be seen as part of his effort to counter German pressure and, he hoped, to contain German expansion. The Polish government's increasingly disdainful attitude toward Hungary was surely a measure of Warsaw's disappointment over the failure of this approach—a failure caused by Berlin rather than Budapest. After the January meetings, Beck still clung to this policy, but even a visit by Count Ciano to Warsaw could not breathe life into a project that was probably incapable of realization from the beginning, could only have worked with the participation of Czechoslovakia rather than on her ruins, and was certainly not capable of life once Germany attained a position of such power that she could direct the policies of Italy, to say nothing of the smaller countries of Southeast Europe.[141]

Two further lines of Polish policy in the face of Germany's demands need to be noted. If it was impossible to develop Polish relations with the

140. The Soviet government has published evidence that there was an expectation and even a hope in the German government that the Poles would reject the demands (*S.U.*, No. 266), but the statements of Bruno Peter Kleist on the views of Hitler and von Ribbentrop to this effect are dated 2 May 1939 and may reflect subsequent reinterpretation. There is, in Kleist's comments, also some confusion of the January and the March German-Polish exchanges.

141. On Beck's continued attempts for his Third Europe scheme, see Cienciala, pp. 175–76. On Ciano's visit to Warsaw, see his *Diplomatic Papers*, pp. 273–75; *Hungarian Documents*, 3, Nos. 187, 283, 327, 345; Szembek, pp. 424–25; Cienciala, p. 189.

Soviet Union to the point where the latter could be a counterweight to Germany, there was at least the theoretical possibility of reviving the alliance with France that had suffered so in the Czechoslovak crisis. There was a similar theoretical possibility of interesting England in the fate of Poland, an idea that the role played by the British government in the Czechoslovak crisis suggested would be as important as it was problematical. The combination of reticence about informing France and Britain concerning the German demands and the soundings, especially in London, about closer relations in the face of a Germany mightier than ever and possibly threatening to everyone should be seen, in my view, as Beck's way of securing Western support if Germany became too insistent. He did not wish the Western Powers to know of Germany's demands, for fear partly of weakening the international position of Poland and partly of being pressured into conceding some of them. After all, the proportion of Germans in Danzig was higher than the proportion of Poles in Těšín. But the longer a crisis in German-Polish relations was postponed, the more likely it was that Germany's continued aggressive actions would either impinge directly on vital interests of the Western Powers or alarm them into a firm stand out of sheer fear of any further strengthening of Germany. In that context, Poland could be seen from London and Paris as a useful counterweight to Germany rather than a burdensome and troublesome dependent. Here too was a reason to let the negotiations with Germany continue quietly; the longer they lasted, the more likely that German action would bring changes in Western attitudes, a speculation that would prove correct.[142] The plans for a trip by Beck to London developed in the winter, but it would take place under circumstances changed by the German action of 15 March.[143]

If Beck was working on securing support against Germany on the one hand, he was also trying to think of ways to work out some agreement with her on the other. If a permanent freezing of the status quo was not possible, was war the *only* alternative? Might there not be some way to provide a prestige success for Hitler that would assuage Poland's powerful western neighbor without threatening Poland's vital interests and, above all, without simply opening the way for further German demands? No thought was ever given to any possible compromise on the German demand that Poland join the Anti-Comintern Pact since this was seen as a derogation of Polish independence in international affairs. The two other German demands, those on Corridor transit and Danzig, however, were in a different category.

142. On Poland's relations with France and England in the period November 1938–February 1939, see Cienciala, pp. 168–206, passim; *B.D.*, 3d, 3, chap. 9; Kennard to Sargent, 23 December 1938, C 27/27/55, FO 371/23129; Strang's notes on *B.D.*, 3d, 3, No. 531, in C 403/54/18, FO 371/23015; Wilson (Paris) tel. 94 of 16 January 1939, State 740.00/546; *Hungarian Documents*, 3, No. 173.
143. *G.D.*, D, 5, Nos. 130, 140.

Before the January meetings, Beck was considering some compromise on the route across the Corridor.[144] He had also considered some new status for Danzig giving the Free City, and hence its National Socialist government, more rights of its own. After his Januarv conversations with Hitler and von Ribbentrop, Beck appears to have been willing to go somewhat further. In mid-January he had his chef de cabinet, Michal Lubiénski, work out a scheme for a German-Polish condominium in Danzig which would leave its inhabitants the option of living under German rule while retaining Poland's special rights in the area. Perhaps under the pressure of others in the Polish government opposed to the idea of concessions to Germany in Danzig, Beck directed that the project be dropped a few days later.[145] When von Ribbentrop was in Warsaw, therefore, no such proposals were discussed; instead, in the face of the German demand for the annexation of Danzig and Poland's reluctance to do more than consider the problem, the two foreign ministers merely agreed on a joint procedure to follow if the League withdrew from its role in the Free City. Beck had, however, not been absolutely negative. His statement that Poland "could not part with tangible rights in exchange for mere guarantees"[146] could be read as a hint for a compromise as much as a rejection of German demands. It was certainly not as clearcut a no as he gave to von Ribbentrop's anti-Soviet schemes.

After von Ribbentrop's Warsaw visit, Beck considered still another possible way out of the dilemma over Danzig. This time the idea was to partition the territory of the Free City with the town of Danzig itself and the eastern two-thirds of the area of the Free City being annexed to East Prussia, while the western projection of the territory into the Corridor would be annexed by Poland.[147] Beck may well have thought that he could secure the endorsement of his own government more easily to such

144. Szembek, *Diary,* 22 November, 6, 7 December 1938, pp. 380, 383, 385; *Biddle Papers,* p. 43. Although the evidence is thin, there would appear to have been consideration of relief for German customs and transit payments, issues that had in prior years caused considerable difficulties.

145. The account in Cienciala, pp. 190–92, is based mainly on Lubienski's account and correspondence with him. It may be noted that L. was very familiar with the technical details of the Danzig question, having previously served as chief of the section for Danzig of the Polish foreign ministry.

146. Szembek, 1 February 1939, p. 414.

147. I have discussed this project in a short article, "A Proposed Compromise over Danzig in 1939?" in *Journal of Central European Affairs,* 14, No. 4 (January 1955), 336–37. Now that the project prepared by Lubienski is known, it is almost certain that the discussion in the Szembek diary of 10 January 1939, pp. 407–8, belongs, as Cienciala believes, in the context of that proposal. This makes it most likely that Beck's authorization for a partition plan to be prepared in the Polish foreign ministry came after von Ribbentrop's visit. When U.S. Ambassador Biddle reported on the partition plan on 7 July 1939, he referred to it as having "gained their [Beck and his associates] serious consideration before the Polish mobilization measures of March 21" (Biddle dispatch 1139 of 7 July 1939, State 760c.62/714). This report by the extremely well-informed Biddle also points to the period between von Ribbentrop's journey and 15 March.

a proposal than to the earlier one because it would open the way for the construction of a more secure railway and possibly a canal to Gdynia entirely within Polish territory, widen the Corridor at its narrowest point, and secure for Poland the small rural Polish population of the Free City. The prospect of obtaining the city of Danzig itself along with most of the land area and population of the territory of the Free City as defined by the peace treaty might have looked attractive to the Germans, had they been seriously interested in a settlement negotiated freely by the two countries.[148] But nothing came of any of these considerations, because the German destruction of Czechoslovakia on 15 March showed all too obviously what would happen to any country that yielded to Germany portions of its territory inhabited by Germans and allowed the Germans to construct extraterritorial routes across its territory. Under the impact of the German move, neither compromise project could be brought forward.

The most obvious sign that all was not well in German-Polish relations was in the field that had been kept quiet during the preceding five years, that of minorities and related incidents. If the years of better German-Polish relations had been characterized by a deliberate effort to restrain the publicity, if not the reality, of nationality conflicts, the evidence of a new atmosphere was there now. The various incidents, troubles, and negotiations ranging from arguments over Polish stamps to brawls about Danzig restaurant signs do not merit detailed examination here. What is important is that issues and emotions that had been repressed by government policy on both sides of the border were in February and March 1939 once again becoming the staple of diplomatic and publicistic controversy. The barometer pointed to storms ahead in public at the same time as secret negotiations were apparently leading to trouble.[149] In the preceding years, the broader policy concerns of the two countries had led them to push such daily irritants to the background. The next few weeks would determine whether that would happen again or whether the past procedure would be reversed with the minorities issue being inflamed rather than dampened to serve other goals.

148. The report by von Moltke on a conversation with Beck on 13 or 14 March should, probably, be read in this context. Beck explained that in his forthcoming London trip he hoped to persuade the British that a vacuum in Danzig should be avoided and that the League should retain a role until Germany and Poland had reached a bilateral agreement. Having just worked out with von Ribbentrop an interim procedure to cover the contingency of League withdrawal, Beck was obviously referring to some long-term solution of the Danzig question when he claimed to hope that an agreement that would do justice to the interests of both parties could be reached (*G.D.*, D, 5, No. 140). See also Ciano's evaluation of Beck's position on Danzig in Ciano, *Diplomatic Papers*, p. 274.

149. On the minorities question and incidents early in 1939, see *G.D.*, D, 5, Nos. 128, 131, 132, 134, 137; 6, No. 125; "Bestellungen aus der Pressekonferenz," 11, 14, 21, 27 February, 6 March 1939, Bundesarchiv, Brammer, Z.Sg. 101/12, ff.45, 47, 52, 60, 65; "Informationsbericht Nr. 15," 27 February 1939, ibid., 101/34, ff.65–67. On 4 March 1939 the Polish general staff decided to prepare an operational "Plan West," having had only a "Plan East" (Forstmeier [ed.], pp. 364–65).

The discussion of German policy toward Czechoslovakia, Poland, and other parts of East and Southeast Europe after Munich has dealt primarily with the short-term aims and methods of German policy. The question that remains and that has only been touched on at certain points in the narrative is the one that asks, What were Hitler's larger perspectives after Munich? With the initiative so clearly in his hands, what did he look forward to doing in the coming years? Austria had been annexed. Large parts of Czechoslovakia had been taken, and the rest of Bohemia and Moravia, Hitler was determined, should follow. But what of the future once Czechoslovakia had entirely disappeared as Hitler had always intended it should? One very important clue has already been touched on in the account of German relations with Poland. This was Germany's insistence on Poland's becoming a vassal of Germany, a fate which was to be practically demonstrated by the new territorial settlement proposed to the Poles in October and that was to be politically acknowledged by adherence to the Anti-Comintern Pact. That leads to the broader question of what Hitler hoped to do once Poland, as well as Hungary, had subordinated themselves to his will. Why, in particular, the insistence that Hungary and Poland, both known to be vehemently anti-Communist— one of which was ruled by a regime that had come to power in violent reaction against a Communist regime and the other led by men who had come to the fore in a war against the Soviet Union—should formally adhere to the Anti-Comintern Pact with its vague denunciation of the Comintern and without any concrete and substantial obligations? It is hardly to be believed that Hitler or von Ribbentrop thought Horthy or Beck would be more anti-Communist after joining the pact than before.

The answer to this puzzle will be found quite readily if it is recognized that for countries like Poland and Hungary (like Spain) joining the Anti-Comintern Pact was purely a formal gesture of political and diplomatic obeisance to Berlin, separating them from any other past or prospective international ties, and having nothing to do with the Soviet Union at all. This is not to say that Hitler had given up his ambition to seize vast portions of Soviet territory; he did indeed expect to do that, but he never looked upon it as a project in which Germany would need the help of all sorts of allies. When the time came, Germany would carry out that task by herself, though others might help if they were so inclined and would be rewarded by slices appropriate to their contribution. The focus of Hitler's intermediate planning, between the immediate destruction of Czechoslovakia and the eventual seizure of huge portions of Russia as *Lebensraum* for German settlers, was aimed against the Western Powers. They had been trying to restrain his activities in Central Europe, and they might become really dangerous if he entered upon his great eastern venture without having settled with France and Britain first. When he did settle with them, he wanted to be able to concentrate all his forces in the west without having to worry about trouble with Poland on his eastern border, and he therefore tried by persuasion and pressure to convert that country into a satellite. All they and the Hungarians had to do was to acknowledge the overlordship of Berlin, share in the Czechoslovak booty, and keep his eastern flank quiet while he dealt with the West.[150] The subsequent fate of Poland and Hungary in this scheme of things was obviously open—they might be totally subjugated or further rewarded. The options were endless, but once the Western Powers had been dealt with, they would be Germany's options, and there was no need to decide ahead of time.

That the focus of Hitler's intentions beyond the immediate one of destroying Czechoslovakia was against the West is clear from a number of other actions taken and policies pursued by Germany after Munich. Because the successful effort to have Hungary and the unsuccessful one to have Poland join the Anti-Comintern Pact have just been reviewed, it may be best to turn first to the long and complicated negotiations by which Germany tried to have its existing Anti-Comintern Pact with Italy and Japan converted into a tripartite military alliance. The earlier stages of this effort have already been mentioned.[151] By August 1938 a deadlock had been reached in the negotiations, with the Japanese insisting on restricting the applicability of any new commitments to the Soviet Union while Germany wanted an alliance directed against all powers. This discrepancy remained after Munich, and here is an important clue to German policy aims. If the Germans wanted an alliance that promised them help against the Western Powers during the crisis over Czechoslovakia, why did they insist on this after the Munich settlement? In a way, Hitler had answered that question when he explained the need for a war to defeat England and France to Mussolini when they met on the way to the Munich meeting.[152] It was thus as a part of his expectation of a showdown with Britain and France as the next project that Hitler wanted a tripartite military alliance even after the Munich conference; in fact von Ribbentrop handed one of a series of drafts of the proposed treaty to Count Ciano at the meeting itself.[153] Unlike Hungary and Poland, Italy and Japan were

150. In this connection, the memorandum for military conversations with Italy that Keitel prepared on instructions from Hitler on 26 November 1938 and transmitted to von Ribbentrop is of considerable interest. Germany and Italy would fight in the west, crushing France first. The attitude of Hungary was expected to be favorable to the Axis while Poland and "the Balkans," presumably meaning Yugoslavia and Rumania, were considered doubtful. One of the tasks expected of Italy was to help keep Germany's eastern and southeastern flank quiet, if necessary by moving jointly with Hungarian forces against Poland (*G.D.*, D, 6, No. 411; cf. *S.U.*, No. 76). Von Ribbentrop explained to Canaris on 14 December that there would be a war with the Western Powers after the disappearance *(Ausschaltung)* of Czechoslovakia and with the closest ties to Poland (*Groscurth Diary*, p. 159).

151. See above, pp. 185–91.

152. Anfuso, pp. 75–79; Ciano, *Diary*, 29–30 September 1938, p. 240.

153. Sommer, pp. 141–45; Toscano, *Origins of the Pact of Steel*, pp. 41–44. These two accounts will be used heavily, and sources cited in them will generally not be referred to here. It should be noted that Toscano's account—the English edition being the last he revised before his death—is especially important for documents from the Italian archives to which he had access and which contain far more on the negotiations than the German archives.

looked upon as active rather than passive associates in the confrontation with the Western Powers.

While the Italians were still thinking about this project, von Ribbentrop was sent to Rome with a new draft treaty. Describing his proposal as a message for Mussolini from Hitler, von Ribbentrop invited himself to Rome by telephone on 23 October, the day before he asked Poland to join the Anti-Comintern Pact, and he discussed his new project in the Italian capital on 27 and 28 October.[154] The lengthy conversations impressed Ciano with the conviction that von Ribbentrop was absolutely determined on war. The German foreign minister told Mussolini that Hitler was certain there would be war with England and France in a few years and that it was now advisable to sign a tripartite alliance. The Japanese, he asserted, appeared to be willing, and opponents of an alliance in Tokyo might at any moment reverse that situation. Czechoslovakia was finished. Germany intended to continue good relations with Poland and to develop closer bonds with Yugoslavia, Rumania, and Hungary. With Russia weak for many years, "all our energies can be directed against the Western Democracies."[155] Although from the German point of view Italy was important to any war with France, the stress von Ribbentrop placed on the tripartite character of any agreement shows that Japan was considered critical for the coming war with England.

Mussolini's response was somewhat disappointing to the Germans. He agreed in principle that war with the Western Powers would indeed come; but he approved of an alliance only in principle, while arguing that the time for a formal signing had not yet arrived. The arguments Mussolini advanced for postponement do not sound particularly convincing, and nothing changed in regard to any of them between late October 1938 and January 1939 when he reversed himself. Mussolini's real reason for wanting to wait was presumably the desire to secure the immediate advantages of having the April agreement with England go into effect, something that was already clearly imminent and would be accomplished on 16 November 1938.[156] The Germans and Italians did agree to arbitrate jointly the territorial claim of Hungary against Czechoslovakia, and this led to the Vienna award of 2 November; but von Ribbentrop had to content himself for the time being with agreement only on the idea of a military alliance, an alliance which, as Mussolini pointed out explicitly, would be an offensive one.

154. Sommer, pp. 145–51; Toscano, *Origins of the Pact of Steel*, pp. 46–70; Ciano, *Diplomatic Papers*, pp. 242–46.
155. Ciano, *Diplomatic Papers*, p. 244. The reference to Poland was not as dishonest as it sounds; von Ribbentrop may well have expected Polish acceptance of the demands he had just presented.
156. *G.D.*, D, 4, Nos. 404, 409; Ciano, *Diary*, 27 October 1938, p. 265; *Harvey Diaries*, 4, 5, 20 October, pp. 209–10, 214–15; Memorandum by Lord Halifax on the Anglo-Italian Agreement, 21 October 1938, R 8513/23/22, FO 371/22414; *D.D.F.*, 2d, 12, Nos. 15, 38, 180, 236, 271.

On returning to Berlin, von Ribbentrop handed the draft alliance to his old friend Oshima Hiroshi, who had just officially become Japanese ambassador to Germany, replacing Togo Shigenori, whose opposition to closer relations with Germany had led to his transfer to Moscow. Like the newly appointed Japanese ambassador to Italy, Shiratori Toshio,[157] Oshima was an ardent believer in signing an alliance with the European Axis, but he would find it impossible to secure even agreement in principle from his government in Tokyo.

The Japanese government included advocates of an alliance with the Axis, but there was strong opposition, especially to the formulation that included the possibility of a war with England, something that was often seen in Japan as also including a possible war with the United States. As has been pointed out in the review of German-Japanese relations in the summer of 1938, there were those in the government who thought that Japan had all she could handle in the never ending war in China. If there was any other possible enemy against whom help might be desired, it was Russia, not England. Though eager to displace Britain's great influence and economic interests in East Asia, particularly in China, these elements still opposed a drastic break with England.

The alliance between the two island kingdoms had long since fallen in ruins, but there was a strong faction within the Tokyo government that saw only dangers and disadvantages in the complete rupture implied in a general alliance with Germany and Italy. In this attitude, they were supported by warnings and urgings from Britain as well as from the United States.[158] The fact that the British government, apparently from cryptographic intelligence or some other very good source, had quite accurate information on the Japanese position in the negotiations was of considerable assistance to them in their efforts to strengthen by discreet urgings those in Japan opposed to the general military alliance.[159] On careful consideration, the British decided that such cautioning was all they could do; there was no sense in trying to buy off Japan by concessions. The Japanese would work with Germany and Italy with or without an alliance if they thought it in their interests to do so, and they would break any alliance they might have if they did not wish to carry out its obligations. The Tokyo government would have to choose without any inducements from Great Britain to influence them.[160]

157. Shiratori did not, however, assume his position in Rome until the end of 1938. Note Ciano's comment on his predecessor, Hotta Masaaki, on his farewell visit of 21 October: "a fine face but as he is somewhat cool and fearful, he does not fit into these new times. We were carrying on a policy of the Triangle [Rome-Berlin-Tokyo], but he was always telling me stories about London" (*Diary*, p. 259).

158. Sommer, pp. 152–62; Drechsler, pp. 112–24. Note, esp., *G.D.*, D, 1, No. 607; *B.D.*, 3d, 8, Nos. 124, 473; *Hungarian Documents*, 2, No. 547.

159. See *B.D.*, 3d, 8, Nos. 254, 295, and the information from a most secret source Halifax gave the cabinet on 15 Februrary 1939, C 2029/421/62, FO 371/22944.

160. *B.D.*, 3d, 8, Nos. 318 (comments in F 13894/71/23, FO 371/22181), 364, 433, 441. Ott was considering a joint German-British mediation in the Sino-Japanese War, but both Berlin and London discouraged the idea; in addition to Sommer, p. 156, see Peck, No. 132.

For some time, the Tokyo authorities simply did not choose; that is, they debated what to do for several months, the key point holding up agreement being the extension of the applicability of the alliance to countries other than the Soviet Union. The Japanese did sign a cultural agreement with Germany on 25 November, the anniversary of the Anti-Comintern Pact; and von Ribbentrop took this as a harbinger of success for his tripartite project. There was, however, no favorable reaction to his draft pact from Tokyo which he might have used to hurry up the Italian government.[161] The delay of the Japanese should have suited the Italians, if not the Germans, but at the turn of the year, Mussolini changed his mind. Instead of delay, he now suddenly wanted a quick agreement.

The reversal of Mussolini's attitude was almost certainly the result of developments in Italy's relations with France. Although interested in securing the advantages of recognition of the Italian empire in East Africa by the implementation of the Anglo-Italian agreement of April 1938, Mussolini distinguished between England and France, his demands upon France being the more immediate. He therefore hardly welcomed the news that Germany, which was proposing a military alliance against England and France, was also planning a joint declaration with France analogous to that Hitler and Chamberlain had signed the day after the Munich conference. At Italy's request, certain changes were made in the planned German-French declaration, but although the Italians were kept informed about the project, they could hardly be expected to like it.[162]

What Mussolini does not appear to have realized for a while was that his alarm was completely unfounded. The German-French talks that produced the declaration of 6 December with von Ribbentrop traveling to Paris for the occasion was, from the point of view of the Germans, purely eyewash. If the French could be lulled into complacency and thereby restrained from a real effort at rearmament, that was all to the good; and Mussolini never quite grasped that in this respect German policy in reality fitted in very well with his own ambitions. Attentive to the propaganda effect, he saw it as crossing his hopes, and it took a few weeks for the Italian leader to recognize that what the Germans were telling both their own press and foreign diplomats was true, namely, that the promise to consult each other included in the declaration by France and Germany had no meaning or importance whatever for Germany. When Berlin said

161. Sommer, pp. 162–64, and esp. n.63; German press conference of 24 November 1938, Bundesarchiv, Traub, Z.Sg. 110/10, ff.155–56. The internal Japanese discussions are well summarized in Morley, pp. 73–78. For German economic activity in East Asia at this time, especially the development of new trade arrangements with Manchukuo, see Office of Military Government for Germany (U.S.), "Report on Deutsche Bank," Exhibits 225–30.

162. A useful account in Walter Bussmann, "Ein deutsch-französischer Verständigungs-versuch vom 6. Dezember 1938," *Nachrichten der Akademie der Wissenschaften in Göttingen*, 1, *Philologisch-Historische Klasse*, 1953, No. 2. The German published documents are in *G.D.*, D, 4, chap. 3; French documents in *D.D.F.*, 2d, 12. See also *Hungarian Documents*, 3, No. 97; *S.U.*, No. 82; "Informationsbericht Nr. 83," 5 December 1938, Bundesarchiv, Brammer, Z.Sg. 101/33, ff.381–83; Adamthwaite, pp. 284–94.

that there was no substance to the agreement, it really meant it.[163] As von Weizsäcker had told the Italian ambassador on 8 November, the thing that counted was the will to carry out a promise, and of this there was none; in the six weeks since the parallel Anglo-German declaration, Germany had not to his knowledge paid any attention to it.[164] As the second man in the German foreign ministry, this was one thing he was in a position to know.

During November 1938 Italian-French relations deteriorated considerably. They had been fraught with tension before, in spite of the temporary rapprochement of 1935, but the situation became far worse as Mussolini turned toward his anti-French objectives. It was this turn, combined with the recognition that England could not be separated from France—a point reinforced by the Anglo-French meeting in Paris on 24 November—that made the Italians so anxious for general staff conversations with the Germans even while they delayed on the alliance project during November and December.[165] The German response to this idea was not overly enthusiastic, partly because of doubts about the military value of Italy's armed forces, and partly because the political situation was still unresolved. The rapid worsening of Italy's relations with France would soon remove the latter obstacle.

Most likely on instructions of Fascist party secretary Achille Starace, acting on a tip from Mussolini, at the conclusion of Ciano's speech of 30 November in the Chamber of Fasces and Corporations the deputies began shouting in unison the specifics of Italy's "national aspirations": Tunis, Corsica, Nice, and Savoy.[166] The reaction of the French government and public to this noisy demonstration was immediate and loud. The vast public uproar actually suggested to some that war was imminent—and the Germans for a while worried that Italy might drag them into war at a time of Rome's rather than Berlin's choosing. This fear was as unwarranted as Mussolini's worry about the Franco-German declaration.[167] Italy was no

163. On the worthlessness of the agreement, see *G.D.*, D, 4, Nos. 337, 343; Dertinger, "Informationsbericht Nr. 78," 24 November 1938, Bundesarchiv, Brammer, Z.Sg. 101/33, ff.367–69 ("Einen realpolitischen Wert für die internationale Lage hat nach hiesiger Auffassung dieser Vertrag ebensowenig wie der zwischen Chamberlain und Hitler"); *Hungarian Documents*, 3, No. 121; *Łukasiewicz Papers*, pp. 152–60. Note Hitler's comment to the new French ambassador, Coulondre on 21 November that the recovery of Alsace-Lorraine would cost too much German blood (Robert Coulondre, *Von Moskau nach Berlin* [Bonn: Athenäum, 1950], p. 309), a form of casualty mathematics characteristic of Hitler but hardly reassuring in its implications. What if the expected casualty statistics were to change?

164. *G.D.*, D, 4, No. 349.

165. A good account of this is in Toscano, *Origins of the Pact of Steel*, pp. 78–85. See Mack Smith, pp. 134–36; *D.D.F.*, 2d, 12; Adamthwaite, pp. 255–58. There was also a German-Italian cultural agreement signed on 22 November 1938.

166. Toscano, *Origins of the Pact of Steel*, pp. 86, 89–96. German press directives of 1, 2, 6, 10 December 1938, Bundesarchiv, Traub, Z.Sg. 110/10, ff.177, 183, 192, 210; *Hungarian Documents*, 3, No. 125; *B.D.*, 3d, 3, Nos. 461, 462, 464, 465.

167. Toscano (p. 96) correctly points out that German worries about Italy rushing into war were greater "than Rome ever imagined." See also *Hungarian Documents*, 3, No. 330.

more about to start a real war than Germany was about to make a real peace with France; although Italy did indeed have demands on France, Mussolini was at that time thinking of making enough noise that the French would accept in quiet relief his planned coup against Albania.[168] Mussolini did, however, also come to the conclusion that a formal alliance with Germany and Japan would now be to Italy's immediate advantage in her confrontation with France. When on 15 December he saw Oshima, whom von Ribbentrop had urged to go to Rome to advocate the tripartite alliance, Mussolini stated that his decision to go ahead with the pact would come between the middle of January and the middle of February, a very substantial change from the indefinite time he had mentioned to von Ribbentrop less than two months before.[169]

In the latter part of December, Mussolini decided to speed up the process; the more he thought about it, the better he liked it. On 23 December he told Ciano that he had decided to accept von Ribbentrop's proposal, and on 1 January he instructed Ciano to inform the Germans that Italy wanted to sign the tripartite alliance during January 1939.[170] The developing tension with France and the accompanying Italian public hostility toward that country were probably the main factors in this speeding up of the timetable.[171] The Germans were delighted by this piece of good news, and von Ribbentrop promised to get Japanese approval in time for a big signature ceremony in Berlin at the end of the month. With a text agreed on by Germany and Italy and with the Japanese ambassadors in Berlin and Rome enthusiastic about the alliance, all looked ready. But these appearances were deceiving. The Japanese government would come to a favorable conclusion in January 1939 no more than it had in the preceding two months. In lengthy internal debates, diplomatic circumlocutions, a conference of Japanese representatives in Europe, and the sending of a special diplomatic mission from Japan to Europe, the Japanese evaded saying yes to the German-Italian proposal.[172]

The critical point, now as before and for the whole spring and summer of 1939, was that the Japanese were willing to participate in new commitments as long as these were restricted in their applicability to the Soviet Union and to no other power; Germany and Italy, however, were interested in precisely the reverse. The succeeding drafts proposed by Berlin and Rome gradually removed previous references to the Comintern and

168. Ciano, *Diary*, 3 December 1938, pp. 291–92.
169. Ibid., 15, 16 December 1938, pp. 196–98.
170. Toscano, *Origins of the Pact of Steel*, pp. 101–8; Sommer, pp. 165–69; *Weizsäcker-Papiere*, p. 149.
171. Mussolini had repeatedly emphasized the negative attitude of many Italians as an obstacle to a formal alliance with Germany; he may well have believed that such objections would be muted if the alliance were signed at a time of obvious tension between Italy and France.
172. Accounts in Toscano, *Origins of the Pact of Steel*, pp. 116–66; Sommer, pp. 171–92; Morley, pp. 78–90, 273–82; see also *Hungarian Documents*, 3, No. 326.

other language suggesting that the pact was directed against Russia, and instead stressed the comprehensive nature of the obligations to be assumed. Conversely, the drafts discussed by the Tokyo cabinet stressed the primacy of hostility to Russia and allowed for the alliance to be directed against other countries only if these were acting jointly with Russia or had themselves turned communist. Von Ribbentrop long remained optimistic about the chances of his scheme. He was encouraged in this by Oshima, while Shiratori, though personally an advocate of signing, was more realistic in his assessment of the situation in Tokyo and hence more accurate in his expressions to the Italian government. There was some hope that by delaying a frank communication to the German government of the attitude in Tokyo, there would be an opportunity for the elements in the Japanese government who favored the alliance directed as much against England and France—and by implication the United States—as against the Soviet Union to win out in the agonizing debate. Although a variety of formulas was tried, none could be found that reconciled the incompatible. Since the advocates of a general alliance could not get their way, especially in the face of the emperor's siding with those opposed to it,[173] the German and Italian governments became increasingly convinced that agreement on a tripartite alliance was at least for the time being impossible.[174]

The turn toward a bilateral German-Italian alliance in view of the failure of tripartite negotiations would not come until after 15 March and will, therefore, be discussed in the next chapter. Two aspects of the German-Italian negotiations, however, must be examined at this point because they provide considerable insight into the policies of both countries, especially of Germany, in the winter of 1938–39. The first of these is an implicit but highly revealing aspect of the tripartite negotiations. If the Germans and Italians had at any time been willing to settle for an agreement directed against Russia, they would have secured the immediate and enthusiastic participation of Japan. The fact that the two Axis powers were willing to let the negotiations drag on and eventually fail over their insistence on a treaty whose provisions were also directed against the Western Powers surely illuminates the priorities of Berlin and Rome during those months. It is in this regard that the tripartite pact negotiations must be seen in the same context as the German insistence that Poland and Hungary join the Anti-Comintern Pact; as German satellites, those two countries would keep Germany's eastern flank quiet while Germany in alliance with Italy and Japan fought the Western Powers.[175] By 15

173. Okata Tokushiro's reading of the evidence in Morley, pp. 85–87, appears to me to be conclusive on this point.
174. As in late 1938, the British and Americans again urged Japan not to burn her bridges to the West; see *B.D.*, 3d, 8, Nos. 467, 479, 488, 491, 501, 519, 523, 526, 536, 543; 9, Nos. 20, 24; *U.S., Japan*, 2:161–63.
175. Note *Hungarian Documents*, 3, Nos. 272, 371.

March, neither of these schemes had much prospect of success: Poland had declined to join the Anti-Comintern Pact, and the Japanese were unwilling to face war with the West. On neither of these projects, however, had the German government given up all hope of success; and the new decisions required by Berlin's recognition of these failures were therefore not taken until after 15 March.[176]

The other aspect that should be noted is that as the Italians agreed to align themselves militarily with Germany, they raised some practical problems in the relationship between the two countries which they hoped to have settled in the framework of their new partnership status. There were problems in regard to the foreign exchange that Italy was required to pay for a small proportion of her imports from Germany, the balance being settled in a clearing account. Italy was desperately short of foreign exchange and wanted the requirement dropped, but Germany was in about the same situation and did not feel it could do without what Italy was obliged to provide. Both Hitler and Mussolini became involved personally in the decisions made in this controversy, which was eventually resolved by a compromise, but which showed that a desire for closer relations did not automatically solve all problems.[177]

The other question was the old one of South Tyrol. The Germans had expressed a willingness to accept a mass transfer of the South Tyrol inhabitants who thought of themselves as Germans; but it had hardly been appropriate to develop and implement plans to accomplish such a transfer of population at a time when the presence of a similar element, larger but better treated, within Czechoslovakia was to provide the political excuse for the destruction of that country. Discussion of the South Tyrol issue had, therefore, been muted in the summer and early fall of 1938. Appropriately, Hitler himself appears to have raised the issue again with the Italians at the Munich conference, which ended the cause of earlier diffidence. When subsequently the Italians decided to go ahead with the alliance project von Ribbentrop had suggested, they simultaneously thought it best to take up this question with the Germans, especially in regard to those persons in South Tyrol who held German (or had until recently held Austrian) citizenship.

Von Ribbentrop, who was obdurate on the foreign exchange question, was certainly willing to be accommodating on this matter. He could repeat Hitler's decision that there could be no South Tyrol question between Italy and Germany. Many South Tyroleans could be quietly transferred to Germany right away, though a total transfer would have to await Germany's acquisition of appropriate living space for them. Since Hitler and von Ribbentrop, at any rate, did not expect this contingency to be far off,

176. Toscano (p. 124) appears to me to have turned this around when he argues that Poland's refusal thwarted the anti-Soviet plans of Germany at that time. Had German policy been directed against the Soviet Union in the winter of 1938–39, why let the negotiations with Japan fail when that country was more than willing to go along with such a policy?

177. Documents on this issue may be found in *G.D.*, D, 4, chap. 4.

the problem did not look particularly difficult to them. As for some small-scale immediate transfers, the Germans could and did begin on that promptly.[178] The Berlin government found it easier to make concesssions to their Italian ally when mere people, not hard cash, were the subject of discussion.

By late February and early March 1939, Germany and Italy were moving toward a general alliance with each other. On Italy's side the major motivating factors were the claims against France and the decision to move to the seizure of Albania, probably early in April.[179] On the German side, it was the expectation of war with the Western Powers. Either with or without such a war, Hitler expected the return of Germany's prewar colonial empire. But this was to be a return free of conditions, restrictions, or German diplomatic concessions; and the soundings from the West in this regard were all waved aside.[180] On 25 January 1939 Hitler would phrase this attitude in terms appropriate to his listener by telling the Italian fascist leader Roberto Farinacci that he would not loosen Germany's ties to Italy in return for the colonies.[181] He simply expected to get them back, and the desultory preliminary preparations for colonies made earlier in 1938 were replaced by far more precise and determined planning in the winter of 1938–39.[182]

The details of colonial preparations reveal little about German foreign policy at this time, but the general decisions Hitler made and communicated to the agencies and individuals involved certainly reflect both his general concern with the whole question and his attitude toward relations with the West. By early December 1938 Hitler had decided that Germany would demand all her colonies back, that he would offer no compensation in any form, and that he expected to organize a state colonial office out of the National Socialist party's Colonial Policy Office.[183] In view of the

178. Ibid., Nos. 427, 444; Toscano, *Origins of the Pact of Steel*, pp. 109–10, 117, 119; Latour, pp. 28–30.
179. Toscano, *Origins of the Pact of Steel*, pp. 127–31; for Italian interest in prompt staff talks with the Germans, see ibid., pp. 162–65.
180. Although not as significant as the publicity attendant upon it might lead one to believe, the approach of South African minister Oswald Pirow belongs in this context. On Pirow's trip and Hitler's rejection of the conditions attached to the Pirow proposals, see *Wiener Library Bulletin*, 12, Nos. 5–6 (1958), 53; *G.D.*, D, 4, Nos. 268, 270–72; C 14063/84/18, FO 371/21683; *D.D.F.*, 2d, 12, Nos. 217, 294, 295, 324, 411; Gilbert (Berlin) tel. 758 of 28 December 1938, State 741.62/325; Oswald Pirow comments on 16 November 1951, Munich, Institut für Zeitgeschichte, ZS 283; and the document cited in n.183, below. Note also the account of the Hitler–Karl Haushofer conversation of November referred to in James Douglas-Hamilton, *Motive for a Mission* (New York: St. Martin's, 1971), p. 84 (the same meeting as that mentioned in *G.D.*, D, 5, No. 99, cited in n.81, above).
181. See the letter of Farinacci to Ciano of 25 January 1939 cited in Toscano, *Origins of the Pact of Steel*, p. 122, n.102. On this day Hitler also met with the leadership of the National Socialist party ("Daten aus alten Notizbüchern," p. 37); in the evening the leaders of the army, navy, and air force were shown the new chancellery (Domarus, 2:1045).
182. See Weinberg, "German Colonial Plans and Policies," pp. 464–68; Hildebrand, pp. 594–98. Cf. *D.D.B.*, 4, No. 42.
183. Memorandum of 6 December 1938 on a conference in the OKW, Wehrwirtschafts- und Rüstungsamt, T-77, 642/1838570–72.

negotiations with Japan for a tripartite military alliance, the Pacific portion of the former German colonial empire was quickly excluded from the discussion, and it was assumed that Germany would insist on the return only of her African colonies.[184] On 13 February, Hitler told the head of the party's Colonial Policy Office that his agency would have charge of Germany's colonies; and in subsequent weeks he laid down some basic guidelines that Franz Ritter von Epp was to follow in preparing the administration of Germany's restored colonial empire.[185] This was one field of endeavor in which Hitler believed there would be no change of direction after 15 March 1939; Germany was to go ahead with her plans.[186] Not long after strict directives were issued that the term "South Tyrol" was to disappear from German maps and publications,[187] instructions also went out that the German colonies should henceforth be referred to as such—no longer as "former" colonies.[188]

Hitler certainly did not expect that crushing France and humbling England would require no effort on Germany's part. By the diplomatic moves just reviewed he hoped to strengthen Germany's position substantially, but as in the past he depended primarily on Germany's own armed might.[189] At the very time in October 1938 that the mobilization of the German army for an attack against Czechoslovakia was being reversed, Hitler ordered a new program to build up the German air force for use against England.[190] Originally scheduled as a fivefold increase, this enormous program had to be scaled down in practice even while it was being nominally affirmed, but the general thrust was clear: Munich was not an end to the danger of war but the prelude to hostilities with the Western Powers.[191] The strategic planning of the German air force during the winter of 1938–39 was accordingly directed toward plans for war against England,[192] and the National Defense Council (*Reichs-*

184. See the report on a conference in the Naval High Command on 25 January 1939, ibid., frame 1838549, and "Bericht 1 über den Stand der kolonialen Vorarbeiten," 27 January 1939, ibid., frames 1838561–64.

185. Details in Weinberg, "Colonial Plans and Policies," pp. 466–68. See also Joel C. Hudson (U.S. consul Berlin), Report 1268, "German Colonial Questions," 21 March 1939, State 862.014/456.

186. "Bericht 3 über den Stand der kolonialen Vorarbeiten," 18 April 1939, T-77, 642/1838577–78.

187. *G.D.*, D, 4, No. 453; "Informationsbericht Nr. 18," 3 March 1939, Bundesarchiv, Brammer, Z.Sg. 101/34, f.83.

188. Instructions of 24 April 1939 in T-77, 642/1838555.

189. Von Ribbentrop's summary of Hitler's opinions on this subject is recorded in Ciano, *Diplomatic Papers*, p. 243.

190. See the record of Göring's conference of 14 October 1938, *TMWC*, 27:160–64; cf. Irving, *Milch*, p. 67.

191. The details can be followed in Homze, pp. 222–27.

192. See ibid., pp. 242–44; *TMWC*, 35:562–63; Karl Gundelach, "Gedanken über die Führung eines Luftkrieges gegen England bei der Luftflotte 2 in den Jahren 1938/1939," *Wehrwissenschaftliche Rundschau*, 10 (1960), 33–46. The appointment of Hans Jeschonnek as chief of staff of the Luftwaffe as of 1 February 1939 was Göring's way of assuring compliance with Hitler's wishes for rapid expansion; the ambitious young general was a devoted supporter of Hitler and any and all inspirations of the Führer (see Homze, pp.

verteidigungsrat) created in 1933 held its first meeting on 18 November 1938 to hear Göring hold forth on the need for Germany to build up her armaments.[193]

The German navy, like the air force, was ordered to speed up its construction program. On 1 November Hitler told Raeder to move the construction program forward as rapidly as possible,[194] and during the subsequent weeks a whole new program was developed. With Hitler pushing for the maximum possible naval program, what came to be known as the "Z-Plan" was prepared and then approved on 17 January 1939.[195] It was understood, of course, that it would take several years for the larger ships provided by the Z-Plan to be completed, but Hitler was at this time thinking of a war against the West that was still some time off. To make sure that within the tight limits of Germany's resources the navy could be made ready in the shortest possible time, the new construction program was given priority over all other projects, including those of the army and air force, by a special decree issued by Hitler on 27 January.[196] On the same day, naval aviation was turned over to the jurisdiction of the German air force; this and the decision to concentrate on the construction of battleships to the exclusion of aircraft carriers were the price the German navy had to pay to Göring for its priority position. These two concessions would make it essential for the German air force to participate in any war against England by attacks on English shipping as well as on land targets. The navy's Z-Plan would be only barely initiated in the few months remaining before the outbreak of war, but it shows the real thrust of Hitler's policy in the period after his promise to Chamberlain that the Anglo-German Naval Treaty along with the Munich agreement would set the tone for Germany's future relations with England.[197]

If new expansion programs seemed appropriate for the German navy and air force in Hitler's eyes, the army was expected to continue to grow along previously established lines.[198] The main concern of the Führer in regard to this branch of the armed forces was its loyalty and absolute obedience to his commands and inspiration. A series of generals who had

---

235–37). As it became obvious that the Luftwaffe was failing, he would commit suicide on 18/19 August 1943.

193. *TMWC*, 32:411–15.

194. Ibid., 35:567; Dülffer, p. 492.

195. The best summary is in Dülffer, pp. 492–501; the full text of the navy's 25 October 1938 memorandum on a naval war with England is in Salewski, 3:27–63. See also Thiess, pp. 130–31, 187.

196. Dülffer, p. 502; *G.D.*, D, 7:556.

197. For the problems relating to the Z-Plan until 1 September 1939, see Dülffer, pp. 503ff. This book also contains a discussion of the last Anglo-German naval discussions. For an example of the interrelations of the navy's priority and other programs, in this case that of antiaircraft guns, see Homze, p. 229.

198. There was some experimentation on the seized Czechoslovak fortifications as a sample of how to break through the Maginot Line.

been particularly outspoken in their criticism of the military risks Germany ran in the Czechoslovak crisis were retired from duty, and the others were overawed, lectured to, and generally argued into line.[199] With von Brauchitsch more subservient than ever and Halder willing to go along, Hitler could feel confident that there would be no repetition of the doubts and hesitations he had contended with in the summer of 1938. The quiet acceptance by the army of the barbaric events in Germany on 9 and 10 November attested to a moral bankruptcy already revealed after 30 June 1934. Hitler, naturally enough, preferred enthusiasm to acquiescence, and he personally undertook an effort to generate that. In a series of talks to selected officers, he tried to show how Germany's strong racial core gave it greater strength than any of its potential enemies, even including the United States. As the first of the operations Hitler expected to carry out in 1939 approached, he lectured the higher officers of the army on 10 February 1939 on the need for their absolute obedience and total devotion in a state that he expected to lead into war with England and France.[200]

In view of the reaction of the German public to the obvious danger of war at the height of the crisis at the end of September and their enthusiastic applause for Chamberlain and Daladier who seemed to them to be peacemakers, Hitler was especially concerned about getting the German public into a more bellicose mood.[201] Always very much interested in the issue of home-front morale, he set about ways to correct what appeared to him to be a major deficiency in Germany's preparations for war. Hitler's vehement speeches denouncing England right after Munich, which will be discussed subsequently, were probably a part of his campaign to prepare the German public for the paths along which he planned to lead them; but his main emphasis in the weeks after Munich was on a press campaign. On 20 October the German press was instructed to stress the need for increases in armaments in order to raise the war willingness of the population.[202] On 10 November, Hitler personally spoke at length to several hundred German journalists. A few hours after authorizing the great pogrom, Hitler reviewed his tactics in 1938 for the journalists, attacked the critics of his policies, and called for greater efforts in the future.[203]

199. Müller, pp. 381–87.

200. Ibid., p. 383. There is a full account of the speech in Jochen Thies, *Architekt der Weltherrschaft* (Düsseldorf: Droste, 1976), pp. 79–80, 112–18. Other speeches of a similar nature by Hitler early in 1939 are discussed, ibid., pp. 119–20. Göring also spoke to a group of high army officers about this time.

201. For the continuation of this attitude, see Gilbert report 480 of 5 December 1938, State 862.00/3806.

202. "Informationsbericht Nr. 71," 20 October 1938, Bundesarchiv, Brammer, Z.Sg. 101/33, f.319.

203. The text of a recording has been edited by Wilhelm Treue, "Rede Hitlers vor der deutschen Press (10. November 1938)," *Vierteljahrshefte für Zeitgeschichte,* 6, No. 2 (April 1958), 175–91. Dertinger, who was one of those present, prepared a report which is in

The central points in Hitler's speech were clearly a general disregard of any and all prospects for international peace and the need to have the press work hard to bring the public solidly behind the regime in any future war, regardless of the purposes of such a war and any possible setbacks in it. The very fact that in the early years of his rule Hitler had felt obliged to stress the peaceful nature of German policy he now cited as a reason for the press to redouble its efforts. The propaganda campaign in the press would have the double task of correcting any temporary illusions of peace growing out of the recent peaceful settlement of a major dispute as well as removing any still lingering effects at home of those assertions of peaceful intent that Hitler had once used to lull suspicion abroad. Here was the domestic propaganda program preparing the public to call for war and accept its sacrifices at the same time as the military and diplomatic preparations were also under way.[204] It is only when this range of preparations and policies is looked at as a whole that one can deduce from Hitler's actions in a great variety of foreign and domestic fields some understanding of his determination to move forward in 1939.

Reports of Hitler's speech of 10 November soon reached the government in London[205] and presumably other governments as well, not a surprising development since hundreds were present and no one was pledged to secrecy. What had been the British and French reaction to the European developments after Munich? Chamberlain saw the reports on Hitler's comments at the end of November 1938; by that time the hope for peace raised by the Munich agreement had already largely evaporated.

In the days immediately after the Munich conference, the sense of relief over the avoidance of war mingled in England with several other strains of thought. There was a feeling of shame over the treatment of Czechoslovakia, over its sacrifice to the fear of war.[206] There was considerable sentiment for a more vigorous program of rearmament to make up the deficiencies revealed in the crisis and assure a stronger position for En-

---

Bundesarchiv, Brammer, Z.Sg. 101/33, ff.357–61, to which he referred in his "Informationsbericht Nr. 49," of 16 May 1939, ibid., 101/34, f.251. Note also Dertinger's postwar comments in Institut für Zeitgeschichte, ZS 870.

A report based on information given the *Times* correspondent in Germany was sent to the Foreign Office by the British chargé in Berlin, Sir George Ogilvie-Forbes, on 18 November 1938 (C 14136/42/18, FO 371/21658); a more detailed report by one of the correspondents present, Count von Toggenburg, was given to an official in the Foreign Office on 23 November (C 14476/1941/18, FO 371/21746). Together with a secret service report on the speech, these documents were sent to Chamberlain.

204. The speech of Heinrich Himmler to SS officers on 8 November with its wild anti-Semitism and insistence on the common aims of Germany and Italy fits in here; see Bradley F. Smith and Agnes F. Peterson (eds.), *Heinrich Himmler: Geheimreden 1933 bis 1945* (Frankfurt/M: Propyläen, 1974), pp. 25–49.

205. See n.203, above.

206. For a similar reaction in Australia, see Andrews, pp. 149ff. A very interesting and positive evaluation from the Canadian side is in *Documents on Canadian External Relations*, 6, No. 903.

gland in any future crisis caused by Germany.[207] Many of those who had not been supporters of rearmament earlier now changed their position wholly or in part.[208] The record shows Lord Halifax as especially insistent on building up England's armed forces.[209] A related factor was the concern over French weakness, especially in the air; and the London government did what it could to spur the French to remedy a grave deficiency of which the French were themselves very conscious indeed.[210]

Another area in which the British government hoped to shore up its defenses was the diplomatic-economic one. As early as the summer of 1938, as a result of the German annexation of Austria, some consideration had been given by London to the problem of assisting the countries of Southeast Europe to maintain their independence of Germany by new trade procedures that might offer them alternative markets for those products that Germany was accepting as part of her effort to dominate the area.[211] After Munich, measures of this kind seemed more urgent than ever. Although it was recognized that to some extent the complementary trade relations between Germany and the countries of Southeast Europe were natural, and that the possibilities open to England were relatively limited, there were some steps that could and should be taken. If Britain did nothing, these countries would have little choice but to enter the German orbit. As one memorandum on the effects of Munich on Southeast Europe put it, "the immutability of public taste" could no longer be brought forward as a reason for not buying Greek tobacco; English smokers would just have to develop a taste for it.[212] In this and other related matters, the British government attempted to assist the countries of Southeast Europe in maintaining an economic independence of Germany.[213] Without going into great detail, however, it would be fair to say

207. *Pownall Diary*, 3 October 1938ff., pp. 164ff.; Cabinet 48 (38) of 3 October 1938, C 11611/540/62, FO 371/21633; C 13298/429/62, FO 371/21632; C 12505, C 12571/1425/18, FO 371/21710; *Ironside Diary*, 2 November 1938, p. 70. The appointment of Sir John Anderson as lord privy seal with special responsibility for air raid precautions (ARP) on 1 November 1938 belongs in this context (Wheeler-Bennet, *Sir John Anderson*, pp. 211–15).

208. The Labor party finally dropped its opposition to rearmament, though they would remain opposed to conscription. On Lord Lothian's views, see Butler, *Lord Lothian*, p. 226.

209. This is evident from the cabinet and the Committee on Foreign Policy minutes and Lord Halifax's pushing for a national register and then conscription in the winter of 1938–39. See CAB 27/624; Gibbs, pp. 510–11.

210. French air rearmament after Munich is discussed below; on British urging of such French steps, see C 11641/55/17, FO 371/21600.

211. C 2777/1941/18, FO 371/21715 (commentary on *B.D.*, 3d, 1, No. 121); R 5338, R 5362/94/67, FO 371/22342.

212. Nicholls to Mallet, 24 October 1938, C 12915/772/18, FO 371/21705. For other documents on British efforts to support Greece by taking part of the Greek tobacco crop, see R 8368, R 8384, R 9728/361/19, FO 371/22363; 33d meeting of the cabinet Committee on Foreign Policy, 21 November 1938, CAB 27/624.

213. C 14616/541/18, FO 371/21704; C 13864, C 13865/772/18, FO 371/21705; R 8044, R 8690/94/67, FO 371/22344; R 9045/94/67, FO 371/22345. See also R 8921/626/21, FO 371/22380; 37th meeting of the cabinet Committee on Foreign Policy, 8 February 1939, CAB 27/624; *Cadogan Diary*, 17 and 18 October 1938, p. 121.

that only in the cases of Rumania, Greece, and Turkey did these measures attain any real measure of success.[214]

The push for rearmament and the effort to counter German economic domination of Southeast Europe were not, however, the only, and at first certainly not the most, important reaction to Munich in the British government.[215] There was considerable hope that the agreement reached at Munich and the Anglo-German Declaration signed the day after might open up a new era in which there would in fact be better relations between England and Germany. If Hitler's last territorial demand in Europe had been met, there was perhaps an opportunity to reopen the conversations looking toward a general European settlement that had been broken off after the Hitler-Henderson meeting of 3 March 1938, at which Hitler had ignored the British approach suggesting colonial concessions in return for the maintenance of the political status quo in Central and Eastern Europe. The annexation of Austria had put a halt to conversations about an Anglo-German settlement, and the hopeful sign that some in London thought they had seen in the conversation with Wiedemann had turned out to be a mirage.

Now, in the aftermath of Munich, optimism revived, and Chamberlain himself was one of those most determined not to allow to slip by what might be a real opportunity. From a perspective of several decades, one has only to think of the moves toward a lessening of tensions after the Cuban missile crisis to see how the averting of war can lead those on the brink in other directions; the English government of 1938 could look back to the Dogger Bank incident of 1904, which had brought England face to face with war with Russia and from which those two long-term antagonists had moved toward an entente. Within the British government, the possibility of a new approach to Germany was studied with care in the aftermath of the Czechoslovak crisis.[216] Since the colonial issue had been brought up by the British themselves on 3 March, and since it was believed to be one of the few, if not the only, issue actually outstanding between London and Berlin, the earlier British ideas on this subject were

214. On British efforts to compete with Germany in regard to Turkish trade credits, see *G.D.*, D, 5, Nos. 552, 553; E 555/9/44, FO 371/23283; E 1177/43/44, FO 371/23284. For the British economic counteroffensive in Rumania and its successes at this time, see Marguerat, pp. 103–19.

215. There was some discussion of a reorganization of the cabinet, which Lord Halifax urged but Chamberlain would not agree to.

216. Note the 15 December 1938 internal Foreign Office explanation of a letter of 5 October on the censorship of anti-Nazi plays: "As we then hoped that, as a result of the Munich Agreement, we were entering upon an era of more friendly relations with Germany, and as we had in mind the possibility of getting the German Government to co-operate in facilitating the emigration of Jews, we were particularly anxious not to cause unnecessary harm in our relations with Germany." C 15573/528/18, FO 371/21701. The general situation is reviewed in Donald Lammers, "From Whitehall after Munich: The Foreign Office and the Future Course of British Policy," *Historical Journal*, 16, No. 4 (Dec. 1973), 831–56. See also *D.D.F.*, 2d, 12, Nos. 41, 88, 219, 226, 280.

reviewed to consider the possibility of perhaps reopening the question and discussing it with Germany.[217]

These hopes and expectations were quickly and thoroughly dashed by Berlin. In response to the reports from the German embassy in London on British desires for better relations with Germany, State Secretary von Weizsäcker explained that there was absolutely no interest in any such ideas in Berlin, where all plans and projects were moving in an exactly opposite direction.[218] While von Weizsäcker was quietly discouraging, Hitler was positively violent in public. A vehement anti-British speech at Saarbrücken on 8 October set the theme for a continuing anti-British tone in the German press and in the speeches of other German leaders.[219] This campaign certainly had its effects in England, and any hopes which survived that barrage were eliminated by the impact of the anti-Jewish pogrom of November.[220] German persecution of the Jews had affected the tone of Anglo-German relations in the past, but there had been a countervailing force in the argument that such behavior on the part of Germany might be in part a reaction to the troubles Germany had suffered as a result of war, defeat, a hard peace treaty, and the depression. The fact that the most violent persecution followed Germany's greatest diplomatic triumph gave the lie to all such excuses, and the remnants of pro-German sympathies in England burned up in the flames and smoke that destroyed the synagogues in Germany.[221]

Before the turn of British policy away from consideration of a general settlement with Germany and the implications of this turn are examined in detail, it might be best to review briefly the role of the November pogrom in the evolution of policy in the one other major power where the government and public were definitively turned against the Third Reich by that conspicuous sign of a reversion to barbarism, the United States.

The relations of Germany with the United States had continued to be rather poor during 1938. The American public was alarmed by the antics

217. C 14471/42/18, FO 371/21659; introductory notes to the memorandum on the colonial problem in C 1305/184/18, FO 371/21679; C 13430, C 13657/184/18, FO 371/21682; *U.S.*, 1938, 1:95–97; *Cadogan Diary*, pp. 116–20, 122–24; *D.D.F.*, 2d, 12, Nos. 258, 280, 306; German information from London of 21 October 1938, Bundesarchiv, Brammer, Z.Sg. 101/33, f.327. Pirow's trip to Germany touched on colonial matters although by then the question was no longer actively considered in London. Note Arnold J. Toynbee's proposal of 15 October 1938 that all of Germany's colonies be returned to her with her Pacific colonial empire increased to include all of New Guinea and part or all of Borneo as a means of securing German support against Japan in East Asia, C 13691/42/18, FO 371/21658. For Toynbee's suggestion of concessions to Germany in 1936, see Weinberg, *Foreign Policy*, p. 259, n.85.

218. *G.D.*, D, 4, Nos. 250–54, 260; 5, No. 73.

219. The Saarbrücken speech is in Domarus, 1:954–56 (but dated to 9 October). See also Wilson to Moffat, 22 October 1938, Moffat Papers, Vol. 14; von Hassell, 15 October 1938, p. 27; *D.D.F.*, 2d, 12, Nos. 60, 110.

220. See Haim Shamir, "Die Kristallnacht, die Notlage der deutschen Juden und die Haltung Englands," *Jahrbuch des Instituts für Deutsche Geschichte*, 1 (1972), 171–214; *Harvey Diaries*, 13 November 1938, pp. 217–19.

221. Note Dirksen's report of 17 November, *G.D.*, D, 4, No. 269; cf. *Hungarian Documents*, 3, No. 49; Irving (ed.), *Breach of Security*, pp. 50–51.

of the German-American Bund, and the American government was concerned about the signs of German aggression in Europe.[222] There was,
furthermore, a number of minor issues in dispute between the two countries, ranging from American refusal to sell the Germans helium for their
dirigibles to the German refusal to continue payments on the Austrian
debts to American creditors although all other creditors were being
paid.[223] German diplomats assumed that in view of the bad state of
German-American relations, any war that broke out as a result of the
Czechoslovak crisis would, sooner or later, see the United States entering
on the side of Germany's enemies. The Munich agreement ended this
particular danger, but it left the American government worried about the
growing might of Germany.[224]

The whole problem of Jewish and other refugees from Germany had
received considerable attention—if little helpful action—from the Washington government even before the November 1938 pogrom.[225] The reaction to the pogrom itself was extremely violent. Public opinion turned
finally and definitively against Germany, and the government reflected
popular dismay.[226] The American ambassador to Germany was recalled
to Washington to the accompaniment of a strong statement personally
made more pointed by President Roosevelt, and the Germans retaliated
by recalling Dieckhoff from Washington to the accompaniment of propaganda attacks on the United States.[227] Relations deteriorated to the
point where it looked as if they might be broken off altogether,[228] and
although this did not happen, the situation remained very strained and the
refugee problem helped to keep it so.[229]

As before, the economic aspects of German-American relations quickly
reflected the basic political and ideological clash. Even in late October
1938 the possibility of an agreement with Germany under the Reciprocal
Trade Agreements Act was still being considered in the State Department.[230] A new German proposal was, however, turned down in Decem-

222. See above, pp. 249–52.

223. "Bestellungen aus der Pressekonferenz," 12 May 1938, Bundesarchiv, Brammer,
Z.Sg. 101/11, f.361; *U.S.,* 1938, 2:494–500; *Hungarian Documents,* 3, No. 466. See also
Offner, pp. 234ff.

224. Moffat to Gilbert, 3 October 1938, Moffat Papers, Vol. 13; Moffat to Wilson, 5
October 1938, ibid., Vol. 14.

225. *U.S.,* 1938, 1:791–92, 794–96, 799–801, 809; 2:446–51; cf. ibid., 1938, 2:596–98.

226. Günther Moltmann, "America's Reaction to the November 1938 Pogrom," *Wiener
Library Bulletin,* 16, No. 4 (Oct. 1962), 70–71.

227. *U.S.,* 1938, 2:396–99, 401–2, 405, 451–53, 456–57; *Moffat Papers,* pp. 221–22;
Roosevelt's emendations on the draft of the 15 November 1938 statement in Hyde Park, PSF
Germany; "Bestellungen aus der Pressekonferenz," 9 January 1939, Bundesarchiv, Brammer, Z.Sg. 101/12, f.10. The two ambassadors remained officially accredited until Germany
declared war on the United States in 1941.

228. Note by Hugh Wilson, 3 December 1938, State 611.623/330½; Roosevelt memoranda
for Hull, 10, 23 December 1938, Hyde Park, OF 198-A; *Moffat Papers,* pp. 222–24; *U.S.,*
1938, 2:453–55.

229. *U.S.,* 1938, 1:819–22, 824–25, 839–46, 856–57, 860, 871–80; Gilbert to Moffat, 10
December, and Moffat to Gilbert, 28 December 1938, Moffat Papers, Vol. 13.

230. See Alvin H. Hansen to Francis B. Sayre, 26 October 1938, State 611.0031/3942½.

ber; the basis for the decision was that fruitful conversations were simply not possible under the then current circumstances.[231] In fact, President Roosevelt was apparently thinking of restrictions or retaliatory action in the economic field.[232] It was precisely at this time that the American government was in the final stages of negotiating a trade agreement with England, signed on 17 November, of which Washington with good reason believed Chamberlain to be the only supporter within the British government.[233] Similarly, this was the time when President Roosevelt, who participated on 14 November in a top-level conference on the construction of a large American air force, decided to do what he could to assist the French in remedying the deficiencies in their air armaments.[234] The alignments of the future were already becoming apparent, at least in outline.

There were still some contrary currents. Hugh Wilson was very much in favor of endeavoring to repair the difficulties in United States relations with Germany,[235] and there were those in Germany who urged restraint in the anti-American propaganda campaign.[236] In spite of Germany's withdrawal from the United States–German Mixed Claims Commission on 1 March 1939 when it became obvious that the bulk of the German case in the sabotage claims dispute rested on forgery,[237] there was considerable discussion within the American government about the possibility of having Hugh Wilson return to his ambassadorial post in Berlin. By the time this question was nearing a favorable decision, the German occupation of Czechoslovakia on 15 March destroyed the opportunity. Thereafter the key question was to be whether the American neutrality legislation would be revised, and ambassadors would not be exchanged again until after a world war had intervened.[238]

231. *U.S.*, 1938, 2:427–31.

232. Welles to Roosevelt, 23 December 1938, and Morgenthau to Roosevelt, 17 January 1939, Hyde Park, PSF Germany. See also *U.S.*, 1938, 2:479–81.

233. *U.S.*, 1938, 2:57–60, 65–71; cf. *Moffat Papers*, pp. 220–21; Roosevelt to Hull and Welles, 17 October 1938, Hyde Park, OF-20.

234. On the 14 November meeting, see General H. H. Arnold's memorandum of 15 November in Hyde Park, OF 25-T; Haight, pp. 55–59. The French purchases of planes in the United States are discussed below.

235. See the report of the Hungarian minister in Washington on Hugh Wilson in *Hungarian Documents*, 3, No. 278.

236. Gilbert tels. 36 and 37 of 14 January 1939, State 711.62/201; Gilbert tel. 85 of 2 February 1939, State 762.00/237; but see "Bestellungen aus der Pressekonferenz," 2 February 1939, Bundesarchiv, Brammer, Z.Sg. 101/12, f.35.

237. American Commissioner, Mixed Claims Commission, to Roosevelt, 26 January 1939, p. 5, Hyde Park, OF 198-C. For the earlier development of this issue, see Weinberg, *Foreign Policy*, pp. 152–54.

On American concern about admitting Wiedemann as consul general in San Francisco, the post to which Hitler had banished him, see Moffat diary, 6 March 1939, Moffat Papers, Vol. 42; Welles to Roosevelt, 6 March 1939, Hyde Park, OF 198.

238. *Moffat Papers*, pp. 229, 230, 232; Moffat diary, 13 and 15 February 1939, Moffat Papers, Vol. 42; Moore to Bullitt, 27 February 1939, Hyde Park, R. Walton Moore Papers; *U.S.*, 1939, 1:25–26. These discussions were in part influenced by the sudden death of the American chargé in Berlin, Prentiss Gilbert, on 24 February.

The repercussions of the pogrom on England were not as spectacular as on the relations of the United States with Germany, but combined with the general rejection by the German government of any prospect of better relations with Britain after Munich, they were of great and lasting significance all the same. When the cabinet Committee on Foreign Policy met on 14 November, Lord Halifax in reviewing developments stated that the public reaction in Germany to the obvious danger of war and the relief over Munich had apparently infuriated Hitler, who now wanted to depict England as Germany's main enemy and who also now might believe that von Ribbentrop had been right after all in saying that England would not fight. Combined with the "happenings in Germany of the last few days" this meant that only a resolute attitude backed by a display of strength was appropriate. "He had reluctantly come to the conclusion that in present circumstances no useful purpose would be served by a resumption at the present time of the contemplated Anglo-German conversations."[239] At the meeting of the cabinet two days later, the prime minister explained that "the colonial issue could only be discussed as part of a general settlement. Such a settlement was clearly impossible in present circumstances, and it followed that there could be no question of returning colonies to Germany."[240] The critical issue now was rearmament.[241]

The British leaders did still have some hope that there might be a way to either weaken the Axis or to restrain Hitler by developing relations with Italy which had, after all, clearly shown a reluctance to follow Germany into a world war in the crisis over Czechoslovakia. As already mentioned, the Anglo-Italian agreement of April was formally implemented on 16 November, and plans were made for Chamberlain and Halifax to visit Rome in January 1939.[242] As a practical matter, however, this made little difference. Since Britain was quite unwilling to abandon her alliance with France, there was no way to reconcile Italy and her demands on France with the Western Powers. The British and French could discuss common

239. 32d meeting of the cabinet Committee on Foreign Policy, 14 November 1938, C 14396/42/18, FO 371/21658; *Harvey Diaries,* 16 November 1938, p. 220.

240. Cabinet meeting 55 (38) of 16 November 1938, C 14063/184/18, FO 371/21683. On 18 November Lord Lothian wrote to Malcolm MacDonald, the secretary of state for Dominion affairs and secretary of state for the colonies, that though he had once favored some restoration of colonies to Germany, he now opposed any such steps because of Germany's racial policies (Lothian Papers, GD 40/17/374/636–37).

241. See Chamberlain's comments at the 14 and 16 November meetings cited above, and C 14277/36/17, FO 371/21597. As Lord Halifax minuted on 22 November: "And if the Question came up, state that it was quite impossible in the present atmosphere which they [the Germans] had created to talk of colonies. And press on with rearming" (C 14561/62/18, FO 371/21665). Cf. *Hungarian Documents,* 3, Nos. 118, 139, 141; *D.D.F.,* 2d, 12, Nos. 295, 312.

242. See esp. the entry in Ciano, *Diary,* 16 November 1938, p. 281; *B.D.,* 3d, 3, No. 456; R 10221/240/22, FO 371/22429. As von Mackensen reported from Rome on 7 December 1938, the program of the Italians for the visit was "to have no program" (tel. 323, German embassy Rome [Quirinal], Pol 2, Italien-England, Bd. 5, Bonn, Pol. Archiv of AA).

approaches to Italy when the British leaders went to Paris for talks, but neither their conversations of 24 November nor the subsequent parallel efforts of the British through regular diplomatic channels nor those of the French through Paul Baudouin could resolve the problem presented by Mussolini's decision to press the aspirations of Italy against France.[243]

A major issue that emerged from the Franco-British meeting was in the field of defense preparations. While the British had been urging the French for some time to rebuild their air force, the French now began to insist on a larger contribution by the British on land. With the disappearance of the Czechoslovak army from Germany's eastern border, the French argued that only England could make up the difference; and there was increasing recognition within the British government that however unpalatable the prospect, a new large British land army for deployment on the continent would have to be created. This issue would be debated with increasing concern in London.[244] By 22 February 1939 the cabinet had decided one of the key issues in principle: a substantial expeditionary force rather than a token couple of divisions would have to be sent to France alongside the advanced striking bomber force if it came to war.[245] The other major hurdle was the issue of peacetime conscription to provide the manpower for such an army on an assured basis and with the necessary replacements; but on this question the prime minister was not yet prepared to move, especially in the face of the united and vehement opposition of the Labor party, the Liberal party, and the entire labor movement of the country.

These British discussions of military options were, of course, related to expectations of future German moves. In a negative sense, it was obvious enough that Germany did not want good relations with England; but what did she want? There were few doubts that Germany expected to exert control over the remainder of Czechoslovakia, though it was by no means clear whether she planned to do this by indirect pressure or total occupation. There was much embarrassed talk about the guarantee Britain along with France had promised the Czechs. There was little economic aid to

243. The British record of the Anglo-French talks is in *B.D.*, 3d, 3, No. 325; the French in *D.D.F.*, 2d, 12, No. 390. See also ibid., Nos. 314, 334–36, 344; R 8506/361/19, FO 317/22363; *U.S.*, 1938, 1:106; *Hungarian Documents*, 2, No. 98; Adamthwaite, pp. 246–50; *Pownall Diary*, 28 November 1938, pp. 170–72; *Harvey Diaries*, 24 November 1938, pp. 223–25; Osuský tel. 1331 of 25 November 1938, Czechoslovak document in T-120, 1039/1809/412222–23. For other aspects of Italy's role in relation to France and England at this time, see C 14365/5302/18, FO 371/21779; *Cadogan Diary*, 12 December 1938, p. 129; *Harvey Diaries*, 11 December 1938, p. 227; *Hungarian Documents*, 3, Nos. 113, 143; Adamthwaite, pp. 260–61.

244. C 15175, C 16018/36/17, FO 371/21597; C 314, C 1503/136/14, FO 371/22915; C 300, C 358, C 940, C 1978/281/17, FO 371/22922; *Pownall Diary*, 5 December 1938ff., pp. 172ff.; Gibbs, chap. 13; Adamthwaite, pp. 252–53; *D.D.F.*, 2d, 12, Nos. 280, 293, 360, 375, 376.

245. Cabinet meeting 8 (39) of 22 February 1939, C 2606/281/17, FO 371/22923; cf. C 2505/15/18, FO 371/22966.

the crippled state, though there was much talk about that subject as well.[246]

One cannot read the record of the discussions in London on these topics without drawing the conclusion that the British government was determined to run no risks and make no sacrifices for those they had urged to sacrifice themselves. It could be and was argued that any other policy would encourage the Czechs and enrage Hitler to no useful purpose, but the other side of this argument surely was that Britain had indeed an obligation to Czechoslovakia and that the credibility of any obligation she assumed in the future might well be measured by her fidelity to the most recent one. These matters must by their nature remain speculative, but I believe that the irritation over the endless delays of the Czechoslovak government in the face of years of British warnings combined with a sense of shame over Munich to make the Czechs personae non grata in London.[247] They were certainly treated that way, in regard to both the promised guarantee and the possibility of economic assistance. The psychological converse of this would be evident after 15 March: there could be no softening of adherence to the British obligation to Poland, and any *future* Anglo-German agreement would first have to provide for the return of the promised independence to the Czechs.[248]

If there was no serious effort to maintain the independence of Czechoslovakia in the face of German pressure, what other German moves were expected and how did the London government see itself reacting to them? A variety of reports reached London predicting all manner of German plans. Some of these pointed to anticipated German moves eastward, others expected aggression in the west, and still others predicted some combination of the two. Though read with care in London, the impact of most of these was simply to reinforce the belief that continued rearmament was the only possible course and that an accommodation with Germany was impossible under the circumstances.[249] The information which

246. On this issue, see *B.D.*, 3d, 3 and 4, passim; cabinet meeting 57 (38) of 30 November 1938, C 14903/111169/18, FO 371/21789; 34th meeting of the cabinet Committee on Foreign Policy, 6 December 1938, CAB 27/624; Král, *München*, No. 275; Osuský tels. 1240 of 2 November and 1245 of 3 November 1938, Czechoslovak documents in T-120, 1039/1809/412208 and 412036; Černy (Paris) tel. 1276 of 15 November 1938, ibid., frame 412211; *D.D.F.*, 2d, 12, Nos. 32, 40, 93, 125, 189.

247. See the comments of the British ambassador in Tokyo reported in Král, *München*, No. 279.

248. The role of a restored Czech independence as a British demand after 15 March 1939 will be discussed in the review of Anglo-German informal soundings in the summer of 1939. The failure of Bernd Martin to understand its significance in English policy after the outbreak of war is only one of the basic flaws in his study *Friedensinitiativen und Machtpolitik im Zweiten Weltkrieg, 1939–1942* (Düsseldorf: Droste, 1974).

249. See W 15502/104/98, FO 371/22538; C 15689/93/62, FO 371/21627; cf. *S.U.*, No. 90. Note the description of German aims as "world domination" by Major von Schwerin, the new head of the British Empire section of German army intelligence, on 26 January 1939 (C 1291/15/18, FO 371/22963) which was given to Lord Halifax for the 1 February 1939 cabinet meeting.

London received from opponents of Hitler did not lead to different con-clusions. Schacht's report that Hitler was not to be trusted, that he con-sidered the Munich agreement worthless, and that no one really in-fluenced him was hardly surprising by mid-December 1938.[250] Some new schemes from Carl Goerdeler and others met with a frigid reception from the British government; Goerdeler proposed that England arrange the cession of Danzig and the Corridor to Germany, the return of Germany's colonies, and a very large loan, in return for which a new German gov-ernment would behave nicely. He ruined the credibility of the German opposition by nationalistic demands that were considered preposterous in Britain.[251] That all such men in any case had no influence in Germany was increasingly obvious from London; there was no sign that the generals would ever find the courage needed to change the course of a regime they served faithfully, and Schacht himself was dismissed from his Reichsbank post in January for warning against the costs of new projects.[252]

In regard to two areas of possible German action the news received by London was more specific and appeared to call for more definite re-actions. Early in 1939, the British government received reports of a planned German attack on Holland. The discussion of these reports in late January and early February, culminating in a decision shared by France to go to war if Germany invaded either Holland or Switzerland (Belgium being already covered by the 1937 pledge), is significant in two ways.[253] The combination of urgency and determination, with the British govern-ment deciding in a period of about ten days to go to war at the next

250. C 15642/62/18, FO 371/27666; see also C 14398/541/18, FO 371/21704. Earlier, Kirkpatrick had sent Strang a list of Hitler's broken promises which the Foreign Office had printed with a few additions. Kirkpatrick, who thought that Chamberlain's Munich actions were correct, added that "it is a paradox that whilst England and U.S. are angry with the P.M. for having given way to Hitler, Hitler is angry with the P.M. for not letting him have his way" (C 15228/528/18, FO 371/21701).

251. C 15084/42/18, FO 371/21659; C 14809, C 15438/62/18, FO 371/21665; C 938/15/18, FO 371/22961; C 1290/15/18, FO 371/22963; *Harvey Diaries,* 11 December 1938, pp. 226–27; *Cadogan Diary,* 10, 11 December 1938, pp. 128–29. Goerdeler's foreign policy demands from the British in 1938–39 are very intelligently discussed by Hermann Graml, "Resistance Thinking in Foreign Policy," in *The German Resistance to Hitler* (Berkeley: University of California Press, 1970), pp. 6–14.

252. *TMWC,* 36:365–75; Wiedemann (who was dropped the same day), pp. 234–35.

253. The relevant exchanges have been largely published in *B.D.,* 3d, 4. Additional mate-rial will be found in the records of the 35th, 36th, and 37th meetings of the cabinet Committee on Foreign Policy, 23 and 26 January and 8 February 1939, CAB 27/624; Cabinet 2 (39) of 25 January 1939, C 1065/15/18, FO 371/22962; meeting of Lord Halifax and Mr. MacDonald with the Dominions representatives, 28 January 1939, Halifax Papers, FO 800/310; C 1822/13/18, FO 371/22958; C 1292/15/18, FO 371/22963; *Harvey Diaries,* 15–16 and 24–29 January 1939, pp. 245, 247–48; *Pownall Diary,* 23 January 1939, pp. 183–84; *Cadogan Diary,* pp. 139–47; *U.S.,* 1939, 1:2–7; Johnson (chargé London) tels. 117 of 28 January and 175 and 176 of 7 February 1939, State 740.00/553, 570, 571.

The Belgians, in line with their general policy, preferred what they called an "in-dependent" course, meaning that they would help no one, stay neutral until attacked them-selves, then fight if attacked and expect others to help them; *D.D.B.,* 5, Nos. 50, 52–56; Overstraeten, pp. 317–22; *Harvey Diaries,* 12 February 1939, p. 253.

German move then anticipated, on the sole condition that the country attacked defend itself, surely signifies a hardening of opinion. The key issue now, as the British told the Belgians on 16 February, was the "attempt of Germany to dominate Europe by force."[254] It was this fundamental issue, rather than any specific German demand, that exercised the British government, and it did not make much difference in what direction the Germans moved. Just a short time before the English leaders had warned Mussolini during the conversations in Rome on 12 January about the dangers of a German move eastward toward the Ukraine about which there were also rumors.[255] Having as they saw it agreed to a German demand at Czechoslovakia's expense which had some justification as implementing the principle of self-determination, and having agreed to it under circumstances where it was presented as Germany's last territorial demand and as completing the unification under Berlin's control of the German population outside the borders of the Reich, an issue in which Hitler had claimed to be interested, the British now saw *any* further German move automatically as belonging to an entirely different category, by Hitler's as well as by their own standards. That category was denial of self-determination to others, not assertion of it for Germans; and this meant expansion for control of Europe—precisely what London was determined to resist.

The second aspect of this decision which must be noted is that it represented what had become so much a shared assumption of the British leaders that it was applied almost automatically to a contingency which did not arise. Later reactions to news about possible German moves against Rumania and Poland can be understood more easily if it is remembered that British entrance into a war was practically assumed if two conditions were met: a German attack on another country and forcible resistance by the country attacked. The Dutch were to be spared for little over a year; the Swiss were on Hitler's agenda for the period after a German victory which never came;[256] the Lithuanians were not expected to fight for Memel; and the Czechs—about whose possible fate word was beginning to reach London in February—were also thought unlikely to

254. *D.D.B.*, 5, No. 56. The same point had been made to the U.S. on 28 January. Late in 1938, the Foreign Office had been asked to prepare an "Appreciation of the Situation in the Event of War in April, 1939." The text is in C 16090/1941/18, FO 371/21747. It assumes Britain and France fighting Germany, Italy joining the latter after a short delay, with all other countries remaining neutral though with varying degrees of sympathy for one side or the other.

255. *B.D.*, 3d, 3, No. 500, p. 525. Mario Toscano in *Designs in Diplomacy* (Baltimore: Johns Hopkins University Press, 1970), pp. 56–60 describes the Soviet government's turning this around into an imaginary British plot to encourage the Germans to seize the Ukraine. On the Rome trip, see also Halifax, pp. 205–6; *Harvey Diaries*, pp. 231, 238–44; *Hungarian Documents*, 3, Nos. 210, 217.

256. Norman Rich, *Hitler's War Aims: The Establishment of the New Order* (New York: Norton, 1974), pp. 401–2.

fight after what had happened to them the year before.[257] The indications reaching London about German demands on Poland, however, opened up other perspectives.

Even before the German demands on Poland were presented to Lipski by von Ribbentrop, the position of Poland and the likelihood of German demands on her were being discussed in London.[258] Although Beck tried to keep the German demands secret for a while, the British minister to Warsaw was sending rather accurate information to London the day after the von Ribbentrop–Lipski meeting on 24 October.[259] There was concern that the French alliance with Poland might confront London with a dilemma analogous to that created by the French alliance with Czechoslovakia, but from the beginning there were important differences. In the first place, the concern over French policy now reflected worry about French weakness and lack of resolution rather than the other way around. In the second place, there was a greater belief that Poland would fight rather than make major concessions—though the latter possibility was not entirely excluded. In the third place, though there were doubts about the proper handling of Danzig, there was a general recognition that the population of the Corridor was overwhelmingly *Polish* so that German demands and Polish firmness in regard to that area were seen from London in an entirely different perspective from that in which the Sudeten area with its millions of Germans had been seen earlier.[260]

Although interested in the Danzig question in a special way because of its relationship to the League and Lord Halifax's chairmanship of the special League committee charged with watching developments in the Free City, the British government watched the whole range of problems in German-Polish relations with great care. Relatively accurately informed about the German-Polish negotiations, the British were, nevertheless, troubled by what they considered the inadequacy of their knowledge, and they decided to invite Beck to London both to learn more from him and to discuss the situation.[261] Their invitation coincided with Beck's desire, and while his trip had originally been scheduled for January or February, in fact it was postponed until after 15 March.

If the prospects for the maintenance of peace looked slim from London's point of view, there was also a reluctance to give up all hope. The

257. C 1822/13/18, FO 371/22958; C 2209/15/18, FO 371/22965; C 3234/15/18, FO 371/22966; *Cadogan Diary*, 11 and 13 March 1939, pp. 155, 156.

258. Note *B.D.*, 3d, 3, No. 206; C 12277/2168/55, FO 371/21808.

259. *B.D.*, 3d, 3, No. 223. London received a full report based on Forster's account to Burckhardt on 13 December 1938, C 15395/197/55, FO 371/21804.

260. See *B.D.*, 3d, 3, No. 385, n.1; C 14878, C 16019/2688/55, FO 371/21809; C 14170/267/18, FO 371/21697; C 16018/36/17, FO 371/21597.

261. 35th meeting of the cabinet Committee on Foreign Policy, 23 January 1939, CAB 27/624; memorandum by Makins, "Proposed Visit of Colonel Beck to England," 27 February 1939, C 2607/92/55, FO 371/23133; cf. *Hungarian Documents*, 3, No. 380.

likelihood of war was too terrible to accept with simple resignation, and various avenues of exploration were still thought possible. These were primarily of an economic nature. Some efforts in this direction had been started in the late fall of 1938 but without much success.[262] These were resumed early in 1939, and for a short time it looked as if some progress were being made.[263] If these faint indications misled both Chamberlain and Henderson into excessively optimistic forecasts that soon sounded ridiculous,[264] such anticipation surely reflected their eagerness for success. The German directives to the press that nothing was expected to come from this at all proved more accurate.[265] The culmination of the preliminary talks was intended to be a visit by the British minister of overseas trade to Berlin; scheduled for 15 March, it was among the first casualties of Germany's aggression that day.

The British attempts at better economic relations as a possible preliminary to better political relations with Germany were not the only such projects destroyed by the German action. A series of proposals for increasing Franco-German trade had also been under discussion for some time. These included plans for joint ventures of major proportions in the French colonial empire and for raising the level of trade and travel between the two countries.[266] The condition for such long-range projects, of course, was that "both governments be convinced that during this time [of three or more years] there would be no unexpected developments."[267] This comment, made on 10 March 1939 by Lucien Lamoureux, a former minister of finance and close associate of Daladier and Bonnet, demonstrated both the hopes of the French and the impossibility of their realization. A brief survey of French policy after Munich must, however, also include several other important issues.

In France as in England there was a short period of hope after the Munich conference, of hope that the age of threats and dangers was over and that better relations with Germany might open a period of peace and stability in Europe. If this lasted a few weeks longer in Paris than in London, it was because of two elements in the situation peculiar to France. In the first place, the talks inaugurated by François-Poncet for a

262. *G.D.*, D, 4, Nos. 257, 259, 261ff.
263. A useful account in Wendt, *Economic Appeasement*, pp. 536–72. See also Biddle dispatch 950 of 15 February 1939, State 862.014/446; *U.S.*, 1939, 1:14–17; C. A. MacDonald, "Economic Appeasement and the German Moderates, 1937–39: An Introductory Essay," *Past and Present*, 56 (Aug. 1972), 119–27.
264. *B.D.*, 3d, 4, Nos. 118 (comments in C 2139/15/18, FO 371/22965), 162 (comments in C 2533/15/18, FO 371/22966), 195 (comments in C 3184/15/18, FO 371/3184), appendix 1, No. 3. See also *Harvey Diaries*, 10–13 March 1939, pp. 260–61; *Cadogan Diary*, 10 March 1939, p. 155; Feiling, pp. 396–97.
265. "Bestellungen aus der Pressekonferenz," 22 February 1939, Bundesarchiv, Brammer, Z.Sg. 101/12, f.55; "Informationsbericht Nr. 15," 27 February 1939, "Nr. 18," 3 March 1939, ibid., 101/34, ff.69–71, 85.
266. *G.D.*, D, 4, Nos. 371–98, passim; Adamthwaite, pp. 294–98.
267. *G.D.*, D, 4, No. 397.

Franco-German declaration analogous to the Anglo-German agreement of 30 September which lasted for several weeks and culminated in von Ribbentrop's Paris visit of 6 December suggested the possibility of an era of improved relations. That all this was purely an optical illusion has already been explained.[268] The other element was the personality and policy of French Foreign Minister Georges Bonnet. Bonnet had been the most persistent advocate of concessions to Germany before Munich and continued to follow this line thereafter. Unlike Lord Halifax, who became slowly but steadily more determined to resist further German demands, Bonnet moved in the opposite direction.

The evidence suggests that in the last months of 1938 Bonnet would have preferred that France abdicate any role in Europe altogether if Germany would leave her alone. He appears to have wanted to drop the French tie to Poland lest it confront France with the same dilemma that the French treaty with Czechoslovakia had produced, and he was similarly willing to abandon completely the French treaty with the Soviet Union. This view might color French perspectives on the European situation for a while, but it did not have major practical results because Bonnet himself was afraid to raise the question with either Poland or the Soviet Union.[269]

There were contrary currents in France. The major concern of many led by Prime Minister Daladier was to remedy the obvious deficiencies in the French armed forces, the most conspicuous being in regard to the French air force.[270] Strenuous efforts were made to speed up the construction of modern planes. It was apparent, however, that France was too far behind in this field to catch up within the foreseeable future by domestic production, and so the French government returned on a large scale to a possibility already explored in a small way earlier: the purchase of airplanes from the United States.

In a project sponsored by Daladier himself and avidly supported by Ambassador Bullitt, a special air mission under Jean Monnet was sent to the United States with Roosevelt's approval.[271] The president saw the relationship between French weakness in the air and her policy toward Germany very clearly; he also saw how French orders and investments could assist in the building up of the American military aircraft industry

268. See above, pp. 507–8.
269. *U.S.*, 1938, 1:83–84, 98; *Hungarian Documents*, 3, No. 592; C 12161/1050/17, FO 371/21612; C 16019/2688/55, FO 371/21809; Phipps to Sargent, 31 December 1938, C 150/90/17, FO 371/22912. See also the Foreign Office comments about this issue on Kennard's 28 November 1938 report on Franco-Polish relations in C 14878/2688/55, ff.253–56; Adamthwaite, pp. 265, 270–78; *D.D.F.*, 2d, 12, Nos. 89, 158, 216, 335.
270. See Gamelin, 2:364ff.; Bullitt tel. 1736 of 11 October 1938, State 740.00/490.
271. The account here is based on the excellent study by Haight, chaps. 2 and 4. Haight was able to secure access to the papers of several French participants; one of the key French documents is the record of the 5 December 1938 meeting of the Permanent Committee of National Defence in Gamelin, 2:371–78. See also Lindbergh, pp. 80–92, passim; *D.D.F.*, 2d, 12, Nos. 160, 171.

which, like all American war production capacity, had been pretty effectively dismantled after the World War. In the face of some reluctance on the part of the American army chief of staff, Malin C. Craig, the president insisted on a vast expansion of America's air force in what came to be the real beginning of the United States rearmament program presented by the president to Congress at the beginning of 1939. Roosevelt saw in this, combined with large-scale sales of planes to France and a revision of the neutrality laws to permit the sale of weapons in time of war, the most likely deterrent to future adventures by Germany leading to a new world war. Whether he was correct in this belief—the converse of Hitler's view that he had to begin a war while Germany still had a head start in rearmament—will never be known. Time ran out before American rearmament had made substantial progress, and unexpected obstacles interfered even in the little time available. An airplane accident on 23 January revealed the negotiations to sell the newest American warplanes to France and produced such a storm of criticism among isolationists in and out of Congress that the president had to pull back, leaving the question of neutrality legislation to his supporters in the Congress, where opposition proved too strong. Nevertheless, substantial orders were placed by the French for American warplanes, thus contributing to the increased preparedness of both countries.

There was also some hardening of French opinion after von Ribbentrop's visit as it became evident that there was no substance to the anticipated rapprochement with Germany.[272] The main factor making for a firmer attitude by the French government, however, was the behavior of Italy. Ironically it was the threatening and bellicose talk from Rome that aroused French public opinion and provided a focus for the French government to become resolute in the face of danger. This danger was not as acute in reality as it appeared to be, but the demands for territory which the French considered integral parts of their country and cherished portions of their colonial empire brought home the dangers of weakness in a way that the Czechoslovak question never had.[273] In the first months of 1939, therefore, the French appeared to be recovering at least to some extent from the loss of nerve so evident in the Czechoslovak crisis. The fact that Bonnet was increasingly under attack from both left and right was a symptom of the way France might react if there were indeed "unexpected developments."[274]

272. Wilson (Paris) tel. 2076 of 8 December 1938, State 751.62/514; *Hungarian Documents*, 3, Nos. 134, 282; *Łukasiewicz Papers*, pp. 151–60.

273. The minutes of the 24 February 1939 meeting of the Permanent Committee of National Defence (Gamelin, 2:391–401) show it devoted entirely to the problem of defense against possible Italian actions. See also Adamthwaite, pp. 262–63.

274. Note the observant reports of the Hungarian minister in Paris, *Hungarian Documents*, 3, Nos. 247, 270, 352; and the report of the Czechoslovak minister in Král, *München*, No. 298.

If the alliance of France with Poland was in disarray after the participation of Poland in the partition of Czechoslovakia, that with the Soviet Union was clouded by even more mistrust than before Munich. The Soviet government denounced the Munich agreement and reexamined its own options, a process that was redoubled when Litvinov returned to Moscow from Geneva in early October. A strong isolationist tone was sounded by Stalin and Molotov at the celebration of the November Revolution, a tone that was noted by German, British, and French diplomats.[275] The very description of the conflict—the "Second Imperialist War"—confidently predicted by Moscow as coming soon, suggested a sense of distance from developments. A slight improvement in relations with Poland was agreed to by Moscow,[276] but this too could be interpreted as a means of isolating the Soviet Union from developments elsewhere in Europe by encouraging Poland to be more independent of Germany in her policy. Other than in this regard, rumors of changes in policy and personalities probably outran reality, except for the continuation of the purge in the Commissariat for Foreign Affairs as well as elsewhere.

There is little information about French relations with the Soviet Union in the winter of 1938–39; the two countries with an apparently more active relationship with Russia were Germany and Great Britain. The Germans had agreed with the Soviet government in October that the press in both countries would be restrained in its attacks on the other. A more substantial factor was German interest in a new economic agreement with the Soviet Union. Negotiations involving a large German trade credit had broken down in March 1938, and in October the Germans wanted to reopen the question. All the evidence points to economic factors being critical in this decision on the German side, though obviously a credit involving a long-term pattern of repayment implied at least some continuation of peaceful relations. The Soviet government, however, appears to have seen the question primarily in political terms, having the matter taken up enthusiastically by its ambassador to Germany and insisting that at least some of the negotiations take place in Moscow, not as in the past in Berlin. The Germans, who wanted a trade agreement, offered the compromise of sending their chief negotiator, Karl Schnurre, to Moscow; but just as the Russians prepared to welcome their guest, von Ribbentrop responded to exaggerated French press accounts by canceling the trip scheduled for the end of January 1939.[277]

What is revealing for the importance attached to the issue by Moscow is the attitude of the Soviet government when the German ambassador was

275. Weinberg, *Germany and the Soviet Union*, p. 7. Much of the following account is based on that book, and sources cited there on pp. 6–13 will not again be cited here. Important French reports in *D.D.F.*, 2d, 12, Nos. 164, 366, 460.

276. The Polish-Soviet Communiqué of 26 November 1938 has already been discussed.

277. The evidence on this incident is listed in Weinberg, *Germany and the Soviet Union*, p. 10, n.33. No new evidence that sheds light on the matter has appeared since.

instructed to present a draft credit and trade agreement in the absence of the expected Schnurre.[278] The negotiations took place with Foreign Trade Commissar Anastas Mikoyan himself; and in a series of meetings in February, the Soviet representative step by step came to agree to the major elements in the German plan.[279] As the Russians agreed to the great scope of raw materials deliveries that the Germans were requesting, the Germans themselves looked more closely at the impact on their other needs of the required export of manufactured goods to pay for all this, and concluded reluctantly that they could not implement in practice what they had themselves proposed in the negotiations.[280] If no success was attained at that time, therefore, it was German, not Soviet, policies that were responsible. The Russians were quite willing to work out a large-scale mutually satisfactory economic arrangement with Germany on terms very much along lines the Germans had proposed but saw the prospect foundering on obstacles of German creation; they would be more cautious when the Germans approached them again later. That caution should be seen as a logical reaction to the Soviet government's having observed the Germans go back on their own plans twice in the most recent past; what is more revealing about the *underlying* Soviet position is the willingness even to entertain another approach from Berlin in the face of such disappointing experiences.

There is an interesting contrast between this attitude and that displayed by the Soviet government in the face of approaches from London. The discussion of possible Soviet participation in the projected new guarantee of Czechoslovakia did not lead to anything,[281] but in other areas there was greater British interest. In view of the signs of Soviet withdrawal from European problems and a deterioration of Anglo-Soviet relations, there was a desire to improve those relations and a willingness to take new steps in that direction. In the face of an increasingly hostile tone in the Soviet press (by contrast with the German-Soviet press truce), the British government hoped to develop better ties with Russia and planned to send a cabinet minister to Moscow.[282] In the same days of late February 1939 that Mikoyan was moving gradually to meet German economic wishes, the Russians were indicating that Robert S. Hudson of the Department of Overseas Trade would not, as requested, be received by Stalin when in Moscow.[283] Hudson's meeting with Ambassador Maisky before his trip

278. This instruction is presumably Berlin tel. 12 of 4 Februrary 1939 (*G.D.*, D, 4, No. 490, n.2); see von Schulenburg to von Weizsäcker, 6 February 1939, ibid., No. 487.
279. Ibid., Nos. 490, 491, 493.
280. Ibid., Nos. 494, 495.
281. See, e.g., ibid., No. 249; *B.D.*, 3d, 3, No. 325; Král, *München*, No. 264.
282. N 57, N 1029/57/38, FO 371/23677; *Harvey Diaries*, 17 February 1939, p. 255; cf. C 15569/5302/18, FO 371/21779. On the origins and purposes of Hudson's trip to Scandinavia and Moscow in 1939 see also the file N 64/63 in FO 371/23653, passim.
283. London tel. 22 to Seeds, 23 February 1939, and Seeds tel. 29 of 28 February 1939, N 1001 and N 1087/64/63, FO 371/23653; cf. *G.D.*, D, 4, No. 325; Fierlinger tel. 186 of 3 March 1939, Czechoslovak document in T-120, 1316/2376/D 497036.

was quite discouraging; unlike the Soviet ambassador to Germany, who had been instructed to express a wish for better Soviet-German relations, Maisky had received very different guidelines from Moscow.[284] On 14 March Halifax briefed Hudson for his journey to Moscow with emphasis on doing nothing that might encourage a Soviet withdrawal into an isolationist stance.[285] By then, however, Stalin had already adopted a very different line.

The Soviet position on the international situation was outlined by Stalin in public on 10 March 1939. Although by that time the economic negotiations with Germany were being aborted by the Germans, Stalin left open the possibility of better trade relations with "all countries." His denunciations were directed at the Western Powers for their attempts to embroil the Soviet Union with Germany, a conflict for which he professed to see no visible grounds. Although this should surely not be interpreted as showing that Stalin had already decided to sign up with Germany by 10 March 1939, it does show that he was willing to consider the possibility seriously, and it would be so interpreted by the Germans.[286] Stalin appears to have thought it likely that Germany would turn next against either Poland and Rumania or the Western Powers, or both, and such steps on Germany's part need not provide "visible grounds" for a German-Soviet conflict.[287]

Soviet intelligence was receiving from Richard Sorge in Japan generally accurate reports on the German attempt to secure Japanese adherence to a generalized, as distinct from an exclusively anti-Soviet, alliance, as well as on the divisions within the Japanese government about this issue. From Rudolf von Scheliha, a high official in the German embassy in Warsaw who had been in Soviet pay since at least early in 1938, the Russians were receiving reports on the German demands on Poland.[288] Soon after the 10 March speech, the Soviet government appears to have received a report on a conversation of 13 March of a close associate of von Ribbentrop, Peter Kleist, that Hitler's war plans were directed against the West, that he expected to settle first the Czechoslovak question (letting the Carpatho-Ukraine fall to Hungary as Russia preferred), then to take care of

284. See the excerpt from Litvinov's letter to Maisky of 19 Februrary 1939, *S.U.*, No. 128; cf. ibid., Nos. 140, 141.
285. N 1342, N 1389/57/38, FO 371/23677; *Harvey Diaries*, 9 March 1939, pp. 259–60; *S.U.*, Nos. 129–31; *B.D.*, 3d, 4, Nos. 121, 125, 128.
286. Weinberg, *Germany and the Soviet Union*, pp. 12–13; *U.S.*, *Soviet Union 1933–1939*, pp. 744–45. Large parts of Rosso's 12 March report on the speech now appear in English in Toscano, *Designs in Diplomacy*, pp. 52–53.
287. See Kirk (Moscow) tel. 85 of 23 February 1939, State 761.62/497; *Hungarian Documents*, 3, No. 284; Osuský report 8 of 23 January 1939, Czechoslovak document in T-120, 1039/1809/412392; Fierlinger report 68 of 14 February 1939, ibid., 1040/1809/412714–23.
288. Some reports of both Sorge and von Scheliha are included in the official Soviet publication of diplomatic documents. On Sorge, see Frederick W. Deakin and G. R. Storry, *The Case of Richard Sorge* (London: Chatto & Windus, 1966); on Rudolf von Scheliha, see Heinz Höhne, *Codeword "Direktor"* (New York: Coward, McCann & Geoghegan, 1971), pp. 39, 148–49, 165–67, 191.

Poland, thereafter to crush the Western Powers, and finally to turn on the Soviet Union.[289]

This kind of information reinforced what was evident from a look at the map; before Germany could turn against the Soviet Union, she would have to deal with a number of other obstacles. From Stalin's perspective there were apparently good reasons to explore the possibility of postponing the evil day—possibly forever—by standing aside or assisting Germany rather than by aligning Russia with those directly affected by Germany's immediate ambitions.

When in early March Hitler moved to take over the rest of Czechoslovakia, he was confident that no one would interfere, and he had given instructions to the Hungarians to participate. Since the Poles had not been willing to fall in with his plans, they were not notified. Probably because of fears that the information would leak out, he also refrained from giving advance notice to his Italian ally; in fact von Ribbentrop and von Weizsäcker deliberately misled the inquiring Italian ambassador.[290] Having misled the Axis partner, Hitler was not about to give notice to the other two parties to the Munich agreement, England and France.[291] He had been warned of possible repercussions; Sir Horace Wilson mentioned that these would be great if German troops marched into the country.[292]

Hitler, however, was determined to go his own way. It was no longer possible to use the remaining Germans in Czechoslovakia as a plausible excuse: while the German press was inventing new atrocities, the German legation in Prague reported that a representative of the Germans "deplores the perfectly correct, even accommodating, attitude of the Czechs everywhere."[293] In view of this situation, the Slovaks were required to provide the needed pretext for what was to have been an ultimatum from Berlin; at the last moment, threats made personally by Hitler to the Czech president, Emil Hácha, were substituted.[294] By the time the browbeaten Hácha had agreed to German occupation of his country as a means of averting the threatened bloodshed, the Germans had already crossed the border marking Hitler's "last territorial demand." What had looked to many to be a sign of German triumph had been discarded as a reluctantly accepted temporary obstacle.

289. *S.U.*, No. 149. The Soviet informant in this case is identified as a "German Journalist." This extremely interesting document reflects Hitler's and von Ribbentrop's views in early March 1939 with great accuracy, and there is no reason to believe that Kleist knew himself to be speaking to a Soviet informant. He had accompanied von Ribbentrop on his visit to Warsaw and was used by the latter for his first soundings with the Soviet embassy in Berlin in April.

290. *G.D.*, D, 4, Nos. 205, 214; see also ibid., No. 224.

291. Hans Fritzsche claims that he tried to have Goebbels persuade Hitler to consult England and France; he claims that von Ribbentrop opposed the idea and that Hitler was doubtful and eventually negative. Hildegard Springer (ed.), *Es sprach Hans Fritzsche* (Stuttgart: Thiele-Verlag, 1949), pp. 207–9.

292. *G.D.*, D, 4, No. 219.

293. Ibid., No. 181.

294. Hoensch, *Slowakei*, p. 292; *G.D.*, D, 4, No. 228; Gajan and Kvaček, No. 56; Král, *Die Deutschen*, Nos. 278, 279.

13   The Road to War

The German triumph over Czechoslovakia seemed to be complete and unchallenged. Hitler himself gloated over his conquest in Prague, and German commandos seized the remaining weapons of the Czechs even as the great Skoda arms factory fell under German control. The Slovaks, who might have thought that their subservience to German schemes would assure them favorable treatment, were soon disabused of their expectations. Not only did the Germans allow some additional Slovak territory to be annexed by Hungary in connection with that country's occupation of the Carpatho-Ukraine,[1] but the main area of Slovakia itself was to be under German control. The nominal independence of the new Slovak state was compromised at birth by a treaty of protection with Germany; furthermore, wherever and whenever the Germans chose to go beyond that treaty's terms in military occupation or political control, Berlin would reject all Slovak protests.[2]

The status of being Hitler's client was hardly a comfortable one. In the first months of pseudo-independence, there was always the possibility that Germany might trade parts or all of the "country" to Poland or Hungary in pursuit of her own policies;[3] a bit

1. See *Hungarian Documents*, 3, Nos. 470, 553, 560; 4, Nos. 8, 13, 56; *G.D.*, D, 6, Nos. 111, 120; Vnuk, pp. 138–49; Dertinger, "Informationsbericht Nr. 29," 25 March 1939, Bundesarchiv, Brammer, Z.Sg. 101/34, f.151; Kennan, No. 14.
2. A good summary in Hoensch, *Die Slowakei*, pp. 334–50; see also *Hungarian Documents*, 3, Nos. 447, 478, 489; *Keitel Papers*, pp. 203–4; *G.D.*, D, 6, Nos. 40, 95, 98, 554.
3. Note Hitler's response to Horthy's desire for pieces of Slovakia in *G.D.*, D, 6, Nos. 111, 120. Cf. Dertinger, "Informationsbericht Nr. 44," 2 May 1939, Bundesarchiv, Brammer, Z.Sg. 101/34, ff.209–11. Vnuk (p. 127) notes that von Ribbentrop delayed signing the protection treaty with Slovakia until 23 March in part in hopes of an agreement with Poland (which might have required a revision of that treaty).

later, Slovakia would be both a base and a partner in the attack on Poland. While this role in the war would bring some small accretion of territory, it would also tie the Slovaks even more permanently to the German juggernaut.[4]

If Hitler was in full control of Bohemia and Moravia and in effective control of Slovakia, he was now also ready for other territorial gains. Memel had been the one piece of land he was confident of seizing in 1939,[5] and the Lithuanians were pressured into yielding it to Germany on 22 March.[6] Hitler himself went to the city Germany had lost after the war, but the original idea of combining the seizure of Memel with that of Danzig had had to be abandoned.[7] This did not mean, however, that Hitler had lost interest in the demands on Poland; only a temporary postponement seemed indicated. The outflanking of Poland's position from the south by the extension of German military power to Slovakia and the possible further outflanking of Poland from the north by the reduction of Lithuania to the status of a German satellite once its port was in German hands might in fact render the Warsaw government more willing to give in to German demands.[8]

The obvious accretion of German strength would have precisely such an effect on Rumania, Poland's southern ally. The negotiations for a new German-Rumanian trade agreement had been initiated before the 15 March coup, but it was only after that startling event that the German representative, Helmuth Wohlthat, was able to drive a bargain so favorable to Germany that it practically delivered the riches of Rumania's oil and agriculture into the hands of the Third Reich. The international repercussions of aspects of the German pressure on Rumania will be reviewed in the context of British and French reactions to the Prague coup; what is relevant to an understanding of German policy is that Wohlthat was able to convert the stronger German position immediately into a great further advance. The concessions made by the Rumanians were so extensive and extraordinary that both Hungary and Bulgaria would come to suspect that the Germans had secured the economic treaty of 23 March by promising to guarantee Rumania's territorial integrity.[9] It would take a while for these worried associates of Berlin to become convinced that not

4. On Slovak participation in the attack on Poland at Germany's request and the resultant territorial cessions, see *G.D.,* D, 7, Nos. 214, 237, 468, 488; Victor S. Mamatey and Radomír Luža (eds.), *A History of the Czechoslovak Republic, 1918–1948* (Princeton, N.J.: Princeton University Press, 1973), p. 280, n.16.

5. Note Dertinger, "Informationsbericht Nr. 2," 10 January 1939, Bundesarchiv, Brammer, Z.Sg. 101/34, f.213.

6. See above, p. 486; Dr. Kausch, "Sonderbestellungen," 22 March 1939, Bundesarchiv, Brammer, Z.Sg. 101/12, f.90; Dertinger, "Informationsbericht Nr. 27," 22 March 1939, ibid., 101/34, ff.137–39.

7. Hitler had thought of combining the naval trip to Memel with one to Danzig; after von Ribbentrop's visit to Warsaw in January it was obvious that this would not be possible. The Hitler-Greiser talk of 24 February 1939 about naval visits to Danzig in 1939 reflects the shift in Hitler's perspective (*G.D.,* D, 6, No. 261 and n.1).

8. Note *Hungarian Documents,* 4, No. 20.

9. Ibid., No. 27; *G.D.,* D, 6, Nos. 67, 97, 110, 219.

political promises but raw pressure had won for Berlin the subservience of Rumania.[10]

There was, thus, some reason for the German government to believe that its greatly strengthened prestige and improved strategic position might yet be converted into Polish and not only Rumanian concessions. Although there is some later evidence indicating that Hitler had never had any hope of Polish agreement to his renewed demands handed to the Poles on 21 March, and that he expected and even preferred for these to be turned down, this would seem to overstate the case.[11] From his point of view, the position of Poland may have appeared so hopeless as to suggest at least the possibility of a reconsideration by Warsaw of its earlier negative stand. A surrender by Poland right after the destruction of Czechoslovakia and simultaneous with or immediately following those of Rumania and Lithuania would have assured quiet on Germany's eastern front while she faced Britain and France. The Germans were to learn quickly that Poland's leaders would not follow the example of Prague, Kovno, and Bucharest.

Although Polish Foreign Minister Josef Beck had returned discouraging answers to German approaches in prior months, there were indications that he was willing to explore possible new approaches to the Danzig question, and his comments at the conference in the Polish foreign ministry on 24 March show that he might well have been willing to return to them at some calmer time;[12] but the aftermath of the German occupation of Prague was hardly such a moment. Not only had the Czechoslovak government yielded to Germany the areas inhabited by Germans and allowed German extraterritorial routes across its territory—only to have these concessions pave the way for total German domination—but the very way in which the Germans assumed effective control of Slovakia was resented in Warsaw and perceived quite correctly as aimed at Poland.[13]

10. Hillgruber is so determined to disprove the ultimatum report of Viorel Tilea, the Rumanian minister in London, that his account (pp. 42–48) misses the main point. See *G.D.*, D, 6, Nos. 30, 31, 78, 131; *Hungarian Documents*, 3, Nos. 508, 509, 531, 546; Marguerat, pp. 132–35. Note the ecstatic comment of the quartermaster general of the German army, Eduard Wagner, in *Der Generalquartiermeister*, p. 85.

11. *S.U.*, No. 266. See also *Hungarian Documents*, 4, Nos. 28, 29; and Hitler's comments to Lipski on 1 March, *Lipski Papers*, No. 135.

12. The memorandum on this conference quotes Beck as saying: "The line [at which Poland would fight] also involves the nonacceptance by our state, regarding the drastic spot that Danzig has always been, of any unilateral suggestion to be imposed on us. And, regardless of what Danzig is worth as an object (in my opinion it may perhaps be worth quite a lot, but this is of no concern at the moment), under the present circumstances it has become a symbol" (*Lipski Papers*, No. 138). In this connection Beck's comments on Danzig while in London on 4 April should also be noted with care: "this [the Danzig question] was not yet in negotiable shape. Poland, in any event, would not be prepared to discuss it under threat or to accept any imposed solution" (*B.D.*, 3d, 5, No. 1, p. 3). Cf. *G.D.*, D, 6, No. 74. One has only to compare these discussions of Danzig with Beck's language in turning down anything he absolutely rejected to see the difference.

13. *Lipski Papers*, Nos. 136, 137; *G.D.*, D, 5, No. 139; 6, Nos. 4, 12; *Hungarian Documents*, 3, Nos. 410, 444, 454; 4, Nos. 21, 32; Cienciala, pp. 208–9.

When von Ribbentrop reiterated the Germans' demand for Danzig and the extraterritorial routes across the Corridor in exchange for a guarantee of Poland's western border, he also hinted at concessions in regard to Slovakia, invited Beck to follow Hácha to Berlin for the signing of a treaty—with the end of Poland by German-Soviet agreement threatened as the alternative.[14] The Polish government answered indirectly by military moves in the Corridor, showing its willingness to respond militarily to any German attempt for a fait accompli.[15] The direct reply was a polite no.[16] Though ready to discuss minor adjustments in the situation, the Poles would not meet the German demands, especially under circumstances that would both establish Poland's status as a client state of Germany—in the same way that joining the Anti-Comintern Pact would have—and open the way for further German demands, as in the case of Czechoslovakia, which had also been promised a German guarantee of the borders the German army had crossed the week before. The Germans came to think that the Polish government decided on 24–25 March to work out an agreement with England which now appeared feasible and to respond negatively to the German proposals.[17] Beck was in fact skeptical about Britain's willingness to fight Germany.[18] In replying firmly but politely, the Polish foreign minister was trying to stave off a German move but without provoking Berlin. He hoped that the recognition of Polish firmness would lead the Germans to reconsider the advisability of starting what would be a war rather than a diplomatic action, while simultaneously showing the British government that Poland would stand up for her own rights. He had already seen some signs that such a posture would find support in Britain and anticipated that a resulting Polish-British combination of some sort would restrain Germany and create a different international atmosphere.[19] Hitler, in the meantime, pondered the question of whether or not this Polish refusal should be considered final; for a short time he hesitated to consider it final, as, like Beck, he wanted to observe the development of British policy.[20] As Hitler told the commander-in-chief of the German army on 25 March, the possibility of a coup in Danzig was tied to some sign from Poland that such a step would be accepted, under protest but accepted nevertheless; a plan for military operations

14. *G.D.*, D, 6, No. 61; *Polish White Book*, No. 61; Szembek, pp. 433, 434; *Biddle Papers*, pp. 43–44. See also *G.D.*, D, 6, No. 73 for another, but not communicated, form of the German demands.

15. *Biddle Papers*, p. 46; *U.S.*, 1939, 1:102; *Hungarian Documents*, 4, Nos. 40, 43, 49, 50; *G.D.*, D, 6, No. 85; Hans Roos, "Die militärpolitische Lage und Planung Polens gegenüber Deutschland von 1939," *Wehrwissenschaftliche Rundschau*, 7, No. 4 (1957), 194. For a report on the sort of thing the Poles feared in Danzig, in this case with reference to Liechtenstein, see *G.D.*, D, 6, No. 141.

16. *Lipski Papers*, Nos. 138, 139; Szembek, pp. 438–39.

17. *G.D.*, D, 6, No. 299, p. 318.

18. Biddle tel. 30 of 18 March 1939, State 740.00/631.

19. The evidence is reviewed in Cienciala, pp. 214–18.

20. *G.D.*, D, 6, No. 99; Dertinger, "Informationsbericht Nr. 30," 25 March 1939, Bundesarchiv, Brammer, Z.Sg. 101/34, ff.153–57.

against Poland was to be prepared, but its execution would depend on factors yet to be developed. These factors, once it became clear from the Polish reply that a coup in Danzig would lead to more than protests,[21] would necessarily involve the German government's reading of the policies with which other nations responded to the events of 15 March.

With both Warsaw and Berlin looking in the direction of London, the development of policy there must now be traced. News of possible German moves against the truncated Czecho-Slovak state had reached London in early March 1939 from a variety of sources, but no action to defend what was perceived as a lost cause against what looked like internal dissolution under outside pressure was taken or even seriously contemplated.[22] The earlier alarms pointing to a sudden German attack in the west had led to firm decisions in London, but then had been followed by skepticism of such alarms and new hopes for the future when the anticipated German moves failed to occur.[23] Now the situation had again changed, the Munich settlement lay in ruins, the first mass of non-Germans had been subjected to Hitler's control.

The leaders of Britain were stunned in spite of the warnings received. If Chamberlain spoke cautiously in the House of Commons on 15 March, this was in part due to the need for a short time to assess the situation; what could be done or said when Czecho-Slovakia herself was obviously gone? This question would be answered soon after, but in his first public statement the prime minister alluded to the loss of confidence resulting from the German action, an issue of critical importance to the whole policy now coming to an end.[24] The steps taken immediately were few and minor. The trade talks were ended and the planned visit of the president of the board of trade, Oliver Stanley, to Germany was canceled. There was a great deal of debate about the recall of Ambassador Henderson, and it was finally decided to summon him back to London for consultations. Similarly, a formal protest was filed in Berlin, but primarily at French urging. The debate over these measures, however, points to a reluctance over reopening discussion of the details as opposed to the fundamental issues of the Czechoslovak question; they give little clue to the more basic reorientation in British policy maturing during the third week of March.[25]

21. The angry German referral throughout the 1939 negotiations to the Polish military steps in the Corridor in late March suggests that these constituted the omen read by Hitler as precluding Polish acceptance under protest of a German seizure of Danzig.

22. The evidence is summarized in Sidney Aster, *1939: The Making of the Second World War* (London: André Deutsch, 1973), pp. 21–23, 28–29; earlier information gathered by the Czechoslovak government is summarized by Luža, *Transfer*, pp. 174–75.

23. See above, pp. 525–27. There is a longer account in Aster, chap. 2.

24. Aster, pp. 28–32. An impression of the collapse of support for the policy of appeasement in the House of Commons by one of its strongest adherents may be found in Robert Rhodes James (ed.), *Chips: The Diary of Sir Henry Channon* (London: Weidenfeld & Nicholson, 1967), pp. 185–86.

25. On the immediate repercussions of 15 March on the British government, see Aster, pp. 29–37; Julian C. Doherty, *Das Ende des Appeasement* (Berlin: Colloquium, 1973), pp. 103–8; *G.D.*, D, 4, No. 244; 5, Nos. 11, 16, 35; Strang minute of 16 March on Henderson's

In the cabinet and other internal discussions of 15 and 16 March as well as in Lord Halifax's strong comments to German Ambassador von Dirksen there are evident the themes that would appear in Chamberlain's speech in Birmingham on 17 March. The British leaders believed that they had tried to work for a peaceful settlement of European disputes, giving the clearest evidence of their determination by agreeing to the cession to Germany of those portions of Czechoslovakia inhabited by Germans. Now Hitler, without provocation, excuse, or negotiations had seized the areas inhabited by his own admission overwhelmingly by Czechs. He had broken not only his promise that the Sudeten area was his last territorial demand but also the basis of his case for the unification of German peoples under German control. Thus the whole assessment of German aims on which British policy had been based was altered. As Chamberlain asked: "Is this the end of an old adventure or is it the beginning of a new? Is this the last attack upon a small State, or is it to be followed by others? Is this, in fact, a step in the direction of an attempt to dominate the world by force?"[26] The very defense Chamberlain presented of his policy at Munich pointed to a policy now terminated by German initiative. The indications were that the new policy to take its place would be less compromising, that the old German argument would simply not be accepted any more, and that an entirely different line would be taken. The process of defining that new line would be quicker than might have been expected, but that was due to a fact then hidden from public view, namely, that the discussion of a firm policy if Germany moved into Holland, as rumored earlier in the year, helped to shape the thinking of those in the British government who had participated in it.

The precipitating element around which the new British policy crystallized with astonishing rapidity was the allegation that Germany was threatening to move into Rumania. As in the case of the Morocco scare of January 1937 and the May Crisis over Czechoslovakia in 1938, there would subsequently be much agitated discussion of the real or imaginary character of the German threat. In this instance, I read the evidence as showing that the Rumanians had excellent reasons for believing that Wohlthat was pressuring for concessions, and that those in the Rumanian government and diplomatic service who did not want their country to fall under German domination dramatized this pressure to an extent not entirely warranted by the situation but without substantial distortion.

No. 110 of 15 March 1939 and Cadogan note of 16 March 1939, C 3123 and C 3313/19/18, FO 371/22993; *B.D.*, 3d, 6, Nos. 247, 264 (comments in C 3102/15/18, FO 371/22966), 308, 401; Cabinet 11 (39) of 15 March 1939, C 3353/19/18, FO 371/22993; Colvin, *None So Blind*, pp. 294–95; Johnson (chargé London) tel. 351 of 17 March 1939, State 740.00/628.

26. Full text in Chamberlain, *The Struggle for Peace*, pp. 413–20. Aster (p. 35) refers to this as Chamberlain's most important speech of 1939 and adds: "When Chamberlain spoke in public, he may have been discreet, . . . but he was always honest." Cf. *G.D.*, D, 6, No. 23.

Rumania faced threats and pressures, though not the immediate danger of invasion.[27]

Whether or not the danger was as immediate and dramatic as suggested by the Rumanian minister in London, Viorel Tilea, and at first believed by the British government, is really of secondary importance. As the German intervention in Spain in the summer and fall of 1936 had first made plausible the rumors of German landings in Morocco; as the invasion of Austria had made credible the rumors of German troop movements in May of 1938—and had left the authorities in London skeptical in May of German denials exactly like the false denials of March—so the reports of German threats to move against Rumania sounded plausible immediately after German troops had suddenly moved into Bohemia and Moravia. The fact that Hungary had moved troops into the Carpatho-Ukraine in obvious concert with Germany and that Hungary was known to be antagonistic to Rumania suggested the obvious possibility of Germany's securing the right to send troops across Hungary into Rumania in exchange for the territorial expansion of Hungary at Rumania's expense.[28] Such an arrangement would not be worked out by the Germans until the following year, but it is hardly surprising that it looked very likely from the perspective of London in 1939.

From London, previously alerted to possible German moves on Rumania, currently perturbed by intelligence reports on German military concentrations in Bohemia that were hardly warranted in the absence of Czech resistance, and knowing of Hungarian and Bulgarian revisionist aspirations against Rumania, the imminent threat to the latter could cause anxiety even if the Rumanian government itself came to downplay the danger. The fact that a few days after almost repudiating Tilea the Rumanians signed an agreement with Germany so favorable to Germany's economic and political interests as to lead Hungary and Bulgaria to suspect that only German guarantees *against* revision had secured Rumanian acquiescence, would leave the British certain that their initial concern had been essentially correct, whatever the precise nature of the negotiations

27. Aster, chap. 3, covers the story in great detail, partly on the basis of information provided by Viroel V. Tilea, the Rumanian minister in London, who played a key role in it. See also *Hungarian Documents*, 3, Nos. 495, 496, 502, 504; 4, Nos. 22, 25; *U.S., 1939*, 1:72, 74–75, 79–80; Kennedy tel. 380 of 18 March 1939, State 740.00/630; Bullitt tel. 539 of 22 March 1939, State 762.71/49; James, *Chips*, pp. 186–96; *Pownall Diary*, pp. 192–93; Doherty, pp. 108–11; Chanady and Jensen, pp. 211–17; Irving, *Breach of Security*, p. 28; C 3538, C 3563/3356/18, FO 371/23060 (on the latter of these documents, which pertains to the Reuters report on the Rumanian denial that there had been an ultimatum, there is the annotation "Compare my message received from 'C.' this morning"—a reference to a Secret Service report, ibid., f.79); Sir Reginald Hoare to Ingram, 19 March 1939, C 4655/3356/18, FO 371/23062; *S.U.*, No. 155; *G.D.*, D, 6, No. 42. Note that the Rumanian ambassador in Warsaw also referred to a German ultimatum, Biddle tel. 28 of 18 March 1939, State 762.71/35; cf. Bullitt tel. 514 of 18 March 1939, State 762.71/40; MacMurray (Ankara) tel. 20 of 27 March 1939, State 740.00/693.

28. See *Hungarian Documents*, 4, No. 7.

between Berlin and Bucharest.[29] The international uproar which followed Tilea's deliberate leaking of the ultimatum story to the press very likely stiffened the Rumanian government against even greater concessions to Germany; and in this case there were immediate as well as long-range effects from the way in which the Rumanian minister had drawn attention to the renewed persistence with which Wohlthat pushed the Rumanian government after 15 March.[30] It is the impact of the Rumanian issue on broader questions of British policy, as contrasted with the details of German-Rumanian relations, however, that must be examined.

When the cabinet met in London on the evening of 18 March, Chamberlain presented his ideas on policy.[31] The minutes deserve quotation at some length.

> The Prime Minister said that up till a week ago we had proceeded on the assumption that we should be able to continue with our policy of getting on to better terms with the Dictator Powers, and that although those powers had aims, those aims were limited . . . . he had now come definitely to the conclusion that Herr Hitler's attitude made it impossible to continue to negotiate on the old basis . . . . No reliance could be placed on any of the assurances given by the Nazi leaders . . . . it was on the basis of this conclusion . . . that he had made his speech at Birmingham on the 17th March . . . . he regarded his speech as a challenge to Germany on the issue whether or not Germany intended to dominate Europe by force. It followed that if Germany took another step in the direction of dominating Europe, she would be accepting the challenge. A German attempt to dominate Roumania was, therefore, more than a question whether Germany would thereby improve her strategical position; it raised the whole question whether Germany intended to obtain domination over the whole of South Eastern Europe. He agreed, therefore, with the Foreign Secretary's view that if Germany were to proceed with this course after warning had been given, we had no alternative but to take up the challenge. On this basis our next course was to ascertain what friends we had who would join with us in resisting aggression. Asked whether we alone should resist German aggression, the Prime Minister said that this was not in his mind. He added that he thought that at least we could rely on the co-operation of the French . . . . he was not asking the Cabinet to determine there and then whether we should declare war on Germany if Germany invaded Roumania. What he wished to ascertain was whether the Cabinet agreed generally with the change of policy which he had outlined.

29. Note the comment by F. K. Roberts of the Foreign Office on 24 March on the record of the Cadogan-Tilea meeting of 20 March: "The account of German-Rumanian Agreement which has appeared in the press seems to justify M. Tilea" (C 3709/3356/18, FO 371/23061). Chanady and Jensen, pp. 214 and 216, come to essentially the same conclusion, stressing Rumanian perception of the reality of a military threat.

30. Gunther (Bucharest) dispatches 830 of 4 April and 834 of 5 April 1939, State 762.71/87 and 89.

31. Cabinet 12 (39) in C 3632/15/18, FO 371/22967.

The chancellor of the exchequer, Sir John Simon, who had been foreign secretary when Hitler came to power in Germany, "said that he was in entire agreement." The Dominions secretary reported that in a meeting with the Dominions high commissioners that afternoon he had heard their agreement with the prime minister's Birmingham speech. Oliver Stanley, the president of the board of trade, also agreed with the prime minister's speech and analysis. Stressing that "the real point was, not whether we could prevent Roumania from being overrun, but whether, if we went to war with Germany, we could defeat her," he noted that the last war had shown that the temporary overrunning of one country "would not affect the final outcome." He thought it especially important that "in approaching other countries not to lay too much emphasis on the fact that our attitude would depend on theirs." The fact that after stressing that "we should make it clear that we were in favor of action to resist German aggression" Stanley was to be included in the group designated to draft the telegrams that were to be sent out to the countries of East and Southeast Europe is noteworthy.

Lord Halifax agreed with the view that the British approach should not be confined to the question of an attack on Rumania. His perception is expressed in the minutes as follows:

> The real issue was Germany's attempt to obtain world domination, which it was in the interest of all countries to resist. He agreed that we were the only country who could organize such resistance. It was, no doubt, equally difficult for this country to find effective means of attacking Germany, whether Germany attacked Roumania or Holland. The attitude of the German government was either bluff, in which case it would be stopped by a public declaration on our part; or it was not bluff, in which case it was necessary that we should all unite to meet it, and the sooner we united the better. Otherwise we might see one country after another absorbed by Germany.

Chamberlain's view was

> that the real point at issue was whether we could obtain sufficient assurances from other countries to justify us in a public pronouncement that we should resist any further act of aggression on the part of Germany. He thought that such an announcement might deter Germany at any rate for a period, and that we should take full advantage of the breathing-space thus offered. He thought that Poland was very likely the key to the situation . . . . we should explain . . . that we thought that the time had now come for those who were threatened by German aggression (whether immediately or ultimately) to get together. We should enquire how far Poland was prepared to go along these lines.

The prime minister did not think that an immediate attack on Rumania was likely, but even so Britain should approach a series of countries—Russia, Poland, Yugoslavia, Turkey, Greece, and Rumania were mentioned—to see whether support would be forthcoming from them "in order that we could make a strong pronouncement of our determination to resist further German aggression with the knowledge that we should be supported in such action." The cabinet agreed that in concert with the French government such approaches should be made, and that if satisfactory assurances could be obtained, a public announcement of British intention to resist any new act of German aggression in Southeast Europe should be made.

In the next few days, these projects would be implemented, and as the implementation was affected by the responses of others and new British perceptions of dangers in Europe, there would be some modifications. None of these, however, went far outside the framework set by Chamberlain and his cabinet on 18 March. The government in London would try to recruit allies; and there was hope that Germany either might be bluffing or would be deterred by an impressive anti-aggression front; but if the Germans moved in new aggressive action, the situation would clearly be one in which England would fight. In 1938 the London government had hoped to avoid war by postponing commitment to the last minute: if Czechoslovakia and France were left in doubt of British help, they might make greater concessions; if the Germans were left to worry about possible British intervention if they went to war, they might prefer to make a peaceful agreement. When this strategy appeared to work, first, because Czechoslovakia made enormous concessions and, second, because Hitler at the last moment shrank from testing British resolve and refrained from attacking Czechoslovakia, there had appeared to be hope of continued peace. Now that the Germans had destroyed that settlement, an entirely new approach would be tried. The British warning would come at the beginning, not the end, of negotiations; and the Germans would be left the choice of restraint or war, while potential victims of German aggression could yield if they were so minded or resist in the knowledge that they could count on British help.[32] The exact location—and hence the local details which might be stressed by German propaganda—made no difference in the basic British policy; nothing makes this more obvious than Lord Halifax's combining Holland and Rumania at a meeting of the cabinet that had agreed a few weeks earlier to go to war if Germany invaded the former. From the perspective of both geography and prior British views of their own vital interests, the two countries coupled in this fashion were far apart; but in the policy of restraining a German drive for European or world domination they were in the same category.

The cabinet deliberations reflected a general shift of British public opinion which reacted very strongly to the breaking of the Munich agree-

---

32. The British decision to protest the annexation of Memel without considering that action as aggression like the feared German moves against Poland or Rumania can be understood in this framework. *B.D.*, 3d, 4, No. 441; Collier minute of 21 March 1939 on this document in N 1500/30/59, FO 371/23600.

ment. In all walks of life, there was a distinct breach with the past. As the British Legion, the main English veterans organization, phrased it on 25 March in declining an invitation to a meeting to be held in Berlin: "The events of the last few weeks have aroused the most profound resentment in every section of the community in Great Britain, and not least among ex-service men."[33]

In some ways the reaction in Paris, at least of Daladier himself, but to a great extent of the French public and of many in the government as well, was similar. If the French humiliation over abandoning their Czechoslovak ally at Munich had been greater, and the willingness of many both in prominent positions and among ordinary people simply to write off French interests in all of Eastern Europe had also been greater than such currents in England, the French had been recalled to a firmer position by the publicity attendant upon Italy's aspirations for expansion. The fact that these aspirations, whether or not Rome intended to pursue them with force, involved not only allies or colonial areas but portions of metropolitan France brought home the danger of Axis aggression in a way nothing else could. Hitler's constant public reiteration of his renunciation of any claim to Alsace-Lorraine was based on an assessment of the French that was far shrewder than Mussolini's. The tearing up of the Munich agreement, coming so soon after the voicing of demands by Germany's Italian partner for Nice, Corsica, and Savoy would really alarm the French.

The trade talks between France and Germany were broken off as abruptly as the English-German ones.[34] Not only was it at French insistence that protests were delivered in Berlin, but the whole pattern of reaction in Paris was at first stunned and then angry. As reported to London, Berlin, and Washington, the French government—even including Bonnet—had "had it."[35] When the British ambassador before leaving for England saw Daladier on 18 March, he was asked to tell Chamberlain and Halifax that France would speed up her rearmament, stand firm, and resist any further aggression.[36] At lunch with American Ambassador Bullitt the same day, Daladier expressed his preference for dropping Bonnet. He voiced a certain determination to go to war if Germany moved on Danzig or Poland and discussed the possibilities of real help for Poland and Rumania from the Soviet Union with Bullitt, who had been ambassador in Moscow

33. Wotton, p. 253. See also Sven Hedin's noting of the changed views of Lord Londonderry from 12 to 20 March in his *Ohne Auftrag in Berlin* (Tübingen: Internationaler Universitäts-Verlag, 1950), p. 38. For a Canadian assessment of the British policy change, speculating that it was perhaps designed to impress the United States, see *Canadian Documents,* 6, No. 946. An analysis by the French ambassador to London of 4 April 1939 is summarized in Adamthwaite, pp. 305–6.

34. *G.D.,* D, 6, No. 11.

35. Ibid., 4, No. 244; 6, Nos. 20, 22; *B.D.,* 3d, 4, Nos. 270, 276, 278, 280, 281; Phipps tel. 136 Saving of 17 March 1939, C 3393/130/17, FO 371/22916; *Hungarian Documents,* 3, Nos. 492, 534. Adamthwaite (pp. 129, 134–35, 301–2) stresses the extent to which the government was stiffened by the Chamber which, for once, was in session at the time of crisis.

36. Phipps tel. 111 of 18 March 1939, C 3377/90/17, FO 371/22912.

before his assignment to Paris. Bullitt cautioned about Russian duplicity but said France should negotiate for assistance anyway. Poland and Rumania, he was certain, would fight if the Red Army entered, but he thought that it might be possible to arrange for arms, munitions, and planes to be supplied to them by the Soviet Union in case of war.[37] Although the issues which would dominate the diplomacy of subsequent weeks are touched on here, one further point must be made about Daladier's expression of determination. He had sounded similarly determined at times in 1938, and his weakening as conveyed to London in September had contributed to the British decision to arrange a settlement on the basis of a territorial transfer. Would such a weakening occur again? An interesting clue to this question is in a report on the views of Pierre-Etienne Flandin sent to Berlin on 22 March. The great French advocate of appeasing Germany and cutting French commitments lamented the collapse of the earlier policy and noted the complete change in France as well as England. There would be no return to past policies after the situation had calmed down, and any in Germany who thought so, or who thought that Germany's stronger position would restrain France and England, were deluding themselves. The democracies, and especially the British democracy, react slowly, Flandin asserted, but once the English had decided to act, nothing would hold them back.[38] There would be no new Munich, as the French explained to the Vatican in June when the new Pope Pius XII urged a conference. First Hitler would have to restore the promise of the last Munich—an independent Czechoslovakia—before any thought could be given to a new one.[39]

The details of how to act and in what manner to proceed were changed during the last two weeks of March. The London government kept the initiative but moved in concert with the French. Their first approach was to the countries listed above (p. 543), asking them what they would do to help Rumania if she were attacked. The responses were to a large extent questions about what England proposed to do. A variety of schemes was canvassed in London, and some of these were tried out on various governments; but views on three points crystallized during these days of diplomatic maneuvering.[40] Throughout the British governmental discussions, the redefining of a new policy of warning Germany that Britain

37. The full text of Bullitt's tel. 513 of 18 March is in 740.00/632; only excerpts are printed in *Bullitt Papers*, pp. 323–25. It should be noted that in this conversation Daladier expressed doubts about Bullitt's certainty that Poland would fight rather than yield to Germany. The French prime minister thought Beck "completely in the hands of the Germans"; by 31 March he was delighted to see the opposite and that "he had been wrong in his opinion of Beck" (Bullitt tel. 605, State 740.00/715). Cf. *Bullitt Papers*, p. 332.

38. *G.D.*, D, 6, No. 69. For signs of a weaker French position, however, see Cienciala, pp. 215–16.

39. *Le Saint Siège et la guerre en Europe*, 1, Nos. 59, 73.

40. The details cannot be recounted here. They are covered by the recent works of Aster (chap. 4) and Doherty (pp. 114–27) as well as the earlier books by Namier, Hofer, and Beloff.

would go to war if Germany attacked another country became increasingly precise. If on 18 March Chamberlain had still thought of awaiting the support of others before committing England, he increasingly turned to the view that a firm British commitment to act was in England's own interest, was more likely to rally others to her side, and would offer a greater hope of saving the peace by deterring aggression.[41]

A second point already stressed in the cabinet meeting of 18 March and increasingly evident thereafter was the key role of Poland. Not only did Poland appear to be a likely victim of German demands and possible aggression, she was also a country known to have close ties with Rumania, the country which appeared to be subject to immediate German demands and whose oil and grain resources would be critical to any allied plans for blockading Germany in case of war. If Poland gave in to German demands and became subservient to the Third Reich, Hitler could turn all his forces on the West, a factor as obvious to London in March 1939 as it had been to Berlin in the months since October 1938 when von Ribbentrop on Hitler's instructions had first tried to implement such a policy. The Poles themselves, however, while they wanted British and French support against German demands, still hoped that Germany might temporize rather than attack, and they wished to do nothing that might provoke a war.

41. Meeting of ministers at 10 Downing Street, 19 March 1939, C 3858, C 3859/15/18, FO 371/22961; Cabinet 13 (39) of 20 March and Cabinet 14 (39) of 22 March, C 3598 and C 3889/15/18, ibid.; 38th meeting of the cabinet Committee on Foreign Policy, CAB 27/624; Feiling, pp. 401–3, 407; *G.D.*, D, 6, No. 48; Halifax, p. 209. Conferences with the French on 21–22 March played a part in the deliberations, see Aster, pp. 87–88; *Harvey Diaries*, p. 297.

Note Dalton's impression of the prime minister's briefing of Labor leaders on the situation in the negotiations: "We all get the impression that the P.M. now realized that his 'appeasement' policy has been a failure; that he is completely disillusioned with Hitler, and very apprehensive about the future" (Dalton Diary, 23 March 1939, London School of Economics). Chamberlain recorded himself as responding in a private talk with Irish Prime Minister Eamon de Valera two days later to the statement that de Valera "hoped very much that what had happened would not deflect me from the policy of appeasement even though methods had to some extent to be altered. In particular, he hoped that I should not be tempted to embark upon a preventive war. I replied that I would never do that and that in my view the policy was still the same, namely, the securing of peace by the removal of reasonable causes of war, whilst pursuing a programme of re-armament, but I said that, Hitler having now demonstrated that his word could not be relied on, it was at present hopeless to engage in any negotiations with him or [for?] a settlement of grievances and, on the contrary, it was necessary in my view to see what steps could be taken to prevent his pursuing any further his policy of swallowing neighbouring small states. With all this Mr. de Valera agreed, though with deep regret and reluctance. He said, however, that he much feared that we should find it impossible to stop Hitler's further advance in Eastern Europe since we should be faced with the crumbling of the resistance of the smaller states who would be so frightened that they would make agreements with Germany, the effect of which would be to subject them to her domination. I replied that I fully appreciated this point, but that we hoped, that if we could give certain specific assurances, to strengthen the will to resistance on the part of those who otherwise would be the next victims of German aggression" (Memorandum by Chamberlain of 27 March 1939 in Halifax Papers, FO 800/310, ff.220–21). Cf. the analyses of the Hungarian ministers in London and Berlin (*Hungarian Documents*, 3, Nos. 525, 555).

Although German diplomats and propagandists would proclaim loudly and repeatedly that Poland was reckless and provocative, the facts were the exact opposite. Throughout the negotiations the Polish government erred, if at all, on the side of caution, to such an extent that in the end they would be attacked before they had completed their own mobilization. While caution lest Germany be provoked was one element in Poland's refusal to participate in a common front with the Soviet Union, certainly another was her fear that the Red Army, if once in the country, would never leave.[42] Most of Poland's leaders in 1939 were not only anti-Communist in political orientation but had participated in the war against Russia from 1918 to 1920. This recent experience, combined with a hatred and fear of Russia derived from centuries of war, partition, and abortive uprisings, made the leaders of Poland—as well as the vast majority of the nationally Polish segment of the population—most dubious about Russian good faith and Soviet help. As they had refused to align themselves formally with Germany for fear of falling under her control, so the Polish government would decline any formal alignment with the Soviet Union. If the British and French had any doubts on this score, they would quickly be disabused.

While the Western Powers either already recognized or soon learned that the Poles did not wish to be associated in a common front with the Soviet Union, they themselves had very mixed feelings about close cooperation with Russia, the third of the critical issues of late March.[43] They had grave doubts that effective cooperation between Poland and Rumania on the one hand and the Soviet Union on the other was possible, and they were very doubtful that the Russians were in any position to provide much more than supplies to their neighbors. The assessment of Soviet military power by the British and French military and political leaders in 1939 was remarkably uniform: the Russians would defend themselves vigorously if attacked; they were not in any condition after the purges and in view of the communication and transportation system near their borders to develop any strong offensive beyond those borders. Although the French appear to have changed their opinions of Soviet military power—somewhat raising it in the summer of 1939 and then lowering it in the winter of 1939–40—the British held to the same view consistently. As Chamberlain wrote on 1 January 1940, when the inability of the Red Army to defeat Finland in the time it had taken Germany to defeat Poland appeared to give substance to the prior assessment at the same time as it aroused more vehement anti-Soviet sentiments throughout the world: "I

42. Litvinov's suggestion of mid-March for a partition of the Baltic States into Soviet and Polish spheres of influence along the line of the Dvina River was likely to increase rather than decrease Polish apprehensions (Budurowycz, p. 145).

43. Note the argument between Cadogan and Vansittart over the relative demerits of Italy and the Soviet Union as a potential ally of Britain in late March 1939, in C 3865/19/18, FO 371/22996.

still regard Germany as the Public Enemy No. 1, and I cannot take Russia very seriously as an aggressive force though no doubt formidable if attacked in her own country."[44]

The concept that Soviet help to the Poles was not likely to be particularly effective reinforced the knowledge that it would not be especially welcome. Stalin's determined efforts to appease Hitler until the very moment of the German attack in 1941 suggest that the Soviet leader's assessment of his country's military power was not so far different from that entertained in the West. What all this meant for Soviet policy in 1939 will be examined in a moment; but the view from London, here discussed first, certainly suggested that the Soviet government might contribute to the deterrent effect of a British commitment to aid Poland or Rumania by a similar promise, with the implementation of any such promise if war did come being left as vague as the implementation of the commitment from London. Faced with the reality, as opposed to the theoretical contingency, of a German attack, all sorts of problems would look different both to the victims of invasion and to the prospective allies of the latter.

What the internal deliberations of the British government reveal is both confusion and ambivalence about the best way to obtain from Moscow a promise to assist any future victim of German aggression, in the hope that the deterrent effect of a British-French anti-aggression front would be strengthened by Soviet support, under circumstances and in a form which would not have the opposite effect of either directly provoking a German attack or indirectly inviting such an attack through the repercussions of an alignment with Russia on the very countries to be protected against attack. If these problems were never resolved, as the interminable discussions within the British and French governments and between them and the Soviet government throughout the spring and summer of 1939 would reveal, one must, in my opinion, keep constantly in mind a fundamental difference in the appreciation of the situation as seen from London on the one hand and from Moscow on the other.

In London the constantly reiterated belief that a war, once started anywhere, would surely involve Great Britain meant that the emphasis should be on such measures as might avoid a war altogether and those which would strengthen the side Britain would fight on if war started after all. Such a war, it was assumed in a complete reversal of the pre-1914 beliefs, was sure to be a long one; and the hope was that at the end the Allies would again triumph over Germany. Whether war started in the east or in the west, it was important for the hope of such a victory that a maximum possible strain be imposed on Germany on both fronts since initial German military superiority was assumed and only Germany's divided exertions had exhausted her in the World War to a point where, with the United States replacing Russia, the Allies had finally triumphed.

44. Quoted in Feiling, pp. 427–28.

From London, as from Paris, the hope of victory in what was believed would be a lengthy and difficult war was closely associated with the two-front concept—and it was simultaneously hoped that by presenting Hitler with the prospect of such a war he just might be convinced to desist from launching one.[45]

From the perspective of Moscow, the situation was rather different. Nothing suggests that Stalin was not also worried about German military strength and the prospects of a war with such a powerful adversary, and nothing suggests that he too did not want all the allies he could get if the Soviet Union were ever involved in a war with Germany; but there is considerable evidence to show that Stalin did not share the opinion that a war started by Germany *anywhere* would necessarily involve the Soviet Union on the opposing side—it might, but it might not. Stalin's famous speech of 10 March cannot be interpreted, as some have tried to do, as the reflection of a decision to align himself with Germany, but it certainly does express a view that a war in Europe need not involve the Soviet Union at all. The Soviet Union might remain aloof from such a war—at least until a time of its own choosing—and a German aggressive move need not necessarily bring on a general conflict.[46]

If we ask what led Stalin to this view and what sort of war not involving the Soviet Union he may have visualized, we are confronted with the fact that the available evidence is necessarily indirect and incomplete. The ideological predisposition to believe that so-called capitalist-imperialist states were destined to fight each other or gang up for a joint attack on Soviet Russia would suggest the possibility of an option: a war within the capitalist camp from which the Soviet Union could remain aloof. The geographic realities almost forced a frame around this broader view. If Germany attacked in the west, there would certainly be an option for Russia to join in or abstain from the conflict as Stalin thought best; there is no evidence that Stalin believed a war in Western Europe, which he appears to have thought would be a long, drawn-out struggle, *necessarily*

45. This calculation never assumed that Germany would be *held* in the east, only that she would be strained by fighting there as well as in the west. This point was made slightly differently by Lord Halifax in the cabinet Committee on Foreign Policy on 27 March: "He argued that there was probably no way in which France and ourselves could prevent Poland and Rumania from being overrun. We were faced with the dilemma of doing nothing or entering into a devastating war. If we did nothing, this in itself would mean a great accession to Germany's strength and a great loss to ourselves of sympathy and support in the United States, in the Balkan countries and in other parts of the world. In those circumstances if we had to choose between two great evils he favored our going to war" (CAB 27/624, f.213). Lord Chatfield, the minister for the coordination of defense, expressed agreement with these views; they are reflected fairly accurately in his not always very informative memoirs, *The Navy and Defence*, 2 (London: W. Heinemann, 1947), 175.

46. The text of his speech is in Joseph V. Stalin, *Leninism* (New York: International Publishers, 1940), pp. 619–70; important sections in Beloff, 2:221–23. The opinion that this speech reflects a previous decision by Stalin to sign with Germany is advanced in Angelo Rossi (pseud. of Angelo Tasca), *Deux ans d'alliance germano-soviétique* (Paris: Plon, 1949), p. 217. For a list of contemporary diplomatic reports and interpretations, see Weinberg, *Germany and the Soviet Union*, p. 13, n.48. See also Toscano, *Designs*, pp. 52–53.

involved a role for Russia. The concept of a two-front war as an absolute requirement for the defeat of Germany did not occur to Stalin until June 1941 after a second front had existed twice only to be erased while Russia aided the Third Reich. If Germany attacked in the east, and that meant if she attacked Poland, then the critical question would be whether the attack was just a sort of transit operation leading to an attack on the Soviet Union itself—in which case there would clearly be no option—or whether it might be a separable act which, especially if Germany became involved in a war in the west because of the attack on Poland, would give Moscow the choice between joining Germany's enemies, remaining aloof altogether, or joining with Germany.

The information received by Moscow in the winter of 1938–39 was undoubtedly analyzed with great care. We do not know—and are unlikely to know for many decades, if ever—what all the information was and how it was interpreted; but there are some very important clues. The Soviet government has itself published some of the reports from agents in locations critical for an assessment of German plans. In 1937 the Russians had recruited Rudolf von Scheliha, counsellor of embassy in the German embassy in Warsaw, who supplied the Soviet government with information from there until the outbreak of war.[47] While a number of von Scheliha's reports have been published, it is difficult to believe that there were no others.[48] Certainly whatever else he reported and Moscow believed or discounted, the Moscow government could learn two things from Scheliha: the Germans were making demands on Poland, and the Poles had not agreed to fulfill them. On these two key issues Stalin was apparently as well, if not better, informed by March 1939 than either London or Paris, which Beck had tried to keep in the dark about his difficulties with the Germans as long as possible.

The other key informant was the long-time Soviet agent Richard Sorge, who supplied Moscow with information from the German embassy in Tokyo.[49] Again we probably do not have a full run of Sorge's reports, but again two things stand out in those of his reports from Tokyo in the winter of 1938–39 which have been published. The Germans were trying to secure an alliance with Japan; but while the Japanese were willing to make an alliance as long as it was directed against the Soviet Union, the Germans kept insisting, and the Japanese kept refusing, that such an alliance be extended to apply to the Western Powers. We do not know what interpretation Stalin placed on these reports, and on similar ones then appearing in the press as a result of leaks in Tokyo, but it is reasonable to assume that the information pointed to the possibility that Germany was not

47. Von Scheliha continued thereafter to send reports from Berlin until his arrest in October 1942; he was executed in December of that year (Höhne, *Codeword Direktor*, pp. 148–49, 165–67, 191, 202).

48. *S.U.*, Nos. 45, 79, 83, 84, 276, 388.

49. A new scholarly work on Sorge is needed; the best work is Frederick W. Deakin and G. R. Storry, *The Case of Richard Sorge* (London: Chatto & Windus, 1966).

thinking of an attack on Poland as merely a preliminary to an invasion of Russia—in which case an alliance with Japan against Russia would surely have been desired by Berlin—but was at least as much concerned with the possibility of a war with the Western Powers.

Stalin's 10 March speech, whether based on such information and assessments or not, certainly reflected a view of the international situation in which Russia might have, and hence could explore, a range of alternative courses of action.[50] Certainly there was nothing in either this speech or in any other speech or action of the Soviet leaders which in any way resembled the often expressed view of the British leaders that a war anywhere in Europe would quickly spread as the World War had spread from the Balkans to engulf the world. If the Soviet government had once accepted the view expressed by Litvinov to the effect that peace was indivisible, there were no signs of it in 1939.

The Soviet reaction to the German destruction of Czechoslovakia on 15 March a few days after Stalin's speech confirms the sense of isolated observation with an eye to alternatives just described. As the Germans, who had long denounced Czechoslovakia as the Central European outpost of Moscow, noted with interest, Soviet reaction to the events of 15–16 March was mild indeed: a mixture of polite disapproval over the German occupation of Bohemia and Moravia with a sense of relief over the Hungarian occupation of the Carpatho-Ukraine.[51] The reaction of Moscow to the immediately ensuing changes in British and French policy is even more revealing. While the exchanges about British and Russian proposals concerning the possibility of support for the next victims of German aggression were in progress,[52] the Soviet government was establishing an interpretation of Western policy which would subsequently never vary and has remained the official line of Soviet historiography until the present. Although Maisky appears to have reported accurately on British reaction to the German move of 15 March, he was told by Litvinov that this was all a passing mood and that Britain and France would go back to the line that Soviet propaganda ascribed to them, that of trying to get Hitler to attack in the east.[53] At the very time that the British

50. The first part of March 1939 was a time when the Soviet government began efforts at securing several Finnish islands in the Gulf of Finland in exchange for parts of Soviet Karelia. Was this a part of a program of Stalin for sealing the Soviet Union off from developments in Central Europe? See *G.D.*, D, 5, No. 470; 6, Nos. 60, 257, n.3; *Moffat Papers*, pp. 238–39; *U.S.*, 1939, 1:953–54, 954–55, 957. Perhaps Litvinov's sounding of the Polish ambassador in March (n.42, above) belongs in this context.

51. See esp. *G.D.*, D, 6, No. 51. The Soviet Union was the only non-Axis power to accord de jure recognition to Slovakia.

52. A substantial selection of the relevant documents has been published in *B.D.*, 3d, 4, chaps. 5 and 6. See also *S.U.*, Nos. 160–64.

53. An abridged text of Litvinov's letter of 19 March is in *S.U.*, No. 167. Although this letter appears to be a response to reports from Maisky on British reactions, only one of these asserting that the British were taking the threat to Rumania seriously, regardless of whether or not there had been a German ultimatum, has been published (ibid., No. 165). The first report of Surits from Paris appears to have been similarly accurate (see ibid., No. 189).

government was casting about for ways to deter Hitler from moving east or to make sure he faced strong resistance if he did so, the Russian government was determined to interpret this policy as meaning the exact opposite, and to use this explanation to explain a free hand for itself.[54]

In the negotiations of 20–30 March, therefore, in which the British government tried to find a way to harmonize a common front against German aggression with Poland and Rumania on the one hand with the Soviet Union on the other, the official Soviet line—now voiced by Maisky in response to Litvinov's coaching—was that Chamberlain was not yet willing to accept military obligations in Eastern Europe although he said he was.[55] As is well known, Chamberlain was to do precisely that on 31 March and to lead his country into war pursuant to the obligation then assumed. The fact that the British step of 31 March would leave the Soviet government less, not more, inclined to cooperate with England and France as well as the whole lengthy diplomatic bargaining of 1939 can be understood only if one recognizes that this deliberate and continuing misinterpretation of British and French policy in Moscow had been formulated as an accompaniment to exploring options for staying out of a war with Germany, options which appeared to the Soviet leaders to have been made conceivable by what they knew or thought they had reason to believe about German plans and intentions. While they would explore the latter most cautiously in the spring and summer of 1939, the very steps that the Western Powers took to confirm their opposition to German expansion eastward only increased the possibility that a German attack on Poland might result in a European war from which the Soviet Union would try to profit without the danger of major participation. It is at least possible that in this Stalin was influenced by the situation in East Asia, where the Soviet Union was relieved to see Japan embroiled in an apparently endless war in China and where a trickle of aid to the Chinese Nationalist government seemed to pay enormous dividends for a minimal investment.

As already mentioned, there were agitated discussions in London about the fate of Rumania in late March while the Rumanian government tried unsuccessfully to secure a small share of the Carpatho-Ukraine. When that failed in the face of Hungarian greed backed by German might, Bucharest tried to keep on the best possible terms with Germany in spite of the pleasure over British interest.[56] The discussions and negotiations about Rumania, which had included concern about Poland from the start, were to crystallize into a public formulation of policy as a result of reports

54. See ibid., No. 171 and n.85.

55. Ibid., No. 187; other relevant documents, ibid., Nos. 176–94, passim; *B.D.*, 3d, 4, chap. 6; C 3727/3356/18, FO 371/23061. See also *Les relations franco-britanniques*, pp. 403–11.

56. On the Hungarian-Rumanian tension over the Carpatho-Ukraine, see above, p. 497; see also *Hungarian Documents*, 3, Nos. 450, 469, 481, 484, 503, 507, 510–13, 517, 519, 520, 537, 549, 551, 559, 561; 4, Nos. 1–27, passim. On Rumanian efforts to stay on good terms with Berlin, see *G.D.*, D, 6, Nos. 80, 92, 153.

reaching London about German-Polish relations while the formation of an
anti-aggression front was being considered.

The Germans had presented their demands to the Poles again on 21
March only to have them politely declined on 26 March. The Polish dec-
lination had been worded in such a manner as to leave open the possibility of further negotiations.[57] The German government recognized this fact
but, as will be seen, preferred not to follow up on such an opening. The
German record of this episode was, therefore, doctored with special care
before wartime publication in the *German White Book*.[58] In the mounting
and obvious tension of those days, the Germans decided as part of their
pressure on Poland to make a diplomatic issue of some incidents of 26
March at Bromberg.[59] Von Ribbentrop protested to Lipski on the following day,[60] while the German newspaper accounts of it suggested to Ian
Colvin, the Berlin correspondent of the *News Chronicle,* that a repetition
of the kind of press campaign that had preceded the destruction of
Czechoslovakia was about to be launched. At the suggestion of the British
military attaché in Berlin, Colvin flew to London on 28 March, and Rex
Leeper, the press officer of the Foreign Office, arranged for him to meet
Undersecretary Cadogan and Lord Halifax, who took him to the prime
minister on the 29th.[61] The fact that Colvin's information on German
plans in 1938 had proved correct now lent some strength to his warning of
an imminent German thrust at Poland.[62]

There was some skepticism in London about the imminence of a German attack; but since the government had already drawn from the negotiations of the last two weeks the conclusion that it would be exceedingly
difficult to construct a multilateral anti-aggression front as long as the
Soviet Union made Polish participation a prerequisite for its signature and

57. *G.D.,* D, 6, Nos. 101, 103; *Lipski Papers,* No. 139; *Biddle Papers,* pp. 47–48; *U.S.,*
1939, 1:102; Biddle tel. 57 of 30 March 1939, State 760c.62/481.

58. See *White Book,* No. 208. The same thing was done with the record of the subsequent
meeting of von Moltke with Beck (cf. *G.D.,* D, 6, No. 118 and *White Book,* No. 211). Since
the German propaganda line would be that Polish "intransigence" was responsible for the
outbreak of war, and was in turn the product of English policy, at this point and in many
other instances extensive "surgery" had to be performed on the documents published by the
German foreign ministry. The commission of surgeons operated under the leadership of von
Moltke, who, as ambassador to Poland in the crucial months, was especially well versed in
the ways the record had to be operated upon to fit in with German propaganda.

59. On this, see Dertinger, "Informationsbericht Nr. 31," of 27 March and "Nr. 32" of 28
March 1939, Bundesarchiv, Brammer, Z.Sg. 101/34, ff.159–63; "Bestellungen aus der
Pressekonferenz," 28 and 29 March 1939, ibid., 101/12, ff.95–96.

60. *G.D.,* D, 6, No. 108.

61. Colvin, *None So Blind,* pp. 299–310; *Cadogan Diary,* 29, 30 March 1939, pp. 164–66;
Harvey Diaries, 29, 30 March 1939, p. 271.

62. For Polish alarm at this point, see *G.D.,* D, 6, No. 115; Bullitt tel. 595 of 30 March
1939, noon (State 740.00/709) reporting the conversation he had just had with the Polish
ambassador, who had told him "that he was in communication with Warsaw a few minutes
ago and that the tension between Berlin and Warsaw is greater than ever; that no progress
whatsoever has been made in the conversations between Berlin and Warsaw and that the
Polish government believes it to be possible that Hitler will attack Poland tomorrow or
Sunday in order to attempt to finish Poland before Beck can have time to sign a definite
alliance with Great Britain."

the Polish government refused to join any pact to which the Soviet Union was a partner, the possibility of a separate step concerning Poland was already under review.[63] In fact the concept of a guarantee of Poland as a means of both encouraging her not to cave in without resistance and of deterring Hitler from even trying had developed in Chamberlain's thinking to a point where on 27 March he expressed himself as willing to make a commitment to Poland even if Poland would not assume a similar obligation toward Great Britain. "If Poland declined to entertain a commitment of this kind then nevertheless we should be prepared to give her the unilateral assurance as regards the Eastern Front seeing that our object was to check and defeat Germany's attempt at world domination."[64] In view of this attitude, Colvin's warning precipitated the public announcement of a policy already being formulated. The rapidity with which the cabinet Committee on Foreign Policy and the cabinet agreed, the Dominions were informed, the French were involved, and the official announcement was made in Parliament on 31 March must be seen as the final stage in a process of defining a policy developed over a period of two weeks.[65]

The phraseology of Chamberlain's formula of 31 March was designed to cover the period while Britain engaged in negotiations for some common front against aggression. He stated:

In order to make perfectly clear the position of His Majesty's Government before those consultations are concluded, I now have to inform the House that during that period in the event of any action which clearly threatened Polish independence, and which the Polish Government accordingly considered it vital to resist with their national forces, His Majesty's Government would feel themselves bound at once to lend the Polish Government all support in their power.

Efforts would be made to supplement this promise by other commitments of aid, beyond the existing Franco-Polish treaty, but Great Britain had taken her stand. Parliament and public supported the policy; perhaps the diary entry of General Pownall summarized the position: "A continental commitment with a vengeance! But I'm sure it's the right policy."[66]

63. *Cadogan Diary*, 22, 26, 27 March 1939, pp. 163–64.

64. 38th meeting of the cabinet Committee on Foreign Policy, 27 March 1939, CAB 27/624, f.204. The choice of language with its reference to an "Eastern Front" is particularly revealing. This evidence and other materials cited by the author lead to an interpretation very different from that in Cienciala, chap. 7.

65. Minute by Mr. Speaight, "Possibility of a German Coup in Danzig," 29 March 1939, C 4859/54/18, FO 371/23016; Cabinet 15 (39) of 29 March, Cabinet 16 (39) of 30 March, Cabinet 17 (39) of 31 March 1939, C 4552, C 4736, C 4656/15/18, FO 371/22968; 39th and 40th meetings of the cabinet Committee on Foreign Policy, CAB 27/624; C 5265/15/18, FO 371/22969; C 4525/54/18, FO 371/23015; Chiefs of Staff Paper 870, 28 March 1939, CAB 53/47; Strang, p. 161; *Cadogan Diary*, 30, 31 March 1939, pp. 165–66; Hoare, pp. 347–50; *Harvey Diaries*, 25 March 1939, p. 268; *Łukasiewicz Papers*, p. 183.

66. *Pownall Diary*, 3 April 1939, p. 197. Note the entry in Jones, 2 April 1939, pp. 430–32. Christopher Thorne, *The Approach of War, 1938–39* (New York: St. Martin's, 1968), p. 220, prints a Gallup Poll of 4 August 1939 in which the question "If Germany and Poland go to

It would prove easier to secure reciprocity from Poland than some form of participation by the Soviet Union. Plans for Polish Foreign Minister Beck to come to London went back some months; the visit took place on 4–6 April, a few days after the developments just described.[67] The Polish government was quite agreeable to an exchange of commitments pending a final settlement of the precise terms of a treaty. Pressed hard by Chamberlain,[68] Beck maintained his objection to combinations involving the Soviet Union and would only go so far as to say that "he had no opinion to express and no objection to raise" if the British government worked out a system under which help from Russia could be expected in case of war. Even so, he stressed the danger that any alignment of Britain with the Soviet Union might precipitate the very conflict all still hoped to avoid.

None of this would keep the British government from trying. The negotiations with the Soviet Union would continue until the German-Soviet Pact made the whole time and paper-consuming process as ridiculous as it had become futile. No effort will be made here to recount these long negotiations; they will only be referred to from time to time. The pattern projected before 31 March would be reinforced, not altered, by the British step; and then the focus shifted to German plans toward Poland and the Soviet Union. The Russian government had been given a preliminary view of the guarantee concept on 29 March; on the 30th Arthur Greenwood of the Labor party had leaked the intended announcement in Parliament to Maisky; and on the 31st Lord Halifax officially informed Maisky before Chamberlain's statement was made.[69]

The official reaction of the Soviet government to the British policy was negative from the beginning.[70] Had it been positive, the road to some agreement would have been open, but this was precisely what Moscow wanted to avoid, at least until the alternative of an agreement with Germany had been explored. After all, once London had committed itself, it might either break that promise—in which case the Soviet Union would find itself perceived as an enemy along with Poland—or it might honor

---

war over Danzig, should we fulfill our pledge to fight on Poland's side?" was answered 76 percent yes, 13 percent no, and 11 percent don't know. Though of a later date, the focus of this question on the Danzig issue in its narrowest form surely indicates broad public backing for Britain's guarantee of Poland.

67. The British records are in *B.D.*, 3d, 5, Nos. 1, 2, 10, 11, 16.

68. See esp. ibid., pp. 11–13.

69. See ibid., No. 3, summarizing the record; *S.U.*, No. 198 on Greenwood's information, and No. 200 on the Maisky-Halifax talk. Adam B. Ulam, *Expansion and Coexistence: Soviet Foreign Policy, 1917–1973*, 2d ed. (New York: Praeger, 1974), p. 275, suggests that the only way for the British to secure Soviet support would have been to turn the phraseology around, that is, to announce that they would *not* help defend Poland unless the Soviet Union agreed to do so also. The speculation is intriguing, but as Ulam himself admits is far removed from the real options of the time.

70. *B.D.*, 3d, 4, No. 597; *S.U.*, No. 203.

that promise—in which case there was the possibility of a general war from which Russia with its differing view of that contingency might abstain if Germany gave signs of limiting her ambitions in the east.[71] Exploring such possibilities would take time, and the Soviet government's long-term device for securing that time was to make its initial demands for agreement high and to raise new demands during the course of negotiations; in the short run it was to prevent a meeting between Lord Halifax and Deputy Commissar for Foreign Affairs Vladimir Potemkin originally scheduled for 15 May.[72] By that date, the first signs of a possible deal with the aggressor were already evident to Moscow, but the realization of such a deal necessarily depended on the evolution of German plans and policies. As for any early Soviet joining of Britain, that was made less likely by the very steps London took to show its determination to stand by Poland. The doubling of the territorial army and finally the introduction of conscription against the solid opposition of the Labor and Liberal parties reassured the French and the Poles about the reality of Chamberlain's commitment, but it suggested to Moscow the possibility of even greater concessions if Russia refused to join the defenders of Hitler's prospective victim.[73]

The very same days in which the British government developed and, in a process speeded up by concern over a possibly imminent German attack on Poland, formulated and announced its determination to stand by Poland were also the days when Hitler gave up whatever hopes he might have entertained of securing Poland's peaceful submission to his will. The evidence on this process in the last days of March and the first days of April is by no means entirely clear, but there is enough to establish firm outlines.

On 10 February Hitler had explained to some assembled officers his general determination to launch a war. He had been obliged to pull back in September 1938 and had not reached his goal. But he had to fight a war still in his lifetime; no German would ever again be held in such complete confidence by the people; so he alone was capable of leading them into a war. The aims of war were to be first domination in Europe and then world hegemony. The first war toward such goals would have to be

71. Weinberg, *Germany and the Soviet Union*, p. 15.
72. On Potemkin's travels in April and May, see ibid., pp. 16–20. See also the documents published in *S.U.*, such as Nos. 264, 265; Biddle dispatch 1058 of 12 May 1939, State 740.00/1576. Note Litvinov's letter to Maisky of 4 April 1939, *S.U.*, No. 210.
73. On the importance of the armaments and especially the conscription issue, see Weinberg, *Germany and the Soviet Union*, pp. 14–15; *Pownall Diary*, 17 April 1939, p. 199; *Hore-Belisha Papers*, pp. 187, 195–99; Hoare, pp. 337–39; Cadogan minute of 27 March 1939, C 3247/130/17, FO 371/22921; Bullitt tel. 588 of 28 March 1939, State 740.00/697; Kirkpatrick minute of 21 April 1939, C 5610/15/18, FO 371/22970; Aster, pp. 98–99. The government's decision to introduce conscription legislation was announced on 26 April; both the French and the American governments had been pushing the British discreetly but insistently in this direction. New British-French staff talks had already been authorized by the cabinet on 8 February; for an account of their development, see Gibbs, chap. 17. Chamberlain, however, refused to enlarge the basis of his cabinet by including representatives of the Conservative opposition like Eden or Churchill.

launched soon because of the rearmament of others which might enable them to overtake Germany.[74] Such general perspectives, however interpreted by his audience, do not yet point with precision to an attack on Poland as the first war to be started. Hitler subsequently explained the details of this decision twice, once on 22 August and once on 23 November 1939. In his August speech, discussed later in this chapter, Hitler said that "it was clear to me that a conflict with Poland had to come sooner or later. I had already made this decision in the spring, but I thought I would first turn against the West in a few years, and only afterwards against the East. But the sequence could not be fixed. One cannot close one's eyes before a threatening situation. I wanted to establish an acceptable relationship with Poland in order to fight first against the West. But this plan, which was agreeable to me, could not be executed since essential points had changed. It became clear to me that Poland would attack us in case of conflict with the West."[75] In November, after the Polish campaign, Hitler phrased this account slightly differently but in a basically similar fashion: "The decision to march into Bohemia was made. Then followed the erection of the Protectorate [of Bohemia and Moravia on 15 March] and with that a basis for action against Poland was laid, but it was not quite clear at that time whether I should start first against the East and then the West or vice versa. Moltke often made the same calculations in his time.[76] Under pressure the decision came to fight with Poland first."[77]

Hitler was on these two occasions speaking to military commanders whose enthusiasm he knew was for an attack on Poland alone.[78] His explanation, which makes that attack not a primary project for the recovery of land lost in 1919—as the military would have it, but as Hitler never even mentions—but instead an unfortunate necessity preliminary to starting a war against England and France, about which the military, as Hitler also knew, were quite unenthusiastic, may in fact be taken as a reasonably accurate reflection of his real thinking. The demands that had been made of Poland in October 1938 would have made Poland subservient to Germany and incapable of carrying out her obligations under the Franco-Polish Pact when Germany turned against the West—what Hitler

74. *Groscurth Diary*, pp. 166–67; Müller, p. 98, n.62; Thiess, pp. 112ff. Halder's account of Hitler's views to the American consul general in Berlin, Geist, on 12 April as being a desire for *Lebensraum* in the east and his turning against Britain and France because they would not allow him to realize his eastern aims shows how clearly the new chief of staff of the German army understood Hitler's perspective at the time (Geist tel. 247 of 13 April 1939, State 740.00/794).

75. Text in Nuremberg document 798-PS, *TMWC*, 26:338–39.

76. The reference is to the various deployment plans of the elder Moltke; they are summarized in Peter Rassow, *Der Plan Moltkes für den Zweifrontenkrieg (1871–1890)* (Breslau: Priebatschs Buchhandlung, 1938).

77. 789-PS, *TMWC*, 26:329.

78. Even after World War II von Brauchitsch was certain that the war on Poland had been necessary; see his affidavit, ibid., 32:464–65; cf. *Groscurth Diary*, p. 41.

described as "an acceptable relationship." Poland had refused those demands. Hitler may well have thought that with the destruction of the rest of Czechoslovakia in 1939 he might have acquired just the stick and carrot for another bloodless triumph: the stick of a stronger strategic position toward Poland and the carrot of Slovakia to offer as bait. After 15 March both were waved in front of the Poles by von Ribbentrop in the meetings already mentioned. Before the Polish polite refusal of 26 March, Hitler had, to Italian Ambassador Attolico, described the Polish attitude as unclear.[79]

The evidence on Hitler's views in the days immediately following is indirect, but everything points in the direction of a rapidly forming decision to attack Poland unless there were a prompt surrender. The fact that Beck might still hope for agreement with Germany was recognized,[80] but since surrender was not forthcoming, the alternative was to be not negotiation but war. The closer relations of Poland with England, especially the British guarantee followed by Beck's visit to London, calmed the situation in Poland,[81] and gave Beck the hope that in a newly stabilized situation negotiations leading to some compromise could be resumed now that Poland could negotiate—and hence presumably make concessions—from a position of strength.[82] The same developments had the opposite effects on Hitler, who concluded that Poland would respond to neither the stick nor the carrot in acceding to German wishes but instead would try to retain her independence at the risk of war if necessary.[83] Concessions on

79. G.D., D, 6, No. 52, p. 49.

80. See n.57, above; Dertinger, "Informationsbericht Nr. 32," 28 March 1939, Bundesarchiv, Brammer, Z.Sg. 101/34, f.163.

81. G.D., D, 6, No. 154. For obvious reasons, this document was omitted from the German White Book.

82. For evidence of this attitude, see Beck's comments to Kennedy in London (U.S., 1939, 1:112–13), to Łukasiewicz (Łukasiewicz Papers, pp. 185–86), and to Lipski and the Polish military attaché in Berlin (Lipski Papers, pp. 529–30; Antoni Szymanski, "Als polnischer Militärattaché in Berlin, 1932–1939," Politische Studien, 13 [1962], 180–81; cf. Hungarian Documents, 4, No. 76). For Beck's effort to start moving along this line, see the important feeler of Count Michal Lubiénski, Beck's chef de cabinet, on 6 April, in G.D., D, 6, No. 167, and his comments to Bullitt in U.S., 1939, 1:117–19. Of interest is the similarly moderate line taken by the Polish ambassador in London, Count Edward Raczýnski, on 2 April 1939 (Dalton Diary, LSE). Polish military planning at the time was purely defensive. For a good analysis of Beck's general view of concessions, see B.D., 3d, 6, No. 223. The specific concessions Beck appears to have had in mind at this time concerned partitioning not the territory of the Free City but its functions. He was apparently considering giving up the representation of Danzig in foreign affairs and its ties to the Polish postal system (ibid., 5, No. 263, in which Arciszewski lists concessions Poland would make, leaving open the possibility of a few more; cf. ibid., 4, No. 547). The British added the idea of representation for the Free City in the Reichstag (ibid., 5, Nos. 285 [p. 324], 569, 580, 631). Nothing came of any of this since the Germans were never interested in discussing a compromise with Poland. The contrast between Beck's attitude after his visit to London and that of Beneš after the May Crisis is, however, instructive and perhaps relevant to the way in which the policies of the two were seen by London.

83. See Walter Warlimonet, Im Hauptquartier der deutschen Wehrmacht (Bonn: Athenäum, 1964), p. 34; Helmuth Greiner, Die oberste Wehrmachtführung, 1939–1943 (Wiesbaden: Limes, 1951), p. 30.

transit problems or changes in the status of Danzig would, of course, not make any difference in this regard, as neither would make Poland a German satellite if arrived at in the traditional form of negotiation. As a shrewd and well-informed German observer explained on 5 April: the German-Polish contacts of recent weeks had led to the conclusion that a peaceful solution was not possible. "The Corridor and Danzig questions are only superficially the points of dispute."[84] From Hitler's point of view, the subordination of Poland as the desired preliminary to an attack in the west could be secured only by war.

In the military sphere, this meant that orders had to be issued to prepare a military attack on Poland; the first of these came out on 3 April, having been drafted in the immediately preceding days. It called for preparations to be completed by 1 September, ordered a variety of technical military details in the interim, and, as in the case of the preceding year's plan for an attack on Czechoslovakia, emphasized that an effort would be made to isolate Poland politically. This effort would, again as in the preceding year, be aided by strengthening the defenses in the west and by so arranging German military action as to assure a speedy crushing of Poland's armed forces.[85]

In the diplomatic field, the immediate implications of this decision for the German government were to break off all talks with Poland, to strengthen the alignment with Italy, and to try to secure additional support for the isolation of Poland. The first of these was quick and simple, since it depended solely on the German government itself. Although at times posturing as an advocate of peace, the state secretary in the German foreign ministry, Ernst von Weizsäcker, was an obvious person to implement this policy, not only because of his official position but also because of his strong anti-Polish sentiments. As early as 29 March he had informed the Danzig authorities that Germany would follow a policy of pressure to the point of destruction (Zermürbungspolitik) toward Poland and instructed them on the steps they were to take accordingly.[86] On 5 April von Weizsäcker informed the German ambassador to Poland that the German government had decided to drop its proposals; he was to avoid any and all negotiations with the Poles. Lipski would be told the same thing, a chore von Weizsäcker performed with great relish on the following day.[87]

84. Dertinger, "Informationsbericht Nr. 34," 5 April 1939, Bundesarchiv, Brammer, Z.Sg. 101/34, f.175. The text reads "Die Korridor- und Danziger Frage [sic] sind nur Themen des äusseren Anlasses."

85. G.D., D, 6, Nos. 149, 185. Note that the one section of the plan which looked to the possible occupation of portions of the Baltic States, and thus might have clashed with Russian ambitions, was struck from the order by a directive dated 13 April 1939, ibid., p. 187, n.3. Cf. Henke, pp. 242–44.

86. G.D., D, 6, Nos. 124, 126. Von Moltke had practically given up hope for success in the negotiations by 31 March (see Hungarian Documents, 3, No. 565) but was not in accord with the idea of cutting off contacts entirely.

87. G.D., D, 6, Nos. 159, 169. Lipski's account in Polish White Book, No. 70, as corrected in Lipski Papers, p. 528. In the talk with Lipski, von Weizsäcker reminded him that Poland

It is inconceivable that this strategy of avoiding any talks with Poland, a strategy inaugurated in early April and adhered to until the end of August, was a joint whim of von Ribbentrop and von Weizsäcker.[88] We do not have Hitler's instructions to this effect; but given his close attention to matters pertaining to Poland, we must assume that as in so many important cases, he gave them orally either on 1 April when he was in Wilhelmshaven, gave a speech on foreign policy, and talked with von Ribbentrop, or on 4 April when he stopped in Berlin on his way from Hamburg to Munich, more likely on the former occasion.[89] Since this strategy differed radically from that of 1938, when a process of escalating demands by the Sudeten Germans had been utilized and negotiations of one kind or another had gone forward during the whole period from March to August, one can only conclude that Hitler deliberately decided to do things differently in this regard. The reason is easy to see; in this sphere his 1938 strategy had simply not worked. He had in 1938 been required to settle for his ostensible demands, and he was not about to take a chance on that happening again. If you did not want a negotiated settlement, and wished to avoid the risk of being nudged into one against your own preferences, the safest thing to do was not to negotiate at all.[90] The clear and consistent adherence of Germany to this line in the face of Polish efforts to revive substantive conversations on an equal basis during the summer of 1939 surely reflects a clearly enunciated order by Hitler that his diplomats fully understood and, given their own attitude toward Poland, found congenial and simple to implement. The risk of war with the Western Powers was consciously assumed. If it could be avoided, well and good; but if it could not, that only showed how urgent and essential a

---

could have shared in the Slovak booty if only . . . Von Weizsäcker's rabid anti-Polish views and his extreme anger over the British guarantee of Poland were by no means unique. When the British military attaché in Berlin reported on the anti-British feelings in German public and official circles, the chargé agreed with the assessment. Sir Orme Sargent minuted on 15 April: "So much for so-called moderate opinion in Germany. Last year we were repeatedly told that moderate opinion was disappointed and discouraged because H.M.G. was not standing up to Hitler. Now that H.M.G. are standing up to Hitler we hear that this same moderate opinion is disgusted with us and can't understand why H.M.G. are standing up to Hitler" (C 4897/13/18, FO 371/22958).

88. Cf. von Scheliha's report in *S.U.*, No. 308.

89. Hitler had gone to Wilhelmshaven for the launching of the *Tirpitz* on 1 April and had then taken a trip to Heligoland on the *Robert Ley*, returning to Hamburg on 4 April. On the anti-British speech of 1 April, see Henke, pp. 239–40. Keitel signed the military order on Hitler's instructions on 3 April. The British chargé in Berlin reported on 6 April that before leaving for Berchtesgaden again Hitler had given instructions "that the Polish question was to be reserved entirely to himself" (*B.D.*, 3d, 5, No. 14).

90. This interpretation runs counter to that advanced by Henke (pp. 242–45) and others that Hitler had not decided on a military conquest of Poland until sometime in May. Like Müller (p. 391) I believe that the evidence better supports the interpretation advanced here. If Hitler seriously considered a peaceful solution on terms Poland might be willing to accept, why the ending of conversations in early April and the denunciation of the 1934 pact with Poland on 28 April? Henke in part contradicts his own theory (p. 246).

war against the Western Powers, and especially England, really was. In any case, Germany would not pull back from its insistence on making Poland a subservient client state, since this was designed precisely to clear Germany's rear for the coming war in the West.[91]

The isolation of Poland was to be in part the work of German propaganda. In 1938, German propaganda had stressed the strength of German defenses in the West as a means of deterring the Western Powers from helping Czechoslovakia, and on the sufferings supposedly inflicted on the Sudeten Germans as a means of undermining Czechoslovakia's political and moral position with the Western Powers. The noisy emphasis on the western fortifications continued in 1939, highlighted by Hitler's tour of the area and the accompanying bombastic speeches in late May.[92] A general trumpeting of German military strength was to serve the purpose of discouraging any and all who might consider aiding Poland. This campaign was tied in part to Hitler personally, the enormous military parade on his fiftieth birthday on 20 April being designed to impress both the foreign visitors present and those who could see the pictures and newsreels, a medium of special importance in the 1930s.[93] There was, furthermore, to be an international propaganda campaign against Poland. The foreign ministry had developed plans for this by 17 April, but implementation was delayed until mid-May.[94] This slow beginning of the campaign was clearly specified in the directives to the German press.[95] Caution in the early stages appears to have been due to concern that the campaign divide England from Poland rather than push them closer together as the first appearance of articles about incidents in Poland had done at the end of March. The way to accomplish the desired objective, in German eyes, was first to attack England and its policy of building up a front against aggression both to consolidate opinion within Germany and to frighten off the British.[96] The second line would be to stress Polish intransigence, with special emphasis on the Danzig issue, on the assumption that this was the weakest point in the British perception of their new tie to Poland. As Danzig Senate President Greiser explained on 5 May, the German plan was to make lots of noise about Danzig in order to separate Britain from Poland and then in or after August to collapse the whole Polish position when Germany was ready to move.[97]

91. Henke, pp. 245–48.

92. On Hitler's trip, see *Groscurth Diary,* p. 175, n.339; Domarus, 2:1189–91.

93. Fritz Terveen, "Der Bildbericht über Hitlers 50. Geburtstag," *Vierteljahrshefte für Zeitgeschichte,* 7, No. 1 (Jan. 1959), 75–84; *B.D.,* 3d, 5, No. 275; Vauhnik, pp. 24–25. On propaganda about German military strength, see the directives to the press of 27 April, 8, 9 May 1939, Bundesarchiv, Brammer, Z.Sg. 101/12, f.107; 101/13, ff.10, 12.

94. *G.D.,* D, 6, No. 367 and n.2. For a general account, in need of correction at some points, see Hagemann, pp. 390–411.

95. The directives are in Bundesarchiv, Brammer, Z.Sg. 101/13, passim. See also *Hungarian Documents,* 4, No. 69.

96. A good brief account in Henke, pp. 239–41.

97. *S.U.,* No. 295.

Closer ties with Italy would also strengthen the German position and offer the chance that others would think twice before interfering with Germany's moves. The German action of 15 March temporarily cast a pall over German-Italian relations. This step was not only taken without prior notice to Mussolini, who prided himself on having sponsored the Munich conference, but it also had deeper ramifications.[98] There was the Italian public to consider; never enthusiastic about the tie to Germany, it now saw the Germans gathering more gains while Italy stood by unrewarded.[99] More significant from the point of view of Mussolini and Ciano was the possibility that Germany's greatly strengthened position in Southeast Europe would be exploited by her at the weakest spots adjacent to Germany. The Italian leaders saw Hungary more indebted to Germany than ever for the permission she had received to occupy the Carpatho-Ukraine.[100] They feared that Germany would now use the Croatian problem inside Yugoslavia to bring about the disintegration of that country and as a result appear on the shore of the Adriatic.[101] The Italian reaction to the coup of 15 March was actually obvious enough to give the British and French, but especially the British, the idea that there might be a chance to detach Italy from Germany's side and that they might make efforts in that direction.[102] The failure of these efforts, at least in the short run, was due primarily to the steps Berlin took to mend its fences.

The Germans very quickly reassured the Italians. With Hitler's view of allocated spheres of *Lebensraum,* in which Germany would move east while Italy dominated the Mediterranean, it was easy enough to promise Rome that Germany considered Yugoslavia in Italy's sphere and to issue instructions and distribute assurances accordingly.[103] These assurances did not, however, include a precise definition of the lines dividing the

98. *G.D.,* D, 6, Nos. 86, 87, 140; Toscano, *Origins of the Pact of Steel,* pp. 168–70; Siebert, pp. 115–17. Economic difficulties in German-Italian relations at this time did not help the situation (*G.D.,* D, 6, Nos. 44, 62, 174, 175, 360).

99. *G.D.,* D, 6, Nos. 37, 52; *Hungarian Documents,* 3, Nos. 526, 548.

100. Note Attolico's emphasis on this in his report of 18 March 1939 quoted in Toscano, *Origins of the Pact of Steel,* p. 174; full text in Mario Toscano (ed.), "Report of the Italian Ambassador in Berlin to Count Ciano 18 March 1939," *Bulletin of the Institute of Historical Research,* 26 (1953), 218–23.

101. *G.D.,* D, 6, Nos. 15, 45; *Hungarian Documents,* 3, Nos. 521, 524; 4, No. 34a–c; Siebert, pp. 117–18; Toscano, *Origins of the Pact of Steel,* pp. 170–72, 175–76. On 21 March, Ciano told the Hungarian minister that when Yugoslavia was partitioned, there should be a common Italian-Hungarian border (*Hungarian Documents,* 4, Nos. 15, 46).

102. On British efforts, see Aster, pp. 81, 83–85; *Harvey Diaries,* 20 March 1939, p. 265; *Cadogan Diary,* p. 162; *Łukasiewicz Papers,* p. 184; *G.D.,* D, 6, No. 114; Toscano, *Origins of the Pact of Steel,* pp. 176–77, 180–81, 200; Siebert, pp. 124–28, 154; R 1845/57/22, FO 371/23808; R 3002/1/22, FO 371/23785. On the French effort, see Adamthwaite, p. 306.

103. *G.D.,* D, 6, Nos. 55, 86, 87, 94, 100, 207; Toscano, *Origins of the Pact of Steel,* pp. 177–86, passim, and p. 200, n.44; Siebert, pp. 118–22; "Bestellungen aus der Pressekonferenz," 27, 29 March, 5 April 1939, Bundesarchiv, Brammer, Z.Sg. 101/12, ff.94, 96, 102; Dertinger, "Informationsbericht Nr. 34," 5 April 1939, ibid., 101/34, ff. 171–73. Mussolini's speech of 26 March reflects his perception of German loyalty to this division, see *G.D.,* D, 6:105.

spheres of the two powers.[104] The coordination of the two powers, instead, took the form of exchanges of support on specific issues. The Germans, who had delayed staff talks with the Italians because they did not wish to encourage Italy to start a war with France at a time inconvenient to themselves,[105] now decided that the time for staff talks had come.[106] Basic strategy was not to be discussed, but some talks that would make the Italians feel better could go forward. When Keitel and Pariani met in Innsbruck on 5–6 April, they exchanged technical information, political nonsense, and silence. The technical information concerned their armaments and communications; the political nonsense was an exchange of assertions that war with the West was necessary but should be postponed for a couple of years; the silence concerned the respective real intentions of the two countries. Keitel was as careful to refrain from mentioning the directive for preparing an attack on Poland that he had just signed as Pariani was to avoid reference to the occupation of Albania scheduled for the following days.[107] All once again looked well, though the foundations for later misunderstanding had been laid.

The Italians, who were about to seize Albania in any case, now moved on the assumption, which proved correct, that the Germans would back them in this action which, though planned long before 15 March, now looked like Rome's consolation prize.[108] Once again an Italian adventure linked her more firmly to Germany, this time by provoking British and French guarantees of Greece and Rumania. Whatever opportunities for a turn toward the West might have existed, Mussolini himself would not turn away from the ambitious course he was steering, and which he could steer only in Germany's wake.[109]

104. Toscano (*Origins of the Pact of Steel*, pp. 188–92) has properly emphasized this point and has shown how this differed from the Anglo-French entente of 1904.

105. This is surely partly responsible for Hitler's emphasizing to Attolico on 20 March that war with the West had best be postponed for a year or two (*G.D.*, D, 6, No. 52).

106. Ibid., No. 57.

107. Ibid., p. 930. On the talks in early April, see ibid., pp. 932–34; Rintelen, p. 60; Toscano, *Origins of the Pact of Steel*, pp. 214–32; Mack Smith, pp. 147–48.

108. *G.D.*, D, 6, Nos. 140, 143, 150, 158, 164, 166, 170–72; *Hungarian Documents*, 4, No. 70; *Engel Diary*, 8 April 1939, p. 45; Siebert, pp. 128–43; Toscano, *Origins of the Pact of Steel*, pp. 232–34. The Hungarians had offered on 4 April to join in a war on Yugoslavia if Italo-Yugoslav hostilities developed out of the Italian action in Albania (*Hungarian Documents*, 4, No. 58). Mack Smith's account of the seizure of Albania (chap. 11) stresses its impact on Rome's more realistic assessment of Italy's military deficiencies (p. 153).

109. The guarantees of Rumania and Greece were announced on 13 April. There had been lengthy and fruitless efforts to persuade Poland to join in the guarantee of Rumania; in the end French insistence played a major role in the British decision to go ahead in the new crisis created by the Italian seizure of Albania. See *B.D.*, 3d, 5, chaps. 1 and 2; Toscano, *Origins of the Pact of Steel*, pp. 235–40; *G.D.*, D, 6, Nos. 195, 197, 203; *U.S.*, 1939, 1:129; 42d meeting of the cabinet Committee on Foreign Policy, 11 April 1939, CAB 27/624. Adamthwaite, pp. 308–10, 313, stresses the extent to which Italy's move reinforced earlier French worries about her own Mediterranean and North African interests. The guarantees ended the possibilities explored in the negotiations documented in n.100, above; see esp. Siebert, p. 162. The Hungarians were quick to note, all the same, that the British government

In addition, Mussolini now raised the question of transferring German-speaking South Tyroleans to Germany once more; and there were promptly new discussions of this subject.[110] While the German diplomats were still a bit skeptical about the total resettlement the Italians seemed to have in mind, Hitler clearly wanted to accommodate Rome's preferences. In line with his earlier views on the subject, in late March he ordered Heinrich Himmler to start the transfer proceedings; and in April or May Hitler instructed him to organize a total transfer operation. The details do not need to be recounted here; the critical point is that whenever questions were raised or problems occurred, Hitler insisted on the transfer going forward.[111] Himmler was in Hitler's eyes the right man for this job—and he would receive vastly greater responsibilities of this kind in 1939. Important for German-Italian relations in the summer of 1939 is that Hitler was absolutely determined to remove any and all possible irritants to Italy on this score; when a minor incident brought the matter to his attention again in June, he exploded in rage, banned the very term "South Tyrol," and ordered the transfer to proceed.[112]

If these matters of specific and immediate concern were solved to the at least apparent satisfaction of both Berlin and Rome, that merely restored the nature of their relationship to what it had been before 15 March. The desire of the Germans to isolate Poland and the desire of Mussolini to gain a stronger position for extorting concessions from France would animate their joint movement forward with the old project of converting the Anti-Comintern Pact into a firm military alliance against Britain, France, and eventually the United States. In April and early May these negotiations continued; but in spite of von Ribbentrop's periodic revival of hopes, the project continued to founder on the unwillingness of the Japanese government, in the face of strong opposition from the Japanese navy, to agree to anything other than an alliance against the Soviet Union.[113] The latter was precisely what the German government did not want; Berlin wished to use the Japanese threat to immobilize the Western Powers and thereby possibly isolate Poland. The various texts prepared

---

carefully differentiated between the de jure recognition of Albania's disappearance as contrasted with the refusal of London to recognize the disappearance of Czechoslovakia (*Hungarian Documents*, 4, No. 79).

110. Latour, pp. 31–37, cites the published documents and some important papers from the unpublished Himmler files. Cf. "Bestellungen aus der Presskonferenz," 26 May 1939, Bundesarchiv, Brammer, Z.Sg. 101/13, f.33.

111. Latour, pp. 37–42.

112. *Hassell Diary*, 21 June 1939, p. 61. The 22 May German-Italian alliance contained a reference to the final character of the boundary between the two countries.

113. Von Ribbentrop became so anxious to have his project succeed that he was even willing to have the German ambassador in Japan, Eugen Ott, involved in the negotiations and sent him a detailed summary of the whole record (*G.D.*, D, 6, No. 270). Although it is not certain that Sorge passed on a copy of this to Moscow—as a friend of Ott's he presumably knew about it—the Soviet collection does contain an earlier report (*S.U.*, No. 214) of 9 April which gives a very accurate picture of the situation.

by the Japanese were all deficient on this critical point; and although von Ribbentrop in particular continued to hope for an eventual agreement with Japan, the evident reluctance of the Japanese to assume obligations tied to European developments[114] hastened the emergence of two new lines of policy as substitutes for the tripartite military alliance.[115]

One project that evolved out of the impossibility of harmonizing the anti-Western thrust of German and Italian policy with the anti-Russian direction of Japanese policy was a bilateral alliance between the two Axis partners. The conversations of Göring in Rome in mid-April had appeared to show a harmony of German with Italian intentions, although the Italians were worried about the tone of the German leader's references to Poland.[116] Since Mussolini really did want several years of peace to prepare for the war against the Western Powers, he was in any case less interested than Germany in the role of Japan as a global counter to England and more interested at that time in a clear demarcation of German and Italian interests in Europe and the assurance of Berlin's full support.[117] Ironically the very concern of the Italians over some possible German project against Poland and German worry about a possible Italian attack on France led the two powers to work out what looked temporarily like a united front.[118]

On 6 and 7 May at a meeting in Milan, von Ribbentrop and Count Ciano agreed to sign a military alliance whose exact terms were yet to be worked out but which was to be specifically and exclusively directed against Britain and France. Unlike the various texts for a tripartite pact that had been discussed, this treaty would be a firm alliance for offensive as well as defensive purposes. Once the Italians had indicated that a bilateral

114. To judge by Hitler's comments on 20 March, he appears to have recognized this fact before von Ribbentrop (*G.D.*, D, 6, No. 52). In the end the still divided Japanese merely congratulated Germany and Italy on the signing of their alliance (ibid., Nos. 425, 427). They had warned the British that a general—as opposed to a limited—Anglo-Soviet alliance would lead them to sign a broad alliance with Germany and Italy.

115. The account in Toscano, *Origins of the Pact of Steel*, pp. 198–213 and 257–89, is particularly good and detailed. Many otherwise not accessible Italian documents are quoted at length or at least cited. The account in Sommer, pp. 193–229, stresses von Ribbentrop's personal role and illusory hopes and provides more information on the internal discussions in Japan; it also covers in considerable detail the American and British efforts to discourage Japan from aligning herself with the Axis. Additional details on the internal Japanese debates may be found in Morley, pp. 90–105.

116. Accounts of the conversations of Göring with Mussolini and Ciano in *G.D.*, D, 6, Nos. 205, 211, 252; Ciano, *Diary*, 15–17 April 1939, pp. 66–67. The Italian minutes of these talks, referred to by Ciano in his diary, appear to be lost. Ciano, who had himself recently been in Poland, was sure the Poles would fight rather than give in. His conclusion on 17 April: "The Germans should not think that in Poland they will make a triumphant entrance as they have done elsewhere; if attacked, the Poles will fight. The Duce also sees it in this way."

117. Attolico, who was most worried about a German attack on Poland, was especially insistent on both delimiting spheres of interest very precisely and securing a clear picture of German intentions.

118. Good accounts in Toscano, *Origins of the Pact of Steel*, pp. 289–370; Siebert, chap. 4. See also Mack Smith, pp. 162–64.

alliance was agreeable to them, Hitler wanted it as firm as possible. There were also to be consultations on future policy, but there was neither a specific delimitation of precise spheres of influence in the Balkans nor an explicitly written as opposed to verbal agreement that the Axis would keep peace for two or three years. The Germans, who still hoped to bring in Japan, were happy to have Italy officially aligned with them without having to commit themselves to a peaceful settlement with Poland.[119] On the contrary, they could hope that the existence of the alliance with Italy enhanced the possibility that their attack on Poland would lead to an isolated rather than a general war.[120] The Italians, or at least Mussolini, could believe that the might of Germany had been lined up behind Italy's aspirations. Since von Ribbentrop had not implemented his ministry's advice that he prepare Italy for a German-Polish war, the Italian leader could imagine that his country might look forward to wonderful years of peaceful gains followed by even more wonderful years of gains in war.[121]

By the time the final text of the Axis alliance, the Pact of Steel as it was called for propaganda effect, had been signed on 22 May, there were already some indications of progress along the second line of policy to emerge from the tripartite negotiations. As von Ribbentrop had indicated to the Italians, a new tripartite pact of the sort the Japanese wanted, namely, one "restricted within the framework of the anti-Communist idea," "would be absolutely valueless."[122] On the contrary, if Germany faced Britain and France as intermediate enemies who might or might not aid Poland (the Soviet Union being perceived as the later enemy from whom Germany would seize the *Lebensraum* she wanted), then far from wanting an alliance *against* the Soviet Union in 1939, Germany could well

119. Sommer's reconstruction (pp. 227–29) of the Hitler–von Ribbentrop discussion of this matter on 10–11 May is most reasonable. Siebert (pp. 180–81) correctly stresses that the German draft prepared before the Milan meeting had included a clause protecting one party against precipitate action by the other, which had been designed to keep Italy from dragging Germany into a war with France at a time of Italy's choosing. Now that the Germans knew that Mussolini had no such intention, that clause was omitted from their draft for the alliance so as not to give Italy an escape clause if Germany moved against Poland without consulting Rome.

120. Von Ribbentrop had expressed the view that Britain would not mobilize one soldier in case of a German-Polish war (*G.D.*, D, 6, No. 209; *Weizsäcker-Papiere*, p. 153).

121. It was, of course, precisely because the Japanese were unwilling to do with open eyes what the Italians allowed themselves to be inveigled into with closed eyes that the alliance had two rather than three members. Ciano failed to secure clarity on the Polish question, the very one which had contributed to Italian urgings that the meeting of the Axis foreign ministers be held. It is hard to imagine any of his predecessors being quite so foolish.

122. Magistrati to Ciano, 27 March 1939, quoted in Toscano, *Origins of the Pact of Steel*, p. 200, n.44. This was why the German counter to the Japanese proposal for notifying Britain, France, and America that they were excluded from the application of the alliance specified "that, under absolutely no conditions, should any written or oral communication be made to either England or France" (Attolico to Ciano, 4 April 1939, quoted ibid., p. 213). The Axis alliance was, as Ciano told the Soviet chargé in Rome, in no way directed against the Soviet Union (*Diary*, 8 May 1939, p. 79).

use an alignment *with* Russia. This would completely isolate Poland and facilitate the destruction of that country as well as the defeat of the Western Powers, who would be tackled later unless they came to Poland's aid.

The weeks between Stalin's 10 March speech and Vyacheslav Molotov's address of 31 May saw the two powers move gingerly toward each other. There is not much point to the argument over who took the initiative in this process. It might be said that the Soviets gave the hints and the Germans took the specific steps, but the process was really one of feeling each other out, at least in the early stages. The Soviet Union had made repeated efforts to establish better relations with National Socialist Germany over the years, but these had invariably been warded off by Hitler, who clearly felt that the Russians had nothing to offer him at that time.[123] This would now change as there was interest on both sides: Stalin to stay out of a European war, strengthen the Soviet Union, and deal with Japan's expansionist policies in East Asia; Hitler to remove the possibility of an alignment of the Soviet Union with the Western Powers and to isolate Poland, which, unlike Czechoslovakia, had a very long border indeed with Russia.[124] If the earliest hints—such as Stalin's speech itself, Potemkin's opening to the Italian ambassador in Moscow a few days later,[125] and the Tass communiqué of 3 April denying that the Soviet Union had agreed to aid Poland with war materials and to stop selling war materials to Germany in case of war[126]—all came from the Soviet side, this may have been due to the fact that the Russian government was better informed about German intentions than the other way around. In any case, in the following days there were soundings from the German side,[127] and in Göring's conversation with Mussolini on 16 April there was a detailed review of the possibility of improved relations of the Axis with Russia as a means of isolating Poland. While both favored the idea, there was concern about Japan's attitude toward such a project, which was discussed as one combining a trade treaty with a promise of nonaggression.[128] On the following day, von Weizsäcker had a friendly conversation with the Soviet ambassador to Germany in which general themes— Russia's desire to isolate herself from a European war and German anx-

123. Weinberg, *Foreign Policy*, pp. 76–81, 181–82, 220–23, 310–12. It should be noted that Georgei Astakhov, one of the figures in these earlier Soviet moves as representative of the people's commissariat of foreign affairs in Tiflis, Georgia, would play a critical role in 1939 as the Soviet chargé in Berlin (ibid., p. 222, n.66).

124. Hitler had explained that possibility as a means of not having to fight too many enemies at one time as early as June 1931: "and if it should be necessary, there will be peace for a while even with Stalin." Edouard Calic, *Ohne Maske* (Frankfurt/M: Societäts-Druckerei, 1968), p. 80.

125. See Rosso to Ciano, 18 March 1939, in Toscano, *Designs in Diplomacy*, p. 53.

126. *G.D.*, D, 6, No. 161; Rosso to Ciano, 3 April 1939, in Toscano, *Designs in Diplomacy*, p. 55.

127. Weinberg, *Germany and the Soviet Union*, pp. 22–23.

128. *G.D.*, D, 6, No. 211. See Toscano, *Designs in Diplomacy*, pp. 61–64. Both Göring and Mussolini referred to Stalin's speech.

iety over a new Triple Entente that would make an attack on Poland very hazardous—as well as a specific Soviet request for deliveries from the Skoda arms works were touched upon.[129]

In those very days the Germans were trying hard to have Japan agree to a tripartite military pact preferably in time for Hitler to announce in his 28 April speech, and von Ribbentrop did not hesitate to use the possibility of a rapprochement with the Soviet Union as a means of pressuring the Japanese on 20 April.[130] The Japanese, however, were not to be moved from their objections to an alliance directed against the West, both the German desire and the Japanese refusal being known to Moscow.[131] Here, of course, was also a complicating factor for English and American diplomacy. The British, not wanting their negotiations with Russia to throw a reluctant Japan completely into Germany's arms, tried to work out the terms of their proposed alignment with the Soviet Union and their responses to Soviet insistence on an alliance along lines suggested by Moscow in such a fashion as to keep Japan from dropping her objections to the German proposals.[132] British diplomatic efforts fared very poorly during April. In the face of Litvinov's and Maisky's asserted belief that the British government was trying hard to steer German aggression into the Soviet Union via Rumania—at the very time when London, trying to find ways of blocking a German seizure of Rumania, issued its guarantee of that country—there was not much prospect of securing an agreement.[133]

The negotiations were going so badly, with the Soviet government rejecting each Western proposal in turn, that even leaders of the Labor party who were vociferous supporters of a treaty with Russia were beginning to think that perhaps the Russians were at least partly at fault.[134] Though increasingly dubious about the possibility and even advisability of an agreement with Russia, the British government kept trying, hoping at least to keep the Soviet Union neutral if she would not agree to help

129. *G.D.*, D, 6, Nos. 215, 217.

130. Sommer, p. 202; Attolico to Ciano, 25 April 1939, Toscano, *Origins of the Pact of Steel*, p. 264. The Japanese ambassador to Italy subsequently referred to his warnings to Tokyo after this meeting and the one of 16 June as having been discounted as preposterous in the Japanese government (*G.D.*, D, 8, No. 11).

131. See Sorge's reports of 9 and 15 April 1939 (*S.U.*, Nos. 214, 235).

132. See *B.D.*, 3d, 9, Nos. 25, 26; and the evidence cited in n.142, below.

133. See *S.U.*, Nos. 211, n.99, 217. Maisky suggested on 9 April that Britain might not go to war with Germany even if the latter occupied France and the French empire (ibid., No. 218).

134. Dalton diary, 12 April 1939, LSE. Maisky claimed to be more optimistic when he saw Dalton again on 17 April (ibid.); the British guarantee of Rumania had helped. On the negotiations, see *B.D.*, 3d, 5, chaps. 3 and 4; *S.U.*, Nos. 207, 214, 223, 224, 226, 227, 231, 233, 237; 41st meeting of the cabinet Committee on Foreign Policy, 10 April 1939, CAB 27/624. The French received negative replies similar to those given England, see *S.U.*, Nos. 215, 222, 232. The many accounts of the Anglo-French-Soviet negotiations in the existing literature are now added to by Adamthwaite, pp. 310–13, 323–27; and Gibbs, chap. 19; neither has drawn on the published Soviet documents.

Poland.[135] Though originally skeptical about the possibility that the Soviet Union might actually side with the Germans,[136] the British were no longer so sure of this by early May and hence made new efforts for an accommodation.[137] Moscow's negative and distrustful attitude to all proposals from London and Paris hardly augured for success in spite of modifications made in response to Russian criticisms.[138] There can be no doubt that Prime Minister Chamberlain was hesitant about an alliance with the Soviet Union; but it is surely of interest to note that as he dropped his objections, the Russian government did its utmost to create new difficulties in the negotiations—the exact opposite, as we shall see, of its procedure in the negotiations with Berlin. In any case by the time the new Western proposals were presented to Moscow, there had been a significant change in personnel. On 3 May, the resignation of Litvinov and his replacement by Molotov was announced.[139]

The significance and import of this Soviet move was at once widely discussed. In the middle of important negotiations, the man who had represented the Soviet Union on the international stage for years was suddenly dismissed. In the absence of direct evidence, one can only speculate on the reasons for this dramatic move by Stalin. Nothing suggests motives of domestic policy. In foreign policy, as between Soviet relations with European powers on the one hand and East Asian powers on the other, there is again nothing in Soviet relations with China or Japan in those months that seems relevant to this step; the fisheries negotiations with Japan, the border troubles with Manchukuo, the aid to China over

135. A Soviet alliance proposal of 17 April, so worded as to invite rejection by requiring all sorts of policy actions not only by England and France but also by Poland and Rumania, particularly set back the negotiations, see *B.D.*, 3d, 5, No. 201 (comments on it in C 5460/15/18, FO 371/22969); *S.U.*, Nos. 238–40; 43d and 44th meetings of the cabinet Committee on Foreign Policy, 19 and 25 April 1939, CAB 27/624; COS Paper 887 of 24 April 1939, CAB 53/48; Cabinet 21 (39) of 19 April 1939, C 5747/3356/18, FO 371/23064; Cabinet 24 (39) of 26 April 1939, C 6204/15/18, FO 371/22971. The Italian ambassador to Moscow, reviewing the negotiations on 5 May, summarized the developments of April as showing "Moscow had begun to feel it was not really threatened by Germany and that, therefore, it was no longer in the position of having to solicit but, rather in the position of being solicited . . . . I believe that the Soviet proposals were made in the conviction that, given their all-encompassing nature, the British government would never agree to accept them" (Rosso to Ciano, 5 May 1939, in Toscano, *Designs in Diplomacy*, p. 67).

Some skepticism about Soviet capabilities for more than defensive operations appears to have resulted from Hudson's Moscow visit in March, see Cabinet 18 (39) of 5 April 1939, C 5028/54/18, FO 371/23016. For evidence that Hudson had been authorized by Lord Halifax to go well beyond trade talks, see N 1929/64/63, FO 371/23654. Cf. *G.D.*, D, 6, No. 183.

136. See Davies, 3 April 1939, p. 440; C 4517/19/18, FO 371/22996; C 5460/15/18, FO 371/22969.

137. See n.142, below.

138. C 5430/3356/18, FO 371/23063; *S.U.*, Nos. 249, 252, 253, 256, 261, 262; *G.D.*, D, 6, No. 257.

139. For other changes in the people's commissariat of foreign affairs after Litvinov's dismissal, see *U.S.*, *Soviet Union 1933–1939*, pp. 770–72. See also Teddy J. Uldricks, "The Impact of the Great Purges on the People's Commissariat of Foreign Affairs," *Slavic Review*, 36, No. 2 (June 1977), 187–204.

the difficult Sinkiang route, in regard to none of these issues is there any apparent link to the change at the People's Commissariat for Foreign Affairs.

In the relations between Soviet Russia and the European powers, the process of elimination clearly points to Germany. Poland can be excluded easily, for since the slight rapprochement of November 1938, there had been no change in the frosty relationship between the two countries nor were there any signs of any. Once the Polish rejection of the German advances to her, combined with the British guarantee, had relieved Moscow of any anxiety that there might be a German-Polish alliance against Russia, Litvinov had felt as free to scold the Poles as Molotov would.[140] In the negotiations with Britain and France, Litvinov had the experience of years of prior contacts, full familiarity with the details of current negotiations, and the reputation of having in prior years advocated an alignment with the Western Powers by contrast with his predecessor's, George Chicherin's, identification with the Rapallo policy of alignment with Germany. Had Stalin wanted an agreement with the West, Litvinov would have been the obvious person to secure it. The handling of the talks with England and France, however, shows that Stalin did not particularly want such an agreement; and the published Soviet documents demonstrate both Stalin's reluctance and Litvinov's faithful implementation of the dictator's policy.[141] If the possibility of an agreement with Germany was to be explored seriously, on the other hand, and the soundings in Berlin and Soviet knowledge of German intentions suggested that this might be a good idea, then Litvinov, however pliant and obedient, was obviously not the man for such negotiations. His very reputation as the Soviet spokesman in Geneva would stand in the way. The fact that he was Jewish, furthermore, would raise an unnecessary obstacle to talks with the Germans. The ideological differences might be bridged as the relations between fascist Italy and Soviet Russia in the 1920s and early 1930s had shown, and as Potemkin as former ambassador to Rome frequently recalled; but Stalin could well believe that Hitler would find it easier to explore the possibilities of agreement with the Soviet Union if he did not have to conduct negotiations through a minister of Jewish background who had long been the object of ridiculing cartoons in the National Socialist press.

If one makes the safe assumption that Stalin was shrewd enough to know that so spectacular a step would be taken as a sign of possible Russian policy changes, he may have thought of it as a test of German

140. *S.U.*, Nos. 204, 205, 211; cf. ibid., No. 277. Bodurowycz points to some trade talks but little else.

141. As this and the following paragraphs show, I have modified the views expressed in my earlier study of the subject (*Germany and the Soviet Union*, p. 24) that the replacement merely opened alternatives, primarily because the Soviet documents published since that book and its reprint appeared show a much clearer determination not to sign with the West on Litvinov's part—obviously under direction from above—than was previously evident.

intentions. If they did not respond to this broad hint by some serious step in Russia's direction, perhaps they were just not interested; and he would have to see what made the best policy under such circumstances. If they did respond, then he would be free to work out the best approach to that situation. The sure way to give the Germans an opportunity to respond to the hint from Moscow was to make certain that nothing happened in the days immediately following the replacement of Litvinov by Molotov that could be taken in Berlin as a closer edging of Moscow toward the West with the implication that there was no chance for Germany to form a new relationship with the Soviet Union. This consideration appears to me as the most likely explanation of the two first actions of the new commissar. The British had just developed a new proposal in response to the Soviet alliance project, and this greeted Molotov on his assumption of office. He immediately denounced this proposal on the basis of what can only have been a deliberate misinterpretation of a key point of the British proposal.[142] It was perhaps symbolic of the situation that on the day, 10 May, Chamberlain announced in the House of Commons that Britain was prepared to agree that "if the Soviet Government wished to make their own intervention contingent on that of Great Britain and France, His Majesty's Government for their part would have no objection," Tass published a Soviet communiqué denouncing the Western Powers for trying to push Russia by herself into a war with Germany.[143]

The opportunity to resolve real or imagined misunderstandings had appeared to be provided by the forthcoming meeting of the League Council in Geneva where it would be Russia's turn to assume the chair. Potemkin was scheduled to attend, and Maisky had been pushing for Lord Halifax to go, hinting that Litvinov would appear if Lord Halifax did.[144] The British government was most interested in the idea of Lord Halifax having a chance to discuss matters with either Potemkin or Molotov, who would now be expected to go.[145] It looked as if such a meeting would take place; while on his Balkan and East European trip in the preceding weeks, Potemkin not only heard advice to the effect that all should get together to hold Germany in check[146] but he even worked out a possible method for

142. See the evidence cited in Weinberg, *Germany and the Soviet Union*, pp. 19–20; Cabinet 26 (39) of 3 May 1939, C 6546/54/18, FO 371/23017 and C 6595/3356/18, FO 371/23065; 45th meeting of the cabinet Committee on Foreign Policy, 5 May 1939, CAB 27/624; *S.U.*, Nos. 278, 280, 281, 283. Interesting is Maisky's long letter to Molotov of 10 May, ibid., No. 284.

143. Chamberlain in Hansard, *Parliamentary Debates*, 5th series, 347 (1939), c. 454; Tass text in *S.U.*, No. 282. This was also the day on which the British government began its parliamentary fight for the conscription bill.

144. C 6743/3356/18, FO 371/23065. Maisky had operated via the *Daily Herald* on this occasion; he would do so again repeatedly in May and June 1939, C 7108/3356/18, FO 371/23066; C 7468, C 8701/3356/18, FO 371/23068.

145. Halifax to Seeds No. 105 of 10 May 1939, C 6753/3356/18, FO 371/23065; Cabinet 27 (39) of 10 May 1939, C 7106/3356/18, FO 371/23066.

146. See the record of his talk with Turkish President Ismet Inönü, 5 May 1939, *S.U.*, No. 273.

cooperation with Poland.[147] Instead of going to Geneva from Warsaw, however, Potemkin returned to Moscow to confer with the newly appointed Molotov, the Council meeting being postponed to accommodate his travel plans. On 16 May Moscow announced that the Soviet Union would be represented by Ambassador Maisky, neither Potemkin nor Molotov making the trip.[148] The Soviet government could now await the German reaction to Litvinov's dismissal, the rejection of the most recent British-French proposals as well as the refusal of Potemkin to go to Geneva being known to Berlin.

In the German capital, the change in the Soviet government was taken precisely the way Stalin appears to have meant it, namely, as a sign of Soviet willingness to work out some sort of rapprochement.[149] The German press was immediately instructed to cease all polemics against the Soviet Union and against Bolshevism, a directive whose importance must be seen in the context of a society in which this had long been one of the main themes of government propaganda.[150] On 5 May, Karl Schnurre, the head of the East European department of the German foreign ministry's economic policy section, could tell the Soviet chargé Astakhov that the Soviet request for deliveries from Skoda would be granted; the happy chargé tried to find out whether Germany would change her attitude toward the Soviet Union now that Litvinov was gone and asked whether Germany would not resume the economic negotiations broken off in February.[151] It is difficult to believe that Astakhov would have asked questions of this sort without authorization from Moscow.

On 6 and 7 May, von Ribbentrop and Ciano agreed at their meeting at Milan to work for an improvement in relations with the Soviet Union.[152] On 6 May Hitler asked to be briefed on the Soviet Union,[153] and on the same day Ambassador von der Schulenburg was summoned to brief von Ribbentrop.[154] The belief of the ambassador that "the Soviet Union had been seeking a rapprochement with Germany for some time," that the

147. See Weinberg, *Germany and the Soviet Union*, p. 19; *S.U.*, No. 285.

148. Weinberg, *Germany and the Soviet Union*, p. 20; *G.D.*, D, 6, No. 401. Lord Halifax, therefore, met Maisky in Geneva (*S.U.*, No. 303; *B.D.*, 3d, 5, Nos. 581, 582), but hardly needed to go there to see him.

149. *G.D.*, D, 6, No. 325; "Informationsbericht Nr. 45," 4 May 1939, Bundesarchiv, Brammer, Z.Sg. 101/34, ff.219–23.

150. Weinberg, *Germany and the Soviet Union*, pp. 23–24; "Bestellungen aus der Pressekonferenz," 4, 5, 6 May 1939, Bundesarchiv, Brammer, Z.Sg. 101/13, ff.3, 5, 6. With the German-sponsored occupation of the Carpatho-Ukraine by Hungary, the Ukrainian question had earlier disappeared from the German press (ibid., 101/12, f.102), although German intelligence operations there continued (*Hungarian Documents*, 3, No. 557).

151. Weinberg, *Germany and the Soviet Union*, p. 25, n.58; *G.D.*, D, 6, No. 332. Note the fact that Greiser knew the details of the Skoda question correctly on the same day (*S.U.*, No. 295).

152. *G.D.*, D, 6, No. 341; Toscano, *Designs in Diplomacy*, pp. 65–66.

153. Kordt, *Wahn und Wirklichkeit*, p. 158; Kleist, pp. 37–38; Hilger, pp. 293–97.

154. *G.D.*, D, 6, No. 325, n.4; *U.S.*, 1939, 1:318–21. The informant of the U.S. embassy was Hans Heinrich Herwarth von Bittenfeld, see Charles E. Bohlen, *Witness to History, 1929–1969* (New York: Norton, 1973), pp. 69–87.

action of Britain and the attitude of Poland could lead to war in the east, and that Stalin wanted "an understanding with the Rome-Berlin Axis" appears to have had some impact on the German foreign minister.[155] There was actually enough discussion of a possible agreement between Germany and the Soviet Union in those days for leaks, both deliberate and otherwise, to reach most capitals and for the German government to prohibit any press discussion of a German-Soviet rapprochement.[156] Although the former Austrian minister in Moscow who was working in the eastern section of the German foreign ministry recommended in response to a renewed feeler from Astakhov to Schnurre that Germany not move toward acceptance of the approaches from Moscow, von Ribbentrop, undoubtedly with Hitler's approval, decided otherwise.[157]

On 18 May, the day after Astakhov had asserted that there were no quarrels between Germany and the Soviet Union, that sure measures could be found to remove the distrust of Germany still existing in Moscow, and that the negotiations between England and the Soviet Union were hardly likely to lead to the result England desired, von Ribbentrop personally instructed von der Schulenburg in Berlin that he was to go immediately to Moscow and suggest to Molotov that economic negotiations be resumed in the hope of reaching a new trade agreement but that he was to be most reticent otherwise.[158] Molotov responded in a friendly manner (very much unlike his reception of approaches from London or Paris) but insisted that "political bases" were needed for any resumed economic negotiations.[159]

What did Molotov mean by this demand which both he and Potemkin refused to explain when asked? Von der Schulenburg and Augusto Rosso, the Italian ambassador in Moscow, both thought some formal political guarantee of nonaggression was implied, something both believed difficult to reconcile with the Axis hopes for a military alliance with Japan. There is much to be said for this interpretation. What else could the Soviets

155. Von der Schulenburg gave his views to the Italian minister in Teheran on 8 May before flying to Germany; Petrucci to Ciano, 8 May 1939, in Toscano, *Designs in Diplomacy*, p. 69.

156. On the leaks, see Weinberg, *Germany and the Soviet Union*, p. 25; Stehlin, pp. 147–52, 375–79 (erroneously dated to 30 April rather than 6 May); note by Strang on Goerdeler's warning through Dr. Schairer, 6 May 1939, C 6794/15/18, FO 371/22972. See also Renzetti to Attolico, 7 May 1939, in Toscano, *Designs in Diplomacy*, pp. 70–71. The press directive is in "Bestellungen aus der Pressekonferenz," 12 May 1939, Bundesarchiv, Brammer, Z.Sg. 101/13, f.18; for Soviet recognition of it, see *G.D.*, D, 6, No. 351.

157. *G.D.*, D, 6, No. 406 is the record of the Schnurre-Astakhov meeting; the recommendation against responding, ibid., n.5.

158. Information on the instruction is from von der Schulenburg's letter to von Weizsäcker of 22 May (ibid., p. 464) and his comment to Italian Ambassador Rosso in *D.D.I.*, 12, No. 13 (also in Toscano, *Designs in Diplomacy*, p. 72). See also Kordt, *Wahn und Wirklichkeit*, p. 158; Kleist, pp. 38–39. For von Ribbentrop's comments on a possible German rapprochement with the Soviet Union to the Papal Nuncio, see *Saint Siège*, 1, No. 47.

159. *G.D.*, D, 6, Nos. 414, n.2, 424; *D.D.I.*, 12, No. 13; *U.S.*, 1939, 1:321–22.

want, especially since they themselves would not specify what they wanted? As they and all others had noted, Hitler had ceased attacking Russia in his speeches and the German press had dropped its anti-Soviet line; so there was nothing to ask for in regard to the political atmosphere. Quiet and unofficial reassurance about German intentions Moscow did not need; it was getting full and reassuring reports on this subject from Warsaw and Tokyo. On 5 May Sorge had reported on the Japanese government's refusal to accept the German proposal for an alliance directed against the West; on 7 May von Scheliha had informed the Soviet government that Germany had expected the Poles to turn down the German offer, would accept no proposal from Warsaw, had occupied Slovakia as part of an anti-Polish strategy, and after destroying Poland would defeat England and France, with the Soviet Union reserved for a later war.[160] Since 11 and 12 May were the days when fighting between Russian and Japanese troops was beginning on the border between Manchuria and Outer Mongolia in what is generally known as the Nomonhan incident,[161] it is hardly surprising that the Soviet government would expect some political gesture from Germany, especially since it was the Germans who had broken off the earlier economic talks.

In the days from 21 to 29 May the German government pondered Molotov's reply. Although the idea of a tripartite military alliance had now been deferred in favor of the Pact of Steel, signed on 22 May, von Ribbentrop had still not given up on bringing in the Japanese. In line with his strong anti-Western attitude, he appears to have thought out at this time the concept of something like a four-power association in which the European Axis powers would use their good offices to effect a reconciliation between the Soviet Union and Japan in a grand design which would harmonize a tripartite military alliance against the West with an improved relationship of the Axis to Russia.[162] Nothing came of this brainchild of von Ribbentrop then—or when he pushed it again in 1940. As Oshima told the German foreign minister, any proposals of this sort sent to Tokyo would mean cutting the ground away from under any hopes for a tripartite pact, since the proposed Japanese reassurance to Russia that she had nothing to fear from Japan ran directly counter to the views of those in Japan who supported a three-power pact.[163] In the face of the

160. *S.U.*, Nos. 274 (Sorge), 276 (von Scheliha).

161. Molotov had complained about the incident to the Japanese ambassador in Moscow the day before he met von der Schulenburg (ibid., No. 299). On the Nomonhan fighting, see Chiyoko Sasaki, *Der Nomonhan Konflict* (diss., Bonn, 1968), with the account of the military events beginning on p. 54 and that of negotiations for an armistice beginning on p. 97. Sasaki's account is more complete than that in Morley, pp. 157–78.

162. See also *G.D.*, D, 6, No. 441 of about 25 May.

163. *D.D.I.*, 12, No. 48; also in Toscano, *Designs in Diplomacy*, pp. 75–76; cf. ibid., p. 80. Note that von Ribbentrop was so upset by Oshima's veto that he told Göring about it (*D.D.I.*, 12, No. 231).

unwillingness of the Japanese to meet the German desire for an alliance, however,[164] and in view of what were considered to be alarming indications of a possible agreement between Russia and the Western Powers,[165] von Ribbentrop decided to have State Secretary von Weizsäcker explore with the Soviet chargé the possibility of better German-Soviet relations, starting with resumed economic negotiations.[166] On 30 May von Weizsäcker and Astakhov had a long conversation marking a major German step forward.[167] Hitler had approved this step, a point von Weizsäcker was careful to explain to Astakhov; and with that essentially political gesture in which appropriate reference was again made to the absence of any quarrels between the two powers, the Germans hoped to get the trade negotiations resumed in a context clearly as political as it was economic.[168] The reason for Hitler's willingness to take this step will be discussed in a moment; the Soviet reaction must first be noted.

After Moscow's rejection of the British proposal of early May, the London government in consultation with the French tried again, this time making further concessions to the Russian point of view.[169] It was in fact the British public expression of confidence that they had now met the principal Soviet wishes and hence could expect prompt agreement that had played a role in the German internal deliberations of late May. When the new Anglo-French proposal was handed to Molotov on 27 May, however, the latter again deliberately misunderstood it, denouncing the plan

164. On the negotiations with Japan between 4 and 30 May, see *G.D.*, D, 6, Nos. 326, 339, 344, 345, 363, 382, 400, 447; Sommer, pp. 229–39; *U.S., Japan 1931–1941*, 2:2–3; Toscano, *Origins of the Pact of Steel*, pp. 332–38, 355–66. On the relationship of any British-Soviet agreement *not* covering the Far East to Japan's abstention from an alliance with the Axis, see *B.D.*, 3d, 9, Nos. 52, 62, 76, 94. For an effort by Japanese Prime Minister Hiranuma of 23 May to have the United States help him out of the dilemma of Japanese diplomacy, see Cordell Hull, "Memorandum for the President," 1 July 1939, Hyde Park, PSF Japan.

165. The Germans had been able to follow the Anglo-French-Russian negotiations from the constant public discussion in the west as well as from a leak in London; see *G.D.*, D, 6, Nos. 233, 239, 269, 343; *Cadogan Diary*, 26 January 1940, p. 249.

166. Weinberg, *Germany and the Soviet Union*, pp. 26–31; *G.D.*, D, 6, Nos. 437, 441, 442, 446, 449, 450; *D.D.I.*, 12, No. 53; cf. Szymanski, pp. 184–85.

167. *G.D.*, D, 6, Nos. 451, 452.

168. See ibid., Nos. 446, n.3, 453.

169. On the British internal deliberations, see Aster, chap. 6 (though I do not think his interpretation valid); Vansittart memorandum of 16 May 1939, C 7169/3356/18, FO 371/23066; 47th and 48th meetings of the cabinet Committee on Foreign Policy, 16 and 19 May 1939, CAB 27/655; Cabinet 28 (39) of 17 May and 30 (39) of 24 May 1939, C 7400, C 7727/3356/18, FO 371/23066 and 23067; Cadogan to Halifax, 23 May 1939, C 7469/3356/18, FO 371/23066; Chips, pp. 199–201; *S.U.*, Nos. 298, 309; *G.D.*, D, 6, No. 458. When at the cabinet meeting of 24 May the secretary of state for the Dominions passed on the request of the high commissioners voiced on the preceding day that after the signing of the treaty with Russia and the attainment of a strong position by Britain, the search for appeasement should be renewed, Chamberlain countered that such ideas were premature: "It was necessary not merely that we should be strong but that others should realize the fact." Furthermore, public opinion was not ready for such a move (C 7678/15/18, FO 371/22973). Note that the British were so confident that agreement was imminent that they handed a copy of the text to the Belgians (*D.D.B.*, 5, No. 67).

for a provision it did not even contain.[170] Clearly the Soviet government was determined not to bind itself in that direction. The signs from Germany were awaited first.

The signing of the Pact of Steel on 22 May was in a way one signal Moscow could read. This was not a tripartite pact; the Axis negotiations with Japan had evidently foundered on the divergence between the aggressive thrusts of the proposed European and Asiatic partners: if Japan would not bind herself against the West, clearly the Germans were unwilling to subordinate their designs on Poland and against England and France to Japan's hopes for an alliance against Russia. In an indirect, but for Moscow very important, way, the Germans had confirmed that the Soviet Union was *not* enemy No. 1. On 30 May the Russians received the second and now direct signal from Berlin in the form of von Weizsäcker's talk with Astakhov.[171] Here was the word not from a subordinate economic negotiator but from the second man in the German foreign ministry, speaking for Hitler. On the following day, Molotov responded in public in a speech to the Supreme Soviet by announcing that economic negotiations with Germany might be resumed.[172] Whether or not the "political bases" were complete, the Soviet government obviously thought that the possibility of fruitful negotiations with Germany existed.

In his thinking about isolating Poland, Hitler appears to have been less sanguine about Japan than von Ribbentrop. Perhaps racial predilections, perhaps a more realistic assessment of Japanese military capabilities, perhaps just his general impatience had made Hitler skeptical about Japan's joining a military alliance well before von Ribbentrop became doubtful about the prospects for success. Hitler's comments on the subject to Attolico on 20 March suggest that by then he had concluded from the negotiations already under way for many months that a firm commitment of Japan to the Axis was not to be expected in the near future.[173] The very brief reference to Japan in Hitler's foreign policy speech of 28 April was hardly a sign of great expectations.[174] In that speech, Hitler had formally denounced the 1934 agreement with Poland and the 1935 naval agreement with England, with most of his denunciations aimed at the United Kingdom.[175]

Hitler had also used the Reichstag forum for a lengthy ridiculing and denunciation of a public suggestion by President Roosevelt that Hitler and

170. Weinberg, *Germany and the Soviet Union*, pp. 31–32; *S.U.*, Nos. 311, 312.
171. The Tass communiqué of 29 May may have been another hint to Berlin; see Weinberg, *Germany and the Soviet Union*, p. 32.
172. Vyacheslav M. Molotov, *The International Situation and Soviet Foreign Policy* (Moscow, 1939), pp. 10–11; *S.U.*, No. 314; *G.D.*, D, 6, No. 463; *B.D.*, 3d, 5, No. 689; *D.D.I.*, 12, Nos. 73, 77, 80, 86; Toscano, *Designs in Diplomacy*, pp. 80–81.
173. *G.D.*, D, 6, No. 52, pp. 48–49.
174. Lipski attributed the short mention to Japan's refusal to sign a military alliance against England and France (*Lipski Papers*, p. 533).
175. Text in Domarus, 2:1148–79. Cf. Henke, pp. 251–53; *G.D.*, D, 6, No. 290.

Mussolini help calm the excited international atmosphere by promising not to try to take over a long list of countries. That appeal, issued on 14 April, was one of a number of steps taken by the Roosevelt administration in the spring of 1939 after the march on Prague.[176] It grew out of a combination of hopes: that a war might be avoided altogether, but that if it came, the Western Powers would stick together, if possible in concert with the Soviet Union. Such a prospect could only be heightened by measures to strengthen the Western Powers militarily,[177] by diplomatic encouragement of an anti-aggression front,[178] by trade moves designed to weaken Germany,[179] and by an amendment of the neutrality laws that would open up to the members of the anti-aggression front the possibility of purchasing war supplies from American industry.[180] The last of these in particular was to fail in the face of isolationist opposition, but even without that sign of American reluctance to provide substantial assistance to his potential enemies, Hitler thought he could feel confident in ignoring the United States at least in 1939.[181]

The denunciation of the German-Polish agreement in the speech was the public sign of the earlier turn in German policy,[182] and as already indicated, Hitler was so determined on war with Poland that he had at the

176. *Moffat Papers,* pp. 231–39; Adolf A. Berle, *Navigating the Rapids,* pp. 211–13; Morgenthau Papers, Presidential Diary, 11 April 1939, Vol. 1, p. 59, Hyde Park; Günther Moltmann, "Franklin D. Roosevelts Friedensappell vom 14. April 1939: Ein fehlgeschlagener Versuch zur Friedenssicherung," *Jahrbuch für Amerikastudien,* 9 (1964), 91–109; Bullitt tel. 748 of 15 April 1939, State 740.00/820; *G.D.,* D, 6, Nos. 34, 107, 200, 228, 250; "Informationsbericht Nr. 38," 14 April 1939, Bundesarchiv, Brammer, Z.Sg. 101/34, ff.187–93.

177. The best source on American assistance in the building up of the French air force is Haight.

178. Henke, pp. 250–51; *U.S.,* 1939, 1:248–51; *S.U.,* No. 297; *G.D.,* D, 6, No. 403. Roosevelt urged Stalin through Oumansky, the Soviet ambassador in Washington, to work out an agreement with Britain and France, telling Oumansky on 30 June that if the Soviet Union joined Hitler, the latter would turn on the Soviet Union as soon as he had defeated France (Davies, pp. 449–50). Oumansky's report on the conversation as printed (*S.U.,* No. 359) mentions Roosevelt's urging an agreement, but not the warning. See also *G.D.,* D, 6, No. 750). The repetition of Roosevelt's warning about German intentions and the importance of a Soviet agreement with the Western Powers when the new American ambassador went to Moscow in August is discussed in the text, p. 608 below.

179. *G.D.,* D, 6, Nos. 14, 24, 27, 33, 56, 71, 89, 104, 130, 157; *U.S.,* 1939, 2:567–74.

180. The proposed amendment to the neutrality law was introduced by Senator Pittman on 20 March 1939. The administration's perspective is reflected in chap. 45, "Neutrality Disaster," of Hull's memoirs.

181. Note that even Hans Thomsen, the German chargé in Washington, placed the whole burden of his comments on possible American intervention on the person of Roosevelt— without warnings about the potential power of the United States and with idiotic speculations about American unwillingness to entrust troop convoying to foreigners in spite of the contrary experience of 1917–18 (*G.D.,* D, 6, No. 403). Hitler in any case was inclined to listen to the German military attaché in Washington, General Friedrich von Bötticher, whose assessment of the United States was even lower than Thomsen's; see Weinberg, "Hitler's Image of the United States," p. 1012; *Engel Diary,* June 1939, p. 47. Thomsen's report on the defeat of the neutrality law revision is in *G.D.,* D, 6, No. 650. See also the comments of Hitler and von Ribbentrop about the United States right after Hitler's 28 April speech, ibid., Nos. 295, 296.

182. See *Biddle Papers,* pp. 51–55.

beginning of April instructed his diplomats not to engage in any negotiations with Warsaw. Beck's speech of 5 May responded to Hitler with a clear but polite defense of the Polish position; whenever in April, May, and June the Polish government tried to reopen discussions, the Germans waved them off.[183] Polish hopes that their distant attitude toward the Soviet Union would be recognized in Berlin as a sign of a continued policy of balance were not realized;[184] on the contrary, by 25 or 26 May von Ribbentrop was already thinking of partitioning Poland with Russia.[185] Efforts by the Italians, who were impressed by England's determination to fight alongside Poland, to mediate between Berlin and Warsaw were rejected.[186] Similarly, the efforts of the Japanese—who saw Germany's desire to destroy a nationalist Poland in 1939 very much the way the Germans had seen Japan's China policy in 1937, namely, as a breach of the barriers containing the Soviet Union—were also rejected by the Germans just as the Japanese themselves had rejected the German warnings two years earlier.[187] As Hitler told some of his leading military officers on 23 May, he was determined to attack Poland at the first opportune moment.[188]

This particular meeting had been occasioned by questions about priorities in raw materials allocation, growing particularly out of Hitler's earlier decision to give first priority to the navy's Z-Plan for new con-

183. *G.D.*, D, 6, Nos. 247, 334, 350, 355, 387, 429, 464, 492; Krauel (Geneva) to the German Foreign Ministry, Pol V 4551 of 22 May 1939, T-120, 1315/2371/D 496277–78; *Hungarian Documents*, 4, Nos. 202, 221; Cienciala, pp. 239–41; Burckhardt, pp. 280–309; Biddle dispatches 1057 of 19 May (State 760c.62/631), 1069 of 1 June (State 860K.01/187), and 1139 of 7 July 1939 (State 760c.62/714); Biddle to Roosevelt, 10 June 1939, Hyde Park, PSF Poland. Under these circumstances, British steps to restrain Poland or urging her to be conciliatory were hardly needed; *B.D.*, 3d, 5, Nos. 237, 459 (comments in C 6910/54/18, FO 371/23018), 713 (comments in C 8102/54/18, FO 371/23020); *G.D.*, D, 6, No. 278. It should be remembered that this situation was known in Moscow. See esp. von Scheliha's report of 25 May (*S.U.*, No. 308) which describes the situation very accurately: Poland interested in the possibility of negotiations with Germany, Germany *not* wanting such approaches but having decided to fight Poland and bring about her complete collapse, Hitler interested in working out a way to limit the war and in any case fully in charge of this whole policy himself. Similarly, the German ambassador to Warsaw realized that the Poles would fight if attacked but preferred to avoid war and would not provoke one (*G.D.*, D, 6, No. 622; note that this report was shown to Hitler).

184. *G.D.*, D, 6, Nos. 227 (p. 234), 225, 389; *S.U.*, No. 289.

185. See paragraph 7 of the draft of von Ribbentrop to von der Schulenburg of 25 or 26 May 1939, *G.D.*, D, 6, No. 441; cf. Weinberg, *Germany and the Soviet Union*, pp. 25–26.

186. *G.D.*, D, 6, Nos. 297, 429. On the deliberate British leaking of information to Germany and Italy affirming her intention to stand by Poland, see *B.D.*, 3d, 5, Nos. 431, 489, 525; *G.D.*, D, 6, Nos. 377, 385; Siebert, p. 182.

187. *G.D.*, D, 6, Nos. 394, 429; Szembek, pp. 397, 399–400; *B.D.*, 3d, 9, No. 36; *S.U.*, No. 321; Biddle to Hull, 20 May, 10 June, 17 June 1939, Cordell Hull Papers, folders 116, 117, Library of Congress; Biddle to Roosevelt, 20 May and 10 June 1939, Hyde Park, PSF Poland.

188. *G.D.*, D, 6, No. 433; also in *TMWC*, 37:546–56. The conference is discussed further in the text. On the document itself, see Hildebrand, p. 610, n.592; Henke, p. 257, n.45. Like a number of other key documents that do not fit his ideological preconceptions, this one has been questioned by Hans-Günther Seraphim; like the others, this one can now be accepted as authentic.

struction.[189] Hitler not only upheld his earlier decision in favor of the navy[190] but took the occasion to explain his general thinking about the future. Just after the signing of the Pact of Steel and the report of von der Schulenburg on his talk with Molotov, Hitler was explicit on his desire to attack Poland, not for Danzig, but for living space in the east. He warned against colonies as no solution to the problem of feeding the population; as always, Hitler used the term *Lebensraum* to refer to agriculturally usable land.[191]

He explained that he would prefer to crush Poland without simultaneously fighting England; but he was quite explicit that England was the main enemy and would have to be defeated sooner or later anyway. If she intervened, or later if she did not, England would be crushed by the cutting off of her vital trade routes, something to be accomplished by the conquest of the Low Countries and the Atlantic coast of France as bases (with the audience left to infer that the navy needed its priority so that it would have its ships ready to use the conquered bases for their designated purpose). The latter operation, the conquest of the French coastline, discussed by Hitler as simply incidental to the defeat of England, was not seen as particularly difficult (a point on which Hitler differed from his generals). The war as a whole, whether fought in a single phase or preferably in two, would he hoped be short, but preparations for a long war were necessary all the same. In any case, whether Poland could be destroyed in an isolated action or not, the power that had to be defeated as the primary enemy of German expansion was England.[192]

Noteworthy is Hitler's reference or lack of reference to other countries. The United States is not mentioned. Italy, though an ally, was not to be told of German intentions, a decision that was to have important consequences. Japan was similarly to be kept uninformed, and her reluctance to be more closely allied with Germany was recognized as a fact of the international situation.[193] In regard to the Soviet Union, Hitler without referring to the source of the idea asserted that economic relations would be possible only when political relations had improved. Far from rejecting the latter as a possibility as he had done in previous years, Hitler now mentioned the possibility that Russia might disinterest herself in the destruction of Poland. While he left open the option of a closer anti-Russian alignment with Japan if the Soviet Union were to follow an anti-German

189. See Dülffer, pp. 507, 510, 529–30.

190. See his answer to Göring's question at the end of the record.

191. This did not mean a renunciation of acquiring colonies for other raw materials; in fact he had just explained to Ritter von Epp his colonial plans which assumed the acquisition of African territories—presumably from a defeated England and France—in the coming year (Geldern report on the Reichskolonialtagung of 15–18 May 1939, T-77, 642/1838551–54).

192. This summary is essentially similar to the one by Henke, pp. 255–58. Hitler's thoughts about a war against England and France as presented here are surely astonishingly similar to the German strategy a year later!

193. Note that von Ribbentrop on 15 May had quoted Hitler to Ott as having repeatedly criticized the Japanese attitude in the tripartite negotiations (*G.D.*, D, 6, No. 383, p. 410).

policy, this was now clearly the less desirable alternative. Hitler's references to economic warfare, blockade, and preparations for a war of ten to fifteen years' duration surely suggest that the possibility of breaching any British blockade as well as the hope of isolating Poland contributed to his thinking about economic and political agreements with the Soviet Union.

Hitler had concluded that Poland could not be relied upon to remain a subservient client state while he fought the West: "The problem of 'Poland' cannot be separated from the conflict with the West."[194] The question now was whether the Soviet Union would be a helpful neutral or associate while he fought the West and Poland, successively or jointly. He had been ready to explore this possibility when von Ribbentrop was still trying to harmonize such a project with his favorite idea of an alliance with Japan. As soon as the German foreign minister recognized that this was not a likely possibility in the near future, he and von Weizsäcker could go ahead on the exploration of relations with the Soviet Union with Hitler's prompt approval.[195]

German foreign policy in the summer of 1939 was thus directed mainly to the preparation of an attack on Poland.[196] Subsidiary to the military preparations—it being expected that Poland would fight to defend herself—were several lines of policy in foreign affairs. First, an effort would be made to secure the assistance or neutrality of lesser powers whose acquiescence in German plans might not make much difference individually but whose collective joining with the British-French front against Germany would not only cause diplomatic difficulties but would seriously affect Germany's economic ability to wage anything but a very short war. In this category were Sweden, Hungary, Rumania, Yugoslavia, Bulgaria, Turkey, and Belgium, Hitler having recognized that Franco's Spain was still too weak from the civil war just ended to provide anything but a helpful neutrality to Germany.[197]

194. "Das Problem 'Polen' ist von der Auseinandersetzung mit dem Westen nicht zu trennen."

195. Von Ribbentrop was not present at the 23 May meeting. There is no evidence that the delay of several days in which von Ribbentrop's original response to Molotov's comment was held up while the Japanese angle was explored was due to Hitler's orders. On the contrary, von Ribbentrop appears to have had the Führer's agreement to going ahead but to have cast about first for some way to harmonize the new policy toward Russia with his old one toward Japan.

196. Note Richard Meinertzhagen, *Middle East Diary, 1917–1956* (London: Crescent Press, 1959), 28 June 1939, pp. 159–60. On 19 June the counsellor of the German legation at the Hague said that around 20 August there would be an incident in German-Polish relations, so staged by Germany as to convince the German public of the need for war and, it was hoped, to isolate Poland (*Canadian Documents*, 6, No. 974). The general nature of Hitler's intentions was apparently known more widely among German officials than has often been thought likely.

197. This would appear to have been the import of a letter Hitler wrote Franco in March 1939 (see *G.D.*, D, 6, No. 605) in response to Franco's letter of 11 January (ibid., 7:501–4); but the Germans did not want Franco to relieve British and French anxieties in this regard before war broke out (ibid., 6, No. 605). Ciano spoke to Franco along similar lines on 12 July 1939 (ibid., No. 663; *D.D.I.*, 12, No. 611).

Second, without informing either Italy or Japan of what was really intended, Hitler expected the military assistance of the former as a result of the Pact of Steel and a neutrality benevolent to Germany and malevolent toward the Western Powers from Japan because of that country's own national interest.

In the third place, Germany would explore the possibility of an agreement with the Soviet Union. Such an agreement would assure that country's not lining up with the West until the defeat of the West had left her alone to face the subsequent German attack to the east, an attack made easier by the prior destruction of Poland. On the positive side, agreement with the Soviet Union would not only cut off Poland from any outside aid but would have the reverse effect of breaking any blockade of Germany. The disappearance of Poland would give Germany a common border with Russia and thereby enable her to secure needed raw materials from the Soviet Union by trade during that intervening war with the West before seizing them through conquest afterwards.[198]

In the fourth place, Hitler would as soon separate the attack on Poland from a simultaneous war in the west, but since the former was in any case only preliminary to the latter, the risk of a wider war would be run this time. Only if Britain and France were willing to stand aside completely while Germany crushed Poland would they be given a short respite of perhaps a year. But nothing that they might pressure Poland into conceding or might offer themselves would make any difference. Hitler would under no circumstances allow negotiations with either Poland or the West to develop which might conceivably deprive him of a war. Everything was to be subordinated to this requirement of a war at all costs, limited if possible, but with both Poland and the West if necessary. If the Western Powers did join in, that would not only confirm Hitler's belief in the necessity to fight them but had the advantage of having the war start before British and French rearmament programs made any more progress. And there was a time schedule which would dominate everything. The choice of a fall campaign in 1938 and 1939 was not accidental. Hitler wished to move after the harvest and before bad weather set in; he wanted enough time for his own first campaign but with a winter immediately afterward separating that campaign from any offensive by the Western Powers. In 1938 he had at the last moment recoiled from war; in 1939 the calendar would be more rigid both because Hitler was more determined and because the autumn rains in Poland made any postponement beyond the 1 September date he had tentatively set extremely dangerous. Hitler would, as will be seen, move that date forward if he could, and that shorter timetable was to have its own important repercussions, especially

198. The transshipment of key raw materials purchased elsewhere in the world across the Soviet Union, using her ports and railways, to Germany was to become a matter of great importance later, but there is no evidence that this point was given much thought in Germany before the fall of 1939. A brief introduction in Weinberg, *Germany and the Soviet Union*, pp. 72–73.

on the negotiations with the Soviet Union as long as it was in effect, but barring the most extraordinary developments, he would not set it back.[199]

The major practical project to which, therefore, German energies were bent in the summer of 1939 was the projected attack on Poland. The plans for the army, navy, and air force were worked out in detail. Hitler himself appears to have stayed out of the air force planning. He reviewed the army plans in detail, but without making drastic changes of his own.[200] The naval plans, however, were more affected by Hitler's personal preferences because he wanted to combine actions of the German navy directly with the opening of hostilities. Having once hoped to pick up Danzig as a bonus on the way back by warship from Memel, Hitler still planned to bring the navy into the Danzig aspect of the attack on Poland. The project of a naval visit to Danzig, perhaps on 25 August, was being canvassed early in May.[201] Hitler personally discussed the idea with Raeder in June.[202] Consideration of a fleet visit to Danzig went on all during the summer; eventually one of the old battleships previously retired to the status of training ship was sent to Danzig in August, anchored opposite the Polish position of the Westerplatte in the Danzig harbor, and given the dubious distinction of formally starting World War II by opening fire in the early morning of 1 September.[203]

If Danzig, as Hitler had said, was not the object of war, but *Lebensraum*, this did not mean that Danzig could not play an important part in the preparations. In addition to the naval aspect just described, Danzig was to be important in setting the diplomatic stage for a war in which the German public was to be united and the potential enemies of Germany might be disunited.[204] Hitler, therefore, worked out carefully a variety of plans with Albert Forster, who repeatedly met with him in 1939 to receive

199. On awareness in informed circles in Berlin that specific and concrete plans with precise dates were discussed by Hitler and Forster, see Dertinger's "Informationsbericht Nr. 52" of 25 May and his "Informationsbericht Nr. 62" of 15 June 1939, Bundesarchiv, Brammer, Z.Sg. 101/34, ff.269 and 313. After a stay in Berlin in June, Groscurth noted in his diary (p. 177) that the date for the attack on Poland was set for 25 August.

200. On the detailed German military plans, see *TMWC*, 30:180–200; 34:428–43. There appears to have been a leak on the military plans from Halder's office, see Szymanski, pp. 319–20. For Germany's need for her most modern weapons, as opposed to exporting them, see *G.D.*, D, 6, No. 703. On the economic preparations, see Hitler's order of 10 May in *TMWC*, 34:403–8; 2d session of the Reichsverteidigungsrat under Göring on 23 June 1939, ibid., 33:145–60. There were also plans for disrupting Poland internally by contacts with ethnic Germans and Ukrainians inside the country. Though of intrinsic interest, these projects do not shed much light on the general lines of German policy.

201. See *G.D.*, D, 6, Nos. 361, 378. Salewski's account (1:92–94) is superficial.

202. *G.D.*, D, 6, No. 558. Cf. ibid., No. 635 and *TMWC*, 34:200–204.

203. The discussions revolved in part around the concern that the blame for the outbreak of war be pushed on the Poles, as von Weizsäcker expressed it (*G.D.*, D, 6, No. 687). On this issue, see also ibid., No. 705; *Weizsäcker Papiere*, pp. 155–56. For Hitler's readiness to sacrifice the *Schleswig-Holstein* and its crew, see the account of Hitler's discussion with Raeder on 22 August 1939 in the Liebmann notes, *Vierteljahrshefte für Zeitgeschichte*, 16, No. 2 (Apr. 1968), 143.

204. Note the finding that the German public was most solidly behind Hitler in the summer of 1939 in Marlis G. Steinert, *Hitler's War and the Germans* (Athens, Ohio: Ohio University Press, 1977), p. 40.

detailed and specific instructions.[205] Not only was German propaganda always to stress the Danzig question on the assumption that it was the weakest link in the chain between Poland and the West,[206] but quarrels were to be created in Danzig so that international attention might be focused on the alleged injustice inherent in the status of the Free City as opposed to the German plans for the destruction of Poland. Of the various categories of issues that might be created, Berlin picked the one of customs inspectors. Presumably this issue was chosen because it affected Polish rights in the Free City and could accordingly be utilized to provoke Poland, while other internal matters in Danzig might leave Warsaw as unconcerned as had so many prior violations of the Danzig constitution. In July and August, therefore, the focal point of news and attention was the reaction of the Poles to a series of provocative steps taken by the Danzig authorities on instructions from Berlin, provocations designed to "keep the pot boiling"[207] but always under enough restraint to keep it from boiling over. The time for action was to be picked by Berlin, not Warsaw; and the cautious restraint of the Polish government left the German leaders confident that they could keep up the barking until the day and hour when they were ready to bite.[208]

An integral part of German military planning was the use of Slovakia as a base for attacking Poland's southern flank; whatever objections the Slovaks might have were rudely overruled.[209] Whether Lithuania might be an auxiliary on the northern, as Slovakia was on the southern, flank was apparently considered somewhat later. In any case, the Lithuanian

205. See n.199, above; *G.D.*, D, 6, Nos. 693, 785; "Informationsbericht Nr. 77," 18 July 1939, Bundesarchiv, Brammer, Z.Sg. 101/34, f.391.

206. For propaganda instructions, see "Bestellungen aus der Pressekonferenz," 16 June, 8, 13, 18, 19 July 1939, Bundesarchiv, Brammer, Z.Sg. 101/13, ff.53, 74, 78, 82, 83; "Informationsbericht Nr. 81," 24 July 1939, ibid., 101/34, ff.401–3; "S.I. Nr. 149/39, Kampagnen der deutschen Presse," 6 July 1939, Bundesarchiv, Oberheitmann, Z.Sg. 109/1, ff.20–21. For British concern over this matter, see Cabinet 30 (39) of 24 May and the special meeting of ministers on 25 May 1939, C 7694, C 7728/54/18, FO 371/23019.

207. The quotation is from "Bestellungen aus der Pressekonferenz," 23 June 1939, Bundesarchiv, Brammer, Z.Sg. 101/13, f.61.

208. The whole dreary dispute over customs inspectors will not be reviewed here. That it was all engineered from Berlin is obvious from *G.D.*, D, 6, No. 774, which comes from von Weizsäcker's files. The state secretary was especially vigorous in fanning the flames of this trumped up issue at the time and continued to do so in his memoirs. The document on the subject originally published in Weinberg, *Germany and the Soviet Union*, pp. 44–45, has now been printed as *G.D.*, D, 7, No. 119 (von Ribbentrop's approval of it, ibid., No. 139). It shows the fear of the Germans that Polish concessions might deprive them of what they imagined was a propaganda advantage. The various collections of diplomatic documents are filled to overflowing with material on this matter. A very good summary was sent by U.S. Consul Kuykendall in his dispatch 221 of 11 August 1939, State 760c.62/1284. Burckhardt's memoirs recount the dispute, often from the German perspective. Only at one point (p. 326) does he come close to understanding the tactic Hitler and Forster were following. See also Herbert S. Levine, "The Mediator: Carl J. Burckhardt's Efforts to Avert a Second World War," *Journal of Modern History*, 45, No. 3 (Sept. 1973), 453. For Polish gestures of accommodation in Danzig, see *G.D.*, D, 6, No. 686; for Roosevelt's hint to Poland not to let the Germans provoke them on the customs issue, see *U.S.*, 1939, 1:211, 213–14.

209. See above, pp. 535–36; cf. *G.D.*, D, 6, Nos. 644, 667, 768; 7, Nos. 3, 100, 165.

government was treated with the utmost courtesy during the summer of 1939; at least that would keep Kovno from drawing closer to Warsaw.[210] Of the Scandinavian countries, Sweden was by far the most important to Germany because of the Third Reich's dependence on Swedish iron.[211] Neither the Four-Year Plan's processing of the Salzgitter "potting soil" nor the acquisition of iron works in Austria and Czechoslovakia had eliminated, or even substantially reduced, that dependence. It should under these circumstances not be surprising that as war approached in 1939, German diplomacy paid special attention to efforts to assure supplies of Swedish iron ore in case of war.[212] Although not successful in securing formal promises from Sweden on the question, the Germans did feel confident that in practice they would get what they needed; and the experience of war would prove this expectation correct. Sweden would provide the matériel essential to Germany's conduct of war.

The other important countries—in addition to the Soviet Union— having a common border with Poland were Hungary and Rumania. While the Hungarians had just acquired a common border with Poland thanks to German action against Czechoslovakia, they were cautious in their dealings with Berlin. In the crisis of 1939, as in that of 1938, Hungary followed a tortuous path, made even more difficult because on the one hand they had tied themselves more closely to Germany while on the other hand the Poles were even more their traditional friends than the Czechs had become their enemies. Their anxious friendship for Germany was therefore tempered by concern over being drawn into a war with Poland; furthermore, the Hungarian leaders continued to believe that in a general war Germany would eventually lose. Under these circumstances Hungary followed a double policy in 1939. They continued to do their best to cooperate with Germany, maintaining close ties with Berlin and Rome and hoping for the maintenance of such a relationship if war did come.[213] The obvious danger of war, reinforced by the comments of Hitler on 29 April and 1 May when Hungarian Prime Minister Teleki and Foreign Minister Csáky were in Germany, suggested that some reinsurance was needed. In those conversations, the German leaders stressed Germany's

210. See above, p. 536; *G.D.*, D, 6, Nos. 292, 328, 408, 445, 421; Kirk (Berlin) tel. 546 of 23 June 1939, State 760c.62/658.

211. I have not otherwise reviewed Germany's relations with the Scandinavian countries. Although there were important ideological issues inherent in the idea of "Nordic" or "Aryan" cooperation—some of which would have an impact on developments during World War II—as a practical matter even the border dispute with Denmark over North Schleswig had little if any significance for the broader concerns of German foreign policy before 1939 or the origins of the war. See Hilke Lenzing, *Die deutsche Volksgruppe in Dänemark und das nationalsozialistische Deutschland (1933–1939)*, (diss., Bonn, 1973). To keep the Scandinavian states from lining up with England, Germany offered nonaggression pacts to them (*G.D.*, D, 6, No. 284).

212. Ibid., Nos. 187, 229, 242.

213. *Hungarian Documents*, 3, Nos. 399, 523; 4, Nos. 103 a and b, 114, 123, 133, 140, 149; *G.D.*, D, 6, Nos. 248, 436, 578, 595, 641, 706, 717; "Bestellungen aus der Pressekonferenz," 13 April 1939, Bundesarchiv, Brammer, Z.Sg. 101/12, f.107.

strength, Poland's suicidal obstinacy, the weakness of Britain and France, and the ability of Japan by her actions in Asia to keep the United States from any substantial military role in Europe.[214] The Hungarian government had already found a way to assure the United States through Ambassador Bullitt that they would not join Germany if it came to war.[215] They even considered special steps for establishing something like a government in exile if Germany were to occupy Hungary as punishment for not joining her in a war on Poland.[216]

It is clear that this double line disturbed Prime Minister Teleki, the man who though a devout Catholic would commit suicide in 1941 rather than lead his country into war with Yugoslavia with which he had shortly before signed a treaty of friendship. On 24 July Teleki wrote Hitler, expressing his desire to work closely with the Axis but warning that Hungary would not fight Poland.[217] This step annoyed the Germans and Italians greatly. As a fuming Hitler told the Hungarian foreign minister on 8 August, Hungary was repeating her attitude of 1938. Germany would crush Poland, regardless of whether or not the Western Powers intervened, but in any case all would win or lose together. If, as he certainly did not anticipate, Germany were to lose, Hungary would just become a portion of an enlarged Czechoslovakia. Perhaps aware of the fact that warnings from within the German army had reached Budapest in 1938, Hitler assured Count Csáky that the prospect of war against Poland had pulled the whole German army together behind himself. As for other countries intervening, there was an excellent chance that Russia would stay out and share in the booty. Hungary would do best to remember who her friends were.[218] One wonders, however, whether such frankness as

214. *G.D.*, D, 6, Nos. 295, 296, 300; *Hungarian Documents*, 4, Nos. 115, 116. The Hungarians warned the Germans against sending to Rumania weapons which would be used against the Germans themselves later (*G.D.*, D, 6, No. 585; *Hungarian Documents*, 4, Nos. 196, 209). On Mussolini's telling the Hungarian military attaché in Rome on 1 May that he intended to attack Greece if there were a general war, see ibid., No. 109.

215. Bullitt tel. 759 of 17 April 1939, State 740.00/906; cf. *B.D.*, 3d, 5, No. 565; *Hungarian Documents*, 3, No. 522.

216. For relevant documents, see John Pelényi, "The Secret Plan for a Hungarian Government in Exile in the West at the Outbreak of World War II," *Journal of Modern History*, 36, No. 2 (June 1964), 170–77 and note following p. 243. By 24 June the Hungarian minister in Berlin had information that the Germans were planning to attack Poland in August–September 1939 (*Hungarian Documents*, 4, No. 198).

217. *G.D.*, D, 6, Nos. 712, 739 and notes; *Hungarian Documents*, 4, Nos. 215, 227, 244, 246, 253, 255, 260, 261, 265; cf. *B.D.*, 3d, 6, No. 408. Note that Ciano's *initial* reaction had been positive (*Hungarian Documents*, 4, No. 240).

218. *G.D.*, D, 6, No. 784; Henke, p. 276. There is no record of this conversation in *Hungarian Documents*, 4, but see Nos. 303 and 372, which reflect the German views, and No. 267, which refers to the Hungarian foreign minister's trip. The Hungarian minister to Paris, who returned to his post from Budapest on 23 August, repeated to the American ambassador Csáky's account of a talk in Berlin with German Interior Minister Frick. Frick had talked "in a hair raising manner and had stated that Hitler was convinced that he could starve England to death by airplane attacks on British merchant shipping. Frick also had indicated that Hitler was likely to make war on Poland the end of this week" (Bullitt tel. 1557 of 23 August 1939, 6:00 p.m., State 760c.62/939).

Teleki's letter if practiced by the Axis powers with each other would not have served them better. In any case, as the Germans would discover when they pressed the Hungarians on the subject in late August, Hungary simply would not help in military operations against Poland, though Germany could count on economic support in a general war—support that was to prove of considerable importance.[219] At the beginning of the war, however, Hungary, though offered a share of the territorial booty, like Lithuania but unlike Slovakia refused to attack her Polish neighbor.[220]

Since Rumania had long been an ally of Poland, the Germans never expected her to participate directly in any war against Poland. What they wanted instead was the assurance that Rumania would not join the front Britain and France were trying to build up against them, because in war, even more than in peacetime, Germany would need Rumanian oil. In spite of the great progress made by the German synthetic oil industry, the growth of the German air force, the expansion of the German navy, and the increased mechanization of her army made very substantial imports of petroleum products critical for the Third Reich.[221] Those from the Western Hemisphere would be cut off by any British blockade, and there was as yet no assurance that the Soviet Union would supply Germany's needs. The imports of oil derived from oil shale in Estonia were steady and substantial, but covered only a small portion of Germany's needs.[222] Rumania was, therefore, from Germany's point of view the most important country of Southeast Europe.[223]

As for the Rumanian alliance with Poland, it was directed only against Russia, and all efforts of the British and French to have it revised explicitly to cover Germany as well failed. The Poles did not want to change the alliance because Beck was certain that such action would drive Hungary completely into German arms and thus open up still another front against his country. Rumania was reluctant to take the requested step for fear of provoking Germany and being drawn into the developing confrontation

219. Ibid.; *G.D.*, D, 7, Nos. 175, 498, 519, 520, 533; *Hungarian Documents*, 4, Nos. 314, 315, 317, 327, 328, 332, 339, 341, 342, 347, 350; *B.D.*, 3d, 7, Nos. 85, 95, 494; Macartney, 1:364–67. Note Ciano's advice to the Hungarians on 2 September: the outcome of the war was doubtful, and they had best be careful (*Hungarian Documents*, 4, No. 338). Teleki, however, told Mussolini that at any conference Hungary would push her territorial demands against Rumania and would do so even beyond the ethnographic line (ibid., Nos 345, a–d, 351).

220. Ibid., Nos. 353, 354, 358, 374, 377–79, 381, 385, 389; *G.D.*, D, 8, Nos. 45, 48, 49, 51, 67.

221. Marguerat, p. 138.

222. Wilhelm Meier-Dörnberg, *Die Ölversorgung der Kriegsmarine, 1935 bis 1945* (Freiburg: Rombach, 1973), pp. 33–34.

223. When Germany and Russia partitioned Poland in 1939, one of the special concessions Germany most wanted from the Soviet Union was assistance in the transportation of Rumanian oil by railway across what had been eastern Poland. Berlin was worried about shipment delays in general and about the effects of a section of the railway route being converted to the wider Russian gauge in particular (see Weinberg, *Germany and the Soviet Union*, pp. 66, 68; *U.S.*, 1939, 1:498).

between that country and Poland.[224] In any case, Rumania had enough to worry about with the revisionist demands of her Hungarian and Bulgarian neighbors and was even more afraid of any peacetime alignment with the Soviet Union.[225] Russia had territorial claims against Rumania, and the Rumanians had learned the hard way in the nineteenth century that being allied with Russia in no way protected Rumania against those claims. Furthermore, the Rumanian government had feared and continued to fear that any German-Russian war would be fought over their territory with Rumania losing her independence to the winner.[226] If Germany did attack Rumania, the Rumanians would be happy for any help they could get from anywhere; but until that moment arrived, they preferred to do nothing which they feared might draw them into any conflict.

Perhaps because Rumanian Foreign Minister Grigore Gafencu was a charming man who made an excellent impression in London and Paris, perhaps because he was not only one of the first East European leaders to publish his memoirs but to do so in German and English at that, the fact that it was Gafencu who had given way to pressure in March 1939 and had signed over his country's economic future to Berlin has often been over-looked. Although eventually dismissed as too pro-Western, Gafencu played a role in 1939 that assisted German interests far more than is often realized. He wanted and received a British and French guarantee for his country; but unlike Beck, who refused to make one-sided agreements with *either* Germany or the Soviet Union, Gafencu had made one with Germany, and during the crisis of 1939 did his best to keep on good terms with Berlin.[227] These efforts, and the great concessions he had made, did not, however, preserve the Rumanian government from both continued German pressure and constant German distrust.[228] The German government was careful not to support Hungarian and Bulgarian aspirations on Rumanian territory openly, but that was about the only concession Berlin would make.[229] Otherwise, unremitting demands for political support and economic concessions reached Bucharest. At the same time as they were taking an increasing proportion of Rumanian oil, the Germans were also

224. Beck, *Dernier rapport*, p. 321; *B.D.*, 3d, 5, Nos. 1, 2, 10, 278. I have considerable doubts about Léger's communication to Bullitt of an alleged Beck-Gafencu secret under-standing that the two countries would join each other if attacked by Germany (*Bullitt Papers*, pp. 348–49).

225. *B.D.*, 3d, 5, Nos. 279, 285; Cabinet 24 (39) of 26 April 1939, C 6244/3356/18, FO 371/23065.

226. Weinberg, *Foreign Policy*, pp. 231, 323; *B.D.*, 3d, 5:331.

227. *G.D.*, D, 6, Nos. 227, 234, 375. Chanady and Jensen (pp. 214–16) attribute all this to German and Hungarian threats and British weakness. Note the comment of the British minister in Bucharest, Sir Reginald Hoare, that the prime minister, Armand Calinescu, was firmer than Gafencu (Hoare to Cadogan, 19 May 1939, R 4488/22/37, FO 371/23840).

228. The German distrust was particularly evident in the deliberate failure to meet com-mitments for armaments deliveries in exchange for Rumanian wheat and oil, see *G.D.*, D, 6, Nos. 337, 354, 376, 398, 703, 738; Marguerat, pp. 149–51. For German pressure on Rumania, see *G.D.*, D, 6, Nos. 488, 504, 662, 631, 651.

229. Ibid., Nos. 319, 625, 627, 633; Marguerat, p. 139.

building up their economic power within the country by special banking ventures.[230] As the German timetable called for war, Germany could be on the whole very satisfied by the way she was converting Rumania into an economic satellite that might well feed the voracious German war machine about as steadily as Sweden.[231]

There was, so it seemed, no need for Germany to woo Bulgaria. The Bulgarian government on the contrary was apparently so inspired by Germany's destruction of Czechoslovakia as to believe that a complete reversal of the peace settlement was just around the corner. For Bulgaria that meant dreams of all sorts of territorial gains. There was some consideration in 1939 of the idea, pushed independently by Britain and the Soviet Union, that Rumanian cession of at least a portion of the southern Dobruja might rally Bulgaria to the side of the Balkan entente. The evidence indicates that it was too late for schemes of this type, and Gafencu's rejection of such concessions as merely likely to whet Bulgarian and Hungarian appetites is amply supported by the record.[232]

The Bulgarian government was asking Germany for extensive arms deliveries and credits to cover their cost. Since, like Hungary, Bulgaria had started rearming later than Germany, Sofia was almost frantically insistent on receiving vast quantities of weapons; and these Bulgarian requests and the German efforts to meet them constitute the main theme of German-Bulgarian relations in 1939.[233] The Bulgarian government explained to Berlin that there was no chance of their agreeing to the sort of deal for joining the Balkan entente then mentioned; Bulgaria expected to regain her borders of 1913. While the German government thought this was just fine, they let it be known that they could not say so in public.[234] The desire for cooperation with Bulgaria was there, however, as Bulgarian Prime Minister George Kiosseivanov learned on his visit to Berlin on 5 July.[235] Hitler assured Kiosseivanov that he much preferred to fight a war at his present age than to fight one later, that Bulgaria was certainly perceived as Germany's friend, and that he would do his very best to help Bulgaria build up her armed forces. Convinced that he could really count on this country, Hitler gave orders for Bulgarian arms wishes to be met generously, and as a result of this directive, real efforts were made in

230. Ibid., pp. 140–41, 146–47; OMGUS, "Report on the Investigation of the Deutsche Bank," Exhibits 394, 395.

231. *G.D.*, D, 6, Nos. 621, 632, 638, 639, 742; 7, Nos. 77 and n.1, 94. Marguerat, pp. 141–48, stresses the persistent limitations on German economic control.

232. *B.D.*, 3d, 5, No. 278, pp. 307–9; *G.D.*, D, 6, No. 375. The Germans appear to have been seriously concerned about the efforts to move Bulgaria into the antiaggression front, see Irving, *Breach of Security*, pp. 27, 65–67.

233. See *G.D.*, D, 6, Nos. 17, 63, 67, 218, 243, 392, 415, 566, 656.

234. Ibid., Nos. 320, 346, 476, 479, 480; cf. Hoptner, pp. 162–64. The Bulgarian demands would have involved territories held in 1939 by Yugoslavia, Greece, and Rumania.

235. On Kiosseivanov's Berlin visit, see *G.D.*, D, 6, Nos. 500, 508, 617; "Vertrauliche Informationen des Reichsministeriums für Volksaufklärung und Propaganda für die Presse," 4 July 1939, Bundesarchiv, Oberheitmann, Z.Sg. 109/1, f.12.

Germany, at a time when Germany was herself straining her resources, to assist Bulgaria in rebuilding its military strength.[236] Berlin understood the old friendship of Bulgaria for Russia, but since the immediate plans called for a war with Poland and with the West before any conflict with Russia, the prospect of a faithful satellite in the Balkans was an inviting one. From the perspective of Berlin, there were many advantages to helping that satellite build up its power. When and how that would be used could be left until later; in the meantime, the known subservience of Bulgaria to Berlin could be utilized as a potential threat to keep Rumania in line, to surround Yugoslavia, and to warn the Turks.

For Yugoslavia, the disappearance first of Czechoslovakia and then of Albania was especially shocking. The former had been its ally in the Little Entente, and although that alliance had lost most of its political and military importance, the shock of one of the successor states disintegrating and disappearing was considerable.[237] The Italian occupation of Albania moreover left Yugoslavia practically cut off from the outside world, facing Italy on two fronts as well as Germany and a newly enlarged Hungary on the north. It is hardly surprising that under these circumstances the government of Alexander Cincar-Marković, which had replaced that of Stojadinović only in February, steered a cautious course in the European crisis. It was understood in England that Yugoslavia had to be extremely careful and could hardly be expected to expose itself to great risks.[238]

The German government wanted two things from Belgrade: that Yugoslavia place her mineral resources at the service of the German war machine, and that Yugoslavia not only refrain from joining the British anti-aggression front but move more closely to the Axis. On the first of these issues, the Germans had the advantage of an entrenched position in the Yugoslav economy, acquired in earlier years, that could be expanded by the leverage that Belgrade's desire for arms from Germany gave Berlin. In this regard, therefore, Germany made considerable progress, with Göring's Four-Year Plan, air force deliveries, and his representative Neuhausen as the local negotiator playing key parts.[239]

As for pulling Yugoslavia closer to the Axis, even the leverage exerted in connection with the arms delivery question did not enable Berlin to secure the desired degree of compliance. The Yugoslav leaders, both the new prime minister and Prince Paul, the regent, wanted to keep their relations with Germany as good as possible, but they were unwilling to go

236. *G.D.*, D, 6, No. 618, p. 717, Nos. 659, 703, 728, 738; 7, Nos. 1, 11, 78, 102.
237. *Hungarian Documents*, 3, Nos. 443, 473, 506.
238. R 1443, R 2701, R 2915/409/92, FO 371/22883; Hoptner, pp. 144–45.
239. On the arms trade, its problems, and its use by the Germans for political pressure, see *G.D.*, D, 6, Nos. 21, 128, 142, 176, 210, 245, 262, 279, 573, 586, 615, 620, 683, 703, 738; 7, Nos. 81, 102, 240, 241; Göring conference of 25 July 1939 in *TMWC*, 38:367–70; OMGUS, "Deutsche Bank," Exhibit 403; *U.S.*, 1939, 1:199; cf. Roland Schönfeld, "Deutsche Rohstoffsicherungspolitik in Jugoslawien, 1934–1944," *Vierteljahrshefte für Zeitgeschichte*, 24, No. 3 (July 1976), 218–19; Hoptner, pp. 158–60. The Yugoslav government moved the bulk of its gold reserve to England and the United States, ibid., p. 156.

any further.[240] In regard to Yugoslavia the Germans with the support of Italy tried to do what they had so successfully done earlier with Hungary, namely, to obtain a kind of ritual purification and identification by having the country leave the League of Nations and join the Anti-Comintern Pact. In spite of every effort, including personal pressure by Hitler and von Ribbentrop on both Prince Paul and Cincar-Marković when they visited Germany in April and June, Yugoslavia would not break formally with its old policy and march in cadence to Germany's tune.[241] Belgrade would do its utmost to stay neutral, providing some economic resources for Germany, but remained unwilling to join either Germany's enemies or the Axis.[242]

Both because of its strategic location and the need of Germany's arms industry for its chrome, Turkey was considered exceptionally important by Hitler. The effort to keep Turkey from aligning herself with the anti-aggression front was entrusted to a man thought capable of the necessary finesse and intrigue. After his experiences in Vienna, Franz von Papen was recalled from temporary retirement by Hitler in April 1939 and sent to Ankara.[243] Perhaps the fact that he had hardly covered himself with glory in Turkey in the World War made him all the more eager to do his best this time around. Two recent developments would make it exceedingly difficult to restore in any future war the relationship Germany and Turkey had maintained—enjoyed is hardly the correct term—in the previous conflict. The territorial settlement by which France returned to Turkey the area around Alexandretta opened up the possibility of a Franco-Turkish alignment.[244] Second, the Italian action in Albania appeared to threaten Turkey directly. The maintenance of a large Italian garrison there was taken as an indication of further Italian aggressive intentions in the direction of the eastern Mediterranean and thereby pushed Turkey toward the British anti-aggression front out of fear of Germany's Axis partner.[245]

In the face of this situation even the repeated blandishments of von Papen, alternating with veiled threats and underlined by German refusals to carry out delivery contracts on armaments for Turkey could not keep the Turkish government from aligning itself with Great Britain.[246] Turkey, like Yugoslavia, wanted to maintain good relations with Germany, and

240. See *G.D.*, D, 6, Nos. 191, 192, 198, 256.

241. Ibid., Nos. 262, 271, 431, 474, 720, 733, 745; 7, No. 16.

242. Ibid., 6, Nos. 609, 691; *Hungarian Documents*, 4, No. 155.

243. The post had been vacant since late November 1938; the developments after 15 March 1939 obviously called the problem to Berlin's attention. See Krecker, pp. 27–28.

244. *G.D.*, D, 6, Nos. 59, 72. On the other hand, the Franco-Turkish negotiations were incredibly protracted, a fact cited by Adamthwaite (p. 328) as characteristic of the "general dilatoriness which infected the main branches of the French government."

245. See Irving, *Breach of Security*, pp. 58–62; Krecker, pp. 29–34.

246. *G.D.*, D, 6, Nos. 259, 281, 286, 288, 289, 303, 305, 315, 317, 324, 336, 413, 475, 483, 489, 495, 496, 512, 513, 518, 533; *S.U.*, No. 269; Siebert, pp. 144–49; Glasneck and Kircheisen, pp. 40–46; Pratt, pp. 156ff.; Krecker, pp. 36–40. On the arms deliveries issue and the decisions of Hitler and Göring not to send the weapons ordered and ready for shipment but to try to keep some trade continuing because Germany needed chrome, see *G.D.*, D, 6, Nos. 321, 435, 454, 472, 703, 782; 7, No. 80; Krecker, pp. 41–43.

she would send Germany the much-needed chrome until the last stages of World War II, but officially Ankara was on the side of the West.[247] That in practice the Turks themselves would see to it that this alignment meant little or nothing could hardly be foreseen by Berlin.[248] Unlike Bulgaria, which seemed almost eager to repeat its role of a subordinate ally of Germany, Turkey steered a course of cautious neutrality though with nominal ties to the West.

From Hitler's point of view, the most important smaller country in Western Europe was Belgium. As already mentioned, he intended to occupy that country—along with Holland and Luxembourg—as part of his planned campaign in the west against Great Britain; but he certainly did not want the Belgians to join Britain and France until he was ready to launch a full-scale attack in the west. Any Belgian (from Germany's point of view) premature alignment with the Western Powers could be very dangerous to Germany because of Belgium's proximity to Germany's most important industrial area. Hitler was therefore most interested in having the Belgian government adhere to its "independent" but in reality neutral policy. That policy, adopted formally in 1936, not only screened German ambitions against Poland but also would make it much easier for the German armed forces to crush Belgium quickly when Germany was ready to do so. The Belgians would have denied themselves the opportunity to coordinate their defensive strategy with England and France, a self-denial based in part on the principle of an independent policy, in part on memories of the propaganda repercussions of pre-1914 staff contacts with the British, and in part on the basis that in the years of close staff contacts with France the Belgians had not in fact learned anything useful about French operational planning—mainly because there was nothing useful to learn, but the Belgians did not know that. In any case, in spite of insistent urgings from London, Belgium allowed only minimal staff contacts and refused to open general staff conversation with the Western Powers.[249]

Under these circumstances it will hardly surprise anyone that the German government in 1939 was free with the most explicit reassurances to Belgium, reassurances at times accompanied by threats of the dire consequences that would befall Belgium if she were to abandon her independent

247. A British-Turkish declaration of mutual support in the Mediterranean was issued on 12 May. Relevant documents in *B.D.*, 3d, 5, chaps. 3, 4, 6, 7; see also 46th meeting of the cabinet Committee on Foreign Policy, 10 May 1939, CAB 27/655.

248. It must be remembered that the relatively firmer position of Turkey in the spring and summer of 1939 was based on two factors which would soon change: the greater distance from German power, and the assumption that the Soviet Union would join the anti-aggression front.

249. *D.D.B.*, 5, Nos. 65, 66, 70, 71, 74. On Belgium's prewar contacts with the British, see Brian Bond, *France and Belgium, 1939–1940* (London: Davis-Poynter, 1975), pp. 26–36; note *B.D.*, 3d, 6, No. 196; *Harvey Diaries*, 27 May 1939, pp. 292–93. The Belgians did think that staff talks with Holland might be useful for them (*D.D.B.*, 5, No. 57).

stance and cooperate with England and France.[250] All discussion of revisionist aspirations for the territories of Eupen and Malmedy that Belgium had acquired at the end of the World War was banned from the German press; once Belgium was occupied, those lands could be seized easily enough.[251] In the meantime, Hitler himself would personally reassure the Belgians of his good intentions toward them.[252] The Belgian ambassador to Paris saw very clearly that German interest in Belgium was solely due to Germany's intention of invading Belgium and worry lest the attacked country find a way to defend herself effectively, but such warnings were not heeded in Brussels.[253] King Leopold, who certainly hoped to spare his country the terrors of another occupation, thought the best way to avoid that was to give the Germans no room to doubt Belgium's innocence of any ties to Berlin's enemies and to assist in avoiding war altogether by a special appeal for peace launched together with Queen Wilhelmina of the Netherlands.[254] As noble as it was futile, that gesture would neither restrain Hitler from attacking Poland nor, when he thought the time right, from invading Belgium.

By way of summary, therefore, it can be said that German policy aims toward the smaller powers in 1939 were largely, if not entirely, attained. Even if Hungary, Yugoslavia, and Turkey had not aligned themselves as closely with Germany as the Berlin government would have liked, on the critical strategic issues the Germans could feel that they had accomplished much. They could go to war reasonably certain of receiving the needed iron ore from Sweden, oil and wheat from Rumania, chrome from Turkey, and various minerals but especially copper from Yugoslavia. They could be fairly certain that none except possibly Turkey would openly join the circle of Germany's enemies, and that Belgium would screen the industrial heart of Germany against attack until the German army was ordered to march to the Channel coast. This record, of course, reflected not only the accomplishments of German diplomacy in 1939 but the strong position Germany had acquired by her actions of previous years. In the hope of reintegrating Germany into a peaceful European

250. *D.D.B.*, 5, Nos. 63, 80, 81; *G.D.*, D, 6, Nos. 516, 517, 694, 697, 701; "Bestellung für die Schriftleitung," 18 August 1939, Bundesarchiv, Brammer, Z.Sg. 101/13, f.112.

251. "Bestellungen aus der Pressekonferenz," 27 March, 3 April 1939, ibid., 101/12, ff.94, 100. The German annexations of Belgian territory are reviewed in Arnold H. Price, "The Belgian-German Frontier during World War II," *Maryland Historian*, 1, No. 2 (Fall 1970), 145–53.

252. *D.D.B.*, 5, No. 62.

253. Ambassador Pol Le Tellier in commenting on German press articles on 4 July 1939 wrote: "La violence de ces réactions, loin de me convaincre de la pureté des intentions de l'Allemagne à notre égard me porte plutôt a croire que le Reich n'a pas renoncé à violer notre sol si les circonstances le persuadent, comme en août 1914, que la voie belge est la plus sûre pour frapper ses grands ennemis. Dès lors, l'intérêt de l'Allemagne est d'empêcher par tour les moyens que nous organisions d'avance avec nos garants français et anglais une défense efficace des frontières belges contre une agression eventuelle allemande" (ibid., No. 76).

254. Leopold had developed this project by 27 July (Overstraeten, pp. 339–42). The Belgian documents on the appeal are to be found in *D.D.B.*, 5, Nos. 87ff.

system, the Western Powers had for years quite deliberately steered away from dividing Europe into ideological blocks. Now when they tried to reverse that policy and to rally the smaller countries against Berlin, they found such a policy extremely difficult to implement in the short time left available, and the German leadership was for that very reason determined to keep the time as short as possible.

If he hoped to obtain raw materials and political support from a number of smaller countries, or at least to keep them from joining his enemies, Hitler counted on direct and active military aid from Italy. Although he did not tell the Italian leaders of his plans for an attack on Poland, Hitler assumed that he had successfully tied Italy to Germany by the Pact of Steel with its clear and unmistakable wording, wording that had met with full Italian approval after a few minor changes requested by Rome.[255] Shortly after signing the pact, Mussolini had reiterated in writing to Hitler his strategic concepts for the forthcoming joint war against the West and his belief that the Axis first needed several years of peace, together with the reasons for his opinion. Hitler neither agreed in writing nor argued with the details of the letter handed to him on 31 May. Perhaps the two leaders could discuss their views personally later that year.[256]

Hitler had, as noted, decided not to take the Italians into his confidence; although there is no evidence linking the two issues, everything that had gone before makes it plausible that Hitler's determined action on the transfer of the South Tyrolean Germans in the summer of 1939 was his way of making sure that the Italians would have no complaints when the critical moment arrived.[257] On the key issue of timing, Hitler, who had already decided to strike that year, would simply confront Mussolini with a fait accompli.[258] As for military staff contacts, these went forward but without the precise commitments that one might have expected owing to the combined effects of German secrecy and the divergent timetables of the prospective wartime allies. Few details could be discussed under these circumstances;[259] and when they were, discrepancies became obvious. In the naval talks, the Italians revealed that their main concern would have to be the protection of the supply route from Italy to Libya—an issue that would indeed play a dominant role in the whole Med-

255. See *G.D.*, D, 6, Nos. 371, 386; Toscano, *Origins of the Pact of Steel*, pp. 349–70; Siebert, pp. 178–84.

256. A full account is in Toscano, *Origins of the Pact of Steel*, pp. 376–88. Note that Mussolini had not taken the option, offered to him at the time, of increasing his independence of Germany by some degree of rapprochement with France (see esp. Siebert, pp. 188–98).

257. Hitler would not, however, allow great publicity about the transfer scheme; that might embarrass the German propaganda campaign about the ill treatment of Germans in Poland (see *G.D.*, D, 6, Nos. 624, 643, nn.1 and 2). In any case, the land for the South Tyrolean Germans to settle on had first to be conquered (see Siebert, p. 233, n.80).

258. Note Keitel's comments to Ciano about this in December 1942 (Ciano, *Diary*, p. 557).

259. *G.D.*, D, 6:936–42, No. 660; "Bestellungen aus der Pressekonferenz," 22 June 1939, Bundesarchiv, Brammer, Z.Sg. 101/13, f.60.

iterranean and North African theater during World War II.[260] As for the possibility of combined offensive operations against Great Britain, the key was to be the building up of a naval base at Kismayu from which submarines and cruisers would be able to raid the British supply routes in the Indian Ocean. Italy, however, had only acquired this area, the Jubaland portion of Italian Somaliland, from Britain in 1925; and by the time war broke out little had been done to prepare the base for its ambitious role.[261] Economic negotiations between the Axis partners also continued to be beset by difficulties;[262] propaganda and myth rather than hard planning and substance constituted the bond between Germany and Italy. Although for a short time it looked as if there might be some rapprochement between Germany and the Vatican, a development greatly desired and often urged on the Germans by their Italian and Spanish friends, nothing substantial beyond a temporary press truce came out of this project. No strengthening of the Axis was to be expected as a result of lessened tension between the new pope, Pius XII, and the authorities in Berlin.[263]

Although Mussolini and Ciano were worried about the possibility of war over Danzig and the Polish question generally, they preferred to have some years of peace.[264] The Duce was, however, in a particularly difficult position, largely of his own making. He had committed Italy in writing and in public to the German side; he did not think Italy ready to honor that promise for some years to come; but he was most reluctant to tell the Germans frankly, as Teleki did, that Italy could not yet go to war. The memory of 1915, the self-esteem of Mussolini and his hope that some exercise of a moderating influence on Hitler might yet avert or postpone war, struggled with a recognition of what war with the West would be

260. *G.D.*, D, 6:943–48. Ciano would bring up this subject at Salzburg in August, ibid., 7:36. The Italians never did follow up hints that there might be oil in Libya (Mack Smith, p. 122).

261. See the description of the situation at Kismayu during the East African campaign in I. S. O. Playfair, *The Mediterranean and Middle East*, 1 (London: H.M. Stationery Office, 1954): 415–16.

262. *G.D.*, D, 6, No. 423; Siebert, p. 228.

263. On this whole episode, as well as on the new pope's suggestion of a conference to settle the dispute over Danzig, see William M. Harrigan, "Pius XII's Effort to Effect a Détente in German-Vatican Relations, 1939–1940," *Catholic Historical Review*, 49, No. 2 (July 1963), 173–91; *Saint Siège*, 1:8–18, Nos. 18ff.; Note by Udet of 11 April 1939 for Göring on his meeting with Hitler on 7 April 1939 about Ciano's request that Göring see the pope while in Rome, London, Imperial War Museum, Milch Papers, folder 65, frames 7391–92; "Informationsbericht Nr. 43," 27 April 1939, Bundesarchiv, Brammer, Z.Sg. 101/34, f.205; "Bestellung für die Redaktion," 5 May 1939, ibid., 101/13, f.5; Osborne report of 17 July 1939, C 10227/54/18, FO 371/22023; Ciano, *Diary*, 13 June 1939, p. 98. For other perspectives on the new pope, see Klieforth to Moffat, 3 March 1939, Moffat Papers, Vol. 16; *D.D.B.*, 5, No. 90.

264. Note Prince Paul's comments on his Rome visit of 10–11 May 1939 in R 4495/409/92, FO 371/23884. Cf. Ciano, *Diary*, pp. 79–80; *Hungarian Documents*, 4, No. 147; and the evidence of inadequate Italian military preparations in Mack Smith, chap. 13, and Angela Raspin's article in Forstmeier (ed.), pp. 202–21.

likely to do to Italy in the immediate future. With Ciano, under prodding from Attolico, becoming increasingly alarmed,[265] the Italians tried to get the Germans to give them a more specific picture of their intentions. Under the terms of the Pact of Steel, the partners were supposed to keep each other informed, and the Italians naturally believed that this applied to the greatest crisis of the moment, the one over Danzig and Poland. The various Italian requests for information and the discussion of a possible Hitler-Mussolini meeting during the summer of 1939 must be seen in this context.[266]

At the same time as the Italian worries might have alerted Hitler to the real state of mind of his prospective ally, however, Rome was also sending very different signals. The Italians not only joined in the condemnation of Teleki's warning that Hungary would not participate in an attack on Poland;[267] they took a variety of steps to assure the Germans of Italy's complete loyalty to the Pact of Steel. On numerous occasions they defended the German position on the Polish question and made sure that Berlin knew it.[268] Both when asking for the details of Germany's plans in regard to Danzig and when arranging the Hitler-Mussolini meeting scheduled for 4 August the Italians explicitly reiterated their promise to fight alongside Germany if war did break out.[269] Though the Germans, therefore, came to understand that Mussolini preferred some diplomatic settlement of their dispute with Poland, perhaps by some conference of the Munich type at which Mussolini himself could shine, they had no reason to anticipate—and Hitler in particular had no reason to assume—that the Italians would not fulfill their treaty obligations.[270]

There may well have been an element of wishful thinking in the expectation of Mussolini and Ciano that there might be a peaceful settlement after all.[271] Perhaps the troubles England was having at Tientsin with Japan in the summer of 1939 led Rome to hope that in spite of British warnings and their own repeatedly expressed opinion, England would not

265. See *G.D.*, D, 6, No. 601; *D.D.I.*, 12, No. 427; *D.D.B.*, 5, No. 79. For Ciano's initial doubts about Attolico's prodding, see his diary entires for 19, 21, and 22 July 1939.

266. *D.D.I.*, 12, No. 130; *B.D.*, 3d, 6, Nos. 546, 711; *Weizsäcker-Papiere*, pp. 155–56. See also *Hungarian Documents*, 4, No. 195.

267. Ciano, *Diary*, 24–26 July 1939, pp. 112–13.

268. See *G.D.*, D, 6, Nos. 456, 629; *D.D.I.*, 12, Nos. 463, 505; *B.D.*, 3d, 6, Nos. 234, 261; Ciano, *Diary*, 7 July 1939, pp. 109–10.

269. See Ciano's letter to Attolico of 2 July 1939, Ciano, *Diplomatic Papers*, p. 288; *G.D.*, D, 6, Nos. 711, 718. Since the request for information from Rome came just before Ciano's visit to Franco, von Ribbentrop was especially careful to provide a deliberately distorted picture of the situation, something that must be remembered as background for Ciano's final break with von Ribbentrop when the two met at Salzburg a month later, and Ciano learned the truth. *G.D.*, D, 6, No. 636; *D.D.I.*, 12, Nos. 503, 504; Siebert, pp. 211–13.

270. *G.D.*, D, 6, Nos. 718, 737; *D.D.I.*, 12, No. 717; Ciano, *Diary*, 19–22 July 1939, pp. 110–12; *Weizsäcker-Papiere*, pp. 156–57; Siebert, pp. 220–21; "Informationsbericht Nr. 84," 11 August 1939, Bundesarchiv, Brammer, Z.Sg. 101/34, ff.405–15.

271. Especially revealing are the reports of the Belgian ambassador in Rome, *D.D.B.*, 5, Nos. 77, 83; cf. ibid., No. 79.

fight in 1939 after all.[272] The very aggravation over Germany's failure to send the promised modern weapons may have reassured Rome that a conflict was hardly imminent; if Berlin expected the Italians to join them in a few weeks in a war certain to determine the fate of their two countries, surely they would want Italy to be as strong as possible.[273] Although the Italian leaders had urged along the German-Soviet rapprochement and were given some information on it from Berlin and even more from the German embassy in Moscow,[274] they certainly did not expect any rapid conclusion of a German-Soviet agreement. In view of von Ribbentrop's repeated assertions that all was well and the similar opinion of Ciano's brother-in-law, Massimo Magistrati, the first counsellor of the Italian embassy in Berlin, the Italians themselves on 28 July suggested a cancellation of the scheduled Hitler-Mussolini meeting.[275]

As more and more alarming reports came to Rome in the following days, however,[276] Ciano began to doubt that all was as calm and peaceful as he had thought, whereas Ambassador Attolico had been sounding the alarm all along. The mixed news from Berlin in the first week of August led Ciano to think of a meeting with von Ribbentrop as a way of clarifying the situation once and for all. With Mussolini's cooperation and approval, he prepared himself to argue for a period of peace and to suggest once again Mussolini's idea of a conference to settle outstanding issues.[277] A meeting in Germany was accordingly arranged, and the Italian foreign minister left Rome fully briefed on the need to avert war for the time being and certain that the Duce was "more than ever convinced of the necessity of delaying the conflict."[278]

When Ciano arrived at Salzburg and met with von Ribbentrop at Fuschl, the castle the German foreign minister had expropriated for his own use from a murdered Austrian nobleman, he immediately discovered that Attolico had been right in warning him.[279] Although Ciano would present to von Ribbentrop and subsequently to Hitler the array of arguments he and the Duce had thought up to urge postponement of war, the

272. See B.D., 3d, 9, No. 244; Lee, chap. 7; Shai, chap. 6.

273. G.D., D, 6, Nos. 703, 738.

274. Ibid., Nos. 480, 523; Toscano, Designs in Diplomacy, pp. 76ff.

275. See esp. Ciano, Diary, 26–31 July 1939, pp. 113–15. Note also Ciano's continued negative comments on Attolico's insistence that war was coming and that Italy should act to head off German action, ibid., 2 and 3 August, pp. 115–16. See also Siebert, pp. 213–23.

276. D.D.I., 12, Nos. 750, 767. The information was provided by Admiral Canaris; see also ibid., No. 648.

277. G.D., D, 6, No. 777; Siebert, pp. 225–28; Ciano, Diary, 2–10 August 1939, pp. 115–18. The section of the Ciano diary for the last week of July and the first week of August 1939 appears to me a particularly convincing proof that Ciano did not retouch the text. He is here revealed as badly misled and rather foolishly deceiving himself; then he changes his mind slowly and against his own preferences.

278. Ibid., 10 August 1939, p. 118.

279. The day before von Ribbentrop had been boasting to Admiral Canaris about Italy's loyalty to the Pact of Steel (Abshagen, p. 198).

German leaders were obviously set on war.[280] Ciano's impression from
the 11 and 12 August conversations was that "the decision to fight is
implacable. He [von Ribbentrop] rejects any solution which might give
satisfaction to Germany and avoid the struggle. I am certain that even if
the Germans were given more than they ask for they would attack just the
same, because they are possessed by the demon of destruction."[281] Hitler
was as determined as his foreign minister. "He, too, is impassive and
implacable in his decision . . . . He has decided to strike, and strike he will.
All our arguments will not in the least avail to stop him."[282] Hitler and
von Ribbentrop also argued that Britain and France were unlikely to go to
war to support Poland; but that if they did, as Ciano was sure they would,
this was probably the best time to fight them anyway. Both Hitler and the
Duce were still young; and any British and French intervention would
itself show that these powers did not mean to allow the Axis the additional
years of preparation that Italy preferred to have. Furthermore, Hitler
argued—one must say with considerable accuracy—that the Western
Powers were also likely to add to their own strength; and that their catch-
ing up in armaments could offset such accretions of strength as might
come to the Axis from their own programs, from the greater aggressiveness of Japan once she had finished in China, and from the isolation of
America once a lull in Europe had obviated the possibility of a third term
for Roosevelt as the Italian arguments for postponement suggested.

Hitler explained with great care why timing was so important. War
would begin by the end of August at the latest because the first major
battles would take a few weeks to be followed by a few more weeks of
mopping up. By the beginning of October, all of that operation had to be
completed because thereafter, and especially after 15 October, the fall
rains would render the armored columns on which he relied for deep
penetrations immobile and would make it impossible for his air force to
use advanced airfields.[283] The blow destroying Poland was necessary in
any case to clear the rear of the Axis for the coming war with the West. In
this connection, both Hitler and von Ribbentrop repeatedly urged the
Italians to use the opportunity provided by Germany's move to do
essentially the same thing themselves by crushing Yugoslavia. Since Italy
could hardly be expected to participate in a quick campaign against Poland, such action would firmly commit her to Germany's side, offer her
the opportunity for great spoils, and free her rear for the coming show-

280. Ciano, *Diary*, 11–13 August 1939, pp. 118–20; Ciano, *Diplomatic Papers*, pp. 297–
304; *D.D.I.*, 13, Nos. 1, 4, 21; *G.D.*, D, 7, Nos. 43, 47; *Weizsäcker-Papiere*, pp. 158, 180–81;
Magistrati, pp. 394–403; Schmidt, pp. 438–40; Kirk tel. 827 of 18 August and Biddle tel. 184
of 18 August 1939, State 760c.62/862 and 867. There are useful accounts in Siebert, chap. 7;
Henke, pp. 278–79; Mack Smith, pp. 192–93.
281. Ciano, *Diary*, 11 August 1939, p. 119; cf. ibid., p. 582; Weizsäcker, *Erinnerungen*, p.
246.
282. Ciano, *Diary*, 12 August 1939, p. 119.
283. For Hitler's discussion of these tactical problems and their relation to the timing of an
attack, see *G.D.*, D, 7:44.

down on Italy's border with France.[284] The Soviet Union would in any case stay out; Moscow was fully aware of Germany's plans, and if Russia gained some territory out of the situation, that was all right too.[285] As for Poland, it would be utterly crushed, and Hitler used the fact that he had agreed to transfer the South Tyrolean Germans to justify to Count Ciano his absolute determination to make no peaceful settlement with Poland.

In the face of this barrage of arguments, Ciano dropped the idea of a communiqué designed to show that there was still the possibility of a peaceful resolution of outstanding issues. He had brought along a draft, but Hitler and von Ribbentrop objected, so that nothing of the sort was issued. Ciano did not even bring up another proposal, a suggested partition of Danzig. This project had been worked on in Warsaw months earlier, but Ciano did not know that.[286] It had now come to the attention of the Italian ambassador to Poland, who sent it to Salzburg for Ciano.[287] The Italian foreign minister knew that the Polish government would not simply yield to German demands but was interested in resuming negotiations with Berlin;[288] he could, however, hardly advocate a plan to partition Danzig with a Hitler determined to destroy Poland. He had Ambassador Attolico give von Weizsäcker a memorandum on the project, but that was a decent burial rather than a formal proposal.[289] At a time when the German propaganda campaign against Poland was being moved at Hitler's direction from the back pages to page two and then to page one of the newspapers,[290] when the German ambassador to Warsaw had been forbidden by von Ribbentrop to go to the country to which he was nominally accredited,[291] and when the line publicly taken by Germany was that there could be no compromise whatever,[292] projects like the partition plan were of no interest to Berlin. What Hitler did have in mind for the final stage of the German-Polish drama will be discussed later.

Ciano returned to Rome permanently disillusioned with the Germans. He was certain that Hitler would start a war, that it would be disastrous for Italy to join Germany, and that the obvious German misleading of Italy

284. This would be in part Yugoslavia's punishment for refusing to ally herself with the Axis; see ibid., p. 35.
285. Further information on German-Soviet relations was provided Italy a few days later; Ciano merely replied "très bien." *G.D.*, D, 7, Nos. 76, 98.
286. See above, pp. 501–2.
287. Weinberg, "Proposed Compromise," p. 338.
288. Biddle tel. 184 of 18 August 1939, State 760c.62/867; *B.D.*, 3d, 6, No. 629.
289. *G.D.*, D, 7, No. 59. Von Weizsäcker had played a part in alerting Attolico and also believed that England and France would move in support of Poland (Siebert, pp. 213–15).
290. "Bestellungen aus der Pressekonferenz," 8, 11, 19 August 1939, Bundesarchiv, Brammer, Z.Sg. 101/13, ff.100, 103, 113; "Vertrauliche Informationen," 11, 14, 17 August 1939, Bundesarchiv, Oberheitmann, Z.Sg. 109/2, ff.43, 52–53, 69.
291. *G.D.*, D, 7, No. 2. Perhaps von Ribbentrop was also upset about von Moltke's comprehensive report of 1 August, ibid., 6, No. 754. The ambassador was desperate to return to Warsaw and very angry over being prohibited from going to his post; ibid., 7, No. 82; Hassell, p. 85; see also *G.D.*, D, 7, No. 44.
292. "Bestellungen aus der Pressekonferenz," 16, 17 August 1939, Bundesarchiv, Brammer, Z.Sg. 101/13, ff.107, 109. See also Kennard's letter to Cadogan of 17 August 1939, *B.D.*, 3d, 7, No. 48.

600   **The Road to War**

provided a fair basis for Rome to assert that it was Germany who had broken the alliance. He would do all in his power to convince Mussolini of this line and to dissuade him from entering the conflict.[293] The Duce was torn between recognition of Italy's incapacity to wage war on the one hand and fear of appearing cowardly on the other. He was also worried lest an angry and disappointed Germany turn against Italy. On the other hand, if there were a peaceful settlement after all, he wanted his share of the cheap booty, thinking of parts of Yugoslavia to be acquired by internal disruption and external pressure rather than by war.[294] If a general war did come, however, he agreed with Count Ciano that Italy should find a way to stay out, at least in the beginning. In this there is some evidence showing that he was influenced by concern that in the early stages of war Italy would find herself having to play a role not unlike that of Austria-Hungary in the first months of war in 1914. At that time the Germans had concentrated their troops in the west and had left the Austrians to face the Russian armies essentially unaided, while this time Germany would attack in the east, leaving Italy to bear the brunt of the fighting with England and France, a prospect that the otherwise belligerent Duce found no more inviting than did his son-in-law.[295] However, just as Ciano had avoided giving the Germans a clear statement that Italy would not join them in a general war, so no specific warning was sent from Rome after the Salzburg meeting either.[296] The Duce went back and forth between wanting to assure Hitler of full support and announcing that he could not do so.[297] He finally agreed to Ciano's idea of another meeting of the two foreign ministers, the assumption being that Ciano would specify Italian neutrality in a general war initiated by a German attack on Poland. By the time Mussolini had reached this decision, the meeting planned for 22 August could not be held because von Ribbentrop was leaving for Moscow.[298] The question of Italy's role in the war Hitler planned to start a few days later was again open.

As for Japan, even if von Ribbentrop might still have had some hope that the Japanese would yet come around to a general alliance, Hitler

293. Anfuso, p. 103; Ciano, *Diary,* 13 August ff.; *B.D.,* 3d, 7, Nos. 71, 72; *U.S.,* 1939, 1:221; Siebert, pp. 249–51; cf. *G.D.,* D, 7, No. 146. He would later learn about a deliberate lie by von Ribbentrop about his correspondence concerning French policy with Bonnet, see Siebert, p. 239, n.3.
294. Hoptner, pp. 166–69, summarizes the evidence on Mussolini's consideration of war against Yugoslavia at this time.
295. See *G.D.,* D, 7, No. 226; Siebert, pp. 247–48. This possibility was recognized as clearly in Paris and London as in Rome, and some in the Western capitals argued that this would be one advantage of Italy's going to war at the side of Germany.
296. Note esp. *G.D.,* D, 7, No. 98.
297. Mussolini was again warned by Canaris via the Italian military attaché, General Roatta (*D.D.I.,* 13, Nos. 10, 67). Canaris hoped that a clear no from Mussolini would lead Hitler to forgo the attack on Poland. The office of the Italian military attaché in Berlin was at no time very enthusiastic about a military alliance with Germany; see also *D.D.F.,* 2d, 9, No. 181.
298. *G.D.,* D, 7, Nos. 154, 190, 220; Ciano, *Diary,* 20–22 August 1939, pp. 124–26; Siebert, pp. 251–55, 261–63; Kirk tel. 837 of 19 August 1939, State 760c.62/877.

himself was more realistic. The negotiations continued in a desultory fashion through the summer, with the Japanese still insisting on a differentiation in their alliance obligations between those against the Soviet Union and those against the Western Powers.[299] The Germans, for reasons previously explained, were completely uninterested in such a project—they wanted the exact opposite—and they warned the Japanese, though without being very explicit about it, that Japan's attitude would incline them to sign a pact with the Soviet Union themselves.[300] At a time when the Japanese were involved in serious frontier incidents with Russia, this must have sounded unreal, coming as it was from the originator of the Anti-Comintern Pact. Furthermore, the Japanese were having quite enough trouble with the Western Powers. Their pressure on the British position in China, symbolized in June 1939 by the incidents at Tientsin, was considered by Tokyo as part of the preparation for the installation of the Wang Ching-wei puppet regime in occupied China,[301] with the British trying hard to handle the situation in such a fashion as to avoid pushing Japan into the arms of the Axis.[302] In order to restrain Japan, President Roosevelt had returned the bulk of the American fleet to the Pacific; and when the Germans once more tried to obtain a clear picture of the situation in Tokyo at the end of June, the Japanese response was in effect a repeated no with reference to the Japanese navy's concern about economic pressure or a war with the United States.[303]

In July and August of 1939 the Germans, who now recognized that Japan would not agree to an alliance directed against Britain and France in time for the projected attack on Poland, if ever, lost interest in the alliance negotiations, while the Japanese, ignorant of Hitler's timetable, continued their internal debates on the subject. The American denunciation of the Japanese-American trade agreement, the news of the British and French military missions to Moscow, and the escalating fighting on the border between Manchuria and Outer Mongolia all suggested that it might be useful for Japan to draw closer to the Axis if there were a way to do it without increasing rather than decreasing Tokyo's risks.[304] From the perspective of Berlin, on the other hand, von Ribbentrop's earlier ideas of harmonizing an agreement with Russia and the Axis relationship with Japan once again became important, accentuated by Russian interest in such a project.[305] Naturally this, too, looked very different from Tokyo.

299. The negotiations are traced in Sommer, pp. 238–42, 248–56; Morley, pp. 105–11.
300. *G.D.*, D, 6, No. 537; 7, No. 11.
301. *G.D.*, D, 6, Nos. 528, 735.
302. See n.272, above.
303. *G.D.*, D, 6, Nos. 591, 597, 619. It is very likely that this query was occasioned by what looked to Berlin like a stalling of their negotiations with Russia; if so, the reply from Tokyo could only encourage them to court Moscow all the harder. The general nature of the Japanese position was known in Moscow, see *S.U.*, No. 342. On the British request that the United States move its fleet back to the Pacific, see Pratt, pp. 176–77.
304. Sommer, pp. 263–74.
305. Note *Weizsäcker-Papiere*, 18 June 1939, p. 154; *D.D.I.*, 12, No. 376; *G.D.*, D, 6, No. 618.

There the idea of a German-Soviet rapprochement was viewed with considerable alarm, especially if Germany were to provide the Soviet Union not only with political reassurance in Europe but with critical machine tools that Germany had declined to provide to Japan.[306] For a German government that had set itself a deadline for war with Poland such concerns were necessarily subsidiary. The earlier Japanese attempts to mediate between Poland and Germany were entirely unappreciated. The idea that the Japanese, who continued their refusal of a preferential position for Germany in the economy of occupied China and were busy squeezing German interests out of that area, should presume to tell the Reich how to conduct its trade negotiations with other countries provoked only anger in Berlin.[307]

The possibility of a real bird in the Moscow bush as opposed to flocks of elusive hopes in the Japanese garden made the choice look easy for the German government. That there would be trouble with Japan in case of a German-Soviet agreement was recognized in Berlin; but if Germany and Russia could be reconciled, perhaps Russia and Japan could be also. But if Japan, once finished with her long involvement in China, could turn her full energies against the West, surely while so involved, she could not line up with the Western Powers. Even if Germany could not secure Japan's full support, she need not fear the possibility of her enmity. The war in China would keep Japan alienated from the Western Powers the way the civil war in Spain had alienated Italy from her allies of the World War.

The third line of German policy, the exploration of the possibility of agreement with the Soviet Union, must now be examined. By the end of May, the preliminary soundings from both sides had prepared the way for substantive negotiations; but that did not mean that the process in June and July was simple. From the point of view of the Germans, the great publicity attendant upon the negotiations between the Western Powers and Russia suggested on the one hand that they would do well to move quickly if they hoped to forestall an agreement of Russia with the West, whereas on the other hand it raised the possibility that the Soviet Union was merely toying with them, stringing Berlin along while driving a better bargain with the West by threatening to turn to Germany. From the point of view of the Soviet Union, there was the apparently attractive prospect of staying out of a European war which might damage others while profiting her, and there was a further incentive to free herself from danger in Europe to cope with current incidents along the border between her Far Eastern satellite of Outer Mongolia and the Japanese satellite of Manchukuo. On the other hand, there was always the possibility that the Germans, though serious about a war on Poland, were *not* serious about an agreement with the Soviet Union. Not only had Berlin rejected all

306. *G.D.*, D, 6, Nos. 688, 704; Sommer, pp. 278–80.
307. See above, pp. 182–85; for the Japanese position in August 1939, see *G.D.*, D, 6, No. 756. Note Göring's comments to Renzetti reported by Attolico on 14 June in *D.D.I.*, 12, No. 231 (English text in Toscano, *Designs in Diplomacy*, pp. 87–88), and *G.D.*, D, 7, No. 292.

previous Soviet attempts at improved relations—a fact of which the Russians would repeatedly remind the German negotiators in 1939—but the
most recent project, that of a trip by Karl Schnurre to Moscow, had been
canceled by the Germans at the last minute under circumstances
humiliating to Moscow—another fact of which the Soviets repeatedly
reminded the Germans. Perhaps the Schnurre trip had been merely a
German maneuver to frighten Poland; perhaps now the Germans were
merely trying to keep the Soviet Union from aligning herself with the
West. Once that alliance project had been aborted, Germany might refuse
to sign an agreement with Moscow, leaving herself the option of continuing eastward after destroying Poland, with the help or tacit acquiescence
of the Western Powers. Under these circumstances, it behooved Stalin to
be very cautious, and so he was.[308]

The preliminary economic talks of June and early July 1939 were
marked by hesitation on both sides.[309] The Russians made clear to the
Germans that this time there would be no repetition of the January fiasco
of the canceled Schnurre trip; agreement would have to be reached on the
basis of the last Soviet proposals. The idea of a trip by Schnurre to
Moscow was canvassed again, but the talks moved slowly.[310] The Russians wanted, in effect, a preliminary assurance that the talks would really
lead to an agreement. The Germans were not entirely certain that they
would or could do everything the Russians asked for, and during June not
only von der Schulenburg but also the commercial counsellor of the German embassy in Moscow and the military attaché, General Ernst Köstring, were in Berlin for consultations, with Köstring having a lengthy
meeting with Hitler on 21 June.[311] In the last days of June, immediately
after these internal discussions, the Germans decided to meet most of the
Soviet economic demands, to assure the Soviet government that Germany
had no hostile intentions toward the Soviet Union, and to try to work out
some form of economic and political agreement.[312] They assumed that the
signs from Moscow were such that, once they had met the Russians' basic

308. Note the observation of the American chargé in Moscow, Alexander Kirk, that in
1939 as opposed to 1938 the Soviet Union was much more cautious; in 1938 Russia was safe
from a really big war over a country which had no common border with Russia, while in 1939
the danger was real (*U.S., Soviet Union 1933–1939*, p. 751; cf. ibid., pp. 773–75).

309. Weinberg, *Germany and the Soviet Union*, pp. 33–37. Many of the German documents cited there have since appeared in *G.D.*, D, 6; some of the Italian ones in English
translation in Toscano, *Designs in Diplomacy*, pp. 81–87.

310. See now also *G.D.*, D, 6, Nos. 462, 478, 490, 491, 499, 514, 530, 543, 568–70, 576;
"Informationsbericht Nr. 67," 23 June 1939, Bundesarchiv, Brammer, Z.Sg. 101/34, f.337;
U.S., 1939, 1:322–24.

311. *G.D.*, D, 6, Nos. 499, 540, 614; *D.D.I.*, 12, No. 386. Köstring described his meeting
with Hitler to Oron J. Hale in an interrogation on 30–31 August 1945; the record is in the
Office of the Chief of Military History. In "Daten aus alten Notizbüchern," there is an entry
on 21 June 1939 listing a conference of Hitler with von Brauchitsch and Köstring.

312. Weinberg, *Germany and the Soviet Union*, pp. 34–35; Toscano, *Designs in Diplomacy*, pp. 90–92; *G.D.*, D, 6, Nos. 574, 579, 583, 588, 596, 614; *U.S.*, 1939, 1:324–29. The
Germans and Italians partially coordinated their approach at this time, see *G.D.*, D, 6, Nos.
536, 613; *D.D.I.*, 12, Nos. 317, 451; Weinberg, *Germany and the Soviet Union*, p. 36;
Toscano, *Designs in Diplomacy*, pp. 94–95.

economic and political prerequisites, agreement would indeed be reached. In Hamburg on 2 July, Hitler felt so confident about an agreement with the Soviet Union that he mentioned it in a speech to party officials in which he also assured them he would settle with Poland once and for all.[313] When von Ribbentrop talked with the Bulgarian prime minister on 5 July during the latter's state visit, he expounded his hopes for an agreement with the Soviet Union and the possibility of reconciling Japan and Russia as well.[314] These hopes and the German expectations of moving forward during July were stimulated by Soviet feelers obviously put forward under instructions from Moscow.[315] The Russian government let it be known that they much preferred an agreement with Germany to all other possibilities open to them, but this did not mean that Moscow was in the same hurry as Berlin.

While the Germans were working with a deadline, the Soviet government was not; and what made their negotiating position easier was that by about 20 June at the latest the Russians knew not only the general thrust of German policy but the timetable that went with it.[316] In response to the new German instruction to their Moscow embassy of 7 July,[317] the Soviet government delayed briefly. The decision-making process within the Soviet government in the second week of July is clouded in obscurity, but two facts are evident from the information available. The Soviet government, and that surely means Stalin, decided by 17 July that an economic agreement with Germany was possible, that is, that the Germans were really serious this time, that their offers were adequate for Soviet purposes, that the Soviet Union could and would make the concessions on its part still needed for an agreement, and—perhaps most important—that the political implications of signing such an agreement during the diplomatic crisis of 1939 were favorable. On the other hand, the Russians now wanted the final stages of the economic negotiations to take place in Berlin, not Moscow, a step the Germans thought likely to reduce the political effect somewhat. In the absence of direct evidence, this procedural demand appears to have been designed to keep control of the timing in Soviet hands. A German special negotiator in Moscow would have to secure a signed agreement within a few days; the permanent

313. Vauhnik, p. 29. Hitler was in Hamburg for the funeral of General Knochenauer; "Daten aus alten Notizbüchern," p. 44; Domarus, 2:1216.

314. G.D., D, 6, No. 618, p. 715. Although von Ribbentrop often misled his visitors, his statements to Kiosseivanov contain many themes about the Soviet Union that von Ribbentrop would subsequently repeat with great frequency. See also his comments to Attolico on 6 July in D.D.I., 12, No. 503.

315. The most famous of these was that of Astakhov to the Bulgarian minister in Berlin on 14 June (G.D., D, 6, No. 529); but Astakhov had spoken in a similar vein to the Estonian minister two weeks earlier (ibid., No. 469); and comments clearly reflecting analogous directives were made by the Soviet air attaché in London directly to the German assistant air attaché two weeks later (ibid., No. 581).

316. See S.U., No. 333 in which Kleist, a close associate of von Ribbentrop, had given an accurate account of German policy and scheduling to a man, presumably von Scheliha, who passed the information on to Moscow.

317. G.D., D, 6, No. 628; cf. ibid., No. 661; U.S., 1939, 1:330.

Soviet trade delegation in Berlin could always plead the need for instructions from Moscow.[318] The Germans, in no position to object, could secure the needed publicity and its political effects by other means and were willing to go ahead. A public announcement of the resumption of formal economic negotiations between Germany and the Soviet Union was issued in Moscow on 21 July.

It has sometimes been suggested that the Soviet decision to go forward and also to announce publicly the economic negotiations with Germany was caused by leaks to the press on 22 July about a meeting between the British minister for overseas trade, Robert Hudson, and Göring's assistant Helmuth Wohlthat on 20 July. That meeting will be discussed later in this chapter, but there can be no more doubt that the Soviet decision communicated to the Germans on 18 July was entirely independently arrived at.[319] Even the public announcement, issued before the news leaks, represents an independent decision by Moscow. The reasons for that step could have been to pressure the Western Powers into greater concessions which in turn could be used to secure more from the Germans, or to reassure Germany of Soviet sincerity in spite of the reversal of location for the talks which the Russians had originally agreed to hold in Moscow and now insisted take place in Berlin. In any case, the road to a German-Soviet economic agreement was now clearly open with both sides expecting a conclusion in the near future because the major differences on terms had already been resolved and because both parties were confident that the "political bases" that Molotov had talked about now existed.

From the perspective of Germany, time was of the essence. Just as soon as the resumption of formal negotiations had been agreed to, the German government not only expected these to lead to a quick agreement, but also wanted to have the political questions settled as soon as possible.[320] In the last days of July, Hitler, von Ribbentrop, and von Weizsäcker worked out the general outlines of a settlement with the Soviet Union in which there would be a partition of Poland and a partition of the Baltic States as well, though von Weizsäcker did not favor the latter idea.[321] Such partitions would provide the Soviet Union with substantial additional territory in Europe, and Germany with an at least geograph-

318. The key document is *G.D.*, D, 6, No. 685. For the intervening negotiations, see ibid., Nos. 642, 648, 677; *D.D.I.*, 12, No. 674. Molotov's telegram to Maisky and Surits of 17 July (*S.U.*, No. 376) appears to reflect the same decision to sign with Germany.

319. I suggested this in 1954 (*Germany and the Soviet Union*, pp. 37–38), when the evi-evidence was rather fragmentary. Now that we have a fuller German and Soviet record, the Soviet decision then dated to have been taken on or before 21 July can be dated to on or before 17 July, with 16 or 17 July the most likely dates (though the early morning hours of 18 July are conceivable).

320. *G.D.*, D, 6, No. 700. Cf. ibid., Nos. 714, 727; Weinberg, *Germany and the Soviet Union*, p. 39, n.31.

321. *G.D.*, D, 6, Nos. 729, 736, 757; *Weizsäcker-Papiere*, pp. 157, 181. When von Weizsäcker refers to the German decision on peace or war depending on whether or not the Soviet Union signed with the Western Powers, he was presumably citing Hitler.

ically isolated Poland to attack plus a share of the Baltic States. The Russians were obviously very much interested in these prospects; but they had to be concerned about the Far East as well, and they would repeatedly stress their desire for German steps to restrain Japan.[322] When Molotov and von der Schulenburg met on 3 August the Soviet representative was most favorable but not as concerned as the Germans about speed, while the Germans became increasingly frantic about the timing.[323] Berlin pushed for the quickest possible agreement in the economic talks. This necessitated new instructions for the Soviet negotiators; these arrived in stages, quite possibly geared to Soviet knowledge of the German intention to attack Poland right after 25 August but in any case meeting the remaining German wishes.[324] In response to German insistence, the Soviet government on 12 August sent new instructions to Astakhov to the effect that Russia was now ready for the political negotiations to be held in Moscow, and in which the broad political issues informally discussed up to then could be embodied in a political agreement.[325] News of this step, which reached Berlin while Ciano was in Salzburg,[326] showed the Germans that agreement with Russia was practically certain. Only two things remained to be settled: the precise terms of an agreement and the speedy conclusion Germany wanted. Since Hitler was eager for a prompt settlement and was willing to make whatever concessions were necessary, he could see no reason for further delay.

At first, on 13 August, Hitler planned to have Hans Frank go to Moscow, as he had once gone to Rome in preparation for the Axis, to secure both final economic and political agreements.[327] He quickly changed his mind however; with war on Poland to start in less than two weeks, he decided in the afternoon or evening of 14 August that von Ribbentrop, whom he considered "the best Foreign Minister that Europe had seen since Bismarck,"[328] should go to Moscow in person. The preparations for

322. *G.D.*, D, 6, Nos. 715, 729, 766; 7, No. 61; cf. *U.S., Soviet Union 1933–1939*, pp. 775–79.

323. *G.D.*, D, 6, Nos. 744, 758–61, 766; *D.D.I.*, 12, No. 118; *U.S.*, 1939, 1:332–33.

324. On the economic negotiations in these days, see *G.D.*, D, 6, Nos. 761, 772, 775; *U.S.*, 1939, 1:333–34. On Soviet knowledge as of 7 August of the German attack schedule, see *S.U.*, No. 402. For German press instructions to keep news of the trade negotiations quiet, see "Bestellungen aus der Pressekonferenz," 5 August 1939, Bundesarchiv, Brammer, Z.Sg. 101/13, f.98; "Vertrauliche Informationen," 5 August 1939, Bundesarchiv, Oberheitmann, Z.Sg. 109/2, f.22.

325. *G.D.*, D, 7, Nos. 18, 20, 50.

326. Weinberg, *Germany and the Soviet Union*, p. 40, n.41; Toscano, *Designs in Diplomacy*, p. 109.

327. *G.D.*, D, 7, No. 62. Ciano's visit may have influenced Hitler's thinking along these lines; for Frank's role in the negotiations leading to the formation of the Axis, see Weinberg, *Foreign Policy*, pp. 266–67, 333–34. The idea of having Schnurre accompany Frank, as originally planned, can be explained by Schnurre's familiarity with both the political and the economic talks, in neither of which Frank had been involved in any way.

328. Hitler had so described von Ribbentrop to Princess Olga of Yugoslavia; see Campbell to Cadogan, 17 June 1939, R 5148/409/92, FO 371/23885. When recounting the comment to Henderson, she had quoted the description as limited to *German* foreign ministers (*B.D.*, 3d, 6, No. 8).

the incident that Hitler had ordered staged as the excuse for his attack on Poland—a faked attack on the German radio station at Gleiwitz and related provocations—had already been under way for several days.[329] In these circumstances, Hitler was not willing to risk any delays. As he explained to the commander-in-chief, chief of staff, and other high officers on that same 14 August, he wanted to settle things with Poland by a quick war. The Soviet Union would stand aside because he planned to work out a division of spheres of interest with her.[330] He did not think England would risk war, but his main concern was that the British might make it difficult for him to start a war on Poland by last-minute offers. Germany would stay on the defensive in the west should Britain and France intervene; but the war with Poland, certain in any case, was to be inaugurated with a prompt military offensive preceded by the seizure of the key bridge over the Vistula at Tczew (Dirschau) and was to be arranged in such a fashion that it could be postponed on forty-eight hours' notice.[331] These details will be discussed later; the comments on Poland and the Soviet Union show Hitler's concept of the planned trip of von Ribbentrop to Moscow ordered on the same day.

The German ambassador in Moscow was accordingly instructed to offer the Soviet Union a formal visit by von Ribbentrop, who would spend a short time in the Russian capital and would expect to meet Stalin as well as Molotov to work out a German-Soviet agreement that would include a partition of Eastern Europe.[332] Here was the key issue: while Britain and France hoped that an anti-aggression front would protect the independence of the states of Eastern Europe that had emerged from the defeat of all the great empires of Central and Eastern Europe in the World War, Germany wanted to terminate that independence; and it was her willingness to share the spoils with the Soviet Union that decided the latter to opt for agreement with Germany as opposed to simply standing aside in the

329. The whole Gleiwitz provocation will not be reviewed in detail here; see Jürgen Runzheimer, "Der Überfall auf den Sender Gleiwitz im Jahre 1939," Vierteljahrshefte für Zeitgeschichte, 10, No. 4 (Oct. 1962), 408–26. Alfred Naujocks, the man in change of the operation, had been sent to Gleiwitz on orders of Reinhard Heydrich on 10 August (ibid., p. 419). Heydrich's plans for this faked operation, with concentration camp inmates in Polish uniforms to be killed as "evidence" of Poland's aggression, were far enough advanced by 17 August to be discussed by Admiral Canaris with Halder (Franz Halder, Kriegstagebuch [Stuttgart: Kohlhammer, 1962] [hereafter cited as Halder Diary], 17 August 1939) and Keitel (Canaris diary entry for 17 August in TMWC, 26:337–38; cf. Abshagen, pp. 195–96). There is a review of the incident in Höhne, Orden unter dem Totenkopf, pp. 241–46.
330. Since the Russians had not yet agreed to receive a negotiator, Hitler merely mentioned the possibility that a prominent German might go to Moscow to work things out.
331. Halder Diary, 14 August 1939; Liebmann notes, Vierteljahrshefte für Zeitgeschichte, 16, No. 2 (Apr. 1968), 162; Hassell Diary, 15 August 1939, p. 74; Henke, pp. 279–80; Helmut Krausnick, "Legenden um Hitlers Aussenpolitik," Vierteljahrshefte für Zeitgeschichte, 2, No. 3 (Oct. 1954), 233. On the Dirschau bridge project, see also Halder Diary, 19 August 1939. In the end the Poles succeeded in blowing up the bridge as the Germans raced to seize it. A full account is included in Herbert Schindler, Mosty und Dirschau: Zwei Handstreiche der Wehrmacht vor Beginn des Polenfeldzuges (Freiburg: Rombach, 1971).
332. G.D., D, 7, No. 56.

approaching conflict.[333] Moscow, like Berlin, had wanted an end to the independence of the new countries, wanted Germany to take the initiative, was especially interested in terminating the freedom of Poland, and had only waited for clear signs that Berlin was indeed ready to pay for Soviet cooperation by an appropriate division of the booty. Molotov was, therefore, most pleased on 15 August by von Ribbentrop's message; the Soviet Union had wanted good relations with Germany for years and was happy to see that feeling finally reciprocated. There should indeed be a nonaggression pact, and in addition to wanting help for better relations with Japan, Molotov had some other specific questions. Even before receiving a full report on the 15 August meeting, von Ribbentrop responded by a blanket agreement to all Molotov's requests, indicated that Hitler wanted to move quickly, and offered to fly to Moscow anytime from 18 August on, preferably finishing the matter before 22 August.[334]

The day after his meeting with von der Schulenburg, Molotov saw the new American ambassador, Laurence Steinhardt. The ambassador followed up on Roosevelt's earlier conversation with Russian Ambassador Constantine Oumansky in which the president had urged the Soviet Union to work with the Western Powers, warning of the dangers of an Axis victory for all countries, including the Soviet Union.[335] Stalin, however, had made up his mind to sign with Germany, not Britain and France, and ignored this warning from Washington as he would later disregard American information about the German plans to attack the Soviet Union.

By the time Molotov gave von der Schulenburg Stalin's generally favorable response on the evening of 17 August, the ambassador had the German positive answer to all Molotov's queries of 15 August. The Soviet dictator's proposal for a more leisurely pace than the Germans wanted touched off a series of frantic telegrams from Berlin.[336] War was imminent, and all the details of a nonaggression pact and secret protocol would be worked out in Moscow during von Ribbentrop's stay. Under the impact of the German importunities—clearly derived from their military

333. See on this also Georg Vigrabs, "Die Stellungnahme der Westmächte und Deutschland zu den baltischen Staaten im Frühling und Sommer 1939," *Vierteljahrshefte für Zeitgeschichte*, 7, No. 3 (July 1959), 261–79; Hans Rothfels, "Das Baltikum als Problem internationale Politik," *Zur Geschichte und Problematik der Demokratie: Festgabe für Hans Herzfeld* (Berlin: Duncker & Humblot, 1958), pp. 608–12.

334. *G.D.*, D, 7, Nos. 70, 73, 75, 79, 89, 92; *D.D.I.*, 13, No. 69.

335. *S.U.*, No. 427; *U.S.*, 1939, 1:293–94, 296; Bullitt to Steinhardt, 12 August 1939, Library of Congress, Steinhardt Papers, 1939, V–Z. The American embassy in Moscow had received a full account of the Molotov–von der Schulenburg meeting of 15 August (*U.S.*, 1939, 1:334–35), and the information was passed on to the British (*B.D.*, 3d, 7, No. 41; Steinhardt tel. 486 of 30 August, State 761.6211/149; see n.154, above). The Turkish government, like the American, sent a message from the president urging Moscow to make an agreement with the Western Powers; this message was delivered on 20 August (*B.D.*, 3d, 7, No. 499).

336. *G.D.*, D, 7, Nos. 105, 111, 113, 125, 132, 133. Ironically the absence of Hitler and von Ribbentrop from Berlin during much of August interfered somewhat with their own insistence on speed. One may well wonder whether the Soviet government had matched Sorge's reports with the code texts of German telegrams, broken the German code, and hence followed the German schedule precisely.

timetable—the Russians began to move more quickly; in a negotiating procedure opposite to the one they followed with the Western Powers, the Soviet leaders became more, not less, accommodating as the negotiations moved along, reflecting their desire for a successful outcome of this set of talks. As late as 4:00 p.m. on 19 August the Russian negotiators in Berlin were still stalling on signing the economic treaty which had been completed the preceding day. Later that evening, clearly in response to new instructions from Moscow, where von der Schulenburg saw Molotov twice that day, the Soviet trade delegate agreed to sign the treaty, a decision which was publicly announced on 20 August.[337] At a time when the world expected the momentary outbreak of war in Europe, Germany and the Soviet Union had agreed on a long-term trade treaty with the provisions for two years of increased economic interchange financed in part by German credits.[338]

With that step out of the way, the political treaty was next. In spite of von der Schulenburg's insistence, Molotov had been unwilling to agree to a date earlier than 26 or 27 August for von Ribbentrop's Moscow trip. As soon as this became known in Berlin on 20 August, Hitler himself wrote Stalin urging that von Ribbentrop be received on 22 or 23 August at the latest.[339] That made an impression in Moscow. Stalin must have recognized that he could either agree to Hitler's schedule or pass up the opportunity of a deal with Germany at least for that year. On 21 August Stalin agreed to von Ribbentrop's coming on the 23d, and on the 22d a public announcement that the German foreign minister was coming to Moscow to sign a nonaggression pact was issued to the press.[340]

The announcement itself made a major impact in the world. Its repercussions on the German government and on Britain, France, Poland, and other countries will have to be discussed, but first a brief word should be said about the nonaggression pact itself.[341] The pact, since it was designed to deal with the contingency of German aggression against Poland, did not contain the clause included in all earlier Soviet nonaggression treaties, that the treaty would be invalid if either party attacked a third power.[342] Since the aggression that the pact was designed to protect was scheduled to occur right away, the pact was to become effective not

337. Ibid., Nos. 123, 132, 135; *U.S.*, 1939, 1:335–36; *D.D.I.*, 13, Nos. 100, 102; "Vertrauliche Informationen," 21 August 1939, Bundesarchiv, Oberheitmann, Z.Sg. 109/2, ff.85–86.
338. Text in *G.D.*, D, 7, No. 131; an analysis, ibid., No. 436. See also Weinberg, *Germany and the Soviet Union*, pp. 43–44.
339. *G.D.*, D, 7, Nos. 142, 149; Weinberg, *Germany and the Soviet Union*, p. 45.
340. *G.D.*, D, 7, Nos. 157–60. On Hitler's reception of the message from Stalin, see Speer, *Erinnerungen*, p. 176.
341. Weinberg, *Germany and the Soviet Union*, pp. 46–49; *G.D.*, D, 7, Nos. 170, 191, 205, 206, 213, 228, 229; *D.D.I.*, 13, No. 264; *U.S.*, 1939, 1:342–43; "Vertrauliche Informationen," 22, 23, 24 August 1939, Bundesarchiv, Oberheitmann, Z.Sg. 109/2, ff.89–90, 94–95, 102, 105–6.
342. This was so extraordinary a departure from past practice that the Soviet chargé in Rome thought it inconceivable as late as 23 August (memorandum by Phillips, 23 August 1939, Houghton Library, Phillips Papers, Vol. 36).

when ratified but as soon as it was signed. As in the case of the Pact of
Steel, special pains were taken to adjust the terms of the treaty to the
extraordinary situation of Germany, a major power determined on attacking a neighbor and wanting treaties worded to accommodate that
project, the difference being that the Russians, unlike the Italians, had
delayed signing and so obtained an appropriate reward.

Added to the pact was a secret protocol providing for the partitioning of
Poland along the Pissa, Narev, Vistula, and San rivers.[343] The Germans
had planned to leave Finland and Estonia to the Soviet Union, claim
Lithuania enlarged by the Vilna area for themselves, and partition Latvia
along the Dvina River. Stalin, however, wanted all of Latvia, and with
Hitler's approval von Ribbentrop agreed to this. The section on the Balkans was less explicit, with Soviet claims to Bessarabia recognized and
Germany declaring her complete political disinterest in the whole area. In
this regard, both sides appear to have preferred a degree of vagueness.
Had Stalin asked for more, he would almost certainly have received it, but
he was apparently reluctant to push his luck in that area. Certainly on the
Polish and Baltic portions of the settlement Stalin wished to be very
specific, and he would watch German observance of the new lines with
great vigilance.[344] Not since the invasion of Georgia in 1921 had the
possibility of territorial expansion been so real and apparently without
risk for the Soviet Union, and not since 1870 had Germany been so hopeful of securing a war on one front.

For Hitler, the partition of Eastern Europe opened up what he considered the ideal situation for war. As he had told a number of the higher
military leaders on 14 August, he now on 22 August explained to a large
assembly of generals and admirals his plan to strike at Poland immediately, most likely on 26 August.[345] This was the time to start a war:
he himself was the man to do it, and with Mussolini in Italy and Franco in

343. In the hurry to draft the text, the Pissa River was omitted. This and other oversights
were corrected by a subsequent protocol; Weinberg, *Germany and the Soviet Union*, pp. 48,
51; *G.D.*, D, 7, No. 284.

344. See the discussion in Weinberg, *Germany and the Soviet Union*, pp. 54–57. According to the unpublished memoirs of von Below (see chap. 2, n.80), Hitler consulted an atlas
when von Ribbentrop called from Moscow for authority to yield the other half of Latvia to
the Soviet Union.

345. The most important source for this talk is the account of Admiral Canaris in *G.D.*, D,
7, Nos. 192, 193. The best discussion of the sources is that of Winfried Baumgart, "Zur
Ansprache Hitlers vor den Führern der Wehrmacht am 22. August 1939," *Vierteljahrshefte
für Zeitgeschichte*, 16, No. 2 (Apr. 1968), 120–49, and 19, No. 3 (July 1971), 294–304, where
two more accounts are added to the previously published ones listed by Baumgart. Other
useful discussions are in Bracher, *Machtergreifung*, pp. 759–62; Henke, pp. 281–85; Krausnick, "Legenden," p. 233; *Vollmacht des Gewissens*, 1:376–79.

Additional evidence used here: *Engel Diary*, pp. 58–59; Institut für Zeitgeschichte, ZS 545
(Erich Kordt); and the interrogation of Walter Warlimont by Harold Deutsch on 18 September 1945 in the State Department Special Interrogation Mission Papers (DeWitt C. Poole),
National Archives, which is especially important because of its antedating the discussion at
the Nuremberg trial. The ribbon copy of the text handed by Louis Lochner to the British
embassy in Berlin, almost certainly prepared in the Abwehr, and published in *B.D.*, 3d, 7,
No. 314 (cf. ibid., No. 399) is located in the Henderson Papers, FO 800/270, ff.288–91. The

Spain, there was an opportunity that might never recur, though he recognized that only the neutrality of Spain could be secured. All factors, of which he listed a considerable number, made this the best moment to strike. He was hopeful that Britain and France would stay out, and he listed the reasons for this expectation, but he also discussed at length why he would go ahead even if Britain and France intervened. Here the forthcoming treaty with the Soviet Union, publicly just announced, would be of great assistance. Poland would be hopelessly isolated and any British blockade broken by the opening to the east. In this regard, the pact with the Soviet Union would be helpful to Germany whether the war with the Western Powers took place simultaneously with the one against Poland or subsequent to it. The presence of von Ribbentrop for at least part of the meeting just before his departure for Moscow underlined the significance of this point.

The war with Poland would be started on some propaganda pretext, whether anyone believed it was irrelevant.[346] The war would be fought to the utter destruction not only of Poland's armed forces but of the country as a whole with the utmost brutality. As Hitler had said on 14 August, his main worry was that the British might make it difficult for him to start a war by some last-minute offer. He would find a way to protect himself against that "danger" in obvious revulsion against the way he thought he had been tricked out of war in 1938. This time no "S.O.B." was going to keep him from war against Poland by pushing for a compromise proposal.[347] He would start a war one way or another; having discussed various types of incidents that might be manufactured in Danzig with Forster on the day before and knowing that faked border incidents with Poland were also being prepared, Hitler was confident by 22 August that he would have the pretext to serve his purpose.[348]

---

reference in the report handed to the British mentioning an eastern border Reval, Lublin, Kaschau, mouth of the Danube as the partition line in Eastern Europe appears to reflect the Abwehr's knowledge of the original rough line Hitler discussed with von Ribbentrop before the latter left for Moscow; the statement ascribed to Hitler that von Ribbentrop was instructed to make any needed offer and accept all Soviet demands is equally close to what is known of Hitler's views. The same thing is true for his comments on the delays of the Japanese. These are the main specifics contained in this version that do not appear in the others. It is certainly entirely conceivable that Hitler made them and that Canaris mentioned them orally to his associates in the Abwehr when showing them his written account and expressing his horror, reflected in Groscurth's diary: "One is crushed. Everything is lying and deception; not a word of truth. Quite correctly [Canaris's diary] read, 'there is absolutely no ethical foundation'" (Groscurth Diary, 24 August 1939, p. 179).

346. Again the text handed the British was more specific, alluding to the use of Polish uniforms, an addition also pointing to the Abwehr as source of the document and likewise referred to in the Groscurth diary (ibid., p. 180). See also Speer, Erinnerungen, p. 179.

347. The German is "Schweinehund" in the Canaris account; it is "Saukerl" in the record handed to the British (where Chamberlain is mentioned by name in this connection). It is worth noting that Hitler voiced extraordinarily similar sentiments in 1941 when he said that his only political worry was that Stalin might make a last-minute cooperative gesture (Weizsäcker-Papiere, 18 June 1941, p. 260).

348. G.D., D, 7, Nos. 176, 188, 244.

It should be obvious from the foregoing account that Hitler's preference for fighting Poland separately from the subsequent war against the West at no time allowed for a compromise on his Polish demands as part of an accommodation with the West. If the Poles gave in completely, that of course would be acceptable as an easy step on the road to victory in the west, but Hitler did not expect such a surrender. He clearly understood, however, that any agreed, as opposed to a German-dictated, solution of the German-Polish controversy would involve concessions on his part, and these he was unwilling to make. As he had explained in his 14 August talk,[349] and as he would repeatedly insist in the last days of peace, any German agreement with England would have to follow, not precede, the crushing of Poland; and only on these terms was he willing to try to isolate the war against Poland.

An analysis of British policy in the summer of 1939 will show that, as the Italians warned Hitler, and as he himself thought possible but unlikely, Hitler's planned sequence of events was out of the question from the perspective of London. In the British view independence, not the partition of the countries of Eastern Europe, was the prerequisite for any agreement; and since the German action of 15 March had destroyed one of those countries as well as confidence in the word of the German government, whatever contacts took place between Britain and Germany repeatedly emphasized the need for a German step to restore some measure of independence to Czechoslovakia as a key to the restoration of confidence. That a Hitler who was obsessed with the desire to go the next step forward even at the risk of war with England and France would ever seriously consider a step backward was quite out of the question; and the sense of unreality which characterizes the contacts between England and Germany during the last months of peace reflects this total incompatibility of German and British policies.

Through June, July, and August, the British government pursued its efforts for an agreement with the Soviet Union. Since the Russian government has not released any of the reports it received from an agent in the coding section of the British Foreign Office,[350] as it has for the reports of Sorge and von Scheliha, we do not know the full extent to which Moscow was aware of the details of the British negotiating strategy; but the general outlines were clear in any case from the actual conduct of the negotiations, from discussions in Parliament, from press leaks, and from the often deliberately unhelpful comments of such Englishmen as David Lloyd George.[351] In those months, the London government gradually agreed to additional concessions to Soviet demands, most of which were newly communicated to the British and French negotiators when they

349. *Halder Diary*, 14 August 1939.
350. See Aster, p. 317, on Captain John Herbert King; cf. Hoptner, p. 125, n.41.
351. *S.U.*, No. 372. There is a special irony in Lloyd George's claiming that Chamberlain wanted an agreement with Germany, not the Soviet Union, when he himself would be the most prominent advocate of peace with Hitler in 1940.

informed Molotov of the latest concession. Instead of recounting this tedious process, the latter stages of which took place weeks after the Soviet government had informed Berlin that it would sign an agreement with Germany, it may be more useful to examine the motives of the parties to these talks.[352]

The British government was interested in three objectives. All staff studies, whether conducted by the British themselves or in coordination with the French, showed that it would be impossible for England and France to do anything substantial for Poland in the early stages of a conflict. Support from the Soviet Union, especially in matériel, would be essential to Poland's defense. The only other hope for Poland was a Western victory over Germany with the revival of Poland after such a war. This prospect was contemplated in London with nothing like the alarm such a contingency had aroused in regard to Czechoslovakia in 1938 because the German minority in Poland was small compared to that in Czechoslovakia and was, after the German occupation of Prague, in any case of no special interest.[353] Nevertheless, the guarantees already given to Poland and Rumania would be greatly strengthened if the Soviet Union agreed in one way or another to assist those countries in resisting German aggression. The Anglo-Polish staff talks of late May only served to confirm this point.[354]

A second objective, which became increasingly important as the negotiations dragged on and which was probably the main reason for their

352. The most recent accounts are those of Sidney Aster and Norman H. Gibbs; both are on the whole very critical of Chamberlain. Important materials, in addition to the published British documents, are S.U., Nos. 322–24, 327, 330, 331, 340, 357, 358, 360, 361, 366, 367; 49th, 50th, 53d, 56th meetings of the cabinet Committee on Foreign Policy, 5, 9, 20 June, 4 July 1939, CAB 27/625; Cabinets 31, 32, 33, 34 (39) of 7, 14, 21, 28 June 1939, C 8219, C 8577, C 8914, C 9158/3356/18, FO 371/23068, 23069; Minute by Chamberlain, probably 4 June 1939, C 9295/3356/18, FO 371/23069; Cabinet Committee on Foreign Policy, "The Negotiations with Russia, Memorandum by the Secretary of State for Foreign Affairs," 8 June 1939, CAB 27/627.

353. There is a striking difference in the cabinet minutes between 1938 and 1939. The real or imagined grievances of the over three million Sudeten Germans loomed large in practically every discussion in 1938; the German minority in Poland was hardly ever mentioned in 1939 except as a possible source of incidents.

354. On the Anglo-French staff talks of 29 March–3 May 1939, see Aster, pp. 143–45; Gibbs, chap. 17; G.D., D, 6, No. 482. On British staff talks with the Poles, see the British brief for the conversations of 15 May 1939, COS No. 903, CAB 53/49; the report of the British delegation in C 9510/427/55, FO 371/23129; COS No. 905, "Anglo-French Action in Support of Poland," 3 June 1939, CAB 53/49. The basis of British strategy, assuming German military superiority at the outset of a war and looking to continued Allied increases in strength, anticipating a long war, and intending for the allies to (1) hold the German offensive, (2) hold Germany and crush Italy, (3) defeat Germany, is spelled out in the "Conclusions on the Broad Strategic Policy for the Conduct of the War," agreed to by the British and French and printed as Annex I to the "Covering Memorandum to the Chiefs of Staff European Appreciation 1939–40," 25 May 1939, COS 915, ibid. A final updating of the assessment is in the War Office's "Appreciation of the Military Situation at beginning of August," 4 August 1939, C 11122/13/18, FO 371/22960.

The inability of the French and British to help Poland did not mean that the reverse was true; at a conference in Warsaw on 24/25 July 1939 the three powers discussed the German "enigma" code machine, and in August the Poles provided England and France each with a machine, a key element in what came to be known as the "ultra" secret.

continuation in the face of ever new demands, was the hope that by signing an agreement with Russia or at least pursuing the negotiations the Western Powers would make it less likely and perhaps impossible for the Soviet Union to ally herself with Germany.[355] As Lord Chatfield said during one of the discussions of a treaty with Russia on 26 June, even if a three-power treaty of mutual guarantee did not cover Poland, it "would at least have the effect that it would prevent Soviet Russia from making a Pact with Germany." Lord Halifax agreed that this was theoretically true, but that there was still nothing to prevent Germany and Russia from making an arrangement to partition Poland once Germany had invaded Poland.[356] In mid-June and again in August members of the German opposition to Hitler warned the British government of a possible German-Soviet pact, hoping that an agreement between the Western Powers and Russia would deter Hitler; but although those warnings were listened to and may well have contributed to British willingness to make concessions to Moscow in those talks, they could not produce any willingness to sign with the West on the part of the Russians.[357] As Lord Halifax commented in the cabinet after the British had agreed to include the Baltic States in the scope of any treaty while the Russians refused to include Holland and Switzerland, "the wheel had thus come full circle from the early days of the negotiations, when Russia had pressed for full reciprocity."[358] All the same, the cabinet did not want to break off the talks; there was great public pressure for a treaty and, as Chamberlain explained in urging agreement to the idea, unprecedented for England, of starting military conversations with another country even before any political treaty had been signed, the talks would at least keep the Soviet Union from aligning herself with Germany.[359] That prophecy of 10 July would prove mistaken, but it does help explain British policy.[360]

355. There are repeated references to this in the *Cadogan Diary*, e.g., 16 May 1939, p. 180.

356. 54th meeting of the cabinet Committee on Foreign Policy, CAB 27/625.

357. The 16 June 1939 warning in *B.D.*, 3d, 6:705 (iii) is marked on the original for the prime minister and was initialed by him (FO 371/22973). On the warnings from the German opposition, see Aster, pp. 274–75; Weinberg, *Germany and the Soviet Union*, p. 40, n.43, and p. 42, n.5. For a British assessment of a possible German-Soviet rapprochement of 4 July 1939, see N 3335/243/38, FO 371/23686.

358. Cabinet 35 (39) of 5 July 1939, C 9573/3356/18, FO 371/23070. The way in which the concessions made by Britain and France led to an increasingly one-sided text favoring Soviet interests, but one London and Paris agreed to in the hope of securing a common front that would deter Hitler, is also stressed in Halifax, pp. 54–56. A summary of the active role of Hoare in pushing for an agreement with Russia is in John Arthur Hoare, *Sir Samuel Hoare* (London: Cape, 1977), pp. 294–98.

359. 57th meeting of the cabinet Committee on Foreign Policy, 10 July 1939, CAB 27/625.

360. A review prepared in the Foreign Office on 26 August of the information that had been available to London and the impressions drawn there concluded that the Soviet Union had no interest in aiding Germany and would, therefore, either sign with Britain and France or go into isolation (N 4146/243/38, FO 371/23686). It could well be argued that this was a shrewder analysis of Soviet interests than that made by Stalin himself—and would certainly be proved so by events—but it differed on a key point from reality: Stalin's preference for aiding Germany if he thought the price was right.

Chamberlain at that time still thought the Russians really wanted an agreement with Britain,[361] but many were doubtful.[362] The Soviet rejection of the British-French proposal of 17 July changed Chamberlain's view to where "he now doubted whether the Soviet Government really desired any agreement with us,"[363] and had he had access to the text of Molotov's telegrams to Maisky and Surits of 17 July he would have been certain of Moscow's disinterest, a disinterest doubtless connected with the simultaneous decision by Stalin to resume formal economic negotiations with Germany.[364] In spite of Chamberlain's doubts and his skepticism about a possible German-Soviet alliance,[365] the talks were continued; concern over the political repercussions from a rupture of the much publicized negotiations and the possible encouragement such a rupture might give Germany joined with the hope of restraining the Soviet Union from signing with Germany as motives for further concessions.[366] As Chamberlain minuted on 12 August in approving the proposal of Lord Halifax that in spite of prior inclinations, London now accommodate at least part way the Soviet insistence on a guarantee against their being threatened by German "indirect aggression" through the Baltic States: "I agree with the S.[ecretary] of S.[tate] that we might accept any of the alternatives which do not appear to give Russia a right, covered by our guarantee, to interfere in the internal affairs of other states."[367] Here, of course, was the fundamental issue: was the independence of the new nations of Eastern Europe to be protected or ended? If it was to be protected, London was willing to go a long way. They would eventually pressure Poland to agree in peacetime to the transit of Soviet troops if Germany attacked,[368] but while Poland eventually agreed to a compromise on this point also,[369] the Russian government was interested in partic-

361. Cabinet 37 (39) of 12 July 1939, C 9969/3356/18, FO 371/23070.

362. See *Pownall Diary,* 17 July 1939, p. 214. The usually well-informed Italian ambassador to Moscow was sure the Soviet government did not want an agreement and kept raising its price for that reason (Rosso report of 13 June, *D.D.I.,* 12, No. 201, English in Toscano, *Designs in Diplomacy,* p. 85); cf. Crolla's (London) report of 29 June, *D.D.I.,* 12, No. 402, Toscano, p. 93, n.93.

363. 58th meeting of the cabinet Committee on Foreign Policy, 19 July 1939, CAB 27/625.

364. *S.U.,* No. 376. If the wording of this document is authentic as published, it should end all discussion of serious Soviet interest in an agreement with the West as of 17 July at the latest and reflects the decision, referred to in n.319 above, to sign with Germany. Note that Maisky quickly fell in with the new line, ibid., No. 381.

365. Cabinet 38 (39), of 19 July 1939, C 10225/3356/18, FO 371/23071.

366. 59th and 60th meetings of the cabinet Committee on Foreign Policy, 26 July and 1 August 1939, CAB 27/625; Cabinet 39 (39) of 26 July 1939, C 10629/3356/18, FO 371/23071; Cabinet 40 (39) of 2 August 1939, C 10926/3356/18, FO 371/23072; British staff talks plans, COS 952 of 29 July 1939, CAB 53/53. Note Lord Halifax's detailed defense of the British conduct of the negotiations to Sir Bernard Pares of 27 July 1939 in Halifax Papers, FO 800/309; cf. *D.D.B.,* 5, No. 93.

367. C 11524/3356/18, FO 371/23072, f.173.

368. Committee of Imperial Defence, Deputy Chiefs of Staff Sub-Committee, 16 August 1939, C 11506/3356/18, FO 371/23072.

369. *B.D.,* 3d, 7, Nos. 150, 176, 198; Bonnet, *Fin d'une Europe,* pp. 289–90; *Łukasiewicz Papers,* pp. 255–57.

ipating in the destruction, not the defense, of those threatened by Germany and had already so promised Berlin.[370]

The third factor contributing significantly to British perseverance in the search for an agreement with Moscow was the hope that the deterrent effect on Germany of the guarantee of Poland would be enormously enhanced by a British–French–Russian united front. If Germany faced the prospect that an attack on Poland would involve her in a war against Britain, France, and the Soviet Union at the same time, surely Hitler would think long and hard about the risks of such an adventure. In view of what is known about Hitler's interest in an agreement with the Soviet Union, this perception of the British leaders cannot simply be dismissed as unrealistic even if it was never tested.

If this was the British government's view of the reasons for trying to secure an agreement with the Soviet Union, London's perception of relations with Germany was very different. The government was certain that no one planned to attack Germany or even to provoke her. As the British were able to reassure themselves, Poland was being most cautious not to provide Berlin with any excuse for complaint;[371] and although in public the Germans pretended to the contrary, in secret Hitler himself thought the Poles so conciliatory and nonprovocative that he explained Polish behavior as caused by doubts of Britain's firmness.[372] Even on the Danzig issue itself there was no cause for concern; as the British assured themselves by a special mission of General Ironside to Warsaw, the Polish government was exercising the utmost restraint in responding to German provocations in the Free City.[373] Here too, whatever German propaganda trumpeted in public, in secret the major concern of the German government was how to stage incidents of sufficient gravity to force a Polish reaction.[374] There was, therefore, no doubt in the British cabinet that Danzig was purely a German pretext for any acts that might be planned against Poland, that on this as on other matters no Polish provocation

370. Hofer, pp. 56–58.

371. See Aster, pp. 203–4, 407; cf. Margesson to Wenner-Gren, 27 June 1939, *B.D.*, 3d, 6:740.

372. Halder's account of Hitler's comments on 14 August: "Dafür dass von englischer Seite kein entscheidendes Handeln zu erwarten ist, spricht vor allem auch die Haltung Polens. Polen wäre noch viel frecher wenn es sich auf England verlassen könne."

373. On Ironside's mission to Poland, in part to find out what Polish intentions about Danzig might be, and the resulting reassurance to London that the Polish leaders were being most careful not to let the Germans provoke them into rash acts, see *B.D.*, 3d, 6, Nos. 250, 319, 350, 361, 374, 397; Kennard minute, 3 July 1939, C 9348/54/18, FO 371/23021; Foreign Office minute of 12 July 1939, C 9748/54/18, FO 371/23022; Ironside's report of 28 July 1939, C 10949/54/18, FO 371/23024; 55th meeting of the cabinet Committee on Foreign Policy, 4 July 1939, CAB 27/625 (at this meeting Kennard alluded to the Polish government's consideration of a plan to partition Danzig); Cabinet 35 (39) of 5 July 1939, C 9820/15/18, FO 371/22974; *Pownall Diary*, 10 July 1939, p. 213; *Ironside Diary*, 4, 10, 18 July 1939, pp. 76, 77–78, 81–82; Aster, pp. 212–13; *Biddle Papers*, p. 64; Cabinet 39 (39) of 26 July 1939, C 10628/54/18, FO 371/23024.

374. See above, n.348.

need be feared, and that, on the contrary, if Germany ever quit threatening the world with war, that subject could also be a topic for negotiation.[375] A war if it came would be about the independence of Poland, whatever German propaganda might say about Danzig.[376] Naturally, if the British took a firm stand they would be accused of provoking Germany, while if they did not, they would be damned for letting Berlin think that London would not honor its promise to Poland.[377] The only hope seemed to lie in a stance of quiet firmness, which, especially if an agreement could be reached with Russia, might restrain Germany enough so that in a calmer atmosphere negotiations might someday be resumed on such issues as might be of European concern.[378]

It was, in view of this policy, almost certainly a mistake for the British government to send Sir Nevile Henderson back to Berlin.[379] Recalled after 15 March, he was sent back in late April; but Henderson's inclinations and indiscretions could only undermine the import of the message he carried with him on returning to Berlin, namely, that Great Britain for the first time in her history was about to introduce conscription in peacetime.[380] Despairing over the danger of war, personally affected by the clear signs that his own government had lost confidence in him,[381] and knowing that he suffered from the cancer that would kill him in 1942, Henderson cast about for ways to save the peace. These usually involved concessions by Poland to Germany, and Henderson's arguing along these lines brought only rebukes on the subject and efforts to buck him up from London; but his proclivity for speaking his mind in Berlin hardly fitted with London's effort to have the Germans recognize that any aggression would lead to a general war.[382] In the last days before the outbreak of war,

375. See Chamberlain's statement in the House of Commons on 10 July, *British Bluebook*, No. 35; Lord Halifax to the Dominion High Commissioners, 11 July 1939, C 10101/15/18, FO 371/22975; Halifax to the Earl of Bessborough, 20 July 1939, Halifax Papers, FO 800/316; cf. *B.D.*, 3d, 9, No. 323.

376. Cabinet 40 (39) of 2 August 1939, C 1095/54/18, FO 371/23024. As early as 27 July Philip Conwell-Evans reported the comment of the German assistant air attaché in London that Germany would not be satisfied with Danzig but expected a fourth partition of Poland (C 10611/15/18, FO 371/22975).

377. The British failure to follow up vigorously on General Ironside's advice that extensive financial aid be given to Poland probably reflected a reluctance to commit funds to what was seen as a surely losing cause but was dangerously short-sighted in disregarding the morale and political aspects of the issue, a point reflected in Hitler's use of this on 14 and 22 August as one indication of Britain's reluctance to honor the guarantee of Poland. See *Ironside Diary*, 18 July 1939, pp. 81–82; *Biddle Papers*, pp. 64–65, 67.

378. Note Halifax's Chatham House speech of 29 June (*British Bluebook*, No. 25; *G.D.*, D, 6, No. 593) and his letter to Ponsonby of 6 July 1939, Halifax Papers, FO 800/328.

379. *Harvey Diaries*, 6 April, 27 May, 9 July 1939, pp. 274, 293, 302.

380. Henderson, pp. 230–31; *B.D.*, 3d, 5, Nos. 288, 289; *G.D.*, D, 6, No. 272. For background, see Cabinets 18 (39) of 5 April and 21 (39) of 19 April 1939, C 5027, C 6167/19/18, FO 371/22997; *U.S.*, 1939, 1:171–72; *B.D.*, 3d, 5, No. 227.

381. *Cadogan Diary*, 6 April, 22 May 1939, pp. 170, 182.

382. Aster, pp. 201–4; cf. *Hungarian Documents*, 4, Nos. 197, 222. Revealing are Henderson's letters published in *B.D.*, 3d, 5–7, to which should be added his letter of 9 May to Sir Horace Wilson and the latter's effort of 12 May to get him onto firmer ground (Henderson

Henderson would succeed in making the British position clear, but a new ambassador might have found this easier.[383] Since the French did make such a change, replacing André François-Poncet with Robert Coulondre to no discernible effect, it may also be that it all made no difference. Certainly Lord Halifax did his best to coordinate the presentation of a firm posture to Berlin.[384]

What direct contacts there were between British and German official and unofficial representatives only emphasized the incompatibility of the basic approaches of Chamberlain and Hitler. With the breach of Munich, Chamberlain's confidence in Hitler's word was gone. As Sidney Aster had expressed it, after 15 March there was a crisis of confidence. "During the next five and a half months prior to the outbreak of war, never once did Chamberlain weaken in his distrust of Hitler. He repeatedly stated that 'no undertakings by Hitler would be of any use.' Hitler would have to prove in some concrete way, therefore, that he had finally abandoned the use of force."[385]

In late April or early May, Ernst von Weizsäcker and others in the German foreign ministry worked out a plan whereby Germany would restore the independence of Czechoslovakia except for the Sudetenland but receive some parts of Poland.[386] Adam von Trott zu Solz took this project to England in the first week of June, though he appears to have made no reference at first to the suggestion about territorial concessions from Poland. In his report, which through Walter Hewel was submitted to Hitler, he ascribed the idea of a restored Czech state as the necessary basis for any Anglo-German agreement to Lord Lothian (who would from what we know have been sympathetic to it).[387] He reported Chamberlain as insisting on a dramatic German step as the essential prerequisite to any serious discussion without specificity as to what that step had to be.[388]

Papers, FO 800/270, ff.72–75, 82–83). Compare the comment from the British embassy in Warsaw in *B.D.*, 3d, 5, No. 301. Henderson's former companion in urging concessions to Germany, Lord Lothian, had completely changed his views and now wanted a firm line taken; see his letters to Felix Frankfurter of 10 May, Lothian Papers, GD 40/17/382/316; to Vansittart of 11 May, GD 40/17/387/840; to T. C. P. Catchpool of 15 May 1939, GD 40/17/389/116.

383. For examples of Henderson's weak presentation, see *G.D.*, D, 6, Nos. 572, 671; 7, No. 66; but see also ibid., No. 114, and his letter to Lord Halifax of 1 August, *B.D.*, 3d, 6:719.

384. See Conwell-Evans's warning to Lord Halifax on 12 July about the comments of Lord Brockett and the warning Lord Halifax sent to the latter on 13 July 1939, Halifax Papers, FO 800/316.

385. Aster, p. 217. Cf. Abshagen report to the German Überseedienst, 13 June 1939, Institut für Zeitgeschichte, ED 104.

386. Christopher Sykes, *Tormented Loyalty: The Story of a German Aristocrat Who Defied Hitler* (New York: Harper & Row, 1969), pp. 236–38.

387. Ibid., pp. 239–40, 246–48, 252–55; *G.D.*, D, 6, No. 497; Jones, 6 June 1939, pp. 436–37.

388. Note Ismay's similar comment to Robin M. A. Hankey (then in Poland) on 16 June 1939: "I agree with you entirely about Danzig; it is no longer a place but a principle, and in

When von Trott zu Solz returned to Germany, neither von Ribbentrop nor Hitler wanted to see him—this was certainly not the direction in which they wanted to move.[389]

Chamberlain had made the same point about the need for a dramatic German action to a Swedish businessman, Axel Wenner-Gren, who tried his hand at mediation in the summer.[390] In correspondence and in person, the Swede tried to get Göring to understand this point and eventually developed a detailed program which included the restoration of Czechoslovak independence, the end of concentration camps, and restored religious freedom in Germany. It is certainly noteworthy that Göring, who himself would probably have preferred the maintenance of peace, commented in his written reply of 2 August on only one of the specific points mentioned: the restoration of Czechoslovakia's independence.[391] Such an action, Göring asserted, was impossible for Hitler; there was no point in Wenner-Gren's discussing his project with Hitler if the suggested program were to be the basis of discussion. On the contrary, a victorious German war with Poland was soon coming anyway and was no threat to England. As for Hitler's having broken his word so that his promises could not be trusted, that too was a false assertion. There would be no dramatic step backward to reestablish confidence, quite the contrary. As Chamberlain himself had the day before inserted into a letter destined for Hitler, all depended on the existence of confidence and "there is no question whatever as to the fact that confidence here does not at the moment exist."[392] The discrepancy between the successful creation of "political bases" for negotiations between Germany and the Soviet Union on the one hand, and the absence of confidence with no willingness to re-create it between Germany and England on the other, is perhaps the most striking characteristic of the diplomatic situation of the summer of 1939 and goes far to illuminate the configuration of Europe at the beginning of World War II.

---

my opinion, we should make no more concessions of any kind unless and until Hitler himself makes a real *geste de rapprochement*. If he did that, and I thought it could be trusted, I would go a very long way to meet him." University of London, Ismay Papers, IV/Han/20.

389. Sykes, pp. 256–58. Von Trott subsequently returned for another visit to England in which he merely confused things (ibid., pp. 258–64). Suggestions by Carl Goerdeler at the end of May also created confusion rather than interest in London (C 8004/15/18, FO 371/22973; Aster, p. 230). An approach bordering on the idiotic was made by Albrecht Haushofer, who turned the history of Poland upside down to urge British concession (Haushofer to the Duke of Hamilton, 16 July 1939, James Douglas-Hamilton, *Motive for a Mission* [New York: St. Martin's, 1971], pp. 91–95).

390. Chamberlain's record of 6 June 1939 is in *B.D.*, 3d, 6:736–38; the phraseology the prime minister used was that "it was for Herr Hitler to undo the mischief he had done."

391. A photocopy of Göring's letter is attached as exhibit 10 to the "Petition for Delisting" submitted on Wenner-Gren's behalf to the U.S. secretary of state on 30 January 1943; a copy of this brief, which supplements the documents in *B.D.*, 3d, 6, appendix III, is in Hyde Park, PPF 3474. See also the discussion of the Czechoslovak issue by von Hassell and Henderson in mid-August, *B.D.*, 3d, 7, No. 46.

392. Wilhelm Lenz and Lothar Kettenacker (eds.), "Lord Kemsleys Gespräche mit Hitler Ende Juli 1939," *Vierteljahrshefte für Zeitgeschichte*, 19, No. 3 (July 1971), 321.

It is with the basic difference between England and Germany in mind that one can understand the semiofficial and unofficial soundings between the two countries that all led to nothing.[393] If confidence in German pledges was absent from London, there were those in Germany who did think that the British pledge to Poland would be fulfilled and who hoped that signs of British willingness to see Germany settle her differences with Poland peacefully would lead to the adoption of a policy of peaceful change by Hitler. If he could be convinced that England would stand by a Poland attacked by Germany, but was willing to see concessions made to Germany in normal diplomatic negotiations, he might desist from his planned offensive. The German ambassador to London, Herbert von Dirksen, was a key figure in aiding and encouraging such attempts. Ironically, in earlier years as head of the eastern division of the German foreign ministry he had been an ardent advocate of German steps to revise the eastern border of Germany at Poland's expense, but his continued hope for such a development did not blind him to the fact that an Anglo-German war would certainly follow a German attack on Poland. He therefore warned von Ribbentrop of the drastic change in British public opinion and official policy after 15 March, stressing the absolute certainty of a British declaration of war on Germany in accordance with the promise to Poland; simultaneously he pointed to those signs in London which indicated continued interest in a peaceful solution as a counter to that line of National Socialist propaganda asserting that England was determined to fight Germany under any handy pretext, a line alternating with the opposite contention that the English were sure to desert their allies at any opportunity.[394]

In the face of von Dirksen's reports, von Ribbentrop, who knew that Hitler was determined to attack Poland, continued to argue that England would not fight—and any signs of British preference for a peaceful settlement of the German-Polish dispute were erroneously taken as proof of this position. The German foreign minister disregarded or obstructed all suggestions that Germany refrain from attacking Poland. The ambassador's insistence had the opposite effect of what he intended. Far from convincing his superiors that peace was possible and that negotiations could succeed, it suggested that von Dirksen was not in sympathy with the basic thrust of German policy, namely, to destroy Poland regardless of

393. The account of Helmut Metzmacher, "Deutsch-englische Ausgleichsbemühungen im Sommer 1939," ibid., 14, No. 4 (Oct. 1966), 369–412, is very useful in spite of some questionable interpretations. There are additional details in Aster, chap. 9.

394. Dirksen's views are reflected in his memoirs, in spite of many inaccuracies on details; in his papers, published by the Soviet government (D.M., 2); and in numerous reports printed in G.D., D, 6 and 7; see esp. 6, Nos. 564. 608, 645 (D.M., 2, No. 12), 710 (D.M., 2, No. 14). On various ways of looking at the likelihood of British intervention in a German-Polish war, see "Informationsbericht Nr. 74," 7 July 1939, Bundesarchiv, Brammer, Z.Sg. 101/34, ff.373–77; Biddle dispatch 1160 of 15 July 1939, State 760c.62/745; Kirk tels. 789 and 848 of 12 and 23 August 1939, State 760c.62/806, 897; Fritzsche, pp. 212–13; Engel Diary, 28 July 1939, p. 56.

whether or not England intervened. Von Dirksen was therefore recalled to Germany, where neither von Ribbentrop nor Hitler would receive him, where neither paid the slightest attention to his advice, and where he could only brood on his Silesian estate about the coming disaster.[395]

The burden of von Dirksen's messages from London, that the British would fight if Germany attacked Poland but preferred a peaceful settlement, reached Berlin through a variety of channels but had no effect whatever because Hitler was uninterested in negotiations.[396] The very references to limits on German expansion, explicit or implicit in the discussions, simply ruled discussion out of consideration for a Hitler who wanted a free hand either with England's acquiescence or after her defeat, but in any case without restraints on his plans.[397] The informal contacts established by Helmuth Wohlthat partly on his own initiative and partly with Göring's authorization similarly led nowhere, the precondition of British willingness to talk being invariably the abandonment of Hitler's intention of attacking Poland.[398] The uproar caused in London by Robert Hudson's leaks concerning these talks was matched by von Ribbentrop's annoyance over their having occurred in the first place.[399] The fear in some circles in London that the government was planning another Munich was matched by Hitler's repeatedly expressed concern about compromise proposals, but actually the British government would make no concessions itself and would urge none on Poland under German threats, while the German government wanted not concessions but war.

Göring, like the Italians, would have preferred a compromise settle-

395. *G.D.*, D, 6, Nos. 723, 752, 753; 7, Nos. 58, 138 (draft in *D.M.*, 2, No. 27); *B.D.*, 3d, 6, No. 533; *D.M.*, 2, Nos. 24, 25. When von Dirksen discussed the situation frankly with the Italian ambassador in Berlin, the Germans intercepted the report of the latter and von Ribbentrop reprimanded von Dirksen (*D.M.*, 2, No. 26; *D.D.I.*, 13, No. 44; *G.D.*, D, 7, No. 115). Von Dirksen's conclusion in his memoirs (p. 255): "During my term of office in London Hitler never once took the trouble to deal with British offers of negotiations—even if only in pretence. He never even answered."

396. See *G.D.*, D, 6, No. 630; cf. "Informationsbericht Nr. 73," 5 July 1939, Bundesarchiv, Brammer, Z.Sg. 101/34, ff.365–71.

397. Henke, pp. 268–71.

398. On the Wohlthat talks, see, in addition to Metzmacher and Aster, *G.D.*, D, 6, No. 380; Kennedy tel. 1031 of 20 July 1939, State 740.00/1935; Dalton Diary, 21, 24 July 1939; C 10521/16/18, FO 371/22987; R. A. B. Butler to Wilson, 2 August, and minute by Wilson, 4 August 1939, Premier 1/330; Memorandum on Myron Taylor conversation with Wohlthat on 21 July 1939, Hyde Park, PSF Palestine; Chamberlain note of 4 August 1939 on the document *B.D.*, 3d, 7, No. 533, in Premier 1/330, f.1. Wohlthat and von Dirksen both exaggerated the conciliatory attitude of London in order to impress their superiors, but both accurately reported that Germany's refraining from aggression against Poland was the key to any Anglo-German negotiations. See also Hofer, pp. 58–60. When reviewing the situation with von Dirksen before the latter returned to Germany on leave, Sir Horace Wilson returned to the question of a concrete action by Hitler to restore confidence and suggested "some form of autonomy or home rule for Bohemia and Moravia" (*B.D.*, 3d, 6, No. 533). On Hudson's views, see his letter to Churchill of 30 June 1939 quoted in Gilbert, *Churchill*, 5:1077–78, and placing him in the camp of the latter.

399. *G.D.*, D, 6, No. 743; cf. Memorandum by Wilson on a conversation with Hesse, 20 August 1939, Premier 1/331A.

ment on the Munich model;[400] but all he heard from London through Wenner-Gren and another Swedish intermediary, Birger Dahlerus, was that England would fight rather than make or urge concessions, while Hitler, as Göring fully understood, wanted a war with Poland.[401] A special representative of von Ribbentrop, Fritz Hesse, the press adviser of the German embassy in London, even told Sir Horace Wilson on 20 August on behalf of Hitler and von Ribbentrop that all the informal contacts were meaningless since Hitler preferred to settle with Poland, a subject he would not discuss with England at all, and to make any offer to England only *afterwards*. Hesse asserted that Hitler and von Ribbentrop were both certain that Britain would indeed fight to implement the guarantee of Poland and that constant repetition of the warnings to Berlin to this effect only served to irritate Hitler.[402] While Chamberlain and Halifax sadly recognized the accuracy of the former statements describing the uselessness of the efforts of various intermediaries to establish some basis for negotiations, they did not, as will be seen, heed Hesse's advice that no further warnings be sent to Germany.

As word reached London that von Ribbentrop was about to fly to Moscow to sign a nonaggression pact, the prime minister and his major advisers were conferring about a projected special letter of warning from Chamberlain to Hitler. On 18 August Vansittart's sources had provided him with the date on which Germany planned to attack Poland as falling between 25 and 28 August, and on the following two days numerous drafts of a final warning to Hitler were worked over at 10 Downing Street and in the Foreign Office.[403] At one time Henderson had suggested that such a letter might be delivered by General Ironside, who spoke fluent German, but the announcement of the forthcoming Nazi-Soviet pact suggested that there was not time for such a mission.[404] The letter was accordingly amended to include a reference to the expected pact's having no effect whatever on the validity of the British guarantee and sent to Henderson to

400. Note that at the end of July Göring warned the French assistant air attaché to have his ambassador return to Berlin by mid-August, while Göring's aide, General Bodenschatz, said that if Britain and France went to war over Poland, Stehlin's job would end on 1 September (Stehlin, pp. 162–63).

401. On Wenner-Gren, see n.391, above; on Dahlerus, see his memoirs, *Der letzte Versuch* (Munich: Nymphenburger Verlagshandlung, 1948), and the accounts by Aster and Hofer. See also the notes in C 9288, C 11573/15/18, 30 June and 15 August 1939, FO 371/22974 and 22976.

402. Minute by Wilson, 20 August 1939, Premier 1/331A; on this document, see the discussion in Henke, pp. 271–75.

403. A collection of drafts is in Premier 1/331A. For background, note Chamberlain's comment at a meeting of the Committee of Imperial Defence on 25 February 1935 when, in connection with the discussion of the air pact then under consideration, he stressed the importance of the deterrent effect of letting an aggressor know beforehand that a quick strike or knockout blow at the beginning of a war would not be the end of that war (C 1904/55/18, FO 371/18829, p. 4).

404. Note *B.D.*, 3d, 7, No. 83.

deliver to Hitler.[405] The cabinet was in full agreement on the text of the warning letter and the need for some immediate military preparations.[406] The British had long hoped that their warning to Hitler of 31 March would be reinforced by an agreement with the Soviet Union; it was now clear even to the most persistent optimist that this was not to be. If anyone thought that British policy had changed because of the Nazi-Soviet pact about to be signed, they were to be disabused, or, as the letter phrased it: "No greater mistake could be made." The message continued:

> Whatever may prove to be the nature of the German-Soviet Agreement, it cannot alter Great Britain's obligation to Poland which His Majesty's Government have stated in public repeatedly and plainly and which they are determined to fulfil.
>
> It has been alleged that, if His Majesty's Government had made their position more clear in 1914, the great catastrophe would have been avoided. Whether or not there is any force in that allegation, His Majesty's Government are resolved that on this occasion there shall be no such tragic misunderstanding.
>
> If the case should arise, they are resolved, and prepared, to employ without delay all the forces at their command, and it is impossible to foresee the end of hostilities once engaged. It would be a dangerous illusion to think that, if war once starts, it will come to an early end even if a success on any one of the several fronts on which it will be engaged should have been secured.[407]

The veiled allusion to the idea that an early defeat of Poland by Germany would in no way mean a quick end to the war had been made much more explicit in a warning sent to Rome on 19 August[408] even before a copy of the 22 August letter to Hitler was handed to the Italian government in the hope that Mussolini would exert his influence on Hitler to restrain the German dictator or at least himself stay out of what would surely be a long war.[409] The Italian leader would draw from the Nazi-Soviet pact some rather different conclusions, but he himself was very much impressed by the British attitude of firmness. Chamberlain had practically given up all hope for peace; the portion of his letter referring to

405. Important for the sequence, especially the receipt in London of the news of the intended German attack, of the forthcoming German-Soviet pact, and the drafting and delivery of the letter, is Lord Halifax's "A Record of Events before the War, 1939," written in late September or October 1939, C 20648/15/18, FO 371/22990; extracts from the diary of Sir Alexander Cadogan, forwarded to Lord Halifax 28 October 1939, C 12122/15/18, FO 371/22978, now in *Cadogan Diary*, pp. 196ff. For the decision to have Henderson deliver the letter, see *B.D.*, 3d, 7, No. 142. A good brief account in Hofer, pp. 165–66.

406. Cabinet 41 (39) of 22 August 1939, C 11924/15/18, FO 371/22977; C 11925/3356/18, FO 371/23073. The text of the public announcement is in *B.D.*, 3d, 7, No. 140, n.3.

407. Ibid., No. 145.

408. Ibid., No. 79.

409. Ibid., No. 190; *D.D.I.*, 13, No. 167; *U.S.*, 1939, 1:230–32. For earlier documents on British efforts with Italy, see *B.D.*, 3d, 5–7, passim, esp. 7, Nos. 160, 166, 192; FO comments in R 4399/1/22, FO 371/23785, and R 4517/57/22, FO 371/23808.

a possible cooling off period to be followed by German negotiations with Poland sounds like a formality rather than the anticipation of a real possibility.[410] As the prime minister told the American ambassador on 23 August, the situation was pretty hopeless, with war clearly imminent.[411] Whether the British warning would serve to deter Hitler was still something of an open question as far as London was concerned, but most of the British leaders were quite doubtful, for all the signs pointed to war.

In making concessions to the Soviet point of view during the negotiations of the spring and summer of 1939 the London government had been influenced by the obvious eagerness of the French to secure Russian aid for Poland. As previously mentioned, the French government had reacted to the event of 15 March in a manner rather similar to that of the British. There was certainly no enthusiasm for war in Paris; there was instead a combination of resignation and determination. The resignation was to the apparent inevitability of war; the determination was to stand fast against any further concessions to Germany. German diplomats reported quite accurately on these attitudes, and they were equally evident to other observers.[412] Although there were some signs of weakness, symbolized in the government by the waverings of Foreign Minister Bonnet,[413] Prime Minister Daladier was absolutely firm. Like Chamberlain, the French prime minister carried the burden of Munich. As he told the German ambassador on 11 July, their first meeting since 15 March, he had helped three and a half million Germans to join Germany only to have twice that many Czechs end up under German rule.[414] As far as he was concerned, there could be no return to policies Germany herself had repudiated.

France was already allied with Poland. The question now facing the French was what to do to make that alliance operative. There were Franco-Polish talks on arms deliveries and other types of military cooperation,[415] and at the end of the talks on 19 May a secret military agreement was signed. It provided for a major French offensive in the west to start on the fifteenth day of war if Germany concentrated her forces against Poland in the initial stages of a war.[416] Not only were there troubles about the new political agreement that was to be signed thereafter,[417] but the

410. A draft Henderson had sent had explicitly called for the restoration of an independent Czechoslovakia as a prerequisite for a change in British policy ("if the original ground for its initiation was once and for all definitely eliminated"), *B.D.*, 3d, 7, No. 118.

411. *U.S.*, 1939, 1:355–56. Note that at 3:45 p.m. on 23 August Chamberlain discussed with Hankey the construction of a war cabinet (Roskill, *Hankey*, 3:413–14).

412. *G.D.*, D, 6, Nos. 188, 379, 409, 501, 602, 603; *U.S.*, 1939, 1:177–78, 180–81; *B.D.*, 3d, 6, No. 212; *D.D.I.*, 12, No. 464.

413. See *U.S.*, 1939, 1:193–94; Bullitt tel. 993 of 23 May 1939, State 751.60c/148.

414. *G.D.*, D, 6, No. 658.

415. Ibid., No. 399; Gamelin, 2:413–23; Beck, p. 345.

416. Beck, pp. 345–46; Bullitt tel. 965 of 19 May 1939, State 751.60c/145; *Łukasiewicz Papers*, pp. 210–18.

417. *U.S.*, 1939, 1:189–91, 279–80; Bullitt tels. 987, 1016, 1017, and 1032 of 23, 25, and 30 May 1939, State 751.60c/147, 149–51; *Łukasiewicz Papers*, pp. 188–95, 202–10, 218–23. The whole muddle is reviewed in Adamthwaite, pp. 319–23; Henryk Batowski, "Le dernier traité

French government appears to have had no intention whatever of carrying out its obligations under the military agreement. During the Anglo-French staff talks earlier that month, the British had asked what the French would do if Germany attacked Poland and stood on the defensive in the west while Italy remained neutral. General Lelong responded that this was "a thorny problem . . . and France could not attack Germany on land without long preparation."[418] This situation did not have the political repercussions in London that the French plans to invade Libya if Germany attacked Czechoslovakia had had in 1938—the British had taken their stand and would not budge. It did, however, disturb General Ironside when he learned in July that the Poles had been lied to.[419] There was not much that the British, who had just begun to organize a continental army, could do about this, but they may have understood that this French policy contained an element contributing to the desperate pressure from Paris for an agreement with Russia in order to secure help for Poland from the east.

For some time the French urged the English to greater concessions to the Soviet point of view in order to obtain a treaty.[420] Then, in June, the French were alarmed that Soviet demands for guarantees of the Baltic States against "indirect aggression" implied that the independence of the countries of Eastern Europe was to be terminated rather than protected.[421] Nevertheless, they were so worried about the need for helping Poland and for building up a strong eastern front against Germany that they pushed for further concessions and persuaded themselves that the Russians really wanted an agreement.[422] When the Russians followed up on their demand of June that agreement on a military convention precede the political treaty by insisting in August that Polish agreement prior to the outbreak of war to the transit of Soviet troops had to precede a military agreement, the French tried desperately to find ways to accommodate them—though the Russians had by then agreed to work out a pact with the Germans.[423]

---

d'alliance franco-polonais (4 septembre 1939)," *Les relations franco-allemands, 1933–1939*, pp. 353–62.

418. COS 900 of 3 May 1939, CAB 53/48. One is inclined to suspect that the French promised an offensive they had no intention of carrying out to avoid a defection by Poland, very much the way Germany had promised Austria-Hungary an offensive southward from East Prussia before 1914 and had carefully refrained from enlightening her ally about the equally imaginary character of that operation.

419. *Ironside Diary*, 11, 26 July 1939, pp. 78–80, 84–85. On the other hand, the French and British did work out a unified command and additional details, see *Pownall Diary*, 5 June, 3, 10 July 1939, pp. 206–8, 210–11, 211–13. The simultaneous troubles over British credits to Poland have already been mentioned; an account of this issue in relation to French credits is in Łukasiewicz Papers, pp. 223–33.

420. *U.S.*, 1939, 1:248–51, 254–55; *S.U.*, Nos. 316, 332, 371; *B.D.*, 3d, 6 and 7, passim.

421. *U.S.*, 1939, 1:266–71, 281–82, 282–84; Note *S.U.*, Nos. 377, 378.

422. See *U.S.*, 1939, 1:205, 213, 217. In France, as in England, the Russian ambassador could use those especially favorable to an agreement with the Soviet Union to bring pressure on the government (*S.U.*, No. 395).

423. A number of important French documents on this have been published by the Soviet government (presumably from copies made by the Germans and captured from the latter),

The prospect of a new war with Germany was particularly abhorrent to the nation that had borne the heaviest burden in the preceding conflict and was certain to face a new German onslaught practically unaided, but there were signs of resolution to accompany the search for Soviet aid. In spite of the most vehement protests, von Ribbentrop's special personal representative in France, Otto Abetz, was expelled when he became too indiscreet.[424] Partly to set the record straight, partly perhaps to salve his own guilty conscience, Foreign Minister Bonnet wrote formally to von Ribbentrop on 1 July, reminding him of the French commitment to Poland which was untouched by the agreement reached when von Ribbentrop had been in Paris the preceding December, and he upheld this line when the German foreign minister replied in unusually truculent language.[425] The information that the French received after the Salzburg meeting between Ciano and Hitler and von Ribbentrop indicated that the Germans had decided to go to war, but that Italy would stay out. The Italian government was known to prefer an international conference, but after Munich it was hard to see how France and Britain could possibly agree to such a procedure unless Germany first evacuated Czechoslovakia, the same point that had been made from the other side of the Channel.[426] The French continued to warn Berlin of their determination to honor the pledge to Poland.[427]

The announcement that von Ribbentrop was going to Moscow to sign a nonaggression pact struck Paris like a bombshell.[428] The prospects for France in a war with Germany now looked dim indeed—it had taken the combined might of France, England, the United States, Russia, Italy, and Japan to defeat Germany in 1914–18—but there seemed to be no alternative to war in the opinion of most of those in the French government. It was expected that Hitler would attack Poland just as soon as the pact with Russia had been signed,[429] and this belief was not confined to Paris. In

---

S.U., Nos. 416, 418, 419, 424, 430–35. See also Adamthwaite, pp. 335–38; Łukasiewicz Papers, pp. 249–53; U.S., 1939, 1:225–26; Hore-Belisha Papers, 21 August 1939, pp. 215–16; Hofer, pp. 176–78.

424. G.D., D, 6, Nos. 640, 658, 664, 676, 690, 767; 7, Nos. 22, 49, 65; Bullitt tel. 1231 of 30 June 1939, State 760c.62/660; "Bestellungen aus der Pressekonferenz," 24 July 1939, Bundesarchiv, Brammer, Z.Sg. 101/13, f.86.

425. G.D., D, 6, Nos. 602, 669, 722 (this document of 25 July is dated 21 July in the French Yellow Book, No. 168). When Lord Halifax sent copies of the correspondence to Chamberlain, the latter commented on 1 August that "the brutality of Ribbentrop's language is very characteristic" (C 10813/824/55, FO 371/23144); cf. Łukasiewicz Papers, pp. 245–46.

426. U.S., 1939, 1:215–17. On 21 August the French (and Americans) like the British learned that the attack on Poland was scheduled for 25 August (Bullitt tel. 1536 of 21 August 1939, State 760c.62/904).

427. G.D., D, 7, No. 64; French Yellow Book, No. 194. The firmness shown by the French may have been influenced by advice from German State Secretary von Weizsäcker, who wanted his superiors deterred from war (see Coulondre's report of 17 August in Weizsäcker-Papiere, p. 328).

428. For a summary of the impressions in Paris, see Hofer, pp. 172–76.

429. U.S., 1939, 1:301–4; Adamthwaite, pp. 339–41.

Moscow the war Germany was about to begin had been the occasion for agreeing to divide the spoils with Hitler; Stalin had decided that encouraging Germany to move was preferable both to opposing Germany and to leaving her in doubt about the Soviet position. In Rome a German attack on Poland was assumed imminent. In London as in Paris the green light Hitler had received from Moscow was thought to be the almost certain prelude to German action.

The country most directly affected by the spectacular turn of events was, of course, Poland. Though leaks and rumors about a possible German-Soviet agreement had reached Warsaw, the Poles had discounted them.[430] In the final weeks of the diplomatic crisis, Soviet assurances of economic support for Poland if she were attacked by Germany alternated with information about a possible fourth partition of Poland.[431] When the agreement was announced, the Polish government could point out to their Western allies the correctness of their own doubts about Soviet intentions—they had been asked to allow the Red Army into Poland at the very time that Moscow and Berlin were negotiating about an agreement obviously directed against them. As for adjustments in policy, there appeared to be no room for any at all. If the Russians stood aside when Germany attacked, little would change from what the Poles had expected anyway. If the Russians went beyond this to a breach of their non-aggression treaty with Poland, there was still very little that Warsaw could do about it. In the choice between surrender and a desperate fight, the experience of Poland in the years from 1772 to 1919 suggested that fighting was the only, even if hopeless, alternative.

In what were generally recognized as the last days of peace, the major and minor powers alike looked with apprehension toward Berlin. If Hitler struck, as all expected, what should, what could, they do? Each country had to make its choice among alternatives fraught with enormous risks, not for this or that specific policy issue, but for its very existence and for the lives of its inhabitants.

430. Note Szymanski, p. 313; *D.D.B.*, 5, No. 85.
431. *U.S.*, 1939, 1:196; *G.D.*, D, 7, No. 42; *Lipski Papers*, No. 150.

14   Hitler Gets His War

**ith a green light** from Moscow, Hitler was hopeful that he could both have his war with Poland now and so upset Britain and France that they would not intervene in that conflict. For several days, German propaganda had been putting special stress on the strength of Germany's fortifications in the west;[1] what could the Western Powers now possibly do for Poland? Procedures for coordinating the political situation in Danzig were well in hand, and instructions were given for the naval bombardment of the Polish base at the Westerplatte in Danzig harbor that was to open hostilities.[2] These plans, like those for the German army and for German diplomats and agents in Poland were all based on one assumption: Poland would neither attack nor provoke Germany, and no contingency plans for such possibilities existed.[3] Germany would strike at a moment of her own choosing, and, as previously mentioned, a fake Polish attack would be engineered at the appropriate moment by the Germans themselves.

1. See "Vertrauliche Informationen," 18, 21 August 1939, Bundesarchiv, Oberheitmann, Z.Sg. 109/2, ff.71–72, 86; Dertinger, "Bestellung für die Schriftleitung," 18 August 1939, Bundesarchiv, Brammer, Z.Sg. 101/13, ff.111–12. Much noise was also made about alleged Polish atrocities against the German minority in Poland, but after the experience of 1938 no one took this seriously.

2. *G.D.*, D, 7, Nos. 138, 167, 188, 194, n.2, 197, 225; *TMWC*, 34:448, 452–53. The *Schleswig-Holstein*, an obsolete warship used mainly for training, was substituted at the last moment for the cruiser *Königsberg*, presumably to avoid any risk of losing the more valuable ship and to have the use of the bigger guns of the *Schleswig-Holstein*. The visit of the *Königsberg* on 25 August had been announced to the Polish government at the end of June (*B.D.*, 3d, 7, No. 209).

3. *G.D.*, D, 7, No. 166. Note that the leader of the German minority in Poland, Rudolf Wiesner, was instructed to leave Poland and was not to be used the way Henlein had been; Hitler preferred to stage-manage the whole scenario directly (ibid., Nos. 195, 196). Was this another of the "lessons" Hitler had learned from the 1938 procedure when the incidents of 13 September had helped bring on Chamberlain's trip (*D.D.F.*, 2d, 11, Nos. 151, 171)?

The appropriate moment appeared to be at hand. In his eagerness for a war on Poland, Hitler had been willing to make the most extensive concessions to the Soviet Union; more even than Stalin thought to ask for, so that once von Ribbentrop's interim report from Moscow showed that an agreement would be reached, Hitler was ready to move.[4] Hitler was confident that the Chamberlain government would fall as a result of the diplomatic defeat England had suffered, and he always assumed that France would not move without England's support.[5] On 23 August, even before von Ribbentrop and Stalin had signed the nonaggression pact and secret protocol, Hitler directed that the attack on Poland begin early on 26 August.[6] His final diplomatic preparations would be made in the two intervening days.

Before these are discussed, it is important to note that on 23 and 24 August, at a time when the news of the German-Soviet pact was reverberating around the world, Hitler still thought that the war with Poland might well be isolated. Neither the British cabinet announcement that the pact in no way affected England's obligations to Poland nor Chamberlain's letter of 22 August absolutely convinced him that the English government would both stay in power and carry out its pledge to Poland.[7] He did apparently have some doubts on the subject, but basically he thought that London was bluffing.[8] If the English were serious, however, that was their misfortune; as he told Henderson on the 23d when discussing Chamberlain's letter, if there was going to be a big war, he much preferred fighting it at age fifty than at age fifty-five or even sixty.[9] The great military demonstration on Hitler's birthday that year may have reminded others of German might, but it reminded Hitler of his age.

On 24 August, Hitler left Berchtesgaden for Berlin and met von Ribbentrop on his return from Moscow. The two conferred at length. Von Ribbentrop reported on his trip, and the two reviewed the international situation. The foreign minister already knew about Chamberlain's let-

4. The possibility that the right moment for war might well come *before* the 1 September date by which German preparations were to be completed had long been in Hitler's mind and communicated in his behalf to the armed forces. Admiral Raeder had so warned the naval staffs as early as 16 May 1939 (Hubatsch, *Weisungen*, p. 19). Von Ribbentrop's request for authorization to yield all of Latvia to the Soviet Union (*G.D.*, D, 7, No. 205) also made it clear that an agreement with the Soviet Union was imminent.

5. *Weizsäcker-Papiere*, 23 August 1939, pp. 159–60. Von Weizsäcker, who spoke with Hitler repeatedly in these critical days because of von Ribeentrop's absence in Moscow, predicted otherwise and also warned that Italy would not join Germany.

6. *Halder Diary*, 26 August 1939.

7. On the situation in Berlin before Henderson's delivery of the letter, see Kirk tel. 874 of 23 August 1939, 9:00 p.m., State 760c.62/945; von Vormann notes in Institut für Zeitgeschichte quoted in Sykes, p. 283, and Hofer, pp. 167–68; Kordt, *Nicht aus den Akten*, p. 332.

8. Jodl diary, 24 August 1939, *TMWC*, 28:390; cf. Lane (Belgrade) tel. 216 of 24 August 1939, 11:00 p.m., State 760c.62/989.

9. For the Hitler-Henderson meeting of 23 August and Hitler's reply, see *G.D.*, D, 7, Nos. 200, 201; *B.D.*, 3d, 7, Nos. 178, 200, 207, 208, 211, 213, 248. (Hitler had referred to his own age before; he now added an oath that he had not been bluffing in 1938.) There was a meeting of Göring with Lipski on 24 August, but its import is unclear (*B.D.*, 3d, 7, No. 263; *Biddle Papers*, p. 76; *Lipski Papers*, pp. 565–66, 590–92; cf. Irving, *Breach of Security*, pp. 92–120).

ter and still discounted the possibility of England's entering the conflict, a point on which Stalin had not been nearly so certain.[10] In their discussions that day, Hitler and von Ribbentrop apparently worked out the details of the last-minute diplomatic preparations. With war scheduled for 26 August, the next day would be the last day of peace and hence the final opportunity for bringing in allies on Germany's side and eliminating help for Poland.[11]

Of the possible allies, Japan had obviously been eliminated by Germany's pact with the Soviet Union. The signature of the pact was a shock to the Japanese, leading to the resignation of the Hiranuma cabinet, and a violation of the secret protocol to the Anti-Comintern Pact. The German government would do what it could to calm down the agitated Japanese, especially by stressing their hopes of assisting with the improvement of Soviet-Japanese relations and by emphasizing the common enmity of Germany and Japan toward the Western Powers; but for the time being, a holding operation was indicated.[12] The successful effort to involve Slovakia formally in war with Poland and the failure to implicate Lithuania have already been mentioned. From Hitler's point of view, here were countries that could in 1939 play the role he had set for Poland and Hungary in 1938: participation in a combined attack on the prospective victim would both speed the process and assist in deterring possible supporters of the victim. An even more important role could be played by the other prospective ally on whom Hitler counted, namely, Italy.

Hitler spent considerable time on 24 August preparing a letter for Mussolini to be hand-carried to Rome the following day—the day before the outbreak of war—by Hans Frank, who was called in from Danzig and briefed on the situation.[13] Mussolini was to be informed of Hitler's belief that Poland had to be crushed promptly and was to be asked for the support that the text of the Pact of Steel specified. He was to be told that England was bluffing and that the Western Powers would not intervene. Now was the time to strike. Hitler decided at the last minute not to send Frank; instead von Ribbentrop called Ciano in the middle of the night of 24–25 August to warn the Italians that war was imminent, and the letter

10. *G.D.*, D, 7, No. 200, n.3. For the discussion of the letter by von Ribbentrop and Stalin on the night of 23–24 August, see ibid., p. 190. For Maisky's report that the British government would be compelled to fight if Poland did so, see *S.U.*, No. 440.

11. *Weizsäcker-Papiere*, 24 August 1939, p. 160.

12. Sommer, pp. 282–92. See *G.D.*, D, 7, Nos. 183, 262, 329, 556; *B.D.*, 3d, 9, No. 584. It is not clear whether the last-minute hints of the Japanese minister in Warsaw, Sakoh, about a possible exchange of Memel for concessions elsewhere had been authorized by Tokyo (Biddle tel. 231 of 30 August 1939, noon, State 760c.62/1200).

13. Frank, p. 343. I have been unable to find external evidence corroborating Frank's account, but internal evidence suggests that it is generally reliable on this issue. The fact that Frank at no time refers to Hitler's earlier plan to send him to Moscow need not invalidate his story since there is no evidence that Frank was told about that quickly discarded project. It is, however, clear on other evidence that Frank had indeed been in Danzig at a legal meeting (*B.D.*, 3d, 7, Nos. 100, 183, 186).

was delivered by Ambassador von Mackensen on the 25th.[14] In it Hitler gave a short and not particularly accurate explanation of the agreement with Russia, stressing the impact of that agreement on Turkey and especially on Rumania, which would now have to stay out of any hostile coalition. Hitler announced that hostilities could begin at any moment—not disclosing that the attack had already been ordered for the morning of the following day. It was clearly Hitler's assumption that Mussolini would join Germany now that the agreement with the Soviet Union had altered the whole situation so greatly to the benefit of the Axis.

Before the Italian reaction is examined, the other preparatory steps Hitler took on 25 August must be reviewed so that the orchestration of developments from Berlin can be understood. To reinforce the propaganda about the fortifications in the west, the German ministers in Holland, Belgium, Luxembourg, and Switzerland were instructed to promise German respect for the neutrality of these countries and to threaten war and destruction if any of them failed to protect Germany's rear by abandoning neutrality in favor of the Western Powers.[15] The Belgians, because of their strategic position, were given both the most solemn assurances and the most dire threats, and were thereby inspired to renewed pledges of neutrality and frantic appeals for the maintenance of peace.[16]

Hitler wanted his newfound Soviet friends to assist in underlining the isolation of Poland—thereby discouraging the Western Powers from intervening—by gestures that would give public expression to the new diplomatic situation. For months there had been no Soviet ambassador in Berlin; and in view of the forthcoming campaign against Poland, a Soviet military representative in Berlin was also needed. Von Ribbentrop and Molotov had discussed this matter in Moscow, and on 25 August the Russians were requested most urgently to implement their agreement to dispatch these officials to Berlin immediately.[17] There would be considerable correspondence and discussion about this issue and about German requests for Soviet pressure on Poland's eastern border in the following days as part of the general campaign to isolate Poland; and although taking a few days to comply, the Russian government did agree to help the Germans in this regard.[18] By that time, the Germans had, as will be explained, postponed the attack on Poland for a short time; but during those days, they continued to play the Soviet card. To the other powers,

14. *G.D.*, D, 7, Nos. 263, 266; *D.D.I.*, 13, Nos. 225, 245; Ciano, *Diary*, 25 August 1939.

15. *G.D.*, D, 7, No. 272.

16. *D.D.B.*, 5, Nos. 118, 120, 121, 126; Overstraeten, 26 August 1939, p. 350. Documents on the appeal of King Leopold and Queen Wilhelmina may be found in the major collections of diplomatic documents.

17. *G.D.*, D, 7, No. 285.

18. Ibid., Nos. 360, 381–83, 387, 388, 413, 414, 424, 425, 446, 453, 456, 471, 480, 514, 532; "Bestellungen aus der Pressekonferenz," 2, 3 September 1939, Bundesarchiv, Brammer, Z.Sg. 101/14, ff.7, 16.

the Germans explained their insistence that the Soviet Union participate in any new settlement in Eastern Europe, and to the Russians they provided the main details of the last-minute negotiations.[19] To obviate any negative repercussions of the bargain with Moscow, Berlin denied the existence of any secret protocol to the pact and coordinated its denials with Stalin.[20] In other military and diplomatic ways Germany and the Soviet Union cooperated in the last days of peace and the first days of war, though it would be two weeks before their new friendship could be "sealed in blood," as Stalin expressed it, in common war against Poland.[21]

Hitler's agreement with the Soviet Union was to have served as a major argument in his dealing with England. In response to the firm speeches in Parliament of Neville Chamberlain and Lord Halifax on 24 August Hitler decided a further step was necessary.[22] He asked Henderson to see him on the 25th, and at their meeting at 1:30 p.m. offered England an alliance to be worked out *after* the settlement of the German-Polish dispute. If England intervened in that dispute, the resulting war would weaken Britain, not Germany. Reminding the British government that the blockade weapon had been broken by the pact with Russia which not only eliminated any real eastern front but opened up vast trade opportunities, Hitler dangled before the British the prospect of an alliance with Germany and even an agreement on arms limitations as alternatives to another world war under circumstances far less favorable to the Western Powers than those of 1914. With its renewed promise to make no territorial demands in the west and to be moderate in German colonial requests, this offer was to be carried by Henderson to London in person. This procedure was suggested by Hitler himself; it meant that according to the Führer's timetable the cabinet in London would have in front of them on the morning of 26 August Hitler's alliance offer as they met to consider the German attack on Poland that would by then already have been under way for several hours.[23]

The purpose of this project should be obvious. As a whole catalogue of offers and promises had accompanied the remilitarization of the Rhineland, so a new collection would be placed before the British to accompany the invasion of Poland. Hitler had tried to pave the way for this offer two weeks before when he had arranged to fly the League high commissioner

19. *G.D.*, D, 7, Nos. 431, 440.

20. Ibid., Nos. 332, 339, 511, 550. The promise to deny the existence of the secret protocol was not only kept by Stalin but has been observed by Soviet historians since.

21. The text of Stalin's message of 22 December 1939 is reprinted in Roman Umiastowski, *Russia and the Polish Republic, 1918–1945* (London: Aquafondata, 1945), p. 182. The reference is to Red Army casualties in the fighting against Poland. Von Ribbentrop had begun urging a Russian advance on 3 September (*G.D.*, D, 7, No. 567).

22. Texts of the British statements in *British War Blue Book*, Nos. 64, 65. On Hitler's reception of the news of this development in the morning of 25 August, see Kordt, *Wahn und Wirklichkeit*, p. 194; Schmidt, p. 449.

23. *G.D.*, D, 7, No. 265; *B.D.*, 3d, 7, Nos. 283, 284, 286, 288, 310, 312, 313.

in Danzig, Carl Burckhardt, to the Obersalzberg for a conversation designed for British and French ears but including a special appeal to the English. Nothing much had come of that gesture.[24] Now that the hour Hitler had picked for war was nearing, a more direct means of diverting the British had to be used.

Hitler hoped that once again he would be allowed to move forward without a general war. As for the promises and commitments offered, these were all for the period *after* a German-Polish war. Quite apart from their very dubious nature—new promises about future German territorial demands sounded almost as funny as an implied offer to send German troops to Malaya to defend Singapore against the Japanese—they were presumably intended to have the same fate as the offers of March 1936.[25] As Hitler's explanations of 23 May and 22 August about a war with the West as soon as the Polish question had been settled to his satisfaction show, there was nothing more substantial to the offer of an alliance than there had been to his 1936 offer to return to the League of Nations. The comparison between his earlier offer to settle the Polish question with the Soviet Union in accordance with the preferences of the latter and his insistence on total disregard for Britain's preferences on the same question reveals all too clearly which offer was to lead to serious negotiations and which was purely a tactical ploy with no substantive significance, a contrast too many have ignored. All that counted was to discourage England from intervening in the war Hitler intended to start on the following morning.[26] If the British were willing to spend the time that war lasted on negotiations about an alliance with Germany, that would be most agreeable to Hitler. If they were foolish enough to declare war, publication of his offer to the British would provide a fine propaganda line for the German public. Hitler, however, anticipated that the British would play into his hands, and so, later, when the London government refused to

24. On Burckhardt's trip and meeting with Hitler, see *B.D.*, 3d, 6, Nos. 36, 601, 604, 659; 7, Nos. 3, 4; Aster, pp. 322–24; Burckhardt, pp. 338–49; Kuykendall (Danzig) tel. of 15 August 1939, 3:00 p.m., and Biddle tel. 174 of 16 August 1939, State 760c.62/823, 844. The meeting had, of course, preceded the signature of the pact with Russia. Hitler had told Burckhardt that if the Western Powers would not give him a free hand in the east, he would first align himself with Russia to defeat the West and thereafter turn against the Soviet Union since he needed the Ukraine. Burckhardt did not pass on this comment to the British and French. A useful summary and evaluation in Herbert S. Levine, "The Mediator: Carl J. Burckhardt's Efforts to Avert a Second World War," *Journal of Modern History*, 45, No. 3 (Sept. 1973), 453–55.

25. On this point, see Weinberg, *Foreign Policy*, pp. 250–51.

26. The phraseology in von Weizsäcker's diary is revealing: "Efforts are still aimed at separating England from the Poles. Henderson is to receive a proposal corresponding [to this]—something done between 1 and 2 p.m.—which by far-reaching and tempting offers for the time after an isolated settlement of the Polish question is to deter her from [becoming involved in] the latter" (*Weizsäcker-Papiere*, p. 160). Henke, pp. 287ff., completely misconstrues the offer. He can do so only by inverting the chronology: by making the alliance go along with, rather than come after the attack on Poland, and by moving the recall of the attack order from 25 August to 24 August (p. 290).

behave as he had planned, additional propaganda themes had to be devised.[27]

After giving Henderson the alliance offer and sending him off to London, Hitler learned that the reply from Mussolini had not yet arrived.[28] The French ambassador, Robert Coulondre, was to come later that afternoon, but here a problem in the German timetable required a decision by Hitler. If the attack on Poland was indeed to be launched in the morning of 26 August, the final order to go forward with the attack had to be issued by 3:00 p.m. on the 25th so that the regular units could move toward the border, the special sabotage units could start crossing the border, and all other last-minute steps could be taken as planned. Hitler had, as mentioned, written to Mussolini, but by the 3:00 p.m. deadline—which of course had not been communicated to the Italians—still had received no answer. Hitler assumed that the answer would be favorable, or, if he had any doubts, decided to disregard them,[29] a point of some significance for assessing Hitler's preference for war. By the afternoon deadline he had issued his offer to England, which he had every reason to believe would be discussed in London on the following day. He had not yet got in touch with the French, but he had already arranged to do so later that day, and he was always confident that British reluctance to act would reinforce the known pacific preferences of France. Hitler was ready to move; as an eyewitness, the army representative on the spot, recorded, Hitler gave the order to go ahead at two minutes after 3:00 p.m., and this order was immediately transmitted to the high command of the army.[30] The official mobilization order was also issued secretly that day with 26 August as the first day on the mobilization schedule.[31] The whole machinery of government from the projected rationing procedures to the soldiers near the Polish border began its move toward 4:30 a.m. on 26 August when war was to start.

As part of the effort to isolate the war, Hitler saw the French ambassador later in the afternoon of 25 August, asking Coulondre to inform Daladier that Germany did not want war with France and had no claims against her, that the situation in regard to Poland was intolerable, and that it was up to the French to decide whether they wanted a war with Germany or not.[32] Here, too, the obvious purpose was to discourage French

27. On 24 August Göring activated Dahlerus, who, unlike Göring, did not know of Hitler's intention of attacking Poland on the 26th.

28. Attolico was to be at the chancellery at 2:30 p.m. (*D.D.I.*, 13, No. 258). Henderson had been there from 1:30 to about 2:30.

29. Hofer, p. 237.

30. Von Vormann's report is quoted ibid., p. 274.

31. *Halder Diary*, 25 August 1939. The Germans hoped that by keeping their own mobilization secret, they could surprise the Poles more effectively, an expectation realized at least in part since the Poles, in order to avoid provoking Germany and in response to British requests, deferred their mobilization.

32. A summary in Hofer, p. 275. Coulondre replied that France would certainly honor her commitment to Poland, that the accounts of Polish atrocities to which Hitler referred were greatly exaggerated, and that after 15 March France had had no choice but to tighten her alliances.

intervention in the war Hitler had already ordered started. His fair words would be before the French cabinet when it made its decision the next morning. It was his hope that the already recorded defection of Russia from the Franco-Soviet alliance, the anticipated defection of England that he himself thought he had assisted by the alliance offer, and the known pacifist sentiments within France would combine to keep the French government from a decision to honor its promise of aid for Poland.

Hardly had Coulondre left the chancellery when Hitler learned that two of his assumptions about the situation were wrong: Mussolini responded that he would not join Germany in a war at that time; and the news of the signature of the Anglo-Polish alliance treaty in the afternoon of 25 August showed that England was not adopting the course Hitler anticipated. Even Hitler could see that London was unlikely to break an alliance the day after signing it. What had happened, and what did Hitler decide to do about it?

In Rome, the situation after Ciano's return from the Salzburg meeting had been one of contradictory currents, with Ciano eventually being authorized by Mussolini to arrange another meeting with von Ribbentrop. Five hours after Ciano had called the German foreign minister to arrange that meeting, von Ribbentrop called back to tell Ciano that he was going to Moscow to sign a pact with Russia; the two foreign ministers agreed to have their meeting afterwards.[33] For a moment, Mussolini and Ciano abandoned their certainty that the Western Powers would intervene. Under the immediate impact of what looked like a possible localization of war, they promptly turned to the idea that the Germans had been pushing: an Italian operation against Yugoslavia to run parallel with that of Germany against Poland.[34]

Very quickly, however, first Ciano and then the Duce returned to their earlier view that a German attack on Poland would lead to a general war. The public and private pronouncements from London and Paris carried conviction in Rome if not in Berlin.[35] As Count Ciano told the German minister of finance, who happened to be in Rome on the morning of 23 August, he was certain that England and France would fight alongside Poland in spite of the announced German pact with Russia. The time was not yet correct for war since the Axis was not prepared for the long war that was to be expected. Even before the German treaty with the Soviet Union was actually signed, the Italian foreign minister was sure that even this great coup would not deter England and France and that Hitler was mistaken if he thought otherwise.[36]

33. Ciano, *Diary*, 21 and 22 August 1939, pp. 125–26; *G.D.*, D, 7, Nos. 154, 190; Siebert, pp. 263–65.

34. Compare *G.D.*, D, 7, No. 190, with Ciano, *Diary*, 22 August 1939, p. 126. Note also the reference in von Mackensen's letter to von Weizsäcker of 23 August 1939, *G.D.*, D, 7, No. 226, p. 203; Siebert, pp. 266–68.

35. *D.D.I.*, 13, Nos. 147, 153, 154, 167, 182; *B.D.*, 3d, 7, Nos. 166, 171, 190, 192, 214, 215, 220.

36. *G.D.*, D, 7, No. 227; cf. ibid., Nos. 211, 212. The German minister of finance also met Mussolini, who expressed hope that war might be avoided but doubted that it would (*Saint*

If Ciano was certain that a general war was imminent and that Italy should stay out, the Duce was wavering between his bellicose inclinations and his fear of appearing to betray his German ally on the one hand and his recognition of Italian unpreparedness, exhaustion of resources in fighting for four years in Ethiopia and Spain, and opposition to war on the part of almost all his advisers on the other.[37] He authorized Ciano to work on a compromise formula under which Germany would receive Danzig as a down payment and other concessions in some sort of conference that, like the Munich one, he would grace with his presence; but he would soon discover that neither side was interested. The English did not trust Hitler to keep his word after his recent breach of the Munich agreement and did not in any case want to urge concessions on Poland in the face of German threats,[38] while a peaceful settlement was the last thing Hitler wanted.

The different view Italy took of the situation and the possibility that in the face of Western determination Italy might abstain from war were known in London and Paris, and during the days after 23 August every effort was made to encourage this development.[39] In line with a suggestion of French Prime Minister Daladier, President Roosevelt also appealed to the Italians to use their influence for the maintenance of peace. With the defeat of the administration's effort to have the neutrality law amended, neither this appeal nor a subsequent one to Hitler could have much effect; but in addition to focusing public attention on Germany's determination to start a war, this American initiative did serve to remind the Italian government of the dangerous implications of a wider conflict.[40]

Into this situation came von Ribbentrop's telephone call of the night of 24–25 August, as a result of which Ciano first succeeded and then failed to secure a decision by Mussolini to stay out of the coming war for the time being. The "strong man" of Italy swung back and forth repeatedly; Hitler's letter of 25 August reached him during the hours of alternating moods.[41] Now he had to decide on an unequivocal answer. He could

---

Siège, No. 118; Schwerin von Krosigk to von Weizsäcker, 26 August 1939, Bundesarchiv, R 2/24243, ff.15–17). On this trip, see Lutz Schwerin von Krosigk, *Memoiren* (Stuttgart: Seewald, 1977), pp. 192–95. The Germans were careful never to tell the Italians about the secret protocol to their pact with the Soviet Union since it went far beyond what the Germans and Italians had earlier discussed as possible in a rapprochement with Russia (Siebert, pp. 277–78).

37. Summary in Hofer, pp. 232–33. Note the analysis of the situation by the British ambassador, Sir Percy Loraine, on 20 August (*B.D.*, 3d, 7, Nos. 96–97); by 2:30 on 23 August he was confident that Italy would not join Germany (ibid., No. 173). Cf. *G.D.*, D, 7, No. 438. A summary of the Italian military deficiencies in Siebert, pp. 290–94.

38. Siebert, pp. 282–84.

39. Hofer, pp. 33–35. See also COS 965, "Attitude of Italy in War," 24 August 1939, CAB 53/54.

40. For German reaction to the defeat of the proposed neutrality law revision, see "Vertrauliche Informationen," 19 July 1939, Bundesarchiv, Oberheitmann, Z.Sg. 109/1, f.62. On Roosevelt's appeal to the king of Italy, see Hofer, pp. 234–35; *Moffat Papers*, pp. 253–54; Welles to Bullitt tel. 639 of 23 August 1939, 11:00 a.m., State 760c.62/1009A; Langer and Gleason, pp. 188–90.

41. Siebert, pp. 295–98.

promise Germany Italian assistance under circumstances Italy had not foreseen and Germany had kept secret until the last moment—even now the Germans did not reveal that war was to start fourteen hours after von Mackensen delivered Hitler's letter. Or he could follow the advice of Ciano, the king, and many others by telling Hitler that for the time being, Italy would have to stay out. Ciano persuaded the Duce to follow the latter course; and with a heavy heart Mussolini wrote to Hitler, explaining that in view of the war coming much earlier than had been expected when the Pact of Steel was signed, Italy could not join until she had the equipment and the raw materials she needed.[42] The most important single factor leading to the Italian decision had been the certainty of both Mussolini and Ciano that Britain and France would fight alongside Poland; at 5:30 p.m. the Italian answer was phoned to Attolico for transmittal to the impatient Germans. As soon as Hitler had finished his conversation with Coulondre, he learned of the Italian reply. In view of his anticipation of Mussolini's full support,[43] Hitler was stunned. But this was not the only bad news: practically simultaneously with Mussolini's letter Hitler received the news that England had signed an alliance with Poland.[44]

This symbol of the determination of England, of which the Italians had been convinced much earlier, finally suggested to Hitler that his calculations were not as accurate as he had thought. The signature of the Anglo-Polish alliance at this moment was partly a deliberate answer to the German government's possible doubts about England's position and partly a coincidental matter of timing. The discussions for a formal Anglo-Polish pact had been continuing for some time, with much of the delay due to the desire of London so to phrase the treaty as to make it fit with the anticipated treaty of England with the Soviet Union. The Anglo-Polish was seen as subordinate to the Anglo-Soviet treaty text,[45] and as the negotiations for the latter dragged on endlessly through the summer, those for the former were practically suspended.[46] Now that it was obvious there

---

42. *G.D.*, D, 7, No. 271; Ciano, *Diary*, 25 August 1939, pp. 128–29. For von Mackensen's report on Mussolini's certainty that war would be general, see *G.D.*, D, 7, No. 280. I cannot agree with Hofer (p. 279) that the British decision to sign with Poland and the Italian decision to abstain from war were entirely independent of each other except in the narrowest and most technical way. Mussolini and Ciano would hardly have been so worried if they had thought there was a real likelihood that a German-Polish war could be isolated. Siebert's opinion (p. 318) that the British would have been more conciliatory in the final days if they had not known of Italy's intention to abstain is certainly incorrect; the *military* advantages for the Western Powers clearly pointed to an attack by them on Italy—as both sides knew.

43. Note Keitel's comments in the Canaris diary for 17 August 1939, *TMWC*, 26:337; and von Ribbentrop's comments in von Weizsäcker's diary for 25 August 1939, *Weizsäcker-Papiere*, pp. 160–61.

44. There are conflicting reports as to which piece of news reached Hitler first; in any case there was little time between them.

45. See Lord Halifax's comment to Bonnet on 20 May 1939, *B.D.*, 3d, 5, No. 569, p. 609.

46. On these, see Cabinet 33 (39) of 21 June 1939, C 8907/27/55, FO 371/23129; Cabinet 41 (39) of 22 August 1939, C 12011/27/55, FO 371/23130; Cabinet Committee on Foreign Policy, "Anglo-Polish Agreement, Memorandum by the Secretary of State for Foreign Affairs," 16 June 1939, CAB 27/627; *B.D.*, 3d, 6, Nos. 521, 610, 613, 661; 7, Nos. 66, 206.

would be no agreement with the Soviet Union at all, quick steps were taken to finalize the text of the Anglo-Polish one.[47] It was ready for signature on 25 August, the final stages having been hurried because of the obvious urgency of the international situation.[48] Public announcement of the signature at 5:35 p.m. on 25 August thus reached Hitler after he had given Henderson the alliance offer to take to England and had already issued the final order to attack Poland on the next day.

Faced by the two unpleasant surprises, Italian defection and British resolution, both of which were surprises only because he had himself miscalculated, Hitler checked with the military to see whether the attack could still be called off. When the high command of the army responded that they thought this was possible, Hitler ordered the troops back to their stations around 7:30 p.m. Almost all the units could be recalled and the naval action at Danzig could also be stopped in time, but a number of incidents and preparatory steps gave many the clear indication that war had indeed been scheduled for 26 August.[49]

The discussion of the outbreak of World War II has recorded the recall of the order to attack Poland without fully taking into account the implications of the circumstances for an understanding of Hitler's actions in the final days of peace. It must be noted that Hitler had first asked the military whether a recall was even possible, a question that obviously implies his being prepared for the answer that it was already too late; whenever Hitler was certain in his own mind what ought to be done, he told rather than asked his generals. Hitler's decision to go to war, thus, was a real one, not a diplomatic bluff, and he was quite prepared to stick with it in spite of the two pieces of bad news he had received, if the military situation demanded proceeding with it. Since the army's leaders thought they could halt the German war machine in time, however, Hitler had a few days for further diplomatic moves before striking.

When the Führer called off the attack on 25 August, he was by no means abandoning his intention of starting a war against Poland. He had originally called for the army to be ready by 1 September, had then moved up the date to 26 August because he wanted to start as early as possible; he explained to the high command of the army that in his opinion the latest feasible date on which they could start would be 2 September.[50] After the latter date, the previously discussed weather problems would in Hitler's

47. Cabinet Committee on Foreign Policy, "Anglo-Polish Agreement, Memorandum by the Secretary of State for Foreign Affairs," 24 August 1939, CAB 27/627; 61st meeting of the cabinet Committee on Foreign Policy, 25 August 1939, CAB 27/625.

48. The final wording still shows traces of the intended relationship of the Anglo-Polish to the Anglo-Soviet treaty; the text and secret protocol are in Cmd. 6616 of 1945. See also Hofer, pp. 170–72.

49. Hofer, pp. 275–78; *Engel Diary*, 25 August 1939; *Halder Diary*, 25 August 1939. On the German closing of cables on 25 August, see *G.D.*, D, 7, Nos. 331, 334, 335. A quick order to the SS stopped what would have been the premature murder of the concentration camp inmates whose corpses, provided with Polish uniforms, were to be used in the fabricated Polish attack (*Groscurth Diary*, 27 August 1939, p. 188).

50. See *Halder Diary*, 30 August 1939.

opinion prevent victory in the one brief campaign that he wished to wage against Poland. When calling off the operation scheduled for 26 August, therefore, Hitler still felt he had some leeway before the whole project would have had to be scrapped for 1939. As will be seen, he did not in the end use all the days he believed he had available to him but instead ordered the attack when by his own reckoning he could have safely postponed war for one more day. This matter will be discussed later, but first the way Hitler used the days of postponement will be examined briefly.[51]

Hitler postponed the attack only because he had a few days to try to make his original diplomatic strategy work. As General Halder, the army chief of staff, learned on the 26th, Hitler had deferred action in the hope of still isolating Poland by separating Britain and Poland.[52] The alliance offer would, he hoped, arouse sufficient doubts in London or lead the English government so to explore the project that in the process Poland would be abandoned to her fate. Hitler still preferred to fight his wars with Poland and with the Western Powers in sequence rather than at the same time.[53] In a secret speech at the chancellery on 27 August he explained to some of the generals and to members of the Reichstag, who had originally been summoned to hear the war speech Hitler had also postponed, that war was indeed at hand. He was apparently concerned lest any of his associates conclude from what they might have learned about the events of 25 August that there would be no war.[54]

Hitler's negotiating strategy in these days was fairly simple. He checked promptly whether Mussolini's letter declining to join immediately in a war unless Germany provided the needed weapons and war materials was a nominal or a real refusal. He asked what specifically Mussolini wanted, and when he wanted it, only to receive a long list that was partly designed—and looked as if it were designed—to be impossible of fulfillment within any reasonable period of time.[55] As Hitler had explained to Mussolini, he himself was willing to risk war with the West in order to settle accounts with Poland.[56] In the face of the Duce's deep regret over

51. The diplomatic maneuvers of 26 August–3 September 1939 are the subject of an enormous literature, among which Hofer's book stands out as the best. The most recent full treatment, which draws on important new British material, is Aster's. In the account given here, no effort will be made to retrace all the details which, in my opinion, are of only secondary importance anyway. The main purpose of the narrative here is to show the main lines of policies pursued and to illuminate the choices made by key participants.

52. *Halder Diary*, 26 August 1939.

53. *Engel Diary*, 27 August 1939, p. 60; cf. "Bestellungen aus der Pressekonferenz," 26 August 1939, Bundesarchiv, Brammer, Z.Sg. 101/13, f.119.

54. *Halder Diary*, 28 August 1939; Domarus, 2:1276–77; *Hassell Diary*, pp. 79–80; *Groscurth Diary*, pp. 190–91; *Weizsäcker-Papiere*, p. 161. The evidence about this speech of Hitler's is somewhat contradictory, as some of the sources suggest that he expressed a willingness to accept a diplomatic solution as long as Danzig and the Corridor were given to Germany.

55. *G.D.*, D, 7, Nos. 277, 282, 298, 299, 301, 302, 308, 316, 317; Hofer, pp. 238–39; Siebert, pp. 304–7. Ciano wrote in his diary that the list was "enough to kill a bull—if a bull could read it" (26 August 1939, p. 129).

56. Hitler's letter of 26 August 1939, *G.D.*, D, 7, No. 307. Halder cites von Brauchitsch as quoting Hitler on 28 August: "If it comes down to it, I will fight a two front war." Ciano read Hitler's letter as having the same meaning (*Diary*, 27 August 1939, p. 130).

his inability to join in the war, Hitler could only express his acceptance of
Italy's position and ask that Rome at least keep up the pretense that Italy
would fight because Hitler thought that this would contribute to his effort
to keep the Western Powers from intervening. If a general war did break
out, he told Mussolini that Germany would win first in the east and then in
the west, either in the coming winter or in the following spring.[57]

As for Mussolini, he was unhappy enough about Italy's incapacity to
participate in war at that time that he tried to work out new peace plans
and conference proposals during the last days of peace. Without reviewing these projects in detail, one could say by way of summary that his
idea of starting negotiations by the cession of Danzig as a preliminary
concession to Germany was not only unacceptable to the Western Powers
and to Poland,[58] but was totally unacceptable to Hitler. From Berlin the
Duce was discouraged from expecting any possibility of peace and from
thinking that the Germans were at all interested in a negotiated settlement.[59] As Hitler wrote Mussolini on 1 September, he did not want him to
try to mediate.[60]

The Italian dictator did not return to a more belligerent position during
these days of anxious negotiations as he had from time to time in the
period before 25 August. The continued arguments of Ciano, Attolico,
and other figures in the Italian government doubtless contributed to this,
but it is also reasonable to assume that knowledge of Hitler's alliance offer
to England had some part in keeping Mussolini in his less bellicose position. When Hitler had offered to return to the League of Nations in March
1936 right after Italy had left Geneva, there was great resentment in
Rome.[61] Now the Italians learned from London, not from their German
ally, that Germany was offering to defend the British Empire—
presumably against such powers as Italy![62] As Hitler's concentration on
securing his immediate goal of an agreement with Russia had antagonized
the Japanese, so now his single-minded absorption on trying to separate
England from Poland created difficulties with Italy.[63] In the course of
World War II, their aggressive ambitions would bring the three powers
together once again, but hardly out of love for each other.

When, partly in response to British and French appeals to restrain
Germany and partly in hope of stopping a war from which he would have
to abstain, Mussolini tried to halt the spreading conflagration after Ger-

57. *G.D.*, D, 7, Nos. 341, 344–46, 349, 350; Hofer, pp. 239–40.
58. Note *G.D.*, D, 7, No. 351. The Vatican favored this idea; see *Saint Siège*, Nos. 128,
132, 133, 135, 136, 153, 165, 166, 170.
59. *G.D.*, D, 7, Nos. 357, 411, 478; see also ibid., Nos. 395, 417, 418, 444, 467, 474, 500;
D.D.B., 5, No. 142; *D.D.I.*, 13, Nos. 491, 507; Schmidt, p. 456.
60. *G.D.*, D, 7, Nos. 504, 505, 507.
61. Weinberg, *Foreign Policy*, p. 256.
62. In the original statement to Henderson, Hitler had inserted a reservation about his tie
to Italy, but when Göring explained the project to Dahlerus for the enlightenment of the
British government on 27 August, he explicitly referred to any Anglo-Italian conflict in the
Mediterranean as leading to German support of England (Dahlerus, pp. 70–71).
63. Hofer, pp. 312–13. See esp. Ciano's account in his *Diary*, 27 August 1939, pp. 130–31.

many's attack on Poland, his effort would quickly collapse over the issue of German troops pulling back to the pre-hostilities border.[64] From Germany's point of view, any Italian proposal was of use only for possibly affording a few days of additional diplomatic confusion while the German army advanced so rapidly that the war in the east might look to the West as finished and hence not worth joining. But beyond that tactical objective, Berlin was as uninterested in Italy's peace efforts after as before 1 September.[65] Hitler, who had recovered from the surprise of 25 August and continued to have a high regard for the Duce, reassured him on 3 September that any peace would have lasted only a short time, which England and France would have utilized so to strengthen Poland as to make any eastern campaign more time-consuming; now was the best time to fight England and France, and in the final analysis Germany and Italy would have to work and fight together.[66]

Given the evident intention of Mussolini to refrain from joining in the conflict immediately, Hitler could only, as mentioned, try to persuade Italy to keep this fact secret from the Western Powers. There is no evidence that it would have made any difference if he had succeeded in this, but in any case he did not. Late on 31 August, after Hitler had already given the second and final order to attack Poland but when neither Italy nor the Western Powers knew that he had done so, the Italians became so alarmed about the possibility that the resolute British and French would strike at them while Hitler struck at Poland that Ciano by a carefully calculated indiscretion revealed the intention of Italy to stay neutral at that time.[67]

While Hitler awaited the British reply to his alliance offer, he also hoped to continue the process of discouraging France from war in support of Poland. Although he had made no proposal of an alliance to France, he had right after issuing the first order for war given to Coulondre a message for Daladier that he then expected the French government to discuss on the morning of 26 August when hearing of the German invasion of Poland. As it was, Coulondre's report reached Paris late on the night of 25 August, after Hitler had canceled the attack order. There a special meeting of the Committee of National Defense had been held on 23 August to assess the impact of the German-Soviet pact on the French obligation to Poland. There had been unanimous agreement that France should stand by her obligations, that letting Poland down would only confront France with an even more serious situation the following year, and that there was really no alternative to honoring the commitment to fight.[68] There was thus a

64. The accounts of Hofer, Siebert, and Aster cover this abortive project.

65. See *G.D.*, D, 7, Nos. 539, 541.

66. Ibid., No. 565.

67. Ciano, *Diary*, 31 August 1939, pp. 134–35; *B.D.*, 3d, 7, No. 621. Here a comparison of Loraine's telegram with the dramatic account in Ciano's diary supports the reliability of the latter.

68. Text in Bonnet, 2:302–8; Hofer, pp. 217–19. It is worth noting that the French military thought resistance in the east would be prolonged into 1940 (though that calculation did not assume a Soviet invasion of Poland).

general expectation that war was to be expected, and with the possible exception of Bonnet's hope for some action by Mussolini to restrain Hitler, there was little prospect of averting a general war.[69] French perception of the firm position of Britain undoubtedly played a part in contributing to firmness in government circles in Paris.[70] Strength, like weakness, was mutually reinforcing.

Under these circumstances, Daladier's response to Hitler's appeal was a dignified reaffirmation of French determination to honor the existing promise to defend Poland combined with an assurance that all existing problems were susceptible of peaceful resolution. Daladier included a personal appeal of one veteran of the trenches to another not to initiate another conflict certain to be bloody and destructive.[71] As Coulondre reported sadly on his effort to reinforce Daladier's plea for peace in transmitting this letter, Hitler had already made up his mind to attack Poland.[72] Hitler's reply to Daladier's letter was a reiteration of his determination to act against Poland combined with such arguments about the need to revise the peace settlement along the German-Polish border and his prior renunciation of any revision of Germany's western border as he thought might influence the attitude of some French leaders and, when the documents were published on German initiative on 28 August, French public opinion as well.[73] Neither any of this, nor Hitler's reference to the fact that with the new German-Soviet pact Poland faced an entirely new situation and would never be re-created in its old form, nor his hint that French acceptance of a fait accompli by Germany could in the future as in the past make for a "peaceful" adjustment of supposedly unfair portions of the 1919 settlement had any effect in Paris. Peace was still desired there, but not at the price of a new surrender.[74]

In London, the situation was similar. The alliance proposal was discussed there by a cabinet that had been kept briefed on the situation.[75] There was no sign of any inclination to give in to German threats.[76] When Hitler's proposal was studied, therefore, with Henderson in attendance, the effort to try to separate England from Poland was immediately rec-

69. U.S., 1939, 1:356–58. Even Flandin expected the French and British governments to go to war (G.D., D, 7, Nos. 258, 294). On French news about and assessments of the probable actions of other countries if war came, see U.S., 1939, 1:307–8, 365–66. On Bonnet's views, see also D.D.B., 5, No. 116.

70. Note, e.g., U.S., 1939, 1:376.

71. French Yellow Book, No. 253; G.D., D, 7, No. 324; cf. B.D., 3d, 7, No. 343.

72. French Yellow Book, No. 261. No German record of this conversation appears to have survived.

73. G.D., D, 7, Nos. 354, 376; French Yellow Book, No. 267; Bullitt Papers, pp. 360–61. Of interest is Flandin's criticism of Hitler's letter for making no reference to Polish independence or access to the sea (G.D., D, 7, No. 370), both points which even the most ardent advocate of concessions to Germany considered essential.

74. Hofer, chap. 6.

75. Cabinet 42 (39) of 24 August 1939, C 12123/15/18, FO 371/22978; G.D., D, 7, No. 287.

76. Henderson had telegraphed the text of Hitler's offer so that it was being examined in London even before the ambassador arrived there; see Halifax diary for 25–27 August 1939, C 20648/15/18, FO 371/22990; Cadogan Diary, 25 August 1939, p. 201.

ognized. The significance of Hitler's suggesting an Anglo-German agreement *after* Germany had dealt as she saw fit with Poland was also understood. In spite of Göring's attempt to reinforce the impact of Hitler's offer by using Dahlerus as an unwitting agent of pressure, the response prepared in London insisted on reversing the sequence of developments. First there would have to be a peaceful and fairly negotiated settlement of Germany's differences with Poland, and only then could there be any serious consideration of other problems in Anglo-German negotiations. The English were indeed interested in good relations with Germany and did their best to emphasize that interest, but all such prospects would be illusory if a German use of force in relations with Poland led to the general war predicted as the certain result of such action in Chamberlain's letter of 22 August.[77] The government in London, which had carefully kept the Dominions informed on the development of the crisis, now had the bulk of the Commonwealth in favor of its position.[78] Britain's response to Hitler's proposal was taken back to Berlin by Henderson on 28 August.[79]

The alliance offer itself had not been taken seriously as a subject for detailed examination. Hitler's suggestion as interpreted by Göring meant that Germany would support the British Empire against Italy, Japan, and the Soviet Union.[80] An offer of that kind, coming from Italy's ally, Japan's Anti-Comintern Pact partner, and the Soviet Union's newfound friend, did not inspire confidence in London. Instead, the British had succeeded in securing Poland's agreement to direct German-Polish negotiations on outstanding differences, and this agreement was officially communicated to Berlin in the British reply.[81] The choice, as Lord Halifax informed the American ambassador in London, was clearly up to Hitler: he could have friendship with England, a fair deal for Poland, and no war, or, if he preferred, the destruction of Poland and a world war.[82]

Hitler had already made his choice. On the day Henderson returned to Berlin with the British reply, von Brauchitsch told Halder that Hitler had tentatively set 1 September as the date for beginning the war and would

77. The British deliberations are summarized in Hofer, chap. 7, and Aster, chap. 13. Drafts of an answer to Hitler may be found in PREM 1/331. The cabinet discussions of 26 August (No. 43) and 27 August (No. 44) are in C 12549/15/18, FO 371/22980, and C 12405/15/18, FO 371/22979. Messages from Carl Goerdeler urging the British government to hold firm were also received at this time; see Minute by Mr. Jebb, 27 August 1939, C 12211/15/18, FO 371/22978; also C 12878, C 12789/15/18, FO 371/22981.

78. See FO 371/23961, passim; *Canadian Documents,* Nos. 999ff.; Cabinet 43 (39) of 26 August 1939, C 12549/15/18, FO 371/22980. See *G.D.,* D, 7, No. 261, for Mackenzie King's appeal to Hitler of 25 August, warning that Canada would join England in war.

79. Text in *B.D.,* 3d, 7, No. 431.

80. Ibid., No. 408. It should also be remembered that it was on 29 August that the London authorities received a slightly amended version of Hitler's speech to the generals of 22 August (ibid., No. 314; C 12341/15/18, FO 371/22979; see above, chap. 13, nn.345–47). Nothing in Hitler's speech was likely to attract support for a reversal of England's policy in London.

81. *B.D.,* 3d, 7, Nos. 354, 411, 420; Kennedy tels. 1223 of 24 August and 1293 of 28 August 1939, State 760c.62/943, 1103; Hofer, p. 314.

82. Kennedy tel. 1278 of 27 August 1939, State 760c.62/1059.

inform him if there were to be any change. Hitler would still prefer to split Britain and Poland but was determined to attack the latter even at the risk of a wider war.[83] At the time when the German army, therefore, was in the last stages of a secret but full mobilization, which had begun on 26 August even though the attack order had been canceled, the Polish government was still being urged by the Western Powers to defer its mobilization lest the blame for the outbreak of war fall on Poland in any future discussion analogous to that about the sequence of mobilizations in 1914.[84]

When Hitler received the British reply on 28 August, he quickly saw that the projected alliance had not had the effect of driving a wedge between England and Poland as he had hoped and that another approach would be needed for the same purpose. He would now utilize the British statement of Poland's readiness for direct German-Polish negotiations to demand the appearance of a Polish plenipotentiary in Berlin on 30 August, the day after so insisting to Sir Nevile Henderson.[85] If the Poles refused to comply with this repetition of the procedure used with Hácha in March, Hitler could blame his subsequent attack on Poland on the intransigence of the latter and hope that in such a situation Poland would be isolated. If, however, a Polish plenipotentiary did appear in Berlin on 30 August as demanded, the Germans would toss on the table such demands as to assure a breakup of the negotiations on 31 August, with war starting on 1 September just the same and with all blame placed by German propaganda on the obstinacy of the Polish representative and government.[86]

As Hitler put forth the demand for an immediate Polish surrender, the German propaganda machinery was attuned to the situation. The wild German press campaign against England was to be toned down and there were to be no personal attacks on Chamberlain.[87] On the other hand, stories of Polish "atrocities" against Germans in Poland were to dominate the newspapers. Whether or not anybody inside or outside Germany believed in these atrocities was considered unimportant; the critical point was to play them up.[88] While this was the German propaganda posture on 29 August, in the chancellery Hitler took the position among his advisers

83. *Halder Diary*, 28 August 1939; cf. *Groscurth Diary*, 27 August 1939, p. 187.

84. Hofer, pp. 331–32; *Biddle Papers*, p. 83; Biddle tel. 232 of 30 August 1939, State 760c.62/1211; *U.S.*, 1939, 1:388. For the bad effect that this delay had on the Polish military effort, see the report by Major-General A. Carton de Wiart of October 1939 in C 16886/27/55, FO 371/23131.

85. *G.D.*, D, 7, Nos. 384, 421; *B.D.*, 3d, 7, Nos. 450, 455, 490, 493, 501, 502, 508. Hitler was, of course, not interested in exploring the idea of a peaceful settlement of the German-Polish dispute as a first step toward improving Anglo-German relations.

86. This strategy is quoted in summary form in the *Halder Diary* for 29 August.

87. "Vertrauliche Informationen," 29 August 1939, Bundesarchiv, Oberheitmann, Z.Sg. 109/2, ff.128–29; Dertinger, "Anweisungen und Information," 29 August 1939, Bundesarchiv, Brammer, Z.Sg. 101/13, f.123.

88. Dertinger, "Bestellungen aus der Pressekonferenz, 29.8.39, Anweisung Nr. 923 (Vertraulich)," Bundesarchiv, Brammer, Z.Sg. 101/12, f.122.

that he wanted a little war; that if the other powers joined in that would be their fault, but that in any case, *a* war was needed.[89]

Hitler was not to be disappointed this time. Beck wanted peace; and whatever the Polish underassessment of German might, overassessment of their own strength, and overconfidence in the power of their French and British allies, there was a clear understanding of the danger to Poland if war came. But as the British ambassador to Poland commented on the scheme Hitler had given Henderson, "they would certainly sooner fight and perish than submit to such humiliation."[90] Beck was not another Hácha or von Schuschnigg. On the other hand, if Hitler thought that his new tactic would in any way influence London to abandon Poland, he was totally mistaken.[91] On the contrary, the British government immediately let it be known in Berlin that the demand for the appearance of a Polish plenipotentiary in Berlin on 30 August was quite unreasonable in their eyes, and they implicitly conveyed the same opinion to Warsaw by being careful not even to inform Poland officially of this preposterous demand until after the 30 August deadline had already passed.[92] The British government was all in favor of a negotiated settlement arrived at in a neutral location by talks in a calm atmosphere and without threats of war; they were careful to urge both the Germans and the Poles to pursue such a course, but they would not badger the Poles into concessions as Henderson, for example, was urging.[93]

On 30 August, the day on which Hitler expected that either there would be a Polish negotiator to be confronted with impossible demands or, lacking that, a split between England and Poland, he set the schedule for the beginning of war. As already tentatively fixed on 28 August, the attack on Poland was now scheduled for the early morning of 1 September. If the talks with London made a further postponement necessary, the attack could be shifted to 2 September; the army would be informed by 3:00 p.m. on the 31st if the situation called for another day's wait. After 2 September the planned attack would have had to be canceled altogether.[94]

Very revealing, and sometimes overlooked in the literature on the subject, is the fact not only that Hitler held to the 1 September date rather than allow the additional day of negotiations his own schedule permitted but that in the event he could see no reason even to await his 3:00 p.m. deadline on the 31st. The order to attack on 1 September reached the high command of the German army by 6:30 a.m. on 31 August, and by 11:30 a.m.

89. *Engel Diary*, 29 August 1939, pp. 60–61.

90. *B.D.*, 3d, 7, No. 512. See also Biddle tel. 201 of 25 August 1939, State 760c.62/998, and tel. 204 of 24 August 1939, State 760c.62/1021; *Biddle Papers*, p. 85.

91. For indirect evidence that Hitler may have thought this strategy would work, see the comments of Jodl, which von Brauchitsch repeated to Halder at 6:00 p.m. on 29 August, in the latter's diary. Jodl's conclusion about the general impression that England was "soft" in regard to a general war presumably reflects Hitler's views.

92. *B.D.*, 3d, 7, Nos. 504, 538, 539; Hofer, pp. 337, 341.

93. On Henderson's last-minute efforts and motives, note *Lipski Papers*, pp. 569–70.

94. *Halder Diary*, 30 August 1939.

it was also known there that Hitler had decided to attack although intervention of the Western Powers probably could not be avoided.[95] War, even a general war, in other words was not the last resort when all avenues for negotiations had been explored to the last minute, but was rather perceived by Hitler as the desired procedure to be adopted at the earliest moment circumstances seemed to allow.

By the afternoon of 31 August, Hitler had regained some hope of isolating the war with Poland he had already ordered. He thought that the moves now being made by the Soviets, in part at Germany's request, together with the Italian pretense of joining in, as he also had asked, would contribute to deterring the Western Powers from intervening; but he attributed the greatest possible impact to the publicity he intended to give the demands on Poland which he planned to present to the Reichstag the next day when he explained the outbreak of war which would have occurred earlier that morning.[96]

What was this set of demands, the publication of which Hitler expected to have such an enormous effect both at home and abroad?[97] While Hitler waited for the British response to his insistence that a Polish negotiator appear on 30 August with full powers to agree to whatever Germany demanded, a set of proposals was prepared in Berlin by some of the officials in the foreign ministry and with some participation by Hitler himself.[98] Three points concerning this lengthy document are critical. In the first place, it was phrased in such a fashion as to give the appearance of moderation so that it could serve as an excellent propaganda device to enrage the German public at Poland's refusal to agree and simultaneously discourage England and France, or at least elements in each country, from going to war in support of Poland under such circumstances. In view of the few days Hitler believed he had left to start a war in 1939, the utilization of the demands for such propagandistic purposes required that they must assuredly not become the subject of actual negotiations which were certain to take time. Hence the second facet of the use of this document by Hitler was that it would not be given to the Poles either via

95. "Mitwirkung des Westens angeblich nicht zu vermeiden; trotzdem Führerentschluss zum Angriff" (Halder Diary, 31 August 1939). See also the subsequent comments of von Weizsäcker about 30 August in Weizsäcker-Papiere, p. 163.

96. See Halder's account of Hitler's comments to von Brauchitsch repeated by the latter at 6:00 p.m. on 31 August (Halder Diary). It is, of course, possible that Hitler exaggerated his own hopes of limiting the war to calm the doubtful von Brauchitsch; however, the comment attributed to Göring that the impression was that England would stay out suggests that Hitler, while aware of the risk of a general war, really did still have some hopes of a small one (ibid.). Siebert (p. 327) attributes Hitler's early decision to a desire to forestall new peace moves by Mussolini.

97. Halder cites von Brauchitsch as quoting Hitler: "Grösste Wirkung auf deutsches Volk und Welt."

98. Hofer, p. 496, n.73, summarizes the then available scanty and contradictory evidence. Hitler's comment quoted in the Groscurth diary for 29 August (p. 192 and n.437) suggests a substantial role for Hitler himself in the preparation of the document. See also Lipski Papers, p. 601; Weizsäcker-Papiere, p. 162. The document itself is in G.D., D, 7, No. 458.

the German embassy in Warsaw or the Polish embassy in Berlin. Although by a variety of routes the Poles learned unofficially about the document's contents on 31 August, it was not officially handed to the Polish ambassador in Berlin until the evening of 1 September when war had already started.[99] Whether the document would have been handed to a Polish negotiator had one appeared on 30 August is very doubtful, given what is known of Hitler's plans for that contingency.[100] In any case, the third and equally critical requirement, if the document were to serve the purpose Hitler intended, was that it not be transmitted to the English either. There was always the "danger," as Hitler had repeatedly said, that he would be confronted by a last-minute compromise proposal and pushed to the negotiating table as had happened at Munich. The obvious way to avoid the risk of having his proposal accepted or responded to by an alternative offer was to keep it secret, or at least not let it be fully known, until the supposedly generous offer had expired. This last point explains both Hitler's timing and von Ribbentrop's conduct at his most stormy meeting with Henderson.

When Hitler gave Henderson his demand for the prompt appearance of a Polish plenipotentiary, he could not know precisely when the English reply would be delivered. Obviously under the circumstances the London government would move as quickly as possible, but there was no way of knowing whether the answer would be delivered the next day, 30 August, or on 31 August. If it arrived on the latter date, and especially if it came in the afternoon or evening, the attack on Poland would have had to be postponed to 2 September; precisely because the English government was anxious to do everything possible to avoid war and therefore hurried its answer so that it was delivered in the night of 30–31 August, Hitler did not need the extra day and, being in a great hurry, could start the war on 1 September.

At the meeting in which Henderson presented the British reply at midnight on 30–31 August, von Ribbentrop had his instructions from the Führer. In a dramatic conversation Henderson read the British response, which pointed out the impossibility of acting as quickly as the Germans had demanded and called for calm, direct German-Polish negotiations on the German demands in a manner recognizing the vital interests of both with arrangements made to avoid incidents in the interim.[101] The German foreign minister constantly interrupted, and, in accordance with Hitler's instructions read but refused to give Henderson a copy of the German "generous offer" which he declared lapsed. The two men almost came to blows as Henderson, the most sincere and enthusiastic advocate of concessions to Germany, recognized that here was a deliberate effort to

99. See *Lipski Papers*, pp. 569–70, 608–9; Krausnick, "Legenden," p. 235, n.76.

100. See also the perceptive summary by the Belgian minister in Berlin in *D.D.B.*, 5, No. 152.

101. *B.D.*, 3d, 7, Nos. 543, 547.

provoke war and cover aggression with a feeble alibi.[102] If Henderson was both angry and despondent, von Ribbentrop was extremely proud of himself for this performance. As State Secretary von Weizsäcker concluded his diary entry for that day: "So now we again face war. R.[ibbentrop] goes home beaming."[103]

The various last-minute attempts to restart negotiations are of interest only insofar as they illuminate the concern of a number of individuals involved to leave no stone unturned in the search for peace and Hitler's determination to let nothing interfere with his decision to attack Poland on 1 September regardless of what the Poles might or might not be persuaded to do diplomatically and even though the intervention of the Western Powers now looked practically certain.[104] Shortly after noon on 31 August, Hitler formally signed the general directive for the attack on Poland early the next day, late in the evening of the same day von Weizsäcker passed out the communiqué containing Germany's proposals so that they could be broadcast that night, and on the following day Hitler gave his speech to the Reichstag expatiating on the evils of Poland, the generosity of Germany, and the need for Germany to fight.[105] When Hitler spoke, the faked incidents to prove a Polish attack on Germany had already been staged for propaganda exploitation, the guns of the *Schleswig-Holstein* had opened fire on the Polish garrison of the Westerplatte in Danzig, and German troops had everywhere crossed the border into Poland.[106]

102. Official records of this meeting are in *G.D.*, D, 7, No. 461; *B.D.*, 3d, 7, Nos. 570, 571, 574, 588. For Henderson's comments, ibid., No. 628; his subsequent account is in his memoirs, pp. 284–87. The interpreter, Schmidt, has described it in his memoirs, pp. 456–60. Hofer has summarized the accounts of the meeting and comments on it, pp. 338–39, 344–48. On Hitler's instructions to von Ribbentrop not to let the text of the demands out of his hands, see *G.D.*, D, 7, No. 513; *B.D.*, 3d, 7, Nos. 682, 684; *Hassell Diary*, pp. 82, 84; testimony of von Ribbentrop, *TMWC*, 3:279; 10:317. The text of the German demands was sent to the German embassy in London during the same night, but with the instructions to keep them secret (*G.D.*, D, 7, No. 458). Schmidt (p. 460) quotes Hitler as saying subsequently: "I needed an alibi, especially with the German people, in order to show them that I had done everything to maintain peace. For that reason I made this generous proposal for settling the Danzig and Corridor question."

103. "Damit stehen wir von Neuem vor dem Krieg. R. geht strahlend nach Hause" (*Weizsäcker-Papiere*, p. 162). Von Weizsäcker's slightly elaborated subsequent account of the same events is printed ibid., pp. 162–63.

104. The Halder diary for 31 August can be used as a good control because the army had to know whether this time the attack order given that day was likely to be recalled again. It must be remembered that Halder and von Brauchitsch were among the very few who knew that Hitler had left himself the possibility of starting war on 2 September, so that after their experience of 25 August they had to be especially careful. For von Brauchitsch's attitude of total resignation, see *Weizsäcker-Papiere*, p. 164; *Hassell Diary*, p. 75.

105. *G.D.*, D, 7, Nos. 482, 493; *TMWC*, 34:456–59; Domarus, 2:1311–18.

106. On the propaganda exploitation of the faked incidents, see "Vertrauliche Informationen, 4. Ergänzung," 1 September 1939, Bundesarchiv, Oberheitmann, Z.Sg. 109/3, f.13. On developments in Danzig, see Kuykendall dispatch 239 of 11 September 1939, State 760c.62/1302. (Kuykendall had been told on 5 September by the German consul general, Martin von Janson, that the events of 1 September had been planned for the preceding week but had been postponed because of the prospect of talks with England, an indication of the extent to which the German authorities in Danzig had had to be informed by Berlin.)

The Poles, as the Germans had expected, fought to defend themselves; and though defeated in their homeland by the German army, which was joined on 17 September by the Red Army, the armed forces of the Polish state would continue to fight elsewhere until the German surrender of 1945. The only question on 1 September was whether or not Poland's allies would go to war with Germany. Whatever hopes Hitler might still have had in this regard would be proved erroneous. If the German public hardly needed much convincing of the evils of a revived Poland and the desirability of seizing portions of it by force, there was no way of persuading England and France to abandon Poland to the tender mercies of a Hitler who had destroyed Czechoslovakia and whom they suspected, correctly as we now know, of turning on them as soon as he felt ready.

The cabinet in London had been following the crisis carefully; both among the professionals in the Foreign Office and among the ministers themselves the nature of German diplomacy in the final crisis was fully understood.[107] The cabinet had supported a firm line on 28 August and agreed on the following day that Hitler's idea of having a Polish plenipotentiary appear on the 30th was out of the question, Chamberlain being especially firm in this regard.[108] When the cabinet met on 1 September, news of the German attack had already been received, and Chamberlain opened with a statement "that the Cabinet met under the gravest possible conditions. The event against which we had fought so long and so earnestly had come upon us. But our consciences were clear, and there should be no possible question where our duty lay."[109] Neither the deficiencies in England's military preparations[110] nor the basic pacific inclinations of the cabinet affected a consensus that England's going to war was purely a question of timing.

The projects launched by the German and Italian governments quite independently of each other in the next few days would receive the same response from London. The Germans still hoped to separate England from Poland in order to have an isolated war. The Italians hoped to stop the whole war to avoid having to defer their own participation in hostilities. When the German government sent a feeler in the evening of 2 September to invite Sir Horace Wilson to fly to Germany to meet Hitler and von Ribbentrop, Wilson responded that first German troops would have to

107. See the notes made in the Foreign Office on *B.D.*, 3d, 7, Nos. 418 and 467 in C 12234 and 12338/15/18, FO 371/22978 and 22979. The Foreign Office reflection of 22 September 1939 on the outbreak of war was: "Hitler wanted his pretext and would have found it even if he had been dealing with the Archangel Gabriel" (Minute by Sir Orme Sargent, C 14016/54/18, FO 371/23028).

108. Cabinet 45 (39) of 28 August 1939, C 12451, C 12452/15/18, FO 371/22979; Cabinet 46 (39) of 30 August 1939, C 12552/15/18, FO 371/22980. See also the note of Halifax to Cadogan of 30 or 31 August 1939 about any discussion of peace taking place *outside* German territory in PREM 1/331A.

109. Cabinet 47 (39) of 1 September 1939, C 13238/15/18, FO 371/22982.

110. Note General Ironside's comment on Chamberlain in his diary, pp. 388–89. See also Aster, chap. 14.

withdraw from Poland, otherwise England would fight.[111] In response to
the previously mentioned soundings from Rome about a possible peace
conference, the British cabinet took the same line: there would be no
negotiations unless German troops withdrew from Poland and the status
quo were restored in Danzig. Otherwise war was to be declared.[112] It is
true that there was considerable confusion over the timing of an ultimatum to Germany, but in this the critical issue was coordination with
France, not the intent to declare war on Germany. In the event, a dramatic
debate in the House of Commons obliged the government to move a few
hours earlier than planned, to push the French on the issue of timing, and
to declare war on Germany several hours before France. There were,
however, no policy differences in the debates in London.[113]

Chamberlain took a clear stand and led his country into war. As a man
of peace and social reform, such an action went against all his personal
preferences and inclinations.[114] Having struggled against war with
persistence, dedication, and stubbornness, he accepted the need to go to
war, as he saw it; but he took it very personally and might have
done well to consider resigning so that others could take on a task
he found necessary but entirely uncongenial. If he was shaken by
having to make the terrible choice of war, it is difficult not to sympathize
with him; perhaps his haggard appearance does him more credit than did
von Ribbentrop's beaming smile. At stake, as Chamberlain well knew,
were the lives and fortunes of millions; and if he agonized over that in a
way Hitler never did, that was hardly to be condemmed in a public figure.
Furthermore, Chamberlain surely knew that after the terrible strain that
the World War, now beginning to be referred to as World War I, had
imposed on Britain, another such conflict would transform his world beyond recognition. But if the terrible choice had to be made, he would
make it. Nothing suggests that he saw the issues very differently from a
young member of the Foreign Office, much later to become well known as
Sir Gladwyn Jebb when representing Britain in the United Nations in the

111. *G.D.*, D, 7, No. 558; *B.D.*, 3d, 9, App. IV. Dahlerus was also used by Hitler and
Göring to try to separate England from Poland at the last moment (Hofer, pp. 392–93).

112. Cabinet 48 (39) of 2 September 1939, C 13239/15/18, FO 371/22982.

113. The matter has been reviewed exhaustively by Aster. An issue of importance that
was not publicly discussed for obvious reasons at the time was that the British military had
advised the *shortest* possible interval between an ultimatum and a declaration of war—
because of concern over a surprise German air attack—while the French military wanted the
longest possible interval in order to complete the process of mobilization (Cabinet 49 [39] of
2 September 1939, C 13240/15/18, FO 371/22982). For Hitler's deliberate delays in responding to diplomatic approaches in order to get the campaign in Poland moving forward, see
Hofer, p. 388.

114. Robert Boothby, a critic of Chamberlain, commenting on the "transparent sincerity"
of Chamberlain's pacific inclinations as expressed at a Foreign Press Association speech on
14 December 1938, said that he had seen anything similar only in George Lansbury, the
famous pacifist who long led the Labor party. Boothby added: "His hatred of war burns him
up . . . . One would not, at first sight, suspect the Prime Minister of being an emotional man;
but when the question of peace or war arises, his passion knows no bounds. This is at once
impressive, formidable, and dangerous" (Robert Boothby, *I Fight to Live* [London: Gollancz, 1947], p. 181).

summer of 1950, who discussed the situation with the German chargé in
London on the evening of 18 August 1939. When Theo Kordt emphasized
that German economic expansion in Central and Eastern Europe was both
essential and compatible with a very large measure of independence for
the countries there, Jebb observed that "the example of Bohemia was not
particularly encouraging." As for a German attack on Poland, that would
touch off a world war in which eventually "the Third Reich would very
probably be smashed." To Kordt's assertion that only the Soviet Union
and the United States would be victors in a general war, with England
facing the prospect of becoming an American Dominion, Jebb responded
that England "would infinitely prefer to be an American Dominion than a
German Gau."[115]

The French government had followed the negotiations of the days after
the exchange between Daladier and Hitler with a sense of the inevitability
of war. They agreed with the position assumed by London in the negotiations, and when informed of Hitler's ultimatum that a Polish plenipotentiary appear in Berlin on 30 August believed that the time limit was
unacceptable, though they did urge that a plenipotentiary be sent.[116] It is
true that Bonnet wanted to try the Italian conference proposal, but he was
overruled by the cabinet meeting in the late afternoon of 31 August.[117]
The German attack on Poland left even Bonnet resigned to war. He did,
however, join the military in counseling a slow procedure for declaring
war, hoping no doubt that the Italian project might still have a chance of
success.[118] There was some opposition to war from two military members
of the Conseil superior de guerre because the military prospects looked so
grim.[119] Nevertheless, the elements in the French government who opposed war could only delay the process of moving toward it.[120] The extra
hours of delay were especially galling to the Poles, who were naturally
eager for maximum support from their French ally; but since the French
had no intention of making any significant military moves in the fall of 1939
anyway, the delay in formal action affected morale but not the course of
military operations.

Prime Minister Edouard Daladier pulled his cabinet together in the face
of what looked to them an impossible situation: France could not abandon
Poland, but the French knew that they would face alone a German army

115. *B.D.*, 3d, 7:555–57. In his memoirs Sir Gladwyn refers to this conversation as having
taken place in May, but that is surely an error (*The Memoirs of Lord Gladwyn* [London:
Weidenfeld & Nicolson, 1972], p. 90). All the Dominions except Ireland declared war on
Germany.

116. See *U.S.*, 1939, 1:383–84; Hofer, p. 355; Adamthwaite, pp. 343–51.

117. *U.S.*, 1939, 1:398–99; see also *Łukasiewicz Papers*, pp. 262–63.

118. *U.S.*, 1939, 1:403–4; *G.D.*, D, 7, No. 538; Hofer, pp. 344–46, 383.

119. The opponents were Generals Charles-Marie Condé and André Gaston Prételat; the
evidence is summarized in Robert O. Paxton, *Parades and Politics at Vichy* (Princeton,
N.J.: Princeton University Press, 1966), pp. 65–66. Since Gamelin had claimed in 1936 that
the French army could not break through in the Rhineland even before the Germans built
any fortifications (*D.D.F.*, 2d, 1, No. 334), it is easy to understand the doubts of 1939.

120. See the comments of Ambassador Bullitt, well informed as usual, in *U.S.*, 1939,
1:408–10; cf. ibid., pp. 411–12; Hofer, p. 389.

they believed would be larger than their own. After the horrendous disaster that the fighting of 1914–18 had meant for France, they now faced a repetition under vastly more difficult and dangerous circumstances. Daladier had agreed to the concessions of 1938; he was not about to repeat that.[121] He appears to have felt more confident of French military strength than in the year before, especially in regard to the air force. Above all, however, he believed that France had no choice but to fight, and it is surely an indication of Daladier's attitude that he utilized the discrepancy between the British and the French ultimatum procedures at the last minute to move forward by twelve hours the French declaration of war.[122] Though he was upset, as were all his associates, by the defection of Russia from any opposition to aggression, it may be that he remembered the most desperate crisis of the Third Republic since 1918. As prime minister he had faced the great riot of 6 February 1934, when the rightist leagues had tried to storm the Chamber of Deputies and when, as again now, the Communists had joined the opponents of the Republic. He had directed the French government's victory of that day, though at the cost of numerous casualties and his own resignation; perhaps he thought that this crisis too could be surmounted, even if the cost would be infinitely greater. With a heavy heart but a firm hand he led a weakened and divided country into its new ordeal.[123]

All other countries were neutral in the conflict, adopting different strategies in the hope of staying out. At the two extremes were the United States and the Soviet Union. While the United States tried to stay out of war by a policy of aid to the Allies, the Soviet Union followed a policy of staying out by aid to Germany. As the war continued and spread, each escalated its own policy. America by more and more extensive aid to Germany's enemies, especially England, Russia by ever greater assistance to Hitler. By the early summer of 1941 a great volume of war materials was being carried across the Atlantic under the Lend-Lease Act passed in March, while simultaneously extra trains were hauling war supplies for Germany from and across the Soviet Union under new German-Soviet trade agreements signed in April. Neither of the two giants would succeed in avoiding participation in the war; both neutrality policies would fail. Almost every other nation also eventually participated, some as victims of attack, some as eager attackers themselves, some at the last minute to participate in the postwar world organization. A flood of blood and disaster of unprecedented magnitude had been let loose on the world. If the details of military operations and the localities of

121. His speech to the Chamber of Deputies on 2 September is in *French Yellow Book*, No. 356. Note Daladier's statement in declining Mussolini's invitation to a conference that he would resign rather than attend a second "Munich" (*B.D.*, 3d, 7, No. 604).

122. See Hofer, p. 591. This action of Daladier's, though known for a long time, has in my opinion not been sufficiently utilized as a clue to his views.

123. Note that he maneuvered Bonnet out of the French foreign ministry into the ministry of justice, taking Bonnet's former portfolio himself, on 14 September. See also *Łukasiewicz Papers*, p. 329.

combat were often vastly different from those of World War I, the fearful anticipation that a new war would be as horrendous or quite likely even worse than the last proved to be all too accurate.

Some of the developments in this great upheaval were initiated and directed by Hitler's Germany, but many flowed from the reactions or initiatives of other countries. The concept Hitler had tried to implement, of a succession of wars, each started on his own initiative against victims of his choosing, each isolated from the other, but victory in each one facilitating a German victory in the next, fell short of realization from the very beginning, when England and France declared war in support of Poland. The failure of the French to mount an offensive in the west in September 1939 almost enabled him to return to his original concept. Germany attacked in the west in 1940 very much the way Hitler had intended after crushing Poland in an isolated war; and his agreement with the Soviet Union enabled him to conduct the campaign in the west with all his forces on one front for the last time in the whole war. But then his thrust was halted by England and soon thereafter the dimensions of the conflict were increasingly out of his control. Even as he marched his armies to their destruction at the hands of the Red Army by invading the Soviet Union, the United States loomed ever more menacing on the horizon; and Japan's advance in East Asia, urged by Germany as a means of diverting the United States from Europe, only contributed to the eventual arrival of American troops on German soil.

A critical element in Hitler's inability to adjust to the altering world balance around him was the fact that he had set out to change it dramatically himself and was prepared for his country to perish in the attempt rather than turn back. Though some may consider him insane for attempting to implement the doctrine of *Lebensraum,* it was the essence of his policies at all times. Even the reality of internal migration westward did not divert a determined Hitler from attempting to lay the foundation for an external migration eastward. On 1 February 1939 he had felt obliged to issue an edict to try to reverse the process of migration within the existing borders which was denuding Germany's eastern provinces of their "Germanic" population.[124] But even such grudgingly admitted reality was not permitted to intrude upon his long-term aims. As Hitler had explained to his military commanders on 23 May, the object of war was not Danzig but the expansion of Germany's *Lebensraum.*[125]

The concept of revising the peace settlement of 1919 in Germany's favor, which he had ridiculed in his writings, remained for him a foolish and rejected alternative even as he used it in his propaganda. If many contemporary observers and some subsequent historians failed to comprehend this, it was certainly always obvious to Hitler himself. In mid-October 1939, at a time when Germany and the Soviet Union were urging

124. A study of "Hitlers Osterlass vom 1. Februar 1939" by Andrzej Brozek is in *Tradition und Neubeginn,* pp. 367–76.
125. *G.D.,* D, 7, No. 433.

the Western Powers to make peace on the basis of an acceptance of what Germany and Russia had done to Poland, the Swedish explorer Sven Hedin, a great admirer of Germany, visited Hitler. The Führer explained that peace would be possible only if the British gave up "the foolish idea of a restoration of Czechoslovakia."[126] The vital point dividing him from the Western Powers was not that of Germany taking over areas inhabited by Germans but rather the seizure by Germany of lands hitherto inhabited by *other* peoples who were to be enslaved or exterminated and replaced by Germans. Under the diplomatic and geographic circumstances of the time, it so happened that the Czechs were the first and the Poles were the second of these peoples, but the process was both the key point in Hitler's whole program and the galvanizing element in making his attack on Poland the occasion for a war wider than he preferred at that time.[127]

It was precisely because Hitler understood all too well that his aims could be realized only by war that he plunged forward. Because he was always peculiarly conscious of his own mortality, and because he recognized that the limited material resources of the Germany he controlled in peacetime would assure him a head start in rearmament for only a few years before other nations caught up, he was in a hurry to start the first of his wars at the earliest possible moment according to his assessment of the diplomatic and military situation. Given the strides beginning to be made by the rearmament of England and France, one must even concede a certain mad logic to his belief that time was running against his cherished goal.

In view of his preference for war, Hitler conducted his foreign policy in 1939 under the personal trauma of Munich. He had shrunk from war then—and attributed such cowardice to everyone else—so he would not be cheated once again of the war he had always intended.[128] Just as his anger at having been deprived of war in 1938 made him all the more determined to have it in 1939, so his postponement of the attack on 25 August left him all the firmer in an almost hysterical fixation to attack a few days later.[129] He would not back off again; his tirade to Dahlerus on 1

126. Sven Hedin, *Ohne Auftrag in Berlin*, pp. 51–56. The German record in *G.D.*, D, 8, No. 263, contains the same sentiment phrased "Czechoslovakia could not be discussed."

127. In writing Chamberlain on 14 August about the situation in German-Polish relations and the proposal to send General Ironside to see Hitler, Halifax wrote that he saw little point in that project: "inasmuch as Hitler's whole line of thought seems to be the familiar one of the free hand in the East, and, if he really wants to annex land in the East on wh. he can settle Germans to grow wheat, I confess I don't see any way of accommodating him" (PREM 1/331, quoted in Aster, pp. 328–29).

128. Several statements of Hitler to this effect made before the outbreak of war have been cited; he was to repeat his own belief in the need for war after 1 September. See his memorandum of 9 October 1939 (*TMWC*, 37:468) and his speech to the army commanders on 23 November 1939 (ibid., 26:329–30; *Groscurth Diary*, p. 414).

129. Hofer, p. 276, summarizes the evidence on the effect of the recall of the attack order on the military and on Hitler's associates as one of giving them the impression of a setback for Hitler and a weakening of his position. Müller's discussion (pp. 416–19) also examines

September in which he declared himself ready to fight England for ten years if necessary[130] surely reflects the views of a dictator who had once balked before the great risk, had then tried to minimize it, and was under no circumstances willing to pull back again. Without war, his whole program and his whole life made no sense to him. The war he started would destroy both.

There is a grim irony in the fact that most of the precautions Hitler took to make sure there would be no diplomatic settlement of the 1939 crisis, no new Munich, were quite unnecessary. Not having agreed to the Munich agreement in good faith, he could never understand how anybody else could have; and hence although he recognized how deeply the Western Powers were chagrined by his destruction of that settlement, he never fully comprehended that their policies were now based on different assumptions. Chamberlain, in particular, was just as determined, though for opposite reasons, that there would be no new Munich; and even had he wanted it, the British Parliament would never have allowed it after 15 March 1939. The Poles were certain to fight for their independence. If the conciliatory Beck was unwilling to accept subordination to Berlin, surely other Polish leaders were if anything even less likely to consider submission a serious alternative. The tragicomedy of midnight 30–31 August was quite unnecessary, however revealing for participant and historian; the danger of having his ostensible demands granted, to which Hitler had succumbed in 1938, simply did not exist in 1939. Had von Ribbentrop handed the demands to Henderson officially, Hitler would still have had his war.

As for the great propaganda operations, they were hardly any more effective or necessary than the last-minute diplomatic ones. It was not necessary to persuade the German public of the need to fight Poland, and it was practically impossible to persuade them of the need to fight England and France. As for the outside world, all the reports of atrocities and incidents dreamed up by the fertile imagination of a Goebbels or a Heydrich were unlikely to persuade anyone who had lived through the German use of similar tactics a year earlier. Perhaps all this noise was necessary for Hitler's self-induced excitement over the situation on Germany's eastern border, steeling him against doubts that might otherwise have assailed a man who on occasion shifted tactics and procedures. Few others were affected; but then the great tragedy of 1939 was that no one else needed to be affected. Hitler alone made the key decision, though those who had contributed to creating such a situation in so important and powerful a country as Germany, as well as those who carried it out without hesitation, have their share of the responsibility.

---

this matter. Though quite accurate in themselves, these discussions omit what appears to me to be more important, namely, the impact on Hitler himself.

130. Dahlerus, pp. 125–26.

Conclusion

**quarter of a century** after 1914 another world war had begun. Whatever the ambitions and hopes of other countries, no country other than Germany would or could initiate a second international conflagration. How had the defeated Germany of 1918 come to play such a role?

By the winter of 1936–37 the initiative in Europe lay with Germany. Her rearmament had advanced to a stage where not only was no country interested in attacking her—that had been the case for many years—but the German government itself felt entirely confident that its territory was safe from attack. Whatever other planning was being worked on, no one in Berlin was spending any time on plans to defend the country. On the diplomatic scene, Germany had found an associate in Italy, was on good terms with both China and Japan in East Asia, and had either drawn the countries of East and Southeast Europe into her orbit or could be reasonably sure of their abstention from effective action against her. Germany's relations with England, France, the Soviet Union, and the United States were admittedly poor; but the former two were neither willing nor able to consider taking the initiative against Germany, while the latter two were preoccupied with domestic concerns, the Great Purge in the Soviet Union, and the depression and New Deal in the United States. The real power relationships created in Europe by the peace settlement of 1919 were slowly emerging into the light from the obfuscations created by the propaganda of Germany, the delusions of others, and the fleeting ambitions of the newly independent states of East and Southeast Europe. Relatively less weakened by the Great War than any other European power, Germany stood forth not only powerful but ominously threatening.

The power of Germany was directed by Adolf Hitler. Careful analyses by scholars have revealed internal divisions, organizational confusions, jurisdictional battles, institutional rivalries, and local deviations behind the façade of monolithic unity that the Third Reich liked to present to its citizens and to the world in word and picture.[1] The fact remains, however, that the broad lines of policy were determined in all cases by Hitler himself. Where others agreed, or at least did not object strenuously, they were allowed the choice of going along or retreating into silence, but on major issues of policy the Führer went his own way. By 1937 few still imagined, as some once had, that they could control, direct, or at least temper the all-powerful leader who had been sought as a savior for Germany and to whose will vast masses of Germans had cheerfully and enthusiastically surrendered their own. Whither would that will direct the vast energies of Europe's most advanced industrial power, and how could anyone inside or outside Germany attempt to thwart the course he chose?

Hitler was preparing for a series of wars each of which Germany would win by launching a quick campaign against an isolated enemy, with victory in each such war helping prepare for the next one by increasing Germany's resources and terrifying others into submission or at least abstention from intervention. Ultimately this sequence would lead to world domination, a perspective most clearly recognizable in Hitler's naval and architectural planning.[2] Before those more distant visions lay the great agricultural lands of Eastern Europe, controlled for the most part by the Soviet Union, while closest to Germany herself were the immediately adjacent countries of Central Europe.[3] The precise details and sequence would have to be determined as the process went forward, but on several aspects of the approach Hitler appears to have had fixed views.

The purpose of the wars was to acquire land for agricultural settlement by Germans. Any German population already in the conquered land would help replace the casualties incurred by conquest and possibly provide men for additional divisions in the German army. The non-German population might temporarily be used for their labor, but they would under no circumstances be "Germanized" culturally; on the contrary, their fate would be expulsion or extermination.[4]

The demographic preparations for German population expansion had been inaugurated in the first months of the National Socialist regime. Programs to support earlier marriage and larger families for "healthy

1. A brief review of some of the literature is in Gerhard L. Weinberg, "Recent German History: Some Comments and Perspectives," in Alexander Fischer (ed.), *Deutschland-Russland-Amerika: Festschrift für Fritz Epstein* (Wiesbaden: Steiner, 1978), pp. 358–68.

2. The former is best explained by Dülffer; the latter by Thies. See also Weinberg, *Foreign Policy*, p. 7.

3. Andreas Hillgruber has used the term *Stufenplan* or step-by-step procedure to describe Hitler's concept; as the text shows, my view is somewhat different.

4. The experiments with mass, as opposed to individual, sterilization did not start until well into World War II.

Aryans" on the one hand, and procedures requiring the sterilization of those supposedly carrying hereditary defects were both instituted in 1933. On the other hand, insistence that the Jews were the most immediate enemies of internal German racial purity as well as the greatest threat to external territorial expansion meant that the first measures against Jews would also form part of the activities of the new regime in its early months. The processes of consolidation at home and then of expansion abroad would lead to the escalation of both facets of the racial policy.

Population growth was a key subject of German propaganda and the education system during the 1930s; the outbreak of war would see the inauguration of a vast euthanasia program thought too risky in peacetime but considered feasible under the cover of hostilities, as shown by the backdating to the first day of the war of Hitler's late October 1939 directive for the murders of those considered not fit to live. Similarly, the campaign against the Jews escalated steadily in the years before the outbreak of war, and here too the identification of the most extreme measures with war itself was projected by a revealing shifting of dates. In this instance by postdating rather than backdating, Hitler would explain his program for the murder of Europe's Jews by dating to 1 September the portion of his 30 January 1939 speech referring to the "destruction of the Jewish race in Europe" in the next war.[5]

As for the actual fighting of the wars themselves, Hitler intended that to go quickly, in sudden blows, avoiding the long stalemate of trench warfare in the previous conflict. The isolation of one war from another would facilitate speed: the ability of Germany to concentrate on one enemy or small group of enemies at a time, preferably alongside allies, would dramatically reverse the situation of the World War, in which Germany had been obliged to disperse her forces over several fronts against a host of enemies. The use of tanks and planes would also obviate any possible stalemate and its associated exhausting war of attrition. Unlike the artillery of the previous war, which had to be moved forward after each advance, airplanes could operate from the same forward bases for considerable distances. While the use of planes would provide wings for the artillery, tanks would add wheels, treads, and armor to the ground assault forces, enabling them to move forward at a speed far greater than that of the slogging infantry in which Hitler himself had served. Germany built up a major air force and an array of armored vehicles, and Hitler personally urged on these developments.

The expansion of Germany's mechanized forces and air power of course served to increase the danger to Germany from a blockade in time

5. The point is discussed in Martin Broszat, "Hitler und die Genesis der 'Endlösung,'" *Vierteljahrshefte für Zeitgeschichte*, 25, No. 4 (Oct. 1977), 751, n.22. Broszat's suggestion that the misdating was intentional is supported by its repetition in the set of Hitler's speeches edited by the head of his personal secretariat, Philipp Bouhler, *Der grossdeutsche Freiheitskampf*, 3 vols. (Munich: Eher, 1940–44), 2:222; 3:197.

of war unless she could secure adequate quantities of petroleum products by purchase from neighbors or by synthetic processes based on her own rich coal deposits. The German government had begun as early as 1933 with a program for a large-scale synthetic oil industry; and when the foreign exchange crisis of 1936 had suggested to some that a continued program of expanding armaments would bring serious problems, Hitler turned over the matter to Göring with instructions to let no financial or other obstacle stand in his way. Simultaneously, the vastly increased needs for steel would be met by the expansion of domestic sources, using domestic low-grade ores rather than greater ore imports. As for importing oil, that could be done at least in part by shifting purchases to Rumania, which in the past had not been a competitive supplier to Germany because of high costs. In the case of synthetic oil made from coal and of steel made from what German industrialists derisively called "potting-soil," the government simply guaranteed acceptance of whatever was delivered at whatever price was needed. The possibility of importing oil from the Soviet Union would play an important role in the German desire for an agreement with that country in 1939, but like synthetics and the imports from Rumania, Hitler saw this as a short-term expedient. The wars Hitler intended to wage would provide her with the oil resources she would need for later wars.[6] Similarly, the vast construction projects of the German navy looked to a future when Germany commanded not merely her own and her satellites' resources but conquered lands, particularly in the Caucasus area, that would provide the fuel needed for Germany's super-battleships of 56,000 tons.[7]

Hitler knew very well that the construction of such huge ships would take years, which was precisely why he insisted on their early development. In the immediate future, more immediate goals would be attained, goals for which the army and air force units Germany already had or could soon expect to have would be in his judgment entirely adequate. Either before or after the first isolated war he would seize Austria. Quite correctly he foresaw that the Austrian government would be reluctant to use armed forces to defend the country against a German invasion; all that was needed, therefore, was the acquiescence of Italy without whose participation no one could save the small country. The split between England and France on the one hand and Italy on the other over Ethiopia had opened up this possibility, and the joint intervention of Germany and Italy on the side of the rebels in the Spanish Civil War kept that possibility open once Italy had won her war in East Africa. The prospect of gain at the side of an impressive Germany inclined Mussolini in the direction of

6. For a discussion of the great emphasis placed by the Germans on the actually somewhat marginal Polish oil fields and their negotiations over this matter with the Soviet Union, see Weinberg, *Germany and the Soviet Union*, pp. 56, 57, 60, 70.

7. None of these monsters was ever completed, but the keels of the first two had been laid down before 1 September 1939 (Dülffer, p. 570).

Berlin, while signs that the German government would agree to the transfer of the German inhabitants of South Tyrol across the Brenner border served to reduce the Italian government's apprehension over having a strong Germany rather than a weak Austria on the other side of that border.

The available evidence shows that Hitler intended to take advantage of Italy's favorable attitude, as well as the likely disinterest of England and France as long as Italy stood aside, to move to seize Austria in the spring or summer of 1938. An incident was to be staged inside Austria that would provide the excuse for a military intervention that no one would resist. At first Hitler appears to have thought of arranging the murder of the German military attaché or the German ambassador in Vienna; subsequently he intended to have less spectacular but more widespread incidents within the country provoke the Austrian government into repressive measures against which appeals would be sent to Hitler and used as a pretext for invasion. In the event, the interaction between events inside the two countries provided the occasion for German occupation of Austria without the need for staged provocations—though an appeal for troops was faked—but as an approach to action the procedure of using provoked incidents would remain an important part in Hitler's tactical system.

The first war, originally conceived as coming either before or after the annexation of Austria, was to be against Czechoslovakia. In this war, the Hungarians and Poles would be encouraged to join in, their ambitions for territory to be satisfied at the expense of the victim while their joining in would help deter aid for Czechoslovakia by making her appear in a helpless and hopeless position. The diplomatic isolation of the prospective victim of attack would be assisted by the manipulation of her massive German national minority, whose real and imagined grievances would be trumpeted to the world as signs that the new state created at Versailles deserved whatever fate befell her and was in any case undeserving of the great sacrifices that would be required for her defense. Those sacrifices were to be made to appear especially great by much noise about the German fortifications being built on Germany's western frontier and by an alliance policy designed to confront England and France with dangers around the globe should they contemplate intervention.

It was for this reason that Hitler was so interested in discovering in early May 1938 that Mussolini had not only tolerated Germany's annexation of Austria but had no particular objection to whatever Germany might want to do to Czechoslovakia either. Hitler thereupon immediately set out to arrange the attack on Czechoslovakia to take place later the same year, and although the May Crisis soon after caused him to make minor alterations in his procedures, the decision to go ahead had already been taken. The alignment with Mussolini, in spite of the absence as yet of any formal alliance, would conjure up dangers for England and France in the Mediterranean—how could they expect to help Czechoslovakia by the sort of operation the Allies had mounted at Salonika in the World War with a possibly hostile Italy across their line of communication? Furthermore, the Western Powers would be confronted, Hitler hoped, by even greater dangers in East Asia.

The outbreak of war in the Far East in July 1937 had been most unwelcome to Germany, with her ties to both China and Japan. Berlin postponed a choice as long as possible; but once an attempt at mediation had foundered over Japan's insistence on raising ever higher demands, Hitler took the side of Japan because it accorded with his own inclinations as well as the preferences of his favorite foreign policy adviser, Joachim von Ribbentrop, the new German foreign minister. All the rivalries that had characterized Germany's East Asian policies in the earlier years of National Socialist rule ended abruptly as von Ribbentrop sacrificed Germany's position in China and made a major effort to align Japan more closely with the Axis. It was Hitler's and von Ribbentrop's belief that the closer such an alignment, the more effectively Great Britain could be immobilized in Europe by threats from Japan to her colonial empire in Southeast and East Asia, with Germany immobilizing British policy in East Asia by the obvious threat from Germany against the home islands and from Italy to Britain's Mediterranean lifeline. The exposed position of French Indochina would have a similar restraining effect on France, while, also in regard to France, German strength in Europe could only relieve Japan.

The Japanese, however, in 1938 as in 1939 were unwilling to pledge themselves to the risk of war with the Western Powers while still embroiled in hostilities on the mainland with China. Tokyo's menacing pose indeed worried the British, but until Germany had won her great victory in the west in 1940, the lead among the multitudinous contending factions within the Japanese government was held by those opposed to the risk of war with England and most likely the United States, as against those who would stake the future of the Japanese empire on the rising tide of Axis power. The endless debates over this issue would in 1938 leave everyone wondering which way the balance would tilt, and in 1939 would first encourage and then aggravate the Germans.

If the possibility of threats in the Mediterranean and in East Asia would restrain Britain while Germany attacked Czechoslovakia, the effectiveness of the propaganda about millions of Germans within the intended target of the attack was to be reinforced in its impact on Britain by two further elements. The confusion over the nationality issue—it was being made to appear that the problem was the presence of Germans in the country when what really concerned Hitler was the presence of Czechs—would deter the members of the British Commonwealth from participation in war and would confront London with the choice between standing aside or coming in without several of the Dominions. The nationality issue would also provide the immediate occasion for war by setting the framework within which Germany would stage the incidents that Berlin could trumpet to the world as reason for the attack. Hitler was much impressed by the coincidental factors in the timing of the outbreak of the World War: the assassination of Archduke Francis Ferdinand had led to war in the wrong year—earlier would have been better for Germany[8]—as well as at an unanticipated moment. Such accidental factors could not be allowed to recur; Germany would first decide when to strike and then arrange for the staging of appropriate incidents that would provide a pretext at the "right" time. Once again, as in the case of Austria, Hitler's first thought was directly inspired by Sarajevo; perhaps the German minister in Prague could be assassinated. From this idea he shifted to having the army stage appropriate incidents involving the German minority inside Czechoslovakia, and in the final weeks of the crisis turned the task over to a special crew of Sudeten German thugs, organized into a Free Corps and assigned fixed quotas of incidents to be arranged on each segment of the border.

The careful attention to the propagandistic aspects of starting a war came not only from an interest in deterring other powers from intervening but also from special considerations of international and domestic policy. In the international arena, the debate over the responsibility for the outbreak of the World War had so drawn the attention of peoples and governments to the precise circumstances surrounding the initiation of hostilities that Hitler was very much interested in conducting Germany's procedures in such a fashion that what he considered the clumsy German approach of 1914 would not be repeated. The staging of incidents at the appropriate moment in a secretly, as opposed to publicly, ordered mobilization has to be seen in part from this perspective. On the domestic side, there was not only this concern about the "war guilt" question but also the one over internal cohesion and morale. Since it had become an article of faith among National Socialists, all other German nationalists, and most certainly Hitler himself that Germany had lost the war in 1918 because of the collapse of morale at home rather than defeat in battle, there was great interest in the solidity of public support for any future war. National Socialist indoctrination in the schools and propaganda in the media would prepare the population for any sacrifices that war would entail, but beyond this it was most important that the bulk of the people accept the justice of Germany's cause, the absolute necessity of the resort to arms, and the certainty of victory this time as opposed to the memory of what had happened before.

These considerations all meant that special attention had to be devoted to the whipping up of enthusiasm at home, picturing the specific situation leading to war as leaving Germany no alternative but resort to arms,

8. For an early expression of this view, see *Mein Kampf*, 1:155; for a late one, see Hitler's talk of 26 June 1944 quoted in Speer, *Erinnerungen*, p. 539, n.6.

making the most of the incidents fabricated to provide a pretext for attacking, keeping any war as short as possible, and both preparing for war and fighting war with as little imposition of restrictions and sacrifices on the home front as possible so that no memories of the privations leading to collapse in the previous great war might arise among the people. Everything would be reversed: the war would start under circumstances that appeared just to the Germans and to all others, it would be fought quickly, it would involve a minimum rather than a maximum of privation at home, and it would end with the victory of a unified, not the defeat of a divided, population.

There was still another aspect to Hitler's intention of fighting a series of wars that was present at the beginning of the period under review and became increasingly important thereafter. This aspect was a self-generated time pressure. Both material and personal considerations made Hitler think of war not only as an essential tool for the conquests he intended but as preferable sooner rather than later. The material consideration was simple. Once Germany had by her rapid rearmament gained a head start over her neighbors, the sooner she struck the greater the chances for success. The longer war was postponed, the more likely it would be that rearmament programs inaugurated by others in response to the menace from Germany would catch up with and surpass that of the Third Reich. Lacking in her original borders the economic resources for the continued replacement of one set of weapons by more modern ones, Germany could either strike while she had an advantage over others or see the balance of strength shift to her potential adversaries. The very advantage of Germany's head start would become a disadvantage as other powers brought into production on their greater economic bases more recently developed and more numerous weapons. Germany would therefore have to strike before such a situation developed, a point which Hitler made repeatedly to his associates and which indeed represents an essentially accurate assessment of the situation if Germany were to have even the slightest hope of succeeding in the preposterously ambitious schemes of conquest Hitler intended.[9]

The personal element was simply Hitler's own fear of an early death for himself or, alternatively, the preference for leading Germany into war while he was still vigorous rather than aging. Identifying Germany's fate and future with his personal life and role in its history, Hitler preferred to lead the country into war himself, lest his successors lack the will to do so. He also thought of his age as a factor of importance; it is impossible to ignore his repeated extraordinary assertion that he preferred to go to war at the age of fifty to facing war when fifty-five or sixty years old.[10] In this regard one enters a realm yet to be seriously and reliably explored by the

9. Of the many references to this concern, the one quoted from memory by Speer, *Erinnerungen*, p. 178, may serve as an example.

10. *B.D.*, 3d, 7, No. 248; *G.D.*, D, 7, No. 200. See also chap. 11, n.231, above.

psychohistorians, but one can hardly overlook not only the evidence that in 1938 the decision to attack Czechoslovakia within the year came a few days after fear of cancer had induced him to write his last will but also the references to his personal age and role in the final war crisis of 1939. Here, too, one must accept a certain tragic accuracy in Hitler's perception; whether any other German leader would indeed have taken the plunge is surely doubtful, and the very warnings Hitler received from some of his generals can only have reinforced his belief in his personal role as the one man able, willing, and even eager to lead Germany and drag the world into war.

What, if any, were the prospects of halting or diverting this insistence on war? From inside Germany, any such effort was enormously complicated by the massive support Hitler and his movement enjoyed. Though some were doubtful, the overwhelming majority of Germans were either enthusiastic or passive. In the absence of free elections the precise degree of approval the regime enjoyed is difficult to measure, but one has only to consider the attitude of the German public toward the Weimar Republic to be struck by the depth of support for the National Socialist government, a support which hardly cracked until the final days of World War II and even then would produce practically no signs of political disaffection of the sort widespread in Germany in the last weeks of World War I.[11] It in no way denigrates the good sense and courage of those opposed to the Hitler regime—if anything it redounds to their credit—to note that they were a small minority, certainly in the years examined here. The quarrels and rivalries within the German state and the National Socialist party should not be allowed to obscure the wide consensus about basic assumptions and national goals, at least as understood by most. Certainly one of the most fateful aspects of Hitler's Germany was that however extreme the real break with German tradition that characterizes his system, there were strands in it which in their *initial* stages built on prior traditions, preferences, and policies and appealed to a large proportion of those in the established hierarchies of the country. There might eventually be doubts about principle or practice or both in regard to the more extreme applications of these policies, but their early stages met with approval rather than opposition. Whether it was persecution of Jews or massive rearmament, resettlement of population groups or territorial expansion, the governing apparatus consisted mainly of men willing and even eager to go far enough along these routes for Hitler to commit them willingly or unwillingly to the rest of the way.

This question of support or opposition was most critical with regard to the army. Hitler looked forward to the replacement of the higher officer

11. An introduction to this, as yet hardly explored, subject is in Hans-Adolf Jacobsen, "Die deutsche Katastrophe 1945: Impressionen vom inneren Zusammenbruch," in his *Von der Strategie der Gewalt zur Politik der Friedenssicherung* (Düsseldorf: Droste, 1977), pp. 176–86.

corps by men entirely in tune with his personality, approach, and aims; but inside the army such men were as yet few, far between, and not of sufficient seniority and experience, while the armed units of the SS had still to produce a crop of division and corps commanders, to say nothing of even loftier qualifications.[12] Under these circumstances the time pressure under which Hitler believed himself, the insistence that war must come sooner rather than later, meant that in the period of rearmament and the first of his wars the existing senior leadership of the army was essential to him. He would always regret that he had been unable to adopt Stalin's procedure of destroying the higher officer corps; instead Hitler had had to check tendencies in that direction in June 1934 and to proceed to the replacement of the existing upper levels of the military hierarchy by measured and stealthy rather than sudden and dramatic moves. In the meantime he needed them—but they could be exceedingly dangerous. They were the ones who held the weapons now being produced in ever greater numbers, and their prestige in the country made them the only conceivable alternative focus for the support of large segments of the German public. But the vast majority either agreed with Hitler's early measures or deliberately closed their eyes to the direction in which he was moving, or both. And then, at the very moment when Hitler turned to steps which might arouse apprehension and even opposition, and in fact did have that effect on many higher officers, Hitler accomplished by a quick and shabby maneuver much of what Stalin had brought about by a bloodbath.

The Fritsch-Blomberg crisis of January–February 1938 gave Hitler vastly greater power over the army both by enhancing his personal position as the new minister of war and commander-in-chief of the armed forces and by placing at his side two men who were slavish devotees of his will and on whom he could depend for obedience to any order however outrageous or criminal. In Wilhelm Keitel as his chief of staff as commander-in-chief of Germany's armed forces Hitler found a man of great organizational ability and stupendous industry who combined boundless devotion to Hitler with a total lack of moral judgment. It is hardly a coincidence that it was on Keitel's recommendation that Hitler turned to Walther von Brauchitsch to command the German army. As bereft as Keitel of moral judgment or courage, von Brauchitsch assumed and held the position of commander-in-chief of the German army under humiliating conditions which joined injustice to his predecessor with personal financial dependence on Hitler for divorce and remarriage. Impervious to appeals by his chief of staff from below or by the senior German military man, the aged Field Marshal August von Mackensen, from

12. In the army one thinks of Heinz Guderian, Walter Model, and Ferdinand Schörner; in the Waffen-SS of Josef (Sepp) Dietrich, Theodor Eicke, and Felix Steiner.

above,[13] the new commander-in-chief of the German army proved a pliant, if nervous, tool of Hitler in the critical years from the planning of war on Czechoslovakia to the declaration of war on the United States. There might be objections within the armed forces, and within the army in particular, but any serious danger to Hitler was contained for years by the fact that in the final analysis Hitler could always depend on the army's commander-in-chief bending to his will.

If Germany was not diverted from the road to war by internal opposition, was there any prospect of doing so from the outside? Certainly there were hopes of accomplishing this. Many of the smaller countries believed, or tried to persuade themselves into believing, that if they left Germany alone, or assisted her when asked, or refrained from assisting Germany's enemies, they might be left alone themselves to pursue their domestic concerns and national aspirations in peace. For some of them this would prove to be the case, but only because the military exertions of others crushed Germany, not because of any special regard inspired in Hitler by their cooperative policies. Sweden, to take an important and conspicuous example, profited materially from her subservience to Germany and managed to stay out of the war; but if the iron deliveries and troop transit facilities provided by Sweden to Germany had resulted in the victory over England and the Soviet Union that Berlin anticipated from them, the swastika would eventually have flown over Stockholm as it did over Oslo and Copenhagen.

The only major power having a common border with Germany in 1937 was France. Terribly weakened by the ordeal of the World War, the French had laboriously rebuilt their economy. But there appeared to be no way to regain the tenuous domestic solidarity that had emerged out of the upheaval of the Dreyfus affair in the decade before the war. Civil discord characterized the internal situation. The great riot of 6 February 1934 had been a warning of possible disaster; and for those who doubted the dangers, the civil war in Spain could long provide a reminder close at hand. As for the military situation, this was characterized by a curious mixture of hope and despair. The hope was that massive fortifications would not only shield the country against surprise attack but could also prevent any repetition of the disastrous impact of fighting inside France with its devastation and occupation of important areas. Such a defensive posture, however, though reinforced by the imagined lessons of the last conflict,[14] had the effect of writing off most of France's allies. If only a lengthy buildup of French and British forces combined with the weakening of Germany by a renewed blockade could pave the way for any of-

13. The appeals of von Brauchitsch's first chief of staff, Ludwig Beck, are examined in chap. 2; that of von Mackensen of 14 February 1940 has been published in Müller, p. 675. For von Brauchitsch's answer to the latter, saying that there was nothing to worry about since he had discussed the mass murders in Poland with Himmler, see ibid., p. 676.

14. I have summarized this point in *Foreign Policy*, pp. 362–63.

fensive action against Germany at some indefinite time after the outbreak of war, the Germans could defeat unmolested and one at a time whatever allies France might have in East and Southeast Europe. If any prospective ally of France learned of this, would they continue their tie to France? If they did remain with their French alliance, would not Germany's quick conquest of them strengthen rather than weaken Germany for the subsequent serious contest of arms in the west? Would not these prospects further restrain the French until it was too late?

There was yet another element in this picture which can be noted but not as yet explained. French intelligence had during the 1920s and early 1930s formed a reasonably accurate picture of Germany's military situation. By 1936, however, the accepted estimates of German strength were so far ahead of reality as to border on the fantastic. This discrepancy between reality and the French imagination grew ever greater: by 1938 the French military leaders seriously claimed to believe that if Germany attacked Czechoslovakia with her main strength, she could still keep fifty divisions on guard against any French attack in the west—when the whole German army had not yet reached fifty divisions! The origins of these delusions remain to be explored; the results are all too obvious. As the French military viewed the prospect of renewed battle with Germany, they were immobilized by despair, an attitude they communicated first to their political leaders and then to their own soldiers.[15]

That French foreign policy was conducted under these circumstances with neither much hope nor great determination is not surprising. The very measures preparatory for a war everyone hoped to avoid because of tragic memories of the last conflict only meant that any new war would necessarily be of long duration and hence more costly. Whether such a war would come was left essentially to the initiative of others; whatever its cause and course, only a long war was seen as offering any hope for France, and only eventual victory in such a long war might bring redemption to the allies of France as it had once brought redemption—and great enlargement—to Serbia. If Paris looked to London for leadership both to avoid war and to win if it were unavoidable, this was in large part due to the weakness of French institutions as well as of the French armed forces.

From the perspective of London, the growing danger in Europe was obvious. Not so obvious was the answer to the question of whether and how war might be avoided. Inherent in the British government's handling of that question were three assumptions of fundamental importance. First, it was assumed that any war with Germany would be terrible and

15. Once the origins of the extraordinary delusions about German strength in the later 1930s have been clarified, it may become easier to understand why so many French military leaders were, after June 1940, willing to fight against England, against other Frenchmen, and against the United States—but under no circumstances against Germany. The publication in 1978 of a French intelligence estimate of late November 1938 referring to a German army at that time of fifty-four divisions (*D.D.F.*, 2d, 12, No. 461) makes the puzzle even more confusing.

long; it would be terrible because of the use of new types of weapons and
long because of Germany's head start in armaments. Only after initial
German offensives had been halted and allied strength built up, could
there be any hope of defeating a Germany weakened by blockade and of
restoring to independent status whatever countries had been conquered
by Germany in the meantime. As this assumption implied, any new war
was believed certain to be general and to involve England regardless of
the precise location and circumstances of its beginning. In complete opposition to Hitler's deduction from the experience of 1914–18, that Germany should fight separate wars against isolated enemies, the British
concluded from the same experience that any future war would surely
spread to all as the last one had, and that it was therefore most sensible to
anticipate that England could not keep out. In other words, it was essential to try to prevent *any* war from starting in Europe because, like the one
originating in distant Serbia, it would soon involve themselves. Tied to
this belief that a European conflict would be general and would be a long
one was the belief that no one had wanted such a thing in 1914 and that
surely no one could possibly desire a repetition of that disaster. What few
could imagine before 1914, all certainly knew after 1918. Accordingly,
every effort had to be made to prevent a recurrence of a general war by
trying to reconcile in some way whatever quarrels seemed most likely to
lead to any war anywhere in Europe.

Added to these assumptions were certain realities of the international
situation within which London had to make its decisions. There was, first
of all, the fact that Britain and her empire were threatened not only in
Europe by Germany but also by Japan in East Asia and by Italy along her
Mediterranean supply route. The famous ten-year rule, that no war
against a major power was to be expected for ten years, had been abandoned in 1932 in response to developments in East Asia. Since then, the
British government had looked with great concern at a range of threats
which could not all be dealt with simultaneously; moreover, action against
one might so commit her in one part of the world as almost to invite an
attack against her elsewhere.

Second, the British were very conscious of the fact that they had disarmed themselves after 1918. On land, they had unilaterally reduced the
enormous army, which had borne the major share of the fighting in the
final year and a half of the last war, to a force about the size of the 100,000
man army set by the peace treaty for Germany. At sea they had scrapped
a large number of warships and limited new construction under a series of
disarmament agreements with the United States and Japan, while in the air
they had dismantled the world's largest air force. Rearmament would take
time. It would also, and here was the third reality, cost vast amounts of
money for a country dependent on world trade for its life and accustomed
by its role in earlier conflicts to thinking of its financial strength as a major
arm of coalition warfare. It is true that this last point would change in a

war in which England was enabled to continue through the financial support of the United States; but it ought to be obvious that at a time when American international financial policy was set by the Johnson Act with its prohibition on lending England a penny in case of war, no one in the London government was prepared to gamble on the possibility of billions of dollars of a not yet invented Lend-Lease program. Rearmament was, therefore, concentrated on air defense first, naval defense second, and the very rudimentary beginnings of rebuilding an army last, with a constant eye to the costs not only in absolute terms but also to their impact on the general trade position of a country still recovering slowly from the depression.

Once inaugurated, rearmament would add some weight to the efforts to resolve difficulties by negotiations, especially if enough time was gained so that eventually the combined strength of England and France might serve to deter Germany from the risk of a war which by British calculation would be sure to involve them all. The converse of Hitler's view—the sooner the better—was the British one—the later the better—in the belief that if war were postponed sufficiently into the future it might never take place at all. If, however, it did start in spite of the efforts to avoid it, these efforts themselves would make the subsequently required sacrifices appear to the British public as unavoidable because of the obstinacy of others rather than incurred through rash actions of their own government. And at least the first stages of the rearmament program would then contribute to success in what in the absence of many of the allies of the last war and the recognized weakness of France was certain to be a hard test of strength.

The avoidance of any long and general war was, therefore, seen as certainly in Britain's interest and susceptible of being shown as being in the interest of others as well. The use by German propaganda in general and Hitler in particular of real or imagined grievances from the peace settlement of 1919 was designed by Berlin to make possible the isolation of German actions, including the first of its series of wars, from interference by others. Until there was clear proof, as opposed to dire warnings, to the contrary, this trumpeting of "grievances" was taken by the British government as a pointer in the direction of issues that might have to be settled by negotiations and concessions if they were not to lead to war. Perhaps others would agree to some changes if these were worked out in negotiations and if German demands were restricted to changes which left other countries their independence—except possibly Austria, which might not really want it. The resulting improvement in the international atmosphere as well as the avoidance of war would be in the interest of all, and such a happy prospect might be the more readily secured if the British themselves, as well as the French, made a contribution to such a new general settlement by concessions to Germany in the colonial field, the area of German "grievances" from 1919 in which

England and the Dominions had been the chief beneficiaries of the settlement.

Originally formulated in the winter of 1935–36 by Sir Robert Vansittart, the idea of a general settlement with Germany, in which colonial and other economic concessions by the Western Powers would be exchanged for German acceptance of the status quo with possibly only minor alterations in Central Europe, eventually became almost an obsession with British leaders.[16] If all contributed their share, Germany might be peacefully reintegrated into the European state system as a nation satisfied enough to cease being a menace to its neighbors, with those neighbors benefiting from the maintenance of peace and Germany from concessions which, if not all she had wanted, were still preferable to the hazards of a new war. The eagerness of the British government to secure such a settlement was not confined to Prime Minister Chamberlain, though he played a major role in formulating and attempting to implement the policy. It was shared by all in the cabinet. Winston Churchill indicated that he would follow a similar policy were he in the government, and when Foreign Secretary Anthony Eden resigned, to be replaced by Lord Halifax, it was over the subsidiary issue of whether and how Mussolini might be detached from Hitler's side rather than the fundamental one of the desirability of attempting an accommodation with Germany.

It was, however, precisely such an accommodation that Germany did not want. Some historians have emphasized Hitler's periodic expressions of hope for an agreement with England and disregard not only his at least equally frequent denunciations of England but, more significantly, his consistent rejection of any and all efforts to bring about an Anglo-German settlement. Having destroyed at the earliest opportunity the Locarno agreement with its provision for English protection against any future French action like the occupation of the Ruhr, Hitler was not about to become involved in any new settlement of a comprehensive nature. In regard to England as in regard to others Hitler naturally preferred subservience to defiance. He would have preferred that Poland submit rather than fight—though hardly out of great fondness for the Poles as German policy in occupied Poland ought now to have made clear to all. He would pursue his policy of external conquest and he would adhere to his policy of murdering Europe's Jews; and the test he applied to other countries was whether they were prepared to subordinate their policies and preferences to Germany's policies on these matters at any given time. In prewar as in wartime Europe, that meant joining Hitler or at least not objecting to his actions in the conquest for space regardless of who might live in the affected area and what the preference of those people might be. This was the test he applied to Italy, to Japan, to the Soviet Union, to Hungary, to Poland, to Yugoslavia, and to others whom at one time or another Hitler

16. The first stages of this project are described in Weinberg, *Foreign Policy*, pp. 244–45.

considered appropriate—if temporary—helpmates for his foreign policy aims of the moment. Similarly, once the machinery for murdering Europe's Jews had been set in motion, the test he applied to the satellites of Berlin was their willingness—or reluctance—to turn over the Jews from their jurisdiction to the Germans to be killed.

These tactical and temporary arrangements, however, must not be confused, as they sometimes are, with any serious willingness on Hitler's part to accommodate his long-term aims and policies to the interests and preferences of any other power or interest. His concordat with the Vatican did not imply any regard for the maintenance of Catholicism any more than the transfer agreement for Jews emigrating to Palestine meant Hitler had become a Zionist. Innumerable other examples, from the agreement with Poland in January 1934 to the nonaggression pact with the Soviet Union in August 1939, could be added to the list. The only foreign leader and power with whom Hitler was prepared to make any real accommodation was Mussolini's Italy; he saw a certain kinship in his relations with the Duce, and he believed that Italy's expansionist ambitions could be harmonized with his own. But as would become obvious the moment the Italians suggested during World War II that Germany abandon her expansionist ambitions in Eastern Europe in order to arrive at a new accommodation with Stalin, Hitler's regard for Italian aspirations in the Mediterranean would never be extended to the point where his own drive for *Lebensraum* in the east might be subordinated to it. And once Mussolini himself had been deposed by the Italians, Germany would seize vast portions of northern Italy, not just the minuscule area of South Tyrol.

It was because Hitler recognized quite correctly that the British proposals for a general settlement involved acquiescence by Germany in a Europe modified too slightly to resemble even remotely his vast ambitions that he evaded with great care every British attempt to involve him in negotiations for any such arrangement. Having denounced those in Germany whose ambitions were limited to revision of the Versailles settlement, which would leave Germany with borders essentially as inadequate as those of 1937, he was not about to be enticed into something very similar by foreign leaders; the noise about the 1919 settlement was to prepare not for its revision but for a total restructuring of Europe and the whole world. That meant war, not talk.

The one time that Hitler eventually became entrapped in the negotiating process only reinforced his disinclination to accept the British approach. In the crisis over Czechoslovakia, Hitler found himself first entrapped by Chamberlain's offer to come to Germany, an offer which he could hardly refuse without putting himself in the wrong at home and abroad, risking both a general war and a dubious home front. He had then tried desperately to avoid a negotiated settlement by activating Poland and Hungary and staging appropriate incidents, only to pull back at the last moment in view of Mussolini's urging, contrary advice from his closest associates, a

British warning, and a sense that the German public was not with him in this project. Having had to settle for what he had felt able to ask in public, rather than what he had wanted in private, left him angry and determined never to allow a repetition of such a process. Not only did English talk of further rearmament after Munich remind him of the fact that the British policy of working for the peaceful settlement of disputes gave his prospective enemies more time to rearm, but the very fact that war had eluded him because of the diplomacy of others and his own hesitation reinforced his earlier preference for war. If the worldwide relief over the drawing back from hostilities in 1938 did not lead to the kind of detente which evolved after the Cuban missile crisis of 1962 it was because Hitler regretted that war had been averted rather than being alarmed that it had been so close.

The British government had on this occasion found a way to avoid war but at great sacrifice of prestige for both England and France and of major territorial amputations for Czechoslovakia. If there really had followed a period of relaxation, then the road to a more peaceful Europe might have been open; but it soon became obvious that this was not the case. Although the rumors that Germany's next move would be to invade Holland proved false, the fact that Berlin was dissatisfied rather than calmed down after Munich showed that war, not peace, was likely. The destruction of the Munich agreement by Germany herself only underlined what many had suspected but until then no one could prove: the German grievances and demands were not related to any attempt to correct those grievances or satisfy the announced demands but were propaganda instruments designed to isolate one victim from future ones. It therefore became critical for other powers to counter that German strategy and only subsequently deal with specific issues, rather than the other way around.

How did other major powers perceive the danger of war? The Soviet Union saw war as a natural and inherently inevitable concomitant of capitalist society, with which she considered herself in something of a war anyway; and she greatly preferred that capitalist nations fight among themselves rather than gang up on Russia. As for any threat from Germany, that was still at a distance as long as the Germans were still in the center of Europe, far removed from the Soviet Union. If others could be persuaded to fight Germany, that was all to the good; and it would weaken both parties to such a conflict while leaving Russia aside, with even the possibility of gain from the confusion. Such a policy could work until Germany turned against a country that had a common boundary with Russia and thus opened up the possibility of an invasion route eastward. At that point the intentions of Germany would become critical. Stalin feared German strength and had repeatedly attempted to secure better relations with the Third Reich. Once Germany turned toward new goals after Munich he was all the more worried. If others would fight Germany, his country might escape participation in a war which could possibly end his rule of the country as the last war had ended the rule of the Romanovs. If possible, therefore, Russia would stand aside from such a war entirely, or, if Germany needed encouragement to strike at others, Russia could perhaps provide that stimulus.

When the Western Powers turned to the concept of a general front against German moves after 15 March 1939, therefore, the Soviet government was cautiously reluctant. Since they had good reason for believing that Germany was attacking Poland only as a preliminary to fighting the West, the Russian government thought it had no interest in joining in such an endeavor. The focus in subsequent scholarship on the military issues in the talks between the Western Powers and Russia is a coincidence of timing rather than a matter of substance. The German timetable required an agreement with the Soviet Union in August and the issue then under discussion between Moscow, London, and Paris happened to be that of allowing Russian troops into Poland. Had the Western Powers delayed their agreement to the Soviet demand for guarantees against indirect aggression, that would have been the subject when the negotiations broke off; had they secured full Polish concurrence on the troop transit issue, the negotiations would have been focused on the next Soviet demand which, to judge by evidence in the record of the talks, was likely to be either Soviet bases in the Baltic States or the dispatch of British warships into the Baltic. The critical point was that in Stalin's eyes Germany was prepared to pay a good price for Soviet aid, but that without the cooperation of the Soviet Union Germany might not go to war at all, since the Russians knew of Japan's refusal to sign with Germany. Having an agreement with the Soviet Union offering cooperation in Eastern Europe and a breach of any blockade, Hitler felt sufficiently encouraged to move.

The Japanese had needed no encouragement from Moscow to embroil themselves in a war with China. It was, therefore, fully in accord with the defensive posture of the Soviet government in the 1930s to provide some assistance to the Chinese Nationalist government in its struggle against Japan. Inside Manchuria, the Russian government had been willing to appease Japan by the sale in 1935 of its interests to the Manchukuo puppet government the Japanese had established there. On the borders of the Soviet Far Eastern provinces and the Soviet client state of Outer Mongolia, however, the Russians bloodied rather than appeased the Japanese. This was all that was needed, given Japan's involvement in war with China. Thereafter, as long as Germany was primarily interested in having Japan threaten the Western Powers, the Soviet Union could readily contain or divert Japan.

This combination of policies—assisting the victim of Japanese aggression in East Asia while siding with Germany in Europe—seemed to the leader of the Soviet Union the best way to preserve his rule of the country without external danger or with a minimum of risk. The calculation would prove disastrously mistaken and leave the Soviet Union exposed to attack under particularly dangerous conditions, but Stalin apparently preferred the risks of postponement with booty to those of alignment with the Western Powers in 1939. President Roosevelt's warning that a Germany triumphant in Western Europe would then threaten the safety of the Soviet Union as well as of the United States was prophetic but in vain.

The American president, like large parts of the American public, observed developments in Europe with growing concern. The whole direction of change appeared to challenge American beliefs, values, and hopes by pointing toward a world modeled on a dictatorial rather than a democratic pattern. The estrangement between Germany and the United States had moved with great rapidity after 1933; from the major countries with the best relations they had quickly become the major countries with the worst. Ideological and political factors predominated in this process, the specific problems at issue being of more symbolic than substantive importance. With much of the American public increasingly convinced that participation in the World War had been an aberration not to be repeated, and a president who strongly preferred to keep the United States out of war, the distaste and even repugnance for Germany that was developing in the United States had, however, little immediate practical effect. Having disarmed after the war very much the way England had, the country was in any case incapable of playing any significant direct role for years in any conflict Germany might start; and the president encouraged, rather than discouraged, the hopes of those who tried to reconcile Germany to a peaceful role in Europe.[17]

President Roosevelt, however, became increasingly convinced that only a strengthened England and France, preferably joined by other countries including the Soviet Union, could restrain Germany from wild adventures or defeat her if she could not be restrained. He therefore not only denounced Germany's actions in public but began to help the rearmament of France, tried to educate the American public to the dangers ahead, and urged some steps toward America's own rearmament. The failure of the administration's attempt to revise the neutrality laws in a manner that would allow England and France to purchase munitions and weapons in the United States in time of war came simultaneously with Roosevelt's failure to persuade Stalin that the best hope of safety lay in an alignment with the Western Powers. There was always the chance that a combination of success in both endeavors might discourage Germany from war altogether; but by the time Roosevelt's foreign hopes were shattered by

17. The point is conveyed by the titles of two important works on the subject: Arnold Offner's *American Appeasement: United States Foreign Policy and Germany, 1933–1938*, and Francis Loewenheim's "The Diffidence of Power—Some Notes and Reflections on the American Road to Munich." The relationship of American disarmament after 1918 to American diplomacy before 1939 and during the war itself, as well as its impact on American strategy until 1944, has generally been ignored by European scholars dealing with the subject. The chronology is instructive: Germany begins building up her army in the spring of 1933; England in the spring of 1939; the United States in the fall of 1940.

the Nazi-Soviet pact, his domestic hopes had already been dashed by congressional defeat of his neturality law revision. Only appeals for peace and when those failed a call to refrain from bombing civilian targets emanated from Washington in the last days of peace and the first days of war. The answer from Berlin was simple and eloquent: one of the first German bombs landed in the grounds of the villa Ambassador Biddle had rented as a refuge for the clerks and women of the American embassy in Warsaw.

It had originally not been a part of Hitler's plan to attack Poland in 1939. After Munich, he intended to destroy what remained of Czechoslovakia, but that was not expected to involve hostilities. His first war was to be in the west, destroying France and crushing England so that they could not interfere with his ambitions in Eastern Europe. Starting a war in the west, however, meant making sure of quiet in the east—just as the earlier plan for an attack on Czechoslovakia had been accompanied by efforts to neutralize the West. The plan to make certain that all was quiet on the eastern front failed. The Hungarians fell into line, but the Poles simply would not do so. From October 1938 on, the German government tried to entice, coax, overawe, and bully the Poles into a position of subservience to Germany, so that in alliance with Italy and Japan Germany could turn west without having to worry about Poland's either requiring a diversion of German forces or taking advantage of German preoccupation elsewhere. As it became clear to Hitler that the Poles were not willing to give up their status as an independent country without a fight—and this rather than specific details of German-Polish relations was the key issue—he reversed his planned sequence of actions and with it the procedure for securing quiet on the other front.

He was now determined to fight Poland so that the total crushing of Germany's eastern neighbor would make it safe for Germany to attack in the west. Here would be the lovely little war of which he had been cheated in 1938. The prospective alliance with Italy and Japan would now serve to deter rather than directly threaten England and France. A repeat performance of the 1938 propaganda campaign about poor, persecuted Germans would serve to isolate Poland from diplomatic support by the Western Powers, whose defeat in war was now postponed until 1940 or 1941, while Slovakia, Lithuania, and even Hungary would be invited to join in and help themselves to parts of Poland just as Poland and Hungary had been urged to share in the Czechoslovak booty in 1938. In practice, the Japanese proved still hesitant about an alliance, while Mussolini was willing to commit Italy by treaty and fine words though hardly by action. The Soviet Union, however, could from Hitler's perspective make a perfect substitute for Japan in the diplomacy of isolating Poland as well as relieving Germany if war with the West did come. As for junior partners, Hitler would find the Slovaks ready but neither the Lithuanians nor the Hungarians willing, but again that would be more than made up by the participation of the Red Army in the conquest of Poland.

If in these respects Hitler tried to repeat the pattern of action he had followed in 1938, in others the approach was deliberately changed. In 1938, negotiations had continued throughout the year, and in the end Hitler had been unable to break loose from them into hostilities. There would, therefore, be no negotiations with Poland in the summer of 1939, and to make certain that there could be no unintentional and unwelcome slippage into negotiations, the German ambassadors in Warsaw and London were recalled and forbidden to return to their posts in the last critical weeks. In 1938 Germany had in the end been forced by circumstances to settle for its propagandistically defensible ostensible demands. Hitler would take no chance on any repetition of such a development in 1939; demands which would be used in German propaganda to explain her going to war were indeed formulated, but von Ribbentrop was personally instructed by Hitler under no circumstances to let these out of his hands. If there were again to be incidents at the proper time to provide a pretext for Germany's attack, staging them would on this critical occasion be entrusted neither to the army nor to any possibly unreliable and inexperienced recruits from the German minority abroad. This time the German secret police apparatus itself would stage the incidents with Reinhard Heydrich, the head of the security service, personally issuing instructions. Hitler would have his war, and this time no one would stop him, least of all the British who had tricked him out of it, as he thought, the year before. If they showed signs of hesitation, it would make an attack on Poland look safe; if they demonstrated firmness, that only showed them determined to fight Germany in any case. The choice for war came first, and whatever others did would be interpreted or misinterpreted to support adherence to that decision and the procedures adopted to implement it.

It had also actually been the hope of the British government that a reversal of *their* 1938 procedure might work to maintain peace once again. Then they had waited until the last possible moment to threaten Germany with a general war if Germany attacked Czechoslovakia, anticipating that the anxiety of Czechoslovakia and France over the question of whether they could count on English support would produce maximum concessions to Germany, while the anxiety of Germany lest England come in would induce Berlin to accept less than they would otherwise prefer to obtain. Now, in 1939, the British took their stand early rather than late, hoping both to rally others and to deter Germany by a show of strength and unity. Unable to persuade the Soviet Union to stand with them in this position, the British—and the France in their wake—stood their ground.

Although Hitler had ordered war to begin as soon as he was sure that the pact with Russia was about to be signed, he found that it was still possible to call off the attack and try once more to separate the Western Powers from Poland. As soon as it was evident that this could not be accomplished, he ordered the attack to go forward regardless of the risks in the west and the knowledge that Mussolini would not as yet come in on Germany's side. He was so impatient to start the war that he would not wait the one day that his own schedule still allowed for the initiation of hostilities in 1939; there could be no question of calling off war altogether.

It takes only one side to start a war. Only an internal coup could have kept Hitler from launching one; and the first serious attempt, the bomb which went off in the Munich beer hall in November 1939, was ironically the work of a loner and was frustrated by the fact that Hitler had cut short his stay in order to confer in Berlin on the forthcoming offensive in the west.[18] In November the war was already under way. In August, when it counted, the German military leaders had been either enthusiastic or willing—the attack on Poland looked to many like the right thing to do, and the agreement with the Soviet Union appeared to be a stroke of genius assuring a one-front war. The German public was by all accounts dubious, and there was no repetition of the mass enthusiasm of August 1914 in Germany any more than in any other European country. There was, however, a new *Burgfrieden,* a new domestic consensus, in the one place where it counted in the Germany of 1939: the top of her military hierarchy.[19]

Under these circumstances, the leader of Europe's most powerful country could unleash the great disaster. In the oceans of tears and blood let loose upon the world millions and millions would drown. If the war did not follow the course Hitler and his associates and assistants preferred, that was due to the exertions of others and to their own mistakes. They would be able to take many initiatives and thus participate in shaping the contours of the war, but the only portion they could entirely control was the opening: the faked incidents in the German borderlands and the opening salvo from the guns of the *Schleswig-Holstein.* As German soldiers raced to seize the important railway bridge over the Vistula at Tczew, the Poles blew it up in their faces.

18. Lothar Gruchmann (ed.), *Autobiographie eines Attentäters: Johann Georg Elser* (Stuttgart: Deutsche Verlags-Anstalt, 1970), p. 9. See also Anton Hoch, "Das Attentat auf Hitler im Münchner Bürgerbräukeller 1939," *Vierteljahrshefte für Zeitgeschichte,* 17, No. 4 (Oct. 1969), 383–413. All other opposition projects up to this point had consisted of plans and talks, but no direct action. Warnings were issued inside and outside the country, but the first attempt to overthrow the Hitler regime took place in March 1943.

19. Note also Speer's entry of 20 December 1946 in his prison diary (p. 48). On what must have been 22 or 23 August 1939, Hitler after his first order to attack Poland said that this time much blood would flow. Germany would fall to destruction with him if the war were not won. In 1946 Speer clearly recalled that neither he himself nor anyone else had been repulsed by such expressions.

Bibliography

Introductory Comments on Archives

German Archives

Extensive portions of the German archives were microfilmed after World War II; the most comprehensive collection of such films is in the National Archives in Washington. These films are cited by their National Archives microcopy numbers. The National Archives also holds important original German documents collected for, but not used at, the Nuremberg trials as well as postwar interrogations of German officials. Related materials, now largely transferred to the National Archives, were used at what was then the Foreign Studies Branch of the Office of the Chief of Military History. There are some German documents in the Manuscripts Division and the Prints and Photographs Division of the Library of Congress. Microfilms from the Berlin Document Center are largely in the National Archives, but a group of materials from the NSDAP Hauptarchiv was filmed—though rather poorly—for the Hoover Institution. Among records held at the German Federal Archives in Koblenz that were not processed by the various filming operations those most important for this study are the collections of instructions for the German press, the papers of General Ludwig Beck (now at the Military Archives in Freiburg), and records of the ministry of finance. There are small groups of papers and numerous postwar interrogations at the Institut für Zeitgeschichte (IfZ) in Munich. A microfilm of important papers of Field Marshal Erhard Milch is held by the Imperial War Museum in London. German records that fell into Soviet hands and are now for the most part in East Germany are cited by the file number of the Central Archive of the German Democratic Republic (DZA) at Potsdam in such cases where I have been able to obtain copies and are otherwise cited at second hand from publications by East German scholars.

Italian Archives

The Italian archives for the 1930s have not generally been available to scholars,[1] but an important group of papers was microfilmed by the Allies in World War II; these have been used at the National Archives where they are listed as microcopy T-586. The other Italian films there (T-821)

1. An important exception is John Coverdale; see his book listed below.

678

pertain mainly to the period of World War II and to prewar military affairs.

Czechoslovak Archives

The archives of Czechoslovakia were seized practically intact by the Germans, who had a team that prepared and sent to Berlin translations of many documents. Those translations that were found after the war in the German foreign ministry archives captured by the Western Allies were microfilmed; they are described in considerable detail in the data sheets covering them that were prepared by Fritz T. Epstein.[2] This important collection includes both copies of diplomatic dispatches and telegrams and the summaries of periodic briefing reports given by Kamil Krofta, Czechoslovakia's foreign minister, to the section chiefs of the foreign ministry. These documents are cited as "Czechoslovak document in T-120" with container, serial, and frame numbers. The internal evidence as to their authenticity and the general reliability of the translations into German is now confirmed by the fact that those translations were used as the textual basis for the majority of the items in a collection of documents published under the auspices of the present government of Czecho-slovakia.[3] Doctoring of the translated documents for political purposes had been left to von Ribbentrop's propagandist, Friedrich Berber.[4]

American Archives

United States archives have proved extremely valuable in the preparation of this work. American diplomats in the 1930s were often extremely well informed—even if the government in Washington did little with their re-ports except file them. American diplomats often obtained information difficult or impossible to obtain elsewhere, and the Central Files of the Department of State as a result contain important material on such mat-ters as the Danzig question, the foreign policies of France and Poland, and developments in Austria. The papers of the special State Department mission to postwar Germany under DeWitt C. Poole are also useful.

Records at the National Archives must be supplemented by important collections elsewhere. The Franklin D. Roosevelt papers at Hyde Park contain much of interest; the Henry Morgenthau, R. Walton Moore, and Clairborne Pell papers there were less important for this work. The Jay Pierrepont Moffat and William Phillips papers are at Harvard. At the

2. T-120, 1039/1809/411884–927; 1143/2028/444168–183; 1316/2376/D 496875–880.
3. Václav Král (ed.), *Das Abkommen von München 1938: Tschechoslowakische dip-lomatische Dokumente 1937–1939* (Prague: Academia, 1968), p. 43.
4. Friedrich Berber (ed.), *Europäische Politik 1933–1938 im Spiegel der Prager Akten,* 3d ed. (Essen: Essener Verlagsanstalt, 1942). Cross-references have been provided in the footnotes where a document on microfilm can be compared with what appears in this collection.

Library of Congress I have consulted the papers of Wilbur J. Carr, Norman H. Davis, William E. Dodd, Cordell Hull, Breckinridge Long, and Laurence A. Steinhardt. The George S. Messersmith papers are at the University of Delaware.

British Archives

The shift from a fifty- to a thirty-year rule has opened extensive British records to scholars, though it must be noted that many documents and whole files are being kept closed until 1990, 2015, and even later. Most important for this project have been the voluminous papers of the Foreign Office at the Public Record Office; also used have been cabinet papers, prime minister's papers, the records of such cabinet committees as the Committee of Imperial Defence and the Committee on Foreign Policy, and the papers of Lord Halifax, Sir Nevile Henderson, Sir John Simon, Sir Alexander Cadogan, Sir Archibald Clark Kerr, and Viscount Runciman in the FO 800 series.

At Cambridge University I have used the Baldwin and Templewood papers; at the Beaverbrook Libary the Lloyd George papers; at the London School of Economics the Dalton papers; at King's College the Ismay papers; and at the Scottish Record Office the Lothian muniments.

Other Archives

The Soviet archives are closed. Some French archives have been made available to certain scholars, but there has been as yet no general opening similar to the American or British. Publications of documents from Soviet and French, as well as other, archives are listed in the bibliography.

No effort has been made to make this bibliography exhaustive. Only works actually cited in this book are included, together with a *small* selection of other works whose general ideas, organizing concepts, or supplementary details were of real significance in shaping the account. The bibliographies listed in section I and many of the secondary works in section IV provide additional listings.

I. Bibliographies, Guides, Archives Inventories, and Other Reference Works

American Historical Association, Committee for the Study of War Documents, and National Archives and Records Service. "Guides to German Records Microfilmed at Alexandria, Va." Washington: National Archives, 1958–.

Bauer, Yehuda (ed.). *Guide to Unpublished Materials of the Holocaust Period.* Vol. 3. Jerusalem: Hebrew University, 1975.

Bibliothek für Zeitgeschichte, Stuttgart (formerly the Weltkriegsbücherei). *Jahresbibliographie* (formerly *Bücherschau der Weltkriegsbücherei*).

————. *Kataloge der Bibliothek für Zeitgeschichte*. Boston: G. K. Hall, 1968. This printed card catalog, together with the annual supplements, constitutes the most useful bibliographic tool for twentieth-century European history.

Das Deutsche Führerlexikon 1934/1935. Berlin: Stollberg, 1934.

Facius, Friedrich; Booms, Hans; Boberach, Heinz. *Das Bundesarchiv und seine Bestände*. 2d ed. Boppard: Boldt, 1968.

Great Britain, Foreign Office. *Index to the Correspondence of the Foreign Office, 1937–1939*. 4 vols. per year. Nendeln/Liechtenstein: Kraus Reprint, 1969.

————, Public Record Office. *The Records of the Foreign Office, 1782–1939*. London: H.M. Stationery Office, 1969.

Heinz, Grete, and Peterson, Agnes F. *NSDAP Hauptarchiv: Guide to the Hoover Institution Microfilm Collection*. Stanford: Hoover Institution, 1964.

Higham, Robin (ed.). *A Guide to the Sources of British Military History*. Berkeley: University of California Press, 1972.

Kent, George O. *A Catalog of the Files and Microfilms of the German Foreign Ministry Archives, 1920–1945*. Stanford: Hoover Institution, 1962–72.

Laqueur, Walter (ed.). *Fascism: A Reader's Guide*. Berkeley: University of California Press, 1976.

Lötzke, Helmut. *Übersicht über die Bestände des Deutschen Zentralarchivs Potsdam*. Berlin (East): Rütten & Loening, 1957.

Neuburger, Otto. *Official Publications of Present-Day Germany*. Washington: Government Printing Office, 1944.

Robinson, Jacob, and Friedman, Philip. *Guide to Jewish History under Nazi Impact*. New York: Yivo, 1960. Very wide bibliographic coverage.

Smyth, Howard M. *Secrets of the Fascist Era*. Carbondale, Ill.: Southern Illinois University Press, 1975. Important on the fate of the Italian archives.

Toynbee, Arnold J. (ed.). *Survey of International Affairs*. 1937–1939. London: Oxford University Press.

Weinberg, Gerhard L., et al. *Guide to Captured German Documents*. Montgomery: Air University, 1952. *Supplement*. Washington: National Archives, 1959.

Wolfe, Robert (ed.). *Captured German and Related Records: A National Archives Conference*. Athens, Ohio: Ohio University Press, 1974. Papers on many aspects of the fate of the German archives.

II.   Publications of Documents, Speeches, etc.

A.   Major collections, organized by country

AUSTRALIA
Documents on Australian Foreign Policy, 1937–1949. Vol. 1, *1937–1938*. Canberra: Australian Government Publishing Service, 1975. Includes documents from British as well as Australian archives. Cited as *Australian Documents*.

BELGIUM
Documents diplomatiques belges, 1920–1940. Vols. 4 and 5, *La politique de sécurité extérieure, 1936–1940*. Brussels: Académie royale, 1965–66. Cited as *D.D.B.*

CANADA
Documents on Canadian External Relations. Vol. 6, *1936–1939*. Ottawa: Department of External Affairs, 1972.

FRANCE
Documents diplomatiques français, 1932–1939. 2d series, 1936–1939. Vols. 3–12. Paris: Imprimerie Nationale, 1967–78. Cited as *D.D.F.*

Les Evenements survenues en France de 1933 à 1945: Temoignages et documents recueilles par la commission d'enquête parlementaire. 9 vols. Paris: Presses

Universitaires, 1947.

Le Livre jaune français: documents diplomatiques, 1938–1939. Paris: Imprimerie Nationale, 1939. Cited as *French Yellow Book*.

GERMANY

Documents on German Foreign Policy, 1918–1945. German edition: *Akten zur deutschen auswärtigen Politik 1918–1945*. Series C, 1933–1937, is cited from the English-language edition, Washington: Government Printing Office, 1957–. Series D, 1937–1941, is cited from the German-language edition, Baden-Baden: Imprimerie Nationale, later P. Keppler, 1950–70. For the period covered by this book, only vol. 6 of Series C remains to be published. Cited as *G.D.*

Documents and Materials Relating to the Eve of the Second World War. 2 vols. Moscow: Foreign Languages Publishing House, 1948. Cited as *D.M.*

Documents secrets du ministère des affaires étrangère, de l'Allemagne. 2, Hongrie: La politique allemande, 1937–1943. 3, La politique allemande en Espagne, 1936–1943. Translated by Madeleine and Michel Eristov. Paris, 1946.

United States Office of Military Government for Germany, Finance Division. "Report on the Investigation of the Deutsche Bank." 4 vols. OMGUS, 1946. Annex. OMGUS, 1947.

Zweites Weissbuch der deutschen Regierung. Basel: Birkhäuser, 1939. Cited as *German White Book*.

GREAT BRITAIN

Documents on British Foreign Policy, 1919–1939. 3d series, *1938–1939*. 9 vols. London: H.M. Stationery Office, 1949–55. Cited as *B.D.*

Documents concerning German-Polish Relations and the Outbreak of Hostilities between Great Britain and Germany on September 3, 1939. New York: Farrar & Rinehart, 1939. Cited as *British War Blue Book*.

HUNGARY

Diplomáciai iratok magyarország külpolitikájáhaz 1936–1945. Vols. 1–4, Budapest: Akadémiai kiadó, 1962–66. These volumes contain German-language summaries of each document. In cases where the full document has appeared elsewhere in a Western language, that is indicated in the footnote where the document is cited from this collection. Cited as *Hungarian Documents*.

Allianz Hitler-Horthy-Mussolini: Dokumente zur ungarischen Aussenpolitik (1933–1944). Budapest: Akadémiai kiadó, 1966. Cited as *Allianz*.

The Confidential Papers of Admiral Horthy. Budapest: Corvina Press, 1965.

ITALY

I Documenti diplomatici italiani. 8th series, 1935–1939. Rome: Libreria dello stato, 1952–. Cited as *D.D.I.*

Ciano, Galeazzo. *Ciano's Diplomatic Papers*. Edited by Malcolm Muggeridge. Translated by Stuart Hood. London: Odhams, 1948. Cited as Ciano, *Papers*.

POLAND

Weissbuch der Polnischen Regierung. Basel: Birkhäuser, 1939. Important corrections in *Lipski Papers*. Cited as *Polish White Book*.

UNION OF SOVIET SOCIALIST REPUBLICS

The major Soviet collection of diplomatic documents, *Dokumenty vneshney politiki SSSR*, reached 1937 too late for consideration in this work. The USSR Ministry of Foreign Affairs has published:

Soviet Peace Efforts on the Eve of World War II (September 1938–August 1939). 2 vols. Moscow: Novosti, 1973. Cited as *S.U.*

Soviet Documents on Foreign Policy, 1917–1941. Edited by Jane Degras. 3 vols. London: Oxford University Press, 1951–53.

UNITED STATES

Foreign Relations of the United States. Washington: Government Printing Office.

All volumes for the years covered by this book have appeared together with several supplementary volumes. The latter include the title of the main series in their titles except for:
Peace and War: United States Foreign Policy 1931–1941. Washington: Government Printing Office, 1943. The main series is cited as *U.S.,* followed by the year or title of supplement.
Important documentary collections from the Roosevelt papers are: *F.D.R.: His Personal Letters, 1928–1945.* Edited by Elliot Roosevelt. 2 vols. New York: Duell, Sloan & Pearce, 1950.
Franklin D. Roosevelt and Foreign Affairs, January 1933–January 1937. Edited by Edgar B. Nixon. 3 vols. Cambridge, Mass.: Harvard University Press, 1969.
THE VATICAN
Actes et documents du Saint Siège relatifs à la seconde guerre mondiale. Vol. 1. Vatican City: Libreria Editrice Vaticana, 1965. Cited as *Saint Siège.*

B.   Other documents and collections, organized by editor

Ádám, Magda (ed.). "Documents relatifs à la politique étrangère de la Hongrie dans la période de la crise tchécoslovaque (1938–1939)," *Acta Historica,* 10, Nos. 1–2 (1963), 89–116; Nos. 3–4 (1964), 373–91.
Allen, William S. (ed.). *The Infancy of Nazism: The Memoirs of Ex-Gauleiter Albert Krebs, 1923–1933.* New York: Franklin Watts, 1976.
Anordnungen des Stellvertreters des Führers. Munich: Eher, 1937.
Berber, Friedrich (ed.). *Europäische Politik 1933–1938 im Spiegel der Prager Akten.* 3d ed. Essen: Essener Verlagsanstalt, 1942.
Bond, Brian (ed.). *Chief of Staff: The Diaries of Lieutenant-General Sir Henry Pownall.* Vol. 1, *1933–1940.* Hamden, Conn.: Archon Books, 1973. Cited as *Pownall Diary.*
Bouhler, Philipp (ed.). *Der grossdeutsche Freiheitskampf: Reden Adolf Hitlers.* 3 vols. Munich: Eher, 1940–44.
Brügel, Johann W. (ed.). *Stalin und Hitler: Pakt gegen Europa.* Vienna: Europa-Verlag, 1973.
Bullitt, Orville (ed.). *For the President–Personal and Secret: Correspondence between Franklin D. Roosevelt and William C. Bullitt.* Boston: Houghton Mifflin, 1972. Cited as *Bullitt Papers.*
Calic, Edouard (ed.). *Ohne Maske: Hitler-Breiting Geheimgespräche 1931.* Frankfurt/M: Societäts-Verlag, 1968.
Cannistraro, Philip V., et al. (eds.). *Poland and the Coming of the Second World War.* Columbus: Ohio State University Press, 1976. Cited as *Biddle Papers.*
Dilks, David (ed.). *The Diaries of Sir Alexander Cadogan, 1938–1945.* New York: G. P. Putnam's Sons, 1972. Cited as *Cadogan Diary.*
Dodd, William E., Jr., and Dodd, Martha (eds.). *Ambassador Dodd's Diary, 1933–1938.* New York: Harcourt Brace, 1941.
Domarus, Max (ed.). *Hitler: Reden und Proklamationen, 1932–1945.* 2 vols. Neustadt a.d. Aisch: Verlagsdruckerei Schmidt, 1962.
Emessen, Theodor R. (ed.). *Aus Görings Schreibtisch.* Berlin: Allgemeiner Deutscher Verlag, 1947. Important documents now in the German Democratic Republic.
Gajan, Koloman, and Kvaček, Robert (eds.). *Germany and Czechoslovakia, 1918–1945: Documents on German Policies.* Prague: Orbis, 1965.
Görlitz, Walter (ed.). *Generalfeldmarschall Keitel, Verbrecher oder Offizier?* Göttingen: Musterschmidt, 1961. Cited as *Keitel Papers.*

Gruchmann, Lothar (ed.). *Autobiographie eines Attentäters, Johann Georg Elser*. Stuttgart: Deutsche Verlags-Anstalt, 1970.

Heiber, Helmut (ed.). *Hitlers Lagebesprechungen: Die Protokollfragmente seiner militärischen Konferenzen, 1942–1945*. Stuttgart: Deutsche Verlags-Anstalt, 1962.

Hess, Rudolf. *Reden*. Munich: Eher, 1938.

Hill, Leonidas (ed.). *Die Weizsäcker-Papiere, 1933–1950*. Frankfurt/M: Propyläen, 1974. Cited as *Weizsäcker-Papiere*.

Der Hochverratsprozess gegen Dr. Guido Schmidt vor dem Wiener Volksgericht. Vienna: Österreichische Staatsdruckerei, 1947. Cited as *Guido Schmidt Trial*.

Hooker, Nancy Harvison (ed.). *The Moffat Papers: Selections from the Diplomatic Journals of Jay Pierrepont Moffat, 1919–1943*. Cambridge, Mass.: Harvard University Press, 1956. Cited as *Moffat Papers*.

Hubatsch, Walther (ed.). *Hitlers Weisungen für die Kriegführung, 1939–1945*. Frankfurt/M: Bernard & Graefe, 1962.

International Military Tribunal. *Trial of the Major War Criminals*. 42 vols. English-language edition. Nuremberg, 1946–48. Cited as *TMWC*.

Irving, David (ed.). *Breach of Security: The German Secret Intelligence File on Events Leading to the Second World War*. London: William Kimber, 1968.

Jacobsen, Hans-Adolf (ed.). *Hans Steinacher, Bundesleiter des VDA, 1933–1937*. Boppard: Boldt, 1970.

James, Robert Rhodes (ed.). *Chips: The Diaries of Sir Henry Channon*. London: Weidenfeld & Nicolson, 1967.

———. *Memoirs of a Conservative: J.C.C. Davidson's Memoirs and Papers, 1910–1937*. New York: Macmillan, 1970.

Jedrzejewicz, Wacław (ed.). *Diplomat in Berlin, 1933–1939: Papers and Memoirs of Józef Lipski, Ambassador of Poland*. New York: Columbia University Press, 1968. Cited as *Lipski Papers*.

———. *Diplomat in Paris, 1936–1939: Memoirs of Juliusz Lukasiewicz, Ambassador of Poland*. New York: Columbia University Press, 1970. Cited as *Łukasiewicz Papers*.

Kerekes, Lajos (ed.). "Akten des ungarischen Ministeriums des Äusseren zur Vorgeschichte der Annexion Österreichs." *Acta Historica*, 7, Nos. 3–4 (1960), 355–90.

Král, Václav (ed.). *Das Abkommen von München 1938: Tschechoslowakische diplomatische Dokumente 1937–1939*. Prague: Academia, 1968. Cited as Král, *München*.

———. *Die Deutschen in der Tschechoslowakei, 1933–1947*. Prague: Československé Akademie Věd, 1964. Cited as Král, *Die Deutschen*.

Lenz, Wilhelm, and Kettenacker, Lothar (eds.). "Lord Kemsleys Gespräche mit Hitler Ende Juli 1939." *Vierteljahrshefte für Zeitgeschichte*, 19, No. 3 (July 1971), 305–21.

Macleod, Roderick, and Kelly, Denis (eds.). *Time Unguarded: The Ironside Diaries, 1937–1940*. New York: David McKay, 1962. Cited as *Ironside Diaries*.

Meier-Welcker, Hans (ed.). "Zur deutsch-italienischen Militärpolitik und Beurteilung der italienischen Wehrmacht vor dem Zweiten Weltkrieg." *Militärgeschichtliche Mitteilungen*, 1970, No. 1, pp. 59–93.

Meyer, Georg (ed.). *Generalfeldmarschall Wilhelm Ritter von Leeb: Tagebuchaufzeichnungen und Lagebetrachtungen aus zwei Weltkriegen*. Stuttgart: Deutsche Verlags-Anstalt, 1976.

Minney, Rubeigh James. *The Private Papers of Hore-Belisha*. London: Collins, 1960. Cited as *Hore-Belisha Papers*.

Mnichov v dokumentech [Munich in documents]. 2 vols. Prague: Orbis, 1958.

New Documents on the History of Munich. Prague: Orbis, 1958. Documents from Soviet and Czechoslovak archives.

Picker, Henry, et al. (eds.). *Hitlers Tischgespräche im Führerhauptquartier 1941–1942*. Stuttgart: Seewald, 1965. A better edition than the one of Gerhard Ritter (Bonn: Athenäum, 1951), but marred by numerous errors and the failure to consult texts in the Library of Congress.

Smith, Bradley F., and Peterson, Agnes F. (eds.). *Heinrich Himmler, Geheimreden 1933 bis 1945*. Frankfurt/M: Propyläen, 1974.

Speidel, Hans (ed.). *Ludwig Beck: Studien*. Stuttgart: K. F. Koehler, 1955.

Springer, Hildegard (ed.). *Es sprach Hans Fritzsche*. Stuttgart: Thiele, 1949.

Strong, H. C. T. "The Czechoslovak Army and the Munich Crisis: A Personal Memorandum." *War and Society: A Yearbook of Military History*, 1975, pp. 162–77.

Toscano, Mario (ed.). "Report of the Italian Ambassador in Berlin to Count Ciano, 18 March 1939." *Bulletin of the Institute of Historical Research*, 26 (1953), 218–23.

Treue, Wilhelm (ed.). "Rede Hitlers vor der deutschen Presse (10. November 1938)." *Vierteljahrshefte für Zeitgeschichte*, 6, No. 2 (April 1958), 175–91.

Trevor-Roper, Hugh R. (ed.). *Hitler's Table Talk, 1941–1944*. London: Weidenfeld & Nicolson, 1953.

―――. *The Testament of Adolf Hitler: The Hitler-Bormann Documents*. London: Cassell, 1961. This book, and the Heiber edition of the situation conferences, must be supplemented by the *Lagebesprechungen* of 23, 25, and 27 April 1945 in *Der Spiegel*, 10 January 1966, pp. 30–46.

"Verhandlungen der Militärmissionen der UdSSR, Grossbritanniens und Frankreichs in Moskau im August 1939." *Deutsche Aussenpolitik*, 4 (1959), 541–50, 674–715.

Weinberg, Gerhard L. (ed.). "Die geheimen Abkommen zum Antikominternpakt." *Vierteljahrshefte für Zeitgeschichte*, 2, No. 2 (April 1954), 193–201.

―――. "Hitler's Private Testament of May 2, 1938." *Journal of Modern History*, 27, No. 4 (Dec. 1955), 415–19.

Zsigmond, László (ed.). "Ungarn und das Münchener Abkommen." *Acta Historica*, 6, Nos. 3–4 (1959), 251–85.

III. Diaries, Memoirs, Collected Papers, and Other Works by Key Participants

Abetz, Otto. *Das Offene Problem: Ein Rückblick auf zwei Jahrzehnte deutscher Frankreichpolitik*. Cologne: Greven-Verlag, 1951.

Aga Khan III. *The Memoirs of Aga Khan*. New York: Simon & Schuster, 1954.

Anfuso, Filippo. *Rom-Berlin im diplomatischen Spiegel*. Translated by Egon Hyman. Essen: Pohl, 1951.

Beck, Joseph. *Dernier rapport, politique polonaise, 1926–1939*. Neuchâtel: Editions de la Baconnière, 1951.

Berle, Adolf A. *Navigating the Rapids, 1918–1971*. Edited by Beatrice Bishop Berle and Travis Beal Jacobs. New York: Harcourt Brace Jovanovich, 1973.

Bialer, Seweryn (ed.). *Stalin and His Generals: Soviet Military Memoirs of World War II*. New York: Pegasus, 1969.

Bleyer-Härtl, Hans. *Ringen um Reich und Recht: Zwei Jahrzehnte politischer Anwalt in Österreich*. Berlin: Traditions-Verlag, 1939.

Blücher, Wipert von. *Gesandter zwischen Diktatur und Demokratie: Erinnerungen aus den Jahren 1935–1944*. Wiesbaden: Limes, 1951.

Bohlen, Charles E. *Witness to History, 1929–1969*. New York: Norton, 1973.

Bonnet, Georges. *De Washington au Quai d'Orsay*. Geneva: Les Editions du Cheval Ailé, 1946.

Boothby, Robert. *I Fight to Live*. London: Gollancz, 1947.

Bräutigam, Otto. *So hat es sich zugetragen: Ein Leben als Soldat und Diplomat*. Würzburg: Holzner, 1968. Not as revealing as the diary in the Manuscripts Division of the Library of Congress.

Burckhardt, Carl J. *Meine Danziger Mission, 1937–1939*. Munich: Callwey, 1960.

Chamberlain, Neville. *The Struggle for Peace*. London: Hutchinson, 1939. Speeches edited by Arthur Bryant.

Chatfield, Admiral Sir Ernle. *The Navy and Defence. 2: It Might Happen Again*. London: W. Heinemann, 1947.

Ciano, Galeazzo. *The Ciano Diaries, 1939–1943*. Edited by Hugh Gibson. Garden City, N.Y.: Doubleday, 1946. Cited as Ciano, *Diary*.

————. *Tagebücher, 1937–1938*. Translated by Hans Mollier and Maximilian Wiesel. Hamburg: Krüger, 1949. Cited as Ciano, *Diary*. Since there are various editions in different languages, the date is given in all citations from the two published sections of the Ciano diary.

Comnène, Nicolas M. *Preludi del grande dramma*. Rome: Edizioni Leonardo, 1947.

Cooper, Alfred Duff (Lord Norwich). *Old Men Forget*. New York: E. P. Dutton, 1954.

Cot, Pierre. *Le Procès de la république*. 2 vols. New York: Editions de la Maison Français, 1944. This important defense by a former cabinet member includes some documents.

Coulondre, Robert. *Von Moskau nach Berlin*. Bonn: Athenäum, 1950.

Dahlerus, Birger. *Der letzte Versuch*. Munich: Nymphenburger Verlagshandlung, 1948.

Daniels, Josephus. *Shirt-Sleeve Diplomat*. Chapel Hill, N.C.: University of North Carolina Press, 1947.

Davies, Joseph E. *Mission to Moscow*. New York: Simon & Schuster, 1941.

Davignon, Jacques. *Berlin 1936–1940: Souvenirs d'une mission*. Brussels: Editions universitaires, 1951.

Dietrich, Otto. *12 Jahre mit Hitler*. Cologne: Atlas, 1955.

Dirksen, Herbert von. *Moskau-Tokio-London: Erinnerungen und Betrachtungen zu 20 Jahren deutscher Aussenpolitik, 1919–1939*. Stuttgart: Kohlhammer, 1950.

Durčansky, Ferdinand. "Mit Tiso bei Hitler." *Politische Studien*, 7 (1956), 1–10.

Eden, Anthony (Earl of Avon). *Facing the Dictators, 1923–1938*. Boston: Houghton Mifflin, 1962.

Engel, Gerhard. *Heeresadjutant bei Hitler 1938–1943*. Edited by Hildegard von Kotze. Stuttgart: Deutsche Verlags-Anstalt, 1974. Though cited as *Engel Diary*, much of the diary is a subsequent reconstruction.

Faber du Faur, Moriz von. *Macht und Ohnmacht: Erinnerungen eines alten Offiziers*. Stuttgart: Hans E. Günther, 1953.

Fabry, Jean. *J'ai connu, 1935–1945*. Paris: Descamps, 1960.

Feierabend, Ladislav. *Prag-London, vice-versa: Erinnerungen*. Vol. 1. Bonn, Brussels, New York: Edition Atlantic Forum, 1971. Important for the Munich crisis.

Fitz Randolph, Sigismond-Sizzo. *Der Frühstücks-Attaché aus London*. Stuttgart: Hans Riegler, 1954.

François-Poncet, André. *Souvenirs d'une ambassade à Berlin.* Paris: Flammarion, 1946.

Frank, Hans. *Im Angesicht des Galgens.* Munich: Friedrich Alfred Beck, 1953.

Gamelin, Maurice. *Servir.* 3 vols. Paris: Plon, 1946. Documents as well as memoirs.

Gauché, Maurice. *Le deuxième bureau au travail (1935–1940).* Paris: Amiot-Dumont, 1953.

Gedye, G. E. R. *Betrayal in Central Europe: Austria and Czechoslovakia: The Fallen Bastions.* New York: Harper, 1939.

Gladwyn, Lord (Sir Gladwyn Jebb). *The Memoirs of Lord Gladwyn.* London: Weidenfeld & Nicolson, 1972.

Griffiths, James. *Pages from Memory.* London: J. M. Dent, 1969.

Grobba, Fritz. *Männer und Mächte im Orient.* Göttingen: Musterschmidt, 1967.

Groscurth, Helmuth. *Tagebücher eines Abwehroffiziers, 1938–1940.* Edited by Helmut Krausnick and Harold C. Deutsch. Stuttgart: Deutsche Verlags-Anstalt, 1970. Cited as *Groscurth Diary.*

Guariglia, Raffaele. *Ricordi, 1922–1946.* Naples: Edizioni scientifiche italiene, 1949.

Guderian, Heinz. *Erinnerungen eines Soldaten.* Heidelberg: Vowinckel, 1951.

Halder, Franz. *Kriegstagebuch.* Edited by Hans-Adolf Jacobsen. Vol. 1. Stuttgart: Kohlhammer, 1962. Cited as *Halder Diary.*

Halifax, Lord. *Fullness of Days.* New York: Dodd Mead, 1957.

Harvey, Oliver. *The Diplomatic Diaries of Oliver Harvey, 1937–1940.* Edited by John Harvey. London: Collins, 1970. Cited as *Harvey Diaries.*

Hassell, Ulrich von. *Vom anderen Deutschland.* Zurich: Atlantis, 1946.

Hedin, Sven. *Ohne Auftrag in Berlin.* Tübingen: Internationaler Universitäts-Verlag, 1950.

Heinkel, Ernst. *Stürmisches Leben.* Stuttgart: Mundus-Verlag, 1953.

Henderson, Nevile. *Failure of a Mission: Berlin, 1937–1939.* New York: G. P. Putnam's Sons, 1940.

Hentig, Werner Otto von. *Mein Leben eine Dienstreise.* Göttingen: Vandenhoeck & Ruprecht, 1962.

Hesse, Fritz. *Das Spiel um Deutschland.* Munich: Paul List, 1953.

Hilger, Gustav. *Wir und der Kreml: Deutsch-sowjetische Beziehungen 1918–1941.* Bonn: Athenäum, 1964.

Hitler, Adolf. *Mein Kampf.* 2 vols. Munich: Eher, 1933 edition.

Hitlers zweites Buch: Ein Dokument aus dem Jahr 1928. Edited by Gerhard L. Weinberg. Stuttgart: Deutsche Verlags-Anstalt, 1969.

Hoare, Sir Samuel (Lord Templewood). *Nine Troubled Years.* London: Collins, 1954.

Holtzendorff, Hans von. *Landsknecht und Hofnarr.* Göttingen: Musterschmidt, 1971.

Horthy, Miklos. *Ein Leben für Ungarn.* Bonn: Athenäum, 1953.

Hossbach, Friedrich. *Zwischen Wehrmacht und Hitler.* Wolfenbüttel: Wolfenbütteler Verlagsanstalt, 1949.

Höttl, Wilhelm (pseud. Walter Hagen). *Die geheime Front.* Linz: Niebelungen-Verlag, 1950.

Hull, Cordell. *Memoirs.* 2 vols. New York: Macmillan, 1948.

Jodl, Louise. *Jenseits des Endes: Leben und Sterben des Generaloberst Alfred Jodl.* Vienna: Molden, 1976.

John, Otto. *Twice through the Lines.* New York: Harper & Row, 1972.

Jones, Thomas. *A Diary with Letters, 1931–1950*. London: Oxford University Press, 1954. The full publication of the diary has not yet reached the period of this book.

Kaeckkenbeek, Georges. *The International Experiment of Upper Silesia: A Study in the Workings of the Upper Silesian Settlement, 1922–1937*. Oxford: Oxford University Press, 1942.

Kennan, George F. *From Prague after Munich: Diplomatic Papers, 1938–1940*. Princeton, N.J.: Princeton University Press, 1968.

Kesselring, Albert. *Soldat bis zum letzten Tag*. Bonn: Athenäum, 1935.

Kirkpatrick, Ivone. *The Inner Circle: Memoirs*. New York: St. Martin's, 1959.

Kleist, Bruno Peter. *Zwischen Hitler und Stalin*. Bonn: Athenäum, 1950.

Kordt, Erich. *Nicht aus den Akten*. Stuttgart: Deutsche Verlags-Anstalt, 1950.

Krivitsky, Walter G. *In Stalin's Secret Service*. New York: Harper, 1939.

Krogmann, Carl Vincent. *Es ging um Deutschlands Zukunft, 1932–1939*. Leoni: Druffel, 1976.

Kroll, Hans. *Lebenserinnerungen eines Botschafters*. Cologne: Kiepenheuer, Witsch, 1967.

Labougle, Eduardo. *Mision en Berlin*. Buenos Aires: Guillermo Kraft, 1946.

Leith-Ross, Frederick. *Money Talks: Fifty Years of International Finance*. London: Hutchinson, 1968.

Liddell Hart, Basil H. *Memoirs*. London: Cassell, 1965.

Lindbergh, Charles A. *The Wartime Journals of Charles A. Lindbergh*. New York: Harcourt Brace Jovanovich, 1970.

Macmillan, Harold. *Winds of Change, 1914–1939*. New York: Harper & Row, 1966.

Magistrati, Massimo. *L'Italia a Berlino (1937–1939)*. Verona: Mondadori, 1956.

Maisky, Ivan M. *Who Helped Hitler?* London: Hutchinson, 1964.

Marcus, Ernst. "The German Foreign Office and the Palestine Question in the Period 1933–1939." *Yad Washem Studies in the European Jewish Catastrophe and Resistance*, 2 (1958), 179–201. Memoirs written in 1946.

Massigli, René. *La Turquie devant la guerre: Mission à Ankara, 1939–1940*. Paris: Plon, 1964. Memoirs including excerpts from documents in the author's files.

Meinertzhagen, Richard. *Middle East Diary, 1917–1956*. London: Crescent Press, 1959.

Molotov, Vyacheslav H. *The International Situation and Soviet Foreign Policy*. Moscow, 1939.

Müller, Vincenz. *Ich fand das wahre Vaterland*. Berlin (East): Deutscher Militärverlag, 1963.

Nicolson, Harold. *Diaries and Letters, 1930–1939*. New York: Atheneum, 1966.

Noël, Léon. *L'aggression allemande contre la Pologne*. Paris: Flammarion, 1946.

Overstraeten, Robert von. *Albert I—Leopold III: Vingt ans de politique militaire belge, 1920–1940*. Bruges: Desclée de Brouwer, 1949.

Papen, Franz von. *Der Wahrheit eine Gasse*. Munich: Paul List, 1952.

Pelényi, John. "The Secret Plan for a Hungarian Government in Exile in the West at the Outbreak of World War II." *Journal of Modern History*, 36, No. 2 (June 1964), 170–77, and note following p. 243.

Ribbentrop, Joachim von. *The Ribbentrop Memoir*. London: Weidenfeld & Nicolson, 1954.

Rieckhoff, Herbert Joachim. *Trumpf oder Bluff? 12 Jahre deutsche Luftwaffe*. Geneva: Interavia-Verlag, 1945.

Rintelen, Enno von. *Mussolini als Bundesgenosse: Erinnerungen des deutschen Militärattachés in Rom, 1936–1943*. Tübingen: Rainer Wunderlich, 1951.

Röhricht, Edgar. *Pflicht und Gewissen: Erinnerungen eines deutschen Generals, 1932–1944*. Stuttgart: Kohlhammer, 1965.

Schmidt, Paul. *Statist auf diplomatischer Bühne, 1923–1945*. Bonn: Athenäum, 1950.

Schwerin-Krosigk, Lutz von. *Memoiren*. Stuttgart: Seewald, 1977.

Speer, Albert. *Erinnerungen*. Berlin: Propyläen, 1969.

———. *Spandauer Tagebücher*. Berlin: Propyläen, 1975.

Spier, Eugen. *Focus: A Footnote of the Thirties*. London: Oswald Wolff, 1963.

Stehlin, Paul. *Temoignage pour l'histoire*. Paris: Robert Laffont, 1964.

Strang, William (Lord Strang). *Home and Abroad*. London: André Deutsch, 1956.

Szembek, Jean. *Journal, 1933–1939*. Paris: Plon, 1952. A selection from the original in Polish. Cited as *Szembek Diary*.

Szymánski, Antoni. "Als polnischer Militärattaché in Berlin, 1932–1939." *Politische Studien*, 13, No. 141 (1962), 42–51.

Tennant, Ernest W. D. *True Account*. London: Max Parrish, 1957.

Tournoux, Paul-Emile. *Haute commandement: Gouvernement et défense des frontières du nord et de l'est, 1919–1939*. Paris: Nouvelles Editions Latines, 1960.

Vansittart, Robert. *Bones of Contention*. New York: Knopf, 1945.

———. *The Mist Procession*. London: Hutchinson, 1958.

Vauhnik, Vladimir. *Memoiren eines Militärattachés*. Klagenfurt: Hermagorasbrüderschaft, 1967.

Vogel, Georg. *Diplomat unter Hitler und Adenauer*. Düsseldorf: Econ Verlag, 1969.

Wagner, Eduard. *Der Generalquartiermeister: Briefe und Tagebuch*. Edited by Elisabeth Wagner. Munich: Olzog, 1963.

Warlimont, Walter. *Im Hauptquartier der deutschen Wehrmacht, 1939–1945*. Bonn: Athenäum, 1964.

Weizsäcker, Ernst von. *Erinnerungen*. Munich: Paul List, 1950. See also his papers edited by Leonidas Hill.

Wiedemann, Fritz. *Der Mann der Feldherr werden wollte*. Dortmund: Blick & Bild Verlag, 1964.

Wilson, Hugh R. *A Career Diplomat: The Third Chapter, the Third Reich*. Edited by Hugh R. Wilson, Jr. New York: Vantage Press, 1960.

———. *Diplomat between Wars*. New York: Longmans, Green, 1941.

Wimmer, Lothar C. F. *Expériences et tribulations d'un diplomate austrichien entre deux guerres, 1929–1938*. Translated by Charles Reichard. Neuchâtel: Editions de la Baconnière, c. 1946. Useful for diplomatic reports in addition to those printed in *Guido Schmidt Trial*, pp. 544–56.

Zay, Jean. *Carnet secrèts de Jean Zay (de Munich à la guerre)*. Edited by Philippe Herriot. Paris: Editions de France, 1942. Important though published by a vehement enemy of the author.

Zuylen, Pierre van. *Les mains libres: Politique extérieure de la Belgique, 1914–1940*. Paris: Desclée de Brouwer, 1950.

IV. Secondary Works

Abel, Karl-Dietrich. *Presselenkung im NS-Staat*. Berlin: Colloquium Verlag, 1968.

Abendroth, Hans-Henning. *Hitler in der spanischen Arena*. Paderborn: Ferdinand Schöningh, 1973. Very important study.

Abshagen, Karl Heinz. *Canaris, Patriot und Weltbürger*. Stuttgart: Union Deutsche Verlagsgesellschaft, 1950.

Adam, Colin Forbes. *The Life of Lord Lloyd*. London: Macmillan, 1948.

Adamthwaite, Anthony. *France and the Coming of the Second World War,*

1936–1939. London: Frank Cass, 1977. Author had some access to the French archives.

Addington, Larry H. *The Blitzkrieg Era and the German General Staff, 1865– 1941*. New Brunswick, N.J.: Rutgers University Press, 1971.

Adli, Abolfazl. *Aussenhandel und Aussenwirtschaftspolitik des Iran*. Berlin: Duncker & Humblot, 1960.

Adolph, Walter. *Kardinal Preysing und zwei Diktaturen: Sein Widerstand gegen die totalitäre Macht*. Berlin: Morus, 1971.

Aigner, Dietrich. *Das Ringen um England: Das deutsch-britische Verhältnis, die öffentliche Meinung 1933–1939, Tragödie zweier Völker*. Munich: Bechtle, 1969. Often cited, but hopelessly unreliable.

Anderson, Mosa. *Noel Buxton: A Life*. London: Allen Unwin, 1952. A full defense of appeasement from the record of a Labor peer.

Andrews, Eric Montgomery. *Isolationism and Appeasement in Australia: Reactions to the European Crises, 1935–1939*. Columbia, S.C.: University of South Carolina Press, 1970. Uses British and Australian documents.

Armstrong, John A. *The Politics of Totalitarianism*. New York: Random House, 1961.

———. *Ukrainian Nationalism, 1939–1945*. 2d ed. New York: Columbia University Press, 1963.

Assmann, Kurt. *Deutsche Schicksalsjahre*. Wiesbaden: Brockhaus, 1950.

Aster, Sidney. "Ivan Maisky and Parliamentary Anti-Appeasement 1938–39." In Alan J. P. Taylor (ed.), *Lloyd George: Twelve Essays*, pp. 317–57. London: Hamish Hamilton, 1970.

———. *1939: The Making of the Second World War*. London: André Deutsch, 1973. Very useful and based on extensive work in British archives and private papers.

Bärnthaler, Irmgard. *Die Vaterländische Front: Geschichte und Organisation*. Vienna: Europa-Verlag, 1971.

Bagel-Bohlan, Anja E. *Hitlers industrielle Kriegsvorbereitung, 1936 bis 1939*. Koblenz: Wehr & Wissen, 1975.

Bariéty, Jacques. "Léon Blum et l'Allemagne, 1930–1938." In *Les relations franco-allemandes, 1933–1939*, pp. 33–55. Paris: Editions du Centre National de la Recherche Scientifique, 1976. Absolutely essential for an understanding of Blum's foreign policy.

Barnett, Correlli. *The Collapse of British Power*. New York: William Morrow, 1972. Full of interesting and controversial ideas.

Barros, James. *Betrayal from Within: Joseph Avenol, Secretary-General of the League of Nations, 1933–1940*. New Haven: Yale University Press, 1969.

Batowski, Henryk. "Polnische diplomatische Akten aus den Jahren 1938/39." *Jahrbücher für Geschichte der UdSSR und der Volksdemokratischen Länder*, 8 (1964), 425–45. A helpful introduction.

———. "Le Voyage de Joseph Beck en Roumanie en octobre 1938." *Annuaire polonais des affaires internationales, 1959–1960*, pp. 137–60. Warsaw: Institut Polonais des Affaires Internationales, n.d. Material from Polish and Rumanian archives.

Baum, Walter. "Marine, Nationalsozialismus und Widerstand." *Vierteljahrshefte für Zeitgeschichte*, 11, No. 1 (Jan. 1963), 16–48.

Baumgart, Winfried. "Zur Ansprache Hitlers vor den Führern der Wehrmacht am 22. August 1939." *Vierteljahrshefte für Zeitgeschichte*, 16, No. 2 (Aug. 1968), 120–49; 19, No. 3 (July 1971), 294–304.

Beck, Earl R. *Verdict on Schacht*. Tallahassee: Florida State University Press, 1955.

Bell, Leland V. *In Hitler's Shadow: The Anatomy of American Nazism*. Port

Washington, N.Y.: Kennikat Press, 1973.

Beloff, Max. *The Foreign Policy of Soviet Russia*. 2, *1936–1941*. London: Oxford University Press, 1949.

ben Elissar, Eliahu. *La diplomatie du IIIe Reich et les Juifs (1933–1939)*. Paris: Juilliard, 1969.

Bernardini, Gene. "The Origins and Development of Racial Anti-Semitism in Fascist Italy." *Journal of Modern History*, 49, No. 3 (Sept. 1977), 431–53.

Bialer, Uri. "'Humanization' of Air Warfare in British Foreign Policy on the Eve of the Second World War." *Journal of Contemporary History*, 13, No. 1 (Jan. 1978), 79–96.

Bigler, Robert M. "Heil Hitler and Heil Horthy! The Nature of Hungarian Racist Nationalism and Its Impact on German-Hungarian Relations." *East European Quarterly*, 8, No. 3 (Fall 1974), 251–72.

Binion, Rudolph. "Repeat Performance: A Psycho-Historical Study of Leopold III and Belgian Neutrality." *History and Theory*, 8, No. 2 (1969), 213–59. Kieft's work is more convincing.

Birkenfeld, Wolfgang. *Der synthetische Treibstoff 1933–1945: Ein Beitrag zur nationalsozialistischen Wirtschafts- und Rüstungspolitik*. Göttingen: Musterschmidt, 1964.

Birkenhead, Earl of. *Halifax: The Life of Lord Halifax*. Boston: Houghton Mifflin, 1966.

Blaker, Michael. *Japanese International Negotiating Style*. New York: Columbia University Press, 1977.

Blinkhorn, Martin. *Carlism and Crisis in Spain, 1931–1939*. New York: Cambridge University Press, 1975.

Bloch, Kurt. *German Interests and Policies in the Far East*. New York: Institute of Pacific Relations, 1940. Still useful.

Bodensieck, Heinrich. "Der Plan eines Freundschaftsvertrages zwischen dem Reich und der Tschechoslowakei im Jahre 1938." *Zeitschrift für Ostforschung*, 10 (1961), 462–76.

Boltin, E. A., and Telpuchowski, B. S. (eds.). *Geschichte des Grossen Vaterländischen Krieges der Sowjetunion*. 1, *Die Vorbereitung und Entfesselung des Zweiten Weltkrieges durch die Imperialistischen Mächte*. Berlin (East): Deutscher Militärverlag, 1962.

Bond, Brian. *France and Belgium, 1939–1940*. London: Davis-Poynter, 1975.

Booms, Hans. "Der Ursprung des Zweiten Weltkrieges—Revision oder Expansion?" *Geschichte in Wissenschaft und Unterricht*, 16, No. 6 (June 1965), 329–53.

Borg, Dorothy. "Notes on Roosevelt's 'Quarantine' Speech." *Political Science Quarterly*, 72 (Sept. 1957), 405–33.

———. *The United States and the Far Eastern Crisis of 1933–1938*. Cambridge, Mass.: Harvard University Press, 1964.

Borg, Dorothy, and Okamoto, Shumpei (eds.). *Pearl Harbor as History: Japanese–American Relations 1931–1941*. New York: Columbia University Press, 1973.

Bosl, Karl (ed.). *Die "Burg": Einflussreiche Kräfte um Masaryk und Beneš*. 2 vols. Munich: Oldenbourg, 1974. See esp. the piece by Hoensch in 2:31–57.

———. *Gleichgewicht, Revision und Restauration: Die Aussenpolitik der ersten tschechoslowakischen Republik*. Munich: Oldenbourg, 1976.

Botz, Gerhard. "Wien und Osteuropa nach dem Anschluss: Die Rolle des Wiener Bürgermeisters in der nationalsozialistischen Aussenpolitik des Jahres 1938." *Österreichische Osthefte*, 16, No. 2 (May 1974), 113–22.

———. *Die Eingliederung Österreichs in das Deutsche Reich: Planung und Verwirklichung des politisch-administrativen Anschlusses (1938–1940)*. Vienna:

Europa-Verlag, 1972.

Bracher, Karl Dietrich; Sauer, Wolfgang; and Schulz, Gerhard. *Die national-sozialistische Machtergreifung*. 2d ed. Cologne: Westdeutscher Verlag, 1962.

Braddick, Henderson B. *Germany, Czechoslovakia, and the "Grand Alliance" in the May Crisis, 1938*. Denver: University of Denver, 1969.

Breyer, Richard. *Das Deutsche Reich und Polen, 1932–1937: Aussenpolitik und Volksgruppenfragen*. Würzburg: Holzner, 1955.

Brook-Shepherd, Gordon. *The Anschluss*. Philadelphia: Lippincott, 1963.

Broszat, Martin. "Deutschland-Ungarn-Rumänien: Entwicklung und Grund-faktoren nationalsozialistischer Hegemonial- und Bündnispolitik 1938–1941." *Historische Zeitschrift*, 206, No. 1 (Feb. 1968), 45–96.

———. "Hitler und die Genesis der 'Endlösung.'" *Vierteljahrshefte für Zeit-geschichte*, 25, No. 4 (Oct. 1977), 739–75.

———. *Nationalsozialistische Polenpolitik, 1939–1945*. Stuttgart: Deutsche Verlags-Anstalt, 1961.

———. "Das Sudetendeutsche Freikorps." *Vierteljahrshefte für Zeitgeschichte*, 9, No. 1 (Jan. 1961), 30–49.

Brügel, Johann W. "Der Runciman Bericht." *Vierteljahrshefte für Zeitgeschichte*, 26, No. 4 (Oct. 1978), 652–59.

———. *Tschechen und Deutsche, 1918–1938*. Munich: Nymphenburger Verlags-handlung, 1967.

Bryson, Thomas A. "Roosevelt's Quarantine Speech: The Georgia Press and the Borg Thesis." *Australian Journal of Politics and History*, 21, No. 2 (Aug. 1975), 95–98.

Buchheit, Gert. *Ludwig Beck, ein preussischer General*. Munich: List, 1964.

Budurowycz, Bohdan B. *Polish-Soviet Relations, 1932–1939*. New York: Colum-bia University Press, 1963.

Bullock, Alan. *Hitler: A Study in Tyranny*. London: Odhams Press, 1952, and later editions.

Burns, Richard Dean, and Bennett, Edward H. (eds.). *Diplomats in Crisis: United States–Chinese–Japanese Relations, 1919–1941*. Santa Barbara, Calif.: ABC-Clio, 1974.

Bussmann, Walter. "Ein deutsch-französischer Verständigungsversuch vom 6. Dezember 1938." *Nachrichten der Akademie der Wissenschaften in Göt-tingen*. 1, *Philologisch-Historische Klasse*, 1953, No. 2.

———. "Zur Entstehung und Überlieferung der 'Hossbach Niederschrift.'" *Vierteljahrshefte für Zeitgeschichte*, 16, No. 4 (Oct. 1968), 373–84.

Butler, J. R. M. *Lord Lothian, 1882–1940*. London: Macmillan, 1960.

Butterworth, Susan B. "Daladier and the Munich Crisis: A Reappraisal." *Journal of Contemporary History*, 9, No. 3 (July 1974), 191–216.

Campbell, F. Gregory. *Confrontation in Central Europe: Weimar Germany and Czechoslovakia*. Chicago: University of Chicago Press, 1975.

Campus, Eliza. "La diplomatie roumaine et les relations franco-allemandes pen-dant les années 1933–1939." In *Les relations franco-allemandes 1933–1939*, pp. 335–52. Important for its use of Rumanian archives.

———. "Die Hitlerfaschistische Infiltration Rumäniens, 1939–1940." *Zeitschrift für Geschichtswissenschaft*, 5 (1957), 213–28.

Carr, William. *Arms, Autarchy, and Aggression: A Study in German Foreign Policy, 1933–1939*. New York: Norton, 1972.

Carroll, Berenice A. *Design for Aggression: Arms and Economics in the Third Reich*. The Hague: Mouton, 1968. A distinctly superior work.

Carsten, Francis L. *Fascist Movements in Austria: From Schönerer to Hitler*. London: Sage, 1977. A preliminary summary.

Cattell, David I. *Soviet Diplomacy and the Spanish Civil War*. Berkeley: University of California Press, 1957.

Celovsky, Boris. *Das Münchener Abkommen von 1938*. Stuttgart: Deutsche Verlags-Anstalt, 1958.

Chanady, A., and Jensen, J. "Germany, Rumania, and the British Guarantees of March-April, 1939." *Australian Journal of Politics and History*, 16, No. 2 (Aug. 1970), 201–17.

Churchill, Winston S. *The Second World War*. 1, *The Gathering Storm*. Boston: Houghton Mifflin, 1948.

Cienciala, Anna M. "Poland and the Munich Crisis, 1938: A Reappraisal." *East European Quarterly*, 3, No. 2 (June 1969), 201–19.

———. *Poland and the Western Powers, 1938–1939*. London: Routledge & Kegan Paul, 1968.

Cierva, Ricardo de la. *Historia de la guerra civil española*. 1, *Perspectivas y antecedentes, 1898–1936*. Madrid: San Martin, 1969. Important material from Spanish archives.

Clarke, Jeffrey J. "The Nationalization of War Industries in France, 1936–1937: A Case Study." *Journal of Modern History*, 49, No. 3 (Sept. 1977). Access to archives of Renault.

Clifford, Nicholas R. *Retreat from China: British Policy in the Far East, 1937–1941*. Seattle: University of Washington Press, 1967.

Cohen, Michael J. "Appeasement in the Middle East: The British White Paper on Palestine, May 1939." *Historical Journal*, 16, No. 3 (Sept. 1973), 571–96.

———. "British Strategy and the Palestine Question, 1936–1939." *Journal of Contemporary History*, 7, Nos. 3–4 (July–Oct. 1972), 157–83.

Colvin, Ian. *None So Blind: A British Diplomatic View of the Origin of World War II*. New York: Harcourt, Brace & World, 1965.

Conway, John S. *The Nazi Persecution of the Churches, 1933–1945*. London: Weidenfeld & Nicolson, 1968.

———. "The Vatican, Great Britain, and Relations with Germany, 1938–1940." *Historical Journal*, 16, No. 1 (Jan. 1973), 147–67.

Coox, Alvin D. *The Anatomy of a Small War: The Soviet-Japanese Struggle for Changkufeng-Khasan, 1938*. Westport, Conn.: Greenwood Press, 1977. Very detailed.

Coverdale, John F. *Italian Intervention in the Spanish Civil War*. Princeton, N.J.: Princeton University Press, 1975. Author had access to Italian archives.

Cowling, Maurice. *The Impact of Hitler, British Politics, and British Policy, 1933–1940*. London: Cambridge University Press, 1975. Interesting but not always successful effort to relate domestic to foreign policy.

Craig, Gordon. *The Politics of the Prussian Army, 1640–1945*. New York: Oxford University Press, 1956.

Craig, Gordon, and Gilbert, Felix (eds.). *The Diplomats*. Princeton, N.J.: Princeton University Press, 1953.

Cross, John A. *Sir Samuel Hoare: A Political Biography*. London: Cape, 1977.

Crowley, James B. *Japan's Quest for Autonomy: National Security and Foreign Policy, 1930–1938*. Princeton, N.J.: Princeton University Press, 1966.

Dallin, Alexander. *German Rule in Russia, 1941–1945*. New York: St. Martin's, 1957.

Deakin, Frederick W., and Storry, G. R. *The Case of Richard Sorge*. London: Chatto & Windus, 1966.

Dekel, Efraim. *Shai: The Exploits of Hagana Intelligence*. New York: Thomas Yoseloff, 1959.

Delfiner, Henry. *The Vienna Broadcasts to Slovakia: A Case Study in Subversion*. New York: Columbia University Press, 1974.

Delzell, Charles F. (ed.). *The Papacy and Totalitarianism between the Two World*

Wars. New York: Wiley, 1974.

――――. "Pius XII, Italy and the Outbreak of War." *Journal of Contemporary History,* 2, No. 4 (1967), 137–61.

Denne, Ludwig. *Das Danzig-Problem in der deutschen Aussenpolitik 1934–39.* Bonn: Röhrscheid, 1959.

Dennis, Peter. *Decision by Default: Peacetime Conscription and British Defence, 1919–1939.* Durham, N.C.: Duke University Press, 1972.

Detwiler, Donald S. *Hitler, Franco und Gibraltar: Die Frage des spanischen Eintritts in den Zweiten Weltkrieg.* Wiesbaden: Steiner, 1962.

Deutsch, Harold C. *Hitler and His Generals: The Hidden Crisis, January–June 1938.* Minneapolis: University of Minnesota Press, 1974.

Diamond, Sander. *The Nazi Movement in the United States, 1924–1941.* Ithaca, N.Y.: Cornell University Press, 1974.

Divine, Robert A. *Roosevelt and World War II.* Baltimore: Johns Hopkins University Press, 1969.

Doherty, Julian C. *Das Ende des Appeasement.* Berlin: Colloquium Verlag, 1973.

Dolezel, Stephan. "Deutschland und die Rest-Tschechoslowakei (1938–1939): Besatzungspolitische Vorstellungen vor dem deutschen Einmarsch." In Karl Bosl (ed.), *Gleichgewicht, Revision und Restauration,* pp. 253–64.

Dolmanyos, Istvan. "Die diplomatischen Beziehungen Horthy-Ungarns zur UdSSR im Spiegel eines Tagebuches (1920–1939)." *Jahrbuch für Geschichte der sozialistischen Länder Europas,* 13, pt. 2 (1969), 123–40.

Donaldson, Frances. *Edward VIII.* New York: Lippincott, 1975.

Douglas, Roy. "Chamberlain and Eden, 1937–38." *Journal of Contemporary History,* 13, No. 1 (Jan. 1978), 97–116.

Douglas-Hamilton, James. *Motive for a Mission: The Story behind Hess's Flight to Britain.* New York: St. Martin's, 1971.

Drechsler, Karl. *Deutschland–China–Japan, 1933–1939: Das Dilemma der deutschen Fernostpolitik.* Berlin (East): Akademie-Verlag, 1964.

Dreifort, John E. "The French Popular Front and the Franco-Soviet Pact, 1936–37: A Dilemma in Foreign Policy." *Journal of Contemporary History,* 11, Nos. 2–3 (July 1976), 217–36.

――――. *Yvon Delbos at the Quai d'Orsay.* Lawrence, Kans.: University Press of Kansas, 1973.

Dreisziger, Nandor A. F. "Civil-Military Relations in Nazi Germany's Shadow: The Case of Hungary." In Adrian Preston (ed.), *Swords and Covenants,* pp. 216–47. London: Croom Helm, 1976.

――――. *Hungary's Way to World War II.* Astor Park, Fla.: Danubian Press, 1968.

Dülffer, Jost. *Weimar, Hitler und die Marine: Reichspolitik und Flottenbau 1920 bis 1939.* Düsseldorf: Droste, 1973. A very helpful work.

Eayrs, James. *In Defence of Canada: Appeasement and Rearmament.* Toronto: University of Toronto Press, 1965. Important material from Canadian archives.

Ebel, Arnold. *Das Dritte Reich und Argentinien: Die diplomatischen Beziehungen unter besonderer Berücksichtigung der Handelspolitik (1933–1939).* Cologne: Böhlau, 1971.

Edouard Daladier, chef de gouvernement. Paris: Presses de la Fondation nationale des sciences politiques, 1977. Pieces by René Girault and François Bédaride on foreign policy.

Einhorn, Marion. *Die ökonomischen Hintergründe der faschistischen deutschen Intervention in Spanien 1936–1939.* Berlin (East): Akademie-Verlag, 1962.

Engel-Jánosi, Friedrich. *Vom Chaos zur Katastrophe: Vatikanische Gespräche 1918 bis 1938: Vornehmlich auf Grund der Berichte der österreichischen Gesandten beim Heiligen Stuhl.* Vienna: Herold, 1971.

Erickson, John. *The Soviet High Command.* London: Macmillan, 1962.

Eubank, Keith. *Munich*. Norman, Okla.: University of Oklahoma Press, 1963.

Europäische Publikation. *Die Vollmacht des Gewissens*. Vol. 1. Munich: Hermann Rinn, 1956.

Feilchenfeld, Werner; Michaelis, Dolf; and Pinner, Ludwig. *Haavara-Transfer nach Palästina und Einwanderung deutscher Juden 1933–1939*. Tübingen: Mohr, 1972.

Feiling, Keith. *The Life of Neville Chamberlain*. London: Macmillan, 1946.

Felice, Renzo de. "Betrachtungen zu Mussolinis Aussenpolitik." *Saeculum*, 24, No. 4 (1973), 314–27.

————. *Storia degli ebrei italiani sotto il fascismo*. 3d ed. Turin: Einaudi, 1972.

Fest, Joachim C. *Hitler: Eine Biographie*. Berlin: Propyläen, 1973. Note the particularly thoughtful critique by Hermann Graml in *Vierteljahrshefte für Zeitgeschichte*, 22, No. 1 (Jan. 1974), 76–92.

Förster, Otto-Wilhelm. *Das Befestigungswesen*. Neckargemünd: Vohwinkel, 1960. Contains Hitler's memorandum on fortifications.

Foerster, Wolfgang. *Ein General kämpft gegen den Krieg: Aus den nachgelassenen Papieren des Generalstabchefs Ludwig Beck*. Munich: Münchener-Dom Verlag, 1949.

Foertsch, Hermann. *Schuld und Verhängnis: Die Fritschkrise im Februar 1938*. Stuttgart: Deutsche Verlags-Anstalt, 1951.

Forstmeier, Friedrich, and Volkmann, Hans-Erich (eds.). *Wirtschaft und Rüstung am Vorabend des Zweiten Weltkrieges*. Düsseldorf: Droste, 1975. An important collection of papers.

France, Centre national de la recherche scientifique. *Les relations franco-allemandes, 1933–1939*. Paris: Editions du Centre, 1976. A collection of papers.

————. *Les relations franco-britanniques, 1935–1939*. Paris: Editions du Centre, 1975. A collection of papers.

Fridenson, Patrick, and Lewin, Jean. *La France et la Grand Bretagne face au problèmes aériens (1935–mai 1940)*. Vincennes: Service Historique de l'Armée de l'Air, 1976.

Frye, Alton. *Nazi Germany and the American Hemisphere, 1933–1941*. New Haven: Yale University Press, 1967.

Funke, Manfred (ed.). *Hitler, Deutschland und die Mächte: Materialien zur Aussenpolitik des Dritten Reiches*. Düsseldorf: Droste, 1977.

Gackenholz, Hermann. "Reichskanzlei, 5. November 1937." In *Forschungen zu Staat und Verfassung: Festgabe für Fritz Hartung*, pp. 59–84. Berlin: Duncker & Humblot, 1959.

Gannon, Franklin Reid. *The British Press and Germany 1936–1939*. Oxford: Clarendon Press, 1971. Author had access to archives of *Times*, *Guardian*, and some journalists' papers.

Gehl, Jürgen. *Austria, Germany, and the Anschluss, 1931–1938*. London: Oxford University Press, 1963.

Geiss, Imanuel, and Wendt, Bernd-Jürgen (eds.). *Deutschland und die Weltpolitik des 19. and 20. Jahrhunderts*. Düsseldorf: Bertelsmann, 1973.

Gemzell, Carl-Axel. *Raeder, Hitler und Skandinavien: Der Kampf für einen maritimen Operationsplan*. Lund: Gleerup, 1965.

Gentzen, Felix-Heinrich. "Die Rolle der 'Deutschen Stiftung' bei der Vorbereitung der Annexion des Memellandes im März 1939." *Jahrbuch für Geschichte der UdSSR und der Volksdemokratischen Länder*, 5 (1961), 71–94.

Genzel, Fritz. "Die deutsch-kanadischen Beziehungen." In Manfred Funke (ed.), *Hitler, Deutschland und die Mächte*, pp. 327–38.

Gibbs, Norman H. *Grand Strategy*. 1, *Rearmament Policy*. London: H.M. Stationery Office, 1976.

Gilbert, Martin. *Winston S. Churchill*. 5, *1922–1939: The Prophet of Truth*. Boston: Houghton Mifflin, 1977. Very one-sided, but containing much useful material.

Gilbert, Martin, and Gott, Richard. *The Appeasers*. Boston: Houghton Mifflin, 1963.

Glasneck, Johannes, and Kircheisen, Inge. *Türkei und Afghanistan—Brennpunkte der Orientpolitik im Zweiten Weltkrieg*. Berlin (East): VEB Deutscher Verlag der Wissenschaften, 1968.

Graml, Hermann, et al. *The German Resistance to Hitler*. Berkeley: University of California Press, 1970.

Gregor, A. James. *The Ideology of Fascism*. New York: Free Press, 1969.

Greiner, Helmuth. *Die oberste Wehrmachtführung, 1939–1943*. Wiesbaden: Limes, 1951.

Gromada, Thaddeus V. "Poland and Slovakia during the September–October Crisis of 1938." In Damian S. Wandycz (ed.), *Studies in Polish Civilization*, pp. 117–28. New York: Columbia University Press, 1966.

——— (ed.). *Essays on Poland's Foreign Policy, 1918–1939*. New York: Józef Pilsudski Institute of America, 1970. See in this collection the editor's "The Slovaks and the Failure of Beck's 'Third Europe' Scheme," pp. 59–68.

Gun, Nerin E. *Eva Braun, Hitler's Mistress*. London: Leslie Frewin, 1968.

Gundelach, Karl. "Gedanken über die Führung eines Luftkrieges gegen England bei der Luftflotte 2 in den Jahren 1938/39: Ein Beitrag zur Vorgeschichte der Luftschlacht um England." *Wehrwissenschaftliche Rundschau*, 10, No. 1 (Jan. 1960), 33–46.

Guttmann, Allen. *The Wound in the Heart: America and the Spanish Civil War*. New York: Random House, 1962.

Haag, John. "'Knights of the Spirit': The Kameradschaftsbund." *Journal of Contemporary History*, 8, No. 3 (July 1973), 113–32.

Hagemann, Walter. *Publizistik im Dritten Reich*. Hamburg: Hamburger Gildenverlag, 1948.

Haight, John M., Jr. *American Aid to France, 1938–1940*. New York: Atheneum, 1970. Access to some French archives.

Harms-Baltzer, Käte. *Die Nationalisierung der deutschen Einwanderer und ihrer Nachkommen in Brasilien als Problem der deutsch-brasilianischen Beziehungen 1930–1938*. Berlin: Colloquium Verlag, 1970. Much broader than title indicates.

Harper, Glenn T. *German Economic Policy in Spain during the Spanish Civil War, 1936–1939*. The Hague: Mouton, 1967.

Harrigan, William M. "Pius XI and Nazi Germany, 1937–1939." *Catholic Historical Review*, 51, No. 4 (Jan. 1966), 457–86.

———. "Pius XII's Effort to Effect a *Détente* in German-Vatican Relations, 1939–40." *Catholic Historical Review*, 49, No. 2 (July 1963), 173–91.

Hegemann, Margot. "Die 'Deutsche Volksgruppe in Rumänien'—eine Fünfte Kolonne des deutschen Imperialismus in Südosteuropa." *Jahrbuch für Geschichte der UdSSR und der Volksdemokratischen Länder*, 4 (1960), 371–81.

Hell, Jürgen. *Der deutsche Faschismus in Lateinamerika, 1933–1943*. Berlin (East): Humboldt-Universität, 1966.

Heller, Richard. "East Fulham Revisited." *Journal of Contemporary History*, 6, No. 3 (1971), 172–96.

Helmreich, Jonathan E. *Belgium and Europe: A Study in Small Power Diplomacy*. The Hague: Mouton, 1976.

Henke, Josef. *England in Hitlers politischem Kalkül, 1935–1939*. Boppard: Boldt, 1973.

Henrikson, Göran. "Das Nürnberger Dokument 386-PS (das 'Hossbach-Protokoll')." *Lund Studies in International History*, 2 (1970), 151–94.

Herzfeld, Hans. "Zur Problematik der Appeasement-Politik." In *Geschichte und Gegenwartsbewusstsein: Festschrift für Hans Rothfels*, pp. 161–97. Göttingen: Vandenhoeck & Ruprecht, 1963.

Hiden, John. *Germany and Europe, 1919–1939*. New York: Longmans, 1977. A useful introduction.

————. "The Weimar Republic and the Problem of the Auslandsdeutsche." *Journal of Contemporary History*, 12, No. 2 (April 1977), 273–89.

Hildebrand, Klaus. *Deutsche Aussenpolitik 1933–1945: Kalkül oder Dogma?* Stuttgart: Kohlhammer, 1971.

————. *Vom Reich zum Weltreich: Hitler, NSDAP und koloniale Frage, 1919–1945*. Munich: Fink, 1969.

Hill, Leonidas. "Three Crises, 1938–39." *Journal of Contemporary History*, 3, No. 1 (Jan. 1968), 113–44. Reviews the contribution of the Weizsäcker papers to the Munich, Prague, and Polish crises.

Hillgruber, Andreas. *Deutsche Grossmacht- und Weltpolitik im 19. und 20. Jahrhundert*. Düsseldorf: Droste, 1977. A useful collection of the author's previously published pieces. Note "Der Faktor Amerika in Hitlers Strategie 1938–1941," pp. 197–22.

————. *Hitler, König Carol und Marschall Antonescu: Die deutsch-rumänischen Beziehungen 1938–1944*. Wiesbaden: Steiner, 1954.

————. *Hitlers Strategie: Politik und Kriegführung 1940–1941*. Frankfurt/M: Bernard & Graefe, 1965. A most important study.

Hilton, Stanley E. *Brazil and the Great Powers, 1930–1939: The Politics of Trade Rivalry*. Austin: University of Texas Press, 1975. Based on extraordinary use of Brazilian (as well as U.S., British, and German) archives.

Hirszowicz, Lukacz. *The Third Reich and the Arab East*. London: Routledge & Kegan Paul, 1966.

Hoch, Anton. "Das Attentat auf Hitler im Münchener Bürgerbräukeller 1939." *Vierteljahrshefte für Zeitgeschichte*, 14, No. 4 (Oct. 1969), 383–413.

Höhne, Heinz. *Codeword "Direktor"*. New York: Coward, McCann & Geoghegan, 1971. Pertains to Soviet espionage in Germany.

————. *Der Orden unter dem Totenkopf: Die Geschichte der SS*. Essen: Bertelsmann, 1969.

Hoensch, Jörg K. "Revision und Expansion, Überlegungen zur Zielsetzung, Methode und Planung der Tschechoslowakei-Politik Hitlers." *Bohemia*, 9 (1968), 208–28; response by Johann W. Brügel, 11 (1971), 365–74.

————. *Die Slowakei in Hitlers Ostpolitik*. Cologne: Böhlau, 1965. Cited as Hoensch, *Slowakei*.

————. *Der ungarische Revisionismus und die Zerschlagung der Tschechoslowakei*. Tübingen: Mohr, 1967. Cited as Hoensch, *Ungarische Revisionismus*.

Hofer, Walter. *Die Entfesselung des Zweiten Weltkrieges: Eine Studie über die internationalen Beziehungen im Sommer 1939*. 3d ed. Frankfurt/M: S. Fischer, 1964.

Holmes, Blair R. "Europe and the Habsburg Restoration in Austria, 1930–1938." *East European Quarterly*, 9, No. 2 (Summer 1974), 173–84.

Homze, Edward L. *Arming the Luftwaffe: The Reich Air Ministry and the German Aircraft Industry, 1919–1939*. Lincoln: University of Nebraska Press, 1976. A most useful work.

Hoptner, Jacob B. *Yugoslavia in Crisis, 1934–1941*. New York: Columbia University Press, 1962. Author had access to some Yugoslav materials.

Howard, Michael. *The Continental Commitment: The Dilemma of British Defence Policy in the Era of the Two World Wars*. London: Temple Smith, 1972.

Hütter, Joachim, et al. (eds.). *Tradition und Neubeginn: Internationale*

Forschungen zur deutschen Geschichte im 20. Jahrhundert. Cologne: Heymann, 1975.

Hughes, Judith M. *To the Maginot Line: The Politics of French Military Preparations in the 1920's.* Cambridge, Mass.: Harvard University Press, 1971.

Hughes, William R. *Indomitable Friend: The Life of Corder Catchpool, 1883–1952.* London: Housman, 1964.

Humbel, Kurt. *Nationalsozialistische Propaganda in der Schweiz, 1931–1939.* Bern: Haupt, 1976.

Hutchinson, Bruce. *The Incredible Canadian.* Toronto: Longmans, Green, 1953. On Mackenzie King.

Huter, Franz (ed.). *Südtirol: Eine Frage des europäischen Gewissens.* Munich: Oldenbourg, 1965.

Institut für Zeitgeschichte. *Gutachten des Instituts für Zeitgeschichte.* Vol. 1. Munich: Selbstverlag, 1958.

Jacobs, Travis Beal. "Roosevelt's 'Quarantine Speech.'" *The Historian,* 24 (Aug. 1962), 489–99.

Jacobsen, Hans-Adolf. *Nationalsozialistische Aussenpolitik 1933–1938.* Frankfurt/M: Alfred Metzner, 1968.

———. *Von der Politik der Gewalt zur Politik der Friedenssicherung.* Düsseldorf: Droste, 1977. Collection of papers.

Jäger, Jörg-Johannes. *Die wirtschaftliche Abhängigkeit des Dritten Reiches vom Ausland dargestellt am Beispiel der Stahlindustrie.* Berlin: Berlin Verlag, 1969.

James, Robert Rhodes. *Churchill: A Study in Failure, 1900–1939.* New York: World Publishing Co., 1970.

Jedlicka, Ludwig, and Neck, Rudolf (eds.). *Österreich 1927 bis 1938.* Munich: Oldenbourg, 1973.

Johnson, Niel M. *George Sylvester Viereck, German-American Propagandist.* Urbana, Ill.: University of Illinois Press, 1972.

Johnston, Verle B. *Legions of Babel: The International Brigades in the Spanish Civil War.* University Park, Pa.: Pennsylvania State University Press, 1967.

Jonas, Manfred. *Isolationism in America, 1935–1941.* Ithaca, N.Y.: Cornell University Press, 1966. A very fine study.

———. "Prophet without Honor: Hans Heinrich Dieckhoff's Reports from Washington." *Mid-America,* 47 (July 1965), 222–33.

Jones, F. C. *Japan's New Order in East Asia: Its Rise and Fall 1937–45.* London: Oxford University Press, 1954.

Joseph, Richard A. "The German Question in French Cameroun, 1919–1939." *Comparative Studies in Society and History,* 17 (Jan. 1975), 65–90.

Kahn, David. *The Codebreakers.* New York: Macmillan, 1967.

Kieft, David Own. *Belgium's Return to Neutrality.* Oxford: Clarendon Press, 1972.

Kielmansegg, Peter. "Die militärisch-politische Tragweite der Hossbach-Besprechung." *Vierteljahrshefte für Zeitgeschichte,* 8, No. 3 (July 1960), 268–74.

Kimball, Warren F. "Dieckhoff and America: A German's View of German-American Relations." *The Historian,* 27 (Feb. 1965), 218–43.

———. "Lend-Lease and the Open Door: The Temptation of British Opulence, 1937–1942." *Political Science Quarterly,* 86, No. 2 (June 1971), 232–59.

Kipphan, Klaus. *Deutsche Propaganda in den Vereinigten Staaten, 1933–1941.* Heidelberg: Carl Winter, 1971.

Kitsikis, Dimitri. "La Grèce entre l'Angleterre et l'Allemagne de 1936 à 1941." *Revue historique,* 238 (July–Sept. 1967), 85–116. Author had access to Greek archives.

Kleine-Ahlbrandt, William L. *The Policy of Simmering: A Study of British Policy during the Spanish Civil War, 1936–1939.* The Hague: Nijhoff, 1962.

Kluke, Paul. "Hitler und das Volkswagenprojekt." *Vierteljahrshefte für Zeitgeschichte,* 8, No. 4 (Oct. 1960), 341–83.

———. "Politische Form und Aussenpolitik des Nationalsozialismus." In *Geschichte und Gegenwartsbewusstsein: Festschrift für Hans Rothfels,* pp. 428–61.

Knipping, Franz. *Die amerikanische Russlandpolitik in der Zeit des Hitler-Stalin Pakts, 1939–1941.* Tübingen: Mohr, 1974.

Kochwasser, Friedrich. *Iran und Wir: Geschichte der deutsch-iranischen Handels- und Wirtschaftsbeziehungen.* Herrenalb/Schwarzwald: Horst Erdmann, 1961.

Koerner, Ralf Richard. *So haben sie es damals gemacht: Die Propagandavorbereitungen zum Österreichanschluss durch das Hitlerregime 1933–1938.* Vienna: Gesellschaft zur Förderung wissenschaftlicher Forschung, 1958.

Komjathy, Anthony T. *The Crises of France's East Central European Diplomacy, 1933–1938.* New York: Columbia University Press, 1976.

Kordt, Erich. *Wahn und Wirklichkeit: Die Aussenpolitik des Dritten Reiches.* 2d ed. Stuttgart: Union Deutsche Verlagsgesellschaft, 1948.

Krausnick, Helmut. "Legenden um Hitlers Aussenpolitik." *Vierteljahrshefte für Zeitgeschichte,* 2, No. 3 (July 1954), 217–39.

Krecker, Lothar. *Deutschland und die Türkei im Zweiten Weltkrieg.* Frankfurt/M: Klostermann, 1964.

Krekeler, Norbert. *Revisionsanspruch und geheime Ostpolitik der Weimarer Republik: Die Subventionierung der deutschen Minderheit in Polen, 1919–1939.* Stuttgart: Deutsche Verlags-Anstalt, 1973.

Kühne, Horst. "Ziele und Ausmass der militärischen Intervention des deutschen Faschismus in Spanien (1936–1939)." *Zeitschrift für Militärgeschichte,* 8 (1969), 273–87. Some material from East German archives.

Kuhn, Axel. *Hitlers aussenpolitisches Programm: Entstehung und Entwicklung 1919–1939.* Stuttgart: Klett, 1945.

Kutakov, Leonid N. *Japanese Foreign Policy on the Eve of the Pacific War: A Soviet View.* Edited by George A. Lensen. Tallahassee, Fla.: Diplomatic Press, 1972.

Kvaček, Robert. "Zur Beziehung zwischen der Tschechoslowakei und den Westmächten vor dem Münchener Diktat." *Acta Universitatis Carolinas, Philosophica et historica,* 1968, pp. 209–33.

Lakowski, Richard, and Wunderlich, Werner. "Seekriegsplanung und Flottenrüstung des deutschen Imperialismus vor dem zweiten Weltkrieg." *Militärgeschichte,* 13, No. 6 (1974), 669–78.

Lammers, Donald M. *Explaining Munich: The Search for Motive in British Policy.* Stanford: Hoover Institution, 1966.

———. "Fascism, Communism, and the Foreign Office, 1937–39." *Journal of Contemporary History,* 6, No. 3 (1971), 66–86.

———. "From Whitehall after Munich: The Foreign Office and the Future Course of British Policy." *Historical Journal,* 16, No. 4 (Dec. 1973), 831–56.

Langer, William L., and Gleason, S. Everett. *The Challenge to Isolation, 1937–1940.* New York: Harper, 1952.

Latour, Conrad F. *Südtirol und die Achse Berlin-Rom, 1938–1945.* Stuttgart: Deutsche Verlags-Anstalt, 1962.

Lee, Bradford A. *Britain and the Sino-Japanese War, 1937–1939: A Study in the Dilemmas of British Decline.* Stanford: Stanford University Press, 1973.

Leitner, Hans Erwin. *Das haben wir damals nicht gewusst.* Eschwege: Werra-Verlagsgesellschaft, 1949. Good for atmosphere.

Lenzing, Hilke. *Die deutsche Volksgruppe in Dänemark und das nationalsozial-*

istische Deutschland (1933–1939). Dissertation. Bonn, 1973.

Leuschner, Joachim. *Volk und Raum: Zum Stil der nationalsozialistischen Aussenpolitik*. Göttingen: Vandenhoeck & Ruprecht, 1958.

Levine, Herbert S. *Hitler's Free City: The History of the Nazi Party in Danzig, 1925–39*. Chicago: University of Chicago Press, 1973.

———. "The Mediator: Carl J. Burckhardt's Efforts to Avert a Second World War." *Journal of Modern History*, 45, No. 3 (Sept. 1973), 439–55.

Li, Lincoln. *The Japanese Army in North China, 1937–1941*. Tokyo: Oxford University Press, 1975.

Liang, Hsi-Huey. *The Sino-German Connection: Alexander von Falkenhausen between China and Germany, 1900–1941*. Amsterdam: Van Gorcum Assen, 1978.

Liu, James T. C. "German Mediation in the Sino-Japanese War, 1937–1938." *Far Eastern Quarterly*, 8, No. 2 (Feb. 1949), 157–81.

Loewenheim, Francis L. "The Diffidence of Power—Some Notes and Reflections on the American Road to Munich." *Rice University Studies*, 58, No. 4 (Fall 1972), 11–79.

———. "An Illusion that Shaped History: New Light on the History and Historiography of American Peace Efforts before Munich." In *Some Pathways in Twentieth Century History: Essays in Honor of Reginald Charles McGrane*, edited by Daniel R. Beaver, pp. 177–220. Detroit: Wayne State University Press, 1969.

Louis, William Roger. *British Strategy in the Far East, 1919–1939*. Oxford: Clarendon Press, 1971.

Luža, Radomír. *Austro-German Relations in the Anschluss Era*. Princeton, N.J.: Princeton University Press, 1975.

———. *The Transfer of the Sudeten Germans: A Study of Czech-German Relations, 1933–1962*. New York: New York University Press, 1964.

Macartney, Carlyle A. *October Fifteenth: A History of Modern Hungary*. 2 vols. Edinburgh: University Press, 1956.

MacDonald, C. A. "Economic Appeasement and the German Moderates, 1937–39: An Introductory Essay." *Past and Present*, 56 (Aug. 1972), 105–35.

Mack Smith, Denis. *Mussolini's Roman Empire*. New York: Penguin Books, 1977.

Maier, Klaus A. *Guernica, 26.4.1937: Die deutsche Intervention in Spanien und der "Fall Guernica."* Freiburg: Rombach, 1975.

Mamatey, Victor, and Luža, Radomír (eds.). *A History of the Czechoslovak Republic, 1918–1948*. Princeton, N.J.: Princeton University Press, 1973.

Marguerat, Philippe. *Le IIIe Reich et le pétrole roumain, 1938–1940*. Geneva: A. W. Sijthoff, 1977. Very helpful work.

Marwick, Arthur. *Clifford Allen, the Open Conspirator*. Edinburgh: Oliver & Boyd, 1964.

Mason, Timothy W. *Sozialpolitik im Dritten Reich: Arbeiterklasse und Volksgemeinschaft*. Opladen: Westdeutscher Verlag, 1977.

Mastny, Vojtech. "Design or Improvisation? The Origins of the German Protectorate of Bohemia and Moravia." In Andrew W. Cordier (ed.), *Columbia Essays in International Affairs: The Dean's Papers 1965*, pp. 127–53. New York: Columbia University Press, 1965.

———. *The Czechs under Nazi Rule: The Failure of National Resistance, 1939–1942*. New York: Columbia University Press, 1971.

Maure, Robert. "The British Decision for Alliance with Russia, May 1939." *Journal of Contemporary History*, 8, No. 3 (July 1974), 3–26.

McCann, Frank D., Jr. *The Brazilian-American Alliance, 1937–1945*. Princeton, N.J.: Princeton University Press, 1973.

McCarthy, J. M. "Australia and Imperial Defence: Co-operation and Conflict 1918–1939." *Australian Journal of Politics and History*, 17, No. 1 (Apr. 1971), 19–32.

McKale, Donald. *The Swastika outside Germany*. Kent, Ohio: Kent State University Press, 1977. History of the AO, the foreign section of the National Socialist party.

McLachlan, Donald. *Room 39: A Study in Naval Intelligence*. New York: Atheneum, 1968.

Meier-Dörnberg, Wilhelm. *Ölversorgung der Kriegsmarine, 1935 bis 1945*. Freiburg: Rombach, 1973.

Merkes, Manfred. *Die deutsche Politik im spanischen Bürgerkrieg 1936–1939*. 2d ed. Bonn: Röhrscheid, 1969. Much improved over 1st ed. but hardly definitive.

Meskill, Johanna M. *Hitler and Japan: The Hollow Alliance*. New York: Atheneum, 1966.

Metzmacher, Helmut. "Deutsch-englische Ausgleichbemühungen im Sommer 1939." *Vierteljahrshefte für Zeitgeschichte*, 14, No. 4 (Oct. 1966), 369–412.

Meyers, Reinhard. *Britische Sicherheitspolitik 1934–1938*. Düsseldorf: Droste, 1976. Extremely helpful.

Michaelis, Meir. *Mussolini and the Jews: German-Italian Relations and the Jewish Question in Italy, 1922–1945*. London: Oxford University Press, 1978.

Middlemas, Keith. *The Strategy of Appeasement: The British Government and Germany, 1937–1939*. Chicago: Quadrangle Books, 1972.

Middlemas, Keith, and Barnes, John. *Baldwin*. London: Weidenfeld & Nicolson, 1969.

Miege, Wolfgang. *Das Dritte Reich und die Deutsche Volksgruppe in Rumänien 1933–1938: Ein Beitrag zur nationalsozialistischen Volkstumspolitik*. Frankfurt/M: Peter Lang, 1972.

Milward, Alan S. *The German Economy at War*. London: Athlone Press, 1965.

Minart, Jacques. *Le drame du désarmement française (ses aspects politiques et techniques): La revanche allemande, 1918–1939*. Paris: La Nef, 1959. A very useful study of French disarmament policy and its implications.

Moltmann, Günther. "America's Reaction to the November 1938 Pogrom." *Wiener Library Bulletin*, 16, No. 4 (Oct. 1962), 70–71.

———. "Franklin D. Roosevelts Friedensappell vom 14. April 1939: Ein fehlgeschlagener Versuch zur Friedenssicherung." *Jahrbuch für Amerikastudien*, 9 (1964), 91–109.

Morley, James W. (ed.). *Deterrent Diplomacy: Japan, Germany, and the USSR 1935–1940*. New York: Columbia University Press, 1976. Contains translations of important Japanese studies.

Müller, Klaus-Jürgen. *Das Heer und Hitler: Armee und nationalsozialistisches Regime 1933–1940*. Stuttgart: Deutsche Verlags-Anstalt, 1969.

Myake, Masaki. "Die Achse Berlin-Rom-Tokio im Spiegel der japanischen Quellen." *Mitteilungen des österreichischen Staatsarchivs*, 21 (1968), 408–45. Useful discussion of the Japanese sources.

Mysyrowicz, Ladislas. *Autopsie d'une défaite: Origines de l'effrondrement militaire français de 1940*. Lausanne: Editions l'Age d'Hommes, 1973.

Namier, Lewis. *Diplomatic Prelude, 1938–1939*. New York: Macmillan, 1948.

———. *Europe in Decay*. London: Macmillan, 1950.

———. *In the Nazi Era*. London: Macmillan, 1952.

Naylor, John F. *Labour's International Policy: The Labour Party in the 1930's*. London: Weidenfeld & Nicolson, 1969.

Néré, Jacques. *The Foreign Policy of France from 1914 to 1945*. London: Routledge & Kegan Paul, 1975.

Neumann, H. J. *Arthur Seyss-Inquart*. Graz: Styria, 1970.

Newman, Simon. *March 1939: The British Guarantee to Poland*. Oxford: Clarendon Press, 1976.

Niedhart, Gottfried. "Appeasement: Die britische Antwort auf die Krise des Weltreichs und des internationalen Systems vor dem Zweiten Weltkrieg." *Historische Zeitschrift*, 226, No. 1 (Feb. 1978), 67–88. Good survey of the literature and interesting ideas.

————. *Grossbritannien und die Sowjetunion 1934–1939: Studien zur britischen Politik der Friedenssicherung zwischen den beiden Weltkriegen*. Munich: Fink, 1972.

———— (ed.). *Kriegsbeginn 1939: Entfesselung oder Ausbruch des Zweiten Weltkriegs?* Darmstadt: Wissenschaftliche Buchgesellschaft, 1976. Collection of pieces.

Nieh, Yu-Hsi. *Die Entwicklung des chinesisch-japanischen Konfliktes in Nordchina und die deutschen Vermittlungsbemühungen, 1937–38*. Hamburg: Institut für Asienkunde, 1970.

Noguères, Henri. *Munich ou la drôle de paix*. Paris: Robert Laffant, 1963.

Offner, Arnold A. *American Appeasement: United States Foreign Policy and Germany, 1933–1938*. Cambridge, Mass.: Harvard University Press, 1969.

————. "Appeasement Revisited: The United States, Great Britain, and Germany, 1933–1940." *Journal of American History*, 64, No. 2 (Sept. 1977), 373–93.

Ovendale, Ritchie. *"Appeasement" and the English Speaking World: The United States, the Dominions, and the Policy of "Appeasement," 1937–1939*. Cardiff: University of Wales Press, 1975.

Overy, R. J. "Transportation and Rearmament in the Third Reich." *Historical Journal*, 16, No. 2 (June 1973), 389–409. A new look at *Autobahnen* and *Volkswagenwerk*.

Paikert, Geza C. *The Danube Swabians: German Populations in Hungary, Rumania and Yugoslavia and Hitler's Impact on their Patterns*. The Hague: Nijhoff, 1967.

Paxton, Robert O. *Parades and Politics at Vichy*. Princeton, N.J.: Princeton University Press, 1966. Important for the French army.

Peck, Joachim. *Kolonialismus ohne Kolonien: Der deutsche Imperialismus und China 1937*. Berlin (East): Akademie-Verlag, 1961. Contains important documents.

Pelz, Stephen E. *Race to Pearl Harbor: The Failure of the Second London Naval Conference and the Onset of World War II*. Cambridge, Mass.: Harvard University Press, 1974.

Perman, Dagmar H. *The Shaping of the Czechoslovak State*. Leyden: Brill, 1962.

Petersen, Jens. *Hitler-Mussolini: Die Entstehung der Achse Berlin-Rom 1933–1936*. Tübingen: Niemeyer, 1973.

————. "Italien in der aussenpolitischen Konzeption Hitlers." In Kurt Jürgensen and Reimer Hansen (eds.), *Historisch-politische Streiflichter*, pp. 206–20. Neumünster: Wachholtz, 1971.

Petzina, Dieter. *Autarkiepolitik im Dritten Reich: Der nationalsozialistische Vierjahresplan*. Stuttgart: Deutsche Verlags-Anstalt, 1968.

Plieg, Ernst-Albrecht. *Das Memelland 1920–1939*. Würzburg: Holzner, 1962.

Pommerin, Reiner. *Das Dritte Reich und Lateinamerika: Die deutsche Politik gegenüber Süd- und Mittelamerika, 1939–1942*. Düsseldorf: Droste, 1977.

Potemkin, Vladimir P. *Politika umirotvorenia agressorov i borba Sovetskogo Soyuza za mir* [The policy of appeasing the aggressors and the struggle of the Soviet Union for peace]. Moscow, 1946.

Pratt, Lawrence R. "The Anglo-American Naval Conversations on the Far East of January 1938." *International Affairs*, 47, No. 4 (Oct. 1971), 745–63.

————. *East of Malta, West of Suez: Britain's Mediterranean Crisis, 1936–1939.* Cambridge: Cambridge University Press, 1975. A very helpful study.

Presseisen, Ernst L. *Germany and Japan: A Study in Totalitarian Diplomacy, 1933–1941.* The Hague: Nijhoff, 1958.

Preston, Adrian (ed.). *General Staffs and Diplomacy before the Second World War.* London: Croom Helm, 1978.

Price, Arnold H. "The Belgian-German Frontier during World War II." *Maryland Historian,* 1, No. 2 (Fall 1970), 145–53.

Procházka, Theodore. "The Delimitation of the Czechoslovak-German Frontiers after Munich." *Journal of Central European Affairs,* 21, No. 2 (July 1961), 200–218.

Rabenau, Friedrich von. *Seeckt: Aus seinen Leben, 1918–1936.* Leipzig: Hase & Koehler, 1940.

Radant, Hans. "Die IG Farbenindustrie AG und Südosteuropa bis 1938." *Jahrbuch für Wirtschaftsgeschichte,* 1966, 3:146–95.

Rahn, Werner. "Ibiza und Almeria: Eine Dokumentation der Ereignisse vom 29. bis 31. Mai 1937." *Marine-Rundschau,* 68, No. 7 (July 1973), 389–406.

Rasmussen, Jorgen S. "Government and Intra-Party Opposition: Dissent within the Conservative Parliamentary Party in the 1930's." *Political Studies,* 19, No. 2 (June 1971), 172–83. Useful summary of the ineffective opposition.

Reichert, Günter. *Das Scheitern der Kleinen Entente: Internationale Beziehungen im Donauraum von 1933 bis 1938.* Munich: Fides, 1971.

Reimann, Viktor. *Innitzer, Kardinal zwischen Hitler und Rom.* Vienna: Fritz Molden, 1967.

Rhodes, Anthony. *The Vatican in the Age of the Dictators, 1922–1945.* London: Hodder & Stoughton, 1973. A thoughtful defense.

Rich, Norman. *Hitler's War Aims.* 1, *Ideology, the Nazi State, and the Course of Expansion.* New York: Norton, 1973. A fine survey.

Riedel, Matthias. *Eisen und Kohle für das Dritte Reich: Paul Pleigers Stellung in der NS-Wirtschaft.* Göttingen: Musterschmidt, 1974.

Riekhoff, Harald von. *German-Polish Relations, 1918–1933.* Baltimore: Johns Hopkins University Press, 1971.

Ritschel, Karl Heinz. *Diplomatie um Südtirol.* Stuttgart: Seewald, 1964.

Ritter, Harry R. "Hermann Neubacher and the Austrian Anschluss Movement, 1918–1940." *Central European History,* 8, No. 4 (Dec. 1975), 348–69.

Robertson, Esmonde M. (ed.). *The Origins of the Second World War: Historical Interpretations.* New York: St. Martin's, 1971.

Rock, William R. *Appeasement on Trial: British Foreign Policy and Its Critics, 1938–1939.* Hamden, Conn.: Archon Books, 1966.

————. *British Appeasement in the 1930's.* New York: Norton, 1977.

Rönnefarth, Helmuth K. G. *Die Sudetenkrise in der internationalen Politik.* 2 vols. Wiesbaden: Steiner, 1961.

Roos, Hans. "Die militärpolitische Lage und Planung Polens gegenüber Deutschland von 1939." *Wehrwissenschaftliche Rundschau,* 7, No. 4 (1957), 181–202.

————. *Polen und Europa: Studien zur polnischen Aussenpolitik 1931–1939.* Tübingen: Mohr, 1957.

Rosar, Wolfgang. *Deutsche Gemeinschaft: Seyss-Inquart und der Anschluss.* Vienna: Europa Verlag, 1971.

Roskill, Stephen. *Hankey, Man of Secrets.* 3, *1931–1963.* New York: St. Martin's, 1974.

Rothfels, Hans. "Das Baltikum als Problem internationaler Politik." In *Zur Geschichte und Problematik der Demokratie: Festgabe für Hans Herzfeld,* pp. 608–12. Berlin: Duncker & Humblot, 1958.

Runzheimer, Jürgen. "Der Überfall auf den Sender Gleiwitz im Jahre 1939." *Vierteljahrshefte für Zeitgeschichte,* 10, No. 4 (Oct. 1962), 408–26.

Sabiliūnas, Leona. *Lithuania in Crisis: Nationalism to Communism 1939–1940.* Bloomington, Ind.: Indiana University Press, 1972.

Sakmyster, Thomas L. "Army Officers and Foreign Policy in Interwar Hungary, 1938–1941." *Journal of Contemporary History,* 10, No. 1 (Jan. 1975), 19–40.

————. "The Hungarian State Visit to Germany of August 1938: Some New Evidence on Hungary in Hitler's Pre-Munich Policy." *Canadian Slavic Studies,* 3, No. 4 (Winter 1969), 677–91. Very important article.

————. "Hungary and the Munich Crisis: The Revisionist Dilemma." *Slavic Review,* 32, No. 4 (Dec. 1973), 725–40.

Salewski, Michael. *Die deutsche Seekriegsleitung, 1935–1945.* 1, *1935–1941.* Frankfurt/M: Bernard & Graefe, 1970.

Sanke, Heinz (ed.). *Der deutsche Faschismus in Lateinamerika, 1933–1943.* Berlin (East): Humboldt-Universität, 1966.

Sasaki, Chiyoko. *Der Nomonhan Konflikt.* Dissertation. Bonn, 1968.

Schapiro, Leonard. *The Communist Party of the Soviet Union.* 2d ed. New York: Random House, 1971.

Scheurig, Bodo. *Ewald von Kleist-Schmenzin: Ein Konservativer gegen Hitler.* Oldenburg: Stalling, 1968.

Schieder, Wolfgang, and Dipper, Christof (eds.). *Der Spanische Bürgerkrieg in der internationalen Politik.* Munich: Nymphenburg, 1976. A collection of papers. See esp. Schieder's "Spanischer Bürgerkrieg und Vierjahresplan," pp. 162–90.

Schiefer, Hans. "Deutschland und die Tschechoslowakei vom September 1938 bis März 1939." *Zeitschrift für Ostforschung,* 4 (1955), 48–66.

Schindler, Herbert. *Mosty und Dirschau, 1939: Zwei Handstreiche der Wehrmacht vor Beginn des Polenfeldzuges.* Freiburg: Rombach, 1971.

Schmitz-Esser, Winfried. "Hitler-Mussolini: Das Südtiroler Abkommen von 1939." *Aussenpolitik,* 13, No. 6 (June 1962), 397–409.

Schönfeld, Roland. "Deutsche Rohstoffsicherungspolitik in Jugoslawien 1934–1944." *Vierteljahrshefte für Zeitgeschichte,* 24, No. 3 (July 1976), 215–58.

Schramm, Wilhelm von. *Sprich von Frieden, wenn du den Krieg willst: Die psychologischen Offensiven Hitlers gegen die Franzosen 1933 bis 1939.* Mainz: Hase & Köhler, 1973.

Schramm von Thadden, Ehrengard. *Griechenland und die Grossmächte im Zweiten Weltkrieg.* Wiesbaden: Steiner, 1955.

Schroeder, Hans-Jürgen. *Deutschland und die Vereinigten Staaten 1933–1939: Wirtschaft und Politik in der Entwicklung des deutsch-amerikanischen Gegensatzes.* Wiesbaden: Steiner, 1970.

Schroeder, Paul W. "Munich and the British Tradition." *Historical Journal,* 19, No. 1 (Jan. 1976), 223–43.

Schwoerer, Lois G. "Lord Halifax's Visit to Germany, November 1937." *The Historian,* 32, No. 3 (May 1970), 353–75.

Scott, William C. "Neville Chamberlain and Munich: Two Aspects of Power." In L. Krieger and F. Stern (eds.), *The Responsibility of Power: Historical Essays in Honor of Hajo Holborn,* pp. 381–99. Garden City, N.Y.: Doubleday, 1969.

Seraphim, Hans-Günther. "Nachkriegsprozesse und zeitgeschichtliche Forschung." In *Mensch und Staat in Recht und Geschichte: Festschrift für Herbert Kraus,* pp. 436–55. Kitzingen/M: Holzner, 1954.

Shamir, Haim. "Die Kristallnacht, die Notlage der deutschen Juden und die Haltung Englands." *Jahrbuch des Instituts für Deutsche Geschichte* (Tel Aviv), 1 (1972), 171–214.

Shay, Robert P., Jr. *British Rearmament in the Thirties.* Princeton, N.J.: Princeton University Press, 1977.

Sheldon, William. "Die amerikanische Aussenpolitik gègenüber der Tschecho-slowakei 1938." In Karl Bosl (ed.). *Gleichgewicht, Revision und Restauration*, pp. 35–60. Interpretation different from that of Loewenheim and Offner.

Siebert, Ferdinand. *Italiens Weg in den Zweiten Weltkrieg*. Bonn: Athenäum, 1962.

Silva, Hélio. *1938: Terrorismo em Campo Verde*. Rio de Janeiro: Civilização Brasileira, 1971.

Smelser, Ronald M. *The Sudeten Problem, 1933–1939: Volkstumspolitik and the Formulation of Nazi Foreign Policy*. Middletown, Conn.: Wesleyan University Press, 1975.

Smith, Arthur L., Jr. *The Deutschtum of Nazi Germany and the United States*. The Hague: Nijhoff, 1965.

Smith, Bradley F. *Reaching Judgement at Nuremberg*. New York: Basic Books, 1977.

Smith, Janet Adam. *John Buchan: A Biography*. Boston: Little Brown, 1966.

Sohl, Klaus. "Die Kriegsvorbereitungen des deutschen Imperialismus in Bulgar-ien am Vorabend des zweiten Weltkrieges." *Jahrbücher für Geschichte der UdSSR und der Volksdemokratischen Länder*, 3 (1959), 91–119.

Sommer, Theo. *Deutschland und Japan zwischen den Mächten 1935–1940*. Tübingen: Mohr, 1962.

Southworth, Herbert R. *Guernica! Guernica! A Study of Journalism, Diplomacy, Propaganda, and History*. Berkeley: University of California Press, 1977.

Spielhagen, Franz (pseud. of Otto Katz). *Spione und Verschwörer in Spanien*. Paris: Editions du Carrefour, 1936.

Sprenger, Heinrich. *Heinrich Sahm, Kommunalpolitiker und Staatsmann*. Col-ogne: Grote, 1969.

Steinert, Marlis G. *Hitler's War and the Germans*. Athens, Ohio: Ohio University Press, 1977.

Stigliani, Nicholas A., and Margotto, Antonette. "Fascist Antisemitism and the Italian Jews." *Wiener Library Bulletin*, 28, Nos. 35–36 (1975), 41–49.

Strauch, Rudi. *Sir Nevile Henderson, Britischer Botschafter in Berlin, 1937 bis 1939*. Bonn: Röhrscheid, 1959.

Sugar, Peter (ed.). *Native Fascism in the Successor States 1918–1945*. Santa Barbara, Calif.: ABC-Clio, 1971.

Sykes, Christopher. *Tormented Loyalty: The Story of a German Aristocrat Who Defied Hitler*. New York: Harper & Row, 1969. On Adam von Trott zu Solz, based on private papers and interviews.

Tasca, Angelo (pseud. Angelo Rossi). *Deux ans d'alliance germano-soviétique*. Paris: Plon, 1949.

Teichova, Alice. *An Economic Background to Munich: International Business and Czechoslovakia, 1918–1938*. London: Cambridge University Press, 1974.

————. "Die geheimen britisch-deutschen Ausgleichsversuche am Vorabend des zweiten Weltkrieges." *Zeitschrift für Geschichtswissenschaft*, 7 (1959), 755–96.

Terveen, Fritz. "Der Bildbericht über Hitlers 50. Geburtstag." *Vierteljahrshefte für Zeitgeschichte*, 7, No. 1 (Jan. 1959), 73–84.

Teske, Hermann. *General Ernst Köstring: Der militärische Mittler zwischen dem Deutschen Reich und der Sowjetunion, 1921–1941*. Frankfurt/M: Mittler, 1966.

Thies, Jochen. *Architekt der Weltherrschaft: Die "Endziele" Hitlers*. Düsseldorf: Droste, 1976. An extremely important and informative book.

Thomas, Hugh. *The Spanish Civil War*. 2d ed. New York: Harper & Row, 1977.

Thompson, Laurence. *The Greatest Treason: The Untold Story of Munich*. New York: William Morrow, 1968.

Thompson, Neville. *The Anti-Appeasers: Conservative Opposition in the 1930's*. Oxford: Clarendon Press, 1971.

Thorne, Christopher. *The Approach of War, 1938–1939*. New York: St. Martin's, 1968.

———. *The Limits of Foreign Policy: The West, the League, and the Far Eastern Crisis of 1931–1933*. New York: G. P. Putnam's Sons, 1973.

Tihanyi, János. "Deutsch-ungarische Aussenhandelsbeziehungen im Dienste der faschistischen Aggressionspolitik 1933 bis 1944." *Jahrbuch für Wirtschaftsgeschichte*, 1972, 1:65–73.

Tilkovsky, L. "Volksdeutsche Bewegung und ungarische Nationalitätenpolitik (1938–1941)." *Acta Historica*, 12, Nos. 1–2 (1966), 59–112.

The *Times*. *The History of the Times*. 4, *The 150th Anniversary and Beyond, 1912–1948*. Part II. Nendeln/Liechtenstein: Kraus Reprint, 1971 [1952].

Toscano, Mario. *Designs in Diplomacy*. Baltimore: Johns Hopkins University Press, 1970.

———. *The Origins of the Pact of Steel*. Baltimore: Johns Hopkins University Press, 1964.

———. *Pagine di storia diplomatica contemporanea*. 2 vols. Milan: Gieffrè, 1963.

———. *Storia diplomatica della questione dell'Alto Adige*. Bari: Laterza, 1967. Like all the works of Toscano listed, includes important material from Italian archives.

Treue, Wilhelm. "Das Dritte Reich und die Westmächte auf dem Balkan." *Vierteljahrshefte für Zeitgeschichte*, 1, No. 1 (Apr. 1953), 45–64.

Treue, Wilhelm, and Uebbing, Helmut. *Die Feuer verlöschen nie: August Thyssen-Hütte 1926–1966*. Düsseldorf: Econ-Verlag, 1969.

Truckanovskii, Vladimir G. (ed.). *Geschichte der internationalen Beziehungen 1917–1939*. Translated by Peter Hoffman and Gabriele and Günter Rosenfeld. Berlin (East): Rütten & Loening, 1963.

Tyrell, Albrecht. *Vom Trommler zum "Führer": Der Wandel von Hitlers Selbstverständnis zwischen 1919 und 1924 und die Entwicklung der NSDAP*. Munich: Wilhelm Fink, 1975. A fine analysis of the early development of Hitler's ideas and policies.

Ulam, Adam B. *Expansion and Coexistence: Soviet Foreign Policy, 1917–1973*. 2d ed. New York: Praeger, 1974.

Uldricks, Teddy J. "The Impact of the Great Purges on the People's Commissariat of Foreign Affairs." *Slavic Review*, 36, No. 2 (June 1977), 187–204. An important analysis.

Umiastowski, Roman. *Russia and the Polish Republic, 1918–1945*. London: Aquafondata, 1945.

U.S., Office of Naval Intelligence. "German Naval Air, 1933 to 1945: A Report Based on German Naval Staff Documents." Washington: ONI, 1947, mimeographed.

Urban, Rudolf. *Demokratenpresse im Lichte Prager Geheimakten*. Prague: Orbis, 1943.

Vigrabs, Georg. "Die Stellungnahme der Westmächte und Deutschlands zu den baltischen Staaten im Frühling und Sommer 1939." *Vierteljahrshefte für Zeitgeschichte*, 7, No. 3 (July 1959), 261–79.

Vital, David. "Czechoslovakia and the Powers, September 1938." *Journal of Contemporary History*, 1, No. 4 (Oct. 1966), 37–67.

Vnuk, František. "Munich and the Soviet Union." *Journal of Central European Affairs*, 21, No. 3 (Oct. 1961), 285–304.

———. "Slovakia's Six Eventful Months (October 1938–March 1939)." *Slovak Studies*, 4, *Historica*, 2 (1966), 7–164.

Völker, Karl-Heinz. *Die Deutsche Luftwaffe 1933–1939: Aufbau, Führung, Rüs-*

tung. Stuttgart: Deutsche Verlags-Anstalt, 1967. Largely replaced by Homze, but some useful details.

Volkmann, Hans-Erich. "Aussenhandel und Aufrüstung in Deutschland, 1933 bis 1939." In Friedrich Forstmeier and Hans-Erich Volkmann (eds.), *Wirtschaft und Rüstung am Vorabend des Zweiten Weltkrieges,* pp. 81–131.

————. "Ökonomie und Machtpolitik: Lettland und Estland im politisch-ökonomischen Kalkül des Dritten Reiches (1933–1940)." *Geschichte und Gesellschaft,* 2, No. 4 (1976), 471–500.

Volland, Klaus. *Das Dritte Reich und Mexico.* Frankfurt/M: Peter Lang, 1976.

Vormann, Nikolaus von. *Der Feldzug 1939 in Polen: Die Operationen des Heeres.* Weissenburg: Prinz Eugen-Verlag, 1958.

Waites, Neville (ed.). *Troubled Neighbours: Franco-British Relations in the Twentieth Century.* London: Weidenfeld & Nicolson, 1971.

Wallace, William V. "New Documents on the History of Munich: A Selection from the Soviet and Czechoslovak Archives." *International Affairs,* 35, No. 4 (1959), 447–54.

Wallach, Jehuda (ed.). *Germany and the Middle East, 1835–1939.* Supplement 1 of the *Jahrbuch des Instituts für Deutsche Geschichte.* Tel Aviv: Israel Press, 1975.

Walsh, Billie K. "The German Military Mission in China, 1928–38." *Journal of Modern History,* 46, No. 3 (Sept. 1974), 502–13.

Wandycz, Damian S. (ed.). *Studies in Polish Civilization.* New York: Polish Institute of Arts and Sciences in America, 1969.

Watt, Donald C. "Anglo-German Naval Negotiations on the Eve of the Second World War." *Journal of the Royal United Service Institution,* 103 (1958), 201–7, 384–91.

————. "An Earlier Model for the Pact of Steel: The Draft Treaties Exchanged between Germany and Italy during Hitler's Visit to Rome in May 1938." *International Affairs,* 33, No. 2 (Apr. 1957), 185–97.

————. "Hitler's Visit to Rome and the May Weekend Crisis: A Study in Hitler's Response to External Stimuli." *Journal of Contemporary History,* 9, No. 1 (Jan. 1974), 23–32.

————. "The Initiation of the Negotiations Leading to the Nazi-Soviet Pact: A Historical Problem." In C. Abransky (ed.), *Essays in Honour of E. H. Carr,* pp. 157–70. Hamden, Conn.: Archon Books, 1974.

————. "The May Crisis of 1938: A Rejoinder to Mr. Wallace." *Slavonic and East European Review,* 44, No. 103 (July 1966), 475–80.

————. *Personalities and Policies.* Notre Dame, Ind.: University of Notre Dame Press, 1965.

————. "The Rome-Berlin Axis, 1936–1940, Myth and Reality." *Review of Politics,* 22, No. 4 (1960), 519–43.

————. *Too Serious a Business: European Armed Forces and the Approach to the Second World War.* Berkeley: University of California Press, 1975.

Weinberg, Gerhard L. "The Defeat of Germany in 1918 and the European Balance of Power." *Central European History,* 2, No. 3 (1969), 248–60.

————. "Deutsch-japanische Verhandlungen über das Südseemandat, 1937–1938." *Vierteljahrshefte für Zeitgeschichte,* 4, No. 4 (Oct. 1956), 390–98. Cited as Weinberg, "Südseemandat."

————. *The Foreign Policy of Hitler's Germany: Diplomatic Revolution in Europe, 1933–1936.* Chicago: University of Chicago Press, 1970. Cited as Weinberg, *Foreign Policy.*

————. "German Colonial Plans and Policies, 1938–1942." In *Geschichte und Gegenwartsbewusstsein: Festschrift für Hans Rothfels,* pp. 462–91.

————. "German Recognition of Manchoukuo." *World Affairs Quarterly,* 28,

No. 2 (July 1957), 149–64. Cited as Weinberg, "Recognition."

———. "Germany and Czechoslovakia, 1933–1945." In *Czechoslovakia Past and Present*, edited by Miloslav Rechcigl, 1:760–69. The Hague: Mouton, 1969.

———. *Germany and the Soviet Union, 1939–1941*. Leyden: Brill, 1954, 1972.

———. "Hitler's Image of the United States." *American Historical Review*, 69, No. 4 (July 1964), 1006–21.

———. "The May Crisis 1938." *Journal of Modern History*, 29, No. 3 (Sept. 1957), 213–25.

———. "A Proposed Compromise over Danzig in 1939?" *Journal of Central European Affairs*, 14, No. 4 (Jan. 1955), 334–38.

———. "Recent German History: Some Comments and Perspectives." In *Deutschland–Russland–Amerika: Festschrift für Fritz Epstein*, pp. 358–68. Wiesbaden: Steiner, 1978.

Wendt, Bernd-Jürgen. *Economic Appeasement: Handel und Finanz in der britischen Deutschland-Politik 1933–1939*. Düsseldorf: Bertelsmann, 1971.

———. *München 1938: England zwischen Hitler und Preussen*. Frankfurt/M: Europäische Verlagsanstalt, 1965.

Whaley, Robert. "How Franco Financed His War—Reconsidered." *Journal of Contemporary History*, 12, No. 1 (Jan. 1977), 133–52. Material from Spanish archives.

Wheeler-Bennet, John W. *John Anderson, Viscount Waverley*. New York: St. Martin's, 1962.

———. *Munich, Prologue to Tragedy*. New York: Viking, 1964.

Whittam, John. "The Italian General Staff and the Coming of the Second World War." In Adrian Preston (ed.), *General Staffs and Diplomacy before the Second World War*, pp. 77–97.

Wieland, Volker. *Zur Problematik der französischen Militärpolitik und Militärdoktrin in der Zeit zwischen den Weltkriegen*. Boppard: Boldt, 1973.

Winchester, Betty Jo. "Hungary and the 'Third Europe' in 1938." *Slavic Review*, 32, No. 4 (Dec. 1973), 741–56.

Wiskemann, Elizabeth. *The Rome/Berlin Axis*. 2d ed. London: Collins, 1966.

Wojciechowski, Marian. *Die Polnisch-deutschen Beziehungen 1933–1938*. Translated by Norbert Damerau. Leyden: Brill, 1971.

Wootton, Graham. *The Official History of the British Legion*. London: Macdonald & Evans, 1956.

Wrench, Evelyn. *Geoffrey Dawson and Our Times*. London: Hutchinson, 1955.

Yisraeli, David. "The Third Reich and the Transfer Agreement." *Journal of Contemporary History*, 6, No. 2 (1971), 129–48.

Young, Robert T. "La Guerre de Longue Durée: Some Reflections on French Strategy and Diplomacy in the 1930's." In Adrian Preston (ed.), *General Staffs and Diplomacy before the Second World War*, pp. 41–64.

———. "Le haut commandement français au moment de Munich." *Revue d'histoire moderne et contemporaine*, 24 (Jan.–Mar. 1977), 110–29.

———. "The Strategic Dream: French Air Doctrine in the Inter-War Period, 1919–1939." *Journal of Contemporary History*, 9, No. 4 (Oct. 1974), 57–76.

Zhivkova, Liudmila. *Anglo-Turkish Relations, 1933–1939*. London: Secker & Warburg, 1976. Material from Bulgarian archives.

Zorach, Jonathan. "The British View of the Czechs in the Era before the Munich Crisis." *Slavonic and East European Review*, 57, No. 1 (Jan. 1979), 56–70.

———. "Czechoslovakia's Fortifications: Their Development and Role in the Munich Crisis." *Militärgeschichtliche Mitteilungen*, 17, No. 2 (1976), 81–94.

Index

NOTE: Colonial territories are listed under the names used at the time rather than the current names of independent states.

Abetz, Otto, 626
Abshagen, Karl-Heinz, 421 n.186
Adam, Wilhelm, 279, 418
Addison, Sir John, 325 n.39
Afghanistan, 167, 247 n.233
Aga Khan, 115
Alba, Duke of, 151 n.36
Albania, 411, 509, 512, 564, 590, 591
Alexandretta, 242, 591
Almería, 99
Altenburg, Günther, 277 n.70, 293, 303 n.190
Anderson, Sir John (Viscount Waverley), 517 n.207
Anfuso, Filippo, 279
Anglo-German Naval Agreement (1935), 29, 514, 577; (1937), 29, 514 n.197
Anglo-German Society, 421
Anglo-Italian Agreement (1937), 145; (1938), 134, 304, 410, 505, 507, 522
Angola, 121, 131–32
Anschluss: England and, 103, 140; Hungary and, 227, 228–29, 231, 301; plebiscite of 10 April 1938, 257, 259, 300–301, 305, 307, 337, 338; Poland and, 202–3, 204–5, 264, 282; United States and, 251, 252 n.10; Yugoslavia and, 215, 219, 223, 301. See also Austria: England and, France and, Germany and, Italy and
Anti-Comintern Pact, 11, 12, 13, 104, 117–18, 160–62, 168, 170ff., 189, 256, 285, 481, 484, 489, 494, 495–96, 498, 500, 503, 504, 591, 630
AO (Auslandsorganisation). See under NSDAP
APA (Aussenpolitisches Amt). See under NSDAP

Arabs: and Germany, 243ff.
Arcziszewski, Mierosław, 559 n.82
Argentina: and Germany, 259
Armed Forces Office. See under Germany, Wehrmachtamt
Arone, Pietro, 599
Astakhov, Georgei, 568 n.123, 573, 574, 576, 577, 604 n.315, 606
Astor, Michael, 120, 427
Astor, Waldorf, 140, 381 n.16
Atherton, Ray, 15
Attlee, Clement, 441 n.264
Attolico, Bernardo, 145 n.9, 187, 411, 412, 413, 453 n.301, 457, 563 n.100, 566 n.117, 596, 597, 599, 637, 640
Australia, 14–15, 427–28, 516 n.206. See also Dominions
Austria, 36, 61, 65, 103, 122, 130, 136, 272; Czechoslovakia and, 266, 274, 284; England and, 103, 140, 274–75, 283–84, 292, 294–95, 297–98, 344, 517; Fatherland Front, 267 n.24, 278, 296; France and, 130 n.120, 266, 275, 282, 283, 292, 294–95, 298, 324; Germany and, 33, 36–37, 39–41, 42, 46, 78, 122, 126, 130, 136, 140, 201–2, 215ff., chap. 9; Hungary and, 273, 292, 295, 296; Italy and, 261–62, 264, 267, 270–72, 280, 283, 286–87, 292, 294, 295, 296, 298; National Socialists, 265, 272, 275, 277, 278–79, 284, 288ff., 296, 297, 299; Socialists, 266–67, 296. See also Habsburg restoration
Avon, Earl of. See Eden, Anthony

Bad Godesberg. See under Chamberlain, Neville
Balbo, Italo, 412

Baldwin, Stanley, 53, 60, 62, 63, 64, 66,
    96, 107, 108
Balearic Islands, 38, 163, 343 n.114
Baltic Sea, 24
Baltic States, 548 n.42, 605. *See also*
    Estonia; Latvia; Lithuania
Barcelona, 155, 164–65
Basque area, 149, 150
Baudoin, Paul, 523
Beck, Josef, 34 n.56, 193ff., 208–9, 228
    n.156, 231, 237, 402 n.100, 403 n.104,
    435, 436 n.243, 450 n.290, 474 n.29,
    478, 480ff., 489–90, 497ff., 527,
    537ff., 556, 559, 579, 587, 645, 655;
    Third Europe project, 193, 204–5,
    323, 405, 499
Beck, Ludwig, 31ff., 56 n.12, 297, 314,
    338, 364–65, 366, 371, 383, 384–86,
    388, 389, 390 n.51; Paris visit, 34
Belgian Congo, 121, 131
Belgium, 81–85, 125, 133, 208, 341–42,
    428, 449 n.287, 525 n.253, 526, 576
    n.169, 592–93, 631; England and, 78,
    83, 84–85, 525–26, 576 n.169, 592;
    France and, 81–85, 341–42, 428, 449
    n.287, 592; Germany and, 81–85, 91,
    92 n.140, 379, 581, 592–93, 631
Beneš, Eduard, 81, 124, 327, 328, 356,
    361, 362, 364 n.200, 376 n.246, 377,
    391, 397, 398, 401, 425, 438, 439,
    440–42, 444, 445, 446 n.277, 460, 461
    n.330, 559 n.82; "Fourth Plan,"
    418–19, 420, 422, 427, 429, 442
Berchtesgaden. *See under* Chamber-
    lain, Neville
Bernhardt, Johannes, 146, 147, 148,
    152, 153, 154, 155, 162 n.74
Bernheim case, 195
Bessarabia, 79, 237, 352 n.156, 610
Biddle, Anthony J. Drexel, Jr., 208
    n.66, 489
Bilbao, 149, 150
Bingham, Robert W., 107
Bismarck (ship), 29, 388
Bled Agreement (23 August 1938), 223,
    232, 237, 406, 407
Blitzkrieg, 19–21, 26–27
Blomberg, Werner von, 3, 31, 32ff.,
    43–51, 98 n.6, 143, 165, 170, 176, 228,
    276–77
Blum, Léon, 96, 441; and Czechoslo-
    vakia, 86, 341–43, 350, 441; and
    Germany, 67, 68, 71, 74, 76, 89ff., 97,

103 n.22; and Italy, 263; and
    U.S.S.R., 85–86; speech of 24 Janu-
    ary 1937, 91
Bodenschatz, Karl-Heinz, 22 n.14, 394
    n.70, 400 n.94, 440 n.261, 622 n.400
Boehm-Tettelbach, Hans, 396
Bömer, Karl, 369 n.214
Böttcher, Viktor, 482
Bötticher, Friedrich von, 578 n.181
Bohle, Ernst Wilhelm, 269
Bonnet, Georges, 350, 361, 528, 529,
    530, 545, 624, 626, 642, 650, 652
    n.123; and Czechoslovakia, 363–64,
    375, 376 n.247, 383, 398, 401, 416
    n.169, 422 n.192, 423, 428, 441 n.262,
    442 n.265
Boothby, Robert, 397 n.81, 650 n.114
Boris (king of Bulgaria), 239
Bratianu, Georges, 235, 492, 493
Brauchitsch, Walther von, 48, 49, 365,
    378, 384–86, 388, 515, 538, 558 n.78,
    607, 639 n.56, 643, 646 n.96, 648
    n.104
Braun, Eva, 308
Brazil: Germany and, 9, 255–59; Ger-
    man minority, 255ff.; Integralists,
    257, 258
British Commonwealth. *See*
    Dominions
British Legion, 450 n.290, 545
British West Indies, 132
Brockett, Lord, 618 n.384
Brunet, René, 441 n.262
Brussels conference (1937), 109, 115
    n.61, 173, 174–75
Bülow-Schwante, Vicco von, 246, 308
Bürckel, Josef, 300, 337, 338
Bulgaria: England and, 589; France
    and, 240 n.201, 490; Germany and,
    238–40, 490, 581, 589–90; rearma-
    ment, 239, 490, 589–90; Rumania
    and, 239, 490, 536, 541, 589;
    U.S.S.R. and, 589; Yugoslavia and,
    238
Bullitt, William C., 39, 69 n.60, 77 n.69,
    85–86, 90 n.129, 275, 324, 325, 363,
    375 n.243, 428 n.219, 529, 545–46,
    586 n.218, 651 n.120
Burckhardt, Carl J., 113, 197, 198, 200,
    202, 380 n.12, 426, 482 n.63, 483 n.67,
    489, 584 n.208, 632–33
Burgenland, 228–29
Butler, R. A. B., 134, 321 n.22

Cadogan, Sir Alexander, 98, 110, 129,
    347–48, 350 n.141, 373–74, 380 n.12,
    382, 438 n.251, 439 n.255, 548 n.41,
    554
Calinescu, Armand, 588 n.227
Cameroons, 28, 71, 74, 75, 77, 127, 131,
    355 nn.165, 166. See also Germany:
    colonial question
Canada, 14, 16, 346, 427–28, 516 n.206,
    545 n.33, 610 n.345. See also
    Dominions
Canaris, Wilhelm, 209 n.68, 407, 413,
    451 n.295, 475 n.32, 597 nn.276, 279,
    600 n.297, 607 n.329, 610 n.345
Carol (king of Rumania), 234, 235, 236,
    237, 477 n.42, 491, 492, 493
Carpatho-Ukraine, 228, 231, 402 n.100,
    405, 408, 436, 470, 472–78, 480, 484,
    487, 492, 494, 497–98, 535, 552, 553,
    563
Cazalet, Victor, 351 n.151
Cerruti, Vittorio, 163 n.77, 285
Chamberlain, Neville, 58, 65; general
    views, 60, 61–62, 75, 111–12, 114–15,
    125, 128, 542, 546 n.41, 650–51; and
    Czechoslovakia, 328–29, 346–47,
    348–49, 352, 358–59, 361–62, 373,
    380–82, 392–93, 394, 395, 396–97, 421
    n.189, 422–23, 425ff., 437ff., 454,
    455, 457, 458, 463, 525 n.250, 539,
    618–19; and France, 6, 96; and Ger-
    many, 66, 68, 69, 71 n.66, 73, 77,
    chaps. 3 and 4 passim, 302, 438, 448
    n.282, 463 n.337, 515 n.203, 516, 518,
    522, 528, 542–43, 546, 548–49, 576 n.
    169, 617 n.375, 618–19, 622–24, 632,
    649–51, 655; and Italy, 96, 111; and
    Poland, 543, 554, 555, 556, 623; and
    rearmament, 52–55, 57, 522, 523; and
    U.S.S.R., 96, 548–49, 556, 570, 572,
    614, 615; and United States, 107ff.,
    134, 521; meeting with Hitler at
    Berchtesgaden, 425–26, 428–32, 437,
    438, 439, 440, 450 n.290, 475, 484;
    meeting with Hitler at Bad Godes-
    berg, 434, 437, 444, 445, 446–48, 454,
    455, 460; speech of 8 April 1938, 352;
    speech of 17 March 1939, 540, 542,
    543
Changkufeng (Lake Khasan) incident,
    188–89
Charles-Roux, François, 78
Chatfield, Lord, 58 n.23, 550 n.45, 614

Chautemps, Camille, 96, 123, 132, 140
    n.168
Chiang Kai-shek, 11, 167, 170, 176, 182
Chile: Germany and, 257 n.34, 259
Chilston, Lord, 214, 415 n.168
China: Germany and, 11–13, 50–51,
    chap. 6; German military advisers,
    170, 181, 182; U.S.S.R. and, 169,
    174, 213, 553
Chinese Eastern Railway, 189
Christie, Graham, 329 n.59, 374 n.239,
    457 n.319
Churchill, Winston S., 52–53, 57,
    63–65, 114, 342, 363, 380 n.10, 391
    n.56, 395, 428, 464
Chvalkovsky, František, 466, 468
Ciano, Galeazzo, 170–71, 177 n.37, 237,
    270, 273, 274, 275, 276, 287, 295
    n.150; and Czechoslovakia, 323, 412,
    413, 414, 455, 456; and England, 117;
    and Germany, 117, 261, 273, 275, 276,
    279, 285, 286, 304, 305, 306, 307ff.,
    563, 566–67, 596, 599–600, 630–31,
    635–37, 639 nn.55, 56, 640, 641; and
    Germany, at Salzburg meeting,
    595 n.260, 596 n.269, 597–
    600, 606, 626; and Hungary, 586
    n.217, 587 n.219; and Poland, 499,
    502 n.148, 566 n.116, 595; and Spain,
    158 n.59; and Tripartite Military
    Alliance, 185–91, 504–12; and
    U.S.S.R., 567 n.122, 573; and Yugo-
    slavia, 217, 218, 273, 563, 635
Cincar-Marković, Aleksander, 490,
    590, 591
Clive, Sir Robert, 342
Cliveden, 362, 427 n.215
Codreanu, Cornelius, 234, 235 n.174,
    493
Collier, Laurence, 417 n.173
Colvin, Ian, 554, 555
Comnen, Nicolae Petrescu-, 235, 236,
    353, 416 n.169, 491 n.104
Condé, Charles-Marie, 651 n.119
Condor Legion, 145, 146, 149, 151–52,
    154, 160, 162 n.72, 163, 268
Congo Basin Treaties, 131
Conwell-Evans, Philip, 99, 421, 423
    n.195, 617 n.376, 618 n.384
Coulondre, Robert, 415 n.167, 618, 634,
    635, 641, 642
Craig, Malin C., 530
Craigie, Sir Robert, 185 n.66, 524 n.247

Cranborne, Lord, 134
Croatian nationalism, 215–16, 563
Cryptography and codes, 13 n.37, 62
n.32, 173 n.20, 236 n.181, 301 n.180,
506, 608 n.336, 612, 613 n.355
Csáky, Istvan, 494, 495, 496, 585–86
Czechoslovakia: Activist parties, 319,
327; army and fortifications, 362–63,
368 n.213, 369, 370; Austria and, 266,
274, 284; Dominions and, 15, 124,
421; England and, 104, 124–25, 242
n.216, 324, 325ff., 335, 336, 339,
344ff., 354ff., 368, 372–73, 374,
390ff., 419ff., 437ff., 444–45, 448–49,
459, 460, 472, 516, 523–24, 526, 539,
612, 618, 619, 621 n.398, 654; France
and, 78–80, 81, 83, 85, 86–87, 124–25,
127, 132, 315, 323–25, 326, 328–29,
336, 339, 341–43, 344ff., 350, 354ff.,
363–64, 368, 372–73, 375, 392 n.62,
397ff., 416, 419, 422–23, 428–29,
439ff., 444–45, 448–50, 452–53, 455
n.310, 459, 460, 463, 472, 546, 626;
Germany and, 32–33, 36–37, 39–41,
42, 65 n.44, 69, 73, 76, 78, 124–26,
188, 201–2, 232, 237, chaps. 10 and
11, 465ff., 498–99, 535; Hungarian
minority, 402 n.100, 405, 406, 436;
Hungary and, 209 n.68, 226–27,
228ff., 309, 315, 322, 333–34, 339, 392
n.62, 404ff., 436–37, 441 n.264,
443–44, 444 n.271, 452, 459, 461, 494;
International Commission (on
boundaries), 459, 466, 468 n.11; Italy
and, 37, 306, 307, 308, 309, 310, 312,
323, 340, 411–14, 452ff.; May crisis,
302, 318, 338, 340, 341, 360, 364,
366–70, 372, 373, 375, 381, 391, 393,
402–3; Munich conference, 455ff.,
460, 461, 462, 463, 464, 465, 467, 472,
490, 491, 525 n.250, 531; Poland and,
87 n.115, 203, 206–9, 315, 322, 339,
363–64, 375, 401–3, 408, 416 n.169,
435–36, 443–44, 444 n.271, 450, 459,
461, 470, 478–89; Rumania and,
352–53, 402, 473, 474, 491; Skoda
works, 464, 474, 535, 569, 573;
U.S.S.R. and, 86–89, 318, 329, 341,
348 n.134, 351, 352–54, 402, 414–18,
439 n.255, 449, 450, 460, 461, 552;
Yugoslavia and, 322, 590. See also
Sudeten area; Sudeten Germans;
Sudeten German party

Dahlerus, Birger, 622, 634 n.27, 640
n.62, 643, 650 n.111, 654–55
Daily Herald, 572 n.144
Daladier, Edouard, 341 n.105, 350, 355,
356, 358, 361, 528, 529, 636, 642,
651–52; and Czechoslovakia, 358,
363, 399ff., 428–29, 439ff., 445 n.272,
455, 458, 624; and Germany, 545,
546, 624, 634; and Poland, 546 n.37
Dalton, Hugh, 53, 61 n.29, 380 n.10,
438 n.254, 446 n.276, 547 n.41
Daluege, Kurt, 269
Dampierre, Robert de, 79–80
Danzig, 61, 65, 193–94, 197–201, 202,
206, 288, 289, 348, 380, 403, 404,
435–36, 480, 481, 482, 483, 487, 488,
489, 498, 500–502, 527, 537–39, 559
n.82, 562, 580, 583–84, 595, 596, 599,
611, 628, 648 n.106, 653; Jewish
population, 198, 200, 202, 482
Darányi, Kálmán, 40, 222, 226, 228,
230, 470, 471, 477, 481–82
Darlan, Jean F. X., 79 n.80
Darré, R. Walther, 26
Davies, Joseph, 354 n.161, 417
Davila, Charles A., 236
Davis, Norman H., 107
Davis, William Rhodes, 260 n.47
Dawson, Geoffrey, 120, 354 n.164, 422
de Gaulle, Charles, 22
Delbos, Yvon, 76, 81, 89 n.126, 96,
123–24, 132, 206 n.57, 221, 236 n.184,
275, 324, 327, 328, 331, 333 n.77, 363
n.199
Denmark, and Germany, 585 n.211
Deutsche Stiftung, 210 n.75
Deutschland (ship), 437 n.250; bombing
incident, 99–101, 150, 164 n.84
Dieckhoff, Hans Heinrich, 11, 252
n.11, 254, 520
Dienststelle Ribbentrop, 167, 172. See
also Ribbentrop, Joachim von
Dietrich, Otto, 46 n.103, 269
Dirksen, Herbert von, 47, 100 n.11,
135, 175, 177, 178 n.39, 181, 286
n.108, 380, 381 n.16, 389 n.49, 391,
423, 540, 620–21
Disarmament, 73, 79 n.80, 107, 130,
137; limitations on air warfare, 130
Djuvara, Mircea, 235
Dobruja, 239, 589
Dodd, William E., 61, 253, 254
Dönitz, Karl, 31

Dominions, 13–16, 37, 74, 99, 124, 127, 283, 316–17, 347 n.125, 374, 421, 427–28, 430, 448 n.282, 449, 455, 543, 555, 576 n.169, 643, 651
Draganov, Parvan, 239 n.200, 604 n.315
Duff Cooper, Alfred (Lord Norwich), 421 n.189, 430, 438–39, 449
Durango (Spain), 149

Ebbutt, Norman, 38 n.72, 120
Ebro (battle), 157, 158
Eden, Anthony (Earl of Avon), 6 n.13, 34 n.56, 43 n.94, 88, 91, chaps. 3 and 4 passim, 274, 282, 344 n.119, 428; and Czechoslovakia, 325, 331 n.69; and Lord Halifax, 114, 122; and Nevile Henderson, 60, 61 n.29; Leamington address (1936), 78 n.77; resignation, 133 n.125, 134–35; and United States, 107–11
Edward VII (king of England), 63
Edward VIII, Duke of Windsor, 53, 62–65
Egypt, 56, 247
Eisenlohr, Ernst, 332, 339 n.94
Engerau, 472 n.25
England: air force, 1 n.1, 56–57, 350, 358, 399 n.91, 427, 430 n.224; Air Ministry, 350 n.141; air-raid defense, 56, 345, 430 n.224, 463, 517 n.207; Anti-Comintern Pact and, 104, 118, 160, 161; army, 5, 54–55, 343, 427, 523, 557, 623; Austria and, 103, 140, 274–75, 283–84, 292, 294–95, 297–98, 344, 517; Belgium and, 78, 83, 84–85, 525–26, 576 n.169, 592; Bulgaria and, 589; cabinet, composition, 518 n.215, 557 n.73, policy, 56, 71, 83, 112, 122, 127, 128, 133, 138, 139, 345–47, 350–51, 355, 356, 372 n.230, 374, 395, 421, 428, 429, 430, 438–39, 443, 444, 445, 446, 447 n.280, 448, 449, 452 n.300, 522, 523, 540, 544, 555, 557 n.73, 613 n.353, 614, 616–17, 623, 642, 649, 650; chiefs of staff, 56–57, 58, 128, 133, 345, 430 n.224, 453 n.304; China and, 174 n.26; colonial question, 14–15, 67ff., 104, 110, 124–25, 126, 127ff., 354–55, 362 n.190, 518–19, 522; conscription, 53, 517 n.209, 523, 557, 572 n.143, 617; Conservative party, 64; Czechoslovakia and, 104, 124–25, 242 n.216,

324, 325ff., 336, 339, 344ff., 354ff., 368, 372–73, 374, 390ff., 419ff., 437ff., 444–45, 448–49, 459, 460, 472, 516, 523–24, 526, 539, 612, 618, 619, 621 n.398, 654; Czechoslovakia, guarantee of, 124, 331, 349, 391 n.56, 392, 421 n.188, 430, 439, 442–43, 444, 446, 457, 523–24; Czechoslovak-Polish relations and, 80, 402, 403; Danzig and, 488, 527, 616–17, 650; economic issues, 67, 95; Foreign Office, 20, 29, 56, 60–61, 62, 68, 70, 71 n.66, 77, 83, 97, 108 n.35, 121–22, 133, 296, 325, 329, 331, 342, 345ff., 350 n.141, 351, 362, 378, 390 n.55, 392 nn.60, 63, 402 n.102, 415 n.168, 421 n.188, 439 n.255, 453 n.304, 518 n.216, 612, 614 n.360, 623 n.409, 649; Foreign Office, general views, 98, 372 n.230; foreign policy, 5–7, 55–57, 102–5, 526, 612, 667–70, 676; foreign trade, 9, 517–18, 528; France and, 5–6, 55, 56 n.14, 57–59, 68, 69, 70–71, 72, 74–75, 78, 80, 100, 122ff., 132–33, 138, 342–43, 345ff., 354ff., 373, 383, 397, 422–23, 427, 439, 442, 508, 517, 522–23, 527, 542, 544, 547 n.41, 555, 557 n.73, 624, 642, 651; France and, staff talks, military cooperation, 133, 343, 349, 357, 358 n.178, 427, 557 n.73, 613, 625; Germany and, 5–7, 9 n.21, 19, 23 n.16, 29, 36–37, 41, 43, chaps. 3 and 4, 177, 178–79, 275, 294–95, 344, 354ff., 360–61, 368, 379ff., 393–94, 395, 431, 466, 495, 510, 516–28, 539–46, 565–69, 582, 598–99, 613, 616–24, 636, 642–43, 645, 647, 649–51; Germany and, Anglo-German Declaration, 461, 465, 508, 518; Germany, war warning to, 139 n.161, 345ff., 354, 359, 368–69, 373, 393–94, 395, 397, 421–22, 423–24, 425, 426–27, 428, 430, 431, 449, 450, 451, 456, 544, 546, 622–24; Greece and, 217, 240, 517–18, 543, 564; Holland and, 525–26, 540; Hungary and, 229, 232, 443–44, 450 n.290; Italy and, 38, 56, 57, 58, 62 n.32, 66 n.48, 110–11, 133–35, 142–43, 163, 270, 271, 274–75, 295, 304, 310, 344 n.119, 410, 450, 454–55, 505, 510, 522–23, 526, 563, 623, 636–37, 641, 649, 650; Japan and, 13 n.37, 56,

57, 58, 170–71, 179, 184–85, 188ff.,
506, 509–10, 565–69, 575–76, 596–97,
601; Labour party, 53, 65 n.41, 428,
438 n.254, 440 n.264, 443 n.269, 517
n.208, 523, 547 n.41, 557, 569; Liberal party, 53, 523, 557; Memel and,
484; navy, 29, 56, 427, 449, 452; Near
East and, 243; Poland and, 203, 206,
208, 348, 402, 403, 450, 478, 500, 502
n.148, 524, 527, 538, 543, 546,
554–55, 559, 579 nn.183, 186, 613,
615, 616, 617, 621, 636, 642–43, 645,
649–51; Poland and, alliance, 635,
637–38; Poland and, guarantee, 555,
559, 616, 620, 622; Poland and, staff
talks, 613 (see also Ironside, Edmund, trip to Warsaw); press, 121,
130 n.118, 138; rearmament, 52–54,
57, 68, 107, 128, 349, 516–17, 524;
Rumania and, 236, 238 n.194, 492,
493, 494 n.116, 517–18, 540–44,
546–47, 553, 564, 569, 588; Spain
and, 148–49, 150–51; Turkey and,
217, 240–41, 517–18, 543, 591–92;
U.S.S.R. and, 80, 87, 88, 104,
163–64, 348 n.134, 415–18, 429, 449,
526, 532–33, 543, 548ff., 553, 554,
556–57, 568–70, 572–73, 574, 576–77,
612–16, 623, 637; United States and,
54, 58, 69, 96–97, 98, 105ff., 138,
139–40, 347 n.125, 358, 422 n.192,
526 n.254, 557 n.73, 578, 601 n.303;
United States and, Trade Agreement
(17 November 1938), 97, 107, 111,
521; view of war, 103–5, 141, 345–46,
549–50, 552, 613 n.354; Yugoslavia
and, 62 n.32, 80, 216, 217, 221, 543,
590
Epp, Franz Ritter von, 513, 580 n.191
Estonia, 8 n.19, 587, 610
Eupen-Malmedy, 91, 92 n.140, 593

Faber du Faur, Moriz, 140, 144 n.5
Fabricius, Wilhelm, 491
Faupel, Wilhelm, 143, 144, 150, 154,
155, 156
Fierlinger, Zdeněk, 415 nn.167, 168,
416 n.170
Finland: Germany and, 610; U.S.S.R.
and, 548, 552 n.50, 610
Fischel, Hermann von, 101
Fitz Randolph, Sigismond-Sizzo, 380
n.11, 452 n.296

Flandin, Pierre-Etienne, 546, 642
nn.69, 73
Forster, Albert, 46–47, 198–99, 200,
204, 209 n.69, 288, 289, 379–80, 404,
426, 482, 483 n.67, 484 n.72, 489 n.99,
583–84, 611; trip to England, 379–80,
381, 391
France, 5–7, 59; air force, 5, 58–59, 126
n.104, 133, 358, 399, 460 n.328, 523,
529–30; army, 57–58, 78–79, 323–24,
342–43, 386 n.34, 399–401, 449–50,
529, 545, 651; Austria and, 130 n.120,
266, 275, 282, 283, 292, 294–95, 298,
324; Belgium and, 81–85, 341–42,
428, 449 n.287, 592; Bulgaria and, 240
n.201, 490; colonial question, 124–26,
127, 354–55 (see also Schacht, Hjalmar, colonial question); Czechoslovakia and, 78–80, 81, 83, 85, 86–87,
124–25, 127, 132, 315, 323–25, 326,
328–29, 336, 339, 341–43, 344ff., 350,
354ff., 363–64, 368, 372–73, 375, 392
n.62, 397ff., 416, 419, 422–23,
428–29, 439ff., 444–45, 448–50,
452–53, 455 n.310, 459, 460, 463, 472,
546, 626; Danzig and, 488, 545; England and, 5–6, 55, 56 n.14, 57–59,
68, 69, 70–71, 72, 74–75, 78, 80, 100,
122ff., 132–33, 138, 342–43, 345ff.,
354ff., 373, 383, 397, 422–23, 427,
439, 442, 508, 517, 522–23, 527, 542,
544, 547 n.41, 555, 557 n.73, 624, 642,
651; foreign policy, 78ff., 125, 141,
461, 550, 666–67; Germany and, 23
n.16, 28–29, 33, 36–37, 42, 52, 59, 67,
69, 70–71, 76ff., 89ff., 178–79,
294–95, 354ff., 368, 399, 431, 460
n.328, 461, 466, 495, 507–9, 510, 515,
528–30, 545–46, 565–69, 582, 598–99,
618, 624–27, 634–35, 641–42, 651–52;
Germany and, Franco-German declaration (December 1938), 461, 487,
507–8, 528–29; Germany and, war
scare over Spanish Morocco (January 1937), 91, 145, 152, 368, 369;
government, 98; Greece and, 564;
and Halifax visit, 115 n.63, 117,
122ff.; Hungary and, 443–44; Italy
and, 38, 142–43, 163, 263, 280, 304,
342–43, 410, 450, 455, 507ff., 510,
512, 522–23, 530, 563, 564 n.109, 566,
567 n.119, 596–97, 636–37, 641, 649;
Japan and, 565, 575–76; Little En-

tente and, 79–81, 85, 217–18, 236;
Poland and, 83, 85, 86, 194 n.8, 203,
206, 208, 315, 401–3, 443–44, 450,
479, 500, 527, 529, 545, 613, 624–27,
641–42, 651–52; Poland and, military
cooperation, 624–25; Popular Front,
96; rearmament, 78–79, 133; Rumania and, 236, 238 n.194, 342, 491,
564, 588; Spanish Civil War and,
90–91, 96, 157, 160, 161; Turkey and,
240–42, 591–92; U.S.S.R. and,
86–89, 163–64, 214, 352–54, 363,
415–18, 450 n.289, 529, 531, 545, 548,
549, 568ff., 576–77, 612–16, 624–27;
United States and, 69, 105, 106, 133,
254, 358, 521, 529–30, 578; Yugoslavia and, 79–80, 216, 217, 218,
220–21, 342
Franco, Francisco, 38, 144, 151, 154,
155, 158ff., 275, 581 n.197. *See also*
Spanish Civil War
François-Poncet, André, 76, 77, 92, 386
n.32, 428 n.219, 528–29, 618; and
Czechoslovakia, 361, 364 n.201, 368
n.213, 396 n.78, 397–98, 437 n.250,
438 n.253, 452–53, 457 n.320; general
views, 92
Francqui, Emile, 109 n.38
Frank, Hans, 46, 47, 269, 272, 282, 285,
411 n.147, 424 n.202, 606, 630
Frank, Karl Hermann, 375 n.244, 418
French Equatorial Africa, 131
French Indochina, 179
Frère, Maurice, 91, 92
Frick, Wilhelm, 364 n.204, 586 n.218
Friends of the New Germany, 249–50
Fritsch, Werner von, 31ff., 144 n.5,
318, 384–85; Fritsch-Blomberg crisis,
43–51, 385
Fritzsche, Hans, 534 n.291
Fuller, Samuel R., Jr., 254
Funck, Hans von, 154
Funk, Walther, 26, 44 n.97

Gafencu, Grigore, 493, 588, 589
Gambia, 75, 77, 132
Gamelin, Maurice, 34 n.56, 85–86, 323
n.31, 341 n.105, 342–43, 355, 356, 358
n.178, 397 n.84, 399–401, 428 n.219,
450, 651 n.119
Gandhi, Mohandas K., 114, 120
Gauché, Maurice, 324
Gdynia, 502

Geneva Convention (1922), 195ff.
George II (king of Greece), 240
George V (king of England), 63
George VI (king of England), 62
Gerl, Franz, 372 n.230
German-American Bund, 249–51, 252,
253 n.15
German East Africa, 15, 121, 132
German News Agency (DNB), 117
German-Polish Society, 404 n.112
German Southwest Africa, 15, 136
Germany: Abwehr, 394, 475 (*see also*
Canaris, Wilhelm); agriculture, 26;
air force, 1 n.1, 2, 22–23, 28–29,
30–31, 41, 56, 164–65, 339, 350, 364
n.204, 387–88, 428, 513–14, 583, 590
(*see also* Condor Legion); Arabs
and, 243ff.; Argentina and, 259;
army, 2–3, 21–22, 28–29, 30ff., 43–51,
58, 316, 339, 370–71, 384–86, 390,
396–97, 407, 417, 418, 419, 424, 431,
434, 452, 462, 464, 467, 469, 475,
514–15, 560, 581, 583, 628, 638, 644,
645, 654 n.129, 677; Austria and, 33,
36–37, 39–40, 42, 46, 78, 122, 126,
130, 136, 140, 201–2, 215ff., chap. 9;
German-Austrian Agreement of 11
July 1936, 264–65, 266, 267, 270, 271;
Belgium and, 81–85, 91, 92 n.140,
379, 581, 592–93, 631; Brazil and, 9,
255–59; Bulgaria and, 238–40, 490,
581, 589–90; Carpatho-Ukraine and,
474ff., 573 n.150; China and, 11–13,
50–51, chap. 6; church struggle, 20,
252; colonial question, 14–15, 27–28,
33 n.55, 36, 61, 67ff., 136ff., 512–13;
Czechoslovakia and, 32–33, 36–37,
39–41, 42, 65 n.44, 69, 73, 76, 78,
124–26, 188, 201–2, 232, 237, chaps.
10 and 11, 465ff., 498–99, 535; Denmark and, 585 n.211; domestic situation, 2–3, 19, 20–21, 302–3, 386–87,
424–25, 451, 458, 515, 562, 573, 583,
619, 646, 662–63; economy, 19, 23ff.,
41, 67, 69 n.57, 128 n.114, 301, 339,
386–87, 389, 579–80, 583 n.200, 587,
654 (*see also* Germany: foreign trade,
Four-Year Plan); England and, 5–7, 9
n.21, 19, 23 n.16, 29, 36–37, 41, 43,
chaps. 3 and 4, 177, 178–79, 275,
294–95, 344, 354ff., 360–61, 368,
379ff., 393–94, 395, 431, 466, 495,
510, 515, 516–28, 539–45, 565–69,

582, 598–99, 613, 616–24, 636, 642–43, 645, 647, 649–51 (see also England, Germany and, Anglo-German Declaration; Halifax, Lord: and Germany, visit to; Hossbach conference); Estonia and, 8 n.19, 587, 610; Finland and, 610; foreign ministry, 27 n.30, 45–47, 167, 169, 172, 173, 197, 199, 200, 243, 244, 246, 254, 279, 307, 309, 335, 475, 562, 567, 618, 646; foreign trade, 8–9, 12, 23, 25, 26, 143, 147–48, 149ff., 170, 182ff., 216, 218–19, 227, 233, 237–39, 240–41, 242ff., 251, 256, 258, 491ff., 507 n.161, 511, 520–21, 531ff., 536, 573, 574, 576, 577, 585, 587–89, 590, 591, 603, 609; Forschungsamt, 440 n.261, 466 n.1; Four-Year Plan, 23–28, 31, 34, 147, 153, 168, 239, 267, 268, 387, 585, 590; France and, 23 n.16, 28–29, 33, 36–37, 42, 52, 59, 67, 69, 70–71, 76ff., 89ff., 178–79, 294–95, 354ff., 368, 399, 413, 460 n.328, 461, 466, 495, 507–9, 510, 515, 528–30, 545–46, 565–69, 582, 598–99, 624–27, 634–35, 641–42, 651–52; Greece and, 240; High Command of the Armed Forces (OKW), 47, 384, 475 (see also Germany, army; Keitel, Wilhelm); Holland and, rumors of German invasion plans, 525–26, 631; Hungary and, 223, 224–32, 235, 301, 333–34, 405–9, 431, 435, 436–37, 447, 452, 457, 470ff., 494–97, 535 n.35, 563, 581, 585–87; Iran and, 247 n.234; Iraq and, 243 n.218, 245; Italy and, 4, 12, 35, 38, 46, 80, 100, 116 n.67, 123, 142–43, 149, 163, 186–88, 236 n.181, 244, 247, chap. 9, 339–40, 366–67, 407 n.125, 409–14, 452ff., 472, 476, 504–12, 516 n.204, 534, 563–67, 594–600, 623, 630–31, 635–37, 639–41, 649; Italy and, military cooperation, 594–95; Japan and, 11–13, 50, 51, 116 n.67, 136, 137, chap. 6, 504–10, 565–69, 575–76, 600–602, 630; Jews, 195, 244–48, 252, 254, 311, 486–87, 658 (see also Germany, pogrom of November 1938); Latin America and, 7–8, 255–60; Latvia and, 8 n.19, 610; Lithuania and, 205–6, 209–11, 484–86, 536, 584–85, 610; Manchukuo and, 50–51, 180, 181, 507

n.161; Mexico and, 8 n.18, 259–60; ministry of economics, 26; ministry of war, 31ff., 167, 172 (see also Fritsch-Blomberg crisis); National Defense Council (Reichsverteidigungsrat), 513–14; naval aviation, 28, 514; navy, 2, 8 n.18, 19, 28–31, 34, 37, 40, 41, 152, 339, 371–72, 388–89, 514, 579–80, 583; navy, Z-Plan, 514, 579–80; Olympic games, 1; opposition to Hitler, 49, 373, 386, 393–97, 407, 412, 419, 421, 426, 428, 431, 458, 459, 462, 525, 560 n.87, 610 n.345, 614, 618 (see also Gördeler, Carl); pogrom of November 1938, 303, 486–87, 515, 519–20, 522; Poland and, 4, 37, 86, 193–209, 315, 318, 322, 401, 402, 403–5, 435–36, 447, 452 n.297, 457, 475, 478–90, 497–504, 536ff., 548–49, 554–55, 559ff., 566, 567, 568, 578ff., 610, 627, 628ff., 638ff., 643ff., 648–49, 655; Polish minority, 196–97, 200–201, 202, 203, 404, 502; Portugal and, 28; press and propaganda, 18, 20, 41, 115, 136, 170, 176 n.35, 181 n.52, 195, 196, 197 n.21, 204 n.51, 210, 211, 321, 329, 332, 333, 345 n.122, 364 n.204, 378, 390, 409, 424–25, 434, 441, 451–52, 463, 466, 468 n.12, 482, 488 n.90, 489, 493, 507, 515, 519, 520, 521, 528, 534, 548, 554 n.58, 562, 573, 574, 575, 584, 599, 606, 616, 620, 628, 633, 644, 646, 655; rearmament, 1, 19ff., 30ff., 52 (see also Germany, army; Hitler, concept of war); Reichsarbeitsdienst, 379; Reichsnährstand, 26; Reichswerke Hermann Göring, 25 (see also Germany, Four-Year Plan); Rumania and, 233–38, 490, 491–94, 536–37, 540–42, 553, 581, 587–89, 631; Saudi Arabia and, 243–44; Scandinavia and, 585; Sino-Japanese war and, 50–51, chap. 6 passim; Slovakia and, 499, 535–36, 538; Spain, Spanish Civil War and, 1, 4, 8 n.18, 28, 38, chap. 5, 581; Sweden and, 24, 581, 585; Turkey and, 240–42, 581, 591–92, 631; Union of South Africa and, 136; U.S.S.R. and, 4, 28, 33, 37, 69, 73, 75, 76, 88–89, 162, 205, 211–15, 352, 403, 414–18, 475, 495

n.128, 510, 531–34, 552, 557, 560
n.85, 568–77, 587 n.223, 601, 602–10,
619, 631–32, 652, 672–74; United
States and, 9, 10–11, 69, 249–55, 387,
519–21, 530, 565, 577–78, 652,
674–75; Vatican and, 10, 20–21, 595;
Wehrmachtamt (Armed Forces
Office), 31ff.; Westwall (Siegfried
Line), 42, 85, 317, 318, 324, 340, 341,
343, 370, 371, 378–79, 385, 389, 394,
400, 401 n.95, 418, 560, 562, 628;
Yugoslavia and, 4, 79, 80, 101,
215–24, 230–31, 301, 490–91, 563,
581, 590–91
Gibson, Hugh, 254
Gilbert, Prentiss, 521 n.238
Glaise-Horstenau, Edmund von, 267,
274 n.53, 289, 290, 300
Gleiwitz provocation, 607, 611, 628,
638 n.49, 648
Goebbels, Joseph, 28 n.36, 120, 300,
380 n.11, 452 n.296, 452
Gömbös, Julius, 224, 225
Goerdeler, Carl, 36 n.64, 43, 351, 394,
396, 457 n.319, 525, 574 n.156, 619
n.389, 643 n.77
Göring, Herbert, 212 n.85
Göring, Hermann, 15 n.47, 35, 43, 47,
49 n.119, 98, 399, 515 n.200, 580
n.190; and air force, 22–23, 41, 387,
513–14; and Austria, 112, 267, 268,
270–72, 278, 283 n.97, 284, 287, 289,
293 n.145, 297, 298, 299; and China,
12, 167–68, 172, 173, 181; and
Czechoslovakia, 39–40, 112, 272,
302, 332 n.71, 334, 345, 379, 387, 406,
451 n.294, 452, 457, 619; and England, 100, 102, 103 n.22, 112–13,
382, 387–88, 440 n.261, 452, 619,
621–22, 634 n.27, 640 n.62, 643, 646
n.96, 650 n.111; and England, possible trip to, 122 n.91, 129 n.117,
381–82, 383; and Four-Year Plan,
23–28; and France, 91; and Hungary,
228, 230, 406, 409 n.136, 431; and
Italy, 268, 270–72, 274, 275, 276–77,
287, 305, 411, 412, 414, 566, 568, 595
n.263; and Japan, 167–68, 172, 181,
602 n.307; and Poland, 194, 199, 201,
204, 228 n.156, 295, 404, 436, 475,
479 n.51, 481, 619, 621–22; and Rumania, 233, 492; and Spain, 147, 148,
152, 153, 268; and Turkey, 591 n.246;

and U.S.S.R., 568; and United
States, 251; and Yugoslavia, 223
n.132, 230, 590
Goga, Octavian, 226 n.144, 234, 235–36
Gold Coast, 132
Grabowski, Witold, 194
Greece: England and, 217, 240, 517–18,
543, 564; France and, 564; Germany
and, 240
Greenwood, Arthur, 556
Greiser, Arthur, 47 n.107, 198–99, 482,
562, 573 n.151
Groscurth, Helmuth, 407, 419 n.180,
423, 451 n.292, 452 n.299, 463 n.335,
583 n.199
Grundherr, Werner von, 485 n.77
Guadalajara, battle of, 149, 166
Guderian, Heinz, 22
Guernica, 23, 149–50
Guse, Günther, 386, 388

Haavara agreement, 245–47, 248
Habicht, Theo, 298
Habsburg restoration, 33, 215, 265,
266–67, 273, 274, 296–97
Hácha, Emil, 469, 534, 538
Haldane, Lord, 115 n.63, 127
Halder, Franz, 424 n.201, 515, 558
n.74, 583 n.200, 607, 639, 643, 648
n.104
Halifax, Lord, 39, 40, 62, 130, 134, 139,
140, 302, 320 n.20, 342; general
views, 70, 114–15, 550 n.45; and
Czechoslovakia, 344–45, 346–47,
348, 349–50, 351, 361, 363–64, 373,
374, 380–82, 390 n.54, 392–93, 395,
421, 422–23, 426, 438–39, 448, 452
n.300, 457 n.319; and Danzig, 348,
527; and Eden, 114; and Germany,
522, 529, 540, 542–43, 544, 550 n.45,
617 n.378, 618, 622, 632, 643, 649
n.108, 654 n.127; and Germany, visit
to, 110, 113ff., 145, 175, 285, 331; and
Poland, 348, 550 n.45, 554, 649 n.108;
and rearmament, 517; and Rumania,
543, 545, 550 n.45; and U.S.S.R.,
533, 556, 557, 570 n.135, 572, 614, 615
Hankey, Sir Maurice, 320 n.20, 345,
624 n.411
Hansen, Erich, 408 n.130, 466 n.1
HAPRO (Handelsgesellschaft für
industrielle Produkte m.b.H.), 12
n.30, 168, 181

Harvey, Oliver, 60 n.25
Hassell, Ulrich von, 46, 50, 269 n.38,
    273, 276, 285–86, 619 n.391
Haushofer, Albrecht, 13 n.37, 452
    n.298, 619 n.389
Haushofer, Karl, 35
Headlam-Morley, James W., 320 n.20
Hedilla, Manuel, 156
Hedin, Sven, 545 n.33, 654
Heinkel 177 (plane), 30 n.43
Helfand, Leon, 609 n.342
Henderson, Sir Nevile, 43, 49 n.119,
    62, 77, 99, 100, 101, 103 n.22, 112–13,
    116, 125, 126, 140, 211, 302, 395 n.76;
    general views, 60–61, 65, 135; ap-
    pointment, 60, 617; Czechoslovakia,
    347 n.128, 351, 352, 361, 372 n.230,
    378, 390 n.55, 391, 421, 422 n.190,
    426, 458–59, 619 n.391, 624 n.410;
    and Germany, 528, 539, 617–18, 622,
    629, 632, 642, 644, 647–48; meeting
    with Hitler 3 March 1938, 130,
    138–40, 518; and Poland, 617–18, 645
Henlein, Konrad, 314, 325 n.42, 328,
    329, 330, 333, 334–36, 338, 344, 351,
    356, 363, 368, 370–71, 374, 375, 376,
    377, 391, 392, 419, 420, 423–24, 425,
    431, 434; Karlovy Vary (Carlsbad)
    speech (24 April 1938), 335, 356, 361,
    370, 373–74, 418
Hertzog, J. B. M., 15, 16, 136, 359
    n.184
Herwarth von Bittenfeld, Hans Hein-
    rich, 573 n.154
Hess, Rudolf, 28 n.36, 35, 250, 282,
    285, 288, 378
Hesse, Fritz, 622
Hessen, Prince of, 285, 286 n.108, 299,
    304, 305, 413, 454, 456
Hewel, Walter, 618
Heydrich, Reinhard, 269, 607 n.329
Heye, Helmuth, 386 n.32
Hilger, Gustav, 603
Himmler, Heinrich, 269, 278, 289
    n.124, 498 n.139, 516 n.204, 565
Hindenburg, Paul von, 45
Hindenburg (dirigible), 11
Hiranuma, Kiichiro, 576 n.164, 630
Hirohito (emperor), 510
Hirota, Koki, 175
Hirsch, Helmut, 10
Hisma (Compañía Hispano-Marroquí
    de Transportes), 146, 147, 148, 151,
    152, 153, 154, 157
Hitler, Adolf, 2, 15 n.47, 98–99, 111;

    general views, 3, 16, 18–19, 59, 65,
    92–94, 112–13, 118–19, 140–41,
    201–2, 228–29, 247–48, 262, 316,
    389–90, 465–66, 503–4, 516, 557–58,
    580, 653–55, 657ff., 675–77 (see also
    Hossbach conference); and army
    (see Germany, army); and Austria,
    228, 269, 272, 278–79, 287–88,
    292–93, 294–95, 296, 297, 298–99, 303
    (see also Hossbach conference); and
    Austria, meeting with von Schusch-
    nigg, 130, 136; and Belgium, 83–85,
    92 n.140, 580, 592, 593; and Brazil,
    259; and Bulgaria, 589–90; and
    Carpatho-Ukraine, 470, 474–78, 481,
    484, 492, 496, 497, 497–98; and
    China, 12, 137, 168, 170, 172; and
    colonies, 70, 77, 115, 119, 126 n.107,
    138–39, 512–13, 580; concept of war,
    18ff., 104–5, 366–67, 389–90, 581,
    598, 653; and Czechoslovakia, 306,
    307, 312, 313, 314, 316–17, 334–41,
    365, 366–67, 369–71, 379, 383, 396,
    408–9, 418–19, 421, 423ff., 433ff.,
    446ff., 450ff., 462–63, 468, 496, 534,
    619 (see also Hossbach conference);
    and Czechoslovakia, Munich agree-
    ment, 462–64, 465–69, 496, 497, 525
    n.250, 654, 655; and Danzig, 580,
    653; and England, 59, 63–65, 70,
    100–101, 104–5, 113, 118–20, 122–23,
    126 n.107, 137ff., 178–79, 187, 301–2,
    303–4, 371, 380, 383, 388–90, 423–24,
    431–32, 450ff., 457, 463, 466, 482,
    503–4, 505, 512–13, 514, 515, 519,
    534, 538–39, 561–62, 577, 580–81,
    607, 611, 612, 616, 617 n.377, 618–19,
    621, 622, 628–29, 632–33, 637, 639,
    644–45, 646, 647, 650 n.111, 654, 655
    (see also Hossbach conference); and
    France, 142–44, 371, 383, 423–24,
    457, 466, 481, 503–4, 505, 508 n.163,
    512–13, 515, 534, 561–62, 580–81,
    607, 611, 612, 628–29, 633, 634–35,
    641–42, 646 (see also Hossbach con-
    ference); and Holland, 580; and
    Hungary, 223, 226, 228–29, 230, 232,
    408–9, 436–37, 463, 470ff., 476–78,
    496–97, 498, 503–4, 535 n.3, 586; and
    Italy, 261, 262, 275–76, 281, 282, 298,
    299, 303–4, 307, 311–12, 339–40, 412
    n.153, 413, 414, 424, 452ff., 511, 534,
    563, 565, 580, 582, 594ff., 610,
    630–31, 637, 639–40; and Italy, visit
    to Rome, 283, 286, 304, 305–11,

339–40; and Japan, 137, 168, 170, 172, 176, 177, 178–79, 180–81, 187, 577, 580, 582, 586, 600–601 (*see also* Hitler, and Tripartite Military Alliance); and Jewish emigration, 247; and Latvia, 610; and Lithuania, 210, 485–86, 536; and motorization, 22–23; and Memel, 485–86, 536; opposition to (*see* Germany, opposition to Hitler); personal life, 35–36, 307, 389–90, 432 n.231, 463 n.336, 562, 589, 629, 654; and Poland, 193, 194, 196, 197, 199, 200–202, 204, 206 n.58, 209, 435–36, 463, 470, 471, 476, 477, 479, 481–82, 484, 486–87, 489–90, 496, 497–98, 499, 503–4, 536–39, 557–62, 577, 578–79, 580–84, 598–99, 605, 607, 611, 612, 616, 617 n.377, 622, 628–29, 631, 634, 638ff., 643–45, 648; and Rumania, 235, 492–93; and Saudi Arabia, 244; and Slovakia, 470–72, 484; and Spain, Spanish Civil War, 142–44, 146, 150, 581 n.197, 611; and Tripartite Military Alliance, 185ff., 504ff., 566 n.114, 567, 577, 580–81, 600–601; and Turkey, 591; and U.S.S.R., 190, 214–15, 476–77, 503–4, 568, 573, 574, 575, 576, 577, 580–81, 582–83, 599, 603, 604, 605, 606, 607, 609, 629, 631, 633 n.24; and United States, 11, 187, 250–51, 252–53, 254, 255, 515, 577–78, 580, 586; and Yugoslavia, 591, 598–99; memorandum on fortifications, 318, 379; speech of 30 January 1937, 84, 91; speech of October 1937, 34 n.58; speech of 21 November 1937, 34 n.58; speech of 23 November 1937, 34 n.58, 123; speech of 20 February 1938, 136, 137, 180, 201, 208, 293, 295, 302; speech of 13 March 1938, 304 n.192; speech of 7 May 1938, 308; talk to generals on 28 May 1938, 371, 382; talk to generals on 13 June 1938, 385; speech of 12 September 1938, 211, 379, 404, 423, 424, 425, 428; speech of 26 September 1938, 451, 483, 484; speech of 8 October 1938, 519; talk to press of 10 November 1938, 424–25, 515–16; talk to officers of 10 February 1939, 515, 557–58; speech of 28 April 1939, 569, 577–78; talk to generals on 23 May 1939, 579–81, 653; talk to generals on 14 August 1939, 607, 610, 611, 612, 616

n.372, 617 n.377; talk to generals on 22 August 1939, 463, 558, 610–12, 617 n.377, 643 n.80; speech of 27 August 1939, 639; speech of 1 September 1939, 646, 648; talk to generals on 23 November 1939, 558

Hoare, Oliver, 381 n.15
Hoare, Sir Reginald, 588 n.227
Hoare, Sir Samuel (Lord Templewood), 66, 88 n.119, 351 n.142, 380 n.12, 426 n.206, 438 n.251, 614 n.358
Hodgson, Sir Robert, 151 n.36, 165–66
Hodža, Milan, 273, 332 n.71, 361, 375 n.244, 376 n.249, 391, 440 n.260, 441, 444, 471
Hohenlohe, Princess Stephanie, 381
Hohler, Sir Thomas, 450 n.290
Holland, war scare January–February 1939, 525–26, 540
Hore-Belisha, Leslie, 5 n.11, 55, 343, 356, 421 n.189
Horthy, Miklós, 209, 225–26, 230, 232, 406–8, 470, 497 n.135, 535 n.3
Hossbach, Friedrich, 40 n.80, 50
Hossbach conference (5 November 1937), 16, 34–43, 45, 49, 64, 118, 123, 144, 201, 228, 287, 301, 316–17, 318, 365
Hotblack, Elliot, 20, 43
Hotta, Masaaki, 506 n.157
Hudson, Robert S., 532–33, 570 n.135, 605, 621
Hull, Cordell, 251, 255
Hungary, 79; *Anschluss* and, 202–3, 227, 228–29, 231; and Anti-Comintern Pact, 494, 495–96; Arrow Cross movement, 232; Austria and, 273, 292, 295, 296; and Carpatho-Ukraine, 473ff., 487, 494, 497, 535; Czechoslovakia and, 209 n.68, 226–27, 228ff., 309, 315, 322, 333–34, 339, 392 n.62, 404ff., 436–37, 441 n.264, 443–44, 444 n.271, 452, 459, 461, 494; England and, 229, 232, 443–44, 450 n.290; France and, 443–44; German minority, 225, 226, 234, 495; Germany and, 223, 224–32, 235, 301, 333–34, 405–9, 431, 435, 436–37, 447, 452, 457, 470ff., 494–97, 535 n.35, 563, 581, 585–87; and Germany, Hungarian state visit of August 1938, 223, 230, 232, 406–9; Italy and, 280, 406 nn.121, 124, 411, 453, 457, 472, 476, 495, 496, 563, 564

n.108, 585, 586, 587 n.219; Poland
and, 203, 207, 208, 231, 322, 404–5,
436, 437 n.249, 471, 473ff., 480, 481,
487, 495 n.125, 496, 499, 586–87; rearmament, 226, 406–7, 494 n.117;
Rumania and, 226, 227, 228, 230, 235,
406, 450 n.290, 491, 494, 496, 497,
536, 541, 543, 586 n.214, 587 n.219;
Slovakia and, 470–72, 473 n.26, 497,
535; U.S.S.R. and, 474, 495, 496
n.129; United States and, 229, 586;
Yugoslavia and, 207, 215, 218, 220,
221–23, 224, 228, 229, 230–31, 405–6,
444, 490, 497, 564 n.108, 590
Hurtwood, Lord Allen of, 459 n.324
Husayni, Haj Amin al-, 245

Ickes, Harold, 11
Imperial Conference, 1937, 14–16, 37,
77 n.71, 102–3
Imrédy, Béla, 230, 231–32, 406–8,
411–12, 436, 494 n.119
India, 14, 65, 114–15, 120
Ingersoll, Ralph, 109
Innitzer, Theodor, 300–301
Inönü, Ismet, 572 n.146, 608 n.335
Inskip, Sir Thomas, 57 n.18
Iran: Germany and, 247 n.234
Iraq: Germany and, 243 n.218, 245
Ironside, Edmund, 43 n.94, 57, 439
n.255, 622, 625, 649 n.110; trip to
Warsaw 1939, 616, 617 n.377
Ismay, Hastings Lionel, 618 n.388
Italy: Albania and, 411, 509, 512, 564,
590, 591; and Anti-Comintern Pact,
12, 13, 170–73, 285; Anti-Semitic
laws, 311, 411; Austria and, 261–62,
264, 267, 270–72, 280, 283, 286–87,
292, 294, 295, 296, 298; China and,
170–71; Czechoslovakia and, 37, 306,
307, 308, 309, 310, 312, 323, 340,
411–14, 452ff.; England and, 38, 56,
57, 58, 62 n.32, 66 n.48, 110–11,
133–35, 142–43, 163, 270, 271,
274–75, 295, 304, 310, 344 n.119, 410,
450, 454–55, 505, 510, 522–23, 526,
563, 623, 636–37, 641, 649, 650;
Ethiopian war, 3–4, 15; foreign trade,
511; France and, 38, 142–43, 163,
263, 280, 304, 342–43, 410, 450, 455,
507ff., 510, 512, 522–23, 530, 563, 564
n.109, 566, 567 n.119, 596–97,
636–37, 641, 649; Germany and, 4,
12, 35, 38, 46, 80, 100, 116 n.67, 123,
142–43, 149, 163, 186–88, 236 n.181,

244, 247, chap. 9, 339–40, 366–67,
407 n.125, 409–14, 452ff., 472, 476,
504–12, 516 n.204, 534, 563–67, 594–
600, 623, 630–31, 635–37, 639–41,
649; Hungary and, 280, 406 nn.121,
124, 411, 453, 457, 472, 476, 495, 496,
563, 564 n.108, 585, 586, 587 n.219,
596; Japan and, 170–71, 172–73, 187,
410, 411, 504–12, 563–69; Poland
and, 499, 566, 567, 579; Spain,
Spanish Civil War and, 142–43, 144,
149, 156 n.51, 160, 162, 163, 165–66,
323, 410, 453, 596 n.269; Turkey and,
591; U.S.S.R. and, 571, 597, 603
n.312; Yugoslavia and, 79, 216–18,
224, 231, 273, 286, 287, 411, 414, 563,
590, 598–99, 600, 635

Jaeckh, Ernst, 26 n.29, 39 n.76, 63 n.36
Janson, Martin von, 648 n.106
Japan: England and, 13 n.37, 56, 57, 58,
170–71, 179, 184–85, 188ff., 506, 509–
10, 565–69, 575–76, 596–97, 601;
France and, 565, 575–76; German colonies and, 74, 136–37, 513; Germany
and, 11–13, 50, 51, 116 n.67, chap. 6,
504–10, 565–69, 575–76, 600–602,
630; Italy and, 170–71, 172–73, 187,
410, 411, 504–12, 563–69; Poland
and, 579, 602, 630 n.12; U.S.S.R.
and, 37, 188–90, 213, 504, 506,
509–10, 565, 568, 575, 601–2, 606,
608; United States and, 109, 187ff.,
506, 510, 569, 576 n.164, 601
Jebb, Sir Gladwyn, 66, 650–51
Jeschonnek, Hans, 513 n.192
Jodl, Alfred, 31ff., 49, 136, 155 n.47,
337 n.87, 364, 389, 413, 418 n.176,
419 n.181, 424, 645 n.91; diary, 337
n.87, 370 n.219, 390 n.51
Johnson, Hershel, 135 n.137

Kandelaki, David, 214
Kánya, Kálmán de, 40, 222, 225–26,
228, 230, 232, 295, 334–35, 406–8, 409
n.136, 411–12, 431 n.227, 436, 494,
495 n.122
Keitel, Wilhelm, 31ff., 47, 48, 49, 292,
333, 337–38, 339, 364, 365, 366, 369,
370, 408, 424, 456, 475 n.32, 504
n.150, 561 n.89, 564, 607 n.329, 637
n.43
Kennan, George F., 469
Kennard, Sir Howard, 527, 616 n.373,
645

Kennedy, Joseph, 301, 430, 624, 643
Kenya, 130
Keppler, Wilhelm, 278–79, 287, 289, 295 n.155, 301
Keresztes-Fischer, Lajos, 408 n.130
Kesselring, Albert, 22
Keynes, John Maynard, 320
King, John Herbert, 612 n.350
King, Mackenzie, 16, 111, 351, 643 n.78
Kionga, 121
Kiosseivanov, George, 589, 604
Kirk, Alexander, 603 n.308
Kirkpatrick, Sir Ivone, 39 n.77, 525 n.250
Kismayu, 595
Klein, Hans, 12 n.30
Kleist, Bruno Peter, 477 n.41, 499 n.140, 533–34, 604 n.316
Kleist-Schmenzin, Ewald von, 394–96
Koch, Erich, 210 n.75, 219
Königsberg (ship), 628 n.2
Köstring, Ernst, 212–13, 603
Konoye, Fumimaro, 176
Konradi, Arthur, 492
Kopp, Federico Colin, 258 n.37
Kordt, Theo, 396, 426, 651
Kriebel, Hermann, 46, 47
Krofta, Kamil, 361, 419 n.182
Krupp steel works, 34
Kung, Hsiang-hsi, 12

Labougle, Eduardo, 259 n.44
Lacroix, Victor de, 326, 327, 360 n.186, 398, 440, 441
La Guardia, Fiorello, 10
Lamoureux, Lucien, 528
Latin America: Germany and, 7–8, 255–60
Latvia: Germany and, 8 n.19, 610
Laval, Pierre, 89
League of Nations, 3, 61, 67, 69, 73, 74, 85, 123, 173, 195, 275, 285, 342, 416, 495, 572–73, 591; Danzig and, 197, 198, 199, 200, 202, 488, 501, 502 n.148, 527; mandates system, 74, 131; mission in Hungary, 224, 226
Leeper, Sir Reginald, 554
Léger, Alexis, 360 n.186, 588 n.224
Leipzig (ship): supposed incident, 100–101, 116, 150
Leith-Ross, Sir Frederick, 69, 70, 91, 97
Lelong, Albert, 625
Leopold, Josef, 265, 278, 279, 288, 293
Leopold (king of the Belgians), 133,

342, 428 n.219, 593, 631 n.16. See also Belgium
LeRond, Henri, 389 n.49
Lersner, Kurt von, 91 n.135
Lester, Sean, 197
LeTellier, Pol, 398 n.88, 593
Levetzow, Werner von, 258 n.42
Libya, 342–43
Liddell Hart, Sir Basil, 400 n.94
Liebitzky, Emil, 296
Liechtenstein, 538 n.15
Lindbergh, Charles, 373 n.234, 398 n.85, 428, 450 n.290
Lindsay, Sir Ronald, 110 n.42
Lipski, Josef, 194 n.5, 199, 200, 201, 404, 408 n.131, 431 n.229, 436, 452 n.297, 476, 481, 482, 483, 487, 488, 489, 497, 554, 560, 577 n.174, 647
Lithuania: Germany and, 205–6, 209–11, 484–86, 536, 584–85, 610; Poland and, 204–6, 485, 486, 584–85; U.S.S.R. and, 213, 353 n.160, 486
Little Entente, 79, 215, 217, 220, 222, 223, 226, 227, 229, 230, 236, 237, 242, 315, 323, 406, 407, 408, 590
Litvinov, Maxim, 252, 253–54, 363–64, 415 n.167, 531, 533 n.284, 548 n.41, 552, 553, 569, 570, 571, 572
Ljotić, Dimitrije, 219
Lloyd, Lord, 394, 397 n.84
Lloyd George, David, 612
Locarno Agreements, 58–59, 67, 73, 78, 81, 89
Lochner, Louis, 610 n.345
Lörzer, Bruno, 22 n.14
Londonderry, Lord, 545 n.33
Loraine, Sir Percy, 242 n.216, 636 n.37
Lothian, Lord, 15 n.47, 65–66, 77, 99–100, 120, 125, 140 n.168, 351, 517 n.208, 522 n.240, 617 n.382, 618
Lubiénski, Michal, 501, 559 n.82
Luftwaffe. See under Germany, air force
Łukasiewicz, Juliusz, 359 n.183, 403 n.104, 416 n.169, 554 n.62
Luxembourg, 83 n.94, 631

MacDonald, Malcolm, 543, 576 n.169
Maček, Vládko, 216
Mackensen, Hans Georg von, 46, 118, 138, 176–77, 178 n.39, 225, 279, 281, 286, 304, 332 n.71, 337, 522 n.242, 631, 637 n.42
Maginot line, 78, 79, 83

Magistrati, Massimo, 276, 305, 597
Maisky, Ivan M., 354 n.163, 417 n.172, 532, 533, 552, 553, 556, 569, 572, 573, 615, 630 n.10
Majorca, 38, 148, 310
Málaga, 149
Mallet, Victor, 395 n.72, 396 n.78
Manchukuo, 50–51, 177, 178, 179, 180, 181, 183, 189, 285, 495–96, 507 n.161
Manstein, Erich von, 390 n.51
Markau, Karl, 251 n.3
Marras, Luigi, 410 n.144
Masařík, Hubert, 332 n.71, 468–69
Masaryk, Jan, 344–45, 347 n.125, 351 n.142, 362, 363 n.197, 374, 381 n.15, 440 n.261, 446 n.277
Masirevich, Constantin de, 225
Mason-Macfarlane, Frank Noel, 362, 554
Massey, Vincent, 402 n.100, 448 n.282
Mastný, Vojtěch, 302, 332, 364 n.201
May crisis. *See under* Czechoslovakia
Memel, 61, 65, 205, 209–11, 484, 485–86, 536, 544 n.32
Menemencioglu, Numan, 241
Merekalov, Aleksei, 212, 533, 568–69
Messersmith, George S., 37 n.68, 61, 254–55, 292 n.136
Metaxas, Jean, 240
Mexico: Germany and, 8 n.18, 259–60
Miklas, Wilhelm, 297, 298, 299
Mikoyan, Anastas, 532
Milch, Erhard, 269
Moffat, Jay Pierrepont, 15
Molotov, Vyacheslav M., 531, 570, 571, 572, 573, 574, 576, 577, 606, 607, 608, 609, 613, 615, 631; speech of 31 May 1939, 577
Moltke, Hans Adolf von, 46 n.103, 196, 197, 200, 479–80, 487, 489, 497, 502 n.148, 554 n.58, 560, 579 n.183, 599
Monnet, Jean, 529
Montreux convention, 241
Moravská Ostrava (Mährisch-Ostrau): area, 479, 498; incidents, 419, 420
Morell, Theodor, 390 n.52
Morgenthau, Henry, 96, 107
Mozambique, 121
Muff, Wolfgang, 289 n.124
Mundelein, George, 10, 11
Munich conference. *See under* Czechoslovakia
Mushakoji, Kintomo, 172

Mussert, Anton Adriaan, 265 n.16
Mussolini, Benito, 35, 263, 458 n.322, 566; and Austria, 266, 270–72, 277, 280, 286, 296, 298, 299, 303; and Czechoslovakia, 411–14; and England, 134, 163, 304, 410; and France, 263, 594 n.256; and Germany, 261, 275, 304, 305, 308, 309, 310, 410, 411, 452ff., 563, 565, 594ff., 600, 630–31, 635–37, 639–40; and Germany, visit to, 272, 275–76, 279–83, 284; and Greece, 587 n.214; and Japan, 171; and Poland, 595; and Spain, Spanish Civil War, 143, 145, 149, 156 n.51, 163, 166, 263–64; and Tripartite Military Alliance, 504ff.; and U.S.S.R., 568; and Yugoslavia, 600, 635

Nadolny, Rudolf, 21
Naujocks, Alfred, 607 n.329
Nauru, 137
Nečas, Jaromír, 441, 442 n.265
Neuhausen, Franz, 218–19, 590
Neumann, Ernst, 211, 485, 496
Neurath, Constantin von, 11, 28 n.36, 35, 38–39, 40, 41 n.83, 45, 50–51, 77, 112, 118, 126, 132, 173, 275–76, 286; and Austria, 266 n.19, 269 nn.35, 37, 272–73, 279, 281, 291; Balkan trip of 1937, 101, 219, 220, 226, 239; and Belgium, 84; and China, 170, 176–77; and Czechoslovakia, 332, 372 n.230, 457; and England, 77, 137–38; and England, proposed visit to, 95 n.1, 99–105, 280; and France, 90, 92; and Hungary, 228, 230, 275; and Italy, 275–76; and Poland, 195, 199, 200–201; and Rumania, 237, 275; and Spain, 145 n.9, 275; and Yugoslavia, 220, 230
Neuwirth, Hans, 467 n.8
New Guinea, 137
New Hebrides, 75, 132
New Zealand, 14–15. *See also* Dominions
News Chronicle, 329, 330, 554
Newton, Basil, 330 n.64, 360 n.187, 440
Nigeria, 131, 132
Nin, Andrés, 156 n.50
Nine-Power Pact, 171
Noé, Ludwig, 380 n.12
Noël, Léon, 355 n.165, 403 n.104

Nomonhan incidents, 575, 601, 602
Norway, 24, 29 n.39
NSDAP, 278; AO (Auslands-
    Organisation), 8 n.17, 167, 246, 256,
    259, 332 n.71; APA (Aussen-
    politisches Amt), 167, 234, 243, 247
    n.233, 475; Colonial Policy Office,
    512–13; Hitler Youth, 210 n.75;
    NSK (Nationalsozialistische Presse-
    Korrespondenz), 116
Nuremberg trial, 29 n.39, 39 n.76
Nyon Conference, 112, 164, 171, 214

Oderberg (Bohumin), 479
Ogilvie-Forbes, Sir George, 116, 515
    n.203, 560 n.87, 561 n.89
Olga (princess of Yugoslavia), 606
    n.328
Olympic games, 1
O'Malley, Sir Owen, 62 n.32
Orlov, Alexander, 155 n.50
Orlov, Admiral V. M., 87–88
Ormsby-Gore, William, 133 n.129
Oshima, Hiroshi, 172, 173, 178, 181,
    183, 184, 187, 188, 189, 506, 509, 510,
    575
Osuský, Stefan, 81, 342 n.111, 361, 398,
    416 n.169, 445 nn.272, 273
Ott, Eugen, 178, 182, 187, 506 n.160,
    565 n.113
Oumansky, Constantine, 578 n.178, 608

Pacelli, Eugenio (Pius XII), 301, 357
    n.176, 546, 595
Palairet, Michael, 297
Palestine, 56, 244–48
Papen, Franz von, 39 n.74, 46, 50, 61,
    119, 265, 273, 277, 278, 279, 281,
    287ff., 591
Pares, Sir Bernard, 615 n.366
Pariani, Alberto, 411, 456, 564
Paris International Exposition of 1937,
    76
Paul (Prince Regent of Yugoslavia),
    101, 216, 217, 223 n.133, 590, 591,
    595 n.264
Paul-Boncour, Joseph, 349, 355 n.165
Pavelić, Ante, 216
Peel Commission, 244
Perth, Earl of, 458 n.322
Pfeffer, Franz von, 251
Phipps, Sir Eric, 60, 62, 69–70, 76, 283,

423, 446 n.276, 545
Picasso, Pablo, 23
Pirow, Oswald, 16, 512 n.180, 519 n.217
Pius XII (Eugenio Pacelli), 546, 595
Poland: and Anti-Comintern Pact, 481,
    483–84, 489, 499, 500; Austria and,
    see Anschluss, Poland and; Corridor,
    65 n.44, 194, 205, 209, 232, 436, 481,
    482, 483, 488, 498, 500, 501, 502, 527,
    538, 539 n.21; Czechoslovakia and,
    87 n.115, 203, 206–9, 315, 322, 339,
    363–64, 375, 401–3, 408, 416 n.169,
    435–36, 443–44, 444 n.271, 450, 459,
    461, 470, 478–79; England and, 203,
    206, 208, 348, 402, 403, 450, 478, 500,
    502 n.148, 524, 527, 538, 543, 546,
    554–55, 559, 579 nn.183, 186, 613,
    615, 616, 617, 621, 636, 642–43, 645,
    649–51; France and, 83, 85, 86, 194
    n.8, 203, 206, 208, 315, 401–3,
    443–44, 450, 479, 500, 527, 545, 613,
    624–27, 641–42, 651–52; German
    minority, 194–97, 200–201, 203, 404,
    479 n.50, 486, 502, 583 n.200, 613,
    628 nn.1, 3, 644; Germany and, 4, 37,
    86, 193–209, 315, 318, 322, 401, 402,
    503–5, 435–36, 447, 452 n.297, 457,
    475, 478–90, 497–504, 536ff., 548–49,
    554–55, 559ff., 566, 567, 568, 578ff.,
    610, 627ff., 638ff., 643ff., 648–49,
    655; Hungary and, 203, 207, 208, 231,
    322, 404–5, 436, 437 n.249, 471,
    473ff., 480, 481, 487, 495n.125, 496,
    499, 586–87; Italy and, 499, 566, 567,
    579; Japan and, 579, 602, 630 n.12;
    Lithuania and, 204–6, 485, 486,
    584–85; military, 502 n.149, 538, 539
    n.21, 548, 634 n.31, 644, 649; and
    proposed Western Pact, 59 n.24, 200
    n.28; and Munich, 478, 480 n.56;
    Rumania and, 203, 207, 402, 474, 547,
    564 n.109, 587–88; Slovakia and, 472,
    499, 535–36, 537, 538, 584; U.S.S.R.
    and, 86–87, 208, 352–53, 363–64, 402,
    403, 415, 416 nn.169, 170, 474, 495,
    499, 531, 548–49, 554–55, 615, 627,
    649; U.S.S.R. and, Polish-Soviet
    Declaration of 27 November 1938,
    474, 499, 531; United States and, 478
Popitz, Johannes, 451 n.292
Portugal, 121, 125, 133
Potemkin, Vladimir, 88, 557, 568, 571,
    572–73, 574

POUM, 155
Pownall, Sir Henry, 401 n.95, 555
Prételat, André Gaston, 651 n.119
Prinz Eugen (ship), 407
Prunas, Renato, 286
Puttkammer, Jesko von, 388 n.45

Raczynski, Edward, 559 n.82
Raeder, Erich, 28–30, 31, 35, 40, 41, 49
    n.119, 371 n.224, 372, 386, 388, 389,
    514, 583, 629 n.4
Rátz, Jeno, 407, 408
Raumer, Hans von, 172, 173, 179
Rechenberg, Bernhard G. von, 253, 255
Reichenau, Walter von, 31, 45, 48, 56
    n.12, 292, 396, 467
Renondeau, Gaston, 22 n.13
Renzetti, Giuseppe, 305, 602 n.307
Reynaud, Paul, 362 n.190
Rhineland remilitarization, 58–59, 78
Ribbentrop, Joachim von, 38, 43, 46,
    47, 50–51, 70–71, 112, 126, 138–39,
    241, 258, 333, 386, 432; and Anti-
    Comintern Pact, 13, 117, 118,
    160–62, 503; and Austria, 139; and
    Czechoslovakia, 421, 422 n.190, 426,
    447, 452, 456, 469 n.14, 477 n.42; and
    England, 64, 135, 382, 566, 567, 619,
    620, 621, 622, 629–30, 647–48; and
    England, in London, 61, 63, 64, 70,
    98 n.6, 101, 117–18, 118 n.74, 139,
    301–2, 344; and France, 565, 566,
    626; and France, Paris visit of De-
    cember 1938, 461, 525, 626; and
    Hungary, 407, 408, 431, 494, 496; and
    Italy, 117, 171ff., 285, 307ff., 411,
    412–13, 596 n.269, 597, 630–31, 637
    n.43 (*see also* Ciano, Salzburg
    meeting); and Japan, 117, 167, 171ff.,
    177ff., 185ff., 411, 601; and Poland,
    204, 481, 482, 484, 487, 488, 489,
    497–98, 499, 501, 505 n.155, 538, 554,
    561, 567, 579, 598, 599, 605, 620, 622,
    647; and Rumania, 491; and Saudi
    Arabia, 244; and Slovakia, 471 n.21,
    535 n.3, 538; and Tripartite Military
    Alliance, 185–91, 504–12, 565–69,
    575–76, 580 n.193, 581, 601; and
    U.S.S.R., 190, 531, 538, 567–68,
    573–74, 576, 579, 581, 601, 604, 605,
    631; and U.S.S.R., trip to Moscow in
    August 1939, 606–10, 629–30; and
    United States, 578 n.181; and Yugo-
slavia, 230
Rintelen, Enno von, 312
Ripka, Hubert, 391 n.56
Rieckhoff, Herbert Joachim, 23
Rio Tinto copper mines, 148, 149 n.25
Ritter, Karl, 257–58, 259, 485 n.77
Roatta, Mario, 600 n.297
Röver, Karl, 364 n.204
Rome Protocols Powers (Italy, Hun-
    gary, Austria), 268–69, 276, 284
Roosevelt, Franklin D., 11, 15 n.48, 43
    n.93, 69, 99, 106, 236 n.253, 254, 255,
    301, 454, 520, 521, 529–30, 636; ap-
    peal of 14 April 1939, 577–78; and
    Japan, 601; and Munich, 454, 458;
    and Poland, 478 n.47; proposals for a
    new European settlement 1936 and
    1938, 107ff., 134, 135 n.136, 139–40;
    and U.S.S.R., 578, 608; speech of 5
    October 1937, 109
Rosenberg, Alfred, 51 n.122, 167, 475,
    477
Rosso, Augusto, 570 n.135, 574, 615
    n.362
Rowak (Rohstoffe- und Waren-
    Einkaufsgesellschaft), 146, 147, 148,
    239
Ruanda-Urundi, 74, 132, 133 n.129
Rudnay de, 39 n.74, 229 n.158
Rumania, 79, 86–87, 546, 587; Bulgaria
    and, 239, 490, 536, 541, 589;
    Carpatho-Ukraine and, 474, 491, 492,
    493 n.114, 497, 553; Czechoslovakia
    and, 352–53, 402, 473, 474, 491; En-
    gland and, 236, 238 n.194, 492, 493,
    494 n.116, 517–18, 540–44, 546–47,
    553, 564, 569, 588; France and, 236,
    238 n.194, 342, 491, 564, 588; German
    minority, 233–34, 492; Germany and,
    233–38, 490, 491–94, 536–37, 540–42,
    553, 581, 587–89, 631; Hungary and,
    226, 227, 228, 230, 235, 406, 450 n.290,
    491, 494, 496, 497, 536, 541, 553, 586
    n.214, 587 n.219; Iron Guard, 234,
    235, 236, 237, 493; Poland and, 203,
    207, 402, 474, 547, 564 n.109, 587–88;
    U.S.S.R. and, 79, 86–87, 233, 236–37,
    352–53, 415, 491, 588
Runciman, Lord, 111 n.47, 392, 419–20,
    430, 437–38, 446
Ruthenia. *See* Carpatho-Ukraine
Rydz-Smigły, Edward, 193, 206 nn.56,
    57, 402 n.102

Sakoh, Shyui Chi, 630 n.12
Sargent, Sir Orme, 34 n.56, 63 n.36, 103, 339 n.94, 392 n.60, 397 n.81, 445–46, 447 n.280, 458 n.323, 560 n.87, 649 n.107
Saud, Ibn, 243, 244
Saudi Arabia: England and, 243; Germany and, 243–44
Schacht, Hjalmar, 12, 15 n.47, 26–27, 98, 148, 214, 525; negotiations on colonial issue, 67–78, 89–94, 97, 103 n.22, 104, 113, 121, 132 n.123
Schairer, Reinhold, 574 n.156
Scheliha, Rudolf von, 533, 551, 575, 579 n.183, 604 n.316
Schirach, Baldur von, 269
Schleicher, Kurt von, 3, 47 n.112
Schleswig-Holstein (ship), 583 n.203, 628 n.2, 648
Schmidt, Guido, 267–68, 269, 274, 279, 293
Schmidt, Paul, 433, 648 n.102
Schmundt, Rudolf, 50, 337 n.90, 338, 366, 369, 370 n.218, 447
Schniewind, Otto, 388
Schnurre, Karl, 531, 573, 574, 603, 606 n.327
Schulenburg, Friedrich Werner von der, 213 n.89, 531–32, 573–74, 603, 606, 607, 608, 609
Schuschnigg, Kurt von, 136, 228, 264ff., 269, 272, 273, 274, 278, 281, 283, 284, 289ff.; meeting with Hitler 12 February 1938, 130, 136, 289ff., 334 n.82; plebiscite project, 293–97, 303
Schwerin, Gerhard von, 524 n.249
Schwerin von Krosigk, Lutz, 28 n.36, 422 n.190, 635
Seeckt, Hans von, 45
Seyss-Inquart, Arthur, 278, 284, 289, 290, 292, 293, 296ff.
Shanghai, 169, 171, 174
Shigemitsu, Mamuro, 188 n.82
Shiratori, Toshio, 506, 509, 510, 569 n.130
Siemens, Leopold, 427
Simon, Sir John, 380 n.12, 421, 422, 426, 438 n.251, 543
Sino-Japanese war, 109, chap. 6, 506 n.160; German mediation attempt, 174–76, 178. See also Brussels conference

Skoda works. See Czechoslovakia
Slávik, Juraj, 450 n.290
Slovakia, Slovak autonomist movement, 207, 228, 231, 315, 319, 402 n.100, 405, 408, 409, 436, 467, 469, 470–72, 478, 484, 486 n.80, 499, 534, 535–36, 538, 552 n.51, 584
Snowden, Lady, 381 n.15
Solomon Islands, 137
Sorge, Richard, 533, 551, 565 n.113, 569 n.131, 575
South Tyrol, 35, 262, 270–71, 273, 281, 286–87, 299, 304–5, 306, 308, 309, 311, 410, 511–12, 513, 565, 594, 599. See also Germany, Italy and
Spain: and Anti-Comintern Pact, 160–62, 503; Carlists, 156; Civil War, 4, 8 n.18, 38, 89–90, 96, 99–101, chap. 5; Civil War, possible German-French mediation, 90–91; England and, 150–51, 160–61; Falange, 155, 156; France and, 151; International Brigades, 143; Non-Intervention Committee, 99, 146 n.15, 150, 275; and Munich crisis, 158–59. See also Nyon Conference
Spanish Morocco, crisis of January 1937, 91, 145, 152, 368, 369
Sperrle, Hugo, 155, 156, 292
Srbik, Ritter von, 300
SS (Schutz-Staffel), 35
Stalin, Joseph, 190, 416–17, 531, 534, 568; and England, 533–34, 570–72, 608, 615, 630; and France, 570–72, 608; and Germany, 4, 214–15, 417, 549, 550–53, 568, 570–72, 604–5, 607ff., 615, 627, 632; and Latvia, 610, view of war, 550–53; speech of 10 March 1939, 533, 550, 552, 568
Stallforth, Federico, 251 n.3
Stanley, Oliver, 528, 539, 543
Starace, Achille, 508
Steed, Wickham, 109 n.39, 373
Stehlin, Paul, 400 n.94, 622 n.400
Steinacher, Hans, 35, 329 n.59, 332 n.71
Steinhardt, Laurence A., 578 n.178, 608
Stilwell, Joseph, 174 n.25
Stohrer, Eberhard von, 50 n.120, 153 n.43, 154, 156 n.51
Stojadinović, Milan, 79, 217ff., 230, 286, 490–91

Strong, H. C. Travell, 362 n.193
Sudeten area, 61, 348, 390, 422, 425,
    432, 434, 437, 441, 444, 447, 457, 459,
    460, 527
Sudeten German Free Corps, 419, 425,
    434, 437, 446 n.276, 447
Sudeten German party, 314, 327, 329,
    331ff., 351, 360, 376–77, 419, 420, 425
Sudeten Germans, 41, 124, 126, 132,
    203, 309, 317, 319–24, 325ff., 339,
    346, 349, 351, 356, 359, 361, 362,
    373ff., 380, 390, 391, 392, 398, 404,
    420, 440, 441, 442, 460, 467
Suetsugo, Nobumasa, 190 n.88
Sugimura, Yotaro, 12 n.35, 71, 78
Surits, Iakov Z., 552 n.53, 615, 625
    n.422
Sweden: Germany and, 24, 581, 585
Switzerland: Germany and, 631
Syria, 242
Sztójay, Döme, 225, 302, 334, 364
    n.204, 366 n.207, 467 n.5, 586 n.216

Tanganyika, 15, 74, 125, 127, 130, 132
Tass. See U.S.S.R.
Tatarescu, Gheorghe, 235, 242
Tauschitz, Stephan, 61
Tavs, Leopold, 288, 289 n.124
Tczew (Dirschau), 607, 677
Teleki, Pál, 585–87, 596
Templers, 245, 246 n.228
Teruel, 157
Těšín (Teschen), 87 n.115, 206–7, 315,
    401, 408, 416 n.169, 435, 470, 478–79
Thailand, 9 n.21
Theben, 472 n.25
Thoma, Wilhelm Ritter von, 155 n.47
Thomas, Georg, 19, 27, 28 n.34
Thomsen, Hans, 578 n.191
Tientsin incident, 596–97, 601
Tilea, Viorel V., 537 n.10, 541, 542
Times (London), 38 n.72, 120, 354
    n.164, 422, 515 n.203
Tippelskirch, Kurt von, 209 n.68
Tirpitz (ship), 29, 388
Tiso, Josef, 471
Titulescu, Nicolae, 233, 237
Todt, Fritz, 318, 371, 379, 482
Toggenburg, Count von, 515 n.203
Togo (former German colony), 71, 74,
    75, 77, 127, 131, 132
Togo, Shigenori, 181, 183, 184, 189, 506
Tonningen, Rost van, 265 n.16

Toynbee, Arnold J., 330, 519 n.217
Transylvania, 226, 235, 238
Trautmann, Oskar, 175, 176, 177 n.37,
    181, 182, 183
Tripartite Pact (1940), 137
Trott zu Solz, Adam von, 618–19
Troubridge, Thomas H., 29
Tukhachevsky, Mikhail, 87
Turkey: England and, 217, 240–41,
    517–18, 543, 591–92; France and,
    240–42, 591–92; Germany and,
    240–42, 581, 591–92, 631; Italy and,
    591; U.S.S.R. and, 608

Udet, Ernst, 22 n.14
Ukraine, Ukrainian nationalism,
    Ukrainian question, 473ff., 487, 583
    n.200
"Ultra" secret, 613 n.354
Union of South Africa, 15–16, 136, 346,
    359 n.184, 427–28
U.S.S.R., 579 n.183; armed forces,
    416–18; Baltic States and, 548 n.42;
    Bulgaria and, 589; and Carpatho-
    Ukraine, 474, 495, 552; China and,
    169, 174, 213, 553; Czechoslovakia
    and, 86–89, 318, 329, 341, 348 n.134,
    351, 352–54, 402, 414–18, 439 n.255,
    449, 450, 460, 552; England and, 80,
    87, 88, 104, 163–64, 348 n.134,
    415–18, 429, 449, 526, 532–33, 543,
    548ff., 553, 554, 556–57, 568–70,
    572–73, 574, 576–77, 612–16, 623,
    637; Estonia and, 610; Finland and,
    548, 552 n.50, 610; France and,
    86–89, 163–64, 214, 352–54, 363,
    415–18, 450 n.289, 529, 531, 545, 548,
    549, 553, 568ff., 576–77, 612–16, 624–
    27; Germany and, 4, 28, 33, 37, 69,
    73, 75, 76, 86–89, 162, 205, 211–15,
    352, 403, 414–18, 475, 495 n.128, 510,
    531–34, 552, 557, 560 n.85, 568–77,
    587 n.223, 601, 602–10, 619, 631–32,
    652, 672–74; Hungary and, 474, 495,
    496 n.129; Italy and, 571, 597, 603
    n.312; Japan and, 37, 188–90, 213,
    504, 506, 509–10, 565, 568, 575,
    601–2, 606, 608; Latvia and, 610;
    Lithuania and, 486; Poland and,
    86–87, 208, 352–53, 363–64, 402, 403,
    415, 416 nn.169, 170, 474, 495, 499,
    531, 548–49, 554–55, 568, 571,
    572–73, 610, 627, 649; and Polish-

Lithuanian dispute, 213, 353 n.160;
purge, 87–88, 89, 190, 212–13, 531;
Red Army, 87–88, 548, 549; Red
Navy, 87–88, 89; Rumania and, 79,
86–87, 233, 236–37, 352–53, 415, 491,
588; Slovakia and, 552 n.51; and
Spanish Civil War, 155, 164, 213–14;
Tass news agency, 568, 572; Turkey
and, 608; United States and, 578, 608
United States: aircraft industry, 133,
521, 529–31; and Anti-
Comintern Pact, 256; England and,
54, 58, 69, 96–97, 98, 105ff., 138,
139–40, 347 n.125, 358, 422 n.192,
526 n.254, 557 n.73, 578, 601 n.303;
and England, trade agreement, 97,
107, 111, 521; France and, 69, 105,
106, 133, 254, 358, 521, 529–30, 578;
Germany and, 9, 10–11, 69, 249–55,
387, 519–21, 530, 565, 577–78, 652,
674–75; Hungary and, 229, 586;
Japan and, 109, 187ff., 506, 510, 569,
576 n.164, 601; Latin American policy, 257, 260; and Munich, 454, 458,
461–62, 525 n.250; neutrality laws,
14, 54, 97, 105–6, 133, 358, 521, 530,
578, 636; Poland and, 478; rearmament, 530; and Spanish Civil War,
163–64; U.S.S.R. and, 578, 608
Upper Silesia, 61, 194–97
Ustasha, 216, 217

Valera, Eamon de, 547 n.41
Valle, Giuseppe, 456
Vansittart, Sir Robert, 43 nn.93, 94, 60,
67, 68 n.56, 88, 103, 129, 274, 548
n.43, 622; and Czechoslovakia
(Sudeten issue), 325, 330, 350 n.141,
363, 374, 380 nn.10, 12, 391, 392 n.60,
395, 396, 402 n.102, 421 n.185, 438
n.251, 457 n.319; and Halifax visit,
115 nn.61, 63, 116 n.68, 122; and
United States, 108, 110 n.42
Vargas, Getulio, 255ff., 453 n.304
Vatican: Germany and, 10, 20–21, 301,
306, 546, 595, 640 n.58
Veesenmayer, Edmund, 295 n.155
Veltjens, Josef, 22 n.14, 147
Vereinigte Stahlwerke, 25 n.23
Versailles, Treaty of, 7, 18, 20, 21, 29,
65, 89, 199, 201, 205–6, 232, 303, 320,
417, 460, 502, 642, 653
Victor Emmanuel III (of Italy), 308, 637

Vienna award of 2 November 1938,
472, 474, 487, 505
Vilna, 205, 484, 610
Volksbund für das Deutschtum im
Ausland (VDA), 35, 210 n.74, 332
n.71
Volksdeutsche Mittelstelle (Vomi), 210
n.75
Vuillemin, Joseph, 399

Wagner, Eduard, 537 n.10
Wang Ching-wei, 601
Weizsäcker, Ernst von, 64 n.39, 188,
190, 279, 281, 298 n.169, 309, 310,
339 n.95, 432, 629 n.5, 646 n.95, 648;
and Czechoslovakia, 340, 366 n.207,
368 n.213, 376 n.251, 394, 412, 426,
452, 457, 462 n.334, 466 n.1, 466–67,
618; and England, 102, 118, 137, 380
n.12, 386, 394, 426, 508, 519, 560
n.87, 599 n.289, 618, 629 n.5; and
France, 508, 599 n.289, 626 n.427;
and Hungary, 431; and Poland,
467–68, 479, 489 n.96, 560, 561, 583
n.203, 584 n.208, 605, 618; and
U.S.S.R., 568–69, 576, 577, 581, 605
Welczek, Johannes von, 90–91, 155,
423, 624
Wenner-Gren, Axel, 619, 622
Western Pact, 59, 81, 126, 200 n.28
Westerplatte, 583, 628, 648
Wiechmann, Hans, 199–200
Wiedemann, Fritz, 11 n.29, 250,
253, 380–81, 388 n.42, 521 n.237, 525
n.252; trip to London, 380–83, 389
n.49, 391, 412, 420
Wiesner, Rudolf, 628 n.3
Wietersheim, Gustav Anton von, 418
Wilhelmina (queen of Holland), 593,
631 n.16
Wilson, Sir Horace, 129 n.117, 380
n.12, 426, 438 n.251, 449ff., 455
n.311, 534, 617 n.382, 621 n.398, 622,
649–50
Wilson, Hugh, 51 n.121, 252 n.8, 303,
520, 521
Wimmer, Lothar, 39 n.76
Windsor, Duchess of (Wallis Simpson),
63, 64
Windsor, Duke of. See Edward VIII
Woermann, Ernst, 63 n.36, 368 n.213,
471 n.23, 478 n.45, 487 n.84
Wohlthat, Helmuth, 238, 426 n.209, 492

n.111, 493–94, 536, 540, 542, 605, 621
World Raw Materials Conference
(Geneva 1937), 26
World War I, 5–6, 7, 18–19, 21, 22, 32,
52, 54–55, 56, 59, 63, 78, 82, 89 n.125,
91, 93, 103, 105, 127, 157, 158, 165,
357, 358, 393, 400, 408, 412, 418, 424,
425, 431, 458, 548, 552, 600, 623,
653, 662
World War II, 87 n.112, 88 n.121, 104,
144 n.5, 146 n.16, 152, 165, 245, 261,
652–53
Wysocki, Alfred, 206 n.58

Yugoslavia: *Anschluss* of Austria, 230,
266; Bulgaria and, 238; Czechoslovakia and, 322, 590; England and, 62
n.32, 80, 216, 217, 221, 543, 590;
France and, 79–80, 216, 217, 218,
220–21, 342; German minority, 219;
Germany and, 4, 79, 80, 101, 215–24,
230–31, 301, 490–91, 563, 581,
590–91; Hungary and, 207, 215, 218,
220, 221–23, 224, 228ff., 405–6, 444,
490, 497, 564 n.108, 590; Italy and,
79, 216–18, 224, 231, 273, 286, 287,
411, 414, 563, 590, 598–99, 600, 635;
United States and, 590; Zbor movement, 219

Zeeland, Paul van, 91, 97
Zeitzler, Kurt, 366 n.208
Zernatto, Guido, 278, 290, 292